Tenth Edition

MODERN DATABASE MANAGEMENT

Jeffrey A. Hoffer
University of Dayton

V. Ramesh
Indiana University

Heikki Topi
Bentley University

PEARSON

Delhi • Chennai • Chandigarh

Credits and acknowledgments borrowed from other sources and reproduced, with permission, in this textbook appear on appropriate page within text.

Authorized adaptation from the United States edition, entitled *Modern Database Management System 10th Edition*, ISBN: 9780136088394 by Hoffer, Jeffrey A., Ramesh, V., Topi, Heikki; published by Pearson Education, Inc., publishing as Prentice Hall © 2011.

Indian Subcontinent Adaptation

ISBN 978-81-317-6143-4

First Impression

This edition is manufactured in India and is authorized for sale only in India, Bangladesh, Bhutan, Pakistan, Nepal, Sri Lanka and the Maldives.

Published by Dorling Kindersley (India) Pvt. Ltd., licensees of Pearson Education in South Asia.

Head Office: 7th Floor, Knowledge Boulevard, A-8(A), Sector 62, Noida 201309, UP, India.
Registered Office: 11 Community Centre, Panchsheel Park, New Delhi 110 017, India.

Printed in India by Rahul Print O Pack

To Patty, for her sacrifices, encouragement, and support for over 28 years of being a textbook author widow. To my students and colleagues, for being receptive and critical and for challenging me to be a better teacher.

—J.A.H.

To Gayathri, for her sacrifices and patience these past 20 years. To my parents for letting me make the journey abroad, and to my cat, Raju, for being a part of our family for almost 20 years.

—V.R.

To Anne-Louise, for her loving support, encouragement, and patience. To Leila, whose laughter and joy of life continue to teach me about what is truly important. To my teachers, colleagues, and students, from whom I continue to learn every day.

—H.T.

Fred R. McFadden
1933–2009

Founding author of Modern Database Management, *Fred McFadden, passed away on August 9, 2009. Fred was a dedicated educator for 30 years in the College of Business at the University of Colorado, Colorado Springs. He received his bachelor's degree in Mechanical Engineering from Michigan State University, his MBA from the University of California, Los Angeles, and his PhD in Industrial Engineering from Stanford University. He began writing* Modern Database Management *in 1980 and was considered a leading information systems educator in database management, systems analysis, and decision support, all areas in which he was a scholarly author. Fred's work on the initial design of this textbook was pioneering, as few books existed then to present information technology to business students.*

Fred was an inspiration to his students and colleagues. An outstanding communicator with a strong sense of clarity and the needs of students, he was a mentor to his co-authors. Fred's first concern was always what was best for the students using the book, and he worked tirelessly to make passages succinct, readable, and motivating. He taught through examples and imaginatively told stories with graphics. He was skilled at blending the latest and best industry practices with leading research results into material accessible to all readers, whether undergraduate or graduate students. Fred was encouraging to his co-authors, always prepared to take on any writing assignment, yet never so prideful of his writing as to not accept comments with respect. Fred was actively involved in writing this text through the 8th edition, and he remained a confidant and guide after he ceased active writing.

Besides his professional contributions, Fred more than anything else was a caring, gentle, passionate person. Growing up on a farm in Michigan taught him to love the outdoors and to have a strong sense of caring for his neighbor, whom Fred saw as everyone.

The co-authors of Modern Database Management, *10th edition, are humbled to dedicate this edition to Fred R. McFadden, our friend and colleague.*

BRIEF CONTENTS

CONTENTS

PINE VALLEY FURNITURE

ONLINE CHAPTERS

PREFACE

This text is designed to be used with an introductory course in database management. Such a course is usually required as part of an information systems curriculum in business schools, computer technology programs, and applied computer science departments. The Association for Information Systems (AIS), the Association for Computing Machinery (ACM), and the International Federation of Information Processing Societies (IFIPS) curriculum guidelines (e.g., IS 2010) all outline this type of database management course. Previous editions of this text have been used successfully for more than 27 years at both the undergraduate and graduate levels, as well as in management and professional development programs.

WHAT'S NEW IN THIS EDITION?

This 10th edition of *Modern Database Management* updates and expands materials in areas undergoing rapid change due to improved managerial practices, database design tools and methodologies, and database technology. Later we detail changes to each chapter. The themes of this 10th edition reflect the major trends in the information systems field and the skills required of modern information systems graduates:

- Data quality and database processing accuracy, which are extremely important with the national and international regulations such as the Sarbanes-Oxley Act, Basel II, COSI, and HIPAA that now require organizations to comply with standards for reporting accurate financial data and ensuring data privacy. Material on data quality and master data management has been updated with a stronger coverage of the people, process, and technology aspects and internationally accepted best practices for information systems development and management (specifically, ITIL).
- Integration of data from multiple internal and external databases and data sources, which is now common for building data warehouses and other types of enterprise systems, and dealing with the rapid organizational changes in information systems brought on by corporate reorganizations, mergers, and acquisitions. These first two bullets are implemented with the revised Chapter 10 on data quality and integration, which updates and improves the focus of the material and introduces the latest principles in these areas.
- Demonstrating knowledge of how to use databases in the context of developing database applications in two and three-tier client/server environments. In this 10th edition (in Chapters 8 and 14), we provide examples of how to connect to databases from popular programming languages such as Java and VB.NET as well Web development languages such as Java Server Pages (JSP), ASP.NET, and PHP. Coverage of XML has also been revised to emphasize the role of XML in data storage and retrieval.
- Linking object-oriented information systems development environments (such as Java Technology and Microsoft .NET) with mainstream technology for maintaining organizational data—relational databases—and in the process dealing with significant paradigm differences between object-oriented and relational frameworks. This major change that was introduced for the ninth edition and has been updated for the 10th edition reflects what is a rapidly changing environment for database processing.

Specific improvements to the textbook have been made in the following areas:

- Arranged the Problems and Exercises into roughly increasing order of difficulty to make it easier for instructors and students to select problems and exercises for practice and assignments.
- Applied standard data naming conventions throughout the book to make it easier for students to distinguish data elements from conceptual to physical forms.

- Clarified system requirements through systems modeling and design and outlined a process to use the increasingly popular industry and business function commercial data models to speed up the systems development process. The new material focuses on changes to the database development process when an organization uses packaged data models. Students are now better prepared to understand why these data models are important and how to read and work with (tailor) them.
- Expanded coverage of SQL, with a few more frequently used components of the language. We have also created new figures to graphically depict the set processing logic of SQL queries, which gives students, especially visual learners, new tools to use when writing queries.
- Included new screen captures to reflect the latest database technologies and an updated Web Resources section in each chapter that lists Web sites that can provide the student with information on the latest database trends and expanded background details on important topics covered in the text.
- Reduced the length of the printed book, which we began doing with the eighth edition. The reduced length is more consistent with what our reviewers say can be covered in a database course today, given the need for depth of coverage in the most important topics. Specifically, for the 10th edition, we combined the first two chapters from the ninth edition into one, so that students can more quickly cover/review background topics and then dig into the material central to database management. We have also combined the two chapters from the ninth edition on client/server and Internet databases into one chapter addressing database issues in a multitier computing environment. We continue to update the chapters on distributed databases, the object-oriented data model, and using relational databases to provide object persistence, including an overview in the printed textbook and full versions on the textbook's Web site. Care has been given to the layout of figures and tables to also reduce the length of the book, while adding some new figures and figure elements to better link the text narrative with the figures. The reduced length should encourage more students to purchase and read the text, without any loss of coverage and learning. The book is also now available through CourseSmart, an innovative e-book delivery system.

MODERN DATABASE MANAGEMENT: A RETRO AND FUTURE PERSPECTIVE

This 10th edition is a humbling milestone. We are extremely grateful for the support of adopters, reviewers, students, colleagues, editors, and publisher staff who have been with us for some or, in a few cases, all of the past 27 years. Database technology has "grown up" over these years, from a resource for only the most sophisticated organizations to being a mainstay of almost any computing environment. Some topics, such as relational databases, have been a central part of the text from the beginning; other topics, such as data warehousing, business intelligence, object-oriented databases, and databases on the Internet, are newer topics. One of the original authors of this text is still a co-author, while a newer generation of database academic experts now contributes to these pages with zest and creativity. The original book authors were educated in fields other than business information systems, whereas today our newer authors are experienced and educated in this rich field central to the success of modern organizations.

As a book that we believe has succeeded in leading the database management textbook market, this book is positioned to continue (in some printed or electronic form) for at least another 27 years. Writing this book has been and remains an awesome responsibility. We authors realize that the course that this text supports will be the foundation for student careers with databases. Over the years, we've seen students reading our book on airplanes while traveling on business, and, believe it or not, reading it on a Florida beach during spring break. The authors remain committed to presenting material with sound pedagogy, including topics (both easy and difficult, traditional and emerging) that are critical for the practical success of database professionals, and being informed by research that reveals what will be the "next big thing" in database management. It is in this spirit that we celebrate our milestone edition, and lay the foundation for many more editions to come.

FOR THOSE NEW TO MODERN DATABASE MANAGEMENT

Modern Database Management has been a leading text since its first edition in 1983. In spite of this market leadership position, some instructors have used other good database management texts. Why might you want to switch at this time? There are several good reasons to switch to *Modern Database Management*, including:

- One of our goals, in every edition, has been to lead other books in coverage of the latest principles, concepts, and technologies. See what we have added for the 10th edition in "What's New in This Edition." In the past, we have led in coverage of object-oriented data modeling and UML, Internet databases, data warehousing, and the use of CASE tools in support of data modeling. For the 10th edition, we are taking the lead on database development for Internet-based applications, data quality and integration, the linking of object-oriented development environments with relational databases, and the increasingly important role of packaged database model as a component of agile, rapid development of information systems. We also have for the first time Camtasia-produced tutorial videos to accompany the book, with more to come for future editions.
- While remaining current, this text focuses on what leading practitioners say is most important for database developers. We work with many practitioners, including the professionals of the Data Management Association (DAMA) and The Data Warehousing Institute (TDWI), leading consultants, technology leaders, and authors of articles in the most widely read professional publications. We draw on these experts to ensure that what the book includes is important and covers not only important entry-level knowledge and skills, but also those fundamentals and mindsets that lead to long-term career success.
- In this highly successful book in its 10th edition, material is presented in a way that has been viewed as very accessible to students. Our methods have been refined through continuous market feedback for over 27 years, as well as through our own teaching. Overall, the pedagogy of the book is sound. We use many illustrations that help to make important concepts and techniques clear. We use the most modern notations. The organization of the book is flexible, so you can use chapters in whatever sequence makes sense for your students. We supplement the book with data sets to facilitate hands-on, practical learning, and with new media resources to make some of the more challenging topics more engaging.
- You may have particular interest in introducing SQL early in your course. Our text can accommodate this. First, we cover SQL in depth, devoting two full chapters to this core technology of the database field. Second, we include many SQL examples in early chapters. Third, many instructors have successfully used the two SQL chapters early in their course. Although logically appearing in the life cycle of systems development as Chapters 6 and 7, part of the implementation section of the text, many instructors have used these chapters immediately after Chapter 1 or in parallel with other early chapters. Finally, we use SQL throughout the book, for example, to illustrate Web application connections to relational databases in Chapter 8, online analytical processing in Chapter 9, and accessing relational databases from object-oriented development environments in Chapter 14.
- We have the latest in supplements and Web site support for the text. See the supplement package for details on all the resources available to you and your students.
- This text is written to be part of a modern information systems curriculum with a strong business systems development focus. Topics are included and addressed

so as to reinforce principles from other typical courses, such as systems analysis and design, networking, Web site design and development, MIS principles, and computer programming. Emphasis is on the development of the database component of modern information systems and on the management of the data resource. Thus, the text is practical, supports projects and other hands-on class activities, and encourages linking database concepts to concepts being learned throughout the curriculum the student is taking.

SUMMARY OF ENHANCEMENTS TO EACH CHAPTER

The following sections present a chapter-by-chapter description of the major changes in this edition. Each chapter description presents a statement of the purpose of that chapter, followed by a description of the changes and revisions that have been made for the 10th edition. Each paragraph concludes with a description of the strengths that have been retained from prior editions.

Part I: The Context of Database Management

CHAPTER 1: THE DATABASE ENVIRONMENT AND DEVELOPMENT PROCESS This chapter discusses the role of databases in organizations and previews the major topics in the remainder of the text. This chapter has undergone extensive reorganization for the 10th edition because it is a consolidation of two previous chapters, allowing students to more quickly cover material that previews the rest of the book. After presenting a brief introduction to the basic terminology associated with storing and retrieving data, the chapter presents a well organized comparison of traditional file-processing systems and modern database technology. The chapter then introduces the core components of a database environment and the range of database applications that are currently in use within organizations—personal, two-tier, multitier, and enterprise applications. The explanation of enterprise databases includes databases that are part of enterprise resource planning systems and data warehouses. A brief history of the evolution of database technology, from pre-database files to modern object-relational technologies, is also presented. The chapter then goes on to explain the process of database development in the context of structured life cycle, prototyping, and agile methodologies. The presentation remains consistent with the companion systems analysis text by Hoffer, George, and Valacich. The chapter also discusses important issues in database development, including management of the diverse group of people involved in database development and frameworks for understanding database architectures and technologies (e.g., the three-schema architecture). Reviewers frequently note the compatibility of this chapter with what students learn in systems analysis and design classes.

Part II: Database Analysis

CHAPTER 2: MODELING DATA IN THE ORGANIZATION This chapter presents a thorough introduction to conceptual data modeling with the entity-relationship (E-R) model. The chapter title emphasizes the reason for the entity-relationship model: to unambiguously document the rules of the business that influence database design. Specific subsections explain in detail how to name and define elements of a data model, which are essential in developing an unambiguous E-R diagram. In the 10th edition, we have provided some new problems and exercises, improved an example from Pine Valley Furniture to show the relationship of conceptual database design with implementation, and provided more annotations in figures to better highlight key elements and better link text to figures. The chapter continues to proceed from simple to more complex examples, and it concludes with a comprehensive E-R diagram for the Pine Valley Furniture Company.

CHAPTER 3: THE ENHANCED E-R MODEL This chapter presents a discussion of several advanced E-R data model constructs, primarily supertype/subtype relationships.

A major change in this chapter is the elimination of the section on business rules, which many adopters and reviewers said they did not have time to cover in class. The most significant addition is a more thorough description of how to conduct a data modeling project when using a packaged data model; this new material better prepares students for working with commercial off-the-shelf (COTS) software and purchased data models, which support major efforts to implement patterns and reusability for application deployment in organizations. As in Chapter 2, figures have been improved with more annotations to clarify important data modeling structures. The chapter continues to present a thorough coverage of supertype/subtype relationships and includes a comprehensive example of an extended E-R data model for the Pine Valley Furniture Company.

Part III: Database Design

CHAPTER 4: LOGICAL DATABASE DESIGN AND THE RELATIONAL MODEL This chapter describes the process of converting a conceptual data model to the relational data model, as well as how to merge new relations into an existing normalized database. It provides a conceptually sound and practically relevant introduction to normalization, emphasizing the importance of the use of functional dependencies and determinants as the basis for normalization. Concepts of normalization and normal forms are extended in Appendix B. The chapter features a discussion of the characteristics of foreign keys and introduces the important concept of a nonintelligent enterprise key. Enterprise keys (also called surrogate keys for data warehouses) are being emphasized as some concepts of object-orientation migrate into the relational technology world. A number of new review questions and problems and exercises are included, and revision also has further clarified the presentation of some of the key concepts. The chapter continues to emphasize the basic concepts of the relational data model and the role of the database designer in the logical design process.

CHAPTER 5: PHYSICAL DATABASE DESIGN AND PERFORMANCE This chapter describes the steps that are essential in achieving an efficient database design, with a strong focus on those aspects of database design and implementation that are typically within the control of a database professional in a modern database environment. The revised chapter is significantly shorter than the previous one, but we believe the reduction in length has been achieved without loss of significant content. The cuts are in areas that are either not relevant anymore because of changes in technology or not directly related to database design (e.g., storage technologies). Consequently, the chapter has a stronger and clearer focus on the core concepts. Several new review questions and problems and exercises are included. The chapter contains an emphasis on ways to improve database performance, with references to specific techniques available in Oracle and other DBMSs to improve database processing performance. The discussion of indexes includes descriptions of the types of indexes (primary and secondary indexes, join index, hash index table) that are widely available in database technologies as techniques to improve query processing speed. Appendix C provides excellent background on fundamental data structures for programs of study that need coverage of this topic. The chapter continues to emphasize the physical design process and the goals of that process.

Part IV: Implementation

CHAPTER 6: INTRODUCTION TO SQL This chapter presents a thorough introduction to the SQL used by most DBMSs (SQL:1999) and introduces the changes that are included in the latest proposed standard (SQL:200n). The coverage of SQL is extensive and divided into this and the next chapter. This chapter includes examples of SQL code, using mostly SQL:1999 and SQL:200n syntax, as well as some Oracle 11g and Microsoft SQL Server syntax. Some unique features of MySQL are mentioned. Views, both dynamic and materialized, are also covered. Chapter 6 explains the SQL commands needed to create and maintain a database and to program single-table queries. The history and SQL technology environment sections have been streamlined for the 10th edition. Coverage of dual-table, IS NULL/IS NOT NULL, more built-in functions, derived tables, and rules for aggregate functions and the GROUP BY clause are included or improved. New problems and exercises have been added to the chapter. It continues to use the Pine Valley Furniture Company case to illustrate a wide variety of practical queries and query results.

CHAPTER 7: ADVANCED SQL This chapter continues the description of SQL, with a careful explanation of multiple-table queries, transaction integrity, data dictionaries, triggers and stored procedures (the differences between which are now more clearly explained), and embedded SQL in other programming language programs. All forms of the OUTER JOIN command are covered. Standard SQL is also used in Chapter 7. This chapter illustrates how to store the results of a query in a derived table, the CAST command to convert data between different data types, and the CASE command for doing conditional processing in SQL. The chapter reduces its coverage of online analytical processing (OLAP) features of SQL:200n, which are also covered in Chapter 9. A new section on self-joins and an explanation of when to use EXISTS (NOT EXISTS) versus IN (NOT IN) are now included. The explanation of cursors with embedded SQL is enhanced. Emphasis continues on the set-processing style of SQL compared with the record-processing of programming languages with which the student may be familiar. New problems and exercises have been added to the chapter. The chapter continues to contain a clear explanation of subqueries and correlated subqueries, two of the most complex and powerful constructs in SQL.

CHAPTER 8: DATABASE APPLICATION DEVELOPMENT This chapter provides a modern discussion of the concepts of client/server architecture and applications, middleware, and database access in contemporary database environments. Technologies that are commonly used to create two- and three-tier applications are presented. Many figures are included to show the options in multitiered networks, including application and database servers, database processing distribution alternatives among network tiers, and browser (thin) clients. New to this edition is the presentation of sample application programs that demonstrate how to access databases from popular programming languages such as, Java, VB.NET, ASP.NET, JSP, and PHP. This chapter lays the technology groundwork for the Internet topics presented in the remainder of the text and highlights some of the key considerations in creating three-tier Internet-based applications. The chapter also presents expanded coverage of the role of Extensible Markup Language (XML) and related technologies in data storage and retrieval. Topics covered include basics of XML schemas, XQuery, and XSLT. The chapter concludes with an overview of Web services, associated standards and technologies, and their role in seamless, secure movement of data in Web-based applications. A brief introduction to service-oriented architecture (SOA) is also presented. Security topics, including Web security, are covered in Chapter 11.

CHAPTER 9: DATA WAREHOUSING This chapter describes the basic concepts of data warehousing, the reasons data warehousing is regarded as critical to competitive advantage in many organizations, and the database design activities and structures unique to data warehousing. An updated section reviews best practices for determining requirements for a dimensional model. A short new section introduces the emerging column databases technology, which has been developed especially for data warehousing applications. New exercises provide hands-on practice with a data mart, using SQL and a BI tool called MicroStrategy that is supported on Teradata University Network. Topics include alternative data warehouse architectures and the dimensional data model (or star schema) for data warehouses. Coverage of architectures has been streamlined consistent with trends in data warehousing, and a deep explanation of how to handle slowly changing dimensional data is provided. Operational data store; independent, dependent, and logical data marts; and various forms of online analytical processing (OLAP) are defined (including the SAMPLE SQL command, which is useful for analyzing data from market research activities). User interfaces, including OLAP, data visualization, business performance management and dashboards, and data mining are also described.

Part V: Advanced Database Topics

CHAPTER 10: DATA QUALITY AND INTEGRATION This chapter, first introduced in the ninth edition, has been reorganized to better reflect the nature of enterprise data management (EDM) activities in organizations. The principles of data governance, which are at the core of EDM activities, are introduced first. This is followed by coverage of data quality. This chapter describes the need for an active program to manage data quality in organizations and outlines the steps that are considered today to be best practices for data quality management. Quality data are defined, and reasons for poor-quality data are identified. Methods for data quality improvement, such as data auditing, improving data capturing (a key part of database design), data stewardship and governance, TQM principles, modern data management technologies, and high-quality data models are all discussed. The current hot topic of master data management, one approach to integrating key business data, is motivated and explained. Different approaches to data integration are overviewed, and the reasons for each are outlined. The ETL process for data warehousing is discussed in detail. The authors believe that the material covered in this chapter continues to represent a major step forward in database management textbooks.

CHAPTER 11: DATA AND DATABASE ADMINISTRATION This chapter presents a thorough discussion of the importance and roles of data and database administration and describes a number of the key issues that arise when these functions are performed. This chapter emphasizes the changing roles and approaches of data and database administration, with emphasis on data quality and high performance. It contains a thorough discussion of database backup procedures, as well as extensively expanded and consolidated coverage of data security threats and responses, and data availability. The data security topics include database security policies, procedures, and technologies (including encryption and smart cards). New to this edition is expanded coverage of the role of databases in Sarbanes-Oxley compliance. We have again added to our discussion of open source DBMS to cover more on the benefits and hazards of this technology and how to choose an open source DBMS. In addition, the topic of heartbeat queries is included in the coverage of database performance improvements. The chapter continues to emphasize the critical importance of data and database management in managing data as a corporate asset.

CHAPTER 12: DISTRIBUTED DATABASES This chapter reviews the role, technologies, and unique database design opportunities of distributed databases. The objectives and trade-offs for distributed databases, data replication alternatives, factors in selecting a data distribution strategy, and distributed database vendors and products are covered. This chapter provides thorough coverage of database concurrency access controls. The revision of the chapter introduces several technical updates that are related to the significant advancements in both data management and networking technologies, which form the context for distributed database. An overview of this chapter is included in the printed textbook, and the full version of this chapter has been moved to the textbook's Web site. Many reviewers indicated that they seldom are able to cover this chapter in an introductory course, but having the material available is critical for advanced students or special topics. Having an overview in the printed text with the full chapter available to students provides the greatest flexibility and economy.

CHAPTER 13: OBJECT-ORIENTED DATA MODELING This chapter presents an introduction to object-oriented modeling using Object Management Group's Unified Modeling Language (UML). This chapter has been carefully reviewed to ensure consistency with the latest UML notation and best industry practices. UML provides an industry-standard notation for representing classes and objects. The chapter continues to emphasize basic object-oriented concepts, such as inheritance, encapsulation, composition, and polymorphism. The revised version of the chapter also includes several brand-new modeling exercises. As with Chapters 12 and 14, the full version of this chapter is available on the textbook's Web site, with a brief overview included in the printed text.

CHAPTER 14: USING RELATIONAL DATABASES TO PROVIDE OBJECT PERSISTENCE This chapter presents an up-to-date approach to how relational databases are used with object-oriented development environments, such as Java EE and Microsoft .NET. Object-oriented and relational approaches have critical design mismatches, which are outlined in the chapter, along with ways database and application developers can deal with these issues. The chapter reviews call-level application program interfaces, SQL query mapping frameworks, and object-relational mapping frameworks as approaches to providing object persistence, which is an essential need in modern development environments that integrate object-oriented development and relational databases. The chapter has been revised to take into account the changing landscape of object-relational mapping (ORM) technologies and the strengthening of the Java Persistence API (JPA) standard. Object-relational mapping is illustrated using the XML mapping files of Hibernate, the most popular ORM framework and the most widely used implementation of the JPA standard. As with Chapters 12 and 13, the full version of this chapter is available on the textbook's Web site, with a brief overview included in the printed text.

Appendices

The 10th edition contains three appendices intended for those who wish to explore certain topics in greater depth.

APPENDIX A: DATA MODELING TOOLS AND NOTATION This appendix addresses a need raised by many readers—how to translate the E-R notation in the text into the form used by the CASE tool or DBMS used in class. Specifically, this appendix compares the notations of CA ERwin Data Modeler r7.3, Oracle Designer 10g, Sybase PowerDesigner 15, and Microsoft Visio Pro 2003. Tables and illustrations show the notations used for the same constructs in each of these popular software packages.

APPENDIX B: ADVANCED NORMAL FORMS This appendix presents a description (with examples) of Boyce-Codd and fourth normal forms, including an example of BCNF to show how to handle overlapping candidate keys. Other normal forms are briefly introduced. The Web Resources section includes a reference for information on many advanced normal form topics.

APPENDIX C: DATA STRUCTURES This appendix describes several data structures that often underlie database implementations. Topics include the use of pointers, stacks, queues, sorted lists, inverted lists, and trees.

PEDAGOGY

A number of additions and improvements have been made to chapter-end materials to provide a wider and richer range of choices for the user. The most important of these improvements are the following:

1. ***Review Questions*** Questions have been updated to support new and enhanced chapter material.
2. ***Problems and Exercises*** This section has been reviewed in every chapter, and many chapters contain new problems and exercises to support updated chapter material. Of special interest are questions in many chapters that give students opportunities to use the data sets provided for the text. Also, Problems and Exercises have be re-sequenced into roughly increasing order of difficulty, which should help instructors and students to find exercises appropriate for what they want to accomplish.
3. ***Field Exercises*** This section provides a set of "hands-on" minicases that can be assigned to individual students or to small teams of students. Field exercises

range from directed field trips to Internet searches and other types of research exercises.

4. *Case* The Mountain View Community Hospital (MVCH) case was updated for the 10th edition only to the extent that chapters have been combined from the ninth edition. In each chapter, the case begins with a description of a realistic, modern hospital situation as it relates to that chapter. The case then presents a series of case questions and exercises that focus on specific aspects of the case. The final section includes project assignments, which tie together some issues and activities across chapters. These project assignments can be completed by individual students or by small project teams. This case provides an excellent means for students to gain hands-on experience with the concepts and tools they have studied.

5. *Web Resources* Each chapter contains a list of updated and validated URLs for Web sites that contain information that supplements the chapter. These Web sites cover online publication archives, vendors, electronic publications, industry standards organizations, and many other sources. These sites allow students and instructors to find updated product information, innovations that have appeared since the printing of the book, background information to explore topics in greater depth, and resources for writing research papers.

We have also updated the pedagogical features that helped make the 10th edition widely accessible to instructors and students. These features include the following:

1. ***Learning objectives*** appear at the beginning of each chapter, as a preview of the major concepts and skills students will learn from that chapter. The learning objectives also provide a great study review aid for students as they prepare for assignments and examinations.
2. ***Chapter introductions and summaries*** both encapsulate the main concepts of each chapter and link material to related chapters, providing students with a comprehensive conceptual framework for the course.
3. ***The chapter review*** includes the Review Questions, Problems and Exercises, and Field Exercises discussed earlier, also contains a Key Terms list to test the student's grasp of important concepts, basic facts, and significant issues.
4. ***A running glossary*** defines key terms in the page margins as they are discussed in the text. These terms are also defined at the end of the text, in the Glossary of Terms. Also included is the end-of-book Glossary of Acronyms for abbreviations commonly used in database management.

ORGANIZATION

We encourage instructors to customize their use of this book to meet the needs of both their curriculum and student career paths. The modular nature of the text, its broad coverage, extensive illustrations, and its inclusion of advanced topics and emerging issues make customization easy. The many references to current publications and Web sites can help instructors develop supplemental reading lists or expand classroom discussion beyond material presented in the text. The use of appendices for several advanced topics allows instructors to easily include or omit these topics.

The modular nature of the text allows the instructor to omit certain chapters or to cover chapters in a different sequence. For example, an instructor who wishes to emphasize data modeling may cover Chapter 13 on object-oriented data modeling along with or instead of Chapters 2 and 3. An instructor who wishes to cover only basic entity-relationship concepts (but not the enhanced E-R model) may skip Chapter 3 or cover it after Chapter 4 on the relational model. Three of the advanced topic chapters—Chapters 12 through 14—are provided in overview form in the printed text and in full version on the book's Companion Web site; this gives the instructor added flexibility to cover these advanced topics at different levels.

We have contacted many adopters of *Modern Database Management* and asked them to share with us their syllabi. Most adopters cover the chapters in sequence, but several alternative sequences have also been successful. These alternatives include:

- Some instructors cover Chapter 11 on data and database administration immediately after Chapter 5 on physical database design and the relational model.
- To cover SQL as early as possible, instructors have effectively covered Chapters 6 and 7 immediately after Chapter 4; some have even covered Chapter 6 immediately after Chapter 1.
- Many instructors have students read appendices along with chapters, such as reading Appendix A on data modeling notations with Chapters 2 or 3 on E-R modeling, Appendix B on advanced normal forms with Chapter 4 on the relational model, and Appendix C on data structures with Chapter 5.

CASE TOOLS

Modern Database Management, 10th edition, offers adopters the option of acquiring outstanding CASE tools software packages from Microsoft and Oracle. Students can purchase this book packaged with the full editions of Microsoft Visio Pro and Oracle 11g at a greatly reduced fee. We are proud to offer such highly valued, powerful software packages to students at such a low cost. These packages can be used to draw data models, generate normalized relations from conceptual data models, and generate database definition code, among other tasks. These tools are also useful in other courses on information systems development.

FOR INSTRUCTORS The following resources are available to instructors:

- The *Instructor's Resource Manual* by Chelley Vician, University of St. Thomas, provides chapter-by-chapter instructor objectives, classroom ideas, and answers to Review Questions, Problems and Exercises, Field Exercises, and Project Case Questions. The Instructor's Resource Manual is available for download on the instructor area of the text's Web site.
- The *Test Item File* by John P. Russo, Wentworth Institute of Technology, includes a comprehensive set of test questions in multiple-choice, true/false, and short-answer format, ranked according to level of difficulty and referenced with page numbers and topic headings from the text. The Test Item File is available in Microsoft Word.
- *PowerPoint presentation slides* by Michel Mitri, James Madison University, feature lecture notes that highlight key terms and concepts. Instructors can customize the presentation by adding their own slides or editing existing ones.
- The *Image Library* is a collection of the text art organized by chapter. It includes all figures, tables, and screenshots (as permission allows) and can be used to enhance class lectures and PowerPoint slides.
- *Accompanying databases* are also provided. Two versions of the Pine Valley Furniture Company case have been created and populated for the 10th edition. One version is scoped to match the textbook examples. A second version is fleshed out with more data and tables, and sample forms, reports, and modules coded in Visual Basic. This version is not complete, however, so that students can create missing tables and additional forms, reports, and modules. Databases are provided in several formats (ASCII tables, Oracle script, and Microsoft Access), but formats vary for the two versions. Some documentation of the databases is also provided. Both versions of the PVFC database are also provided on Teradata University Network.
- A white paper by Willard Baird, Progress Telecom, *Achieving Optimal Database Performance*, provides supplemental reading for students interested in tuning an Oracle database. This paper provides a real-world perspective from a very experienced database administrator. It offers students and instructors an opportunity to consider the differences between material taught in classrooms and the hands-on experience gained through professional database administration.

COURSESMART eTEXTBOOK

CourseSmart is an exciting new choice for students looking to save money. As an alternative to purchasing the print textbook, students can purchase an electronic version of the same content and save up to 50% off the suggested list price of the print text. With a CourseSmart eTextbook, students can search the text, make notes online, print out reading assignments that incorporate lecture notes, and bookmark important passages for later review. For more information, or to purchase access to the CourseSmart eTextbook, visit **www.coursesmart.com**.

ACKNOWLEDGMENTS

We are grateful to numerous individuals who contributed to the preparation of *Modern Database Management*, 10th edition. First, we wish to thank our reviewers for their detailed suggestions and insights, characteristic of their thoughtful teaching style. As always, analysis of topics and depth of coverage provided by the reviewers was crucial. Our reviewers and others who gave us many useful comments to improve the text include Tamara Babaian, Bentley University; Gary Baram, Temple University; Timothy Bridges, University of Central Oklahoma; Bijoy Bordoloi, Southern Illinois University, Edwardsville; Traci Carte, University of Oklahoma; Wingyan Chung, Santa Clara University; Jon Gant, Syracuse University; Jinzhu Gao, University of the Pacific; Monica Garfield, Bentley University; Rick Gibson, American University; William H. Hochstettler III, Franklin University; Weiling Ke, Clarkson University; Dongwon Lee, Pennsylvania State University; Ingyu Lee, Troy University; Brian Mennecke, Iowa State University; Dat-Dao Nguyen, California State University, Northridge;Lara Preiser-Houy, California State Polytechnic University, Pomona; John Russo, Wentworth Institute of Technology; Ioulia Rytikova, George Mason University; Richard Segall, Arkansas State University; Chelley Vician, University of St. Thomas; and Daniel S. Weaver, Messiah College.

We received excellent input from people in industry, including Todd Walter, Carrie Ballinger, Rob Armstrong, and Dave Schoeff (all of Teradata Corp); Chad Gronbach and Philip DesAutels (Microsoft Corp.); Peter Gauvin (Ball Aerospace); Mridvika Raisinghani (Ernst & Young); Nisha Subramanian (Cook Medical, Inc.); Paul Longhurst (Overstock.com); Derek Strauss (Gavroshe International); Richard Hackathorn (Bolder Technology); and Michael Alexander (Open Access Technology, International).

We also thank Klara Nelson at the University of Tampa, who authored the Mountain View Community Hospital case study. This extensive real-world situation is a notable addition to the text. Linda Jayne, formerly operations manager of Suncoast Hospital, Largo, Florida, provided many relevant stories and validation of the situations faced by Mountain View Community Hospital, introduced in the eighth edition. We appreciate her taking the time to meet with us and to review the existing case.

Thanks are also due Willard Baird, Progress Telecom, a highly experienced Oracle database administrator, who has co-authored the Web site piece *Achieving Optimal Database Performance* with us. Willard is able to convey trends in database administration to us very clearly and in a timely fashion, and his experience with the trend toward more holistic approaches to database optimization that have occurred over the past few years have led to our decision to put up a piece on the Web site for students and instructors who desire a deeper understanding of this area.

We have special admiration for and gratitude to Chelley Vician of University of St. Thomas, author of the *Instructor's Resource Manual*. Chelley has been extremely careful in preparing the *Instructor's Resource Manual* and in the process has helped us clarify and fix various parts of the text. Chelley has added great value to this book. Christina Cooper, Indiana University, has been of considerable assistance to Chelley Vician, to ensure notational changes in the *Instructor's Resource Manual*. We also thank Sven Aelterman, Troy University, for his many excellent suggestions for improvements and clarifications throughout the text. And we thank Pragya Seth, an MS in Information Systems (MSIS) student at Indiana University, for help in reviewing material in several chapters.

We are also grateful to the staff and associates of Pearson Prentice Hall for their support and guidance throughout this project. In particular, we wish to thank Executive Editor Bob Horan, who coordinated the planning for the text, Editorial Project Manager Kelly Loftus, who kept us on track and made sure everything was complete, Production Project Manager Becca Richter, Senior Marketing Manager Anne Fahlgren, Media Project Manager Denise Vaughn, and Marketing Assistant Melinda Jensen. We extend special thanks to Jen Carley at PMG, whose supervision of the production process was excellent.

Finally, we give immeasurable thanks to our spouses, who endured many evenings and weekends of solitude for the thrill of seeing a book cover hang on a den wall. In particular, we marvel at the commitment of Patty Hoffer, who has lived the lonely life of a textbook author's spouse through 10 editions over more than 28 years of late-night and weekend writing. Anne-Louise Klaus knew this time what to expect, and we want to sincerely thank her for being willing to continue her wholehearted support for Heikki's involvement in the project. For Gayathri Mani, this was the first time, but her unwavering support and understanding are equally appreciated. Much of the value of this text is due to their patience, encouragement, and love, but we alone bear the responsibility for any errors or omissions between the covers.

Jeffrey A. Hoffer

V. Ramesh

Heikki Topi

The publishers would like to thank Malathi Sriram, Associate Professor, SDM Institute for Management Development, Mysore, for her valuable suggestions and inputs in enhancing the content of this book to suit the requirements of Indian universities

PART

I

The Context of Database Management

Chapter 1
The Database Environment and Development Process

AN OVERVIEW OF PART ONE

In this chapter and opening part of the book, we set the context and provide basic database concepts and definitions used throughout the text. In this part, we portray database management as an exciting, challenging, and growing field that provides numerous career opportunities for information systems students. Databases continue to become a more common part of everyday living and a more central component of business operations. From the database that stores contact information in your personal digital assistant (PDA) or smartphone to the very large databases that support enterprise-wide information systems, databases have become the central points of data storage that were envisioned decades ago. Customer relationship management and Internet shopping are examples of two database-dependent activities that have developed in recent years. The development of data warehouses that provide managers the opportunity for deeper and broader historical analysis of data also continues to take on more importance.

We begin by providing basic definitions of *data, database, metadata, database management system, data warehouse,* and other terms associated with this environment. We compare databases with the older file management systems they replaced and describe several important advantages that are enabled by the carefully planned use of databases. We describe the major components of the database environment and the types of applications, as well as two-tier, multitier, and enterprise databases. Enterprise databases include those that are used to support enterprise resource planning systems and data warehouses.

The chapter in this introductory part of the book also describes the general steps followed in the analysis, design, implementation, and administration of databases. Further, this chapter also illustrates how the database development process fits into the overall information systems development process. Database development for both structured life cycle and prototyping methodologies is explained. We introduce enterprise data modeling, which sets the range and general contents of organizational databases. This is often the first step in database development. We introduce the concept of schemas and the three-schema architecture, which is the dominant approach in modern database systems. Finally, we describe the roles of the various people who are typically involved in a database development project. The Pine Valley Furniture Company case is introduced and used to illustrate many of the principles and concepts of database management. This case is used throughout the text as a continuing example of the use of database management systems.

CHAPTER

1

The Database Environment and Development Process

Learning Objectives

After studying this chapter, you should be able to:

- Concisely define each of the following key terms: **data, database, database management system, data model, information, metadata, enterprise data model, entity, relational database, enterprise resource planning (ERP) system, database application, data warehouse, data independence, repository, user view, enterprise data modeling, systems development life cycle (SDLC), prototyping, agile software development, computer-aided software engineering (CASE), conceptual schema, logical schema,** and **physical schema.**
- Name several limitations of conventional file processing systems.
- Explain at least ten advantages of the database approach, compared to traditional file processing.
- Identify several costs and risks of the database approach.
- List and briefly describe nine components of a typical database environment.
- Identify four categories of applications that use databases and their key characteristics.
- Describe the life cycle of a systems development project, with an emphasis on the purpose of database analysis, design, and implementation activities.
- Explain the prototyping and agile-development approaches to database and application development.
- Explain the roles of individuals who design, implement, use, and administer databases.
- Explain the differences between external, conceptual, and internal schemas and the reasons for the three-schema architecture for databases.

DATA MATTER!

Perfume Marketing Pvt Ltd. (PMPL) is the marketing front of a larger firm, Perfumes International. Perfumes International is a pioneer in manufacturing various types of perfumes catering to different segments of the industry. Perfumes International is a family-owned business established in 1981.

PMPL started its IT implementation in a small way in June 2002. Since its sales were increasing, a growing need for automating its sales force and services was felt. At its warehouses, PMPL already had a rudimentary inventory and invoice generation software Tally. This software was thought to be versatile enough to take care of the day-to-day activities of a single warehouse. But, this solution, at their warehouses was islets of data that never contributed to the overall national sales picture of PMPL on a "real-time" basis. The IT Manager, to whom the CEO, PMPL gave the responsibility of implementing IT, had a good and long innings at PMPL to understand its intricacies of working. He took up this task with great vigour. A complete system study was what the IT Manager had in mind, **data warehouse, sales force information system.**

Also, the rapid expansion of business made the access to latest data necessary for decision makers and field marketing personnel. It was thought that the legacy data available in the flat file (CSV) format could the basis for building an ERP solution. With this in mind, PMPL started this venture of "IT-ization". The company wanted to invest in the IT implementation in a phased manner. The kind of complex reports required for analysis and interpretation, leading to the right kind of decision making.

A team of four IT professionals were put to this task of implementing IT in a manner suitable to the overall mission and vision of the company. The team started by documenting the existing processes to automate them in the first phase. The team did not expect miracles overnight. At the end of the first year (December 2003), some of the departmental processes were automated with end-users satisfied with the initial enthusiasm. Will the IT team at PMPL be successful in building an enterprise-wide data model that in turn will be the building block of the software that will help PMPL in making better decisions regarding inventory levels at various depots, better budgeting, profitability analysis, sales-to-expense ratio, etc.?

INTRODUCTION

Over the past two decades there has been enormous growth in the number and importance of database applications. Databases are used to store, manipulate, and retrieve data in nearly every type of organization, including business, health care, education, government, and libraries. Database technology is routinely used by individuals on personal computers, by workgroups accessing databases on network servers, and by employees using enterprise-wide distributed applications. Databases are also accessed by customers and other remote users through diverse technologies, such as automated teller machines, Web browsers, smartphones, and intelligent living and office environments. Most Web-based applications depend on a database foundation.

Following this period of rapid growth, will the demand for databases and database technology level off? Very likely not! In the highly competitive environment of the early 2000s, there is every indication that database technology will assume even greater importance. Managers seek to use knowledge derived from databases for competitive advantage. For example, detailed sales databases can be mined to determine customer buying patterns as a basis for advertising and marketing campaigns. Organizations embed procedures called *alerts* in databases to warn of unusual conditions, such as impending stock shortages or opportunities to sell additional products, and to trigger appropriate actions.

Although the future of databases is assured, much work remains to be done. Many organizations have a proliferation of incompatible databases that were developed to meet immediate needs rather than based on a planned strategy or a well-managed evolution. Enormous amounts of data are trapped in older, "legacy" systems, and the data are often of poor quality. New skills are required to design and manage data warehouses and to integrate databases with Internet applications. There is a shortage of skills in areas such as database analysis, database design, data administration, and database administration. We address these and other important issues in this textbook to equip you for the jobs of the future.

A course in database management has emerged as one of the most important courses in the information systems curriculum today. Many schools have added an additional elective course in data warehousing or database administration to provide in-depth coverage of these important topics. As information systems professionals, you must be prepared to analyze database requirements and design and implement databases within the context of information systems development. You also must be prepared to consult with end users and show them how they can use databases (or data warehouses) to build decision support systems and executive information systems for competitive advantage. And, the widespread use of databases attached to Web sites that return dynamic information to users of these sites requires that you understand not only how to link databases to the Web-based applications but also how to secure those databases so that their contents can be viewed but not compromised by outside users.

In this chapter, we introduce the basic concepts of databases and database management systems (DBMSs). We describe traditional file management systems and some of their shortcomings that led to the database approach. Next, we consider the benefits, costs, and risks of using the database approach. We review of the range of technologies used to build, use, and manage databases, describe the types of applications that use databases—personal, two-tier, three-tier, and enterprise—and describe how databases have evolved over the past five decades.

Because a database is one part of an information system, this chapter also examines how the database development process fits into the overall information systems development process. The chapter emphasizes the need to coordinate database development with all the other activities in the development of a complete information system. It includes highlights from a hypothetical database development process at Pine Valley Furniture Company. Using this example, the chapter introduces tools for developing databases on personal computers and the process of extracting data from enterprise databases for use in stand-alone applications.

There are several reasons for discussing database development at this point. First, although you may have used the basic capabilities of a database management system, such as Microsoft Access, you may not yet have developed an understanding of how these databases were developed. Using simple examples, this chapter briefly illustrates what you will be able to do after you complete a database course using this text. Thus, this chapter helps you to develop a vision and context for each topic developed in detail in subsequent chapters.

Second, many students learn best from a text full of concrete examples. Although all of the chapters in this text contain numerous examples, illustrations, and actual database designs and code, each chapter concentrates on a specific aspect of database management. We have designed this chapter to help you understand, with minimal technical details, how all of these individual aspects of database management are related and how database development tasks and skills relate to what you are learning in other information systems courses.

Finally, many instructors want you to begin the initial steps of a database development group or individual project early in your database course. This chapter gives you an idea of how to structure a database development project sufficient to begin a course exercise. Obviously, because this is only the first chapter, many of the examples and notations we will use will be much simpler than those required for your project, for other course assignments, or in a real organization.

One note of caution: You will not learn how to design or develop databases just from this chapter. Sorry! We have purposely kept the content of this chapter introductory and simplified. Many of the notations used in this chapter are not exactly like the ones you will learn in subsequent chapters. Our purpose in this chapter is to give you a general understanding of the key steps and types of skills, not to teach you specific techniques. You will, however, learn fundamental concepts and definitions and develop an intuition and motivation for the skills and knowledge presented in later chapters.

BASIC CONCEPTS AND DEFINITIONS

We define a **database** as an organized collection of logically related data. Not many words in the definition, but have you looked at the size of this book? There is a lot to do to fulfill this definition.

Database
An organized collection of logically related data.

A database may be of any size and complexity. For example, a salesperson may maintain a small database of customer contacts—consisting of a few megabytes of data—on her laptop computer. A large corporation may build a large database consisting of several terabytes of data (a *terabyte* is a trillion bytes) on a large mainframe computer that is used for decision support applications (Winter, 1997). Very large data warehouses contain more than a petabyte of data. (A *petabyte* is a quadrillion bytes.) (We assume throughout the text that all databases are computer based.)

Data

Historically, the term *data* referred to facts concerning objects and events that could be recorded and stored on computer media. For example, in a salesperson's database, the data would include facts such as customer name, address, and telephone number. This type of data is called *structured* data. The most important structured data types are numeric, character, and dates. Structured data are stored in tabular form (in tables, relations, arrays, spreadsheets, etc.) and are most commonly found in traditional databases and data warehouses.

The traditional definition of data now needs to be expanded to reflect a new reality: Databases today are used to store objects such as documents, e-mails, maps, photographic images, sound, and video segments in addition to structured data. For example, the salesperson's database might include a photo image of the customer contact. It might also include a sound recording or video clip about the most recent product. This type of data is referred to as unstructured data, or as multimedia data. Today structured and unstructured data are often combined in the same database to create a true multimedia environment. For example, an automobile repair shop can combine structured data (describing customers and automobiles) with multimedia data (photo images of the damaged autos and scanned images of insurance claim forms).

An expanded definition of **data** that includes structured and unstructured types is "a stored representation of objects and events that have meaning and importance in the user's environment."

Data
Stored representations of objects and events that have meaning and importance in the user's environment.

Data Versus Information

The terms *data* and *information* are closely related, and in fact are often used interchangeably. However, it is useful to distinguish between data and information. We define **information** as data that have been processed in such a way that the knowledge of the person who uses the data is increased. For example, consider the following list of facts:

Information
Data that have been processed in such a way as to increase the knowledge of the person who uses the data.

Bohra, Kiran D.	180991
Singh, Seema	179878
Arora, Ankit	231456
Chakraborty, Sunad	239807
Sharma, Arun	789342

These facts satisfy our definition of data, but most people would agree that the data are useless in their present form. Even if we guess that this is a list of people's names paired with their Social Security numbers, the data remain useless because we have no idea what the entries mean. Notice what happens when we place the same data in a context, as shown in Figure 1-1a.

By adding a few additional data items and providing some structure, we recognize a class roster for a particular course. This is useful information to some users, such as the course instructor and the registrar's office. Of course, as general awareness of the importance of strong data security has increased, few organizations still use Social Security numbers as identifiers. Instead, most organizations use an internally generated number for identification purposes.

Another way to convert data into information is to summarize them or otherwise process and present them for human interpretation. For example, Figure 1-1b shows summarized student enrollment data presented as graphical information. This information could be used as a basis for deciding whether to add new courses or to hire new faculty members.

In practice, according to our definitions, databases today may contain either data or information (or both). For example, a database may contain an image of the class roster document shown in Figure 1-1a. Also, data are often preprocessed and stored in summarized form in databases that are used for decision support. Throughout this text we use the term *database* without distinguishing its contents as data or information.

FIGURE 1-1 Converting data to information
(a) Data in context

Class Roster

Course: MGT 500 Business Policy   Semester: Spring 2010

Section: 2

Name	ID	Major	GPA
Bohra, Kiran D.	180991	MGT	2.9
Singh, Seema	179878	MKT	3.4
Arora, Ankit	231456	PRM	2.8
Chakraborty, Sunad	239807	MGT	3.7
Sharma, Arun	789342	IS	2.9

(b) Summarized data

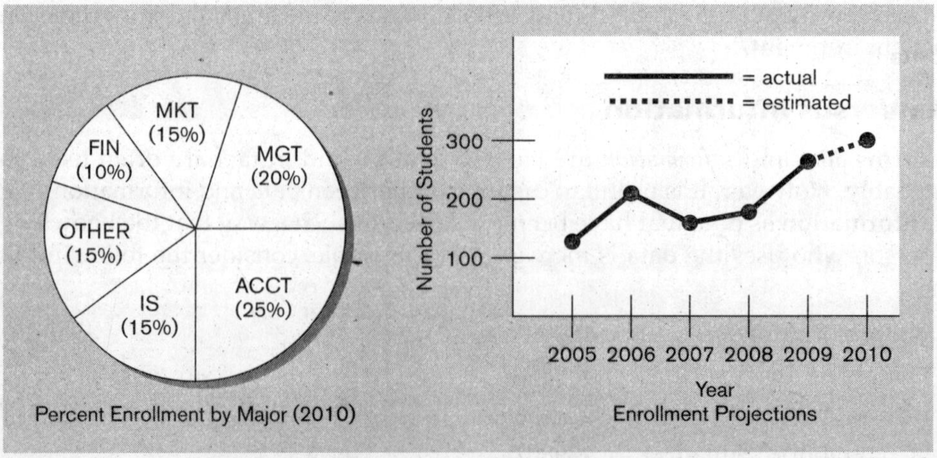

Metadata

As we have indicated, data become useful only when placed in some context. The primary mechanism for providing context for data is metadata. **Metadata** are data that describe the properties or characteristics of end-user data and the context of that data. Some of the properties that are typically described include data names, definitions, length (or size), and allowable values. Metadata describing data context include the source of the data, where the data are stored, ownership (or stewardship), and usage. Although it may seem circular, many people think of metadata as "data about data."

Metadata
Data that describe the properties or characteristics of end-user data and the context of those data.

Some sample metadata for the Class Rster (Figure 1-1a) are listed in Table 1-1. For each data item that appears in the Class Roster, the metadata show the data item name, the data type, length, minimum and maximum allowable values (where appropriate), a brief description of each data item, and the source of the data (sometimes called the *system of record*). Notice the distinction between data and metadata. Metadata are once removed from data. That is, metadata describe the properties of data but are separate from that data. Thus, the metadata shown in Table 1-1 do not include any sample data from the Class Roster of Figure 1-1a. Metadata enable database designers and users to understand what data exist, what the data mean, and how to distinguish between data items that at first glance look similar. Managing metadata is at least as crucial as managing the associated data because data without clear meaning can be confusing, misinterpreted, or erroneous. Typically, much of the metadata are stored as part of the database and may be retrieved using the same approaches that are used to retrieve data or information.

Data can be stored in files or in databases. In the following sections we examine the progression from file processing systems to databases and the advantages and disadvantages of each.

TRADITIONAL FILE PROCESSING SYSTEMS

When computer-based data processing was first available, there were no databases. To be useful for business applications, computers had to store, manipulate, and retrieve large files of data. Computer file processing systems were developed for this purpose. Although these systems have evolved over time, their basic structure and purpose have changed little over several decades.

As business applications became more complex, it became evident that traditional file processing systems had a number of shortcomings and limitations (described next).

TABLE 1-1 Example Metadata for Class Roster

Data Item	Metadata					
Name	**Type**	**Length**	**Min**	**Max**	**Description**	**Source**
Course	Alphanumeric	30			Course ID and name	Academic Unit
Section	Integer	1	1	9	Section number	Registrar
Semester	Alphanumeric	10			Semester and year	Registrar
Name	Alphanumeric	30			Student name	Student IS
ID	Integer	9			Student ID (SSN)	Student IS
Major	Alphanumeric	4			Student major	Student IS
GPA	Decimal	3	0.0	4.0	Student grade point average	Academic Unit

As a result, these systems have been replaced by database processing systems in most business applications today. Nevertheless, you should have at least some familiarity with file processing systems since understanding the problems and limitations inherent in file processing systems can help you avoid these same problems when designing database systems.

PINE VALLEY FURNITURE

File Processing Systems at Pine Valley Furniture Company

Early computer applications at Pine Valley Furniture (during the 1980s) used the traditional file processing approach. This approach to information systems design met the data processing needs of individual departments rather than the overall information needs of the organization. The information systems group typically responded to users' requests for new systems by developing (or acquiring) new computer programs for individual applications such as inventory control, accounts receivable, or human resource management. No overall map, plan, or model guided application growth.

Three of the computer applications based on the file processing approach are shown in Figure 1-2. The systems illustrated are Order Filling, Invoicing, and Payroll. The figure also shows the major data files associated with each application. A file is a collection of related records. For example, the Order Filling System has three files: Customer Master, Inventory Master, and Back Order. Notice that there is duplication of some of the files used by the three applications, which is typical of file processing systems.

TABLE 1-2 Disadvantages of File Processing Systems
Program-data dependence
Duplication of data
Limited data sharing
Lengthy development times
Excessive program maintenance

Disadvantages of File Processing Systems

Several disadvantages associated with conventional file processing systems are listed in Table 1-2 and described briefly below. It is important to understand these issues because if we don't follow the database management practices described in this book, some of these disadvantages can also become issues for databases as well.

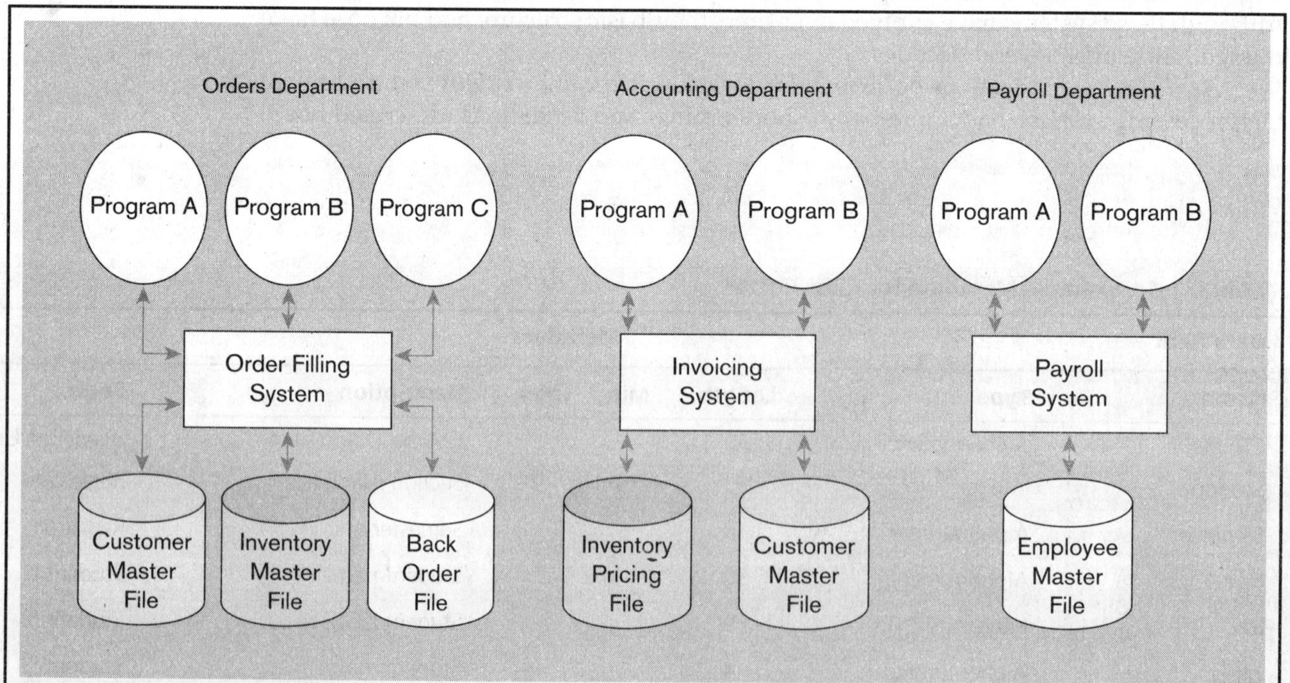

FIGURE 1-2 Old file processing systems at Pine Valley Furniture Company

PROGRAM-DATA DEPENDENCE File descriptions are stored within each **database application** program that accesses a given file. For example, in the Invoicing System in Figure 1-2, Program A accesses the Inventory Pricing File and the Customer Master File. Because the program contains a detailed file description for these files, any change to a file structure requires changes to the file descriptions for all programs that access the file.

Database application
An application program (or set of related programs) that is used to perform a series of database activities (create, read, update, and delete) on behalf of database users.

Notice in Figure 1-2 that the Customer Master File is used in the Order Filling System and the Invoicing System. Suppose it is decided to change the customer address field length in the records in this file from 30 to 40 characters. The file descriptions in each program that is affected (up to five programs) would have to be modified. It is often difficult even to locate all programs affected by such changes. Worse, errors are often introduced when making such changes.

DUPLICATION OF DATA Because applications are often developed independently in file processing systems, unplanned duplicate data files are the rule rather than the exception. For example, in Figure 1-2 the Order Filling System contains an Inventory Master File, whereas the Invoicing System contains an Inventory Pricing File. These files contain data describing Pine Valley Furniture Company's products, such as product description, unit price, and quantity on hand. This duplication is wasteful because it requires additional storage space and increased effort to keep all files up to date. Data formats may be inconsistent or data values may not agree (or both). Reliable metadata are very difficult to establish in file processing systems. For example, the same data item may have different names in different files, or conversely, the same name may be used for different data items in different files.

LIMITED DATA SHARING With the traditional file processing approach, each application has its own private files, and users have little opportunity to share data outside their own applications. Notice in Figure 1-2, for example, that users in the Accounting Department have access to the Invoicing System and its files, but they probably do not have access to the Order Filling System or to the Payroll System and their files. Managers often find that a requested report requires a major programming effort because data must be drawn from several incompatible files in separate systems. When different organizational units own these different files, additional management barriers must be overcome.

LENGTHY DEVELOPMENT TIMES With traditional file processing systems, each new application requires that the developer essentially start from scratch by designing new file formats and descriptions and then writing the file access logic for each new program. The lengthy development times required are inconsistent with today's fast-paced business environment, in which time to market (or time to production for an information system) is a key business success factor.

EXCESSIVE PROGRAM MAINTENANCE The preceding factors all combined to create a heavy program maintenance load in organizations that relied on traditional file processing systems. In fact, as much as 80 percent of the total information system's development budget might be devoted to program maintenance in such organizations. This in turn means that resources (time, people, and money) are not being spent on developing new applications.

It is important to note that many of the disadvantages of file processing we have mentioned can also be limitations of databases if an organization does not properly apply the database approach. For example, if an organization develops many separately managed databases (say, one for each division or business function) with little or no coordination of the metadata, then uncontrolled data duplication, limited data sharing, lengthy development time, and excessive program maintenance can occur. Thus, the database approach, which is explained in the next section, is as much a way to manage organizational data as it is a set of technologies for defining, creating, maintaining, and using these data.

THE DATABASE APPROACH

So, how do we overcome the flaws of file processing? No, we don't call Ghostbusters, but we do something better: We follow the database approach. We first begin by defining some core concepts that are fundamental in understanding the database approach to managing data. We then describe how the database approach can overcome the limitations of the file processing approach.

Data Models

Data model
Graphical systems used to capture the nature and relationships among data.

Designing a database properly is fundamental to establishing a database that meets the needs of the users. **Data models** capture the nature of and relationships among data and are used at different levels of abstraction as a database is conceptualized and designed. The effectiveness and efficiency of a database is directly associated with the structure of the database. Various graphical systems exist that convey this structure and are used to produce data models that can be understood by end users, systems analysts, and database designers. Chapters 2 and 3 are devoted to developing your understanding of data modeling, as is Chapter 13, which addresses a different approach using object-oriented data modeling. A typical data model is made up entities, attributes, and relationships and the most common data modeling representation is the entity-relationship model. A brief description is presented below. More details will be forthcoming in Chapters 2 and 3.

Entity
A person, a place, an object, an event, or a concept in the user environment about which the organization wishes to maintain data.

ENTITIES Customers and orders are objects about which a business maintains information. They are referred to as "entities." An **entity** is like a noun in that it describes a person, a place, an object, an event, or a concept in the business environment for which information must be recorded and retained. CUSTOMER and ORDER are entities in Figure 1-3a. The data you are interested in capturing about the entity (e.g., Customer Name) is called an *attribute*. Data are recorded for many customers. Each customer's information is referred to as an *instance* of CUSTOMER.

RELATIONSHIPS A well-structured database establishes the *relationships* between entities that exist in organizational data so that desired information can be retrieved. Most relationships are one-to-many (*1:M*) or many-to-many (*M:N*). A customer can place (the Places relationship) more than one order with a company. However, each order is usually associated with (the Is Placed By relationship) a particular customer. Figure 1-3a shows the *1:M* relationship of customers who may place one or more orders; the *1:M* nature of the relationship is marked by the crow's foot attached to the rectangle (entity) labeled ORDER. This relationship appears to be the same in Figures 1-3a and 1-3b. However, the relationship between orders and products is *M:N*. An order may be for one or more products, and a product may be included on more than one order. It is worthwhile noting that Figure 1-3a is an enterprise-level model, where it is necessary to include only the higher-level relationships of customers, orders, and products. The project-level diagram shown in Figure 1-3b includes additional level of details, such as the further details of an order.

Relational Databases

Relational database
A database that represents data as a collection of tables in which all data relationships are represented by common values in related tables.

Relational databases establish the relationships between entities by means of common fields included in a file, called a relation. The relationship between a customer and the customer's order depicted in the data models in Figure 1-3 is established by including the customer number with the customer's order. Thus, a customer's identification number is included in the file (or relation) that holds customer information such as name, address, and so forth. Every time the customer places an order, the customer

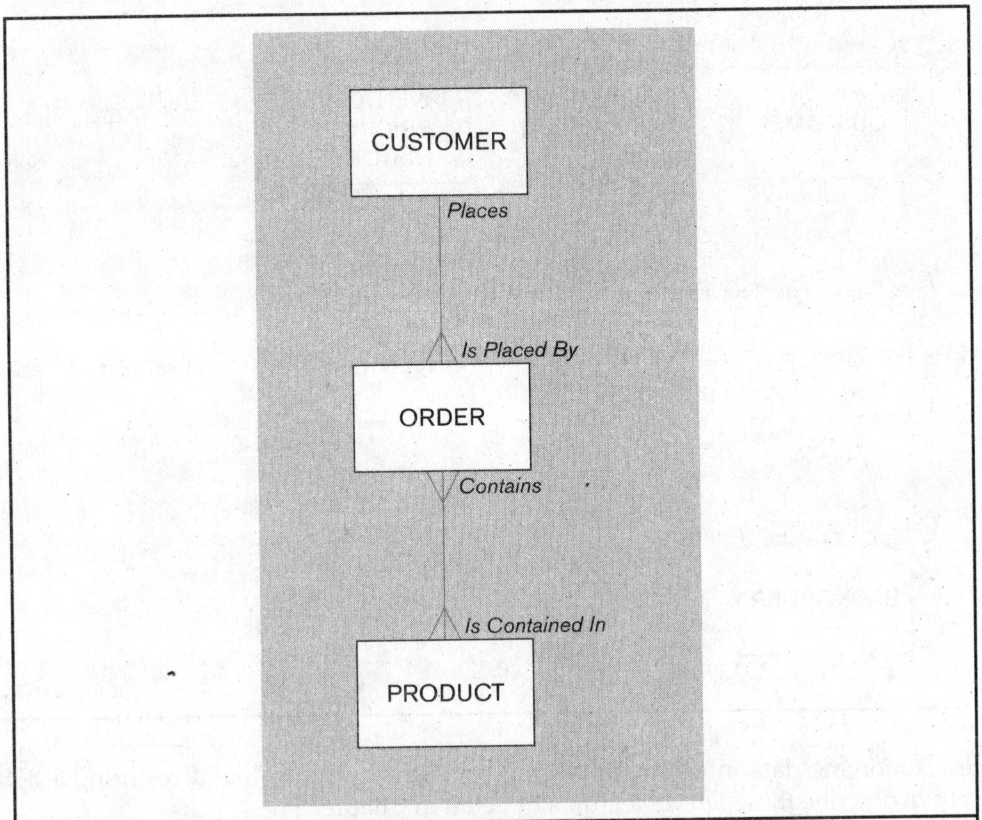

FIGURE 1-3 Comparison of enterprise and project level data models
(a) Segment of an enterprise data model

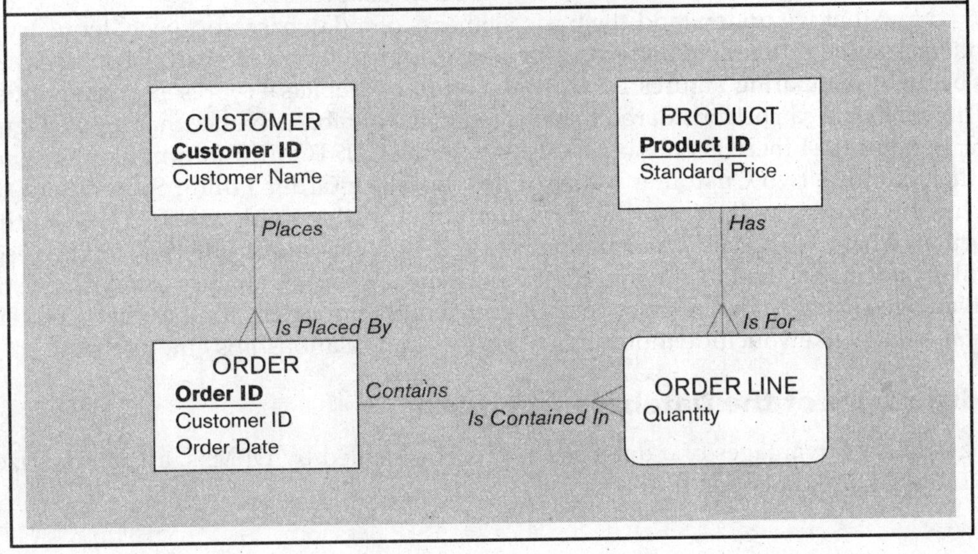

(b) Segment of a project data model

identification number is also included in the relation that holds order information. Relational databases use the identification number to establish the relationship between customer and order.

Database Management Systems

A **database management system (DBMS)** is a software system that enables the use of a database approach. The primary purpose of a DBMS is to provide a systematic method of creating, updating, storing, and retrieving the data stored in a database. It enables end users and application programmers to share data, and it enables data to be shared among multiple applications rather than propagated and stored in new files for every new application (Mullins, 2002). A DBMS also provides facilities for controlling data

Database management system (DBMS)
A software system that is used to create, maintain, and provide controlled access to user databases.

FIGURE 1-4 Enterprise model for Figure 1-3 segments

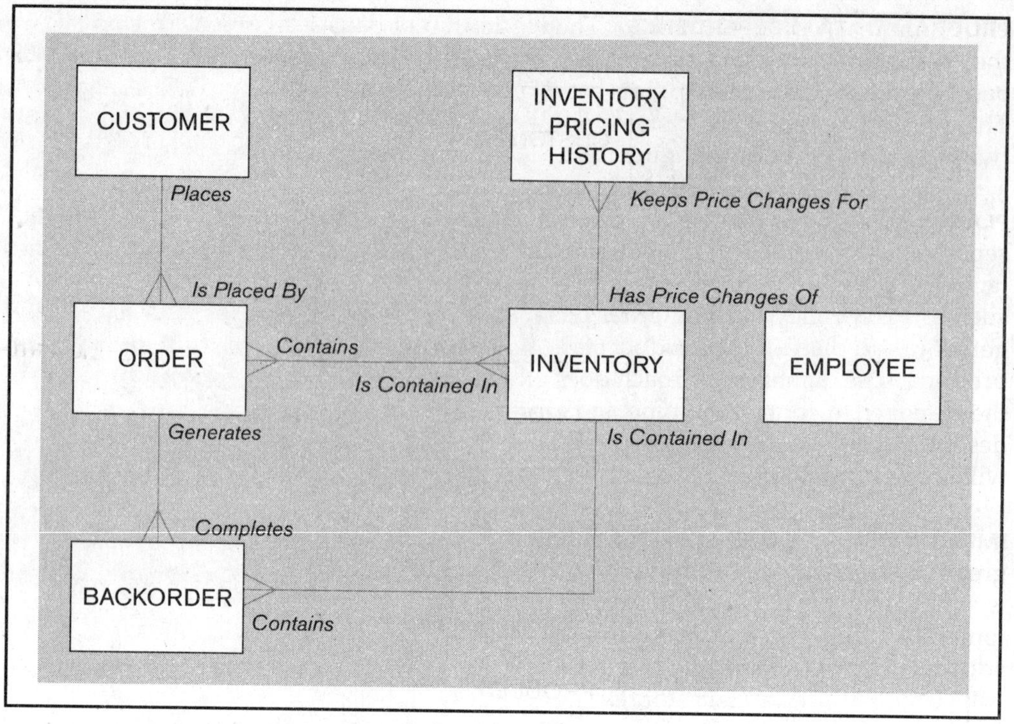

access, enforcing data integrity, managing concurrency control, and restoring a database. We describe these DBMS features in detail in Chapter 11.

Now that we understand the basic elements of a database approach, let us try to understand the differences between a database approach and file-based approach. Let us begin by comparing Figures 1-2 and 1-4. Figure 1-4 depicts a representation (entities) of how the data can be considered to be stored in the database. Notice that unlike Figure 1-2, in Figure 1-4 there is only one place where the CUSTOMER information is stored rather than the two Customer Master Files. Both the Order Filling System and the Invoicing System will access the data contained in the single CUSTOMER entity. Further, what CUSTOMER information is stored, how it is stored and how it is accessed is likely not closely tied to either of the two systems. All of this enables us to achieve the advantages listed in the next section. Of course, it is important to note that a real life database will likely include thousands of entities and relationships among them.

Advantages of the Database Approach

The primary advantages of a database approach, enabled by DBMSs, are summarized in Table 1-3 and described next.

TABLE 1-3 Advantages of the Database Approach
Program-data independence
Planned data redundancy
Improved data consistency
Improved data sharing
Increased productivity of application development
Enforcement of standards
Improved data quality
Improved data accessibility and responsiveness
Reduced program maintenance
Improved decision support

PROGRAM-DATA INDEPENDENCE The separation of data descriptions (metadata) from the application programs that use the data is called **data independence**. With the database approach, data descriptions are stored in a central location called the *repository*. This property of database systems allows an organization's data to change and evolve (within limits) without changing the application programs that process the data.

Data independence
The separation of data descriptions from the application programs that use the data.

PLANNED DATA REDUNDANCY Good database design attempts to integrate previously separate (and redundant) data files into a single, logical structure. Ideally, each primary fact is recorded in only one place in the database. For example, facts about a product, such as Pine Valley oak computer desk, its finish, price, and so forth are recorded together in one place in the Product table, which contains data about each of Pine Valley's products. The database approach does not eliminate redundancy entirely, but it enables the designer to control the type and amount of redundancy. At other times it may be desirable to include some limited redundancy to improve database performance, as we will see in later chapters.

IMPROVED DATA CONSISTENCY By eliminating or controlling data redundancy, we greatly reduce the opportunities for inconsistency. For example, if a customer's address is stored only once, we cannot disagree about the customer's address. When the customer's address changes, recording the new address is greatly simplified because the address is stored in a single place. Finally, we avoid the wasted storage space that results from redundant data storage.

IMPROVED DATA SHARING A database is designed as a shared corporate resource. Authorized internal and external users are granted permission to use the database, and each user (or group of users) is provided one or more user views into the database to facilitate this use. A **user view** is a logical description of some portion of the database that is required by a user to perform some task. A user view is often developed by identifying a form or report that the user needs on a regular basis. For example, an employee working in human resources will need access to confidential employee data; a customer needs access to the product catalog available on Pine Valley's Web site. The views for the human resources employee and the customer are drawn from completely different areas of one unified database.

User view
A logical description of some portion of the database that is required by a user to perform some task.

INCREASED PRODUCTIVITY OF APPLICATION DEVELOPMENT A major advantage of the database approach is that it greatly reduces the cost and time for developing new business applications. There are three important reasons that database applications can often be developed much more rapidly than conventional file applications:

1. Assuming that the database and the related data capture and maintenance applications have already been designed and implemented, the application developer can concentrate on the specific functions required for the new application, without having to worry about file design or low-level implementation details.
2. The database management system provides a number of high-level productivity tools, such as forms and report generators, and high-level languages that automate some of the activities of database design and implementation. We describe many of these tools in subsequent chapters.
3. Significant improvement in application developer productivity, estimated to be as high as 60 percent (Long, 2005), is currently being realized through the use of Web services, based on the use of standard Internet protocols and a universally accepted data format (XML). Web services and XML are covered in Chapter 8.

ENFORCEMENT OF STANDARDS When the database approach is implemented with full management support, the database administration function should be granted single-point authority and responsibility for establishing and enforcing data standards. These standards will include naming conventions, data quality standards, and uniform procedures for accessing, updating, and protecting data. The data repository provides database administrators with a powerful set of tools for developing and enforcing these standards. Unfortunately, the failure to implement a strong database administration function is perhaps the most common source of database failures in organizations. We describe the database administration (and related data administration) functions in Chapter 11.

IMPROVED DATA QUALITY Concern with poor quality data is a common theme in strategic planning and database administration today. In fact, a recent report by The Data Warehousing Institute (TDWI) estimated that data quality problems currently cost U.S. businesses some $600 billion each year (**www.tdwi.org/research/display.asp?ID=6589**). The database approach provides a number of tools and processes to improve data quality. Two of the more important are the following:

Constraint
A rule that cannot be violated by database users.

1. Database designers can specify integrity constraints that are enforced by the DBMS. A **constraint** is a rule that cannot be violated by database users. We describe numerous types of constraints (also called "business rules") in Chapters 2 and 3. If a customer places an order, the constraint that ensures that the customer and the order remain associated is called a "relational integrity constraint," and it prevents an order from being entered without specifying who placed the order.
2. One of the objectives of a data warehouse environment is to clean up (or "scrub") operational data before they are placed in the data warehouse (Jordan, 1996). Do you ever receive multiple copies of a catalog? The company that sends you three copies of each of its mailings could recognize significant postage and printing savings if its data were scrubbed, and its understanding of its customers would also be enhanced if it could determine a more accurate count of existing customers. We describe data warehouses in Chapter 9 and the potential for improving data quality in Chapter 10.

IMPROVED DATA ACCESSIBILITY AND RESPONSIVENESS With a relational database, end users without programming experience can often retrieve and display data, even when it crosses traditional departmental boundaries. For example, an employee can display information about computer desks at Pine Valley Furniture Company with the following query:

```
SELECT *
FROM Product_T
WHERE ProductDescription = "Computer Desk";
```

The language used in this query is called Structured Query Language, or SQL. (You will study this language in detail in Chapters 6 and 7.) Although the queries constructed can be *much* more complex, the basic structure of the query is easy for even novice, nonprogrammers to grasp. If they understand the structure and names of the data that fit within their view of the database, they soon gain the ability to retrieve answers to new questions without having to rely on a professional application developer. This can be dangerous; queries should be thoroughly tested to be sure they are returning accurate data before relying on their results, and novices may not understand that challenge.

REDUCED PROGRAM MAINTENANCE Stored data must be changed frequently for a variety of reasons: new data item types are added, data formats are changed, and so on. A celebrated example of this problem was the well-known "year 2000" problem, in which common two-digit year fields were extended to four digits to accommodate the rollover from the year 1999 to the year 2000.

In a file processing environment, the data descriptions and the logic for accessing data are built into individual application programs (this is the program-data dependence issue described earlier). As a result, changes to data formats and access methods inevitably result in the need to modify application programs. In a database environment, data are more independent of the application programs that use them. Within limits, we can change either the data or the application programs that use the data without necessitating a change in the other factor. As a result, program maintenance can be significantly reduced in a modern database environment.

IMPROVED DECISION SUPPORT Some databases are designed expressly for decision support applications. For example, some databases are designed to support customer relationship management, whereas others are designed to support financial analysis or supply chain management. You will study how databases are tailored for different decision support applications and analytical styles in Chapter 9.

Cautions About Database Benefits

The previous section identified 10 major potential benefits of the database approach. However, we must caution you that many organizations have been frustrated in attempting to realize some of these benefits. For example, the goal of data independence (and, therefore, reduced program maintenance) has proven elusive due to the limitations of older data models and database management software. Fortunately, the relational model and the newer object-oriented model provide a significantly better environment for achieving these benefits. Another reason for failure to achieve the intended benefits is poor organizational planning and database implementation; even the best data management software cannot overcome such deficiencies. For this reason, we stress database planning and design throughout this text.

TABLE 1-4 Costs and Risks of the Database Approach

New, specialized personnel
Installation and management cost and complexity
Conversion costs
Need for explicit backup and recovery
Organizational conflict

Costs and Risks of the Database Approach

A database is not a silver bullet, and it does not have the magic power of Harry Potter. As with any other business decision, the database approach entails some additional costs and risks that must be recognized and managed when it is implemented (see Table 1-4).

NEW, SPECIALIZED PERSONNEL Frequently, organizations that adopt the database approach need to hire or train individuals to design and implement databases, provide database administration services, and manage a staff of new people. Further, because of the rapid changes in technology, these new people will have to be retrained or upgraded on a regular basis. This personnel increase may be more than offset by other productivity gains, but an organization should recognize the need for these specialized skills, which are required to obtain the most from the potential benefits. We discuss the staff requirements for database management in Chapter 11.

INSTALLATION AND MANAGEMENT COST AND COMPLEXITY A multiuser database management system is a large and complex suite of software that has a high initial cost, requires a staff of trained personnel to install and operate, and has substantial annual maintenance and support costs. Installing such a system may also require upgrades to the hardware and data communications systems in the organization. Substantial training is normally required on an ongoing basis to keep up with new releases and upgrades. Additional or more sophisticated and costly database software may be needed to provide security and to ensure proper concurrent updating of shared data.

CONVERSION COSTS The term *legacy system* is widely used to refer to older applications in an organization that are based on file processing and/or older database technology. The cost of converting these older systems to modern database technology—measured in terms of dollars, time, and organizational commitment—may often seem prohibitive to an organization. The use of data warehouses is one strategy for continuing to use older systems while at the same time exploiting modern database technology and techniques (Ritter, 1999).

NEED FOR EXPLICIT BACKUP AND RECOVERY A shared corporate database must be accurate and available at all times. This requires that comprehensive procedures be developed and used for providing backup copies of data and for restoring a database when damage occurs. These considerations have acquired increased urgency in today's security-conscious environment. A modern database management system normally automates many more of the backup and recovery tasks than a file system. We describe procedures for security, backup, and recovery in Chapter 11.

ORGANIZATIONAL CONFLICT A shared database requires a consensus on data definitions and ownership, as well as responsibilities for accurate data maintenance. Experience has shown that conflicts on data definitions, data formats and coding, rights to update shared data, and associated issues are frequent and often difficult to resolve. Handling these issues requires organizational commitment to the database approach, organizationally astute database administrators, and a sound evolutionary approach to database development.

If strong top management support of and commitment to the database approach is lacking, end-user development of stand-alone databases is likely to proliferate. These databases do not follow the general database approach that we have described, and they are unlikely to provide the benefits described earlier. In the extreme, they may lead to a pattern of inferior decision making that threatens the well-being or existence of an organization.

COMPONENTS OF THE DATABASE ENVIRONMENT

Now that you have seen the advantages and risks of using the database approach to managing data, let us examine the major components of a typical database environment and their relationships (see Figure 1-5). You have already been introduced to some (but not all) of these components in previous sections. Following is a brief description of the nine components shown in Figure 1-5:

Computer-aided software engineering (CASE) tools
Software tools that provide automated support for some portion of the systems development process.

Repository
A centralized knowledge base of all data definitions, data relationships, screen and report formats, and other system components.

1. ***Computer-aided software engineering (CASE) tools*** **CASE tools** are automated tools used to design databases and application programs. These tools help with creation of data models and in some cases can also help automatically generate the "code" needed to create the database. We reference the use of automated tools for database design and development throughout the text.
2. ***Repository*** A **repository** is a centralized knowledge base for all data definitions, data relationships, screen and report formats, and other system components. A repository contains an extended set of metadata important for managing databases as well as other components of an information system. We describe the repository in Chapter 11.

FIGURE 1-5 Components of the database environment

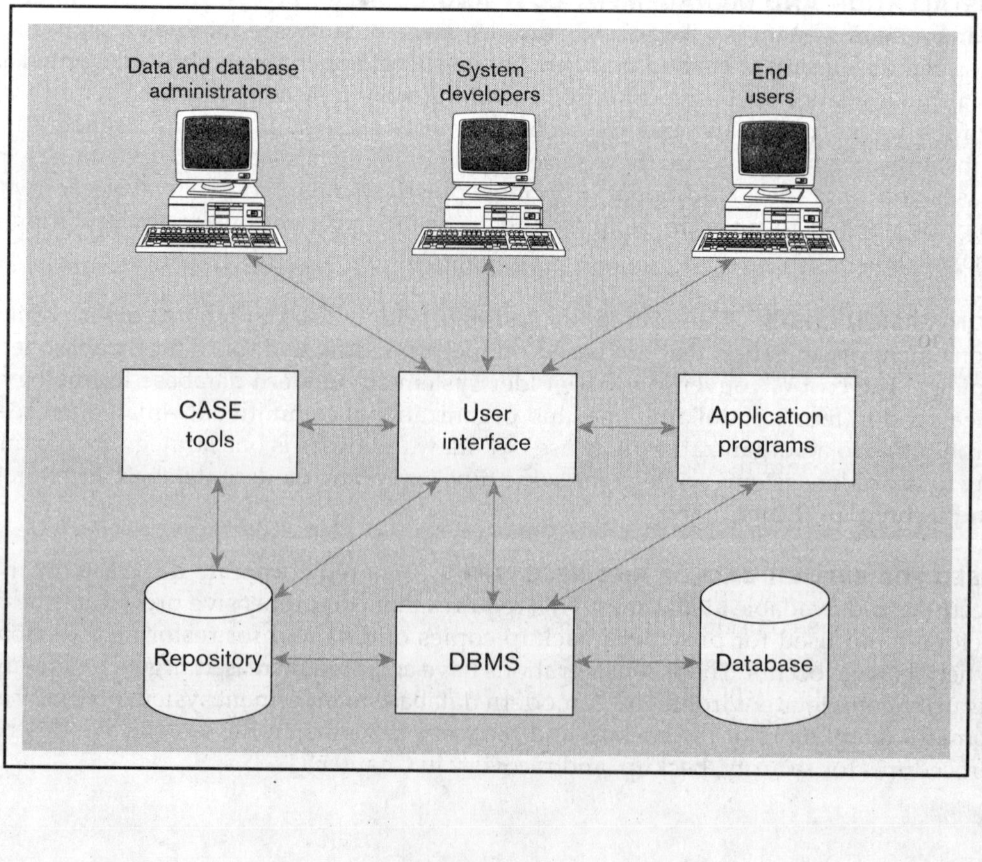

3. ***DBMS*** A DBMS is a software system that is used to create, maintain, and provide controlled access to user databases. We describe the functions of a DBMS in Chapter 11.
4. ***Database*** A database is an organized collection of logically related data, usually designed to meet the information needs of multiple users in an organization. It is important to distinguish between the database and the repository. The repository contains definitions of data, whereas the database contains occurrences of data. We describe the activities of database design in Chapters 4 and 5 and of implementation in Chapters 6 through 9.
5. ***Application programs*** Computer-based application programs are used to create and maintain the database and provide information to users. Key database-related application programming skills are described in Chapters 6 through 9 and Chapter 14.
6. ***User interface*** The user interface includes languages, menus, and other facilities by which users interact with various system components, such as CASE tools, application programs, the DBMS, and the repository. User interfaces are illustrated throughout this text.
7. ***Data and database administrators*** Data administrators are persons who are responsible for the overall management of data resources in an organization. Database administrators are responsible for physical database design and for managing technical issues in the database environment. We describe these functions in detail in Chapter 11.
8. ***System developers*** System developers are persons such as systems analysts and programmers who design new application programs. System developers often use CASE tools for system requirements analysis and program design.
9. ***End users*** End users are persons throughout the organization who add, delete, and modify data in the database and who request or receive information from it. All user interactions with the database must be routed through the DBMS.

In summary, the database operational environment shown in Figure 1-5 is an integrated system of hardware, software, and people, designed to facilitate the storage, retrieval, and control of the information resource and to improve the productivity of the organization.

THE RANGE OF DATABASE APPLICATIONS

What can databases help us do? Figure 1-5 shows that there are several methods for people to interact with the data in the database. First, users can interact directly with the database using the user interface provided by the DBMS. In this manner users can issues commands (called *queries*) against the database and examine the results or potentially even store this inside a Microsoft Excel spreadsheet or Word document. This method of interaction with the database is referred to ad-hoc querying and requires a level of understanding the query language on the part of the user.

Because most business users do not possess this level of knowledge, the second and more common mechanism for accessing the database is using application programs. An application program consists of two key components. A graphical user interface that is used to accept the users' request (e.g., to input, delete, or modify data) and/or provide a mechanism for displaying the data retrieved from the database. The business logic contains the programming logic necessary to act on the users' commands. The machine that runs the user interface (and sometimes the business logic) is referred to as the client. The machine the runs the DBMS and contains the database is referred to as the *database server*.

It is important to understand that the applications and the database need not to reside on the same computer (and, in most cases, they don't). In order to better understand the range of database applications, we divide them into three categories, based on the location of the client (application) and the database software itself: personal, two-tier, and multitier databases. We introduce each category with a typical example, followed by some issues that generally arise within that category of use.

Personal Databases

Personal databases are designed to support one user. Personal databases have long resided on personal computers (PCs), including laptops, and increasingly on smartphones and PDAs. The purpose of these databases is to provide the user with ability to manage (store, update, delete, and retrieve) small amounts of data in an efficient manner. Simple database applications that store customer information and the details of contacts with each customer can be used from a PC and easily transferred from one device to the other for backup and work purposes. For example, consider a company that has a number of salespersons who call on actual or prospective customers. A database of customers and a pricing application can enable the salesperson to determine the best combination of quantity and type of items for the customer to order.

Personal databases are widely used because they can often improve personal productivity. However, they entail a risk: The data cannot easily be shared with other users. For example, suppose the sales manager wants a consolidated view of customer contacts. This cannot be quickly or easily provided from an individual salesperson's databases. This illustrates a very common problem: If data are of interest to one person, they probably are or will soon become of interest to others as well. For this reason, personal databases should be limited to those rather special situations (e.g., in a very small organization) where the need to share the data among users of the personal database is unlikely to arise.

Two-Tier Client/Server Databases

As noted above, the utility of a personal (single-user) database is quite limited. Often, what starts off as a single-user database evolves into something that needs to be shared among several users. A workgroup is a relatively small team of people (typically fewer than 25 persons) who collaborate on the same project or application or on a group of similar projects or applications. These persons might be engaged (for example) with a construction project or with developing a new computer application and need to share data amongst the group.

The most common method of sharing data for this type of need is based on creating a two-tier client/server application as shown in Figure 1-6. Each member of the workgroup has a computer, and the computers are linked by means of network (wired or wireless LAN). In most cases, each computer has a copy of a specialized application (client) which provides the user interface as well as the business logic through which the data is manipulated. The database itself and the DBMS are stored on a central device

FIGURE 1-6 Two-tier database with local area network

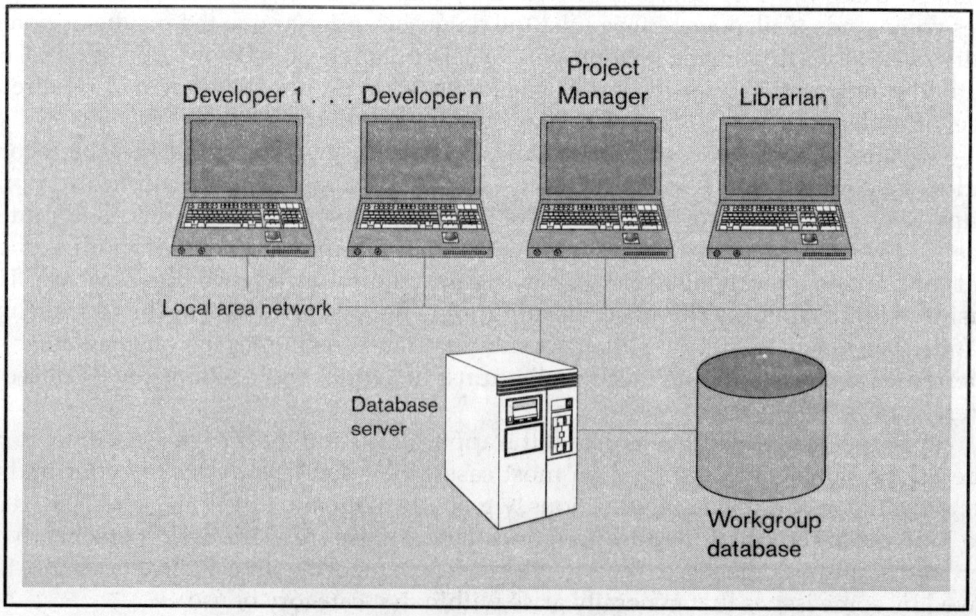

called the "database server," which is also connected to the network. Thus, each member of the workgroup has access to the shared data. Different types of group members (e.g., developer or project manager) may have different user views of this shared database. This arrangement overcomes the principal objection to PC databases, which is that the data are not easily shared. This arrangement, however, introduces many data management issues not present with personal (single-user) databases, such as data security and data integrity when multiple users attempt to change and update data at the same time.

Multitier Client/Server Databases

One of the drawbacks of the two-tier database architecture is that the amount of functionality that needs to be programmed into the application on the users' computer can be pretty significant because it needs to contain both the user interface logic as well as the business logic. This, of course, means that the client computers need to be powerful enough to handle the programmed application. Another drawback is that each time there is a change to either the business logic or user interface, each client computer that has the application needs to be updated.

To overcome these limitations, most modern applications that need to support a large number of users are built using the concept of multitiered architecture. In most organizations, these applications are intended to support a department (such as marketing or accounting) or a division (such as a line of business), which is generally larger than a workgroup (typically between 25 and 100 persons).

An example of a company that has several multitier applications is shown in Figure 1-7. In a three-tiered architecture, the user interface is accessible on the individual users' computer. This user interface may either be Web browser based or written using programming languages such as Visual Basic.NET, Visual C#, or Java. The application layer/Web server layer contains the business logic required to accomplish the business transactions requested by the users. This layer in turn talks to the database server. The

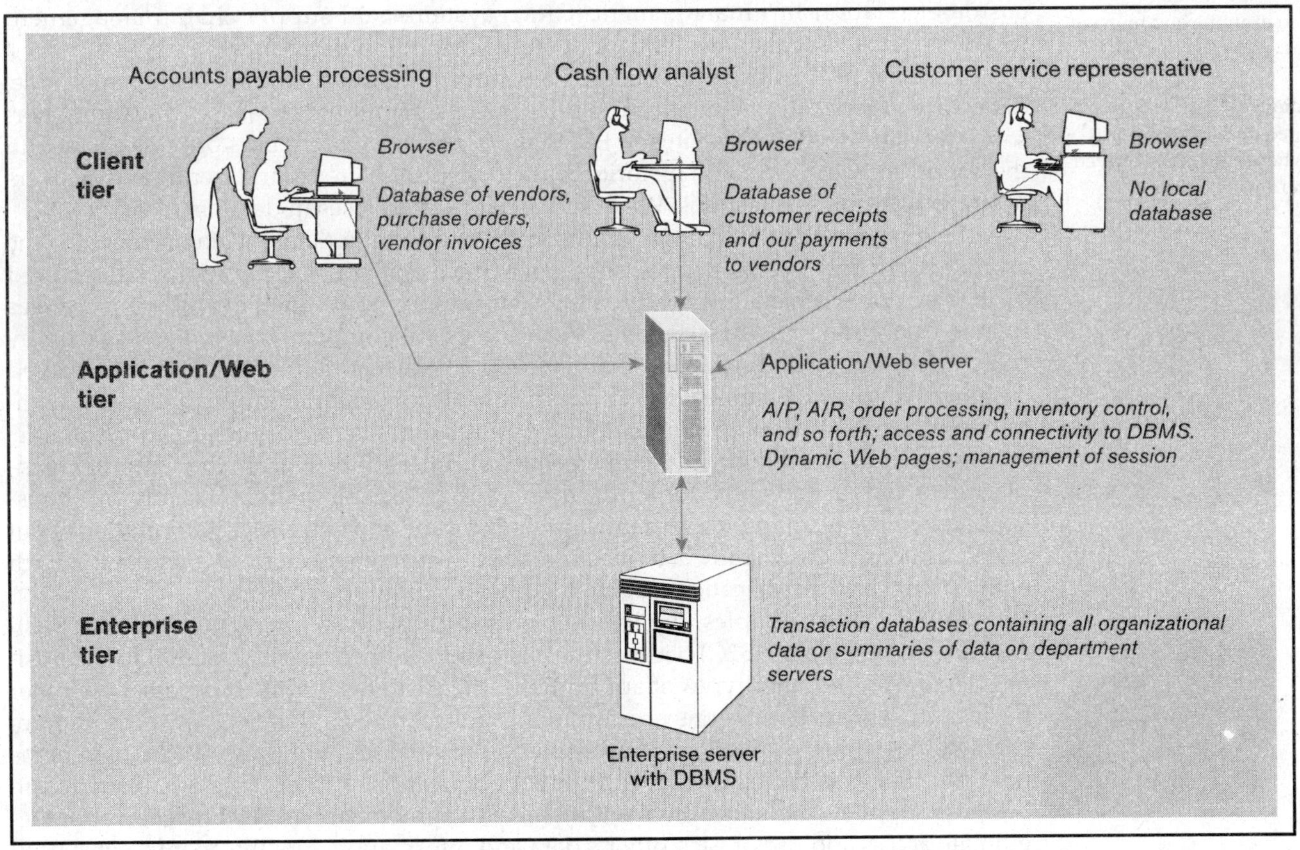

FIGURE 1-7 Three-tiered client/server database architecture

most significant implication for database development from the use of multitier client/server architectures is the ease of separating the development of the database and the modules that maintain the data from the information systems modules that focus on business logic and/or presentation logic. In addition, this architecture allows us to improve performance and maintainability of the application and database. We will consider both two and multitier client/server architectures in more detail in Chapter 8.

Enterprise Applications

An enterprise (that's small "e", not capital "E," as in *Starship*) application/database is one whose scope is the entire organization or enterprise (or, at least, many different departments). Such databases are intended to support organization-wide operations and decision making. Note that an organization may have several enterprise databases, so such a database is not inclusive of all organizational data. A single operational enterprise database is impractical for many medium to large organizations due to difficulties in performance for very large databases, diverse needs of different users, and the complexity of achieving a single definition of data (metadata) for all database users. An enterprise database does, however, support information needs from many departments and divisions. The evolution of enterprise databases has resulted in two major developments:

1. Enterprise resource planning (ERP) systems
2. Data warehousing implementations

Enterprise resource planning (ERP)
A business management system that integrates all functions of the enterprise, such as manufacturing, sales, finance, marketing, inventory, accounting, and human resources. ERP systems are software applications that provide the data necessary for the enterprise to examine and manage its activities.

Data warehouse
An integrated decision support database whose content is derived from the various operational databases.

Enterprise resource planning (ERP) systems have evolved from the material requirements planning (MRP) and manufacturing resource planning (MRP-II) systems of the 1970s and 1980s. These systems scheduled the raw materials, components, and subassembly requirements for manufacturing processes, and also scheduled shop floor and product distribution activities. Next, extension to the remaining business functions resulted in enterprise-wide management systems, or ERP systems. All ERP systems are heavily dependent on databases to store the integrated data required by the ERP applications. In addition to ERP systems, there are several specialized applications, such as customer relationship management (CRM) systems and supply chain management (SCM) systems, that also are dependent on data stored in databases.

Whereas ERP systems work with the current operational data of the enterprise, **data warehouses** collect content from the various operational databases, including personal, workgroup, department, and ERP databases. Data warehouses provide users with the opportunity to work with historical data to identify patterns and trends and answers to strategic business questions. We describe data warehouses in detail in Chapter 9.

Finally, one change that has dramatically affected the database environment is the ascendance of the Internet, and the subsequent development of applications that are used by the masses. Acceptance of the Internet by businesses has resulted in important changes in long-established business models. Very successful companies have been shaken by competition from new businesses that have employed the Internet to provide improved customer information and service, to eliminate traditional marketing channels and distribution channels, and to implement employee relationship management. For example, customers configure and order their personal computers directly from the computer manufacturers. Bids are accepted for airline tickets and collectables within seconds of submission, sometimes resulting in substantial savings for the end consumer. Information about open positions and company activities is readily available within many companies. Each of these Web-based applications highlighted use databases extensively.

In the above examples, the Internet is used to facilitate interaction between business and the customer (B2C) because the customers are necessarily external to the business However, for other types of applications, the customers of the businesses are other businesses. Those interactions are commonly referred to as B2B relationships and are enabled by extranets. An extranet uses Internet technology, but access to the extranet is not universal as is the case with an Internet application. Rather, access is restricted to business suppliers and customers with whom an agreement has been reached about legitimate access and use of each other's data and information. Finally, an intranet is used by employees' of the firm to access applications and databases within the company.

TABLE 1-5 Summary of Database Applications

Type of Database / Application	Typical Number of Users	Typical Size of Database
Personal	1	Megabytes
Two-tier	5–100	Megabytes–gigabytes
Three-tier	100–1000	Gigabytes
Enterprise resource planning	>100	Gigabytes–terabytes
Data warehousing	>100	Terabytes–petabytes

Allowing such access to a business database raises data security and integrity issues that are new to the management of information systems, where data have traditionally been closely guarded and secured within each company. These issues are covered in more detail in Chapters 8 and 10.

Table 1-5 presents a brief summary of the different types of databases outlined in this section.

EVOLUTION OF DATABASE SYSTEMS

Database management systems were first introduced during the 1960s and have continued to evolve during subsequent decades. Figure 1-8a sketches this evolution by highlighting the database technology (or technologies) that were dominant during each decade. In most cases, the period of introduction was quite long, and the technology was first introduced during the decade preceding the one shown in the figure. For example, the relational model was first defined by E. F. Codd, an IBM research fellow, in a paper published in 1970 (Codd, 1970). However, the relational model did not realize widespread commercial success until the 1980s. For example, the challenge of the 1970s where programmers needed to write complex programs to access data was addressed by the introduction of the Structured Query Language (SQL) in the 1980s.

Figure 1-8b shows a visual depiction of the organizing principle underlying each of the major database technologies. For example, in the hierarchical model, files are organized in a top-down structure that resembles a tree or genealogy chart, whereas in the network model, each file can be associated with an arbitrary number of other files. The relational model (the primary focus of this book) organizes data in the form of tables and relationships among them. The object-oriented model is based on object classes and relationships among them. As shown in Figure 1-8b, an object class encapsulates attributes and methods. Object-relational databases are a hybrid between object-oriented and relational databases. Finally, multidimensional databases, which form the basis for data warehouses, allow us to view data in the form of cubes or a star schema; we discuss this in more detail in Chapter 9. Database management systems were developed to overcome the limitations of file processing systems, described in a previous section. To summarize, some of the following four objectives generally drove the development and evolution of database technology:

1. The need to provide greater independence between programs and data, thereby reducing maintenance costs
2. The desire to manage increasingly complex data types and structures
3. The desire to provide easier and faster access to data for users who have neither a background in programming languages nor a detailed understanding of how data are stored in databases
4. The need to provide ever more powerful platforms for decision support applications

1960s

File processing systems were still dominant during this period. However, the first database management systems were introduced during this decade and were used

FIGURE 1-8 The range of database technologies: past and present

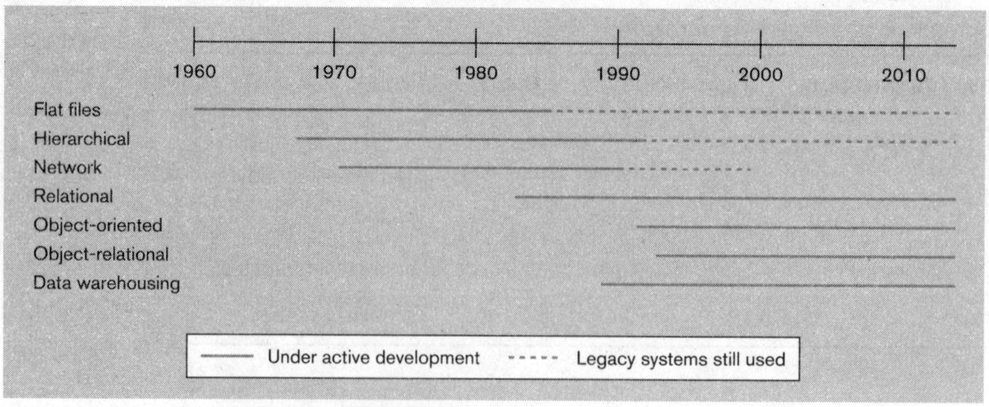

(a) Evolution of database technologies

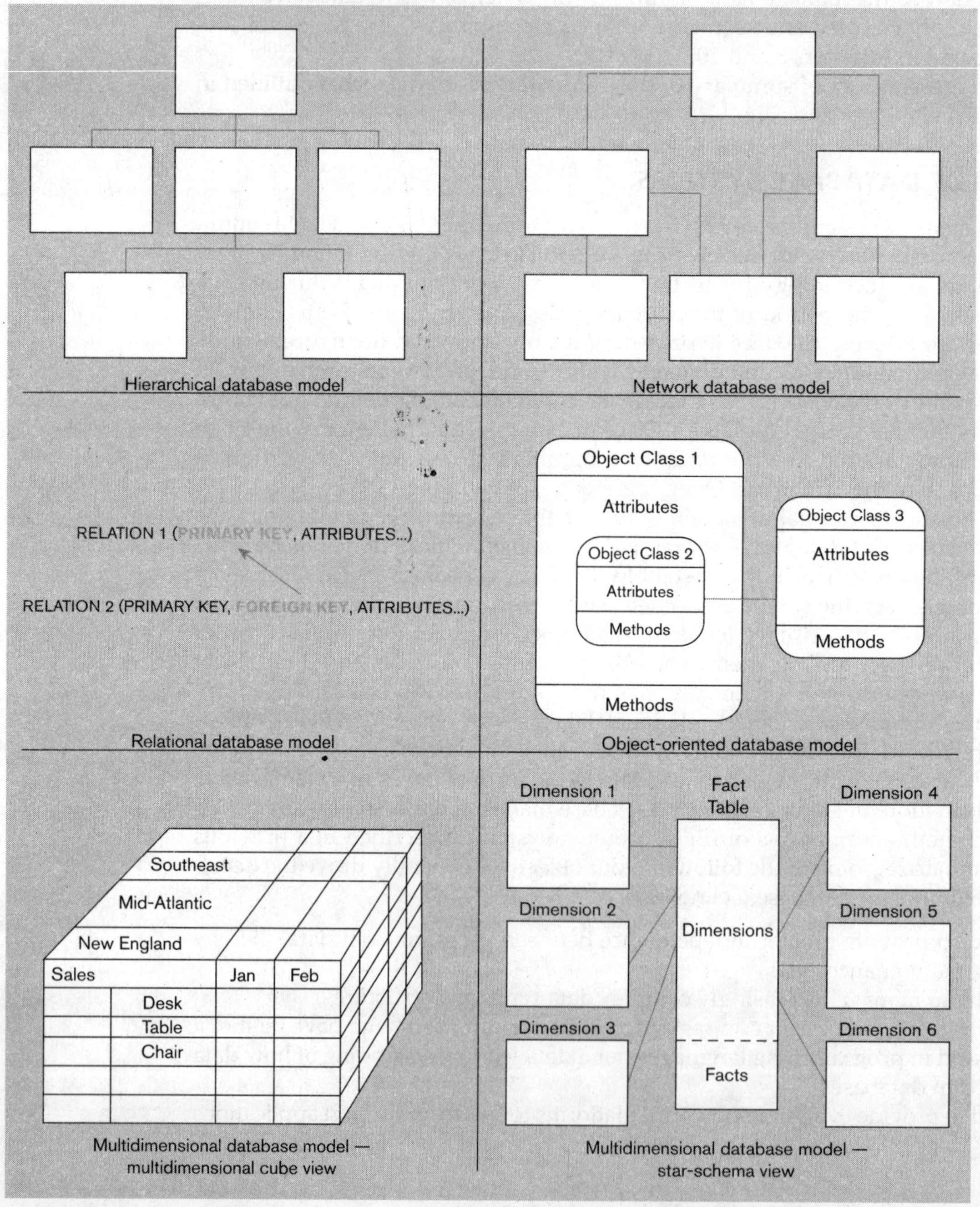

(b) Database architectures

primarily for large and complex ventures such as the Apollo moon-landing project. We can regard this as an experimental "proof-of-concept" period in which the feasibility of managing vast amounts of data with a DBMS was demonstrated. Also, the first efforts at standardization were taken with the formation of the Data Base Task Group in the late 1960s.

1970s

During this decade the use of database management systems became a commercial reality. The hierarchical and network database management systems were developed, largely to cope with increasingly complex data structures such as manufacturing bills of materials that were extremely difficult to manage with conventional file processing methods. The hierarchical and network models are generally regarded as first-generation DBMS. Both approaches were widely used, and in fact many of these systems continue to be used today. However, they suffered from the same key disadvantages as file processing systems: limited data independence and lengthy development times for application development.

1980s

To overcome these limitations, E. F. Codd and others developed the relational data model during the 1970s. This model, considered second-generation DBMS, received widespread commercial acceptance and diffused throughout the business world during the 1980s. With the relational model, all data are represented in the form of tables. Typically, SQL is used for data retrieval. Thus, the relational model provides ease of access for nonprogrammers, overcoming one of the major objections to first-generation systems. The relational model has also proven well suited to client/server computing, parallel processing, and graphical user interfaces (Gray, 1996).

1990s

The 1990s ushered in a new era of computing, first with client/server computing, and then with data warehousing and Internet applications becoming increasingly important. Whereas the data managed by a DBMS during the 1980s were largely structured (such as accounting data), multimedia data (including graphics, sound, images, and video) became increasingly common during the 1990s. To cope with these increasingly complex data, object-oriented databases (considered third generation) were introduced during the late 1980s (Grimes, 1998).

Because organizations must manage a vast amount of structured and unstructured data, both relational and object-oriented databases are of great importance today. In fact, some vendors are developing combined object-relational DBMSs that can manage both types of data. We describe object-relational databases in Chapter 13.

2000 and Beyond

Currently, the major type of database that is still most widely used is the relational database. However, object-oriented and object-relational databases are also garnering some attention, especially as the growth in unstructured content continues. This growth is partially fueled by Web 2.0 applications such as blogs, wikis, and social networking sites (Facebook, MySpace, Twitter, LinkedIn, etc.) and partially by how easy it has become to create unstructured data such as pictures and images. Developing effective database practices to deal with these diverse types of data is going to continue to be of prime importance as we move into the next decade. As larger computer memory chips become cheaper, new database technologies to manage in-memory databases are emerging. This trend opens up new possibilities for even faster database processing.

Recent regulations such as Sarbanes-Oxley, HIPAA, and the Basel Convention have highlighted the importance of good data management practices and the ability to reconstruct historical positions has gained prominence. This has led to developments in computer forensics with increased emphasis and expectations around discovery of electronic evidence. The importance of good database administration capabilities also continues to rise because effective disaster recovery and adequate security are mandated by these regulations.

THE DATABASE DEVELOPMENT PROCESS

Enterprise data modeling
The first step in database development, in which the scope and general contents of organizational databases are specified.

How do organizations start developing a database? In many organizations, database development begins with **enterprise data modeling**, which establishes the range and general contents of organizational databases. Its purpose is to create an overall picture or explanation of organizational data, not the design for a particular database. A particular database provides the data for one or more information systems, whereas an enterprise data model, which may encompass many databases, describes the scope of data maintained by the organization. In enterprise data modeling, you review current systems, analyze the nature of the business areas to be supported, describe the data needed at a very high level of abstraction, and plan one or more database development projects.

PINE VALLEY FURNITURE

Figure 1-3a showed a segment of an enterprise data model for Pine Valley Furniture Company, using a simplified version of the notation you will learn in Chapters 2 and 3. Besides such a graphical depiction of the entity types, a thorough enterprise data model would also include business-oriented descriptions of each entity type and a compendium of various statements about how the business operates, called business rules, which govern the validity of data. Relationships between business objects (business functions, units, applications, etc.) and data are often captured using matrixes and complement the information captured in the enterprise data model. Figure 1-9 shows an example of such a matrix.

Enterprise data modeling as a component of a top-down approach to information systems planning and development represents one source of database projects. Such projects often develop new databases to meet strategic organizational goals, such as improved customer support, better production and inventory management, or more accurate sales forecasting. Many database projects arise, however, in a more bottom-up fashion. In this case, projects are requested by information systems users, who need certain information to do their jobs, or from other information systems professionals, who see a need to improve data management in the organization.

A typical bottom-up database development project usually focuses on the creation of one database. Some database projects concentrate only on defining, designing, and implementing a database as a foundation for subsequent information systems development. In

FIGURE 1-9 Example business function-to-data entity matrix

Business Functions \ Data Entity Types	Customer	Product	Raw Material	Order	Work Center	Work Order	Invoice	Equipment	Employee
Business Planning	X	X						X	X
Product Development		X	X		X			X	
Materials Management		X	X	X	X	X		X	
Order Fulfillment	X	X	X	X	X	X	X	X	X
Order Shipment	X	X		X	X		X		X
Sales Summarization	X	X		X			X		X
Production Operations		X	X	X	X	X		X	X
Finance and Accounting	X	X	X	X	X		X	X	X

X = data entity is used within business function

most cases, however, a database and the associated information processing functions are developed together as part of a comprehensive information systems development project.

Systems Development Life Cycle

As you may know from other information systems courses you've taken, a traditional process for conducting an information systems development project is called the **systems development life cycle (SDLC)**. The SDLC is a complete set of steps that a team of information systems professionals, including database designers and programmers, follow in an organization to specify, develop, maintain, and replace information systems. Textbooks and organizations use many variations on the life cycle and may identify anywhere from 3 to 20 different phases.

Systems development life cycle (SDLC)
The traditional methodology used to develop, maintain, and replace information systems.

The various steps in the SDLC and their associated purpose are depicted in Figure 1-10 (Hoffer et al., 2010). The process appears to be circular and is intended to convey the iterative nature of systems development projects. The steps may overlap in time, they may be conducted in parallel, and it is possible to backtrack to previous steps

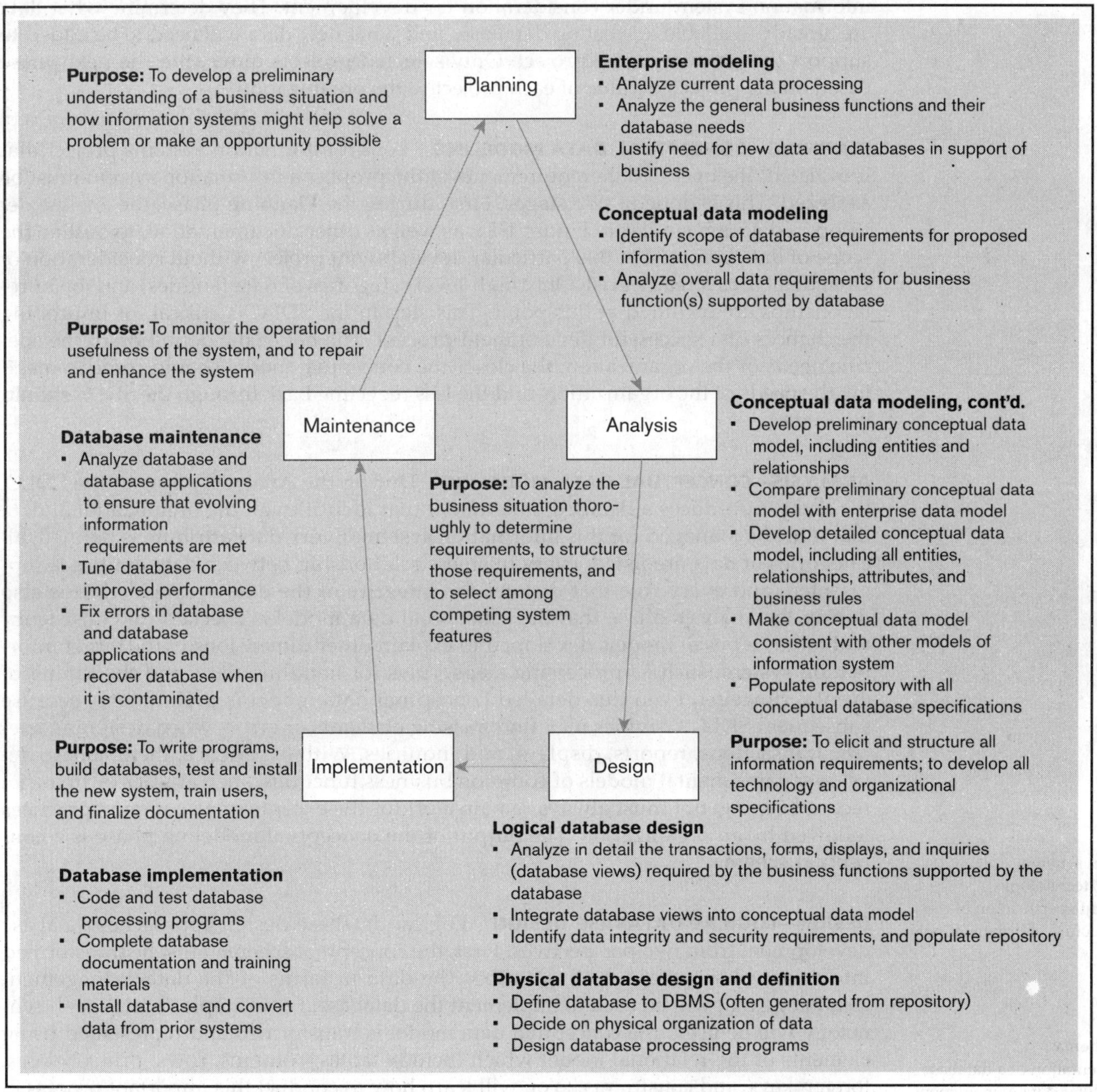

FIGURE 1-10 Database development activities during the systems development life cycle (SDLC)

when prior decisions need to be reconsidered. Some feel that the most common path through the development process is to cycle through the steps depicted in Figure 1-10, but at more detailed levels on each pass, as the requirements of the system become more concrete.

Figure 1-10 also provides an outline of the database development activities typically included in each phase of the SDLC. Note that there is not always a one-to-one correspondence between SDLC phases and database development steps. For example, conceptual data modeling occurs in both the Planning and the Analysis phases. We will briefly illustrate each of these database development steps for Pine Valley Furniture Company later in this chapter.

PLANNING—ENTERPRISE MODELING The database development process begins with a review of the enterprise modeling components that were developed during the information systems planning process. During this step, analysts review current databases and information systems, analyze the nature of the business area that is the subject of the development project, and describe, in very general terms, the data needed for each information system under consideration for development. They determine what data are already available in existing databases and what new data will need to be added to support the proposed new project. Only selected projects move into the next phase based on the projected value of each project to the organization.

PLANNING—CONCEPTUAL DATA MODELING For an information systems project that is initiated, the overall data requirements of the proposed information system must be analyzed. This is done in two stages. First, during the Planning phase, the analyst develops a diagram similar to Figure 1-3a, as well as other documentation, to outline the scope of data involved in this particular development project without consideration of what databases already exist. Only high-level categories of data (entities) and major relationships are included at this point. This step in the SDLC is critical for improving the chances of a successful development process. The better the definition of the specific needs of the organization, the closer the conceptual model should come to meeting the needs of the organization, and the less recycling back through the SDLC should be needed.

ANALYSIS—CONCEPTUAL DATA MODELING During the Analysis phase of the SDLC, the analyst produces a detailed data model that identifies all the organizational data that must be managed for this information system. Every data attribute is defined, all categories of data are listed, every business relationship between data entities is represented, and every rule that dictates the integrity of the data is specified. It is also during the analysis phase that the conceptual data model is checked for consistency with other types of models developed to explain other dimensions of the target information system, such as processing steps, rules for handling data, and the timing of events. However, even this detailed conceptual data model is preliminary, because subsequent SDLC activities may find missing elements or errors when designing specific transactions, reports, displays, and inquiries. With experience, the database developer gains mental models of common business functions, such as sales or financial record keeping, but must always remain alert for the exceptions to common practices followed by an organization. The output of the conceptual modeling phase is a **conceptual schema**.

Conceptual schema
A detailed, technology-independent specification of the overall structure of organizational data.

DESIGN—LOGICAL DATABASE DESIGN Logical database design approaches database development from two perspectives. First, the conceptual schema must be transformed into a logical schema, which describes the data in terms of the data management technology that will be used to implement the database. For example, if relational technology will be used, the conceptual data model is transformed and represented using elements of the relational model which include tables, columns, rows, primary keys, foreign keys, and constraints. (You will learn how to conduct this important process in Chapter 4.) This representation is referred to as the **logical schema**.

Logical schema
The representation of a database for a particular data management technology.

Then, as each application in the information system is designed, including the program's input and output formats, the analyst performs a detailed review of the transactions, reports, displays, and inquiries supported by the database. During this so-called bottom-up analysis, the analyst verifies exactly what data are to be maintained in the database and the nature of those data as needed for each transaction, report, and so forth. It may be necessary to refine the conceptual data model as each report, business transaction, and other user view is analyzed. In this case, one must combine, or integrate, the original conceptual data model along with these individual user views into a comprehensive design during logical database design. It is also possible that additional information processing requirements will be identified during logical information systems design, in which case these new requirements must be integrated into the previously identified logical database design.

The final step in logical database design is to transform the combined and reconciled data specifications into basic, or atomic, elements following well-established rules for well-structured data specifications. For most databases today, these rules come from relational database theory and a process called normalization, which we will describe in detail in Chapter 4. The result is a complete picture of the database without any reference to a particular database management system for managing these data. With a final logical database design in place, the analyst begins to specify the logic of the particular computer programs and queries needed to maintain and report the database contents.

DESIGN—PHYSICAL DATABASE DESIGN AND DEFINITION A **physical schema** is a set of specifications that describe how data from a logical schema are stored in a computer's secondary memory by a specific database management system. There is one physical schema for each logical schema. Physical database design requires knowledge of the specific DBMS that will be used to implement the database. In physical database design and definition, an analyst decides on the organization of physical records, the choice of file organizations, the use of indexes, and so on. To do this, a database designer needs to outline the programs to process transactions and to generate anticipated management information and decision-support reports. The goal is to design a database that will efficiently and securely handle all data processing against it. Thus, physical database design is done in close coordination with the design of all other aspects of the physical information system: programs, computer hardware, operating systems, and data communications networks.

Physical schema
Specifications for how data from a logical schema are stored in a computer's secondary memory by a database management system.

IMPLEMENTATION—DATABASE IMPLEMENTATION In database implementation, a designer writes, tests, and installs the programs/scripts that access, create, or modify the database. The designer might do this using standard programming languages (e.g., Java, C#, or Visual Basic.NET), in special database processing languages (e.g., SQL), or use special-purpose nonprocedural languages to produce stylized reports and displays, possibly including graphs. Also, during implementation, the designer will finalize all database documentation, train users, and put procedures into place for the ongoing support of the information system (and database) users. The last step is to load data from existing information sources (files and databases from legacy applications plus new data now needed). Loading is often done by first unloading data from existing files and databases into a neutral format (such as binary or text files) and then loading these data into the new database. Finally, the database and its associated applications are put into production for data maintenance and retrieval by the actual users. During production, the database should be periodically backed up and recovered in case of contamination or destruction.

MAINTENANCE—DATABASE MAINTENANCE The database evolves during database maintenance. In this step, the designer adds, deletes, or changes characteristics of the structure of a database in order to meet changing business conditions, to correct errors in database design, or to improve the processing speed of database applications. The designer might also need to rebuild a database if it becomes contaminated or destroyed due to a program or computer system malfunction. This is typically the longest step of database development, because it lasts throughout the life of the database and its associated applications. Each time the database evolves, view it as an abbreviated database development process in which conceptual data modeling, logical and physical database design, and database implementation occur to deal with proposed changes.

Alternative IS Development Approaches

The systems development life cycle or slight variations on it are often used to guide the development of information systems and databases. The SDLC is a methodical, highly structured approach, which includes many checks and balances to ensure that each step produces accurate results and the new or replacement information system is consistent with existing systems with which it must communicate or for which there needs to be consistent data definitions. Whew! That's a lot of work! Consequently, the SDLC is often criticized for the length of time needed until a working system is produced, which occurs only at the end of the process. Instead, organizations increasingly use rapid application development (RAD) methods, which follow an iterative process of rapidly repeating analysis, design, and implementation steps until they converge on the system the user wants. These RAD methods work best when most of the necessary database structures already exist, and hence for systems that primarily retrieve data, rather than for those that populate and revise databases.

Prototyping
An iterative process of systems development in which requirements are converted to a working system that is continually revised through close work between analysts and users.

One of the most popular RAD methods is **prototyping**, which is an iterative process of systems development in which requirements are converted to a working system that is continually revised through close work between analysts and users. Figure 1-11 shows the prototyping process. This figure includes annotations to indicate roughly which database development activities occur in each prototyping phase. Typically, you make only a very cursory attempt at conceptual data modeling when the information system problem is identified. During the development of the initial prototype, you simultaneously design the displays and reports the user wants while

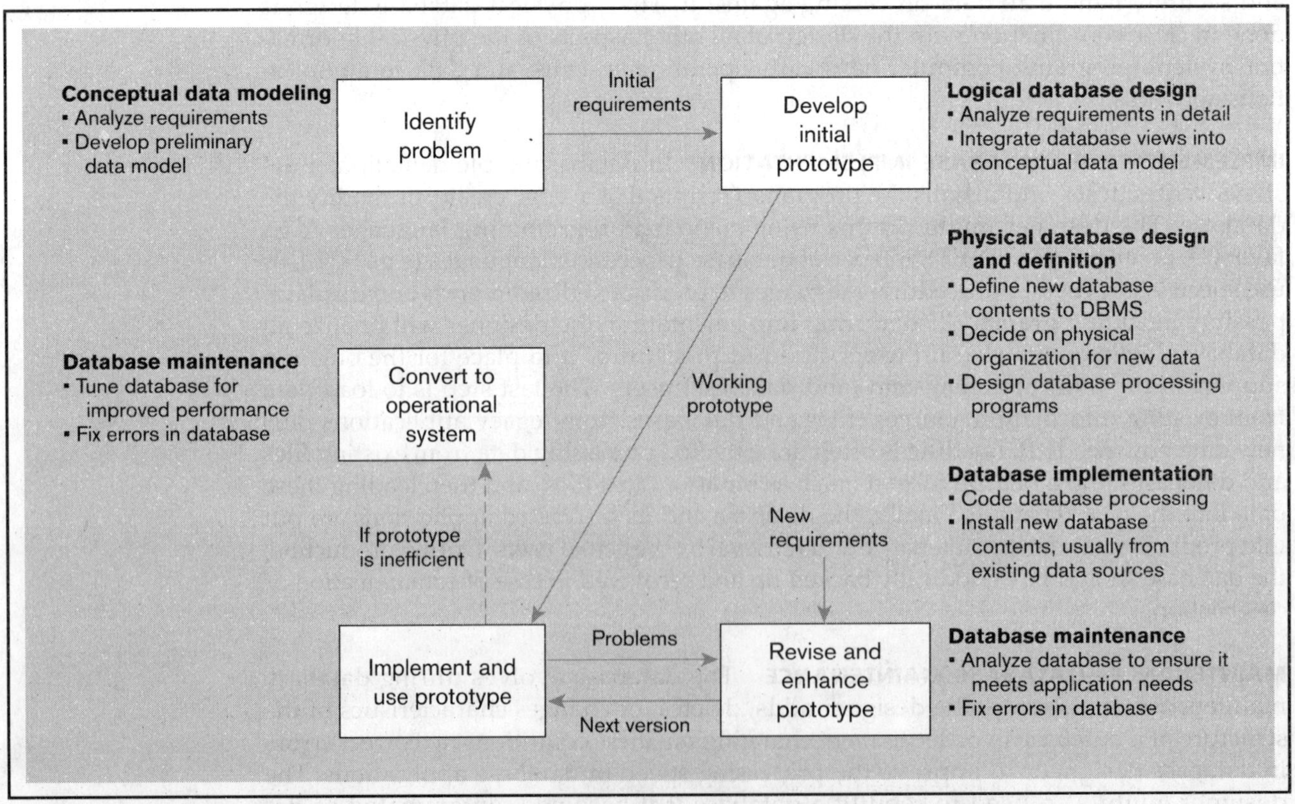

FIGURE 1-11 The prototyping methodology and database development process

understanding any new database requirements and defining a database to be used by the prototype. This is typically a new database, which is a copy of portions of existing databases, possibly with new content. If new content is required, it will usually come from external data sources, such as market research data, general economic indicators, or industry standards.

Database implementation and maintenance activities are repeated as new versions of the prototype are produced. Often security and integrity controls are minimal because the emphasis is on getting working prototype versions ready as quickly as possible. Also, documentation tends to be delayed until the end of the project, and user training occurs from hands-on use. Finally, after an accepted prototype is created, the developer and the user decide whether the final prototype, and its database, can be put into production as is. If the system, including the database, is too inefficient, the system and database might need to be reprogrammed and reorganized to meet performance expectations. Inefficiencies, however, have to be weighed against violating the core principles behind sound database design.

With the increasing popularity of visual programming tools (such as Visual Basic, Java, or C#) that make it easy to modify the interface between user and system, prototyping is becoming the systems development methodology of choice to develop new applications internally. With prototyping, it is relatively easy to change the content and layout of user reports and displays.

The benefits from iterative approaches to systems development demonstrated by RAD and prototyping approaches have resulted in further efforts to create ever more responsive development approaches. In February 2001, a group of 17 individuals interested in supporting these approaches and created "The Manifesto for Agile Software Development." For them, **agile software development** practices include valuing (**www.agilemanifesto.org**):

Individuals and interactions over processes and tools
Working software over comprehensive documentation
Customer collaboration over contract negotiation, and
Responding to change over following a plan

Agile software development
An approach to database and software development that emphasizes **"individuals and interactions** over processes and tools, **working software** over comprehensive documentation, **customer collaboration** over contract negotiation, and **response to change** over following a plan."

Emphasis on the importance of people, both software developers and customers, is evident in their phrasing. This is in response to the turbulent environment within which software development occurs, as compared to the more staid environment of most engineering development projects from which the earlier software development methodologies came. The importance of the practices established in the SDLC continues to be recognized and accepted by software developers including the creators of The Manifesto for Agile Software Development. However, it is impractical to allow these practices to stifle quick reactions to changes in the environment that change project requirements.

The use of agile or adaptive processes should be considered when a project involves unpredictable and/or changing requirements, responsible and collaborative developers, and involved customers who understand and can contribute to the process (Fowler, 2005). If you are interested in learning more about agile software development, investigate agile methodologies such as eXtreme Programming, Scrum, the DSDM Consortium, and feature-driven development.

Three-Schema Architecture for Database Development

The explanation earlier in this chapter of the database development process referred to several different, but related, models of databases developed on a systems development project. These data models and the primary phase of the SDLC in which they are developed are summarized below:

- Enterprise data model (during the Information Systems Planning phase)
- External schema or user view (during the Analysis and Logical Design phases)
- Conceptual schema (during the Analysis phase)

FIGURE 1-12 Three-schema architecture

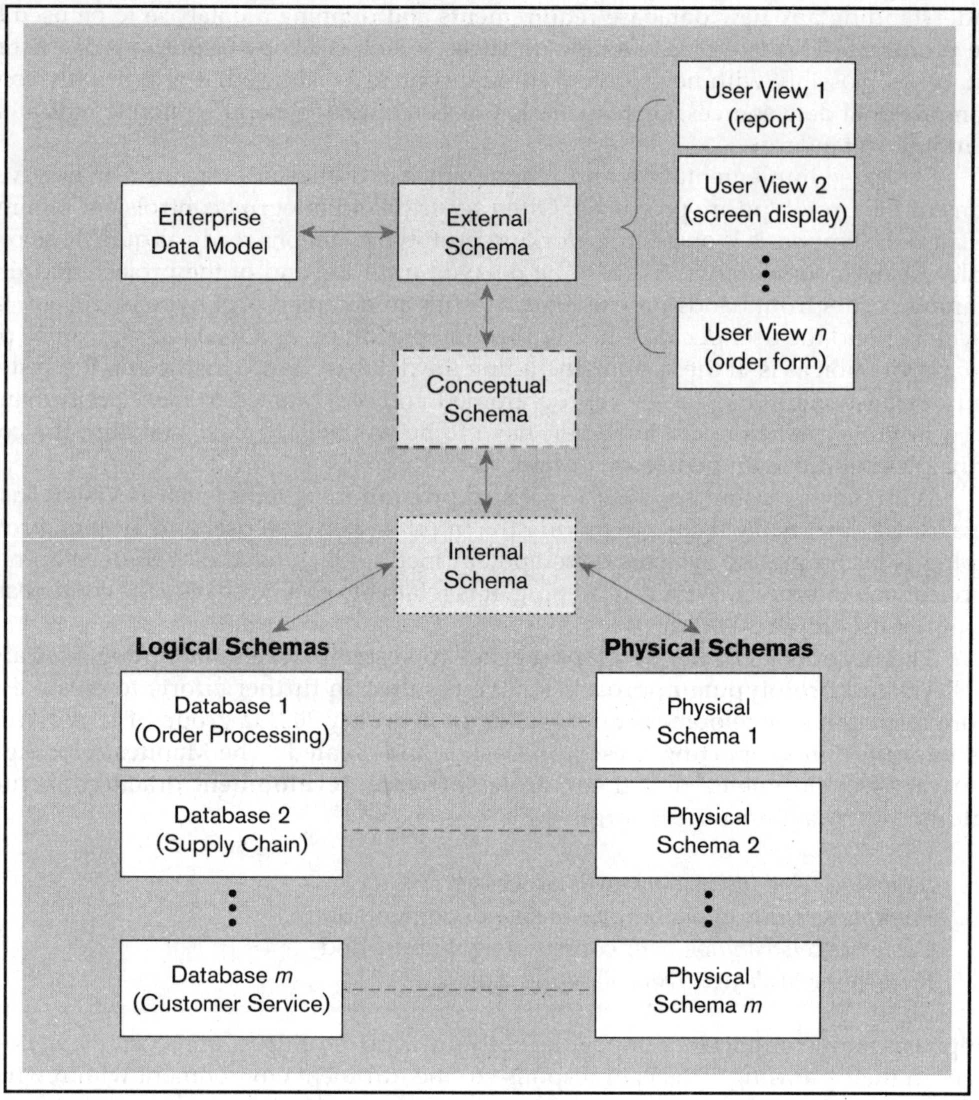

- Logical schema (during the Logical Design phase)
- Physical schema (during the Physical Design phase)

In 1978, an industry committee commonly known as ANSI/SPARC published an important document that described three-schema architecture—external, conceptual and internal schemas—for describing the structure of data. Figure 1-12 shows the relationship between the various schemas developed during the SDLC and the ANSI three-schema architecture. It is important to keep in mind that all these schemas are just different ways of visualizing structure of the same database by different stakeholders.

The three schemas as defined by ANSI (depicted down the center of Figure 1-12) are as follows:

1. ***External schema*** This is the view (or views) of managers and other employees who are the database users. As shown in Figure 1-12, the external schema can be represented as a combination of the enterprise data model (a top-down view) and a collection of detailed (or bottom-up) user views.
2. ***Conceptual schema*** This schema combines the different external views into a single, coherent, and comprehensive definition of the enterprise's data. The conceptual schema represents the view of the data architect or data administrator.
3. ***Internal schema*** As shown in Figure 1-12, an internal schema today really consists of two separate schemas: a logical schema and a physical schema. The logical schema is the representation of data for a type of data management technology

(e.g., relational). The physical schema describes how data are to be represented and stored in secondary storage using a particular DBMS (e.g., Oracle).

Managing the People Involved in Database Development

Isn't it always ultimately about people working together? As implied in Figure 1-10, a database is developed as part of a project. A **project** is a planned undertaking of related activities to reach an objective that has a beginning and an end. A project begins with the first steps of the Project Initiation and Planning phase and ends with the last steps of the Implementation phase. A senior systems or database analyst will be assigned to be project leader. This person is responsible for creating detailed project plans as well as staffing and supervising the project team.

Project
A planned undertaking of related activities to reach an objective that has a beginning and an end.

A project is initiated and planned in the Planning phase, executed during Analysis, Logical Design, Physical Design, and Implementation phases, and closed down at the end of implementation. During initiation the project team is formed. A systems or database development team can include one or more of the following:

- ***Business analysts*** These individuals work with both management and users to analyze the business situation and develop detailed system and program specifications for projects.
- ***Systems analysts*** These individuals may perform business analyst activities but also specify computer systems requirements and typically have a stronger systems development background than business analysts.
- ***Database analysts and data modelers*** These individuals concentrate on determining the requirements and design for the database component of the information system.
- ***Users*** Users provide assessments of their information needs and monitor that the developed system meets their needs.
- ***Programmers*** These individuals design and write computer programs that have commands to maintain and access data in the database embedded in them.
- ***Database architects*** These individuals establish standards for data in business units, striving to attain optimum data location, currency, and quality.
- ***Data administrators*** These individuals have responsibility for existing and future databases and ensure consistency and integrity across databases, and as experts on database technology, provide consulting and training to other project team members.
- ***Project managers*** Project managers oversee assigned projects, including team composition, analysis, design, implementation, and support of projects.
- ***Other technical experts*** Other individuals are needed in areas such as networking, operating systems, testing, data warehousing, and documentation.

It is the responsibility of the project leader to select and manage all of these people as an effective team. See Hoffer et al. (2010) for details on how to manage a systems development project team. See Henderson et al. (2005) for a more detailed description of career paths and roles in data management. The emphasis on people rather than roles when agile development processes are adopted means that team members will be less likely to be constrained to a particular role. They will be expected to contribute and collaborate across these roles, thus using their particular skills, interests, and capabilities more completely.

DEVELOPING A DATABASE APPLICATION FOR PINE VALLEY FURNITURE COMPANY

PINE VALLEY FURNITURE

Pine Valley Furniture Company was introduced earlier in this chapter. By the late 1990s, competition in furniture manufacturing had intensified, and competitors seemed to respond more rapidly than Pine Valley Furniture to new business opportunities. While there were many reasons for this trend, managers felt that the computer information systems they had been using (based on traditional file processing)

FIGURE 1-13 Computer System for Pine Valley Furniture Company

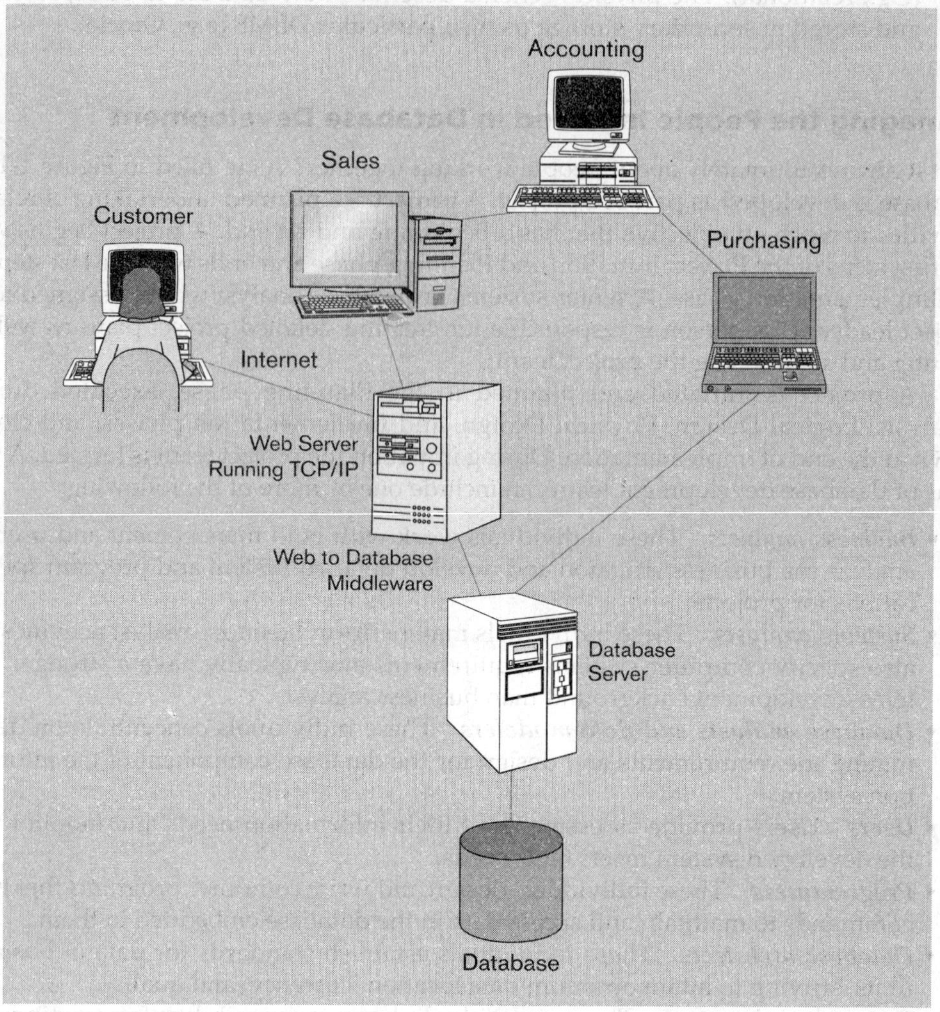

had become outdated. After attending an executive development session led by Fred McFadden and Jeff Hoffer (we wish!), the company started a development effort that eventually led to adopting a database approach for the company. Figure 1-13 displays a general schematic of the computer network within Pine Valley Furniture Company.

Data previously stored in separate files have been integrated into a single database structure. Also, the metadata that describe these data reside in the same structure. The DBMS provides the interface between the various database applications for organizational users and the database (or databases). The DBMS allows users to share the data and to query, access, and update the stored data.

Before addressing a request that has been received for direct access to sales data from Helen Jarvis, product manager for home office furniture, let's review the process that Pine Valley Furniture Company followed as they originally moved into a database environment. Pine Valley Furniture Company's first step in converting to a database approach was to develop a list of the high-level entities that support the business activities of the organization. You will recall that an entity is an object or concept that is important to the business. Some of the high-level entities identified at Pine Valley Furniture were the following: CUSTOMER, PRODUCT, EMPLOYEE, CUSTOMER ORDER, and DEPARTMENT. After these entities were identified and defined, the company proceeded to develop an enterprise data model. Remember that an enterprise data model is a graphical model that shows the high-level entities for the organization and associations among those entities.

The results of preliminary studies convinced management of the potential advantages of the database approach. After additional data modeling steps had been completed, the company decided to implement a modern relational database management system that views all data in the form of tables. (We cover relational databases in more detail in Chapter 4.) A simplified segment of the project data model used is discussed next.

Simplified Project Data Model Example

A segment of the project data model containing four entities and three pertinent associations is shown in Figure 1-3b. The entities shown in this model segment are the following:

CUSTOMER	A person or an organization that buys or may potentially buy products from Pine Valley Furniture
ORDER	The purchase of one or more products by a customer
PRODUCT	The items Pine Valley Furniture makes and sells
ORDER LINE	Details about each product sold on a particular customer order (such as quantity and price)

The three associations (called *relationships* in database terminology) shown in the Figure 1-3b (represented by the three lines connecting entities) capture three fundamental business rules, as follows:

1. Each CUSTOMER *Places* any number of ORDERs. Conversely, each ORDER *Is Placed By* exactly one CUSTOMER.
2. Each ORDER *Contains* any number of ORDER LINEs. Conversely, each ORDER LINE *Is Contained In* exactly one ORDER.
3. Each PRODUCT *Has* any number of ORDER LINEs. Conversely, each ORDER LINE *Is For* exactly one PRODUCT.

Places, Contains, and Has are called one-to-many relationships because, for example, one customer places potentially many orders and one order is placed by exactly one customer.

Notice the following characteristics of the project data model:

1. It is a model of the organization that provides valuable information about how the organization functions, as well as important constraints.
2. The project data model focuses on entities, relationships, and business rules. It also includes attribute labels for each piece of data that will be stored in each entity. Many entities would include more attributes than we list in Figure 1-3b, but we have included a sufficient number to help you begin to understand how the data will be stored in a database.

Figure 1-14 shows the following four tables with sample data: Customer, Product, Order, and OrderLine. Notice that these tables represent the four entities shown in the project data model (Figure 1-3b). Each column of a table represents an attribute (or characteristic) of an entity. For example, the attributes shown for Customer are CustomerID and CustomerName. Each row of a table represents an instance (or occurrence) of the entity. An important property of the relational model is that it represents relationships between entities by values stored in the columns of the corresponding tables. For example, notice that CustomerID is an attribute of both the Customer table and the Order table. As a result, we can easily link an order to its associated customer. For example, we can determine that OrderID 1003 is associated with CustomerID 1. Can you determine which ProductIDs are associated with OrderID 1004? In subsequent chapters, you will learn how to retrieve data from these tables by using a powerful query language, SQL, which exploits these linkages.

To facilitate the sharing of data and information, Pine Valley Furniture Company uses a local area network (LAN) that links employee workstations in the various departments to a database server, as shown in Figure 1-13. During the early 2000s, the company mounted a two-phase effort to introduce Internet technology. First, to improve intracompany communication and decision making, an intranet was installed

FIGURE 1-14 Four relations (Pine Valley Furniture Company)

(a) Order and Order Line Tables

Order_T

OrderID	OrderDate	CustomerID
1001	10/21/2010	
1002	10/21/2010	
1003	10/22/2010	
1004	10/22/2010	
1005	10/24/2010	
1006	10/24/2010	
1007	10/27/2010	
1008	10/30/2010	
1009	11/5/2010	
1010	11/5/2010	

Record: 1 of 10 No Filter Search

OrderLine_T

OrderID	ProductID	OrderedQuantity
1001	1	2
1001	2	2
1001	4	1
1002	3	5
1003	3	3
1004	6	2
1004	8	2
1005	4	4
1006	4	1
1006	5	2
1006	7	2
1007	1	3
1007	2	2
1008	3	3
1008	8	3
1009	4	2
1009	7	3
1010	8	10
* 0	0	0

Record: 1 of 18 No Filter Search

Customer_T

CustomerID	CustomerName
1	Contemporary Casuals
2	Value Furniture
3	Home Furnishings
4	Eastern Furniture
5	Impressions
6	Furniture Gallery
7	Period Furniture
8	Calfornia Classics
9	M and H Casual Furniture
10	Seminole Interiors
11	American Euro Lifestyles
12	Battle Creek Furniture
13	Heritage Furnishings
14	Kaneohe Homes
15	Mountain Scenes
* (New)	

(b) Customer table

Product_T

ProductID	ProductStandardPrice
1	$175.00
2	$200.00
3	$375.00
4	$650.00
5	$325.00
6	$750.00
7	$800.00
8	$250.00
* (New)	$0.00

(c) Product table

that allows employees fast Web-based access to company information, including phone directories, furniture design specifications, e-mail, and so forth. In addition, Pine Valley Furniture Company also added a Web interface to some of its business applications, such as order entry, so that more internal business activities that require access to data in the database server can also be conducted by employees through its intranet. However, most applications that use the database server still do not have a Web interface and require that the application itself be stored on employees' workstations.

Although the database quite adequately supports daily operations at Pine Valley Furniture Company, managers soon learned that the same database is often inadequate for decision support applications. For example, following are some types of questions that cannot be easily answered:

1. What is the pattern of furniture sales this year, compared with the same period last year?
2. Who are our 10 largest customers, and what are their buying patterns?
3. Why can't we easily obtain a consolidated view of any customer who orders through different sales channels, rather than viewing each contact as representing a separate customer?

To answer these and other questions, an organization often needs to build a separate database that contains historical and summarized information. Such a database is usually called a *data warehouse* or, in some cases, a *data mart*. Also, analysts need specialized decision support tools to query and analyze the database. One class of tools used for this purpose is called online analytical processing (OLAP) tools. We describe data warehouses, data marts, and related decision support tools in Chapter 9. There you will learn of the interest in building a data warehouse that is now growing within Pine Valley Furniture Company.

A Current Pine Valley Furniture Company Project Request

A trait of a good database is that it does and can evolve! Helen Jarvis, product manager for home office furniture at Pine Valley Furniture Company, knows that competition has become fierce in this growing product line. Thus, it is increasingly important to Pine Valley Furniture that Helen be able to analyze sales of her products more thoroughly. Often these analyses are ad hoc, driven by rapidly changing and unanticipated business conditions, comments from furniture store managers, trade industry gossip, or personal experience. Helen has requested that she be given direct access to sales data with an easy-to-use interface so that she can search for answers to the various marketing questions she will generate.

Chris Martin is a systems analyst in Pine Valley Furniture's information systems development area. Chris has worked at Pine Valley Furniture for five years, and has experience with information systems from several business areas within Pine Valley. With this experience, his information systems education at Western Florida University, and the extensive training Pine Valley has given him, he has become one of Pine Valley's best systems developers. Chris is skilled in data modeling and is familiar with several relational database management systems used within the firm. Because of his experience, expertise, and availability, the head of information systems has assigned Chris to work with Helen on her request for a marketing support system.

Because Pine Valley Furniture has been careful in the development of its systems, especially since adopting the database approach, the company already has databases that support its operational business functions. Thus, it is likely that Chris will be able to extract the data Helen needs from existing databases. Pine Valley's information systems architecture calls for such systems as Helen is requesting to be built on stand-alone databases so that the unstructured and unpredictable use of data will not interfere with the access to the operational databases needed to support efficient transaction processing systems.

Further, because Helen's needs are for data analysis, not creation and maintenance, and are personal, not institutional, Chris decides to follow a combination of prototyping and life-cycle approaches in developing the system Helen has requested. This means that Chris will follow all the life-cycle steps, but focus his energy on the steps that are integral to prototyping. Thus, he will very quickly address project planning, then use an iterative cycle of analysis, design, and implementation to work closely with Helen to develop a working prototype of the system she needs. Because the system will be personal and likely will require a database with limited scope, Chris hopes the prototype will end up being the actual system Helen will use. Chris has chosen to develop the system using Microsoft Access, Pine Valley's preferred technology for personal databases.

Project Planning

Chris begins the project by interviewing Helen. Chris asks Helen about her business area, taking notes about business area objectives, business functions, data entity types, and other business objects with which she deals. At this point, Chris listens more than he talks so that he can concentrate on understanding Helen's business area; he interjects questions and makes sure that Helen does not try to jump ahead to talk about what she thinks she needs with regards to computer screens and reports from the information system. Chris asks very general questions, using business and marketing terminology as much as possible. For example, Chris asks Helen what issues she faces managing the home office products; what people, places, and things are of interest to her in her job; how far back in time she needs data to go to do her analyses; and what events occur in the business that are of interest to her. Chris pays particular attention to Helen's objectives as well as the data entities that she is interested in.

Chris does two quick analyses before talking with Helen again. First, he identifies all of the databases that contain data associated with the data entities Helen mentioned. From these databases, Chris makes a list of all of the data attributes from these data entities that he thinks might be of interest to Helen in her analyses of the home office furniture market. Chris's previous involvement in projects that developed Pine Valley's standard sales tracking and forecasting system and cost accounting system helps him to speculate on the kinds of data Helen might want. For example, the objective to exceed sales goals for each product finish category of office furniture suggests that Helen wants product annual sales goals in her system; also, the objective of achieving at least an 8 percent annual sales growth means that the prior year's orders for each product need to be included. He also concludes that Helen's database must include all products, not just those in the office furniture line, because she wants to compare her line to others. However, he is able to eliminate many of the data attributes kept on each data entity. For example, Helen does not appear to need various customer data such as address, phone number, contact person, store size, and salesperson. Chris does, though, include a few additional attributes, customer type and zip code, which he feels might be important in a sales forecasting system.

Second, from this list, Chris draws a graphic data model that represents the data entities with the associated data attributes, as well as the major relationships between these data entities. Chris's hope is that he can reduce the time for the analysis phase of the systems development process (and hence the time to do conceptual data modeling) by presenting this data model to Helen. A graphic of the data model for the preliminary database that Chris produces appears in Figure 1-15. The data attributes

FIGURE 1-15 Preliminary data model for Home Office product line marketing support system

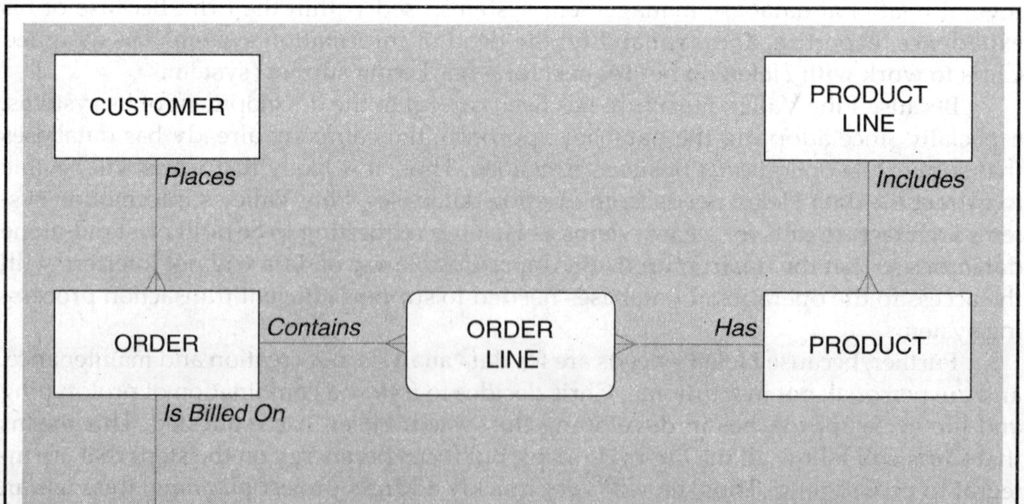

TABLE 1-6 Data Attributes for Entities in the Preliminary Data Model (Pine Valley Furniture Company)

Entity Type	Attribute
Customer	Customer Identifier
	Customer Name
	Customer Type
	Customer Zip Code
Product	Product Identifier
	Product Description
	Product Finish
	Product Price
	Product Cost
	Product Annual Sales Goal
	Product Line Name
Product Line	Product Line Name
	Product Line Annual Sales Goal
Order	Order Number
	Order Placement Date
	Order Fulfillment Date
	Customer Identifier
Ordered Product	Order Number
	Product Identifier
	Order Quantity
Invoice	Invoice Number
	Order Number
	Invoice Date
Payment	Invoice Number
	Payment Date
	Payment Amount

of each entity Chris thinks Helen wants for the system are listed in Table 1-6. Chris lists in Table 1-6 only basic data attributes from existing databases, because Helen will likely want to combine these data in various ways for the analyses she will want to do.

Analyzing Database Requirements

Prior to their next meeting, Chris sends Helen a rough project schedule outlining the steps he plans to follow and the estimated length of time each step will take. Because prototyping is a user-driven process, in which the user says when to stop iterating on the new prototype versions, Chris can provide only rough estimates of the duration of certain project steps. For this reason, Chris's boss has decided that this project should be billed to Helen's department on a consulting time basis, not at a fixed cost.

Chris does more of the talking at this second meeting, but he pays close attention to Helen's reactions to his initial ideas for the database application. He methodically walks through each data entity in Figure 1-15, explaining what it means, what each data attribute associated with it (in Table 1-6) means, and what business policies and procedures are represented by each line between entities. For example, Chris explains that each order is billed on one invoice and each invoice is a bill for exactly one order. An Order Number uniquely identifies each order, and an order is placed by one customer. Other data about an order Chris thinks Helen might want to know include the date when the order was placed and the date when the order was filled. (This would be the latest shipment date for the products on the order.) Chris also explains that the Payment Date attribute represents the most recent date when the customer made any payments, in full or partial, for the order.

Maybe because Chris was so well prepared or so enthusiastic, Helen is excited about the possibilities, and this excitement leads her to tell Chris about some additional data she wants (the number of years a customer has purchased products from Pine Valley Furniture Company and the number of shipments necessary to fill each order). Helen also notes that Chris has only one year of sales goals indicated for a product line. She reminds him that she wants these data for both the past and current years. As she reacts to the data model, Chris asks her how she intends to use the data she wants. Chris does not try to be thorough at this point, because he knows that Helen has not worked with an information set like the one being developed; thus, she may not yet be positive what data she wants or what she wants to do with the data. Rather, Chris's objective is to understand a few ways in which Helen intends to use the data so he can develop an initial prototype, including the database and several computer displays or reports. The final list of attributes that Helen agrees she needs appears in Table 1-7.

Designing the Database

Because Chris is following a prototyping methodology, and because the first two sessions with Helen quickly identified the data Helen might need, Chris is able to immediately begin to build the prototype. First, Chris extracts from the corporate databases the data entities and attributes that Helen suggested. Chris is able to create all of these files using the SQL query language. Some of the data Helen wants are computed from raw, operational data (e.g., Customer Years), but SQL makes it easy for Chris to specify these calculations. This extracting results in a single ASCII file for each data entity; each row in a file contains all of the data attributes associated with that data entity in the data model, and the rows are different instances of the entity. For example, each row of the ASCII file for the PRODUCT LINE data entity contains data for product line names and the annual sales goals for the past and current years.

Second, Chris translates the final data model from his discussion with Helen into a set of tables for which the columns are data attributes and the rows are different sets of values for those attributes. Tables are the basic building blocks of a relational database, which is the database style for Microsoft Access. The definitions of the ProductLine and Product tables Chris created, including associated data attributes, are shown in Figures 1-16 and 1-17. The tables are defined using SQL. It is customary to add the suffix _T to a table name. Also note that because relational databases do not allow for spaces between names, the individual words in the attributes from the data model have now been concatenated. Hence, Product Description in the data model has become ProductDescription in the table. Chris did this translation so that each table had an attribute, called the table's "primary key," which will be distinct for each row in the table. The other major properties of each

TABLE 1-7 Data Attributes for Entities in Final Data Model (Pine Valley Furniture Company)

Entity Type	Attribute
Customer	Customer Identifier
	Customer Name
	Customer Type
	Customer Zip Code
	Customer Years
Product	Product Identifier
	Product Description
	Product Finish
	Product Price
	Product Cost
	Product Prior Year Sales Goal
	Product Current Year Sales Goal
	Product Line Name
Product Line	Product Line Name
	Product Line Prior Year Sales Goal
	Product Line Current Year Sales Goal
Order	Order Number
	Order Placement Date
	Order Fulfillment Date
	Order Number of Shipments
	Customer Identifier
Ordered Product	Order Number
	Product Identifier
	Order Quantity
Invoice	Invoice Number
	Order Number
	Invoice Date
Payment	Invoice Number
	Payment Date
	Payment Amount

*Changes from preliminary list of attributes appear in italics.

table are that there is only one value for each attribute in each row, and if we know the value of the identifier, there can be only one value for each of the other attributes. For example, for any product line, there can be only one value for the current year's sales goal.

The design of the database includes specifying the format, or properties, for each attribute (MS Access calls attributes *fields*). These design decisions were easy in this

FIGURE 1-16 SQL definition of ProductLine table

```
CREATE TABLE ProductLine_T
(ProductLineID        VARCHAR (40) NOT NULL PRIMARY KEY,
PlPriorYearGoal       DECIMAL,
PlCurrentYearGoal     DECIMAL);
```

FIGURE 1-17 SQL definition of Product table

```
CREATE TABLE Product_T
(ProductID                 NUMBER(11,0) NOT NULL PRIMARY KEY
ProductDescription         VARCHAR (50),
ProductFinish              VARCHAR (20),
ProductStandardPrice       DECIMAL(6,2),
ProductCost                DECIMAL,
ProductPriorYearGoal       DECIMAL,
ProductCurrentYearGoal     DECIMAL,
ProductLineID              VARCHAR (40),
FOREIGN KEY                (ProductLineID) REFERENCES ProductLine_T (ProductLineID));
```

case because most of the attributes were already specified in the corporate data dictionary.

The other major decision Chris has to make about database design is how to physically organize the database to respond fastest to the queries Helen will write. Because the database will be used for decision support, neither Chris nor Helen can anticipate all of the queries that will arise; thus, Chris must make the physical design choices from experience rather than precise knowledge of the way the database will be used. The key physical database design decision that SQL allows a database designer to make is on which attributes to create indexes. (An index is like a card catalog in the library, through which rows with common characteristics can be quickly located.) All primary key attributes (like OrderNumber for the Order_T table)—those with unique values across the rows of the table—are indexed. In addition to this, Chris uses a general rule of thumb: Create an index for any attribute that has more than 10 different values and that Helen might use to segment the database. For example, Helen indicated that one of the ways she wants to use the database is to look at sales by product finish. Thus, it might make sense to create an index on the Product_T table using the Product Finish attribute.

However, Pine Valley uses only six product finishes, or types of wood, so this is not a useful index candidate. On the other hand, OrderPlacementDate (called a secondary key because there may be more than one row in the Order_T table with the same value of this attribute), which Helen also wants to use to analyze sales in different time periods, is a good index candidate.

Figure 1-18 shows the prototype project data model developed by Chris for the home office marketing database. Each box represents one table in the database; the attributes of a table are listed inside the associated box. The project data model shows how the relations will be linked by including common fields, or foreign keys. The foreign keys have a dashed underline in the model. For example, the attribute Product Line is the primary identifier in the PRODUCT LINE relation, and is also included in the PRODUCT relation. This linkage makes it possible to compare current sales to sales goals by product line.

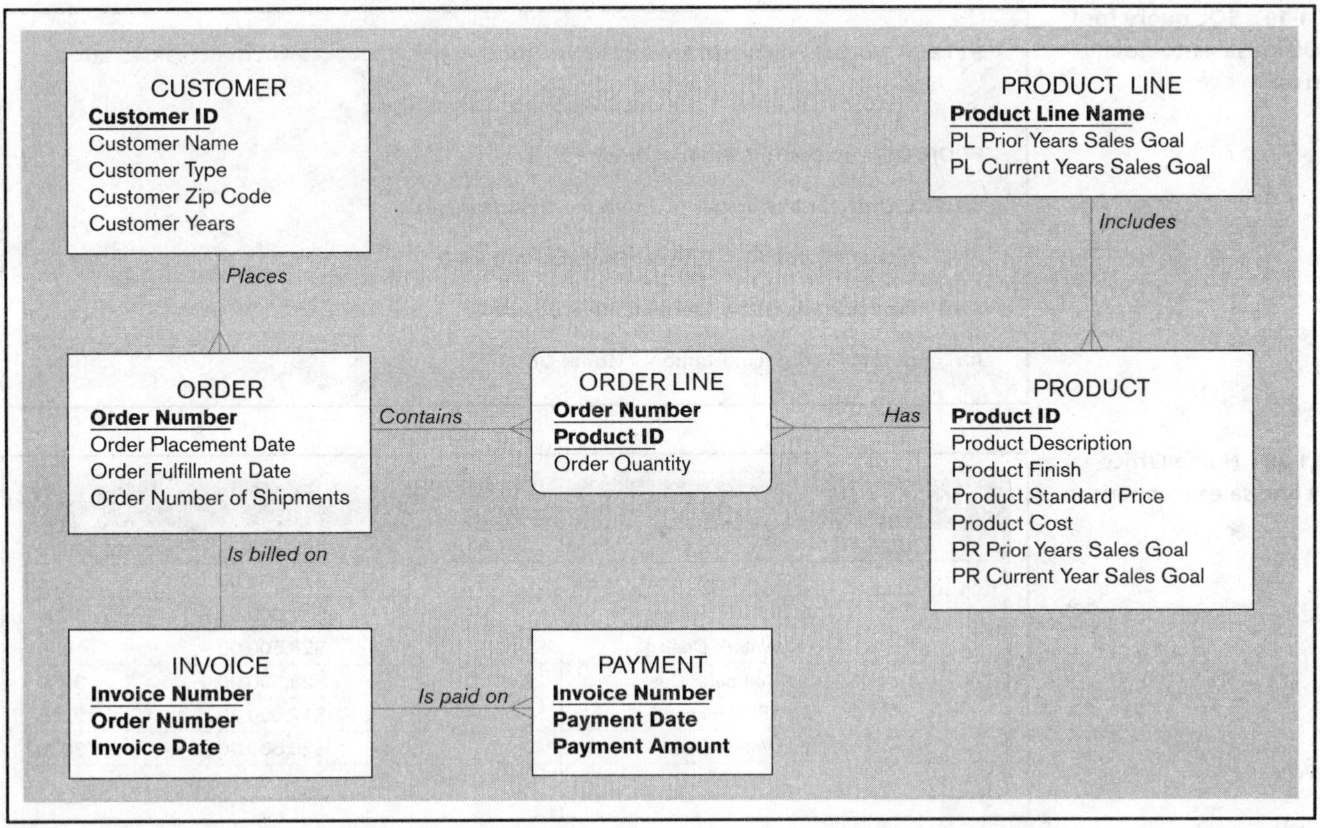

FIGURE 1-18 Project data model for Home Office product line marketing support system

Using the Database

Helen will use the database Chris has built mainly for ad hoc questions, so Chris will train her so that she can access the database and build queries to answer her ad hoc questions. Helen has indicated a few standard questions she expects to ask periodically. Chris will develop several types of prewritten routines (forms, reports, and queries) that can make it easier for Helen to answer these standard questions (so she does not have to program these questions from scratch).

During the prototyping development process, Chris may develop many examples of each of these routines as Helen communicates more clearly what she wants the system to be able to do. At this early stage of development, however, Chris wants to develop one routine to create the first prototype. One of the standard sets of information Helen says she wants is a list of each of the products in the Home Office line showing each product's total sales to date compared with its current year sales goal. Helen may want the results of this query to be displayed in a more stylized fashion—an opportunity to use a report—but for now Chris will present this feature to Helen only as a query.

The query to produce this list of products appears in Figure 1-19, with sample output in Figure 1-20. The query in Figure 1-19 uses SQL. You can see three of the six standard SQL clauses in this query: SELECT, FROM, and WHERE. SELECT indicates which attributes will be shown in the result. One calculation is also included and given the label "Sales to Date." FROM indicates which tables must be accessed to retrieve data. WHERE defines the links between the tables and indicates that results from only the Home Office product line are to be included. Only limited data are included for this example, so the Total Sales results in Figure 1-20 are fairly small, but the format is the result of the query in Figure 1-19.

Chris is now ready to meet with Helen again to see if the prototype is beginning to meet her needs. Chris shows Helen the system. As Helen makes suggestions, Chris is able to make a few changes online, but many of Helen's observations will have to wait for more careful work at his desk.

FIGURE 1-19 SQL query for Home Office sales-to-goal comparison

```
SELECT Product.ProductID, Product.ProductDescription, Product.PRCurrentYearSalesGoal,
        (OrderQuantity * ProductPrice) AS SalesToDate
FROM Order.OrderLine, Product.ProductLine
WHERE Order.OrderNumber = OrderLine.OrderNumber
AND Product.ProductID = OrderedProduct.ProductID
AND Product.ProductID = ProductLine.ProductID
AND Product.ProductLineName = "Home Office";
```

FIGURE 1-20 Home Office product line sales comparison

Home Office Sales to Date : Select Query

Product ID	Product Description	PR Current Year Sales Goal	Sales to Date
3	Computer Desk	$23,500.00	5625
10	96" Bookcase	$22,500.00	4400
5	Writer's Desk	$26,500.00	650
3	Computer Desk	$23,500.00	3750
7	48" Bookcase	$17,000.00	2250
5	Writer's Desk	$26,500.00	3900

Space does not permit us to review the whole project to develop the Home Office marketing support system. Chris and Helen ended up meeting about a dozen times before Helen was satisfied that all the attributes she needed were in the database; that the standard queries, forms, and reports Chris wrote were of use to her; and that she knew how to write queries for unanticipated questions. Chris will be available to Helen at any time to provide consulting support when she has trouble with the system, including writing more complex queries, forms, or reports. One final decision that Chris and Helen made was that the performance of the final prototype was efficient enough that the prototype did not have to be rewritten or redesigned. Helen was now ready to use the system.

Administering the Database

The administration of the Home Office marketing support system is fairly simple. Helen decided that she could live with weekly downloads of new data from Pine Valley's operational databases into her Microsoft Access database. Chris wrote a C# program with SQL commands embedded in it to perform the necessary extracts and wrote an MS Access program in Visual Basic to rebuild the Access tables from these extracts; he scheduled these jobs to run every Sunday evening. Chris also updated the corporate information systems architecture model to include the Home Office marketing support system. This step was important so that when changes occurred to formats for data included in Helen's system, the corporate CASE tool could alert Chris that changes might have to be made also in her system.

Summary

Over the past two decades there has been enormous growth in the number and importance of database applications. Databases are used to store, manipulate, and retrieve data in every type of organization. In the highly competitive environment of the 2000s, there is every indication that database technology will assume even greater importance. A course in modern database management is one of the most important courses in the information systems curriculum.

A database is an organized collection of logically related data. We define *data* as stored representations of objects and events that have meaning and importance in the user's environment. Information is data that have been processed in such a way that the knowledge of the person who uses the data increases. Both data and information may be stored in a database.

Metadata are data that describe the properties or characteristics of end-user data and the context of that data. A database management system (DBMS) is a software system that is used to create, maintain, and provide controlled access to user databases. A DBMS stores metadata in a repository, which is a central storehouse for all data definitions, data relationships, screen and report formats, and other system components.

Computer file processing systems were developed early in the computer era so that computers could store, manipulate, and retrieve large files of data. These systems (still in use today) have a number of important limitations such as dependence between programs and data, data duplication, limited data sharing, and lengthy development times. The database approach was developed to overcome these limitations. This approach emphasizes the integration and sharing of data across the organization. Advantages of this approach include program-data independence, improved data sharing, minimal data redundancy, and improved productivity of application development.

Database applications can be arranged into the following categories: personal databases, two-tier databases, multitier, and enterprise databases. Enterprise databases include data warehouses and integrated decision support databases whose content is derived from the various operational databases. Enterprise resource planning (ERP) systems rely heavily on enterprise databases. A modern database and the applications that use it may be located on multiple computers. Although any number of tiers may exist (from one to many), three tiers of computers relate to the client/server architecture for database processing: (1) the client tier, where database contents are presented to the user; (2) the application/Web server tier, where analyses on database contents are made and user sessions are managed; and (3) the enterprise server tier, where the data from across the organization are merged into an organizational asset.

Database development begins with enterprise data modeling, during which the range and general contents of organizational databases are established. In addition to the relationships among the data entities themselves their relationship to other organizational planning objects: organizational units, locations, business functions, and information systems, also need to be established. Relationships between data entities and the other organizational planning objects can be represented at a high level by planning matrixes, which can be manipulated to understand patterns of relationships. Once the need for a database is identified, either from a planning exercise or from a specific request (such as the one from Helen Jarvis for a Home Office products marketing support system), a project team is formed to develop all elements. The project team follows a systems development process, such as the systems development life cycle or prototyping. The systems development life cycle can be represented by five methodical steps: (1) planning, (2) analysis, (3) design, (4) implementation, and (5) maintenance. Database development activities occur in each of these overlapping phases, and feedback may occur that causes a project to return to a prior phase. In prototyping, a database and its applications are iteratively refined through a close interaction of systems developers and users. Prototyping works best when the database application is small and stand-alone, and a small number of users exist.

Those working on a database development project deal with three views, or schemas, for a database: (1) a conceptual schema, which provides a complete, technology-independent picture of the database; (2) an internal schema, which specifies the complete database as it will be stored in computer secondary memory in terms of a logical schema and a physical schema; and (3) an external schema or user view, which describes the database relevant to a specific set of users in terms of a set of user views combined with the enterprise data model.

We closed the chapter with the review of a hypothetical database development project at Pine Valley Furniture Company. This system to support marketing a Home Office furniture product line illustrated the use of a personal database management system and SQL coding for developing a retrieval-only database. The database in this application contained data extracted from the enterprise databases and then stored in a separate database on the client tier. Prototyping was used to develop this database application because the user, Helen Jarvis, had rather unstructured needs that could best be discovered through an iterative process of developing and refining the system. Also, her interest and ability to work closely with Chris was limited.

Chapter Review

Key Terms

Agile software development *29*
Computer-aided software engineering (CASE) tools *16*
Conceptual schema *26*
Constraint *14*
Data *5*
Data independence *13*
Data model *10*
Data warehouse *20*
Database *5*
Database application *9*
Database management system (DBMS) *11*
Enterprise data modeling *24*
Enterprise resource planning (ERP) *20*
Entity *10*
Information *5*
Logical schema *26*
Metadata *7*
Physical schema *27*
Project *31*
Prototyping *28*
Relational database *10*
Repository *16*
Systems development life cycle (SDLC) *25*
User view *13*

Review Questions

1. Define each of the following terms:
   a. data
   b. information
   c. metadata
   d. database application
   e. data warehouse
   f. constraint
   g. database
   h. entity
   i. database management system
   j. client/server architecture
   k. systems development life cycle (SDLC)
   l. agile software development
   m. enterprise data model
   n. conceptual data model
   o. logical data model
   p. physical data model
2. Match the following terms and definitions:

____ data	a. data placed in context or summarized
____ database application	b. application program(s)
____ constraint	c. facts, text, graphics, images, etc.
____ repository	d. a graphical model that shows the high-level entities for the organization and the relationships among those entities
____ metadata	e. organized collection of related data
____ data warehouse	f. includes data definitions and constraints
____ information	g. centralized storehouse for all data definitions
____ user view	h. separation of data description from programs
____ database management system	i. a business management system that integrates all functions of the enterprise
____ data independence	j. logical description of portion of database
____ database	k. a software application that is used to create, maintain, and provide controlled access to user databases
____ enterprise resource planning (ERP)	l. a rule that cannot be violated by database users
____ systems development life cycle (SDLC)	m. integrated decision support database
____ prototyping	n. consist of the enterprise data model and multiple user views
____ enterprise data model	o. a rapid approach to systems development
____ conceptual schema	p. consists of two data models: a logical model and a physical model
____ internal schema	q. a comprehensive description of business data
____ external schema	r. a structured, step-by-step approach to systems development

3. Contrast the following terms:
   a. data dependence; data independence
   b. structured data; unstructured data
   c. data; information
   d. repository; database
   e. entity; enterprise data model
   f. data warehouse; ERP system
   g. two-tier databases; multitier databases
   h. systems development life cycle; prototyping
   i. enterprise data model; conceptual data model
   j. prototyping; agile software development
4. List five disadvantages of file processing systems.
5. List the nine major components in a database system environment.
6. How are relationships between tables expressed in a relational database?
7. What does the term *data independence* mean, and why is it an important goal?
8. List 10 potential benefits of the database approach over conventional file systems.
9. List five costs or risks associated with the database approach.
10. Define a three-tiered database architecture.
11. In the three-tiered database architecture, is it possible for there to be no database on a particular tier? If not, why? If yes, give an example.
12. Name the five phases of the traditional systems development life cycle, and explain the purpose and deliverables of each phase.
13. In which of the five phases of the SDLC do database development activities occur?
14. Are there procedures and processes that are common to the use of SDLC, prototyping, and agile methodologies? Explain any that you can identify and then indicate why the methodologies are considered to be different even though fundamental procedures and processes are still included.
15. Explain the differences between user views, a conceptual schema, and an internal schema as different perspectives of the same database.
16. In the three-schema architecture:
    a. The view of a manager or other type of user is called the ______ schema.
    b. The view of the data architect or data administrator is called the ______ schema.
    c. The view of the database administrator is called the ______ schema.
17. Why might Pine Valley Furniture Company need a data warehouse?
18. As the ability to handle large amounts of data improves, describe three business areas where these very large databases are being used effectively.
19. Why is the traditional file-processing system disadvantageous?
20. Why are data models very important for designing a database?
21. Name and explain at least five different roles that people need to play for the development of the database systems.

Problems and Exercises

1. For each of the following pairs of related entities, indicate whether (under typical circumstances) there is a one-to-many or a many-to-many relationship. Then, using the shorthand notation introduced in the text, draw a diagram for each of the relationships.
   a. STUDENT and COURSE (students register for courses)
   b. BOOK and BOOK COPY (books have copies)
   c. COURSE and SECTION (courses have sections)
   d. SECTION and ROOM (sections are scheduled in rooms)
   e. INSTRUCTOR and COURSE
2. Reread the definitions for *data* and *database* in this chapter. Database management systems only recently began to include the capability to store and retrieve more than numeric and textual data. What special data storage, retrieval, and maintenance capabilities do images, sound, video, and other advanced data types require that are not required or are simpler with numeric and textual data?
3. Table 1-1 shows example metadata for a set of data items. Identify three other columns for these data (i.e., three other metadata characteristics for the listed attributes) and complete the entries of the table in Table 1-1 for these three additional columns.
4. In the section "Disadvantages of File Processing Systems," the statement is made that the disadvantages of file processing systems can also be limitations of databases, depending on how an organization manages its databases. First, why do organizations create multiple databases, not just one all-inclusive database supporting all data processing needs? Second, what organizational and personal factors are at work that might lead an organization to have multiple, independently managed databases (and, hence, not completely follow the database approach)?
5. Consider a student club or organization in which you are a member. What are the data entities of this enterprise? List and define each entity. Then, develop an enterprise data model (such as Figure 1-3a) showing these entities and important relationships between them.
6. A driver's license bureau maintains a database of licensed drivers. State whether each of the following represents data or metadata. If it represents data, state whether it is structured or unstructured data. If it represents metadata, state whether it is a fact describing a property of data or a fact describing the context of data.
   a. Driver's name, address, and birth date
   b. The fact that the driver's name is a 30-character field
   c. A photo image of the driver
   d. An image of the driver's fingerprint
   e. The make and serial number of the scanning device that was used to scan the fingerprint
   f. The resolution (in megapixels) of the camera that was used to photograph the driver
   g. The fact that the driver's birth date must precede today's date by at least 16 years
7. Great Lakes Insurance would like to implement a relational database for both its in-house and outside agents. The outside agents will use notebook computers to keep track of customers and policy information. Based on what you have learned in this chapter, what type (or types) of database(s) would you recommend for this application?

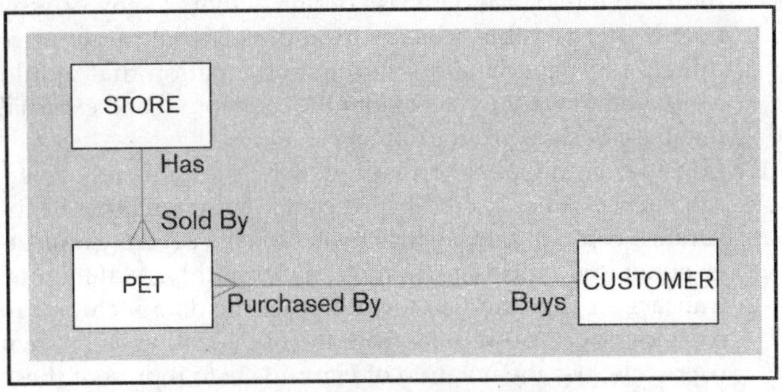

FIGURE 1-21 Data model for Problem and Exercise 8

8. Figure 1-21 shows an enterprise data model for a pet store.
   a. What is the relationship between Pet and Store (one-to-one, many-to-many, or one-to-many)?
   b. What is the relationship between Customer and Pet?
   c. Do you think there should be a relationship between Customer and Store?
9. Consider Figure 1-7, which depicts a hypothetical three-tiered database architecture. Identify potential duplications of data across all the databases listed on this figure. What problems might arise because of this duplication? Does this duplication violate the principles of the database approach outlined in this chapter? Why or why not?
10. What is your reaction to the representation of the systems development life cycle included in this chapter? Explain any problems you have with it.
11. List three additional entities that might appear in an enterprise data model for Pine Valley Furniture Company (Figure 1-3a).
12. Consider your business school or other academic unit as a business enterprise.
    a. Define several major data entity types and draw a preliminary enterprise data model (similar in notation to Figure 1-3a).
    b. Would your business school or academic unit benefit from a multiple-tiered architecture for data? Why or why not?
13. Contrast the top-down nature of database development during conceptual data modeling with the bottom-up nature of database development during logical database design. What major differences exist in the type of information considered in each of these two database development steps?
14. The objective of the prototyping systems development methodology is to rapidly build and rebuild an information system as the user and systems analyst learn from use of the prototype what features should be included in the evolving information system. Because the final prototype does not have to become the working system, where do you think would be an ideal location to develop a prototype: on a personal computer, department server, or enterprise server? Does your answer depend on any assumptions?
15. Explain the differences between an enterprise data model and a conceptual data model. How many databases does each represent? What scope of the organization does each address? What are other salient differences?

16. Is it possible that during the physical database design and creation step of database development you might want to return to the logical database design activity? Why or why not? If it is possible, give an example of what might arise during physical database design and creation that would cause you to want to reconsider the conceptual and external database designs from prior steps.
17. Consider an organization with which you frequently interact, such as a bank, credit card company, university, or insurance company, from which you receive several computer-generated messages, such as monthly statements, transaction slips, and so forth. Depict the data included in each message you receive from the organization as its own user view; use the notation of Figure 1-3a to represent these views. Now, combine all of these user views together into one conceptual data model, also using the notation of Figure 1-3a. What did you observe about the process of combining the different user views? Were there inconsistencies across the user views? Once you have created the conceptual data model, would you like to change anything about any of the user views?
18. Consider Figure 1-15. Explain the meaning of the line that connects ORDER to INVOICE and the line that connects INVOICE to PAYMENT. What does this say about how Pine Valley Furniture Company does business with its customers?
19. Answer the following questions concerning Figures 1-16 and 1-17:
    a. What will be the field size for the ProductLineName field in the Product table? Why?
    b. In Figure 1-17, how is the ProductID field in the Product table specified to be required? Why is it a required attribute?
    c. In Figure 1-17, explain the function of the FOREIGN KEY definition.
20. Consider the SQL query in Figure 1-19.
    a. How is Sales to Date calculated?
    b. How would the query have to change if Helen Jarvis wanted to see the results for all of the product lines, not just the Home Office product line?
21. Helen Jarvis wants to determine the most important customers for Home Office products. She requests a listing of total dollar sales year-to-date for each customer who bought these products, as revealed by invoiced payments. The list is to be sorted in descending order, so that the largest customer heads the list.
    a. Look at Figure 1-18 and determine what entities are required to produce this list.
    b. Which entities will be involved in the SQL query that will give Helen the information she needs?
22. In this chapter, we described four important data models and their properties: enterprise, conceptual, logical, and physical. In the following table, summarize the important properties of these data models by entering a Y (for Yes) or an N (for No) in each cell of the table.
23. A FMCG marketing company wants to release its new product in the market; a market survey needs to be done. It wants to employ an outside agency for carrying out the survey. What data needs to be collected internally and externally from the organization? Based on this information, what type of databases would you recommend for this survey?
24. An automobile accessories dealer has been in the business for around eight to ten years. But the sales have been stagnating over a couple of years. While the company has been using IT for its accounting-related business processes, it has not implemented IT for its sales. Sales personnel were taking a long time to complete the sales transactions manually. The sales data was found wanting and was incomplete to take any decisions. The CEO feels that having a proper database of the transacted and projected sales would help. What would be your recommendations to the CEO regarding analysis of the database requirements for the sales-related database?
25. A multiplex screening movies has hosted its ticketing system online. At the end of the day, the theater manager wants to analyze the counter collections with respect to the screening of the movies. Apart from the standard queries, the theater manager wants to use many ad hoc queries. As a database analyst and designer, how would you go about helping the theater manager using the database?

Table for Problem and Exercise 22

	All Entities?	All Attributes?	Technology Independent?	DBMS Independent?	Record Layouts?
Enterprise					
Conceptual					
Logical					
Physical					

Field Exercises

For Questions 1 through 7, choose an organization with a fairly extensive information systems department and set of information system applications. You should choose one which you are familiar, possibly your employer, your university, or an organization where a friend works. Use the same organization for each question.

1. Investigate whether the organization follows more of a traditional file processing approach or the database approach to organizing data. How many different databases does the organization have? Try to draw a figure, similar to Figure 1-2, to depict some or all of the files and databases in this organization.
2. Talk with a database administrator or designer from the organization. What type of metadata does this organization maintain about its databases? Why did the organization choose to keep track of these and not other metadata? What tools are used to maintain these metadata?

3. Determine the company's use of intranet, extranet, or other Web-enabled business processes. For each type of process, determine its purpose and the database management system that is being used in conjunction with the networks. Ask what the company's plans are for the next year with regard to using intranets, extranets, or the Web in their business activities. Ask what new skills they are looking for in order to implement these plans.
4. Consider a major database in this organization, such as one supporting customer interactions, accounting, or manufacturing. What is the architecture for this database? Is the organization using some form of client/server architecture? Interview information systems managers in this organization to find out why they chose the architecture for this database.
5. Interview systems and database analysts at this organization. Ask them to describe their systems development process. Does it resemble more the systems development life cycle or prototyping? Do they use methodologies similar to both? When do they use their different methodologies? Explore the methodology used for developing applications to be used through the Web. How have they adapted their methodology to fit this new systems development process?
6. Interview a systems analyst or database analyst and ask questions about the typical composition of an information systems development team. Specifically, what role does a database analyst play in project teams? Is a database analyst used throughout the systems development process or is the database analyst used only at selected points?
7. Interview a systems analyst or database analyst and ask questions about how that organization uses CASE tools in the systems development process. Concentrate your questions on how CASE tools are used to support data modeling and database design and how the CASE tool's repository maintains the information collected about data, data characteristics, and data usage. If multiple CASE tools are used on one or many projects, ask how the organization attempts to integrate data models and data definitions. Finally, inquire how satisfied the systems and database analysts are with CASE tool support for data modeling and database design.
8. You may want to keep a personal journal of ideas and observations about database management while you are studying this book. Use this journal to record comments you hear, summaries of news stories or professional articles you read, original ideas or hypotheses you create, uniform resource locators (URLs) for and comments about Web sites related to databases, and questions that require further analysis. Keep your eyes and ears open for anything related to database management. Your instructor may ask you to turn in a copy of your journal from time to time in order to provide feedback and reactions. The journal is an unstructured set of personal notes that will supplement your class notes and can stimulate you to think beyond the topics covered within the time limitations of most courses.

References

Anderson-Lehman, R., H. J. Watson, B. Wixom, and J. A. Hoffer. 2004. "Continental Airlines Flies High with Real-Time Business Intelligence." *MIS Quarterly Executive* 3,4 (December).

Codd, E. F. 1970. "A Relational Model of Data for Large Shared Data Banks." *Communications of the ACM* 13,6 (June): 377–87.

Fowler, M. 2005. "The New Methodology" available at **www.martinfowler.com/articles/newMethodology.html** (access verified February 20, 2010).

Gray, J. 1996. "Data Management: Past, Present, and Future." *IEEE Computer* 29,10: 38–46.

Grimes, S. 1998. "Object/Relational Reality Check." *Database Programming & Design* 11,7 (July): 26–33.

Henderson, D., B. Champlin, D. Coleman, P. Cupoli, J. Hoffer, L. Howarth et al. 2005. "Model Curriculum Framework for Post Secondary Education Programs in Data Resource Management." The Data Management Association International Foundation Committee on the Advancement of Data Management in Post Secondary Institutions Sub Committee on Curriculum Framework Development. DAMA International Foundation.

Hoffer, J. A., J. F. George, and J. S. Valacich. 2010. *Modern Systems Analysis and Design*, 6th ed. Upper Saddle River, NJ: Prentice Hall.

Jordan, A. 1996. "Data Warehouse Integrity: How Long and Bumpy the Road?" *Data Management Review* 6,3 (March): 35–37.

Long, D. 2005. Presentation. ".Net Overview," Tampa Bay Technology Leadership Association, May 19, 2005.

Mullins, C. S. 2002. *Database Administration: The Complete Guide to Practices and Procedures*. New York: Addison-Wesley.

Ritter, D. 1999. "Don't Neglect Your Legacy." *Intelligent Enterprise* 2,5 (March 30): 70, 72.

Further Reading

Ballou, D. P., and G. K. Tayi. 1999. "Enhancing Data Quality in Data Warehouse Environments." *Communications of the ACM* 42,1 (January): 73–78.

Date, C. J. 1998. "The Birth of the Relational Model, Part 3." *Intelligent Enterprise* 1,4 (December 10): 45–48.

Kimball, R., and M. Ross. 2002. The *Data Warehouse Toolkit: The Complete Guide to Dimensional Data Modeling*, 2d ed. New York: Wiley. Ritter, D. 1999. "The Long View." *Intelligent Enterprise* 2,12 (August 24): 58, 63, 67.

Silverston, L. 2001a. *The Data Model Resource Book, Vol. 1: A Library of Universal Data Models for all Enterprises*. New York: Wiley.

Silverston, L. 2001b. *The Data Model Resource Book, Vol 2: A Library of Data Models for Specific Industries*. New York: Wiley.

Winter, R. 1997. "What, After All, Is a Very Large Database?" *Database Programming & Design* 10,1 (January): 23–26.

Web Resources

www.dbazine.com An online portal for database issues and solutions.

www.webopedia.com An online dictionary and search engine for computer terms and Internet technology.

www.techrepublic.com A portal site for information technology professionals that users can customize to their own particular interests.

www.zdnet.com A portal site where users can review recent articles on information technology subjects.

www.information-management.com DM Review magazine Web site, with the tagline "Covering Business Intelligence, Integration and Analytics." Provides a comprehensive list of links to relevant resource portals in addition to providing many of the magazine articles online.

www.dbta.com Data Base Trends & Applications magazine Web site. Addresses enterprise-level information issues.

http://databases.about.com A comprehensive site with many feature articles, links, interactive forum, chat rooms, and so forth.

http://thecaq.aicpa.org/Resources/Sarbanes+Oxley AICPA site for current information regarding Sarbanes-Oxley legislation.

www.basel.int United Nations page offering an overview of the Basel Convention, which addresses global waste issues.

www.usdoj.gov/jmd/irm/lifecycle/table.htm The Department of Justice Systems Development Life Cycle Guidance Document. This is an example of a systems methodology that you may want to look over.

http://groups.google.com/group/comp.software-eng?lnk=gsch&hl=en The software engineering archives for a Google group that focuses on software engineering and related topics. This site contains many links that you may want to explore.

www.acinet.org/acinet America's Career InfoNet, which provides information about careers, outlook, requirements, and so forth.

www.collegegrad.com/salaries/index.shtml A site for finding recent salary information for a wide range of careers, including database-related careers.

www.essentialstrategies.com/publications/methodology/zachman.htm David Hay's Web site, which has considerable information on universal data models as well as how database development fits into the Zachman information systems architecture.

www.inmondatasystems.com Web site for one of the pioneers of data warehousing.

www.agilemanifesto.org Web site that explains the viewpoints of those who created The Manifesto for Agile Software Development

CASE

Mountain View Community Hospital

Introduction

This case is included to provide you an opportunity to apply the concepts and techniques you will learn in each chapter. The case can also be used to support a semester-long database project built throughout the term that results in a complete application. We have selected a hospital for this case because it is a type of organization that is at least somewhat familiar to most persons and because health-care institutions are of such importance in our society today. A segment of the case is included at the end of each chapter in this text. Each segment includes a brief description of the case as it relates to the material in the chapter followed by questions and exercises related to the material. Additional requirements, assignments, and project deliverables are provided in support of a semester project.

Case Description

Mountain View Community Hospital (MVCH) is a not-for-profit, short-term, acute care general hospital. It is a relatively small hospital, with some 150 beds. Mountain View Community Hospital strives to meet the needs of a community of about 60,000 with an annual growth rate of 10 percent, a trend that is expected to continue since the surrounding area is attracting many retirees. To serve the health-care needs of this growing community, Mountain View Community Hospital plans to expand its capacity by adding another 50 beds over the next five years, and opening a managed care retirement center with independent apartments and assisted living facilities. The basic goal is to provide high-quality, cost-effective health-care services for the surrounding community in a compassionate, caring, and personalized manner.

Within the last fiscal year, the hospital performed more than one million laboratory procedures and over 110,000 radiology procedures. During that time, the hospital had 9,192 admissions and 112,230 outpatient visits, brought 1,127 babies into the world, and performed 2,314 inpatient and 1,490 outpatient surgeries. Patients who receive outpatient surgeries do not remain in the hospital overnight. With an average of 2,340 patients a month, the emergency department experienced approximately 28,200 visits throughout the year. Approximately 30 percent of the patients admitted to the hospital were first treated in the emergency room, and about 13 percent of emergency room visits resulted in hospital admission. The hospital employs 740 full-time and 439 part-time personnel, among them 264 full-time and 176 part-time registered nurses, and 10 full-time and 6 part-time licensed practical nurses. The hospital's active medical staff includes over 250 primary physicians, specialists, and subspecialists. Volunteers are an integral part of MVCH's culture and contribute greatly to the well-being of patients and their families. Approximately 300 volunteers from different backgrounds and of all ages devote their time, energy, and talents to many areas of the hospital. They greet visitors and patients and help them find their way through the hospital, deliver mail and flowers to patient rooms, escort patients, aid staff with clerical duties, work in the gift shop, assist at community and fund-raising events, and help out in a host of other areas.

Mountain View Community Hospital provides a number of key services, including general medical and surgical care, general intensive care, a cardiology department, open-heart surgery, a neurology department, pediatric medical and surgical care, obstetrics, an orthopedics department, oncology, and a 24-hour emergency department. The hospital also offers a wide range of diagnostic services. A specialty service within the neurology department is the recently opened Multiple Sclerosis (MS) Center, which provides comprehensive and expert care for patients with multiple sclerosis in order to improve their quality of life. Using an interdisciplinary team approach, the center emphasizes all aspects of MS care from diagnosis and treatment of MS symptoms and secondary complications, to individual and family counseling, rehabilitation therapy, and social services. Headed by Dr. Zequida, called Dr. "Z" by staff and patients, the MS Center is a member of a consortium of MS centers.

The current organizational chart for Mountain View Community Hospital is shown in MVCH Figure 1-1. Like most other general hospitals, Mountain View Community is divided into two primary organizational groups. The physicians, headed by Dr. Browne (chief of staff), are responsible for the quality of medical care provided to their patients. The group headed by Ms. Baker (CEO and president) provides the nursing, clinical, and administrative support the physicians need to serve their patients. According to Ms. Baker, the most pressing issues affecting the hospital within the last year have been financial challenges such as bad debt, personnel shortages (particularly registered nurses and imaging technicians), and malpractice insurance. Other critical issues are the quality of care, patient safety, compliance with HIPAA, and technological innovation, which is seen as a major enabler for decreasing costs and improving quality. The trend toward managed care and the need to maintain costs while maintaining/improving clinical outcomes requires the hospital to track and analyze both clinical and financial data related to patient care services.

Goals and Critical Success Factors

In response to the steady growth and expansion plans at Mountain View Community Hospital, a special study team including Mr. Heller, Mr. Lopez, Dr. Jefferson, and a consultant has been developing a long-term strategic plan, including an information systems plan for the hospital. Their work is not complete, but they have begun to identify many of the elements necessary to build the plan. To meet the goals of high-quality health care, cost containment, and expansion into new services, the team concluded that the hospital has four critical success factors (CSFs): quality of medical care, control of operating costs, control of capital costs, and recruitment and retention of skilled personnel. The development of improved information systems is viewed as an enabler in dealing with each of these CSFs.

The team is currently at work to generate two to four short- or long-term objectives for each CSF. So far they have developed the following four objectives related to the control of the operating costs CSF:

1. Reduce costs for purchased items
2. More efficiently schedule staff
3. Lower cost of liability insurance
4. Expand volunteer services

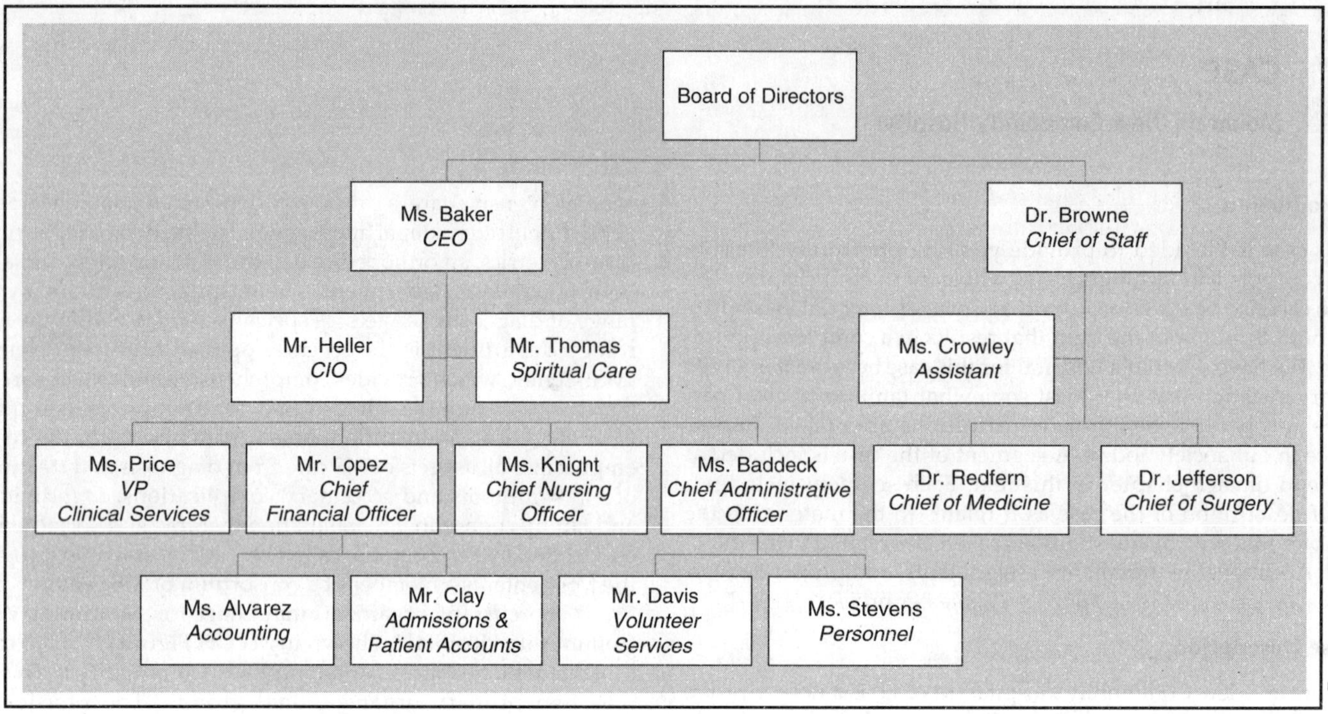

MVCH FIGURE 1-1 Organizational chart

The study team has developed a preliminary list of business functions that describe the administrative and medical activities within the hospital. These functions consider the organizational goals and CSFs explained in the prior section. At this point, the study team has identified five major business functions that cut across all of the organizational units:

1. ***Patient care administration*** Manage the logistical and record-keeping aspects of patient care
2. ***Clinical services*** Provide laboratory testing and procedures, and patient monitoring and screening
3. ***Patient care services*** Provide patients with medical care and support services
4. ***Financial management*** Manage the financial resources and operations of the hospital
5. ***Administrative services*** Provide general management and support services not directly related to patient care

The study team has been able to break each of these high-level business functions into lists of more detailed functions (see MVCH Figure 1-2), but the team knows that these lists are not complete nor well defined at this point.

Mountain View Community Hospital has computer applications that support the following areas (among others): patient care administration, clinical services, financial management, and administrative services. Many of these applications have been purchased from outside vendors, but a few have been developed internally. Most of the computer applications are implemented using relational database and client/server technology. In the client/server environment, the client runs the database applications that request the data. The server runs the DBMS software, which fulfills the requests and handles the functions required for concurrent, shared data access to the database. Most of the databases (as well as the applications) are two tier, using the classification introduced in this chapter.

Patient care administration	**Clinical services**	**Patient care services**	**Financial management**	**Administrative services**
Patient scheduling	Electrodiagnosis	Dietary/Nutrition	Patient accounting · *Bill patient* · *Account for receivables*	Purchasing
Patient registration · *Admit patient* · *Assign patient to bed* · *Transfer patient* · *Discharge patient*	Psychiatric testing	Nursing Surgery	Cost accounting	Inventory control
Physician orders	Patient monitoring	Rehabilitation · *Perform physical therapy*	Payroll	Housekeeping
Laboratory reporting	Multiphasic screening	Blood banking	General accounting	Personnel
	Radiology · *Perform X-rays*		Risk management	Volunteering · *Recruit volunteers* · *Schedule volunteers* · *Evaluate volunteers*
	Laboratory · *Perform blood tests*			

MVCH FIGURE 1-2 Business functions

Enterprise Modeling

The study team identified a preliminary set of 11 entity types that describe the data required by the hospital in support of the various business functions: FACILITY, PHYSICIAN, PATIENT, DIAGNOSTIC UNIT, WARD, STAFF, ORDER, SERVICE/DRUG, MEDICAL/SURGICAL ITEM, SUPPLY ITEM, and VENDOR. From discussions with hospital staff, reviewing hospital documents, and studying existing information systems, the study team developed a list of business rules describing the policies of the hospital and nature of the hospital's operation that govern the relationships between these entities. Some of these rules are:

1. A FACILITY maintains one or more DIAGNOSTIC UNITS (radiology, clinical laboratory, cardiac diagnostic unit, etc.).
2. A FACILITY contains a number of WARDs (obstetrics, oncology, geriatrics, etc.).
3. Each WARD is assigned a certain number of STAFF members (nurses, secretaries, etc.); a STAFF member may be assigned to multiple WARDs.
4. A FACILITY staffs its medical team with a number of PHYSICIANs. A PHYSICIAN may be on the staff of more than one FACILITY.
5. A PHYSICIAN treats PATIENTs, and a PATIENT is treated by any number of PHYSICIANs.
6. A PHYSICIAN diagnoses PATIENTs, and a PATIENT is diagnosed by any number of PHYSICIANs.
7. A PATIENT may be assigned to a WARD (outpatients are not assigned to a WARD). The hospital cares only about the current WARD a patient is assigned to (if assigned at all).
8. A PATIENT uses MEDICAL/SURGICAL ITEMS, which are supplied by VENDORs. A VENDOR also provides SUPPLY ITEMs that are used for housekeeping and maintenance purposes.
9. A PHYSICIAN writes one or more ORDERS for a PATIENT. Each ORDER is for a given PATIENT, and a PATIENT may have many ORDERs.
10. An ORDER can be for a diagnostic test (lab tests such as lipid profile, CBC, liver function tests; diagnostic imaging such as MRIs and X-rays) or a drug.

They recognized that certain business functions, such as risk management and volunteering, were not adequately represented in the set of data entities and business rules, but they decided to deal with these and other areas later. The study team stored descriptions of these data entities and the business rules in the CASE repository for later analysis. Using the identified entities and business rules, the study team developed a preliminary enterprise data model (see MVCH Figure 1-3). Again, this conceptual model is preliminary and does not follow all the conventions used in the information systems department for drawing data models, but the purpose of this enterprise model is to give only a general overview of organizational data.

Case Questions

1. The goal of Mountain View Community Hospital is to provide high-quality, cost-effective health-care services for the surrounding community in a compassionate, caring, and personalized manner. Give some examples of how the use of databases in the hospital might improve health-care quality or contain costs. How else could a well-managed database help the hospital achieve its mission?
2. How can database technology be used to help Mountain View Community Hospital comply with the security standards of the Health Insurance Portability and Accountability Act of 1996 (HIPAA)? HIPAA requires health-care providers to maintain reasonable and appropriate administrative, technical, and physical safeguards to ensure that the integrity, confidentiality, and availability of electronic health information they collect, maintain, use, or transmit is protected. (For more details on HIPAA, visit www.hhs.gov/ocr/privacy.)
3. What are some of the costs and risks of using databases that the hospital must manage carefully?
4. How critical are data quality requirements in the hospital environment? For which applications might quality requirements be more restrictive?
5. At present, Mountain View Community Hospital is using relational database technology. Although this technology is

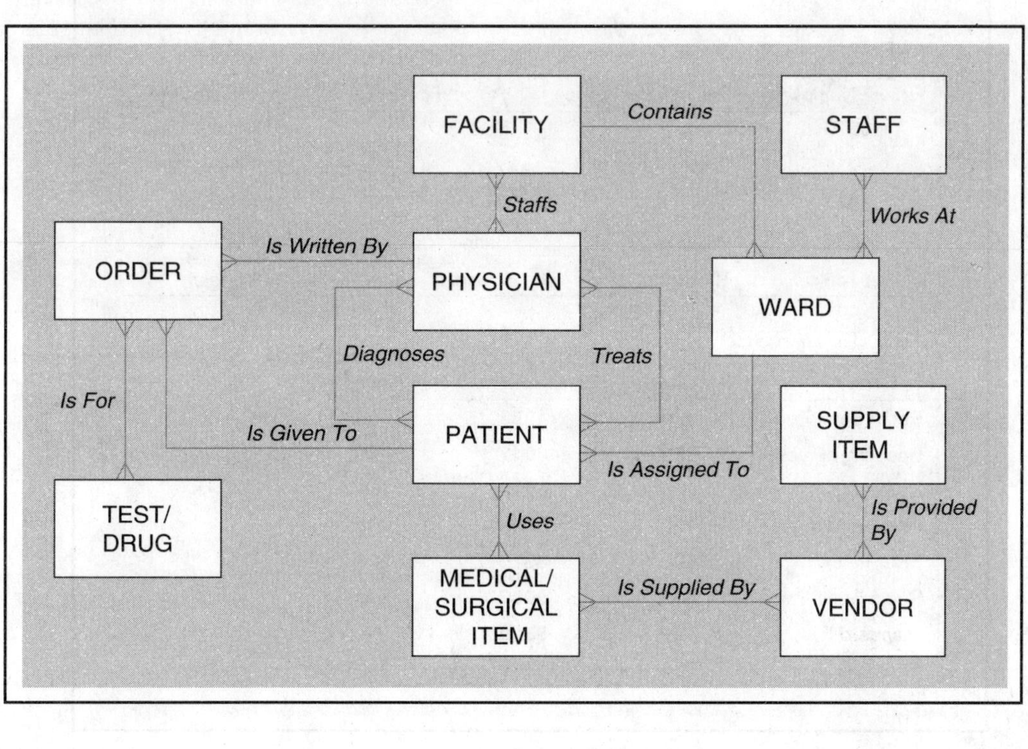

MVCH FIGURE 1-3 Preliminary enterprise data model

appropriate for structured data, such as patient or accounting data, it is less well-suited to unstructured data, such as graphical data and images. Can you think of some types of data maintained by a hospital that fit this latter category? What types of database technology rather than relational might be better suited to these data types?

6. How could the hospital use Web-based applications? What are some of the benefits and risks associated with Web-based applications for the hospital?
7. The case description lists 10 business rules. The study team used these rules to develop MVCH Figure 1-3. Are there any other business rules implied by or depicted in that figure? What are they?

Case Exercises

1. The relational databases at Mountain View Community Hospital contain a number of tables. Two of these tables, with some sample data, are shown in MVCH Figure 1-4. The PATIENT table contains data concerning current or recent patients at the hospital, whereas the PATIENT CHARGES table contains data describing charges that have been incurred by those patients. Interestingly, the PATIENT CHARGES table is not captured in the preliminary enterprise data model shown in Figure 1-3.
   - **a.** Using the notation introduced in this chapter, draw a diagram showing the relationship between the entities PATIENT and PATIENT CHARGES.
   - **b.** Develop a metadata chart for the data attributes in the PATIENT and PATIENT CHARGES tables using (at minimum) the columns shown in Table 1-1. You may include other metadata characteristics that you think are appropriate for the management of data at Mountain View Community Hospital.
2. One of the important outputs from the "bill patient" business function is the Patient Bill. Following is a highly simplified version of this bill (MVCH Figure 1-5).
   - **a.** Using the data from MVCH Figure 1-4, add missing data that would typically appear on a patient bill.
   - **b.** Using your result from part a), verify that the enterprise data model in MVCH Figure 1-3 contains the data necessary to generate a patient bill. Explain what you have to do to perform this verification. What did you discover from your analysis?
3. Using the notation introduced in this chapter, draw a single diagram that represents the following relationships in the hospital environment.
   - A HOSPITAL has on its staff one or more PHYSICIANs. A PHYSICIAN is on the staff of only one HOSPITAL.
   - A PHYSICIAN may admit one or more PATIENTs. A PATIENT is admitted by only one PHYSICIAN.
   - A HOSPITAL has one or more WARDs. Each WARD is located in exactly one HOSPITAL.
   - A WARD has any number of EMPLOYEEs. An EMPLOYEE may work in one or more WARDs.
4. Using a DBMS suggested by your instructor, such as Microsoft Access or SQL Server, you may begin to prototype a database for Mountain View Community Hospital. Here are some suggestions to guide you:
   - **a.** Develop a metadata chart for an EMPLOYEE table similar to Table 1-1.
   - **b.** What types of relationships (*1:1*, *1:M*, or *M:N*) are likely to exist between your PATIENT table and other tables in the database? How did you determine that?
   - **c.** MVCH hospital administrators regularly need information about their patient population. Based on the distinction between data and information discussed in this

MVCH FIGURE 1-4 Two database tables from Mountain View Community Hospital

PATIENT

Patient Number	Patient Last Name	Patient First Name	Patient Address
8379	Dimas	Selena	617 Valley Vista
4238	Dolan	Mark	818 River Run
3047	Larreau	Annette	127 Sandhill
5838	Wiggins	Brian	431 Walnut
6143	Thomas	Wendell	928 Logan

PATIENT CHARGES

Item Description	Item Code	Patient Number	Amount
Room Semi-Priv	200	4238	1600
Speech Therapy	350	3047	750
Radiology	275	4238	150
Physical Therapy	409	5838	600
EKG Test	500	8379	200
Room Semi-Priv	200	3047	800
Standard IV	470	8379	150
EEG Test	700	4238	200

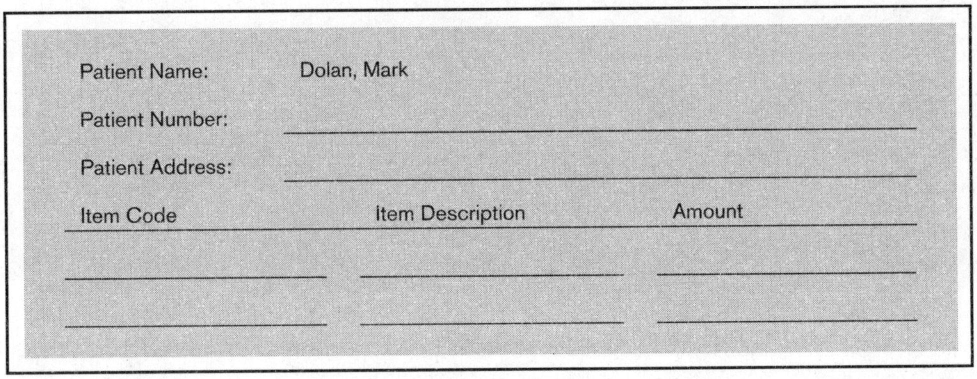
Patient Name: Dolan, Mark

Patient Number: ____________

Patient Address: ____________

Item Code	Item Description	Amount

MVCH FIGURE 1-5 Partial patient bill

chapter, explain why a printout of a PATIENT table will not satisfy these information needs.

   d. Create a report that organizes the data from your PATIENT table to provide hospital administrators with useful information about the patient population at MVCH.

5. Earlier in this chapter, we showed an SQL query that displays information about computer desks at Pine Valley Furniture Company:

```
SELECT *
FROM Product
WHERE ProductDescription="Computer Desk";
```

   Following this example, create an SQL query for your PATIENT table that displays information about the outpatients.

6. The manager of the risk management area, Ms. Jamieson, is anxious to receive computerized support for her activities. The hospital is increasingly facing malpractice claims and litigation, and she does not believe she can wait for improved information services until the information systems and database plans are set. Specifically, Ms. Jamieson wants a system that will track claims, legal suits, lawyers, judges, medical staff, disbursements against claims, and judgments. How would you proceed to deal with this request for improved information services? What methodology would you apply to design or acquire the systems and databases she needs? Why?
7. Consider again the request of the manager of risk management from Case Exercise 6. On what tier or tiers would you recommend the system and database she needs be developed? Why?

Project Assignments

P1. The study team's activities described in this case study are still in the very early stages of information system and database development. Outline the next steps that should be followed within the Information Systems unit to align current systems and databases to the future information systems needs of the hospital.

P2. The patient bill is an example of a view that would be of interest in a hospital environment. Identify and list other user views that could occur in a hospital environment.

P3. Carefully read through the case description, exercises, and questions again and:

   a. Modify the enterprise data model shown in MVCH Figure 1-3 to include any additional entities and relationships that you identify.
   b. Modify the list of business rules from the case description to include the additional entities and relationships you identified.
   c. Draw a context diagram of MVCH's improved information system similar to the one for a burger restaurant shown in MVCH Figure 1-6. A context diagram provides the highest-level view of a system and shows the system boundaries, external entities that interact with the system, and major information flows between the entities and the system.

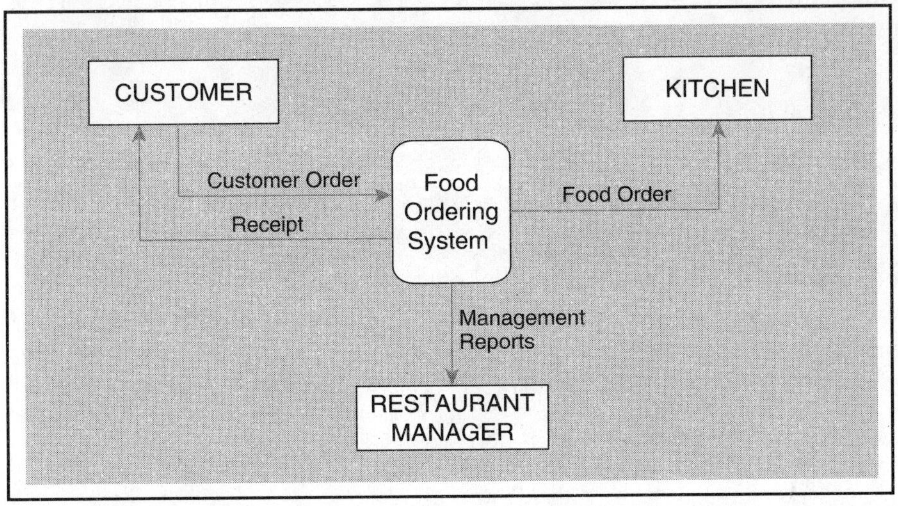

MVCH FIGURE 1-6 Context diagram example

Source: Adapted from Hoffer et al. (2010).

PART II

Database Analysis

Chapter 2
Modeling Data in the Organization

Chapter 3
The Enhanced E-R Model

AN OVERVIEW OF PART TWO

The first step in database development is database analysis, in which we determine user requirements for data and develop data models to represent those requirements. The two chapters in Part II describe in depth the de facto standard for conceptual data modeling—entity-relationship diagramming. A conceptual data model represents data from the viewpoint of the organization, independent of any technology that will be used to implement the model.

Chapter 2 ("Modeling Data in the Organization") begins by describing business rules, which are the policies and rules about the operation of a business that a data model represents. Characteristics of good business rules are described, and the process of gathering business rules is discussed. General guidelines for naming and defining elements of a data model are presented within the context of business rules.

Chapter 2 introduces the notations and main constructs of this modeling technique, including entities, relationships, and attributes; for each construct, we provide specific guidelines for naming and defining these elements of a data model. We distinguish between strong and weak entity types and the use of identifying relationships. We describe different types of attributes, including required versus optional attributes, simple versus composite attributes, single-valued versus multivalued attributes, derived attributes, and identifiers. We contrast relationship types and instances and introduce associative entities. We describe and illustrate relationships of various degrees, including unary, binary, and ternary relationships. We also describe the various relationship cardinalities that arise in modeling situations. We discuss the common problem of how to model time-dependent data. Finally, we describe the situation in which multiple relationships are defined between a given set of entities. The E-R modeling concepts are illustrated with an extended example for Pine Valley Furniture Company. This final example, as well as a few other examples throughout the chapter, is presented using Microsoft Visio, which shows how many data modeling tools represent data models.

Chapter 3 ("The Enhanced E-R Model") presents advanced concepts in E-R modeling; these additional modeling features are often required to cope with the increasingly complex business environment encountered in organizations today.

The most important modeling construct incorporated in the enhanced entity-relationship (EER) diagram is supertype/subtype relationships. This facility allows us to model a general entity type (called a supertype) and then subdivide it into several specialized entity types called subtypes. For example, sports cars and sedans are subtypes of automobiles. We introduce a simple notation for representing supertype/subtype relationships and several refinements. We also introduce generalization and specialization as two contrasting techniques for identifying supertype/subtype relationships. Supertype/subtype notation is necessary for the increasingly popular universal data model, which is motivated and explained in Chapter 3. The comprehensiveness of a well-documented relationship can be overwhelming, so we introduce a technique called entity clustering for simplifying the presentation of an E-R diagram to meet the needs of a given audience.

The concept of patterns has become a central element of many information systems development methodologies. The notion is that there are reusable component designs that can be combined and tailored to meet new information system requests. In the database world, these patterns are called universal data models, prepackaged data models, or logical data models. These patterns can be purchased or may be inherent in a commercial off-the-shelf package, such as an ERP or CRM application. Increasingly, it is from these patterns that new databases are designed. In Chapter 3 we describe the usefulness of such patterns and outline a modification of the database development process when such patterns are the starting point. Universal industry or business function data models extensively use the extended entity-relationship diagramming notations introduced in this chapter.

There is another, alternative notation for data modeling: the Unified Modeling Language class diagrams for systems developed using object-oriented technologies. This technique is presented later in the book, in Chapter 13. It is possible to read Chapter 13 immediately after Chapter 3 if you want to compare these alternative, but conceptually similar, approaches.

The conceptual data modeling concepts presented in the two chapters in Part II provide the foundation for your career in database analysis and design. As a database analyst you will be expected to apply the E-R notation in modeling user requirements for data and information.

CHAPTER

2

Modeling Data in the Organization

Learning Objectives

After studying this chapter, you should be able to:

- Concisely define each of the following key terms: **business rule, term, fact, entity-relationship model (E-R model), entity-relationship diagram (E-R diagram), entity, entity type, entity instance, strong entity type, weak entity type, identifying owner, identifying relationship, attribute, required attribute, optional attribute, composite attribute, simple attribute, multivalued attribute, derived attribute, identifier, composite identifier, relationship type, relationship instance, associative entity, degree, unary relationship, binary relationship, ternary relationship, cardinality constraint, minimum cardinality, maximum cardinality,** and **time stamp.**
- State reasons why many system developers believe that data modeling is the most important part of the systems development process.
- Write good names and definitions for entities, relationships, and attributes.
- Distinguish unary, binary, and ternary relationships and give a common example of each.
- Model each of the following constructs in an E-R diagram: composite attribute, multivalued attribute, derived attribute, associative entity, identifying relationship, and minimum and maximum cardinality constraints.
- Draw an E-R diagram to represent common business situations.
- Convert a many-to-many relationship to an associative entity type.
- Model simple time-dependent data using time stamps and relationships in an E-R diagram.

INTRODUCTION

You have already been introduced to modeling data and the entity-relationship (E-R) data model through simplified examples in Chapter 1. (You may want to review, for example, the E-R models in Figures 1-3 and 1-4.) In this chapter, we formalize data modeling based on the powerful concept of business rules and describe the E-R data model in detail. This chapter begins your journey of learning how to design and use databases. It is exciting to create information systems that run organizations and help people do their jobs well.

Business rules, the foundation of data models, are derived from policies, procedures, events, functions, and other business objects, and they state constraints on the organization. Business rules represent the language and fundamental structure of an organization (Hay, 2003). Business rules formalize the understanding of the organization by organization owners, managers, and leaders with that of information systems architects.

Business rules are important in data modeling because they govern how data are handled and stored. Examples of basic business rules are data names and definitions. This chapter explains guidelines for the clear naming and definition of data objects in a business. In terms of conceptual data modeling, names and definitions must be provided for the main data objects: entity types (e.g., Customer), attributes (Customer Name), and relationships (Customer Places Orders). Other business rules may state constraints on these data objects. These constraints can be captured in a data model, such as an entity-relationship diagram, and associated documentation. Additional business rules govern the people, places, events, processes, networks, and objectives of the organization, which are all linked to the data requirements through other system documentation.

After decades of use, the E-R model remains the mainstream approach for conceptual data modeling. Its popularity stems from factors such as relative ease of use, widespread computer-aided software engineering (CASE) tool support, and the belief that entities and relationships are natural modeling concepts in the real world.

The E-R model is most used as a tool for communications between database designers and end users during the analysis phase of database development (described in Chapter 1). The E-R model is used to construct a conceptual data model, which is a representation of the structure and constraints of a database that is independent of software (such as a database management system).

Some authors introduce terms and concepts peculiar to the relational data model when discussing E-R modeling; the relational data model is the basis for most database management systems in use today. In particular, they recommend that the E-R model be completely normalized, with full resolution of primary and foreign keys. However, we believe that this forces a premature commitment to the relational data model. In today's database environment, the database may be implemented with object-oriented technology or with a mixture of object-oriented and relational technology. Therefore, we defer discussion of normalization concepts to Chapter 4.

The E-R model was introduced in a key article by Chen (1976), in which he described the main constructs of the E-R model—entities and relationships—and their associated attributes. The model has subsequently been extended to include additional constructs by Chen and others; for example, see Teorey et al. (1986) and Storey (1991). The E-R model continues to evolve, but unfortunately there is not yet a standard notation for E-R modeling. Song et al. (1995) present a side-by-side comparison of 10 different E-R modeling notations, explaining the major advantages and disadvantages of each approach. Because data modeling software tools are now commonly used by professional data modelers, we adopt for use in this text a variation of the notation used in professional modeling tools. Appendix A will help you translate between our notation and other popular E-R diagramming notations.

As said in a popular travel service TV commercial, "we are doing important stuff here." Many systems developers believe that data modeling is the most important part of the systems development process for the following reasons (Hoffer et al., 2010):

1. The characteristics of data captured during data modeling are crucial in the design of databases, programs, and other system components. The facts and rules captured during the process of data modeling are essential in assuring data integrity in an information system.

2. Data rather than processes are the most complex aspect of many modern information systems and hence require a central role in structuring system requirements. Often the goal is to provide a rich data resource that might support any type of information inquiry, analysis, and summary.
3. Data tend to be more stable than the business processes that use that data. Thus, an information system design that is based on a data orientation should have a longer useful life than one based on a process orientation.

In an actual work environment, you may not have to develop a data model from scratch. Because of the increased acceptance of packaged software (for example, enterprise resource planning with a predefined data model) and purchased business area or industry data models (which we discuss in Chapter 3), your job of data modeling has a jump start. This is good because such components and patterns give you a starting point based on generally accepted practices. However, your job is not done for several reasons:

1. There are still many times when a new, custom-built application is being developed along with the associated database. The business rules for the business area supported by this application need to be modeled.
2. Purchased applications and data models need to be customized for your particular setting. Predefined data models tend to be very extensive and complex; hence, they require significant data modeling skill to tailor the models to be effective and efficient in a given organization. Although this effort can be much faster, thorough, and accurate than starting from scratch, the ability to understand a particular organization to match the data model to its business rules is an essential task.

In this chapter, we present the main features of E-R modeling, using common notation and conventions. We begin with a sample E-R diagram, including the basic constructs of the E-R model—entities, attributes, and relationships—and then we introduce the concept of business rules, which is the foundation for all the data modeling constructs. We define three types of entities that are common in E-R modeling: strong entities, weak entities, and associative entities; a few more entity types are defined in Chapter 3. We also define several important types of attributes, including required and optional attributes, single- and multivalued attributes, derived attributes, and composite attributes. We then introduce three important concepts associated with relationships: the degree of a relationship, the cardinality of a relationship, and participation constraints in a relationship. We conclude with an extended example of an E-R diagram for Pine Valley Furniture Company.

THE E-R MODEL: AN OVERVIEW

An **entity-relationship model (E-R model)** is a detailed, logical representation of the data for an organization or for a business area. The E-R model is expressed in terms of entities in the business environment, the relationships (or associations) among those entities, and the attributes (or properties) of both the entities and their relationships. An E-R model is normally expressed as an **entity-relationship diagram (E-R diagram, or ERD)**, which is a graphical representation of an E-R model.

Entity-relationship model (E-R model)
A logical representation of the data for an organization or for a business area, using entities for categories of data and relationships for associations between entities.

Entity-relationship diagram (E-R diagram, or ERD)
A graphical representation of an entity-relationship model.

Sample E-R Diagram

To jump-start your understanding of E-R diagrams, Figure 2-1 presents a simplified E-R diagram for a small furniture manufacturing company, Pine Valley Furniture Company. (This figure, which does not include attributes, is often called an *enterprise data model*, which we introduced Chapter 1.) A number of suppliers supply and ship different items to Pine Valley Furniture. The items are assembled into products that are sold to customers who order the products. Each customer order may include one or more lines corresponding to the products appearing on that order.

FIGURE 2-1 Sample E-R diagram

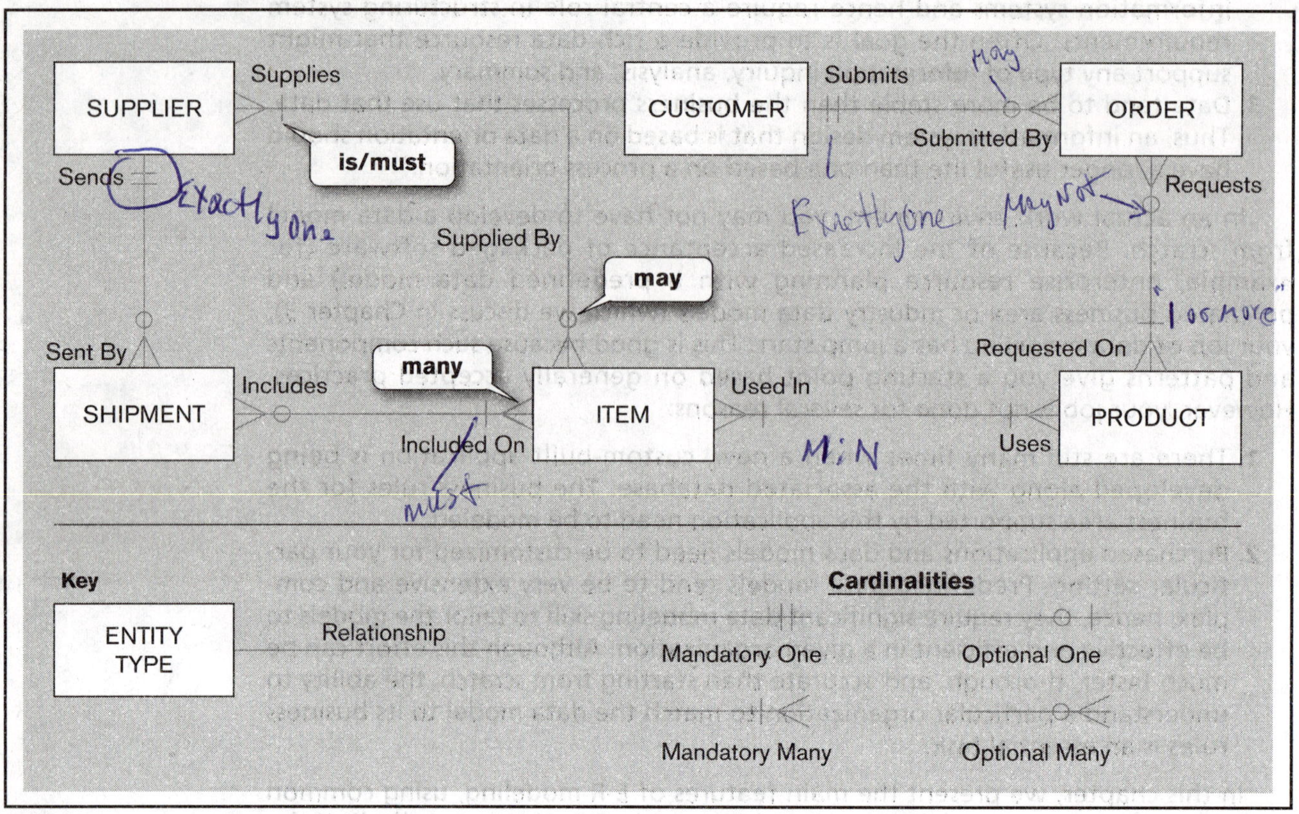

The diagram in Figure 2-1 shows the entities and relationships for this company. (Attributes are omitted to simplify the diagram for now.) Entities (the objects of the organization) are represented by the rectangle symbol, whereas relationships between entities are represented by lines connecting the related entities. The entities in Figure 2-1 are:

CUSTOMER	A person or an organization that has ordered or might order products. *Example*: L. L. Fish Furniture.
PRODUCT	A type of furniture made by Pine Valley Furniture that may be ordered by customers. Note that a product is not a specific bookcase, because individual bookcases do not need to be tracked. *Example*: A 6-foot, 5-shelf, oak bookcase called O600.
ORDER	The transaction associated with the sale of one or more products to a customer and identified by a transaction number from sales or accounting. *Example*: The event of L. L. Fish buying one product O600 and four products O623 on September 10, 2010.
ITEM	A type of component that goes into making one or more products and can be supplied by one or more suppliers. *Example*: A 4-inch ball-bearing caster called I-27–4375.
SUPPLIER	Another company that may provide items to Pine Valley Furniture. *Example*: Sure Fasteners, Inc.
SHIPMENT	The transaction associated with items received in the same package by Pine Valley Furniture from a supplier. All items in a shipment appear on one bill-of-lading document. *Example*: The receipt of 300 I-27-4375 and 200 I-27-4380 items from Sure Fasteners, Inc., on September 9, 2010.

Note that it is important to clearly define, as metadata, each entity. For example, it is important to know that the CUSTOMER entity includes persons or organizations that have not yet purchased products from Pine Valley Furniture. It is common for different departments in an organization to have different meanings for the same term (homonyms). For example, Accounting may designate as customers only those persons or organizations who have ever made a purchase, thus excluding potential customers, whereas Marketing designates as customers anyone they have contacted or who has purchased from Pine Valley Furniture or any known competitor. An accurate and thorough ERD without clear metadata may be interpreted in different ways by different people. We outline good naming and definition conventions as we formally introduce E-R modeling throughout this chapter.

The symbols at the end of each line on an ERD specify relationship cardinalities, which represent how many entities of one kind relate to how many entities of another kind. On examining Figure 2-1, we can see that these cardinality symbols express the following business rules:

1. A SUPPLIER may supply many ITEMs (by "may supply," we mean the supplier may not supply any items). Each ITEM is supplied by any number of SUPPLIERs (by "is supplied," we mean that the item must be supplied by at least one supplier). See annotations in Figure 2-1 that correspond to underlined words.
2. Each ITEM must be used in the assembly of at least one PRODUCT and may be used in many products. Conversely, each PRODUCT must use one or more ITEMs.
3. A SUPPLIER may send many SHIPMENTs. However, each shipment must be sent by exactly one SUPPLIER. Notice that sends and supplies are separate concepts. A SUPPLIER may be able to supply an item, but may not yet have sent any shipments of that item.
4. A SHIPMENT must include one (or more) ITEMs. An ITEM may be included on several SHIPMENTs.
5. A CUSTOMER may submit any number of ORDERs. However, each ORDER must be submitted by exactly one CUSTOMER. Given that a CUSTOMER may not have submitted any ORDERs, some CUSTOMERs must be potential, inactive, or some other customer possibly without any related ORDERs.
6. An ORDER must request one (or more) PRODUCTs. A given PRODUCT may not be requested on any ORDER, or may be requested on one or more orders.

There are actually two business rules for each relationship, one for each direction from one entity to the other. Note that each of these business rules roughly follows a certain grammar:

<entity> <minimum cardinality> <relationship> <maximum cardinality> <entity>

For example, rule 5 is:

<CUSTOMER> <may> <Submit> <any number> <ORDER>

This grammar gives you a standard way to put each relationship into a natural English business rule statement.

E-R Model Notation

The notation we use for E-R diagrams is shown in Figure 2-2. As indicated in the previous section, there is no industry-standard notation (in fact, you saw a slightly simpler notation in Chapter 1). The notation in Figure 2-2 combines most of the desirable features of the different notations that are commonly used in E-R drawing tools today and also allows us to model accurately most situations that are encountered in practice.

FIGURE 2-2 Basic E-R notation

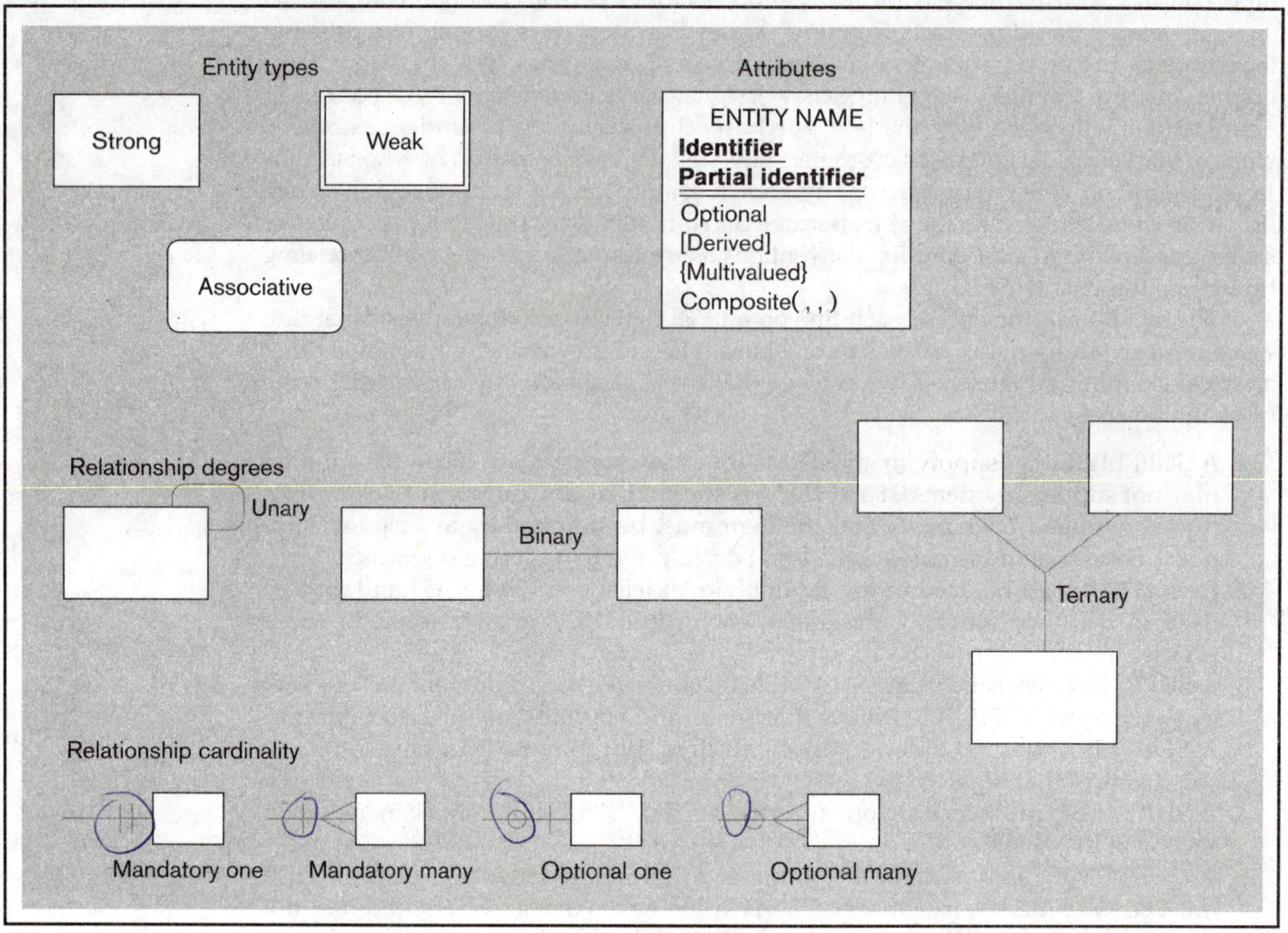

We introduce additional notation for enhanced entity-relationship models (including class-subclass relationships) in Chapter 3.

In many situations, however, a simpler E-R notation is sufficient. Most drawing tools, either stand-alone ones such as Microsoft Visio or those in CASE tools such as Oracle Designer, CA ERwin, or PowerDesigner, do not show all the entity and attribute types we use. It is important to note that any notation requires special annotations, not always present in a diagramming tool, to show all the business rules of the organizational situation you are modeling. We will use the Visio notation for a few examples throughout the chapter and at the end of the chapter so that you can see the differences. Appendix A llustrates the E-R notation from several commonly used guidelines and diagramming tools. This appendix may help you translate between the notations in the text and the notations you use in classes.

MODELING THE RULES OF THE ORGANIZATION

Now that you have an example of a data model in mind, let's step back and consider more generally what a data model is representing. We will see in this and the next chapter how to use data models, in particular the entity-relationship notation, to document rules and policies of an organization. *In fact, documenting rules and policies of an organization that govern data is exactly what data modeling is all about*. Business rules and policies govern creating, updating, and removing data in an information processing and storage system; thus they must be described along with the data to which they are related. For example, the policy "every student in the university must have a faculty adviser" forces data (in a database) about each student to be associated with data about some student adviser. Also, the statement "a student is any person who has applied for admission or taken a course or training program from any credit or noncredit unit of the university" not only defines the concept of "student" but also states a policy of the university (e.g., implicitly, alumni are students, and a high school student who attended a college fair but has not applied is not a student, assuming the college fair is not a noncredit training program).

Business rules and policies are not universal; different universities may have different policies for student advising and may include different types of people as students. Also, the rules and policies of an organization may change (usually slowly) over time; a university may decide that a student does not have to be assigned a faculty adviser until the student chooses a major.

Your job as a database analyst is to

- Identify and understand those rules *that govern data*
- Represent those rules so that they can be unambiguously understood by information systems developers and users
- Implement those rules in database technology

Data modeling is an important tool in this process. Because the purpose of data modeling is to document business rules about data, we introduce the discussion of data modeling and the entity-relationship notation with an overview of business rules. Data models cannot represent all business rules (and do not need to, because not all business rules govern data); data models along with associated documentation and other types of information system models (e.g., models that document the processing of data) represent all business rules that must be enforced through information systems.

Overview of Business Rules

A **business rule** is "a statement that defines or constrains some aspect of the business. It is intended to assert business structure or to control or influence the behavior of the business . . . rules prevent, cause, or suggest things to happen" (GUIDE Business Rules Project, 1997). For example, the following two statements are common expressions of business rules that affect data processing and storage:

Business rule
A statement that defines or constrains some aspect of the business. It is intended to assert business structure or to control or influence the behavior of the business.

- "A student may register for a section of a course only if he or she has successfully completed the prerequisites for that course."
- "A preferred customer qualifies for a 10 percent discount, unless he has an overdue account balance."

Most organizations (and their employees) today are guided by thousands of combinations of such rules. In the aggregate, these rules influence behavior and determine how the organization responds to its environment (Gottesdiener, 1997; von Halle, 1997). Capturing and documenting business rules is an important, complex task. Thoroughly capturing and structuring business rules, then enforcing them through database technologies, helps to ensure that information systems work right and that users of the information understand what they enter and see.

THE BUSINESS RULES PARADIGM The concept of business rules has been used in information systems for some time. There are many software products that help organizations manage their business rules (for example, JRules from ILOG, an IBM company). In the database world, it has been more common to use the related term *integrity constraint* when referring to such rules. The intent of this term is somewhat more limited in scope, usually referring to maintaining valid data values and relationships in the database.

A business rules approach is based on the following premises:

- Business rules are a core concept in an enterprise because they are an expression of business policy and guide individual and aggregate behavior. Well-structured business rules can be stated in natural language for end users and in a data model for systems developers.

- Business rules can be expressed in terms that are familiar to end users. Thus, users can define and then maintain their own rules.
- Business rules are highly maintainable. They are stored in a central repository, and each rule is expressed only once, then shared throughout the organization. Each rule is discovered and documented only once, to be applied in all systems development projects.
- Enforcement of business rules can be automated through the use of software that can interpret the rules and enforce them using the integrity mechanisms of the database management system (Moriarty, 2000).

Although much progress has been made, the industry has not realized all of these objectives to date (Owen, 2004). Possibly the premise with greatest potential benefit is "Business rules are highly maintainable." The ability to specify and maintain the requirements for information systems as a set of rules has considerable power when coupled with an ability to generate automatically information systems from a repository of rules. Automatic generation and maintenance of systems will not only simplify the systems development process but also will improve the quality of systems.

Scope of Business Rules

In this chapter and the next, we are concerned with business rules that impact only an organization's databases. Most organizations have a host of rules and/or policies that fall outside this definition. For example, the rule "Friday is business casual dress day" may be an important policy statement, but it has no immediate impact on databases. In contrast, the rule "A student may register for a section of a course only if he or she has successfully completed the prerequisites for that course" is within our scope because it constrains the transactions that may be processed against the database. In particular, it causes any transaction to be rejected that attempts to register a student who does not have the necessary prerequisites. Some business rules cannot be represented in common data modeling notation; those rules that cannot be represented in a variation of an entity-relationship diagram are stated in natural language, and some can be represented in the relational data model, which we describe in Chapter 4.

GOOD BUSINESS RULES Whether stated in natural language, a structured data model, or other information systems documentation, a business rule will have certain characteristics if it is to be consistent with the premises outlined previously. These characteristics are summarized in Table 2-1. These characteristics will have a better chance of being satisfied if a business rule is defined, approved, and owned by business, not technical, people. Businesspeople become stewards of the business rules. You, as the database analyst, facilitate the surfacing of the rules and the transformation of ill-stated rules into ones that satisfy the desired characteristics.

GATHERING BUSINESS RULES Business rules appear (possibly implicitly) in descriptions of business functions, events, policies, units, stakeholders, and other objects. These descriptions can be found in interview notes from individual and group information systems requirements collection sessions, organizational documents (e.g., personnel manuals, policies, contracts, marketing brochures, and technical instructions), and other sources. Rules are identified by asking questions about the who, what, when, where, why, and how of the organization. Usually, a data analyst has to be persistent in clarifying initial statements of rules because initial statements may be vague or imprecise (what some people have called "business ramblings"). Thus, precise rules are formulated from an iterative inquiry process. You should be prepared to ask such questions as "Is this always true?" "Are there special circumstances when an alternative occurs?" "Are there distinct kinds of that person?" "Is there only one of those or are there many?" and "Is there a need to keep a history of those, or is the current data all that is useful?" Such questions can be useful for surfacing rules for each type of data modeling construct we introduce in this chapter and the next.

TABLE 2-1 Characteristics of a Good Business Rule

Characteristic	Explanation
Declarative	A business rule is a statement of policy, not how policy is enforced or conducted; the rule does not describe a process or implementation, but rather describes what a process validates.
Precise	With the related organization, the rule must have only one interpretation among all interested people, and its meaning must be clear.
Atomic	A business rule marks one statement, not several; no part of the rule can stand on its own as a rule (that is, the rule is indivisible, yet sufficient).
Consistent	A business rule must be internally consistent (that is, not contain conflicting statements) and must be consistent with (and not contradict) other rules.
Expressible	A business rule must be able to be stated in natural language, but it will be stated in a structured natural language so that there is no misinterpretation.
Distinct	Business rules are not redundant, but a business rule may refer to other rules (especially to definitions).
Business-oriented	A business rule is stated in terms businesspeople can understand, and because it is a statement of business policy, only businesspeople can modify or invalidate a rule; thus, a business rule is owned by the business.

Source: Based on Gottesdiener (1999) and Plotkin (1999).

Data Names and Definitions

Fundamental to understanding and modeling data are naming and defining data objects. Data objects must be named and defined before they can be used unambiguously in a model of organizational data. In the entity-relationship notation you will learn in this chapter, you have to give entities, relationships, and attributes clear and distinct names and definitions.

DATA NAMES We will provide specific guidelines for naming entities, relationships, and attributes as we develop the entity-relationship data model, but there are some general guidelines about naming any data object. Data names should (Salin, 1990; ISO/IEC, 2005)

- ***Relate to business, not technical (hardware or software), characteristics;*** so, Customer is a good name, but File10, Bit7, and Payroll Report Sort Key are not good names.
- ***Be meaningful,*** almost to the point of being self-documenting (i.e., the definition will refine and explain the name without having to state the essence of the object's meaning); you should avoid using generic words such as *has, is, person,* or *it*.
- ***Be unique*** from the name used for every other distinct data object; words should be included in a data name if they distinguish the data object from other similar data objects (e.g., Home Address versus Campus Address).
- ***Be readable,*** so that the name is structured as the concept would most naturally be said (e.g., Grade Point Average is a good name, whereas Average Grade Relative To A, although possibly accurate, is an awkward name).
- ***Be composed of words taken from an approved list;*** each organization often chooses a vocabulary from which significant words in data names must be chosen (e.g., maximum is preferred, never upper limit, ceiling, or highest); alternative, or alias names, also can be used as can approved abbreviations (e.g., CUST for CUSTOMER), and you may be encouraged to use the abbreviations so that data names are short enough to meet maximum length limits of database technology.
- ***Be repeatable,*** meaning that different people or the same person at different times should develop exactly or almost the same name; this often means that there is a standard hierarchy or pattern for names (e.g., the birth date of a student

would be Student Birth Date and the birth date of an employee would be Employee Birth Date).
- ***Follow a standard syntax,*** meaning that the parts of the name should follow a standard arrangement adopted by the organization.

Salin (1990) suggests that you develop data names by

1. Preparing a definition of the data. (We talk about definitions next.)
2. Removing insignificant or illegal words (words not on the approved list for names); note that the presence of AND and OR in the definition may imply that two or more data objects are combined, and you may want to separate the objects and assign different names.
3. Arranging the words in a meaningful, repeatable way.
4. Assigning a standard abbreviation for each word.
5. Determining whether the name already exists, and if so, adding other qualifiers that make the name unique.

We will see examples of good data names as we develop a data modeling notation in this chapter.

Term
A word or phrase that has a specific meaning for the business.

Fact
An association between two or more terms.

DATA DEFINITIONS A definition (sometimes called a *structural assertion*) is considered a type of business rule (GUIDE Business Rules Project, 1997). A definition is an explanation of a term or a fact. A **term** is a word or phrase that has a specific meaning for the business. Examples of terms are *course, section, rental car, flight, reservation,* and *passenger*. Terms are often the key words used to form data names. Terms must be defined carefully and concisely. However, there is no need to define common terms such as *day, month, person,* or *television,* because these terms are understood without ambiguity by most persons.

A **fact** is an association between two or more terms. A fact is documented as a simple declarative statement that relates terms. Examples of facts that are definitions are the following (the defined terms are underlined):

- "A <u>course</u> is a module of instruction in a particular subject area." This definition associates two terms: *module of instruction* and *subject area*. We assume that these are common terms that do not need to be further defined.
- "A <u>customer</u> may request a <u>model of car</u> from a <u>rental branch</u> on a particular <u>date</u>." This fact, which is a definition of *model rental request,* associates the four underlined terms (GUIDE Business Rules Project, 1997). Three of these terms are business- specific terms that would need to be defined individually (date is a common term).

A fact statement places no constraints on instances of the fact. For example, it is inappropriate in the second fact statement to add that a customer may not request two different car models on the same date. Such constraints are separate business rules.

GOOD DATA DEFINITIONS We will illustrate good definitions for entities, relationships, and attributes as we develop the entity-relationship notation in this and the next chapters. There are, however, some general guidelines to follow (Aranow, 1989; ISO/IEC, 2004):

- Definitions (and all other types of business rules) are gathered from the same sources as all requirements for information systems. Thus, systems and data analysts should be looking for data objects and their definitions as these sources of information systems requirements are studied.
- Definitions will usually be accompanied by diagrams, such as entity-relationship diagrams. The definition does not need to repeat what is shown on the diagram but rather supplement the diagram.
- Definitions will be stated in the singular and explain what the data is, not what it is not. A definition will use commonly understood terms and abbreviations and stand alone in its meaning and not embed other definitions within it. It should be concise and concentrate on the essential meaning of the data, but it may also state such characteristics of a data object as
  - Subtleties
  - Special or exceptional conditions

- Examples
- Where, when, and how the data are created or calculated in the organization
- Whether the data are static or changes over time
- Whether the data are singular or plural in its atomic form
- Who determines the value for the data
- Who owns the data (i.e., who controls the definition and usage)
- Whether the data are optional or whether empty (what we will call null) values are allowed
- Whether the data can be broken down into more atomic parts or are often combined with other data into some more composite or aggregate form

If not included in a data definition, these characteristics need to be documented elsewhere, where other metadata are stored.

- A data object should not be added to a data model, such as an entity-relationship diagram, until after it has been carefully defined (and named) and there is agreement on this definition. But expect the definition of the data to change once you place the object on the diagram because the process of developing a data model tests your understanding of the meaning of data. (In other words, *modeling data is an iterative process.*)

There is an unattributed phrase in data modeling that highlights the importance of good data definitions: "He who controls the meaning of data controls the data." It might seem that obtaining concurrence in an organization on the definitions to be used for the various terms and facts should be relatively easy. However, this is usually far from the case. In fact, it is likely to be one of the most difficult challenges you will face in data modeling or, for that matter, in any other endeavor. It is not unusual for an organization to have multiple definitions (perhaps a dozen or more) for common terms such as *customer* or *order*.

To illustrate the problems inherent in developing definitions, consider a data object of Student found in a typical university. A sample definition for Student is "a person who has been admitted to the school and who has registered for at least one course during the past year." This definition is certain to be challenged, because it is probably too narrow. A person who is a student typically proceeds through several stages in relationship with the school, such as the following:

1. Prospect—some formal contact, indicating an interest in the school
2. Applicant—applies for admission
3. Admitted applicant—admitted to the school and perhaps to a degree program
4. Matriculated student—registers for at least one course
5. Continuing student—registers for courses on an ongoing basis (no substantial gaps)
6. Former student—fails to register for courses during some stipulated period (now may reapply)
7. Graduate—satisfactorily completes some degree program (now may apply for another program)

Imagine the difficulty of obtaining consensus on a single definition in this situation! It would seem you might consider three alternatives:

1. ***Use multiple definitions to cover the various situations.*** This is likely to be highly confusing if there is only one entity type, so this approach is not recommended (multiple definitions are not good definitions). It might be possible to create multiple entity types, one for each student situation. However, because there is likely considerable similarity across the entity types, the fine distinctions between the entity types may be confusing, and the data model will show many constructs.
2. ***Use a very general definition that will cover most situations.*** This approach may necessitate adding additional data about students to record a given student's actual status. For example, data for a student's status, with values of prospect, applicant, and so forth might be sufficient. On the other hand, if the same student could hold multiple statuses (e.g., prospect for one degree and matriculated for another degree), this might not work.

3. ***Consider using multiple, related, data objects for Student.*** For example, we could create a general entity type for Student and then other specific entity types for kinds of students with unique characteristics. We describe the conditions that suggest this approach in Chapter 3.

MODELING ENTITIES AND ATTRIBUTES

The basic constructs of the E-R model are entities, relationships, and attributes. As shown in Figure 2-2, the model allows numerous variations for each of these constructs. The richness of the E-R model allows designers to model real-world situations accurately and expressively, which helps account for the popularity of the model.

Entities

Entity
A person, a place, an object, an event, or a concept in the user environment about which the organization wishes to maintain data.

An **entity** is a person, a place, an object, an event, or a concept in the user environment about which the organization wishes to maintain data. Thus, an entity has a noun name. Some examples of each of these *kinds* of entities follow:

Person: EMPLOYEE, STUDENT, PATIENT
Place: STORE, WAREHOUSE, STATE
Object: MACHINE, BUILDING, AUTOMOBILE
Event: SALE, REGISTRATION, RENEWAL
Concept: ACCOUNT, COURSE, WORK CENTER

Entity type
A collection of entities that share common properties or characteristics.

Entity instance
A single occurrence of an entity type.

ENTITY TYPE VERSUS ENTITY INSTANCE There is an important distinction between entity types and entity instances. An **entity type** is a collection of entities that share common properties or characteristics. Each entity type in an E-R model is given a name. Because the name represents a collection (or set) of items, it is always singular. We use capital letters for names of entity type(s). In an E-R diagram, the entity name is placed inside the box representing the entity type (see Figure 2-1).

An **entity instance** is a single occurrence of an entity type. Figure 2-3 illustrates the distinction between an entity type and two of its instances. An entity type is described just once (using metadata) in a database, whereas many instances of that entity type may be represented by data stored in the database. For example, there is one EMPLOYEE entity type in most organizations, but there may be hundreds (or even thousands) of instances of this entity type stored in the database. We often use the single term *entity* rather than *entity instance* when the meaning is clear from the context of our discussion.

Entity type: EMPLOYEE			
Attributes	**Attribute Data Type**	**Example Instance**	**Example Instance**
Employee Number	CHAR (10)	642-17-8360	534-10-1971
Name	CHAR (25)	Michelle Brady	David Johnson
Address	CHAR (30)	100 Pacific Avenue	450 Redwood Drive
City	CHAR (20)	San Francisco	Redwood City
State	CHAR (2)	CA	CA
Zip Code	CHAR (9)	98173	97142
Date Hired	DATE	03-21-1992	08-16-1994
Birth Date	DATE	06-19-1968	09-04-1975

FIGURE 2-3 Entity type EMPLOYEE with two instances

ENTITY TYPE VERSUS SYSTEM INPUT, OUTPUT, OR USER A common mistake people make when they are learning to draw E-R diagrams, especially if they are already familiar with data process modeling (such as data flow diagramming), is to confuse data entities with other elements of an overall information systems model. A simple rule to avoid such confusion is that a true data entity will have many possible instances, each with a distinguishing characteristic, as well as one or more other descriptive pieces of data.

Consider Figure 2-4a, which might be drawn to represent a database needed for a college sorority's expense system. (For simplicity in this and some other figures, we show only one name for a relationship.) In this situation, the sorority treasurer manages accounts, receives expense reports, and records expense transactions against each account. However, do we need to keep track of data about the Treasurer (the TREASURER entity type) and her supervision of accounts (the Manages relationship) and receipt of reports (the Receives relationship)? The Treasurer is the person entering data about accounts and expenses and receiving expense reports. That is, she is a user of the database. Because there is only one Treasurer, TREASURER data do not need to be kept. Further, is the EXPENSE REPORT entity necessary? Because an expense report is computed from expense transactions and account balances, it is the result of extracting data from the database and received by the Treasurer. Even though there will be multiple instances of expense reports given to the Treasurer over time, data needed to compute the report contents each time are already represented by the ACCOUNT and EXPENSE entity types.

Another key to understanding why the ERD in Figure 2-4a might be in error is the nature of the *relationship names*, Receives and Summarizes. These relationship names refer to business activities that transfer or translate data, not to simply the association of one kind of data with another kind of data. The simple E-R diagram in Figure 2-4b shows entities and a relationship that would be sufficient to handle the sorority expense system as described here. See Problem and Exercise 19 for a variation on this situation.

STRONG VERSUS WEAK ENTITY TYPES Most of the basic entity types to identify in an organization are classified as strong entity types. A **strong entity type** is one that exists independently of other entity types. (Some data modeling software, in fact, use the term *independent entity*.) Examples include STUDENT, EMPLOYEE, AUTOMOBILE, and COURSE.

Strong entity type
An entity that exists independently of other entity types.

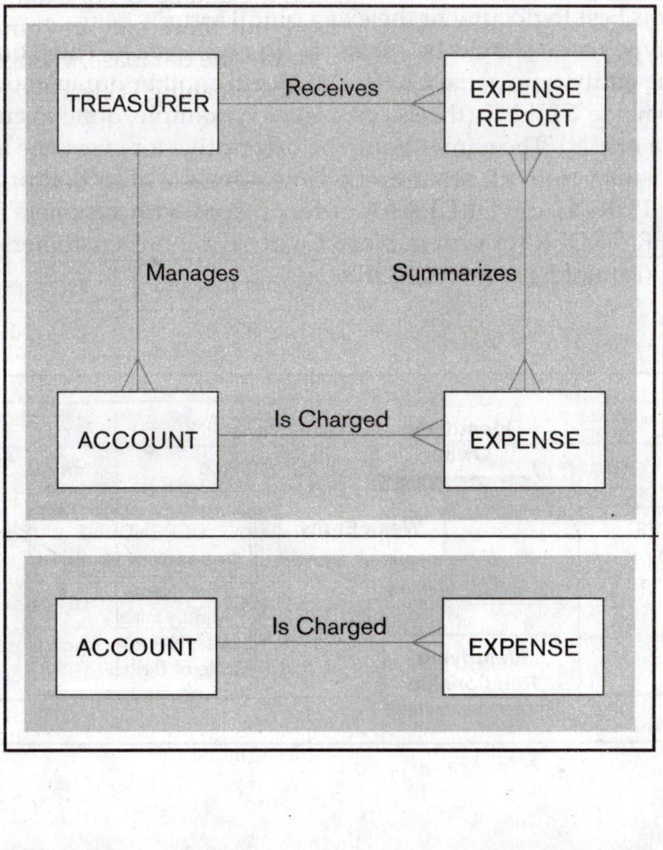

FIGURE 2-4 Example of inappropriate entities
(a) System user (Treasurer) and output (Expense Report) shown as entities

(b) E-R diagram with only the necessary entities

Instances of a strong entity type always have a unique characteristic (called an *identifier*)—that is, an attribute or a combination of attributes that uniquely distinguish each occurrence of that entity.

Weak entity type
An entity type whose existence depends on some other entity type.

Identifying owner
The entity type on which the weak entity type depends.

In contrast, a **weak entity type** is an entity type whose existence depends on some other entity type. (Some data modeling software, in fact, use the term *dependent entity*.) A weak entity type has no business meaning in an E-R diagram without the entity on which it depends. The entity type on which the weak entity type depends is called the **identifying owner** (or simply *owner* for short). A weak entity type does not typically have its own identifier. Generally, on an E-R diagram, a weak entity type has an attribute that serves as a *partial* identifier. During a later design stage (described in Chapter 4), a full identifier will be formed for the weak entity by combining the partial identifier with the identifier of its owner or by creating a surrogate identifier attribute.

Identifying relationship
The relationship between a weak entity type and its owner.

An example of a weak entity type with an identifying relationship is shown in Figure 2-5. EMPLOYEE is a strong entity type with identifier Employee ID (we note the identifier attribute by underlining it). DEPENDENT is a weak entity type, as indicated by the double-lined rectangle. The relationship between a weak entity type and its owner is called an **identifying relationship.** In Figure 2-5, Carries is the identifying relationship (indicated by the double line). The attribute Dependent Name serves as a *partial* identifier. (Dependent Name is a composite attribute that can be broken into component parts, as we describe later.) We use a double underline to indicate a partial identifier. During a later design stage, Dependent Name will be combined with Employee ID (the identifier of the owner) to form a full identifier for DEPENDENT.

NAMING AND DEFINING ENTITY TYPES In addition to the general guidelines for naming and defining data objects, there are a few special guidelines for *naming* entity types, which follow:

- An entity type name is a *singular noun* (such as CUSTOMER, STUDENT, or AUTOMOBILE); an entity is a person, a place, an object, an event, or a concept, and the name is for the entity type, which represents a set of entity instances (i.e., STUDENT represents students Hank Finley, Jean Krebs, and so forth). It is common to also specify the plural form (possibly in a CASE tool repository accompanying the E-R diagram), because sometimes the E-R diagram is read best by using plurals. For example, in Figure 2-1, we would say that a SUPPLIER may supply ITEMs. Because plurals are not always formed by adding an *s* to the singular noun, it is best to document the exact plural form.
- An entity type name should be *specific to the organization*. Thus, one organization may use the entity type name CUSTOMER and another organization may use the entity type name CLIENT (this is one task, for example, done to customize a purchased data model). The name should be descriptive for everyone in the organization and distinct from all other entity type names within that organization. For example, a PURCHASE ORDER for orders placed with suppliers is distinct from CUSTOMER ORDER for orders placed with us by our customers. Both of these entity types cannot be named ORDER.

FIGURE 2-5 Example of a weak entity and its identifying relationship

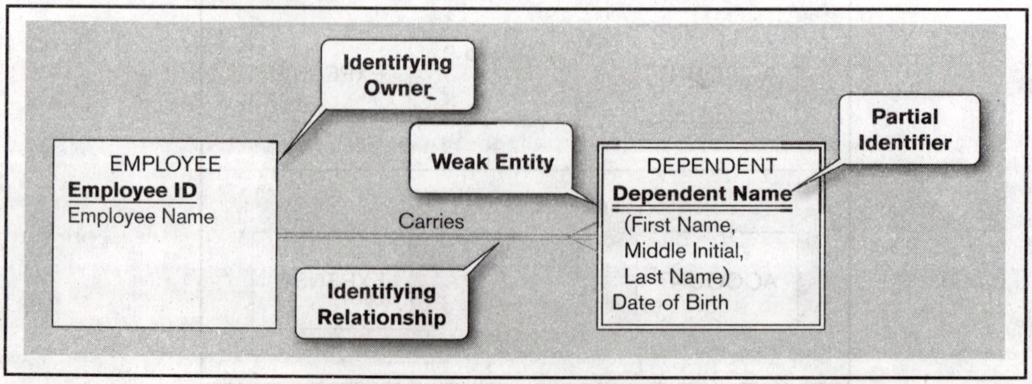

- An entity type name should be *concise*, using as few words as possible. For example, in a university database, an entity type REGISTRATION for the event of a student registering for a class is probably a sufficient name for this entity type; STUDENT REGISTRATION FOR CLASS, although precise, is probably too wordy because the reader will understand REGISTRATION from its use with other entity types.
- An *abbreviation*, or a *short name*, should be specified for each entity type name, and the abbreviation may be sufficient to use in the E-R diagram; abbreviations must follow all of the same rules as do the full entity names.
- *Event entity types* should be named for the result of the event, not the activity or process of the event. For example, the event of a project manager assigning an employee to work on a project results in an ASSIGNMENT, and the event of a student contacting his or her faculty adviser seeking some information is a CONTACT.
- The *name* used for the same entity type *should be the same* on all E-R diagrams on which the entity type appears. Thus, as well as being specific to the organization, the name used for an entity type should be a standard, adopted by the organization for all references to the same kind of data. However, some entity types will have aliases, or alternative names, which are synonyms used in different parts of the organization. For example, the entity type ITEM may have aliases of MATERIAL (for production) and DRAWING (for engineering). Aliases are specified in documentation about the database, such as the repository of a CASE tool.

There are also some specific guidelines for *defining* entity types, which follow:

- *An entity type definition usually starts with* "An X is. . . ." This is the most direct and clear way to state the meaning of an entity type.
- An entity type definition should *include a statement of what the unique characteristic is for each instance of the entity type.* In many cases, stating the identifier for an entity type helps to convey the meaning of the entity. An example for Figure 2-4b is "An expense is a payment of the purchase of some good or service. An expense is identified by a journal entry number."
- An entity type definition should make it clear what *entity instances are included and not included* in the entity type; often, it is necessary to list the kinds of entities that are excluded. For example, "A customer is a person or organization that has placed an order for a product from us or one that we have contacted to advertise or promote our products. A customer does not include persons or organizations that buy our products only through our customers, distributors, or agents."
- An entity type definition often includes a description of *when an instance of the entity type is created and deleted*. For example, in the previous bullet point, a customer instance is implicitly created when the person or organization places its first order; because this definition does not specify otherwise, implicitly a customer instance is never deleted, or it is deleted based on general rules that are specified about the purging of data from the database. A statement about when to delete an entity instance is sometimes referred to as the retention of the entity type. A possible deletion statement for a customer entity type definition might be "A customer ceases to be a customer if it has not placed an order for more than three years."
- For some entity types, the definition must specify *when an instance might change into an instance of another entity type*. For example, consider the situation of a construction company for which bids accepted by potential customers become contracts. In this case, a bid might be defined by "A bid is a legal offer by our organization to do work for a customer. A bid is created when an officer of our company signs the bid document; a bid becomes an instance of contract when we receive a copy of the bid signed by an officer of the customer." This definition is also a good example to note how one definition can use other entity type names (in this case, the definition of bid uses the entity type name CUSTOMER).
- For some entity types, the definition must specify *what history is to be kept about instances of the entity type*. For example, the characteristics of an ITEM in Figure 2-1

may change over time, and we may need to keep a complete history of the individual values and when they were in effect. As we will see in some examples later, such statements about keeping history may have ramifications about how we represent the entity type on an E-R diagram and eventually how we store data for the entity instances.

Attributes

Attribute
A property or characteristic of an entity or relationship type that is of interest to the organization.

Each entity type has a set of attributes associated with it. An **attribute** is a property or characteristic of an entity type that is of interest to the organization. (Later we will see that some types of relationships may also have attributes.) Thus, an attribute has a noun name. Following are some typical entity types and their associated attributes:

STUDENT	Student ID, Student Name, Home Address, Phone Number, Major
AUTOMOBILE	Vehicle ID, Color, Weight, Horsepower
EMPLOYEE	Employee ID, Employee Name, Payroll Address, Skill

In naming attributes, we use an initial capital letter followed by lowercase letters. If an attribute name consists of more than one words, we use a space between the words and we start each word with a capital letter; for example Employee Name or Student Home Address. In E-R diagrams, we represent an attribute by placing its name in the entity it describes. Attributes may also be associated with relationships, as described later. Note that an attribute is associated with exactly one entity or relationship.

Notice in Figure 2-5 that all of the attributes of DEPENDENT are characteristics only of an employee's dependent, not characteristics of an employee. In traditional E-R notation, an entity type (not just weak entities but any entity) does not include attributes of entities to which it is related (what might be called foreign attributes). For example, DEPENDENT does not include any attribute that indicates to which employee this dependent is associated. This nonredundant feature of the E-R data model is consistent with the shared data property of databases. Because of relationships, which we discuss shortly, someone accessing data from a database will be able to associate attributes from related entities (e.g., show on a display screen a Dependent Name and the associated Employee Name).

Required attribute
An attribute that must have a value for every entity (or relationship) instance with which it is associated.

Optional attribute
An attribute that may not have a value for every entity (or relationship) instance with which it is associated.

REQUIRED VERSUS OPTIONAL ATTRIBUTES Each entity (or instance of an entity type) potentially has a value associated with each of the attributes of that entity type. An attribute that must be present for each entity instance is called a **required attribute**, whereas an attribute that may not have a value is called an **optional attribute**. For example, Figure 2-6 shows two STUDENT entities (instances) with their respective

FIGURE 2-6 Entity type STUDENT with required and optional attributes

Entity type: STUDENT

Attributes	Attribute Data Type	Required or Optional	Example Instance	Example Instance
Student ID	CHAR (10)	Required	876-24-8217	822-24-4456
Student Name	CHAR (40)	Required	Michael Grant	Melissa Kraft
Home Address	CHAR (30)	Required	314 Baker St.	1422 Heft Ave
Home City	CHAR (20)	Required	Centerville	Miami
Home State	CHAR (2)	Required	OH	FL
Home Zip Code	CHAR (9)	Required	45459	33321
Major	CHAR (3)	Optional	MIS	

attribute values. The only optional attribute for STUDENT is Major. (Some students, specifically Melissa Kraft in this example, have not chosen a major yet; MIS would, of course, be a great career choice!) However, every student must, by the rules of the organization, have values for all the other attributes; *that is, we cannot store any data about a student in a STUDENT entity instance unless there are values for all the required attributes.* In various E-R diagramming notations, a symbol might appear in front of each attribute to indicate whether it is required (e.g., *) or optional (e.g., o), or required attributes will be in **boldface**, whereas optional attributes will be in normal font (the format we use in this text); in many cases, required or optional is indicated within supplemental documentation. In Chapter 3, when we consider entity supertypes and subtypes, we will see how sometimes optional attributes imply that there are different types of entities. (For example, we may want to consider students who have not declared a major as a subtype of the student entity type.) An attribute without a value is said to be null. Thus, each entity has an identifying attribute, which we discuss in a subsequent section, plus one or more other attributes. If you try to create an entity that has only an identifier, that entity is likely not legitimate. Such a data structure may simply hold a list of legal values for some attribute, which is better kept outside the database.

SIMPLE VERSUS COMPOSITE ATTRIBUTES Some attributes can be broken down into meaningful component parts (detailed attributes). A common example is Name, which we saw in Figure 2-5; another is Address, which can usually be broken down into the following component attributes: Street Address, City, State, and Postal Code. A **composite attribute** is an attribute, such as Address, that has meaningful component parts, which are more detailed attributes. Figure 2-7 shows the notation that we use for composite attributes applied to this example. Most drawing tools do not have a notation for composite attributes, so you simply list all the component parts.

Composite attribute
An attribute that has meaningful component parts (attributes).

Composite attributes provide considerable flexibility to users, who can either refer to the composite attribute as a single unit or else refer to individual components of that attribute. Thus, for example, a user can either refer to Address or refer to one of its components, such as Street Address. The decision about whether to subdivide an attribute into its component parts depends on whether users will need to refer to those individual components, and hence, they have organizational meaning. Of course, the designer must always attempt to anticipate possible future usage patterns for the database.

A **simple (or atomic) attribute** is an attribute that cannot be broken down into smaller components that are meaningful for the organization. For example, all the attributes associated with AUTOMOBILE are simple: Vehicle ID, Color, Weight, and Horsepower.

Simple (or atomic) attribute
An attribute that cannot be broken down into smaller components that are meaningful to the organization.

SINGLE-VALUED VERSUS MULTIVALUED ATTRIBUTES Figure 2-6 shows two entity instances with their respective attribute values. For each entity instance, each of the attributes in the figure has one value. It frequently happens that there is an attribute that may have more than one value for a given instance. For example, the EMPLOYEE entity type in Figure 2-8 has an attribute named Skill, whose values record the skill (or skills) for that employee. Of course, some employees may have more than one skill,

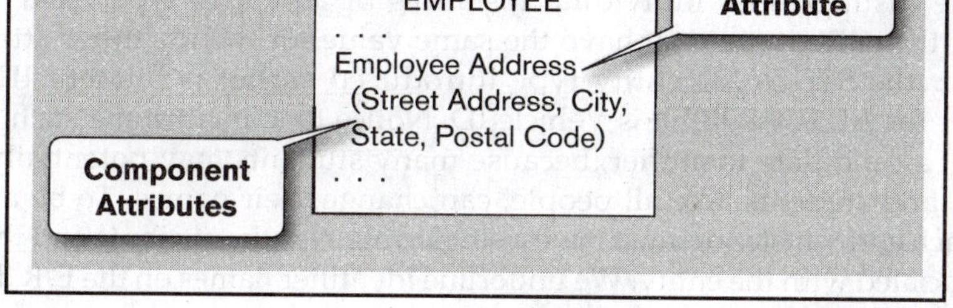

FIGURE 2-7 A composite attribute

FIGURE 2-8 Entity with multivalued attribute (Skill) and derived attribute (Years Employed)

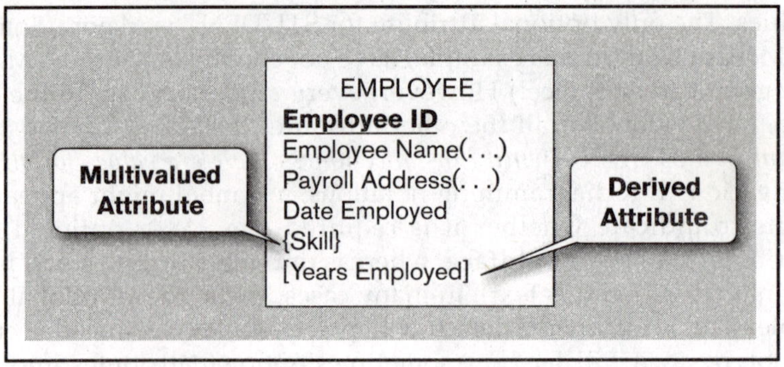

Multivalued attribute
An attribute that may take on more than one value for a given entity (or relationship) instance.

such as PHP Programmer and C++ Programmer. A **multivalued attribute** is an attribute that may take on more than one value for a given entity (or relationship) instance. In this text we indicate a multivalued attribute with curly brackets around the attribute name, as shown for the Skill attribute in the EMPLOYEE example in Figure 2-8. In Microsoft Visio, once an attribute is placed in an entity, you can edit that attribute (column), select the Collection tab, and choose one of the options. (Typically, MultiSet will be your choice, but one of the other options may be more appropriate for a given situation.) Other E-R diagramming tools may use an asterisk (*) after the attribute name, or you may have to use supplemental documentation to specify a multivalued attribute.

Multivalued and composite are different concepts, although beginner data modelers often confuse these terms. Skill, a multivalued attribute, may occur multiple times for each employee; Employee Name and Payroll Address are both likely composite attributes, each of which occurs once for each employee, but which have component, more atomic attributes, which are not shown in Figure 2-8 for simplicity. See Problem and Exercise 14 to review the concepts of composite and multivalued attributes.

STORED VERSUS DERIVED ATTRIBUTES Some attribute values that are of interest to users can be calculated or derived from other related attribute values that are stored in the database. For example, suppose that for an organization, the EMPLOYEE entity type has a Date Employed attribute. If users need to know how many years a person has been employed, that value can be calculated using Date Employed and today's date. A **derived attribute** is an attribute whose values can be calculated from related attribute values (plus possibly data not in the database, such as today's date, the current time, or a security code provided by a system user). We indicate a derived attribute in an E-R diagram by using square brackets around the attribute name, as shown in Figure 2-8 for the Years Employed attribute. Some E-R diagramming tools use a notation of a forward slash (/) in front of the attribute name to indicate that it is derived. (This notation is borrowed from UML for a virtual attribute.)

Derived attribute
An attribute whose values can be calculated from related attribute values.

In some situations, the value of an attribute can be derived from attributes in related entities. For example, consider an invoice created for each customer at Pine Valley Furniture Company. Order Total would be an attribute of the INVOICE entity, which indicates the total dollar amount that is billed to the customer. The value of Order Total can be computed by summing the Extended Price values (unit price times quantity sold) for the various line items that are billed on the invoice. Formulas for computing values such as this are one type of business rule.

Identifier
An attribute (or combination of attributes) whose value distinguishes instances of an entity type.

IDENTIFIER ATTRIBUTE An **identifier** is an attribute (or combination of attributes) whose value distinguishes individual instances of an entity type. That is, no two instances of the entity type may have the same value for the identifier attribute. The identifier for the STUDENT entity type introduced earlier is Student ID, whereas the identifier for AUTOMOBILE is Vehicle ID. Notice that an attribute such as Student Name is not a candidate identifier, because many students may potentially have the same name, and students, like all people, can change their names. To be a candidate identifier, each entity instance must have a single value for the attribute and the attribute must be associated with the entity. We underline identifier names on the E-R diagram, as

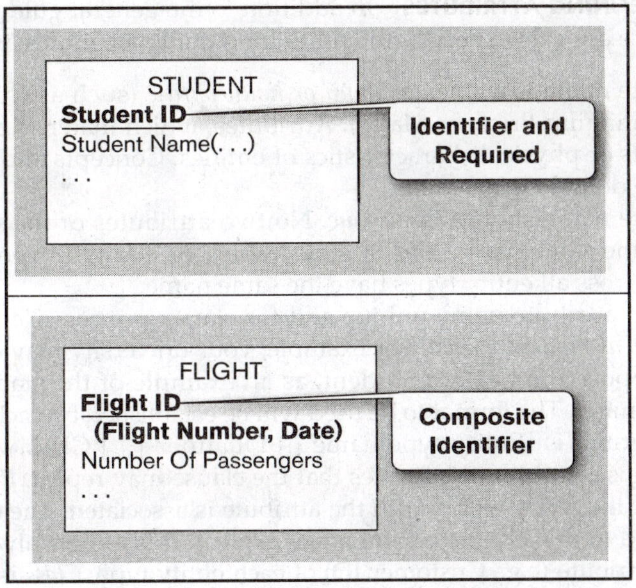

FIGURE 2-9 Simple and composite identifier attributes
(a) Simple identifier attribute

(b) Composite identifier attribute

shown in the STUDENT entity type example in Figure 2-9a. To be an identifier, the attributed is also required (so the distinguishing value must exist), so an identifier is also in bold. Some E-R drawing software will place a symbol, called a stereotype, in front of the identifier (e.g., <<ID>> or <<PK>>).

For some entity types, there is no single (or atomic) attribute that can serve as the identifier (i.e., that will ensure uniqueness). However, two (or more) attributes used in combination may serve as the identifier. A **composite identifier** is an identifier that consists of a composite attribute. Figure 2-9b shows the entity FLIGHT with the composite identifier Flight ID. Flight ID in turn has component attributes Flight Number and Date. This combination is required to identify uniquely individual occurrences of FLIGHT. We use the convention that the composite attribute (Flight ID) is underlined to indicate it is the identifier, while the component attributes are not underlined. Some data modelers think of a composite identifier as "breaking a tie" created by a simple identifier. Even with Flight ID, a data modeler would ask a question, such as "Can two flights with the same number occur on the same date?" If so, yet another attribute is needed to form the composite identifier and to break the tie.

Composite identifier
An identifier that consists of a composite attribute.

Some entities may have more than one candidate identifier. If there is more than one candidate identifier, the designer must choose one of them as the identifier. Bruce (1992) suggests the following criteria for selecting identifiers:

1. Choose an identifier that will not change its value over the life of each instance of the entity type. For example, the combination of Employee Name and Payroll Address (even if unique) would be a poor choice as an identifier for EMPLOYEE because the values of Employee Name and Payroll Address could easily change during an employee's term of employment.
2. Choose an identifier such that for each instance of the entity, the attribute is guaranteed to have valid values and not be null (or unknown). If the identifier is a composite attribute, such as Flight ID in Figure 2-9b, make sure that all parts of the identifier will have valid values.
3. Avoid the use of so-called intelligent identifiers (or keys), whose structure indicates classifications, locations, and so on. For example, the first two digits of an identifier value may indicate the warehouse location. Such codes are often changed as conditions change, which renders the identifier values invalid.
4. Consider substituting single-attribute surrogate identifiers for large composite identifiers. For example, an attribute called Game Number could be used for the entity type GAME instead of the combination of Home Team and Visiting Team.

NAMING AND DEFINING ATTRIBUTES In addition to the general guidelines for naming data objects, there are a few special guidelines for naming attributes, which follow:

- An attribute name is a *singular noun or noun phrase* (such as Customer ID, Age, Product Minimum Price, or Major). Attributes, which materialize as data values, are concepts or physical characteristics of entities. Concepts and physical characteristics are described by nouns.
- An attribute name should be *unique*. No two attributes of the same entity type may have the same name, and it is desirable, for clarity purposes, that no two attributes across all entity types have the same name.
- To make an attribute name unique and for clarity purposes, *each attribute name should follow a standard format*. For example, your university may establish Student GPA, as opposed to GPA of Student, as an example of the standard format for attribute naming. The format to be used will be established by each organization. A common format is [Entity type name { [Qualifier] }] Class, where [. . .] is an optional clause, and { . . . } indicates that the clause may repeat. *Entity type name* is the name of the entity with which the attribute is associated. The entity type name may be used to make the attribute name explicit. It is almost always used for the identifier attribute (e.g., Customer ID) of each entity type. *Class* is a phrase from a list of phrases defined by the organization that are the permissible characteristics or properties of entities (or abbreviations of these characteristics). For example, permissible values (and associated approved abbreviations) for Class might be Name (Nm), Identifier (ID), Date (Dt), or Amount (Amt). Class is, obviously, required. *Qualifier* is a phrase from a list of phrases defined by the organization that are used to place constraints on classes. One or more qualifiers may be needed to make each attribute of an entity type unique. For example, a qualifier might be Maximum (Max), Hourly (Hrly), or State (St). A qualifier may not be necessary: Employee Age and Student Major are both fully explicit attribute names. Sometimes a qualifier is necessary. For example, Employee Birth Date and Employee Hire Date are two attributes of Employee that require one qualifier. More than one qualifier may be necessary. For example, Employee Residence City Name (or Emp Res Cty Nm) is the name of an employee's city of residence, and Employee Tax City Name (or Emp Tax Cty Nm) is the name of the city in which an employee pays city taxes.
- *Similar attributes* of different entity types *should use the same qualifiers and classes*, as long as those are the names used in the organization. For example, the city of residence for faculty and students should be, respectively, Faculty Residence City Name and Student Residence City Name. Using similar names makes it easier for users to understand that values for these attributes come from the same possible set of values, what we will call *domains*. Users may want to take advantage of common domains in queries (e.g., find students who live in the same city as their adviser), and it will be easier for users to recognize that such a matching may be possible if the same qualifier and class phrases are used.

There are also some specific guidelines for defining attributes, which follow:

- An attribute definition states *what the attribute is and possibly why it is important*. The definition will often parallel the attribute's name; for example, Student Residence City Name could be defined as "The name of the city in which a student maintains his or her permanent residence."
- An attribute definition should make it clear *what is included and not included* in the attribute's value; for example, "Employee Monthly Salary Amount is the amount of money paid each month in the currency of the country of residence of the employee exclusive of any benefits, bonuses, reimbursements, or special payments."
- Any *aliases*, or alternative names, for the attribute can be specified in the definition, or may be included elsewhere in documentation about the attribute, possibly stored in the repository of a CASE tool used to maintain data definitions.
- It may also be desirable to state in the definition *the source of values for the attribute*. Stating the source may make the meaning of the data clearer. For example, "Customer Standard Industrial Code is an indication of the type of business for

the customer. Values for this code come from a standard set of values provided by the Federal Trade Commission and are found on a CD we purchase named SIC provided annually by the FTC."

- An attribute definition (or other specification in a CASE tool repository) also should indicate *if a value for the attribute is required or optional*. This business rule about an attribute is important for maintaining data integrity. The identifier attribute of an entity type is, by definition, required. If an attribute value is required, then to create an instance of the entity type, a value of this attribute must be provided. Required means that an entity instance must always have a value for this attribute, not just when an instance is created. Optional means that a value may not exist for an instance of an entity instance to be stored. Optional can be further qualified by stating whether once a value is entered, a value must always exist. For example, "Employee Department ID is the identifier of the department to which the employee is assigned. An employee may not be assigned to a department when hired (so this attribute is initially optional), but once an employee is assigned to a department, the employee must always be assigned to some department."
- An attribute definition (or other specification in a CASE tool repository) may also indicate *whether a value for the attribute may change* once a value is provided and before the entity instance is deleted. This business rule also controls data integrity. Nonintelligent identifiers may not change values over time. To assign a new nonintelligent identifier to an entity instance, that instance must first be deleted and then re-created.
- For a multivalued attribute, the attribute definition should indicate *the maximum and minimum number of occurrences of an attribute value for an entity instance*. For example, "Employee Skill Name is the name of a skill an employee possesses. Each employee must possess at least one skill, and an employee can choose to list at most 10 skills." The reason for a multivalued attribute may be that a history of the attribute needs to be kept. For example, "Employee Yearly Absent Days Number is the number of days in a calendar year the employee has been absent from work. An employee is considered absent if he or she works less than 50 percent of the scheduled hours in the day. A value for this attribute should be kept for each year in which the employee works for our company."
- An attribute definition may also indicate *any relationships that attribute has with other attributes*. For example, "Employee Vacation Days Number is the number of days of paid vacation for the employee. If the employee has a value of 'Exempt' for Employee Type, then the maximum value for Employee Vacation Days Number is determined by a formula involving the number of years of service for the employee."

MODELING RELATIONSHIPS

Relationships are the glue that holds together the various components of an E-R model. Intuitively, a *relationship* is an association representing an interaction among the instances of one or more entity types that is of interest to the organization. Thus, a relationship has a verb phrase name. Relationships and their characteristics (degree and cardinality) represent business rules, and usually relationships represent the most complex business rules shown in an ERD. In other words, this is where data modeling gets really interesting and fun, as well as crucial for controlling the integrity of a database.

To understand relationships more clearly, we must distinguish between relationship types and relationship instances. To illustrate, consider the entity types EMPLOYEE and COURSE, where COURSE represents training courses that may be taken by employees. To track courses that have been completed by particular employees, we define a relationship called Completes between the two entity types (see Figure 2-10a). This is a many-to-many relationship, because each employee may complete any number of courses (zero, one, or many courses), whereas a given course may be completed by any number of employees (nobody, one employee, many employees). For example, in Figure 2-10b, the employee Milan Shah has completed three courses (.NET, SQL, Perl). The SQL course has been completed by two employees (Chandan Singh and Milan Shah) and the Visual Basic course has not been completed by anyone.

FIGURE 2-10 Relationship type and instances
(a) Relationship type (Complete)
(b) Relationship instances

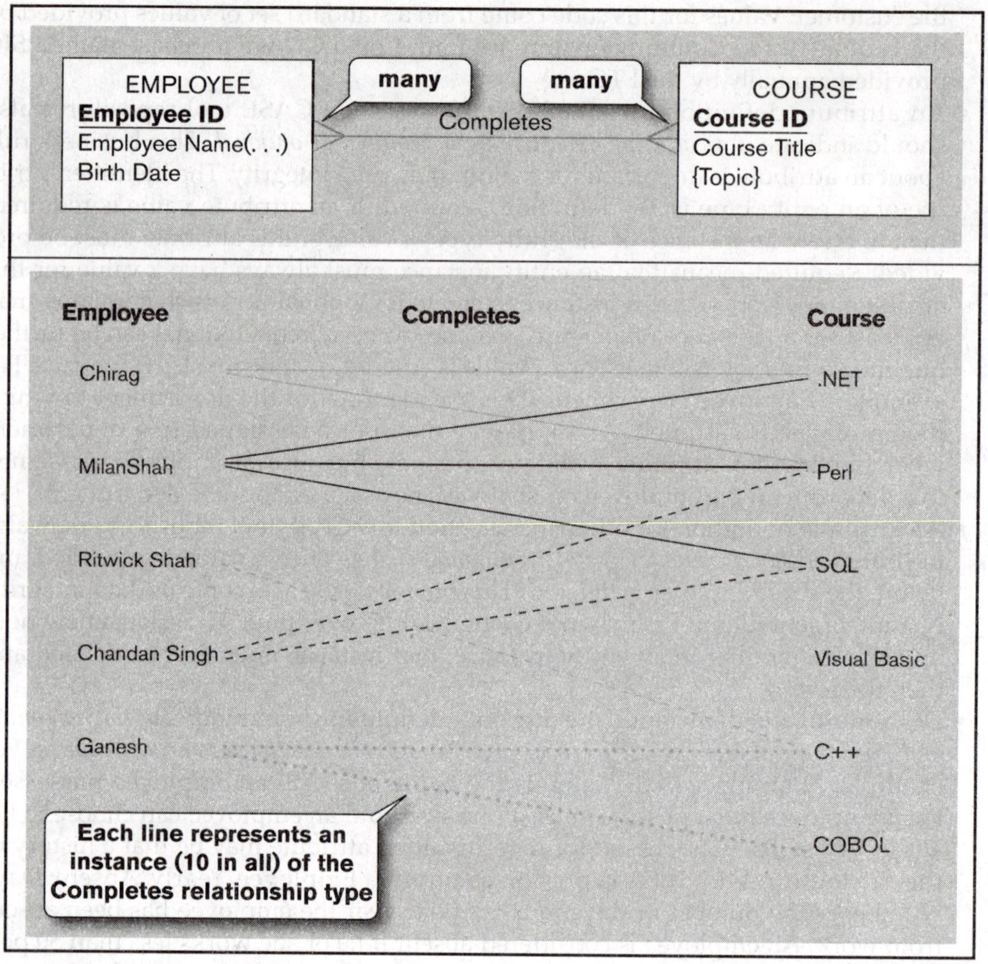

In this example, there are two entity types (EMPLOYEE and COURSE) that participate in the relationship named Completes. In general, any number of entity types (from one to many) may participate in a relationship.

We frequently use in this and subsequent chapters the convention of a single verb phrase label to represent a relationship. Because relationships often occur due to an organizational event, entity instances are related because an action was taken; thus a verb phrase is appropriate for the label. This verb phrase should be in the present tense and descriptive. There are, however, many ways to represent a relationship. Some data modelers prefer the format with two relationship names, one to name the relationship in each direction. One or two verb phrases have the same structural meaning, so you may use either format as long as the meaning of the relationship in each direction is clear.

Basic Concepts and Definitions in Relationships

Relationship type
A meaningful association between (or among) entity types.

A **relationship type** is a meaningful association between (or among) entity types. The phrase *meaningful association* implies that the relationship allows us to answer questions that could not be answered given only the entity types. A relationship type is denoted by a line labeled with the name of the relationship, as in the example shown in Figure 2-10a, or with two names, as in Figure 2-1. We suggest you use a short, descriptive verb phrase that is meaningful to the user in naming the relationship. (We say more about naming and defining relationships later in this section.)

Relationship instance
An association between (or among) entity instances where each relationship instance associates exactly one entity instance from each participating entity type.

A **relationship instance** is an association between (or among) entity instances, where each relationship instance associates exactly one entity instance from each participating entity type (Elmasri and Navathe, 1994). For example, in Figure 2-10b, each of the 10 lines in the figure represents a relationship instance between one employee and one course, indicating that the employee has completed that course. For example, the line between Employee Ritchie to Course Perl is one relationship instance.

TABLE 2-2 Instances Showing Date Completed

Employee Name	Course Title	Date Completed
Chirag	.NET	06/2009
Chirag	Perl	09/2009
Milan Shah	.NET	06/2009
Milan Shah	SQL	02/2010
Milan Shah	Perl	03/2009
Ritwick Mallick	C++	11/2009
Chandan Singh	SQL	03/2009
Chandan Singh	Perl	03/2010
Ganesh	COBOL	09/2009
Ganesh	C++	06/2009

ATTRIBUTES ON RELATIONSHIPS It is probably obvious to you that entities have attributes, but attributes may be associated with a many-to-many (or one-to-one) relationship, too. For example, suppose the organization wishes to record the date (month and year) when an employee completes each course. This attribute is named Date Completed. For some sample data, see Table 2-2.

Where should the attribute Date Completed be placed on the E-R diagram? Referring to Figure 2-10a, you will notice that Date Completed has not been associated with either the EMPLOYEE or COURSE entity. That is because Date Completed is a property of the relationship Completes, rather than a property of either entity. In other words, for each instance of the relationship Completes, there is a value for Date Completed. One such instance (for example) shows that the employee named Milan Shah completed the course titled .NET in 06/2009.

A revised version of the ERD for this example is shown in Figure 2-11a. In this diagram, the attribute Date Completed is in a rectangle connected to the Completes relationship line. Other attributes might be added to this relationship if appropriate, such as Course Grade, Instructor, and Room Location.

It is interesting to note that an attribute cannot be associated with a one-to-many relationship, such as Carries in Figure 2-5. For example, consider Dependent Date, similar to Date Completed above, for when the DEPENDENT begins to be carried by the EMPLOYEE. Because each DEPENDENT is associated with only one EMPLOYEE, such a date is unambiguously a characteristic of the DEPENDENT (i.e., for a given DEPENDENT, Dependent Date cannot vary by EMPLOYEE). So, if you ever have the urge to associate an attribute with a one-to-many relationship, "step away from the relationship!"

FIGURE 2-11 An associative entity

(a) Attribute on a relationship

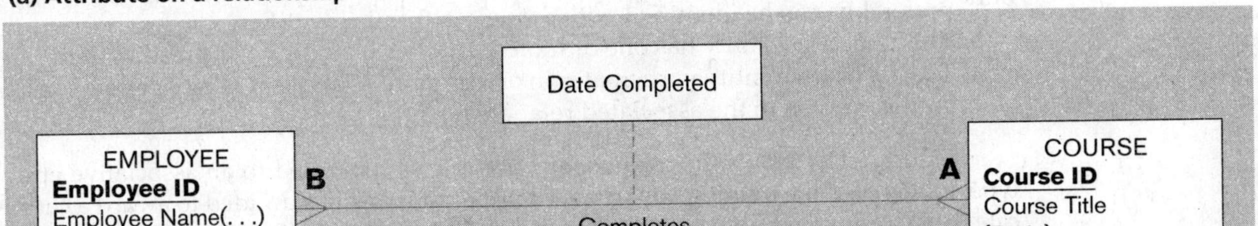

(continued)

FIGURE 2-11 ***(continued)***

(b) An associative entity (CERTIFICATE)

(c) An associative entity using Microsoft VISIO

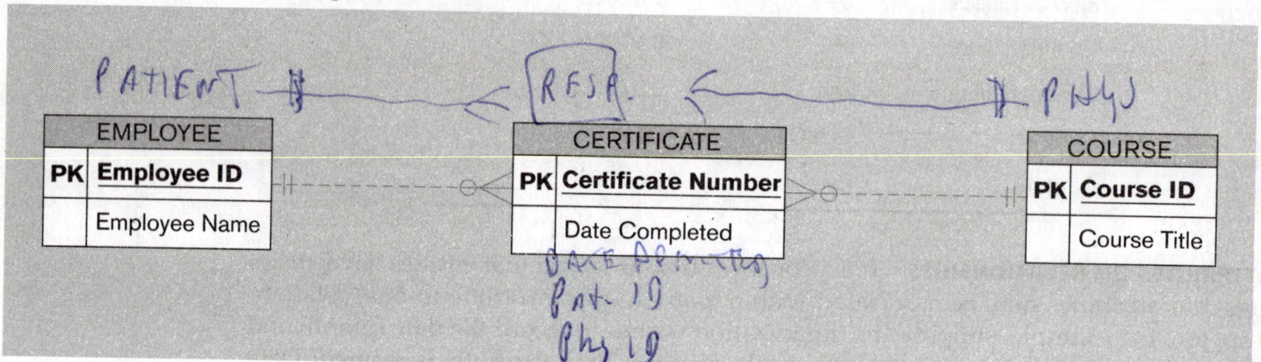

Associative entity
An entity type that associates the instances of one or more entity types and contains attributes that are peculiar to the relationship between those entity instances.

ASSOCIATIVE ENTITIES The presence of one or more attributes on a relationship suggests to the designer that the relationship should perhaps instead be represented as an entity type. To emphasize this point, most E-R drawing tools require that such attributes be placed in an entity type. An **associative entity** is an entity type that associates the instances of one or more entity types and contains attributes that are peculiar to the relationship between those entity instances. The associative entity CERTIFICATE is represented with the rectangle with rounded corners, as shown in Figure 2-11b. Most E-R drawing tools do not have a special symbol for an associative entity. Associative entities are sometimes referred to as gerunds, because the relationship name (a verb) is usually converted to an entity name that is a noun. Note in Figure 2-11b that there are no relationship names on the lines between an associative entity and a strong entity. This is because the associative entity represents the relationship. Figure 2-11c shows how associative entities are drawn using Microsoft Visio, which is representative of how you would draw an associative entity with most E-R diagramming tools. In Visio, the relationship lines are dashed because CERTIFICATE does not include the identifiers of the related entities in its identifier. (Certificate Number is sufficient.)

How do you know whether to convert a relationship to an associative entity type? Following are four conditions that should exist:

1. All the relationships for the participating entity types are "many" relationships.
2. The resulting associative entity type has independent meaning to end users and, preferably, can be identified with a single-attribute identifier.
3. The associative entity has one or more attributes in addition to the identifier.
4. The associative entity participates in one or more relationships independent of the entities related in the associated relationship.

Figure 2-11b shows the relationship Completes converted to an associative entity type. In this case, the training department for the company has decided to award a certificate to each employee who completes a course. Thus, the entity is named CERTIFICATE, which certainly has independent meaning to end users. Also, each certificate has a number (Certificate Number) that serves as the identifier. The attribute Date Completed is also included. Note also in Figure 2-11b and the Visio version of Figure 2-11c that both EMPLOYEE and COURSE are mandatory participants in the two relationships with CERTIFICATE. This is exactly what occurs when you have to represent a many-to-many relationship (Completes in Figure 2-11a) as two one-to-many relationships (the ones associated with CERTIFICATE in Figures 2-11b and 2-11c).

Notice that converting a relationship to an associative entity has caused the relationship notation to move. That is, the "many" cardinality now terminates at the associative entity, rather than at each participating entity type. In Figure 2-11, this shows that an employee, who may complete one or more courses (notation A in Figure 2-11a), may be awarded more than one certificate (notation A in Figure 2-11b); and that a course, which may have one or more employees complete it (notation B in Figure 2-11a), may have many certificates awarded (notation B in Figure 2-11b). See Problem and Exercise 18 for an interesting variation on Figure 2-11a, which emphasizes the rules for when to convert a many-to-many relationship, such as Completes, into an associative entity.

Degree of a Relationship

The **degree** of a relationship is the number of entity types that participate in that relationship. Thus, the relationship Completes in Figure 2-11 is of degree 2, because there are two entity types: EMPLOYEE and COURSE. The three most common relationship degrees in E-R models are unary (degree 1), binary (degree 2), and ternary (degree 3). Higher-degree relationships are possible, but they are rarely encountered in practice, so we restrict our discussion to these three cases. Examples of unary, binary, and ternary relationships appear in Figure 2-12. (Attributes are not shown in some figures for simplicity.)

Degree
The number of entity types that participate in a relationship.

As you look at Figure 2-12, understand that any particular data model represents a specific situation, not a generalization. For example, consider the Manages relationship in Figure 2-12a. In some organizations, it may be possible for one employee to be managed by many other employees (e.g., in a matrix organization). It is important when you develop an E-R model that you understand the business rules of the particular organization you are modeling.

UNARY RELATIONSHIP A **unary relationship** is a relationship between the instances of a *single* entity type. (Unary relationships are also called *recursive relationships*.) Three examples are shown in Figure 2-12a. In the first example, Is Married To is shown as a one-to-one relationship between instances of the PERSON entity type. Because this is a one-to-one relationship, this notation indicates that only the current marriage, if one exists, needs to be kept about a person. What would change if we needed to retain the history of marriages for each person? See Review Question 20 and Problem and Exercise 10 for other business rules and their effect on the Is Married To relationship representation. In the second example, Manages is shown as a one-to-many relationship between instances of the EMPLOYEE entity type. Using this relationship, we could identify, for example, the employees who report to a particular manager. The third example is one case of using a unary relationship to represent a sequence, cycle, or priority list. In this example, sports teams are related by their standing in their league (the Stands After relationship). (Note: In these examples, we ignore whether these are mandatory- or optional-cardinality relationships or whether the same entity instance can repeat in the same relationship instance; we will introduce mandatory and optional cardinality in a later section of this chapter.)

Unary relationship
A relationship between instances of a single entity type.

Figure 2-13 shows an example of another unary relationship, called a *bill-of-materials structure*. Many manufactured products are made of assemblies, which in turn are composed of subassemblies and parts, and so on. As shown in Figure 2-13a, we can represent this structure as a many-to-many unary relationship. In this figure, the entity type ITEM is used to represent all types of components, and we use Has Components for the name of the relationship type that associates lower-level items with higher-level items.

Two occurrences of this bill-of-materials structure are shown in Figure 2-13b. Each of these diagrams shows the immediate components of each item as well as the quantities of that component. For example, item TX100 consists of item BR450 (quantity 2) and item DX500 (quantity 1). You can easily verify that the associations are in fact many-to-many. Several of the items have more than one component type (e.g., item MX300 has three immediate component types: HX100, TX100, and WX240). Also, some of the components are used in several higher-level assemblies. For example, item WX240 is used in both item MX300 and item WX340, even at different levels of the bill-of-materials. The many-to-many relationship guarantees that, for example, the same subassembly structure of WX240 (not shown) is used each time item WX240 goes into making some other item.

FIGURE 2-12 Examples of relationships of different degrees

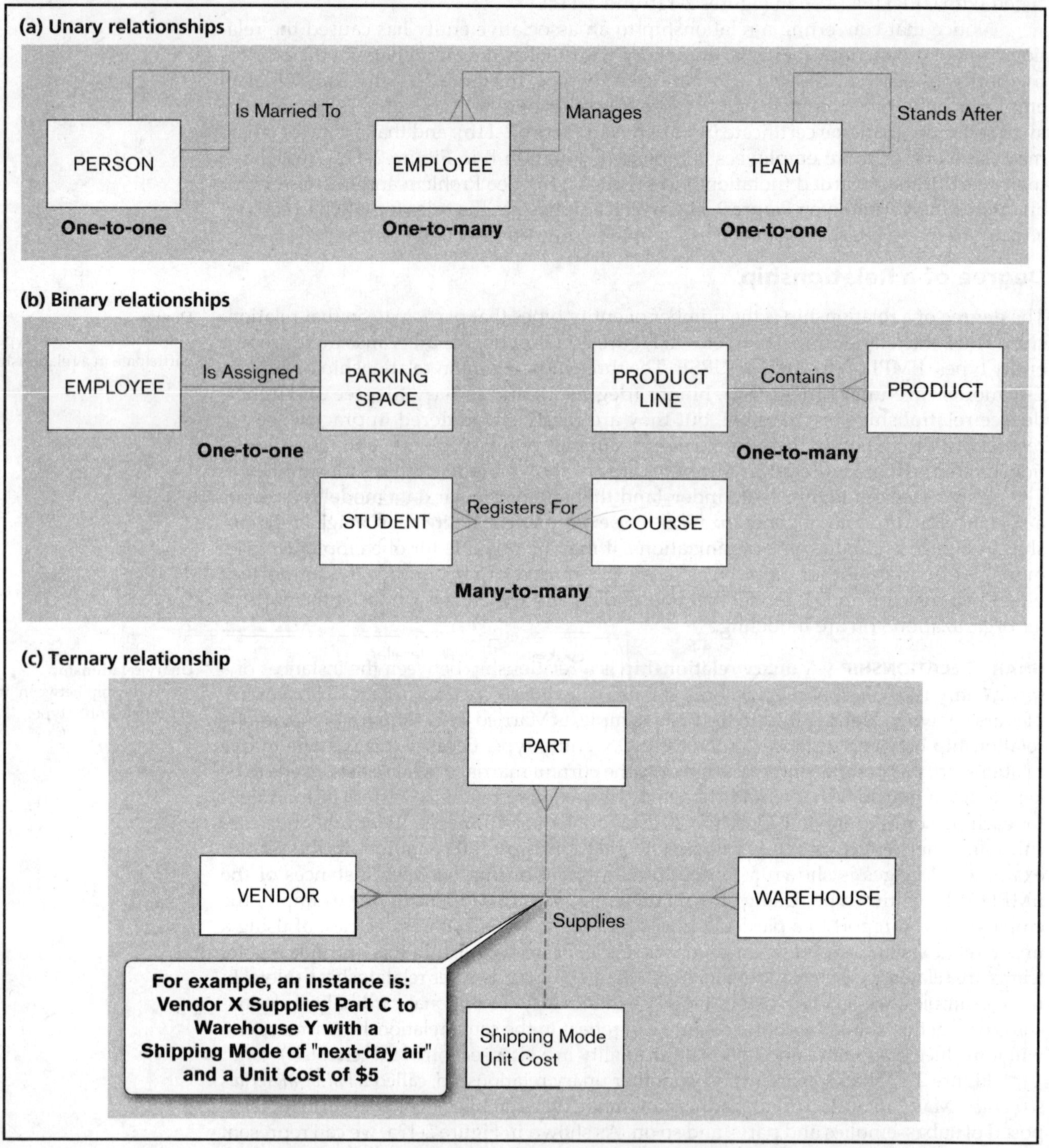

The presence of the attribute Quantity on the relationship suggests that the analyst consider converting the relationship Has Components to an associative entity. Figure 2-13c shows the entity type BOM STRUCTURE, which forms an association between instances of the ITEM entity type. A second attribute (named Effective Date) has been added to BOM STRUCTURE to record the date when this component was first used in the related assembly. Effective dates are often needed when a history of values is required. Other data model structures can be used for unary relationships involving such hierarchies; we show some of these other structures in Chapter 9.

Binary relationship
A relationship between the instances of two entity types.

BINARY RELATIONSHIP A **binary relationship** is a relationship between the instances of two entity types and is the most common type of relationship encountered in data

FIGURE 2-13 Representing a bill-of-materials structure

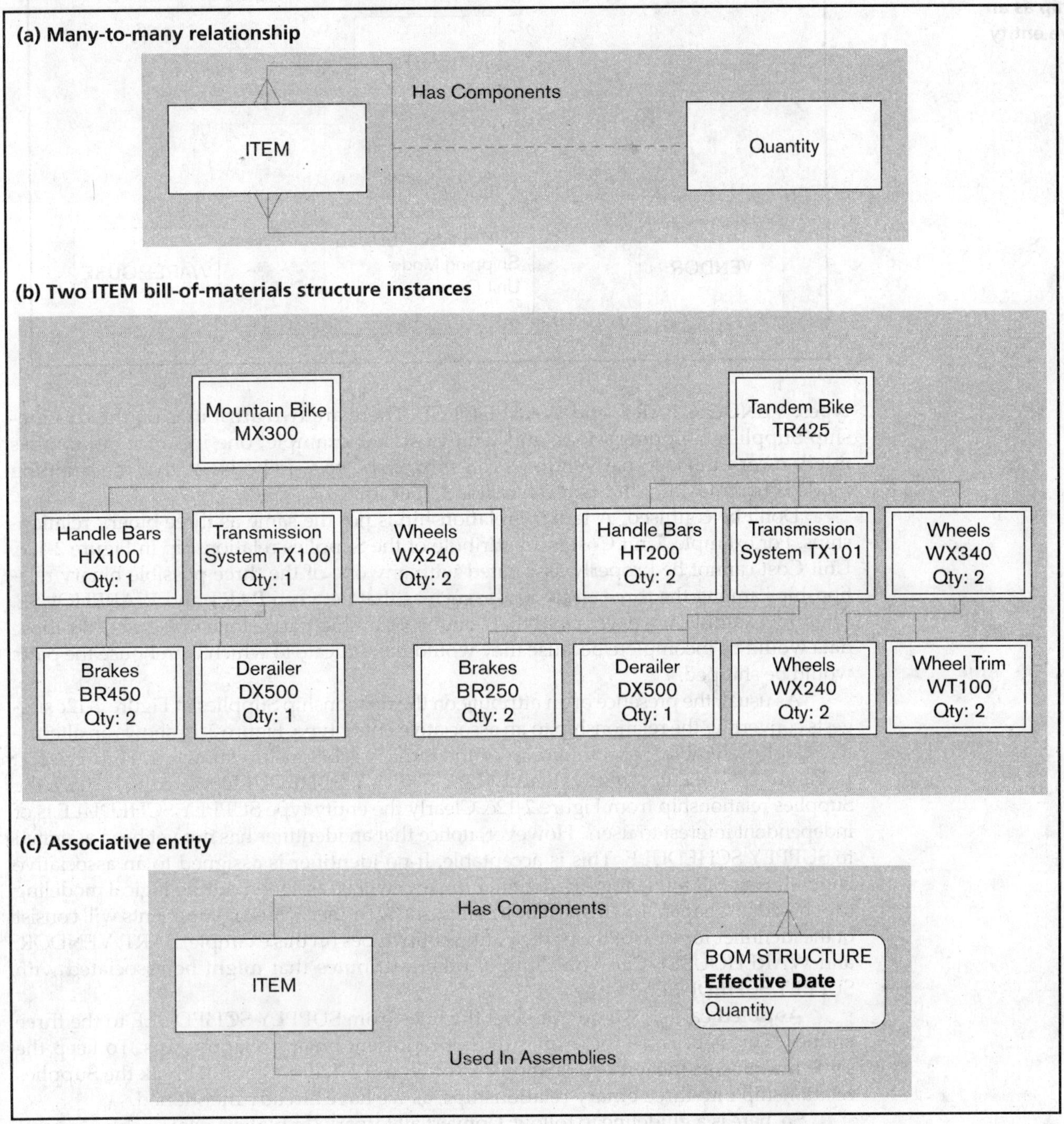

modeling. Figure 2-12b shows three examples. The first (one-to-one) indicates that an employee is assigned one parking place, and that each parking place is assigned to one employee. The second (one-to-many) indicates that a product line may contain several products, and that each product belongs to only one product line. The third (many-to-many) shows that a student may register for more than one course, and that each course may have many student registrants.

Ternary relationship
A simultaneous relationship among the instances of three entity types.

TERNARY RELATIONSHIP A **ternary relationship** is a *simultaneous* relationship among the instances of three entity types. A typical business situation that leads to a ternary relationship is shown in Figure 2-12c. In this example, vendors can supply various parts to warehouses. The relationship Supplies is used to record the specific parts that are supplied by a given vendor to a particular warehouse. Thus there are three entity

FIGURE 2-14 Ternary relationship as an associative entity

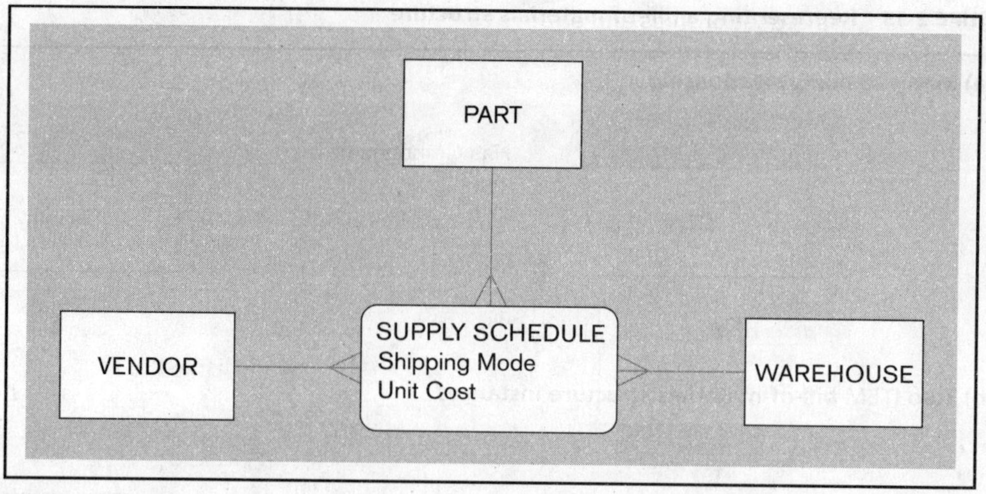

types: VENDOR, PART, and WAREHOUSE. There are two attributes on the relationship Supplies: Shipping Mode and Unit Cost. For example, one instance of Supplies might record the fact that vendor X can ship part C to warehouse Y, that the shipping mode is next-day air, and that the cost is $5 per unit.

Don't be confused: A ternary relationship is not the same as three binary relationships. For example, Unit Cost is an attribute of the Supplies relationship in Figure 2-12c. Unit Cost cannot be properly associated with any one of the three possible binary relationships among the three entity types, such as that between PART and WAREHOUSE. Thus, for example, if we were told that vendor X can ship part C for a unit cost of $8, those data would be incomplete because they would not indicate to which warehouse the parts would be shipped.

As usual, the presence of an attribute on the relationship Supplies in Figure 2-12c suggests converting the relationship to an associative entity type. Figure 2-14 shows an alternative (and preferable) representation of the ternary relationship shown in Figure 2-12c. In Figure 2-14, the (associative) entity type SUPPLY SCHEDULE is used to replace the Supplies relationship from Figure 2-12c. Clearly the entity type SUPPLY SCHEDULE is of independent interest to users. However, notice that an identifier has not yet been assigned to SUPPLY SCHEDULE. This is acceptable. If no identifier is assigned to an associative entity during E-R modeling, an identifier (or key) will be assigned during logical modeling (discussed in Chapter 4). This will be a composite identifier whose components will consist of the identifier for each of the participating entity types (in this example, PART, VENDOR, and WAREHOUSE). Can you think of other attributes that might be associated with SUPPLY SCHEDULE?

As noted earlier, we do not label the lines from SUPPLY SCHEDULE to the three entities. This is because these lines do not represent binary relationships. To keep the same meaning as the ternary relationship of Figure 2-12c, we cannot break the Supplies relationship into three binary relationships, as we have already mentioned.

So, here is a guideline to follow: Convert all ternary (or higher) relationships to associative entities, as in this example. Song et al. (1995) show that participation constraints (described in a following section on cardinality constraints) cannot be accurately represented for a ternary relationship, given the notation with attributes on the relationship line. However, by converting to an associative entity, the constraints can be accurately represented. Also, many E-R diagram drawing tools, including most CASE tools, cannot represent ternary relationships. So, although not semantically accurate, you must use these tools to represent the ternary relationship with an associative entity and three binary relationships, which have a mandatory association with each of the three related entity types.

Attributes or Entity?

Sometimes you will wonder if you should represent data as an attribute or an entity; this is a common dilemma. Figure 2-15 includes three examples of situations when an attribute could be represented via an entity type. We use this textbook's E-R notation in

FIGURE 2-15 Using relationships and entities to link related attributes

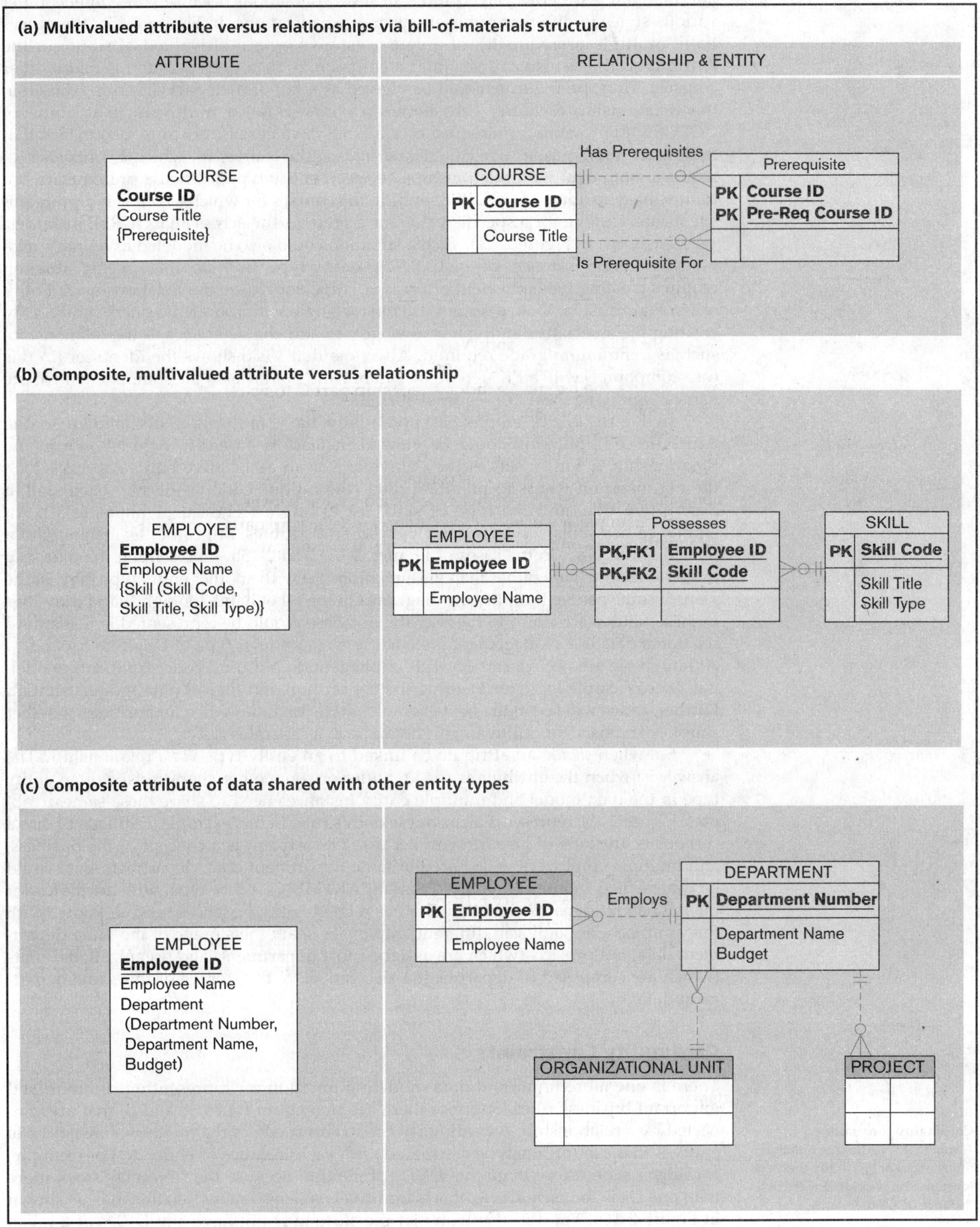

the left column and the notation from Microsoft Visio in the right column; it is important that you learn how to read ERDs in several notations because you will encounter various styles in different publications and organizations. In Figure 2-15a, the potentially multiple prerequisites of a course (shown as a multivalued attribute in the Attribute cell) are also courses (and a course may be a prerequisite for many other courses). Thus, prerequisite could be viewed as a bill-of-materials structure (shown in the Relationship & Entity cell) between courses, not a multivalued attribute of COURSE. Representing prerequisites via a bill-of-materials structure also means that finding the prerequisites of a course and finding the courses for which a course is prerequisite both deal with relationships between entity types. When a prerequisite is a multivalued attribute of COURSE, finding the courses for which a course is a prerequisite means looking for a specific value for a prerequisite across all COURSE instances. As was shown in Figure 2-13a, such a situation could also be modeled as a unary relationship among instances of the COURSE entity type. In Visio, this specific situation requires creating the equivalent of an associative entity (see the Relationship & Entity cell in Figure 2-15a; Visio does not use the rectangle with rounded corners symbol). By creating the associative entity, it is now easy to add characteristics to the relationship, such as a minimum grade required. Also note that Visio shows the identifier (in this case compound) with a PK stereotype symbol and boldface on the component attribute names, signifying these are required attributes.

In Figure 2-15b, employees potentially have multiple skills (shown in the Attribute cell), but skill could be viewed instead as an entity type (shown in the Relationship & Entity cell as the equivalent of an associative entity) about which the organization wants to maintain data (the unique code to identify each skill, a descriptive title, and the type of skill, for example technical or managerial). An employee has skills, which are not viewed as attributes, but rather as instances of a related entity type. In the cases of Figures 2-15a and 2-15b, representing the data as a multivalued attribute rather than via a relationship with another entity type may, in the view of some people, simplify the diagram. On the other hand, the right-hand drawings in these figures are closer to the way the database would be represented in a standard relational database management system, the most popular type of DBMS in use today. Although we are not concerned with implementation during conceptual data modeling, there is some logic for keeping the conceptual and logical data models similar. Further, as we will see in the next example, there are times when an attribute, whether simple, composite, or multivalued, should be in a separate entity.

So, when *should* an attribute be linked to an entity type via a relationship? The answer is: when the attribute is the identifier or some other characteristic of an entity type in the data model and multiple entity instances need to share these same attributes. Figure 2-15c represents an example of this rule. In this example, EMPLOYEE has a composite attribute of Department. Because Department is a concept of the business, and multiple employees will share the same department data, department data could be represented (nonredundantly) in a DEPARTMENT entity type, with attributes for the data about departments that all other related entity instances need to know. With this approach, not only can different employees share the storage of the same department data, but projects (which are assigned to a department) and organizational units (which are composed of departments) also can share the storage of this same department data.

Cardinality Constraints

There is one more important data modeling notation for representing common and important business rules. Suppose there are two entity types, A and B, that are connected by a relationship. A **cardinality constraint** specifies the number of instances of entity B that can (or must) be associated with each instance of entity A. For example, consider a video store that rents DVDs of movies. Because the store may stock more than one DVD for each movie, this is intuitively a one-to-many relationship, as shown in Figure 2-16a. Yet it is also true that the store may not have any DVDs of a given movie in stock at a particular time (e.g., all copies may be checked out). We need a

Cardinality constraint
A rule that specifies the number of instances of one entity that can (or must) be associated with each instance of another entity.

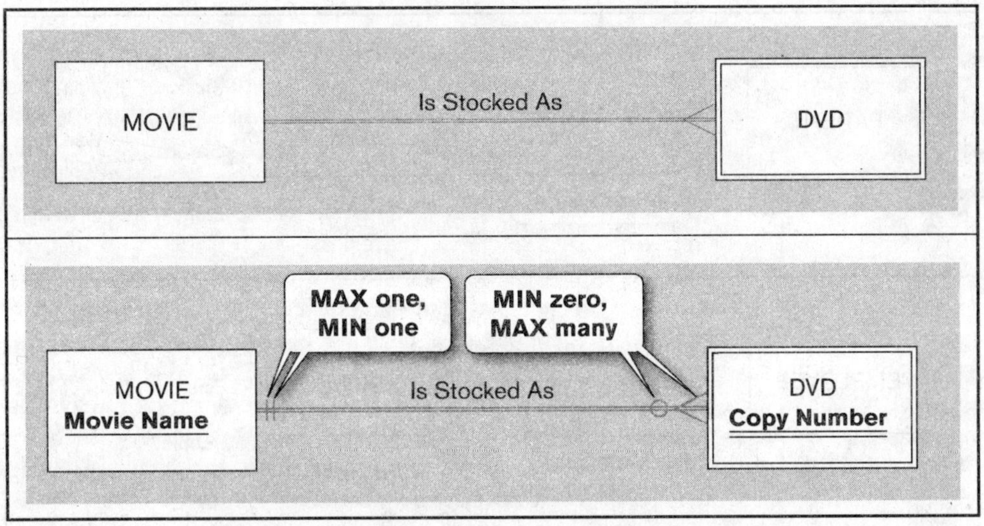

FIGURE 2-16 Introducing cardinality constraints
(a) Basic relationship
(b) Relationship with cardinality constraints

more precise notation to indicate the range of cardinalities for a relationship. This notation was introduced in Figure 2-2, which you may want to review at this time.

MINIMUM CARDINALITY The **minimum cardinality** of a relationship is the minimum number of instances of entity B that may be associated with each instance of entity A. In our DVD example, the minimum number of DVDs for a movie is zero. When the minimum number of participants is zero, we say that entity type B is an optional participant in the relationship. In this example, DVD (a weak entity type) is an optional participant in the Is Stocked As relationship. This fact is indicated by the symbol zero through the line near the DVD entity in Figure 2-16b.

Minimum cardinality
The minimum number of instances of one entity that may be associated with each instance of another entity.

MAXIMUM CARDINALITY The **maximum cardinality** of a relationship is the maximum number of instances of entity B that may be associated with each instance of entity A. In the video example, the maximum cardinality for the DVD entity type is "many"—that is, an unspecified number greater than one. This is indicated by the "crow's foot" symbol on the line next to the DVD entity symbol in Figure 2-16b. (You might find interesting the explanation of the origin of the crow's foot notation found in the Wikipedia entry about the entity-relationship model; this entry also shows the wide variety of notation used to represent cardinality; see **http:/en.wikipedia.org/wiki/Entity-relationship_model**.)

Maximum cardinality
The maximum number of instances of one entity that may be associated with each instance of another entity.

A relationship is, of course, bidirectional, so there is also cardinality notation next to the MOVIE entity. Notice that the minimum and maximum are both one (see Figure 2-16b). This is called a *mandatory one* cardinality. In other words, each DVD of a movie must be a copy of exactly one movie. In general, participation in a relationship may be optional or mandatory for the entities involved. If the minimum cardinality is zero, participation is optional; if the minimum cardinality is one, participation is mandatory.

In Figure 2-16b, some attributes have been added to each of the entity types. Notice that DVD is represented as a weak entity. This is because a DVD cannot exist unless the owner movie also exists. The identifier of MOVIE is Movie Name. DVD does not have a unique identifier. However, Copy Number is a *partial* identifier, which, together with Movie Name, would uniquely identify an instance of DVD.

Some Examples of Relationships and Their Cardinalities

Examples of three relationships that show all possible combinations of minimum and maximum cardinalities appear in Figure 2-17. Each example states the business rule for each cardinality constraint and shows the associated E-R notation. Each example also shows some relationship instances to clarify the nature of the relationship. You should

FIGURE 2-17 Examples of cardinality constraints
(a) Mandatory cardinalities
(b) One optional, one mandatory cardinality
(c) Optional cardinalities

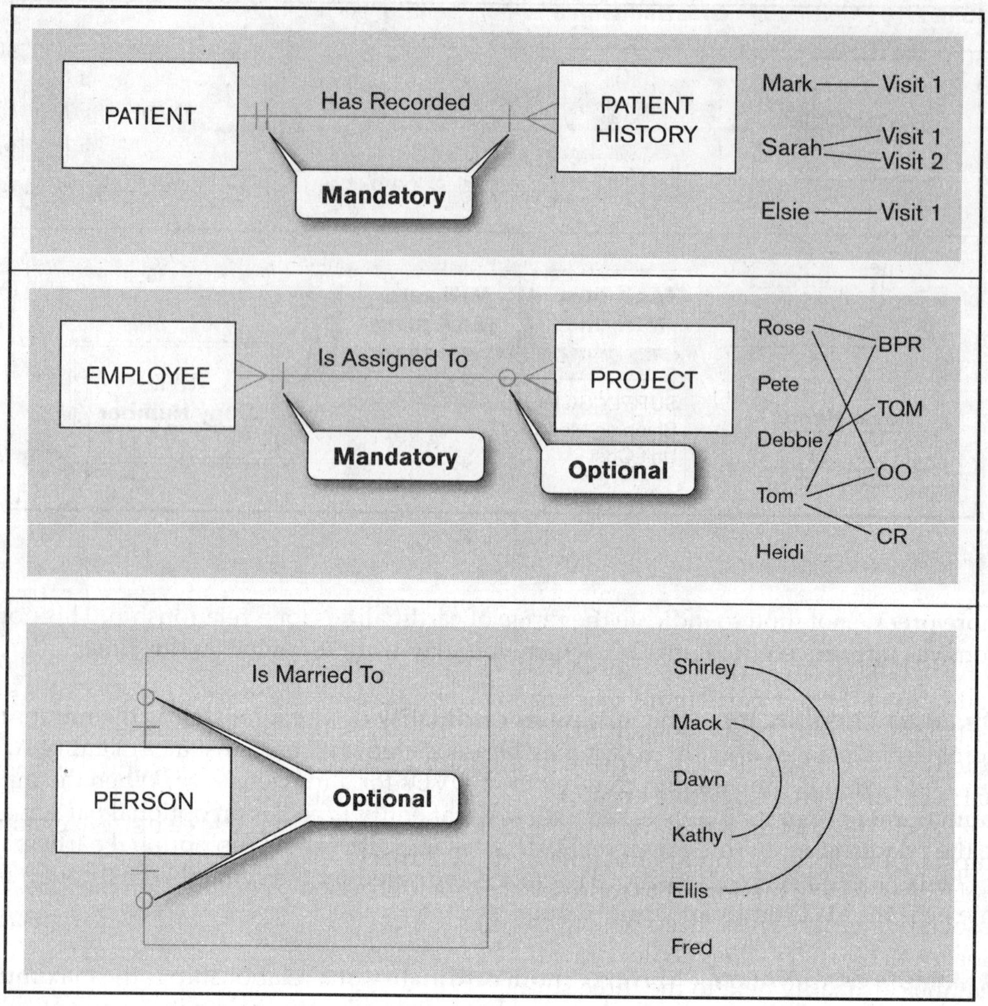

study each of these examples carefully. Following are the business rules for each of the examples in Figure 2-17:

1. *PATIENT Has Recorded PATIENT HISTORY (Figure 2-17a)* Each patient has one or more patient histories. (The initial patient visit is always recorded as an instance of PATIENT HISTORY.) Each instance of PATIENT HISTORY "belongs to" exactly one PATIENT.
2. *EMPLOYEE Is Assigned To PROJECT (Figure 2-17b)* Each PROJECT has at least one EMPLOYEE assigned to it. (Some projects have more than one.) Each EMPLOYEE may or (optionally) may not be assigned to any existing PROJECT (e.g., employee Pete), or may be assigned to one or more PROJECTs.
3. *PERSON Is Married To PERSON (Figure 2-17c)* This is an optional zero or one cardinality in both directions, because a person may or may not be married at a given point in time.

It is possible for the maximum cardinality to be a fixed number, not an arbitrary "many" value. For example, suppose corporate policy states that an employee may work on at most five projects at the same time. We could show this business rule by placing a 5 above or below the crow's foot next to the PROJECT entity in Figure 2-17b.

A TERNARY RELATIONSHIP We showed the ternary relationship with the associative entity type SUPPLY SCHEDULE in Figure 2-14. Now let's add cardinality constraints to this diagram, based on the business rules for this situation. The E-R diagram, with the relevant business rules, is shown in Figure 2-18. Notice that PART and

FIGURE 2-18 Cardinality constraints in a ternary relationship

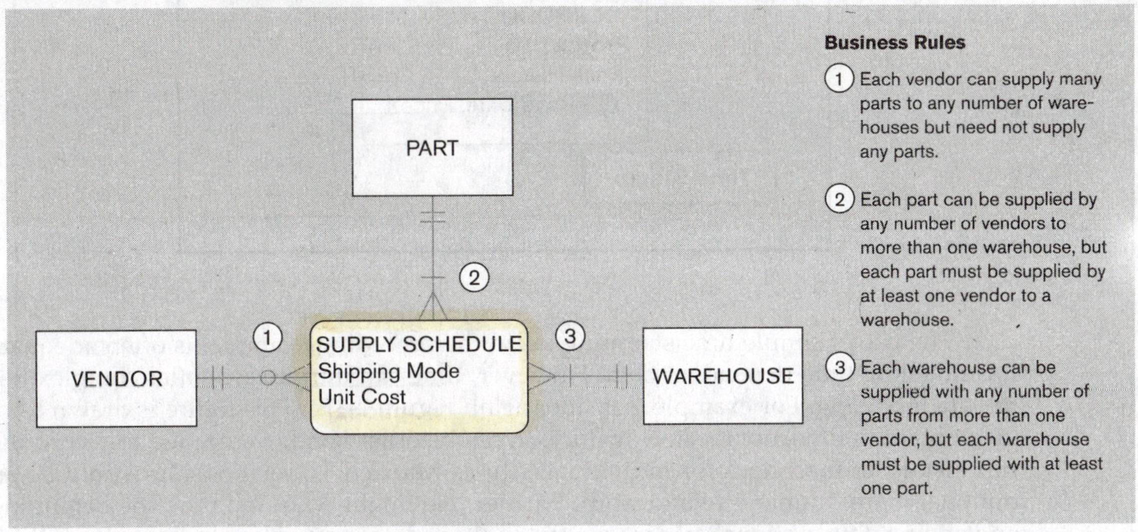

WAREHOUSE must relate to some SUPPLY SCHEDULE instance, and a VENDOR optionally may not participate. The cardinality at each of the participating entities is a mandatory one, because each SUPPLY SCHEDULE instance must be related to exactly one instance of each of these participating entity types. (Remember, SUPPLY SCHEDULE is an associative entity.)

As noted earlier, a ternary relationship is not equivalent to three binary relationships. Unfortunately, you are not able to draw ternary relationships with many CASE tools; instead, you are forced to represent ternary relationships as three binaries (i.e., an associative entity with three binary relationships). If you are forced to draw three binary relationships, then do not draw the binary relationships with names, and be sure that the cardinality next to the three strong entities is a mandatory one.

Modeling Time-Dependent Data

Database contents vary over time. With renewed interest today in traceability and reconstruction of a historical picture of the organization for various regulatory requirements, such as HIPAA and Sarbanes-Oxley, the need to include a time series of data has become essential. For example, in a database that contains product information, the unit price for each product may be changed as material and labor costs and market conditions change. If only the current price is required, Price can be modeled as a single-valued attribute. However, for accounting, billing, financial reporting, and other purposes, we are likely to need to preserve a history of the prices and the time period during which each was in effect. As Figure 2-19 shows, we can conceptualize this requirement as a series of prices and the effective date for each price. This results in the (composite) multivalued attribute named Price History, with components Price and Effective Date. An important characteristic of such a composite, multivalued attribute is that the component attributes go together. Thus, in Figure 2-19, each Price is paired with the corresponding Effective Date.

In Figure 2-19, each value of the attribute Price is time stamped with its effective date. A **time stamp** is simply a time value, such as date and time, that is associated with a data value. A time stamp may be associated with any data value that changes over time when we need to maintain a history of those data values. Time stamps may be recorded to indicate the time the value was entered (transaction time), the time the value becomes valid or stops being valid, or the time when critical actions were performed, such as updates, corrections, or audits. This situation is similar to the employee skill diagrams in Figure 2-15b; thus, an alternative, not shown in Figure 2-19, is to make Price History a separate entity type, as was done with Skill using Microsoft Visio.

Time stamp
A time value that is associated with a data value, often indicating when some event occurred that affected the data value.

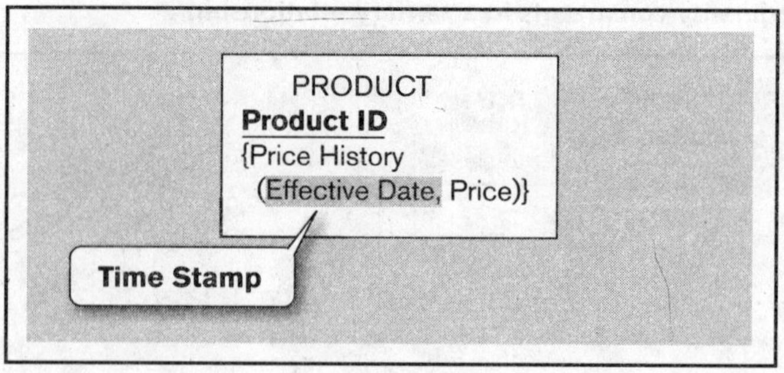

FIGURE 2-19 Simple example of time stamping

The use of simple time stamping (as in the preceding example) is often adequate for modeling time-dependent data. However, time can introduce subtler complexities to data modeling. For example, consider again Figure 2-17c. This figure is drawn for a given point in time, not to show history. If, on the other hand, we needed to record the full history of marriages for individuals, the Is Married To relationship would be an optional many-to-many relationship. Further, we might want to know the beginning and ending date (optional) of each marriage; these dates would be, similar to the bill-of-materials structure in Figure 2-13c, attributes of the relationship or associative entity.

Financial and other compliance regulations, such as Sarbanes-Oxley and Basel II, require that a database maintain history rather than just current status of critical data. In addition, some data modelers will argue that a data model should always be able to represent history, even if today users say they need only current values. These factors suggest that all relationships should be modeled as many-to-many (which is often done in purchased data model). Thus, for most databases, this will necessitate forming an associative entity along every relationship. There are two obvious negatives to this approach. First, many additional (associative) entities are created, thus cluttering ERDs. Second, a many-to-many (*M:N*) relationship is less restrictive than a one-to-many (1:*M*). So, if initially you want to enforce only one associated entity instance for some entity (i.e., the "one" side of the relationships), this cannot be enforced by the data model with an *M:N* relationship. It would seem likely that some relationships would never be *M:N*; for example, would a 1:*M* relationship between customer and order ever become *M:N* (but, of course, maybe someday our organization would sell items that would allow and often have joint purchasing, like vehicles or houses)? The conclusion is that if history or a time series of values might ever be desired or required by regulation, you should consider using an *M:N* relationship.

PINE VALLEY FURNITURE

An even more subtle situation of the effect of time on data modeling is illustrated in Figure 2-20a, which represents a portion of an ERD for Pine Valley Furniture Company. Each product is assigned (i.e., current assignment) to a product line (or related group of products). Customer orders are processed throughout the year, and monthly summaries are reported by product line and by product within product line.

Suppose that in the middle of the year, due to a reorganization of the sales function, some products are reassigned to different product lines. The model shown in Figure 2-20a is not designed to track the reassignment of a product to a new product line. Thus, all sales reports will show cumulative sales for a product based on its current product line rather than the one at the time of the sale. For example, a product may have total year-to-date sales of $50,000 and be associated with product line B, yet $40,000 of those sales may have occurred while the product was assigned to product line A. This fact will be lost using the model in Figure 2-20a. The simple design change shown in Figure 2-20b will correctly recognize product reassignments. A new relationship, called Sales For Product Line, has been added between ORDER and PRODUCT LINE. As customer orders are processed, they are credited to both the correct product (via Sales For Product) and the correct product line (via Sales For Product Line) as of the time of the sale. The approach of Figure 2-20b is similar to what is done in a data warehouse to retain historical records of the precise situation at any point in time. (We will return to dealing with the time dimension in Chapter 9.)

Another aspect of modeling time is recognizing that although the requirements of the organization today may be to record only the current situation, the design of

FIGURE 2-20 Example of time in Pine Valley Furniture product database

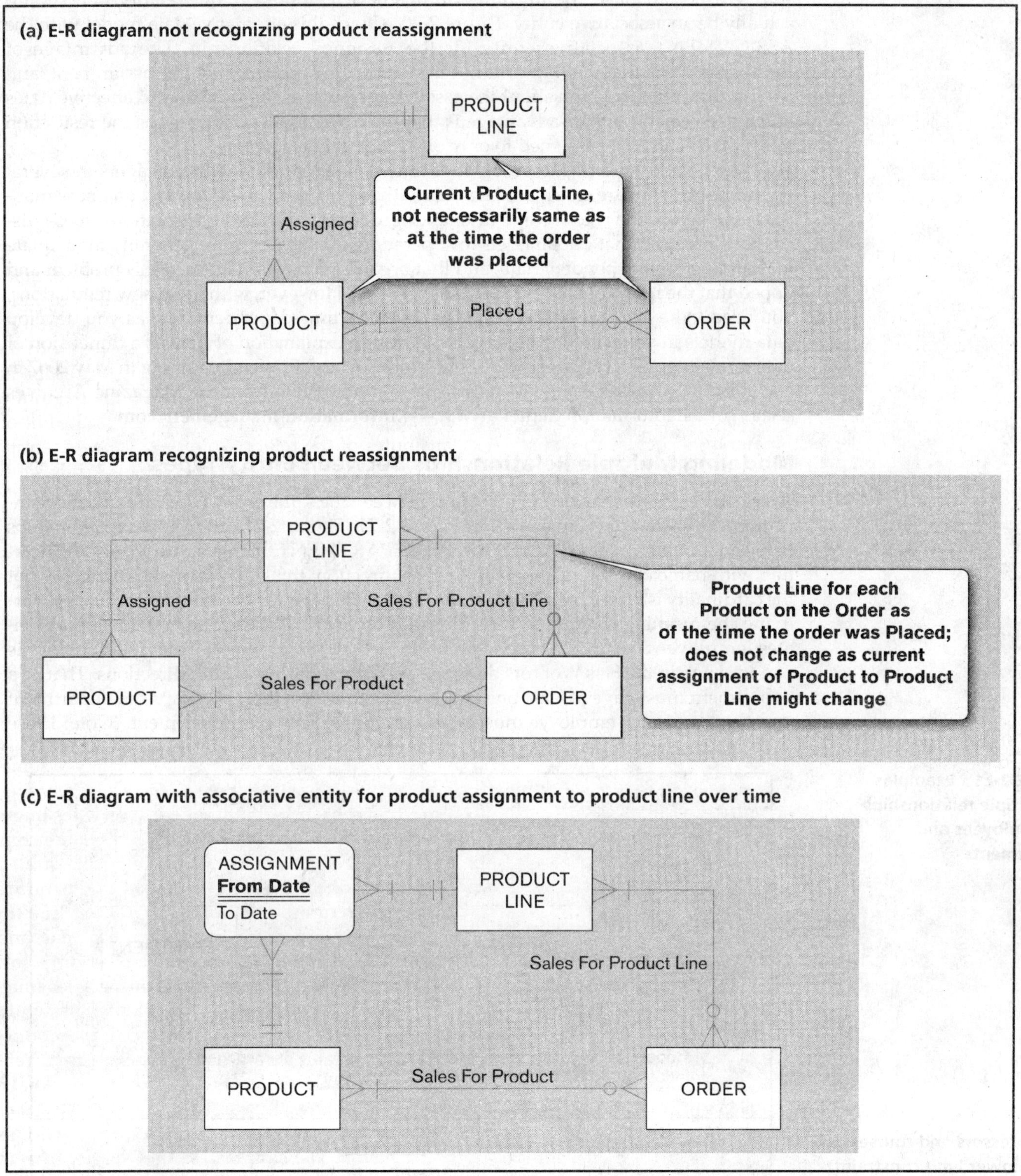

the database may need to change if the organization ever decides to keep history. In Figure 2-20b, we know the current product line for a product and the product line for the product each time it is ordered. But what if the product were ever reassigned to a product line during a period of zero sales for the product? Based on this data model in Figure 2-20b, we would not know of these other product line assignments. A common solution to this need for greater flexibility in the data model is to consider whether a one-to-many relationship, such as Assigned, should become a many-to-many relationship. Further, to allow for attributes on this new relationship, this relationship should actually be an associative entity. Figure 2-20c shows this alternative data model with the ASSIGNMENT associative entity for the Assigned relationship. The advantage of the alternative is that we now will not miss recording any product line assignment, and we can record information about the assignment (such as the from and to effective dates of the assignment); the disadvantage is that the data model no longer has the restriction that a product may be assigned to only one product line at a time.

We have discussed the problem of time-dependent data with managers in several organizations who are considered leaders in the use of data modeling and database management. Before the recent wave of financial reporting disclosure regulations, these discussions revealed that data models for operational databases were generally inadequate for handing time-dependent data, and that organizations often ignored this problem and hoped that the resulting inaccuracies balanced out. However, with these new regulations, you need to be alert to the complexities posed by time-dependent data as you develop data models in your organization. For a thorough explanation of time as a dimension of data modeling, see a series of articles by T. Johnson and R. Weis beginning in May 2007 in *DM Review* (now *Information Management*) and accessible from the Magazine Archives section of the Information Center at of **www.information-management.com**.

Modeling Multiple Relationships Between Entity Types

There may be more than one relationship between the same entity types in a given organization. Two examples are shown in Figure 2-21. Figure 2-21a shows two relationships between the entity types EMPLOYEE and DEPARTMENT. In this figure we use the notation with names for the relationship in each direction; this notation makes explicit what the cardinality is for each direction of the relationship (which becomes important for clarifying the meaning of the unary relationship on EMPLOYEE). One relationship associates employees with the department in which they work. This relationship is one-to-many in the Has Workers direction and is mandatory in both directions. That is, a department must have at least one employee who works there (perhaps the department manager), and each employee must be assigned to exactly one department. (Note: These

FIGURE 2-21 Examples of multiple relationships
(a) Employees and departments
(b) Professors and courses (fixed lower limit constraint)

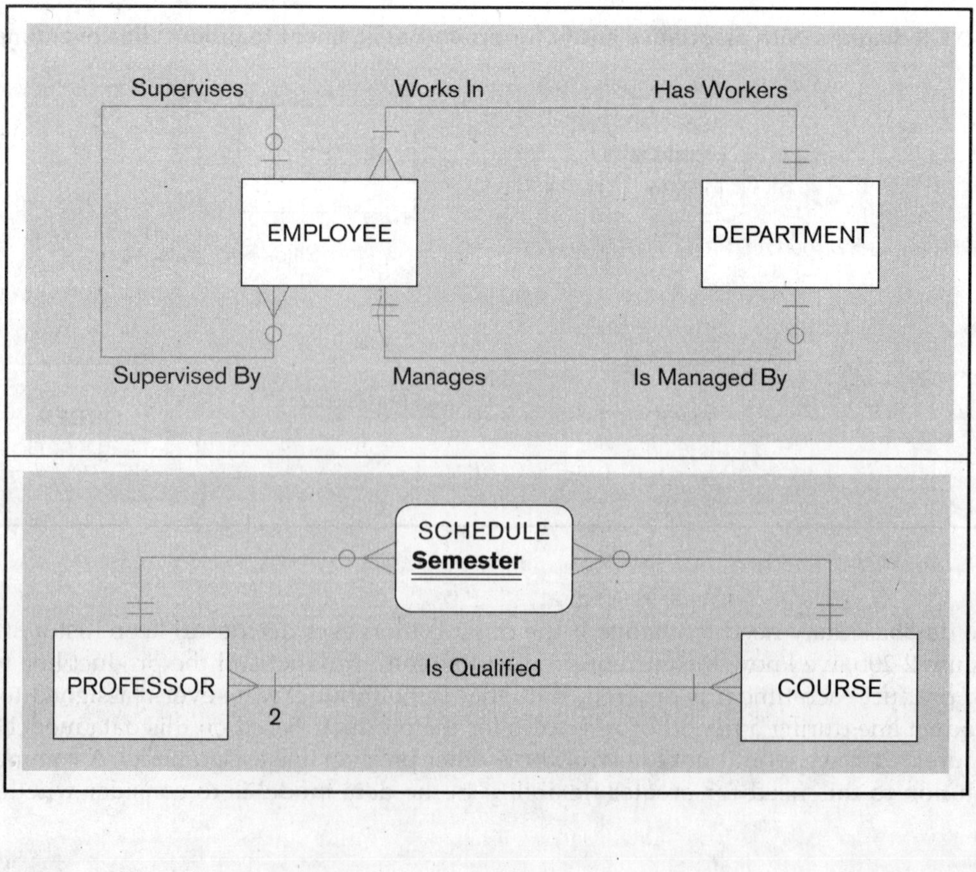

are specific business rules we assume for this illustration. It is crucial when you develop an E-R diagram for a particular situation that you understand the business rules that apply for that setting. For example, if EMPLOYEE were to include retirees, then each employee may not be currently assigned to exactly one department; further, the E-R model in Figure 2-21a assumes that the organization needs to remember in which DEPARTMENT each EMPLOYEE currently works, rather than remembering the history of department assignments. Again, the structure of the data model reflects the information the organization needs to remember.)

The second relationship between EMPLOYEE and DEPARTMENT associates each department with the employee who manages that department. The relationship from DEPARTMENT to EMPLOYEE (called Is Managed By in that direction) is a mandatory one, indicating that a department must have exactly one manager. From EMPLOYEE to DEPARTMENT, the relationship (Manages) is optional because a given employee either is or is not a department manager.

Figure 2-21a also shows the unary relationship that associates each employee with his or her supervisor, and vice versa. This relationship records the business rule that each employee may have exactly one supervisor (Supervised By). Conversely, each employee may supervise any number of employees, or may not be a supervisor.

The example in Figure 2-21b shows two relationships between the entity types PROFESSOR and COURSE. The relationship Is Qualified associates professors with the courses they are qualified to teach. A given course must have at a minimum two qualified instructors (an example of how to use a fixed value for a minimum or maximum cardinality). This might happen, for example, so that a course is never the "property" of one instructor. Conversely, each instructor must be qualified to teach at least one course (a reasonable expectation).

The second relationship in this figure associates professors with the courses they are actually scheduled to teach during a given semester. Because Semester is a characteristic of the relationship, we place an associative entity, SCHEDULE, between PROFESSOR and COURSE.

One final point about Figure 2-21b: Have you figured out what the identifier is for the SCHEDULE associative entity? Notice that Semester is a partial identifier; thus, the full identifier will be the identifier of PROFESSOR along with the identifier of COURSE as well as Semester. Because such full identifiers for associative entities can become long and complex, it is often recommended that surrogate identifiers be created for each associative entity; so, Schedule ID would be created as the identifier of SCHEDULE, and Semester would be an attribute. What is lost in this case is the explicit business rule that the combination of the PROFESSOR identifier, COURSE identifier, and Semester must be unique for each SCHEDULE instance (because this combination is the identifier of SCHEDULE). Of course, this can be added as another business rule.

Naming and Defining Relationships

In addition to the general guidelines for naming data objects, there are a few special guidelines for naming relationships, which follow:

- A relationship name is a *verb phrase* (such as Assigned To, Supplies, or Teaches). Relationships represent actions being taken, usually in the present tense, so transitive verbs (an action on something) are the most appropriate. A relationship name states the action taken, not the result of the action (e.g., use Assigned To, not Assignment). The name states the essence of the interaction between the participating entity types, not the process involved (e.g., use an Employee is *Assigned To* a project, not an Employee is *Assigning* a project).
- You should *avoid vague names*, such as Has or Is Related To. Use descriptive, powerful verb phrases, often taken from the action verbs found in the definition of the relationship.

There are also some specific guidelines for defining relationships, which follow:

- A relationship definition *explains what action is being taken and possibly why it is important*. It may be important to state who or what does the action, but it is not important to explain how the action is taken. Stating the business objects involved in the relationship is natural, but because the E-R diagram shows what entity types are involved in the relationship and other definitions explain the entity types, you do not have to describe the business objects.

- It may also be important to *give examples to clarify the action*. For example, for a relationship of Registered For between student and course, it may be useful to explain that this covers both on-site and online registration and includes registrations made during the drop/add period.
- The definition should explain any *optional participation*. You should explain what conditions lead to zero associated instances, whether this can happen only when an entity instance is first created, or whether this can happen at any time. For example, "Registered For links a course with the students who have signed up to take the course, and the courses a student has signed up to take. A course will have no students registered for it before the registration period begins and may never have any registered students. A student will not be registered for any courses before the registration period begins and may not register for any classes (or may register for classes and then drop any or all classes)."
- A relationship definition should also *explain the reason for any explicit maximum cardinality* other than many. For example, "Assigned To links an employee with the projects to which that employee is assigned and the employees assigned to a project. Due to our labor union agreement, an employee may not be assigned to more than four projects at a given time." This example, typical of many upper-bound business rules, suggests that maximum cardinalities tend not to be permanent. In this example, the next labor union agreement could increase or decrease this limit. Thus, the implementation of maximum cardinalities must be done to allow changes.
- A relationship definition should *explain any mutually exclusive relationships*. Mutually exclusive relationships are ones for which an entity instance can participate in only one of several alternative relationships. We will show examples of this situation in Chapter 3. For now, consider the following example: "Plays On links an intercollegiate sports team with its student players and indicates on which teams a student plays. Students who play on intercollegiate sports teams cannot also work in a campus job (i.e., a student cannot be linked to both an intercollegiate sports team via Plays On and a campus job via the Works On relationship)." Another example of a mutually exclusive restriction is when an employee cannot both be Supervised By and be Married To the same employee.
- A relationship definition should *explain any restrictions on participation in the relationship*. Mutual exclusivity is one restriction, but there can be others. For example, "Supervised By links an employee with the other employees he or she supervises and links an employee with the other employee who supervises him or her. An employee cannot supervise him- or herself, and an employee cannot supervise other employees if his or her job classification level is below 4."
- A relationship definition should *explain the extent of history that is kept in the relationship*. For example, "Assigned To links a hospital bed with a patient. Only the current bed assignment is stored. When a patient is not admitted, that patient is not assigned to a bed, and a bed may be vacant at any given point in time." Another example of describing history for a relationship is "Places links a customer with the orders they have placed with our company and links an order with the associated customer. Only two years of orders are maintained in the database, so not all orders can participate in this relationship."
- A relationship definition should *explain whether an entity instance involved in a relationship instance can transfer participation to another relationship instance*. For example, "Places links a customer with the orders they have placed with our company and links an order with the associated customer. An order is not transferable to another customer." Another example is "Categorized As links a product line with the products sold under that heading and links a product to its associated product line. Due to changes in organization structure and product design features, products may be recategorized to a different product line. Categorized As keeps track of only the current product line to which a product is linked."

E-R MODELING EXAMPLE: PINE VALLEY FURNITURE COMPANY

PINE VALLEY FURNITURE

Developing an E-R diagram can proceed from one (or both) of two perspectives. With a top-down perspective, the designer proceeds from basic descriptions of the business, including its policies, processes, and environment. This approach is most appropriate for developing a high-level E-R diagram with only the major entities and relationships and with a limited set of attributes (such as just the entity identifiers). With a bottom-up approach, the designer proceeds from detailed discussions with users, and from a detailed study of documents, screens, and other data sources. This approach is necessary for developing a detailed, "fully attributed" E-R diagram.

In this section, we develop a high-level ERD for Pine Valley Furniture Company, based largely on the first of these approaches (see Figure 2-22 for a Microsoft Visio version). For simplicity, we do not show any composite or multivalued attributes (e.g., skill is shown as a separate entity type associated with EMPLOYEE via an associative entity, which allows an employee to have many skills and a skill to be held by many employees).

Figure 2-22 provides many examples of common E-R modeling notations, and hence, it can be used as an excellent review of what you have learned in this chapter. In a moment, we will explain the business rules that are represented in this figure. However, before you read that explanation, one way to use Figure 2-22 is to search for typical E-R model constructs in it, such as one-to-many, binary, or unary relationships. Then, ask yourself why the business data was modeled this way. For example, ask yourself

- Where is a unary relationship, what does it mean, and for what reasons might the cardinalities on it be different in other organizations?
- Why is Includes a one-to many relationship, and why might this ever be different in some other organization?
- Does Includes allow for a product to be represented in the database before it is assigned to a product line (e.g., while the product is in research and development)?
- If there were a different customer contact person for each sales territory in which a customer did business, where in the data model would we place this person's name?
- What is the meaning of the Does Business In associative entity, and why does each Does Business In instance have to be associated with exactly one SALES TERRITORY and one CUSTOMER?
- In what way might Pine Valley change the way it does business that would cause the Supplies associative entity to be eliminated and the relationships around it change?

Each of these questions is included in Problem and Exercise 1 at the end of the chapter, but we suggest you use these now as a way to review your understanding of E-R diagramming.

From a study of the business processes at Pine Valley Furniture Company, we have identified the following entity types. An identifier is also suggested for each entity, together with selected important attributes:

- The company sells a number of different furniture products. These products are grouped into several product lines. The identifier for a product is Product ID, whereas the identifier for a product line is Product Line ID. We identify the following additional attributes for product: Product Description, Product Finish, and Product Standard Price. Another attribute for product line is Product Line Name. A product line may group any number of products but must group at least one product. Each product must belong to exactly one product line.
- Customers submit orders for products. The identifier for an order is Order ID, and another attribute is Order Date. A customer may submit any number of orders, but need not submit any orders. Each order is submitted by exactly one customer. The identifier for a customer is Customer ID. Other attributes include Customer Name, Customer Address, and Customer Postal Code.
- A given customer order must request at least one product and only one product per order line item. Any product sold by Pine Valley Furniture may not appear on any order line item or may appear on one or more order line items. An attribute associated with each order line item is Ordered Quantity.

FIGURE 2-22 Data model for Pine Valley Furniture Company in Microsoft Visio notation

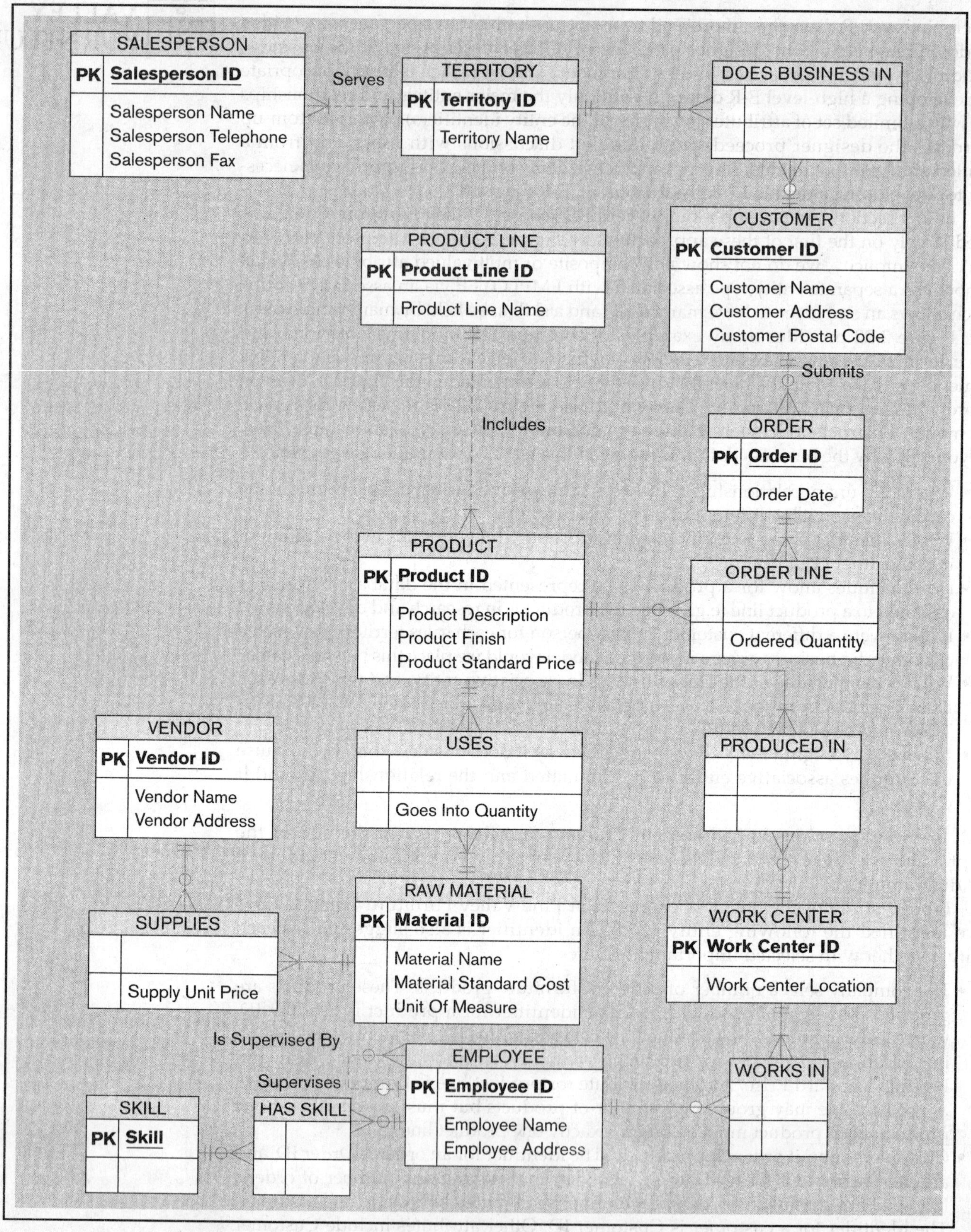

- Pine Valley Furniture has established sales territories for its customers. Each customer may do business in any number of these sales territories or may not do business in any territory. A sales territory has one to many customers. The identifier for a sales territory is Territory ID and an attribute of a Territory Name.
- Pine Valley Furniture Company has several salespersons. The identifier for a salesperson is Salesperson ID. Other attributes include Salesperson Name, Salesperson Telephone, and Salesperson Fax. A salesperson serves exactly one sales territory. Each sales territory is served by one or more salespersons.
- Each product is assembled from a specified quantity of one or more raw materials. The identifier for the raw material entity is Material ID. Other attributes include Unit Of Measure, Material Name, and Material Standard Cost. Each raw material is assembled into one or more products, using a specified quantity of the raw material for each product.
- Raw materials are supplied by vendors. The identifier for a vendor is Vendor ID. Other attributes include Vendor Name and Vendor Address. Each raw material can be supplied by one or more vendors. A vendor may supply any number of raw materials or may not supply any raw materials to Pine Valley Furniture. Supply Unit Price is the unit price a particular vendor supplies a particular raw material.
- Pine Valley Furniture has established a number of work centers. The identifier for a work center is Work Center ID. Another attribute is Work Center Location. Each product is produced in one or more work centers. A work center may be used to produce any number of products or may not be used to produce any products.
- The company has more than 100 employees. The identifier for employee is Employee ID. Other attributes include Employee Name, Employee Address, and Skill. An employee may have more than one skill. Each employee may work in one or more work centers. A work center must have at least one employee working in that center, but may have any number of employees. A skill may be possessed by more than one employee or possibly no employees.
- Each employee has exactly one supervisor; however, a manager has no supervisor. An employee who is a supervisor may supervise any number of employees, but not all employees are supervisors.

DATABASE PROCESSING AT PINE VALLEY FURNITURE

PINE VALLEY FURNITURE

The purpose of the data model diagram in Figure 2-22 is to provide a conceptual design for the Pine Valley Furniture Company database. It is important to check the quality of such a design through frequent interaction with the persons who will use the database after it is implemented. An important and often performed type of quality check is to determine whether the E-R model can easily satisfy user requests for data and/or information. Employees at Pine Valley Furniture have many data retrieval and reporting requirements. In this section, we show how a few of these information requirements can be satisfied by database processing against the database shown in Figure 2-22.

We use the SQL database processing language (explained in Chapters 6 and 7) to state these queries. To fully understand these queries, you will need to understand concepts introduced in Chapter 4. However, a few simple queries in this chapter should help you to understand the capabilities of a database to answer important organizational questions and give you a jump-start toward understanding SQL queries in Chapter 6 as well as in later chapters.

Showing Product Information

Many different users have a need to see data about the products Pine Valley Furniture produces (e.g., salespersons, inventory managers, and product managers). One specific need is for a salesperson who wants to respond to a request from a customer for a list of products of a certain type. An example of this query is

List all details for the various computer desks that are stocked by the company.

The data for this query are maintained in the PRODUCT entity (see Figure 2-22). The query scans this entity and displays all the attributes for products that contain the description Computer Desk.

The SQL code for this query is

```
SELECT *
FROM Product
WHERE ProductDescription LIKE "Computer Desk%";
```

Typical output for this query is

PRODUCTID	PRODUCTDESCRIPTION	PRODUCTFINISH	PRODUCTSTANDARDPRICE
3	Computer Desk 48"	Oak	375.00
8	Computer Desk 64"	Pine	450.00

SELECT * FROM Product says display all attributes of PRODUCT entities. The WHERE clause says to limit the display to only products whose description begins with the phrase Computer Desk.

Showing Product Line Information

Another common information need is to show data about Pine Valley Furniture product lines. One specific type of person who needs this information is a product manager. The following is a typical query from a territory sales manager:

List the details of products in product line 4.

The data for this query are maintained in the PRODUCT entity. As we explain in Chapter 4, the attribute Product Line ID will be added to the PRODUCT entity when a data model in Figure 2-22 is translated into a database that can be accessed via SQL. The query scans the PRODUCT entity and displays all attributes for products that are in the selected product line.

The SQL code for this query is

```
SELECT *
FROM Product
WHERE ProductLineID = 4;
```

Typical output for this query is

PRODUCTID	PRODUCTDESCRIPTION	PRODUCTFINISH	PRODUCTSTANDARDPRICE	PRODUCTONHAND	PRODUCTLINEID
18	Grandfather Clock	Oak	890.0000	0	4
19	Grandfather Clock	Oak	1100.0000	0	4

The explanation of this SQL query is similar to the explanation of the previous one.

Showing Customer Order Status

The previous two queries are relatively simple, involving data from only one table in each case. Often, data from multiple tables are needed in one information request. Although the previous query is simple, we did have to look through the whole database to find the entity and attributes needed to satisfy the request.

To simplify query writing and for other reasons, many database management systems support creating restricted views of a database suitable for the information needs

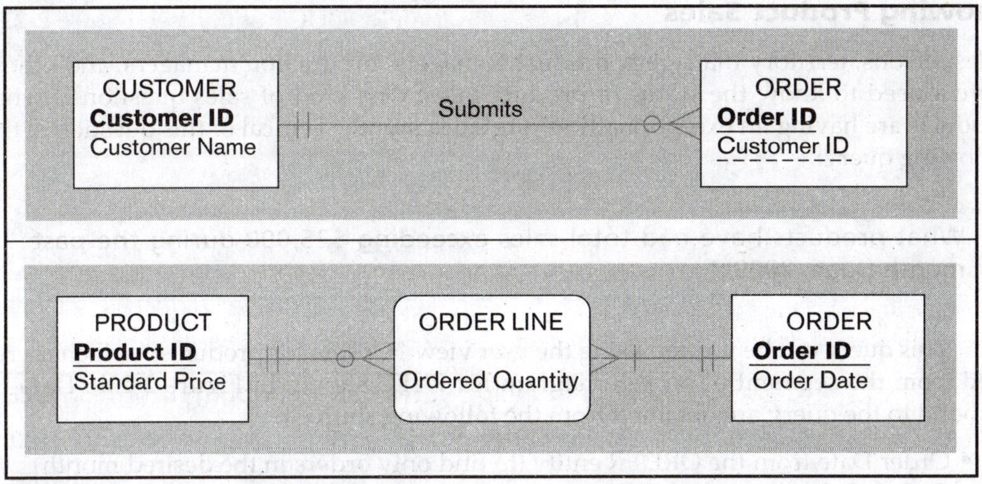

FIGURE 2-23 Two user views for Pine Valley Furniture
(a) User View 1: Orders for customers
(b) User View 2: Orders for products

of a particular user. For queries related to customer order status, Pine Valley utilizes such a user view called "Orders for customers," which is created from the segment of an E-R diagram for PVFC shown in Figure 2-23a. This user view allows users to see only CUSTOMER and ORDER entities in the database, and only the attributes of these entities shown in the figure. For the user, there is only one (virtual) table, ORDERS FOR CUSTOMERS, with the listed attributes. As we explain in Chapter 4, the attribute Customer ID will be added to the ORDER entity (as shown in Figure 2-23a). A typical order status query is

How many orders have we received from Value Furniture?

Assuming that all the data we need are pulled together into this one user view, or virtual entity, called OrdersForCustomers, we can simply write the query as follows:

```
SELECT COUNT(Order ID)
FROM OrdersForCustomers
WHERE CustomerName = "Value Furniture";
```

Without the user view, we can write the SQL code for this query in several ways. The way we have chosen is to compose a query within a query, called a *subquery*. (We will explain subqueries in Chapter 7, with some diagramming techniques to assist you in composting the query.) The query is performed in two steps. First, the subquery (or inner query) scans the CUSTOMER entity to determine the Customer ID for the customer named Value Furniture. (The ID for this customer is 5, as shown in the output for the previous query.) Then the query (or outer query) scans the ORDER entity and counts the order instances for this customer.

The SQL code for this query without the "Orders for customer" user view is as follows:

```
SELECT COUNT (OrderID)
FROM Order
WHERE CustomerID =
    (SELECT CustomerID
    FROM Customer
    WHERE CustomerName = "Value Furniture");
```

For this example query, using a subquery rather than a view did not make writing the query much more complex.

Typical output for this query using either of the query approaches above is

```
COUNT(ORDERID)
      4
```

Showing Product Sales

Salespersons, territory managers, product managers, production managers, and others have a need to know the status of product sales. One kind of sales question is what products are having an exceptionally strong sales month. Typical of this question is the following query:

> What products have had total sales exceeding $25,000 during the past month (June, 2009)?

This query can be written using the user view "Orders for products," which is created from the segment of an E-R diagram for PVFC shown in Figure 2-23b. Data to respond to the query are obtained from the following sources:

- Order Date from the ORDER entity (to find only orders in the desired month)
- Ordered Quantity for each product on each order from the associative entity ORDER LINE for an ORDER entity in the desired month
- Standard Price for the product ordered from the PRODUCT entity associated with the ORDER LINE entity

For each item ordered during the month of June 2009, the query needs to multiply Ordered Quantity by Product Standard Price to get the dollar value of a sale. For the user, there is only one (virtual) table, ORDERS FOR PRODUCTS, with the listed attributes. The total amount is then obtained for that item by summing all orders. Data are displayed only if the total exceeds $25,000.

The SQL code for this query is beyond the scope of this chapter, because it requires techniques introduced in Chapter 7. We introduce this query now only to suggest the power that a database such as the one shown in Figure 2-22 has to find information for management from detailed data. In many organizations today, users can use a Web browser to obtain the information described here. The programming code associated with a Web page then invokes the required SQL commands to obtain the requested information.

Summary

This chapter has described the fundamentals of modeling data in the organization. Business rules, derived from policies, procedures, events, functions, and other business objects, state constraints that govern the organization and, hence, how data are handled and stored. Using business rules is a powerful way to describe the requirements for an information system, especially a database. The power of business rules results from business rules being core concepts of the business, being able to be expressed in terms familiar to end users, being highly maintainable, and being able to be enforced through automated means, mainly through a database. Good business rules are ones that are declarative, precise, atomic, consistent, expressible, distinct, and business oriented.

Examples of basic business rules are data names and definitions. This chapter explained guidelines for the clear naming and definition of data objects in a business. In terms of conceptual data modeling, names and definitions must be provided for entity types, attributes, and relationships. Other business rules may state constraints on these data objects. These constraints can be captured in a data model and associated documentation.

The data modeling notation most frequently used today is the entity-relationship data model. An E-R model is a detailed, logical representation of the data for an organization. An E-R model is usually expressed in the form of an E-R diagram, which is a graphical representation of an E-R model. The E-R model was introduced by Chen in 1976. However, at the present time there is no standard notation for E-R modeling. Notations such as those found in Microsoft Visio are used in many CASE tools.

The basic constructs of an E-R model are entity types, relationships, and related attributes. An entity is a person, a place, an object, an event, or a concept in the user environment about which the organization wishes to maintain data. An entity type is a collection of entities that share common properties, whereas an entity instance is a single occurrence of an entity type. A strong entity type is an entity that has its own identifier and can exist without other entities. A weak entity type is an entity whose existence depends on the existence of a strong entity type. Weak entities do not have their own identifier, although they normally have a partial identifier. Weak entities are identified through an identifying relationship with their owner entity type.

An attribute is a property or characteristic of an entity or relationship that is of interest to the organization. There are several types of attributes. A required attribute must have a value for an entity instance, whereas an optional attribute value may be null. A simple attribute is one that has no component parts. A composite attribute is an attribute that can be broken down into component parts. For example, Person Name can be broken down into the parts First Name, Middle Initial, and Last Name.

A multivalued attribute is one that can have multiple values for a single instance of an entity. For example, the attribute College Degree might have multiple values for an individual. A derived attribute is one whose values can be calculated from other attribute values. For example, Average Salary can be calculated from values of Salary for all employees.

An identifier is an attribute that uniquely identifies individual instances of an entity type. Identifiers should be chosen carefully to ensure stability and ease of use. Identifiers may be simple attributes, or they may be composite attributes with component parts.

A relationship type is a meaningful association between (or among) entity types. A relationship instance is an association between (or among) entity instances. The degree of a relationship is the number of entity types that participate in the relationship. The most common relationship types are unary (degree 1), binary (degree 2), and ternary (degree 3).

In developing E-R diagrams, we sometimes encounter many-to-many (and one-to-one) relationships that have one or more attributes associated with the relationship, rather than with one of the participating entity types. In such cases, we might consider converting the relationship to an associative entity. This type of entity associates the instances of one or more entity types and contains attributes that are peculiar to the relationship. Associative entity types may have their own simple identifier, or they may be assigned a composite identifier during logical design.

A cardinality constraint is a constraint that specifies the number of instances of entity B that may (or must) be associated with each instance of entity A. Cardinality constraints normally specify the minimum and maximum number of instances. The possible constraints are mandatory one, mandatory many, optional one, optional many, and a specific number. The minimum cardinality constraint is also referred to as the participation constraint. A minimum cardinality of zero specifies optional participation, whereas a minimum cardinality of one specifies mandatory participation.

Because many databases need to store the value of data over time, modeling time-dependent data is an important part of data modeling. Data that repeat over time may be modeled as multivalued attributes or as separate entity instances; in each case, a time stamp is necessary to identify the relevant date and time for the data value. Sometimes separate relationships need to be included in the data model to represent associations at different points in time. The recent wave of financial reporting disclosure regulations have made it more important to include time-sensitive and historical data in databases.

Chapter Review

Key Terms

Associative entity *80*
Attribute *72*
Binary relationship *82*
Business rule *63*
Cardinality constraint *86*
Composite attribute *73*
Composite identifier *75*
Degree *81*
Derived attribute *74*
Entity *68*
Entity instance *68*
Entity-relationship diagram (E-R diagram) *59*
Entity-relationship model (E-R model) *59*
Entity type *68*
Fact *66*
Identifier *74*
Identifying owner *70*
Identifying relationship *70*
Maximum cardinality *87*
Minimum cardinality *87*
Multivalued attribute *74*
Optional attribute *72*
Relationship instance *78*
Relationship type *78*
Required attribute *72*
Simple (or atomic) attribute *73*
Strong entity type *69*
Term *66*
Ternary relationship *83*
Time stamp *89*
Unary relationship *81*
Weak entity type *70*

Review Questions

1. Define each of the following terms:
   a. entity type
   b. entity-relationship model
   c. entity instance
   d. attribute
   e. relationship type
   f. identifier
   g. multivalued attribute
   h. associative entity
   i. cardinality constraint
   j. weak entity
   k. identifying relationship
   l. derived attribute
   m. business rule

2. Match the following terms and definitions.

____composite attribute	a. uniquely identifies entity instances
____associative entity	b. relates instances of a single entity type
____unary relationship	c. specifies maximum and minimum number of instances
____weak entity	d. relationship modeled as an entity type
____attribute	e. association between entity types
____entity	f. collection of similar entities
____relationship type	g. number of participating entity types in relationship
____cardinality constraint	h. property of an entity
____degree	i. can be broken into component parts
____identifier	j. depends on the existence of another entity type
____entity type	k. relationship of degree 3
____ternary	l. many-to-many unary relationship
____bill-of-materials	m. person, place, object, concept, event

3. Contrast the following terms:
   a. stored attribute; derived attribute
   b. simple attribute; composite attribute
   c. entity type; relationship type
   d. strong entity type; weak entity type
   e. degree; cardinality
   f. required attribute; optional attribute
   g. composite attribute; multivalued attribute
   h. ternary relationship; three binary relationships
4. Give three reasons why many system designers believe that data modeling is the most important part of the systems development process.
5. Give four reasons why a business rules approach is advocated as a new paradigm for specifying information systems requirements.
6. Explain where you can find business rules in an organization.
7. State six general guidelines for naming data objects in a data model.
8. State four criteria for selecting identifiers for entities.
9. Why must some identifiers be composite rather than simple?
10. State three conditions that suggest the designer should model a relationship as an associative entity type.
11. List the four types of cardinality constraints, and draw an example of each.
12. Give an example, other than those described in this chapter, of a weak entity type. Why is it necessary to indicate an identifying relationship?
13. What is the degree of a relationship? List the three types of relationship degrees described in the chapter and give an example of each.
14. Give an example (other than those described in this chapter) for each of the following, and justify your answer:
    a. derived attribute
    b. multivalued attribute
    c. atomic attribute
    d. composite attribute
    e. required attribute
    f. optional attribute
15. Give an example of each of the following, other than those described in this chapter, and clearly explain why your example is this type of relationship and not of some other degree.
    a. ternary relationship
    b. unary relationship
16. Give an example of the use of effective (or effectivity) dates as attributes of an entity.
17. State a rule that says when to extract an attribute from one entity type and place it in a linked entity type.
18. What are the special guidelines for naming relationships?
19. In addition to explaining what action is being taken, what else should a relationship definition explain?
20. For the Manages relationship in Figure 2-12a, describe one or more situations that would result in different cardinalities on the two ends of this unary relationship. Based on your description for this example, do you think it is always clear simply from an E-R diagram what the business rule is that results in certain cardinalities? Justify your answer.
21. Explain the distinction between entity type and entity instance.
22. Why is it recommended that all ternary relationships be converted into an associative entity?
23. Why does it become important to have a time series of data in context of business today? Illustrate the same with an example.
24. Explain with an example how would you identify and differentiate between an entity and an attribute.
25. Compare and contrast with examples – ternary and binary relationships.

Problems and Exercises

1. Answer the following questions concerning Figure 2-22:
   a. Where is a unary relationship, what does it mean, and for what reasons might the cardinalities on it be different in other organizations?
   b. Why is Includes a one-to many relationship, and why might this ever be different in some other organization?
   c. Does Includes allow for a product to be represented in the database before it is assigned to a product line (e.g., while the product is in research and development)?
   d. If there is a rating of the competency for each skill an employee possesses, where in the data model would we place this rating?
   e. What is the meaning of the DOES BUSINESS IN associative entity, and why does each DOES BUSINESS IN instance have to be associated with exactly one TERRITORY and one CUSTOMER?
   f. In what way might Pine Valley change the way it does business that would cause the Supplies associative entity to be eliminated and the relationships around it to change?
2. There is a bulleted list associated with Figure 2-22 that describes the entities and their relationships in Pine Valley Furniture. For each of the 10 points in the list, identify the subset of Figure 2-22 described by that point.
3. You may have been assigned a CASE or a drawing tool to develop conceptual data models. Using this tool, attempt to redraw all the E-R diagrams in this chapter. What difficulties did you encounter? What E-R notations did not translate well to your tool? How did you incorporate the E-R notation that did not directly translate into the tool's notation?
4. Consider the two E-R diagrams in Figure 2-24, which represent a database of community service agencies and volunteers in two different cities (A and B). For each of the following three questions, place a check mark under City A, City B, or Can't Tell for the choice that is the best answer.

FIGURE 2-24 Diagram for Problem and Exercise 4

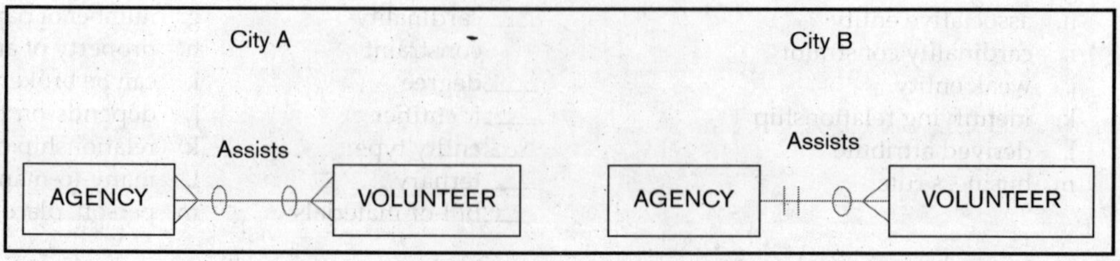

	City A	City B	Can't Tell
a. Which city maintains data about only those volunteers who currently assist agencies?			
b. In which city would it be possible for a volunteer to assist more than one agency?			
c. In which city would it be possible for a volunteer to change which agency or agencies he or she assists?			

5. The entity type STUDENT has the following attributes: Student Name, Address, Phone, Age, Activity, and No of Years. Activity represents some campus-based student activity, and No of Years represents the number of years the student has engaged in this activity. A given student may engage in more than one activity. Draw an ERD for this situation. What attribute or attributes did you designate as the identifier for the STUDENT entity? Why?

6. Are associative entities also weak entities? Why or why not? If yes, is there anything special about their "weakness"?

7. Because Visio does not explicitly show associative entities, it is not clear in Figure 2-22 which entity types are associative. List the associative entities in this figure. Why are there so many associative entities in Figure 2-22?

8. Figure 2-25 shows a grade report that is mailed to students at the end of each semester. Prepare an ERD reflecting the data contained in the grade report. Assume that each course is taught by one instructor. Also, draw this data model using the tool you have been told to use in the course. Explain what you chose for the identifier of each entity type on your ERD.

9. Add minimum and maximum cardinality notation to each of the following figures, as appropriate:
a. Figure 2-5
b. Figure 2-10a
c. Figure 2-11b
d. Figure 2-12 (all parts)
e. Figure 2-13c
f. Figure 2-14

10. The Is Married To relationship in Figure 2-12a would seem to have an obvious answer in Problem and Exercise 9d—that is, until time plays a role in modeling data. Draw a data model for the PERSON entity type and the Is Married To relationship for each of the following variations by showing the appropriate cardinalities and including, if necessary, any attributes:
a. All we need to know is who a person is currently married to, if anyone. (This is likely what you represented in your answer to Problem and Exercise 9d.)
b. We need to know who a person has ever been married to, if anyone.
c. We need to know who a person has ever been married to, if anyone, as well as the date of their marriage and the date, if any, of the dissolution of their marriage.
d. The same situation as in c, but now assume (which you likely did not do in c) that the same two people can remarry each other after a dissolution of a prior marriage to each other.
e. In history, and even in some cultures today, there may be no legal restriction on the number of people to whom one can be currently married. Does your answer to part c of this Problem and Exercise handle this situation or must you make some changes (if so, draw a new ERD).

11. Figure 2-26 represents a situation of students who attend and work in schools and who also belong to certain clubs that are located in different schools. Study this diagram carefully to try to discern what business rules are represented.
a. You will notice that cardinalities are not included on the Works For relationship. State a business rule for this relationship and then represent this rule with the cardinalities that match your rule.
b. State a business rule that would make the Located In relationship redundant (i.e., where the school in which a club is located can be surmised or derived in some way from other relationships).
c. Suppose a student could work for only a school that student attends but might not work. Would the Works For relationship still be necessary, or could you represent whether a student works for the school she attends in some other way (if so, how)?

12. Figure 2-27 shows two diagrams (A and B), both of which are legitimate ways to represent that a stock has a history of

MILLENNIUM COLLEGE
GRADE REPORT
FALL SEMESTER 200X

NAME: Emily Williams ID: 268300458
CAMPUS ADDRESS: 208 Brooks Hall
MAJOR: Information Systems

COURSE ID	TITLE	INSTRUCTOR NAME	INSTRUCTOR LOCATION	GRADE
IS 350	Database Mgt.	Codd	B104	A
IS 465	System Analysis	Parsons	B317	B

FIGURE 2-25 Grade report

FIGURE 2-26 E-R diagram for Problem and Exercise 11

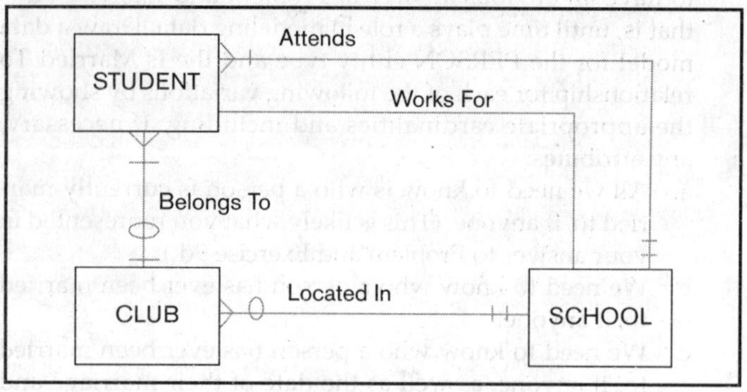

many prices. Which of the two diagrams do you consider a better way to model this situation and why?

13. Modify Figure 2-11a to model the following additional information requirements: The training director decides, for each employee who completes each class, who (what employees) should be notified of the course completion. The training director needs to keep track of which employees are notified about each course completion by a student. The date of notification is the only attribute recorded about this notification.

14. Review Figure 2-8 and Figure 2-22.

a. Identify any attributes in Figure 2-22 that might be composite attributes but are not shown that way. Justify your suggestions. Redraw the ERD to reflect any changes you suggest.

b. Identify any attributes in Figure 2-22 that might be multivalued attributes but are not shown that way. Justify your suggestions. Redraw the ERD to reflect any changes you suggest.

c. Is it possible for the same attribute to be both composite and multivalued? If no, justify your answer; if yes, give an example (Hint: Consider the CUSTOMER attributes in Figure 2-22).

15. Draw an ERD for each of the following situations. (If you believe that you need to make additional assumptions, clearly state them for each situation.) Draw the same situation using the tool you have been told to use in the course.

a. A company has a number of employees. The attributes of EMPLOYEE include Employee ID (identifier), Name, Address, and Birthdate. The company also has several projects. Attributes of PROJECT include Project ID (identifier), Project Name, and Start Date. Each employee may be assigned to one or more projects, or may not be assigned to a project. A project must have at least one employee assigned and may have any number of employees assigned. An employee's billing rate may vary by project, and the company wishes to record the applicable billing rate (Billing Rate) for each employee when assigned to a particular project. Do the attribute names in this description follow the guidelines for naming attributes? If not, suggest better names. Do you have any associative entities on your ERD? If so, what are the identifiers for those associative entities? Does your ERD allow a project to be created before it has any employees assigned to it? Explain. How would you change your ERD if the Billing Rate could change in the middle of a project?

b. A laboratory has several chemists who work on one or more projects. Chemists also may use certain kinds of equipment on each project. Attributes of CHEMIST include Employee ID (identifier), Name, and Phone No. Attributes of PROJECT include Project ID (identifier) and Start Date. Attributes of EQUIPMENT include Serial No and Cost. The organization wishes to record Assign Date—that is, the date when a given equipment item was assigned to a particular chemist working on a specified project. A chemist must be assigned to at least one project and one equipment item. A given equipment item need not be assigned, and a given project need not be assigned either a chemist or an equipment item. Provide good definitions for all of the relationships in this situation.

c. A college course may have one or more scheduled sections, or may not have a scheduled section. Attributes of COURSE include Course ID, Course Name, and Units. Attributes of SECTION include Section Number

FIGURE 2-27 E-R diagram for Problem and Exercise 12

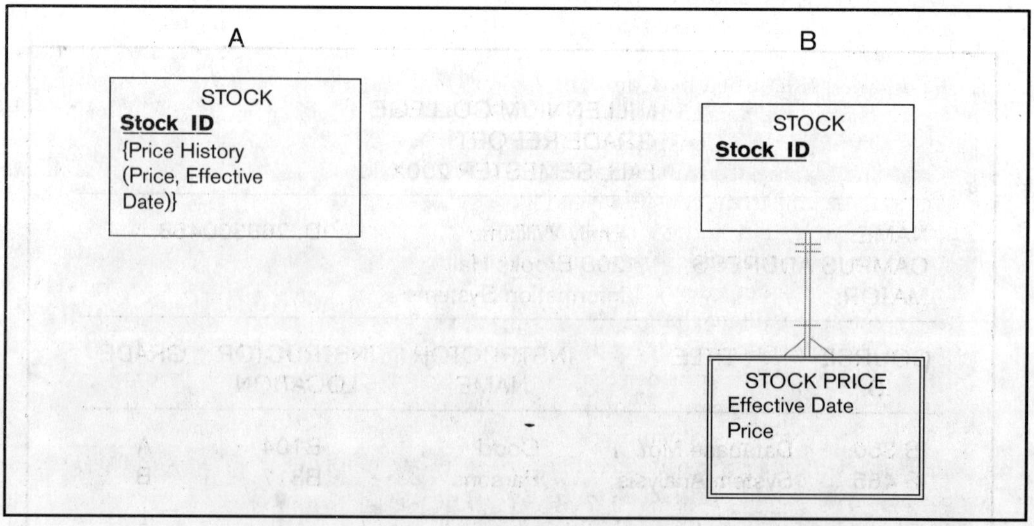

and Semester ID. Semester ID is composed of two parts: Semester and Year. Section Number is an integer (such as 1 or 2) that distinguishes one section from another for the same course but does not uniquely identify a section. How did you model SECTION? Why did you choose this way versus alternative ways to model SECTION?

d. A hospital has a large number of registered physicians. Attributes of PHYSICIAN include Physician ID (the identifier) and Specialty. Patients are admitted to the hospital by physicians. Attributes of PATIENT include Patient ID (the identifier) and Patient Name. Any patient who is admitted must have exactly one admitting physician. A physician may optionally admit any number of patients. Once admitted, a given patient must be treated by at least one physician. A particular physician may treat any number of patients, or may not treat any patients. Whenever a patient is treated by a physician, the hospital wishes to record the details of the treatment (Treatment Detail). Components of Treatment Detail include Date, Time, and Results. Did you draw more than one relationship between physician and patient? Why or why not? Did you include hospital as an entity type? Why or why not? Does your ERD allow for the same patient to be admitted by different physicians over time? How would you include on the ERD the need to represent the date on which a patient is admitted for each time they are admitted?

e. The loan office in a bank receives from various parties requests to investigate the credit status of a customer. Each credit request is identified by a Request ID and is described by a Request Date and Requesting Party Name. The loan office also received results of credit checks. A credit check is identified by a Credit Check ID and is described by the Credit Check Date and the Credit Rating. The loan office matches credit requests with credit check results. A credit request may be recorded before its result arrives; a particular credit result may be used in support of several credit requests. Draw an ERD for this situation. Now, assume that credit results may not be reused for multiple credit requests. Redraw the ERD for this new situation using two entity types, and then redraw it again using one entity type. Which of these two versions do you prefer, and why?

f. Companies, identified by Company ID and described by Company Name and Industry Type, hire consultants, identified by Consultant ID and described by Consultant Name, Consultant Specialty, which is multivalued. Assume that a consultant can work for only one company at a time, and we need to track only current consulting engagements. Draw an ERD for this situation. Now, consider a new attribute, Hourly Rate, which is the rate a consultant charges a company for each hour of his or her services. Redraw the ERD to include this new attribute. Now, consider that each time a consultant works for a company, a contract is written describing the terms for this consulting engagement. Contract is identified by a composite identifier of Company ID, Consultant ID, and Contract Date. Assuming that a consultant can still work for only one company at a time, redraw the ERD for this new situation. Did you move any attributes to different entity types in this latest situation? As a final situation, now consider that although a consultant can work for only one company at a time, we now need to keep the complete history of all consulting engagements for each consultant and company. Draw an ERD for this final situation. Explain why these different changes to the situation led to different data models, if they did.

g. An art museum owns a large volume of works of art. Each work of art is described by an item code (identifier), title, type, and size; size is further composed of height, width, and weight. A work of art is developed by an artist, but the artist for some works is unknown. An artist is described by an artist ID (identifier), name, date of birth, and date of death (which is null for still living artists). Only data about artists for works currently owned by the museum are kept in the database. At any point in time, a work of art is either on display at the museum, held in storage, away from the museum as part of a traveling show, or on loan to another gallery. If on display at the museum, a work of art is also described by its location within the museum. A traveling show is described by a show ID (identifier), the city in which the show is currently appearing, and the start and end dates of the show. Many of the museum works may be part of a given show, and only active shows with at least one museum work of art need be represented in the database. Finally, another gallery is described by a gallery ID (identifier), name, and city. The museum wants to retain a complete history of loaning a work of art to other galleries, and each time a work is loaned, the museum wants to know the date the work was loaned and the date it was returned. As you develop the ERD for this problem, follow good data naming guidelines.

h. Each case handled by the law firm of Dewey, Cheetim, and Howe has a unique case number; a date opened, date closed, and judgment description are also kept on each case. A case is brought by one or more plaintiffs, and the same plaintiff may be involved in many cases. A plaintiff has a requested judgment characteristic. A case is against one or more defendants, and the same defendant may be involved in many cases. A plaintiff or defendant may be a person or an organization. Over time, the same person or organization may be a defendant or a plaintiff in cases. In either situation, such legal entities are identified by an entity number, and other attributes are name and net worth. As you develop the ERD for this problem, follow good data naming guidelines.

i. Each publisher has a unique name; a mailing address and telephone number are also kept on each publisher. A publisher publishes one or more books; a book is published by exactly one publisher. A book is identified by its ISBN, and other attributes are title, price, and number of pages. Each book is written by one or more authors; an author writes one or more books, potentially for different publishers. Each author is uniquely described by an author ID, and we know each author's name and address. Each author is paid a certain royalty rate on each book he or she authors, which potentially varies for each book and for each author. An author receives a separate royalty check for each book he or she writes. Each check is identified by its check number, and we also keep track of the date and amount of each check. As you develop the ERD for this problem, follow good data naming guidelines.

16. Assume that at Pine Valley Furniture each product (described by product number, description, and cost) comprises at least three components (described by component number, description, and unit of measure), and components are used to make one or many products. In addition, assume that components are used to make other components and that raw materials are also considered to be components. In both cases of components, we need to keep track of how many components go into making something else. Draw an ERD for this situation, and place minimum and maximum cardinalities on the diagram. Also, draw a data model for this situation using the tool you have been told to use in your course.

17. Emerging Electric wishes to create a database with the following entities and attributes:
    - Customer, with attributes Customer ID, Name, Address (Street, City, State, Zip Code), and Telephone
    - Location, with attributes Location ID, Address (Street, City, State, Zip Code), and Type (values of Business or Residential)
    - Rate, with attributes Rate Class and RatePerKWH

    After interviews with the owners, you have come up with the following business rules:
    - Customers can have one or more locations.
    - Each location can have one or more rates, depending on the time of day.

    Draw an ERD for this situation and place minimum and maximum cardinalities on the diagram. Also, draw a data model for this situation using the tool you have been told to use in your course. State any assumptions that you have made.

18. Each semester, each student must be assigned an adviser who counsels students about degree requirements and helps students register for classes. Each student must register for classes with the help of an adviser, but if the student's assigned adviser is not available, the student may register with any adviser. We must keep track of students, the assigned adviser for each, and the name of the adviser with whom the student registered for the current term. Represent this situation of students and advisers with an E-R diagram. Also, draw a data model for this situation using the tool you have been told to use in your course.

19. In the chapter, when describing Figure 2-4a, it was argued that the Received and Summarizes relationships and TREASURER entity were not necessary. Within the context of this explanation, this is true. Now, consider a slightly different situation. Suppose it is necessary, for compliance purposes (e.g., Sarbanes-Oxley compliance), to know when each expense report was produced and which officers (not just the treasurer) received each expense report and when they each signed off on that report. Redraw Figure 2-4a, now including any attributes and relationships required for this revised situation.

20. Prepare an ERD for a real estate firm that lists property for sale. Also prepare a definition for each entity type, attribute, and relationship on your diagram. In addition, draw a data model for this situation using the tool you have been told to use in your course. The following describes this organization:
    - The firm has a number of sales offices in several states. Attributes of sales office include Office Number (identifier) and Location.
    - Each sales office is assigned one or more employees. Attributes of employee include Employee ID (identifier) and Employee Name. An employee must be assigned to only one sales office.
    - For each sales office, there is always one employee assigned to manage that office. An employee may manage only the sales office to which he or she is assigned.
    - The firm lists property for sale. Attributes of property include Property ID (identifier) and Location. Components of Location include Address, City, State, and Zip Code.
    - Each unit of property must be listed with one (and only one) of the sales offices. A sales office may have any number of properties listed or may have no properties listed.
    - Each unit of property has one or more owners. Attributes of owners are Owner ID (identifier) and Owner Name. An owner may own one or more units of property. An attribute of the relationship between property and owner is Percent Owned.

21. After completing a course in database management, you are asked to develop a preliminary ERD for a symphony orchestra. You discover the following entity types that should be included:

CONCERT SEASON	The season during which a series of concerts will be performed. Identifier is Opening Date, which includes Month, Day, and Year.
CONCERT	A given performance of one or more compositions. Identifier is Concert Number. Another important attribute is Concert Date, which consists of the following: Month, Day, Year, and Time. Each concert typically has more than one concert date.
COMPOSITION	Compositions to be performed at each concert. Identifier is Composition ID, which consists of the following: Composer Name and Composition Name. Another attribute is Movement ID, which consists of two parts: Movement Number and Movement Name. Many, but not all, compositions have multiple movements.
CONDUCTOR	Person who will conduct the concert. Identifier is Conductor ID. Another attribute is Conductor Name.
SOLOIST	Solo artist who performs a given composition on a particular concert. Identifier is Soloist ID. Another attribute is Soloist Name.

During further discussions you discover the following:

- A concert season schedules one or more concerts. A particular concert is scheduled for only one concert season.
- A concert includes the performance of one or more compositions. A composition may be performed at one or more concerts or may not be performed.
- For each concert there is one conductor. A conductor may conduct any number of concerts or may not conduct any concerts.
- Each composition may require one or more soloists or may not require a soloist. A soloist may perform one or more compositions at a given concert or may not perform any composition. The symphony orchestra wishes to record the date when a soloist last performed a given composition (Date Last Performed).

Draw an ERD to represent what you have discovered. Identify a business rule in this description and explain how this business rule is modeled on the E-R diagram. Also draw a data model for this situation using the tool you have been told to use in your course.

22. Obtain several common user views such as a credit card receipt, credit card statement, and annual summary, or some other common document from one organization with which you interact.
    a. Prepare an ERD for one of these documents. Also prepare a data model for this document, using the tool you have been told to use in your course.
    b. Prepare an ERD for another of these documents. Also prepare a data model for this document, using the tool you have been told to use in your course.
    c. Do you find the same entities, attributes, and relationships in the two ERDs you developed for parts a and b? What differences do you find in modeling the same data entities, attributes, and relationships between the two ERDs? Can you combine the two ERDs into one ERD for which the original two are subsets? Do you encounter any issues in trying to combine the ERDs? Suggest some issues that might arise if two different data modelers had independently developed the two data models.
    d. How might you use data naming and definition standards to overcome the issues you identified in part c?

23. Draw an ERD for the following situation (Batra et al., 1988). Also, develop the list of words for qualifiers and classes that you use to form attribute names. Explain why you chose the words on your list. Also, draw a data model for this situation using the tool you have been told to use in your course.

    Projects, Inc., is an engineering firm with approximately 500 employees. A database is required to keep track of all employees, their skills, projects assigned, and departments worked in. Every employee has a unique number assigned by the firm and is required to store his or her name and date of birth. If an employee is currently married to another employee of Projects, Inc., the date of marriage and who is married to whom must be stored; however, no record of marriage is required if an employee's spouse is not also an employee. Each employee is given a job title (e.g., engineer, secretary, and so on). An employee does only one type of job at any given time, and we only need to retain information for an employee's current job.

    There are 11 different departments, each with a unique name. An employee can report to only 1 department. Each department has a phone number.

    To procure various kinds of equipment, each department deals with many vendors. A vendor typically supplies equipment to many departments. We are required to store the name and address of each vendor and the date of the last meeting between a department and a vendor.

    Many employees can work on a project. An employee can work on many projects (e.g., Southwest Refinery, California Petrochemicals, and so on) but can only be assigned to at most one project in a given city. For each city, we are interested in its state and population. An employee can have many skills (preparing material requisitions, checking drawings, and so on), but she or he may use only a given set of skills on a particular project. (For example, an employee MURPHY may prepare requisitions for the Southwest Refinery project and prepare requisitions as well as check drawings for California Petrochemicals.) Employees use each skill that they possess in at least one project. Each skill is assigned a number, and we must store a short description of each skill. Projects are distinguished by project numbers, and we must store the estimated cost of each project.

24. Draw an ERD for the following situation. (State any assumptions you believe you have to make in order to develop a complete diagram.) Also, draw a data model for this situation using the tool you have been told to use in your course: Stillwater Antiques buys and sells one-of-a-kind antiques of all kinds (e.g., furniture, jewelry, china, and clothing). Each item is uniquely identified by an item number and is also characterized by a description, asking price, condition, and open-ended comments. Stillwater works with many different individuals, called clients, who sell items to and buy items from the store. Some clients only sell items to Stillwater, some only buy items, and some others both sell and buy. A client is identified by a client number and is also described by a client name and client address. When Stillwater sells an item in stock to a client, the owners want to record the commission paid, the actual selling price, sales tax (tax of zero indicates a tax exempt sale), and date sold. When Stillwater buys an item from a client, the owners want to record the purchase cost, date purchased, and condition at time of purchase.

25. Draw an ERD for the following situation. (State any assumptions you believe you have to make in order to develop a complete diagram.) Also, draw a data model for this situation using the tool you have been told to use in your course: The H. I. Topi School of Business operates international business programs in 10 locations throughout Europe. The school had its first class of 9,000 graduates in 1965. The school keeps track of each graduate's student number, name when a student, country of birth, current country of citizenship, current name, and current address, as well as the name of each major the student completed. (Each student has one or two majors.) To maintain strong ties to its alumni, the school holds various events around the world. Events have a title, date, location, and type (e.g., reception, dinner, or seminar). The school needs to keep track of which graduates have attended which events. For an attendance by a graduate at an event, a comment is recorded about information school officials learned from that graduate at that event. The school also keeps in

contact with graduates by mail, e-mail, telephone, and fax interactions. As with events, the school records information learned from the graduate from each of these contacts. When a school official knows that he or she will be meeting or talking to a graduate, a report is produced showing the latest information about that graduate and the information learned during the past two years from that graduate from all contacts and events the graduate attended.

26. Wally Los Gatos, owner of Wally's Wonderful World of Wallcoverings, has hired you as a consultant to design a database management system for his chain of three stores that sell wallpaper and accessories. He would like to track sales, customers, and employees. After an initial meeting with Wally, you have developed a list of business rules and specifications to begin the design of an E-R model:

- Customers place orders through a branch.
- Wally would like to track the following about customers: Name, Address, City, State, Zip Code, Telephone, Date of Birth, and Primary Language.
- A customer may place many orders.
- A customer does not always have to order through the same branch all the time.
- Customers may have one or more accounts, although they may also have no accounts.
- The following information needs to be recorded about accounts: Balance, Last payment date, Last payment amount, and Type.
- A branch may have many customers.
- The following information about each branch needs to be recorded: Branch Number, Location (Address, City, State, Zip Code), and Square Footage.
- A branch may sell all items or may only sell certain items.
- Orders are composed of one or more items.
- The following information about each order needs to be recorded: Order Date and Credit Authorization Status.
- Items may be sold by one or more branches.
- We wish to record the following about each item: Description, Color, Size, Pattern, and Type.
- An item can be composed of multiple items; for example, a dining room wallcovering set (item 20) may consist of wallpaper (item 22) and borders (item 23).
- Wally employs 56 employees.
- He would like to track the following information about employees: Name, Address (Street, City, State, Zip Code), Telephone, Date of Hire, Title, Salary, Skill, and Age.
- Each employee works in one and only one branch.
- Each employee may have one or more dependents. We wish to record the name of the dependent as well as the age and relationship.
- Employees can have one or more skills.

Based upon this information, draw an E-R model. Please indicate any assumptions that you have made. Also, draw a data model for this situation using the tool you have been told to use in your course.

27. Our friend Wally Los Gatos (see Problem and Exercise 26), realizing that his wallcovering business had a few wrinkles in it, decided to pursue a law degree at night. After graduating, he has teamed up with Lyla El Pàjaro to form Peck and Paw, Attorneys at Law. Wally and Lyla have hired you to design a database system based upon the following set of business rules. It is in your best interest to perform a thorough analysis, to avoid needless litigation. Please create an ERD based upon the following set of rules:

- An ATTORNEY is retained by one or more CLIENTS for each CASE.
- Attributes of ATTORNEY are Attorney ID, Name, Address, City, State, Zip Code, Specialty (may be more than one), and Bar (may be more than one).
- A CLIENT may have more than one ATTORNEY for each CASE.
- Attributes of CLIENT are Client ID, Name, Address, City, State, Zip Code, Telephone, and Date of Birth.
- A CLIENT may have more than one CASE.
- Attributes of CASE are Case ID, Case Description, and Case Type.
- An ATTORNEY may have more than one CASE.
- Each CASE is assigned to one and only one COURT.
- Attributes of COURT are Court ID, Court Name, City, State, and Zip Code.
- Each COURT has one or more JUDGES assigned to it.
- Attributes of JUDGE are Judge ID, Name, and Years In Practice.
- Each JUDGE is assigned to exactly one court.

Please state any assumptions that you have made. Also, draw a data model for this situation using the tool you have been told to use in your course.

28. Review your answer to Problem and Exercise 25; if necessary, change the names of the entities, attributes, and relationships to conform to the naming guidelines presented in this chapter. Then, using the definition guidelines, write a definition for each entity, attribute, and relationship. If necessary, state assumptions so that each definition is as complete as possible.

29.

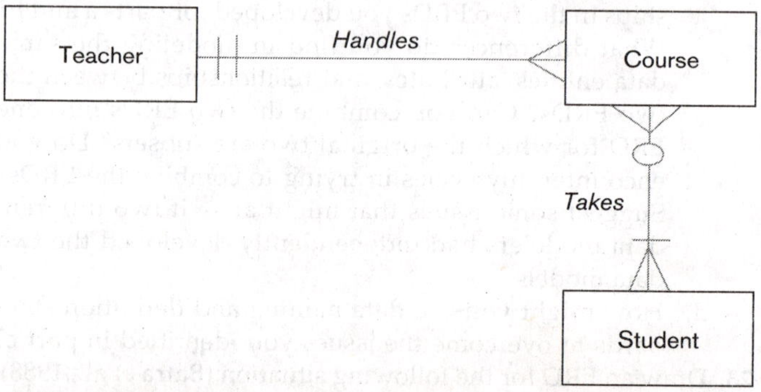

Identify (as bullet points) the business rules applicable to the entities involved in the relationships given above.

30. Mysore One is a single point entry/access application to various local governing revenue payments. Mysore One operates as a kiosk in Mysore city at numerous locations to facilitate the citizens of Mysore to make a one stop payment of the electricity bill, property tax, road tax, water bill, etc. Discuss how you would draw up an enterprise data model for such a scenario.

31. A business school offering post-graduate diploma in management admits students to the PGDM program. You are required to design a DBMS for the admission office. You have developed a list of business rules.

- Students apply to the college by getting the application form from the local branches of a nationalized bank
- Students who have taken the Common Admission Test only are eligible
- Applicant's Details: Application No., Applicant's Name, Applicant's Address, Applicant's DOB, Applicant's Qualification, and CAT No. and CAT Score are stored by the Admission Office.

- An applicant, if eligible, may get admission to any of the campuses of the B-School.
- Eligibility of the student is based on a number of parameters:
  o Applicant's GPA in graduation degree
  o Applicant's performance in high school
  o Applicant's score in CAT
  o Applicants meeting the criteria for the above components are called for a personal interview and group discussion.
- The applicants finally admitted to the college will be evaluated on the following parameters with revised weightages:
  o Applicant's GPA in graduation
  o Applicant's performance in 10th Standard
  o Applicant's score in CAT
  o Applicant's performance in group discussion
  o Applicant's performance in personal interview
  o Each applicant will get admitted into only one of the campuses
- A final list of admitted students along with their photographs will be sent to the PGP Office for further process.

Draw an E-R model for the above business rules and constraints.

32.

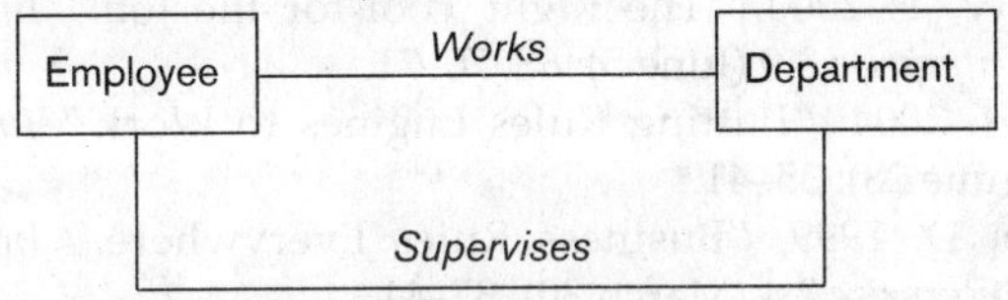

For the above ERD, fill in the minimum and maximum cardinality as appropriate.

Field Exercises

1. Interview a database analyst or systems analyst and document how he or she decides on names for data objects in data models. Does the organization in which this person works have naming guidelines? If so, describe the pattern used. If there are no guidelines, ask whether your contact has ever had any problems because guidelines did not exist. Does the organization use any tool to help management metadata, including data names?
2. Visit two local small businesses, one in the service sector (e.g., dry cleaner, auto repair shop, veterinarian, or bookstore) and one that manufactures tangible goods. Interview employees from these organizations to elicit from them the entities, attributes, and relationships that are commonly encountered in these organizations. Use this information to construct E-R diagrams. What differences and similarities are there between the diagrams for the service- and the product-oriented companies? Does the E-R diagramming technique handle both situations equally well? Why or why not?
3. Ask a database or systems analyst to give you examples of unary, binary, and ternary relationships that the analyst has dealt with personally at his or her company. Ask which is most common and why.
4. Ask a database or systems analyst in a local company to show you an E-R diagram for one of the organization's primary databases. Ask questions to be sure you understand what each entity, attribute, and relationship means. Does this organization use the same E-R notation used in this text? If not, what other or alternative symbols are used and what do these symbols mean? Does this organization model associative entities on the E-R diagram? If not, how are associative entities modeled? What metadata are kept about the objects on the E-R diagram?
5. For the same E-R diagram used in Field Exercise 4 or for a different database in the same or a different organization, identify any uses of time stamping or other means to model time- dependent data. Why are time-dependent data necessary for those who use this database? Would the E-R diagram be much simpler if it were not necessary to represent the history of attribute values?
6. Search on the Internet for products that help document and manage business rules, standards, and procedures. One such site is **www.axisboulder.com**. Choose a couple tools and summarize their capabilities and discuss how they would be useful in managing business rules.

References

Aranow, E. B. 1989. "Developing Good Data Definitions." *Database Programming & Design* 2,8 (August): 36–39.

Batra, D., J. A. Hoffer, and R. B. Bostrom. 1988. "A Comparison of User Performance Between the Relational and Extended Entity Relationship Model in the Discovery Phase of Database Design." *Proceedings of the Ninth International Conference on Information Systems*. Minneapolis, November 30–December 3: 295–306.

Bruce, T. A. 1992. *Designing Quality Databases with IDEF1X Information Models*. New York: Dorset House.

Chen, P. P.-S. 1976. "The Entity-Relationship Model—Toward a Unified View of Data." *ACM Transactions on Database Systems* 1,1(March): 9–36.

Elmasri, R., and S. B. Navathe. 1994. *Fundamentals of Database Systems*. 2d ed. Menlo Park, CA: Benjamin/Cummings.

Gottesdiener, E. 1997. "Business Rules Show Power, Promise." *Application Development Trends* 4,3 (March): 36–54.

Gottesdiener, E. 1999. "Turning Rules into Requirements." *Application Development Trends* 6,7 (July): 37–50.

Hay, D. C. 2003. "What Exactly IS a Data Model?" Parts 1, 2, and 3. *DM Review* Vol 13, Issues 2 (February: 24–26), 3 (March: 48–50), and 4 (April: 20–22, 46).

GUIDE. 1997 (October)."GUIDE Business Rules Project." Final Report, revision 1.2.

Hoffer, J. A., J. F. George, and J. S. Valacich. 2010. *Modern Systems Analysis and Design*. 6th ed. Upper Saddle River, NJ: Prentice Hall.

ISO/IEC. 2004. "Information Technology—Metadata Registries (MDR)—Part 4: Formulation of Data Definitions." July. Switzerland. Available at **http:/metadata-standards.org/11179**.

ISO/IEC. 2005. "Information Technology—Metadata Registries (MDR)—Part 5: Naming and Identification Principles." September. Switzerland. Available at **http:/metadat standards.org/11179**.

Johnson, T. and R. Weis. 2007. "Time and Time Again: Managing Time in Relational Databases, Part 1." May. *DM Review*. Available from Magazine Archives section in the Information Center of **www.information-management.com**. See whole series of articles called "Time and Time Again" in subsequent issues.

Moriarty, T. 2000. "The Right Tool for the Job." *Intelligent Enterprise* 3,9 (June 5): 68, 70–71.

Owen, J. 2004. "Putting Rules Engines to Work." *InfoWorld* (June 28): 35–41.

Plotkin, D. 1999. "Business Rules Everywhere." *Intelligent Enterprise* 2,4 (March 30): 37–44.

Salin, T. 1990. "What's in a Name?" *Database Programming & Design* 3,3 (March): 55–58.

Song, I.-Y., M. Evans, and E. K. Park. 1995. "A Comparative Analysis of Entity-Relationship Diagrams." *Journal of Computer & Software Engineering* 3,4: 427–59.

Storey, V. C. 1991. "Relational Database Design Based on the Entity-Relationship Model." *Data and Knowledge Engineering* 7: 47–83.

Teorey, T. J., D. Yang, and J. P. Fry. 1986. "A Logical Design Methodology for Relational Databases Using the Extended Entity- Relationship Model." *Computing Surveys* 18, 2 (June): 197–221.

von Halle, B. 1997. "Digging for Business Rules." *Database Programming & Design* 8,11: 11–13.

Further Reading

Batini, C., S. Ceri, and S. B. Navathe. 1992. *Conceptual Database Design: An Entity-Relationship Approach*. Menlo Park, CA: Benjamin/Cummings.

Bodart, F., A. Patel, M. Sim, and R. Weber. 2001. "Should Optional Properties Be Used in Conceptual Modelling? A Theory and Three Empirical Tests." *Information Systems Research* 12,4 (December): 384–405.

Carlis, J., and J. Maguire. 2001. *Mastering Data Modeling: A User-Driven Approach*. Upper Saddle River, NJ: Prentice Hall.

Keuffel, W. 1996. "Battle of the Modeling Techniques." *DBMS* 9,8 (August): 83, 84, 86, 97.

Moody, D. 1996. "The Seven Habits of Highly Effective Data Modelers." *Database Programming & Design* 9,10 (October): 57, 58, 60–62, 64.

Teorey, T. 1999. *Database Modeling & Design*. 3d ed. San Francisco, CA: Morgan Kaufman.

Tillman, G. 1994. "Should You Model Derived Data?" *DBMS* 7,11 (November): 88, 90.

Tillman, G. 1995. "Data Modeling Rules of Thumb." *DBMS* 8,8 (August): 70, 72, 74, 76, 80–82, 87.

Web Resources

http://dwr.ais.columbia.edu/info/Data%20Naming%20Standards.html Web site that provides guidelines for naming entities, attributes, and relationships similar to those suggested in this chapter.

www.adtmag.com Web site of *Application Development Trends*, a leading publication on the practice of information systems development.

www.axisboulder.com Web site for one vendor of business rules software.

www.businessrulesgroup.org Web site of the Business Rules Group, formerly part of GUIDE International, which formulates and supports standards about business rules.

http://en.wikipedia.org/wiki/Entity-relationship_model The Wikipedia entry for entity-relationship model, with an explanation of the origins of the crow's foot notation, which is used in this book.

www.intelligententerprise.com•Web site of *Intelligent Enterprise*, a leading publication on database management and related areas. This magazine is the result of combining two previous publications, *Database Programming & Design* and *DBMS*.

http://ss64.com/ora/syntax-naming.html Web site that suggests naming conventions for entities, attributes, and relationships within an Oracle database environment.

www.tdan.com Web site of *The Data Administration Newsletter*, is an online journal that includes articles on a wide variety of data management topics. This Web site is considered a "must follow" Web site for data management professionals.

CASE

Mountain View Community Hospital

Case Description

After completing a course in database management, you have been hired as a summer intern by Mountain View Community Hospital. Your first assignment is to work as part of a team of three people to develop a high-level E-R diagram for the hospital. You conduct interviews with a number of hospital administrators and staff to identify the key entity types for the hospital. You have also seen the preliminary enterprise-level diagram shown in MVCH Figure 1-3 and subsequent revisions. As a result, your team has identified the following entity types:

- Care Center—a treatment center within the hospital. Examples of care centers are maternity, emergency care, or multiple sclerosis center. Each care center has a care center ID (identifier) and a care center name.
- Patient—a person who is either admitted to the hospital or is registered as an outpatient. Each patient has an identifier, the medical record number (MRN), and a name.
- Physician—a member of the hospital medical staff who may admit patients to the hospital and who may administer medical treatments. Each physician has a physician ID (identifier) and name.
- Bed—a hospital bed that may be assigned to a patient who is admitted to the hospital. Each bed has a bed number (identifier), a room number, and a care center ID.
- Item—any medical or surgical item that may be used in treating a patient. Each item has an item number (identifier), description, and unit cost.
- Employee—any person employed as part of the hospital staff. Each employee has an employee number (identifier) and name.
- Diagnosis—a patient's medical condition diagnosed by a physician. Each diagnosis has a diagnosis ID/code and diagnosis name. Mountain View Community Hospital is using the HIPAA-mandated ICD-9-CM Volume 1 diagnosis codes[1] for patient conditions (e.g., 00.50, STAPH FOOD POISONING, 173.3, BASAL CELL CARCINOMA, 200.2, MALIGNANT MELANOMA, BURKITT'S TYPE, or 776.5. CONGENITAL ANEMIA).
- Treatment—any test or procedure ordered by and/or performed by a physician for a patient. Each treatment has a treatment ID/treatment code and treatment name using standard codes. HIPAA-mandated ICD-9-CM Volume 3 Procedure Codes are used for diagnostic and therapeutic procedures (e.g., 03.31, SPINAL TAP, 14.3, REPAIR OF RETINAL TEAR, 87.44, ROUTINE CHEST X-RAY, or 90.5, MICROSCOPIC EXAMINATION OF BLOOD).
- Order—any order issued by a physician for treatment and/or services such as diagnostic tests (radiology, laboratory) and therapeutic procedures (physical therapy, diet orders), or drugs and devices (prescriptions). Each order has an order ID, order date, and order time.

The team next recorded the following information concerning relationships:

- Each hospital employee is assigned to work in one or more care centers. Each care center has at least one employee and may have any number of employees. The hospital records the number of hours per week that a given employee works in a particular care center.
- Each care center has exactly one employee who is designated nurse-in-charge for that care center.
- A given patient may or may not be assigned to a bed (since some patients are outpatients). Occupancy rates are seldom at 100 percent, so a bed may or may not be assigned to a patient.
- A patient may be referred to the hospital by exactly one physician. A physician may refer any number of patients or may not refer any patients.
- A patient must be admitted to the hospital by exactly one physician. A physician may admit any number of patients or may not admit any patients.
- Prior to a patient being seen by a physician, a nurse typically obtains and records relevant information about the patient. This includes the patient's weight, blood pressure, pulse, and temperature. The nurse who assesses the vital signs also records the date and time. Finally, the reasons for the visit and any symptoms the patient describes are recorded.
- Physicians diagnose any number of conditions affecting a patient, and a diagnosis may apply to many patients. The hospital records the following information: date and time of diagnosis, diagnosis code, and description.
- Physicians may order and perform any number of services/treatments for a patient or may not perform any treatment. A treatment or service may be performed on any number of patients, and a patient may have treatments performed or ordered by any number of physicians. For each treatment or service rendered, the hospital records the following information: physician ordering the treatment, treatment date, treatment time, and results.
- A patient may also consume any number of items. A given item may be consumed by one or more patients, or may not be consumed. For each item consumed by a patient, the hospital records the following: date, time, quantity, and total cost (which can be computed by multiplying quantity times unit cost).

Case Questions

1. Why would Mountain View Community Hospital want to use E-R modeling to understand its data requirements? What other ways might the hospital want to model its information requirements?
2. Is Mountain View Community Hospital itself an entity type in the data model? Why or why not?

[1] Note: ICD refers to the International Classification of Diseases, which, in the United States, is the HIPAA-mandated coding system used in medical billing. More information can be found at **www.cms.hhs.gov/medlearn/icd9code.asp**.

3. Do there appear to be any of the following in the description of the Mountain View Community Hospital data requirements? If so, what are they?
   a. weak entities
   b. multivalued attributes
   c. multiple relationships
4. When developing an E-R diagram for Mountain View Community Hospital, what is the significance of the business rule that states that some patients are assigned to a bed, but outpatients are not assigned to a bed?
5. Do you think that *Items* should be split into two separate entities, one for nonreusable and one for reusable items? Why or why not?
6. What quality check(s) would you perform to determine whether the E-R model you developed can easily satisfy user requests for data and/or information?

Case Exercises

1. Study the case description very closely. What other questions would you like to ask to understand the data requirements at Mountain View Community Hospital?
2. Develop an E-R diagram for Mountain View Community Hospital. State any assumptions you made in developing the diagram. If you have been assigned a particular data modeling tool, redraw your E-R diagram using this tool.
3. The case describes an entity type called *Item*. Given your answer to Case Exercise 2, will this entity type also be able to represent in-room TVs as a billable item to patients? Why or why not?
4. Suppose the attribute bed number were a composite attribute, composed of care center ID, room number, and individual bed number. Redraw any parts of your answer to Case Exercise 2 that would have to change to handle this composite attribute.
5. Consider your new E-R diagram for Case Exercise 4. Now, additionally assume that a care center contains many rooms, and each room may contain items that are billed to patients assigned to that room. Redraw your E-R diagram to accommodate this new assumption.
6. Does your answer to Case Exercise 2 allow more than one physician to perform a treatment on a patient at the same time? If not, redraw your answer to Case Exercise 2 to accommodate this situation. Make any additional assumptions you consider necessary to represent this situation.
7. Does your answer to Case Exercise 2 allow the same treatment to be performed more than once on the same patient by the same physician? If not, redraw your answer to Case Exercise 2 to accommodate this situation. Make any additional assumptions you consider necessary in order to represent this situation.

Project Assignments

P1. Develop an E-R diagram for Mountain View Community Hospital, based on the enterprise data model you developed in Chapter 1 and the case description, questions, and exercises presented previously. Using the notation described in this chapter, clearly indicate the different types of entities, attributes (identifiers, multivalued attributes, composite attributes, derived attributes) and relationships that apply in this case.

P2. Develop a list of well-stated business rules for your E-R diagram.

P3. Prepare a list of questions that have arisen as a result of your E-R modeling efforts, and that need to be answered to clarify your understanding of Mountain View Community Hospital's business rules and data requirements.

CHAPTER

3

The Enhanced E-R Model

Learning Objectives

After studying this chapter, you should be able to:

- Concisely define each of the following key terms: **enhanced entity-relationship (EER) model, subtype, supertype, attribute inheritance, generalization, specialization, completeness constraint, total specialization rule, partial specialization rule, disjointness constraint, disjoint rule, overlap rule, subtype discriminator, supertype/ subtype hierarchy, entity cluster, and universal data model.**
- Recognize when to use supertype/subtype relationships in data modeling.
- Use both specialization and generalization as techniques for defining supertype/subtype relationships.
- Specify both completeness constraints and disjointness constraints in modeling supertype/subtype relationships.
- Develop a supertype/subtype hierarchy for a realistic business situation.
- Develop an entity cluster to simplify presentation of an E-R diagram.
- Explain the major features and data modeling structures of a universal (packaged) data model.
- Describe the special features of a data modeling project when using a packaged data model.

INTRODUCTION

The basic E-R model described in Chapter 2 was first introduced during the mid-1970s. It has been suitable for modeling most common business problems and has enjoyed widespread use. However, the business environment has changed dramatically since that time. Business relationships are more complex, and as a result, business data are much more complex as well. For example, organizations must be prepared to segment their markets and to customize their products, which places much greater demands on organizational databases.

To cope better with these changes, researchers and consultants have continued to enhance the E-R model so that it can more accurately represent the complex data encountered in today's business environment. The term **enhanced entity-relationship (EER) model** is used to identify the model that has resulted from extending the original E-R model with these new modeling constructs. These extensions make the EER model semantically similar to object-oriented data modeling, which we cover in Chapter 13.

Enhanced entity-relationship (EER) model
A model that has resulted from extending the original E-R model with new modeling constructs.

The most important modeling construct incorporated in the EER model is supertype/subtype relationships. This facility enables us to model a general entity type (called the *supertype*) and then subdivide it into several specialized entity types (called *subtypes*). Thus, for example, the entity type CAR can be modeled as a supertype, with subtypes SEDAN, SPORTS CAR, COUPE, and so on. Each subtype inherits attributes from its supertype and in addition may have special attributes and be involved in relationships of its own. Adding new notation for modeling supertype/subtype relationships has greatly improved the flexibility of the basic E-R model.

E-R, and especially EER, diagrams can become large and complex, requiring multiple pages (or very small font) for display. Some commercial databases include hundreds of entities. Many users and managers specifying requirements for or using a database do not need to see all the entities, relationships, and attributes to understand the part of the database with which they are most interested. Entity clustering is a way to turn a part of an entity-relationship data model into a more macro-level view of the same data. Entity clustering is a hierarchical decomposition technique (a nesting process of breaking a system into further and further subparts), which can make E-R diagrams easier to read and databases easier to design. By grouping entities and relationships, you can lay out an E-R diagram in such a way that you to give attention to the details of the model that matter most in a given data modeling task.

As introduced in Chapter 2, universal and industry-specific generalizable data models, which extensively utilized EER capabilities, have become very important for contemporary data modelers. These packaged data models and data model patterns have made data modelers more efficient and produce data models of higher quality. The EER features of supertypes/subtypes are essential to create generalizable data models; additional generalizing constructs, such as typing entities and relationships, are also employed. It has become very important for data modelers to know how to customize a data model pattern or data model for a major software package (e.g., enterprise resource planning or customer relationship management), just as it has become commonplace for information system builders to customize off-the-shelf software packages and software components.

REPRESENTING SUPERTYPES AND SUBTYPES

Recall from Chapter 2 that an entity type is a collection of entities that share common properties or characteristics. Although the entity instances that compose an entity type are similar, we do not expect them to have exactly the same attributes. For example, recall required and optional attributes from Chapter 2. One of the major challenges in data modeling is to recognize and clearly represent entities that are almost the same; that is, entity types that share common properties but also have one or more distinct properties that are of interest to the organization.

Subtype
A subgrouping of the entities in an entity type that is meaningful to the organization and that shares common attributes or relationships distinct from other subgroupings.

Supertype
A generic entity type that has a relationship with one or more subtypes.

For this reason, the E-R model has been extended to include supertype/subtype relationships. A **subtype** is a subgrouping of the entities in an entity type that is meaningful to the organization. For example, STUDENT is an entity type in a university. Two subtypes of STUDENT are GRADUATE STUDENT and UNDERGRADUATE STUDENT. In this example, we refer to STUDENT as the supertype. A **supertype** is a generic entity type that has a relationship with one or more subtypes.

In the E-R diagramming we have done so far, supertypes and subtypes have been hidden. For example, consider again Figure 2-22, which is the E-R diagram (in Microsoft Visio) for Pine Valley Furniture Company. Notice that it is possible for a customer to not do business in any territory (i.e., no associated instances of the DOES BUSINESS IN associative entity). Why is this? One possible reason is that there are two types of customers—national account customers and regular customers—and only regular customers are assigned to a sales territory. Thus, in Figure 2-22, the reason for the optional cardinality next to the DOES BUSINESS IN associative entity coming from CUSTOMER is obscured. Explicitly drawing a customer entity supertype and several entity subtypes will help us to make the E-R diagram more meaningful. Later in this chapter, we show a revised E-R diagram for Pine Valley Furniture, which demonstrates several EER notations to make vague aspects of Figure 2-22 more explicit.

Basic Concepts and Notation

The notation that is used for supertype/subtype relationships in this text is shown in Figure 3-1a. The supertype is connected with a line to a circle, which in turn is connected with a line to each subtype that has been defined. The U-shaped symbol on each line connecting a subtype to the circle emphasizes that the subtype is a subset of the supertype. It also indicates the direction of the subtype/supertype relationship. (This U is optional because the meaning and direction of the supertype/subtype relationship is usually obvious; in most examples, we will not include this symbol). Figure 3-1b shows the type of EER notation used by Microsoft Visio (which is very similar to that used in this text), and Figure 3-1c shows the type of EER notation used by some CASE tools (e.g., Oracle Designer); the notation in Figure 3-1c is also the form often used for universal and industry-specific data models. These different formats have identical basic features, and you should easily become comfortable using any of these forms. We primarily use the text notation for examples in this chapter because advanced EER features are more standard with this format.

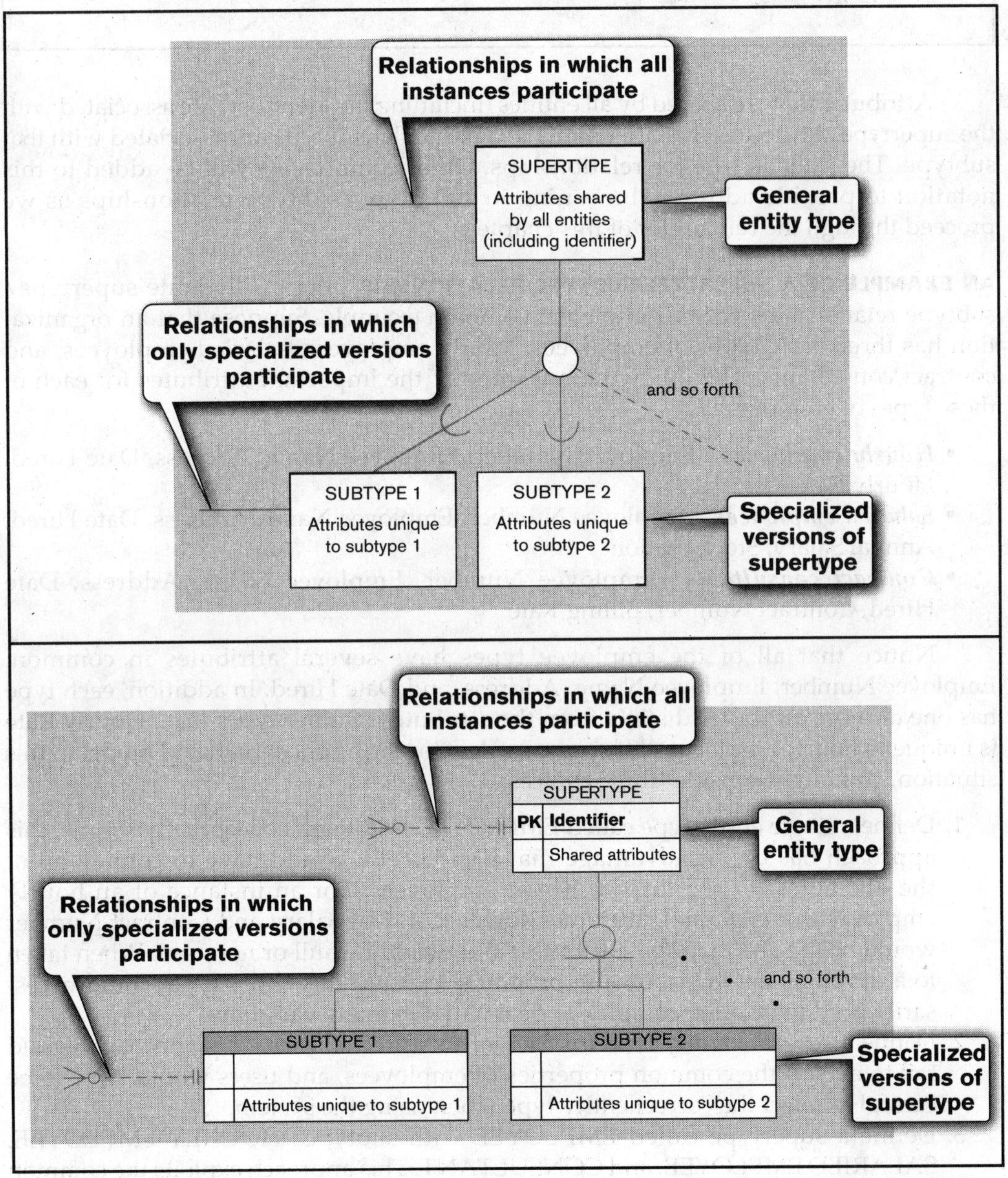

FIGURE 3-1 Basic notation for supertype/subtype relationships

(a) EER notation

(b) Microsoft Visio notation

(continued)

FIGURE 3-1 (*continued*)
(c) Subtypes inside supertypes notation

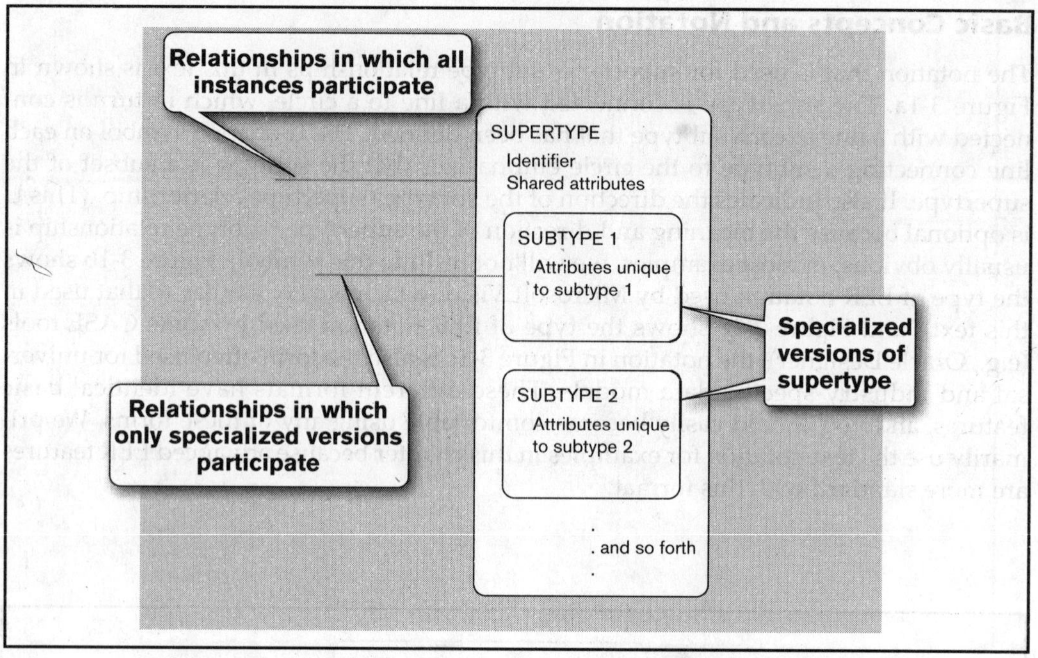

Attributes that are shared by all entities (including the identifier) are associated with the supertype. Attributes that are unique to a particular subtype are associated with that subtype. The same is true for relationships. Other components will be added to this notation to provide additional meaning in supertype/subtype relationships as we proceed through the remainder of this chapter.

AN EXAMPLE OF A SUPERTYPE/SUBTYPE RELATIONSHIP Let us illustrate supertype/subtype relationships with a simple yet common example. Suppose that an organization has three basic types of employees: hourly employees, salaried employees, and contract consultants. The following are some of the important attributes for each of these types of employees:

- ***Hourly employees*** Employee Number, Employee Name, Address, Date Hired, Hourly Rate
- ***Salaried employees*** Employee Number, Employee Name, Address, Date Hired, Annual Salary, Stock Option
- ***Contract consultants*** Employee Number, Employee Name, Address, Date Hired, Contract Number, Billing Rate

Notice that all of the employee types have several attributes in common: Employee Number, Employee Name, Address, and Date Hired. In addition, each type has one or more attributes distinct from the attributes of other types (e.g., Hourly Rate is unique to hourly employees). If you were developing a conceptual data model in this situation, you might consider three choices:

1. Define a single entity type called EMPLOYEE. Although conceptually simple, this approach has the disadvantage that EMPLOYEE would have to contain all of the attributes for the three types of employees. For an instance of an hourly employee (for example), attributes such as Annual Salary and Contract Number would not apply (optional attributes) and would be null or not used. When taken to a development environment, programs that use this entity type would necessarily need to be quite complex to deal with the many variations.
2. Define a separate entity type for each of the three entities. This approach would fail to exploit the common properties of employees, and users would have to be careful to select the correct entity type when using the system.
3. Define a supertype called EMPLOYEE with subtypes HOURLY EMPLOYEE, SALARIED EMPLOYEE, and CONSULTANT. This approach exploits the common properties of all employees, yet recognizes the distinct properties of each type.

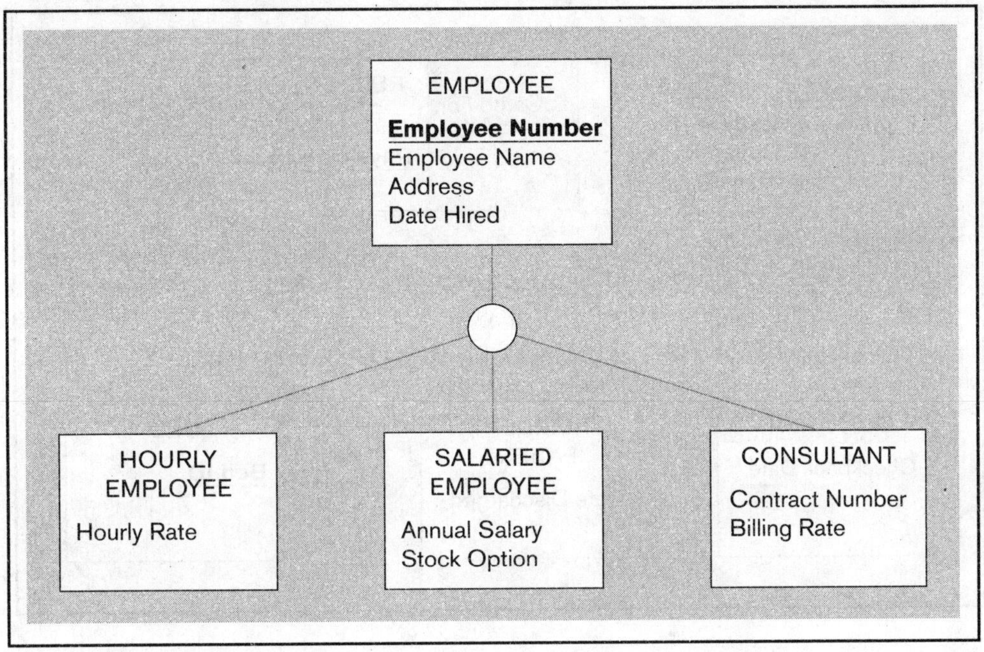

FIGURE 3-2 Employee supertype with three subtypes

Figure 3-2 shows a representation of the EMPLOYEE supertype with its three subtypes, using enhanced E-R notation. Attributes shared by all employees are associated with the EMPLOYEE entity type. Attributes that are peculiar to each subtype are included with that subtype only.

ATTRIBUTE INHERITANCE A subtype is an entity type in its own right. An entity instance of a subtype represents the same entity instance of the supertype. For example, if "Therese Jones" is an occurrence of the CONSULTANT subtype, then this same person is necessarily an occurrence of the EMPLOYEE supertype. As a consequence, an entity in a subtype must possess not only values for its own attributes, but also values for its attributes as a member of the supertype, including the identifier.

Attribute inheritance is the property by which subtype entities inherit values of all attributes and instance of all relationships of the supertype. This important property makes it unnecessary to include supertype attributes or relationships redundantly with the subtypes (remember, when it comes to data modeling, redundancy = bad, simplicity = good). For example, Employee Name is an attribute of EMPLOYEE (Figure 3-2) but not of the subtypes of EMPLOYEE. Thus, the fact that the employee's name is "Therese Jones" is inherited from the EMPLOYEE supertype. However, the Billing Rate for this same employee is an attribute of the subtype CONSULTANT.

Attribute inheritance
A property by which subtype entities inherit values of all attributes and instances of all relationships of their supertype.

We have established that a member of a subtype must be a member of the supertype. Is the converse also true—that is, is a member of the supertype also a member of one (or more) of the subtypes? This may or may not be true, depending on the business situation. (Sure, "it depends" is the classic academic answer, but it's true in this case.) We discuss the various possibilities later in this chapter.

WHEN TO USE SUPERTYPE/SUBTYPE RELATIONSHIPS So, how do you know when to use a supertype/subtype relationship? You should consider using subtypes when either (or both) of the following conditions are present:

1. There are attributes that apply to some (but not all) instances of an entity type. For example, see the EMPLOYEE entity type in Figure 3-2.
2. The instances of a subtype participate in a relationship unique to that subtype.

Figure 3-3 is an example of the use of subtype relationships that illustrates both of these situations. The hospital entity type PATIENT has two subtypes: OUTPATIENT and RESIDENT PATIENT. (The identifier is Patient ID.) All patients have an Admit

FIGURE 3-3 Supertype/subtype relationships in a hospital

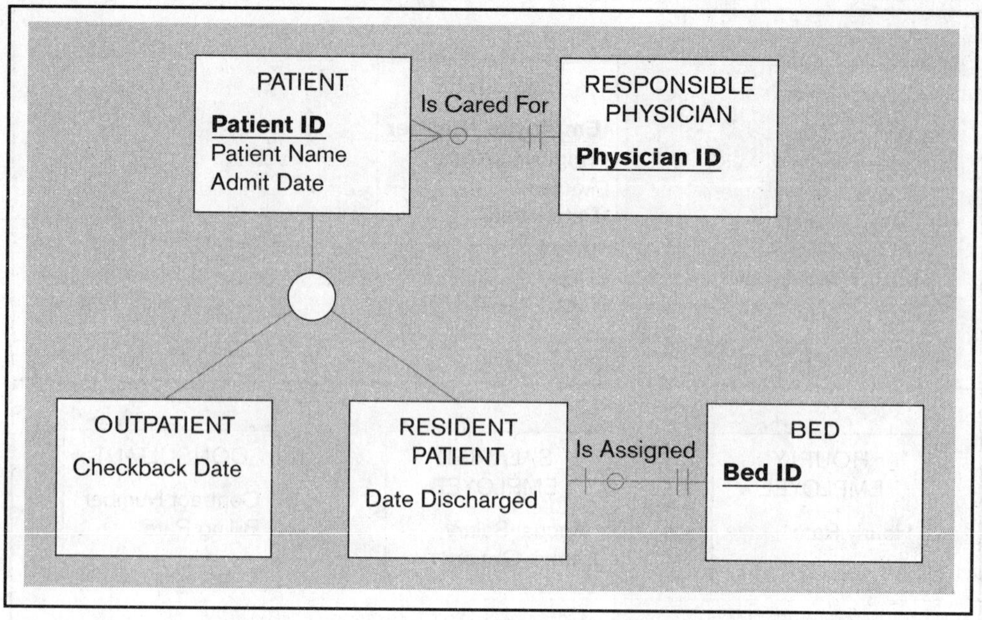

Date attribute, as well as a Patient Name. Also, every patient is cared for by a RESPONSIBLE PHYSICIAN who develops a treatment plan for the patient.

Each subtype has an attribute that is unique to that subtype. Outpatients have Checkback Date, whereas resident patients have Date Discharged. Also, resident patients have a unique relationship that assigns each patient to a bed. (Notice that this is a mandatory relationship; it would be optional if it were attached to PATIENT.) Each bed may or may not be assigned to a patient.

Earlier we discussed the property of attribute inheritance. Thus, each outpatient and each resident patient inherits the attributes of the parent supertype PATIENT: Patient ID, Patient Name, and Admit Date. Figure 3-3 also illustrates the principle of relationship inheritance. OUTPATIENT and RESIDENT PATIENT are also instances of PATIENT; therefore, each Is Cared For by a RESPONSIBLE PHYSICIAN.

Representing Specialization and Generalization

We have described and illustrated the basic principles of supertype/subtype relationships, including the characteristics of "good" subtypes. But in developing real-world data models, how can you recognize opportunities to exploit these relationships? There are two processes—generalization and specialization—that serve as mental models in developing supertype/subtype relationships.

Generalization
The process of defining a more general entity type from a set of more specialized entity types.

GENERALIZATION A unique aspect of human intelligence is the ability and propensity to classify objects and experiences and to generalize their properties. In data modeling, **generalization** is the process of defining a more general entity type from a set of more specialized entity types. Thus generalization is a bottom-up process.

An example of generalization is shown in Figure 3-4. In Figure 3-4a, three entity types have been defined: CAR, TRUCK, and MOTORCYCLE. At this stage, the data modeler intends to represent these separately on an E-R diagram. However, on closer examination, we see that the three entity types have a number of attributes in common: Vehicle ID (identifier), Vehicle Name (with components Make and Model), Price, and Engine Displacement. This fact (reinforced by the presence of a common identifier) suggests that each of the three entity types is really a version of a more general entity type.

This more general entity type (named VEHICLE) together with the resulting supertype/subtype relationships is shown in Figure 3-4b. The entity CAR has the specific attribute No Of Passengers, whereas TRUCK has two specific attributes: Capacity and Cab Type. Thus, generalization has allowed us to group entity types along with

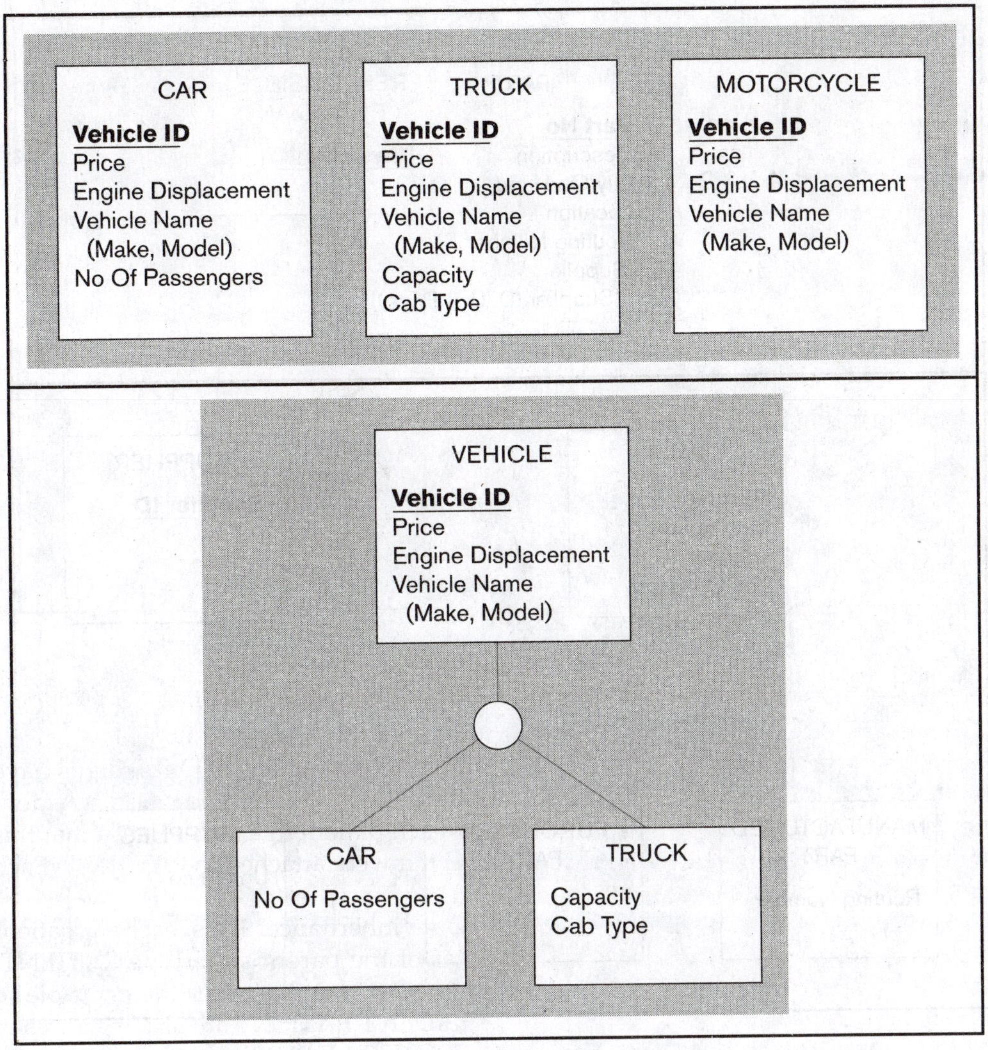

FIGURE 3-4 Example of generalization
(a) Three entity types: CAR, TRUCK, and MOTORCYCLE
(b) Generalization to VEHICLE supertype

their common attributes and at the same time preserve specific attributes that are peculiar to each subtype.

Notice that the entity type MOTORCYCLE is not included in the relationship. Is this simply an omission? No. Instead, it is deliberately not included because it does not satisfy the conditions for a subtype discussed earlier. Comparing Figure 3-4 parts a and b, you will notice that the only attributes of MOTORCYCLE are those that are common to all vehicles; there are no attributes specific to motorcycles. Furthermore, MOTORCYCLE does not have a relationship to another entity type. Thus there is no need to create a MOTORCYCLE subtype.

The fact that there is no MOTORCYCLE subtype suggests that it must be possible to have an instance of VEHICLE that is not a member of any of its subtypes. We discuss this type of constraint in the section on specifying constraints.

SPECIALIZATION As we have seen, generalization is a bottom-up process. Specialization is a top-down process, the direct reverse of generalization. Suppose that we have defined an entity type with its attributes. Specialization is the process of defining one or more subtypes of the supertype and forming supertype/subtype relationships. Each subtype is formed based on some distinguishing characteristic, such as attributes or relationships specific to the subtype.

Specialization
The process of defining one or more subtypes of the supertype and forming supertype/subtype relationships.

An example of specialization is shown in Figure 3-5. Figure 3-5a shows an entity type named PART, together with several of its attributes. The identifier is Part No, and other attributes are Description, Unit Price, Location, Qty On Hand, Routing Number,

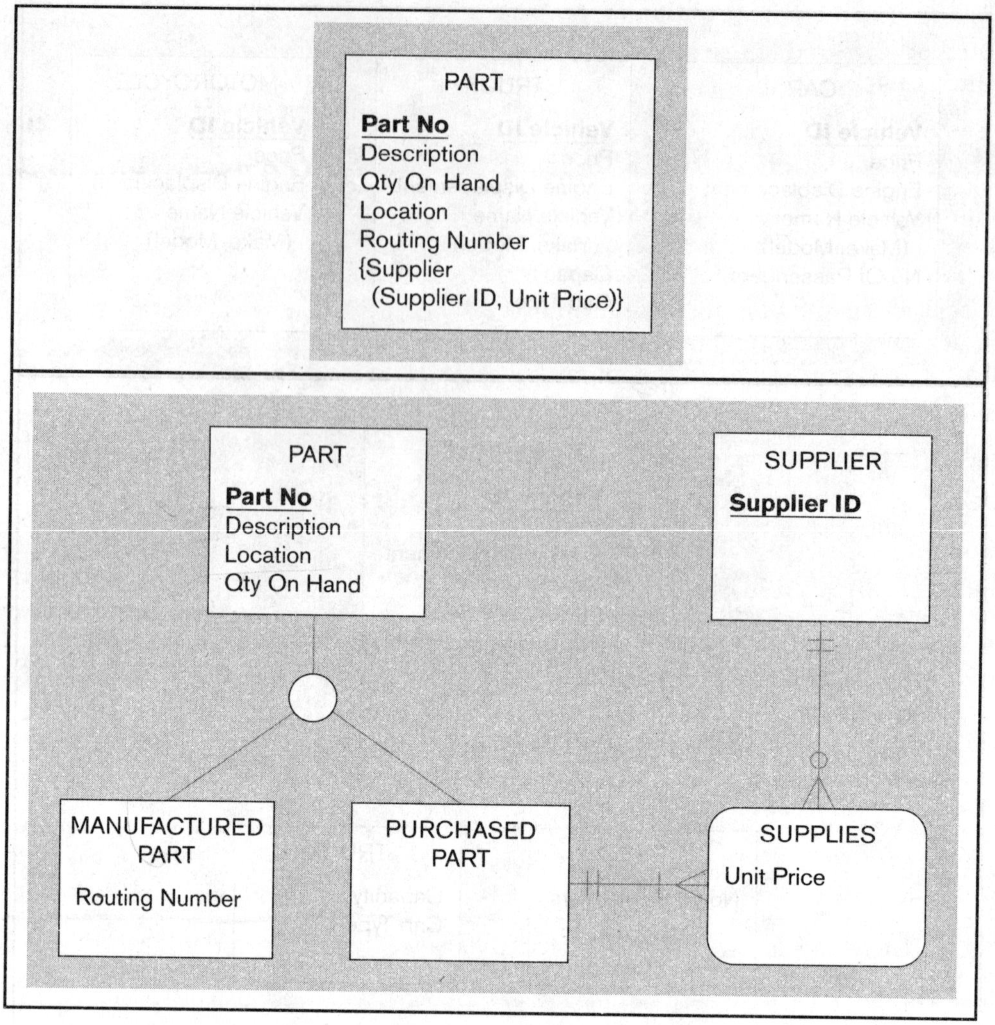

FIGURE 3-5 Example of specialization
(a) Entity type PART
(b) Specialization to MANUFACTURED PART and PURCHASED PART

and Supplier. (The last attribute is multivalued and composite because there may be more than one supplier with an associated unit price for a part.)

In discussions with users, we discover that there are two possible sources for parts: Some are manufactured internally, whereas others are purchased from outside suppliers. Further, we discover that some parts are obtained from both sources. In this case, the choice depends on factors such as manufacturing capacity, unit price of the parts, and so on.

Some of the attributes in Figure 3-5a apply to all parts, regardless of source. However, others depend on the source. Thus Routing Number applies only to manufactured parts, whereas Supplier ID and Unit Price apply only to purchased parts. These factors suggest that PART should be specialized by defining the subtypes MANUFACTURED PART and PURCHASED PART (Figure 3-5b).

In Figure 3-5b, Routing Number is associated with MANUFACTURED PART. The data modeler initially planned to associate Supplier ID and Unit Price with PURCHASED PART. However, in further discussions with users, the data modeler suggested instead that they create a SUPPLIER entity type and an associative entity linking PURCHASED PART with SUPPLIER. This associative entity (named SUPPLIES in Figure 3-5b) allows users to more easily associate purchased parts with their suppliers. Notice that the attribute Unit Price is now associated with the associative entity, so that the unit price for a part may vary from one supplier to another. In this example, specialization has permitted a preferred representation of the problem domain.

COMBINING SPECIALIZATION AND GENERALIZATION Specialization and generalization are both valuable techniques for developing supertype/subtype relationships. The technique you use at a particular time depends on several factors, such as the nature of the problem domain, previous modeling efforts, and personal preference. You should be prepared to use both approaches and to alternate back and forth as dictated by the preceding factors.

SPECIFYING CONSTRAINTS IN SUPERTYPE/SUBTYPE RELATIONSHIPS

So far we have discussed the basic concepts of supertype/subtype relationships and introduced some basic notation to represent these concepts. We have also described the processes of generalization and specialization, which help a data modeler recognize opportunities for exploiting these relationships. In this section, we introduce additional notation to represent constraints on supertype/subtype relationships. These constraints allow us to capture some of the important business rules that apply to these relationships. The two most important types of constraints that are described in this section are completeness and disjointness constraints (Elmasri and Navathe, 1994).

Specifying Completeness Constraints

A **completeness constraint** addresses the question of whether an instance of a supertype must also be a member of at least one subtype. The completeness constraint has two possible rules: total specialization and partial specialization. The **total specialization rule** specifies that each entity instance of the supertype must be a member of some subtype in the relationship. The **partial specialization rule** specifies that an entity instance of the supertype is allowed not to belong to any subtype. We illustrate each of these rules with earlier examples from this chapter (see Figure 3-6).

Completeness constraint
A type of constraint that addresses whether an instance of a supertype must also be a member of at least one subtype.

Total specialization rule
A rule that specifies that each entity instance of a supertype must be a member of some subtype in the relationship.

Partial specialization rule
A rule that specifies that an entity instance of a supertype is allowed not to belong to any subtype.

TOTAL SPECIALIZATION RULE Figure 3-6a repeats the example of PATIENT (Figure 3-3) and introduces the notation for total specialization. In this example, the business rule is the following: A patient must be either an outpatient or a resident patient. (There are no other types of patient in this hospital.) Total specialization is indicated by the *double* line extending from the PATIENT entity type to the circle. (In the Microsoft Visio notation, total specialization is called "Category is complete" and is shown also by a *double* line under the category circle between the supertype and associated subtypes.)

In this example, every time a new instance of PATIENT is inserted into the supertype, a corresponding instance is inserted into either OUTPATIENT or RESIDENT PATIENT. If the instance is inserted into RESIDENT PATIENT, an instance of the relationship Is Assigned is created to assign the patient to a hospital bed.

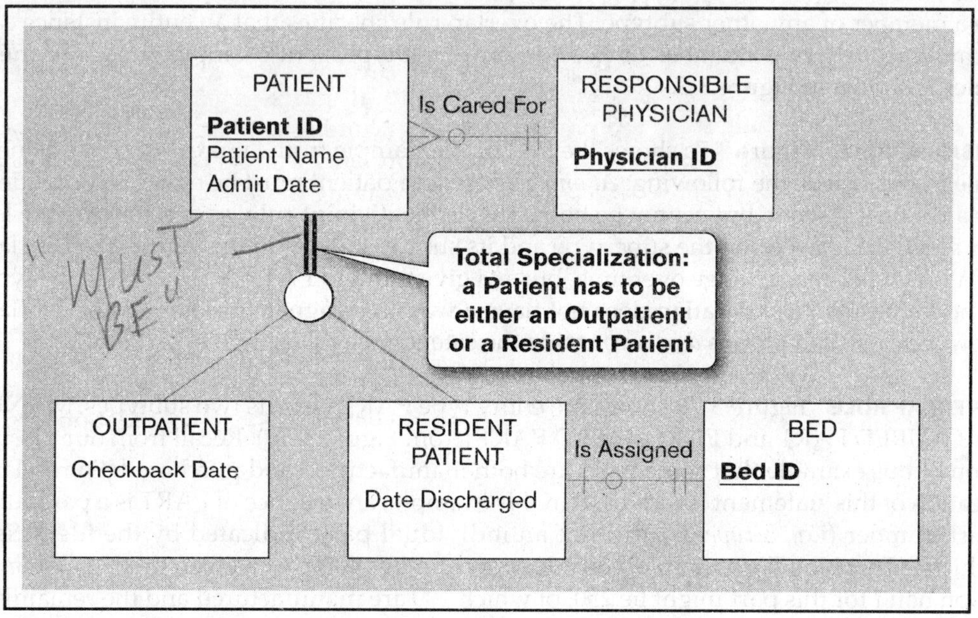

FIGURE 3-6 Examples of completeness constraints
(a) Total specialization rule

(continued)

FIGURE 3-6 ***(continued)***
(b) Partial specialization rule

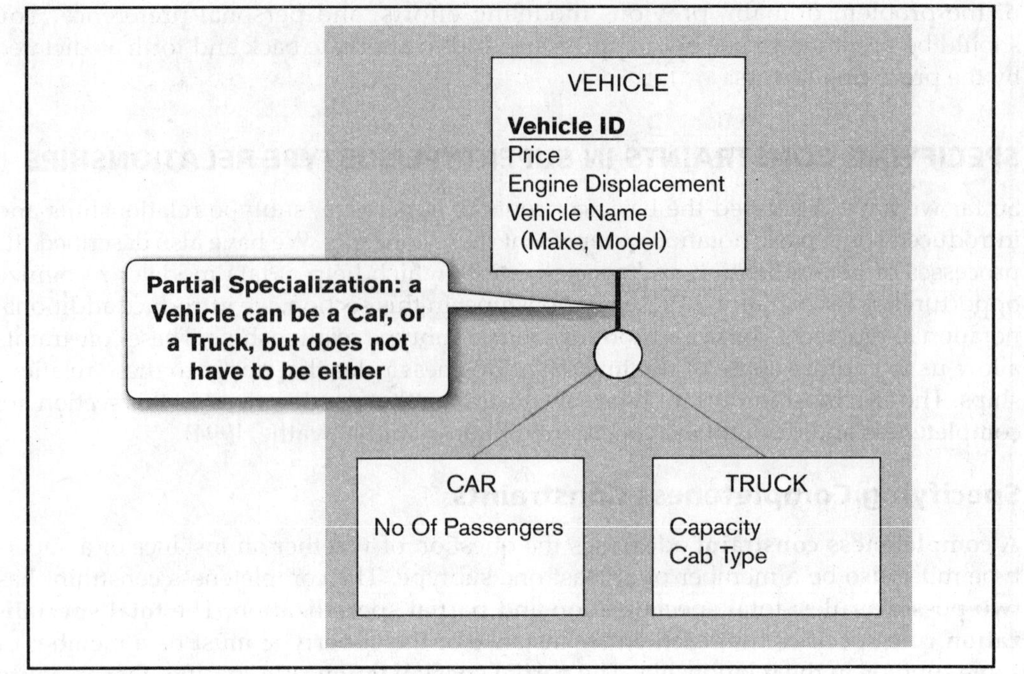

PARTIAL SPECIALIZATION RULE Figure 3-6b repeats the example of VEHICLE and its subtypes CAR and TRUCK from Figure 3-4. Recall that in this example, motorcycle is a type of vehicle, but it is not represented as a subtype in the data model. Thus, if a vehicle is a car, it must appear as an instance of CAR, and if it is a truck, it must appear as an instance of TRUCK. However, if the vehicle is a motorcycle, it cannot appear as an instance of any subtype. This is an example of partial specialization, and it is specified by the single line from the VEHICLE supertype to the circle.

Specifying Disjointness Constraints

Disjointness constraint
A constraint that addresses whether an instance of a supertype may simultaneously be a member of two (or more) subtypes.

A **disjointness constraint** addresses whether an instance of a supertype may simultaneously be a member of two (or more) subtypes. The disjointness constraint has two possible rules: the disjoint rule and the overlap rule. The disjoint rule specifies that if an entity instance (of the supertype) is a member of one subtype, it cannot simultaneously be a member of any other subtype. The overlap rule specifies that an entity instance can simultaneously be a member of two (or more) subtypes. An example of each of these rules is shown in Figure 3-7.

Disjoint rule
A rule that specifies that an instance of a supertype may not simultaneously be a member of two (or more) subtypes.

DISJOINT RULE Figure 3-7a shows the PATIENT example from Figure 3-6a. The business rule in this case is the following: *At any given time*, a patient must be either an outpatient or a resident patient, but cannot be both. This is the **disjoint rule**, as specified by the letter *d* in the circle joining the supertype and its subtypes. Note in this figure, the subclass of a PATIENT may change over time, but at a given time, a PATIENT is of only one type. (The Microsoft Visio notation does not have a way to designate disjointness or overlap; however, you can place a *d* or an *o* inside the category circle using the Text tool.)

OVERLAP RULE Figure 3-7b shows the entity type PART with its two subtypes, MANUFACTURED PART and PURCHASED PART (from Figure 3-5b). Recall from our discussion of this example that some parts are both manufactured and purchased. Some clarification of this statement is required. In this example, an instance of PART is a particular part number (i.e., a *type of part*), not an individual part (indicated by the identifier, which is Part No). For example, consider part number 4000. At a given time, the quantity on hand for this part might be 250, of which 100 are manufactured and the remaining 150 are purchased parts. In this case, it is not important to keep track of individual

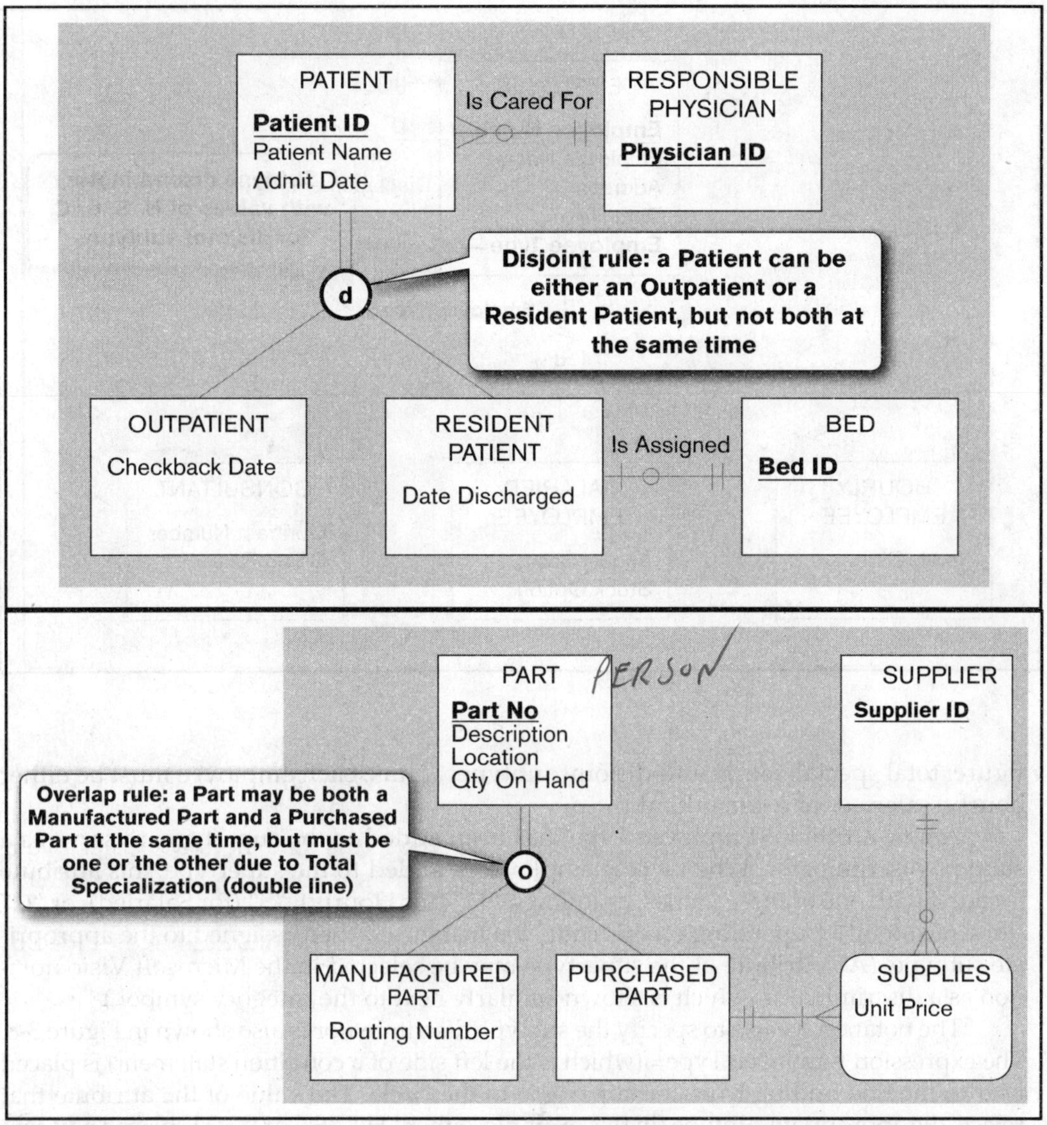

FIGURE 3-7 Examples of disjointness constraints
(a) Disjoint rule
(b) Overlap rule

parts. When tracking individual parts is important, each part is assigned a serial number identifier, and the quantity on hand is one or zero, depending on whether that individual part exists or not.

The **overlap rule** is specified by placing the letter *o* in the circle, as shown in Figure 3-7b. Notice in this figure that the total specialization rule is also specified, as indicated by the double line. Thus, any part must be either a purchased part or a manufactured part, or it may simultaneously be both of these.

Overlap rule
A rule that specifies that an instance of a supertype may simultaneously be a member of two (or more) subtypes.

Defining Subtype Discriminators

Given a supertype/subtype relationship, consider the problem of inserting a new instance of a supertype. Into which of the subtypes (if any) should this instance be inserted? We have already discussed the various possible rules that apply to this situation. We need a simple mechanism to implement these rules, if one is available. Often this can be accomplished by using a subtype discriminator. A **subtype discriminator** is an attribute of a supertype whose values determine the target subtype or subtypes.

Subtype discriminator
An attribute of a supertype whose values determine the target subtype or subtypes.

DISJOINT SUBTYPES An example of the use of a subtype discriminator is shown in Figure 3-8. This example is for the EMPLOYEE supertype and its subtypes, introduced in Figure 3-2. Notice that the following constraints have been added to this

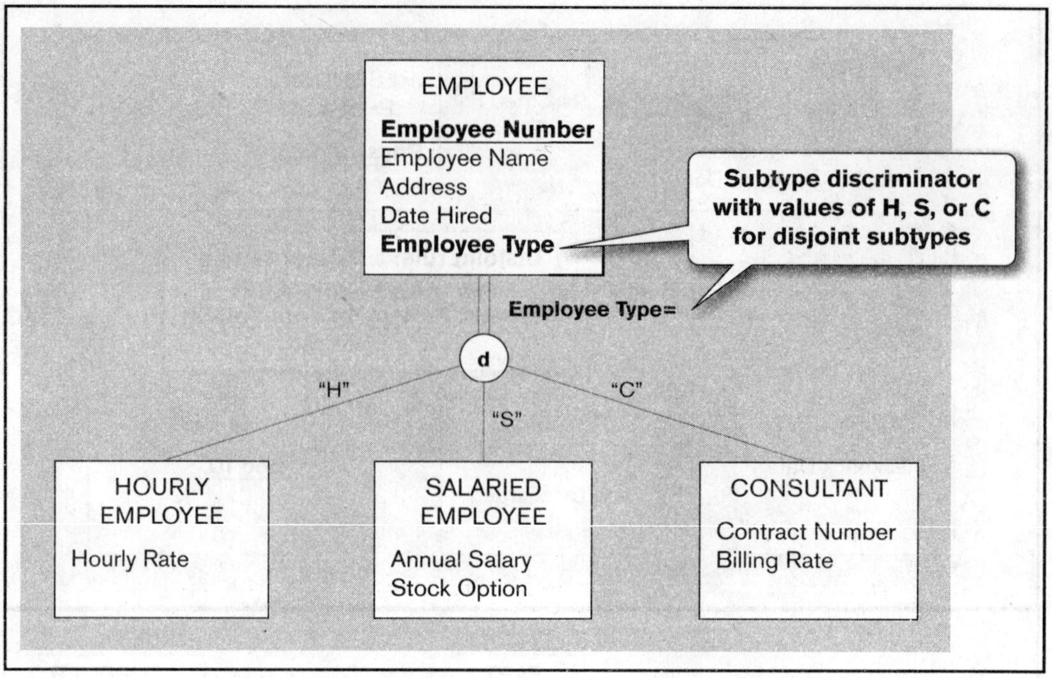

FIGURE 3-8 Introducing a subtype discriminator (disjoint rule)

figure: total specialization and disjoint subtypes. Thus, each employee must be either hourly, salaried, or a consultant.

A new attribute (Employee Type) has been added to the supertype, to serve as a subtype discriminator. When a new employee is added to the supertype, this attribute is coded with one of three values, as follows: "H" (for Hourly), "S" (for Salaried), or "C" (for Consultant). Depending on this code, the instance is then assigned to the appropriate subtype. (An attribute of the supertype may be selected in the Microsoft Visio notation as a discriminator, which is shown similarly next to the category symbol.)

The notation we use to specify the subtype discriminator is also shown in Figure 3-8. The expression Employee Type= (which is the left side of a condition statement) is placed next to the line leading from the supertype to the circle. The value of the attribute that selects the appropriate subtype (in this example, either "H," "S," or "C") is placed adjacent to the line leading to that subtype. Thus, for example, the condition Employee Type="S" causes an entity instance to be inserted into the SALARIED EMPLOYEE subtype.

OVERLAPPING SUBTYPES When subtypes overlap, a slightly modified approach must be applied for the subtype discriminator. The reason is that a given instance of the supertype may require that we create an instance in more than one subtype.

An example of this situation is shown in Figure 2-9 for PART and its overlapping subtypes. A new attribute named Part Type has been added to PART. Part Type is a composite attribute with components Manufactured? and Purchased? Each of these attributes is a Boolean variable (i.e., it takes on only the values yes, "Y," and no, "N"). When a new instance is added to PART, these components are coded as follows:

Type of Part	Manufactured?	Purchased?
Manufactured only	"Y"	"N"
Purchased only	"N"	"Y"
Purchased and manufactured	"Y"	"Y"

The method for specifying the subtype discriminator for this example is shown in Figure 3-9. Notice that this approach can be used for any number of overlapping subtypes.

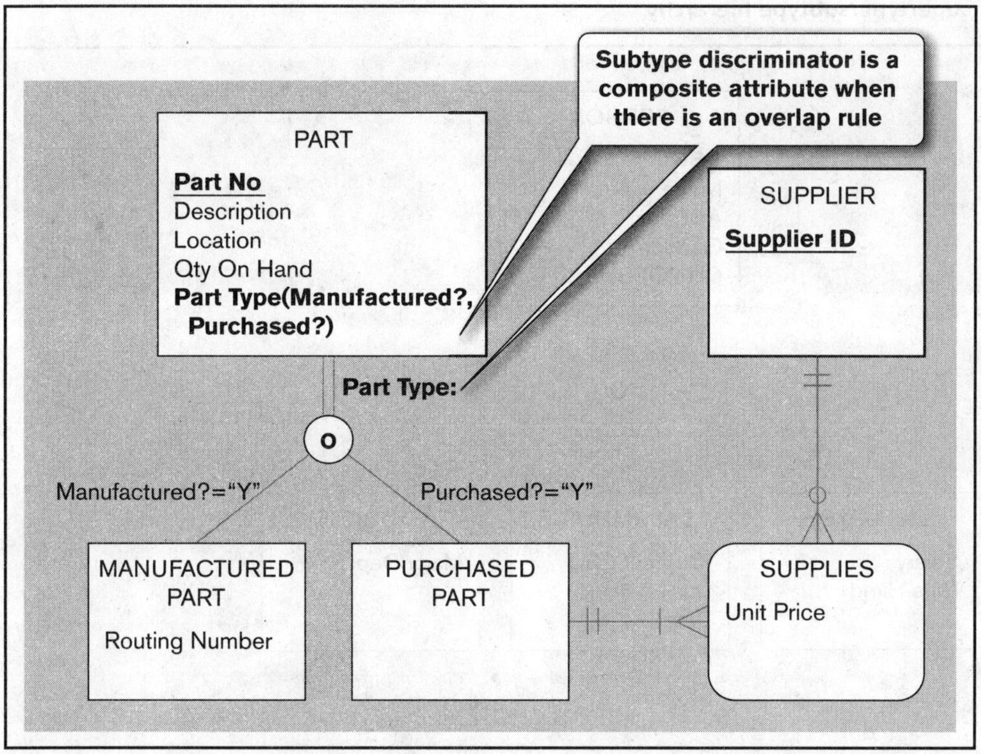

FIGURE 3-9 Subtype discriminator (overlap rule)

Defining Supertype/Subtype Hierarchies

We have considered a number of examples of supertype/subtype relationships in this chapter. It is possible for any of the subtypes in these examples to have other subtypes defined on it (in which case, the subtype becomes a supertype for the newly defined subtypes). A **supertype/subtype hierarchy** is a hierarchical arrangement of supertypes and subtypes, where each subtype has only one supertype (Elmasri and Navathe, 1994).

Supertype/subtype hierarchy A hierarchical arrangement of supertypes and subtypes in which each subtype has only one supertype.

We present an example of a supertype/subtype hierarchy in this section in Figure 3-10. (For simplicity, we do not show subtype discriminators in this and most subsequent examples. See Problem and Exercise 2 and 3.) This example includes most of the concepts and notation we have used in this chapter to this point. It also presents a methodology (based on specialization) that you can use in many data modeling situations.

AN EXAMPLE OF A SUPERTYPE/SUBTYPE HIERARCHY Suppose that you are asked to model the human resources in a university. Using specialization (a top-down approach), you might proceed as follows. Starting at the top of a hierarchy, model the most general entity type first. In this case, the most general entity type is PERSON. List and associate all attributes of PERSON. The attributes shown in Figure 3-10 are SSN (identifier), Name, Address, Gender, and Date Of Birth. The entity type at the top of a hierarchy is sometimes called the *root*.

Next, define all major subtypes of the root. In this example, there are three subtypes of PERSON: EMPLOYEE (persons who work for the university), STUDENT (persons who attend classes), and ALUMNUS (persons who have graduated). Assuming that there are no other types of persons of interest to the university, the total specialization rule applies, as shown in the figure. A person might belong to more than one subtype (e.g., ALUMNUS and EMPLOYEE), so the overlap rule is used. Note that overlap allows for any overlap. (A PERSON may be simultaneously in any pair or in all three subtypes.) If certain combinations are not allowed, a more refined supertype/subtype hierarchy would have to be developed to eliminate the prohibited combinations.

Attributes that apply specifically to each of these subtypes are shown in the figure. Thus, each instance of EMPLOYEE has a value for Date Hired and Salary. Major Dept

FIGURE 3-10 Example of supertype/subtype hierarchy

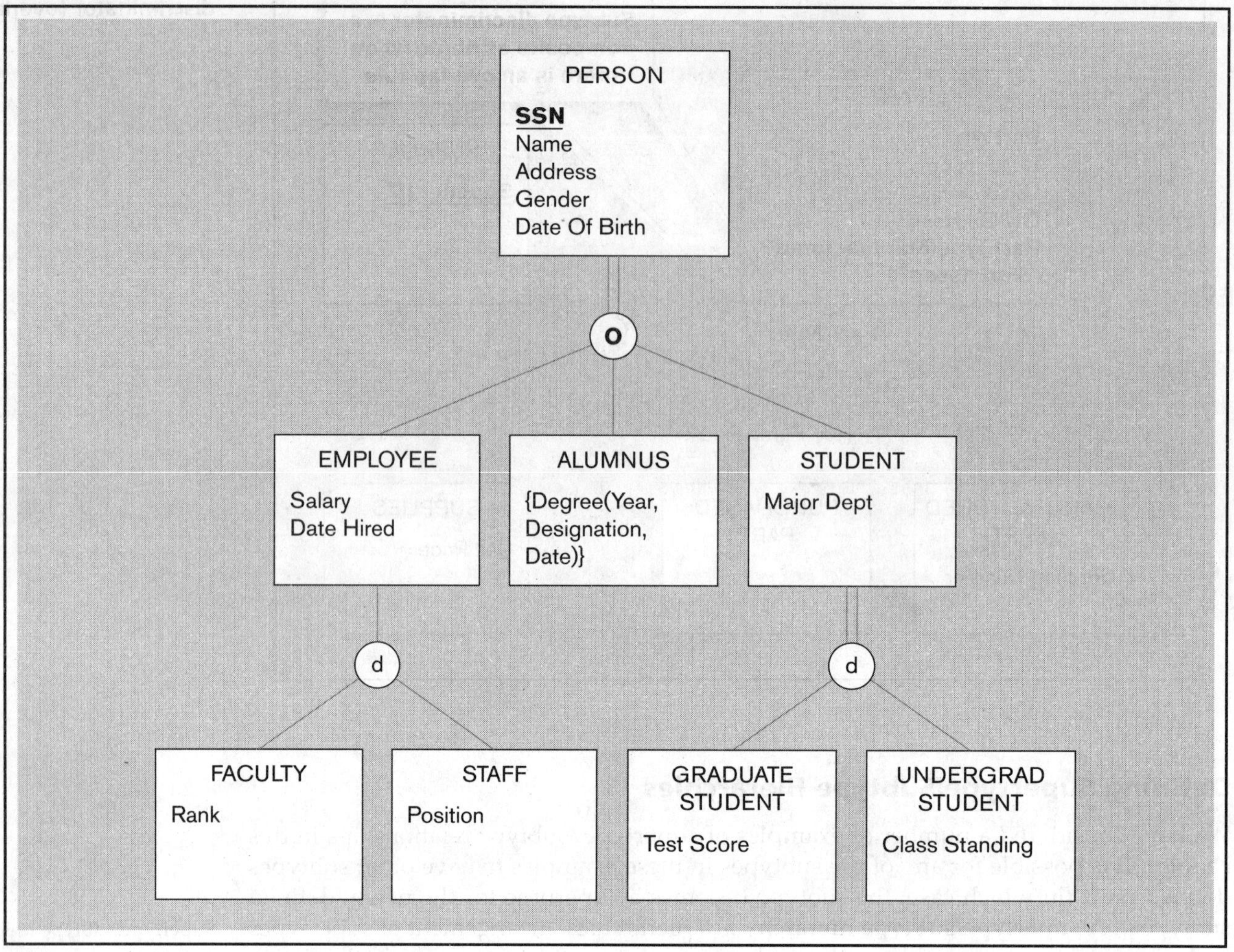

is an attribute of STUDENT, and Degree (with components Year, Designation, and Date) is a multivalued, composite attribute of ALUMNUS.

The next step is to evaluate whether any of the subtypes already defined qualify for further specialization. In this example, EMPLOYEE is partitioned into two subtypes: FACULTY and STAFF. FACULTY has the specific attribute Rank, whereas STAFF has the specific attribute Position. Notice that in this example the subtype EMPLOYEE becomes a supertype to FACULTY and STAFF. Because there may be types of employees other than faculty and staff (such as student assistants), the partial specialization rule is indicated. However, an employee cannot be both faculty and staff at the same time. Therefore, the disjoint rule is indicated in the circle.

Two subtypes are also defined for STUDENT: GRADUATE STUDENT and UNDERGRAD STUDENT. UNDERGRAD STUDENT has the attribute Class Standing, whereas GRADUATE STUDENT has the attribute Test Score. Notice that total specialization and the disjoint rule are specified; you should be able to state the business rules for these constraints.

SUMMARY OF SUPERTYPE/SUBTYPE HIERARCHIES We note two features concerning the attributes contained in the hierarchy shown in Figure 3-10:

1. Attributes are assigned at the highest logical level that is possible in the hierarchy. For example, because SSN (i.e., Social Security Number) applies to all persons, it is assigned to the root. In contrast, Date Hired applies only to employees, so it is assigned to EMPLOYEE. This approach ensures that attributes can be shared by as many subtypes as possible.

2. Subtypes that are lower in the hierarchy inherit attributes not only from their immediate supertype, but from all supertypes higher in the hierarchy, up to the root. Thus, for example, an instance of faculty has values for all of the following attributes: SSN, Name, Address, Gender, and Date Of Birth (from PERSON); Date Hired and Salary (from EMPLOYEE); and Rank (from FACULTY).

In the student case at the end of this chapter, we ask you to develop an enhanced E-R diagram for Mountain View Community Hospital using the same procedure we outlined in this section.

EER MODELING EXAMPLE: PINE VALLEY FURNITURE COMPANY

PINE VALLEY FURNITURE

In Chapter 2, we presented a sample E-R diagram for Pine Valley Furniture. (This diagram, developed using Microsoft Visio, is repeated in Figure 3-11.) After studying this diagram, you might use some questions to help you clarify the meaning of entities and relationships. Three such areas of questions are (see annotations in Figure 3-11 that indicate the source of each question):

1. Why do some customers not do business in one or more sales territories?
2. Why do some employees not supervise other employees, and why are they not all supervised by another employee? And, why do some employees not work in a work center?
3. Why do some vendors not supply raw materials to Pine Valley Furniture?

You may have other questions, but we will concentrate on these three to illustrate how supertype/subtype relationships can be used to convey a more specific (semantically rich) data model.

After some investigation into these three questions, we discover the following business rules that apply to how Pine Valley Furniture does business:

1. There are two types of customers: regular and national account. Only regular customers do business in sales territories. A sales territory exists only if it has at least one regular customer associated with it. A national account customer is associated with an account manager. It is possible for a customer to be both a regular and a national account customer.
2. Two special types of employees exist: management and union. Only union employees work in work centers, and a management employee supervises union employees. There are other kinds of employees besides management and union. A union employee may be promoted into management, at which time that employee stops being a union employee.
3. Pine Valley Furniture keeps track of many different vendors, not all of which have ever supplied raw materials to the company. A vendor is associated with a contract number once that vendor becomes an official supplier of raw materials.

These business rules have been used to modify the E-R diagram in Figure 3-11 into the EER diagram in Figure 3-12. (We have left most attributes off this diagram except for those that are essential to see the changes that have occurred.) Rule 1 means that there is a total, overlapping specialization of CUSTOMER into REGULAR CUSTOMER and NATIONAL ACCOUNT CUSTOMER. A composite attribute of CUSTOMER, Customer Type (with components National and Regular), is used to designate whether a customer instance is a regular customer, a national account, or both. Because only regular customers do business in sales territories, only regular customers are involved in the Does Business In relationship (associative entity).

Rule 2 means that there is a partial, disjoint specialization of EMPLOYEE into MANAGEMENT EMPLOYEE and UNION EMPLOYEE. An attribute of EMPLOYEE, Employee Type, discriminates between the two special types of employees. Specialization is partial because there are other kinds of employees besides these two types. Only union employees are involved in the Works In relationship, but all union employees work in some work center, so the minimum cardinality of next to Works In

FIGURE 3-11 E-R diagram for Pine Valley Furniture Company

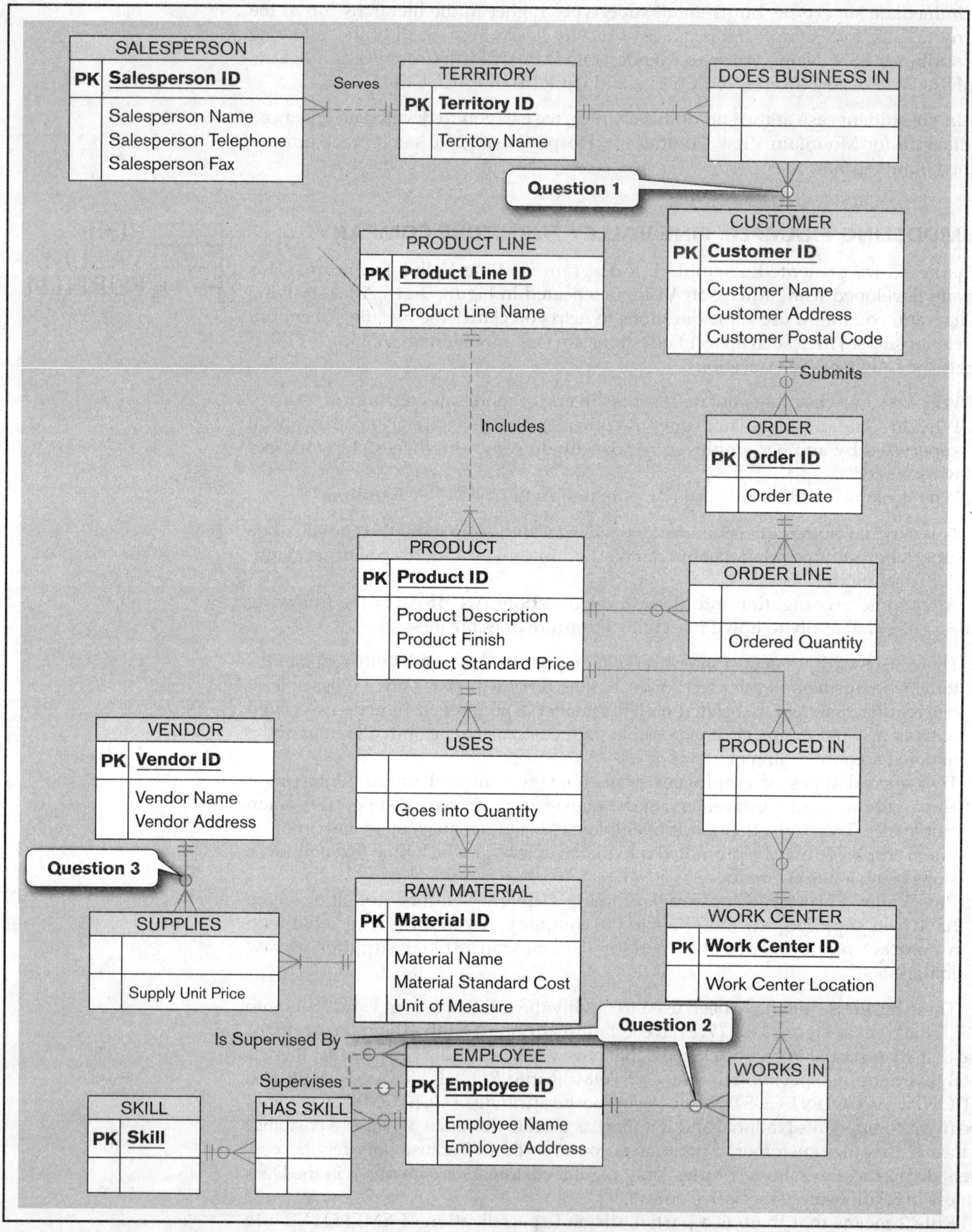

FIGURE 3-12 EER diagram for Pine Valley Furniture Company using Microsoft Visio

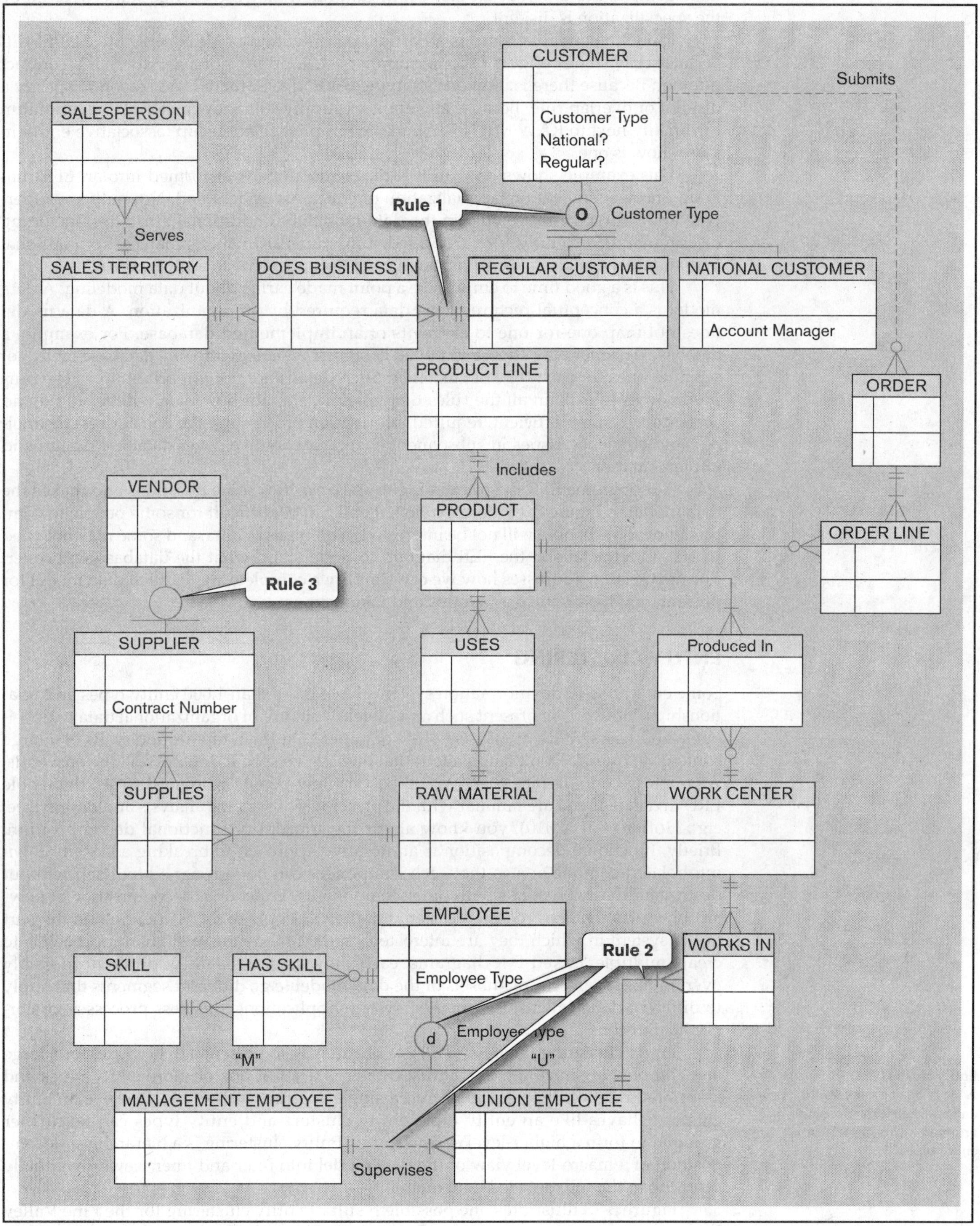

from UNION EMPLOYEE is now mandatory. Because an employee cannot be both management and union at the same time (although they can change status over time), the specialization is disjoint.

Rule 3 means that there is a partial specialization of VENDOR into SUPPLIER because only some vendors become suppliers. A supplier, not a vendor, has a contract number. Because there is only one subtype of VENDOR, there is no reason to specify a disjoint or overlap rule. Because all suppliers supply some raw material, the minimum cardinality next to RAW MATERIAL in the Supplies relationship (associative entity in Visio) now is one.

This example shows how an E-R diagram can be transformed into an EER diagram once generalization/specialization of entities is understood. Not only are supertype and subtype entities now in the data model, but additional attributes, including discriminating attributes, also are added, minimum cardinalities change (from optional to mandatory), and relationships move from the supertype to a subtype.

This is a good time to emphasize a point made earlier about data modeling. A data model is a conceptual picture of the data required by an organization. A data model does not map one-for-one to elements of an implemented database. For example, a database designer may choose to put all customer instances into one database table, not separate ones for each type of customer. Such details are not important now. The purpose now is to explain all the rules that govern data, not how data will be stored and accessed to achieve efficient, required information processing. We will address technology and efficiency issues in subsequent chapters when we cover database design and implementation.

Although the EER diagram in Figure 3-12 clarifies some questions and makes the data model in Figure 3-11 more explicit, it still can be difficult for some people to comprehend. Some people will not be interested in all types of data, and some may not need to see all the details in the EER diagram to understand what the database will cover. The next section addresses how we can simplify a complete and explicit data model for presentation to specific user groups and management.

ENTITY CLUSTERING

Some enterprise-wide information systems have more than 1,000 entity types and relationships. How do we present such an unwieldy picture of organizational data to developers and users? With a *really big* piece of paper? On the wrap-around walls of a large conference room? (Don't laugh about that one; we've seen it done!) Well, the answer is, we don't have to. In fact, there would be very few people who need to see the whole ERD in detail. If you are familiar with the principles of systems analysis and design (see, e.g., Hoffer et al., 2010), you know about the concept of functional decomposition. Briefly, functional decomposition is an iterative approach to breaking a system down into related components so that each component can be redesigned by itself without destroying the connections with other components. Functional decomposition is powerful because it makes redesign easier and allows people to focus attention on the part of the system in which they are interested. In data modeling, a similar approach is to create multiple, linked E-R diagrams, each showing the details of different (possibly overlapping) segments or subsets of the data model (e.g., different segments that apply to different departments, information system applications, business processes, or corporate divisions).

Entity cluster
A set of one or more entity types and associated relationships grouped into a single abstract entity type.

Entity clustering (Teorey, 1999) is a useful way to present a data model for a large and complex organization. An **entity cluster** is a set of one or more entity types and associated relationships grouped into a single abstract entity type. Because an entity cluster behaves like an entity type, entity clusters and entity types can be further grouped to form a higher-level entity cluster. Entity clustering is a hierarchical decomposition of a macro-level view of the data model into finer and finer views, eventually resulting in the full, detailed data model.

Figure 3-13 illustrates one possible result of entity clustering for the Pine Valley Furniture Company data model of Figure 3-12. Figure 3-13a shows the complete data

FIGURE 3-13 Entity clustering for Pine Valley Furniture Company
(a) Possible entity clusters (using Microsoft Visio)

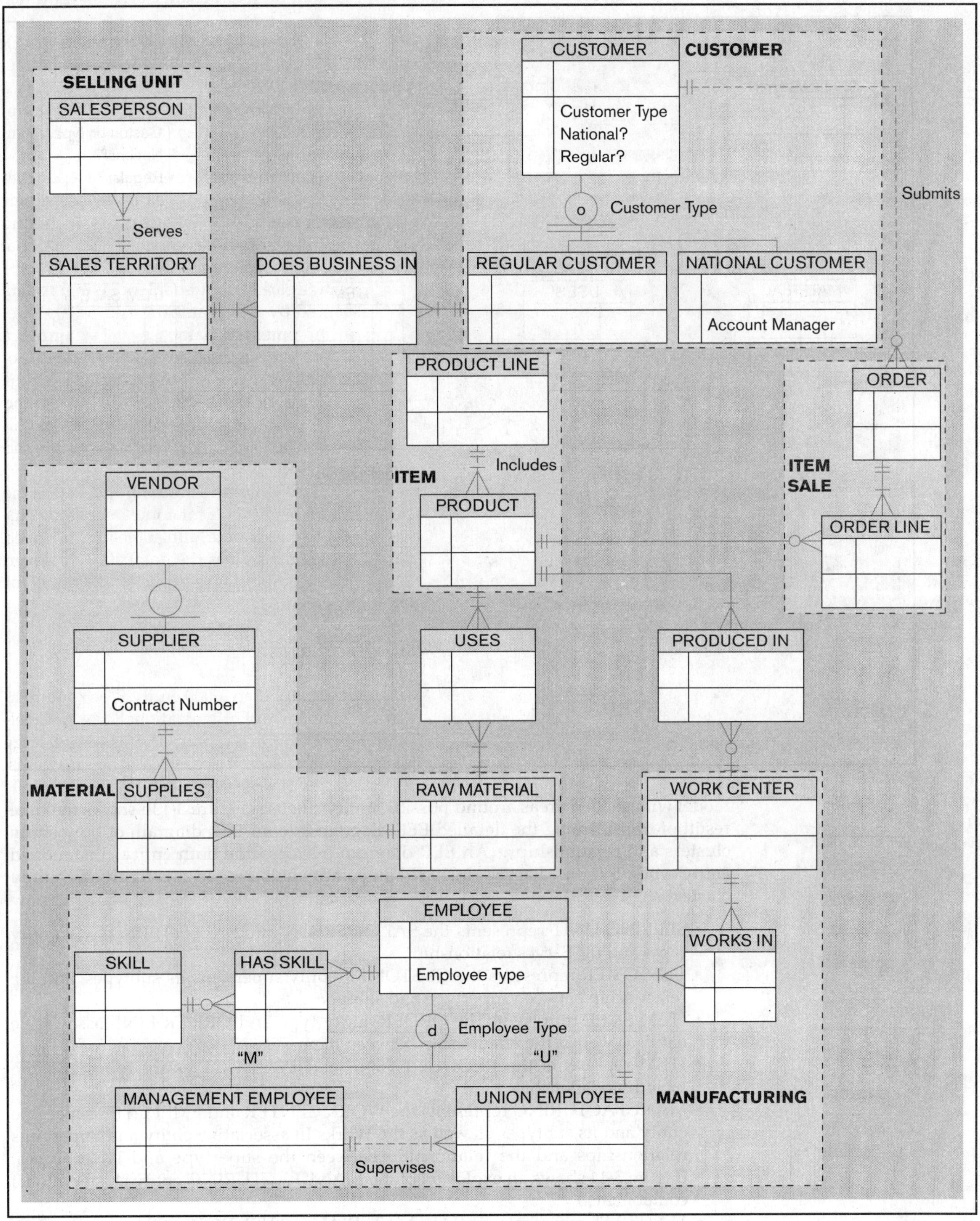

(continued)

FIGURE 3-13 *(continued)*
(b) EER diagram for entity clusters (using Microsoft Visio)

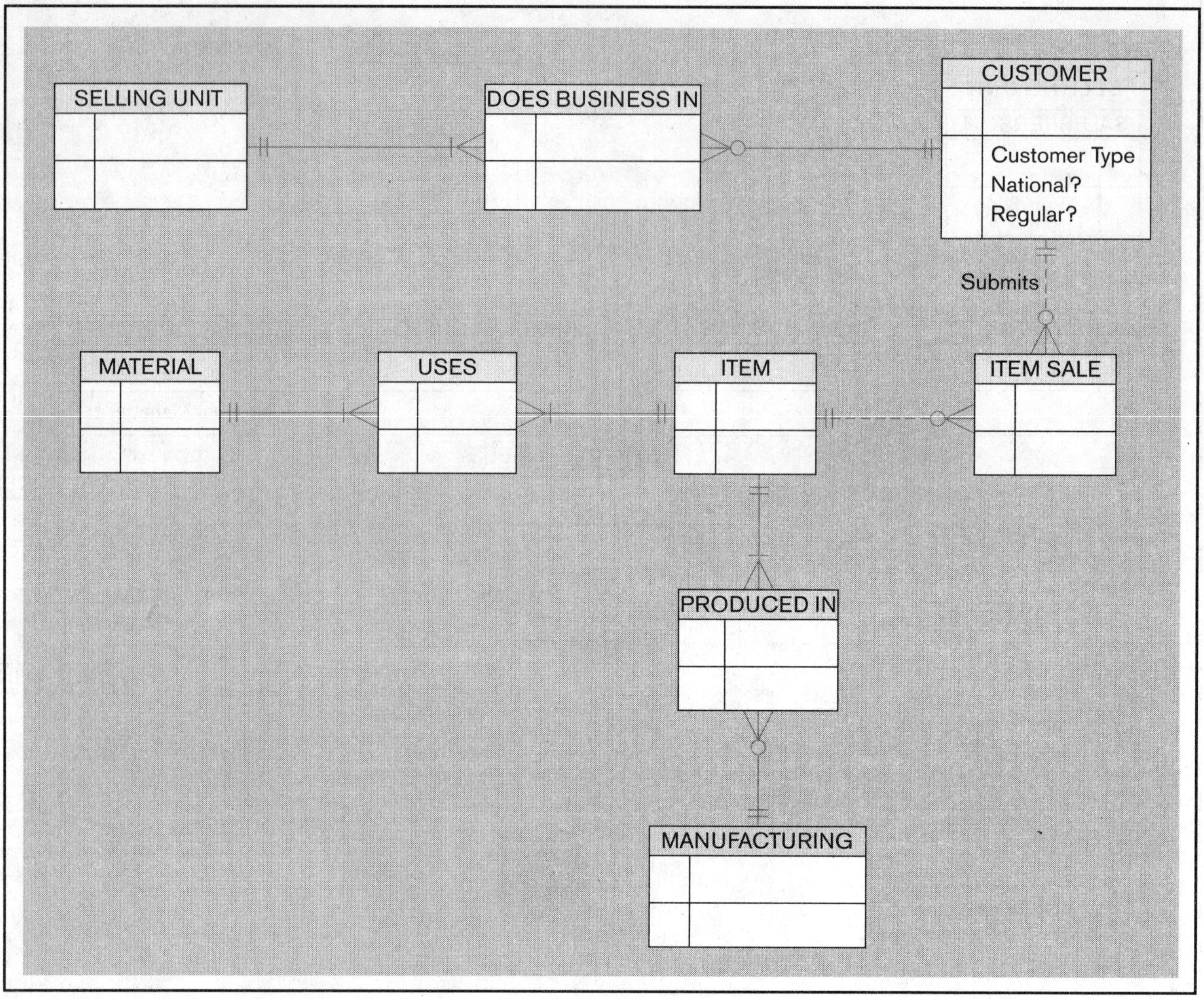

model with shaded areas around possible entity clusters; Figure 3-13b shows the final result of transforming the detailed EER diagram into an EER diagram of only entity clusters and relationships. (An EER diagram may include both entity clusters and entity types, but this diagram includes only entity clusters.) In this figure, the entity cluster

- SELLING UNIT represents the SALESPERSON and SALES TERRITORY entity types and the Serves relationship
- CUSTOMER represents the CUSTOMER entity supertype, its subtypes, and the relationship between supertype and subtypes
- ITEM SALE represents the ORDER entity type and ORDER LINE associative entity as well as the relationship between them
- ITEM represents the PRODUCT LINE and PRODUCT entity types and the Includes relationship
- MANUFACTURING represents the WORK CENTER and EMPLOYEE supertype entity and its subtypes as well as the Works In associative entity and Supervises relationships and the relationship between the supertype and its subtypes. (Figure 3-14 shows an explosion of the MANUFACTURING entity cluster into its components.)
- MATERIAL represents the RAW MATERIAL and VENDOR entity types, the SUPPLIER subtype, the Supplies associative entity, and the supertype/subtype relationship between VENDOR and SUPPLIER.

FIGURE 3-14 MANUFACTURING entity cluster

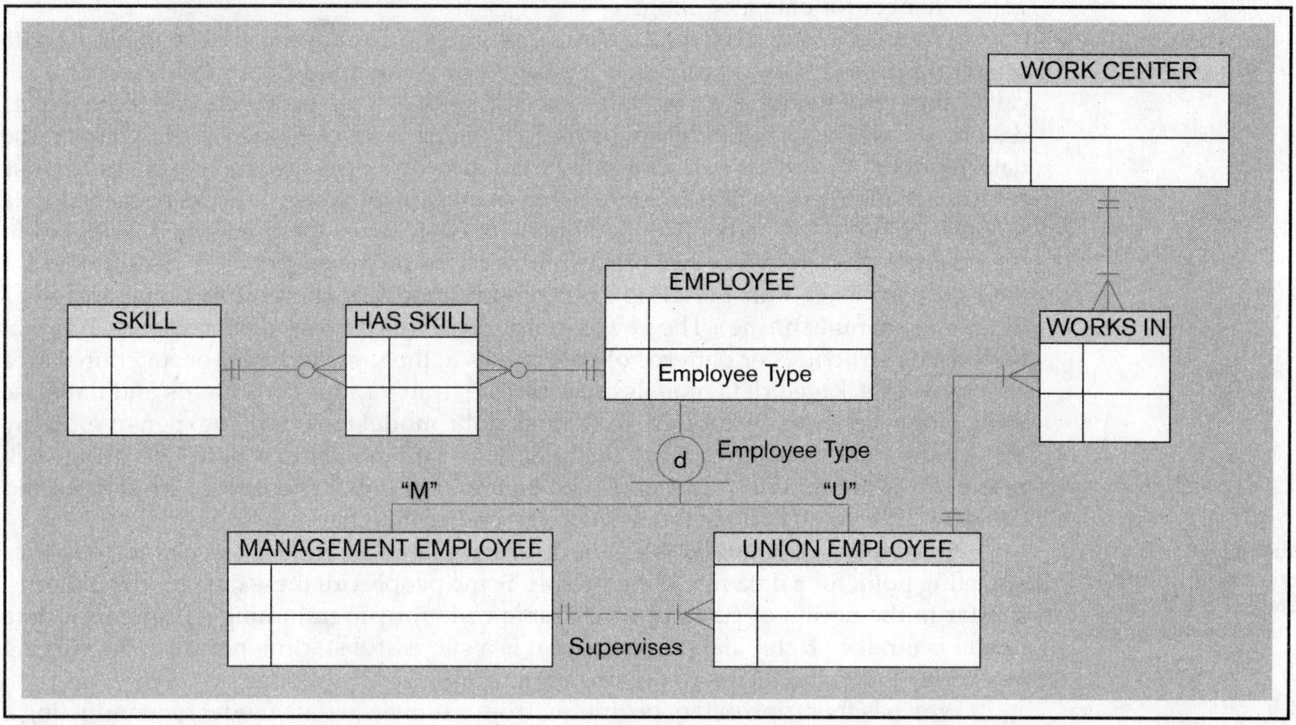

The E-R diagrams in Figures 3-13 and 3-14 can be used to explain details to people most concerned with assembly processes and the information needed to support this part of the business. For example, an inventory control manager can see in Figure 3-13b that the data about manufacturing can be related to item data (the Produced In relationship). Furthermore, Figure 3-14 shows what detail is kept about the production process involving work centers and employees. This person probably does not need to see the details about, for example, the selling structure, which is embedded in the SELLING UNIT entity cluster.

Entity clusters in Figure 3-13 were formed (1) by abstracting a supertype and its subtype (see the CUSTOMER entity cluster) and (2) by combining directly related entity types and their relationships (see the SELLING UNIT, ITEM, MATERIAL, and MANUFACTURING entity clusters). An entity cluster can also be formed by combining a strong entity and its associated weak entity types (not illustrated here). Because entity clustering is hierarchical, if it were desirable, we could draw another EER diagram in which we combine the SELLING UNIT and CUSTOMER entity clusters with the DOES BUSINESS IN associative entity one entity cluster, because these are directly related entity clusters.

An entity cluster should focus on an area of interest to some community of users, developers, or managers. Which entity types and relationships are grouped to form an entity cluster depends on your purpose. For example, the ORDER entity type could be grouped in with the CUSTOMER entity cluster and the ORDER LINE entity type could be grouped in with the ITEM entity cluster in the example of entity clustering for the Pine Valley Furniture data model. This regrouping would eliminate the ITEM SALE cluster, which might not be of interest to any group of people. Also, you can do several different entity clusterings of the full data model, each with a different focus.

PACKAGED DATA MODELS

According to Len Silverston (1998), "The age of the data modeler as artisan is passing. Organizations can no longer afford the labor or time required for handcrafting data models from scratch. In response to these constraints, the age of the data modeler as engineer is dawning." As one executive explained to us, "the acquisition of a [packaged data model] was one of the key strategic things his organization did to gain quick results and long-term success" for the business. Packaged data models are a game-changer for data modeling.

As introduced in Chapter 2, an increasingly popular approach of beginning a data modeling project is by acquiring a packaged or predefined data model, either a so-called universal model or an industry-specific model (some providers call these logical data models [LDMs], but these are really EER diagrams as explained in this chapter; the data model may also be part of a purchased software package, such as an enterprise resource planning or customer relationship management system). These packaged data models are not fixed, rather, the data modeler customizes the predefined model to fit the business rules of his or her organization based on a best-practices data model for their industry (e.g., transportation or communications) or chosen functional area (e.g., finance or manufacturing). The key assumption of this data modeling approach is that underlying structures or patterns of enterprises in the same industry or functional area are similar. Packaged data models are available from various consultants and database technology vendors. Although packaged data models are not inexpensive, many believe the total cost is lower and the quality of data modeling is better by using such resources. Some generic data models can be found in publications (e.g., see articles and books by Hay and by Silverston listed at the end of this chapter).

Universal data model
A generic or template data model that can be reused as a starting point for a data modeling project.

A **universal data model** is a generic or template data model that can be reused as a starting point for a data modeling project. Some people call these data model patterns, similar to the notion of patterns of reusable code for programming. A universal data model is not the "right" data model, but it is a successful starting point for developing an excellent data model for an organization.

Why has this approach of beginning from a universal data model for conducting a data modeling project become so popular? The following are some of the most compelling reasons professional data modelers are adopting this approach (we have developed this reasoning from Hoberman, 2006, and from an in-depth study we have conducted at the leading online retailer Overstock.com, which has adopted several packaged data models from Teradata Corporation):

- Data models can be developed using proven components evolved from cumulative experiences (as stated by the data administrator in the company we studied, "why reinvent when you can adapt?"). These data models are kept up-to-date by the provider as new kinds of data are recognized in an industry (e.g., RFID).
- Projects take less time and cost because the essential components and structures are already defined and only need to be quickly customized to the particular situation. The company we studied stated that the purchased data model was about 80 percent right before customization and that the cost of the package was about equal to the cost of one database modeler for one year.
- Data models are less likely to miss important components or make modeling errors due to not recognizing common possibilities. For example, the company we studied reported that their packaged data models helped them to avoid the temptation of simply mirroring existing databases, with all the historical "warts" of poor naming conventions, data structures customized for some historical purpose, and the inertia of succumbing to the pressure to simply duplicate the inadequate past practices. As another example, one vendor of packaged data models, Teradata, claims that one of its data models was scoped using more than 1,000 business questions and key performance indicators.
- Because of a holistic, enterprise view and development from best practices of data modeling experts found in a universal data model, the resulting data model for a particular enterprise tends to be easier to evolve as additional data requirements are identified for the given situation. A purchased model results in reduced rework in the future because the package gets it correct right out of the box and anticipates the future needs.
- The generic model provides a starting point for asking requirements questions so that most likely all areas of the model are addressed during requirements

determination. In fact, the company we studied said that their staff was "intrigued by all the possibilities" to meet even unspoken requirements from the capabilities of the prepackaged data models.

- Data models of an existing database are easier to read by data modelers and other data management professionals the first time because they are based on common components seen in similar situations.
- Extensive use of supertype/subtype hierarchies and other structures in universal data models promotes reusing data and taking a holistic, rather than narrow, view of data in an organization.
- Extensive use of many-to-many relationships and associative entities even where a data modeler might place a one-to-many relationship gives the data model greater flexibility to fit any situation, and naturally handles time stamping and retention of important history of relationships, which can be important to comply with regulations and financial record-keeping rules.
- Adaptation of a data model from your DBMS vendor usually means that your data model will easily work with other applications from this same vendor or their software partners.
- If multiple companies in the same industry use the same universal data model as the basis for their organizational databases, it may be easier to share data for interorganizational systems (e.g., reservation systems between rental car and airline firms).

A Revised Data Modeling Process with Packaged Data Models

Data modeling from a packaged data model requires no less skill than data modeling from scratch. Packaged data models are not going to put data modelers out of work (or keep you from getting that job as an entry-level data analyst you want now that you've started studying database management!). In fact, working with a package requires advanced skills, like those you are learning in this chapter and Chapter 2. As we will see, the packaged data models are rather complex because they are thorough and developed to cover all possible circumstances. A data modeler has to be very knowledgeable of the organization as well as the package to customize the package to fit the specific rules of that organization.

What do you get when you purchase a data model? What you are buying is metadata. You receive, usually on a CD, a fully populated description of the data model, usually specified in a structured data modeling tool, such as ERwin from Computer Associates or Oracle Designer from Oracle Corporation. The supplier of the data model has drawn the EER diagram, named and defined all the elements of the data model, and given all the attributes characteristics of data type (character, numeric, image), length, format, and so forth. You can print the data model and various reports about its contents to support the customization process. Once you customize the model, you can then use the data modeling tool to automatically generate the SQL commands to define the database to a variety of database management systems.

How is the data modeling process different when starting with a purchased solution? The following are the key differences (our understanding of these differences are enhanced by the interviews we conducted at Overstock.com):

- Because a purchased data model is extensive, you begin by identifying the parts of the data model that apply to your data modeling situation. Concentrate on these parts first and in the most detail. Start, as with most data modeling activities, first with entities, then attributes, and finally relationships. Consider how your organization will operate in the future, not just today.
- You then rename the identified data elements to terms local to the organization rather than the generic names used in the package.
- In many cases, the packaged data model will be used in new information systems that replace existing databases as well as to extend into new areas. So the next step is to map the data to be used from the package to data in current databases. One way this mapping will be used is to design migration plans to convert existing

databases to the new structures. The following are some key points about this mapping process:

- There will be data elements from the package that are not in current systems, and there will be some data elements in current databases not in the package. Thus, some elements won't map between the new and former environments. This is to be expected because the package anticipates information needs you have not, yet, satisfied by your current databases and because you do some special things in your organization that you want to retain but that are not standard practices. However, be sure that each non-mapped data element is really unique and needed. For example, it is possible that a data element in a current database may actually be derived from other more atomic data in the purchased data model. Also, you need to decide if data elements unique to the purchased data model are needed now or can be added on when you are ready to take advantage of these capabilities in the future.
- In general, the business rules embedded in the purchased data model cover all possible circumstances (e.g., the maximum number of customers associated with a customer order). The purchased data model allows for great flexibility, but a general-purpose business rule may be too weak for your situation (e.g., you are sure you will never allow more than one customer per customer order). As you will see in the next section, the flexibility and generalizability of a purchased data model results in complex relationships and many entity types. Although the purchased model alerts you to what is possible, you need to decide if you really need this flexibility and if the complexity is worthwhile.
- Because you are starting with a prototypical data model, it is possible to engage users and managers to be supported by the new database early and often in the data modeling project. Interviews, JAD sessions, and other requirements gathering activities are based on concrete ERDs rather than wish lists. The purchased data model essentially suggests specific questions to be asked or issues to discuss (e.g., "Would we ever have a customer order with more than one customer associated with it?" or "Might an employee also be a customer?"). The purchased model in a sense provides a visual checklist of items to discuss (e.g., Do we need these data? Is this business rule right for us?); further, it is comprehensive, so it is less likely that an important requirement will be missed.
- Because the purchased data model is comprehensive, there is no way you will be able to build and populate the full database or even customize the whole data model in one project. However, you don't want to miss the opportunity to visualize future requirements shown in the full data model. Thus, you will get to a point where you have to make a decision on what will be built first and possible future phases to build out as much of the purchased data model as will make sense. One approach to explaining the build-out schedule is to use entity clustering to show segments of the full data model that will be built in different phases. Future mini-projects will address detailed customization for new business needs and other segments of the data model not developed in the initial project.

You will learn in subsequent chapters of this book important database modeling and design concepts and skills that are important in any database development effort, including those based on purchased data models. There are, however, some important things to note about projects involving purchased data models. Some of these involve using existing databases to guide how to customize a purchased data model, including the following:

- Over time the same attribute may have been used for different purposes—what people call overloaded columns in current systems. This means that the data values in existing databases may not have uniform meaning for the migration to the new database. Oftentimes these multiple uses are not documented and are not known until the migration begins. Some data may no longer be needed (maybe used for a special business project), or there may be hidden requirements that were not formally incorporated into the database design. More on how to deal with this in a moment.

- Similarly, some attributes may be empty (i.e., have no values), at least for some periods of time. For example, some employee home addresses could be missing, or product engineering attributes for a given product line might be absent for products developed a few years ago. This could have occurred because of application software errors, human data entry mistakes, or other reasons. As we have studied, missing data may suggest optional data, and the need for entity subtypes. So missing data need to be studied to understand why the data are sparse.
- A good method for understanding hidden meaning and identifying inconsistencies in existing data models, and hence data and business rules that need to be included in the customized purchased data model, is data profiling. Profiling is a way to statistically analyze data to uncover hidden patterns and flaws. Profiling can find outliers, identify shifts in data distribution over time, and identify other phenomenon. Each perturbation of the distribution of data may tell a story, such as showing when major application system changes occurred, or when business rules changed. Often these patterns suggest poorly designed databases (e.g., data for separate entities were combined to improve processing speed for a special set of queries but the better structure was never restored). Data profiling can also be used to assess how accurate current data are and anticipate the clean-up effort that will be needed to populate the purchased data model with high-quality data.
- Arguably the most important challenge of customizing a purchased data model is determining the business rules that will be established through the data model. A purchased data model will anticipate the vast majority of the needed rules, but each rule must be verified for your organization. Fortunately, you don't have to guess which ones to address; each is laid out by the entities, attributes, and relationships with their metadata (names, definitions, data types, formats, lengths, etc.) in the purchased model. It simply takes time to go through each of these data elements with the right subject matter experts to make sure you have the relationship cardinalities and all other aspects of the data model right.

Packaged Data Model Examples

What, then, do packaged or universal data models look like? Central to the universal data model approach are supertype/subtype hierarchies. For example, a core structure of any universal data model is the entity type PARTY, which generalizes persons or organizations as actors for the enterprise, and an associated entity type PARTY ROLE, which generalizes various roles parties can play at different times. A PARTY ROLE instance is a situation in which a PARTY acts in a particular ROLE TYPE. These notions of PARTY, PARTY ROLE, and ROLE TYPE supertypes and their relationship are shown in Figure 3-15a. We use the supertype/subtype notation from Figure 3-1c because this is the notation most frequently used in publically available universal data models. (Most packaged data models are proprietary intellectual property of the vendor, and, hence, we cannot show them in this textbook.) This is a very generic data model (albeit simple to begin our discussion). This type of structure allows a specific party to serve in different roles during different time periods. It allows attribute values of a party to be "overridden" (if necessary in the organization) by values pertinent to the role being played during the given time period (e.g., although a PERSON of the PARTY supertype has a Current Last Name as of now, when in the party role of BILL TO CUSTOMER a different Current Last Name could apply during the particular time period [From Date to Thru Date] of that role). Note that even for this simple situation, the data model is trying to capture the most general circumstances. For example, an instance of the EMPLOYEE subtype of the PERSON ROLE subtype of PARTY ROLE would be associated with an instance of the ROLE TYPE that describes the employee-person role-party role. Thus, one description of a role type explains all the instances of the associated party roles of that role type.

An interesting aspect of Figure 3-15a is that PARTY ROLE actually simplifies what could be a more extensive set of subtypes of PARTY. Figure 3-15b shows one PARTY supertype with many subtypes covering many party roles. With partial specialization and overlap of subtypes, this alternative would appear to accomplish the same data

FIGURE 3-15 PARTY, PARTY ROLE, and ROLE TYPE in a universal data model

(a) Basic PARTY universal data model

(b) PARTY supertype/subtype hierarchy

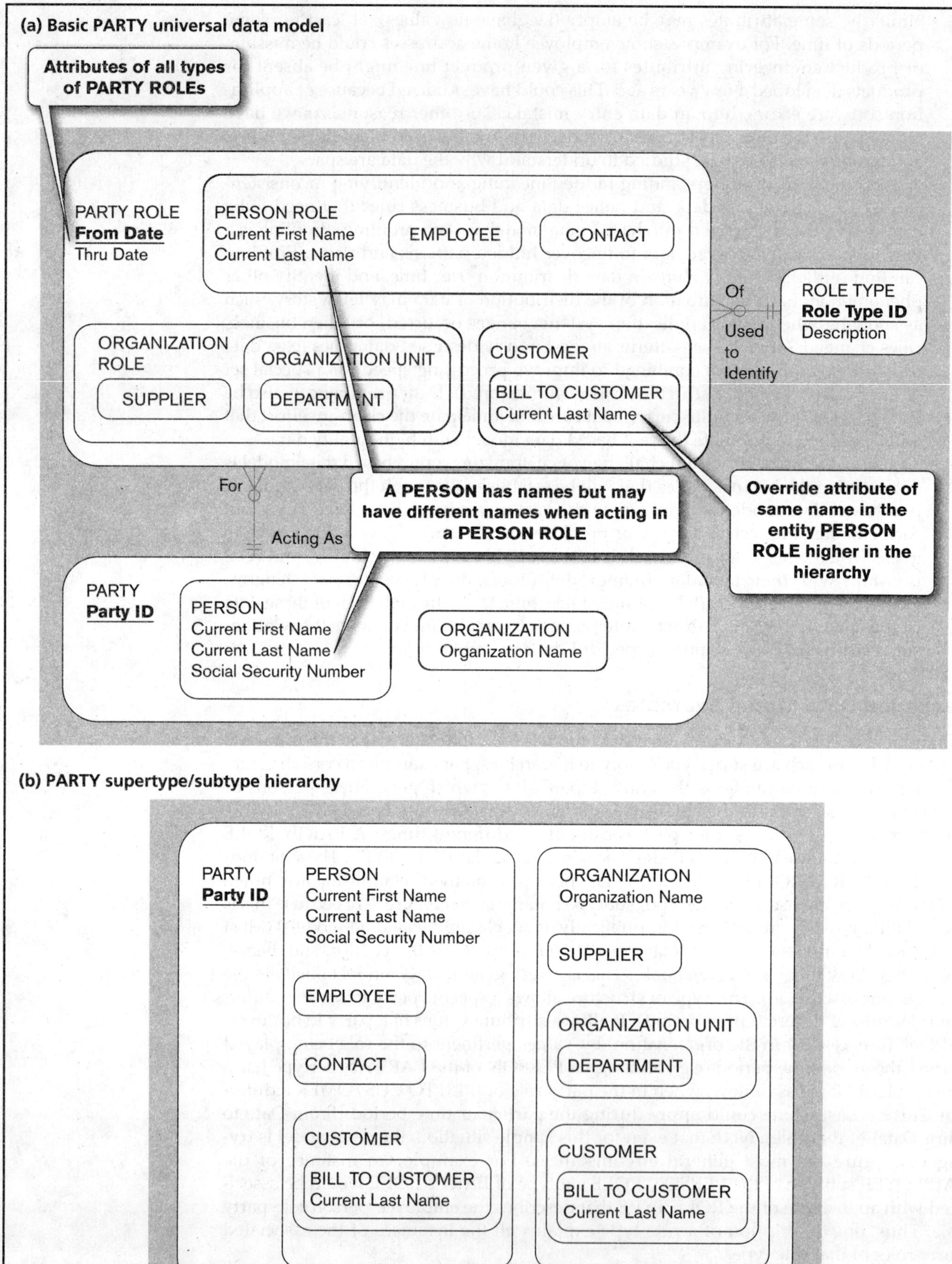

modeling semantics as Figure 3-15a. However, Figure 3-15a recognizes the important distinction between enterprise actors (PARTYs) and the roles each plays from time to time (PARTY ROLEs). Thus, the PARTY ROLE concept actually adds to the generalization of the data model and the universal applicability of the predefined data model.

The next basic construct of most universal data models is the representation of relationships between parties in the roles they play. Figure 3-16 shows this next extension of the basic universal data model. PARTY RELATIONSHIP is an associative entity, which hence allows any number of parties to be related as they play particular roles. Each instance of a relationship between PARTYs in PARTY ROLEs would be a separate instance of a PARTY RELATIONSHIP subtype. For example, consider the employment of a person by some organization unit during some time span, which over time is a many-to-many association. In this case, the EMPLOYMENT subtype of PARTY RELATIONSHIP would (for a given time period) likely link one PERSON playing the role of an EMPLOYEE subtype of PARTY ROLE with one ORGANIZATION ROLE playing some pertinent party role, such as ORGANIZATION UNIT. (That is, a person is

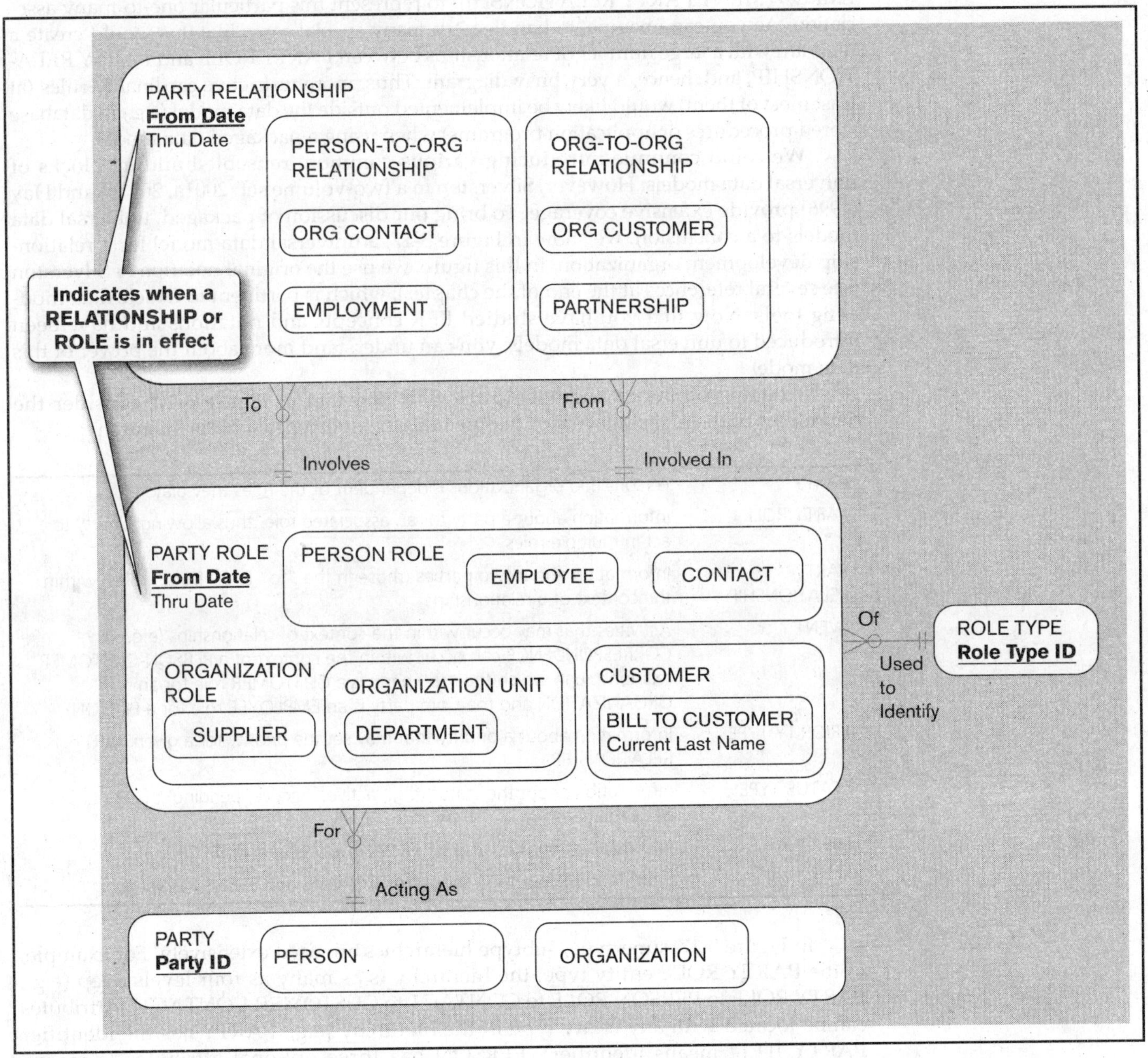

FIGURE 3-16 Extension of a universal data model to include PARTY RELATIONSHIPs

employed in an organization unit during a period of From Date to Thru Date in PARTY RELATIONSHIP.)

PARTY RELATIONSHIP is represented very generally, so it really is an associative entity for a unary relationship among PARTY ROLE instances. This makes for a very general, flexible pattern of relationships. What might be obscured, however, are which subtypes might be involved in a particular PARTY RELATIONSHIP, and stricter relationships that are not many-to-many, probably because we don't need to keep track of the relationship over time. For example, because the Involves and Involved In relationships link the PARTY ROLE and PARTY RELATIONSHIP supertypes, this does not restrict EMPLOYMENT to an EMPLOYEE with an ORGANIZATION UNIT. Also, if the enterprise needs to track only current employment associations, the data model in Figure 3-16 will not enforce that a PERSON PARTY in an EMPLOYEE PARTY ROLE can be associated with only one ORGANIZATION UNIT at a time. We will see in the next section how we can include additional business rule notation on an EER diagram to make this specific. Alternatively, we could draw specific relationships from just the EMPLOYEE PARTY ROLE and the ORGANIZATION UNIT PARTY ROLE to the EMPLOYMENT PARTY RELATIONSHIP to represent this particular one-to-many association. As you can imagine, to handle very many special cases like this would create a diagram with a large number of relationships between PARTY ROLE and PARTY RELATIONSHIP, and, hence, a very busy diagram. Thus, more restrictive cardinality rules (at least most of them) would likely be implemented outside the data model (e.g., in database stored procedures or application programs) when using a packaged data model.

We could continue introducing various common, reusable building blocks of universal data models. However, Silverston in a two-volume set (2001a, 2001b) and Hay (1996) provide extensive coverage. To bring our discussion of packaged, universal data models to a conclusion, we show in Figure 3-17, a universal data model for a relationship development organization. In this figure, we use the original notation of Silverston (see several references at the end of the chapter), which is pertinent to Oracle data modeling tools. Now that you have studied EER concepts and notations and have been introduced to universal data models, you can understand more about the power of this data model.

To help you better understand the EER diagram in Figure 3-17, consider the definitions of the highest-level entity type in each supertype/subtype hierarchy:

PARTY	Persons and organizations independent of the roles they play
PARTY ROLE	Information about a party for an associated role, thus allowing a party to act in multiple roles
PARTY RELATIONSHIP	Information about two parties (those in the "to" and "from" roles) within the context of a relationship
EVENT	Activities that may occur within the context of relationships (e.g., a CORRESPONDENCE can occur within the context of a PERSON-CUSTOMER relationship in which the "to" party is a CUSTOMER role for an ORGANIZATION and the from party is an EMPLOYEE role for a PERSON)
PRIORITY TYPE	Information about a priority that may set the priority for a given PARTY RELATIONSHIP
STATUS TYPE	Information about the status (e.g., active, inactive, pending) of events or party relationships
EVENT ROLE	Information about all of the PARTYs involved in an EVENT
ROLE TYPE	Information about the various PARTY ROLEs and EVENT ROLEs

In Figure 3-17, supertype/subtype hierarchies are used extensively. For example, in the PARTY ROLE entity type, the hierarchy is as many as four levels deep (e.g., PARTY ROLE to PERSON ROLE to CONTACT to CUSTOMER CONTACT). Attributes can be located with any entity type in the hierarchy [e.g., PARTY has the identifier PARTY ID (# means identifier), PERSON has three optional attributes (*o* means optional), and ORGANIZATION has a required attribute (* means required)].

FIGURE 3-17 A universal data model for relationship development

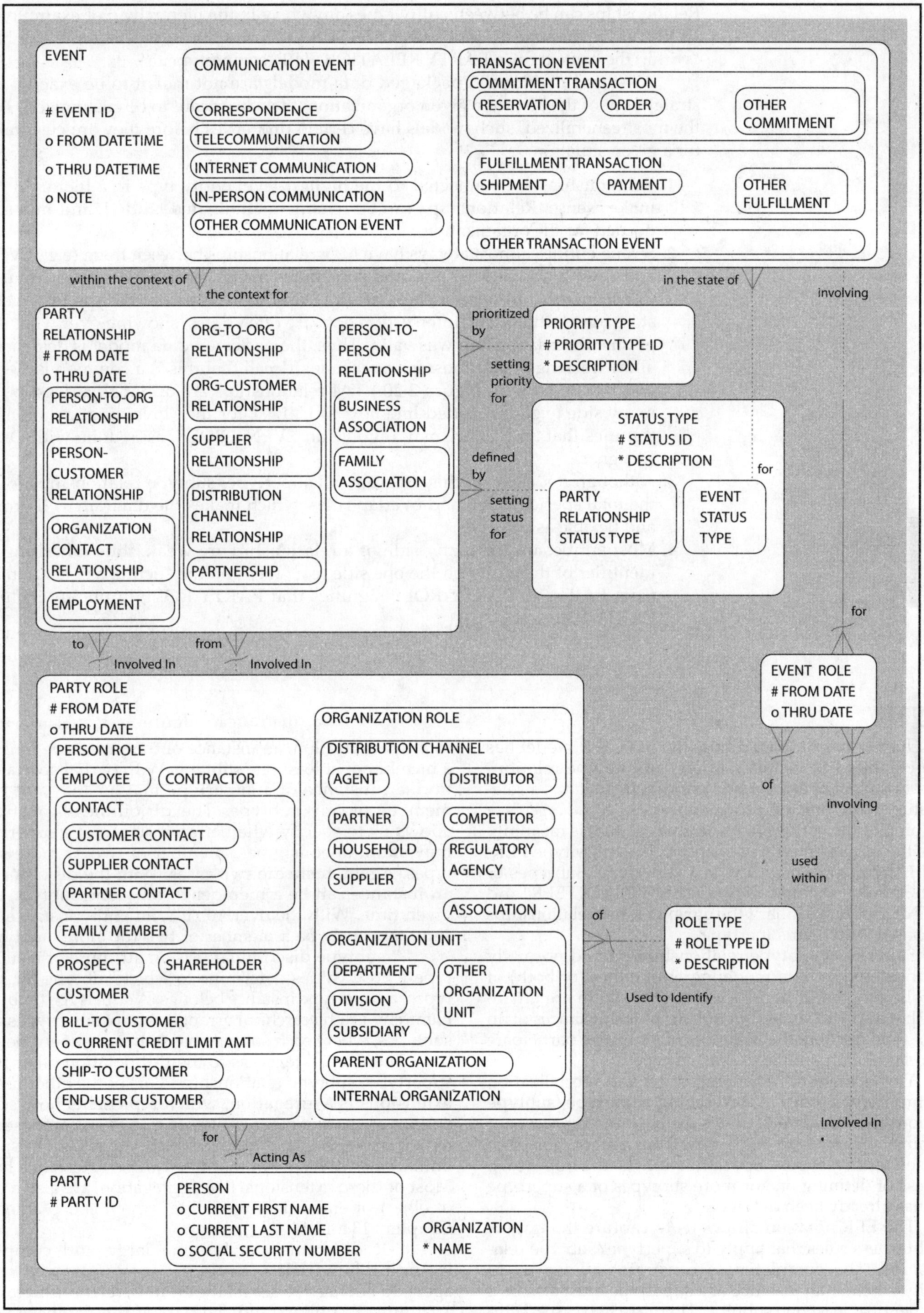

Relationships can be between entity types anywhere in the hierarchy. For example, any EVENT is "in the state of" an EVENT STATUS TYPE, a subtype, whereas any EVENT is "within the context of" a PARTY RELATIONSHIP, a supertype.

As stated previously, packaged data models are not meant to be exactly right straight out of the box for a given organization; they are meant to be customized. To be the most generalized, such models have certain properties before they are customized for a given situation:

1. Relationships are connected to the highest-level entity type in a hierarchy that makes sense. Relationships can be renamed, eliminated, added, and moved as needed for the organization.
2. Strong entities almost always have *M:N* relationships between them (e.g., EVENT and PARTY), so at least one, and sometimes many, associative entities are used. Consequently, all relationships are 1:*M*, and there is an entity type in which to store intersection data. Intersection data are often dates, showing over what span of time the relationship was valid. Thus, the packaged data model is designed to allow tracking of relationships over time. (Recall that this is a common issue that was discussed with Figure 2-20.) 1:*M* relationships are optional, at least on the many side (e.g., the dotted line next to EVENT for the "involving" relationship signifies that an EVENT may involve an EVENT ROLE, as is done with Oracle Designer).
3. Although not clear on this diagram, all supertype/subtype relationships follow the total specialization and overlap rules, which makes the diagram as thorough and flexible as possible.
4. Most entities on the many side of a relationship are weak, thus inheriting the identifier of the entity on the one side (e.g., the ~ on the "acting as" relationship from PARTY to PARTY ROLE signifies that PARTY ROLE implicitly includes PARTY ID).

Summary

This chapter has described how the basic E-R model has been extended to include supertype/subtype relationships. A *supertype* is a generic entity type that has a relationship with one or more subtypes. A *subtype* is a grouping of the entities in an entity type that is meaningful to the organization. For example, the entity type PERSON is frequently modeled as a supertype. Subtypes of PERSON may include EMPLOYEE, VOLUNTEER, and CLIENT. Subtypes inherit the attributes and relationships associated with their supertype.

Supertype/subtype relationships should normally be considered in data modeling with either (or both) of the following conditions present: First, there are attributes that apply to some (but not all) of the instances of an entity type. Second, the instances of a subtype participate in a relationship unique to that subtype.

The techniques of generalization and specialization are important guides in developing supertype/subtype relationships. Generalization is the bottom-up process of defining a generalized entity type from a set of more specialized entity types. Specialization is the top-down process of defining one or more subtypes of a supertype that has already been defined.

The EER notation allows us to capture the important business rules that apply to supertype/subtype relationships. The completeness constraint allows us to specify whether an instance of a supertype must also be a member of at least one subtype. There are two cases: With total specialization, an instance of the supertype must be a member of at least one subtype. With partial specialization, an instance of a supertype may or may not be a member of any subtype. The disjointness constraint allows us to specify whether an instance of a supertype may simultaneously be a member of two or more subtypes. Again, there are two cases. With the disjoint rule, an instance can be a member of only one subtype at a given time. With the overlap rule, an entity instance can simultaneously be a member of two (or more) subtypes.

A subtype discriminator is an attribute of a supertype whose values determine to which subtype (or subtypes) a supertype instance belongs. A supertype/subtype hierarchy is a hierarchical arrangement of supertypes and subtypes, where each subtype has only one supertype.

There are extensions to the E-R notation other than supertype/subtype relationships. One of the other useful extensions is aggregation, which represents how some entities are part of other entities (e.g., a PC is composed of a disk drive, RAM, a motherboard, etc.). Due to space limitations we have not discussed these extensions here. Most of these extensions, like aggregation, are also a part of object-oriented data modeling, which is explained in Chapters 13 and 14.

E-R diagrams can become large and complex, including hundreds of entities. Many users and managers do not need to see all the entities, relationships, and attributes to understand the part of the database with which they are most interested. Entity clustering is a way to turn a part of an entity-relationship data model into a more macro-level view of the same data. An entity cluster is a set of one or more entity types and associated relationships grouped into a single abstract entity type. Several entity clusters and associated relationships can be further grouped into even a higher entity cluster, so entity clustering is a hierarchical decomposition technique. By grouping entities and relationships, you can lay out an E-R diagram to allow you to give attention to the details of the model that matter most in a given data modeling task.

Packaged data models, so called universal and industry-specific data models, extensively utilize EER features. These generalizable data models often use multiple level supertype/subtype hierarchies and associative entities. Subjects and the roles subjects play are separated, creating many entity types; this complexity can be simplified when customized for a given organization, and entity clusters can be used to present simpler views of the data model to different audiences.

The use of packaged data models can save considerable time and cost in data modeling. The skills required for a data modeling project with a packaged data model are quite advanced and are built on the data modeling principles covered in this text. You have to consider not only current needs but also future requirements to customize the general-purpose package. Data elements must be renamed to local terms, and current data need to be mapped to the target database design. This mapping can be challenging due to various forms of mismatches between the data in current databases with those found in the best-practices purchased database model. Fortunately, having actual data models "right out of the box" helps to structure the customization process for completeness and ease of communication with subject matter experts. Overloaded columns, poor metadata, and abuses of the structure of current databases can make the customization and migration processes challenging. Data profiling can be used to understand the current data and uncover hidden meanings and business rules in data for your organization.

Chapter Review

Key Terms

Attribute inheritance *117*
Completeness constraint *121*
Disjoint rule *122*
Disjointness constraint *122*
Enhanced entity-relationship (EER) model *113*
Entity cluster *130*
Generalization *118*
Overlap rule *123*
Partial specialization rule *121*
Specialization *119*
Subtype *114*
Subtype discriminator *123*
Supertype *114*
Supertype/subtype hierarchy *125*
Total specialization rule *121*
Universal data model *134*

Review Questions

1. Define each of the following terms:
   a. supertype
   b. subtype
   c. specialization
   d. entity cluster
   e. completeness constraint
   f. enhanced entity-relationship (EER) model
   g. subtype discriminator
   h. total specialization rule
   i. generalization
   j. disjoint rule
   k. overlap rule
   l. partial specialization rule
   m. universal data model
2. Match the following terms and definitions:

____ supertype	a. subset of supertype
____ entity cluster	b. entity belongs to two subtypes
____ subtype	c. subtype gets supertype attributes
____ specialization	d. generalized entity type
____ subtype discriminator	e. creating subtypes for an entity type
____ attribute inheritance	f. a group of associated entity types and relationships
____ overlap rule	g. locates target subtype for an entity

3. Contrast the following terms:
   a. supertype; subtype
   b. generalization; specialization
   c. disjoint rule; overlap rule
   d. total specialization rule; partial specialization rule
   e. PARTY; PARTY ROLE
   f. entity; entity cluster
4. State two conditions that indicate when a database designer should consider using supertype/subtype relationships.
5. State the reason for entity clustering.
6. Give an example (other than those discussed in the chapter) of a supertype/subtype relationship.
7. What is attribute inheritance? Why is it important?
8. Give an example of each of the following:
   a. a supertype/subtype relationship where the disjoint rule applies
   b. a supertype/subtype relationship where the overlap rule applies
9. What types of business rules are normally captured in an EER diagram?
10. What is the purpose of a subtype discriminator?
11. When would a packaged data model be useful?
12. In what ways is starting a data modeling project with a packaged data model different from starting a data modeling project with a clean sheet of paper?

13. How can data profiling be used during a data modeling project, especially one using a packaged data model?
14. Does a data modeling project using a packaged data model require less or greater skill than a project not using a packaged data model? Why or why not?
15. What do you purchase when you acquire a packaged data model?
16. When might a supertype/subtype hierarchy be useful?
17. When is a member of a supertype always a member of at least one subtype?
18. What is attribute inheritance? How does this affect a subtype?
19. What conditions govern the usage of supertype/subtype relationships? Name and explain in brief the processes that aid in the development of these relationships?
20. Discuss the role of constraints on supertype/subtype relationships. What are the different types of business rules and how do they differ from each other? Explain the various types of action assertions and their classification.

Problems and Exercises

1. Examine the hierarchy for the university EER diagram (Figure 3-10). As a student, you are an instance of one of the subtypes: either UNDERGRAD STUDENT or GRADUATE STUDENT. List the names of all the attributes that apply to you. For each attribute, record the data value that applies to you.
2. Add a subtype discriminator for each of the supertypes shown in Figure 3-10. Show the discriminator values that assign instances to each subtype. Use the following subtype discriminator names and values:
   a. PERSON: Person Type (Employee? Alumnus? Student?)
   b. EMPLOYEE: Employee Type (Faculty, Staff)
   c. STUDENT: Student Type (Grad, Undergrad)
3. For simplicity, subtype discriminators were left off many figures in this chapter. Add subtype discriminator notation in each figure listed below. If necessary, create a new attribute for the discriminator.
   a. Figure 3-2
   b. Figure 3-3
   c. Figure 3-4b
   d. Figure 3-7a
   e. Figure 3-7b
4. Refer to the employee EER diagram in Figure 3-2. Make any assumptions that you believe are necessary. Develop a sample definition for each entity type, attribute, and relationship in the diagram.
5. Refer to the EER diagram for patients in Figure 3-3. Make any assumptions you believe are necessary. Develop sample definitions for each entity type, attribute, and relationship in the diagram.
6. Figure 3-13 shows the development of entity clusters for the Pine Valley Furniture E-R diagram. In Figure 3-13b, explain the following:
   a. Why is the minimum cardinality next to the DOES BUSINESS IN associative entity coming from CUSTOMER zero?
   b. What would be the attributes of ITEM (refer to Figure 2-22)?
   c. What would be the attributes of MATERIAL (refer to Figure 2-22)?
7. A rental car agency classifies the vehicles it rents into four categories: compact, midsize, full-size, and sport utility. The agency wants to record the following data for all vehicles: Vehicle ID, Make, Model, Year, and Color. There are no unique attributes for any of the four classes of vehicle. The entity type vehicle has a relationship (named Rents) with a customer entity type. None of the four vehicle classes has a unique relationship with an entity type. Would you consider creating a supertype/subtype relationship for this problem? Why or why not?
8. At a weekend retreat, the entity type PERSON has three subtypes: CAMPER, BIKER, and RUNNER. Draw a separate EER diagram segment for each of the following situations:
   a. At a given time, a person must be exactly one of these subtypes.
   b. A person may or may not be one of these subtypes. However, a person who is one of these subtypes cannot at the same time be one of the other subtypes.
   c. A person may or may not be one of these subtypes. On the other hand, a person may be any two (or even three) of these subtypes at the same time.
   d. At a given time, a person must be at least one of these subtypes.
9. A bank has three types of accounts: checking, savings, and loan. Following are the attributes for each type of account:
   CHECKING: Acct No, Date Opened, Balance, Service Charge
   SAVINGS: Acct No, Date Opened, Balance, Interest Rate
   LOAN: Acct No, Date Opened, Balance, Interest Rate, Payment

   Assume that each bank account must be a member of exactly one of these subtypes. Using generalization, develop an EER model segment to represent this situation using the traditional EER notation, the Visio notation, or the subtypes inside supertypes notation, as specified by your instructor. Remember to include a subtype discriminator.
10. Refer to your answer to Problem and Exercise 20 in Chapter 2. Develop entity clusters for this E-R diagram and redraw the diagram using the entity clusters. Explain why you chose the entity clusters you used.
11. Refer to your answer to Problem and Exercise 23 in Chapter 2. Develop entity clusters for this E-R diagram and redraw the diagram using the entity clusters. Explain why you chose the entity clusters you used.
12. Draw an EER diagram for the following problem using this textbook's EER notation, the Visio notation, or the subtypes inside supertypes notation, as specified by your instructor.

    A nonprofit organization depends on a number of different types of persons for its successful operation. The organization is interested in the following attributes for all of these persons: SSN, Name, Address, City/State/Zip, and Telephone. Three types of persons are of greatest interest: employees, volunteers, and donors. Employees have only a Date Hired attribute, and volunteers have only a Skill attribute. Donors have only a relationship (named Donates) with an Item entity type. A donor must have donated one or more items, and an item may have no donors, or one or more donors.

There are persons other than employees, volunteers, and donors who are of interest to the organization, so that a person need not belong to any of these three groups. On the other hand, at a given time a person may belong to two or more of these groups (e.g., employee and donor).

13. Add a subtype discriminator (named Person Type) to the diagram you created in Problem and Exercise 12.

14. Develop an EER model for the following situation, using the traditional EER notation, the Visio notation, or the subtypes inside supertypes notation, as specified by your instructor:

A person may be employed by one or more organizations, and each organization may be the employer of one or more persons. An organization can be an internal organizational unit or an external organization. For persons and organizations, we want to know their ID, name, address, and phone number. For persons, we want to know their birth date, and for organizations, we want to know their budget number. For each employment, we want to know the employment date, termination date, and bonus.

Employment of a person by an organization may result in the person holding many positions over time. For each position, we want to know its title, and each time someone holds that position, we need to know the start date and termination date and salary. An organization is responsible for each position. It is possible for a person to be employed by one organization and hold a position for which another organization is responsible.

15. Draw an EER diagram for the following description of a law firm:

Each case handled by the firm has a unique case number; a date opened, date closed, and judgment description are also kept on each case. A case is brought by one or more plaintiffs, and the same plaintiff may be involved in many cases. A plaintiff has a requested judgment characteristic. A case is against one or more defendants and the same defendant may be involved in many cases. A plaintiff or defendant may be a person or an organization. Over time, the same person or organization may be a defendant or a plaintiff in cases. In either situation, such legal entities are identified by an entity number, and other attributes are name and net worth.

16. Develop an EER model for the following situation using the traditional EER notation, the Visio notation, or the subtypes inside supertypes notation, as specified by your instructor:

An international school of technology has hired you to create a database management system to assist in scheduling classes. After several interviews with the president, you have come up with the following list of entities, attributes, and initial business rules:

- Room is identified by Building ID and Room No and also has a Capacity. A room can be either a lab or a classroom. If it is a classroom, it has an additional attribute called Board Type.
- Media is identified by MType ID and has attributes of Media Type and Type Description. Note: Here we are tracking type of media (such as a VCR, projector, etc.), not the individual piece of equipment. Tracking of equipment is outside of the scope of this project.
- Computer is identified by CType ID and has attributes Computer Type, Type Description, Disk Capacity, and Processor Speed. Please note: As with Media Type, we are tracking only the type of computer, not an individual computer. You can think of this as a class of computers (e.g., PIII 900MHZ).
- Instructor has identifier Emp ID and has attributes Name, Rank, and Office Phone.
- Timeslot has identifier TSIS and has attributes Day Of Week, Start Time, and End Time.
- Course has identifier Course ID and has attributes Course Description and Credits. Courses can have one, none, or many prerequisites. Courses also have one or more sections.
- Section has identifier Section ID and attribute Enrollment Limit.

After some further discussions, you have come up with some additional business rules to help you create the initial design:

- An instructor teaches one, none, or many sections of a course in a given semester.
- An instructor specifies preferred time slots.
- Scheduling data are kept for each semester, uniquely identified by semester and year.
- A room can be scheduled for one section or no section during one time slot in a given semester of a given year. However, one room can participate in many schedules, one schedule, or no schedules; one time slot can participate in many schedules, one schedule, or no schedules; one section can participate in many schedules, one schedule, or no schedules. Hint: Can you associate this to anything that you have seen before?
- A room can have one type of media, several types of media, or no media.
- Instructors are trained to use one, none, or many types of media.
- A lab has one or more computer types. However, a classroom does not have any computers.
- A room cannot be both a classroom and a lab. There also are no other room types to be incorporated into the system.

17. Develop an EER model for the following situation using the traditional EER notation, the Visio notation, or the subtypes inside supertypes notation, as specified by your instructor:

Wally Los Gatos and his partner Henry Chordate have formed a new limited partnership, Fin and Finicky Security Consultants. Fin and Finicky consults with corporations to determine their security needs. You have been hired by Wally and Henry to design a database management system to help them manage their business.

Due to a recent increase in business, Fin and Finicky has decided to automate their client tracking system. You and your team have done a preliminary analysis and come up with the following set of entities, attributes, and business rules:

Consultant

There are two types of consultants: business consultants and technical consultants. Business consultants are contacted by a business in order to first determine security needs and provide an estimate for the actual services to be performed. Technical consultants perform services according to the specifications developed by the business consultants.

Attributes of business consultant are the following: Employee ID (identifier), Name, Address (which is composed of Street, City, State, and Zip Code), Telephone, Date Of Birth, Age, Business Experience (which is composed of Number of Years, Type of Business [or businesses], and Degrees Received).

Attributes of technical consultant are the following: Employee ID (identifier), Name, Address (which is composed of Street, City, State, and Zip Code), Telephone, Date Of Birth, Age, Technical Skills, and Degrees Received.

Customer

Customers are businesses that have asked for consulting services. Attributes of customer are Customer ID (identifier), Company Name, Address (which is composed of Street, City, State, and Zip Code), Contact Name, Contact Title, Contact Telephone, Business Type, and Number Of Employees.

Location

Customers can have multiple locations. Attributes of location are Customer ID (identifier), Location ID (which is unique only for each Customer ID), Address (which is composed of Street, City, State, and Zip Code), Telephone, and Building Size.

Service

A security service is performed for a customer at one or more locations. Before services are performed, an estimate is prepared. Attributes of service are Service ID (identifier), Description, Cost, Coverage, and Clearance Required.

Additional Business Rules

In addition to the entities outlined previously, the following information will need to be stored to tables and should be shown in the model. These may be entities, but they also reflect a relationship between more than one entity:

- Estimates, which have characteristics of Date, Amount, Business Consultant, Services, and Customer
- Services Performed, which have characteristics of Date, Amount, Technical Consultant, Services, and Customer

In order to construct the EER diagram, you may assume the following:

A customer can have many consultants providing many services. You wish to track both actual services performed as well as services offered. Therefore, there should be two relationships between customer, service, and consultant, one to show services performed and one to show services offered as part of the estimate.

18. Based on the EER diagram constructed for Problem and Exercise 17, develop a sample definition for each entity type, attribute, and relationship in the diagram.

19. You are working for a large country club. This country club wants to keep a database on its members and their guests. For each member, the club keeps mail and telephone contact information, name, and membership number. When you join this club, you can join as a social member (which allows you two rounds of golf a year as well as privileges to the swimming pool and weight room), a tennis member (which allows you all the privileges of a social member as well as use of the tennis courts and four rounds of golf), or a golfing member (which allows you all the privileges of a tennis member and unlimited use of the golf course). This database needs to track how often a member (who has limited use of the golf course; all golfing members have unlimited use of the golf course) has used the golf course, and how many guests any and each member has brought to the club. All members have guest privileges. The club also wants to attract new members by mailing to all those who came to the club as guests and live in the state. The mailing includes information about their visits (i.e., date of visit and which member was their host for each visit). Once a person becomes a member of any type, information about them as guests is no longer important to retain. Develop an EER diagram for this situation.

20. Draw an EER diagram for the following situation:

TomKat Entertainment is a chain of theaters owned by former husband and wife actors/entertainers who, for some reason, can't get a job performing anymore. The owners want a database to track what is playing or has played on each screen in each theater of their chain at different times of the day. A theater (identified by a Theater ID and described by a theater name and location) contains one or more screens for viewing various movies. Within each theater each screen is identified by its number and is described by the seating capacity for viewing the screen. Movies are scheduled for showing in time slots each day. Each screen can have different time slots on different days (i.e., not all screens in the same theater have movies starting at the same time, and even on different days the same movie may play at different times on the same screen). For each time slot, the owners also want to know the end time of the time slot (assume all slots end on the same day the slot begins), attendance during that time slot, and the price charged for attendance in that time slot. Each movie (which can be either a trailer, feature, or commercial) is identified by a Movie ID and further described by its title, duration, and type (i.e., trailer, feature, or commercial). In each time slot, one or more movies are shown. The owners want to also keep track of in what sequence the movies are shown (e.g., in a time slot there might be two trailers, followed by two commercials, followed by a feature film, and closed with another commercial).

21. Add the following to Figure 3-16: an EMPLOYMENT party relationship is further explained by the positions and assignments to positions during the time a person is employed. A position is defined by an organization unit, and a unit may define many positions over time. Over time, positions are assigned to various employment relationships (i.e., somebody employed by some organization unit is assigned a particular position). For example, a position of Business Analyst is defined by the Systems Development organization unit. Carl Gerber, while employed by the Data Warehousing organization unit, is assigned the position of Systems Analyst. In the spirit of universal data modeling, enhance Figure 3-16 for the most general case consistent with this description.
22. Develop an EER model for the following situation. Identity which of these statements are attributes, entities, and business rules:

    A B-school offers elective courses to its students in their second year. After talking to the PGP Chairperson, the following are the basic list of entities, attributes, and business rules identified:

    - The elective courses are made available in respective areas such as marketing, HR, systems, finance, operations. In future, newer areas could be added depending on the academic council decisions. The elective courses could be of 1, 2, or 3 credits. Each credit entails 10 hours of contact sessions.
    - The second year has three terms of 3 months each.
    - Students have a cap on the number of credits they can opt for in each term.
    - Also, the total number of credits for all the terms put together should not exceed a particular number.
    - Students specialize in a particular area on the basis of a predetermined number of credits opted in that area.
    - Course has course code as identifier and attributes such as its title, evaluation components, the number of credits, the faculty delivering the course, and course description.
    - Student has roll number as identifier and has attributes such as name, courses opted, total credits, credits in each term, and specialization area on the basis of the course credits opted in the area.

Field Exercises

1. Interview a friend or family member to elicit common examples of supertype/subtype relationships they may come into contact with at work. You will have to explain the meaning of this term to the person you are interviewing and provide a common example, such as PROPERTY: RESIDENTIAL, COMMERCIAL or BONDS: CORPORATE, MUNICIPAL. Use the information the person provides to construct an EER diagram segment and present it to the person. Revise, if necessary, until it seems appropriate to you and your friend or family member.
2. Visit two local small businesses, one in the service sector and one in manufacturing. Interview employees from these organizations to obtain examples of both supertype/subtype relationships and business rules (such as "A customer can return merchandise only with a valid sales slip"). In which of these environments is it easier to find examples of these constructs? Why?
3. Ask a database administrator or database or system analyst in a local company to show you an EER (or E-R) diagram for one of the organization's primary databases. Does this organization model have supertype/subtype relationships? If so, what notation is used, and does the CASE tool the company uses support these relationships? Also, what types of business rules are included during the EER modeling phase? How are business rules represented, and how and where are they stored?
4. Read the summary of business rules published by the GUIDE Business Rules Project (1997) and the article by Gottesdiener (1997). Search the Web for additional information on business rules. Then write a three-page executive summary of current directions in business rules and their potential impact on systems development and maintenance.
5. Research universal data models. Find articles on universal (or packaged, industry, or functional area) data models, or find information on some commercial offerings. Identify common features across these models as well as different ways to model the same concepts. Discuss what you think are the advantages and disadvantages of the different ways used to model the same concepts.

References

Elmasri, R., and S. B. Navathe. 1994. *Fundamentals of Database Systems*. Menlo Park, CA: Benjamin/Cummings.

Gottesdiener, E. 1997. "Business Rules Show Power, Promise." *Application Development Trends* 4,3 (March): 36–54.

GUIDE. 1997 (October). "GUIDE Business Rules Project." Final Report, revision 1.2.

Hay, D. C. 1996. *Data Model Patterns: Conventions of Thought*. New York: Dorset House Publishing.

Hoberman, S. 2006. "Industry Logical Data Models." *Teradata Magazine*. Available at **www.teradata.com**.

Hoffer, J. A., J. F. George, and J. S. Valacich. 2010. *Modern Systems Analysis and Design*, 6th ed. Upper Saddle River, NJ: Prentice Hall.

Silverston, L. 1998. "Is Your Organization Too Unique to Use Universal Data Models?" *DM Review* 8,8 (September), accessed at **www.information-management.com/issues/19980901/425-1.html**.

Silverston, L. 2001a. *The Data Model Resource Book, Volume 1*, Rev. ed. New York: Wiley.

Silverston, L. 2001b. *The Data Model Resource Book, Volume 2*, Rev. ed. New York: Wiley.

Silverston, L. 2002. "A Universal Data Model for Relationship Development." *DM Review* 12,3 (March): 44–47, 65.

Teorey, T. 1999. *Database Modeling & Design*. San Francisco: Morgan Kaufman Publishers.

Further Reading

Frye, C. 2002. "Business Rules Are Back." *Application Development Trends* 9, 7 (July): 29–35.

Moriarty, T. "Using Scenarios in Information Modeling: Bringing Business Rules to Life." *Database Programming & Design* 6, 8 (August): 65–67.

Ross, R. G. 1997. *The Business Rule Book*. Version 4. Boston: Business Rule Solutions, Inc.

Ross, R. G. 1998. *Business Rule Concepts: The New Mechanics of Business Information Systems.* Boston: Business Rule Solutions, Inc.

Ross, R. G. 2003. *Principles of the Business Rule Approach.* Boston: Addison-Wesley.

Schmidt, B. 1997. "A Taxonomy of Domains." *Database Programming & Design* 10, 9 (September): 95, 96, 98, 99.

Silverston, L. 2002. Silverston has a series of articles in *DM Review* that discuss universal data models in different settings. See in particular Vol. 12 issues 1 (January) on clickstream analysis, 5 (May) on health care, 7 (July) on financial services, and 12 (December) on manufacturing.

von Halle, B. 1996. "Object-Oriented Lessons." *Database Programming & Design* 9,1 (January): 13–16.

von Halle, B. 2001. von Halle has a series of articles in *DM Review* on building a business rules system. These articles are in Vol. 11, issues 1–5 (January–May).

von Halle, B., and R. Kaplan. 1997. "Is IT Falling Short?" *Database Programming & Design* 10, 6 (June): 15–17.

Web Resources

www.adtmag.com Web site of *Application Development Trends,* a leading publication on the practice of information systems development.

www.brsolutions.com Web site of Business Rule Solutions, the consulting company of Ronald Ross, a leader in the development of a business rule methodology. Or you can check out **www.BRCommunity.com,** which is a virtual community site for people interested in business rules (sponsored by Business Rule Solutions).

www.businessrulesgroup.org Web site of the Business Rules Group, formerly part of GUIDE International, which formulates and supports standards about business rules.

www.databaseanswers.org/data_models A fascinating site that shows over 100 sample E-R diagrams for a wide variety of applications and organizations. A variety of notations are used, so this a good site to also learn about variations in E-R diagramming.

www.intelligententerprise.com Web site of *Intelligent Enterprise,* a leading publication on database management and related areas. This magazine is the result of combining two previous publications, *Database Programming & Design* and *DBMS.*

www.kpiusa.com The homepage for Knowledge Partners International, founded by Barbara von Halle. This site has some interesting case studies and white papers about business rules.

http://researchlibrary.theserverside.net/detail/RES/1214505974_136.html Link to the white paper "Modeling Unstructured Data" by Steve Hoberman. Unstructured data (e.g., e-mails, images, sounds) is an emerging area for databases, and there are some special issues in data modeling for unstructured data.

www.tdan.com Web site of *The Data Administration Newsletter*, which regularly publishes new articles, special reports, and news on a variety of data modeling and administration topics.

www.teradatastudentnetwork.com Web site for Teradata Student Network, a free resource for a wide variety of information about database management and related topics. Go to this site and search on "entity relationship" to see many articles and assignments related to EER data modeling.

CASE

Mountain View Community Hospital

Case Description

After developing a preliminary E-R model and discussing it with the rest of your team, you realize that you need to delve deeper into the interview notes and documentation you obtained to add more detail to the model and possibly add entities and relationships you had overlooked. Several issues need to be addressed.

As a large service organization, Mountain View Community Hospital (MVCH) depends on four major groups of persons for its continued success: employees, physicians, patients, and volunteers. A small number of persons in the hospital community do not belong to any of these four groups. A particular person may belong to two (or more) of these groups at a given time. For example, a volunteer or employee may also be a patient at the hospital at some point in time.

The four groups of people listed previously share many common characteristics such as a unique identifier, Name, Address, City/State/Zip, Birth Date, Phone, and E-mail. Then there are characteristics that apply to only one of these groups. For example, a hire date (Date Hired) is recorded for employees only. Volunteer Services records skills and interests of their volunteers in order to place them appropriately. Physicians have a pager number (Pager#) and a DEA number (a physician needs a DEA registration number from the Drug Enforcement Administration to be able to prescribe controlled substances). For patients, the hospital records the date of first contact with the hospital (Contact Date). There are also characteristics that apply to some, but not all of the groups. For example, both physicians and nurses have a specialty (e.g., pediatrics, oncology, etc.).

In addition to the characteristics already mentioned, the hospital records a number of other characteristics about its patients: emergency contact information (last and first name, relationship to patient, address, and phone), insurance information (insurance company name, policy number, group number, and insurance phone number), information about the insurance subscriber in case the patient is not the insurance subscriber (last and first name, relationship to patient, address, and phone), and contact information for the patient's primary care physician or other physician who referred the patient to the hospital.

At MVCH, each patient has one (and only one) physician responsible for that patient. A given physician may not be responsible for a patient at a given time or may be responsible for one or more patients. The primary patient segments are resident patients and outpatients. Outpatients may come in for many reasons, including routine examinations at an outpatient care center (e.g., the MS Center), ambulatory/outpatient surgery, diagnostic services, or emergency room care. Each outpatient is scheduled for zero or more visits. A visit has several attributes: a unique identifier (Visit#), date, and time. Notice that an instance of visit cannot exist without an outpatient owner entity. Some patients that are seen as outpatients, for example, in the emergency room, are subsequently admitted to the hospital and become resident patients. Each resident patient has a Date Admitted attribute as well as a Discharge Date.

The volunteer application form in MVCH Figure 3-1 shows all the information that Volunteer Services under Mr. Davis requires from persons interested in volunteering. Volunteers work in many areas of the hospital based on their interests and skills. Volunteer Services keeps track of a person's time of service (begin and end date), work unit where a person works as a volunteer, and the volunteer's supervisor. Each volunteer is supervised by an employee or physician, but not all employees and physicians supervise volunteers. Volunteer Services also keep track of a volunteer's number of hours worked and recognizes outstanding volunteers at an annual awards ceremony.

Employees fall into three categories: nurses, technicians, and staff. Each nurse has a certificate/degree indicating his or her qualification as an RN or LPN. (LPNs work under the direction of RNs at MVCH.) Each nurse must also have a current Colorado nursing license and may hold certifications in special fields such as dialysis, pediatrics, anesthesia, critical care, pain management, and so on. Most nurses are assigned to one (and only one) care center at a time, although over time, they may be working in more than one care center. Some nurses are floaters who are not assigned to a specific care center but instead work wherever they are needed. As described earlier, one of the nurses assigned to a care center is appointed nurse-in-charge (Nurse In Charge). Only nurses with an RN certificate can be appointed nurse-in-charge.

Specific job-related competency skills are recorded for the hospital's technicians. A cardiovascular technician for example may be skilled in specific equipment, such as setting up and getting readings from a Holter monitor, a portable device that monitors a patient's EKG for a period of 24 to 48 hours during routine activities. Medical laboratory technicians need to be able to set up, operate, and control equipment, perform a variety of tests, analyze the test data, and summarize test results for physicians who use them to diagnose and treat patients. Emergency room technicians' skills include the ability to perform CPR, or set up an IV. Dialysis technicians, who may be skilled in different types of dialysis, (e.g., pediatric dialysis, outpatient dialysis) need a variety of skills related to setting up treatment, assessing the patient during dialysis, and assessing and troubleshooting equipment problems during dialysis. Each technician is assigned to a work unit in the hospital (a care center, the central medical laboratory, radiology, etc.).

Staff members have a job classification (Job Class), such as secretary, administrative assistant, admitting specialist, collection specialist, and so on. Like the technicians, each staff member is assigned to a work unit in the hospital (a care center, the central medical laboratory, radiology, etc.).

Work units such as a care center have a Name (identifier) and Location. The location denotes the facility (e.g., main building) and floor (e.g., 3 West, 2 South). A care center often has one or more beds (up to any number) assigned to it, but there are also care centers without assigned beds. The only attribute of bed is the identifier Bed ID, which consists of two components: Bed#

Mountain View Community Hospital

VOLUNTEER APPLICATION

Last Name ______ First Name ______ Date of Birth ______

Street Address ______ City ______ State ______ Zip ______

Home Phone: ( ) ______ Work Phone: ( ) ______ E-Mail ______

Have you been *convicted of a felony* within the past seven years?

○ NO ○ YES If YES, please explain ______

Emergency Contact Last Name ______ First Name ______

Relationship ______ Phone: ( ) ______

References (Not Relatives)

Last Name ______	Last Name ______
First Name ______	First Name ______
Relationship ______ Phone ( ) ______	Relationship ______ Phone ( ) ______
Address: ______	Address ______
City ______ State ______ Zip ______	City ______ State ______ Zip ______

Current or Last Employment

Name of Employer ______

Employer Address ______

Position (Type of work) ______ Dates of Employment ______

Prior Volunteer Service

Have you volunteered at Mountain Valley Community Hospital before?

○ NO ○ YES If YES, please list ______

Do you have previous volunteer experience elsewhere?

○ NO ○ YES If YES, please list ______

Interests & Preferences

Why do you want to become a volunteer? ______

What are your hobbies, skills, other interests? ______

Which languages do you speak? ______

What do you envision yourself doing as a volunteer? ______

Please indicate days and times when you are available to volunteer.

	Mon	Tues	Wed	Thur	Fri	Sat	Sun
Morning							
Afternoon							
Evening							

Applicant's Signature ______ Date ______

MVCH FIGURE 3-1 Volunteer application form

and Room#. Each resident patient must be assigned to a bed. Because MVCH doesn't always fill all its beds, a bed may or may not have a resident patient assigned to it at a given time.

Case Questions

1. Is the ability to model supertype/subtype relationships important in a hospital environment such as MVCH? Why or why not?
2. Are there any weak entities, multivalued attributes, or multiple relationships in the description of the data requirements in this case segment? If so, what are they?
3. Can you think of any other business rules (other than the one explicitly described in the case) that are likely to be used in a hospital environment? Can these be represented on an EER diagram for MVCH?
4. Are there any universal data models that can be reused as a starting point for modeling MVCH's data requirements?

Would you recommend using such as model for the MVCH project? Why or why not?

Case Exercises

1. Draw an EER diagram to represent the requirements described in this case segment carefully following the notation from this chapter.
2. Suppose each care center had two nurses-in-charge, one for the day shift, and another one for the evening shift. How would that change the diagram you developed in Case Exercise 1?
3. Develop definitions for each of the following types of objects in your EER diagram from Case Exercise 1. Consult with some member of the hospital or health-care community (if one is available); do some research on the Internet, or otherwise make reasonable assumptions based on your own knowledge and experience.
   a. Entity types
   b. Attributes
   c. Relationships
4. Figure 3-17 shows the following entity types in a universal data model: PARTY, PARTY ROLE, PARTY RELATIONSHIP, EVENT, PRIORITY TYPE, STATUS TYPE, EVENT ROLE, and ROLE TYPE. How would these apply to the MVCH case? Give examples of each entity type based on the information provided in the case descriptions up to this point.
5. Derive and clearly state the business rules that are implicit in the volunteer application form shown in MVCH Figure 3-1.
6. Compare the EER diagram that you developed in this chapter with the E-R diagram you developed in Chapter 2. What are the differences between these two diagrams? Why are there differences?

Project Assignments

P1. Revise the list of business rules you developed in Chapter 2 in light of the information provided in this case segment and your insights from the Case Exercises.

P2. Following the notation from this chapter, merge your Chapter 2 E-R diagram with the EER diagram you developed for Case Exercises 1 and 2 to represent the data requirements for MVCH's new system.

P3. Document and explain the decisions you made during merging.

PART

III

Database Design

Chapter 4
Logical Database Design and the Relational Model

Chapter 5
Physical Database Design and Performance

AN OVERVIEW OF PART THREE

By the end of the database analysis phase of database development, systems and database analysts have a fairly clear understanding of data storage and access requirements. However, the data model developed during analysis explicitly avoids any ties to database technologies. Before we can implement a database, the conceptual data model must be mapped into a data model that is compatible with the database management system to be used.

The activities of database design transform the requirements for data storage developed during database analysis into specifications to guide database implementation. There are two forms of specifications:

1. Logical specifications, which map the conceptual requirements into the data model associated with a specific database management system
2. Physical specifications, which indicate all the parameters for data storage that are then input to database implementation, during which a database is actually defined using a data definition language

In Chapter 4 ("Logical Database Design and the Relational Model"), we describe logical database design, with special emphasis on the relational data model. Logical database design is the process of transforming the conceptual data model (described in Chapters 2 and 3) into a logical data model. Most database management systems in use today use the relational data model, so this data model is the basis for our discussion of logical database design.

In Chapter 4, we first define the important terms and concepts for this model, including *relation*, *primary key* and *surrogate primary key*, *foreign key*, *anomaly*, *normal form*, *normalization*, *functional dependency*, *partial functional dependency*, and *transitive dependency*. We next describe and illustrate the process of transforming an E-R model to the relational model. Many modeling tools support this transformation; however, it is important that you understand the underlying principles and procedures. We then describe and illustrate in detail the important concepts of normalization (the process of designing well-structured relations). Appendix B includes further discussion of normalization. Finally, we describe how to merge relations from separate logical design activities (e.g., different groups within a large project team) while avoiding common pitfalls that may occur in this process. We end this discussion with a presentation of enterprise keys, which make relational keys distinct across relations.

The purpose of physical database design, the topic of Chapter 5 ("Physical Database Design and Performance"), is to translate the logical description of data into the technical specifications for storing and retrieving data. The goal is to create a design for storing data that will provide adequate performance and ensure database integrity, security, and recoverability. Physical database design produces the technical specifications that programmers and others involved in information systems construction will use during the implementation phase, which we discuss in Chapters 6 through 9.

In Chapter 5, you will learn key terms and concepts for physical database design, including *data type*, *page*, *pointer*, *denormalization*, *partitioning*, *indexed file organization*, and *hashed file organization*. You will study the basic steps in developing an efficient physical database design. You will learn about choices for storing attribute values and how to select among these choices. You will also learn why normalized tables do not always form the best physical data files and how you can, if necessary, denormalize the data to achieve data retrieval speed improvements. You will learn about different file organizations and different types of indexes, which are important in speeding the retrieval of data. Appendix C addresses some additional constructs for physical data storage. In addition, you will learn how physical database design choices that improve data quality affect the process of validating the accuracy of financial reporting. These are essential issues today because of government regulations, such as Sarbanes-Oxley, and because of the growing realization that ensuring high data quality makes business sense.

You must carefully perform physical database design because decisions made during this stage have a major impact on data accessibility, response times, security, user friendliness, information quality, and similarly important information system design factors. Database administration (described in Chapter 11) plays a major role in physical database design, so we will return to some advanced design issues in that chapter, and Chapter 12 addresses distributed database design issues.

CHAPTER

4

Logical Database Design and the Relational Model

Learning Objectives

After studying this chapter, you should be able to:

- Concisely define each of the following key terms: **relation, primary key, composite key, foreign key, null, entity integrity rule, referential integrity constraint, well-structured relation, anomaly, surrogate primary key, recursive foreign key, normalization, normal form, functional dependency, determinant, candidate key, first normal form, second normal form, partial functional dependency, third normal form, transitive dependency, synonyms, alias, homonym,** and **enterprise key.**
- List five properties of relations.
- State two essential properties of a candidate key.
- Give a concise definition of each of the following: first normal form, second normal form, and third normal form.
- Briefly describe four problems that may arise when merging relations.
- Transform an E-R (or EER) diagram into a logically equivalent set of relations.
- Create relational tables that incorporate entity integrity and referential integrity constraints.
- Use normalization to decompose a relation with anomalies into well-structured relations.

INTRODUCTION

In this chapter, we describe logical database design, with special emphasis on the relational data model. Logical database design is the process of transforming the conceptual data model (described in Chapters 2 and 3) into a logical data model—one that is consistent and compatible with a specific type of database technology. An experienced database designer often will do logical database design in parallel with conceptual data modeling if he or she knows the type of database technology that will be used. It is, however, important to treat these as separate steps so that you concentrate on each important part of database development. Conceptual data modeling is about understanding the organization—getting the right requirements. Logical database design is about creating stable database structures—correctly expressing the requirements in a technical language. Both are important steps that must be performed carefully.

Although there are other data models, we have two reasons for emphasizing the relational data model in this chapter. First, the relational data model is by far the one most commonly used in contemporary database applications. Second, some of the principles of logical database design for the relational model apply to the other logical models as well.

We have introduced the relational data model informally through simple examples in earlier chapters. It is important, however, to note that the relational data model is a form of logical data model, and as such it is different from the conceptual data models. Thus, an E-R data model is not a relational data model, and an E-R model may not obey the rules for a well-structured relational data model, called *normalization*, which we explain in this chapter. That is okay, because the E-R model was developed for other purposes—understanding data requirements and business rules about the data—not structuring the data for sound database processing, which is the goal of logical database design.

In this chapter, we first define the important terms and concepts for the relational data model. (We often use the abbreviated term *relational model* when referring to the relational data model.) We next describe and illustrate the process of transforming an EER model into the relational model. Many CASE tools support this transformation today at the technical level; however, it is important that you understand the underlying principles and procedures. We then describe the concepts of normalization in detail. Normalization, which is the process of designing well-structured relations, is an important component of logical design for the relational model. Finally, we describe how to merge relations while avoiding common pitfalls that may occur in this process.

The objective of logical database design is to translate the conceptual design (which represents an organization's requirements for data) into a logical database design that can be implemented via a chosen database management system. The resulting databases must meet user needs for data sharing, flexibility, and ease of access. The concepts presented in this chapter are essential to your understanding of the database development process.

THE RELATIONAL DATA MODEL

The relational data model was first introduced in 1970 by E. F. Codd, then of IBM (Codd, 1970). Two early research projects were launched to prove the feasibility of the relational model and to develop prototype systems. The first of these, at IBM's San Jose Research Laboratory, led to the development of System R (a prototype relational DBMS [RDBMS]) during the late 1970s. The second, at the University of California at Berkeley, led to the development of Ingres, an academically oriented RDBMS. Commercial RDBMS products from numerous vendors started to appear about 1980. (See the Web site for this book for links to RDBMS and other DBMS vendors.) Today RDBMSs have become the dominant technology for database management, and there are literally hundreds of RDBMS products for computers ranging from smartphones and personal computers to mainframes.

Basic Definitions

The relational data model represents data in the form of tables. The relational model is based on mathematical theory and therefore has a solid theoretical foundation. However, we need only a few simple concepts to describe the relational model. Therefore, it can be easily understood and used even by those unfamiliar with the underlying theory. The relational data model consists of the following three components (Fleming and von Halle, 1989):

1. ***Data structure*** Data are organized in the form of tables, with rows and columns.
2. ***Data manipulation*** Powerful operations (using the SQL language) are used to manipulate data stored in the relations.
3. ***Data integrity*** The model includes mechanisms to specify business rules that maintain the integrity of data when they are manipulated.

EmpID	Name	DeptName	Salary
100	Malini Srivastav	Marketing	48,000
140	Akash Bahety	Accounting	52,000
110	Chandan shetty	Info Systems	43,000
190	Lakshmi Dave	Finance	55,000
150	Sushma Murthy	Marketing	42,000

EMPLOYEE1

FIGURE 4-1 EMPLOYEE1 relation with sample data

We discuss data structure and data integrity in this section. Data manipulation is discussed in Chapters 6, 7, and 8.

RELATIONAL DATA STRUCTURE A **relation** is a named, two-dimensional table of data. Each relation (or table) consists of a set of named columns and an arbitrary number of unnamed rows. An attribute, consistent with its definition in Chapter 2, is a named column of a relation. Each row of a relation corresponds to a record that contains data (attribute) values for a single entity. Figure 4-1 shows an example of a relation named EMPLOYEE1. This relation contains the following attributes describing employees: EmpID, Name, DeptName, and Salary. The five rows of the table correspond to five employees. It is important to understand that the sample data in Figure 4-1 are intended to illustrate the structure of the EMPLOYEE1 relation; they are not part of the relation itself. Even if we add another row of data to the figure or change any of the data in the existing rows, it is still the same EMPLOYEE1 relation. Nor does deleting a row change the relation. In fact, we could delete all of the rows shown in Figure 4-1, and the EMPLOYEE1 relation would still exist. In other words, Figure 4-1 is an instance of the EMPLOYEE1 relation.

Relation
A named two-dimensional table of data.

We can express the structure of a relation by using a shorthand notation in which the name of the relation is followed (in parentheses) by the names of the attributes in that relation. For EMPLOYEE1 we would have

EMPLOYEE1(EmpID, Name, DeptName, Salary)

RELATIONAL KEYS We must be able to store and retrieve a row of data in a relation, based on the data values stored in that row. To achieve this goal, every relation must have a primary key. A **primary key** is an attribute or a combination of attributes that uniquely identifies each row in a relation. We designate a primary key by underlining the attribute name(s). For example, the primary key for the relation EMPLOYEE1 is EmpID. Notice that this attribute is underlined in Figure 4-1. In shorthand notation, we express this relation as follows:

Primary key
An attribute or a combination of attributes that uniquely identifies each row in a relation.

EMPLOYEE1(EmpID, Name, DeptName, Salary)

The concept of a primary key is related to the term *identifier* defined in Chapter 2. The same attribute or a collection of attributes indicated as an entity's identifier in an E-R diagram may be the same attributes that compose the primary key for the relation representing that entity. There are exceptions: For example, associative entities do not have to have an identifier, and the (partial) identifier of a weak entity forms only part of a weak entity's primary key. In addition, there may be several attributes of an entity that may serve as the associated relation's primary key. All of these situations will be illustrated later in this chapter.

A **composite key** is a primary key that consists of more than one attribute. For example, the primary key for a relation DEPENDENT would likely consist of the combination EmpID and DependentName. We show several examples of composite keys later in this chapter.

Composite key
A primary key that consists of more than one attribute.

Foreign key
An attribute in a relation that serves as the primary key of another relation in the same database.

Often we must represent the relationship between two tables or relations. This is accomplished through the use of foreign keys. A **foreign key** is an attribute (possibly composite) in a relation that serves as the primary key of another relation. For example, consider the relations EMPLOYEE1 and DEPARTMENT:

EMPLOYEE1(EmpID, Name, DeptName, Salary)
DEPARTMENT(DeptName, Location, Fax)

The attribute DeptName is a foreign key in EMPLOYEE1. It allows a user to associate any employee with the department to which he or she is assigned. Some authors emphasize the fact that an attribute is a foreign key by using a dashed underline, like this:

EMPLOYEE1(EmpID, Name, DeptName, Salary)

We provide numerous examples of foreign keys in the remainder of this chapter and discuss the properties of foreign keys under the heading "Referential Integrity."

PROPERTIES OF RELATIONS We have defined relations as two-dimensional tables of data. However, not all tables are relations. Relations have several properties that distinguish them from non-relational tables. We summarize these properties next:

1. Each relation (or table) in a database has a unique name.
2. An entry at the intersection of each row and column is atomic (or single valued). There can be only one value associated with each attribute on a specific row of a table; no multivalued attributes are allowed in a relation.
3. Each row is unique; no two rows in a relation can be identical.
4. Each attribute (or column) within a table has a unique name.
5. The sequence of columns (left to right) is insignificant. The order of the columns in a relation can be changed without changing the meaning or use of the relation.
6. The sequence of rows (top to bottom) is insignificant. As with columns, the order of the rows of a relation may be changed or stored in any sequence.

REMOVING MULTIVALUED ATTRIBUTES FROM TABLES The second property of relations listed in the preceding section states that no multivalued attributes are allowed in a relation. Thus, a table that contains one or more multivalued attributes is not a relation. For example, Figure 4-2a shows the employee data from the EMPLOYEE1 relation extended to include courses that may have been taken by those employees. Because a given employee may have taken more than one course, the attributes CourseTitle and DateCompleted are multivalued attributes. For example, the employee with EmpID 100 has taken two courses. If an employee has not taken any courses, the CourseTitle and DateCompleted attribute values are null. (See the employee with EmpID 190 for an example.)

We show how to eliminate the multivalued attributes in Figure 4-2b by filling the relevant data values into the previously vacant cells of Figure 4-2a. As a result, the table in Figure 4-2b has only single-valued attributes and now satisfies the atomic property of relations. The name EMPLOYEE2 is given to this relation to distinguish it from EMPLOYEE1. However, as you will see, this new relation does have some undesirable properties.

Sample Database

A relational database may consist of any number of relations. The structure of the database is described through the use of a schema (defined in Chapter 1), which is a description of the overall logical structure of the database. There are two common methods for expressing a schema:

a. Short text statements, in which each relation is named and the names of its attributes follow in parentheses. (See the EMPLOYEE1 and DEPARTMENT relations defined earlier in this chapter.)

FIGURE 4-2 Eliminating multivalued attributes

(a) Table with repeating groups

EmpID	Name	DeptName	Salary	CourseTitle	DateCompleted
100	Malini Srivastav	Marketing	48,000	SPSS	6/19/201X
				Surveys	10/7/201X
140	Akash Bahety	Accounting	52,000	Tax Acc	12/8/201X
110	Chandan Shetty	Info Systems	43,000	Visual Basic	1/12/201X
				C++	4/22/201X
190	Lakshmi Dave	Finance	55,000		
150	Sushma Murthy	Marketing	42,000	SPSS	6/16/201X
				Java	8/12/201X

(b) EMPLOYEE2 relation

EMPLOYEE2

EmpID	Name	DeptName	Salary	CourseTitle	DateCompleted
100	Malini Srivastav	Marketing	48,000	SPSS	6/19/201X
100	Malini Srivastav	Marketing	48,000	Surveys	10/7/201X
140	Akash Bahety	Accounting	52,000	Tax Acc	12/8/201X
110	Chandan Shetty	Info Systems	43,000	Visual Basic	1/12/201X
110	Chandan Shetty	Info Systems	43,000	C++	4/22/201X
190	Lakshmi Dave	Finance	55,000		
150	Sushma Murthy	Marketing	42,000	SPSS	6/19/201X
150	Sushma Murthy	Marketing	42,000	Java	8/12/201X

b. A graphical representation, in which each relation is represented by a rectangle containing the attributes for the relation

Text statements have the advantage of simplicity. However, a graphical representation provides a better means of expressing referential integrity constraints (as you will see shortly). In this section, we use both techniques for expressing a schema so that you can compare them.

PINE VALLEY FURNITURE

A schema for four relations at Pine Valley Furniture Company is shown in Figure 4-3. The four relations shown in this figure are CUSTOMER, ORDER, ORDER LINE, and PRODUCT. The key attributes for these relations are underlined, and other important attributes are included in each relation. We show how to design these relations using the techniques of normalization later in this chapter.

Following is a text description of these relations:

CUSTOMER(CustomerID, CustomerName, CustomerAddress,
  CustomerCity, CustomerState, CustomerPostalCode)
ORDER(OrderID, OrderDate, CustomerID)
ORDER LINE(OrderID, ProductID, OrderedQuantity)
PRODUCT(ProductID, ProductDescription, ProductFinish,
  ProductStandardPrice, ProductLineID)

Notice that the primary key for ORDER LINE is a composite key consisting of the attributes OrderID and ProductID. Also, CustomerID is a foreign key in the ORDER relation; this allows the user to associate an order with the customer who submitted the order. ORDER LINE has two foreign keys: OrderID and ProductID. These keys allow the user to associate each line on an order with the relevant order and product.

FIGURE 4-3 Schema for four relations (Pine Valley Furniture Company)

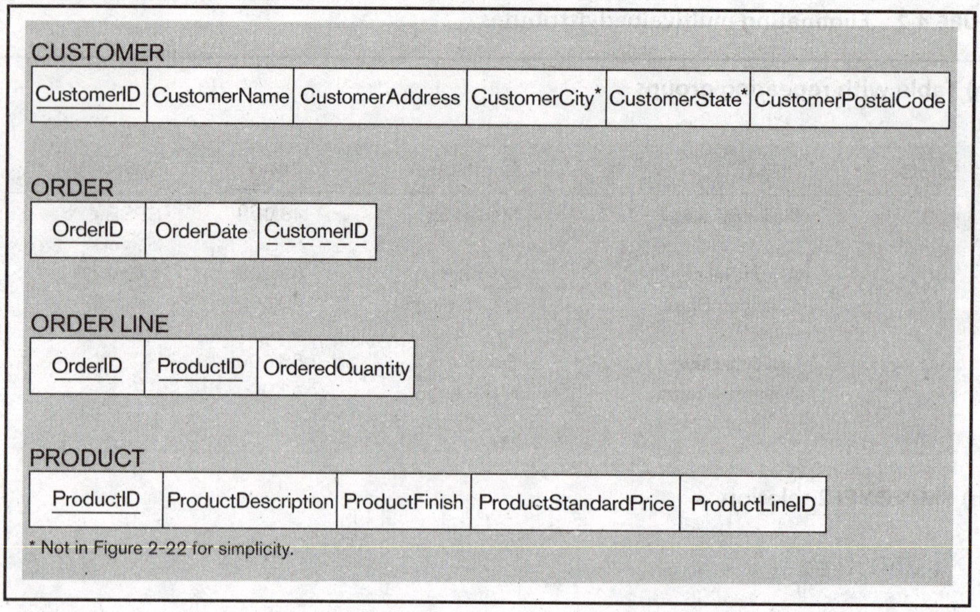

An instance of this database is shown in Figure 4-4. This figure shows four tables with sample data. Notice how the foreign keys allow us to associate the various tables. It is a good idea to create an instance of your relational schema with sample data for four reasons:

1. The sample data allow you to test your assumptions regarding the design.
2. The sample data provide a convenient way to check the accuracy of your design.
3. The sample data help improve communications with users in discussing your design.
4. You can use the sample data to develop prototype applications and to test queries.

INTEGRITY CONSTRAINTS

The relational data model includes several types of constraints, or rules limiting acceptable values and actions, whose purpose is to facilitate maintaining the accuracy and integrity of data in the database. The major types of integrity constraints are domain constraints, entity integrity, and referential integrity.

Domain Constraints

All of the values that appear in a column of a relation must be from the same domain. A domain is the set of values that may be assigned to an attribute. A domain definition usually consists of the following components: domain name, meaning, data type, size (or length), and allowable values or allowable range (if applicable). Table 4-1 (page 162) shows domain definitions for the domains associated with the attributes in Figures 4-3 and 4-4.

Entity Integrity

The entity integrity rule is designed to ensure that every relation has a primary key and that the data values for that primary key are all valid. In particular, it guarantees that every primary key attribute is non-null.

In some cases, a particular attribute cannot be assigned a data value. There are two situations in which this is likely to occur: Either there is no applicable data value or the applicable data value is not known when values are assigned. Suppose, for example, that you fill out an employment form that has a space reserved for a fax number. If you have no fax number, you leave this space empty because it does not apply to you. Or suppose that you are asked to fill in the telephone number of your previous employer. If you do not recall this number, you may leave it empty because that information is not known.

FIGURE 4-4 Instance of a relational schema (Pine Valley Furniture Company)

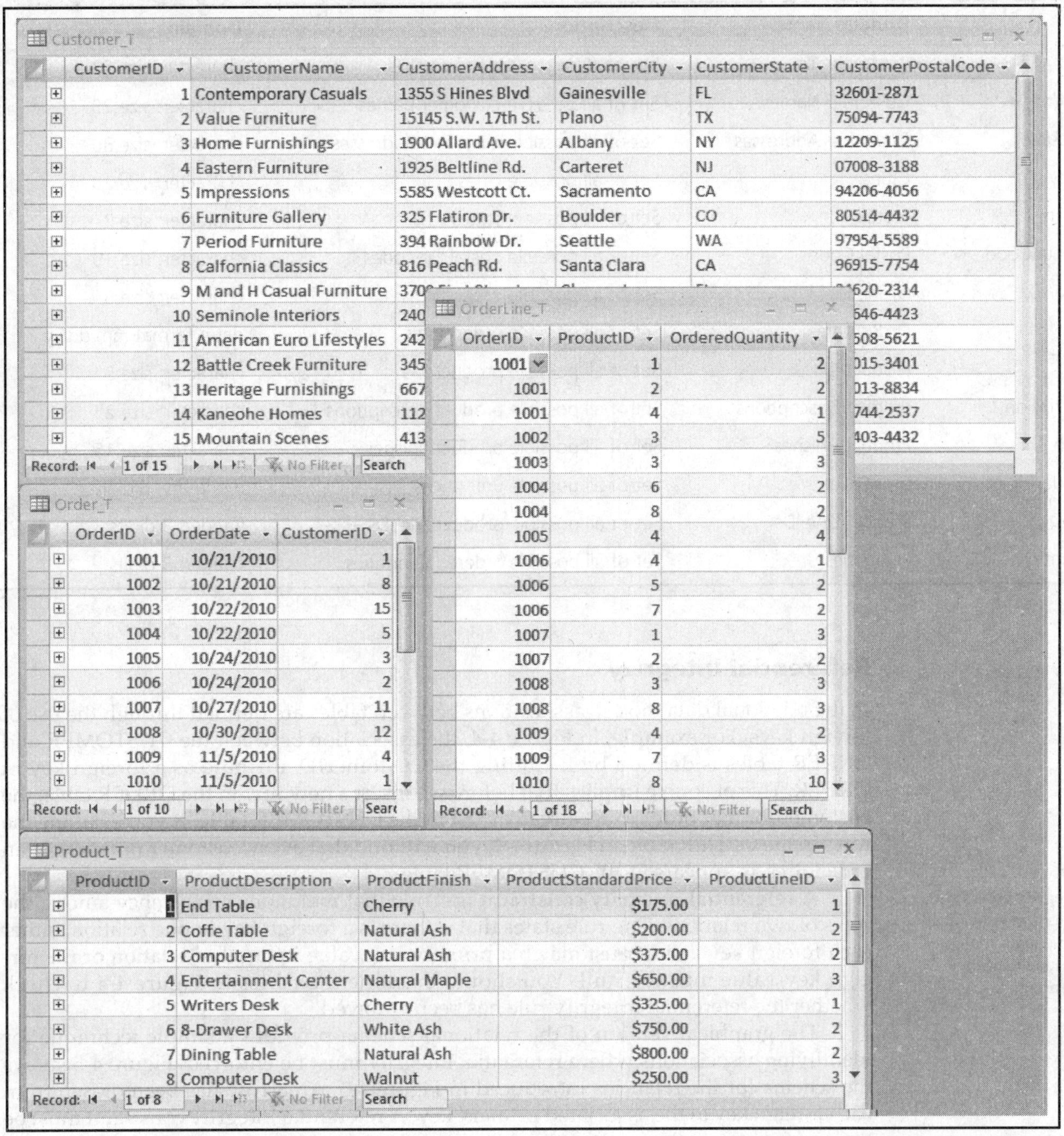

Customer_T

CustomerID	CustomerName	CustomerAddress	CustomerCity	CustomerState	CustomerPostalCode
1	Contemporary Casuals	1355 S Hines Blvd	Gainesville	FL	32601-2871
2	Value Furniture	15145 S.W. 17th St.	Plano	TX	75094-7743
3	Home Furnishings	1900 Allard Ave.	Albany	NY	12209-1125
4	Eastern Furniture	1925 Beltline Rd.	Carteret	NJ	07008-3188
5	Impressions	5585 Westcott Ct.	Sacramento	CA	94206-4056
6	Furniture Gallery	325 Flatiron Dr.	Boulder	CO	80514-4432
7	Period Furniture	394 Rainbow Dr.	Seattle	WA	97954-5589
8	Calfornia Classics	816 Peach Rd.	Santa Clara	CA	96915-7754
9	M and H Casual Furniture	370			620-2314
10	Seminole Interiors	240			546-4423
11	American Euro Lifestyles	242			508-5621
12	Battle Creek Furniture	345			015-3401
13	Heritage Furnishings	667			013-8834
14	Kaneohe Homes	112			744-2537
15	Mountain Scenes	413			403-4432

Record: 1 of 15 No Filter Search

Order_T

OrderID	OrderDate	CustomerID
1001	10/21/2010	1
1002	10/21/2010	8
1003	10/22/2010	15
1004	10/22/2010	5
1005	10/24/2010	3
1006	10/24/2010	2
1007	10/27/2010	11
1008	10/30/2010	12
1009	11/5/2010	4
1010	11/5/2010	1

Record: 1 of 10 No Filter Searc

OrderLine_T

OrderID	ProductID	OrderedQuantity
1001	1	2
1001	2	2
1001	4	1
1002	3	5
1003	3	3
1004	6	2
1004	8	2
1005	4	4
1006	4	1
1006	5	2
1006	7	2
1007	1	3
1007	2	2
1008	3	3
1008	8	3
1009	4	2
1009	7	3
1010	8	10

Record: 1 of 18 No Filter Search

Product_T

ProductID	ProductDescription	ProductFinish	ProductStandardPrice	ProductLineID
1	End Table	Cherry	$175.00	1
2	Coffe Table	Natural Ash	$200.00	2
3	Computer Desk	Natural Ash	$375.00	2
4	Entertainment Center	Natural Maple	$650.00	3
5	Writers Desk	Cherry	$325.00	1
6	8-Drawer Desk	White Ash	$750.00	2
7	Dining Table	Natural Ash	$800.00	2
8	Computer Desk	Walnut	$250.00	3

Record: 1 of 8 No Filter Search

The relational data model allows us to assign a null value to an attribute in the just described situations. A **null** is a value that may be assigned to an attribute when no other value applies or when the applicable value is unknown. In reality, a null is not a value but rather it indicates the absence of a value. For example, it is not the same as a numeric zero or a string of blanks. The inclusion of nulls in the relational model is somewhat controversial, because it sometimes leads to anomalous results (Date, 2003). However, Codd, the inventor of the relational model, advocates the use of nulls for missing values (Codd, 1990).

Null
A value that may be assigned to an attribute when no other value applies or when the applicable value is unknown.

Everyone agrees that primary key values must not be allowed to be null. Thus, the **entity integrity rule** states the following: No primary key attribute (or component of a primary key attribute) may be null.

Entity integrity rule
A rule that states that no primary key attribute (or component of a primary key attribute) may be null.

TABLE 4-1 Domain Definitions for INVOICE Attributes

Attribute	Domain Name	Description	Domain
CustomerID	Customer IDs	Set of all possible customer IDs	character: size 5
CustomerName	Customer Names	Set of all possible customer names	character: size 25
CustomerAddress	Customer Addresses	Set of all possible customer addresses	character: size 30
CustomerCity	Cities	Set of all possible cities	character: size 20
CustomerState	States	Set of all possible states	character: size 2
CustomerPostalCode	Postal Codes	Set of all possible postal zip codes	character: size 10
OrderID	Order IDs	Set of all possible order IDs	character: size 5
OrderDate	Order Dates	Set of all possible order dates	date: format mm/dd/yy
ProductID	Product IDs	Set of all possible product IDs	character: size 5
ProductDescription	Product Descriptions	Set of all possible product descriptions	character: size 25
ProductFinish	Product Finishes	Set of all possible product finishes	character: size 15
ProductStandardPrice	Unit Prices	Set of all possible unit prices	monetary: 6 digits
ProductLineID	Product Line IDs	Set of all possible product line IDs	integer: 3 digits
OrderedQuantity	Quantities	Set of all possible ordered quantities	integer: 3 digits

Referential Integrity

In the relational data model, associations between tables are defined through the use of foreign keys. For example, in Figure 4-4, the association between the CUSTOMER and ORDER tables is defined by including the CustomerID attribute as a foreign key in ORDER. This of course implies that before we insert a new row in the ORDER table, the customer for that order must already exist in the CUSTOMER table. If you examine the rows in the ORDER table in Figure 4-4, you will find that every customer number for an order already appears in the CUSTOMER table.

Referential integrity constraint A rule that states that either each foreign key value must match a primary key value in another relation or the foreign key value must be null.

A **referential integrity constraint** is a rule that maintains consistency among the rows of two relations. The rule states that if there is a foreign key in one relation, either each foreign key value must match a primary key value in another relation or the foreign key value must be null. You should examine the tables in Figure 4-4 to check whether the referential integrity rule has been enforced.

The graphical version of the relational schema provides a simple technique for identifying associations where referential integrity must be enforced. Figure 4-5 shows the schema for the relations introduced in Figure 4-3. An arrow has been drawn from each foreign key to the associated primary key. A referential integrity constraint must be defined for each of these arrows in the schema.

How do you know whether a foreign key is allowed to be null? If each order must have a customer (a mandatory relationship), then the foreign key CustomerID cannot be null in the ORDER relation. If the relationship is optional, then the foreign key could be null. Whether a foreign key can be null must be specified as a property of the foreign key attribute when the database is defined.

Actually, whether a foreign key can be null is more complex to model on an E-R diagram and to determine than we have shown so far. For example, what happens to order data if we choose to delete a customer who has submitted orders? We may want to see sales even if we do not care about the customer any more. Three choices are possible:

1. Delete the associated orders (called a cascading delete), in which case we lose not only the customer but also all the sales history
2. Prohibit deletion of the customer until all associated orders are first deleted (a safety check)

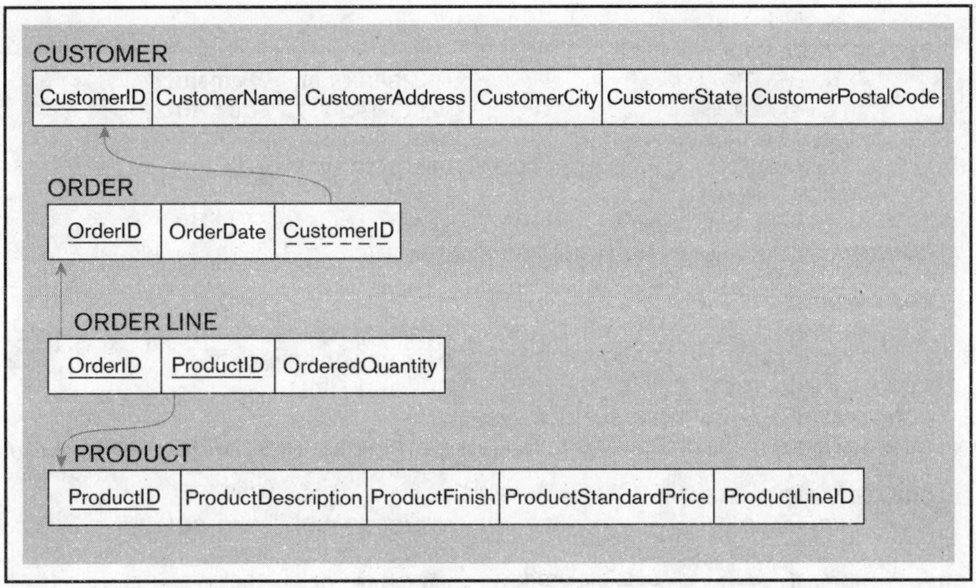

FIGURE 4-5 Referential integrity constraints (Pine Valley Furniture Company)

3. Place a null value in the foreign key (an exception that says although an order must have a CustomerID value when the order is created, CustomerID can become null later if the associated customer is deleted)

We will see how each of these choices is implemented when we describe the SQL database query language in Chapter 6. Please note that in practice, organizational rules and various regulations regarding data retention often determine what data can be deleted and when, and they therefore govern the choice between various deletion options.

Creating Relational Tables

In this section, we create table definitions for the four tables shown in Figure 4-5. These definitions are created using **CREATE TABLE** statements from the SQL data definition language. In practice, these table definitions are actually created during the implementation phase later in the database development process. However, we show these sample tables in this chapter for continuity and especially to illustrate the way the integrity constraints described previously are implemented in SQL.

The SQL table definitions are shown in Figure 4-6. One table is created for each of the four relations shown in the relational schema (Figure 4-5). Each attribute for a table is then defined. Notice that the data type and length for each attribute is taken from the domain definitions (Table 4-1). For example, the attribute CustomerName in the Customer_T table is defined as VARCHAR (variable character) data type with length 25. By specifying **NOT NULL**, each attribute can be constrained from being assigned a null value.

The primary key is specified for each table using the **PRIMARY KEY** clause at the end of each table definition. The OrderLine_T table illustrates how to specify a primary key when that key is a composite attribute. In this example, the primary key of OrderLine_T is the combination of OrderID and ProductID. Each primary key attribute in the four tables is constrained with **NOT NULL**. This enforces the entity integrity constraint described in the previous section. Notice that the **NOT NULL** constraint can also be used with non-primary-key attributes.

Referential integrity constraints are easily defined, using the graphical schema shown in Figure 4-5. An arrow originates from each foreign key and points to the related primary key in the associated relation. In the SQL table definition, a **FOREIGN KEY REFERENCES** statement corresponds to each of these arrows. Thus, for the table Order_T, the foreign key CustomerID references the primary key of Customer_T, which is also called CustomerID. Although in this case the foreign key and primary keys have the same name, this need not be the case. For example, the foreign key attribute could be named CustNo instead of CustomerID. However, the foreign and primary keys must be from the same domain.

FIGURE 4-6 SQL table definitions

```
CREATE TABLE Customer_T
        (CustomerID                 NUMBER(11,0)      NOT NULL,
        CustomerName                VARCHAR2(25)      NOT NULL,
        CustomerAddress             VARCHAR2(30),
        CustomerCity                VARCHAR2(20),
        CustomerState               CHAR(2),
        CustomerPostalCode          VARCHAR2(9),
CONSTRAINT Customer_PK PRIMARY KEY (CustomerID));

CREATE TABLE Order_T
        (OrderID                    NUMBER(11,0)      NOT NULL,
        OrderDate                   DATE DEFAULT SYSDATE,
        CustomerID                  NUMBER(11,0),
CONSTRAINT Order_PK PRIMARY KEY (OrderID),
CONSTRAINT Order_FK FOREIGN KEY (CustomerID) REFERENCES Customer_T (CustomerID));

CREATE TABLE Product_T
        (ProductID                  NUMBER(11,0)      NOT NULL,
        ProductDescription          VARCHAR2(50),
        ProductFinish               VARCHAR2(20),
        ProductStandardPrice        DECIMAL(6,2),
        ProductLineID               NUMBER(11,0),
CONSTRAINT Product_PK PRIMARY KEY (ProductID));

CREATE TABLE OrderLine_T
        (OrderID                    NUMBER(11,0)      NOT NULL,
        ProductID                   NUMBER(11,0)      NOT NULL,
        OrderedQuantity             NUMBER(11,0),
CONSTRAINT OrderLine_PK PRIMARY KEY (OrderID, ProductID),
CONSTRAINT OrderLine_FK1 FOREIGN KEY (OrderID) REFERENCES Order_T (OrderID),
CONSTRAINT OrderLine_FK2 FOREIGN KEY (ProductID) REFERENCES Product_T (ProductID));
```

The OrderLine_T table provides an example of a table that has two foreign keys. Foreign keys in this table reference both the Order_T and Product_T tables.

Well-Structured Relations

Well-structured relation
A relation that contains minimal redundancy and allows users to insert, modify, and delete the rows in a table without errors or inconsistencies.

To prepare for our discussion of normalization, we need to address the following question: What constitutes a well-structured relation? Intuitively, a **well-structured relation** contains minimal redundancy and allows users to insert, modify, and delete the rows in a table without errors or inconsistencies. EMPLOYEE1 (Figure 4-1) is such a relation. Each row of the table contains data describing one employee, and any modification to an employee's data (such as a change in salary) is confined to one row of the table. In contrast, EMPLOYEE2 (Figure 4-2b) is not a well-structured relation. If you examine the sample data in the table, you will notice considerable redundancy. For example, values for EmpID, Name, DeptName, and Salary appear in two separate rows for employees 100, 110, and 150. Consequently, if the salary for employee 100 changes, we must record this fact in two rows (or more, for some employees).

Anomaly
An error or inconsistency that may result when a user attempts to update a table that contains redundant data. The three types of anomalies are insertion, deletion, and modification anomalies.

Redundancies in a table may result in errors or inconsistencies (called **anomalies**) when a user attempts to update the data in the table. We are typically concerned about three types of anomalies:

1. ***Insertion anomaly*** Suppose that we need to add a new employee to EMPLOYEE2. The primary key for this relation is the combination of EmpID and CourseTitle (as noted earlier). Therefore, to insert a new row, the user must supply values for both EmpID and CourseTitle (because primary key values cannot be null or nonexistent). This is an anomaly because the user should be able to enter employee data without supplying course data.
2. ***Deletion anomaly*** Suppose that the data for employee number 140 are deleted from the table. This will result in losing the information that this employee

EmpID	CourseTitle	DateCompleted
100	SPSS	6/19/201X
100	Surveys	10/7/201X
140	Tax Acc	12/8/201X
110	Visual Basic	1/12/201X
110	C++	4/22/201X
150	SPSS	6/19/201X
150	Java	8/12/201X

FIGURE 4-7 EMP COURSE

completed a course (Tax Acc) on 12/8/201X. In fact, it results in losing the information that this course had an offering that completed on that date.

3. ***Modification anomaly*** Suppose that employee number 100 gets a salary increase. We must record the increase in each of the rows for that employee (two occurrences in Figure 4-2); otherwise, the data will be inconsistent.

These anomalies indicate that EMPLOYEE2 is not a well-structured relation. The problem with this relation is that it contains data about two entities: EMPLOYEE and COURSE. We will use normalization theory (described later in this chapter) to divide EMPLOYEE2 into two relations. One of the resulting relations is EMPLOYEE1 (Figure 4-1). The other we will call EMP COURSE, which appears with sample data in Figure 4-7. The primary key of this relation is the combination of EmpID and CourseTitle, and we underline these attribute names in Figure 4-7 to highlight this fact. Examine Figure 4-7 to verify that EMP COURSE is free of the types of anomalies described previously and is therefore well structured.

TRANSFORMING EER DIAGRAMS INTO RELATIONS

During logical design, you transform the E-R (and EER) diagrams that were developed during conceptual design into relational database schemas. The inputs to this process are the entity-relationship (and enhanced E-R) diagrams that you studied in Chapters 2 and 3. The outputs are the relational schemas described in the first two sections of this chapter.

Transforming (or mapping) EER diagrams into relations is a relatively straightforward process with a well-defined set of rules. In fact, many CASE tools can automatically perform many of the conversion steps. However, it is important that you understand the steps in this process for four reasons:

1. CASE tools often cannot model more complex data relationships such as ternary relationships and supertype/subtype relationships. In these situations, you may have to perform the steps manually.
2. There are sometimes legitimate alternatives where you will need to choose a particular solution.
3. You must be prepared to perform a quality check on the results obtained with a CASE tool.
4. Understanding the transformation process helps you understand why conceptual data modeling (modeling the real-world domain) is truly a different activity from representing the results of the conceptual data modeling process in a form that can be implemented using a DBMS.

In the following discussion, we illustrate the steps in the transformation with examples taken from Chapters 2 and 3. It will help for you to recall that we discussed three types of entities in those chapters:

1. ***Regular entities*** are entities that have an independent existence and generally represent real-world objects, such as persons and products. Regular entity types are represented by rectangles with a single line.

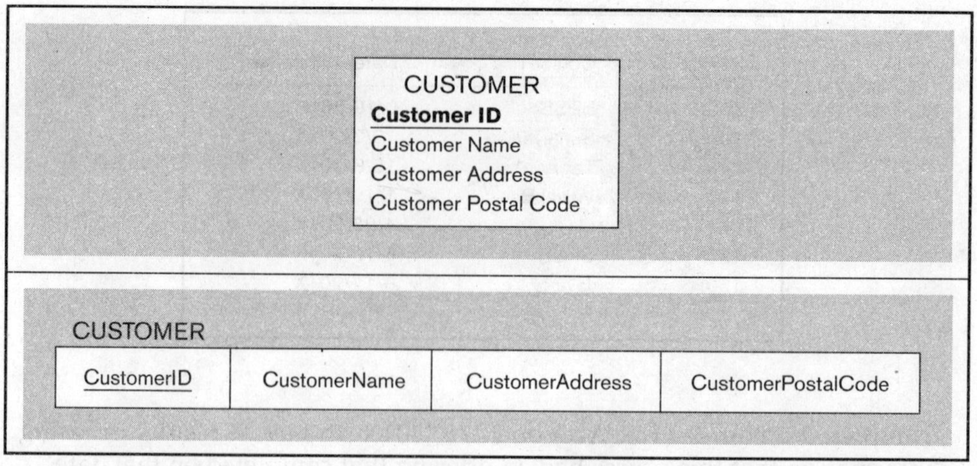

FIGURE 4-8 Mapping the regular entity CUSTOMER
(a) CUSTOMER entity type
(b) CUSTOMER relation

2. ***Weak entities*** are entities that cannot exist except with an identifying relationship with an owner (regular) entity type. Weak entities are identified by a rectangle with a double line.
3. ***Associative entities*** (also called gerunds) are formed from many-to-many relationships between other entity types. Associative entities are represented by a rectangle with rounded corners.

Step 1: Map Regular Entities

Each regular entity type in an E-R diagram is transformed into a relation. The name given to the relation is generally the same as the entity type. Each simple attribute of the entity type becomes an attribute of the relation. The identifier of the entity type becomes the primary key of the corresponding relation. You should check to make sure that this primary key satisfies the desirable properties of identifiers outlined in Chapter 2.

Figure 4-8a shows a representation of the CUSTOMER entity type for Pine Valley Furniture Company from Chapter 2 (see Figure 2-22). The corresponding CUSTOMER relation is shown in graphical form in Figure 4-8b. In this figure and those that follow in this section, we show only a few key attributes for each relation to simplify the figures.

COMPOSITE ATTRIBUTES When a regular entity type has a composite attribute, only the simple components of the composite attribute are included in the new relation as its attributes. Figure 4-9 shows a variation on the example in Figure 4-8, where Customer Address is represented as a composite attribute with components Street, City, and State (see Figure 4-9a). This entity is mapped to the CUSTOMER relation, which contains the simple address attributes, as shown in Figure 4-9b. Although Customer Name is modeled

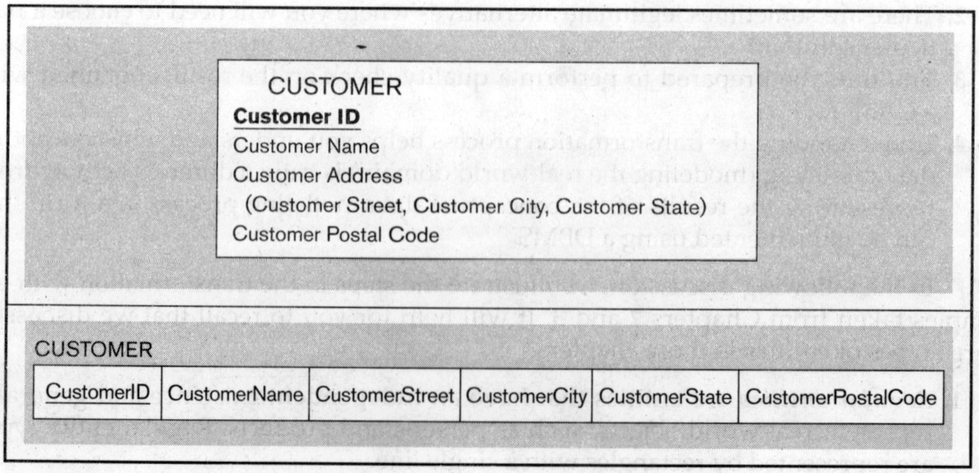

FIGURE 4-9 Mapping a composite attribute
(a) CUSTOMER entity type with composite attribute
(b) CUSTOMER relation with address detail

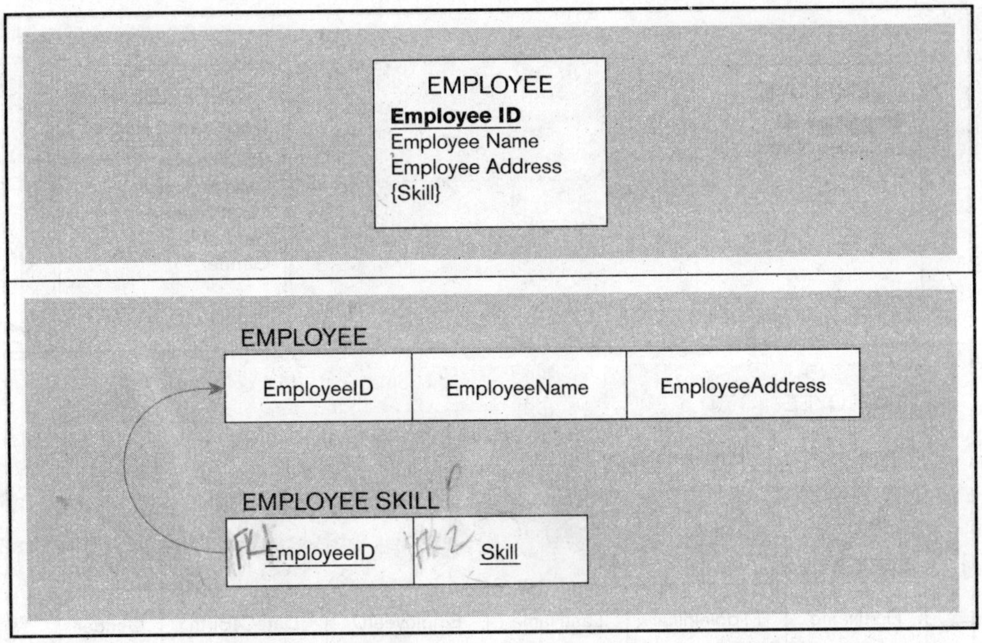

FIGURE 4-10 Mapping an entity with a multivalued attribute
(a) EMPLOYEE entity type with multivalued attribute

(b) Mapping a multivalued attribute

as a simple attribute in Figure 4-9a, you are aware that it instead could have been modeled as a composite attribute with components Last Name, First Name, and Middle Initial. In designing the CUSTOMER relation (Figure 4-9b), you may choose to use these simple attributes instead of CustomerName. Compared to composite attributes, simple attributes improve data accessibility and facilitate maintaining data quality.

MULTIVALUED ATTRIBUTES When the regular entity type contains a multivalued attribute, two new relations (rather than one) are created. The first relation contains all of the attributes of the entity type except the multivalued attribute. The second relation contains two attributes that form the primary key of the second relation. The first of these attributes is the primary key from the first relation, which becomes a foreign key in the second relation. The second is the multivalued attribute. The name of the second relation should capture the meaning of the multivalued attribute.

An example of this procedure is shown in Figure 4-10. This is the EMPLOYEE entity type for Pine Valley Furniture Company. As shown in Figure 4-10a, EMPLOYEE has Skill as a multivalued attribute. Figure 4-10b shows the two relations that are created. The first (called EMPLOYEE) has the primary key EmployeeID. The second relation (called EMPLOYEE SKILL) has the two attributes, EmployeeID and Skill, which form the primary key. The relationship between foreign and primary keys is indicated by the arrow in the figure.

The relation EMPLOYEE SKILL contains no nonkey attributes (also called *descriptors*). Each row simply records the fact that a particular employee possesses a particular skill. This provides an opportunity for you to suggest to users that new attributes can be added to this relation. For example, the attributes YearsExperience and/or CertificationDate might be appropriate new values to add to this relation. See Figure 2-15b for another variation on employee skills.

If an entity type contains multiple multivalued attributes, each of them will be converted to a separate relation.

Step 2: Map Weak Entities

Recall that a weak entity type does not have an independent existence but exists only through an identifying relationship with another entity type called the *owner*. A weak entity type does not have a complete identifier but must have an attribute called a partial identifier that permits distinguishing the various occurrences of the weak entity for each owner entity instance.

FIGURE 4-11 Example of mapping a weak entity
(a) Weak entity DEPENDENT

(b) Relations resulting from weak entity

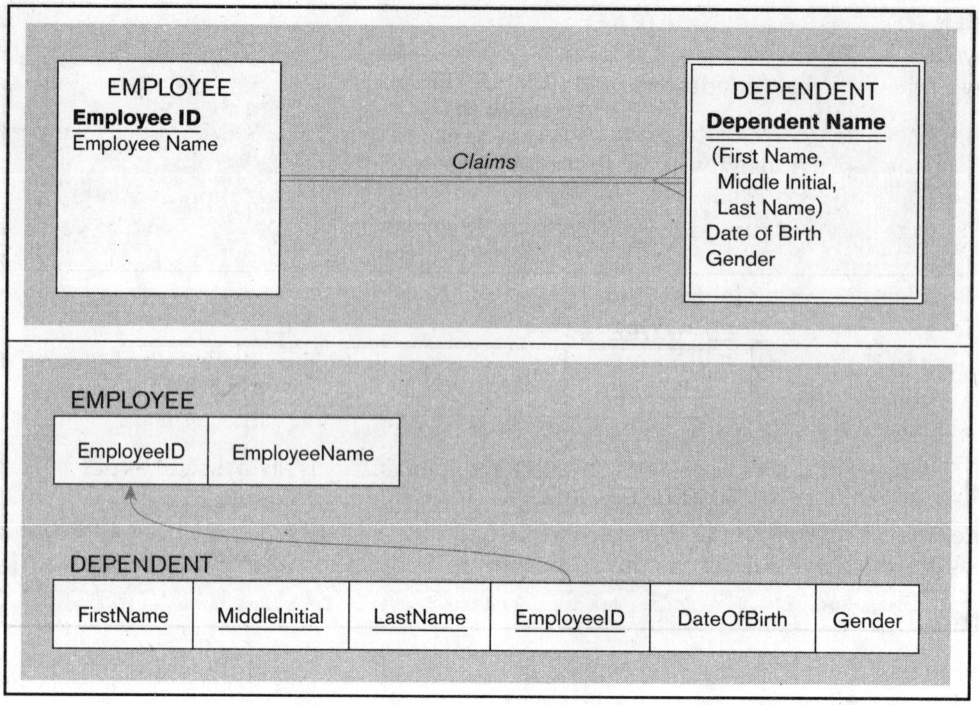

The following procedure assumes that you have already created a relation corresponding to the identifying entity type during Step 1. If you have not, you should create that relation now, using the process described in Step 1.

For each weak entity type, create a new relation and include all of the simple attributes (or simple components of composite attributes) as attributes of this relation. Then include the primary key of the *identifying* relation as a foreign key attribute in this new relation. The primary key of the new relation is the combination of this primary key of the identifying and the partial identifier of the weak entity type.

An example of this process is shown in Figure 4-11. Figure 4-11a shows the weak entity type DEPENDENT and its identifying entity type EMPLOYEE, linked by the identifying relationship Claims (see Figure 2-5). Notice that the attribute Dependent Name, which is the partial identifier for this relation, is a composite attribute with components First Name, Middle Initial, and Last Name. Thus, we assume that, *for a given employee*, these items will uniquely identify a dependent (a notable exception being the case of prizefighter George Foreman, who has named all his sons after himself).

Figure 4-11b shows the two relations that result from mapping this E-R segment. The primary key of DEPENDENT consists of four attributes: EmployeeID, FirstName, MiddleInitial, and LastName. DateOfBirth and Gender are the nonkey attributes. The foreign key relationship with its primary key is indicated by the arrow in the figure.

Surrogate primary key
A serial number or other system-assigned primary key for a relation.

In practice, an alternative approach is often used to simplify the primary key of the DEPENDENT relation: Create a new attribute (called Dependent#), which will be used as a **surrogate primary key** in Figure 4-11b. With this approach, the relation DEPENDENT has the following attributes:

DEPENDENT(Dependent#, EmployeeID, FirstName, MiddleInitial, LastName, DateOfBirth, Gender)

Dependent# is simply a serial number that is assigned to each dependent of an employee. Notice that this solution will ensure unique identification for each dependent (even for those of George Foreman!).

WHEN TO CREATE A SURROGATE KEY A surrogate key is usually created to simplify the key structures. According to Hoberman (2006), a surrogate key should be created when any of the following conditions hold:

- There is a composite primary key, as in the case of the DEPENDENT relation shown previously with the four component primary key.
- The natural primary key (i.e., the key used in the organization and identified in conceptual data modeling as the identifier) is inefficient (e.g., it may be very long and hence costly for database software to handle if it is used as a foreign key that references other tables).
- The natural primary key is recycled (i.e., the key is reused or repeated periodically, so it may not actually be unique over time); a more general statement of this condition is when the natural primary key cannot, in fact, be guaranteed to be unique over time (e.g., there could be duplicates, such as with names or titles).

Whenever a surrogate key is created, the natural key is always kept as nonkey data in the same relation because the natural key has organizational meaning. In fact, surrogate keys mean nothing to users, so they are usually never displayed; rather, the natural keys are shown to the user as the primary keys and used as identifiers in searches.

Step 3: Map Binary Relationships

The procedure for representing relationships depends on both the degree of the relationships (unary, binary, or ternary) and the cardinalities of the relationships. We describe and illustrate the important cases in the following discussion.

MAP BINARY ONE-TO-MANY RELATIONSHIPS For each binary 1:*M* relationship, first create a relation for each of the two entity types participating in the relationship, using the procedure described in Step 1. Next, include the primary key attribute (or attributes) of the entity on the one-side of the relationship as a foreign key in the relation that is on the many-side of the relationship. (A mnemonic you can use to remember this rule is this: The primary key migrates to the many side.)

To illustrate this simple process, we use the Submits relationship between customers and orders for Pine Valley Furniture Company (see Figure 2-22). This 1:*M* relationship is illustrated in Figure 4-12a. (Again, we show only a few attributes for simplicity.) Figure 4-12b shows the result of applying this rule to map the entity types with the 1:*M* relationship. The primary key CustomerID of CUSTOMER (the one side) is included as a foreign key in ORDER (the many side). The foreign key relationship is indicated with an arrow.

PINE VALLEY FURNITURE

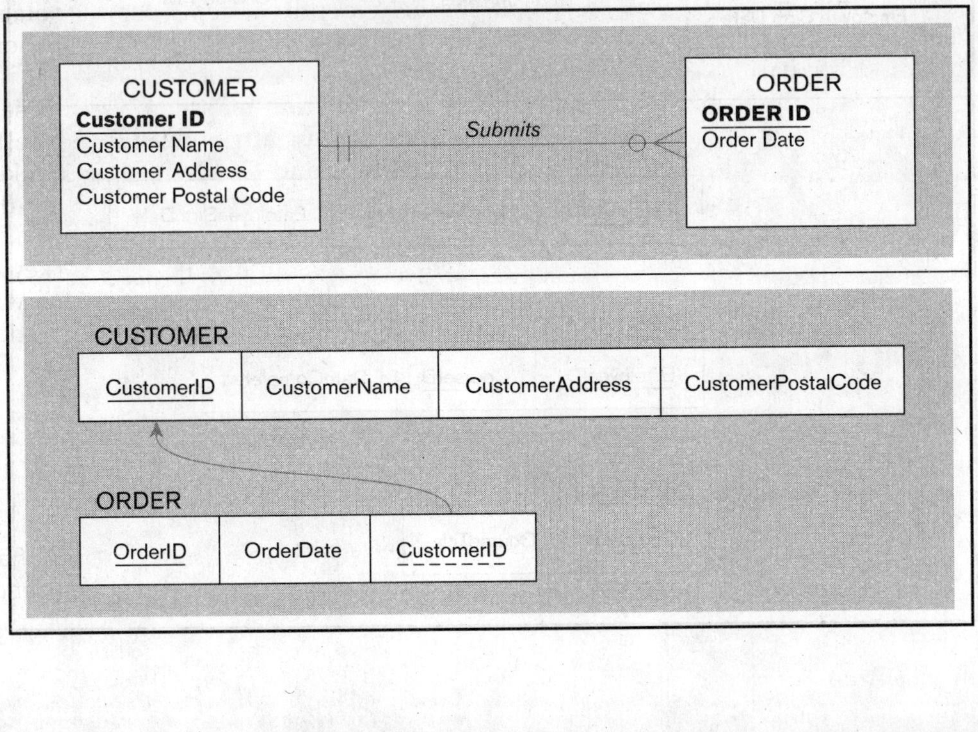

FIGURE 4-12 Example of mapping a 1:*M* relationship
(a) Relationship between customers and orders

(b) Mapping the relationship

MAP BINARY MANY-TO-MANY RELATIONSHIPS Suppose that there is a binary many-to-many (*M:N*) relationship between two entity types, A and B. For such a relationship, create a new relation, C. Include as foreign key attributes in C the primary key for each of the two participating entity types. These attributes together become the primary key of C. Any nonkey attributes that are associated with the *M:N* relationship are included with the relation C.

Figure 4-13 shows an example of applying this rule. Figure 4-13a shows the Completes relationship between the entity types EMPLOYEE and COURSE from Figure 2-11a. Figure 4-13b shows the three relations (EMPLOYEE, COURSE, and CERTIFICATE) that are formed from the entity types and the Completes relationship. If Completes had been represented as an associative entity, as is done in Figure 2-11b, a similar result would occur, but we will deal with associative entities in a subsequent section. In the case of an *M:N* relationship, first, a relation is created for each of the two regular entity types EMPLOYEE and COURSE. Then a new relation (named CERTIFICATE in Figure 4-13b) is created for the Completes relationship. The primary key of CERTIFICATE is the combination of EmployeeID and CourseID, which are the respective primary keys of EMPLOYEE and COURSE. As indicated in the diagram, these attributes are foreign keys that "point to" the respective primary keys. The nonkey attribute DateCompleted also appears in CERTIFICATE. Although not shown here, it might be wise to create a surrogate primary key for the CERTIFICATE relation.

MAP BINARY ONE-TO-ONE RELATIONSHIPS Binary one-to-one relationships can be viewed as a special case of one-to-many relationships. The process of mapping such a relationship to relations requires two steps. First, two relations are created, one for each of the participating entity types. Second, the primary key of one of the relations is included as a foreign key in the other relation.

In a 1:1 relationship, the association in one direction is nearly always an optional one, whereas the association in the other direction is mandatory one. (You can review the notation for these terms in Figure 2-1.) You should include in the relation on the

FIGURE 4-13 Example of mapping a *M:N* relationship
(a) Completes relationship (*M:N*)

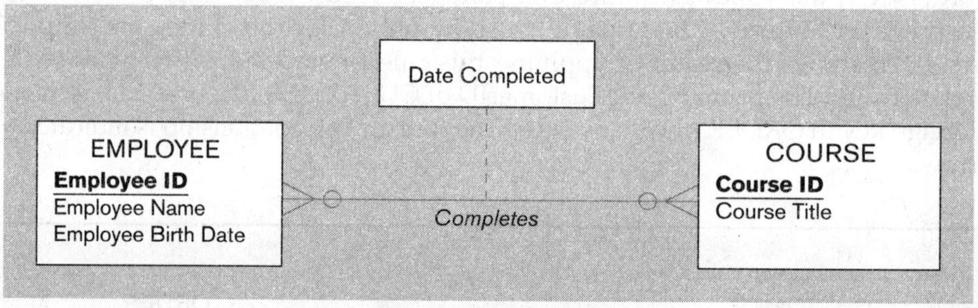

(b) Three resulting relations

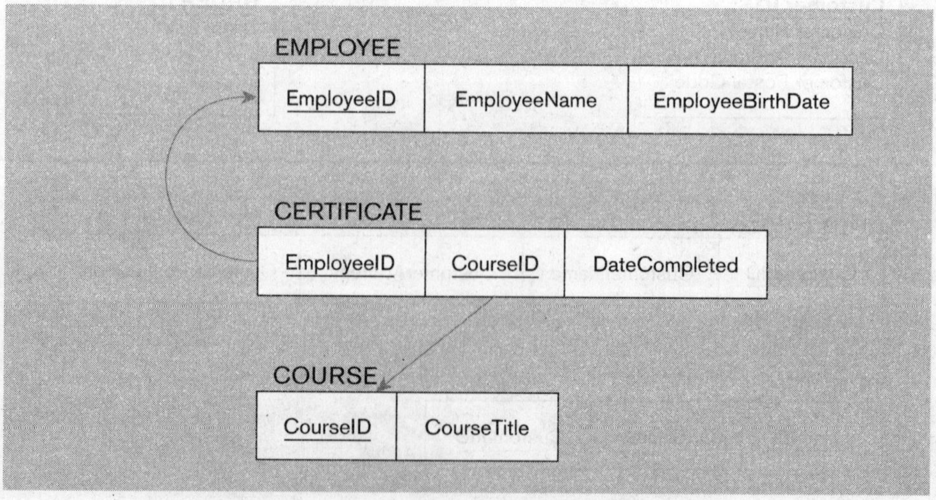

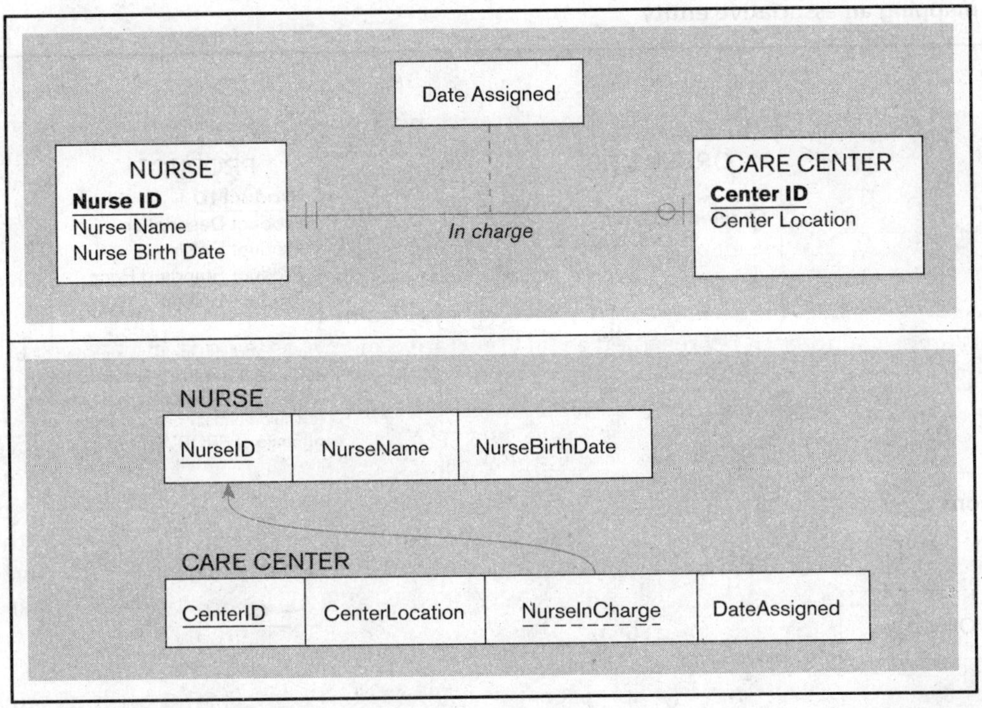

FIGURE 4-14 Example of mapping a binary 1:1 relationship
(a) In Charge relationship (binary 1:1)
(b) Resulting relations

optional side of the relationship the foreign key of the entity type that has the mandatory participation in the 1:1 relationship. This approach will prevent the need to store null values in the foreign key attribute. Any attributes associated with the relationship itself are also included in the same relation as the foreign key.

An example of applying this procedure is shown in Figure 4-14. Figure 4-14a shows a binary 1:1 relationship between the entity types NURSE and CARE CENTER. Each care center must have a nurse who is in charge of that center. Thus, the association from CARE CENTER to NURSE is a mandatory one, whereas the association from NURSE to CARE CENTER is an optional one (since any nurse may or may not be in charge of a care center). The attribute Date Assigned is attached to the In Charge relationship.

The result of mapping this relationship to a set of relations is shown in Figure 4-14b. The two relations NURSE and CARE CENTER are created from the two entity types. Because CARE CENTER is the optional participant, the foreign key is placed in this relation. In this case, the foreign key is NurseInCharge. It has the same domain as NurseID, and the relationship with the primary key is shown in the figure. The attribute DateAssigned is also located in CARE CENTER and would not be allowed to be null.

Step 4: Map Associative Entities

As explained in Chapter 2, when a data modeler encounters a many-to-many relationship, he or she may choose to model that relationship as an associative entity in the E-R diagram. This approach is most appropriate when the end user can best visualize the relationship as an entity type rather than as an *M:N* relationship. Mapping the associative entity involves essentially the same steps as mapping an *M:N* relationship, as described in Step 3.

The first step is to create three relations: one for each of the two participating entity types and a third for the associative entity. We refer to the relation formed from the associative entity as the *associative relation*. The second step then depends on whether on the E-R diagram an identifier was assigned to the associative entity.

IDENTIFIER NOT ASSIGNED If an identifier was not assigned, the default primary key for the associative relation consists of the two primary key attributes from the other two relations. These attributes are then foreign keys that reference the other two relations.

FIGURE 4-15 Example of mapping an associative entity

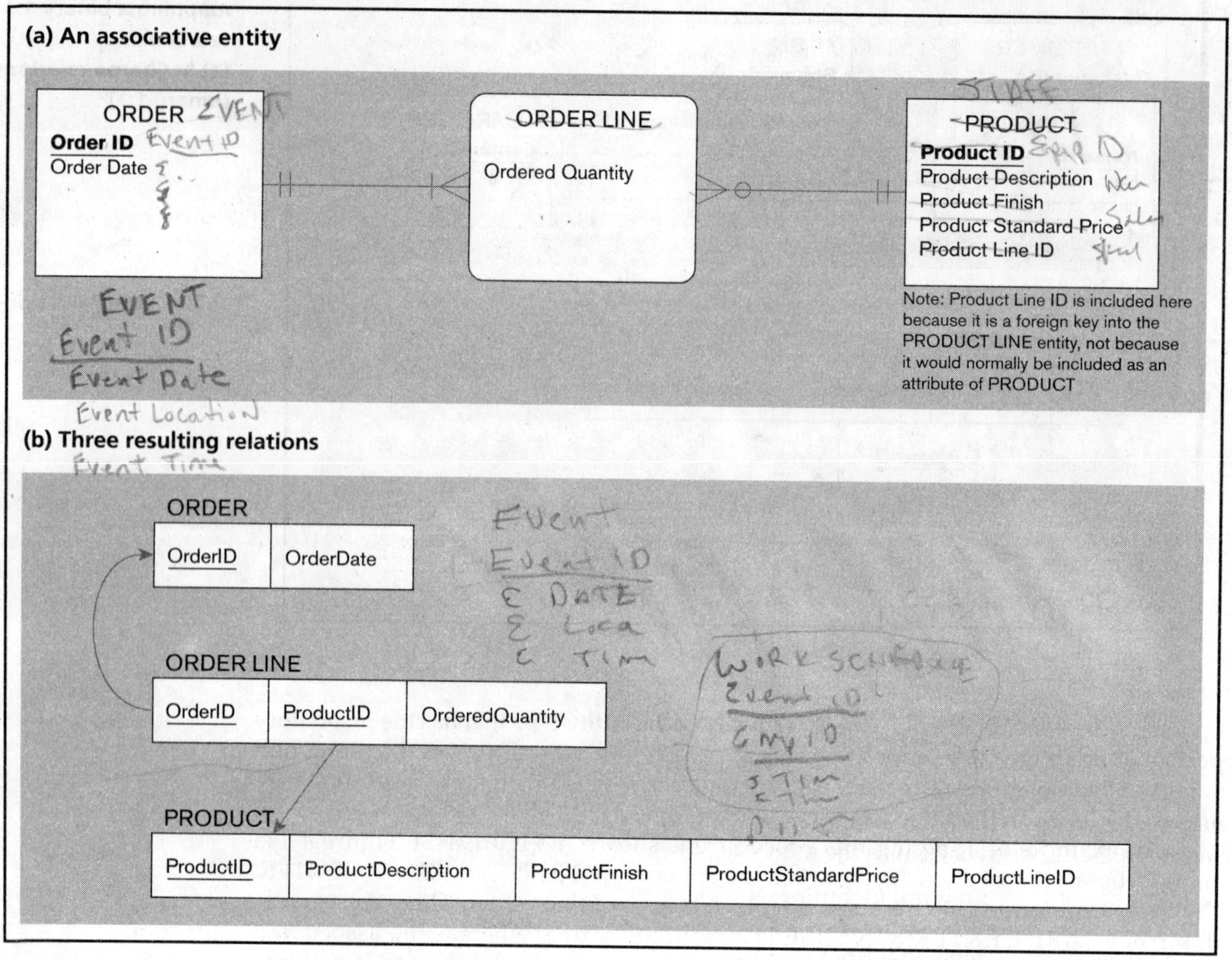

PINE VALLEY FURNITURE

An example of this case is shown in Figure 4-15. Figure 4-15a shows the associative entity ORDER LINE that links the ORDER and PRODUCT entity types at Pine Valley Furniture Company (see Figure 2-22). Figure 4-15b shows the three relations that result from this mapping. Note the similarity of this example to that of an *M:N* relationship shown in Figure 4-13.

IDENTIFIER ASSIGNED Sometimes a data modeler will assign a single-attribute identifier to the associative entity type on the E-R diagram. There are two reasons that may have motivated the data modeler to assign a single-attribute key during conceptual data modeling:

1. The associative entity type has a natural single-attribute identifier that is familiar to end users.
2. The default identifier (consisting of the identifiers for each of the participating entity types) may not uniquely identify instances of the associative entity.

These motivations are in addition to the reasons mentioned earlier in this chapter to create a surrogate primary key.

The process for mapping the associative entity in this case is now modified as follows. As before, a new (associative) relation is created to represent the associative entity. However, the primary key for this relation is the identifier assigned on the E-R diagram (rather than the default key). The primary keys for the two participating entity types are then included as foreign keys in the associative relation.

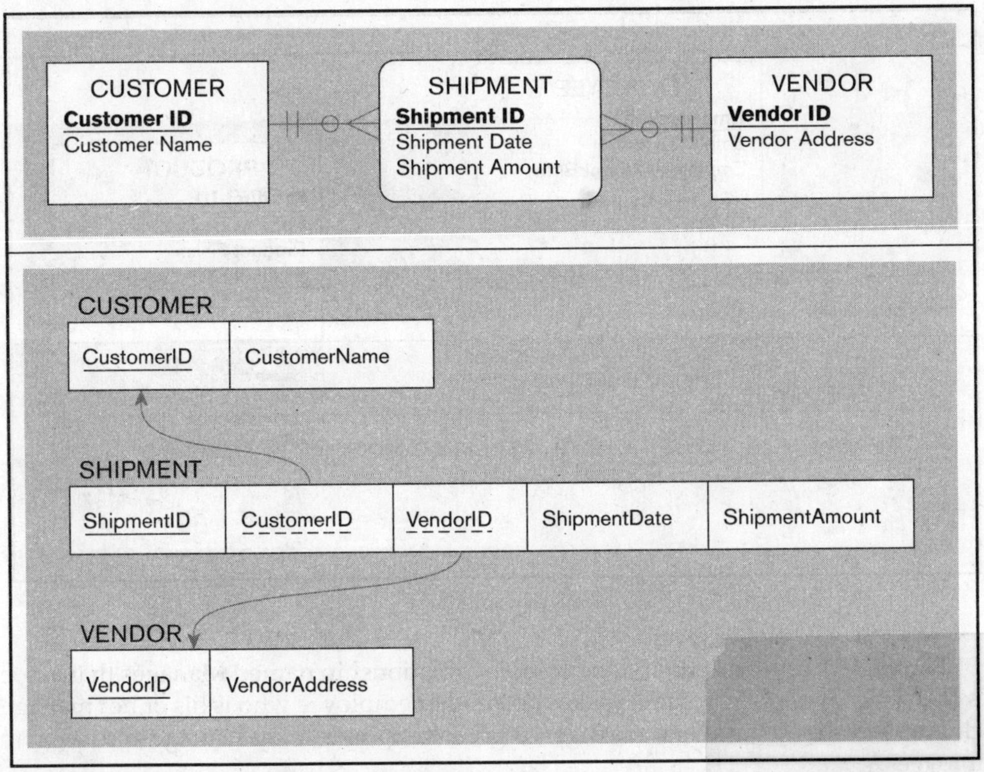

FIGURE 4-16 Example of mapping an associative entity with an identifier
(a) SHIPMENT associative entity
(b) Three resulting relations

An example of this process is shown in Figure 4-16. Figure 4-16a shows the associative entity type SHIPMENT that links the CUSTOMER and VENDOR entity types. Shipment ID has been chosen as the identifier for SHIPMENT for two reasons:

1. Shipment ID is a natural identifier for this entity that is very familiar to end users.
2. The default identifier consisting of the combination of Customer ID and Vendor ID does not uniquely identify the instances of SHIPMENT. In fact, a given vendor typically makes many shipments to a given customer. Even including the attribute Date does not guarantee uniqueness, since there may be more than one shipment by a particular vendor on a given date. The surrogate key ShipmentID will, however, uniquely identify each shipment.

Two nonkey attributes associated with SHIPMENT are Shipment Date and Shipment Amount.

The result of mapping this entity to a set of relations is shown in Figure 4-16b. The new associative relation is named SHIPMENT. The primary key is ShipmentID. CustomerID and VendorID are included as foreign keys in this relation, and ShipmentDate and ShipmentAmount are nonkey attributes.

Step 5: Map Unary Relationships

In Chapter 2, we defined a unary relationship as a relationship between the instances of a single entity type. Unary relationships are also called *recursive relationships*. The two most important cases of unary relationships are one-to-many and many-to-many relationships. We discuss these two cases separately because the approach to mapping is somewhat different for the two types.

UNARY ONE-TO-MANY RELATIONSHIPS The entity type in the unary relationship is mapped to a relation using the procedure described in Step 1. Then a foreign key attribute is added to the same relation; this attribute references the primary key values in the same relation. (This foreign key must have the same domain as the primary key.) This type of a foreign key is called a **recursive foreign key**.

Recursive foreign key
A foreign key in a relation that references the primary key values of the same relation.

FIGURE 4-17 Mapping a unary 1:*N* relationship
(a) EMPLOYEE entity with unary relationship
(b) EMPLOYEE relation with recursive foreign key

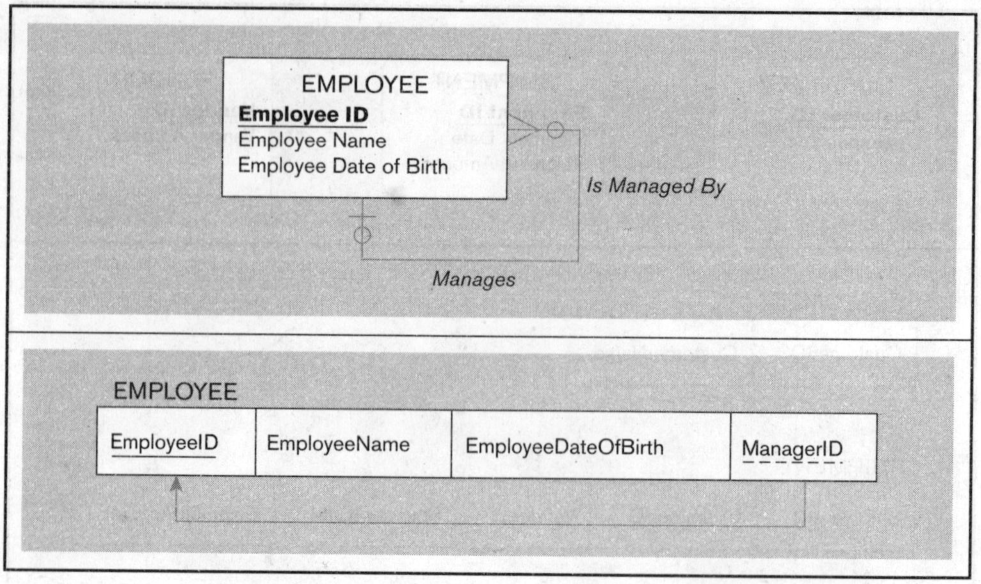

Figure 4-17a shows a unary one-to-many relationship named Manages that associates each employee of an organization with another employee who is his or her manager. Each employee may have one manager; a given employee may manage zero to many employees.

The EMPLOYEE relation that results from mapping this entity and relationship is shown in Figure 4-17b. The (recursive) foreign key in the relation is named ManagerID. This attribute has the same domain as the primary key EmployeeID. Each row of this relation stores the following data for a given employee: EmployeeID, EmployeeName, EmployeeDateOfBirth, and ManagerID (i.e., EmployeeID for this employee's manager). Notice that because it is a foreign key, ManagerID references EmployeeID.

UNARY MANY-TO-MANY RELATIONSHIPS With this type of relationship, two relations are created: one to represent the entity type in the relationship and an associative relation to represent the *M:N* relationship itself. The primary key of the associative relation consists of two attributes. These attributes (which need not have the same name) both take their values from the primary key of the other relation. Any nonkey attribute of the relationship is included in the associative relation.

An example of mapping a unary *M:N* relationship is shown in Figure 4-18. Figure 4-18a shows a bill-of-materials relationship among items that are assembled from other items or components. (This structure was described in Chapter 2, and an example appears in Figure 2-13.) The relationship (called Contains) is *M:N* because a given item can contain numerous component items, and, conversely, an item can be used as a component in numerous other items.

The relations that result from mapping this entity and its relationship are shown in Figure 4-18b. The ITEM relation is mapped directly from the same entity type. COMPONENT is an associative relation whose primary key consists of two attributes that are arbitrarily named ItemNo and ComponentNo. The attribute Quantity is a nonkey attribute of this relation that, for a given item, records the quantity of a particular component item used in that item. Notice that both ItemNo and ComponentNo reference the primary key (ItemNo) of the ITEM relation.

We can easily query these relations to determine, for example, the components of a given item. The following SQL query will list the immediate components (and their quantity) for item number 100:

```
SELECT ComponentNo, Quantity
FROM Component_T
WHERE ItemNo = 100;
```

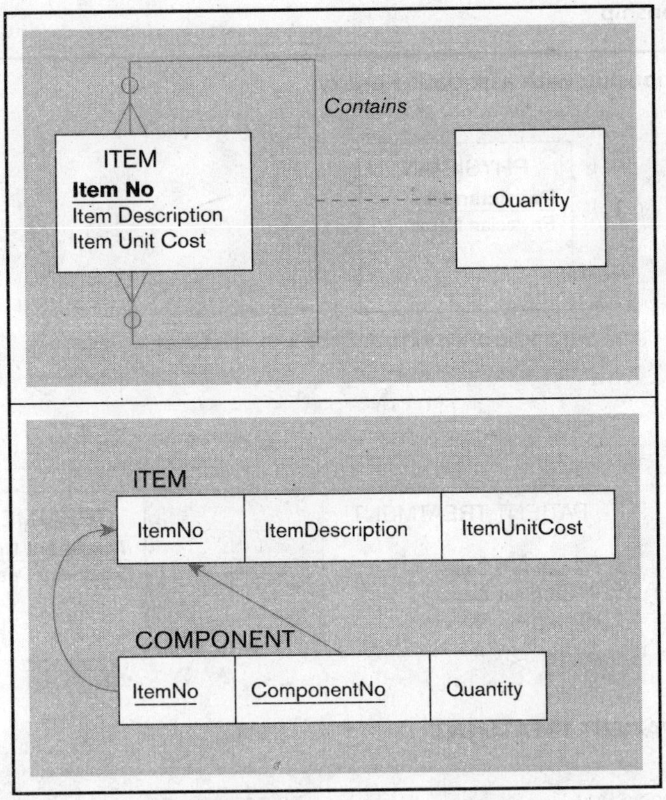

FIGURE 4-18 Mapping a unary *M:N* relationship
(a) Bill-of-materials relationship Contains (*M:N*)

(b) ITEM and COMPONENT relations

Step 6: Map Ternary (and *n*-ary) Relationships

Recall from Chapter 2 that a ternary relationship is a relationship among three entity types. In that chapter, we recommended that you convert a ternary relationship to an associative entity to represent participation constraints more accurately.

To map an associative entity type that links three regular entity types, we create a new associative relation. The default primary key of this relation consists of the three primary key attributes for the participating entity types. (In some cases, additional attributes are required to form a unique primary key.) These attributes then act in the role of foreign keys that reference the individual primary keys of the participating entity types. Any attributes of the associative entity type become attributes of the new relation.

An example of mapping a ternary relationship (represented as an associative entity type) is shown in Figure 4-19. Figure 4-19a is an E-R segment (or view) that represents a *patient* receiving a *treatment* from a *physician*. The associative entity type PATIENT TREATMENT has the attributes PTreatment Date, PTreatment Time, and PTreatment Results; values are recorded for these attributes for each instance of PATIENT TREATMENT.

The result of mapping this view is shown in Figure 4-19b. The primary key attributes PatientID, PhysicianID, and TreatmentCode become foreign keys in PATIENT TREATMENT. The foreign key into TREATMENT is called PTreatmentCode in PATIENT TREATMENT. We are using this column name to illustrate that the foreign key name does not have to be the same as the name of the primary key to which it refers, as long as the values come from the same domain. These three attributes are components of the primary key of PATIENT TREATMENT. However, they do not uniquely identify a given treatment, because a patient may receive the same treatment from the same physician on more than one occasion. Does including the attribute Date as part of the primary key (along with the other three attributes) result in a primary key? This would be so if a given patient receives only one treatment from a particular physician on a given date. However, this is not likely to be the case. For example, a patient may receive a treatment in the morning, then the same treatment again in the afternoon. To resolve this issue, we include PTreatmentDate and PTreatmentTime as part of the primary key. Therefore, the primary key of PATIENT TREATMENT consists of the five attributes

FIGURE 4-19 Mapping a ternary relationship

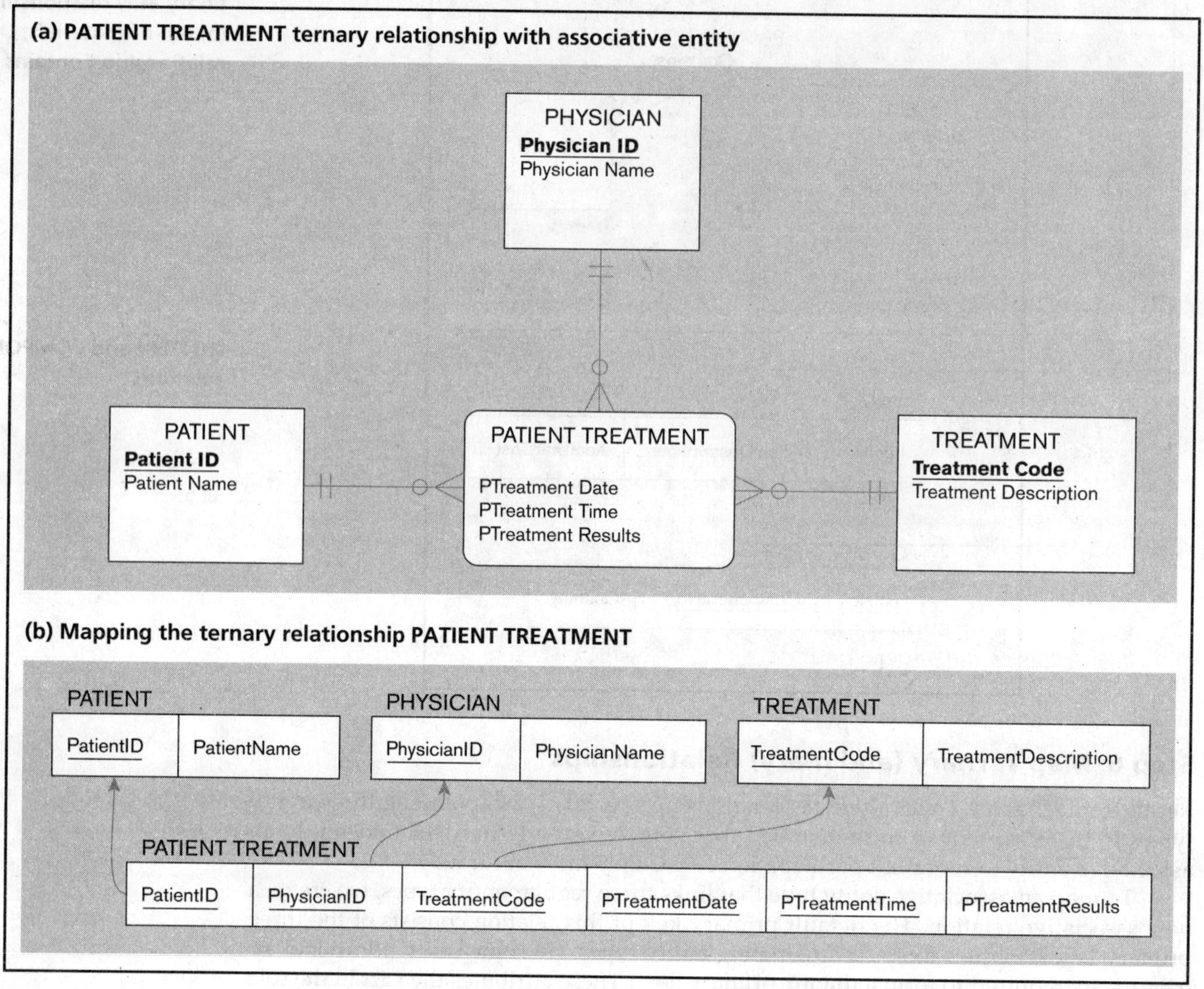

shown in Figure 4-19b: PatientID, PhysicianID, TreatmentCode, PTreatmentDate, and PTreatmentTime. The only nonkey attribute in the relation is PTreatmentResults.

Although this primary key is technically correct, it is complex and therefore difficult to manage and prone to errors. A better approach is to introduce a surrogate key, such as Treatment#, that is a serial number that uniquely identifies each treatment. In this case, each of the former primary key attributes except for PTreatmentDate and PTreatmentTime becomes a foreign key in the PATIENT TREATMENT relation. Another similar approach is to use an enterprise key, as described at the end of this chapter.

Step 7: Map Supertype/Subtype Relationships

The relational data model does not yet directly support supertype/subtype relationships. Fortunately, there are various strategies that database designers can use to represent these relationships with the relational data model (Chouinard, 1989). For our purposes, we use the following strategy, which is the one most commonly employed:

1. Create a separate relation for the supertype and for each of its subtypes.
2. Assign to the relation created for the supertype the attributes that are common to all members of the supertype, including the primary key.
3. Assign to the relation for each subtype the primary key of the supertype and only those attributes that are unique to that subtype.
4. Assign one (or more) attributes of the supertype to function as the subtype discriminator. (The role of the subtype discriminator was discussed in Chapter 3.)

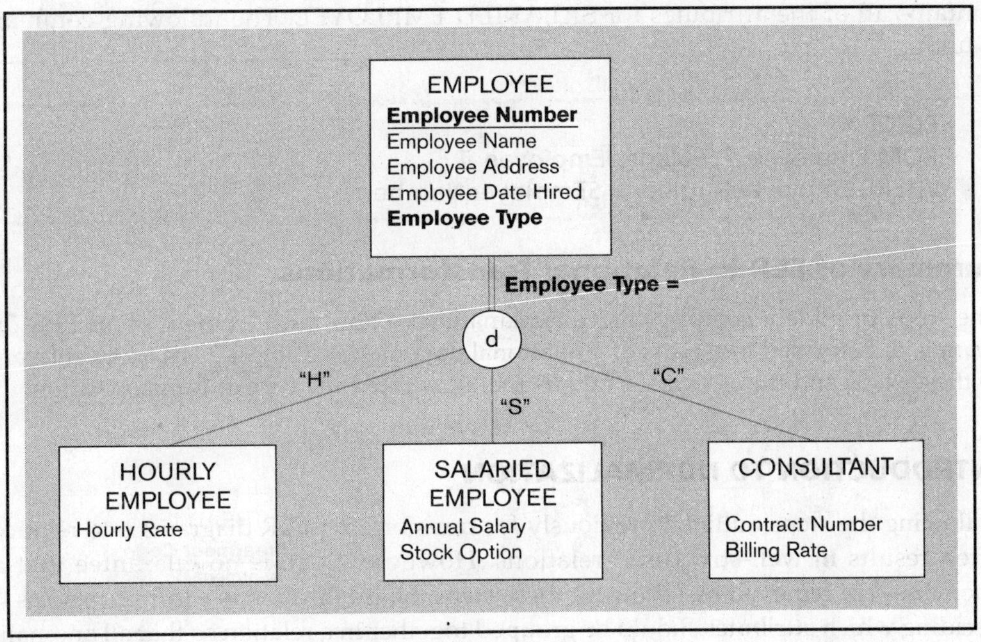

FIGURE 4-20 Supertype/subtype relationships

An example of applying this procedure is shown in Figures 4-20 and 4-21. Figure 4-20 shows the supertype EMPLOYEE with subtypes HOURLY EMPLOYEE, SALARIED EMPLOYEE, and CONSULTANT. (This example is described in Chapter 3, and Figure 4-20 is a repeat of Figure 3-8.) The primary key of EMPLOYEE is Employee Number, and the attribute Employee Type is the subtype discriminator.

The result of mapping this diagram to relations using these rules is shown in Figure 4-21. There is one relation for the supertype (EMPLOYEE) and one for each of the three subtypes. The primary key for each of the four relations is EmployeeNumber. A prefix is used to distinguish the name of the primary key for each subtype. For example, SEmployeeNumber is the name for the primary key of the relation SALARIED EMPLOYEE. Each of these attributes is a foreign key that references the supertype primary key, as indicated by the arrows in the diagram. Each subtype relation contains only those attributes unique to the subtype.

For each subtype, a relation can be produced that contains all of the attributes of that subtype (both specific and inherited) by using an SQL command that joins the subtype with its supertype. For example, suppose that we want to display a table that

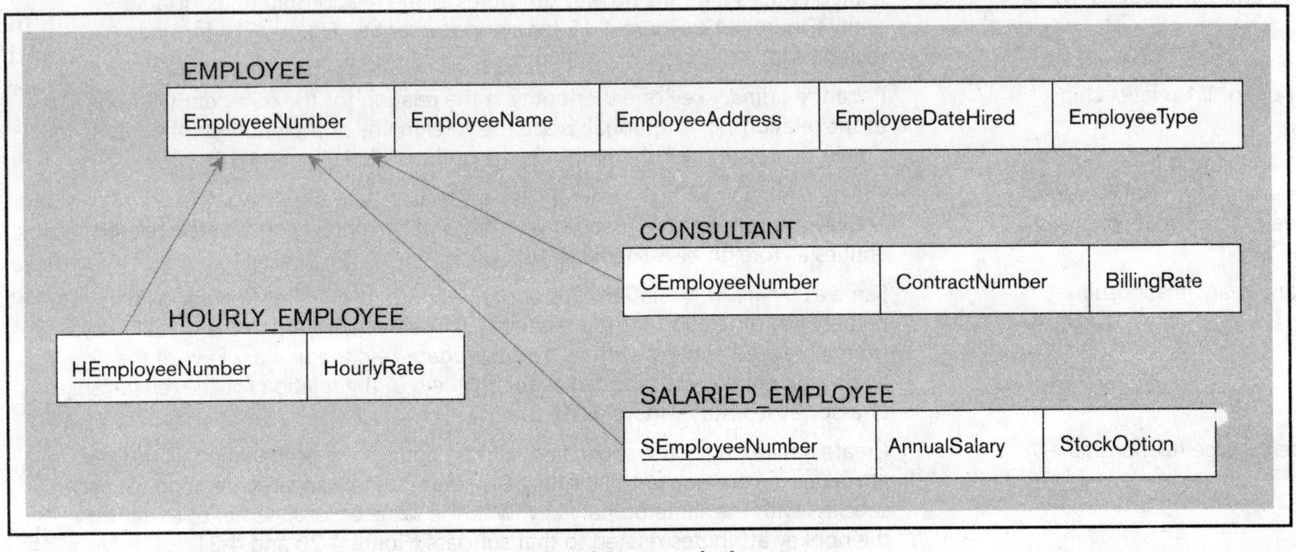

FIGURE 4-21 Mapping supertype/subtype relationships to relations

contains all of the attributes for SALARIED EMPLOYEE. The following command is used:

```
SELECT *
FROM Employee_T, SalariedEmployee_T
WHERE EmployeeNumber = SEmployeeNumber;
```

Summary of EER-to-Relational Transformations

The steps provide a comprehensive explanation of how each element of an EER diagram is transformed into parts of a relational data model. Table 4-2 is a quick reference to these steps and the associated figures that illustrate each type of transformation.

INTRODUCTION TO NORMALIZATION

Following the steps outlined previously for transforming EER diagrams into relations often results in well-structured relations. However, there is no guarantee that all anomalies are removed by following these steps. Normalization is a formal process for deciding which attributes should be grouped together in a relation so that all anomalies are removed. For example, we used the principles of normalization to convert the EMPLOYEE2 table (with its redundancy) to EMPLOYEE1 (Figure 4-1) and EMP COURSE

TABLE 4-2 Summary of EER to Relational Transformations

EER Structure	Relational Representation (Sample Figure)
Regular entity	Create a relation with primary key and nonkey attributes (Figure 4-8)
Composite attribute	Each component of a composite attribute becomes a separate attribute in the target relation (Figure 4-9)
Multivalued attribute	Create a separate relation for multivalued attribute with composite primary key, including the primary key of the entity (Figure 4-10)
Weak entity	Create a relation with a composite primary key (which includes the primary key of the entity on which this entity depends) and nonkey attributes (Figure 4-11)
Binary or unary 1:*N* relationship	Place the primary key of the entity on the one side of the relationship as a foreign key in the relation for the entity on the many side (Figure 4-12; Figure 4-17 for unary relationship)
Binary or unary *M:N* relationship or associative entity without its own key	Create a relation with a composite primary key using the primary keys of the related entities plus any nonkey attributes of the relationship or associative entity (Figure 4-13; Figure 4-15 for associative entity; Figure 4-18 for unary relationship)
Binary or unary 1:1 relationship	Place the primary key of either entity in the relation for the other entity; if one side of the relationship is optional, place the foreign key of the entity on the mandatory side in the relation for the entity on the optional side (Figure 4-14)
Binary or unary *M:N* relationship or associative entity with its own key	Create a relation with the primary key associated with the associative entity plus any nonkey attributes of the associative entity and the primary keys of the related entities as foreign keys (Figure 4-16)
Ternary and *n*-ary relationships	Same as binary *M:N* relationships above; without its own key, include as part of primary key of relation for the relationship or associative entity the primary keys from all related entities; with its own surrogate key, the primary keys of the associated entities are included as foreign keys in the relation for the relationship or associative entity (Figure 4-19)
Supertype/subtype relationship	Create a relation for the superclass, which contains the primary and all nonkey attributes in common with all subclasses, plus create a separate relation for each subclass with the same primary key (with the same or local name) but with only the nonkey attributes related to that subclass (Figure 4-20 and 4-21)

(Figure 4-7). There are two major occasions during the overall database development process when you can usually benefit from using normalization:

1. ***During logical database design (described in this chapter)*** You should use normalization concepts as a quality check for the relations that are obtained from mapping E-R diagrams.
2. ***When reverse-engineering older systems*** Many of the tables and user views for older systems are redundant and subject to the anomalies we describe in this chapter.

So far we have presented an intuitive discussion of well-structured relations; however, we need formal definitions of such relations, together with a process for designing them. **Normalization** is the process of successively reducing relations with anomalies to produce smaller, well-structured relations. Following are some of the main goals of normalization:

Normalization
The process of decomposing relations with anomalies to produce smaller, well-structured relations.

1. Minimize data redundancy, thereby avoiding anomalies and conserving storage space
2. Simplify the enforcement of referential integrity constraints
3. Make it easier to maintain data (insert, update, and delete)
4. Provide a better design that is an improved representation of the real world and a stronger basis for future growth

Normalization makes no assumptions about how data will be used in displays, queries, or reports. Normalization, based on what we will call *normal forms* and *functional dependencies,* defines rules of the business, not data usage. Further, remember that data are normalized by the end of logical database design. Thus, normalization, as we will see in Chapter 5, places no constraints on how data can or should be physically stored or, therefore, on processing performance. Normalization is a logical data modeling technique used to ensure that data are well structured from an organization-wide view.

Steps in Normalization

Normalization can be accomplished and understood in stages, each of which corresponds to a normal form (see Figure 4-22). A **normal form** is a state of a relation that requires that certain rules regarding relationships between attributes (or functional dependencies) are satisfied. We describe these rules briefly in this section and illustrate them in detail in the following sections:

Normal form
A state of a relation that requires that certain rules regarding relationships between attributes (or functional dependencies) are satisfied.

1. ***First normal form*** Any multivalued attributes (also called *repeating groups*) have been removed, so there is a single value (possibly null) at the intersection of each row and column of the table (as in Figure 4-2b).
2. ***Second normal form*** Any partial functional dependencies have been removed (i.e., nonkey attributes are identified by the whole primary key).
3. ***Third normal form*** Any transitive dependencies have been removed (i.e., nonkey attributes are identified by only the primary key).
4. ***Boyce-Codd normal form*** Any remaining anomalies that result from functional dependencies have been removed (because there was more than one possible primary key for the same nonkeys).
5. ***Fourth normal form*** Any multivalued dependencies have been removed.
6. ***Fifth normal form*** Any remaining anomalies have been removed.

We describe and illustrate the first through the third normal forms in this chapter. The remaining normal forms are described in Appendix B. These other normal forms are in an appendix only to save space in this chapter, not because they are less important. In fact, you can easily continue with Appendix B immediately after the section on the third normal form.

Functional Dependencies and Keys

Up to the Boyce-Codd normal form, normalization is based on the analysis of functional dependencies. A **functional dependency** is a constraint between two attributes or two sets of attributes. For any relation R, attribute B is functionally

Functional dependency
A constraint between two attributes in which the value of one attribute is determined by the value of another attribute.

FIGURE 4-22 Steps in normalization

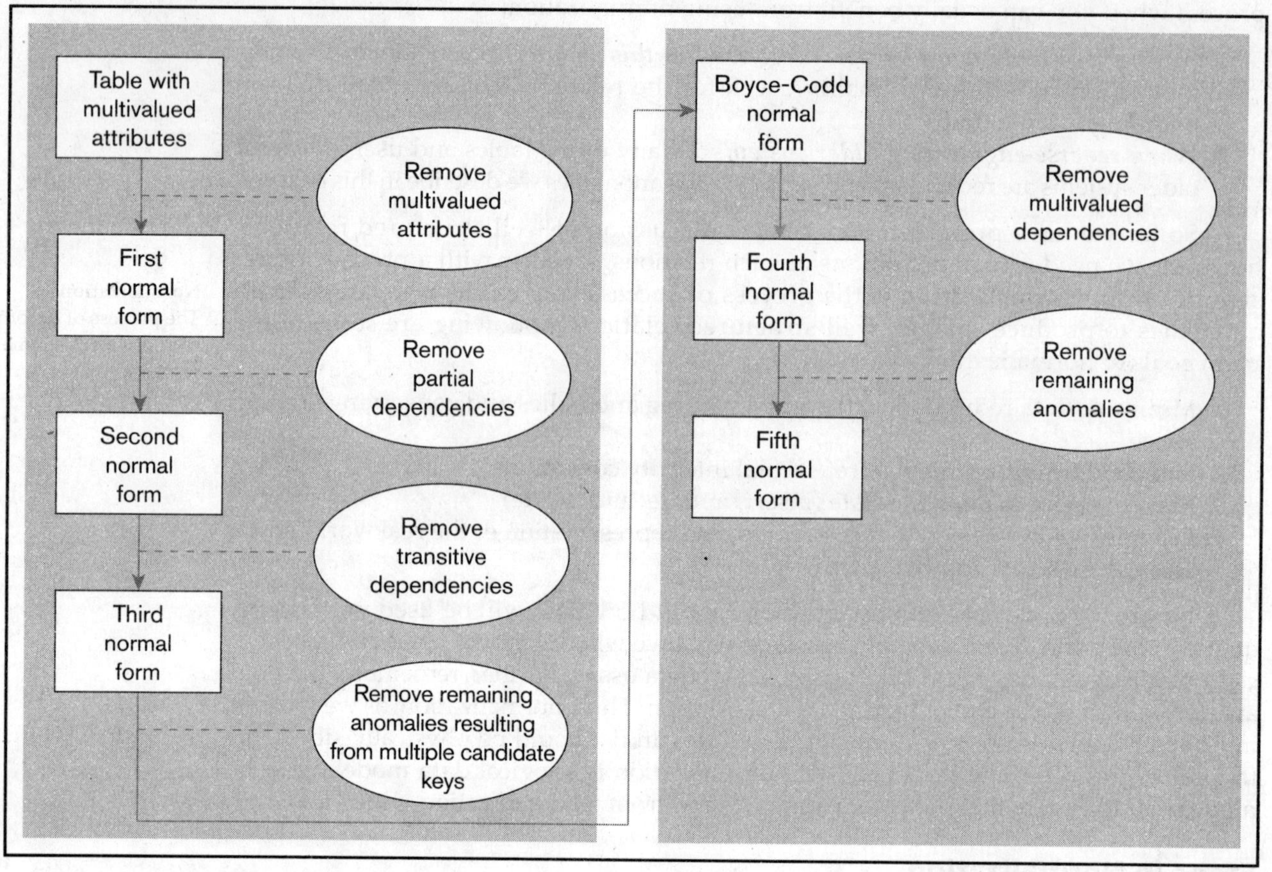

dependent on attribute A if, for every valid instance of A, that value of A uniquely determines the value of B (Dutka and Hanson, 1989). The functional dependency of B on A is represented by an arrow, as follows: A → B. A functional dependency is not a mathematical dependency: B cannot be computed from A. Rather, if you know the value of A, there can be only one value for B. An attribute may be functionally dependent on a combination of two (or more) attributes rather than on a single attribute. For example, consider the relation EMP COURSE (EmpID, CourseTitle, DateCompleted) shown in Figure 4-7. We represent the functional dependency in this relation as follows:

EmpID, CourseTitle → DateCompleted

The comma between EmpID and CourseTitle stands for the logical AND operator, because DateCompleted is functionally dependent on EmpID and CourseTitle in combination.

The functional dependency in this statement implies that the date a course is completed is determined by the identity of the employee and the title of the course. Typical examples of functional dependencies are the following:

1. ***SSN → Name, Address, Birthdate*** A person's name, address, and birth date are functionally dependent on that person's Social Security number (in other words, there can be only one Name, one Address, and one Birthdate for each SSN).
2. ***VIN → Make, Model, Color*** The make, model, and color of a vehicle are functionally dependent on the vehicle identification number (as above, there can be only one value of Make, Model, and Color associated with each VIN).
3. ***ISBN → Title, FirstAuthorName, Publisher*** The title of a book, the name of the first author, and the publisher are functionally dependent on the book's international standard book number (ISBN).

DETERMINANTS The attribute on the left side of the arrow in a functional dependency is called a **determinant**. SSN, VIN, and ISBN are determinants (respectively) in the preceding three examples. In the EMP COURSE relation (Figure 4-7), the combination of EmpID and CourseTitle is a determinant.

Determinant
The attribute on the left side of the arrow in a functional dependency.

CANDIDATE KEYS A **candidate key** is an attribute, or combination of attributes, that uniquely identifies a row in a relation. A candidate key must satisfy the following properties (Dutka and Hanson, 1989), which are a subset of the six properties of a relation previously listed:

Candidate key
An attribute, or combination of attributes, that uniquely identifies a row in a relation.

1. ***Unique identification*** For every row, the value of the key must uniquely identify that row. This property implies that each nonkey attribute is functionally dependent on that key.
2. ***Nonredundancy*** No attribute in the key can be deleted without destroying the property of unique identification.

Let's apply the preceding definition to identify candidate keys in two of the relations described in this chapter. The EMPLOYEE1 relation (Figure 4-1) has the following schema: EMPLOYEE1(EmpID, Name, DeptName, Salary). EmpID is the only determinant in this relation. All of the other attributes are functionally dependent on EmpID. Therefore, EmpID is a candidate key and (because there are no other candidate keys) also is the primary key.

We represent the functional dependencies for a relation using the notation shown in Figure 4-23. Figure 4-23a shows the representation for EMPLOYEE1. The horizontal line in the figure portrays the functional dependencies. A vertical line drops from the primary key (EmpID) and connects to this line. Vertical arrows then point to each of the nonkey attributes that are functionally dependent on the primary key.

For the relation EMPLOYEE2 (Figure 4-2b), notice that (unlike EMPLOYEE1) EmpID does not uniquely identify a row in the relation. For example, there are two rows in the table for EmpID number 100. There are two types of functional dependencies in this relation:

1. EmpID → Name, DeptName, Salary
2. EmpID, CourseTitle → DateCompleted

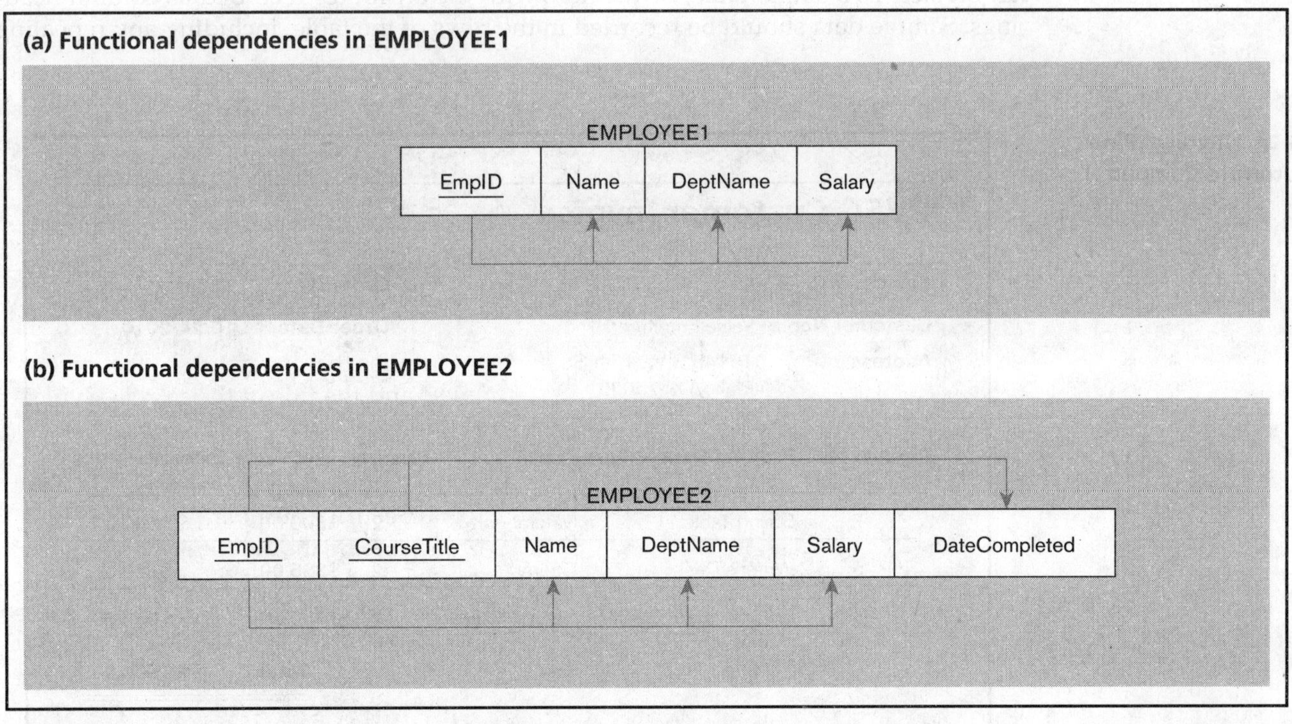

FIGURE 4-23 Representing functional dependencies

The functional dependencies indicate that the combination of EmpID and CourseTitle is the only candidate key (and therefore the primary key) for EMPLOYEE2. In other words, the primary key of EMPLOYEE2 is a composite key. Neither EmpID nor CourseTitle uniquely identifies a row in this relation and therefore (according to property 1) cannot by itself be a candidate key. Examine the data in Figure 4-2b to verify that the combination of EmpID and CourseTitle does uniquely identify each row of EMPLOYEE2. We represent the functional dependencies in this relation in Figure 4-23b. Notice that DateCompleted is the only attribute that is functionally dependent on the full primary key consisting of the attributes EmpID and CourseTitle.

We can summarize the relationship between determinants and candidate keys as follows: A candidate key is always a determinant, whereas a determinant may or may not be a candidate key. For example, in EMPLOYEE2, EmpID is a determinant but not a candidate key. A candidate key is a determinant that uniquely identifies the remaining (nonkey) attributes in a relation. A determinant may be a candidate key (such as EmpID in EMPLOYEE1), part of a composite candidate key (such as EmpID in EMPLOYEE2), or a nonkey attribute. We will describe examples of this shortly.

As a preview to the following illustration of what normalization accomplishes, normalized relations have as their primary key the determinant for each of the nonkeys, and within that relation there are no other functional dependencies.

PINE VALLEY FURNITURE

NORMALIZATION EXAMPLE: PINE VALLEY FURNITURE COMPANY

Now that we have examined functional dependencies and keys, we are ready to describe and illustrate the steps of normalization. If an EER data model has been transformed into a comprehensive set of relations for the database, then each of these relations needs to be normalized. In other cases in which the logical data model is being derived from user interfaces, such as screens, forms, and reports, you will want to create relations for each user interface and normalize those relations.

For a simple illustration, we use a customer invoice from Pine Valley Furniture Company (see Figure 4-24.)

Step 0: Represent the View in Tabular Form

The first step (preliminary to normalization) is to represent the user view (in this case, an invoice) as a single table, or relation, with the attributes recorded as column headings. Sample data should be recorded in the rows of the table, including any repeating

FIGURE 4-24 Invoice (Pine Valley Furniture Company)

PVFC Customer Invoice

Customer ID 2 **Order ID** 1006
Customer Name Value Furniture **Order Date** 10/24/2010
Address 15145 S.W. 17th St.
Plano TX 75022

Product ID	Product Description	Finish	Quantity	Unit Price	Extended Price
7	Dining Table	Natural Ash	2	$800.00	$1,600.00
5	Writer's Desk	Cherry	2	$325.00	$650.00
4	Entertainment Center	Natural Maple	1	$650.00	$650.00
				Total	$2,900.00

FIGURE 4-25 INVOICE data (Pine Valley Furniture Company)

OrderID	Order Date	Customer ID	Customer Name	Customer Address	ProductID	Product Description	Product Finish	Product StandardPrice	Ordered Quantity
1006	10/24/2010	2	Value Furniture	Plano, TX	7	Dining Table	Natural Ash	800.00	2
					5	Writer's Desk	Cherry	325.00	2
					4	Entertainment Center	Natural Maple	650.00	1
1007	10/25/2010	6	Furniture Gallery	Boulder, CO	11	4–Dr Dresser	Oak	500.00	4
					4	Entertainment Center	Natural Maple	650.00	3

groups that are present in the data. The table representing the invoice is shown in Figure 4-25. Notice that data for a second order (OrderID 1007) are included in Figure 4-25 to clarify further the structure of this data.

Step 1: Convert to First Normal Form

A relation is in **first normal form (1NF)** if the following two constraints both apply:

First normal form (1NF) A relation that has a primary key and in which there are no repeating groups.

1. There are no repeating groups in the relation (thus, there is a single fact at the intersection of each row and column of the table).
2. A primary key has been defined, which uniquely identifies each row in the relation.

REMOVE REPEATING GROUPS As you can see, the invoice data in Figure 4-25 contain a repeating group for each product that appears on a particular order. Thus, OrderID 1006 contains three repeating groups, corresponding to the three products on that order.

In a previous section, we showed how to remove repeating groups from a table by filling relevant data values into previously vacant cells of the table (see Figures 4-2a and 4-2b). Applying this procedure to the invoice table yields the new table (named INVOICE) shown in Figure 4-26.

OrderID	Order Date	Customer ID	Customer Name	Customer Address	ProductID	Product Description	Product Finish	Product StandardPrice	Ordered Quantity
1006	10/24/2010	2	Value Furniture	Plano, TX	7	Dining Table	Natural Ash	800.00	2
1006	10/24/2010	2	Value Furniture	Plano, TX	5	Writer's Desk	Cherry	325.00	2
1006	10/24/2010	2	Value Furniture	Plano, TX	4	Entertainment Center	Natural Maple	650.00	1
1007	10/25/2010	6	Furniture Gallery	Boulder, CO	11	4–Dr Dresser	Oak	500.00	4
1007	10/25/2010	6	Furniture Gallery	Boulder, CO	4	Entertainment Center	Natural Maple	650.00	3

FIGURE 4-26 INVOICE relation (1NF) (Pine Valley Furniture Company)

SELECT THE PRIMARY KEY There are four determinants in INVOICE, and their functional dependencies are the following:

OrderID → OrderDate, CustomerID, CustomerName, CustomerAddress
CustomerID → CustomerName, CustomerAddress
ProductID → ProductDescription, ProductFinish, ProductStandardPrice
OrderID, ProductID → OrderedQuantity

Why do we know these are the functional dependencies? These business rules come from the organization. We know these from studying the nature of the Pine Valley Furniture Company business. We can also see that no data in Figure 4-26 violates any of these functional dependencies. But, because we don't see all possible rows of this table, we cannot be sure that there wouldn't be some invoice that would violate one of these functional dependencies. Thus, we must depend on our understanding of the rules of the organization.

As you can see, the only candidate key for INVOICE is the composite key consisting of the attributes OrderID and ProductID (because there is only one row in the table for any combination of values for these attributes). Therefore, OrderID and ProductID are underlined in Figure 4-26, indicating that they comprise the primary key.

When forming a primary key, you must be careful not to include redundant (and therefore unnecessary) attributes. Thus, although CustomerID is a determinant in INVOICE, it is not included as part of the primary key because all of the nonkey attributes are identified by the combination of OrderID and ProductID. We will see the role of CustomerID in the normalization process that follows.

A diagram that shows these functional dependencies for the INVOICE relation is shown in Figure 4-27. This diagram is a horizontal list of all the attributes in INVOICE, with the primary key attributes (OrderID and ProductID) underlined. Notice that the only attribute that depends on the full key is OrderedQuantity. All of the other functional dependencies are either partial dependencies or transitive dependencies (both are defined next).

ANOMALIES IN 1NF Although repeating groups have been removed, the data in Figure 4-26 still contain considerable redundancy. For example, CustomerID, CustomerName, and CustomerAddress for Value Furniture are recorded in three rows (at least) in the table. As a result of these redundancies, manipulating the data in the table can lead to anomalies such as the following:

1. ***Insertion anomaly*** With this table structure, the company is not able to introduce a new product (say, Breakfast Table with ProductID 8) and add it to the database before it is ordered the first time: No entries can be added to the table without both ProductID *and* OrderID. As another example, if a customer calls and requests another product be added to his OrderID 1007, a new row must be inserted in which the order date and all of the customer information must be repeated. This leads to data replication and potential data entry errors (e.g., the customer name may be entered as "Valley Furniture").

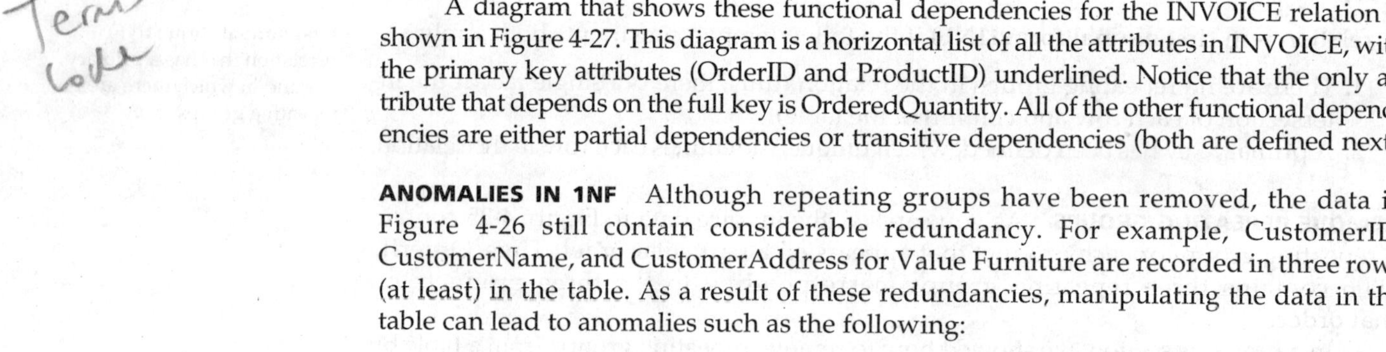

FIGURE 4-27 Functional dependency diagram for INVOICE

2. ***Deletion anomaly*** If a customer calls and requests that the Dining Table be deleted from her OrderID 1006, this row must be deleted from the relation, and we lose the information concerning this item's finish (Natural Ash) and price ($800.00).
3. ***Update anomaly*** If Pine Valley Furniture (as part of a price adjustment) increases the price of the Entertainment Center (ProductID 4) to $750.00, this change must be recorded in all rows containing that item. (There are two such rows in Figure 4-26.)

Step 2: Convert to Second Normal Form

We can remove many of the redundancies (and resulting anomalies) in the INVOICE relation by converting it to second normal form. A relation is in **second normal form (2NF)** if it is in first normal form and contains no partial functional dependencies. A **partial functional dependency** exists when a nonkey attribute is functionally dependent on part (but not all) of the primary key. As you can see, the following partial dependencies exist in Figure 4-27:

Second normal form (2NF)
A relation in first normal form in which every nonkey attribute is fully functionally dependent on the primary key.

Partial functional dependency
A functional dependency in which one or more nonkey attributes are functionally dependent on part (but not all) of the primary key.

OrderID → OrderDate, CustomerID, CustomerName, CustomerAddress
ProductID → ProductDescription, ProductFinish, ProductStandardPrice

The first of these partial dependencies (for example) states that the date on an order is uniquely determined by the order number and has nothing to do with the ProductID.

To convert a relation with partial dependencies to second normal form, the following steps are required:

1. Create a new relation for each primary key attribute (or combination of attributes) that is a determinant in a partial dependency. That attribute is the primary key in the new relation.
2. Move the nonkey attributes that are dependent on this primary key attribute (or attributes) from the old relation to the new relation.

The results of performing these steps for the INVOICE relation are shown in Figure 4-28. Removal of the partial dependencies results in the formation of two new relations: PRODUCT and CUSTOMER ORDER. The INVOICE relation is now left with just the primary key attributes (OrderID and ProductID) and OrderedQuantity, which is functionally dependent on the whole key. We rename this relation ORDER LINE, because each row in this table represents one line item on an order.

As indicated in Figure 4-28, the relations ORDER LINE and PRODUCT are in third normal form. However, CUSTOMER ORDER contains transitive dependencies and therefore (although in second normal form) is not yet in third normal form.

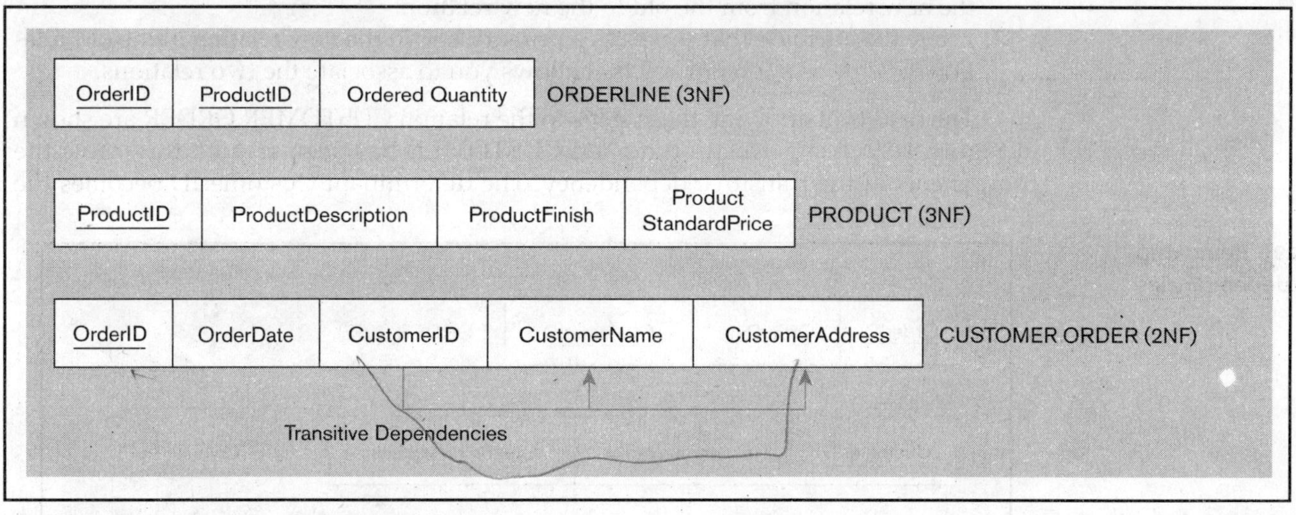

FIGURE 4-28 Removing partial dependencies

A relation that is in first normal form will be in second normal form if any one of the following conditions applies:

1. The primary key consists of only one attribute (e.g., the attribute ProductID in the PRODUCT relation in Figure 4-28). By definition, there cannot be a partial dependency in such a relation.
2. No nonkey attributes exist in the relation (thus all of the attributes in the relation are components of the primary key). There are no functional dependencies in such a relation.
3. Every nonkey attribute is functionally dependent on the full set of primary key attributes (e.g., the attribute OrderedQuantity in the ORDER LINE relation in Figure 4-28).

Step 3: Convert to Third Normal Form

Third normal form (3NF)
A relation that is in second normal form and has no transitive dependencies.

Transitive dependency
A functional dependency between the primary key and one or more nonkey attributes that are dependent on the primary key via another nonkey attribute.

A relation is in **third normal form (3NF)** if it is in second normal form and no transitive dependencies exist. A **transitive dependency** in a relation is a functional dependency between the primary key and one or more nonkey attributes that are dependent on the primary key via another nonkey attribute . For example, there are two transitive dependencies in the CUSTOMER ORDER relation shown in Figure 4-28:

OrderID → CustomerID → CustomerName
OrderID → CustomerID → CustomerAddress

In other words, both customer name and address are uniquely identified by CustomerID, but CustomerID is not part of the primary key (as we noted earlier).

Transitive dependencies create unnecessary redundancy that may lead to the type of anomalies discussed earlier. For example, the transitive dependency in CUSTOMER ORDER (Figure 4-28) requires that a customer's name and address be reentered every time a customer submits a new order, regardless of how many times they have been entered previously. You have no doubt experienced this type of annoying requirement when ordering merchandise online, visiting a doctor's office, or any number of similar activities.

REMOVING TRANSITIVE DEPENDENCIES You can easily remove transitive dependencies from a relation by means of a three-step procedure:

1. For each nonkey attribute (or set of attributes) that is a determinant in a relation, create a new relation. That attribute (or set of attributes) becomes the primary key of the new relation.
2. Move all of the attributes that are functionally dependent on the primary key of the new relation from the old to the new relation.
3. Leave the attribute that serves as a primary key in the new relation in the old relation to serve as a foreign key that allows you to associate the two relations.

The results of applying these steps to the relation CUSTOMER ORDER are shown in Figure 4-29. A new relation named CUSTOMER has been created to receive the components of the transitive dependency. The determinant CustomerID becomes the

FIGURE 4-29 Removing transitive dependencies

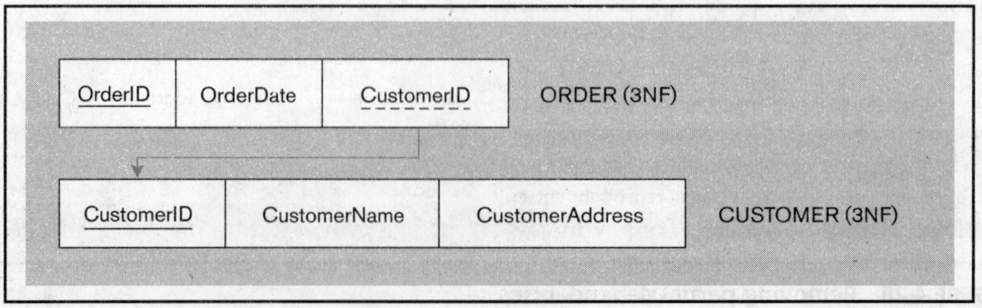

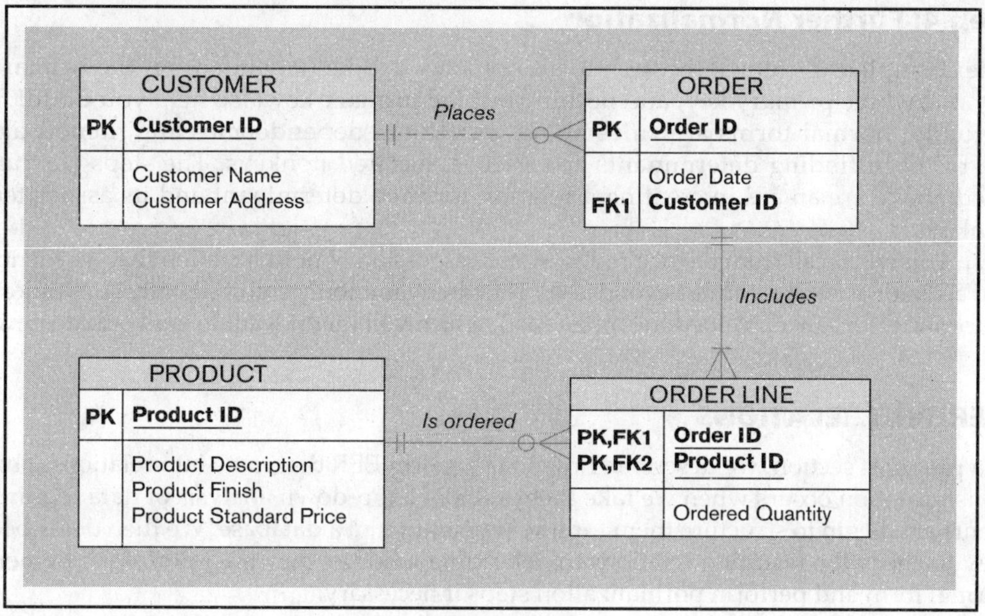

FIGURE 4-30 Relational schema for INVOICE data (Microsoft Visio notation)

primary key of this relation, and the attributes CustomerName and CustomerAddress are moved to the relation. CUSTOMER ORDER is renamed ORDER, and the attribute CustomerID remains as a foreign key in that relation. This allows us to associate an order with the customer who submitted the order. As indicated in Figure 4-29, these relations are now in third normal form.

Normalizing the data in the INVOICE view has resulted in the creation of four relations in third normal form: CUSTOMER, PRODUCT, ORDER, and ORDER LINE. A relational schema showing these four relations and their associations (developed using Microsoft Visio) is shown in Figure 4-30. Note that CustomerID is a foreign key in ORDER, and OrderID and ProductID are foreign keys in ORDER LINE. (Foreign keys are shown in Visio for logical, but not conceptual, data models.) Also note that minimum cardinalities are shown on the relationships even though the normalized relations provide no evidence of what the minimum cardinalities should be. Sample data for the relations might include, for example, a customer with no orders, thus providing evidence of the optional cardinality for the relationship Places. However, even if there were an order for every customer in a sample data set, this would not prove mandatory cardinality. Minimum cardinalities must be determined from business rules, not illustrations of reports, screens, and transactions. The same statement is true for specific maximum cardinalities (e.g., a business rule that no order may contain more than 10 line items).

Determinants and Normalization

We demonstrated normalization through 3NF in steps. There is an easy shortcut, however. If you look back at the original set of four determinants and the associated functional dependencies for the invoice user view, each of these corresponds to one of the relations in Figure 4-30, with each determinant being the primary key of a relation, and the nonkeys of each relation are those attributes functionally dependent on each determinant. There is a subtle but important difference: Because OrderID determines CustomerID, CustomerName, and CustomerAddress and CustomerID determines its dependent attributes, CustomerID becomes a foreign key in the ORDER relation, which is where CustomerName and CustomerAddress are represented. The point is, if you can determine determinants that have no overlapping dependent attributes, then you have defined the relations. Thus, you can do normalization step by step as illustrated for the Pine Valley Furniture invoice, or you can create relations in 3NF straight from determinants' functional dependencies.

Step 4: Further Normalization

After completing steps 0 through 3, all nonkeys will be dependent on the primary key, the whole primary key, and nothing but the primary key ("so help you Codd!"). Actually, normal forms are rules about functional dependencies and, hence, are the result of finding determinants and their associated nonkeys. The steps we outlined above are an aid in creating a relation for each determinant and its associated nonkeys.

You will recall from the beginning of our discussion of normalization that we identified additional normal forms beyond 3NF. The most commonly enforced of these additional normal forms are explained in Appendix B, which you might want to read or scan now.

MERGING RELATIONS

In a previous section, we described how to transform EER diagrams into relations. This transformation occurs when we take the results of a top-down analysis of data requirements and begin to structure them for implementation in a database. We then described how to check the resulting relations to determine whether they are in third (or higher) normal form and perform normalization steps if necessary.

As part of the logical design process, normalized relations may have been created from a number of separate EER diagrams and (possibly) other user views (i.e., there may be bottom-up or parallel database development activities for different areas of the organization as well as top-down ones). For example, besides the invoice used in the prior section to illustrate normalization, there may be an order form, an account balance report, production routing, and other user views, each of which have been normalized separately. The three-schema architecture for databases (see Chapter 1) encourages the simultaneous use of both top-down and bottom-up database development processes. In reality, most medium to large organizations have many reasonably independent systems development activities that at some point need to come together to create a shared database. The result is that some of the relations generated from these various processes may be redundant; that is, they may refer to the same entities. In such cases, we should merge those relations to remove the redundancy. This section describes merging relations (also called *view integration*). An understanding of how to merge relations is important for three reasons:

1. On large projects, the work of several subteams comes together during logical design, so there is often a need to merge relations.
2. Integrating existing databases with new information requirements often leads to the need to integrate different views.
3. New data requirements may arise during the life cycle, so there is a need to merge any new relations with what has already been developed.

An Example

Suppose that modeling a user view results in the following 3NF relation:

EMPLOYEE1(EmployeeID, Name, Address, Phone)

Modeling a second user view might result in the following relation:

EMPLOYEE2(EmployeeID, Name, Address, Jobcode, NoYears)

Because these two relations have the same primary key (EmployeeID), they likely describe the same entity and may be merged into one relation. The result of merging the relations is the following relation:

EMPLOYEE(EmployeeID, Name, Address, Phone, Jobcode, NoYears)

Notice that an attribute that appears in both relations (e.g., Name in this example) appears only once in the merged relation.

View Integration Problems

When integrating relations as in the preceding example, a database analyst must understand the meaning of the data and must be prepared to resolve any problems that may arise in that process. In this section, we describe and briefly illustrate four problems that arise in view integration: *synonyms*, *homonyms*, *transitive dependencies*, and *supertype/subtype relationships*.

SYNONYMS In some situations, two (or more) attributes may have different names but the same meaning (e.g., when they describe the same characteristic of an entity). Such attributes are called **synonyms**. For example, EmployeeID and EmployeeNo may be synonyms. When merging the relations that contain synonyms, you should obtain agreement (if possible) from users on a single, standardized name for the attribute and eliminate any other synonyms. (Another alternative is to choose a third name to replace the synonyms.) For example, consider the following relations:

Synonyms
Two (or more) attributes that have different names but the same meaning.

STUDENT1(<u>StudentID</u>, Name)
STUDENT2(<u>MatriculationNo</u>, Name, Address)

In this case, the analyst recognizes that both StudentID and MatriculationNo are synonyms for a person's student identity number and are identical attributes. (Another possibility is that these are both candidate keys, and only one of them should be selected as the primary key.) One possible resolution would be to standardize on one of the two attribute names, such as StudentID. Another option is to use a new attribute name, such as StudentNo, to replace both synonyms. Assuming the latter approach, merging the two relations would produce the following result:

STUDENT(<u>StudentNo</u>, Name, Address)

Often when there are synonyms, there is a need to allow some database users to refer to the same data by different names. Users may need to use familiar names that are consistent with terminology in their part of the organization. An **alias** is an alternative name used for an attribute. Many database management systems allow the definition of an alias that may be used interchangeably with the primary attribute label.

Alias
An alternative name used for an attribute.

HOMONYMS An attribute name that may have more than one meaning is called a **homonym**. For example, the term *account* might refer to a bank's checking account, savings account, loan account, or other type of account (and therefore *account* refers to different data, depending on how it is used).

Homonym
An attribute that may have more than one meaning.

You should be on the lookout for homonyms when merging relations. Consider the following example:

STUDENT1(<u>StudentID</u>, Name, Address)
STUDENT2(<u>StudentID</u>, Name, PhoneNo, Address)

In discussions with users, an analyst may discover that the attribute Address in STUDENT1 refers to a student's campus address, whereas in STUDENT2 the same attribute refers to a student's permanent (or home) address. To resolve this conflict, we would probably need to create new attribute names, so that the merged relation would become

STUDENT(<u>StudentID</u>, Name, PhoneNo, CampusAddress, PermanentAddress)

TRANSITIVE DEPENDENCIES When two 3NF relations are merged to form a single relation, transitive dependencies (described earlier in this chapter) may result. For example, consider the following two relations:

STUDENT1(<u>StudentID</u>, Major)
STUDENT2(<u>StudentID</u>, Advisor)

Because STUDENT1 and STUDENT2 have the same primary key, the two relations can be merged:

STUDENT(<u>StudentID</u>, Major, Advisor)

However, suppose that each major has exactly one advisor. In this case, Advisor is functionally dependent on Major:

Major → Advisor

If the preceding functional dependency exists, then STUDENT is in 2NF but not in 3NF, because it contains a transitive dependency. The analyst can create 3NF relations by removing the transitive dependency. Major becomes a foreign key in STUDENT:

STUDENT(<u>StudentID</u>, Major)
MAJOR ADVISOR(<u>Major</u>, Advisor)

SUPERTYPE/SUBTYPE RELATIONSHIPS These relationships may be hidden in user views or relations. Suppose that we have the following two hospital relations:

PATIENT1(<u>PatientID</u>, Name, Address)
PATIENT2(<u>PatientID</u>, RoomNo)

Initially, it appears that these two relations can be merged into a single PATIENT relation. However, the analyst correctly suspects that there are two different types of patients: resident patients and outpatients. PATIENT1 actually contains attributes common to all patients. PATIENT2 contains an attribute (RoomNo) that is a characteristic only of resident patients. In this situation, the analyst should create supertype/subtype relationships for these entities:

PATIENT(<u>PatientID</u>, Name, Address)
RESIDENT PATIENT(<u>PatientID</u>, RoomNo)
OUTPATIENT(<u>PatientID</u>, DateTreated)

We have created the OUTPATIENT relation to show what it might look like if it were needed, but it is not necessary, given only PATIENT1 and PATIENT2 user views. For an extended discussion of view integration in database design, see Navathe, Elmasri, and Larson (1986).

A FINAL STEP FOR DEFINING RELATIONAL KEYS

In Chapter 2, we provided some criteria for selecting identifiers: They do not change values over time and must be unique and known, nonintelligent, and use a single attribute surrogate for composite identifier. Actually, none of these criteria must apply until the database is implemented (i.e., when the identifier becomes a primary key and is defined as a field in the physical database). Before the relations are defined as tables, the primary keys of relations should, if necessary, be changed to conform to these criteria.

Recently database experts (e.g., Johnston, 2000) have strengthened the criteria for primary key specification. Experts now also recommend that a primary key be unique across *the whole database* (a so-called **enterprise key**), not just unique within the relational table to which it applies. This criterion makes a primary key more like what in object-oriented databases is called an *object identifier* (see Chapters 13 and 14). With this recommendation, the primary key of a relation becomes a value internal to the database system and has no business meaning.

Enterprise key
A primary key whose value is unique across all relations.

A candidate primary key, such as EmpID in the EMPLOYEE1 relation of Figure 4-1 or CustomerID in the CUSTOMER relation (Figure 4-29), if ever used in the organization, is called a *business key* or *natural key* and would be included in the relation as a nonkey attribute. The EMPLOYEE1 and CUSTOMER relations (and every other relation in the database) then have a new enterprise key attribute (called, say, ObjectID), which has no business meaning.

Why create this extra attribute? One of the main motivations for using an enterprise key is database evolvability—merging new relations into a database after the database is created. For example, consider the following two relations:

EMPLOYEE(<u>EmpID</u>, EmpName, DeptName, Salary)
CUSTOMER(<u>CustID</u>, CustName, Address)

In this example, without an enterprise key, EmpID and CustID may or may not have the same format, length, and data type, whether they are intelligent or nonintelligent. Suppose the organization evolves its information processing needs and recognizes that employees can also be customers, so employee and customer are simply two subtypes of the same PERSON supertype. (You saw this in Chapter 3, when studying universal data modeling.) Thus, the organization would then like to have three relations:

PERSON(<u>PersonID</u>, PersonName)
EMPLOYEE(<u>PersonID</u>, DeptName, Salary)
CUSTOMER(<u>PersonID</u>, Address)

In this case, PersonID is supposed to be the same value for the same person throughout all roles. But if values for EmpID and CustID were selected before relation PERSON was created, the values for EmpID and CustID probably will not match. Moreover, if we change the values of EmpID and CustID to match the new PersonID, how do we ensure that all EmpIDs and CustIDs are unique if another employee or customer already has the associated PersonID value? Even worse, if there are other tables that relate to, say, EMPLOYEE, then foreign keys in these other tables have to change, creating a ripple effect of foreign key changes. The only way to guarantee that each primary key of a relation is unique across the database is to create an enterprise key from the very beginning so primary keys never have to change.

In our example, the original database (without PERSON) with an enterprise key is shown in Figures 4-31a (the relations) and 4-31b (sample data). In this figure, EmpID and CustID are now business keys, and OBJECT is the supertype of all other relations. OBJECT can have attributes such as the name of the type of object (included in this example as attribute ObjectType), date created, date last changed, or any other internal system attributes for an object instance. Then, when PERSON is needed, the database evolves to the design shown in Figures 4-31c (the relations) and 4-31d (sample data). Evolution to the database with PERSON still requires some alterations to existing tables, but not to primary key values. The name attribute is moved to PERSON because it is common to both subtypes, and a foreign key is added to EMPLOYEE and CUSTOMER to point to the common person instance. As you will see in Chapter 6, it is easy to add and delete nonkey columns, even foreign keys, to table definitions. In contrast, changing the primary key of a relation is not allowed by most database management systems because of the extensive cost of the foreign key ripple effect.

FIGURE 4-31 Enterprise key

(a) Relations with enterprise key

OBJECT (OID, ObjectType)
EMPLOYEE (OID, EmpID, EmpName, DeptName, Salary)
CUSTOMER (OID, CustID, CustName, Address)

(b) Sample data with enterprise key

OBJECT

OID	ObjectType
1	EMPLOYEE
2	CUSTOMER
3	CUSTOMER
4	EMPLOYEE
5	EMPLOYEE
6	CUSTOMER
7	CUSTOMER

EMPLOYEE

OID	EmpID	EmpName	DeptName	Salary
1	100	Jennings, Fred	Marketing	50000
4	101	Hopkins, Dan	Purchasing	45000
5	102	Huber, Ike	Accounting	45000

CUSTOMER

OID	CustID	CustName	Address
2	100	Fred's Warehouse	Greensboro, NC
3	101	Bargain Bonanza	Moscow, ID
6	102	Jasper's	Tallahassee, FL
7	103	Desks 'R Us	Kettering, OH

(c) Relations after adding the PERSON relation

OBJECT (OID, ObjectType)
EMPLOYEE (OID, EmpID, DeptName, Salary, PersonID)
CUSTOMER (OID, CustID, Address, PersonID)
PERSON (OID, Name)

(continued)

Summary

Logical database design is the process of transforming the conceptual data model into a logical data model. The emphasis in this chapter has been on the relational data model, because of its importance in contemporary database systems. The relational data model represents data in the form of tables called relations. A relation is a named, two-dimensional table of data. A key property of relations is that they cannot contain multivalued attributes.

In this chapter, we described the major steps in the logical database design process. This process is based on transforming EER diagrams into normalized relations. This process has three steps: Transform EER diagrams into relations, normalize the relations, and merge the relations. The result of this process is a set of relations in third normal form that can be implemented using any contemporary relational database management system.

FIGURE 4-31 (continued)

(d) Sample data after adding the PERSON relation

OBJECT

OID	ObjectType
1	EMPLOYEE
2	CUSTOMER
3	CUSTOMER
4	EMPLOYEE
5	EMPLOYEE
6	CUSTOMER
7	CUSTOMER
8	PERSON
9	PERSON
10	PERSON
11	PERSON
12	PERSON
13	PERSON
14	PERSON

PERSON

OID	Name
8	Jennings, Fred
9	Fred's Warehouse
10	Bargain Bonanza
11	Hopkins, Dan
12	Huber, Ike
13	Jasper's
14	Desks 'R Us

EMPLOYEE

OID	EmpID	DeptName	Salary	PersonID
1	100	Marketing	50000	8
4	101	Purchasing	45000	11
5	102	Accounting	45000	12

CUSTOMER

OID	CustID	Address	PersonID
2	100	Greensboro, NC	9
3	101	Moscow, ID	10
6	102	Tallahassee, FL	13
7	103	Kettering, OH	14

Each entity type in the EER diagram is transformed into a relation that has the same primary key as the entity type. A one-to-many relationship is represented by adding a foreign key to the relation that represents the entity on the many side of the relationship. (This foreign key is the primary key of the entity on the one side of the relationship.) A many-to-many relationship is represented by creating a separate relation. The primary key of this relation is a composite key, consisting of the primary key of each of the entities that participate in the relationship.

The relational model does not directly support supertype/subtype relationships, but we can model these relationships by creating a separate table (or relation) for the supertype and for each subtype. The primary key of each subtype is the same (or at least from the same domain) as for the supertype. The supertype must have an attribute called the subtype discriminator that indicates to which subtype (or subtypes) each instance of the supertype belongs.

The purpose of normalization is to derive well-structured relations that are free of anomalies (inconsistencies or errors) that would otherwise result when the relations are updated or modified. Normalization is based on the analysis of functional dependencies, which are constraints between two attributes (or two sets of attributes). It may be accomplished in several stages. Relations in first normal form (1NF) contain no multivalued attributes or repeating groups. Relations in second normal form (2NF) contain no partial dependencies, and relations in third normal form (3NF) contain no transitive dependencies. We can use diagrams that show the functional dependencies in a relation to help decompose that relation (if necessary) to obtain relations in third normal form. Higher normal forms (beyond 3NF) have also been defined; we discuss these normal forms in Appendix B.

We must be careful when combining relations to deal with problems such as synonyms, homonyms, transitive dependencies, and supertype/subtype relationships. In addition, before relations are defined to the database management system, all primary keys should be described as single-attribute nonintelligent keys and, preferably, as enterprise keys.

Chapter Review

Key Terms

Alias 189
Anomaly 164
Candidate key 181
Composite key 157
Determinant 181
Enterprise key 191
Entity integrity rule 161
First normal form (1NF) 183
Foreign key 158
Functional dependency 179
Homonym 189
Normal form 179
Normalization 179
Null 161
Partial functional dependency 185
Primary key 157
Recursive foreign key 173
Referential integrity constraint 162
Relation 157
Second normal form (2NF) 185
Surrogate primary key 168
Synonyms 189
Third normal form (3NF) 186
Transitive dependency 186
Well-structured relation 164

Review Questions

1. Define each of the following terms:
   a. determinant
   b. functional dependency
   c. transitive dependency
   d. recursive foreign key
   e. normalization
   f. composite key
   g. relation
   h. normal form
   i. partial functional dependency
   j. enterprise key
   k. surrogate primary key
2. Match the following terms to the appropriate definitions:

   ____ well-structured relation
   ____ anomaly
   ____ functional dependency
   ____ determinant
   ____ composite key
   ____ 1NF
   ____ 2NF
   ____ 3NF
   ____ recursive foreign key
   ____ relation
   ____ transitive dependency

   a. constraint between two attributes
   b. functional dependency between the primary key and a nonkey attribute via another nonkey attribute
   c. references the primary key in the same relation
   d. multivalued attributes removed
   e. inconsistency or error
   f. contains little redundancy
   g. contains two (or more) attributes
   h. contains no partial functional dependencies
   i. transitive dependencies eliminated
   j. attribute on left side of functional dependency
   k. named two-dimensional table of data
3. Contrast the following terms:
   a. normal form; normalization
   b. candidate key; primary key
   c. partial dependency; transitive dependency
   d. composite key; recursive foreign key
   e. determinant; candidate key
   f. foreign key; primary key
   g. enterprise key; surrogate key
4. Describe the primary differences between the conceptual and logical data models.
5. Summarize six important properties of relations.
6. Describe two properties that each candidate key must satisfy.
7. Describe three types of anomalies that can arise in a table and the negative consequences of each.
8. Fill in the blanks in each of the following statements:
   a. A relation that has no partial functional dependencies is in ____ normal form.
   b. A relation that has no transitive dependencies is in ____ normal form.
   c. A relation that has no multivalued attributes is in ____ normal form.
9. What is a well-structured relation? Why are well-structured relations important in logical database design?
10. Describe the primary way in which relationships in an E-R diagram are expressed in a corresponding relational data model.
11. Describe how the following components of an E-R diagram are transformed into relations:
    a. regular entity type
    b. relationship (1:*M*)
    c. relationship (*M:N*)
    d. relationship (supertype/subtype)
    e. multivalued attribute
    f. weak entity
    g. composite attribute
12. What is the primary purpose of normalization?
13. Briefly describe four typical problems that often arise in merging relations and common techniques for addressing those problems.
14. List three conditions that you can apply to determine whether a relation that is in first normal form is also in second normal form.
15. Explain how each of the following types of integrity constraints is enforced in the SQL CREATE TABLE commands:
    a. entity integrity
    b. referential integrity
16. What are the benefits of enforcing the integrity constraints as part of the database design and implementation process (instead of doing it in application design)?
17. How are relationships between entities represented in the relational data model?
18. How do you represent a 1:*M* unary relationship in a relational data model?
19. How do you represent an *M:N* ternary relationship in a relational data model?
20. How do you represent an associative entity in a relational data model?

21. What is the relationship between the primary key of a relation and the functional dependencies among all attributes within that relation?
22. Under what conditions must a foreign key not be null?
23. Explain what can be done with primary keys to eliminate key ripple effects as a database evolves.
24. Describe the difference between how a 1:*M* unary relationship and an *M*:*N* unary relationship are implemented in a relational data model.
25. Explain three conditions that suggest a surrogate key should be created for the primary key of a relation.
26. Why is relational data model emphasized more than any other model? What are the advantages of this model?
27. What are multi-valued attributes? How does one eliminate them?
28. What is the purpose of integrity constraints? Explain the different types of integrity constraints needed?
29. What is a well-structured relation? How do anomalies dictate the constitution of a well-structured relation?

Problems and Exercises

1. For each of the following E-R diagrams from Chapter 2:
   I. Transform the diagram to a relational schema that shows referential integrity constraints (see Figure 4-5 for an example of such a schema).
   II. For each relation, diagram the functional dependencies (see Figure 4-23 for an example).
   III. If any of the relations are not in 3NF, transform them to 3NF.
   a. Figure 2-8
   b. Figure 2-9b
   c. Figure 2-11a
   d. Figure 2-11b
   e. Figure 2-15a (relationship version)
   f. Figure 2-15b (attribute version)
   g. Figure 2-16b
   h. Figure 2-19
2. For each of the following EER diagrams from Chapter 3:
   I. Transform the diagram into a relational schema that shows referential integrity constraints (see Figure 4-5 for an example of such a schema).
   II. For each relation, diagram the functional dependencies (see Figure 4-23 for an example).
   III. If any of the relations are not in 3NF, transform them to 3NF.
   a. Figure 3-6b
   b. Figure 3-7a
   c. Figure 3-9
   d. Figure 3-10
   e. Figure 3-11
3. For each of the following relations, indicate the normal form for that relation. If the relation is not in third normal form, decompose it into 3NF relations. Functional dependencies (other than those implied by the primary key) are shown where appropriate.
   a. CLASS(CourseNo, SectionNo)
   b. CLASS(CourseNo, SectionNo, Room)
   c. CLASS(CourseNo, SectionNo, Room, Capacity) [FD: Room → Capacity]
   d. CLASS(CourseNo, SectionNo, CourseName, Room, Capacity) [FD: CourseNo → CourseName; FD: Room → Capacity]
4. For your answers to the following Problems and Exercises from prior chapters, transform the EER diagrams into a set of relational schemas, diagram the functional dependencies, and convert all the relations to third normal form:
   a. Chapter 2, Problem and Exercise 15b
   b. Chapter 2, Problem and Exercise 15g
   c. Chapter 2, Problem and Exercise 15h
   d. Chapter 2, Problem and Exercise 15i
   e. Chapter 2, Problem and Exercise 21
   f. Chapter 2, Problem and Exercise 24
5. Figure 4-32 shows a class list for Millennium College. Convert this user view to a set of 3NF relations using an enterprise key. Assume the following:
   - An instructor has a unique location.
   - A student has a unique major.
   - A course has a unique title.
6. Figure 4-33 (page 196) shows an EER diagram for a simplified credit card environment. There are two types of card accounts: debit cards and credit cards. Credit card accounts accumulate charges with merchants. Each charge is identified by the date and time of the charge as well as the primary keys of merchant and credit card.
   a. Develop a relational schema.
   b. Show the functional dependencies.
   c. Develop a set of 3NF relations using an enterprise key.
7. Table 4-3 (page 196) contains sample data for parts and for vendors who supply those parts. In discussing these data with users, we find that part numbers (but not descriptions) uniquely identify parts and that vendor names uniquely identify vendors.
   a. Convert this table to a relation (named PART SUPPLIER) in first normal form. Illustrate the relation with the sample data in the table.
   b. List the functional dependencies in PART SUPPLIER and identify a candidate key.
   c. For the relation PART SUPPLIER, identify each of the following: an insert anomaly, a delete anomaly, and a modification anomaly.
   d. Draw a relational schema for PART SUPPLIER and show the functional dependencies.
   e. In what normal form is this relation?
   f. Develop a set of 3NF relations from PART SUPPLIER.

MILLENNIUM COLLEGE
CLASS LIST
FALL SEMESTER 201X

COURSE NO.: IS 460
COURSE TITLE: DATABASE
INSTRUCTOR NAME: NORMA L. FORM
INSTRUCTOR LOCATION: B 104

STUDENT NO.	STUDENT NAME	MAJOR	GRADE
38214	Bright	IS	A
40875	Cortez	CS	B
51893	Edwards	IS	A

FIGURE 4-32 Class list (Millennium College)

FIGURE 4-33 EER diagram for bank cards

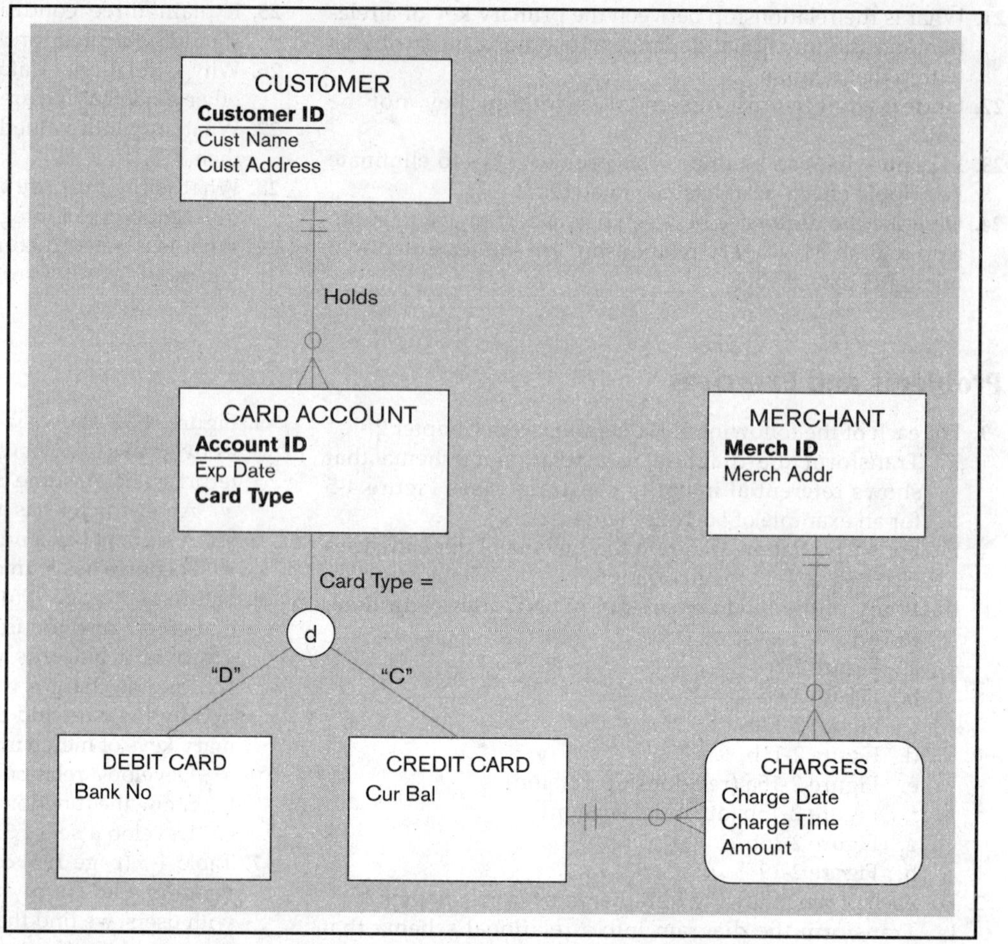

TABLE 4-3 Sample Data for Parts and Vendors

Part No	Description	Vendor Name	Address	Unit Cost
1234	Logic chip	Fast Chips	Cupertino	10.00
		Smart Chips	Phoenix	8.00
5678	Memory chip	Fast Chips	Cupertino	3.00
		Quality Chips	Austin	2.00
		Smart Chips	Phoenix	5.00

g. Show the 3NF relations using Microsoft Visio (or any other tool specified by your instructor).

8. Table 4-4 shows a relation called GRADE REPORT for a university. Your assignment is as follows:
   a. Draw a relational schema and diagram the functional dependencies in the relation.
   b. In what normal form is this relation?
   c. Decompose GRADE REPORT into a set of 3NF relations.
   d. Draw a relational schema for your 3NF relations and show the referential integrity constraints.
   e. Draw your answer to part d using Microsoft Visio (or any other tool specified by your instructor).
9. Table 4-5 shows a shipping manifest. Your assignment is as follows:
   a. Draw a relational schema and diagram the functional dependencies in the relation.
   b. In what normal form is this relation?
   c. Decompose MANIFEST into a set of 3NF relations.
   d. Draw a relational schema for your 3NF relations and show the referential integrity constraints.
   e. Draw your answer to part d using Microsoft Visio (or any other tool specified by your instructor).
10. Transform the relational schema developed in Problem and Exercise 9 into an EER diagram. State any assumptions that you have made.
11. For your answers to the following Problems and Exercises from prior chapters, transform the EER diagrams into a set of relational schemas, diagram the functional dependencies, and convert all the relations to third normal form.
    a. Chapter 3, Problem and Exercise 15
    b. Chapter 3, Problem and Exercise 20
12. Transform Figure 2-15b, attribute version, to 3NF relations. Transform Figure 2-15b, relationship version, to 3NF relations. Compare these two sets of 3NF relations with those in Figure 4-10. What observations and conclusions do you reach by comparing these different sets of 3NF relations?
13. The Public Safety office at Millennium College maintains a list of parking tickets issued to vehicles parked illegally on the campus. Table 4-6 shows a portion of this list for the fall semester. (Attribute names are abbreviated to conserve space.)

TABLE 4-4 Grade Report Relation

Grade Report

StudentID	StudentName	CampusAddress	Major	CourseID	CourseTitle	Instructor Name	Instructor Location	Grade
168300458	Williams	208 Brooks	IS	IS 350	Database Mgt	Codd	B 104	A
168300458	Williams	208 Brooks	IS	IS 465	Systems Analysis	Parsons	B 317	B
543291073	Baker	104 Phillips	Acctg	IS 350	Database Mgt	Codd	B 104	C
543291073	Baker	104 Phillips	Acctg	Acct 201	Fund Acctg	Miller	H 310	B
543291073	Baker	104 Phillips	Acctg	Mkgt 300	Intro Mktg	Bennett	B 212	A

TABLE 4-5 Shipping Manifest

Shipment ID:	**00-0001**	**Shipment Date:**	**01/10/2010**
Origin:	Boston	Expected Arrival:	01/14/2010
Destination:	Brazil		
Ship Number:	39	Captain:	002-15 Henry Moore

Item Number	Type	Description	Weight	Quantity	TOTALWEIGHT
3223	BM	Concrete Form	500	100	50,000
3297	BM	Steel Beam	87	2,000	174,000
				Shipment Total:	224,000

TABLE 4-6 Parking Tickets at Millennium College

Parking Ticket Table

St ID	L Name	F Name	Phone No	St Lic	Lic No	Ticket #	Date	Code	Fine
38249	Brown	Thomas	111-7804	FL	BRY 123	15634	10/17/10	2	$25
						16017	11/13/10	1	$15
82453	Green	Sally	391-1689	AL	TRE 141	14987	10/05/10	3	$100
						16293	11/18/10	1	$15
						17892	12/13/10	2	$25

a. Convert this table to a relation in first normal form by entering appropriate data in the table. What are the determinants in this relation?

b. Draw a dependency diagram that shows all functional dependencies in the relation, based on the sample data shown.

c. Give an example of one or more anomalies that can result in using this relation.

d. Develop a set of relations in third normal form. Include a new column with the heading Violation in the appropriate table to explain the reason for each ticket. Values in this column are: expired parking meter (ticket code 1), no parking permit (ticket code 2), and handicap violation (ticket code 3).

e. Develop an E-R diagram with the appropriate cardinality notations.

14. The materials manager at Pine Valley Furniture Company maintains a list of suppliers for each of the material items purchased by the company from outside vendors. Table 4-7 shows the essential data required for this application.

a. Draw a dependency diagram for this data. You may assume the following:

- Each material item has one or more suppliers. Each supplier may supply one or more items or may not supply any items.
- The unit price for a material item may vary from one vendor to another.
- The terms code for a supplier uniquely identifies the terms of the sale (e.g., code 2 means 10 percent net 30 days, etc.). The terms for a supplier are the same for all material items ordered from that supplier.

b. Decompose this diagram into a set of diagrams in 3NF.
c. Draw an E-R diagram for this situation.

15. Table 4-8 shows a portion of a shipment table for a large manufacturing company. Each shipment (identified by Shipment#) uniquely identifies the shipment Origin, Destination, and Distance. The shipment Origin and Destination pair also uniquely identifies the Distance.
a. Develop a diagram that shows the functional dependencies in the SHIPMENT relation.
b. In what normal form is SHIPMENT? Why?
c. Convert SHIPMENT to third normal form if necessary. Show the resulting table(s) with the sample data presented in SHIPMENT.

16. Figure 4-34 shows an EER diagram for Vacation Property Rentals. This organization rents preferred properties in several states. As shown in the figure, there are two basic types of properties: beach properties and mountain properties.
a. Transform the EER diagram to a set of relations and develop a relational schema.
b. Diagram the functional dependencies and determine the normal form for each relation.
c. Convert all relations to third normal form, if necessary, and draw a revised relational schema.
d. Suggest an integrity constraint that would ensure that no property is rented twice during the same time interval.

17. For your answers to Problem and Exercise 16 from Chapter 3, transform the EER diagrams into a set of relational schemas, diagram the functional dependencies, and convert all the relations to third normal form.

18. Figure 4-35 includes an EER diagram describing a car racing league. Transform the diagram into a relational schema that shows referential integrity constraints (see Figure 4-5 for an example of such a schema). In addition, verify that the resulting relations are in 3NF.

19. Figure 4-36 includes an EER diagram for a medium-size software vendor. Transform the diagram into a relational schema that shows referential integrity constraints (see Figure 4-5 for an example of such a schema). In addition, verify that the resulting relations are in 3NF.

20. Examine the set of relations in Figure 4-37. What normal form are these in? How do you know this? If they are in 3NF, convert the relations into an EER diagram. What assumptions did you have to make to answer these questions?

21. A pet store currently uses a legacy flat file system to store all of its information. The owner of the store, Peter Corona, wants to

TABLE 4-7 Pine Valley Furniture Company Purchasing Data

Attribute Name	Sample Value
Material ID	3792
Material Name	Hinges 3" locking
Unit of Measure	each
Standard Cost	$5.00
Vendor ID	V300
Vendor Name	Apex Hardware
Unit Price	$4.75
Terms Code	1
Terms	COD

TABLE 4-8 Shipment Relation

Shipment#	Origin	Destination	Distance
409	Seattle	Denver	1,537
618	Chicago	Dallas	1,058
723	Boston	Atlanta	1,214
824	Denver	Los Angeles	975
629	Seattle	Denver	1,537

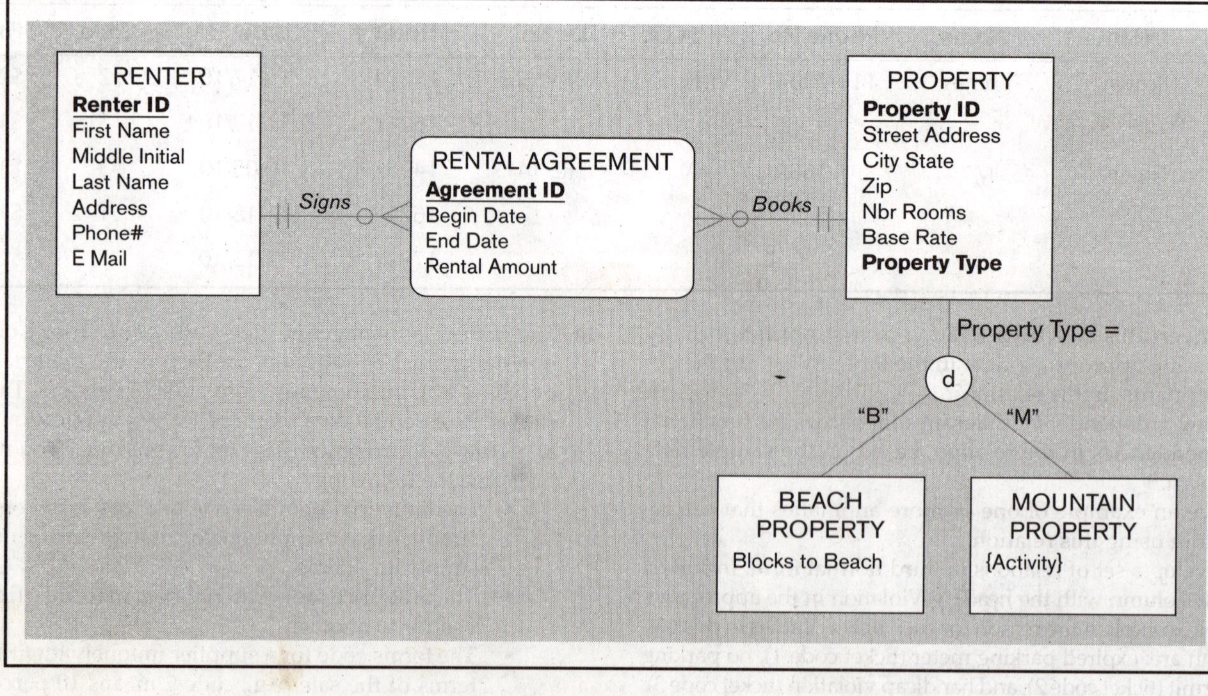

FIGURE 4-34 EER diagram for Vacation Property Rentals

implement a Web-enabled database application. This would enable branch stores to enter data regarding inventory levels, ordering, and so on. Presently, the data for inventory and sales tracking are stored in one file that has the following format:

StoreName, PetName, Pet Description, Price, Cost, SupplierName, ShippingTime, QuantityOnHand, DateOfLastDelivery, DateOfLastPurchase, DeliveryDate1, DeliveryDate2, DeliveryDate3, DeliveryDate4, PurchaseDate1, PurchaseDate2, PurchaseDate3, PurchaseDate4, LastCustomerName, CustomerName1, CustomerName2, CustomerName3, CustomerName4

Assume that you want to track all purchase and inventory data, such as who bought the fish, the date that it was purchased, the date that it was delivered, and so on. The present file format allows only the tracking of the last purchase and delivery as well as four prior purchases and deliveries. You can assume that a type of fish is supplied by one supplier.

a. Show all functional dependencies.
b. What normal form is this table in?
c. Design a normalized data model for these data. Show that it is in 3NF.

22. For Problem and Exercise 21, draw the ER diagram based on the normalized relations.

23. How would Problems and Exercises 21 and 22 change if a type of fish could be supplied by multiple suppliers?

24. Figure 4-38 shows an EER diagram for a university dining service organization that provides dining services to a major university.

a. Transform the EER diagram to a set of relations and develop a relational schema.
b. Diagram the functional dependencies and determine the normal form for each relation.
c. Convert all relations to third normal form, if necessary, and draw a revised relational schema.

25. The following attributes form a relation that includes information about individual computers, their vendors, software packages running on the computers, computer users, and user authorizations. Users are authorized to use a specific software package on a specific computer during a specific timeframe (characterized with attributes UserAuthorization Starts and UserAuthorizationEnds and secured with UserAuthorizationPassword). Software is licensed to be used on specific computers (potentially multiple software packages at the same time) until an expiration time (SoftwareLicenceExpires) at a specific price. Computers are sold by vendors, and each vendor has a support person with an ID, name, and phone extension. Each individual computer has a specific purchase price. The attributes are as follows:

ComputerSerialNbr, VendorID, VendorName, VendorPhone, VendorSupportID, VendorSupportName, VendorSupportExtension, SoftwareID, SoftwareName, SoftwareVendor, SoftwareLicenceExpires, SoftwareLicencePrice, UserID, UserName, UserAuthorizationStarts, UserAuthorizationEnds, UserAuthorizationPassword, PurchasePrice

Based on this information,

a. Identify the functional dependencies between the attributes.
b. Identify the reasons why this relation is not in 3NF.
c. Present the attributes organized so that the resulting relations are in 3NF.

26. The following attributes represent data about a movie copy at a video rental store. Each movie is identified by a movie number and has a title and information about the director and the studio that produced the movie. Each movie has one or several characters, and there is exactly one actor playing the role of each of the characters (but one actor can play multiple roles in each of the movies). A video store has multiple copies of the same movie, and the store differentiates copies with a movie copy number, which is unique within a single movie but not unique between different movies. Each movie copy has a rental status and return date; in addition, each copy has a type (VHS, DVD, or

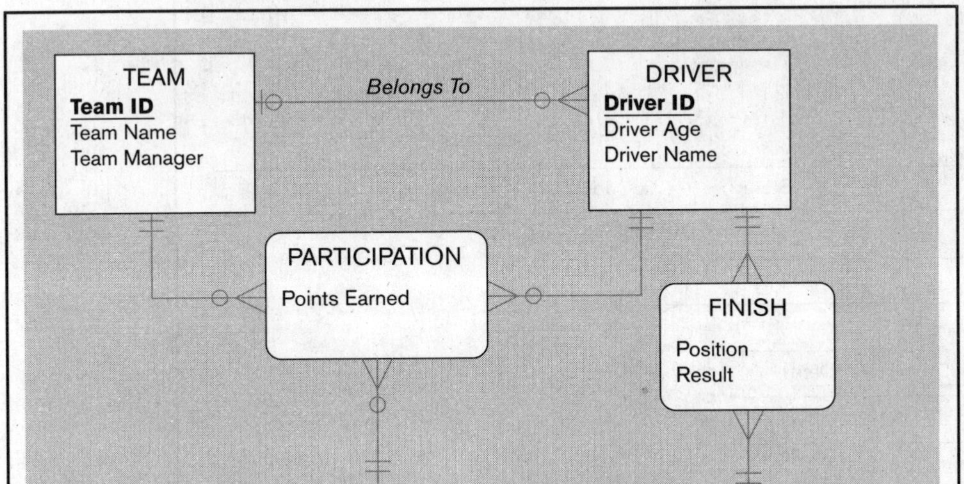

FIGURE 4-35 EER diagram for a car racing league

FIGURE 4-36 EER diagram for a middle-size software vendor

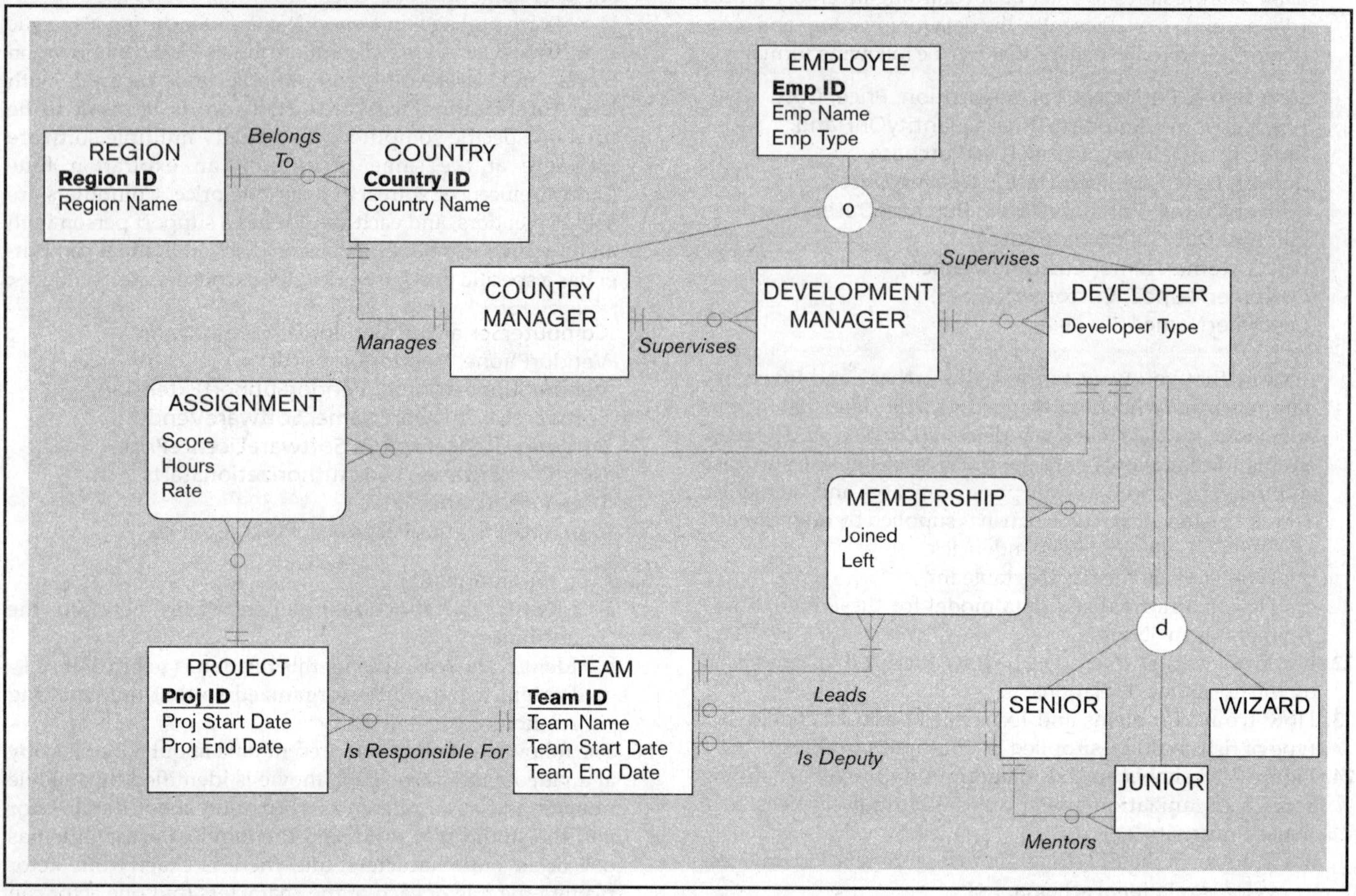

Attorney

AttorneyID	Name	Address	City	State	ZipCode

Speciality

AttorneyID	Speciality

Bar

AttorneyID	Bar

Client

ClientID	Name	Address	City	State	ZipCode	Telephone	DOB

Case

CaseID	Description	CaseType	CourtID

Retains

AttorneyID	CaseID	ClientID	Date

Court

CourtID	CourtName	City	State	ZipCode

Judge

JudgeID	Name	Years	CourtID

FIGURE 4-37 Relations for Problem and Exercise 20

FIGURE 4-38 EER diagram for university dining services

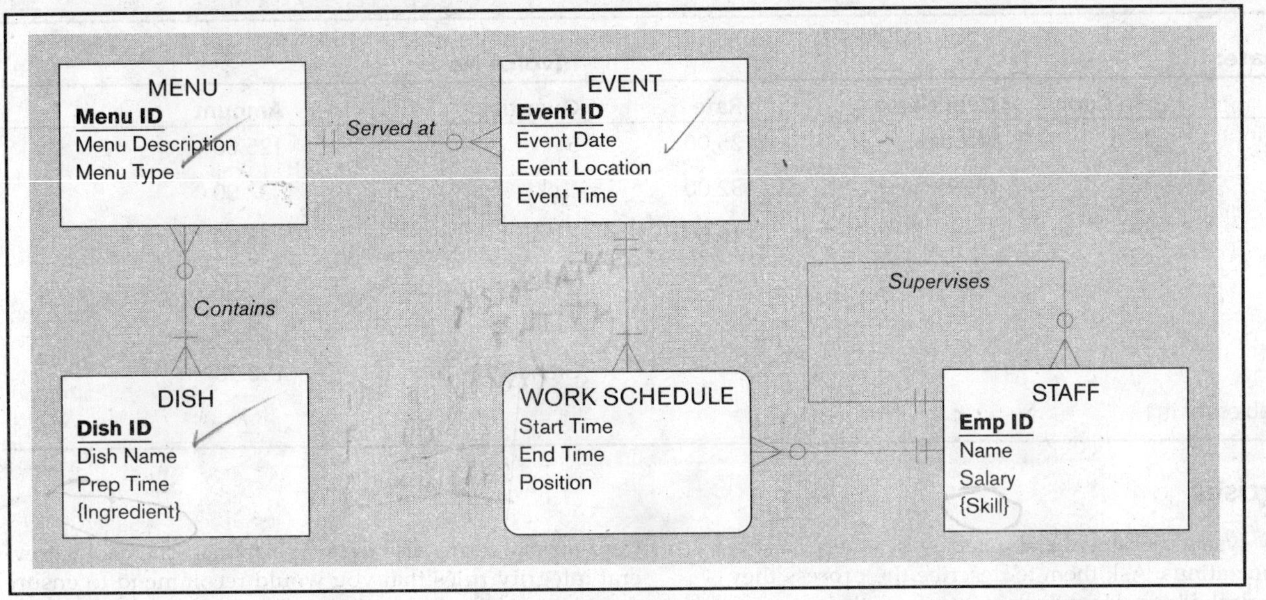

Blu-ray). The rental price depends on the movie and the copy type, but the price is the same for all copies of the same type. The attributes are as follows:

Movie Nbr, Title, Director ID, Director Name, Studio ID, Studio Name, Studio Location, Studio CEO, Character, Actor ID, Name, Movie Copy Nbr, Movie Copy Type, Movie Rental Price, Copy Rental Status, Copy Return Date

A sample data set regarding a movie would be as follows (the data in the curly brackets are character/actor data, in this case for four different characters):

567, "It's a Wonderful Life", 25, "Frank Capra", 234, "Liberty Films", "Hollywood, CA", "Orson Wells", {"George Bailey", 245, "James Stewart" | "Mary Bailey", 236, "Donna Reed" | "Clarence Oddbody", 765, "Henry Travers" | "Henry F. Potter", 325, "Lionel Barrymore" }, 5434, "DVD", 2.95, "Rented", "12/15/2010"

Based on this information,

a. Identify the functional dependencies between the attributes.

b. Identify the reasons why this set of data items is not in 3NF and tell what normal form (if any) it is in.

c. Present the attributes organized into 3NF relations that have been named appropriately.

27. The Table 4-9 below contains the sales data at the West Side Store (Refer to the Table 4-9 given below to answer the questions)

a. Convert the Table 4-9 details into the first normal form.

b. What are the functional dependencies that you can identify? List at least two.

c. Develop the final 3NF for this table enumerating the total number of tables needed for a well-structured relation.

28. A local car dealer, "Friendly Dealers", sells cars from two to three different automobile companies. "Friendly Dealers" maintains the details of manufacturers, so that its employees can interact with the manufacturers, if needed. "Friendly Dealers" also keeps information related to the models of cars they deal with. They maintain information such as list price, price of the dealership paid, model name, series (e.g., Maruti 800, DX, etc). They keep information of the sales that they make with the details of the buyers (such as name, address, contact details, etc), create an ERD, and apply the rules of normalization to arrive at a compact database structure.

29. Table 4-10 shows an invoice for a sales company:

TABLE 4-9 Sales Data at the West Side Store

Sl. No.	Bill No.	Credit Card No.	Customer Name	Customer Contact	Bill Date	Item No.	Item Rate	Qty.	Total Cost
1.	100034	447756130	Seema Das	9448961021	30/06/2010	S101	15.00	6	
						N110	45.00	3	
						T14	110.00	2	
						S102	25.00	3	
2.	100035	Cash payment	Nikunj Patel	9310756667	02/07/2010	B16	450.00	2	
						C108	140.00	5	
3.	100036	Cash payment	Aditya Bhandari		02/07/2010	A111	566.00	1	

TABLE 4-10 ABC Sales Company, Bangalore

Invoice

Invoice Date:				**Invoice No**	
Sl. No	**Item Code**	**Item Name**	**Rate**	**Quantity**	**Amount**
1.	I-234	Noodles	25.00	5	125.00
2.	I-765	Mayonnaise	32.00	1 pkt	32.00
3.	I-541	Brown Bread	19.00	2 loaves	38.00
				Total	195.00
				Tax @ 2%	3.90
				Grand Total	198.90

Develop tables for it.1.

Field Exercises

1. Interview system designers and database designers at several organizations. Ask them to describe the process they use for logical design. How do they transform their conceptual data models (e.g., E-R diagrams) to relational schema? What is the role of CASE tools in this process? Do they use normalization? If they do, how far in the process do they go, and for what purpose?
2. Obtain a common document such as a sales slip, customer invoice from an auto repair shop, credit card statement, etc. Use the normalization steps (steps 0 through 4) described in this chapter to convert this user view to a set of relations in third normal form. Also draw a relational schema. List several integrity rules that you would recommend to ensure the quality of the data in this application.
3. Using Appendix B as a resource, interview a database analyst/designer to determine whether he or she normalizes relations to higher than 3NF. Why or why not does he or she use normal forms beyond 3NF?
4. Find a form or report from a business organization, possibly a statement, bill, or document you have received. Draw an EER diagram of the data in this form or report. Transform the diagram into a set of 3NF relations.

References

Chouinard, P. 1989. "Supertypes, Subtypes, and DB2." *Database Programming & Design* 2,10 (October): 50–57.

Codd, E. F. 1970. "A Relational Model of Data for Large Shared Data Banks." *Communications of the ACM* 13,6 (June): 77–87.

Codd, E. F. 1990. *The Relational Model for Database Management*, Version 2. Reading, MA: Addison-Wesley.

Date, C. J. 2003. *An Introduction to Database Systems*, 8th ed. Reading, MA: Addison-Wesley.

Dutka, A. F., and H. H. Hanson. 1989. *Fundamentals of Data Normalization*. Reading, MA: Addison-Wesley.

Fleming, C. C., and B. von Halle. 1989. *Handbook of Relational Database Design*. Reading, MA: Addison-Wesley.

Hoberman, S. 2006. "To Surrogate Key or Not." *DM Review* 16,8 (August): 29.

Johnston, T. 2000. "Primary Key Reengineering Projects: The Problem" and "Primary Key Reengineering Projects: The Solution." Available at **www.information-management.com**.

Navathe, S., R. Elmasri, and J. Larson. 1986. "Integrating User Views in Database Design." *Computer* 19,1 (January): 50–62.

Further Reading

Elmasri, R., and S. Navathe. 2006. *Fundamentals of Database Systems*, 5th ed. Menlo Park, CA: Benjamin Cummings.

Hoffer, J. A., J. F. George, and J. S. Valacich. 2010. *Modern Systems Analysis and Design*, 6th ed. Upper Saddle River, NJ: Prentice Hall.

Russell, T., and R. Armstrong. 2002. "13 Reasons Why Normalized Tables Help Your Business." *Database Administrator*, April 20, 2002. Available at **http://searchoracle.techtarget.com/tip/13-reasons-why-normalized-tables-help-your-business**

Storey, V. C. 1991. "Relational Database Design Based on the Entity-Relationship Model." *Data and Knowledge Engineering* 7,1 (November): 47–83.

Web Resources

http://en.wikipedia.org/wiki/Database_normalization Wikipedia entry that provides a thorough explanation of first, second, third, fourth, fifth, and Boyce-Codd normal forms.

www.bkent.net/Doc/simple5.htm Web site that presents a summary paper by William Kent titled "A Simple Guide to Five Normal Forms in Relational Database Theory."

www.stevehoberman.com/challenges.htm Web site where Steve Hoberman, a leading consultant and lecturer on database design, periodically creates database design (conceptual and logical) problems and posts them. These are practical (based on real experiences or questions sent to him) situations that make for nice puzzles to solve.

www.troubleshooters.com/codecorn/norm.htm Web page on normalization on Steve Litt's site that contains various troubleshooting tips for avoiding programming and systems development problems.

CASE

Mountain View Community Hospital

Case Description

You have been introduced to the Mountain View Community Hospital (MVCH) case in the preceding chapters. This chapter continues the case, with special emphasis on logical design for the relational data model. Although the hospital will continue to evaluate newer technology (e.g., object-oriented databases, XML, and XML databases), it is expected that relational technology will continue to dominate its systems development over the next few years.

Case Questions

1. Should MVCH continue to use relational technology for its systems development? Why or why not?
2. Should MVCH use normalization in designing its relational databases? Why or why not?
3. Why are entity integrity constraints of importance to the hospital? Based on the case description from previous chapters, which attributes have you encountered that may be null?
4. Why are referential integrity constraints of importance to the hospital?
5. Physicians at MVCH can be uniquely identified by their Social Security number, their license number, their DEA registration number, or hospital-assigned PhysicianID. Which attribute would you suggest using as the primary key for a PHYSICIAN relation? Why? What specific concerns are related to those attributes that you do not recommend be used?
6. The chapter describes the importance of using an *enterprise key*, which is a primary key that is unique across the whole database. Why might this be important in a hospital setting such as MVCH? Explain.
7. Why might you need to revisit and potentially modify the EER model you developed earlier, during the logical design phase?

Case Exercises

1. The assistant administrator at MVCH has asked you to review the data used in the patient billing and accounting systems. Occasional errors have been discovered in patient statements and the patient records maintained by the hospital. As part of this effort, you have selected four user views for analysis. Simplified versions of these views are shown in MVCH Figures 4-1 through 4-4 and described briefly here:
   - ***Patient bill (MVCH Figure 4-1)*** This statement is presented to the patient (or patient representative) when the patient is discharged. Assume that each item on the bill

INVOICE

MOUNTAIN VIEW COMMUNITY HOSPITAL
200 Forest Dr.
Mountain View, CO 80638

Mary Baker
200 Oak St.
Mountain View, CO 806338

INVOICE DATE:	10/24/2010
ACCOUNT NUMBER:	000976555
DUE DATE:	11/14/2010

PATIENT NAME	PATIENT #	DATE ADMITTED	DATE DISCHARGED
Mary Baker	3249	10/15/2010	10/18/2010

CODE	DESCRIPTION	TOTAL CHARGE
200	Room semi-pr	1,800.00
205	Television	75.00
307	X-ray	150.00
413	Lab tests	200.00

TOTAL CHARGES DUE	2,225.00

MVCH FIGURE 4-1 Patient bill

MVCH FIGURE 4-2 Room utilization report (excerpt)

ROOM UTILIZATION REPORT
Short Stay Surgical Ward
10/15/2010

LOCATION	ACCOM	PATIENT #	PATIENT NAME	EXP DISCHARGE DATE
100-1	PR	6213	Rose, David	10/17/2010
101-1	PR	1379	Cribbs, Ron	10/16/2010
102-1	SP			
102-2	SP	1239	Miller, Ruth	10/16/2010
103-1	PR	7040	Ortega, Juan	
104-1	PR			10/19/2010
105-1	SP	3249	Baker, Mary	10/18/2010

MVCH FIGURE 4-3 Patient display

MVCH PATIENT DISPLAY

10/16/2010 12:41 AM

PATIENT #:	3249
PATIENT NAME:	Mary Baker
PATIENT ADDRESS:	300 Oak St.
CITY-STATE-ZIP:	Mountain View, CO 80638
DATE ADMITTED:	10-15-10
DATE DISCHARGED:	
LOCATION:	437-2
EXTENSION:	529
INSURANCE:	Blue Cross/Blue Shield

has a unique description and that the charge for a particular item may vary from one patient to another.

- ***Room utilization report (MVCH Figure 4-2)*** This is a daily report that is distributed to qualified personnel. The information can also be retrieved online by a qualified staff member. It shows the status of each room and bed location in the hospital and is used primarily for scheduling and tracking the utilization of facilities. The Location column in this report records the room number and bed location in the room. The Accom column indicates the type of accommodation (PR = private, SP = semiprivate).
- ***Patient display (MVCH Figure 4-3)*** This display is presented on demand to any qualified doctor, nurse, or other staff member. Assume that for each location there is a unique telephone number.
- ***Daily physician report (MVCH Figure 4-4)*** This report is prepared daily for each physician on the staff of MVCH. It shows the patients who have been treated on that day by the physician and the name of the treatment (or procedure). To simplify the analysis, assume that each patient may receive only one treatment from a given physician on a given day. (We ask you to comment on this assumption later.)

a. Using the normalization steps described in this chapter, develop a set of 3NF relations for each of the four user views.

b. For each user view, draw a relational schema for the 3NF relations you developed in Case Exercise 1a. Be sure to show the functional dependencies and referential integrity constraints for each schema.

c. Merge the relations for the four user views into a single set of 3NF relations, using the guidelines presented in this chapter. Draw a single relational schema for the four user views and show the referential integrity constraints.

d. Suggest any refinements to the design in Case Exercise 1c that would promote data quality and integrity.

e. How would you change your approach to accommodate the rule that a patient may receive multiple treatments from a given physician on a given day?

2. The Multiple Sclerosis (MS) Center, headed by Dr. "Z," has been using a spreadsheet to keep track of information that patients provide upon signing in for a clinic visit. One of the staff members thought it would be better to use a relational database for recording this information and imported the

MVCH FIGURE 4-4 Daily physician report (excerpt)

MOUNTAIN VIEW COMMUNITY HOSPITAL
DAILY PHYSICIAN REPORT
10/17/2010

PHYSICIAN ID:	Gerald Wilcox	PHYSICIAN PHONE:	329-1848
PATIENT #	**PATIENT NAME**	**LOCATION**	**PROCEDURE**
6083	Brown, May	184-2	Tonsillectomy
1239	Miller, Ruth	102-2	Observation
4139	Major, Carl	107-3	Appendectomy
9877	Carlos, Juan	188-2	Herniorrhaphy
1277	Pace, Charles	187-8	Cholecystectomy

spreadsheet as a table into a Microsoft Access database (MVCH Figure 4-5).

a. What would you suggest as the primary key for this table?
b. Is this table a relation? Why or why not?
c. Can you identify any problems with this table structure? Are there any insertion, deletion, or update anomalies?
d. Diagram the functional dependencies for this table.
e. Using the normalization steps described in this chapter, develop a set of 3NF relations.
f. Using a tool such as Microsoft Visio, draw the relational schema, clearly indicating referential integrity constraints.
g. Write CREATE TABLE commands for all relations in your schema. Make reasonable assumptions concerning the data type for each attribute in each of the relations.

3. Dr. Z in the MS Center is using the MS Clinic Management System from an external vendor to keep track of clinical information regarding his patients. The application uses a relational database. Before seeing a patient, Dr. Z reviews a printout of the worksheet shown in MVCH Figure 4-6.

a. Diagram the functional dependencies for this worksheet and develop a set of 3NF relations for the data on this worksheet.
b. Draw the relational schema and clearly show the referential integrity constraints.
c. Draw your answer to part b using Microsoft Visio (or any other tool specified by your instructor).

Project Assignments

After developing conceptual data models for MVCH's new system and reviewing them with your team and key stakeholders

Patient #	Name	First Seen	Social Worker	Visit Date	Visit Time	Reason for Visit	New symptoms	Level of Pain
9844	John Miller	10/1/2008	Matt Baker	10/11/2009	2:30 pm	Severe leg pain	Severe leg pain for past 2 days	4
				10/18/2009	11:30 am	Follow-up, also need flu shot	None	2
				1/3/2010	10 am	Routine	None	0
				3/15/2010	10:30 am	Routine	None	0
4211	Sheryl Franz	1/3/2009	Lynn Riley	1/3/2010	2 pm	Referred by Primary care physician		0
				2/11/2010	9 am	Physical	None	0
				3/22/2010	4:00 pm	Routine and B12 Shot	Greater difficulties with writing & buttoning shirts	1
8766	Juan Ortega	2/2/2009	Matt Baker	2/2/2010	9:30 am	Blurred vision in right eye		0
				2/14/2010	9:30 am	Follow-up		0
				3/18/2010	????	New symptoms	Pins/needles in both legs; trouble with balance	1

MVCH FIGURE 4-5 MS Center patient sign-in data

MVCH FIGURE 4-6 MS Center patient worksheet

Mountain View Community Hospital
MS CENTER PATIENT WORKSHEET

MRN#	PATIENT NAME	Sex	DOB	STAGE	DATE PRINTED
7885	Michael J Olsen	M	June 16, 1949	Secondary Progressive MS	07 July 2010

Presenting Symptoms

Tingling and numbness in both hands;spasticity in both legs, primarily the left one;significant loss of mobility, relies on wheelchair most days;episodes of severe muscular pain, primarily in left leg.

Active Medications

1. Aspirin, 325 mg, QD
2. Simvastatin, 40 mg, QHS
3. Baclofen, 10 mg, TID
4. Betaseron (interferon beta-1b), 250 mcg QOD, sc
5. Amantadine, 100 mg, BID
6. Plendil, 5 mg, QD

Clinical Laboratory Data

Lipid Profile	LDL(<100)	Trig(<200)	HDL(<35)	CHOL(<200)
06/23/2010	54	214	27	183
03/16/2010	54	325	24	217
12/13/2010	62	200	24	166

Radiology Data

Last Brain MRI: 05/23/2010 No new lesions;no expanding lesions

Clinic Data

Blood Pressure (<=120/80)		Weight	
07/07/2010	135/80mmHg	07/07/2010	188
06/07/2010	124/75 mmHg	06/07/2010	190
05/20/2010	140/90 mmHg	05/20/2010	189
03/15/2010	135/86 mmHg	03/15/2010	188
01/17/2010	131/80 mmHg	01/17/2010	191

Last neurological assessment:
03/05 No change

Last Expanded Disability Status Scale (EDSS) Score:
03/05 5.5 (scale:0–10)

Last Fatigue Severity Scale (FSS) Score:
03/05 2 (scale:1–7)

Advisories

06/07/2010	Suggested follow-up lipid profile in 2 weeks
05/20/2010	Suggested follow-up for Triglycerides > 300, consider titrating Simvastatin up to 60 mg before initiating other therapies
03/15/2010	Discontinued Tizanidine;suggested follow-up for medication Baclofen

at the hospital, you are ready to move on to the logical design for the relational database. Your next deliverable is the relational schema. You may also have to modify the EER model you created in Chapter 3.

P1. Map the EER diagram you developed in Chapter 3 to a relational schema, using the techniques described in this chapter. Be sure to underline all primary keys, include all necessary foreign keys, and clearly indicate referential integrity constraints.

P2. Analyze and diagram the functional dependencies in each relation. If any relation is not in 3NF, decompose that relation into 3NF relations, using the steps described in this chapter. Revise the relational schema accordingly.

P3. Create enterprise keys for all relations and redefine all relations. Revise the relational schema accordingly.

P4. If necessary, revisit and modify the EER model you developed in Chapter 3 and explain the changes you made.

CHAPTER

5

Physical Database Design and Performance

Learning Objectives

After studying this chapter, you should be able to:

- Concisely define each of the following key terms: **field, data type, denormalization, horizontal partitioning, vertical partitioning, physical file, tablespace, extent, file organization, sequential file organization, indexed file organization, index, secondary key, join index, hashed file organization, hashing algorithm, pointer,** and **hash index table.**
- Describe the physical database design process, its objectives, and its deliverables.
- Choose storage formats for attributes from a logical data model.
- Select an appropriate file organization by balancing various important design factors.
- Describe three important types of file organization.
- Describe the purpose of indexes and the important considerations in selecting attributes to be indexed.
- Translate a relational data model into efficient database structures, including knowing when and how to denormalize the logical data model.

INTRODUCTION

In Chapters 2 through 4, you learned how to describe and model organizational data during the conceptual data modeling and logical database design phases of the database development process. You learned how to use EER notation, the relational data model, and normalization to develop abstractions of organizational data that capture the meaning of data. However, these notations do not explain how data will be processed or stored. The purpose of physical database design is to translate the logical description of data into the technical specifications for storing and retrieving data. The goal is to create a design for storing data that will provide adequate performance and ensure database integrity, security, and recoverability.

Physical database design does not include implementing files and databases (i.e., creating them and loading data into them). Physical database design produces the technical specifications that programmers, database administrators, and others involved in information systems construction will use during the implementation phase, which we discuss in Chapters 6 through 9.

In this chapter, you study the basic steps required to develop an efficient and high-integrity physical database design; security and recoverability are addressed in Chapter 11. We concentrate in this chapter on the design of a single, centralized database. Later, in Chapter 12, you learn about the design of databases that are stored at multiple, distributed sites. In this chapter, you learn how to estimate the amount of data that users will require in the database and determine how data are likely to be used. You learn about choices for storing attribute values and how to select from among these choices to achieve efficiency and data quality. Because of recent U.S. and international regulations (e.g., Sarbanes-Oxley) on financial reporting by organizations, proper controls specified in physical database design are required as a sound foundation for compliance. Hence, we place special emphasis on data quality measures you can implement within the physical design. You will also learn why normalized tables are not always the basis for the best physical data files and how you can denormalize the data to improve the speed of data retrieval. Finally, you learn about the use of indexes, which are important in speeding up the retrieval of data. In essence, you learn in this chapter how to made databases really "hum."

You must carefully perform physical database design, because the decisions made during this stage have a major impact on data accessibility, response times, data quality, security, user friendliness, and similarly important information system design factors. Database administration (described in Chapter 11) plays a major role in physical database design, so we return to some advanced design issues in that chapter.

RangaManch, a large theater group aided by the state government grants, plans to digitize all its sources of dramas, plays, and street plays. **RangaManch** has a large repository of all the above-mentioned categories in the regular filing format. **RangaManch** has its collaborative members such as Prithvi Theaters in Chennai, National School of Drama in Agra, and RangeenNatak School in Bhopal. The fundamental idea is to pool and share the literature of drama and its repositories among the theaters mentioned. The challenge and opportunity presented here is threefold—one, the type of data format that is required to store this type of data collection; two, the size or space required for such a data storage; and three, the architecture of the shared data dissemination. The database consultant appointed by **RangaManch** already has the logical database design in place. But implementing it physically is a big challenge; especially, the sharing of repositories across the theater groups, response times of the database, security, and administration.

THE PHYSICAL DATABASE DESIGN PROCESS

To make life a little easier for you, many physical database design decisions are implicit or eliminated when you choose the database management technologies to use with the information system you are designing. Because many organizations have standards for operating systems, database management systems, and data access languages, you must deal only with those choices not implicit in the given technologies. Thus, we will cover only those decisions that you will make most frequently, as well as other selected decisions that may be critical for some types of applications, such an online data capture and retrieval.

The primary goal of physical database design is data processing efficiency. Today, with ever-decreasing costs for computer technology per unit of measure (both speed and space measures), it is typically very important to design a physical database to minimize the time required by users to interact with the information system. Thus, we concentrate on how to make processing of physical files and databases efficient, with less attention on minimizing the use of space.

Designing physical files and databases requires certain information that should have been collected and produced during prior systems development phases. The information needed for physical file and database design includes these requirements:

- Normalized relations, including estimates for the range of the number of rows in each table
- Definitions of each attribute, along with physical specifications such as maximum possible length

- Descriptions of where and when data are used in various ways (entered, retrieved, deleted, and updated, including typical frequencies of these events)
- Expectations or requirements for response time and data security, backup, recovery, retention, and integrity
- Descriptions of the technologies (database management systems) used for implementing the database

Physical database design requires several critical decisions that will affect the integrity and performance of the application system. These key decisions include the following:

- Choosing the storage format (called *data type*) for each attribute from the logical data model. The format and associated parameters are chosen to maximize data integrity and to minimize storage space.
- Giving the database management system guidance regarding how to group attributes from the logical data model into *physical records*. You will discover that although the columns of a relational table as specified in the logical design are a natural definition for the contents of a physical record, this does not always form the foundation for the most desirable grouping of attributes.
- Giving the database management system guidance regarding how to arrange similarly structured records in secondary memory (primarily hard disks), using a structure (called a *file organization*) so that individual and groups of records can be stored, retrieved, and updated rapidly. Consideration must also be given to protecting data and recovering data if errors are found.
- Selecting structures (including *indexes* and the overall *database architecture*) for storing and connecting files to make retrieving related data more efficient.
- Preparing strategies for handling queries against the database that will optimize performance and take advantage of the file organizations and indexes that you have specified. Efficient database structures will be of benefit only if queries and the database management systems that handle those queries are tuned to intelligently use those structures.

Physical Database Design as a Basis for Regulatory Compliance

One of the primary motivations for strong focus on physical database design is that it forms a foundation for compliance with new national and international regulations on financial reporting. Without careful physical design, an organization cannot demonstrate that its data are accurate and well protected. Laws and regulations such as the Sarbanes-Oxley Act (SOX) in the United States and Basel II for international banking are reactions to recent cases of fraud and deception by executives in major corporations and partners in public accounting firms. The purpose of SOX is to protect investors by improving the accuracy and reliability of corporate disclosures made pursuant to the securities laws, and for other purposes. SOX requires that every annual financial report include an internal control report. This is designed to show that not only are the company's financial data accurate, but the company has confidence in them because adequate controls (e.g., database integrity controls) are in place to safeguard financial data.

SOX is the most recent regulation in a stream of efforts to improve financial data reporting. The Committee of Sponsoring Organizations (COSO) of the Treadway Commission is a voluntary private-sector organization dedicated to improving the quality of financial reporting through business ethics, effective internal controls, and corporate governance. COSO was originally formed in 1985 to sponsor the National Commission on Fraudulent Financial Reporting, an independent private sector initiative that studied the causal factors that can lead to fraudulent financial reporting and developed recommendations for public companies and their independent auditors, for the SEC and other regulators, and for educational institutions. The Control Objectives for Information and Related Technology (COBIT) is an open standard published by the IT Governance Institute and the Information Systems Audit and Control Association. It is an IT control framework built in part upon the COSO framework. The IT Infrastructure Library (ITIL), published by the Office of Government Commerce in Great Britain, focuses on IT services and is often used to complement the COBIT framework.

These standards, guidelines, and rules focus on corporate governance, risk assessment, and security and controls of data. Although laws such as SOX and Basel II require comprehensive audits of all procedures that deal with financial data, compliance can be greatly enhanced by a strong foundation of basic data integrity controls. Because such preventive controls are applied consistently and thoroughly, if designed into the database and enforced by the DBMS, field-level data integrity controls can be viewed very positively in compliance audits. Other DBMS features, such as triggers and stored procedures, discussed in Chapter 7, as well as audit trails and activity logs, discussed in Chapter 11, provide even further ways to ensure that only legitimate data values are stored in the database. However, even these control mechanisms are only as good as the underlying field data controls. Further, for full compliance, all data integrity controls must be thoroughly documented; defining these controls for the DBMS is a form of documentation. Further, changes to these controls must occur through well-documented change control procedures (so that temporary changes cannot be used to bypass well-designed controls).

Data Volume and Usage Analysis

As mentioned previously, data volume and frequency-of-use statistics are important inputs to the physical database design process, particularly in the case of very large-scale database implementations. Thus, you have to maintain a good understanding of the size and usage patterns of the database throughout its life cycle. In this section, we discuss data volume and usage analysis as if it were a one-time static activity, but in practice, you should continuously monitor significant changes in usage and data volumes.

An easy way to show the statistics about data volumes and usage is by adding notation to the EER diagram that represents the final set of normalized relations from logical database design. Figure 5-1 shows the EER diagram (without attributes) for a simple inventory database in Pine Valley Furniture Company. This EER diagram represents the normalized relations constructed during logical database design for the original conceptual data model of this situation depicted in Figure 3-5b.

Both data volume and access frequencies are shown in Figure 5-1. For example, there are 3,000 PARTs in this database. The supertype PART has two subtypes, MANUFACTURED (40 percent of all PARTs are manufactured) and PURCHASED (70 percent

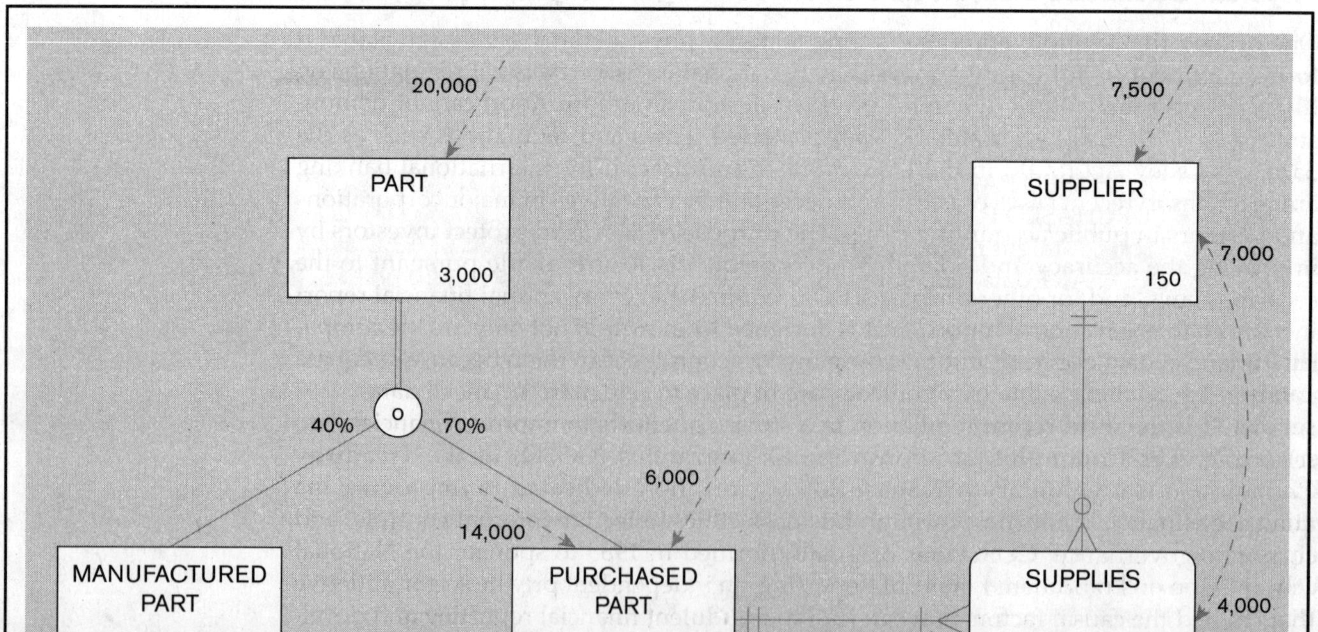

FIGURE 5-1 Composite usage map (Pine Valley Furniture Company)

are purchased; because some PARTs are of both subtypes, the percentages sum to more than 100 percent). The analysts at Pine Valley estimate that there are typically 150 SUPPLIERs, and Pine Valley receives, on average, 40 SUPPLIES instances from each SUPPLIER, yielding a total of 6,000 SUPPLIES. The dashed arrows represent access frequencies. So, for example, across all applications that use this database, there are on average 20,000 accesses per hour of PART data, and these yield, based on subtype percentages, 14,000 accesses per hour to PURCHASED PART data. There are an additional 6,000 direct accesses to PURCHASED PART data. Of this total of 20,000 accesses to PURCHASED PART, 8,000 accesses then also require SUPPLIES data and of these 8,000 accesses to SUPPLIES, there are 7,000 subsequent accesses to SUPPLIER data. For online and Web-based applications, usage maps should show the accesses per second. Several usage maps may be needed to show vastly different usage patterns for different times of day. Performance will also be affected by network specifications.

The volume and frequency statistics are generated during the systems analysis phase of the systems development process when systems analysts are studying current and proposed data processing and business activities. The data volume statistics represent the size of the business and should be calculated assuming business growth over at least a several-year period. The access frequencies are estimated from the timing of events, transaction volumes, the number of concurrent users, and reporting and querying activities. Because many databases support ad hoc accesses, and such accesses may change significantly over time, and known database access can peak and dip over a day, week, or month, the access frequencies tend to be less certain and even than the volume statistics. Fortunately, precise numbers are not necessary. What is crucial is the relative size of the numbers, which will suggest where the greatest attention needs to be given during physical database design in order to achieve the best possible performance. For example, in Figure 5-1, notice that

- There are 3,000 PART instances, so if PART has many attributes and some, like description, would be quite long, then the efficient storage of PART might be important.
- For each of the 4,000 times per hour that SUPPLIES is accessed via SUPPLIER, PURCHASED PART is also accessed; thus, the diagram would suggest possibly combining these two co-accessed entities into a database table (or file). This act of combining normalized tables is an example of denormalization, which we discuss later in this chapter.
- There is only a 10 percent overlap between MANUFACTURED and PURCHASED parts, so it might make sense to have two separate tables for these entities and redundantly store data for those parts that are both manufactured and purchased; such planned redundancy is okay if purposeful. Further, there are a total of 20,000 accesses an hour of PURCHASED PART data (14,000 from access to PART and 6,000 independent access of PURCHASED PART) and only 8,000 accesses of MANUFACTURED PART per hour. Thus, it might make sense to organize tables for MANUFACTURED and PURCHASED PART data differently due to the significantly different access volumes.

It can be helpful for subsequent physical database design steps if you can also explain the nature of the access for the access paths shown by the dashed lines. For example, it can be helpful to know that of the 20,000 accesses to PART data, 15,000 ask for a part or a set of parts based on the primary key, PartNo (e.g., access a part with a particular number); the other 5,000 accesses qualify part data for access by the value of QtyOnHand. (These specifics are not shown in Figure 5-1.) This more precise description can help in selecting indexes, one of the major topics we discuss later in this chapter. It might also be helpful to know whether an access results in data creation, retrieval, update, or deletion. Such a refined description of access frequencies can be handled by additional notation on a diagram such as in Figure 5-1, or by text and tables kept in other documentation.

DESIGNING FIELDS

A **field** is the smallest unit of application data recognized by system software, such as a programming language or database management system. A field corresponds to a simple attribute in the logical data model, and so in the case of a composite attribute, a field represents a single component.

Field
The smallest unit of application data recognized by system software.

The basic decisions you must make in specifying each field concern the type of data (or storage type) used to represent values of this field, data integrity controls built into the database, and the mechanisms that the DBMS uses to handle missing values for the field. Other field specifications, such as display format, also must be made as part of the total specification of the information system, but we will not be concerned here with those specifications that are often handled by applications rather than the DBMS.

Choosing Data Types

Data type
A detailed coding scheme recognized by system software, such as a DBMS, for representing organizational data.

A **data type** is a detailed coding scheme recognized by system software, such as a DBMS, for representing organizational data. The bit pattern of the coding scheme is usually transparent to you, but the space to store data and the speed required to access data are of consequence in physical database design. The specific DBMS you will use will dictate which choices are available to you. For example, Table 5-1 lists some of the data types available in the Oracle 11g DBMS, a typical DBMS that uses the SQL data definition and manipulation language. Additional data types might be available for currency, voice, image, and user defined for some DBMSs.

Selecting a data type involves four objectives that will have different relative levels of importance for different applications:

1. Represent all possible values.
2. Improve data integrity.
3. Support all data manipulations.
4. Minimize storage space.

An optimal data type for a field can, in minimal space, represent every possible value (while eliminating illegal values) for the associated attribute and can support the required data manipulation (e.g., numeric data types for arithmetic operations and character data types for string manipulation). Any attribute domain constraints from the conceptual data model are helpful in selecting a good data type for that attribute. Achieving these four objectives can be subtle. For example, consider a DBMS for which a data type has a maximum width of 2 bytes. Suppose this data type is sufficient to represent a QuantitySold field. When QuantitySold fields are summed, the sum may require a number larger than 2 bytes. If the DBMS uses the field's data type for results of any mathematics on that field, the 2-byte length will not work. Some data types have special manipulation capabilities; for example, only the DATE data type allows true date arithmetic.

TABLE 5-1 Commonly Used Data Types in Oracle 11g

Data Type	Description
VARCHAR2	Variable-length character data with a maximum length of 4,000 characters; you must enter a maximum field length (e.g., VARCHAR2(30) specifies a field with a maximum length of 30 characters). A value less than 30 characters will consume only the required space.
CHAR	Fixed-length character data with a maximum length of 2,000 characters; default length is 1 character (e.g., CHAR(5) specifies a field with a fixed length of 5 characters, capable of holding a value from 0 to 5 characters long).
CLOB	Character large object, capable of storing up to 4 gigabytes of one variable-length character data field (e.g., to hold a medical instruction or a customer comment).
NUMBER	Positive or negative number in the range 10^{-130} to 10^{126}; can specify the precision (total number of digits to the left and right of the decimal point) and the scale (the number of digits to the right of the decimal point) (e.g., NUMBER(5) specifies an integer field with a maximum of 5 digits, and NUMBER(5,2) specifies a field with no more than 5 digits and exactly 2 digits to the right of the decimal point).
INTEGER	Positive or negative integer with up to 38 digits (same as SMALL INT).
DATE	Any date from January 1, 4712 B.C., to December 31, 9999 A.D.; DATE stores the century, year, month, day, hour, minute, and second.
BLOB	Binary large object, capable of storing up to 4 gigabytes of binary data (e.g., a photograph or sound clip).

FIGURE 5-2 Example of a code lookup table (Pine Valley Furniture Company)

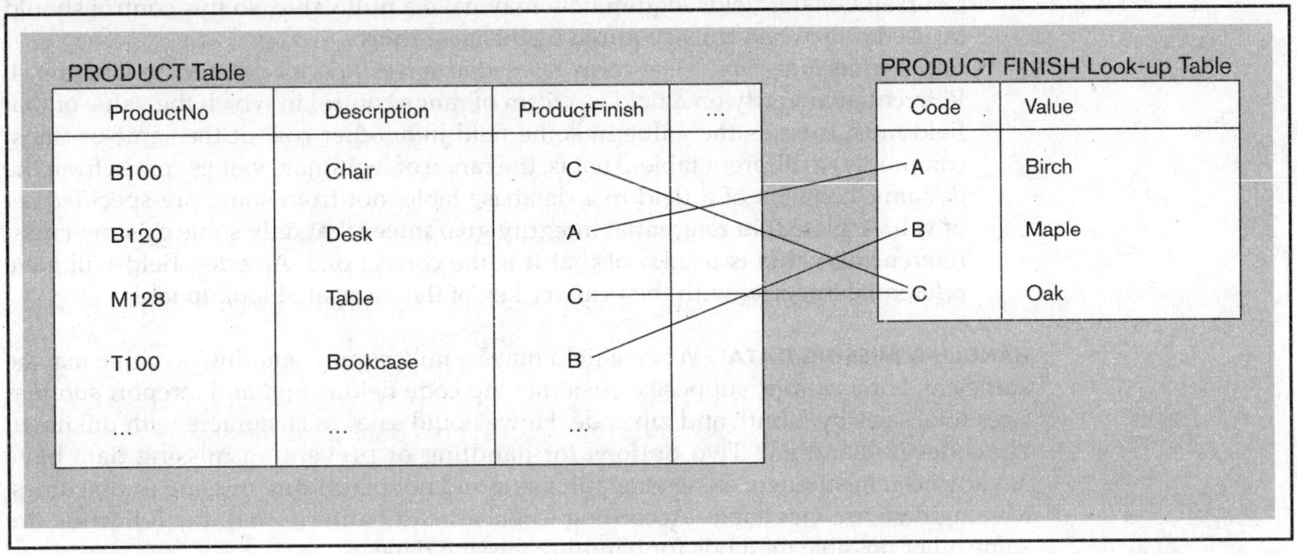

PINE VALLEY FURNITURE

CODING TECHNIQUES Some attributes have a sparse set of values or are so large that, given data volumes, considerable storage space will be consumed. A field with a limited number of possible values can be translated into a code that requires less space. Consider the example of the ProductFinish field illustrated in Figure 5-2. Products at Pine Valley Furniture come in only a limited number of woods: Birch, Maple, and Oak. By creating a code or translation table, each ProductFinish field value can be replaced by a code, a cross-reference to the lookup table, similar to a foreign key. This will decrease the amount of space for the ProductFinish field and hence for the PRODUCT file. There will be additional space for the PRODUCT FINISH lookup table, and when the ProductFinish field value is needed, an extra access (called a join) to this lookup table will be required. If the ProductFinish field is infrequently used or if the number of distinct ProductFinish values is very large, the relative advantages of coding may outweigh the costs. Note that the code table would not appear in the conceptual or logical model. The code table is a physical construct to achieve data processing performance improvements, not a set of data with business value.

Controlling Data Integrity For many DBMSs, data integrity controls (i.e., controls on the possible value a field can assume) can be built into the physical structure of the fields and controls enforced by the DBMS on those fields. The data type enforces one form of data integrity control because it may limit the type of data (numeric or character) and the length of a field value. The following are some other typical integrity controls that a DBMS may support:

- ***Default value*** A default value is the value a field will assume unless a user enters an explicit value for an instance of that field. Assigning a default value to a field can reduce data entry time because entry of a value can be skipped. It can also help to reduce data entry errors for the most common value.
- ***Range control*** A range control limits the set of permissible values a field may assume. The range may be a numeric lower-to-upper bound or a set of specific values. Range controls must be used with caution because the limits of the range may change over time. A combination of range controls and coding led to the year 2000 problem that many organizations faced, in which a field for year was represented by only the numbers 00 to 99. It is better to implement any range controls through a DBMS because range controls in applications may be inconsistently enforced. It is also more difficult to find and change them in applications than in a DBMS.
- ***Null value control*** A null value was defined in Chapter 4 as an empty value. Each primary key must have an integrity control that prohibits a null value. Any other required field may also have a null value control placed on it if that is the policy of the organization. For example, a university may prohibit adding a course

to its database unless that course has a title as well as a value of the primary key, CourseID. Many fields legitimately may have a null value, so this control should be used only when truly required by business rules.

- ***Referential integrity*** The term *referential integrity* was defined in Chapter 4. Referential integrity on a field is a form of range control in which the value of that field must exist as the value in some field in another row of the same or (most commonly) a different table. That is, the range of legitimate values comes from the dynamic contents of a field in a database table, not from some pre-specified set of values. Note that referential integrity guarantees that only some existing cross-referencing value is used, not that it is the correct one. A coded field will have referential integrity with the primary key of the associated lookup table.

HANDLING MISSING DATA When a field may be null, simply entering no value may be sufficient. For example, suppose a customer zip code field is null and a report summarizes total sales by month and zip code. How should sales to customers with unknown zip codes be handled? Two options for handling or preventing missing data have already been mentioned: using a default value and not permitting missing (null) values. Missing data are inevitable. According to Babad and Hoffer (1984), the following are some other possible methods for handling missing data:

- Substitute an estimate of the missing value. For example, for a missing sales value when computing monthly product sales, use a formula involving the mean of the existing monthly sales values for that product indexed by total sales for that month across all products. Such estimates must be marked so that users know that these are not actual values.
- Track missing data so that special reports and other system elements cause people to resolve unknown values quickly. This can be done by setting up a trigger in the database definition. A trigger is a routine that will automatically execute when some event occurs or time period passes. One trigger could log the missing entry to a file when a null or other missing value is stored, and another trigger could run periodically to create a report of the contents of this log file.
- Perform sensitivity testing so that missing data are ignored unless knowing a value might significantly change results (e.g., if total monthly sales for a particular salesperson are almost over a threshold that would make a difference in that person's compensation). This is the most complex of the methods mentioned and hence requires the most sophisticated programming. Such routines for handling missing data may be written in application programs. All relevant modern DBMSs now have more sophisticated programming capabilities, such as case expressions, user-defined functions, and triggers, so that such logic can be available in the database for all users without application-specific programming.

DENORMALIZING AND PARTITIONING DATA

Modern database management systems have an increasingly important role in determining how the data are actually stored on the storage media. The efficiency of database processing is, however, significantly affected by how the logical relations are structured as database tables. The purpose of this section is to discuss denormalization as a mechanism that is often used to improve efficient processing of data and quick access to stored data. It first describes the best-known denormalization approach: combining several logical tables into one physical table to avoid the need to bring related data back together when they are retrieved from the database. Then the section will discuss another form of denormalization called *partitioning*, which also leads to differences between the logical data model and the physical tables, but in this case one relation is implemented as multiple tables.

Denormalization

With the rapid decline in the costs of secondary storage per unit of data, the efficient use of storage space (reducing redundancy), while still a relevant consideration, has become less important than it has been in the past. In most cases, the primary goal of physical record design—efficient data processing—dominates the design process. In other words, speed, not style, matters. As in your dorm room, as long as you can find your favorite sweat shirt when you need it, it doesn't matter how tidy the room looks. (We won't tell your Mom.)

Efficient processing of data, just like efficient accessing of books in a library, depends on how close together related data (books or indexes) are. Often all the attributes that appear within a relation are not used together, and data from different relations are needed together to answer a query or produce a report. Thus, although normalized relations solve data maintenance anomalies and minimize redundancies (and storage space), normalized relations, if implemented one for one as physical records, may not yield efficient data processing.

A fully normalized database usually creates a large number of tables. For a frequently used query that requires data from multiple, related tables, the DBMS can spend considerable computer resources each time the query is submitted in matching up (called *joining*) related rows from each table required to build the query result. Because this joining work is so time-consuming, the processing performance difference between totally normalized and partially normalized databases can be dramatic. Inmon (1988) reports on a study to quantify fully and partially normalized databases. A fully normalized database contained eight tables with about 50,000 rows each; another partially normalized database had four tables with roughly 25,000 rows each; and yet another partially normalized database had two tables. The result showed that the less-than-fully normalized databases could be as much as an order of magnitude faster than the fully normalized one. Although such results depend greatly on the database and the type of processing against it, these results suggest that you should carefully consider whether the physical structure should exactly match the normalized relations for a database.

Denormalization is the process of transforming normalized relations into non-normalized physical record specifications. We will review various forms of, reasons for, and cautions about denormalization in this section. In general, denormalization may partition a relation into several physical records, may combine attributes from several relations together into one physical record, or may do a combination of both.

Denormalization
The process of transforming normalized relations into non-normalized physical record specifications.

OPPORTUNITIES FOR AND TYPES OF DENORMALIZATION Rogers (1989) introduces several common denormalization opportunities (Figures 5-3 through Figure 5-5 show examples of normalized and denormalized relations for each of these three situations):

1. ***Two entities with a one-to-one relationship*** Even if one of the entities is an optional participant, if the matching entity exists most of the time, then it may be wise to combine these two relations into one record definition (especially if the access frequency between these two entity types is high). Figure 5-3 shows student data with optional data from a standard scholarship application a student may complete. In this case, one record could be formed with four fields from the STUDENT and SCHOLARSHIP APPLICATION normalized relations (assuming that ApplicationID is no longer needed). (Note: In this case, fields from the optional entity must have null values allowed.)
2. ***A many-to-many relationship (associative entity) with nonkey attributes*** Rather than join three files to extract data from the two basic entities in the relationship, it may be advisable to combine attributes from one of the entities into the record representing the many-to-many relationship, thus avoiding one of the join operations. Again, this would be most advantageous if this joining occurs frequently. Figure 5-4 shows price quotes for different items from different vendors. In this case, fields from ITEM and PRICE QUOTE relations might be combined into one record to avoid having to join all three tables together. (Note: This may create considerable duplication of data; in the example, the ITEM fields, such as Description, would repeat for each price quote. This would necessitate excessive updating if duplicated data changed. Careful analysis of a composite usage map to study access frequencies and the number of occurrences of PRICE QUOTE per

FIGURE 5-3 A possible denormalization situation: two entities with a one-to-one relationship

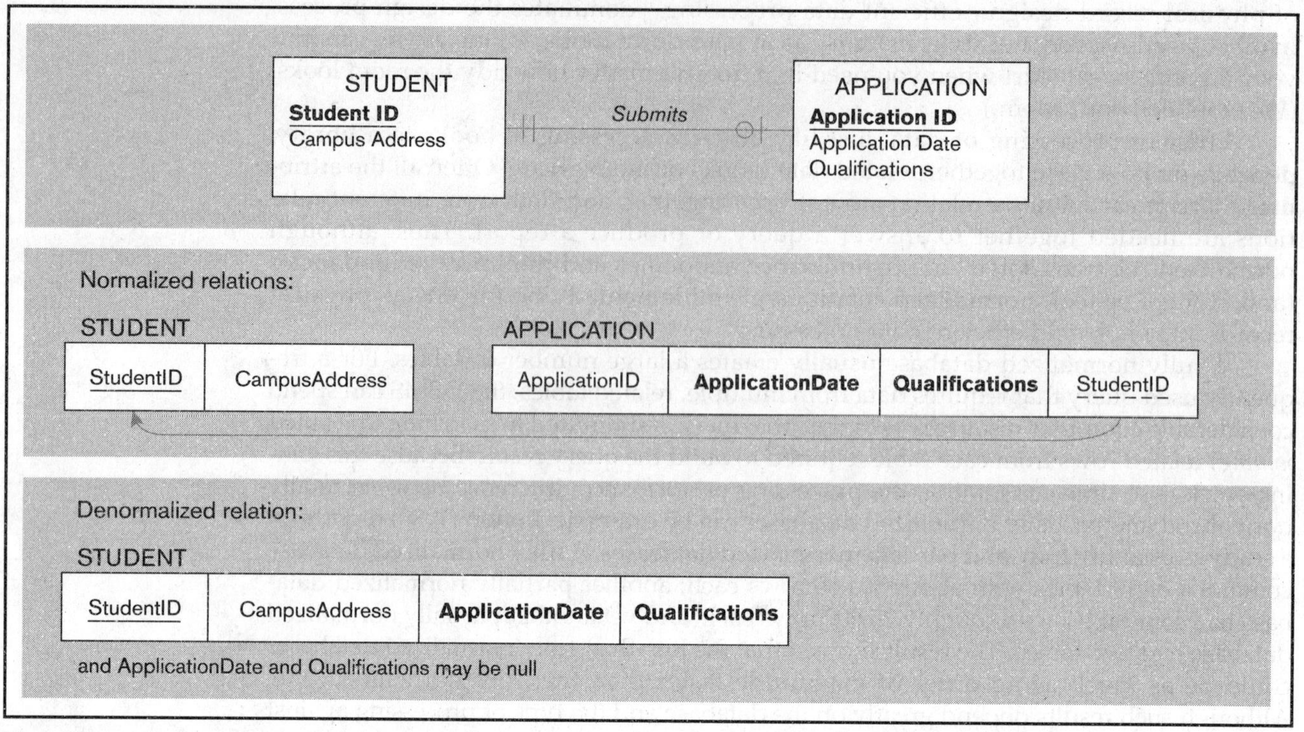

(*Note:* We assume that ApplicationID is not necessary when all fields are stored in one record, but this field can be included if it is required application data.)

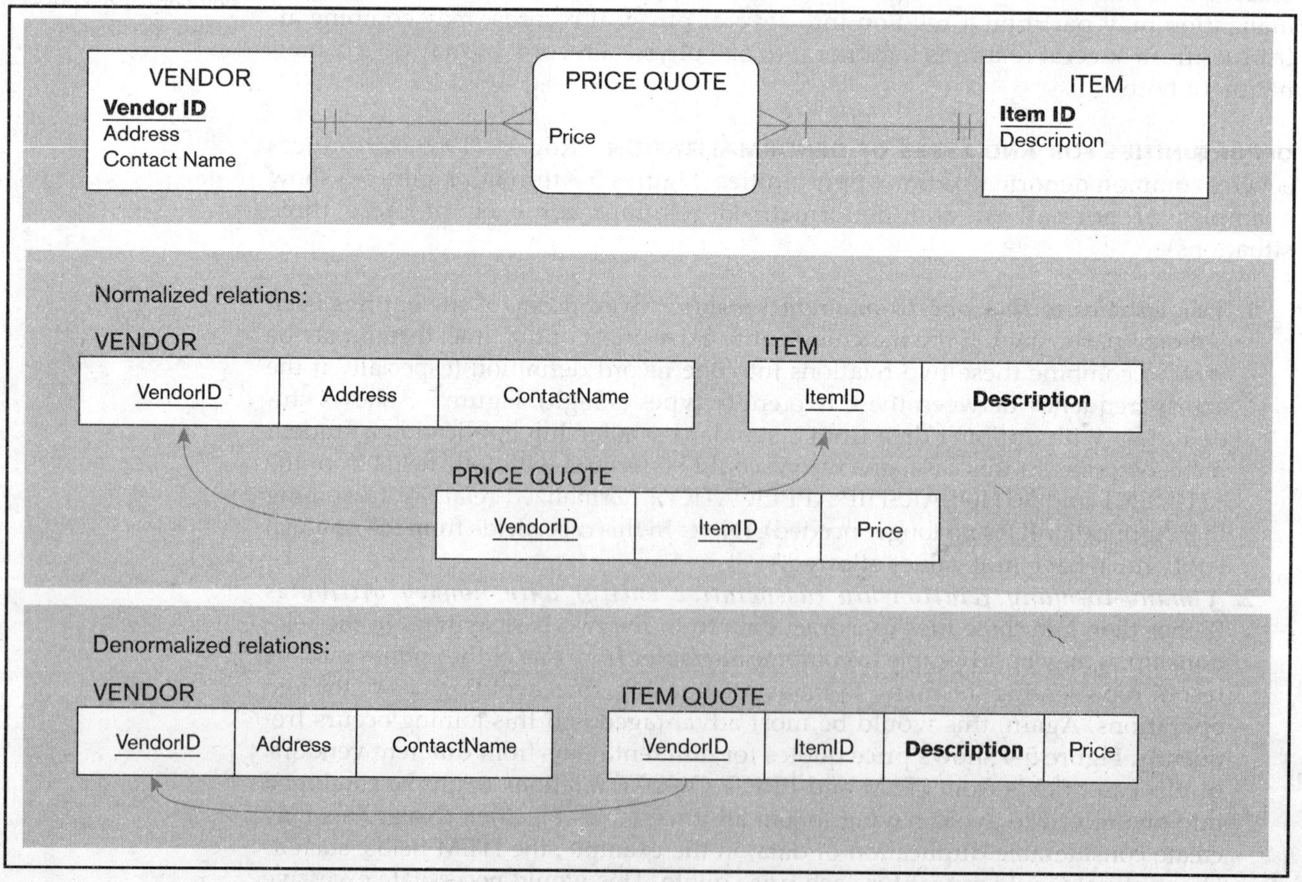

FIGURE 5-4 A possible denormalization situation: a many-to-many relationship with nonkey attributes

FIGURE 5-5 A possible denormalization situation: reference data

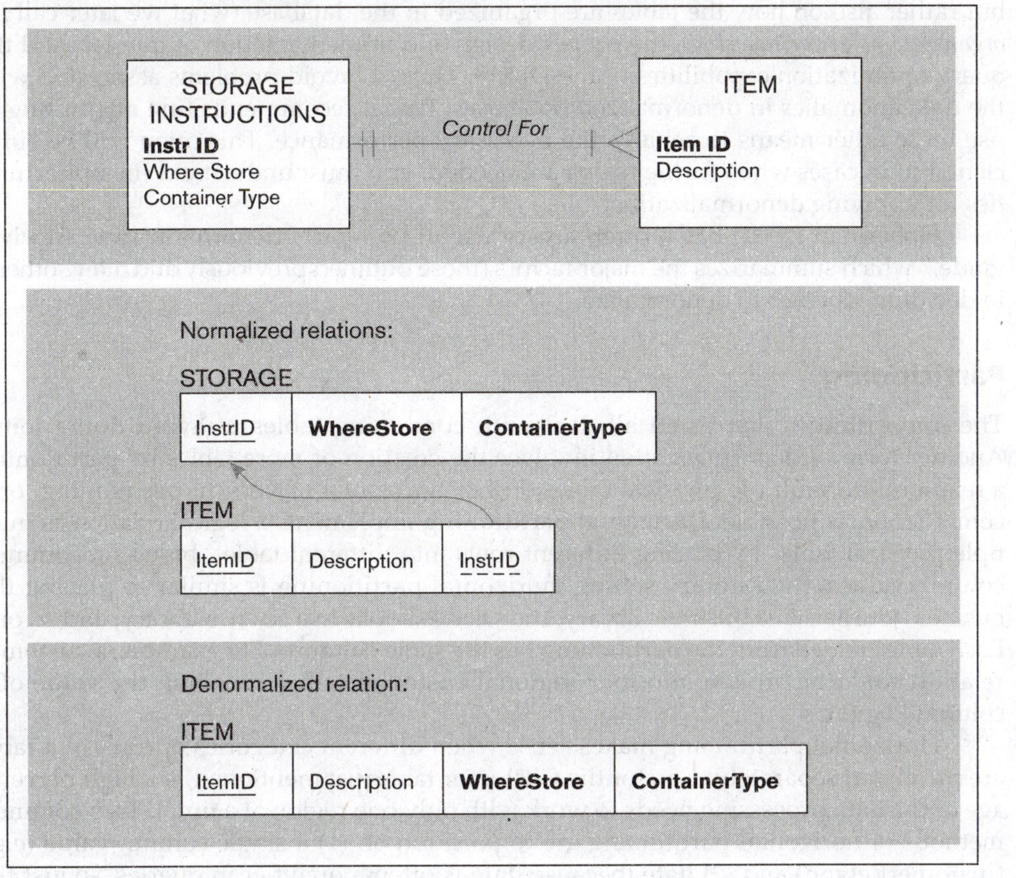

associated VENDOR or ITEM would be essential to understand the consequences of such denormalization.)

3. *Reference data* Reference data exist in an entity on the one side of a one-to-many relationship, and this entity participates in no other database relationships. You should seriously consider merging the two entities in this situation into one record definition when there are few instances of the entity on the many side for each entity instance on the one side. See Figure 5-5, in which several ITEMs have the same STORAGE INSTRUCTIONS, and STORAGE INSTRUCTIONS relates only to ITEMs. In this case, the storage instructions data could be stored in the ITEM record to create, of course, redundancy and potential for extra data maintenance. (InstrID is no longer needed.)

DENORMALIZE WITH CAUTION Denormalization has it critics. As Finkelstein (1988) points out, denormalization can increase the chance of errors and inconsistencies (caused by reintroducing anomalies into the database) and can force the reprogramming of systems if business rules change. For example, redundant copies of the same data caused by a violation of second normal form are often not updated in a synchronized way. And, if they are, extra programming is required to ensure that all copies of exactly the same business data are updated together. Further, denormalization optimizes certain data processing at the expense of other data processing, so if the frequencies of different processing activities change, the benefits of denormalization may no longer exist. Denormalization almost always also leads to more storage space for raw data and maybe more space for database overhead (e.g., indexes). Thus, denormalization should be an explicit act to gain significant processing speed when other physical design actions are not sufficient to achieve processing expectations.

Pascal (2002a, 2002b) passionately reports of the many dangers of denormalization. The motivation for denormalization is that a normalized database often creates many tables, and joining tables slows database processing. Pascal argues that this is not necessarily true, so the motivation for denormalization may be without merit in some cases. Overall, performance does not depend solely on the number of tables accessed but rather also on how the tables are organized in the database (what we later call *file organizations* and *clustering*), the proper design and implementation of queries, and the query optimization capabilities of the DBMS. Thus, to avoid problems associated with the data anomalies in denormalized databases, Pascal recommends first attempting to use these other means to achieve the necessary performance. This often will be sufficient, but in cases when further steps are needed, you must understand the opportunities for applying denormalization.

Hoberman (2002) has written a very useful two-part "denormalization survival guide," which summarizes the major factors (those outlined previously and a few others) in deciding whether to denormalize.

Partitioning

The opportunities just listed all deal with combining tables to avoid doing joins. Another form of denormalization involves the creation of more tables by partitioning a relation into multiple physical tables. Either horizontal or vertical partitioning, or a combination, is possible. **Horizontal partitioning** implements a logical relation as multiple physical tables by placing different rows into different tables, based on common column values. (In a library setting, horizontal partitioning is similar to placing the business journals in a business library, the science books in a science library, and so on.) Each table created from the partitioning has the same columns. For example, a customer relation could be broken into four regional customer tables based on the value of a column Region.

Horizontal partitioning
Distribution of the rows of a logical relation into several separate tables.

Horizontal partitioning makes sense when different categories of rows of a table are processed separately (e.g., for the Customer table just mentioned, if a high percentage of the data processing needs to work with only one region at a time). Two common methods of horizontal partitioning are to partition on (1) a single column value (e.g., CustomerRegion) and (2) date (because date is often a qualifier in queries, so just the needed partitions can be quickly found). (See Bieniek, 2006, for a guide to table partitioning.) Horizontal partitioning can also make maintenance of a table more efficient because fragmenting and rebuilding can be isolated to single partitions as storage space needs to be reorganized. Horizontal partitioning can also be more secure because file-level security can be used to prohibit users from seeing certain rows of data. Also, each partitioned table can be organized differently, appropriately for the way it is individually used. It is likely also faster to recover one of the partitioned files than one file with all the rows. In addition, taking one of the partitioned files out of service because it was damaged or so it can be recovered still allows processing against the other partitioned files to continue. Finally, each of the partitioned files can be placed on a separate disk drive to reduce contention for the same drive and hence improve query and maintenance performance across the database. These advantages of horizontal partitioning (actually, all forms of partitioning), along with the disadvantages, are summarized in Table 5-2.

Note that horizontal partitioning is very similar to creating a supertype/subtype relationship because different types of the entity (where the subtype discriminator is the field used for segregating rows) are involved in different relationships, hence different processing. In fact, when you have a supertype/subtype relationship, you need to decide whether you will create separate tables for each subtype or combine them in various combinations. Combining makes sense when all subtypes are used about the same way, whereas partitioning the supertype entity into multiple files makes sense when the subtypes are handled differently in transactions, queries, and reports. When a relation is partitioned horizontally, the whole set of rows can be reconstructed by using the SQL UNION operator (described in Chapter 6). Thus, for example, all customer data can be viewed together when desired.

The Oracle DBMS supports several forms of horizontal partitioning, designed in particular to deal with very large tables (Brobst et al., 1999). A table is partitioned when it is defined to the DBMS using the SQL data definition language (you will learn about the CREATE TABLE command in Chapter 6); that is, in Oracle, there is one table with

TABLE 5-2 Advantages and Disadvantages of Data Partitioning

Advantages of Partitioning

1. *Efficiency*: Data queried together are stored close to one another and separate from data not used together. Data maintenance is isolated in smaller partitions.
2. *Local optimization*: Each partition of data can be stored to optimize performance for its own use.
3. *Security*: Data not relevant to one group of users can be segregated from data those users are allowed to use.
4. *Recovery and uptime*: Smaller files take less time to back up and recover, and other files are still accessible if one file is damaged, so the effects of damage are isolated.
5. *Load balancing*: Files can be allocated to different storage areas (disks or other media), which minimizes contention for access to the same storage area or even allows for parallel access to the different areas.

Disadvantages of Partitioning

1. *Inconsistent access speed*: Different partitions may have different access speeds, thus confusing users. Also, when data must be combined across partitions, users may have to deal with significantly slower response times than in a non-partitioned approach.
2. *Complexity*: Partitioning is usually not transparent to programmers, who will have to write more complex programs when combining data across partitions.
3. *Extra space and update time*: Data may be duplicated across the partitions, taking extra storage space compared to storing all the data in normalized files. Updates that affect data in multiple partitions can take more time than if one file were used.

several partitions rather than separate tables per se. Oracle 11g has three data distribution methods as basic partitioning approaches:

1. ***Range partitioning,*** in which each partition is defined by a range of values (lower and upper key value limits) for one or more columns of the normalized table. A table row is inserted in the proper partition, based on its initial values for the range fields. Because partition key values may follow patterns, each partition may hold quite a different number of rows. A partition key may be generated by the database designer to create a more balanced distribution of rows. A row may be restricted from moving between partitions when key values are updated.
2. ***Hash partitioning,*** in which data are evenly spread across partitions independent of any partition key value. Hash partitioning overcomes the uneven distribution of rows that is possible with range partitioning. It works well if the goal is to distribute data evenly across devices.
3. ***List partitioning,*** in which the partitions are defined based on predefined lists of values of the partitioning key. For example, in a table partitioned based on the value of the column State, one partition might include rows that have the value "CT," "ME," "MA," "NH," "RI," or "VT," and another partition rows that have the value "NJ" or "NY".

If a more sophisticated form of partitioning is needed, Oracle 11g also offers composite partitioning, which combines aspects of two of the three single-level partitioning approaches.

Partitions are in many cases transparent to the database user. (You need to refer to a partition only if you want to force the query processor to look at one or more partitions.) The part of the DBMS that optimizes the processing of a query will look at the definition of partitions for a table involved in a query and will automatically decide whether certain partitions can be eliminated when retrieving the data needed to form the query results, which can drastically improve query processing performance.

For example, suppose a transaction date is used to define partitions in range partitioning. A query asking for only recent transactions can be more quickly processed by looking at only the one or few partitions with the most recent transactions rather than scanning the database or even using indexes to find rows in the desired range from a non-partitioned table. A partition on date also isolates insertions of new rows to one partition, which may reduce the overhead of database maintenance, and dropping "old" transactions will require simply dropping a partition. Indexes can still be used with a partitioned table and can improve performance even more than partitioning alone. See Brobst et al. (1999) for more details on the pros and cons of using dates for range partitioning.

In hash partitioning, rows are more evenly spread across the partitions. If partitions are placed in different storage areas that can be processed in parallel, then query performance will improve noticeably compared to when all the data have to be accessed sequentially in one storage area for the whole table. As with range partitioning, the existence of partitions typically is transparent to a programmer of a query. **Vertical partitioning** distributes the columns of a logical relation into separate tables, repeating the primary key in each of the tables. An example of vertical partitioning would be breaking apart a PART relation by placing the part number along with accounting-related part data into one record specification, the part number along with engineering-related part data into another record specification, and the part number along with sales-related part data into yet another record specification. The advantages and disadvantages of vertical partitioning are similar to those for horizontal partitioning. When, for example, accounting-, engineering-, and sales-related part data need to be used together, these tables can be joined. Thus, neither horizontal nor vertical partitioning prohibits the ability to treat the original relation as a whole.

Vertical partitioning
Distribution of the columns of a logical relation into several separate physical tables.

Combinations of horizontal and vertical partitioning are also possible. This form of denormalization—record partitioning—is especially common for a database whose files are distributed across multiple computers. Thus, you study this topic again in Chapter 12.

A single physical table can be logically partitioned or several tables can be logically combined by using the concept of a user view, which will be demonstrated in Chapter 6. With a user view, users can be given the impression that the database contains tables other than what are physically defined; you can create these logical tables through horizontal or vertical partitioning or other forms of denormalization. However, the purpose of any form of user view, including logical partitioning via views, is to simplify query writing and to create a more secure database, not to improve query performance. One form of a user view available in Oracle is called a partition view. With a partition view, physically separate tables with similar structures can be logically combined into one table using the SQL UNION operator. There are limitations to this form of partitioning. First, because there are actually multiple separate physical tables, there cannot be any global index on all the combined rows. Second, each physical table must be separately managed, so data maintenance is more complex (e.g., a new row must be inserted into a specific table). Third, the query optimizer has fewer options with a partition view than with partitions of a single table for creating the most efficient query processing plan.

The final form of denormalization we introduce is data replication. With data replication, the same data are purposely stored in multiple places in the database. For example, consider again Figure 5-1. You learned earlier in this section that relations can be denormalized by combining data from an associative entity with data from one of the simple entities with which it is associated. So, in Figure 5-1, SUPPLIES data might be stored with PURCHASED PART data in one expanded PURCHASED PART physical record specification. With data duplication, the same SUPPLIES data might also be stored with its associated SUPPLIER data in another expanded SUPPLIER physical record specification. With this data duplication, once either a SUPPLIER or PURCHASED PART record is retrieved, the related SUPPLIES data will also be available without any further access to secondary memory. This improved speed is worthwhile only if SUPPLIES data are frequently accessed with SUPPLIER and with PURCHASED PART data and if the costs for extra secondary storage and data maintenance are not great.

DESIGNING PHYSICAL DATABASE FILES

Physical file
A named portion of secondary memory (such as a hard disk) allocated for the purpose of storing physical records.

A **physical file** is a named portion of secondary memory (such as a magnetic tape or hard disk) allocated for the purpose of storing physical records. Some computer operating systems allow a physical file to be split into separate pieces, sometimes called *extents*. In subsequent sections, we will assume that a physical file is not split and that each record in a file has the same structure. That is, subsequent sections address how to store and link relational table rows from a single database in physical storage space. In order to optimize the performance of the database processing, the person who administers a database, the database administrator, often needs to know extensive details about how the database management system manages physical storage space. This knowledge is very DBMS specific, but the principles described in subsequent sections are the foundation for the physical data structures used by most relational DBMSs.

Most database management systems store many different kinds of data in one operating system file. By an *operating system file* we mean a named file that would appear on a disk directory listing (e.g., a listing of the files in a folder on the C: drive of your personal computer). For example, an important logical structure for storage space in Oracle is a tablespace. A **tablespace** is a named logical storage unit in which data from one or more database tables, views, or other database objects may be stored. An instance of Oracle 11g includes many tablespaces—for example, two (SYSTEM and SYSAUX) for system data (data dictionary or data about data), one (TEMP) for temporary work space, one (UNDOTBS1) for undo operations, and one or several to hold user business data. A tablespace consists of one or several physical operating system files. Thus, Oracle has responsibility for managing the storage of data inside a tablespace, whereas the operating system has many responsibilities for managing a tablespace, but they are all related to its responsibilities related to the management of operating system files (e.g., handling file-level security, allocating space, and responding to disk read and write errors).

Tablespace
A named logical storage unit in which data from one or more database tables, views, or other database objects may be stored.

Because an instance of Oracle usually supports many databases for many users, a database administrator usually will create many user tablespaces, which helps to achieve database security because the administrator can give each user selected rights to access each tablespace. Each tablespace consists of logical units called *segments* (consisting of one table, index, or partition), which, in turn, are divided into **extents**. These, finally, consist of a number of contiguous *data blocks*, which are the smallest unit of storage. Each table, index, or other so-called schema object belongs to a single tablespace, but a tablespace may contain (and typically contains) one or more tables, indexes, and other schema objects. Physically, each tablespace can be stored in one or multiple data files, but each data file is associated with only one tablespace and only one database.

Extent
A contiguous section of disk storage space.

Modern database management systems have an increasingly active role in managing the use of the physical devices and files on them; for example, the allocation of schema objects (e.g., tables and indexes) to data files is typically fully controlled by the DBMS. A database administrator does, however, have the ability to manage the disk space allocated to tablespaces and a number of parameters related to the way free space is managed within a database. Because this is not a text on Oracle, we do not cover specific details on managing tablespaces; however, the general principles of physical database design apply to the design and management of Oracle tablespaces as they do to whatever the physical storage unit is for any database management system. Figure 5-6 is an EER model that shows the relationships between various physical and logical database terms related to physical database design in an Oracle environment.

File Organizations

A **file organization** is a technique for physically arranging the records of a file on secondary storage devices. With modern relational DBMSs, you do not have to design file organizations, but you may be allowed to select an organization and its parameters for a table or physical file. In choosing a file organization for a particular file in a database, you should consider seven important factors:

File organization
A technique for physically arranging the records of a file on secondary storage devices.

1. Fast data retrieval
2. High throughput for processing data input and maintenance transactions
3. Efficient use of storage space
4. Protection from failures or data loss
5. Minimizing need for reorganization
6. Accommodating growth
7. Security from unauthorized use

FIGURE 5-6 DBMS terminology in an Oracle 11g environment

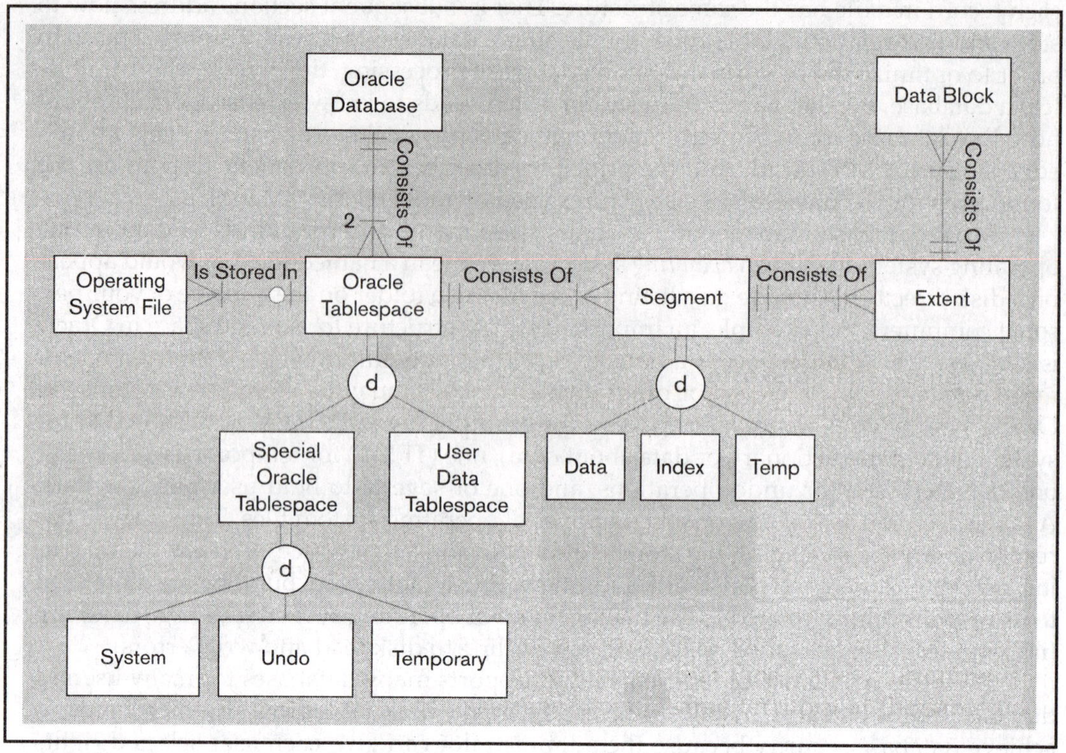

Often these objectives are in conflict, and you must select a file organization that provides a reasonable balance among the criteria within resources available.

In this chapter, we consider the following families of basic file organizations: sequential, indexed, and hashed. Figure 5-7 illustrates each of these organizations, with the nicknames of some university sports teams.

Sequential file organization
The storage of records in a file in sequence according to a primary key value.

SEQUENTIAL FILE ORGANIZATIONS In a **sequential file organization**, the records in the file are stored in sequence according to a primary key value (see Figure 5-7a). To locate a particular record, a program must normally scan the file from the beginning until the desired record is located. A common example of a sequential file is the alphabetical list of persons in the white pages of a telephone directory (ignoring any index that may be included with the directory). A comparison of the capabilities of sequential files with the other two types of files appears later in Table 5-3. Because of their inflexibility, sequential files are not used in a database but may be used for files that back up data from a database.

Indexed file organization
The storage of records either sequentially or nonsequentially with an index that allows software to locate individual records.

Index
A table or other data structure used to determine in a file the location of records that satisfy some condition.

Secondary key
One field or a combination of fields for which more than one record may have the same combination of values. Also called a nonunique key.

INDEXED FILE ORGANIZATIONS In an **indexed file organization**, the records are stored either sequentially or nonsequentially, and an index is created that allows the application software to locate individual records (see Figure 5-7b). Like a card catalog in a library, an **index** is a table that is used to determine in a file the location of records that satisfy some condition. Each index entry matches a key value with one or more records. An index can point to unique records (a primary key index, such as on the ProductID field of a product record) or to potentially more than one record. An index that allows each entry to point to more than one record is called a **secondary key** index. Secondary key indexes are important for supporting many reporting requirements and for providing rapid ad hoc data retrieval. An example would be an index on the ProductFinish column of a Product table. Because indexes are extensively used with relational DBMSs, and the choice of what index and how to store the index entries matters greatly in database processing performance, we review indexed file organizations in more detail than the other types of file organizations.

Some index structures influence where table rows are stored, and other index structures are independent of where rows are located. Because the actual structure of an

FIGURE 5-7 Comparison of file organizations

(a) Sequential

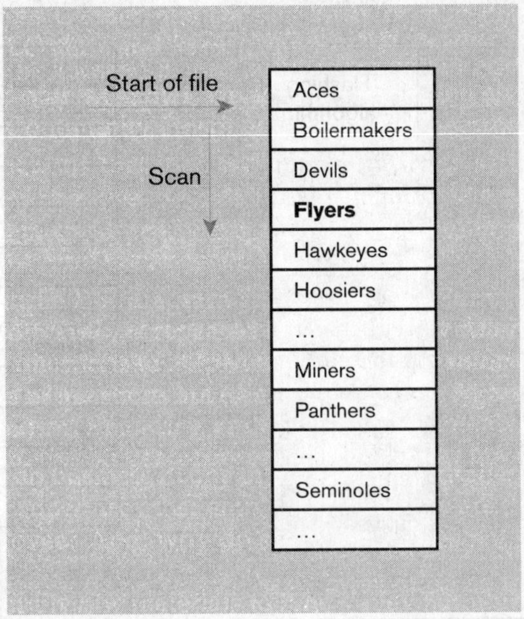

(b) Indexed

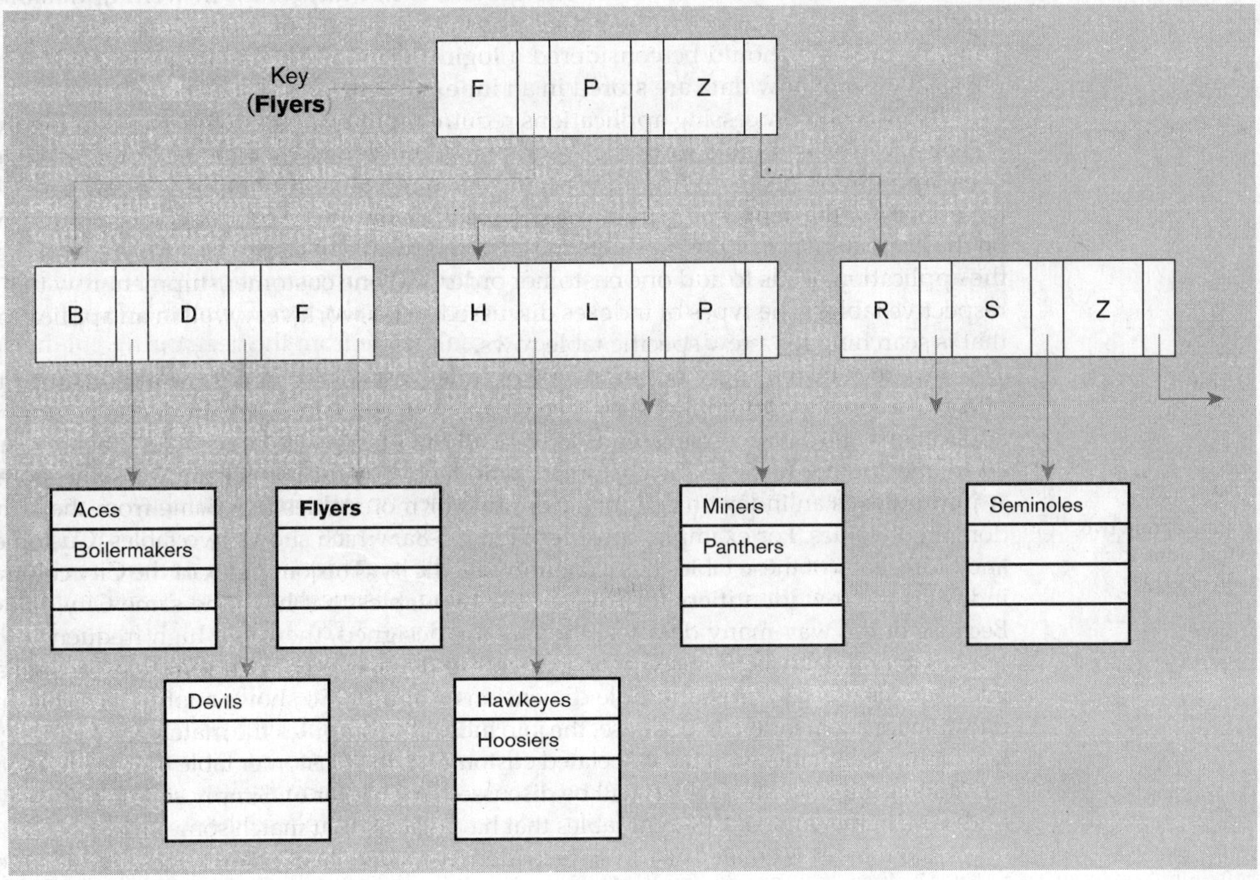

(continued)

FIGURE 5-7 ***(continued)***

(c) Hashed

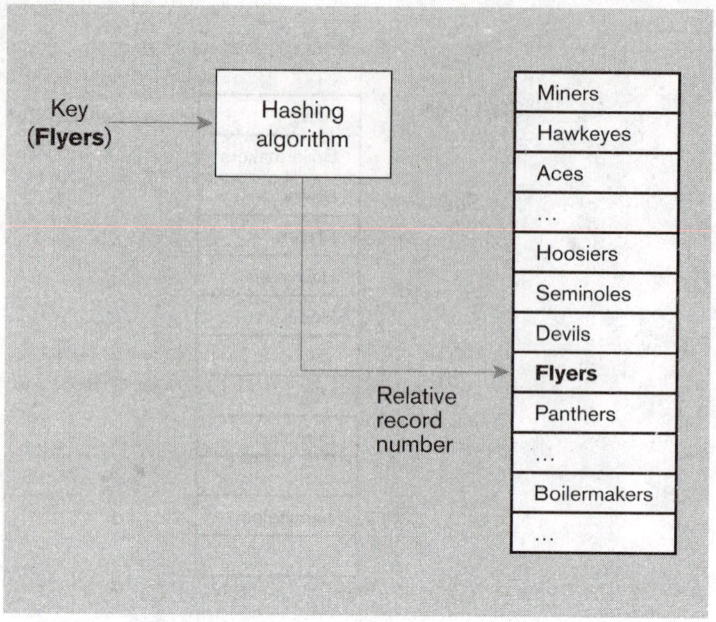

index does not influence database design and is not important in writing database queries, we will not address the actual physical structure of indexes in this chapter. Thus, Figure 5-7b should be considered a logical view of how an index is used, not a physical view of how data are stored in an index structure.

Transaction processing applications require rapid response to queries that involve one or a few related table rows. For example, to enter a new customer order, an order entry application needs to find the specific customer table row rapidly, a few product table rows for the items being purchased, possibly a few other product table rows based on the characteristics of the products the customer wants (e.g., product finish), and then the application needs to add one customer order and one customer shipment row to the respective tables. The types of indexes discussed so far work very well in an application that is searching for a few specific table rows.

Another increasingly popular type of index, especially in data warehousing and other decision support applications (see Chapter 9), is a join index. In decision support applications, the data accessing tends to want all rows from very large tables that are related to one another (e.g., all the customers who have bought items from the same store). A **join index** is an index on columns from two or more tables that come from the same domain of values. For example, consider Figure 5-8a, which shows two tables, Customer and Store. Each of these tables has a column called City. The join index of the City column indicates the row identifiers for rows in the two tables that have the same City value. Because of the way many data warehouses are designed, there is a high frequency for queries to find data (facts) in common to a store and a customer in the same city (or similar intersections of facts across multiple dimensions). Figure 5-8b shows another possible application for a join index. In this case, the join index precomputes the matching of a foreign key in the Order table with the associated customer in the Customer table (i.e., the result of a relational join operator, which will be discussed in Chapter 6). Simply stated, a join says find rows in the same or different tables that have values that match some criterion.

Join index
An index on columns from two or more tables that come from the same domain of values.

A join index is created as rows are loaded into a database, so the index, like all other indexes previously discussed, is always up-to-date. Without a join index in the database of Figure 5-8a, any query that wants to find stores and customers in the same city would have to compute the equivalent of the join index each time the query is run. For very large tables, joining all the rows of one table with matching rows in another possibly large table can be very time-consuming and can significantly delay responding to an online query. In Figure 5-8b, the join index provides one place for the DBMS to find

FIGURE 5-8 Join indexes
(a) Join index for common nonkey columns

Customer

RowID	Cust#	CustName	City	State
10001	C2027	Hadley	Dayton	Ohio
10002	C1026	Baines	Columbus	Ohio
10003	C0042	Ruskin	Columbus	Ohio
10004	C3861	Davies	Toledo	Ohio
...				

Store

RowID	Store#	City	Size	Manager
20001	S4266	Dayton	K2	E2166
20002	S2654	Columbus	K3	E0245
20003	S3789	Dayton	K4	E3330
20004	S1941	Toledo	K1	E0874
...				

Join Index

CustRowID	StoreRowID	Common Value*
10001	20001	Dayton
10001	20003	Dayton
10002	20002	Columbus
10003	20002	Columbus
10004	20004	Toledo
...		

*This column may or may not be included, as needed. Join index could be sorted on any of the three columns. Sometimes two join indexes are created, one as above and one with the two RowID columns reversed.

(continued)

information about related table rows. A join index, similarly to any other index, saves query processing time by finding data meeting a prespecified qualification at the expense of the extra storage space and maintenance of the index. The use of databases for new applications, such as in data warehousing and online decision support, is leading to the development of new types of indexes. We encourage you to investigate the indexing capabilities of the database management system you are using to understand fully when to apply each type of index and how to tune the performance of the index structures.

HASHED FILE ORGANIZATIONS In a **hashed file organization**, the address of each record is determined using a hashing algorithm (see Figure 5-7c). A **hashing algorithm** is a routine that converts a primary key value into a record address. Although there are several variations of hashed files, in most cases the records are located nonsequentially, as dictated by the hashing algorithm. Thus, sequential data processing is impractical.

Hashed file organization
A storage system in which the address for each record is determined using a hashing algorithm.

Hashing algorithm
A routine that converts a primary key value into a relative record number or relative file address.

A typical hashing algorithm uses the technique of dividing each primary key value by a suitable prime number and then using the remainder of the division as the relative storage location. For example, suppose that an organization has a set of

FIGURE 5-8 (*continued*)
(b) Join index for matching a foreign key (FK) and a primary key (PK)

Order

RowID	Order#	Order Date	Cust#(FK)
30001	O5532	10/01/2001	C3861
30002	O3478	10/01/2001	C1062
30003	O8734	10/02/2001	C1062
30004	O9845	10/02/2001	C2027
. . .			

Customer

RowID	Cust#(PK)	CustName	City	State
10001	C2027	Hadley	Dayton	Ohio
10002	C1062	Baines	Columbus	Ohio
10003	C0042	Ruskin	Columbus	Ohio
10004	C3861	Davies	Toledo	Ohio
. . .				

Join Index

CustRowID	OrderRowID	Cust#
10001	30004	C2027
10002	30002	C1062
10002	30003	C1062
10004	30001	C3861
. . .		

approximately 1,000 employee records to be stored on magnetic disk. A suitable prime number would be 997, because it is close to 1,000. Now consider the record for employee 12,396. When we divide this number by 997, the remainder is 432. Thus, this record is stored at location 432 in the file. Another technique (not discussed here) must be used to resolve duplicates (or overflow) that can occur with the division/remainder method when two or more keys hash to the same address (known as a "hash clash").

One of the severe limitations of hashing is that because data table row locations are dictated by the hashing algorithm, only one key can be used for hashing-based (storage and) retrieval. Hashing and indexing can be combined into what is called a hash index table to overcome this limitation. A **hash index table** uses hashing to map a key into a location in an index (sometimes called a *scatter index table*), where there is a **pointer** (a field of data indicating a target address that can be used to locate a related field or record of data) to the actual data record matching the hash key. The index is the target of the hashing algorithm, but the actual data are stored separately from the addresses generated by hashing. Because the hashing results in a position in an index, the table rows can be stored independently of the hash address, using whatever file organization for the data table makes sense (e.g., sequential or first available space). Thus, as with other indexing schemes but unlike most pure hashing schemes, there can be several primary and secondary keys, each with its own hashing algorithm and index table, sharing one data table.

Hash index table
A file organization that uses hashing to map a key into a location in an index, where there is a pointer to the actual data record matching the hash key.

Pointer
A field of data indicating a target address that can be used to locate a related field or record of data.

Also, because an index table is much smaller than a data table, the index can be more easily designed to reduce the likelihood of key collisions, or overflows, than can occur in the more space-consuming data table. Again, the extra storage space for the index adds flexibility and speed for data retrieval, along with the added expense of storing and maintaining the index space. Another use of a hash index table is found in some data warehousing database technologies that use parallel processing. In this situation, the DBMS can evenly distribute data table rows across all storage devices to fairly distribute work across the parallel processors, while using hashing and indexing to rapidly find on which processor desired data are stored.

As stated earlier, the DBMS will handle the management of any hashing file organization. You do not have to be concerned with handling overflows, accessing indexes, or the hashing algorithm. What is important for you, as a database designer, is to understand the properties of different file organizations so that you can choose the most appropriate one for the type of database processing required in the database and application you are designing. Also, understanding the properties of the file organizations used by the DBMS can help a query designer write a query in a way that takes advantage of the file organization's properties. As you will see in Chapters 6 and 7, many queries can be written in multiple ways in SQL; different query structures, however, can result in vastly different steps by the DBMS to answer the query. If you know how the DBMS thinks about using a file organization (e.g., what indexes it uses when and how and when it uses a hashing algorithm), you can design better databases and more efficient queries.

The three families of file organizations cover most of the file organizations you will have at your disposal as you design physical files and databases. Although more complex structures can be built using the data structures outlined in Appendix C, you are unlikely to be able to use these with a database management system.

Table 5-3 summarizes the comparative features of sequential, indexed, and hashed file organizations. You should review this table and study Figure 5-7 to see why each comparative feature is true.

Clustering Files

Some database management systems allow adjacent secondary memory space to contain rows from several tables. For example, in Oracle, rows from one, two, or more related tables that are often joined together can be stored so that they share the same data

TABLE 5-3 Comparative Features of Different File Organizations

	File Organization		
Factor	**Sequential**	**Indexed**	**Hashed**
Storage space	No wasted space	No wasted space for data but extra space for index	Extra space may be needed to allow for addition and deletion of records after the initial set of records is loaded
Sequential retrieval on primary key	Very fast	Moderately fast	Impractical, unless using a hash index
Random retrieval on primary key	Impractical	Moderately fast	Very fast
Multiple-key retrieval	Possible but requires scanning whole file	Very fast with multiple indexes	Not possible unless using a hash index
Deleting records	Can create wasted space or require reorganizing	If space can be dynamically allocated, this is easy but requires maintenance of indexes	Very easy
Adding new records	Requires rewriting a file	If space can be dynamically allocated, this is easy but requires maintenance of indexes	Very easy, but multiple keys with the same address require extra work
Updating records	Usually requires rewriting a file	Easy but requires maintenance of indexes	Very easy

blocks (the smallest storage units). A cluster is defined by the tables and the column or columns by which the tables are usually joined. For example, a Customer table and a customer Order table would be joined by the common value of CustomerID, or the rows of a PriceQuote table (which contains prices on items purchased from vendors) might be clustered with the Item table by common values of ItemID. Clustering reduces the time to access related records compared to the normal allocation of different files to different areas of a disk. Time is reduced because related records will be closer to each other than if the records are stored in separate files in separate areas of the disk. Defining a table to be in only one cluster reduces retrieval time for only those tables stored in the same cluster.

The following Oracle database definition commands show how a cluster is defined and tables are assigned to the cluster. First, the cluster (adjacent disk space) is specified, as in the following example:

```
CREATE CLUSTER Ordering (CustomerID CHAR(25));
```

The term Ordering names the cluster space; the attribute CustomerID specifies the attribute with common values.

Then tables are assigned to the cluster when the tables are created, as in the following example:

```
CREATE TABLE Customer_T (
  CustomerID              VARCHAR2(25) NOT NULL,
  CustomerAddress         VARCHAR2(15)
  )
  CLUSTER Ordering (CustomerID);
CREATE TABLE Order_T (
  OrderID               VARCHAR2(20) NOT NULL,
  CustomerID            VARCHAR2(25) NOT NULL,
  OrderDate             DATE
  )
  CLUSTER Ordering (CustomerID);
```

Access to records in a cluster can be specified in Oracle to be via an index on the cluster key or via a hashing function on the cluster key. Reasons for choosing an indexed versus a hashed cluster are similar to those for choosing between indexed and hashed files (see Table 5-3). Clustering records is best used when the records are fairly static. When records are frequently added, deleted, and changed, wasted space can arise, and it may be difficult to locate related records close to one another after the initial loading of records, which defines the clusters. Clustering is, however, one option a file designer has to improve the performance of tables that are frequently used together in the same queries and reports.

Designing Controls for Files

One additional aspect of a database file about which you may have design options is the types of controls you can use to protect the file from destruction or contamination or to reconstruct the file if it is damaged. Because a database file is stored in a proprietary format by the DBMS, there is a basic level of access control. You may require additional security controls on fields, files, or databases. We address these options in detail in Chapter 11. Briefly, files will be damaged, so the key is the ability to rapidly restore a damaged file. Backup procedures provide a copy of a file and of the transactions that have changed the file. When a file is damaged, the file copy or current file, along with the log of transactions, is used to recover the file to an uncontaminated state. In terms of security, the most effective method is to encrypt the contents of the file so that only programs with access to the decryption routine will be able to see the file contents. Again, these important topics will be covered later, when you study the activities of data and database administration in Chapter 11.

USING AND SELECTING INDEXES

Most database manipulations require locating a row (or collection of rows) that satisfies some condition. Given the terabyte size of modern databases, locating data without some help would be like looking for the proverbial "needle in a haystack"; or, in more contemporary terms, it would be like searching the Internet without a powerful search engine. For example, we might want to retrieve all customers in a given zip code or all students with a particular major. Scanning every row in a table, looking for the desired rows, may be unacceptably slow, particularly when tables are large, as they often are in real-world applications. Using indexes, as described earlier, can greatly speed up this process, and defining indexes is an important part of physical database design.

As described in the section on indexes, indexes on a file can be created for either a primary or a secondary key or both. It is typical that an index would be created for the primary key of each table. The index is itself a table with two columns: the key and the address of the record or records that contain that key value. For a primary key, there will be only one entry in the index for each key value.

Creating a Unique Key Index

The Customer table defined in the section on clustering has the primary key CustomerID. A unique key index would be created on this field using the following SQL command:

```
CREATE UNIQUE INDEX CustIndex_PK ON Customer_T(CustomerID);
```

In this command, CustIndex_PK is the name of the index file created to store the index entries. The ON clause specifies which table is being indexed and the column (or columns) that forms the index key. When this command is executed, any existing records in the Customer table would be indexed. If there are duplicate values of CustomerID, the CREATE INDEX command will fail. Once the index is created, the DBMS will reject any insertion or update of data in the CUSTOMER table that would violate the uniqueness constraint on CustomerIDs. Notice that every unique index creates overhead for the DBMS to validate uniqueness for each insertion or update of a table row on which there are unique indexes. We will return to this point later, when we review when to create an index.

When a composite unique key exists, you simply list all the elements of the unique key in the ON clause. For example, a table of line items on a customer order might have a composite unique key of OrderID and ProductID. The SQL command to create this index for the OrderLine_T table would be as follows:

```
CREATE UNIQUE INDEX LineIndex_PK ON OrderLine_T(OrderID, ProductID);
```

Creating a Secondary (Nonunique) Key Index

Database users often want to retrieve rows of a relation based on values for various attributes other than the primary key. For example, in a Product table, users might want to retrieve records that satisfy any combination of the following conditions:

- All table products (Description = "Table")
- All oak furniture (ProductFinish = "Oak")
- All dining room furniture (Room = "DR")
- All furniture priced below $500 (Price < 500)

To speed up such retrievals, we can define an index on each attribute that we use to qualify a retrieval. For example, we could create a nonunique jndex on the Description field of the Product table with the following SQL command:

```
CREATE INDEX DescIndex_FK ON Product_T(Description);
```

Notice that the term UNIQUE should not be used with secondary (nonunique) key attributes, because each value of the attribute may be repeated. As with unique keys, a secondary key index can be created on a combination of attributes.

When to Use Indexes

During physical database design, you must choose which attributes to use to create indexes. There is a trade-off between improved performance for retrievals through the use of indexes and degraded performance (because of the overhead for extensive index maintenance) for inserting, deleting, and updating the indexed records in a file. Thus, indexes should be used generously for databases intended primarily to support data retrievals, such as for decision support and data warehouse applications. Indexes should be used judiciously for databases that support transaction processing and other applications with heavy updating requirements, because the indexes impose additional overhead.

Following are some rules of thumb for choosing indexes for relational databases:

1. Indexes are most useful on larger tables.
2. Specify a unique index for the primary key of each table.
3. Indexes are most useful for columns that frequently appear in WHERE clauses of SQL commands either to qualify the rows to select (e.g., WHERE ProductFinish = "Oak," for which an index on ProductFinish would speed retrieval) or for linking (joining) tables (e.g., WHERE Product_T.ProductID = OrderLine_T.ProductID, for which a secondary key index on ProductID in the OrderLine_T table and a primary key index on ProductID in the Product_T table would improve retrieval performance). In the latter case, the index is on a foreign key in the OrderLine_T table that is used in joining tables.
4. Use an index for attributes referenced in ORDER BY (sorting) and GROUP BY (categorizing) clauses. You do have to be careful, though, about these clauses. Be sure that the DBMS will, in fact, use indexes on attributes listed in these clauses (e.g., Oracle uses indexes on attributes in ORDER BY clauses but not GROUP BY clauses).
5. Use an index when there is significant variety in the values of an attribute. Oracle suggests that an index is not useful when there are fewer than 30 different values for an attribute, and an index is clearly useful when there are 100 or more different values for an attribute. Similarly, an index will be helpful only if the results of a query that uses that index do not exceed roughly 20 percent of the total number of records in the file (Schumacher, 1997).
6. Before creating an index on a field with long values, consider first creating a compressed version of the values (coding the field with a surrogate key) and then indexing on the coded version (Catterall, 2005). Large indexes, created from long index fields, can be slower to process than small indexes.
7. If the key for the index is going to be used for determining the location where the record will be stored, then the key for this index should be a surrogate key so that the values cause records to be evenly spread across the storage space (Catterall, 2005). Many DBMSs create a sequence number so that each new row added to a table is assigned the next number in sequence; this is usually sufficient for creating a surrogate key.
8. Check your DBMS for the limit, if any, on the number of indexes allowable per table. Some systems permit no more than 16 indexes and may limit the size of an index key value (e.g., no more than 2,000 bytes for each composite value). If there is such a limit in your system, you will have to choose those secondary keys that will most likely lead to improved performance.
9. Be careful of indexing attributes that have null values. For many DBMSs, rows with a null value will not be referenced in the index (so they cannot be found from an *index search* of the attribute = NULL). Such a search will have to be done by scanning the file.

Selecting indexes is arguably the most important physical database design decision, but it is not the only way you can improve the performance of a database. Other ways address such issues as reducing the costs to relocate records, optimizing the use of extra or so-called free space in files, and optimizing query processing algorithms. (See Viehman, 1994, for a discussion of these additional ways to enhance physical database design and efficiency.) We briefly discuss the topic of query optimization in the following section of this chapter because such optimization can be used to overrule how the DBMS would use certain database design options included because of their expected improvement in data processing performance in most instances.

DESIGNING A DATABASE FOR OPTIMAL QUERY PERFORMANCE

The primary purpose today for physical database design is to optimize the performance of database processing. Database processing includes adding, deleting, and modifying a database, as well as a variety of data retrieval activities. For databases that have greater retrieval traffic than maintenance traffic, optimizing the database for query performance (producing online or off-line anticipated and ad hoc screens and reports for end users) is the primary goal. This chapter has already covered most of the decisions you can make to tune the database design to meet the need of database queries (clustering, indexes, file organizations, etc.). In this final section of this chapter, we introduce parallel query processing as an additional advanced database design and processing option now available in many DBMSs.

The amount of work a database designer needs to put into optimizing query performance depends greatly on the DBMS. Because of the high cost of expert database developers, the less database and query design work developers have to do, the less costly the development and use of a database will be. Some DBMSs give very little control to the database designer or query writer over how a query is processed or the physical location of data for optimizing data reads and writes. Other systems give the application developers considerable control and often demand extensive work to tune the database design and the structure of queries to obtain acceptable performance. Sometimes, the workload varies so much and the design options are so subtle that good performance is all that can be achieved. When the workload is fairly focused—say, for data warehousing, where there are a few batch updates and very complex queries requiring large segments of the database—performance can be well tuned either by smart query optimizers in the DBMS or by intelligent database and query design or a combination of both. For example, the Teradata DBMS is highly tuned for parallel processing in a data warehousing environment. In this case, rarely can a database designer or query writer improve on the capabilities of the DBMS to store and process data. This situation is, however, rare, and therefore it is important for a database designer to consider options for improving database processing performance. Chapter 7 will provide additional guidelines for writing efficient queries.

Parallel Query Processing

One of the major computer architectural changes over the past few years is the increased use of multiple processors in database servers. Database servers frequently use symmetric multiprocessor (SMP) technology (Schumacher, 1997). To take advantage of this parallel processing capability, some of the most sophisticated DBMSs include strategies for breaking apart a query into modules that can be processed in parallel by each of the related processors. The most common approach is to replicate the query so that each copy works against a portion of the database, usually a horizontal partition (i.e., sets of rows). The partitions need to be defined in advance by the database designer. The same query is run against each portion in parallel on separate processors, and the intermediate results from each processor are combined to create the final query result as if the query were run against the whole database.

Suppose you have an Order table with several million rows for which query performance has been slow. To ensure that subsequent scans of this table are performed in parallel, using at least three processors, you would alter the structure of the table with the SQL command:

```
ALTER TABLE Order_T PARALLEL 3;
```

You need to tune each table to the best degree of parallelism, so it is not uncommon to alter a table several times until the right degree is found.

Parallel query processing speed can be impressive. Schumacher (1997) reports on a test in which the time to perform a query was cut in half with parallel processing compared to using a normal table scan. Because an index is a table, indexes can also be given the parallel structure, so that scans of an index are also faster. Again, Schumacher (1997) shows an example where the time to create an index by parallel processing was reduced from approximately seven minutes to five seconds!

Besides table scans, other elements of a query can be processed in parallel, such as certain types of joining related tables, grouping query results into categories, combining several parts of a query result together (called *union*), sorting rows, and computing aggregate values. Row update, delete, and insert operations can also be processed in parallel. In addition, the performance of some database creation commands can be improved by parallel processing; these include creating and rebuilding an index and creating a table from data in the database. The Oracle environment must be preconfigured with a specification for the number of virtual parallel database servers to exist. Once this is done, the query processor will decide what it thinks is the best use of parallel processing for any command.

Sometimes the parallel processing is transparent to the database designer or query writer. With some DBMSs, the part of the DBMS that determines how to process a query, the query optimizer, uses physical database specifications and characteristics of the data (e.g., a count of the number of different values for a qualified attribute) to determine whether to take advantage of parallel processing capabilities.

Overriding Automatic Query Optimization

Sometimes, the query writer knows (or can learn) key information about the query that may be overlooked or unknown to the query optimizer module of the DBMS. With such key information in hand, a query writer may have an idea for a better way to process a query. But before you as the query writer can know you have a better way, you have to know how the query optimizer (which usually picks a query processing plan that will minimize expected query processing time, or cost) will process the query. This is especially true for a query you have not submitted before. Fortunately, with most relational DBMSs, you can learn the optimizer's plan for processing the query before running the query. A command such as EXPLAIN or EXPLAIN PLAN (the exact command varies by DBMS) will display how the query optimizer intends to access indexes, use parallel servers, and join tables to prepare the query result. If you preface the actual relational command with the explain clause, the query processor displays the logical steps to process the query and stops processing before actually accessing the database. The query optimizer chooses the best plan based on statistics about each table, such as average row length and number of rows. It may be necessary to force the DBMS to calculate up-to-date statistics about the database (e.g., the Analyze command in Oracle) to get an accurate estimate of query costs. You may submit several EXPLAIN commands with your query, written in different ways, to see if the optimizer predicts different performance. Then, you can submit for actual processing the form of the query that had the best predicted processing time, or you may decide not to submit the query because it will be too costly to run.

You may even see a way to improve query processing performance. With some DBMSs, you can force the DBMS to do the steps differently or to use the capabilities of the DBMS, such as parallel servers, differently than the optimizer thinks is the best plan.

For example, suppose we wanted to count the number of orders processed by a particular sales representative, Smith. In Oracle, parallel table processing works only when a table is scanned, not when it is accessed via an index. So, in Oracle, we might want to force both a full table scan as well as scanning in parallel. The SQL command for this query would be as follows:

```
SELECT /*+ FULL(Order_T) PARALLEL(Order_T,3) */ COUNT(*)
FROM Order_T
WHERE Salesperson = "SMITH";
```

The clause inside the /* */ delimiters is the hint to Oracle. This hint overrides whatever query plan Oracle would naturally create for this query. Thus, a hint is specific to each query, but the use of such hints must be anticipated by altering the structure of tables to be handled with parallel processing.

Summary

During physical database design, you, the designer, translate the logical description of data into the technical specifications for storing and retrieving data. The goal is to create a design for storing data that will provide adequate performance and ensure database integrity, security, and recoverability. In physical database design, you consider normalized relations and data volume estimates, data definitions, data processing requirements and their frequencies, user expectations, and database technology characteristics to establish the specifications that are used to implement the database using a database management system.

A field is the smallest unit of application data, corresponding to an attribute in the logical data model. You must determine the data type, integrity controls, and how to handle missing values for each field, among other factors. A data type is a detailed coding scheme for representing organizational data. Data may be coded to reduce storage space. Field integrity control includes specifying a default value, a range of permissible values, null value permission, and referential integrity.

A process of denormalization transforms normalized relations into non-normalized implementation specifications. Denormalization is done to improve the efficiency of I/O operations by specifying the database implementation structure so that data elements that are required together are also accessed together on the physical medium. Partitioning is also considered a form of denormalization. Horizontal partitioning breaks a relation into multiple record specifications by placing different rows into different tables, based on common column values. Vertical partitioning distributes the columns of a relation into separate files, repeating the primary key in each of the files.

A physical file is a named portion of secondary memory allocated for the purpose of storing physical records. Data within a physical file are organized through a combination of sequential storage and pointers. A pointer is a field of data that can be used to locate a related field or record of data.

A file organization arranges the records of a file on a secondary storage device. The three major categories of file organizations are (1) sequential, which stores records in sequence according to a primary key value; (2) indexed, in which records are stored sequentially or nonsequentially and an index is used to keep track of where the records are stored; and (3) hashed, in which the address of each record is determined using an algorithm that converts a primary key value into a record address. Physical records of several types can be clustered together into one physical file in order to place records frequently used together close to one another in secondary memory.

The indexed file organization is one of the most popular in use today. An index may be based on a unique key or a secondary (nonunique) key, which allows more than one record to be associated with the same key value. A join index indicates rows from two or more tables that have common values for related fields. A hash index table makes the placement of data independent of the hashing algorithm and permits the same data to be accessed via several hashing functions on different fields. Indexes are important in speeding up data retrieval, especially when multiple conditions are used for selecting, sorting, or relating data. Indexes are useful in a wide variety of situations, including for large tables, for columns that are frequently used to qualify the data to be retrieved, when a field has a large number of distinct values, and when data processing is dominated by data retrieval rather than data maintenance.

The introduction of multiprocessor database servers has made possible new capabilities in database management systems. One major new feature is the ability to break apart a query and process the query in parallel against segments of a table. Such parallel query processing can greatly improve the speed of query processing. Also, database programmers can improve database processing performance by providing the DBMS with hints about the sequence in which to perform table operations. These hints override the cost-based optimizer of the DBMS. Both the DBMS and programmers can look at statistics about the database to determine how to process a query. A wide variety of guidelines for good query design were included in the chapter.

This chapter concludes the database design section of this book. Having developed complete physical data specifications, you are now ready to begin implementing the database with database technology. Implementation means defining the database and programming client and server routines to handle queries, reports, and transactions against the database. These are primary topics of the next five chapters, which cover relational database implementation on client platforms, server platforms, client/server environments, and data warehouse technologies.

Chapter Review

Key Terms

Data type *212*
Denormalization *215*
Extent *221*
Field *211*
File organization *221*
Hash index table *226*
Hashed file organization *225*
Hashing algorithm *225*
Horizontal partitioning *218*
Index *222*
Indexed file organization *222*
Join index *224*
Physical file *220*
Pointer *226*
Secondary key *222*
Sequential file organization *222*
Tablespace *221*
Vertical partitioning *220*

Review Questions

1. Define each of the following terms:
   a. file organization
   b. sequential file organization
   c. indexed file organization
   d. hashing file organization
   e. denormalization
   f. composite key
   g. secondary key
   h. data type
   i. join index
2. Match the following terms to the appropriate definitions:

____ extent	a. a detailed coding scheme for representing organizational data
____ hashing algorithm	b. a data structure used to determine in a file the location of a record/records
____ index	c. a named area of secondary memory
____ physical record	d. a contiguous section of disk storage space
____ pointer	e. a field not containing business data
____ data type	f. converts a key value into an address
____ physical file	g. adjacent fields

3. Contrast the following terms:
   a. horizontal partitioning; vertical partitioning
   b. physical file; tablespace
   c. normalization; denormalization
   d. range control; null control
   e. secondary key; primary key
4. What are the major inputs into physical database design?
5. What are the key decisions in physical database design?
6. What decisions have to be made to develop a field specification?
7. Explain how physical database design has an important role in forming a foundation for regulatory compliance.
8. What are the objectives of selecting a data type for a field?
9. Explain why you sometimes have to reserve much more space for a numeric field than any of the initial stored values requires.
10. Why are field values sometimes coded?
11. What options are available for controlling data integrity at the field level?
12. Describe three ways to handle missing field values.
13. Explain why normalized relations may not comprise an efficient physical implementation structure.
14. List three common situations that suggest that relations be denormalized before database implementation.
15. Explain the reasons why some observers are against the practice of denormalization.
16. What are the advantages and disadvantages of horizontal and vertical partitioning?
17. List seven important criteria in selecting a file organization.
18. What are the benefits of a hash index table?
19. What is the purpose of clustering of data in a file?
20. State nine rules of thumb for choosing indexes.
21. Indexing can clearly be very beneficial. Why should you *not* create an index for every column of every table of your database?
22. Explain how parallel processing can improve query performance.
23. What according to you is the primary purpose of physical database design?
24. As the database administrator of a particular type of database environment (MS-SQL/Oracle/MySQL), can you choose the type of file organization for the database?

Problems and Exercises

1. Consider the following two relations for Millennium College:

```
STUDENT(StudentID, StudentName,
  CampusAddress, GPA)
REGISTRATION(StudentID, CourseID, Grade)
```

Following is a typical query against these relations:

```
SELECT Student_T.StudentID, StudentName,
  CourseID, Grade
FROM Student_T, Registration_T
    WHERE Student_T.StudentID =
      Registration_T.StudentID
    AND GPA > 3.0
ORDER BY StudentName;
```

   a. On what attributes should indexes be defined to speed up this query? Give the reasons for each attribute selected.
   b. Write SQL commands to create indexes for each attribute you identified in part a.

Problems and Exercises 2–5 have been written assuming that the DBMS you are using is Oracle. If that is not the case, feel free to modify the question for the DBMS environment that you are familiar with. You can also compare and contrast answers for different DBMSs.

2. Choose Oracle data types for the attributes in the normalized relations in Figure 5-4b.
3. Choose Oracle data types for the attributes in the normalized relations that you created in Problem and Exercise 19 in Chapter 4.
4. Explain in your own words what the precision (p) and scale (s) parameters for the Oracle data type NUMBER mean.
5. Say that you are interested in storing the numeric value 3,456,349.2334. What will be stored, with each of the following Oracle data types:
   a. NUMBER(11)
   b. NUMBER(11,1)
   c. NUMBER(11,-2)
   d. NUMBER(6)
   e. NUMBER
6. Suppose you are designing a default value for the age field in a student record at your university. What possible values would you consider, and why? How might the default vary by other characteristics about the student, such as school within the university or degree sought?
7. When a student has not chosen a major at a university, the university often enters a value of "Undecided" for the major field. Is "Undecided" a way to represent the null value? Should it be used as a default value? Justify your answer carefully.

8. Consider the following normalized relations from a database in a large retail chain:

STORE (StoreID, Region, ManagerID, SquareFeet)
EMPLOYEE (EmployeeID, WhereWork, EmployeeName, EmployeeAddress)
DEPARTMENT (DepartmentID, ManagerID, SalesGoal)
SCHEDULE (DepartmentID, EmployeeID, Date)

What opportunities might exist for denormalizing these relations when defining the physical records for this database? Under what circumstances would you consider creating such denormalized records?

9. Consider the following normalized relations for a sports league:

TEAM(TeamID, TeamName, TeamLocation)
PLAYER(PlayerID, PlayerFirstName, PlayerLastName, PlayerDateOfBirth, PlayerSpecialtyCode)
SPECIALTY(SpecialtyCode, SpecialtyDescription)
CONTRACT(TeamID, PlayerID, StartTime, EndTime, Salary)
LOCATION(LocationID, CityName, CityState, CityCountry, CityPopulation)
MANAGER(ManagerID, ManagerName, ManagerTeam)

What recommendations would you make regarding opportunities for denormalization? What additional information would you need to make fully informed denormalization decisions?

10. What problems might arise from vertically partitioning a relation? Given these potential problems, what general conditions influence when to partition a relation vertically?
11. Is it possible with a sequential file organization to permit sequential scanning of the data, based on several sorted orders? If not, why not? If it is possible, how?
12. Suppose each record in a file were connected to the prior record and the next record in key sequence using pointers. Thus, each record might have the following format:

    Primary key, other attributes, pointer to prior record, pointer to next record

    a. What would be the advantages of this file organization compared with a sequential file organization?
    b. In contrast with a sequential file organization, would it be possible to keep the records in multiple sequences? Why or why not?
13. Assume that a student table in a university database had an index on StudentID (the primary key) and indexes on Major, Age, MaritalStatus, and HomeZipCode (all secondary keys). Further, assume that the university wanted a list of students majoring in MIS or computer science, over age 25, and married OR students majoring in computer engineering, single, and from the 45462 zip code. How could indexes be used so that only records that satisfy this qualification are accessed?
14. Consider Figure 5-7b. Assuming that the empty rows in the leaves of this index show space where new records can be stored, explain where the record for Sooners would be stored. Where would the record for Flashes be stored? What might happen when one of the leaves is full and a new record needs to be added to that leaf?
15. Consider Figure 4-36 and your answer to Problem and Exercise 19 in Chapter 4. Assume that the most important reports that the organization needs are as follows:
    - A list of the current developer's project assignments
    - A list of the total costs for all projects
    - For each team, a list of its membership history
    - For each country, a list of all projects, with projected end dates, in which the country's developers are involved
    - For each year separately, a list of all developers, in the order of their average assignment scores for all the assignments that were completed during that year

    Based on this (admittedly limited) information, make a recommendation regarding the indexes that you would create for this database. Choose two of the indexes and provide the SQL command that you would use to create those indexes.
16. Can clustering of files occur after the files are populated with records? Why or why not?
17. Parallel query processing, as described in this chapter, means that the same query is run on multiple processors and that each processor accesses in parallel a different subset of the database. Another form of parallel query processing, not discussed in this chapter, would partition the query so that each part of the query runs on a different processor, but that part accesses whatever part of the database it needs. Most queries involve a qualification clause that selects the records of interest in the query. In general, this qualification clause is of the following form:

    (condition OR condition OR . . .) AND (condition OR condition OR . . .) AND . . .

    Given this general form, how might a query be broken apart so that each parallel processor handles a subset of the query and then combines the subsets together after each part is processed?

Problems and Exercises 18–21 refer to the large Pine Valley Furniture Company data set provided with the text.

PINE VALLEY FURNITURE

18. Create a join index on the CustomerID fields of the Customer_T and Order_T tables in Figure 4-4.
19. Consider the composite usage map in Figure 5-1. After a period of time, the assumptions for this usage map have changed, as follows:
    - There is an average of 40 supplies (rather than 50) for each supplier.
    - Manufactured parts represent only 30 percent of all parts, and purchased parts represent 75 percent.
    - The number of direct access to purchased parts increases to 7,500 per hour (rather than 6,000).

    Draw a new composite usage map reflecting this new information to replace Figure 5-1.
20. Consider the EER diagram for Pine Valley Furniture shown in Figure 3-12. Figure 5-9 looks at a portion of that EER diagram.

    Let's make a few assumptions about the average usage of the system:
    - There are 50,000 customers, and of these, 80 percent represent regular accounts and 20 percent represent national accounts.
    - Currently, the system stores 800,000 orders, although this number is constantly changing.
    - Each order has an average of 20 products.
    - There are 3,000 products.
    - Approximately 500 orders are placed per hour.

    a. Based on these assumptions, draw a usage map for this portion of the EER diagram.
    b. Management would like employees only to use this database. Do you see any opportunities for denormalization?

FIGURE 5-9 Figure for Problem and Exercise 20

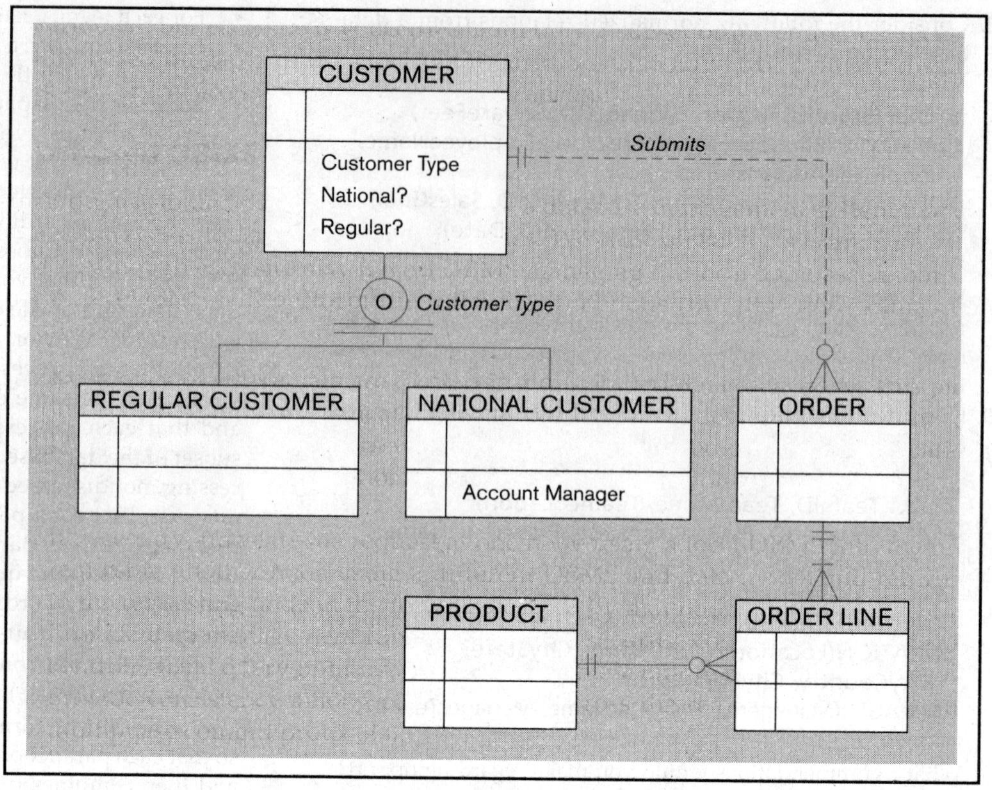

21. Refer to Figure 4-5. For each of the following reports (with sample data), indicate any indexes that you feel would help the report run faster as well as the type of index:
   a. State, by products (user-specified period)

State, by Products Report, January 1, 2010, to March 31, 2010

State	Product Description	Total Quantity Ordered
CO	8-Drawer Dresser	1
CO	Entertainment Center	0
CO	Oak Computer Desk	1
CO	Writer's Desk	2
NY	Writer's Desk	1
VA	Writer's Desk	5

   b. Most frequently sold product finish in a user-specified month

Most Frequently Sold Product Finish Report, March 1, 2010, to March 31, 2010

Product Finish	Units Sold
Cherry	13

   c. All orders placed last month

Monthly Order Report, March 1, 2010, to March 31, 2010

Order ID	Order Date	Customer ID	Customer Name
19	3/5/10	4	Eastern Furniture

Associated Order Details:

Product Description	Quantity Ordered	Price	Extended Price
Cherry End Table	10	$75.00	$750.00
High Back Leather Chair	5	$362.00	$1,810.00

Order_ID	Order Date	Customer IDs	Customer Name
24	3/10/10	1	Contemporary Casuals

Associated Order Details:

Product Description	Quantity Ordered	Price	Extended Price
Bookcase	4	$69.00	$276.00

   d. Total products sold, by product line (user-specified period)

Products Sold by Product Line, March 1, 2010, to March 31, 2010

Product Line	Quantity Sold
Basic	200
Antique	15
Modern	10
Classical	75

22. Central Bureau of Health Intelligence (CBHI) in India, for every City Corporation, maintains and disseminates the National Health Profile on:

- Demographics, Population Statistics
- Health Status, Mortality, Disability

The CBHI intends to track diseases, disabilities, and mortality rates within the jurisdiction of City Corporation in an effort to strengthen its analysis of health care trends and treatment outcomes.

GP_DB details the general practice (GP) – how well a practice is organized, customer experiences, and also includes how diseases are managed, e.g., diabetes. Other sources of data can be the National Diabetes Audit. The GP data set contains records from 3,372 GPs in the City Corporation each with the following attributes:

- GP Code which uniquely identifies a GP in the area.
- Number of disease cases.
- Primary Care Trust (PCT) Code for linking a GP to a PCT.

Needless to say, there is a PCT_DB that has around 4,328 records.

The city population data from the census database – CNS_DB – is linked to the GP_DB. The CNS_DB The CBHI also has a National Health Services Database – NHS_DB.

Approximately, NHS_DB has 1,257 records, which will increase annually by 2–3%.

Every time the CNS_DB is accessed, the GP_DBS and NHS_DB are accessed. The PCT_DB is accessed only when the GP_DB has a link to the Primary Care. Do a data volume and usage analysis.

23. Consider the following relational database for the "Golden Chariot on Wheels'", an initiative of the Tourism Department of Government of Karnataka along with the Southern Railways. The database keeps track of the trains, tours, stations, and tourists on the train (passengers). The 11-day journey of the train Golden Chariot leaves on alternate days in a week traversing from Bangalore–Hampi–Bangalore and Hampi–Bangalore–Hampi.

Note the following facts about the same:

- o The train numbers are unique in the TRAIN table.
- o The train goes on many trips in a week. A trip is associated with a single train.
- o The stations are identified with the station name and the district in which it is located. This is identified by the STATION table.
- o The train either stops at the station or may not. The VISIT table keeps track of the train stopping at that station.
- o The name of the passenger and the PNR number of the ticket are unique in the Passenger table.

Train Table

Train number	Train name	Capacity

Journey Table

Journey ID	Start date	End date	Train number

Station Table

Station number	Station name	Station district

Station_Stops Table

Train number	Station number	Arrival date	Departure date

Passenger Table

Passenger number	Passenger name	PNR number	Train number	Phone number	Address

Understand the following situations and using the physical database design techniques state how and what you would modify in the logical database design to show improved performance or otherwise address it.

a. A frequent need of quickly retrieving the data about a trip with the train details used for the trip.
b. There is a regular need to get the data about a train visits to stations based on the arrival date.
c. There is a need to retrieve the total numbers of passengers who are on a particular train.
d. The start and end dates of train trips needs to be obtained from the database system.
e. Data about passengers from Bangalore and/or Hampi has to accessed more often than data about passengers from elsewhere

Field Exercises

1. Find out which database management systems are available at your university for student use. Investigate which data types these DBMSs support. Compare these DBMSs based on the data types supported and suggest which types of applications each DBMS is best suited for, based on this comparison.
2. Using the Web site for this text and other Internet resources, investigate the parallel processing capabilities of several leading DBMSs. How do their capabilities differ?
3. Denormalization can be a controversial topic among database designers. Some believe that any database should be fully normalized (even using all the normal forms discussed in Appendix B). Others look for ways to denormalize to improve processing performance. Contact a database designer or administrator in an organization with which you are familiar. Ask whether he or she believes in fully normalized or denormalized physical databases. Ask the person why he or she has this opinion.
4. Contact a database designer or administrator in an organization with which you are familiar. Ask what file organizations are available in the various DBMSs used in that organization. Interview this person to learn what factors he or she considers when selecting an organization for database files. For indexed files, ask how he or she decides what indexes to create. Are indexes ever deleted? Why or why not?

References

Babad, Y. M., and J. A. Hoffer. 1984. "Even No Data Has a Value." *Communications of the ACM* 27,8 (August): 748–56.

Bieniek, D. 2006. "The Essential Guide to Table Partitioning and Data Lifecycle Management." *Windows IT Pro* (March) accessed at **www.windowsITpro.com**.

Brobst, S., S. Gant, and F. Thompson. 1999. "Partitioning Very Large Database Tables with Oracle8." *Oracle Magazine* 8,2 (March–April): 123–26.

Catterall, R. 2005. "The Keys to the Database." *DB2 Magazine* 10,2 (Quarter 2): 49–51.

Finkelstein, R. 1988. "Breaking the Rules Has a Price." *Database Programming & Design* 1,6 (June): 11–14.

Hoberman, S. 2002. "The Denormalization Survival Guide—Parts I and II." Published in the online journal *The Data Administration Newsletter*, found in the April and July issues of Tdan.com; the two parts of this guide are available at **www.tdan.com/i020fe02.htm** and **www.tdan.com/i021ht03.htm**, respectively.

Inmon, W. H. 1988. "What Price Normalization." *ComputerWorld* (October 17): 27, 31.

Pascal, F. 2002a. "The Dangerous Illusion: Denormalization, Performance and Integrity, Part 1." *DM Review* 12,6 (June): 52–53, 57.

Pascal, F. 2002b. "The Dangerous Illusion: Denormalization, Performance and Integrity, Part 2." *DM Review* 12,6 (June): 16, 18.

Rogers, U. 1989. "Denormalization: Why, What, and How?" *Database Programming & Design* 2,12 (December): 46–53.

Schumacher, R. 1997. "Oracle Performance Strategies." *DBMS* 10,5 (May): 89–93.

Viehman, P. 1994. "Twenty-four Ways to Improve Database Performance." *Database Programming & Design* 7,2 (February): 32–41.

Further Reading

Ballinger, C. 1998. "Introducing the Join Index." *Teradata Review* 1,3 (Fall): 18–23. (Note: *Teradata Review* is now *Teradata Magazine*.)

Bontempo, C. J., and C. M. Saracco. 1996. "Accelerating Indexed Searching." *Database Programming & Design* 9,7 (July): 37–43.

DeLoach, A. 1987. "The Path to Writing Efficient Queries in SQL/DS." *Database Programming & Design* 1,1 (January): 26–32.

Elmasri, R., and S. Navathe. 2006. *Fundamentals of Database Systems*, 5th ed. Menlo Park, CA: Benjamin Cummings.

Loney, K., E. Aronoff, and N. Sonawalla. 1996. "Big Tips for Big Tables." *Database Programming & Design* 9,11 (November): 58–62.

Oracle. 2008. *Oracle SQL Parallel Execution*. An Oracle White Paper, June 2008. Available at **www.oracle.com/technology/products/bi/db/11g/pdf/twp_bidw_parallel_execution_11gr1.pdf**

Roti, S. 1996. "Indexing and Access Mechanisms." *DBMS* 9,5 (May): 65–70.

Web Resources

www.SearchOracle.com and www.SearchSQLServer.com Sites that contain a wide variety of information about database management and DBMSs. New "tips" are added daily, and you can subscribe to an alert service for new postings to the site. Many tips deal with improving the performance of queries through better database and query design.

www.tdan.com Web site of *The Data Administration Newsletter*, which frequently publishes articles on all aspects of database development and design.

www.teradata.com/tdmo/ A journal for NCR Teradata data warehousing products that includes articles on database design. You can search the site for key terms from this chapter, such as *join index*, and find many articles on these topics.

CASE

Mountain View Community Hospital

Case Description

Up to this point, you have developed the conceptual and logical models for Mountain View Community Hospital's database. After considering several options, the hospital has decided to use Microsoft SQL Server, a relational DBMS, for implementing the database. Before the functional database is actually created, it is necessary to specify its physical design to ensure that the database is effective and efficient. As you have learned, physical database design is specific to the target environment and must conform to the capabilities of the DBMS to be used. It requires a good understanding of the DBMS's features, such as available data types, indexing, support for referential integrity and other constraints, and many more. (You can alternatively assume that MVCH chose another DBMS with which you are familiar and then answer the following questions accordingly.)

Case Questions

1. What additional kinds of information do you need for the physical database design of the MVCH database besides the 3NF relations you developed earlier for this case in Chapter 4?
2. What different types or forms of clinical data are collected at a hospital such as MVCH? Can you identify data that may not be easily accommodated by the standard data types provided by a DBMS? How would you handle that?
3. Are there opportunities for horizontal or vertical partitioning of this database? If you are not sure, what other information would you need to answer this question with greater certainty?
4. Do you see an opportunity for using a join index for this database? Why or why not?
5. Consider the following query against the MVCH database:

   For each treatment ordered in the past two weeks, list by treatment ID and date (in reverse chronological order) the number of times a physician performed that treatment that day, sorted alphabetically by physician name.

   a. Which secondary key indexes would you suggest to optimize the performance of this query? Why? Make any assumptions you need in order to answer this question.
   b. Following the examples in this chapter, write the SQL statements that create these secondary key indexes.
6. This chapter describes the 2002 Sarbanes-Oxley Act, which is not focused on not-for-profit providers such as many community hospitals.
   a. Can you see how MVCH could benefit from voluntarily complying with SOX?
   b. Specifically how can proper physical database design help with compliance and the following:
      - Improving accuracy and completeness of MVCH data
      - Eliminating duplicates and data inconsistencies
      - Improving understandability of MVCH data

Case Exercises

1. In Case Exercise 2 in Chapter 4, you wrote CREATE TABLE commands for each relation of Dr. Z's small database, which was to be created in Microsoft Access. Since then, Dr. Z has decided to use Microsoft SQL Server, consistent with other databases at MVCH. Reconsider your previous CREATE TABLE commands in answering the following questions:
   a. Would you choose different data types for any fields? Why?
   b. Are any fields candidates for coding? If so, what coding scheme would you use for each of these fields?
   c. Which fields require data values? Are there any fields that may take on null values?
   d. Suppose the *reason for a visit* or *the patient's social worker* are not entered. What procedures would you use for handling these missing data? Can you and should you use a default value for this field? Why or why not?
   e. Using Microsoft Visio (or other tool required by your instructor), draw the physical data model that shows the data types, primary keys, and foreign keys.
2. In Case Exercise 3 from Chapter 4, you developed the relational schema for Dr. Z's Multiple Sclerosis (MS) Clinic Management System.
   a. Do you see any opportunities for user-defined data types? Which fields? Why?
   b. Are any fields candidates for coding? If so, what coding scheme would you use for each of these fields?
   c. Are there any fields that may take on a null value? If so, which ones?
   d. Do you see any opportunities for denormalization of the relations you designed in Chapter 4? If not, why not? If yes, where and how might you denormalize?
   e. Do you see an opportunity for using a bitmap index for this database? Why or why not?
   f. Can you think of a situation with this set of tables where you might want to use a join index?
3. MVCH Figure 5-1 shows a portion of the data model for MVCH's database that represents a set of normalized relations based on the enterprise model shown in MVCH Figure 1-1 and additional business rules provided in the Chapter 2 case segment. Recall that TREATMENT refers to any test or procedure ordered by a physician for a patient and that ORDER refers to any order issued by a physician for treatment and/or services such as diagnostic tests (radiology, laboratory).

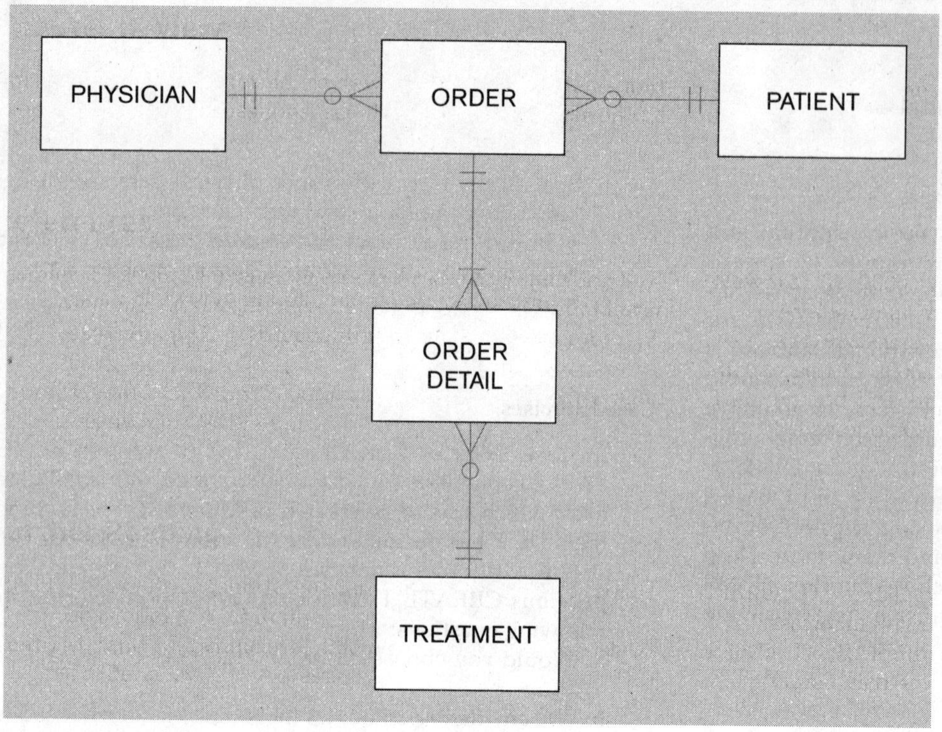

MVCH FIGURE 5-1 Partial data model

Using the information provided below regarding data volume and access frequencies, and following the example provided in Figure 5-1, modify the E-R model shown in MVCH Figure 5-1 to create a preliminary composite usage map.

a. Data volume analysis:
- Recall from an earlier case segment that the hospital performs more than a million laboratory procedures and more than 110,000 radiology procedures annually. Add these two figures to arrive at the number of records for the ORDER DETAIL table.
- There are approximately 250 PHYSICIANS, 20,000 PATIENTS, and 200,000 physician ORDERS in this database.
- ICD-9 procedure codes for treatments (lab procedures, radiology procedures, etc.) fall into approximately 3,500 major categories. Use this number to approximate the number of TREATMENT records.

b. Data access frequencies per hour:
- Across all applications that use the MVCH database, there are approximately 100 direct accesses to PHYSICIAN, 35 to ORDER, 200 to PATIENT, and 150 to TREATMENT.
- Of the 200 accesses to PATIENT, 30 accesses then also require ORDER data, and of these 30, there are 20 subsequent accesses to PHYSICIAN, and 30 accesses to ORDER DETAIL.
- Of the 35 direct accesses to ORDER, 10 accesses then also require PHYSICIAN data, and 20 require access to PATIENT data, ORDER DETAIL data, and TREATMENT data.
- Of the 100 direct accesses to PHYSICIAN, 20 also access ORDER, ORDER DETAIL, and TREATMENT data.
- Of the 150 direct accesses to TREATMENT, 10 also access ORDER DETAIL data and associated ORDER and PHYSICIAN data.

4. In Case Exercise 3, you created a composite usage map for part of the MVCH database, based on MVCH Figure 5-1. Referring to that composite usage map, do you see any opportunities for clustering rows from two or more tables? Why or why not? Is the concept of clustering tables supported in SQL Server? Does it differ from Oracle's implementation? If so, how?

PROJECT ASSIGNMENTS

In Chapter 4, you created the relational schema for the MVCH database. Next, you will develop the specification for database implementation. Specifically, you need to identify and document choices regarding the properties of each data element in the database, using the information provided in the case segments and options available in SQL Server (or other DBMS you may be using for this assignment).

P1. Review the information provided in the case segments and identify the data type for each field in the database.
- Do you see any opportunities for user-defined data types? Which fields? Why?
- Are any fields candidates for coding? If so, what coding scheme would you use for each of these fields?
- Which fields may take on a null value? Why?
- Which fields should be indexed? What type of index?

P2. Create a data dictionary similar to the metadata table shown in Table 1-1 in Chapter 1 to document your choices. For each table in the relational schema you developed earlier, provide the following information for each field/data element: field name, definition/description, data type, format, allowable values, whether the field is required or optional, whether the field is indexed and the type of index, whether the field is a primary key, whether the field is a foreign key, and the table that is referenced by the foreign key field.

P3. Using Microsoft Visio (or similar tool designated by your instructor), create the physical data model for the MVCH relational schema you developed in Chapter 4, clearly indicating data types, primary keys, and foreign keys.

P4. Identify five reports to be generated by the database and create a composite usage map for each.

PART

IV

Implementation

AN OVERVIEW OF PART FOUR

Part IV considers topics associated with implementing relational systems, including Web-enabled Internet applications and data warehouses. Database implementation, as indicated in Chapter 1, includes coding and testing database processing programs, completing database documentation and training materials, and installing databases and converting data, as necessary, from prior systems. Here, at last, is the point in the systems development life cycle for which we have been preparing. Our prior activities—enterprise modeling, conceptual data modeling, and logical and physical database design—are necessary previous stages. At the end of implementation, we expect a functioning system that meets users' information requirements. After that, the system will be put into production use, and database maintenance will be necessary for the life of the system. The chapters in Part IV help develop an initial understanding of the complexities and challenges of implementing a database system.

Chapter 6 describes Structured Query Language (SQL), which has become a standard language (especially on database servers) for creating and processing relational databases. In addition to a brief history of SQL that includes a thorough introduction to SQL:1999, currently used by most DBMSs, along with discussion of the SQL:200n standard that is implemented by many relational systems, the syntax of SQL is explored. Data definition language (DDL) commands used to create a database are included, as are single-table data manipulation language (DML) commands used to query a database. Dynamic and materialized views, which constrain a user's environment to relevant tables necessary to complete the user's work, are also covered.

Chapter 7 continues the explanation of more advanced SQL syntax and constructs. Multiple-table queries, along with subqueries and correlated subqueries, are demonstrated. These capabilities provide SQL with much of its power. Transaction integrity issues and an explanation of data dictionary construction place SQL within a wider context. Additional programming capabilities, including triggers and stored procedures, and embedding SQL in other programming language programs further demonstrate the capabilities of SQL. Online transaction processing (OLTP) is contrasted with online analytical processing (OLAP) features of SQL:1999 and SQL:200n; OLAP queries, necessary for accessing data warehouses, are also covered. Strategies for writing and testing queries, from simple to more complex, are offered.

Chapter 8 provides a discussion of the concepts of client/server architecture, applications, middleware, and database access in contemporary database environments. Technologies that are commonly used in creating two- and three-tier applications are presented, and sample application programs are used to demonstrate how to access databases from popular programming languages such as Java, VB.NET, ASP.NET, JSP, and PHP. The chapter also presents expanded coverage of the emerging role of Extensible Markup Language (XML) and related technologies in data storage and retrieval. Topics covered include basics of XML schemas, XQuery, XSLT, Web services, and service-oriented architecture (SOA).

Chapter 9 describes the basic concepts of data warehousing, the reasons data warehousing is regarded as critical to competitive advantage in many organizations, and the database design activities and structures unique to data warehousing. Topics include alternative data warehouse architectures, types of data warehouse data, and the dimensional data model (star schema) for data marts. Database design for data marts, including surrogate keys, fact table grain, modeling dates and time, conformed dimensions, factless fact tables, and helper/hierarchy/reference tables, is explained and illustrated.

As indicated by this brief synopses of the chapters, Part IV provides both a conceptual understanding of the issues involved in implementing database applications and a practical initial understanding of the procedures necessary to construct a database prototype. The introduction of common strategies, such as client/server, Web enabled, Web services, and data warehousing, equip you to understand expected future developments in databases.

CHAPTER 6

Introduction to SQL

Learning Objectives

After studying this chapter, you should be able to:

- Concisely define each of the following key terms: **relational DBMS (RDBMS), catalog, schema, data definition language (DDL), data manipulation language (DML), data control language (DCL), referential integrity, scalar aggregate, vector aggregate, base table, virtual table, dynamic view,** and **materialized view.**
- Interpret the history and role of SQL in database development.
- Define a database using the SQL data definition language.
- Write single-table queries using SQL commands.
- Establish referential integrity using SQL.
- Discuss the SQL:1999 and SQL:200n standards.

INTRODUCTION

Pronounced "S-Q-L" by some and "sequel" by others, SQL has become the de facto standard language for creating and querying relational databases. (Can the next standard be the sequel to SQL?) The primary purpose of this chapter is to introduce SQL, the most common language for relational systems. It has been accepted as a U.S. standard by the American National Standards Institute (ANSI) and is a Federal Information Processing Standard (FIPS). It is also an international standard recognized by the International Organization for Standardization (ISO). ANSI has accredited the International Committee for Information Technology Standards (INCITS) as a standards development organization; INCITS is working on the next version of the SQL standard to be released.

The SQL standard is like afternoon weather in Florida (and maybe where you live, too)—wait a little while, and it will change. The ANSI SQL standards were first published in 1986 and updated in 1989, 1992 (SQL-92), 1999 (SQL:1999), 2003 (SQL:2003), 2006 (SQL:2006), and 2008 (SQL:2008). SQL:2008 was in final draft form at the time of writing this edition. (See **http://en.wikipedia.org/wiki/SQL** for a summary of this history.) The standard is now generally referred to as SQL:200n (they will need SQL:20nn any day now!).

SQL-92 was a major revision and was structured into three levels: Entry, Intermediate, and Full. SQL:1999 established core-level conformance, which must be met before any other level of conformance can be achieved; core-level conformance requirements are unchanged in SQL:200n. In addition to fixes and enhancements of SQL:1999, SQL:2003 introduced a new set of SQL/XML standards, three new data types, various new built-in functions, and improved methods for generating values automatically. SQL:2006 refined these additions and made them more compatible with XQuery, the XML query language published by the World Wide Web Consortium (W3C). At the time of this writing, most database management systems claim SQL:1992 compliance and partial compliance with SQL:1999 and SQL:200n.

Except where noted as a particular vendor's syntax, the examples in this chapter conform to the SQL standard. Concerns have been expressed about SQL:1999 and SQL:2003/SQL:200n being true standards because conformance with the standard is no longer certified by the U.S. Department of Commerce's National Institute of Standards and Technology (NIST) (Gorman, 2001). "Standard SQL" may be considered an oxymoron (like safe investment or easy payments)! Vendors' interpretations of the SQL standard differ from each other, and vendors extend their products' capabilities with proprietary features beyond the stated standard. This makes it difficult to port SQL from one vendor's product to another. One must become familiar with the particular version of SQL being used and not expect that SQL code will transfer exactly as written to another vendor's version. Table 6-1 demonstrates differences in handling date and time values to illustrate discrepancies one encounters across SQL vendors (IBM DB2, Microsoft SQL Server, MySQL [an open source DBMS], and Oracle).

SQL has been implemented in both mainframe and personal computer systems, so this chapter is relevant to both computing environments. Although many of the PC-database packages use a query-by-example (QBE) interface, they also include SQL coding as an option. QBE interfaces use graphic presentations and translate the QBE actions into SQL code before query execution occurs. In Microsoft Access, for example, it is possible to switch back and forth between the two interfaces; a query that has been built using a QBE interface can be viewed in SQL by clicking a button. This feature may aid you in learning SQL syntax. In client/server architectures, SQL commands are executed on the server, and the results are returned to the client workstation.

The first commercial DBMS that supported SQL was Oracle in 1979. Oracle is now available in mainframe, client/server, and PC-based platforms for many operating systems, including various UNIX, Linux, and Microsoft Windows operating systems. IBM's DB2, Informix, and Microsoft SQL Server are available for this range of operating systems also. See Eisenberg et al. (2004) for an overview of SQL:2003.

TABLE 6-1 Handling Date and Time Values (Arvin, 2005,based on content currently and previously available at http://troelsarvin.blogspot.com/)

TIMESTAMP data type: A core feature, the standard requires that this data type store year, month, day, hour, minute, and second (with fractional seconds; default is six digits).

TIMESTAMP WITH TIME ZONE data type: Extension to TIMESTAMP also stores the time zone.

		Implementation:
Product	**Follows Standard?**	**Comments**
DB2	TIMESTAMP only	Includes validity check and will not accept an entry such as 2010–02–29 00:05:00.
MS-SQL	No	DATETIME stores date and time, with only three digits for fractional seconds; DATETIME2 has a larger date range and greater fractional precision. Validity check similar to DB2's is included.
MySQL	No	TIMESTAMP updates to current date and time when other data in the row are updated and displays the value for the time zone of the user. DATETIME similar to MS-SQL, but validity checking is less accurate and may result in values of zero being stored.
Oracle	TIMESTAMP and TIMESTAMP WITH TIME ZONE	TIMESTAMP WITH TIME ZONE not allowed as part of a unique key. Includes validity check on dates.

ORIGINS OF THE SQL STANDARD

The concepts of relational database technology were first articulated in 1970, in E. F. Codd's classic paper "A Relational Model of Data for Large Shared Data Banks." Workers at the IBM Research Laboratory in San Jose, California, undertook development of System R, a project whose purpose was to demonstrate the feasibility of implementing the relational model in a database management system. They used a language called Sequel, also developed at the San Jose IBM Research Laboratory. Sequel was renamed SQL during the project, which took place from 1974 to 1979. The knowledge gained was applied in the development of SQL/DS, the first relational database management system available commercially (from IBM). SQL/DS was first available in 1981, running on the DOS/VSE operating system. A VM version followed in 1982, and the MVS version, DB2, was announced in 1983.

When System R was well received at the user sites where it was installed, other vendors began developing relational products that used SQL. One product, Oracle, from Relational Software, was actually on the market before SQL/DS (1979). Other products included INGRES from Relational Technology (1981), IDM from Britton-Lee (1982), DG/SQL from Data General Corporation (1984), and Sybase from Sybase, Inc. (1986). To provide some directions for the development of relational DBMSs, ANSI and the ISO approved a standard for the SQL relational query language (functions and syntax) that was originally proposed by the X3H2 Technical Committee on Database (Technical Committee X3H2—Database, 1986; ISO, 1987), often referred to as SQL/86. For a more detailed history of the SQL standard, see the documents available at **www.wiscorp.com**.

The following were the original purposes of the SQL standard:

1. To specify the syntax and semantics of SQL data definition and manipulation languages
2. To define the data structures and basic operations for designing, accessing, maintaining, controlling, and protecting an SQL database
3. To provide a vehicle for portability of database definition and application modules between conforming DBMSs
4. To specify both minimal (Level 1) and complete (Level 2) standards, which permit different degrees of adoption in products
5. To provide an initial standard, although incomplete, that will be enhanced later to include specifications for handling such topics as referential integrity, transaction management, user-defined functions, join operators beyond the equi-join, and national character sets

In terms of SQL, when is a standard not a standard? As explained earlier, most vendors provide unique, proprietary features and commands for their SQL database management system. So, what are the advantages and disadvantages of having an SQL standard, when there is such variations from vendor to vendor? The benefits of such a standardized relational language include the following (although these are not pure benefits because of vendor differences):

- ***Reduced training costs*** Training in an organization can concentrate on one language. A large labor pool of IS professionals trained in a common language reduces retraining for newly hired employees.
- ***Productivity*** IS professionals can learn SQL thoroughly and become proficient with it from continued use. An organization can afford to invest in tools to help IS professionals become more productive. And because they are familiar with the language in which programs are written, programmers can more quickly maintain existing programs.
- ***Application portability*** Applications can be moved from machine to machine when each machine uses SQL. Further, it is economical for the computer software industry to develop off-the-shelf application software when there is a standard language.
- ***Application longevity*** A standard language tends to remain so for a long time; hence there will be little pressure to rewrite old applications. Rather, applications

will simply be updated as the standard language is enhanced or new versions of DBMSs are introduced.

- ***Reduced dependence on a single vendor*** When a nonproprietary language is used, it is easier to use different vendors for the DBMS, training and educational services, application software, and consulting assistance; further, the market for such vendors will be more competitive, which may lower prices and improve service.
- ***Cross-system communication*** Different DBMSs and application programs can more easily communicate and cooperate in managing data and processing user programs.

On the other hand, a standard can stifle creativity and innovation; one standard is never enough to meet all needs, and an industry standard can be far from ideal because it may be the offspring of compromises among many parties. A standard may be difficult to change (because so many vendors have a vested interest in it), so fixing deficiencies may take considerable effort. Another disadvantage of standards that can be extended with proprietary features is that using special features added to SQL by a particular vendor, may result in the loss of some advantages, such as application portability.

The original SQL standard has been widely criticized, especially for its lack of referential integrity rules and certain relational operators. Date and Darwen (1997) express concern that SQL seems to have been designed without adhering to established principles of language design, and "as a result, the language is filled with numerous restrictions, ad hoc constructs, and annoying special rules" (p. 8). They feel that the standard is not explicit enough and that the problem of standard SQL implementations will continue to exist. Some of these limitations will be noticeable in this chapter.

Many products are available that support SQL, and they run on machines of all sizes, from small personal computers to large mainframes. The database market is maturing, and the rate of significant changes in products may slow, but they will continue to be SQL based. The number of relational database vendors with significant market share has continued to consolidate. According to Lai (2007), Oracle controlled over 44 percent of the overall database market in 2007, IBM a little over 21 percent, and Microsoft almost 19 percent. Sybase and Teradata also had significant—albeit much smaller—shares, and open source products, such as MySQL, PostgreSQL, and Ingres, combined for about 10 percent market share. MySQL, an open source version of SQL that runs on Linux, UNIX, Windows, and Mac OS X operating systems, has achieved considerable popularity. (Download MySQL for free from **www.mysql.com**.) The market position of MySQL may be changing; at the time of writing this edition, Oracle had just acquired MySQL as part of its purchase of Sun Microsystems. Opportunities still exist for smaller vendors to prosper through industry-specific systems or niche applications. Upcoming product releases may change the relative strengths of the database management systems by the time you read this book. But all of them will continue to use SQL, and they will follow, to a certain extent, the standard described here.

Because of its significant market share, we most often illustrate SQL in this text using Oracle 11g syntax. We illustrate using a specific relational DBMS not to promote or endorse Oracle but rather so we know that the code we use will work with some DBMS. In the vast majority of the cases, the code will, in fact, work with many relational DBMSs because it complies with standard ANSI SQL. In some cases, we include illustrations using several or other relational DBMSs when there are interesting differences; however, there are only a few such cases, because we are not trying to compare systems, and we want to be parsimonious.

THE SQL ENVIRONMENT

With today's relational DBMSs and application generators, the importance of SQL within the database architecture is not usually apparent to the application users. Many users who access database applications have no knowledge of SQL at all. For example, sites on the Web allow users to browse their catalogs (e.g., see **www.llbean.com**). The information about an item that is presented, such as size, color, description, and availability, is stored in a database. The information has been retrieved using an SQL query, but the user has not issued an SQL command. Rather, the user has used a prewritten program (e.g., written in Java) with embedded SQL commands for database processing.

An SQL-based relational database application involves a user interface, a set of tables in the database, and a relational database management system (RDBMS) with an SQL capability. Within the RDBMS, SQL will be used to create the tables, translate user requests, maintain the data dictionary and system catalog, update and maintain the tables, establish security, and carry out backup and recovery procedures. A **relational DBMS (RDBMS)** is a data management system that implements a relational data model, one where data are stored in a collection of tables, and the data relationships are represented by common values, not links. This view of data was illustrated in Chapter 2 for the Pine Valley Furniture database system and will be used throughout this chapter's SQL query examples.

Relational DBMS (RDBMS)
A database management system that manages data as a collection of tables in which all data relationships are represented by common values in related tables.

Figure 6-1 is a simplified schematic of an SQL environment, consistent with SQL:200n standard. As depicted, an SQL environment includes an instance of an SQL database management system along with the databases accessible by that DBMS and the users and programs that may use that DBMS to access the databases. Each database is contained in a **catalog**, which describes any object that is a part of the database, regardless of which user created that object. Figure 6-1 shows two catalogs: DEV_C and PROD_C. Most companies keep at least two versions of any database they are using. The production version, PROD_C here, is the live version, which captures real business data and thus must be very tightly controlled and monitored. The development version, DEV_C here, is used when the database is being built and continues to serve as a development tool where enhancements and maintenance efforts can be thoroughly tested before being applied to the production database. Typically this database is not as tightly controlled or monitored, because it does not contain live business data. Each database will have a named schema(s) associated with a catalog. A **schema** is a collection of related objects, including but not limited to base tables and views, domains, constraints, character sets, triggers, and roles.

Catalog
A set of schemas that, when put together, constitute a description of a database.

Schema
A structure that contains descriptions of objects created by a user, such as base tables, views, and constraints, as part of a database.

If more than one user has created objects in a database, combining information about all users' schemas will yield information for the entire database. Each catalog must also contain an information schema, which contains descriptions of all schemas in the catalog, tables, views, attributes, privileges, constraints, and domains, along with

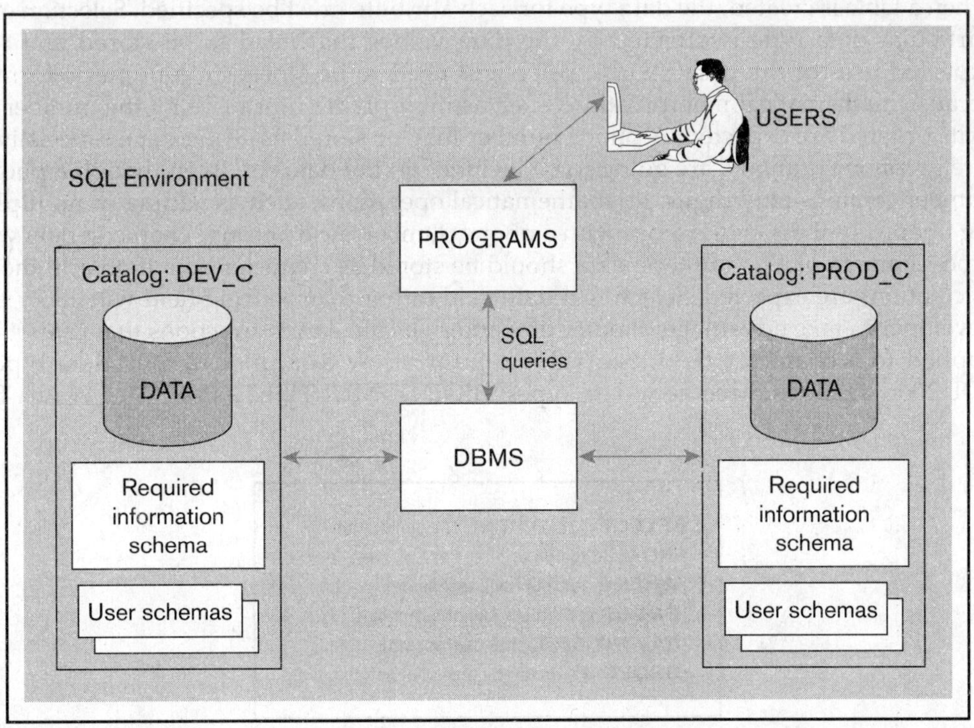

FIGURE 6-1 A simplified schematic of a typical SQL environment, as described by the SQL:2000n standards

other information relevant to the database. The information contained in the catalog is maintained by the DBMS as a result of the SQL commands issued by the users and can be rebuilt without conscious action by the user. It is part of the power of the SQL language that the issuance of syntactically simple SQL commands may result in complex data management activities being carried out by the DBMS software. Users can browse the catalog contents by using SQL SELECT statements.

Data definition language (DDL)
Commands used to define a database, including those for creating, altering, and dropping tables and establishing constraints.

SQL commands can be classified into three types. First, there are **data definition language (DDL)** commands. These commands are used to create, alter, and drop tables, views, and indexes, and they are covered first in this chapter. There may be other objects controlled by the DDL, depending on the DBMS. For example, many DBMSs support defining synonyms (abbreviations) for database objects or a field to hold a specified sequence of numbers (which can be helpful in assigning primary keys to rows in tables). In a production database, the ability to use DDL commands will generally be restricted to one or more database administrators in order to protect the database structure from unexpected and unapproved changes. In development or student databases, DDL privileges will be granted to more users.

Data manipulation language (DML)
Commands used to maintain and query a database, including those for updating, inserting, modifying, and querying data.

Next, there are **data manipulation language (DML)** commands. Many consider the DML commands to be the core commands of SQL. These commands are used for updating, inserting, modifying, and querying the data in the database. They may be issued interactively, so that a result is returned immediately following the execution of the statement, or they may be included within programs written in a procedural programming language, such as C, Java, PHP, or COBOL or with a GUI tool (e.g., SQL Assistant with Teradata or MySQL Query Browser). Embedding SQL commands may provide the programmer with more control over timing of report generation, interface appearance, error handling, and database security (see Chapter 8 on embedding SQL in Web-based programs). Most of this chapter is devoted to covering basic DML commands, in interactive format. The general syntax of the SQL SELECT command used in DML is shown in Figure 6-2.

Data control language (DCL)
Commands used to control a database, including those for administering privileges and committing (saving) data.

Finally, **data control language (DCL)** commands help a DBA control the database; they include commands to grant or revoke privileges to access the database or particular objects within the database and to store or remove transactions that would affect the database.

Each DBMS has a defined list of data types that it can handle. All contain numeric, string, and date/time-type variables. Some also contain graphic data types, spatial data types, or image data types, which greatly increase the flexibility of data manipulation. When a table is created, the data type for each attribute must be specified. Selection of a particular data type is affected by the data values that need to be stored and the expected uses of the data. A unit price will need to be stored in a numeric format because mathematical manipulations such as multiplying unit price by the number of units ordered are expected. A phone number may be stored as string data, especially if foreign phone numbers are going to be included in the data set. Even though a phone number contains only digits, no mathematical operations, such as adding or multiplying phone numbers, make sense with a phone number. And because character data will process more quickly, numeric data should be stored as character data if no arithmetic calculations are expected. Selecting a date field rather than a string field will allow the developer to take advantage of date/time interval calculation functions that cannot be applied to a character field. See Table 6-2 for a few examples of SQL data types. SQL:200n includes three new data types: BIGINT, MULTISET, and XML. Watch for

FIGURE 6-2 General syntax of the SELECT statement used in DML

```
SELECT [ALL/DISTINCT] column_list
FROM table_list
[WHERE conditional expression]
[GROUP BY group_by_column_list]
[HAVING conditional expression]
[ORDER BY order_by_column_list]
```

TABLE 6-2 Sample SQL Data Types

String	CHARACTER (CHAR)	Stores string values containing any characters in a character set. CHAR is defined to be a fixed length.
	CHARACTER VARYING (VARCHAR or VARCHAR2)	Stores string values containing any characters in a character set but of definable variable length.
	BINARY LARGE OBJECT (BLOB)	Stores binary string values in hexadecimal format. BLOB is defined to be a variable length. (Oracle also has CLOB and NCLOB, as well as BFILE for storing unstructured data outside the database.)
Number	NUMERIC	Stores exact numbers with a defined precision and scale.
	INTEGER (INT)	Stores exact numbers with a predefined precision and scale of zero.
Temporal	TIMESTAMPTIMESTAMP WITH LOCAL TIME ZONE	Stores a moment an event occurs, using a definable fraction-of–a-second precision.Value adjusted to the user's session time zone (available in Oracle and MySQL)
Boolean	BOOLEAN	Stores truth values: TRUE, FALSE, or UNKNOWN.

these new data types to be added to RDBMSs that had not previously introduced them as an enhancement of the existing standard.

Given the wealth of graphic and image data types, it is necessary to consider business needs when deciding how to store data. For example, color may be stored as a descriptive character field, such as "sand drift" or "beige." But such descriptions will vary from vendor to vendor and do not contain the amount of information that could be contained in a spatial data type that includes exact red, green, and blue intensity values. Such data types are now available in universal servers, which handle data warehouses, and can be expected to appear in RDBMSs as well. In addition to the predefined data types included in Table 6-2, SQL:1999 and SQL:200n support constructed data types and user-defined types. There are many more predefined data types than those shown in Table 6-2. It will be necessary to familiarize yourself with the available data types for each RDBMS with which you work to achieve maximum advantage from its capabilities.

We are almost ready to illustrate sample SQL commands. The sample data that we will be using are shown in Figure 6-3 (which was captured in Microsoft Access). The data model corresponds to that shown in Figure 2-22. The PVFC database files are available for your use on this book's Web site; the files are available in several formats, for use with different DBMSs, and the database is also available on Teradata Student Network. Instructions for locating them are included inside the front cover of the book. There are two PVFC files. The one used here is named BookPVFC (also called Standard PVFC), and you can use it to work through the SQL queries demonstrated in Chapters 6 and 7. Another file, BigPVFC, contains more data and does not always correspond to Figure 2-22, nor does it always demonstrate good database design. Big PVFC is used for some of the exercises at the end of the chapter.

PINE VALLEY FURNITURE

Each table name follows a naming standard that places an underscore and the letter T (for table) at the end of each table name, such as Order_T or Product_T. (Most DBMSs do not permit a space in the name of a table nor typically in the name of an attribute.) When looking at these tables, note the following:

1. Each order must have a valid customer ID included in the Order_T table.
2. Each item in an order line must have both a valid product ID and a valid order ID associated with it in the OrderLine_T table.
3. These four tables represent a simplified version of one of the most common sets of relations in business database systems—the customer order for products. SQL commands necessary to create the Customer_T table and the Order_T table were included in Chapter 2 and are expanded here.

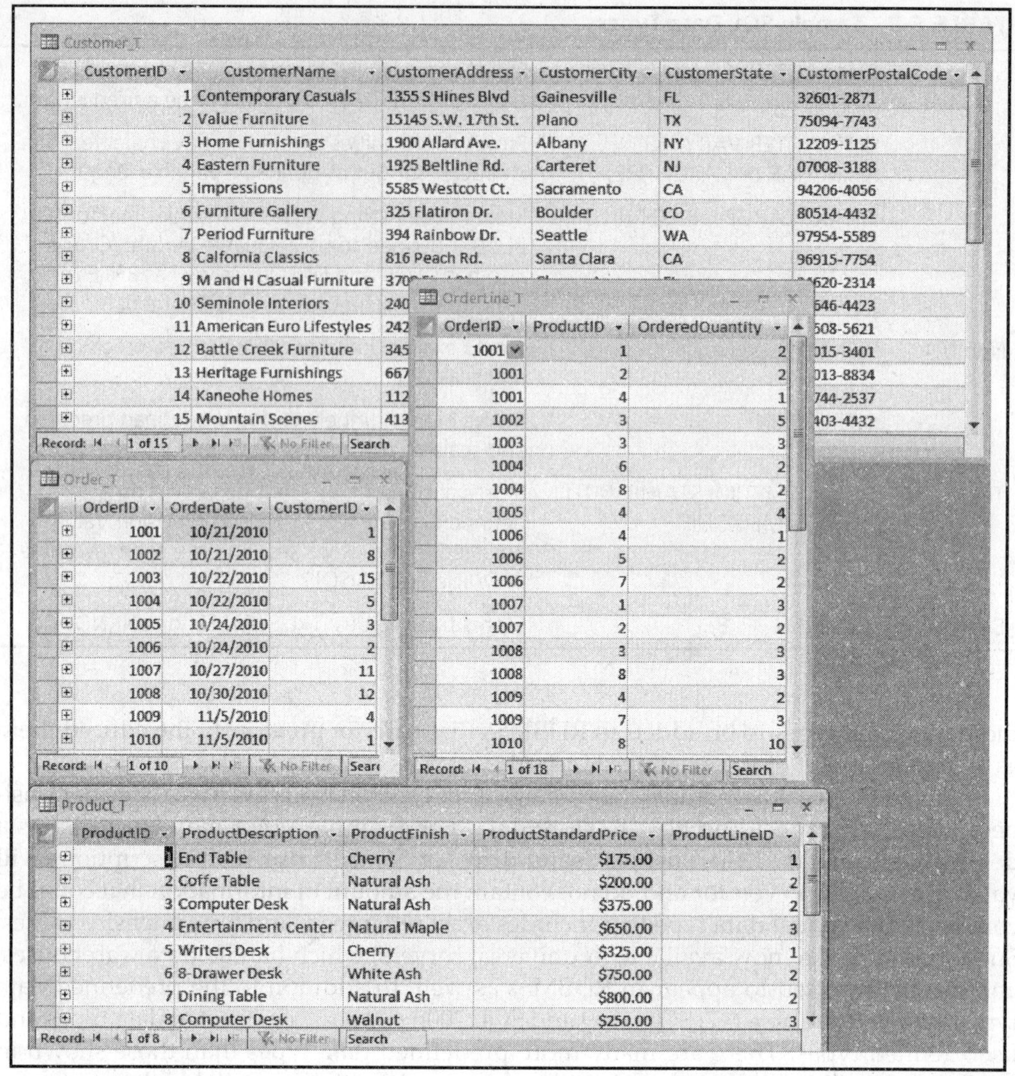

FIGURE 6-3 Sample Pine Valley Furniture Company data

The remainder of the chapter will illustrate DDL, DML, and DCL commands. Figure 6-4 gives an overview of where the various types of commands are used throughout the database development process. We will use the following notation in the illustrative SQL commands:

1. All-capitalized words denote commands. Type them exactly as shown, though capitalization may not be required by the RDBMSs. Some RDBMSs will always show data names in output using all capital letters, even if they can be entered in mixed case. (This is the style of Oracle, which is what we follow except where noted.) Tables, columns, named constraints, and so forth are shown in mixed case. Remember that table names follow the "underscore T" convention. SQL commands do not have an "underscore" and so should be easy to distinguish from table and column names. Also, RDBMSs do not like embedded spaces in data names, so multiple-word data names from ERDs are entered with the words together, without spaces between them. A consequence is that, for example, a column named QtyOnHand will become QTYONHAND when it is displayed by many RDBMSs. (You can use the ALIAS clause in a SELECT to rename a column name to a more readable value for display.)
2. Lowercase and mixed-case words denote values that must be supplied by the user.
3. Brackets enclose optional syntax.
4. An ellipsis (. . .) indicates that the accompanying syntactic clause may be repeated as necessary.

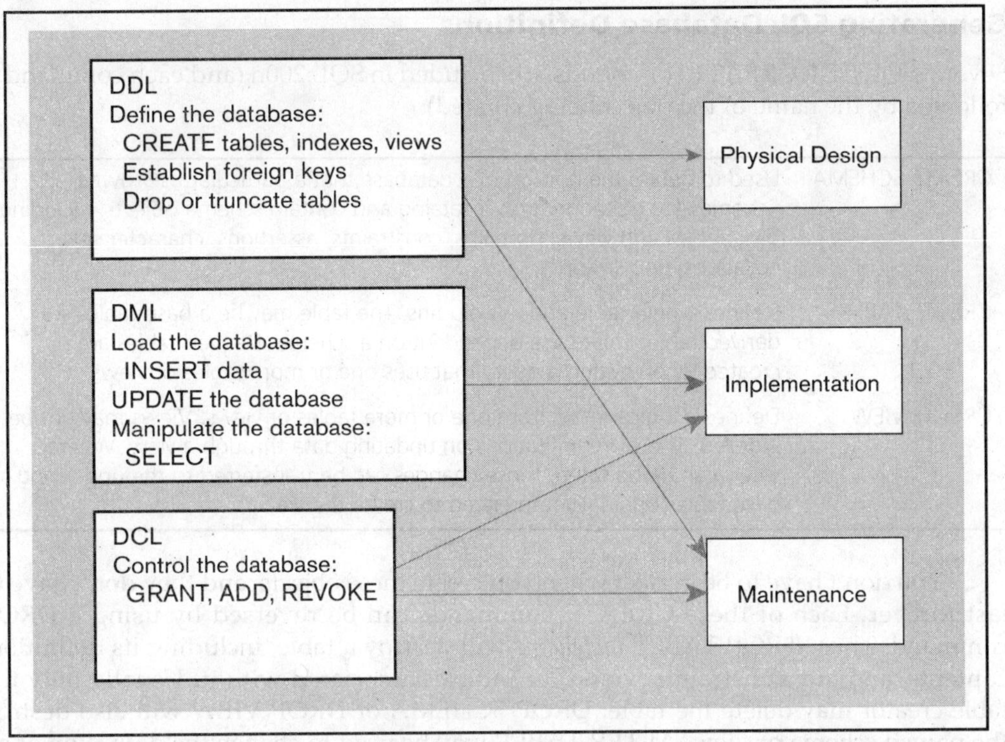

FIGURE 6-4 DDL, DML, DCL, and the database development process

5. Each SQL command ends with a semicolon (;). In interactive mode, when the user presses Enter, the SQL command will execute. Be alert for alternate conventions, such as typing GO or having to include a continuation symbol such as a hyphen at the end of each line used in the command. The spacing and indentations shown here are included for readability and are not a required part of standard SQL syntax.

DEFINING A DATABASE IN SQL

Because most systems allocate storage space to contain base tables, views, constraints, indexes, and other database objects when a database is created, you may not be allowed to create a database. Because of this, the privilege of creating databases may be reserved for the database administrator, and you may need to ask to have a database created. Students at a university may be assigned an account that gives access to an existing database, or they may be allowed to create their own database in a limited amount of allocated storage space (sometimes called *perm space* or *table space*). In any case, the basic syntax for creating a database is

```
CREATE SCHEMA database_name; AUTHORIZATION owner_user id
```

The database will be owned by the authorized user, although it is possible for other specified users to work with the database or even to transfer ownership of the database. Physical storage of the database is dependent on both the hardware and software environment and is usually the concern of the system administrator. The amount of control over physical storage that a database administrator is able to exert depends on the RDBMS being used. Little control is possible when using Microsoft Access, but Microsoft SQL Server 2008 allows for more control of the physical database. A database administrator may exert considerable control over the placement of data, control files, index files, schema ownership, and so forth, thus improving the ability to tune the database to perform more efficiently and to create a secure database environment.

Generating SQL Database Definitions

Several SQL DDL CREATE commands are included in SQL:200n (and each command is followed by the name of the object being created):

CREATE SCHEMA	Used to define the portion of a database that a particular user owns. Schemas are dependent on a catalog and contain schema objects, including base tables and views, domains, constraints, assertions, character sets, collations, and so forth.
CREATE TABLE	Defines a new table and its columns. The table may be a base table or a derived table. Tables are dependent on a schema. Derived tables are created by executing a query that uses one or more tables or views.
CREATE VIEW	Defines a logical table from one or more tables or views. Views may not be indexed. There are limitations on updating data through a view. Where views can be updated, those changes can be transferred to the underlying base tables originally referenced to create the view.

You don't have to be perfect when you create these objects, and they don't have to last forever. Each of these CREATE commands can be reversed by using a DROP command. Thus, DROP TABLE *tablename* will destroy a table, including its definition, contents, and any constraints, views, or indexes associated with it. Usually only the table creator may delete the table. DROP SCHEMA or DROP VIEW will also destroy the named schema or view. ALTER TABLE may be used to change the definition of an existing base table by adding, dropping, or changing a column or by dropping a constraint. Some RDBMSs will not allow you to alter a table in a way that the current data in that table will violate the new definitions (e.g., you cannot create a new constraint when current data will violate that constraint, or if you change the precision of a numeric column you may lose the extra precision of more precise existing values).

There are also five other CREATE commands included in the SQL standards; we list them here but do not cover them in this book:

CREATE CHARACTER SET	Allows the user to define a character set for text strings and aids in the globalization of SQL by enabling the use of languages other than English. Each character set contains a set of characters, a way to represent each character internally, a data format used for this representation, and a collation, or way of sorting the character set.
CREATE COLLATION	A named schema object that specifies the order that a character set will assume. Existing collations may be manipulated to create a new collation.
CREATE TRANSLATION	A named set of rules that maps characters from a source character set to a destination character set for translation or conversion purposes.
CREATE ASSERTION	A schema object that establishes a CHECK constraint that is violated if the constraint is false.
CREATE DOMAIN	A schema object that establishes a domain, or set of valid values, for an attribute. Data type will be specified, and a default value, collation, or other constraint may also be specified, if desired.

Creating Tables

Once the data model is designed and normalized, the columns needed for each table can be defined, using the SQL CREATE TABLE command. The general syntax for CREATE TABLE is shown in Figure 6-5. Here is a series of steps to follow when preparing to create a table:

1. Identify the appropriate data type, including length, precision, and scale, if required, for each attribute.
2. Identify the columns that should accept null values, as discussed in Chapter 5. Column controls that indicate a column cannot be null are established when a

```
CREATE TABLE tablename
( {column definition      [table constraint] } . , . .
[ON COMMIT {DELETE | P RESERVE} ROWS] );

where column definition ::=
column_name
        {domain name| d atatype [(size)] }
        [column_constraint_clause. . .]
        [default value]
        [collate clause]

and table constraint ::=
        [CONSTRAINT constraint_name]
        Constraint_type [constraint_attributes]
```

FIGURE 6-5 General syntax of the CREATE TABLE statement used in data definition language

table is created and are enforced for every update of the table when data are entered.

3. Identify the columns that need to be unique. When a column control of UNIQUE is established for a column, the data in that column must have a different value for each row of data within that table (i.e., no duplicate values). Where a column or set of columns is designated as UNIQUE, that column or set of columns is a candidate key, as discussed in Chapter 4. Although each base table may have multiple candidate keys, only one candidate key may be designated as a PRIMARY KEY. When a column(s) is specified as the PRIMARY KEY, that column(s) is also assumed to be NOT NULL, even if NOT NULL is not explicitly stated. UNIQUE and PRIMARY KEY are both column constraints. Note that a table with a composite primary key, OrderLine_T, is defined in Figure 6-6. The OrderLine_PK constraint includes both OrderID and ProductID in the primary key constraint, thus creating a composite key. Additional attributes may be included within the parentheses as needed to create the composite key.
4. Identify all primary key–foreign key mates, as presented in Chapter 4. Foreign keys can be established immediately, as a table is created, or later by altering the table. The parent table in such a parent–child relationship should be created first so that the child table will reference an existing parent table when it is created. The column constraint REFERENCES can be used to enforce referential integrity (e.g., the Order_FK constraint on the Order_T table).
5. Determine values to be inserted in any columns for which a default value is desired. DEFAULT can be used to define a value that is automatically inserted when no value is inserted during data entry. In Figure 6-6, the command that creates the Order_T table has defined a default value of SYSDATE (Oracle's name for the current date) for the OrderDate attribute.
6. Identify any columns for which domain specifications may be stated that are more constrained than those established by data type. Using CHECK as a column constraint, it may be possible to establish validation rules for values to be inserted into the database. In Figure 6-6, creation of the Product_T table includes a check constraint, which lists the possible values for Product_Finish. Thus, even though an entry of 'White Maple' would meet the VARCHAR data type constraints, it would be rejected because 'White Maple' is not in the checklist.
7. Create the table and any desired indexes, using the CREATE TABLE and CREATE INDEX statements. (CREATE INDEX is not a part of the SQL:1999 standard because indexing is used to address performance issues, but it is available in most RDBMSs.)

PINE VALLEY FURNITURE

Figure 6-6 shows database definition commands using Oracle 11g that include additional column constraints, as well as primary and foreign keys given names. For example, the Customer table's primary key is CustomerID. The primary key constraint is named Customer_PK. In Oracle, for example, once a constraint has been given a

FIGURE 6-6 SQL database definition commands for Pine Valley Furniture Company (Oracle 11g)

```
CREATE TABLE Customer_T
        (CustomerID                 NUMBER(11,0)    NOT NULL,
         CustomerName               VARCHAR2(25)    NOT NULL,
         CustomerAddress            VARCHAR2(30),
         CustomerCity               VARCHAR2(20),
         CustomerState              CHAR(2),
         CustomerPostalCode         VARCHAR2(9),
CONSTRAINT Customer_PK PRIMARY KEY (CustomerID));

CREATE TABLE Order_T
        (OrderID                    NUMBER(11,0)    NOT NULL,
         OrderDate                  DATE DEFAULT SYSDATE,
         CustomerID                 NUMBER(11,0),
CONSTRAINT Order_PK PRIMARY KEY (OrderID),
CONSTRAINT Order_FK FOREIGN KEY (CustomerID) REFERENCES Customer_T(CustomerID));

CREATE TABLE Product_T
        (ProductID                  NUMBER(11,0)    NOT NULL,
         ProductDescription         VARCHAR2(50),
         ProductFinish              VARCHAR2(20)
                    CHECK (ProductFinish IN ('Cherry', 'Natural Ash', 'White Ash',
                                'Red Oak', 'Natural Oak', 'Walnut')),
         ProductStandardPrice       DECIMAL(6,2),
         ProductLineID              INTEGER,
CONSTRAINT Product_PK PRIMARY KEY (ProductID));

CREATE TABLE OrderLine_T
        (OrderID                    NUMBER(11,0)    NOT NULL,
         ProductID                  INTEGER         NOT NULL,
         OrderedQuantity            NUMBER(11,0),
CONSTRAINT OrderLine_PK PRIMARY KEY (OrderID, ProductID),
CONSTRAINT OrderLine_FK1 FOREIGN KEY (OrderID) REFERENCES Order_T(OrderID),
CONSTRAINT OrderLine_FK2 FOREIGN KEY (ProductID) REFERENCES Product_T(ProductID));
```

meaningful name by the user, a database administrator will find it easy to identify the primary key constraint on the customer table because its name, Customer_PK, will be the value of the constraint_name column in the DBA_CONSTRAINTS table. If a meaningful constraint name were not assigned, a 16-byte system identifier would be assigned automatically. These identifiers are difficult to read and even more difficult to match up with user-defined constraints. Documentation about how system identifiers are generated is not available, and the method can be changed without notification. Bottom line: Give all constraints names or be prepared for extra work later.

When a foreign key constraint is defined, referential integrity will be enforced. This is good: We want to enforce business rules in the database. Fortunately, you are still allowed to have a null value for the foreign key (signifying a zero cardinality of the relationship) as long as you do not put the NOT NULL clause on the foreign key column. For example, if you try to add an order with an invalid CustomerID value (every order has to be related to some customer, so the minimum cardinality is one next to Customer for the Submits relationship in Figure 2-22), you will receive an error message. Each DBMS vendor generates its own error messages, and these messages may be difficult to interpret. Microsoft Access, being intended for both personal and professional use, provides simple error messages in dialog boxes. For example, for a referential integrity violation, Access displays the following error message: "You cannot add or change a record because a related record is required in table Customer_T." No record will be added to Order_T until that record references an existing customer in the Customer_T table.

Sometimes a user will want to create a table that is similar to one that already exists. SQL:1999 included the capability of adding a LIKE clause to the CREATE TABLE statement to allow for the copying of the existing structure of one or more tables into a new table. For example, a table can be used to store data that are questionable until the questionable data can be reviewed by an administrator. This exception table has the same structure as the verified transaction table, and missing or conflicting data will be reviewed and resolved before those transactions are appended to the transaction table. SQL:200n has expanded the CREATE . . . LIKE capability by allowing additional information, such as table constraints, from the original table to be easily ported to the new table when it is created. The new table exists independently of the original table. Inserting a new instance into the original table will have no effect on the new table. However, if the attempt to insert the new instance triggers an exception, the trigger can be written so that the data is stored in the new table to be reviewed later.

Oracle, MySQL, and some other RDBMSs have an interesting "dummy" table that is automatically defined with each database—the Dual table. The Dual table is used to run an SQL command against a system variable. For example,

```
SELECT Sysdate FROM Dual;
```

displays the current date, and

```
SELECT 8 + 4 FROM Dual;
```

displays the result of this arithmetic.

Creating Data Integrity Controls

We have seen the syntax that establishes foreign keys in Figure 6-6. To establish referential integrity constraint between two tables with a 1:*M* relationship in the relational data model, the primary key of the table on the one side will be referenced by a column in the table on the many side of the relationship. Referential integrity means that a value in the matching column on the many side must correspond to a value in the primary key for some row in the table on the one side or be NULL. The SQL REFERENCES clause prevents a foreign key value from being added if it is not already a valid value in the referenced primary key column, but there are other integrity issues.

If a CustomerID value is changed, the connection between that customer and orders placed by that customer will be ruined. The REFERENCES clause prevents making such a change in the foreign key value, but not in the primary key value. This problem could be handled by asserting that primary key values cannot be changed once they are established. In this case, updates to the customer table will be handled in most systems by including an ON UPDATE RESTRICT clause. Then, any updates that would delete or change a primary key value will be rejected unless no foreign key references that value in any child table. See Figure 6-7 for the syntax associated with updates.

Another solution is to pass the change through to the child table(s) by using the ON UPDATE CASCADE option. Then, if a customer ID number is changed, that change will flow through (cascade) to the child table, Order_T, and the customer's ID will also be updated in the Order_T table.

A third solution is to allow the update on Customer_T but to change the involved CustomerID value in the Order_T table to NULL by using the ON UPDATE SET NULL option. In this case, using the SET NULL option would result in losing the connection between the order and the customer, which is not a desired effect. The most flexible option to use would be the CASCADE option. If a customer record were deleted, ON DELETE RESTRICT, CASCADE, or SET NULL would also be available. With DELETE RESTRICT, the customer record could not be deleted unless there were no orders from that customer in the Order_T table. With DELETE CASCADE, removing the customer would remove all associated order records from Order_T. With DELETE SET NULL, the order records for that customer would be set to null before the customer's record was deleted. With DELETE SET DEFAULT, the order records for that customer would be set to a default value before the customer's record was deleted. DELETE RESTRICT would probably make the most sense. Not all SQL RDBMSs provide for primary key referential integrity. In that case, update and delete permissions on the primary key column may be revoked.

FIGURE 6-7 Ensuring data integrity through updates

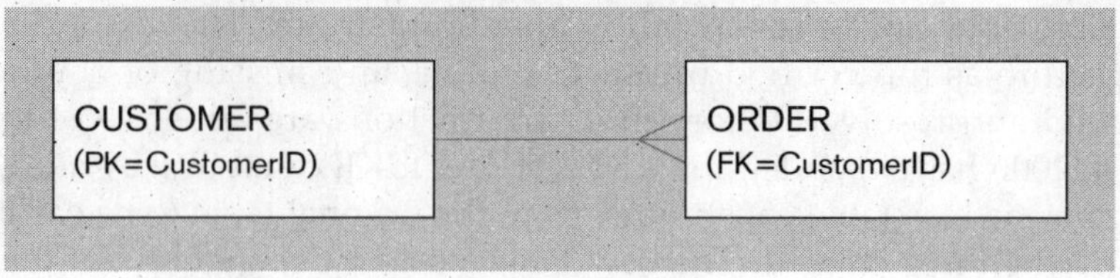

Restricted Update: A customer ID can only be deleted if it is not found in ORDER table.

```
CREATE TABLE CustomerT
        (CustomerID         INTEGER DEFAULT '999'     NOT NULL,
         CustomerName       VARCHAR(40)               NOT NULL,
         ...
CONSTRAINT Customer_PK PRIMARY KEY (CustomerID),
ON UPDATE RESTRICT);
```

Cascaded Update: Changing a customer ID in the CUSTOMER table will result in that value changing in the ORDER table to match.

... ON UPDATE CASCADE);

Set Null Update: When a customer ID is changed, any customer ID in the ORDER table that matches the old customer ID is set to NULL.

... ON UPDATE SET NULL);

Set Default Update: When a customer ID is changed, any customer ID in the ORDER tables that matches the old customer ID is set to a predefined default value.

... ON UPDATE SET DEFAULT);

Changing Table Definitions

Base table definitions may be changed by using ALTER on the column specifications. The ALTER TABLE command can be used to add new columns to an existing table. Existing columns may also be altered. Table constraints may be added or dropped. The ALTER TABLE command may include keywords such as ADD, DROP, or ALTER and allow the column's names, data type, length, and constraints to be changed. Usually, when adding a new column, its null status will be NULL so that data that have already been entered in the table can be dealt with. When the new column is created, it is added to all of the instances in the table, and a value of NULL would be the most reasonable. The ALTER command cannot be used to change a view.

Syntax:

ALTER TABLE table_name alter_table_action;

Some of the alter_table_actions available are:

ADD [COLUMN] column_definition
ALTER [COLUMN] column_name **SET DEFAULT** default-value
ALTER [COLUMN] column_name **DROP DEFAULT**
DROP [COLUMN] column_name **[RESTRICT] [CASCADE]**
ADD table_constraint

Command: To add a customer type column named CustomerType to the Customer table.

```
ALTER TABLE CUSTOMER_T
ADD COLUMN CustomerType VARCHAR2 (2) DEFAULT "Commercial";
```

The ALTER command is invaluable for adapting a database to inevitable modifications due to changing requirements, prototyping, evolutionary development, and mistakes. It is also useful when performing a bulk data load into a table that contains a foreign key. The constraint may be temporarily dropped. Later, after the bulk data load has finished, the constraint can be enabled. When the constraint is reenabled, it is possible to generate a log of any records that have referential integrity problems. Rather than have the data load balk each time such a problem occurs during the bulk load, the database administrator can simply review the log and reconcile the few (hopefully few) records that were problematic.

Removing Tables

To remove a table from a database, the owner of the table may use the DROP TABLE command. Views are dropped by using the similar DROP VIEW command.

Command: To drop a table from a database schema.

```
DROP TABLE Customer_T;
```

This command will drop the table and save any pending changes to the database. To drop a table, you must either own the table or have been granted the DROP ANY TABLE system privilege. Dropping a table will also cause associated indexes and privileges granted to be dropped. The DROP TABLE command can be qualified by the keywords RESTRICT or CASCADE. If RESTRICT is specified, the command will fail, and the table will not be dropped if there are any dependent objects, such as views or constraints, that currently reference the table. If CASCADE is specified, all dependent objects will also be dropped as the table is dropped. Many RDBMSs allows users to retain the table's structure but remove all of the data that have been entered in the table with its TRUNCATE TABLE command. Commands for updating and deleting part of the data in a table are covered in the next section.

INSERTING, UPDATING, AND DELETING DATA

PINE VALLEY FURNITURE

Once tables have been created, it is necessary to populate them with data and maintain those data before queries can be written. The SQL command that is used to populate tables is the INSERT command. When entering a value for every column in the table, you can use a command like the following, which was used to add the first row of data to the Customer_T table for Pine Valley Furniture Company. Notice that the data values must be ordered in the same order as the columns in the table.

Command: To insert a row of data into a table where a value will be inserted for every attribute.

```
INSERT INTO Customer_T VALUES
(001, 'Contemporary Casuals', '1355 S. Himes Blvd.', 'Gainesville', 'FL', 32601);
```

When data will not be entered into every column in the table, either enter the value NULL for the empty fields or specify those columns to which data are to be added. Here, too, the data values must be in the same order as the columns have been specified in the INSERT command. For example, the following statement was used to insert one row of data into the Product_T table, because there was no product line ID for the end table.

Command: To insert a row of data into a table where some attributes will be left null.

```
INSERT INTO Product_T (ProductID,
ProductDescription, ProductFinish, ProductStandardPrice)
    VALUES (1, 'End Table', 'Cherry', 175, 8);
```

In general, the INSERT command places a new row in a table, based on values supplied in the statement, copies one or more rows derived from other database data into a table, or extracts data from one table and inserts them into another. If you want to populate a table, CaCustomer_T, that has the same structure as CUSTOMER_T, with only Pine Valley's California customers, you could use the following INSERT command.

Command: Populating a table by using a subset of another table with the same structure.

```
INSERT INTO CaCustomer_T
SELECT * FROM Customer_T
    WHERE CustomerState = 'CA';
```

In many cases, we want to generate a unique primary identifier or primary key every time a row is added to a table. Customer identification numbers are a good example of a situation where this capability would be helpful. SQL:200n had added a new feature, identity columns, that removes the previous need to create a procedure to generate a sequence and then apply it to the insertion of data. To take advantage of this, the CREATE TABLE Customer_T statement displayed in Figure 6-6 may be modified (emphasized by bold print) as follows:

```
CREATE TABLE Customer_T
(CustomerID INTEGER GENERATED ALWAYS AS IDENTITY
    (START WITH 1
    INCREMENT BY 1
    MINVALUE 1
    MAXVALUE 10000
    NO CYCLE),
CustomerName            VARCHAR2(25) NOT NULL,
CustomerAddress         VARCHAR2(30),
CustomerCity            VARCHAR2(20),
CustomerState           CHAR(2),
CustomerPostalCode      VARCHAR2(9),
CONSTRAINT Customer_PK PRIMARY KEY (CustomerID);
```

Only one column can be an identity column in a table. When a new customer is added, the CustomerID value will be assigned implicitly if the vendor has implemented identity columns.

Thus, the command that adds a new customer to Customer_T will change from this:

```
INSERT INTO Customer_T VALUES
(001, 'Contemporary Casuals', '1355 S. Himes Blvd.', 'Gainesville',
  'FL', 32601);
```

to this:

```
INSERT INTO Customer_T VALUES
('Contemporary Casuals', '1355 S. Himes Blvd.', 'Gainesville', 'FL', 32601);
```

The primary key value, 001, does not need to be entered, and the syntax to accomplish the automatic sequencing has been simplified in SQL:200n.

Batch Input

The INSERT command is used to enter one row of data at a time or to add multiple rows as the result of a query. Some versions of SQL have a special command or utility for entering multiple rows of data as a batch: the INPUT command. For example, Oracle includes a program, SQL*Loader, which runs from the command line and can be used to load data from a file into the database. SQL Server includes a BULK INSERT command with Transact-SQL for importing data into a table or view. (These powerful and feature rich programs are not within the scope of this text.)

Deleting Database Contents

Rows can be deleted from a database individually or in groups. Suppose Pine Valley Furniture decides that it will no longer deal with customers located in Hawaii. Customer_T rows for customers with addresses in Hawaii could all be eliminated using the next command.

Command: Deleting rows that meet a certain criterion from the Customer table.

```
DELETE FROM Customer_T
WHERE CustomerState = 'HI';
```

The simplest form of DELETE eliminates all rows of a table.

Command: Deleting all rows from the Customer table.

```
DELETE FROM Customer_T;
```

This form of the command should be used very carefully!

Deletion must also be done with care when rows from several relations are involved. For example, if we delete a Customer_T row, as in the previous query, before deleting associated Order_T rows, we will have a referential integrity violation, and the DELETE command will not execute. (Note: Including the ON DELETE clause with a field definition can mitigate such a problem. Refer to the "Creating Data Integrity Controls" section in this chapter if you've forgotten about the ON clause.) SQL will actually eliminate the records selected by a DELETE command. Therefore, always execute a SELECT command first to display the records that would be deleted and visually verify that only the desired rows are included.

Updating Database Contents

To update data in SQL, we must inform the DBMS what relation, columns, and rows are involved. If an incorrect price is entered for the dining table in the Product_T table, the following SQL UPDATE statement would establish the correction.

Command: To modify standard price of product 7 in the Product table to 775.

```
UPDATE Product_T
SET ProductStandardPrice = 775
    WHERE ProductID = 7;
```

The SET command can also change a value to NULL; the syntax is SET columname = NULL. As with DELETE, the WHERE clause in an UPDATE command may contain a subquery, but the table being updated may not be referenced in the subquery. Subqueries are discussed in Chapter 7.

The SQL:200n standard has included a new keyword, MERGE, that makes updating a table easier. Many database applications need to update master tables with new data. A Purchases_T table, for example, might include rows with data about new products and rows that change the standard price of existing products. Updating Product_T can be accomplished by using INSERT to add the new products and UPDATE to modify StandardPrice in an SQL-92 or SQL:1999 DBMS. SQL:200n compliant DBMSs can accomplish the update and the insert in one step by using MERGE:

```
MERGE INTO Product_T AS PROD
USING
(SELECT ProductID, ProductDescription, ProductFinish,
ProductStandardPrice, ProductLineID FROM Purchases_T) AS PURCH
    ON (PROD.ProductID = PURCH.ProductID)
WHEN MATCHED THEN UPDATE
    PROD.ProductStandardPrice = PURCH.ProductStandardPrice
```

```
WHEN NOT MATCHED THEN INSERT
    (ProductID, ProductDescription, ProductFinish, ProductStandardPrice,
    ProductLineID)
    VALUES(PURCH.ProductID, PURCH.ProductDescription,
    PURCH.ProductFinish, PURCH.ProductStandardPrice,
      PURCH.ProductLineID);
```

INTERNAL SCHEMA DEFINITION IN RDBMSS

The internal schema of a relational database can be controlled for processing and storage efficiency. The following are some techniques used for tuning the operational performance of the relational database internal data model:

1. Choosing to index primary and/or secondary keys to increase the speed of row selection, table joining, and row ordering. You can also drop indexes to increase speed of table updating. You may want to review the section in Chapter 5 on selecting indexes.
2. Selecting file organizations for base tables that match the type of processing activity on those tables (e.g., keeping a table physically sorted by a frequently used reporting sort key).
3. Selecting file organizations for indexes, which are also tables, appropriate to the way the indexes are used and allocating extra space for an index file so that an index can grow without having to be reorganized.
4. Clustering data so that related rows of frequently joined tables are stored close together in secondary storage to minimize retrieval time.
5. Maintaining statistics about tables and their indexes so that the DBMS can find the most efficient ways to perform various database operations.

Not all of these techniques are available in all SQL systems. Indexing and clustering are typically available, however, so we discuss these in the following sections.

Creating Indexes

Indexes are created in most RDBMSs to provide rapid random and sequential access to base-table data. Because the ISO SQL standards do not generally address performance issues, no standard syntax for creating indexes is included. The examples given here use Oracle syntax and give a feel for how indexes are handled in most RDBMSs. Note that although users do not directly refer to indexes when writing any SQL command, the DBMS recognizes which existing indexes would improve query performance. Indexes can usually be created for both primary and secondary keys and both single and concatenated (multiple-column) keys. In some systems, users can choose between ascending and descending sequences for the keys in an index.

PINE VALLEY FURNITURE

For example, an alphabetical index on CustomerName in the Customer_T table in Oracle is created here.

Command: To create an alphabetical index on customer name in the Customer table.

```
CREATE INDEX Name_IDX ON Customer_T (CustomerName);
```

RDBMs usually support several different types of indexes, each of which assists in different kinds of keyword searches. For example, in MySQL you can create unique (appropriate for primary keys), nonunique (secondary keys), fulltext (used for full-text searches), spatial (used for spatial data types), and hash (which is used for in-memory tables).

Indexes can be created or dropped at any time. If data already exist in the key column(s), index population will automatically occur for the existing data. If an index is defined as UNIQUE (using the syntax CREATE UNIQUE INDEX . . .) and the existing data violate this condition, the index creation will fail. Once an index is created, it will be updated as data are entered, updated, or deleted.

When we no longer need tables, views, or indexes, we use the associated DROP statements. For example, the NAME_IDX index from the previous example is dropped here.

Command: To remove the index on the customer name in the Customer table.

```
DROP INDEX Name_IDX;
```

Although it is possible to index every column in a table, use caution when deciding to create a new index. Each index consumes extra storage space and also requires overhead maintenance time whenever indexed data change value. Together, these costs may noticeably slow retrieval response times and cause annoying delays for online users. A system may use only one index even if several are available for keys in a complex qualification. A database designer must know exactly how indexes are used by the particular RDBMS in order to make wise choices about indexing. Oracle includes an explain plan tool that can be used to look at the order in which an SQL statement will be processed and at the indexes that will be used. The output also includes a cost estimate that can be compared with estimates from running the statement with different indexes to determine which is most efficient.

PROCESSING SINGLE TABLES

"Processing single tables" may seem like Friday night at the hottest club in town, but we have something else in mind. Sorry, no dating suggestions (and sorry for the pun).

Four data manipulation language commands are used in SQL. We have talked briefly about three of them (UPDATE, INSERT, and DELETE) and have seen several examples of the fourth, SELECT. Although the UPDATE, INSERT, and DELETE commands allow modification of the data in the tables, it is the SELECT command, with its various clauses, that allows users to query the data contained in the tables and ask many different questions or create ad hoc queries. The basic construction of an SQL command is fairly simple and easy to learn. Don't let that fool you; SQL is a powerful tool that enables users to specify complex data analysis processes. However, because the basic syntax is relatively easy to learn, it is also easy to write SELECT queries that are syntactically correct but do not answer the exact question that is intended. Before running queries against a large production database, always test them carefully on a small test set of data to be sure that they are returning the correct results. In addition to checking the query results manually, it is often possible to parse queries into smaller parts, examine the results of these simpler queries, and then recombine them. This will ensure that they act together in the expected way. We begin by exploring SQL queries that affect only a single table. In Chapter 7, we join tables and use queries that require more than one table.

Clauses of the SELECT Statement

Most SQL data retrieval statements include the following three clauses:

SELECT	Lists the columns (including expressions involving columns) from base tables, derived tables, or views to be projected into the table that will be the result of the command. (That's the technical way of saying it lists the data you want to display.)
FROM	Identifies the tables, derived tables, or views from which columns will be chosen to appear in the result table and includes the tables, derived tables, or views needed to join tables to process the query.
WHERE	Includes the conditions for row selection within the items in the FROM clause and the conditions between tables, derived tables, or views for joining. Because SQL is considered a set manipulation language, the WHERE clause is important in defining the set of rows being manipulated.

The first two clauses are required, and the third is necessary when only certain table rows are to be retrieved or multiple tables are to be joined. (Most examples for this section are drawn from the data shown in Figure 6-3.) For example, we can display product name and quantity on hand from the PRODUCT view for all Pine Valley Furniture Company products that have a standard price of less than $275.

PINE VALLEY FURNITURE

Query: Which products have a standard price of less than $275?

```
SELECT ProductDescription, ProductStandardPrice
  FROM Product_T
    WHERE ProductStandardPrice < 275;
```

Result:

PRODUCTDESCRIPTION	PRODUCTSTANDARDPRICE
End Table	175
Computer Desk	250
Coffee Table	200

As stated before, in this book we show results (except where noted) in the style of Oracle, which means that column headings are in all capital letters. If this is too annoying for users, then the data names should be defined with an underscore between the words rather than run-on words, or you can use an alias (described later in this section) to redefine a column heading for display.

Every SELECT statement returns a result table (a set of rows) when it executes. So, SQL is consistent—tables in, tables out of every query. This becomes important with more complex queries because we can use the result of one query (a table) as part of another query (e.g., we can include a SELECT statement as one of the elements in the FROM clause, creating a derived table, which we illustrate later in this chapter).

Two special keywords can be used along with the list of columns to display: DISTINCT and *. If the user does not wish to see duplicate rows in the result, SELECT DISTINCT may be used. In the preceding example, if the other computer desk carried by Pine Valley Furniture had also cost less than $275, the results of the query would have had duplicate rows. SELECT DISTINCT ProductDescription would display a result table without the duplicate rows. SELECT *, where * is used as a wildcard to indicate all columns, displays all columns from all the items in the FROM clause.

Also, note that the clauses of a SELECT statement must be kept in order, or syntax error messages will occur and the query will not execute. It may also be necessary to qualify the names of the database objects according to the SQL version being used. If there is any ambiguity in an SQL command, you must indicate exactly from which table, derived table, or view the requested data are to come. For example, in Figure 6-3 CustomerID is a column in both Customer_T and Order_T. When you own the database being used (i.e., the user created the tables) and you want CustomerID to come from Customer_T, specify it by asking for Customer_T.CustomerID. If you want CustomerID to come from Order_T, then ask for Order_T.CustomerID. Even if you don't care which table CustomerID comes from, it must be specified because SQL can't resolve the ambiguity without user direction. When you are allowed to use data created by someone else, you must also specify the owner of the table by adding the owner's user ID. Now a request to SELECT the CustomerID from Customer_T may look like this: OWNER_ID.Customer_T.CustomerID. The examples in this book assume that the reader owns the tables or views being used, as the SELECT statements will be easier to read without the qualifiers. Qualifiers will be included where necessary and may always be included in statements if desired. Problems may occur when qualifiers are left out, but no problems will occur when they are included.

If typing the qualifiers and column names is wearisome (computer keyboards aren't, yet, built to accommodate the two-thumb cellphone texting technique), or if the column names will not be meaningful to those who are reading the reports, establish aliases for data names that will then be used for the rest of the query. Although SQL:1999 does not include aliases or synonyms, they are widely implemented and aid in readability and simplicity in query construction.

Query: What is the address of the customer named Home Furnishings? Use an alias, Name, for the customer name. (The AS clauses are bolded for emphasis only.)

```
SELECT CUST.CustomerName AS Name, CUST.CustomerAddress
  FROM ownerid.Customer_T AS Cust
    WHERE Name = 'Home Furnishings';
```

This retrieval statement will give the following result in many versions of SQL. In Oracle's SQL*Plus, the alias for the column cannot be used in the rest of the SELECT statement, except in a HAVING clause, so in order for the query to run, CustomerName would have to be used in the last line rather than Name. Notice that the column header prints as Name rather than CustomerName and that the table alias may be used in the SELECT clause even though it is not defined until the FROM clause.

Result:

NAME	CUSTOMERADDRESS
Home Furnishings	1900 Allard Ave.

You've likely concluded that SQL generates pretty plain output. Using an alias is a good way to make column headings more readable. (Aliases also have other uses, which we'll address later.) Many RDBMSs have other proprietary SQL clauses to improve the display of data. For example, Oracle has the COLUMN clause of the SELECT statement, which can be used to change the text for the column heading, change alignment of the column heading, reformat the column value, or control wrapping of data in a column, among other properties. You may want to investigate such capabilities for the RDBMS you are using.

When you use the SELECT clause to pick out the columns for a result table, the columns can be rearranged so that they will be ordered differently in the result table than in the original table. In fact, they will be displayed in the same order as they are included in the SELECT statement. Look back at Product_T in Figure 6-3 to see the different ordering of the base table from the result table for this query.

Query: List the unit price, product name, and product ID for all products in the Product table.

```
SELECT ProductStandardPrice, ProductDescription, ProductID
FROM Product_T;
```

Result:

PRODUCTSTANDARDPRICE	PRODUCTDESCRIPTION	PRODUCTID
175	End Table	1
200	Coffee Table	2
375	Computer Desk	3
650	Entertainment Center	4
325	Writer's Desk	5
750	8-Drawer Desk	6
800	Dining Table	7
250	Computer Desk	8

Using Expressions

The basic SELECT . . . FROM . . . WHERE clauses can be used with a single table in a number of ways. You can create expressions, which are mathematical manipulations of the data in the table, or take advantage of stored functions, such as SUM or AVG, to manipulate the chosen rows of data from the table. Mathematical manipulations can be constructed by using the + for addition, – for subtraction, * for multiplication, and / for division. These operators can be used with any numeric columns. Expressions are computed for each row of the result table, such as displaying the difference between the standard price and unit cost of a product, or they can involve computations of columns and functions, such as standard price of a product multiplied by the amount of that product sold on a particular order (which would require summing OrderedQuantities). Some systems also have an operand called modulo, usually indicated by %. A modulo is the integer remainder that results from dividing two integers. For example, 14 % 4 is 2 because 14/4 is 3, with a remainder of 2. The SQL standard supports year–month and day–time intervals, which make it possible to perform date and time arithmetic (e.g., to calculate someone's age from today's date and a person's birthday).

Perhaps you would like to know the current standard price of each product and its future price if all prices were increased by 10 percent. Using SQL*Plus, here are the query and the results.

Query: What are the standard price and standard price if increased by 10 percent for every product?

```
SELECT ProductID, ProductStandardPrice, ProductStandardPrice*1.1 AS
Plus10Percent
  FROM Product_T;
```

Result:

PRODUCTID	PRODUCTSTANDARDPRICE	PLUS10PERCENT
2	200.0000	220.00000
3	375.0000	412.50000
1	175.0000	192.50000
8	250.0000	275.00000
7	800.0000	880.00000
5	325.0000	357.50000
4	650.0000	715.00000
6	750.0000	825.00000

The precedence rules for the order in which complex expressions are evaluated are the same as those used in other programming languages and in algebra. Expressions in parentheses will be calculated first. When parentheses do not establish order, multiplication and division will be completed first, from left to right, followed by addition and subtraction, also left to right. To avoid confusion, use parentheses to establish order. Where parentheses are nested, the innermost calculations will be completed first.

Using Functions

Standard SQL identifies a wide variety of mathematical, string and date manipulation, and other functions. We will illustrate some of the mathematical functions in this section. You will want to investigate what functions are available with the DBMS you are using, some of which may be proprietary to that DBMS. The standard functions include the following:

Mathematical — MIN, MAX, COUNT, SUM, ROUND (to round up a number to a specific number of decimal places), TRUNC (to truncate insignificant digits), and MOD (for modular arithmetic)

String — LOWER (to change to all lower case), UPPER (to change to all capital letters), INITCAP (to change to only an initial capital letter), CONCAT (to concatenate), SUBSTR (to isolate certain character positions), and COALESCE (finding the first not NULL values in a list of columns)

Date — NEXT_DAY (to compute the next date in sequence), ADD_MONTHS (to compute a date a given number of months before or after a given date), and MONTHS_BETWEEN (to compute the number of months between specified dates)

Analytical — TOP (find the top *n* values in a set, e.g., the top 5 customers by total annual sales)

Perhaps you want to know the average standard price of all inventory items. To get the overall average value, use the AVG stored function. We can name the resulting expression with an alias, AveragePrice. Using SQL*Plus, here are the query and the results.

Query: What is the average standard price for all products in inventory?

```
SELECT AVG (ProductStandardPrice) AS AveragePrice
FROM Product_T;
```

Result:

AVERAGEPRICE
440.625

SQL:1999 stored functions include ANY, AVG, COUNT, EVERY, GROUPING, MAX, MIN, SOME, and SUM. SQL:200n adds LN, EXP, POWER, SQRT, FLOOR, CEILING, and WIDTH_BUCKET. New functions tend to be added with each new SQL standard, and more functions have been added in SQL:2003 and SQL:2008, many of which are for advanced analytical processing of data (e.g., calculating moving averages and statistical sampling of data). As seen in the above example, functions such as COUNT, MIN, MAX, SUM, and AVG of specified columns in the column list of a SELECT command may be used to specify that the resulting answer table is to contain aggregated data instead of row-level data. Using any of these aggregate functions will give a one-row answer.

Query: How many different items were ordered on order number 1004?

```
SELECT COUNT (*)
  FROM OrderLine_T
    WHERE OrderID = 1004;
```

Result:

COUNT (*)
2

It seems that it would be simple enough to list order number 1004 by changing the query.

Query: How many different items were ordered on order number 1004, and what are they?

```
SELECT ProductID, COUNT (*)
  FROM OrderLine_T
    WHERE OrderID = 1004;
```

In Oracle, here is the result.

Result:

ERROR at line 1:
ORA-00937: not a single-group group function

And in Microsoft SQL Server, the result is as follows.

Result:

Column 'OrderLine_T.ProductID' is invalid in the select list because
it is not contained in an Aggregate function and there is no
GROUP BY clause.

The problem is that ProductID returns two values, 6 and 8, for the two rows selected, whereas COUNT returns one aggregate value, 2, for the set of rows with ID = 1004. In most implementations, SQL cannot return both a row value and a set value; users must run two separate queries, one that returns row information and one that returns set information.

A similar issue arises if we try to find the difference between the standard price of each product and the overall average standard price (which we calculated above). You might think the query would be

```
SELECT ProductStandardPrice – AVG(ProductStandardPrice)
  FROM Product_T;
```

However, again we have mixed a column value with an aggregate, which will cause an error. Remember that the FROM list can contain tables, derived tables, and views. One approach to developing a correct query is to make the aggregate the result of a derived table, as we do in the following sample query.

Query: Display for each product the difference between its standard price and the overall average standard price of all products.

```
SELECT ProductStandardPrice – PriceAvg AS Difference
  FROM Product_T, (SELECT AVG(ProductStandardPrice) AS PriceAvg
    FROM Product_T);
```

Result:

```
DIFFERENCE
    –240.63
     –65.63
    –265.63
    –190.63
     359.38
    –115.63
     209.38
     309.38
```

Also, it is easy to confuse the functions COUNT (*) and COUNT. The function COUNT (*), used in the previous query, counts all rows selected by a query, regardless of whether any of the rows contain null values. COUNT tallies only rows that contain values; it ignores all null values.

SUM and AVG can only be used with numeric columns. COUNT, COUNT (*), MIN, and MAX can be used with any data type. Using MIN on a text column, for example, will find the lowest value in the column, the one whose first column is closest to the beginning of the alphabet. SQL implementations interpret the order of the alphabet differently. For example, some systems may start with A–Z, then a–z, then 0–9 and special characters. Others treat upper- and lowercase letters as being equivalent. Still others start with some special characters, then proceed to numbers, letters, and other special characters. Here is the query to ask for the first ProductName in Product_T alphabetically, which was done using the AMERICAN character set in Oracle 11g.

Query: Alphabetically, what is the first product name in the Product table?

```
SELECT MIN (ProductDescription)
  FROM Product_T;
```

It gives the following result, which demonstrates that numbers are sorted before letters in this character set. (Note: The following result is from Oracle. Microsoft SQL Server returns the same result but labels the column (No column name) in SQL Query Analyzer, unless the query specifies a name for the result.)

Result:

```
MIN(PRODUCTDESCRIPTION)
8-Drawer Desk
```

Using Wildcards

The use of the asterisk (*) as a wildcard in a SELECT statement has been previously shown. Wildcards may also be used in the WHERE clause when an exact match is not possible. Here, the keyword LIKE is paired with wildcard characters and usually a string containing the characters that are known to be desired matches. The wildcard character, %, is used to represent any collection of characters. Thus, using LIKE '%Desk' when searching ProductDescription will find all different types of desks carried by Pine Valley Furniture. The underscore (_) is used as a wildcard character to represent exactly one character rather than any collection of characters. Thus, using LIKE '_-drawer' when searching ProductName will find any products with specified drawers, such as 3-, 5-, or 8-drawer dressers.

Using Comparison Operators

With the exception of the very first SQL example in this section, we have used the equality comparison operator in our WHERE clauses. The first example used the greater (less) than operator. The most common comparison operators for SQL implementations are listed in Table 6-3. (Different SQL DBMSs can use different comparison operators.) You are used to thinking about using comparison operators with numeric data, but you can also use them with character data and dates in SQL. The query shown here asks for all orders placed after 10/24/2010.

TABLE 6-3 Comparison Operators in SQL

Operator	Meaning
=	Equal to
>	Greater than
>=	Greater than or equal to
<	Less than
<=	Less than or equal to
<>	Not equal to
!=	Not equal to

Query: Which orders have been placed since 10/24/2010?

```
SELECT OrderID, OrderDate
  FROM Order_T
    WHERE OrderDate > '24-OCT-2010';
```

Notice that the date is enclosed in single quotes and that the format of the date is different from that shown in Figure 6-3, which was taken from Microsoft Access. The query was run in SQL*Plus. You should check the reference manual for the SQL language you are using to see how dates are to be formatted in queries and for data input.

Result:

ORDERID	ORDERDATE
1007	27-OCT-10
1008	30-OCT-10
1009	05-NOV-10
1010	05-NOV-10

Query: What furniture does Pine Valley carry that isn't made of cherry?

```
SELECT ProductDescription, ProductFinish
  FROM Product_T
    WHERE ProductFinish != 'Cherry';
```

Result:

PRODUCTDESCRIPTION	PRODUCTFINISH
Coffee Table	Natural Ash
Computer Desk	Natural Ash
Entertainment Center	Natural Maple
8-Drawer Desk	White Ash
Dining Table	Natural Ash
Computer Desk	Walnut

Using Null Values

Columns that are defined without the NOT NULL clause may be empty, and this may be a significant fact for an organization. You will recall that a null value means that a column is missing a value; the value is not zero or blank or any special code—there simply is no value. We have already seen that functions may produce different results when null values are present than when a column has a value of zero in all qualified rows. It is not uncommon, then, to first explore whether there are null values before deciding how to write other commands, or it may be that you simply want to see data about table rows where there are missing values. For example, before undertaking a postal mail advertising campaign, you might want to pose the following query.

Query: Display all customers for whom we do not know their postal code.

```
SELECT * FROM Customer_T WHERE CustomerPostalCode IS NULL;
```

Result:

Fortunately, this query returns 0 rows in the result in our sample database, so we can mail advertisements to all our customers because we know their postal codes. The term IS NOT NULL returns results for rows where the qualified column has a non-null value. This allows us to deal with rows that have values in a critical column, ignoring other rows.

Using Boolean Operators

You probably have taken a course or part of a course on finite or discrete mathematics—logic, Venn diagrams, and set theory, oh my! Remember we said that SQL is a set-oriented language, so there are many opportunities to use what you learned in finite math to write complex SQL queries. Some complex questions can be answered by adjusting the WHERE clause further. The Boolean or logical operators AND, OR, and NOT can be used to good purpose:

AND	Joins two or more conditions and returns results only when all conditions are true.
OR	Joins two or more conditions and returns results when any conditions are true.
NOT	Negates an expression.

If multiple Boolean operators are used in an SQL statement, NOT is evaluated first, then AND, then OR. For example, consider the following query.

Query A: List product name, finish, and standard price for all desks and all tables that cost more than $300 in the Product table.

```
SELECT ProductDescription, ProductFinish, ProductStandardPrice
  FROM Product_T
    WHERE ProductDescription LIKE '%Desk'
      OR ProductDescription LIKE '%Table'
      AND ProductStandardPrice > 300;
```

Result:

PRODUCTDESCRIPTION	PRODUCTFINISH	PRODUCTSTANDARDPRICE
Computer Desk	Natural Ash	375
Writer's Desk	Cherry	325
8-Drawer Desk	White Ash	750
Dining Table	Natural Ash	800
Computer Desk	Walnut	250

All of the desks are listed, even the computer desk that costs less than $300. Only one table is listed; the less expensive ones that cost less than $300 are not included. With

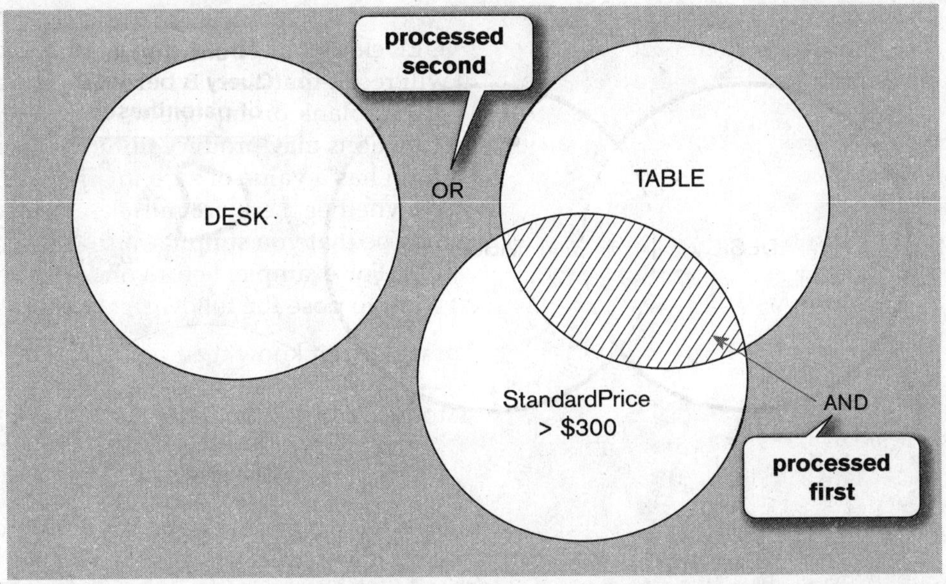

FIGURE 6-8 Boolean query without the use of parentheses
(a) Venn diagram of Query A logic, first process (AND)

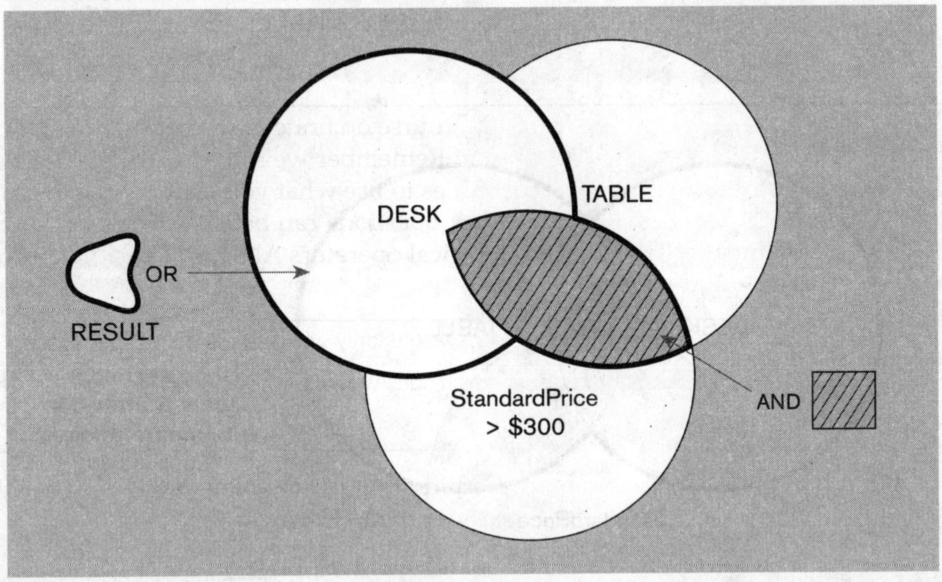

(b) Venn diagram of Query A logic, second process (OR)

this query, the AND will be processed first, returning all tables with a standard price greater than $300 (Figure 6-8a). Then the OR is processed, returning all desks, regardless of cost, and all tables costing more than $300 (Figure 6-8b). This is the area surrounded by the thick OR line in Figure 6-8b.

If we had wanted to return only desks and tables costing more than $300, we should have put parentheses after the WHERE and before the AND, as shown in Query B below. Figures 6-9a and 6-9b show the difference in processing caused by the judicious use of parentheses in the query. The result is all desks and tables with a standard price of more than $300, indicated by the filled area with horizontal lines. The walnut computer desk has a standard price of $250 and is not included.

Query B: List product name, finish, and unit price for all desks and tables in the PRODUCT table that cost more than $300.

```
SELECT ProductDescription, ProductFinish, ProductStandardPrice
  FROM Product_T;
  WHERE (ProductDescription LIKE '%Desk'
    OR ProductDescription LIKE '%Table')
    AND ProductStandardPrice > 300;
```

FIGURE 6-9 Boolean query with use of parentheses
(a) Venn diagram of Query B logic, first process (AND)

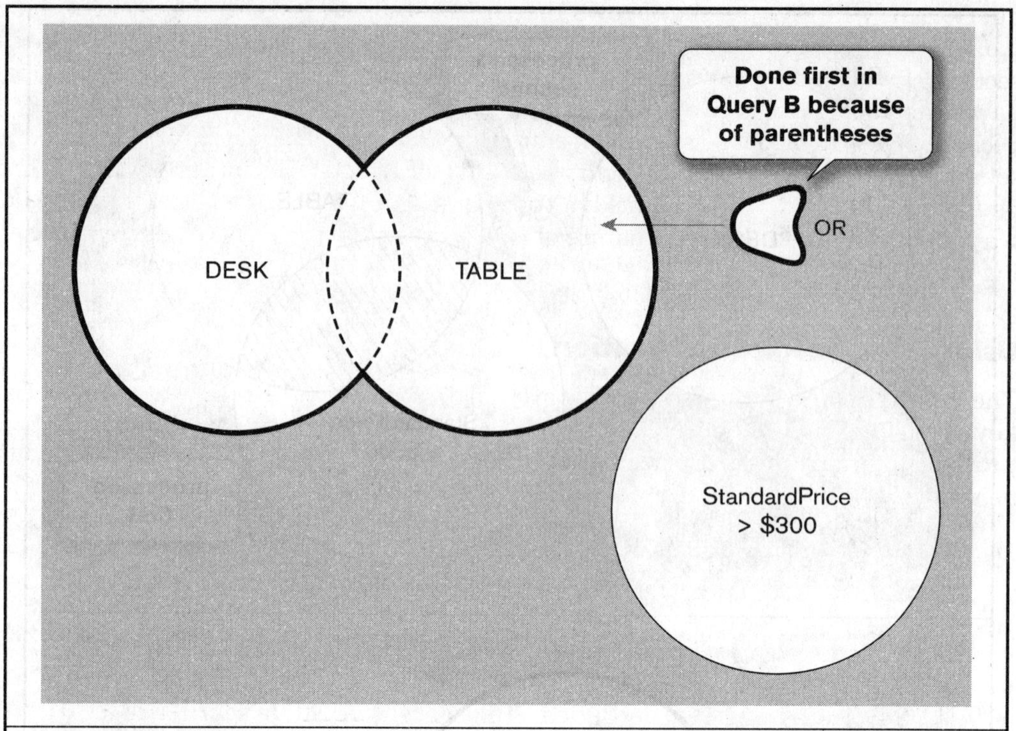

(b) Venn diagram of Query B, second process (OR)

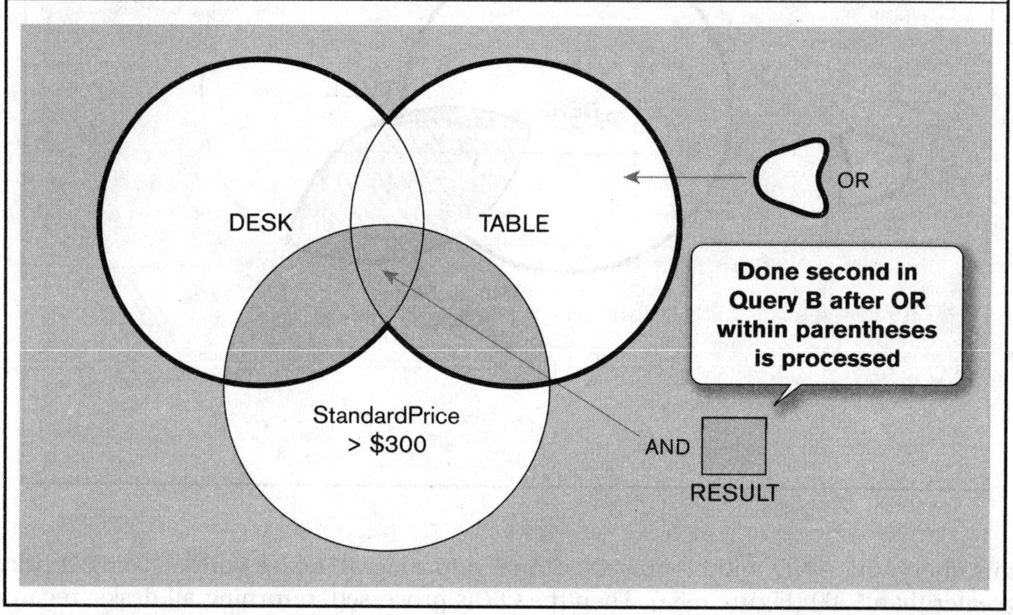

The results follow. Only products with unit price greater than $300 are included.

Result:

PRODUCTDESCRIPTION	PRODUCTFINISH	PRODUCTSTANDARDPRICE
Computer Desk	Natural Ash	375
Writer's Desk	Cherry	325
8-Drawer Desk	White Ash	750
Dining Table	Natural Ash	800

This example illustrates why SQL is considered a set-oriented, not a record-oriented, language. (C, Java, and Cobol are examples of record-oriented languages because they must process one record, or row, of a table at a time.) To answer this query, SQL will find the set of rows that are Desk products, and then it will union (i.e., merge) that set with the set of rows that are Table products. Finally, it will intersect (i.e., find common rows) the resultant set from this union with the set of rows that have a standard price above $300. If indexes can be used, the work is done even faster, because SQL will create sets of index entries that satisfy each qualification and do the set manipulation on those index entry sets, each of which takes up less space and can be manipulated much more quickly. You will see in Chapter 7 even more dramatic ways in which the set-oriented nature of SQL works for more complex queries involving multiple tables.

Using Ranges for Qualification

The comparison operators < and > are used to establish a range of values. The keywords BETWEEN and NOT BETWEEN can also be used. For example, to find products with a standard price between $200 and $300, the following query could be used.

Query: Which products in the Product table have a standard price between $200 and $300?

```
SELECT ProductDescription, ProductStandardPrice
  FROM Product_T
    WHERE ProductStandardPrice > 199 AND ProductStandardPrice < 301;
```

Result:

PRODUCTDESCRIPTION	PRODUCTSTANDARDPRICE
Coffee Table	200
Computer Desk	250

The same result will be returned by the following query.

Query: Which products in the PRODUCT table have a standard price between $200 and $300?

```
SELECT ProductDescription, ProductStandardPrice
  FROM Product_T
    WHERE ProductStandardPrice BETWEEN 200 AND 300;
```

Result: Same as previous query.

Adding NOT before BETWEEN in this query will return all the other products in Product_T because their prices are less than $200 or more than $300.

Using Distinct Values

Sometimes when returning rows that don't include the primary key, duplicate rows will be returned. For example, look at this query and the results that it returns.

Query: What order numbers are included in the OrderLine table?

```
SELECT OrderID
  FROM OrderLine_T;
```

Eighteen rows are returned, and many of them are duplicates because many orders were for multiple items.

Result:

ORDERID
1001
1001
1001
1002
1003
1004
1004
1005
1006
1006
1006
1007
1007
1008
1008
1009
1009
1010

18 rows selected.

Do we really need the redundant OrderIDs in this result? If we add the keyword DISTINCT, then only 1 occurrence of each OrderID will be returned, 1 for each of the 10 orders represented in the table.

Query: What are the distinct order numbers included in the OrderLine table?

```
SELECT DISTINCT OrderID
  FROM OrderLine_T;
```

Result:

ORDERID
1001
1002
1003
1004
1005
1006
1007
1008
1009
1010

10 rows selected.

DISTINCT and its counterpart, ALL, can be used only once in a SELECT statement. It comes after SELECT and before any columns or expressions are listed. If a SELECT statement projects more than one column, only rows that are identical for every column will be eliminated. Thus, if the previous statement also includes OrderedQuantity, 14 rows are returned because there are now only 4 duplicate rows rather than 8. For example, both items ordered on OrderID 1004 were for 2 items, so the second pairing of 1004 and 2 will be eliminated.

Query: What are the unique combinations of order number and order quantity included in the OrderLine table?

```
SELECT DISTINCT OrderID, OrderedQuantity
  FROM OrderLine_T;
```

Result:

ORDERID	ORDEREDQUANTITY
1001	1
1001	2
1002	5
1003	3
1004	2
1005	4
1006	1
1006	2
1007	2
1007	3
1008	3
1009	2
1009	3
1010	10

14 rows selected.

Using IN and NOT IN with Lists

To match a list of values, consider using IN.

Query: List all customers who live in warmer states.

```
SELECT CustomerName, CustomerCity, CustomerState
  FROM Customer_T
    WHERE CustomerState IN ('FL', 'TX', 'CA', 'HI');
```

Result:

CUSTOMERNAME	CUSTOMERCITY	CUSTOMERSTATE
Contemporary Casuals	Gainesville	FL
Value Furniture	Plano	TX
Impressions	Sacramento	CA
California Classics	Santa Clara	CA
M and H Casual Furniture	Clearwater	FL
Seminole Interiors	Seminole	FL
Kaneohe Homes	Kaneohe	HI

7 rows selected.

IN is particularly useful in SQL statements that use subqueries, which will be covered in Chapter 7. The use of IN is also very consistent with the set nature of SQL. Very simply, the list (set of values) inside the parentheses after IN can be literals, as illustrated here, or can be a SELECT statement with a single result column, the result of which will be plugged in as the set of values for comparison. In fact, some SQL programmers always use IN, even when the set in parentheses after IN includes only one item. Similarly, any "table" of the FROM clause can be itself a derived table defined by including a SELECT statement in parentheses in the FROM clause (as we saw earlier, with the query about the difference between the standard price of each product and the average standard price of all products). The ability to include a SELECT statement anyplace within SQL where a set is involved is a very powerful and useful feature of SQL, and, of course, totally consistent with SQL being a set-oriented language, as illustrated in Figures 6-8 and 6-9.

Sorting Results: The ORDER BY Clause

Looking at the preceding results, it may seem that it would make more sense to list the California customers, followed by the Floridians, Hawaiians, and Texans. That brings us to the other three basic parts of the SQL statement:

ORDER BY	Sorts the final results rows in ascending or descending order.
GROUP BY	Groups rows in an intermediate results table where the values in those rows are the same for one or more columns.
HAVING	Can only be used following a GROUP BY and acts as a secondary WHERE clause, returning only those groups that meet a specified condition.

So, we can order the customers by adding an ORDER BY clause.

Query: List customer, city, and state for all customers in the Customer table whose address is Florida, Texas, California, or Hawaii. List the customers alphabetically by state and alphabetically by customer within each state.

```
SELECT CustomerName, CustomerCity, CustomerState
  FROM Customer_T
    WHERE CustomerState IN ('FL', 'TX', 'CA', 'HI')
      ORDER BY CustomerState, CustomerName;
```

Now the results are easier to read.

Result:

CUSTOMERNAME	CUSTOMERCITY	CUSTOMERSTATE
California Classics	Santa Clara	CA
Impressions	Sacramento	CA
Contemporary Casuals	Gainesville	FL
M and H Casual Furniture	Clearwater	FL
Seminole Interiors	Seminole	FL
Kaneohe Homes	Kaneohe	HI
Value Furniture	Plano	TX

7 rows selected.

Notice that all customers from each state are listed together, and within each state, customer names are alphabetized. The sorting order is determined by the order in which the columns are listed in the ORDER BY clause; in this case, states were alphabetized first, then customer names. If sorting from high to low, use DESC as a keyword, placed after the column used to sort. Instead of typing the column names in the ORDER BY clause, you can use their column positions in the select list; for example, in the preceding query, we could have written the clause as

```
ORDER BY 3, 1;
```

For cases in which there are many rows in the result table but you need to see only a few of them, many SQL systems (including MySQL) support a LIMIT clause, such as the following, which would show only the first five rows of the result:

```
ORDER BY 3, 1 LIMIT 5;
```

The following would show five rows after skipping the first 30 rows:

```
ORDER BY 3, 1 LIMIT 30, 5;
```

How are NULLs sorted? Null values may be placed first or last, before or after columns that have values. Where the NULLs will be placed will depend upon the SQL implementation.

Categorizing Results: The GROUP BY Clause

GROUP BY is particularly useful when paired with aggregate functions, such as SUM or COUNT. GROUP BY divides a table into subsets (by groups); then an aggregate function can be used to provide summary information for that group. The single value returned by the previous aggregate function examples is called a **scalar aggregate**. When aggregate functions are used in a GROUP BY clause and several values are returned, they are called **vector aggregates**.

Scalar aggregate
A single value returned from an SQL query that includes an aggregate function.

Vector aggregate
Multiple values returned from an SQL query that includes an aggregate function.

Query: Count the number of customers with addresses in each state to which we ship.

```
SELECT CustomerState, COUNT (CustomerState)
  FROM Customer_T
    GROUP BY CustomerState;
```

Result:

CUSTOMERSTATE	COUNT(CUSTOMERSTATE)
CA	2
CO	1
FL	3
HI	1
MI	1
NJ	2
NY	1
PA	1
TX	1
UT	1
WA	1

11 rows selected.

It is also possible to nest groups within groups; the same logic is used as when sorting multiple items.

Query: Count the number of customers with addresses in each city to which we ship. List the cities by state.

```
SELECT CustomerState, CustomerCity, COUNT (CustomerCity)
  FROM Customer_T
    GROUP BY CustomerState, CustomerCity;
```

Although the GROUP BY clause seems straightforward, it can produce unexpected results if the logic of the clause is forgotten (and this is a common "gotcha" for novice SQL coders). When a GROUP BY is included, the columns allowed to be specified in the SELECT clause are limited. Only a column with a single value for each group can be included. In the previous query, each group is identified by the combination of a city and its state. The SELECT statement includes both the city and state columns. This works because each combination of city and state is one COUNT value. But if the SELECT clause of the first query in this section had also included city, that statement would fail because the GROUP BY is only by state. Because a state can have more than one city, the requirement that each value in the SELECT clause have only one value in the GROUP BY group is not met, and SQL will not be able to present the city information so that it makes sense. *If you write queries using the following rule, your queries will work*: Each column referenced in the SELECT statement must be referenced in the GROUP BY clause, unless the column is an argument for an aggregate function included in the SELECT clause.

Qualifying Results by Categories: The HAVING Clause

The HAVING clause acts like a WHERE clause, but it identifies groups, rather than rows, that meet a criterion. Therefore, you will usually see a HAVING clause following a GROUP BY clause.

Query: Find only states with more than one customer.

```
SELECT CustomerState, COUNT (CustomerState)
  FROM Customer_T
    GROUP BY CustomerState
    HAVING COUNT (CustomerState) > 1;
```

This query returns a result that has removed all states (groups) with one customer. Remember that using WHERE here would not work because WHERE doesn't allow aggregates; further, WHERE qualifies a set of rows, whereas HAVING qualifies a set of groups. As with WHERE, the HAVING qualification can be compared to the result of a SELECT statement, which computes the value for comparison (i.e., a set with only one value is still a set).

Result:

CUSTOMERSTATE	COUNT(CUSTOMERSTATE)
CA	2
FL	3
NJ	2

To include more than one condition in the HAVING clause, use AND, OR, and NOT just as in the WHERE clause. In summary, here is one last command that includes all six clauses; remember that they must be used in this order.

Query: List, in alphabetical order, the product finish and the average standard price for each finish for selected finishes having an average standard price less than 750.

```
SELECT ProductFinish, AVG (ProductStandardPrice)
  FROM Product_T
    WHERE ProductFinish IN ('Cherry', 'Natural Ash', 'Natural Maple',
    'White Ash')
      GROUP BY ProductFinish
        HAVING AVG (ProductStandardPrice) < 750
          ORDER BY ProductFinish;
```

Result:

PRODUCTFINISH	AVG(PRODUCTSTANDARDPRICE)
Cherry	250
Natural Ash	458.333333
Natural Maple	650

Figure 6-10 shows the order in which SQL processes the clauses of a statement. Arrows indicate the paths that may be followed. Remember, only the SELECT and FROM clauses are mandatory. Notice that the processing order is different from the order of the syntax used to create the statement. As each clause is processed, an intermediate results table is produced that will be used for the next clause. Users do not see the intermediate results tables; they see only the final results. A query can be debugged by remembering the order shown in Figure 6-10. Take out the optional clauses and then add them back in one at a time in the order in which they will be processed. In this way, intermediate results can be seen and problems often can be spotted.

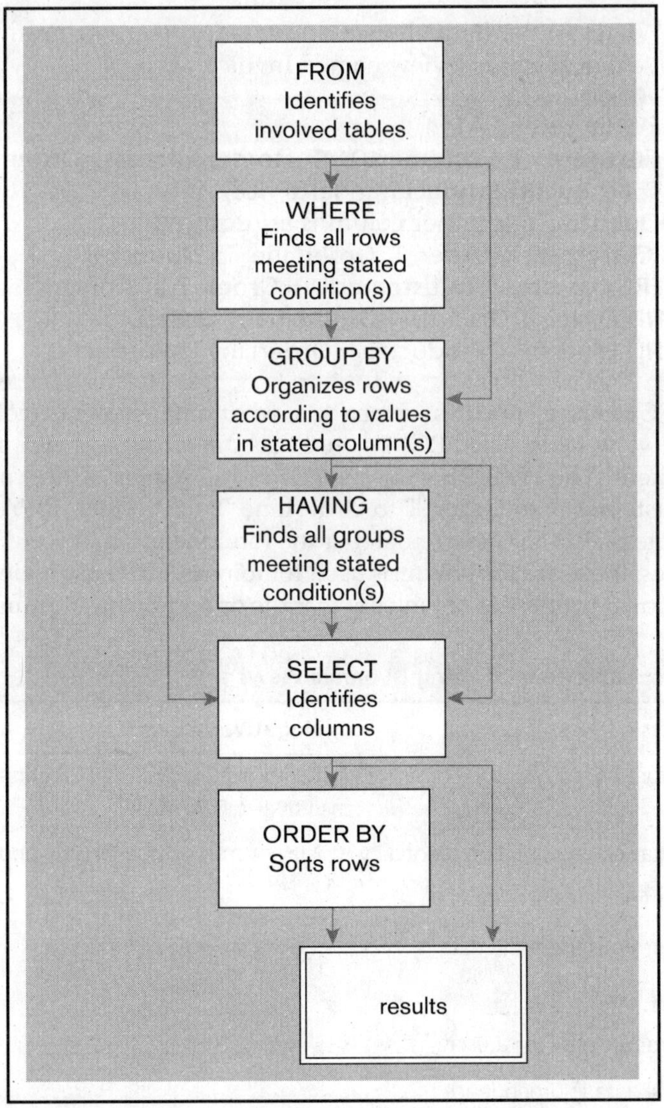

FIGURE 6-10 SQL statement processing order (adapted from van der Lans, 2006, p. 100)

Using and Defining Views

Base table
A table in the relational data model containing the inserted raw data. Base tables correspond to the relations that are identified in the database's conceptual schema.

Virtual table
A table constructed automatically as needed by a DBMS. Virtual tables are not maintained as real data.

Dynamic view
A virtual table that is created dynamically upon request by a user. A dynamic view is not a temporary table. Rather, its definition is stored in the system catalog, and the contents of the view are materialized as a result of an SQL query that uses the view. It differs from a materialized view, which may be stored on a disk and refreshed at intervals or when used, depending on the RDBMS.

Materialized view
Copies or replicas of data, based on SQL queries created in the same manner as dynamic views. However, a materialized view exists as a table and thus care must be taken to keep it synchronized with its associated base tables.

The SQL syntax shown in Figure 6-6 demonstrates the creation of four **base tables** in a database schema using Oracle 11g SQL. These tables, which are used to store data physically in the database, correspond to relations in the logical database design. By using SQL queries with any RDBMS, it is possible to create **virtual tables**, or **dynamic views**, whose contents materialize when referenced. These views may often be manipulated in the same way as a base table can be manipulated, through SQL SELECT queries. **Materialized views**, which are stored physically on a disk and refreshed at appropriate intervals or events, may also be used.

The often-stated purpose of a view is to simplify query commands, but a view may also improve data security and significantly enhance programming consistency and productivity for a database. To highlight the convenience of using a view, consider Pine Valley's invoice processing. Construction of the company's invoice requires access to the four tables from the Pine Valley database of Figure 6-3: Customer_T, Order_T, OrderLine_T, and Product_T. A novice database user may make mistakes or be unproductive in properly formulating queries involving so many tables. A view allows us to predefine this association into a single virtual table as part of the database. With this view, a user who wants only customer invoice data does not have to reconstruct the joining of tables to produce the report or any subset of it. Table 6-4 summarizes the pros and cons of using views.

A view, Invoice_V, is defined by specifying an SQL query (SELECT . . . FROM . . . WHERE) that has the view as its result. If you decide to try this query as is, without selecting additional attributes, remove the comma after OrderedQuantity. The example assumes you will elect to include additional attributes in the query.

Query: What are the data elements necessary to create an invoice for a customer? Save this query as a view named Invoice_V.

```
CREATE VIEW Invoice_V AS
  SELECT Customer_T.CustomerID, CustomerAddress, Order_T.OrderID,
  Product_T.ProductID,ProductStandardPrice,
  OrderedQuantity, and other columns as required
    FROM Customer_T, Order_T, OrderLine_T, Product_T
      WHERE Customer_T.CustomerID = Order_T.CustomerID
        AND Order_T.OrderID = OrderLine_T.OrderD
        AND Product_T.ProductID = OrderLine_T.ProductID;
```

The SELECT clause specifies, or projects, what data elements (columns) are to be included in the view table. The FROM clause lists the tables and views involved in the view development. The WHERE clause specifies the names of the common columns used to join Customer_T to Order_T to OrderLine_T to Product_T. (You'll learn about joining in Chapter 7, but for now remember the foreign keys that were defined to reference other tables; these are the columns used for joining.) Because a view is a table, and one of the relational properties of tables is that the order of rows is immaterial, the rows

TABLE 6-4 Pros and Cons of Using Dynamic Views

Positive Aspects	Negative Aspects
Simplify query commands	Use processing time re-creating the view each time it is referenced
Help provide data security and confidentiality	May or may not be directly updateable
Improve programmer productivity	
Contain most current base table data	
Use little storage space	
Provide a customized view for a user	
Establish physical data independence	

in a view may not be sorted. But queries that refer to this view may display their results in any desired sequence.

We can see the power of such a view when building a query to generate an invoice for order number 1004. Rather than specify the joining of four tables, we can have the query include all relevant data elements from the view table, Invoice_V.

Query: What are the data elements necessary to create an invoice for order number 1004?

```
SELECT CustomerID, CustomerAddress, ProductID,
  OrderedQuantity, and other columns as required
   FROM Invoice_V
     WHERE OrderID = 1004;
```

A dynamic view is a virtual table; it is constructed automatically, as needed, by the DBMS and is not maintained as persistent data. Any SQL SELECT statement may be used to create a view. The persistent data are stored in base tables, those that have been defined by CREATE TABLE commands. A dynamic view always contains the most current derived values and is thus superior in terms of data currency to constructing a temporary real table from several base tables. Also, in comparison to a temporary real table, a view consumes very little storage space. A view is costly, however, because its contents must be calculated each time they are requested (that is, each time the view is used in an SQL statement). Materialized views are now available and address this drawback.

A view may join together multiple tables or views and may contain derived (or virtual) columns. For example, if a user of the Pine Valley Furniture database only wants to know the total value of orders placed for each furniture product, a view for this can be created from Invoice_V. The following example in SQL*Plus illustrates how this is done with Oracle, although this can be done with any RDBMS that supports views.

Query: What is the total value of orders placed for each furniture product?

```
CREATE VIEW OrderTotals_V AS
  SELECT ProductID Product, SUM (ProductStandardPrice*OrderedQuantity)
  Total
   FROM Invoice_V
   GROUP BY ProductID;
```

We can assign a different name (an alias) to a view column rather than use the associated base table or expression column name. Here, Product is a renaming of ProductID, local to only this view. Total is the column name given the expression for total sales of each product. (Total may not be a legal alias with some relational DBMSs because it might be a reserved word for a proprietary function of the DBMS; you always have to be careful when defining columns and aliases not to use a reserved word.) The expression can now be referenced via this view in subsequent queries as if it were a column rather than a derived expression. Defining views based on other views can cause problems. For example, if we redefine Invoice_V so that StandardPrice is not included, then OrderTotals_V will no longer work because it will not be able to locate standard unit prices.

Views can also help to establish security. Tables and columns that are not included will not be obvious to the user of the view. Restricting access to a view with GRANT and REVOKE statements adds another layer of security. For example, granting some users access rights to aggregated data, such as averages, in a view but denying them access to detailed base table data will not allow them to display the base table data. SQL security commands are explained further in Chapter 11.

Privacy and confidentiality of data can be achieved by creating views that restrict users to working with only the data they need to perform their assigned duties. If a clerical worker needs to work with employees' addresses but should not be able to access their compensation rates, they may be given access to a view that does not contain compensation information.

Some people advocate the creation of a view for every single base table, even if that view is identical to the base table. They suggest this approach because views can contribute to greater programming productivity as databases evolve. Consider a situation in which 50 programs all use the Customer_T table. Suppose that the Pine Valley Furniture Company database evolves to support new functions that require the Customer_T table to be renormalized into two tables. If these 50 programs refer directly to the Customer_T base table, they will all have to be modified to refer to one of the two new tables or to joined tables. But if these programs all use the view on this base table, then only the view has to be re-created, saving considerable reprogramming effort. However, dynamic views require considerable run-time computer processing because the virtual table of a view is re-created each time the view is referenced. Therefore, referencing a base table through a view rather than directly can add considerable time to query processing. This additional operational cost must be balanced against the potential reprogramming savings from using a view.

It can be possible to update base table data via update commands (INSERT, DELETE, and UPDATE) against a view as long as it is unambiguous what base table data must change. For example, if the view contains a column created by aggregating base table data, then it would be ambiguous how to change the base table values if an attempt were made to update the aggregate value. If the view definition includes the WITH CHECK OPTION clause, attempts to insert data through the view will be rejected when the data values do not meet the specifications of WITH CHECK OPTION. Specifically, when the CREATE VIEW statement contains any of the following situations, that view may not be used to update the data:

1. The SELECT clause includes the keyword DISTINCT.
2. The SELECT clause contains expressions, including derived columns, aggregates, statistical functions, and so on.
3. The FROM clause, a subquery, or a UNION clause references more than one table.
4. The FROM clause or a subquery references another view that is not updateable.
5. The CREATE VIEW command contains a GROUP BY or HAVING clause.

It could happen that an update to an instance would result in the instance disappearing from the view. Let's create a view named ExpensiveStuff_V, which lists all furniture products that have a StandardPrice over $300. That view will include ProductID 5, a writer's desk, which has a unit price of $325. If we update data using Expensive_Stuff_V and reduce the unit price of the writer's desk to $295, then the writer's desk will no longer appear in the ExpensiveStuff_V virtual table because its unit price is now less than $300. In Oracle, if you want to track all merchandise with an original price over $300, include a WITH CHECK OPTION clause after the SELECT clause in the CREATE VIEW command. WITH CHECK OPTION will cause UPDATE or INSERT statements on that view to be rejected when those statements would cause updated or inserted rows to be removed from the view. This option can be used only with updateable views.

Here is the CREATE VIEW statement for ExpensiveStuff_V.

Query: List all furniture products that have ever had a standard price over $300.

```
CREATE VIEW ExpensiveStuff_V
  AS
    SELECT ProductID, ProductDescription, ProductStandardPrice
      FROM Product_T
        WHERE ProductStandardPrice > 300
        WITH CHECK OPTION;
```

When attempting to update the unit price of the writer's desk to $295 using the following Oracle SQL*Plus syntax:

```
UPDATE ExpensiveStuff_V
SET ProductStandardPrice = 295
  WHERE ProductID = 5;
```

Oracle gives the following error message:

```
ERROR at line 1:
ORA-01402: view WITH CHECK OPTION where-clause violation
```

A price increase on the writer's desk to $350 will take effect with no error message because the view is updateable and the conditions specified in the view are not violated.

Information about views will be stored in the systems tables of the DBMS. In Oracle 11g, for example, the text of all views is stored in DBA_VIEWS. Users with system privileges can find this information.

Query: List some information that is available about the view named EXPENSIVESTUFF_V. (Note that EXPENSIVESTUFF_V is stored in uppercase and must be entered in uppercase in order to execute correctly.)

```
SELECT OWNER,VIEW_NAME,TEXT_LENGTH FROM DBA_VIEWS
  WHERE VIEW_NAME = 'EXPENSIVESTUFF_V';
```

Result:

OWNER	VIEW_NAME	TEXT_LENGTH
MPRESCOTT	EXPENSIVESTUFF_V	110

MATERIALIZED VIEWS Like dynamic views, materialized views can be constructed in different ways for various purposes. Tables may be replicated in whole or in part and refreshed on a predetermined time interval or triggered when the table needs to be accessed. Materialized views can be based on queries from one or more tables. It is possible to create summary tables based on aggregations of data. Copies of remote data that use distributed data may be stored locally as materialized views. Maintenance overhead will be incurred to keep the local view synchronized with the remote base tables or data warehouse, but the use of materialized views may improve the performance of distributed queries, especially if the data in the materialized view are relatively static and do not have to be refreshed very often.

Summary

This chapter has introduced the SQL language for relational database definition (DDL), manipulation (DML), and control (DCL) languages, commonly used to define and query relational database management systems (RDBMSs). This standard has been criticized as having many flaws. In reaction to these criticisms and to increase the power of the language, extensions are constantly under review by the ANSI X3H2 committee and International Committee for Information Technology Standards (INCITS). The current generally implemented standard is SQL:1999, but SQL:2008 is under final draft review.

The establishment of SQL standards and conformance certification tests has contributed to relational systems being the dominant form of new database development. Benefits of the SQL standards include reduced training costs, improved productivity, application portability and longevity, reduced dependence on single vendors, and improved cross-system communication.

The SQL environment includes an instance of an SQL DBMS along with accessible databases and associated users and programs. Each database is included in a catalog and has a schema that describes the database objects. Information contained in the catalog is maintained by the DBMS itself rather than by the users of the DBMS.

The SQL DDL commands are used to define a database, including its creation and the creation of its tables, indexes, and views. Referential integrity is also established through DDL commands. The SQL DML commands are used to load, update, and query the database through use of the SELECT command. DCL commands are used to establish user access to the database.

SQL commands may directly affect the base tables, which contain the raw data, or they may affect a database view that has been created. Changes and updates made to views may or may not be passed on to the base tables. The basic syntax of an SQL SELECT statement contains the following keywords: SELECT, FROM, WHERE, ORDER BY, GROUP BY, and HAVING. SELECT determines which attributes will be displayed in the query results table. FROM determines which tables or views will be used in the query. WHERE sets the criteria of the query, including any joins of multiple tables that are necessary. ORDER BY determines the order in which the results will be displayed. GROUP BY is used to categorize results and may return either scalar aggregates or vector aggregates. HAVING qualifies results by categories.

Understanding the basic SQL syntax presented in this chapter should enable the reader to start using SQL effectively and to build a deeper understanding of the possibilities for more complex querying with continued practice. Advanced SQL topics are covered in Chapter 7.

Chapter Review

Key Terms

Base table 280
Catalog 249
Data control language (DCL) 250
Data definition language (DDL) 250
Data manipulation language (DML) 250
Dynamic view 280
Materialized view 280
Relational DBMS (RDBMS) 249
Scalar aggregate 277
Schema 249
Vector aggregate 277
Virtual table 280

Review Questions

1. Define each of the following terms:
   a. base table
   b. data definition language
   c. data manipulation language
   d. dynamic view
   e. materialized view
   f. referential integrity constraint
   g. relational DBMS (RDBMS)
   h. schema
   i. virtual table
2. Match the following terms to the appropriate definitions:

____ view	a. list of values
____ referential integrity constraint	b. description of a database
____ dynamic view	c. view materialized as a result of a SQL query that uses the view
____ materialized view	d. logical table
____ SQL:200n	e. missing or nonexistent value
____ null value	f. descriptions of database objects of a database
____ scalar aggregate	g. programming language in which SQL commands are embedded
____ vector aggregate	h. established in relational data models by use of foreign keys
____ catalog	i. view that exists as a table
____ schema	j. currently proposed standard relational query and definition language
____ host language	k. single value

3. Contrast the following terms:
   a. base table; view
   b. dynamic view; materialized view
   c. catalog; schema
4. What are SQL-92, SQL:1999, and SQL:200n? Briefly describe how SQL:200n differs from SQL:1999.
5. Describe a relational DBMS (RDBMS), its underlying data model, its data storage structures, and how data relationships are established.
6. List six potential benefits of achieving an SQL standard that is widely accepted.
7. Describe the components and structure of a typical SQL environment.
8. Distinguish among data definition commands, data manipulation commands, and data control commands.
9. Explain how referential integrity is established in databases that are SQL:1999 compliant. Explain how the ON UPDATE RESTRICT, ON UPDATE CASCADE, and ON UPDATE SET NULL clauses differ from one another. What happens if the ON DELETE CASCADE clause is set?
10. Explain some possible purposes of creating a view using SQL. In particular, explain how a view can be used to reinforce data security.
11. Explain why it is necessary to limit the kinds of updates performed on data when referencing data through a view.
12. Describe a set of circumstances for which using a view can save reprogramming effort.
13. Drawing on material covered in prior chapters, explain the factors to be considered in deciding whether to create a key index for a table in SQL.
14. Explain and provide at least one example of how to qualify the ownership of a table in SQL. What has to occur for one user to be allowed to use a table in a database owned by another user?
15. How is the order in which attributes appear in a result table changed? How are the column heading labels in a result table changed?
16. What is the difference between COUNT, COUNT DISTINCT, and COUNT(*) in SQL? When will these three commands generate the same and different results?
17. What is the evaluation order for the Boolean operators (AND, OR, NOT) in an SQL command? How can one be sure that the operators will work in the desired order rather than in this prescribed order?
18. If an SQL statement includes a GROUP BY clause, the attributes that can be requested in the SELECT statement will be limited. Explain that limitation.
19. Describe a situation in which you would need to write a query using the HAVING clause.
20. In what clause of a SELECT statement is an IN operator used? What follows the IN operator? What other SQL operator can sometimes be used to perform the same operation as the IN operator? Under what circumstances can this other operator be used?
21. Explain why SQL is called a set-oriented language.
22. When would the use of the LIKE keyword with the CREATE TABLE command be helpful?
23. What is an identity column? Explain the benefits of using the identity column capability in SQL.
24. SQL:200n has a new keyword, MERGE. Explain how using this keyword allows one to accomplish updating and merging data into a table using one command rather than two.
25. In what order are the clauses of an SQL statement processed?
26. Within which clauses of an SQL statement can a derived table be defined?
27. In an ORDER BY clause, what are the two ways to refer to the columns to be used for sorting the results of the query?
28. Explain the purpose of the CHECK clause within a CREATE TABLE SQL command. Explain the purpose of the WITH CHECK OPTION in a CREATE VIEW SQL command.
29. What can be changed about a table definition, using the ALTER SQL command? Can you identify anything about a

table definition that cannot be changed using the ALTER SQL command?

30. Is it possible to use both a WHERE clause and a HAVING clause in the same SQL SELECT statement? If so, what are the different purposes of these two clauses?

31. What are the basic operations that can be performed on data that is stored?

32. What is the purpose of the GROUP By clause? Why should the attribute used in the GROUP By clause also appear in the SELECT Statement?

33. What is the difference between

a. COUNT() and COUNT(*) functions

b. DELETE and TRUNCATE commands

c. HAVING and WHERE clauses

Problems and Exercises

Problems and Exercises 1 through 9 are based on the class scheduling 3NF relations along with some sample data shown in Figure 6-11. Not shown in this figure are data for an ASSIGNMENT relation, which represents a many-to-many relationship between faculty and sections.

1. Write a database description for each of the relations shown, using SQL DDL (shorten, abbreviate, or change any data names, as needed for your SQL version). Assume the following attribute data types:

StudentID (integer, primary key)
StudentName (25 characters)
FacultyID (integer, primary key)
FacultyName (25 characters)
CourseID (8 characters, primary key)

STUDENT (StudentID, StudentName)

StudentID	StudentName
38214	Letersky
54907	Altvater
66324	Aiken
70542	Marra
...	

QUALIFIED (FacultyID, CourseID, DateQualified)

FacultyID	CourseID	DateQualified
2143	ISM 3112	9/1988
2143	ISM 3113	9/1988
3467	ISM 4212	9/1995
3467	ISM 4930	9/1996
4756	ISM 3113	9/1991
4756	ISM 3112	9/1991
...		

FACULTY (FacultyID, FacultyName)

FacultyID	FacultyName
2143	Birkin
3467	Berndt
4756	Collins
...	

SECTION (SectionNo, Semester, CourseID)

SectionNo	Semester	CourseID
2712	I-2008	ISM 3113
2713	I-2008	ISM 3113
2714	I-2008	ISM 4212
2715	I-2008	ISM 4930
...		

COURSE (CourseID, CourseName)

CourseID	CourseName
ISM 3113	Syst Analysis
ISM 3112	Syst Design
ISM 4212	Database
ISM 4930	Networking
...	

REGISTRATION (StudentID, SectionNo, Semester)

StudentID	SectionNo	Semester
38214	2714	I-2008
54907	2714	I-2008
54907	2715	I-2008
66324	2713	I-2008
...		

FIGURE 6-11 **Class scheduling relations (missing ASSIGNMENT)**

CourseName (15 characters)
DateQualified (date)
SectionNo (integer, primary key)
Semester (7 characters)

2. Use SQL to define the following view:

StudentID	StudentName
38214	Letersky
54907	Altvater
54907	Altvater
66324	Aiken

3. Because of referential integrity, before any row can be entered into the SECTION table, the CourseID to be entered must already exist in the COURSE table. Write an SQL assertion that will enforce this constraint.
4. Write SQL data definition commands for each of the following queries:
   a. How would you add an attribute, Class, to the Student table?
   b. How would you remove the Registration table?
   c. How would you change the FacultyName field from 25 characters to 40 characters?
5. Write SQL commands for the following:
   a. Create two different forms of the INSERT command to add a student with a student ID of 65798 and last name Lopez to the Student table.
   b. Now write a command that will remove Lopez from the Student table.
   c. Create an SQL command that will modify the name of course ISM 4212 from Database to Introduction to Relational Databases.
6. Write SQL queries to answer the following questions:
   a. Which students have an ID number that is less than 50000?
   b. What is the name of the faculty member whose ID is 4756?
   c. What is the smallest section number used in the first semester of 2008?
7. Write SQL queries to answer the following questions:
   a. How many students are enrolled in Section 2714 in the first semester of 2008?
   b. Which faculty members have qualified to teach a course since 1993? List the faculty ID, course, and date of qualification.
8. Write SQL queries to answer the following questions:
   a. Which students are enrolled in Database and Networking? (Hint: Use SectionNo for each class so you can determine the answer from the Registration table by itself.)
   b. Which instructors cannot teach both Syst Analysis and Syst Design?
9. Write SQL queries to answer the following questions:
   a. What are the courses included in the Section table? List each course only once.
   b. List all students in alphabetical order by StudentName.
   c. List the students who are enrolled in each course in Semester I, 2008. Group the students by the sections in which they are enrolled.
   d. List the courses available. Group them by course prefix. (ISM is the only prefix shown, but there are many others throughout the university.)

Problems and Exercises 10 through 15 are based on the relations shown in Figure 6-12. The database tracks an adult literacy program. Tutors complete a certification class offered by the agency. Students complete an assessment interview that results in a report for the tutor and a recorded Read score. When matched with a student, a tutor meets with the student for one to four hours per week. Some students work with the same tutor for years, some for less than a month. Other students change tutors if their learning style does not match the tutor's tutoring style. Many tutors are retired and are available to tutor only part of the year. Tutor status is recorded as Active, Temp Stop, or Dropped.

10. How many tutors have a status of Temp Stop? Which tutors are active?
11. List the tutors who took the certification class in January.
12. How many students were matched with someone in the first five months of the year?
13. Which student has the highest Read score?
14. How long had each student studied in the adult literacy program?
15. What is the average length of time a student stayed (or has stayed) in the program?

PINE VALLEY FURNITURE

Problems and Exercises 16 through 43 are based on the entire ("big" version) Pine Valley Furniture Company database. Note: Depending on what DBMS you are using, some field names may have changed to avoid using reserved words for the DBMS. When you first use the DBMS, check the table definitions to see what the exact field names are for the DBMS you are using. See the Preface and inside covers of this book for instructions on where to find this database on **www.teradatastudentnetwork.com.**

16. Modify the Product_T table by adding an attribute QtyOnHand that can be used to track the finished goods inventory. The field should be an integer field of five characters and should accept only positive numbers.
17. Enter sample data of your own choosing into QtyOnHand in the Product_T table. Test the modification you made in Problem and Exercise 16 by attempting to update a product by changing the inventory to 10,000 units. Test it again by changing the inventory for the product to –10 units. If you do not receive error messages and are successful in making these changes, then you did not establish appropriate constraints in Problem and Exercise 16.
18. Add an order to the Order_T table and include a sample value for every attribute.
    a. First, look at the data in the Customer_T table and enter an order from any one of those customers.
    b. Enter an order from a new customer. Unless you have also inserted information about the new customer in the Customer_T table, your entry of the order data should be rejected. Referential integrity constraints should prevent you from entering an order if there is no information about the customer.
19. Use the Pine Valley database to answer the following questions:
    a. How many work centers does Pine Valley have?
    b. Where are they located?
20. List the employees whose last names begin with an *L*.
21. Which employees were hired during 1999?
22. List the customers who live in California or Washington. Order them by zip code, from high to low.
23. List all raw materials that are made of cherry and that have dimensions (thickness and width) of 12 by 12.
24. List the MaterialID, MaterialName, Material, MaterialStandardPrice, and Thickness for all raw materials

FIGURE 6-12 Adult literacy program (for Problems and Exercises 10 through 15)

TUTOR (TutorID, CertDate, Status)

TutorID	CertDate	Status
100	1/05/2008	Active
101	1/05/2008	Temp Stop
102	1/05/2008	Dropped
103	5/22/2008	Active
104	5/22/2008	Active
105	5/22/2008	Temp Stop
106	5/22/2008	Active

STUDENT (StudentID, Read)

StudentID	Read
3000	2.3
3001	5.6
3002	1.3
3003	3.3
3004	2.7
3005	4.8
3006	7.8
3007	1.5

MATCH HISTORY (MatchID, TutorID, StudentID, StartDate, EndDate)

MatchID	TutorID	StudentID	StartDate	EndDate
1	100	3000	1/10/2008	
2	101	3001	1/15/2008	5/15/2008
3	102	3002	2/10/2008	3/01/2008
4	106	3003	5/28/2008	
5	103	3004	6/01/2008	6/15/2008
6	104	3005	6/01/2008	6/28/2008
7	104	3006	6/01/2008	

made of cherry, pine, or walnut. Order the listing by Material, StandardPrice, and Thickness.

25. Display the product line ID and the average standard price for all products in each product line.
26. For every product that has been ordered, display the product ID and the total quantity ordered (label this result TotalOrdered). List the most popular product first and the least popular last.
27. For each customer, list the CustomerID and total number of orders placed.
28. For each salesperson, display a list of CustomerIDs.
29. Display the product ID and the number of orders placed for each product. Show the results in decreasing order by the number of times the product has been ordered and label this result column NumOrders.

30. For each customer, list the CustomerID and the total number of orders placed in 2010.
31. For each salesperson, list the total number of orders.
32. For each customer who had more than two orders, list the CustomerID and the total number of orders placed.
33. List all sales territories (TerritoryID) that have more than one salesperson.
34. Which product is ordered most frequently?
35. Display the territory ID and the number of salespersons in the territory for all territories that have more than one salesperson. Label the number of salespersons NumSalesPersons.
36. Display the SalesPersonID and a count of the number of orders for that salesperson for all salespersons except salespersons 3, 5, and 9. Write this query with as few clauses or components as possible, using the capabilities of SQL as much as possible.
37. For each salesperson, list the total number of orders by month for the year 2010. (Hint: If you are using Access, use the Month function. If you are using Oracle, convert the date to a string, using the TO_CHAR function, with the format string 'Mon' [i.e., TO_CHAR(order_date,'MON')]. If you are using another DBMS, you will need to investigate how to deal with months for this query.)
38. List MaterialName, Material, and Width for raw materials that are *not* cherry or oak and whose width is greater than 10 inches.
39. List ProductID, ProductDescription, ProductFinish, and ProductStandardPrice for oak products with a ProductStandardPrice greater than $400 or cherry products with a StandardPrice less than $300
40. For each order, list the order ID, customer ID, order date, and most recent date among all orders.
41. For each customer, list the customer ID, the number of orders from that customer, and the ratio of the number of orders from that customer to the total number of orders from all customers combined. (This ratio, of course, is the percentage of all orders placed by each customer.)
42. For products 1, 2, and 7, list in one row and three respective columns that product's total unit sales; label the three columns Prod1, Prod2, and Prod7.
43. Not all versions of this database include referential integrity constraints for all foreign keys. Use whatever commands are available for the RDBMS you are using, investigate if any referential integrity constraints are missing. Write any missing constraints and, if possible, add them to the associated table definitions.
44. Tyler Richardson set up a house alarm system when he moved to his new home in Seattle. For security purposes, he has all of his mail, including his alarm system bill, mailed to his local UPS store. Although the alarm system is activated and the company is aware of its physical address, Richardson receives repeated offers mailed to his physical address, imploring him to protect his house with the system he currently uses. What do you think the problem might be with that company's database(s)?
45. Write the SQL DDL command descriptions for each of the following relations:

Table Name: EMP Table

Attribute	Data Type	Length	Constraint
EMPNO	INTEGER	NA	NOT NULL, PRIMARY KEY
ENAME	CHARACTER	25	
JOB	CHARACTER	15	
JOINDATE	DATE	NA	
SALARY	INTEGER	NA	
DEPTNO	INTEGER	NA	NOT NULL, FOREIGN KEY

Table Name: BONUS Table

Attribute	Data Type	Length	Constraint
EMPNO	INTEGER	NA	NOT NULL, FOREIGN KEY
COMM	INTEGER	NA	

Table Name: DEPT Table

Attribute	Data Type	Length	Constraint
DEPTNO	INTEGER	NA	PRIMARY KEY
DEPTNAME	CHARACTER	15	

Change the data types as needed for your version of SQL.

46. Write an SQL command for each of the following queries (refer to the tables given above for the query to be issued):
    a. How would you list all unique JOB in the EMP table?
    b. Find the employees who are earning salaries between 22,000 and 30,000?
    c. Increase the salary of all the employees by 10%.
47. Write an SQL command for each of the following queries (refer to the tables created in the above question for the query to be issued):
    a. Find the total amount paid as salary to the employees belonging.
    b. List all the employees whose COMM is greater than their SALARY.
    c. Define the following view:

ENAME	JOB	JOINDATE
....	....	....
....	....	....

Field Exercises

1. Arrange an interview with a database administrator in an organization in your area. When you interview the database administrator, familiarize yourself with one application that is actively used in the organization. Focus your interview questions on determining end users' involvement with the application and understanding the extent to which end users must be familiar with SQL. For example, if end users are using SQL, what training do they receive? Do they use an interactive form of SQL for their work, or do they use embedded SQL? How have the required skills of the end users changed over the past few years, as the database user interfaces have changed?

2. Arrange an interview with a database administrator in your area. Focus the interview on understanding the environment within which SQL is used in the organization. Inquire about the version of SQL that is used and determine whether the same version is used at all locations. If different versions are used, explore any difficulties that the DBA has had in administering the database. Also inquire about any proprietary languages, such as Oracle's PL*SQL, that are being used. Learn about possible differences in versions used at different locations and explore any difficulties that occur if different versions are installed.
3. Arrange an interview with a database administrator in your area who has at least seven years of experience as a database administrator. Focus the interview on understanding how DBA responsibilities and the way they are completed have changed during the DBA's tenure. Does the DBA have to generate more or less SQL code to administer the databases now than in the past? Has the position become more or less stressful?

References

Arvin, T. 2005. "Comparison of Different SQL Implementations" this and other information accessed at **http://troelsarvin.blogspot.com**.

Codd, E. F. 1970. "A Relational Model of Data for Large Shared Data Banks." *Communications of the ACM* 13,6 (June): 77–87.

Date, C. J., and H. Darwen. 1997. *A Guide to the SQL Standard*. Reading, MA: Addison-Wesley.

Eisenberg, A., J. Melton, K. Kulkarni, J. E. Michels, and F. Zemke. 2004. "SQL:2003 Has Been Published." *SIGMOD Record* 33,1 (March):119–126.

Gorman, M. M. 2001. "Is SQL a Real Standard Anymore?" *The Data Administration Newsletter* (July), available at **www.tdan.com/i016hy01.htm**.

Lai, E. 2007. "IDC: Oracle Extended Lead Over IBM in 2006 Database Market." *Computerworld* (April 26), available at **www.computerworld.com/action/article.do?command=viewArticleBasic&articleId=9017898&intsrc=news_list**.

van der Lans, R. F. 2006. *Introduction to SQL; Mastering the Relational Database Language*, 4th ed. Workingham, UK: Addison-Wesley.

Further Reading

Bagui, S., and R. Earp. 2006. *Learning SQL on SQL Server 2005*. Sebastopol, CA: O'Reilly Media, Inc.

Bordoloi, B., and D. Bock. 2004. *Oracle SQL*. Upper Saddle River, NJ: Pearson Prentice Hall.

Celko, J. 2006. *Joe Celko's SQL Puzzles & Answers*, 2nd ed. San Francisco: Morgan Kaufmann.

Guerrero, F. G., and C. E. Rojas. 2001. *Microsoft SQL Server 2000 Programming by Example*. Indianapolis: QUE Corporation.

Gulutzan, P., and T. Petzer. 1999. *SQL-99 Complete, Really*. Lawrence, KS: R&D Books.

Nielsen, P. 2003. *Microsoft SQL Server 2000 Bible*. New York: Wiley Publishing, Inc.

Web Resources

http://standards.ieee.org The home page of the IEEE Standards Association.

http://troelsarvin.blogspot.com/ Blog that provides a detailed comparison of different SQL implementations, including DB2, Microsoft SQL, MySQL, Oracle, and PostGreSQL.

www.1keydata.com/sql/sql.html Web site that provides tutorials on a subset of ANSI standard SQL commands.

www.ansi.org Information on ANSI and the latest national and international standards.

www.coderecipes.net Web site that explains and shows examples for a wide range of SQL commands.

www.fluffycat.com/SQL/ Web site that defines a sample database and shows examples of SQL queries against this database.

www.incits.org The home page of the International Committee for Information Technology Standards, which used to be the National Committee for Information Technology Standards, which used to be the Accredited Standard Committee X3.

www.iso.ch International Organization for Standardization Web site, from which copies of current standards may be purchased.

www.itl.nist.gov/div897/ctg/dm/sql_examples.htm Web site that shows examples of SQL commands for creating tables and views, updating table contents, and performing some SQL database administration commands.

www.java2s.com/Code/SQL/CatalogSQL.htm Web site that provides tutorials on SQL in a MySQL environment.

www.mysql.com The official home page for MySQL, which includes many free downloadable components for working with MySQL.

www.paragoncorporation.com/ArticleDetail.aspx?ArticleID=27 Web site that provides a brief explanation of the power of SQL and a variety of sample SQL queries.

www.sqlcourse.com and www.sqlcourse2.com Web sites that provide tutorials for a subset of ANSI SQL, along with a practice database.

www.teradatastudentnetwork.com Web site where your instructor may have created some course environments for you to use Teradata SQL Assistant, Web Edition, with one or more of the Pine Valley Furniture and Mountain View Community Hospital data sets for this text.

www.tizag.com/sqlTutorial/ A set of tutorials on SQL concepts and commands.

www.wiscorp.com/SQLStandards.html Whitemarsh Information Systems Corp., a good source of information about SQL standards, including SQL:2003 and later standards.

CASE

Mountain View Community Hospital

Case Description

This case segment uses the physical designs you constructed for Mountain View Community Hospital (MVCH) in Chapter 5 to complete the case questions and case exercises.

Case Questions

1. What version of SQL and what RDBMS will you use to do the case exercises?
2. Which CASE tools are available for completing the case exercises? Can the CASE tool you are using generate the database schema from the physical data model(s) you created?
3. Can you suggest an easy way to populate your tables if you want to create a large set of test data?
4. How do the actual values you are using help you to test the functionality of your database?

Case Exercises

1. In Case Exercise 1 in Chapter 5, you created the physical data model for Dr. Z's database that keeps track of patients checking in. You may recall that Dr. Z decided to use SQL Server. Instructions for installing SQL Server and SQL Server Management Studio Express are available in the Pine Valley sample database area of this book's Web site.
   a. Using the design you created in Chapter 5, create the database and tables using SQL. Be sure to create the SQL assertions necessary to ensure referential integrity and other constraints.
   b. Populate the database with sample data. (MVCH Figure 4-5 in Chapter 4 provides some sample data, but you need a few more patients and visits for the queries in part c.)
   c. Write and test some queries that will work using your sample data. Write queries that
      i. Select information from only one of the tables (e.g., an alphabetical listing of all patients, an alphabetical listing of all the patients assigned to one of the social workers, etc.).
      ii. Aggregate information from one attribute in a table (e.g., How often has patient 8766 visited the MS Center at MVCH in a given month? How many patients are assigned to each social worker?).
      iii. Try out the various functions, such as MIN, MAX, and AVG (e.g., What is the average level of pain reported by Dr. Z's patients? What is the worst level of pain his patients have experienced?).
2. Using your database from Case Exercise 1, write and test SQL queries that
   a. Select information from only one of the tables.
   b. Aggregate information from one attribute in a table.
   c. Try out the various functions, such as MIN, MAX, and AVG.
   d. Qualify results by category.

Project Assignments

P1. Use the physical data model you created in Chapter 5 to guide you in writing the SQL statements for creating the MVCH database for the relational schema you created in Chapter 4.
   a. Write the SQL statements for creating the tables, specifying data types and field lengths, establishing primary keys and foreign keys, and implementing other constraints you identified.
   b. Following the examples in Chapter 5, write the SQL statements that create the indexes.

P2. Select a portion of your database and populate it with sample data. Be prepared to defend the sample test data that you insert into your database.

P3. Write and execute a variety of queries, based on the introduction to SQL in this chapter to test the functionality of your database. Ensure that your queries are correct and produce the results you expected.

CHAPTER

7

Advanced SQL

Learning Objectives

After studying this chapter, you should be able to:

- Concisely define each of the following key terms: **join, equi-join, natural join, outer join, correlated subquery, user-defined data type, Persistent Stored Modules (SQL/PSM), trigger, function, procedure, embedded SQL,** and **dynamic SQL.**
- Write single- and multiple-table queries using SQL commands.
- Define three types of join commands and use SQL to write these commands.
- Write noncorrelated and correlated subqueries and know when to write each.
- Establish referential integrity using SQL.
- Understand common uses of database triggers and stored procedures.
- Discuss the SQL:200n standard and explain its enhancements and extensions.

INTRODUCTION

The previous chapter introduced SQL and explored its capabilities for querying one table. The real power of the relational model derives from its storage of data in many related entities. Taking advantage of this approach to data storage requires establishing relationships and constructing queries that use data from multiple tables. This chapter examines multiple-table queries in some detail. Different approaches to getting results from more than one table are demonstrated, including the use of subqueries, inner and outer joins, and union joins.

Once an understanding of basic SQL syntax is gained, it is important to understand how SQL is used in the creation of applications. Triggers, small modules of code that include SQL, execute automatically when a particular condition, defined in the trigger, exists. Procedures are similar modules of code but must be called before they execute. SQL commands are often embedded within modules written in a host language, such as C, PHP, .NET, or Java. Dynamic SQL creates SQL statements on the fly, inserting parameter values as needed, and is essential to Web applications. Brief introductions and examples of each of these methods are included in this chapter. Some of the enhancements and extensions to SQL included in SQL:200n are also covered. Oracle, a leading RDBMS vendor, is SQL:1999 compliant.

Completion of this chapter gives the student an overview of SQL and some of the ways in which it may be used. Many additional features, often referred to as "obscure" in more detailed SQL texts, will be needed in particular situations. Practice with the syntax included in this chapter will give you a good start toward mastery of SQL.

PROCESSING MULTIPLE TABLES

PINE VALLEY FURNITURE

Now that we have explored some of the possibilities for working with a single table, it's time to bring out the light sabers, jet packs, and tools for heavy lifting: We will work with multiple tables simultaneously. The power of RDBMSs is realized when working with multiple tables. When relationships exist among tables, the tables can be linked together in queries. Remember from Chapter 4 that these relationships are established by including a common column(s) in each table where a relationship is needed. Often this is accomplished by setting up a primary key–foreign key relationship, where the foreign key in one table references the primary key in another, and the values in both come from a common domain. We can use these columns to establish a link between two tables by finding common values in the columns. Figure 7-1 carries forward two relations from Figure 6-3, depicting part of the Pine Valley Furniture Company database. Notice that CustomerID values in Order_T correspond to CustomerID values in Customer_T. Using this correspondence, we can deduce that Contemporary Casuals placed orders 1001 and 1010 because Contemporary Casuals's CustomerID is 1, and Order_T shows that OrderID 1001 and 1010 were placed by customer 1. In a relational system, data from related tables are combined into one result table or view and then displayed or used as input to a form or report definition.

The linking of related tables varies among different types of relational systems. In SQL, the WHERE clause of the SELECT command is also used for multiple-table operations. In fact, SELECT can include references to two, three, or more tables in the same command. As illustrated next, SQL has two ways to use SELECT for combining data from related tables.

Join
A relational operation that causes two tables with a common domain to be combined into a single table or view.

The most frequently used relational operation, which brings together data from two or more related tables into one resultant table, is called a **join**. Originally, SQL specified a join implicitly by referring in a WHERE clause to the matching of common columns over which tables were joined. Since SQL-92, joins may also be specified in the FROM clause. In either case, two tables may be joined when each contains a column that shares a common domain with the other. As mentioned previously, a primary key from one table and a foreign key that references the table with the primary key will share a common domain and are frequently used to establish a join. Occasionally, joins will be established using columns that share a common domain but not the primary-foreign key relationship, and that also works (e.g., we might join customers and salespersons based on common postal codes, for which there is no relationship in the data model for the database). The result of a join operation is a single table. Selected columns from all the tables are included. Each row returned contains data from rows in the different input tables where values for the common columns match.

Explicit JOIN . . . ON commands are included in the FROM clause. The following join operations are included in the standard, though each RDBMS product is likely to support only a subset of the keywords: INNER, OUTER, FULL, LEFT, RIGHT, CROSS, and UNION. (We'll explain these in a following section.) NATURAL is an optional keyword. No matter what form of join you are using, *there should be one ON or WHERE specification for each pair of tables being joined.* Thus, if two tables are to be combined, one ON or WHERE condition would be necessary, but if three tables (A, B, and C) are to be combined, then two

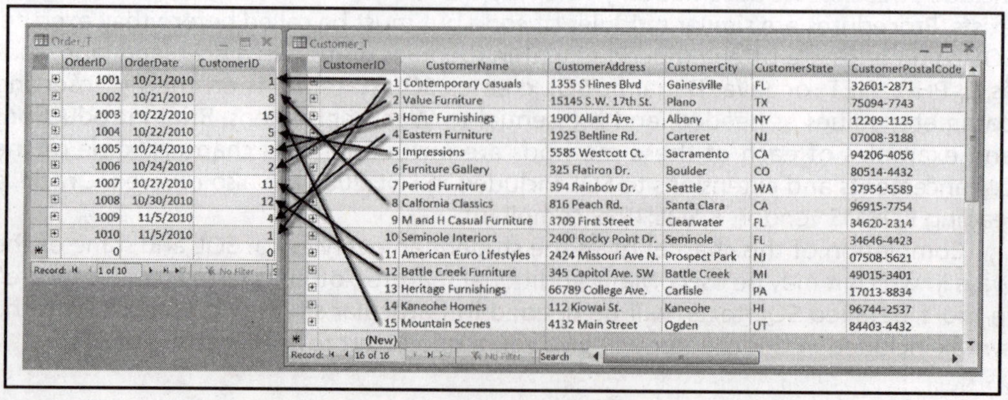
Order_T

OrderID	OrderDate	CustomerID
1001	10/21/2010	1
1002	10/21/2010	8
1003	10/22/2010	15
1004	10/22/2010	5
1005	10/24/2010	3
1006	10/24/2010	2
1007	10/27/2010	11
1008	10/30/2010	12
1009	11/5/2010	4
1010	11/5/2010	1
0		0

Record: 1 of 10

Customer_T

CustomerID	CustomerName	CustomerAddress	CustomerCity	CustomerState	CustomerPostalCode
1	Contemporary Casuals	1355 S Hines Blvd	Gainesville	FL	32601-2871
2	Value Furniture	15145 S.W. 17th St.	Plano	TX	75094-7743
3	Home Furnishings	1900 Allard Ave.	Albany	NY	12209-1125
4	Eastern Furniture	1925 Beltline Rd.	Carteret	NJ	07008-3188
5	Impressions	5585 Westcott Ct.	Sacramento	CA	94206-4056
6	Furniture Gallery	325 Flatiron Dr.	Boulder	CO	80514-4432
7	Period Furniture	394 Rainbow Dr.	Seattle	WA	97954-5589
8	Calfornia Classics	816 Peach Rd.	Santa Clara	CA	96915-7754
9	M and H Casual Furniture	3709 First Street	Clearwater	FL	34620-2314
10	Seminole Interiors	2400 Rocky Point Dr.	Seminole	FL	34646-4423
11	American Euro Lifestyles	2424 Missouri Ave N.	Prospect Park	NJ	07508-5621
12	Battle Creek Furniture	345 Capitol Ave. SW	Battle Creek	MI	49015-3401
13	Heritage Furnishings	66789 College Ave.	Carlisle	PA	17013-8834
14	Kaneohe Homes	112 Kiowai St.	Kaneohe	HI	96744-2537
15	Mountain Scenes	4132 Main Street	Ogden	UT	84403-4432
(New)					

Record: 16 of 16

FIGURE 7-1 Pine Valley Furniture Company Customer_T and Order_T tables, with pointers from customers to their orders

ON or WHERE conditions would be necessary because there are 2 pairs of tables (A-B and B-C), and so forth. Most systems support up to 10 pairs of tables within one SQL command. At this time, core SQL does not support CROSS JOIN, UNION JOIN, FULL [OUTER] JOIN, or the keyword NATURAL. Knowing this should help you understand why you may not find these implemented in the RDBMS you are using. Because they are included in the SQL:200n standard and are useful, expect to find them becoming more widely available.

The various types of joins are described in the following sections.

Equi-join

With an **equi-join**, the joining condition is based on *equality* between values in the common columns. For example, if we want to know data about customers who have placed orders, that information is kept in two tables, Customer_T and Order_T. It is necessary to match customers with their orders and then collect the information about, for example, customer name and order number in one table in order to answer our question. We call the table created by the query the result or *answer table.*

Equi-join
A join in which the joining condition is based on equality between values in the common columns. Common columns appear (redundantly) in the result table.

Query: What are the customer IDs and names of all customers, along with the order IDs for all the orders they have placed?

```
SELECT Customer_T.CustomerID, Order_T.CustomerID,
 CustomerName, OrderID
   FROM Customer_T, Order_T
     WHERE Customer_T.CustomerID = Order_T. CustomerID
     ORDER BY OrderID
```

Result:

CUSTOMERID	CUSTOMERID	CUSTOMERNAME	ORDERID
1	1	Contemporary Casuals	1001
8	8	California Classics	1002
15	15	Mountain Scenes	1003
5	5	Impressions	1004
3	3	Home Furnishings	1005
2	2	Value Furniture	1006
11	11	American Euro Lifestyles	1007
12	12	Battle Creek Furniture	1008
4	4	Eastern Furniture	1009
1	1	Contemporary Casuals	1010

10 rows selected.

The redundant CustomerID columns, one from each table, demonstrate that the customer IDs have been matched and that matching gives one row for each order placed. We prefixed the CustomerID columns with the names of their respective tables so SQL knows which CustomerID column we referenced in each element of the SELECT list; we did not have to prefix CustomerName nor OrderID with their associated table names because each of these columns is found in only one table in the FROM list.

The importance of achieving the match between tables can be seen if the WHERE clause is omitted. That query will return all combinations of customers and orders, or 150 rows, and includes all possible combinations of the rows from the two tables (i.e., an order will be matched with every customer, not just the customer who placed that order). In this case, this join does not reflect the relationships that exist between the tables and is not a useful or meaningful result. The number of rows is equal to the number of rows in each table, multiplied together (10 orders × 15 customers = 150 rows). This is called a *Cartesian join*. Cartesian joins with spurious results will occur when any joining component of a WHERE clause with multiple conditions is missing or erroneous. In the rare case that a Cartesian join is desired, omit the pairings in the WHERE clause. A Cartesian join may be explicitly created by using the phrase CROSS JOIN in the FROM statement. FROM Customer_T CROSS JOIN Order_T would create a Cartesian product of all customers with all orders. (Use this query only if you really mean to because a cross join against a production database can produce hundreds of thousands of rows and can consume significant computer time—plenty of time to receive a pizza delivery!)

The keywords INNER JOIN . . . ON are used to establish an equi-join in the FROM clause. While the syntax demonstrated here is Microsoft Access SQL syntax, note that some systems, such as Oracle and Microsoft SQL Server, treat the keyword JOIN by itself without the word INNER to establish an equi-join:

Query: What are the customer IDs and names of all customers, along with the order IDs for all the orders they have placed?

```
SELECT Customer_T.CustomerID, Order_T.CustomerID,
  CustomerName, OrderID
FROM Customer_T INNER JOIN Order_T ON
  Customer_T.CustomerID = Order_T.CustomerID
ORDER BY OrderID;
```

Result: Same as the previous query.

Simplest of all would be to use the JOIN . . . USING syntax, if this is supported by the RDBMS you are using. If the database designer thought ahead and used identical column names for the primary and foreign keys, as has been done with CustomerID in the Customer_T and Order_T tables, the following query could be used:

```
SELECT Customer_T.CustomerID, Order_T.CustomerID,
  CustomerName, OrderID
FROM Customer_T INNER JOIN Order_T USING CustomerID
ORDER BY OrderID ;
```

Notice that the WHERE clause now functions only in its traditional role as a filter as needed. Since the FROM clause is generally evaluated prior to the WHERE clause, some users prefer using the newer syntax of ON or USING in the FROM clause. A smaller record set that meets the join conditions is all that must be evaluated by the remaining clauses, and performance may improve. All DBMS products support the traditional method of defining joins within the WHERE clause. Microsoft SQL Server supports the INNER JOIN . . . ON syntax, Oracle has supported it since 9i, and MySQL has supported it since 3.23.17.

We again emphasize that SQL is a set-oriented language. Thus, this join example is produced by taking the customer table and the order table as two sets and appending together those rows from Customer_T with rows from Order_T that have equal CustomerID values. This is a set intersection operation, which is followed by appending the selected columns from the matching rows. Figure 7-2 uses set diagrams to display the most common types of two-table joins.

Natural Join

Natural join
A join that is the same as an equi-join except that one of the duplicate columns is eliminated in the result table.

A **natural join** is the same as an equi-join, except that it is performed over matching columns, and one of the duplicate columns is eliminated in the result table. The natural join is the most commonly used form of join operation. (No, a "natural" join is not a more healthy join with more fiber, and there is no un-natural join; but you will find it a natural and essential function with relational databases.) Notice in the command below that CustomerID must still be qualified because there is still ambiguity; CustomerID

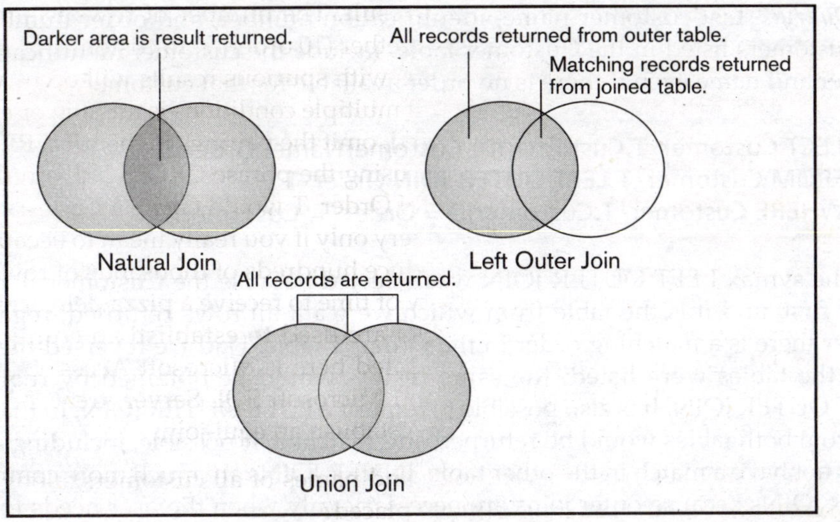

FIGURE 7-2 Visualization of different join types, with the results returned in the shaded area

exists in both Customer_T and Order_T, and therefore it must be specified from which table CustomerID should be displayed. NATURAL is an optional keyword when the join is defined in the FROM clause.

Query: For each customer who has placed an order, what is the customer's ID, name, and order number?

```
SELECT Customer_T.CustomerID, CustomerName, OrderID
FROM Customer_T NATURAL JOIN Order_T ON
Customer_T.CustomerID = Order_T.CustomerID;
```

Note that the order of table names in the FROM clause is immaterial. The query optimizer of the DBMS will decide in which sequence to process each table. Whether indexes exist on common columns will influence the sequence in which tables are processed, as will which table is on the 1 and which is on the M side of 1:*M* relationship. If a query takes significantly different amounts of time, depending on the order in which tables are listed in the FROM clause, the DBMS does not have a very good query optimizer.

Outer Join

In joining two tables, we often find that a row in one table does not have a matching row in the other table. For example, several CustomerID numbers do not appear in the Order_T table. In Figure 7-1 pointers have been drawn from customers to their orders. Contemporary Casuals has placed two orders. Furniture Gallery, Period Furniture, M & H Casual Furniture, Seminole Interiors, Heritage Furnishings, and Kaneohe Homes have not placed orders in this small example. We can assume that this is because those customers have not placed orders since 10/21/2010, or their orders are not included in our very short sample Order_T table. As a result, the equi-join and natural join shown previously do not include all the customers shown in Customer_T.

Of course, the organization may be very interested in identifying those customers who have not placed orders. It might want to contact them to encourage new orders, or it might be interested in analyzing these customers to discern why they are not ordering. Using an **outer join** produces this information: Rows that do not have matching values in common columns are also included in the result table. Null values appear in columns where there is not a match between tables.

Outer join
A join in which rows that do not have matching values in common columns are nevertheless included in the result table.

Outer joins can be handled by the major RDBMS vendors, but the syntax used to accomplish an outer join varies across vendors. The example given here uses ANSI standard syntax. When an outer join is not available explicitly, use UNION and NOT EXISTS (discussed later in this chapter) to carry out an outer join. Here is an outer join.

Query: List customer name, identification number, and order number for all customers listed in the Customer table. Include the customer identification number and name even if there is no order available for that customer.

```
SELECT Customer_T.CustomerID, CustomerName, OrderID
  FROM Customer_T LEFT OUTER JOIN Order_T
  WHERE Customer_T.CustomerID = Order_T. CustomerID;
```

The syntax LEFT OUTER JOIN was selected because the Customer_T table was named first, and it is the table from which we want all rows returned, regardless of whether there is a matching order in the Order_T table. Had we reversed the order in which the tables were listed, the same results would be obtained by requesting a RIGHT OUTER JOIN. It is also possible to request a FULL OUTER JOIN. In that case, all rows from both tables would be returned and matched, if possible, including any rows that do not have a match in the other table. INNER JOINs are much more common than OUTER JOINs because outer joins are necessary only when the user needs to see data from all rows, even those that have no matching row in another table.

It should also be noted that the OUTER JOIN syntax does not apply easily to a join condition of more than two tables. The results returned will vary according to the vendor, so be sure to test any outer join syntax that involves more than two tables until you understand how it will be interpreted by the DBMS being used.

Also, the result table from an outer join may indicate NULL (or a symbol, such as ??) as the values for columns in the second table where no match was achieved. If those columns could have NULL as a data value, you cannot know whether the row returned is a matched row or an unmatched row unless you run another query that checks for null values in the base table or view. Also, a column that is defined as NOT NULL may be assigned a NULL value in the result table of an OUTER JOIN. In the following result, NULL values are shown by an empty value (i.e., a customer without any orders is listed with no value for OrderID).

Result:

CUSTOMERID	CUSTOMERNAME	ORDERID
1	Contemporary Casuals	1001
1	Contemporary Casuals	1010
2	Value Furniture	1006
3	Home Furnishings	1005
4	Eastern Furniture	1009
5	Impressions	1004
6	Furniture Gallery	
7	Period Furniture	
8	California Classics	1002
9	M & H Casual Furniture	
10	Seminole Interiors	
11	American Euro Lifestyles	1007
12	Battle Creek Furniture	1008
13	Heritage Furnishings	
14	Kaneohe Homes	
15	Mountain Scenes	1003

16 rows selected.

It may help you to glance back at Figures 7-1 and 7-2. In Figure 7-2, customers are represented by the left circle and orders are represented by the right. With an INNER JOIN of Customer_T and Order_T, only the 10 rows that have arrows drawn in Figure 7-1 will be returned. The LEFT OUTER JOIN on Customer_T, returns all of the customers along with the orders they have placed, and customers are returned even if they have not placed orders. Because Customer 1, Contemporary Casuals, has placed two orders, a total of 16 rows are returned because rows are returned for both orders placed by Contemporary Casuals.

The advantage of an outer join is that information is not lost. Here, all customer names were returned, whether or not they had placed orders. Requesting a RIGHT OUTER join would return all orders. (Because referential integrity requires that every order be associated with a valid customer ID, this right outer join would only ensure that referential integrity is being enforced.) Customers who had not placed orders would not be included in the result.

> ***Query:*** List customer name, identification number, and order number for all orders listed in the Order table. Include the order number, even if there is no customer name and identification number available.

```
SELECT Customer_T.CustomerID,CustomerName, OrderID
  FROM Customer_T RIGHT OUTER JOIN Order_T ON
    Customer_T.CustomerID = Order_T.CustomerID;
```

Union Join

SQL:1999 and, by extension, SQL:200n also allow for the use of UNION JOIN, which has not yet been implemented in all DBMS products. The results of a UNION JOIN will be a table that includes all data from each table that is joined. The result table will contain all columns from each table and will contain an instance for each row of data included from each table. Thus, a UNION JOIN of the Customer_T table (15 customers and 6 attributes) and the Order_T table (10 orders and 3 attributes) will return a result table of 25 rows (15 + 10) and 9 columns (6 + 3). Assuming that each original table contained no nulls, each customer row in the result table will contain three attributes with assigned null values, and each order row will contain six attributes with assigned null values.

UNION JOINs may not include the keyword NATURAL, an ON clause, or a USING clause. Each of these implies an equivalence that would conflict with the UNION JOIN's inclusion of all the data from each table that is joined. Do not confuse this command with the UNION command that joins multiple SELECT statements and is covered later in this chapter.

Sample Join Involving Four Tables

Much of the power of the relational model comes from its ability to work with the relationships among the objects in the database. Designing a database so that data about each object are kept in separate tables simplifies maintenance and data integrity. The capability to relate the objects to each other by joining the tables provides critical business information and reports to employees. Although the examples provided in Chapters 6 and 7 are simple and constructed only to provide a basic understanding of SQL, it is important to realize that these commands can be and often are built into much more complex queries that provide exactly the information needed for a report or process.

Here is a sample join query that involves a four-table join. This query produces a result table that includes the information needed to create an invoice for order number 1006. We want the customer information, the order and order line information, and the product information, so we will need to join four tables. Figure 7-3a shows an annotated ERD of the four tables involved in constructing this query; Figure 7-3b shows an abstract instance diagram of the four tables with order 1006 hypothetically having two line items for products Px and Py, respectively. We encourage you to draw such diagrams to help conceive the data involved in a query and how you might then construct the corresponding SQL command with joins.

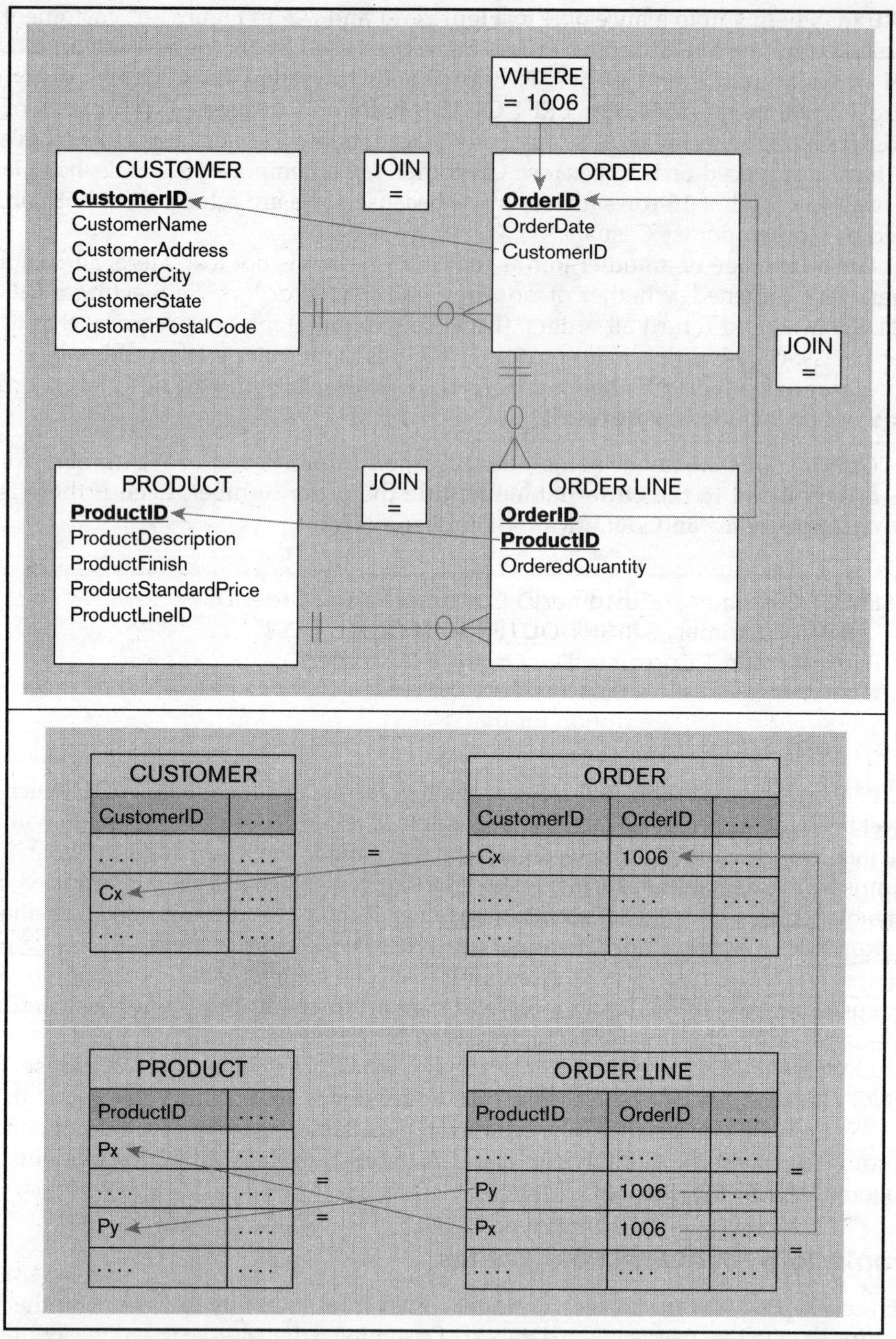

FIGURE 7-3 Diagrams depicting a four-table join
(a) Annotated ERD with relations used in a four-table join

(b) Annotated instance diagram of relations used in a four-table join

Query: Assemble all information necessary to create an invoice for order number 1006.

```
SELECT Customer_T.CustomerID, CustomerName, CustomerAddress,
   CustomerCity, CustomerState, CustomerPostalCode, Order_T.OrderID,
   OrderDate, OrderedQuantity, ProductDescription, StandardPrice,
   (OrderedQuantity * ProductStandardPrice)
FROM Customer_T, Order_T, OrderLine_T, Product_T
   WHERE Order_T.CustomerID = Customer_T.CustomerID
     AND Order_T.OrderID = OrderLine_T.OrderID
     AND OrderLine_T.ProductID = Product_T.ProductID
     AND Order_T.OrderID = 1006;
```

FIGURE 7-4 Results from a four-table join (edited for readability)

CUSTOMERID	CUSTOMERNAME	CUSTOMERADDRESS	CUSTOMER CITY	CUSTOMER STATE	CUSTOMER POSTALCODE
2	Value Furniture	15145 S. W. 17th St.	Plano	TX	75094 7743
2	Value Furniture	15145 S. W. 17th St.	Plano	TX	75094 7743
2	Value Furniture	15145 S. W. 17th St.	Plano	TX	75094 7743

ORDERID	ORDERDATE	ORDERED QUANTITY	PRODUCTNAME	PRODUCT STANDARDPRICE	(QUANTITY* STANDARDPRICE)
1006	24-OCT -10	1	Entertainment Center	650	650
1006	24-OCT -10	2	Writer's Desk	325	650
1006	24-OCT -10	2	Dining Table	800	1600

The results of the query are shown in Figure 7-4. Remember, because the join involves four tables, there are three column join conditions, as follows:

1. Order_T.CustomerID = Customer_T.CustomerID = links an order with its associated customer.
2. Order_T.OrderID = OrderLine_T.OrderID links each order with the details of the items ordered.
3. OrderLine_T.ProductID = Product_T.ProductID links each order detail record with the product description for that order line.

Self-Join

There are times when a join requires matching rows in a table with other rows in that same table—that is, joining a table with itself. There is no special command in SQL to do this, but people generally call this operation a *self-join*. Self-joins arise for several reasons, the most common of which is a unary relationship, such as the Supervises relationship in the Pine Valley Furniture database in Figure 2-22. This relationship is implemented by placing in the EmployeeSupervisor column the EmployeeID (foreign key) of the employee's supervisor, another employee. With this recursive foreign key column, we can ask the following question:

Query: What are the employee ID and name of each employee and the name of his or her supervisor (label the supervisor's name Manager)?

```
SELECT E.EmployeeID, E.EmployeeName, M.EmployeeName AS Manager
  FROM Employee_T E, Employee_T M
  WHERE E.EmployeeSupervisor = M.EmployeeID;
```

Result:

EMPLOYEEID	EMPLOYEENAME	MANAGER
123-44-347	Jim Jason	Robert Lewis

There are two things to note in this query. First, the Employee table is, in a sense, serving two roles: It contains a list of employees and a list of managers. Thus, the FROM clause refers to the Employee_T table twice, once for each of these roles. However, to distinguish these roles in the rest of the query, we give the Employee_T table an alias for each role (in this case, E for employee and M for manager roles, respectively). Then the columns from the SELECT list are clear: first the ID and name of an employee (with prefix E) and then the name of a manager (with prefix M). Which manager? That then is the second point: The WHERE clause joins the "employee" and "manager" tables based on the foreign key from employee (EmployeeSupervisor) to manager (EmployeeID). As far as SQL is concerned, it considers the E and M tables to be two different tables that have identical column names, so the column names must have a suffix to clarify from which table a column is to be chosen each time it is referenced.

It turns out that there are various interesting queries that can be written using self-joins following unary relationships. For example, which employees have a salary greater than the salary of their manager (not uncommon in professional baseball, but generally frowned on in business or government organizations), or (if we had this data in our database) is anyone married to his or her manager (not uncommon in a family-run business but possibly prohibited in many organizations)? Several of the Problems and Exercises at the end of this chapter require queries with a self-join.

As with any other join, it is not necessary that a self-join be based on a foreign key and a specified unary relationship. For example, when a salesperson is scheduled to visit a particular customer, maybe she would want to know who are all the other customers in the same postal code as the customer she is scheduled to visit. Remember, it is possible to join rows on columns from different (or the same) tables as long as those columns come from the same domain of values and the linkage of values from those columns makes sense. For example, even though ProductFinish and EmployeeCity may have the identical data type, they don't come from the same domain of values, and there is no conceivable business reason to link products and employees on these columns. However, one might conceive of some reason to understand the sales booked by a salesperson by looking at order dates of the person's sales relative to his or her hire date. It is amazing what questions SQL can answer (although we have limited control on how SQL displays the results).

Subqueries

The preceding SQL examples illustrate one of the two basic approaches for joining two tables: the joining technique. SQL also provides the subquery technique, which involves placing an inner query (SELECT . . . FROM . . . WHERE) within a WHERE or HAVING clause of another (outer) query. The inner query provides a set of one or more values for the search condition of the outer query. Such queries are referred to as subqueries or nested subqueries. Subqueries can be nested multiple times. Subqueries are prime examples of why SQL is a set-oriented language.

Sometimes, either the joining or the subquery technique can be used to accomplish the same result, and different people will have different preferences about which technique to use. Other times, only a join or only a subquery will work. The joining technique is useful when data from *several relations* are to be retrieved and displayed, and the relationships are not necessarily nested, whereas the subquery technique allows you to display data from only the tables mentioned in the outer query. Let's compare two queries that return the same result. Both answer the question, what is the name and address of the customer who placed order number 1008? First, we will use a join query, which is graphically depicted in Figure 7-5a.

Query: What are the name and address of the customer who placed order number 1008?

```
SELECT CustomerName, CustomerAddress, CustomerCity,
  CustomerState, CustomerPostalCode
FROM Customer_T, Order_T
WHERE Customer_T.CustomerID = Order_T. CustomerID
  AND OrderID = 1008;
```

In set-processing terms, this query finds the subset of the Order_T table for OrderID = 1008 and then matches the row(s) in that subset with the rows in the Customer_T table that have the same CustomerID values. In this approach, it is not necessary that only one order have the OrderID value 1008. Now, look at the equivalent query using the subquery technique, which is graphically depicted in Figure 7-5b.

FIGURE 7-5 Graphical depiction of two ways to answer a query with different types of joins

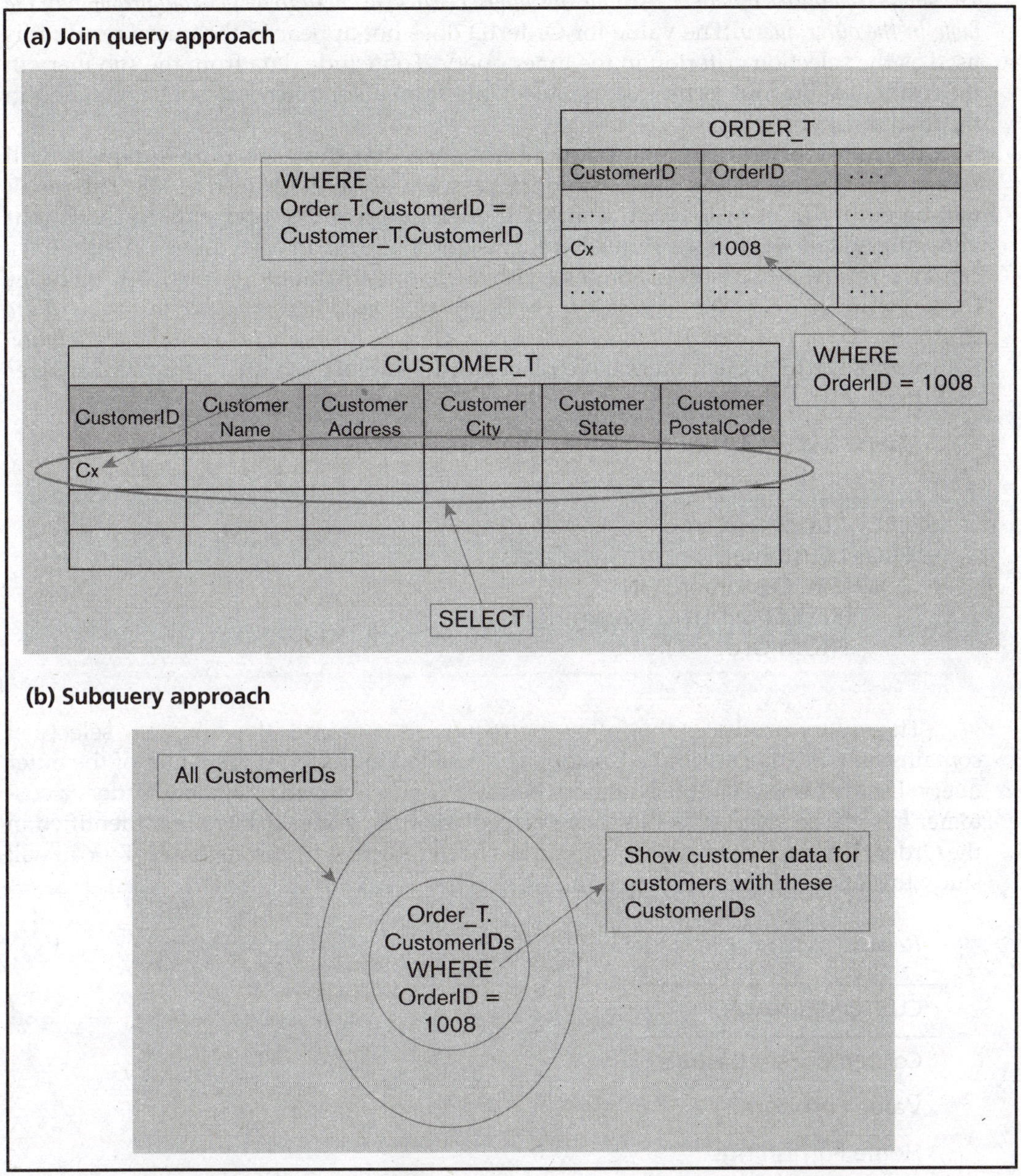

Query: What are the name and address of the customer who placed order number 1008?

```
SELECT CustomerName, CustomerAddress, CustomerCity,
CustomerState, CustomerPostalCode
  FROM Customer_T
    WHERE Customer_T.CustomerID =
      (SELECT Order_T.CustomerID
        FROM Order_T
          WHERE OrderID = 1008);
```

Notice that the subquery, shaded in blue and enclosed in parentheses, follows the form learned for constructing SQL queries and could stand on its own as an independent query. That is, the result of the subquery, as with any other query, is a set of rows— in this case, a set of CustomerID values. We know that only one value will be in the result. (There is only one CustomerID for the order with OrderID 1008.) To be safe, we can, and probably should, use the IN operator rather than = when writing subqueries. *The subquery approach may be used for this query because we need to display data from only the table in the outer query.* The value for OrderID does not appear in the query result; it is used as the selection criterion in the inner query. To include data from the subquery in the result, use the join technique, because data from a subquery cannot be included in the final results.

As noted previously, we know in advance that the preceding subquery will return at most one value, the CustomerID associated with OrderID 1008. The result will be empty if an order with that ID does not exist. (It is advisable to check that your query will work if a subquery returns zero, one, or many values.) A subquery can also return a list (set) of values (with zero, one, or many entries) if it includes the keyword IN. *Because the result of the subquery is used to compare with one attribute (CustomerID, in this query), the select list of a subquery may include only one attribute.* For example, which customers have placed orders? Here is a query that will answer that question.

Query: What are the names of customers who have placed orders?

```
SELECT CustomerName
  FROM Customer_T
    WHERE CustomerID IN
      (SELECT DISTINCT CustomerID
       FROM Order_T);
```

This query produces the following result. As required, the subquery select list contains only the one attribute, CustomerID, needed in the WHERE clause of the outer query. Distinct is used in the subquery because we do not care how many orders a customer has placed, as long as they have placed an order. For each customer identified in the Order_T table, that customer's name has been returned from Customer_T. (You will study this query again in Figure 7-7a.)

Result:

CUSTOMERNAME
Contemporary Casuals
Value Furniture
Home Furnishings
Eastern Furniture
Impressions
California Classics
American Euro Lifestyles
Battle Creek Furniture
Mountain Scenes
9 rows selected.

The qualifiers NOT, ANY, and ALL may be used in front of IN or with logical operators such as = , >, and <. Because IN works with zero, one, or many values from the inner query, many programmers simply use IN instead of = for all queries, even if the equal sign would work. The next example shows the use of NOT, and it also demonstrates that a join can be used in an inner query.

Query: Which customers have not placed any orders for computer desks?

```
SELECT CustomerName
  FROM Customer_T
  WHERE CustomerID NOT IN
  (SELECT CustomerID
    FROM Order_T, OrderLine_T, Product_T
      WHERE Order_T.OrderID = OrderLine_T.OrderID
        AND OrderLine_T.ProductID = Product_T.ProductID
        AND ProductDescription = 'Computer Desk');
```

Result:

```
CUSTOMERNAME
Value Furniture
Home Furnishings
Eastern Furniture
Furniture Gallery
Period Furniture
M & H Casual Furniture
Seminole Interiors
American Euro Lifestyles
Heritage Furnishings
Kaneohe Homes
10 rows selected.
```

The result shows that 10 customers have not yet ordered computer desks. The inner query returned a list (set) of all customers who had ordered computer desks. The outer query listed the names of those customers who were not in the list returned by the inner query. Figure 7-6 graphically breaks out the results of the subquery and main query.

Qualifications such as < ANY or >= ALL instead of IN are also useful. For example, the qualification >= ALL can be used to match with the maximum value in a set. But be careful: Some combinations of qualifications may not make sense, such as = ALL (which makes sense only when the all the elements of the set have the same value).

Two other conditions associated with using subqueries are EXISTS and NOT EXISTS. These keywords are included in an SQL query at the same location where IN would be, just prior to the beginning of the subquery. EXISTS will take a value of *true* if the subquery returns an intermediate result table that contains one or more rows (i.e., a nonempty set) and *false* if no rows are returned (i.e., an empty set). NOT EXISTS will take a value of *true* if no rows are returned and *false* if one or more rows are returned.

So, when do you use EXISTS versus IN, and when do you use NOT EXISTS versus NOT IN? You use EXISTS (NOT EXISTS) when your only interest is whether the subquery returns a nonempty (empty) set (i.e., you don't care what is in the set, just whether it is empty), and you use IN (NOT IN) when you need to know what values are (are not) in the set. Remember, IN and NOT IN return a set of values from only one column, which can then be compared to one column in the outer query. EXISTS and NOT EXISTS returns only a true or false value depending on whether there are any rows in the answer table of the inner query or subquery.

Consider the following SQL statement, which includes EXISTS.

FIGURE 7-6 Using the NOT IN qualifier

```
SELECT CustomerName FROM Customer_T
    WHERE CustomerID NOT IN
        (SELECT CustomerID FROM Order_T, OrderLine_T, Product_T
        WHERE Order_T.OrderID = OrderLine_T.OrderID
        AND OrderLine_T.ProductID = Product_T.ProductID
        AND ProductDescription = 'Computer Desk');
```

1. The subquery (shown in the box) is processed first and an intermediate results table created. It returns the Customer ID for every customer that has purchased at least one computer desk.

CUSTOMERID
1
5
8
12
15

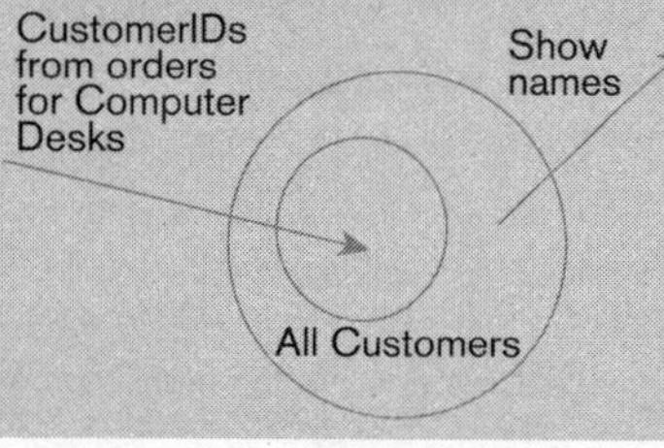

2. The main query is then processed and returns every customer who was **NOT IN** the subquery' results.

CUSTOMERNAME
Value Furniture
Home Furnishings
Eastern Furniture
Furniture Gallery
Period Furniture
M and H Casual Furniture
Seminole Interiors
American Euro Lifestyles
Heritage Furnishings
Kaneohe Homes

Query: What are the order IDs for all orders that have included furniture finished in natural ash?

```
SELECT DISTINCT OrderID FROM OrderLine_T
WHERE EXISTS
  (SELECT *
    FROM Product_T
      WHERE ProductID = OrderLine_T.ProductID
      AND ProductFinish = 'Natural Ash');
```

The subquery is executed for each order line in the outer query. The subquery checks for each order line to see if the finish for the product on that order line is natural ash (indicated by the arrow added to the query above). If this is true (EXISTS), the outer query displays the order ID for that order. The outer query checks this one row at a time for every row in the set of referenced rows (the OrderLine_T table). There have been seven such orders, as the result shows. (We discuss this query further in Figure 7-7b.)

Result:

ORDERID
1001
1002
1003
1006
1007
1008
1009

7 rows selected.

When EXISTS or NOT EXISTS is used in a subquery, the select list of the subquery will usually just select all columns (SELECT *) as a placeholder because it does not matter which columns are returned. The purpose of the subquery is to test whether any rows fit the conditions, not to return values from particular columns for comparison purposes in the outer query. The columns that will be displayed are determined strictly by the outer query. The EXISTS subquery illustrated previously, like almost all other EXISTS subqueries, is a correlated subquery, which is described next. Queries containing the keyword NOT EXISTS will return a result table when no rows are found that satisfy the subquery.

In summary, use the subquery approach when qualifications are nested or when qualifications are easily understood in a nested way. Most systems allow pairwise joining of *one and only one column* in an inner query with one column in an outer query. An exception to this is when a subquery is used with the EXISTS keyword. Data can be displayed only from the table(s) referenced in the outer query. Up to 16 levels of nesting are typically supported. Queries are processed from the inside out, although another type of subquery, a correlated subquery, is processed from the outside in.

Correlated Subqueries

In the first subquery example in the prior section, it was necessary to examine the inner query before considering the outer query. That is, the result of the inner query was used to limit the processing of the outer query. In contrast, **correlated subqueries** use the result of the outer query to determine the processing of the inner query. That is, the inner query is somewhat different for each row referenced in the outer query. In this case, the inner query must be computed for *each* outer row, whereas in the earlier examples, the inner query was computed *only once* for all rows processed in the outer query. The EXISTS subquery example in the prior section had this characteristic, in which the inner query was executed for each OrderLine_T row, and each time it was executed, the inner query was for a different ProductID value—the one from the OrderLine_T row in the outer query. Figures 7-7a and 7-7b depict the different processing order for each of the examples from the previous section on subqueries.

Correlated subquery
In SQL, a subquery in which processing the inner query depends on data from the outer query.

Let's consider another example query that requires composing a correlated subquery.

Query: List the details about the product with the highest standard price.

```
SELECT ProductDescription, ProductFinish, ProductStandardPrice
FROM Product_T PA
  WHERE PA.ProductStandardPrice > ALL
    (SELECT ProductStandardPrice FROM Product_T PB
      WHERE PB.ProductID ! = PA.ProductID);
```

As you can see in the following result, the dining table has a higher unit price than any other product.

Result:

PRODUCTDESCRIPTION	PRODUCTFINISH	PRODUCTSTANDARDPRICE
Dining Table	Natural Ash	800

The arrow added to the query above illustrates the cross-reference for a value in the inner query to be taken from a table in the outer query. The logic of this SQL statement is that the subquery will be executed once for each product to be sure that no other product has a higher standard price. Notice that we are comparing rows in a table to themselves and that we are able to do this by giving the table two aliases, PA and PB; you'll recall we identified this earlier as a self-join. First, ProductID 1, the end table, will be considered. When the subquery is executed, it will return a set of values, which are the standard prices of every product except the one being considered in the outer query (product 1, for the first time it is executed). Then, the outer query will check to see if the standard price for the product being considered is greater than all of the standard prices returned by the subquery. If it is, it will be returned as the result of the query. If not, the next standard price value in the outer query will be considered, and the inner query

FIGURE 7-7 Subquery processing

(a) Processing a noncorrelated subquery

What are the names of customers who have placed orders?

```
SELECT CustomerName
        FROM Customer_T
                WHERE CustomerID IN
                        (SELECT DISTINCT CustomerID
                                FROM Order_T);
```

1. The subquery (shown in the box) is processed first and an intermediate results table created:

CUSTOMERID
1
8
15
5
3
2
11
12
4

9 rows selected.

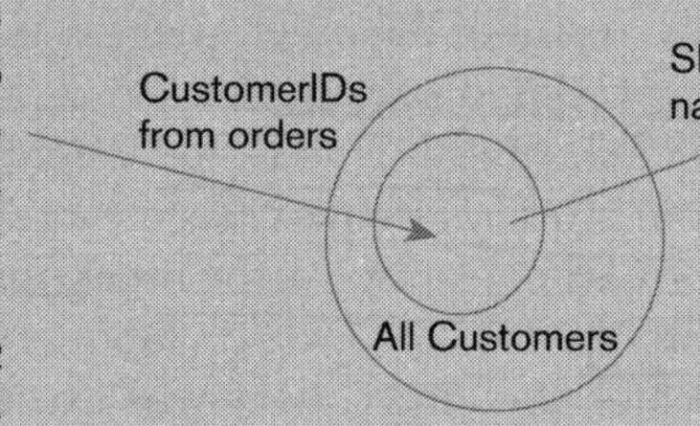

2. The outer query returns the requested customer information for each customer included in the intermediate results table:

CUSTOMERNAME
Contemporary Casuals
Value Furniture
Home Furnishings
Eastern Furniture
Impressions
California Classics
American Euro Lifestyles
Battle Creek Furniture
Mountain Scenes

9 rows selected.

(continued)

will return a list of all the standard prices for the other products. The list returned by the inner query changes as each product in the outer query changes; that makes it a correlated subquery. Can you identify a special set of standard prices for which this query will not yield the desired result (see Problem and Exercise 38)?

Using Derived Tables

Subqueries are not limited to inclusion in the WHERE clause. As we saw in Chapter 6, they may also be used in the FROM clause to create a temporary derived table (or set) that is used in the query. Creating a derived table that has an aggregate value in it, such as MAX, AVG, or MIN, allows the aggregate to be used in the WHERE clause. Here, pieces of furniture that exceed the average standard price are listed.

Query: Show the product description, product standard price, and overall average standard price for all products that have a standard price that is higher than the average standard price.

```
SELECT ProductDescription, ProductStandardPrice, AvgPrice
  FROM
    (SELECT AVG(ProductStandardPrice) AvgPrice FROM Product_T),
       Product_T
  WHERE ProductStandardPrice > AvgPrice;
```

Result:

PRODUCTDESCRIPTION	PRODUCTSTANDARDPRICE	AVGPRICE
Entertainment Center	650	440.625
8-Drawer Dresser	750	440.625
Dining Table	800	440.625

FIGURE 7-7 ***(continued)***

(b) Processing a correlated subquery

What are the order IDs for all orders that have included furniture finished in natural ash?

```
SELECT DISTINCT OrderID FROM OrderLine_T
WHERE EXISTS
      (SELECT *
        FROM Product _T
              WHERE ProductID = OrderLine_T.ProductID
                   AND Productfinish = 'Natural Ash');
```

	OrderID	ProductID	OrderedQuantity
1 →	1001	1	1
	1001	2	2
	1001	4	1
3 →	1002	3	5
	1003	3	3
	1004	6	2
	1004	8	2
	1005	4	4
	1006	4	1
	1006	5	2
	1007	1	3
	1007	2	2
	1008	3	3
	1008	8	3
	1009	4	2
	1009	7	3
	1010	8	10
*	0	0	0

	ProductID	ProductDescription	ProductFinish	ProductStandardPrice	ProductLineID
	1	End Table	Cherry	$175.00	10001
2 →	2	Coffee Table	Natural Ash	$200.00	20001
4 →	3	Computer Desk	Natural Ash	$375.00	20001
	4	Entertainment Center	Natural Maple	$650.00	30001
	5	Writer's Desk	Cherry	$325.00	10001
	6	8-Drawer Dresser	White Ash	$750.00	20001
	7	Dining Table	Natural Ash	$800.00	20001
	8	Computer Desk	Walnut	$250.00	30001
*	(AutoNumber)			$0.00	

1. The first order ID is selected from OrderLine_T: OrderID =1001.
2. The subquery is evaluated to see if any product in that order has a natural ash finish. Product 2 does, and is part of the order. EXISTS is valued as *true* and the order ID is added to the result table.
3. The next order ID is selected from OrderLine_T: OrderID =1002.
4. The subquery is evaluated to see if the product ordered has a natural ash finish. It does. EXISTS is valued as *true* and the order ID is added to the result table.
5. Processing continues through each order ID. Orders 1004, 1005, and 1010 are not included in the result table because they do not include any furniture with a natural ash finish. The final result table is shown in the text on page 302.

So, why did this query require a derived table rather than, say, a subquery? The reason is we want to display both the standard price and the average standard price for each of the selected products. The similar query in the prior section on correlated subqueries worked fine to show data from only the table in the outer query, the product table. However, to show both standard price and the average standard price in each displayed row, we have to get both values into the "outer" query, as is done in the query above.

Combining Queries

Sometimes, no matter how clever you are, you can't get all the rows you want into the single answer table using one SELECT statement. Fortunately, you have a lifeline! The UNION clause is used to combine the output (i.e., union the set of rows) from multiple queries together into a single result table. To use the UNION clause, each query involved must output the same number of columns, and they must be UNION compatible. This means that the output from each query for each column should be of compatible data types. Acceptance as a compatible data type varies among the DBMS products. When performing a union where output for a column will merge two different data types, it is safest to use the CAST command to control the data type conversion yourself. For example, the DATE data type in Order_T might need to be converted into a text data type. The following SQL command would accomplish this:

```
SELECT CAST (OrderDate AS CHAR) FROM Order_T;
```

The following query determines the customer(s) who has in a given line item purchased the largest quantity of any Pine Valley product and the customer(s) who has in a given line item purchased the smallest quantity and returns the results in one table.

Query:

```
SELECT C1.CustomerID, CustomerName, OrderedQuantity,
'Largest Quantity' AS Quantity
FROM Customer_T C1,Order_T O1, OrderLine_T Q1
    WHERE C1.CustomerID = O1.CustomerID
    AND O1.OrderID = Q1.OrderID
    AND OrderedQuantity =
    (SELECT MAX(OrderedQuantity)
    FROM OrderLine_T)
UNION
SELECT C1.CustomerID, CustomerName, OrderedQuantity,
'Smallest Quantity'
FROM Customer_T C1, Order_T O1, OrderLine_T Q1
    WHERE C1.CustomerID = O1.CustomerID
    AND O1.OrderID = Q1.OrderID
    AND OrderedQuantity =
        (SELECT MIN(OrderedQuantity)
        FROM OrderLine_T)
ORDER BY 3;
```

Notice that an expression Quantity has been created in which the strings 'Smallest Quantity' and 'Largest Quantity' have been inserted for readability. The ORDER BY clause has been used to organize the order in which the rows of output are listed. Figure 7-8 breaks the query into parts to help you understand how it processes.

Result:

CUSTOMERID	CUSTOMERNAME	ORDEREDQUANTITY	QUANTITY
1	Contemporary Casuals	1	Smallest Quantity
2	Value Furniture	1	Smallest Quantity
1	Contemporary Casuals	10	Largest Quantity

Did we have to answer this question by using UNION? Could we instead have answered it using one SELECT and a complex, compound WHERE clause with many ANDs and ORs? In general, the answer is sometimes (another good academic answer, like "it depends"). Often, it is simply easiest to conceive of and write a query using several simply SELECTs and a UNION. Or, if it is a query you frequently run, maybe one way will process more efficiently than another. You will learn from experience which approach is most natural for you and best for a given situation.

Now that you remember the union set operation from finite mathematics, you may also remember that there are other set operations—intersect (to find the elements in common between two sets) and minus (to find the elements in one set that are not in

FIGURE 7-8 Combining queries using UNION

```
SELECT C1.CustomerID, CustomerName, OrderedQuantity, 'Largest Quantity' AS Quantity
    FROM Customer_T C1,Order_T O1, OrderLine_T Q1
    WHERE C1.CustomerID = O1.CustomerID
              AND O1.OrderID = Q1.OrderID
              AND OrderedQuantity =
                          (SELECT MAX(OrderedQuantity)
                          FROM OrderLine_T)
```

1. In the above query, the subquery is processed first and an intermediate results table created. It contains the maximum quantity ordered from OrderLine_T and has a value of 10.
2. Next the main query selects customer information for the customer or customers who ordered 10 of any item. Contemporary Casuals has ordered 10 of some unspecified item.

```
SELECT C1.CustomerID, CustomerName, OrderedQuantity, 'Smallest Quantity'
    FROM Customer_T C1, Order_T O1, OrderLine_T Q1
    WHERE C1.CustomerID = O1.CustomerID
              AND O1.OrderID = Q1.OrderID
              AND OrderedQuantity =
                          (SELECT MIN(OrderedQuantity)
                          FROM OrderLine_T)
ORDER BY 3;
```

1. In the second main query, the same process is followed but the result returned is for the minimum order quantity.
2. The results of the two queries are joined together using the UNION command.
3. The results are then ordered according to the value in OrderedQuantity. The default is ascending value, so the orders with the smallest quantity, 1, are listed first.

another set). These operations—INTERSECT and MINUS—are also available in SQL, and they are used just as UNION was above to manipulate the result sets created by two SELECT statements.

Conditional Expressions

Establishing IF-THEN-ELSE logical processing within an SQL statement can now be accomplished by using the CASE keyword in a statement. Figure 7-9 gives the CASE syntax, which actually has four forms. The CASE form can be constructed using either an expression that equates to a value or a predicate. The predicate form is based on three-value logic (true, false, don't know) but allows for more complex operations. The value-expression form requires a match to the value expression. NULLIF and COALESCE are the keywords associated with the other two forms of the CASE expression.

FIGURE 7-9 CASE conditional syntax

```
{CASE expression
{WHEN expression
THEN {expression      | NULL}} ...
| {WHEN predicate
THEN {expression      | NULL}} ...
[ELSE {expression       NULL}]
END }
| ( NULLIF (expression, expression)       }
| ( COALESCE (expression      . . .) }
```

CASE could be used in constructing a query that asks "What products are included in Product Line 1?" In this example, the query displays the product description for each product in the specified product line and a special text, '####' for all other products, thus displaying a sense of the relative proportion of products in the specified product line.

Query:

```
SELECT CASE
    WHEN ProductLine = 1 THEN ProductDescription
    ELSE '####'
END AS ProductDescription
FROM Product_T;
```

Result:

PRODUCTDESCRIPTION
End Table
####
####
####
Writers Desk
####
####
####

Gulutzan & Pelzer (1999, p. 573) indicate that "It's possible to use CASE expressions this way as retrieval substitutes, but the more common applications are (a) to make up for SQL's lack of an enumerated <data type>, (b) to perform complicated if/then calculations, (c) for translation, and (d) to avoid exceptions. We find CASE expressions to be indispensable, and it amazes us that in pre SQL-92 DBMSs they didn't exist."

More Complicated SQL Queries

We have kept the examples used in Chapter 6 and this chapter very simple in order to make it easier for you to concentrate on the piece of SQL syntax being introduced. It is important to understand that production databases may contain hundreds and even thousands of tables, and many of those contain hundreds of columns. While it is difficult to come up with complicated queries from the four tables used in Chapter 6 and this chapter, the text comes with a larger version of the Pine Valley Furniture Company database, which allows for somewhat more complex queries. This version is available at **www.prenhall.com/hoffer** and at **www.teradatastudentnetwork.com**; here are two samples drawn from that database:

Question 1: For each salesperson, list his or her biggest-selling product.

Query: First, we will define a view called TSales, which computes the total sales of each product sold by each salesperson. We create this view to simplify answering this query by breaking it into several easier-to-write queries.

```
CREATE VIEW TSales AS
SELECT SalespersonName,
    ProductDescription,
    SUM(OrderedQuantity) AS Totorders
```

```
FROM Salesperson_T, OrderLine_T, Product_T, Order_T
    WHERE Salesperson_T.SalespersonID=Order_T.SalespersonID
    AND Order_T.OrderID=OrderLine_T.OrderID
    AND OrderLine_T.ProductID=Product_T.ProductID
    GROUP BY SalespersonName, ProductDescription;
```

Next we write a correlated subquery using the view:

```
SELECT SalespersonName, ProductDescription
    FROM TSales AS A
        WHERE Totorders = (SELECT MAX(Totorders) FROM TSales B
        WHERE B.SalesperssonName = A.SalespersonName);
```

Notice that once we had the TSales view, the correlated subquery was rather simple to write. Also, it was simple to conceive of the final query once all the data needed to display were all in the set created by the virtual table (set) of the view. Our thought process was if we could create a set of information about the total sales for each salesperson, we could then find the maximum value of total sales in this set. Then it is simply a matter of scanning that set to see which salesperson(s) has total sales equal to that maximum value. There are likely other ways to write SQL statements to answer this question, so use whatever approach works and is most natural for you. We suggest that you draw diagrams, like those you have seen in figures in this chapter, to represent the sets you think you could manipulate to answer the question you face.

Question 2: Write an SQL query to list all salespersons who work in the territory where the most end tables have been sold.

Query: First, we will create a query called TopTerritory, using the following SQL statement:

```
SELECT TOP 1 Territory_T.TerritoryID,
SUM(OrderedQuantity) AS TopSales
    FROM Territory_T INNER JOIN (Product_T INNER JOIN
      (((Customer_T INNER JOIN DoesBusinessIn_T ON
      Customer_T.CustomerID = DoesBusinessIn_T.CustomerID)
      INNER JOIN Order_T ON Customer_T.CustomerID =
      Order_T.CustomerID) INNER JOIN OrderLine_T ON
      Order_T.OrderID = OrderLine_T.OrderID) ON
      Product_T.ProductID = OrderLine_T.ProductID) ON
      Territory_T.TerritoryID = DoesBusinessIn_T.TerritoryID
      WHERE ((ProductDescription)='End Table')
      GROUP BY Territory_T.TerritoryID
      ORDER BY TotSales DESC;
```

This will give us the territory number of the top-producing territory for sales of end tables.

Next, we will write a query using this query as a derived table. (To save space, we simply insert the name we used for the above query, but SQL requires that the above query be inserted as a derived table where its name appears in the query below. Alternatively, TopTerritory could have been created as a view.)

```
SELECT Salesperson_T.SalespersonID, SalesperspmName
    FROM Territory_T INNER JOIN Salesperson_T ON
      Territory_T.TerritoryID = Salesperson_T.TerritoryID
    WHERE Salesperson_T.TerritoryID IN
      (SELECT TerritoryID FROM TopTerritory);
```

You probably noticed the use of the TOP operator in the TopTerritory query above. TOP, which is compliant with the SQL:2003 standard, specifies a given number or percentage of the rows (with or without ties, as indicated by a subclause) to be returned from the ordered query result set.

TIPS FOR DEVELOPING QUERIES

SQL's simple basic structure results in a query language that is easy for a novice to use to write simple ad hoc queries. At the same time, it has enough flexibility and syntax options to handle complicated queries used in a production system. Both characteristics, however, lead to potential difficulties in query development. As with any other computer programming, you are likely not to write a query correctly the first time. Be sure you have access to an explanation of the error codes generated by the RDBMS. Work initially with a test set of data, usually small, for which you can compute the desired answer by hand as a way to check your coding. This is especially true if you are writing INSERT, UPDATE, or DELETE commands, and it is why organizations have test, development, and production versions of a database, so inevitable development errors do not harm production data.

First, as a novice query writer, you will find it easy to write a query that runs without error. Congratulations, but the results may not be exactly what you intended. Sometimes it will be obvious to you that there is a problem, especially if you forget to define the links between tables with a WHERE clause and get a Cartesian join of all possible combinations of records. Other times, your query will appear to be correct, but close inspection using a test set of data may reveal that your query returns 24 rows when it should return 25. Sometimes it will return duplicates you don't want or just a few of the records you want, and sometimes it won't run because you are trying to group data that can't be grouped. Watch carefully for these types of errors before you turn in your homework. Working through a well-thought-out set of test data by hand will help you to catch your errors. When you are constructing a set of test data, include some examples of common data values. Then think about possible exceptions that could occur. For example, real data might unexpectedly include null data, out-of-range data, or impossible data values.

Certain steps are necessary in writing any query. The graphical interfaces now available make it easier to construct queries and to remember table and attribute names as you work. Here are some suggestions to help you (we assume that you are working with a database that has been defined and created):

- Familiarize yourself with the data model and the entities and relationships that have been established. The data model expresses many of the business rules that may be idiosyncratic for the business or problem you are considering. It is very important to have a good grasp of the data that are available with which to work. As demonstrated in Figures 7-7a and 7-7b, you can draw the segment of the data model you intend to reference in the query and then annotate it to show qualifications and joining criteria. Alternatively you can draw figures such as Figures 7-5 and 7-6 with sample data and Venn diagrams to also help conceive of how to construct subqueries or derived tables that can be used as components in a more complex query.
- Be sure that you understand what results you want from your query. Often, a user will state a need ambiguously, so be alert and address any questions you have after working with users.
- Figure out what attributes you want in your query result. Include each attribute after the SELECT keyword.
- Locate within the data model the attributes you want and identify the entity where the required data are stored. Include these after the FROM keyword.
- Review the ERD and all the entities identified in the previous step. Determine what columns in each table will be used to establish the relationships. Consider what type of join you want between each set of entities.

- Construct a WHERE equality for each link. Count the number of entities involved and the number of links established. Usually there will be one more entity than there are WHERE clauses. When you have established the basic result set, the query may be complete. In any case, run it and inspect your results.
- When you have a basic result set to work with, you can begin to fine-tune your query by adding GROUP BY and HAVING clauses, DISTINCT, NOT IN, and so forth. Test your query as you add keywords to it to be sure you are getting the results you want.
- Until you gain query writing experience, your first draft of a query will tend to work with the data you expect to encounter. Now, try to think of exceptions to the usual data that may be encountered and test your query against a set of test data that includes unusual data, missing data, impossible values, and so forth. If you can handle those, your query is almost complete. Remember that checking by hand will be necessary; just because an SQL query runs doesn't mean it is correct.

As you start to write more complicated queries using additional syntax, debugging queries may be more difficult for you. If you are using subqueries, errors of logic can often be located by running each subquery as a freestanding query. Start with the subquery that is nested most deeply. When its results are correct, use that tested subquery with the outer query that uses its result. You can follow a similar process with derived tables. Follow this procedure until you have tested the entire query. If you are having syntax trouble with a simple query, try taking apart the query to find the problem. You may find it easier to spot a problem if you return just a few crucial attribute values and investigate one manipulation at a time.

As you gain more experience, you will be developing queries for larger databases. As the amount of data that must be processed increases, the time necessary to successfully run a query may vary noticeably, depending on how you write the query. Query optimizers are available in the more powerful database management systems such as Oracle, but there are also some simple strategies for writing queries that may prove helpful for you. The following are some common strategies to consider if you want to write queries that run more efficiently:

- Rather than use the SELECT * option, take the time to include the column names of the attributes you need in a query. If you are working with a wide table and need only a few of the attributes, using SELECT * may generate a significant amount of unnecessary network traffic as unnecessary attributes are fetched over the network. Later, when the query has been incorporated into a production system, changes in the base table may affect the query results. Specifying the attribute names will make it easier to notice and correct for such events.
- Try to build your queries so that your intended result is obtained from one query. Review your logic carefully to reduce the number of subqueries in the query as much as possible. Each subquery you include requires the DBMS to return an interim result set and integrate it with the remaining subqueries, thus increasing processing time.
- Sometimes data that reside in one table will be needed for several separate reports. Rather than obtain those data in several separate queries, create a single query that retrieves all the data that will be needed; you reduce the overhead by having the table accessed once rather than repeatedly. It may help you to recognize such a situation by thinking about the data that are typically used by a department and creating a view for the department's use.

Guidelines for Better Query Design

Now you have some strategies for developing queries that will give you the results you want. But will these strategies result in efficient queries, or will they result in the "query from hell," giving you plenty of time for the pizza to be delivered, to watch the *Star Trek* anthology, or to organize your closet? Various database experts, such as DeLoach (1987) and Holmes (1996), provide suggestions for improving query processing in a variety of settings. Also see the Web Resources at the end of this chapter and prior chapters for links to sites where query design suggestions are continually posted. We summarize here some of their suggestions that apply to many situations:

1. ***Understand how indexes are used in query processing*** Many DBMSs will use only one index per table in a query—often the one that is the most discriminating (i.e., has the most key values). Some will never use an index with only a few values compared to the number of table rows. Others may balk at using an index for which the column has many null values across the table rows. Monitor accesses to indexes and then drop indexes that are infrequently used. This will improve the performance of database update operations. In general, queries that have equality criteria for selecting table rows (e.g., WHERE Finish = "Birch" OR "Walnut") will result in faster processing than queries involving more complex qualifications do (e.g., WHERE Finish NOT = "Walnut") because equality criteria can be evaluated via indexes.
2. ***Keep optimizer statistics up-to-date*** Some DBMSs do not automatically update the statistics needed by the query optimizer. If performance is degrading, force the running of an update-statistics-like command.
3. ***Use compatible data types for fields and literals in queries*** Using compatible data types will likely mean that the DBMS can avoid having to convert data during query processing.
4. ***Write simple queries*** Usually the simplest form of a query will be the easiest for a DBMS to process. For example, because relational DBMSs are based on set theory, write queries that manipulate sets of rows and literals.
5. ***Break complex queries into multiple simple parts*** Because a DBMS may use only one index per query, it is often good to break a complex query into multiple, simpler parts (which each use an index) and then combine together the results of the smaller queries. For example, because a relational DBMS works with sets, it is very easy for the DBMS to UNION two sets of rows that are the result of two simple, independent queries.
6. ***Don't nest one query inside another query*** Usually, nested queries, especially correlated subqueries, are less efficient than a query that avoids subqueries to produce the same result. This is another case where using UNION, INTERSECT, or MINUS and multiple queries may produce results more efficiently.
7. ***Don't combine a table with itself*** Avoid, if possible, using self-joins. It is usually better (i.e., more efficient for processing the query) to make a temporary copy of a table and then to relate the original table with the temporary one. Temporary tables, because they quickly get obsolete, should be deleted soon after they have served their purpose.
8. ***Create temporary tables for groups of queries*** When possible, reuse data that are used in a sequence of queries. For example, if a series of queries all refer to the same subset of data from the database, it may be more efficient to first store this subset in one or more temporary tables and then refer to those temporary tables in the series of queries. This will avoid repeatedly combining the same data together or repeatedly scanning the database to find the same database segment for each query. The trade-off is that the temporary tables will not change if the original tables are updated when the queries are running. Using temporary tables is a viable substitute for derived tables, and they are created only once for a series of references.
9. ***Combine update operations*** When possible, combine multiple update commands into one. This will reduce query processing overhead and allow the DBMS to seek ways to process the updates in parallel.
10. ***Retrieve only the data you need*** This will reduce the data accessed and transferred. This may seem obvious, but there are some shortcuts for query writing that violate this guideline. For example, in SQL the command SELECT * from EMP will retrieve all the fields from all the rows of the EMP table. But, if the user needs to see only some of the columns of the table, transferring the extra columns increases the query processing time.

11. ***Don't have the DBMS sort without an index*** If data are to be displayed in sorted order and an index does not exist on the sort key field, then sort the data outside the DBMS after the unsorted results are retrieved. Usually a sort utility will be faster than a sort without the aid of an index by the DBMS.
12. ***Learn!*** Track query processing times, review query plans with the EXPLAIN command, and improve your understanding of the way the DBMS determines how to process queries. Attend specialized training from your DBMS vendor on writing efficient queries, which will better inform you about the query optimizer.
13. ***Consider the total query processing time for ad hoc queries*** The total time includes the time it takes the programmer (or end user) to write the query as well as the time to process the query. Many times, for ad hoc queries, it is better to have the DBMS do extra work to allow the user to more quickly write a query. And isn't that what technology is supposed to accomplish—to allow people to be more productive? So, don't spend too much time, especially for ad hoc queries, trying to write the most efficient query. Write a query that is logically correct (i.e., produces the desired results) and let the DBMS do the work. (Of course, do an EXPLAIN first to be sure you haven't written "the query from hell" so that all other users will see a serious delay in query processing time.) This suggests a corollary: When possible, run your query when there is a light load on the database, because the total query processing time includes delays induced by other load on the DBMS and database.

All options are not available with every DBMS, and each DBMS has unique options due to its underlying design. You should refer to reference manuals for your DBMS to know which specific tuning options are available to you.

ENSURING TRANSACTION INTEGRITY

RDBMSs are no different from other types of database managers in that one of their primary responsibilities is to ensure that data maintenance is properly and completely handled. Even with extensive testing, as suggested in the prior section, bad things can happen to good data managers: A data maintenance program may not work correctly because someone submitted the job twice, some unanticipated anomaly in the data occurred, or there was a computer hardware, software, or power malfunction during the transaction. Data maintenance is defined in units of work called *transactions*, which involve one or more data manipulation commands. A transaction is a complete set of closely related update commands that must all be done, or none of them done, for the database to remain valid. Consider Figure 7-10, for example. When an order is entered into the Pine Valley database, all of the items ordered should be entered at the same time. Thus, either all OrderLine_T rows from this form are to be entered, along with all the information in Order_T, or none of them should be entered. Here, the business transaction is the complete order, not the individual items that are ordered. What we need are commands to define the boundaries of a transaction, to commit the work of a transaction as a permanent change to the database, and to abort a transaction on purpose and correctly, if necessary. In addition, we need data recovery services to clean up after abnormal termination of database processing in the middle of a transaction. Perhaps the order form is accurate, but in the middle of entering the order, the computer system malfunctions or loses power. In this case, we do not want some of the changes made and not others. It's all or nothing at all if we want a valid database.

When a single SQL command constitutes a transaction, some RDBMSs will automatically commit or roll back after the command is run. With a user-defined transaction, however, where multiple SQL commands need to be run and either entirely committed or entirely rolled back, commands are needed to manage the transaction explicitly. Many systems will have BEGIN TRANSACTION and END TRANSACTION commands, which are used to mark the boundaries of a logical unit of work. BEGIN TRANSACTION creates a log file and starts recording all changes (insertions, deletions, and updates) to the database in this file. END TRANSACTION or COMMIT WORK takes the

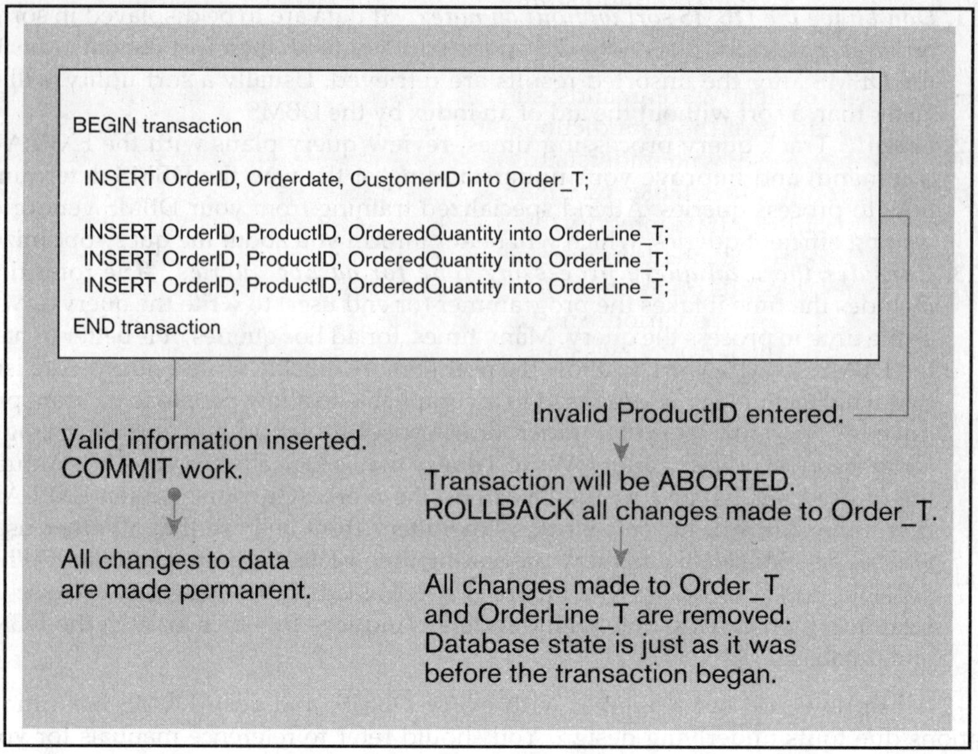

FIGURE 7-10 An SQL transaction sequence (in pseudocode)

contents of the log file and applies them to the database, thus making the changes permanent, and then empties the log file. ROLLBACK WORK asks SQL to empty the log file. Some RDBMSs also have an AUTOCOMMIT (ON/OFF) command that specifies whether changes are made permanent after each data modification command (ON) or only when work is explicitly made permanent (OFF) by the COMMIT WORK command.

User-defined transactions can improve system performance because transactions will be processed as sets rather than as individual transactions, thus reducing system overhead. When AUTOCOMMIT is set to OFF, changes will not be made automatically until the end of a transaction is indicated. When AUTOCOMMIT is set to ON, changes will be made automatically at the end of each SQL statement; this would not allow for user-defined transactions to be committed or rolled back only as a whole.

SET AUTOCOMMIT is an interactive command; therefore, a given user session can be dynamically controlled for appropriate integrity measures. Each SQL INSERT, UPDATE, and DELETE command typically works on only one table at a time. Some data maintenance requires updating of multiple tables for the work to be complete. Therefore, these transaction-integrity commands are important in clearly defining whole units of database changes that must be completed in full for the database to retain integrity.

Further, some SQL systems have concurrency controls that handle the updating of a shared database by concurrent users. These can journalize database changes so that a database can be recovered after abnormal terminations in the middle of a transaction. They can also undo erroneous transactions. For example, in a banking application, the update of a bank account balance by two concurrent users should be cumulative. Such controls are transparent to the user in SQL; no user programming is needed to ensure proper control of concurrent access to data. To ensure the integrity of a particular database, be sensitive to transaction integrity and recovery issues and make sure that application programmers are appropriately informed of when these commands are to be used.

DATA DICTIONARY FACILITIES

RDBMSs store database definition information in secure system-created tables; we can consider these system tables as a data dictionary. Becoming familiar with the systems tables for any RDBMS being used will provide valuable information, whether you are a user or a database administrator. Because the information is stored in tables, it can be accessed by using SQL SELECT statements that can generate reports about system usage, user privileges, constraints, and so on. Also, the RDBMS will provide special SQL (proprietary) commands, such as SHOW, HELP, or DESCRIBE, to display predefined contents of the data dictionary, including the DDL that created database objects. Further, a user who understands the systems-table structure can extend existing tables or build other tables to enhance built-in features (e.g., to include data on who is responsible for data integrity). A user is, however, often restricted from modifying the structure or contents of the system tables directly, because the DBMS maintains them and depends on them for its interpretation and parsing of queries.

Each RDBMS keeps various internal tables for these definitions. In Oracle 11g, there are 522 data dictionary views for DBAs to use. Many of these views, or subsets of the DBA view (i.e., information relevant to an individual user), are also available to users who do not possess DBA privileges. Those view names begin with USER (anyone authorized to use the database) or ALL (any user) rather than DBA. Views that begin with V$ provide updated performance statistics about the database. Here is a list of some of the tables (accessible to DBAs) that keep information about tables, clusters, columns, and security. There are also tables related to storage, objects, indexes, locks, auditing, exports, and distributed environments.

Table	Description
DBA_TABLES	Describes all tables in the database
DBA_TAB_COMMENTS	Comments on all tables in the database
DBA_CLUSTERS	Describes all clusters in the database
DBA_TAB_COLUMNS	Describes columns of all tables, views, and clusters
DBA_COL_PRIVS	Includes all grants on columns in the database
DBA_COL_COMMENTS	Comments on all columns in tables and views
DBA_CONSTRAINTS	Constraint definitions on all tables in the database
DBA_CLU_COLUMNS	Maps table columns to cluster columns
DBA_CONS_COLUMNS	Information about all columns in constraint definitions
DBA_USERS	Information about all users of the database
DBA_SYS_PRIVS	Describes system privileges granted to users and to roles
DBA_ROLES	Describes all roles that exist in the database
DBA_PROFILES	Includes resource limits assigned to each profile
DBA_ROLE_PRIVS	Describes roles granted to users and to other roles
DBA_TAB_PRIVS	Describes all grants on objects in the database

To give an idea of the type of information found in the system tables, consider DBA_USERS. DBA_USERS contains information about the valid users of the database; its 12 attributes include user name, user ID, encrypted password, default tablespace, temporary tablespace, date created, and profile assigned. DBA_TAB_COLUMNS has 31 attributes, including owner of each table, table name, column name, data type, data length, precision, and scale, among others. An SQL query against DBA_TABLES to find out who owns PRODUCT_T follows. (Note that we have to specify PRODUCT_T, not Product_T, because Oracle stores data names in all capital letters.)

Query: Who is the owner of the PRODUCT_T table?

```
SELECT OWNER, TABLE_NAME
  FROM DBA_TABLES
    WHERE TABLE_NAME = 'PRODUCT_T';
```

Result:

OWNER	TABLE_NAME
MPRESCOTT	PRODUCT_T

Every RDBMS contains a set of tables in which metadata of the sort described for Oracle 11g is contained. Microsoft SQL Server 2008 divides the system tables (or views) into different categories, based on the information needed:

- ***Catalog views,*** which return information that is used by the SQL Server database engine. All user-available catalog metadata is exposed through catalog views.
- ***Compatibility views,*** which are implementations of the system tables from earlier releases of SQL Server. These views expose the same metadata available in SQL Server 2000.
- ***Dynamic management views and functions,*** which return server state information that can be used to monitor the health of a server instance, diagnose problems, and tune performance. There are two types of dynamic management views and functions:
  - ***Server-scoped dynamic management views and functions,*** which require VIEW SERVER STATE permission on the server.
  - ***Database-scoped dynamic management views and functions,*** which require VIEW DATABASE STATE permission on the database.
- ***Information schema views,*** which provide an internal system table–independent view of the SQL Server metadata. The information schema views included in SQL Server comply with the ISO standard definition for the INFORMATION_SCHEMA.
- ***Replication views,*** which contain information that is used by data replication in Microsoft SQL Server.

SQL Server metadata tables begin with sys, just as Oracle tables begin with DBA, USER, or ALL.

Here are a few of the Microsoft SQL Server 2008 catalog views:

View	Description
sys.columns	Table and column specifications
sys.computed_columns	Specifications about computed columns
sys.foreign_key_columns	Details about columns in foreign key constraints
sys.indexes	Table index information
sys.objects	Database objects listing
sys.tables	Tables and their column names
sys.synonyms	Names of objects and their synonyms

These metadata views can be queried just like a view of base table data. For example, the following query displays specific information about objects in a SQL Server database that have been modified in the past 10 days:

```
SELECT name as object_name, SCHEMA_NAME (schema_id) AS
  schema_name, type_desc, create_date, modify_date
FROM sys.objects
WHERE modify_date > GETDATE() – 10
ORDER BY modify_date;
```

You will want to investigate the system views and metadata commands available with the RDBMS you are using. They can be life savers when you need critical information to solve a homework assignment or to work exam exercises. (Is this enough motivation?)

SQL:200N ENHANCEMENTS AND EXTENSIONS TO SQL

Chapter 6 and this chapter have demonstrated the power and simplicity of SQL. However, readers with a strong interest in business analysis may have wondered about the limited set of statistical functions available. Programmers familiar with other languages may have wondered how variables will be defined, flow control established, or **user-defined data types (UDTs)** created. And, as programming becomes more object oriented, how is SQL going to adjust? SQL:1999 extended SQL by providing more programming capabilities. SQL:200n has standardized additional statistical functions. With time, the SQL standard will be modified to encompass object-oriented concepts. Other notable additions in SQL:200n include three new data types and a new part, SQL/XML. The first two areas, additional statistical functions within the WINDOW clause, and the new data types, are discussed here. SQL/XML is discussed briefly in Chapter 8.

User-defined data type (UDT) A data type that a user can define by making it a subclass of a standard type or creating a type that behaves as an object. UDTs may also have defined functions and methods.

Analytical and OLAP Functions

SQL:200n added a set of analytical functions, referred to as OLAP (online analytical processing) functions, as SQL language extensions. Most of the functions have already been implemented in Oracle, DB2, Microsoft SQL Server, and Teradata. Including these functions in the SQL standard addresses the needs for analytical capabilities within the database engine. Linear regressions, correlations, and moving averages can now be calculated without moving the data outside the database. As SQL:200n is implemented, vendor implementations will adhere strictly to the standard and become more similar. We discuss OLAP further in Chapter 9, as part of the discussion of data warehousing.

Table 7-1 lists a few of the newly standardized functions. Both statistical and numeric functions are included. Functions such as ROW_NUMBER and RANK will allow the developer to work much more flexibly with an ordered result. For database marketing or customer relationship management applications, the ability to consider

TABLE 7-1 Some Built-in Functions Added in SQL:200n

Function	Description
CEILING	Computes the least integer greater than or equal to its argument—for example, CEIL(100) or CEILING(100).
FLOOR	Computes the greatest integer less than or equal to its argument—for example, FLOOR(25).
SQRT	Computes the square root of its argument—for example, SQRT(36).
RANK	Computes the ordinal rank of a row within its window. Implies that if duplicates exist, there will be gaps in the ranks assigned. The rank of the row is defined as 1 plus the number of rows preceding the row that are not peers of the row being ranked.
DENSE_RANK	Computes the ordinal rank of a row within its window. Implies that if duplicates exist, there will be no gaps in the ranks assigned. The rank of the row is the number of distinct rows preceding the row and itself.
ROLLUP	Works with GROUP BY to compute aggregate values for each level of the hierarchy specified by the group by columns, (The hierarchy is assumed to be left to right in the list of GROUP BY columns.)
CUBE	Works with GROUP BY to create a subtotal of all possible columns for the aggregate specified.
SAMPLE	Reduces the number of rows by returning one or more random samples (with or without replacement). (This function is not ANSI SQL-2003 compliant but is available with many RDBMSs.)
OVER or WINDOW	Creates partitions of data, based on values of one or more columns over which other analytical functions (e.g., RANK) can be computed.

only the top *n* rows or to subdivide the result into groupings by percentile is a welcome addition. Users can expect to achieve more efficient processing, too, as the functions are brought into the database engine and optimized. Once they are standardized, application vendors can depend on them, including their use in their applications and avoiding the need to create their own functions outside of the database.

SQL:1999 was amended to include an additional clause, the WINDOW clause. The WINDOW clause improves SQL's numeric analysis capabilities. It allows a query to specify that an action is to be performed over a set of rows (the window). This clause consists of a list of window definitions, each of which defines a name and specification for the window. Specifications include partitioning, ordering, and aggregation grouping.

Here is a sample query from the paper that proposed the amendment (Zemke et al., 1999, p. 4):

```
SELECT SH.Territory, SH.Month, SH.Sales,
AVG (SH.Sales) OVER W1 AS MovingAverage
    FROM SalesHistory AS SH
      WINDOW W1 AS (PARTITION BY (SH.Territory)
        ORDER BY (SH.Month ASC)
        ROWS 2 PRECEDING);
```

The window name is W1, and it is defined in the WINDOW clause that follows the FROM clause. The PARTITION clause partitions the rows in SalesHistory by Territory. Within each territory partition, the rows will be ordered in ascending order, by month. Finally, an aggregation group is defined as the current row and the two preceding rows of the partition, following the order imposed by the ORDER BY clause. Thus, a moving average of the sales for each territory will be returned as MovingAverage. Although proposed, MOVING_AVERAGE was not included in SQL:1999 or SQL:200n; it has been implemented by many RDBMS vendors, especially those supporting data warehousing and business intelligence. Though using SQL is not the preferred way to perform numeric analyses on data sets, inclusion of the WINDOW clause has made many OLAP analyses easier. Several new WINDOW functions were approved in SQL:200n. Of these new window functions, RANK and DENSE_RANK are included in Table 7-1. Previously included aggregate functions, such as AVG, SUM, MAX, and MIN, can also be used in the WINDOW clause.

New Data Types

SQL:200n includes three new data types and removed two traditional data types. The data types that were removed are BIT and BIT VARYING. Eisenberg et al. (2004) indicate that BIT and BIT VARYING were removed because they had not been widely supported by RDBMS products and were not expected to be supported.

The three new data types are BIGINT, MULTISET, and XML. BIGINT is an exact numeric type of scale 0, meaning it is an integer. The precision of BIGINT is greater than that of either INT or SMALLINT, but its exact definition is implementation specific. However, BIGINT, INT, and SMALLINT must have the same radix, or base system. All operations that can be performed using INT and SMALLINT can be performed using BIGINT, too.

MULTISET is a new collection data type. The previous collection data type is ARRAY, a noncore SQL data type. MULTISET differs from ARRAY because it can contain duplicates. This also distinguishes a table defined as MULTISET data from a relation, which is a set and cannot contain duplicates. MULTISET is unordered, and all elements are of the same element type. The elements can be any other supported data type. INTEGER MULTISET, for example, would define a multiset where all the elements are INTEGER data type. The values in a multiset may be created through INSERT or through a SELECT statement. An example of the INSERT approach would be MULTISET (2,3,5,7) and of the SELECT approach MULTISET (SELECT ProductDescription FROM Product_T WHERE ProductStandardPrice > 200;. MULTISET) reflects the real-world circumstance that some relations may contain duplicates that are acceptable when a subset is extracted from a table.

Other Enhancements

In addition to the enhancements to windowed tables described previously, the CREATE TABLE command has been enhanced by the expansion of CREATE TABLE LIKE options. CREATE TABLE LIKE allows one to create a new table that is similar to an existing table, but in SQL:1999 information such as default values, expressions used to generate a calculated column, and so forth, could not be copied to the new table. Now a general syntax of CREATE TABLE LIKE . . . INCLUDING has been approved. INCLUDING COLUMN DEFAULTS, for example, will pick up any default values defined in the original CREATE TABLE command and transfer it to the new table by using CREATE TABLE LIKE . . . INCLUDING. It should be noted that this command creates a table that seems similar to a materialized view. However, tables created using CREATE TABLE LIKE are independent of the table that was copied. Once the table is populated, it will not be automatically updated if the original table is updated.

An additional approach to updating a table can now be taken by using the new SQL:200n MERGE command. In a transactional database, it is an everyday need to be able to add new orders, new customers, new inventory, and so forth, to existing order, customer, and inventory tables. If changes that require updating information about customers and adding new customers are stored in a transaction table, to be added to the base customer table at the end of the business day, adding a new customer used to require an INSERT command, and changing information about an existing customer used to require an UPDATE command. The MERGE command allows both actions to be accomplished using only one query. Consider the following example from Pine Valley Furniture Company:

PINE VALLEY FURNITURE

```
MERGE INTO Customer_T as Cust
    USING (SELECT CustomerID, CustomerName, CustomerAddress,
    CustomerCity, CustomerState, CustomerPostalCode
      FROM CustTrans_T)
      AS CT
    ON (Cust.CustomerID = CT.CustomerID)
WHEN MATCHED THEN UPDATE
  SET Cust.CustomerName = CT.CustomerName,
    Cust.CustomerAddress = CT.CustomerAddress,
    Cust.CustomerCity = CT.CustomerCity,
    Cust.CustomerState = CT.CustomerState,
    Cust.CustomerPostalCode = CT.CustomerPostalCode
WHEN NOT MATCHED THEN INSERT
  (CustomerID, CustomerName, CustomerAddress, CustomerCity,
  CustomerState, CustomerPostalCode)
    VALUES (CT.CustomerID, CT.CustomerName, CT.CustomerAddress,
    CT.CustomerCity, CT.CustomerState, CT.CustomerPostalCode);
```

Programming Extensions

SQL-92 and earlier standards developed the capabilities of SQL as a data retrieval and manipulation language, and not as an application language. As a result, SQL has been used in conjunction with computationally complete languages such as C, .NET, and Java to create business application programs, procedures, or functions. SQL:1999, however, extended SQL by adding programmatic capabilities in core SQL, SQL/PSM, and SQL/OLB. These capabilities have been carried forward and included in SQL:200n.

The extensions that make SQL computationally complete include flow control capabilities, such as IF-THEN, FOR, WHILE statements, and loops, which are contained in a package of extensions to the essential SQL specifications. This package, called **Persistent Stored Modules (SQL/PSM)**, is so named because the capabilities to create and drop program modules are stored in it. *Persistent* means that a module of code will be stored until dropped, thus making it available for execution across user sessions, just as the base tables are retained until they are explicitly dropped. Each module is stored in a schema as a schema object. A schema does not have to have any program modules, or it may have multiple modules.

Persistent Stored Modules (SQL/PSM)
Extensions defined in SQL:1999 that include the capability to create and drop modules of code stored in the database schema across user sessions.

Each module must have a name, an authorization ID, an association with a particular schema, an indication of the character set to be used, and any temporary table declarations that will be needed when the module executes. Every module must contain one or more SQL procedures—named programs that each execute one SQL statement when called. Each procedure must also include an SQLSTATE declaration that acts as a status parameter and indicates whether an SQL statement has been successfully executed.

SQL/PSM can be used to create applications or to incorporate procedures and functions using SQL data types directly. Using SQL/PSM introduces procedurality to SQL, because statements are processed sequentially. Remember that SQL by itself is a nonprocedural language and that no statement execution sequence is implied. SQL/PSM includes several SQL control statements:

Statement	Description
CASE	Executes different sets of SQL sequences, according to a comparison of values or the value of a WHEN clause, using either search conditions or value expressions. The logic is similar to that of an SQL CASE expression, but it ends with END CASE rather than END and has no equivalent to the ELSE NULL clause.
IF	If a predicate is TRUE, executes an SQL statement. The statement ends with an ENDIF and contains ELSE and ELSEIF statements to manage flow control for different conditions.
LOOP	Causes a statement to be executed repeatedly until a condition exists that results in an exit.
LEAVE	Sets a condition that results in exiting a loop.
FOR	Executes once for each row of a result set.
WHILE	Executes as long as a particular condition exists. Incorporates logic that functions as a LEAVE statement.
REPEAT	Similar to the WHILE statement, but tests the condition after execution of the SQL statement.
ITERATE	Restarts a loop.

SQL/PSM brings the promise of addressing several widely noted deficiencies of essential SQL. It is still too soon to know if programmers are going to embrace SQL/PSM or continue to use host languages, invoking SQL through embedded SQL or via call-level interface (CLI). The standard makes it possible to do the following:

- Create procedures and functions within SQL, thus making it possible to accept input and output parameters and to return a value directly
- Detect and handle errors within SQL rather than having to handle errors through another language
- Use the DECLARE statement to create variables that stay in scope throughout the procedure, method, or function in which they are contained
- Pass groups of SQL statements rather than individual statements, thus improving performance
- Handle the impedance-mismatch problem, where SQL processes sets of data while procedural languages process single rows of data within modules

SQL/PSM has not yet been widely implemented, and therefore we have not included extensive syntax examples in this chapter. Oracle's PL/SQL and Microsoft SQL Server's T-SQL bear some resemblance to the new standard, with its modules of code and BEGIN . . . END, LOOP, and WHILE statements. Although SQL/PSM is not yet widely popular, this situation could change quickly.

TRIGGERS AND ROUTINES

Prior to the issuance of SQL:1999, no support for user-defined functions or procedures was included in the SQL standards. Commercial products, recognizing the need for such capabilities, have provided them for some time, and we expect to see their syntax change over time to be in line with the SQL:1999 requirements, just as we expect to see inclusion of SQL/PSM standards.

Trigger
A named set of SQL statements that are considered (triggered) when a data modification (i.e., INSERT, UPDATE, DELETE) occurs or if certain data definitions are encountered. If a condition stated within a trigger is met, then a prescribed action is taken.

Triggers and routines are very powerful database objects because they are stored in the database and controlled by the DBMS. Thus, the code required to create them is stored in only one location and is administered centrally. As with table and column constraints, this promotes stronger data integrity and consistency of use within the database; it can be useful in data auditing and security to create logs of information about data updates. Not only can triggers be used to prevent unauthorized changes to the database, they can also be used to evaluate changes and take actions based on the nature of the changes. Because triggers are stored only once, code maintenance is also simplified (Mullins, 1995). Also, because they can contain complex SQL code, they are more powerful than table and column constraints; however, constraints are usually more efficient and should be used instead of the equivalent triggers, if possible. A significant advantage of a trigger over a constraint to accomplish the same control is that the processing logic of a trigger can produce a customized user message about the occurrence of a special event, whereas a constraint will produce a standardized, DBMS error message, which often is not very clear about the specific event that occurred.

Both triggers and routines consist of blocks of procedural code. Routines are stored blocks of code that must be called to operate (see Figure 7-11). They do not run automatically. In contrast, trigger code is stored in the database and runs automatically whenever the triggering event, such as an UPDATE, occurs. Triggers are a special type of stored procedure and may run in response to either DML or DDL commands. Trigger syntax and functionality vary from RDBMS to RDBMS. A trigger written to work with an Oracle database will need to be rewritten if the database is ported to Microsoft SQL Server and vice versa. For example, Oracle triggers can be written to fire once per INSERT, UPDATE, or DELETE command or to fire once per row affected by the command. Microsoft SQL Server triggers can fire only once per DML command, not once per row.

Triggers

Because triggers are stored and executed in the database, they execute against all applications that access the database. Triggers can also cascade, causing other triggers to fire. Thus, a single request from a client can result in a series of integrity or logic checks being performed on the server without causing extensive network traffic between client

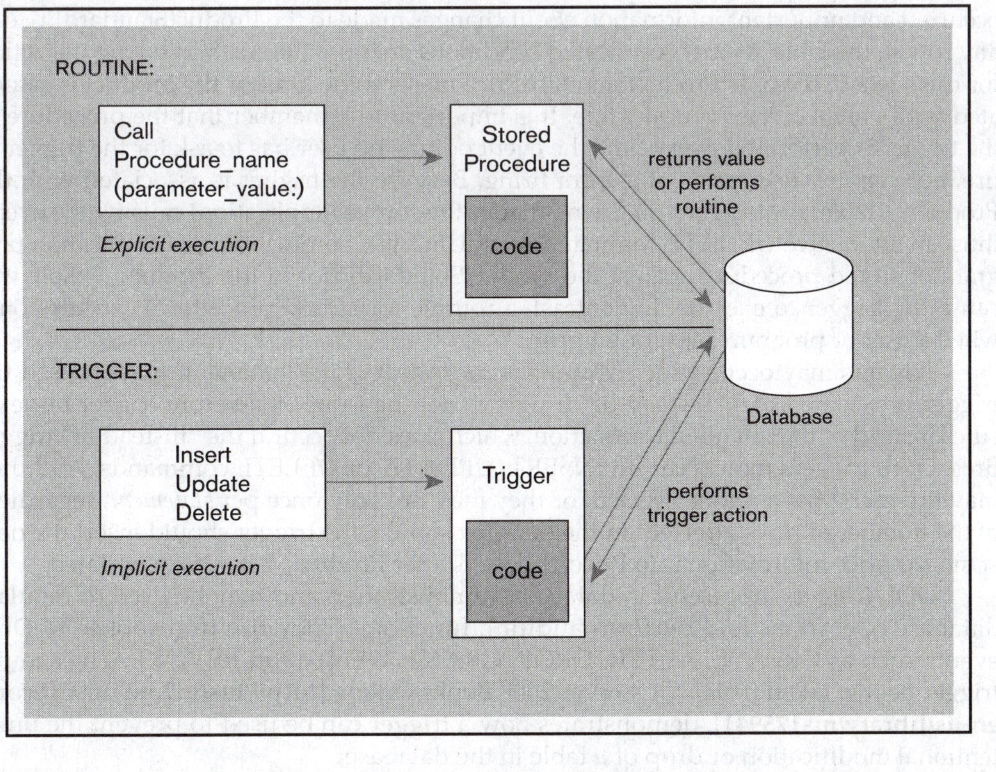

FIGURE 7-11 Triggers contrasted with stored procedures
Source: Based on Mullins (1995).

FIGURE 7-12 Simplified trigger syntax in SQL:200n

```
CREATETRIGGER trigger_name
    {BEFORE| AFTER | INSTEAD OF} {INSERT | DELETE | UPDATE} ON
    table_name
    [FOR EACH {ROW | STATEMENT}] [WHEN ( search condition)]
    <triggered SQL statement here>;
```

and server. Triggers can be used to ensure referential integrity, enforce business rules, create audit trails, replicate tables, or activate a procedure (Rennhackkamp, 1996).

Constraints can be thought of as a special case of triggers. They also are applied (triggered) automatically as a result of data modification commands, but their precise syntax is determined by the DBMS and does not have the flexibility of a trigger.

PINE VALLEY FURNITURE

Triggers are used when you need to perform, under specified conditions, a certain action as the result of some database event (e.g., the execution of a DML statement such as INSERT, UPDATE, or DELETE or the DDL statement ALTER TABLE). Thus, a trigger has three parts—the *event*, the *condition*, and the *action*—and these parts are reflected in the coding structure for triggers. (See Figure 7-12 for a simplified trigger syntax.) Consider the following example from Pine Valley Furniture Company: Perhaps the manager in charge of maintaining inventory needs to know (the action of being informed) when an inventory item's standard price is updated in the Product_T table (the event). After creating a new table, PriceUpdates_T, a trigger can be written that enters each product when it is updated, the date that the change was made, and the new standard price that was entered. The trigger is named StandardPriceUpdate, and the code for this trigger follows:

```
CREATE TRIGGER StandardPriceUpdate
AFTER UPDATE OF ProductStandardPrice ON Product_T
FOR EACH ROW
INSERT INTO PriceUpdates_T VALUES (ProductDescription, SYSDATE,
ProductStandardPrice);
```

In this trigger, the *event* is an update of ProductStandardPrice, the *condition* is FOR EACH ROW (i.e., not just certain rows), and the *action after the event* is to insert the specified values in the PriceUpdates_T table, which stores a log of when (SYSDATE) the change occurred and important information about changes made to the ProductStandardPrice of any row in the table. More complicated conditions are possible, such as taking the action for rows where the new ProductStandardPrice meets some limit or the product is associated with only a certain product line. It is important to remember that the procedure in the trigger is performed every time the event occurs; no user has to ask for the trigger to fire, nor can any user prevent it from firing. Because the trigger is associated with the Product_T table, the trigger will fire no matter the source (application) causing the event; thus, an interactive UPDATE command or an UPDATE command in an application program or stored procedure against the ProductStandardPrice in the Product_T table will cause the trigger to execute. In contrast, a routine (or stored procedure) executes only when a user or program asks for it to run.

Triggers may occur either *before*, *after*, or *instead of* the statement that aroused the trigger is executed. An "instead of" trigger is not the same as a before trigger but executes instead of the intended transaction, which does not occur if the "instead of" trigger fires. DML triggers may occur on INSERT, UPDATE, or DELETE commands. And they may fire each time a *row* is affected, or they may fire only once per *statement*, regardless of the number of rows affected. In the case just shown, the trigger should insert the new standard price information into PriceUpdate_T after Product_T has been updated.

DDL triggers are useful in database administration and may be used to regulate database operations and perform auditing functions. They fire in response to DDL events such as CREATE, ALTER, DROP, GRANT, DENY, and REVOKE. The sample trigger below, taken from SQL Server 2008 Books Online [**http://msdn2.microsoft.com/en-us/library/ms175941**], demonstrates how a trigger can be used to prevent the unintentional modification or drop of a table in the database:

```
CREATE TRIGGER safety
ON DATABASE
FOR DROP_TABLE, ALTER_TABLE
AS
    PRINT 'You must disable Trigger "safety" to drop or alter tables!'
    ROLLBACK;
```

A developer who wishes to include triggers should be careful. Because triggers fire automatically, unless a trigger includes a message to the user, the user will be unaware that the trigger has fired. Also, triggers can cascade and cause other triggers to fire. For example, a BEFORE UPDATE trigger could require that a row be inserted in another table. If that table has a BEFORE INSERT trigger, it will also fire, possibly with unintended results. It is even possible to create an endless loop of triggers! So, while triggers have many possibilities, including enforcement of complex business rules, creation of sophisticated auditing logs, and enforcement of elaborate security authorizations, they should be included with care.

Triggers can be written that provide little notification when they are triggered. A user who has access to the database but not the authority to change access permissions might insert the following trigger, also taken from SQL Server 2008 Books Online [**http://msdn2.microsoft.com/en-us/library/ms191134**]:

```
CREATE TRIGGER DDL_trigJohnDoe
ON DATABASE
FOR ALTER_TABLE
AS
GRANT CONTROL SERVER TO JohnDoe;
```

When an administrator with appropriate permissions issues any ALTER _TABLE command, the trigger DDL_trigJohnDoe will fire without notifying the administrator, and it will grant CONTROL SERVER permissions to John Doe.

Routines

In contrast to triggers, which are automatically run when a specified event occurs, routines must be explicitly called, just as the MIN built-in function is called. SQL-invoked routines can be either procedures or functions. The terms *procedure* and *function* are used in the same manner as they are in other programming languages. A **function** returns one value and has only input parameters. You have already seen the many built-in functions included in SQL, including the newest functions listed in Table 7-1. A **procedure** may have input parameters, output parameters, and parameters that are both input and output parameters. You may declare and name a unit of procedural code using proprietary code of the RDBMS product being used or invoke (via a CALL to an external procedure) a host-language library routine. SQL products had developed their own versions of routines prior to the issuance of SQL:1999, so be sure to become familiar with the syntax and capabilities of any product you use. Some of these proprietary languages, such as Microsoft SQL Server's Transact-SQL and Oracle's PL/SQL, are in wide use and will continue to be available. To give you an idea of how much stored procedure syntax has varied across products, Table 7-2 examines the CREATE PROCEDURE syntax used by three RDBMS vendors; this is the syntax for a procedure stored with the database. This table comes from **www.tdan.com/i023fe03.htm** by Peter Gulutzan (accessed June 6, 2007, but no longer accessible).

Function
A stored subroutine that returns one value and has only input parameters.

Procedure
A collection of procedural and SQL statements that are assigned a unique name within the schema and stored in the database.

The following are some of the advantages of SQL-invoked routines:

- ***Flexibility*** Routines may be used in more situations than constraints or triggers, which are limited to data-modification circumstances. Just as triggers have more code options than constraints, routines have more code options than triggers.
- ***Efficiency*** Routines can be carefully crafted and optimized to run more quickly than slower, generic SQL statements.

TABLE 7-2 Comparison of Vendor Syntax Differences in Stored Procedures

The vendors' syntaxes differ in stored procedures more than in ordinary SQL. For an illustration, here is a chart that shows what CREATE PROCEDURE looks like in three dialects. We use one line for each significant part, so you can compare dialects by reading across the line.

SQL:1999/IBM	MICROSOFT/SYBASE	ORACLE
CREATE PROCEDURE	CREATE PROCEDURE	CREATE PROCEDURE
Sp_proc1	Sp_proc1	Sp_proc1
(param1 INT)	@param1 INT	(param1 IN OUT INT)
MODIFIES SQL DATA BEGIN DECLARE num1 INT;	AS DECLARE @num1 INT	AS num1 INT; BEGIN
IF param1 <> 0	IF @param1 <> 0	IF param1 <> 0
THEN SET param1 = 1;	SELECT @param1 = 1;	THEN param1 :=1;
END IF		END IF;
UPDATE Table1 SET column1 = param1;	UPDATE Table1 SET column1 = @param1	UPDATE Table1 SET column1 = param1;
END		END

Source: Data from *SQL Performance Tuning* (Gulutzan and Pelzer, Addison-Wesley, 2002). Viewed at **www.tdan.com/i023fe03.htm**, June 6, 2007 (no longer available from this site).

- ***Sharability*** Routines may be cached on the server and made available to all users so that they do not have to be rewritten.
- ***Applicability*** Routines are stored as part of the database and may apply to the entire database rather than be limited to one application. This advantage is a corollary to sharability.

The SQL:200n syntax for procedure and function creation is shown in Figure 7-13. As you can see, the syntax is complicated, and we will not go into the details about each clause here. However, a simple procedure follows, to give you an idea of how the code works.

A procedure is a collection of procedural and SQL statements that are assigned a unique name within the schema and stored in the database. When it is needed to run the procedure, it is called by name. When it is called, all of the statements in the procedure will be executed. This characteristic of procedures helps to reduce network traffic, because all of the statements are transmitted at one time, rather than sent individually. A procedure can access database contents and may have local variables. When the procedure accesses database contents, the procedure will generate an error message if the user/program calling the procedure does not have the necessary rights to access the part of the database used by the procedure.

FIGURE 7-13 Syntax for creating a routine, SQL:200n

```
{CREATE PROCEDURE | CREATE FUNCTION} routine_nam e
([parameter [{,parameter} . . .]])
[RETURNS data_type result_cast]   /* for functions only */
[LANGUAGE {ADA | C | COBOL | FORTRAN | MUMPS | PASCAL | PLI | SQL}]
[PARAMETER STYLE {SQL | GENERAL}]
[SPECIFIC specific_name]
[DETERMINISTI C | NOT DETERMINISTIC]
[NO SQL | CONTAINS SQL | READS SQL DATA | MODIFIES SQL DA TA]
[RETURNS NULL ON NULL INPUT | CALLED ON NULL INPUT]
[DYNAMIC RESULT SETS unsigned_integer]      /* for procedures only */
[STATIC DISPATCH]                            /* for functions only */
[NEW SAVEPOINT LEVEL | OLD SA VEPOINT LEVEL]
routine_body
```

To build a simple procedure that will set a sale price, the existing Product_T table in Pine Valley Furniture company is altered by adding a new column, SalePrice, that will hold the sale price for the products:

PINE VALLEY FURNITURE

```
ALTER TABLE Product_T
ADD (SalePrice DECIMAL (6,2));
```

Result:

```
Table altered.
```

This simple procedure will execute two SQL statements, and there are no input or output parameters; if present, parameters are listed and given SQL data types in a parenthetical clause after the name of the procedure, similar to the columns in a CREATE TABLE command. The procedure scans all rows of the Product_T table. Products with a ProductStandardPrice of $400 or higher are discounted 10 percent, and products with a ProductStandardPrice of less than $400 are discounted 15 percent. As with other database objects, there are SQL commands to create, alter, replace, drop, and show the code for procedures. The following is an Oracle code module that will create and store the procedure named ProductLineSale:

```
CREATE OR REPLACE PROCEDURE ProductLineSale
  AS BEGIN
    UPDATE Product_T
      SET SalePrice = .90 * ProductStandardPrice
      WHERE ProductStandardPrice > = 400;
    UPDATE Product_T
      SET SalePrice = .85 * ProductStandardPrice
      WHERE ProductStandardPrice < 400;
END;
```

Oracle returns the comment "Procedure created" if the syntax has been accepted.

To run the procedure in Oracle, use this command (which can be run interactively, as part of an application program, or as part of another stored procedure):

```
SQL > EXEC ProductLineSale
```

Oracle gives this response:

```
PL/SQL procedure successfully completed.
```

Now Product_T contains the following:

PRODUCTLINE	PRODUCTID	PRODUCTDESCRIPTION	PRODUCTFINISH	PRODUCTSTANDARDPRICE	SALEPRICE
10001	1	End Table	Cherry	175	148.75
20001	2	Coffee Table	Natural Ash	200	170
20001	3	Computer Desk	Natural Ash	375	318.75
30001	4	Entertainment Center	Natural Maple	650	585
10001	5	Writer's Desk	Cherry	325	276.25
20001	6	8-Drawer Dresser	White Ash	750	675
20001	7	Dining Table	Natural Ash	800	720
30001	8	Computer Desk	Walnut	250	212.5

We have emphasized numerous times that SQL is a set-oriented language, meaning that, in part, the result of an SQL command is a set of rows. You probably noticed in Figure 7-13 that procedures can be written to work with many different host languages, most of which are record-oriented languages, meaning they are designed to manipulate one record, or row, at a time. This difference is often called an *impedance mismatch* between SQL and the host language that uses SQL commands. When SQL calls an SQL procedure, as in the example above, this is not an issue, but when the procedure is called, for example, by a C program, it can be an issue. In the next section we consider embedding SQL in host languages and some of the additional capabilities needed to allow SQL to work seamlessly with languages not designed to communicate with programs written in other, set-oriented languages.

EMBEDDED SQL AND DYNAMIC SQL

We have been using the interactive, or direct, form of SQL. With interactive SQL, one SQL command is entered and executed at a time. Each command constitutes a logical unit of work, or a transaction. The commands necessary to maintain a valid database, such as ROLLBACK and COMMIT, are transparent to the user in most interactive SQL situations. SQL was originally created to handle database access alone and did not have flow control or the other structures necessary to create an application. SQL/PSM, introduced in SQL:1999, provides for the types of programmatic extensions needed to develop a database application.

Embedded SQL
Hard-coded SQL statements included in a program written in another language, such as C or Java.

Dynamic SQL
Specific SQL code generated on the fly while an application is processing.

Prior to SQL/PSM, two other forms of SQL were widely used in creating applications on both clients and servers; they are referred to as **embedded SQL** and **dynamic SQL**. SQL commands can be embedded in third-generation langagues (3GLs), such as Ada, and COBOL, as well as in C, PHP, .NET, and Java if the commands are placed at appropriate locations in a 3GL host program. Oracle also offers PL/SQL, or SQL Procedural Language, a proprietary language that extends SQL by adding some procedural language features such as variables, types, control structures (including IF-THEN-ELSE loops), functions, and procedures. PL/SQL blocks of code can also be embedded within 3GL programs.

Dynamic SQL derives the precise SQL statement at run time. Programmers write to an application programming interface (API) to achieve the interface between languages. Embedded SQL and dynamic SQL will continue to be used. Programmers are used to them, and in many cases they are still an easier approach than attempting to use SQL as an application language in addition to using it for database creation, administration, and querying.

There are several reasons to consider embedding SQL in a 3GL:

1. It is possible to create a more flexible, accessible interface for the user. Using interactive SQL requires a good understanding of both SQL and the database structure—understanding that a typical application user may not have. Although many RDBMSs come with form, report, and application generators (or such capabilities available as add-ons), developers frequently envision capabilities that are not easily accomplished with these tools but that can be easily accomplished using a 3GL. Large, complex programs that require access to a relational database may best be programmed in a 3GL with embedded SQL calls to an SQL database.
2. It may be possible to improve performance by using embedded SQL. Using interactive SQL requires that each query be converted to executable machine code each time the query is processed. Or, the query optimizer, which runs automatically in a direct SQL situation, may not successfully optimize the query, causing it to run slowly. With embedded SQL, the developer has more control over database access and may be able to create significant performance improvements. Knowing when to rely on the SQL translator and optimizer and when to control it through the program depends on the nature of the problem, and making this trade-off is best accomplished through experience and testing.

3. Database security may be improved by using embedded SQL. Restricted access can be achieved by a DBA through the GRANT and REVOKE permissions in SQL and through the use of views. These same restrictions can also be invoked in an embedded SQL application, thus providing another layer of protection. Complex data integrity checks also may be more easily accomplished, including cross-field consistency checks.

A program that uses embedded SQL will consist of the host program written in a 3GL such as C or COBOL, and there will also be sections of SQL code sprinkled throughout. Each section of SQL code will begin with EXEC SQL, keywords used to indicate an embedded SQL command that will be converted to the host source code when run through the precompiler. You will need a separate precompiler for each host language that you plan to use. Be sure to determine that the 3GL compiler is compatible with your RDBMS's precompiler for each language.

When the precompiler encounters an EXEC SQL statement, it will translate that SQL command into the host program language. Some, but not all, precompilers will check for correct SQL syntax and generate any required error messages at this point. Others will not generate an error message until the SQL statement actually attempts to execute. Some products' precompilers (DB2, SQL/DS, Ingres) create a separate file of SQL statements that is then processed by a separate utility called a binder, which determines that the referenced objects exist, that the user possesses sufficient privileges to run the statement, and the processing approach that will be used. Other products (Oracle, Informix) interpret the statements at run time rather than compiling them. In either case, the resulting program will contain calls to DBMS routines, and the link/editor programs will link these routines into the program.

Here is a simple example, using C as the host language, that will give you an idea of what embedded SQL looks like in a program. This example uses a prepared SQL statement named GETCUST, which will be compiled and stored as executable code in the database. CustID is the primary key of the customer table. GETCUST, the prepared SQL statement, returns customer information (cname, caddress, city, state, postcode) for an order number. A placeholder is used for the order information, which is an input parameter. Customer information is output from the SQL query and stored into host variables using the *into* clause. This example assumes that only one row is returned from the query, what is often called a singleton SELECT. (We'll discuss below how to handle the situation in which it is possible to return more than one row.)

```
    exec sql prepare getcust from
    "select cname, c_address, city, state, postcode
    from customer_t, order_t
    where customer_t.custid = order_t.custid and orderid = ?";
    .
    .
    ./* code to get proper value in theOrder */
  exec sql execute getcust into :cname, :caddress, :city, :state,
  :postcode using theOrder;
  .
  .
  .
```

If a prepared statement returns multiple rows, it is necessary to write a program loop using cursors to return a row at a time to be stored. A cursor is a data structure, internal to the programming environment, that points to a result table row (similarly to how a display screen cursor points to where data would be inserted in a form if you began entering data). Cursors help to eliminate the impedance mismatch between SQL's set-at-a-time processing and procedural languages' record-at-a-time processing. Record-at-a-time languages have to be able to move cursor values forward and backward in the set (FETCH NEXT or FETCH PRIOR), to find the first or last row in a result set (FETCH FIRST and FETCH LAST), to move the cursor to a specific row or one relative to the current position (FETCH ABSOLUTE or FETCH RELATIVE), and to know the number of rows to process and when the end of the result set is reached, which often triggers the end of a programming loop (FOR . . . END FOR). There are different types of cursors, and the number of types and how they are each handled varies by RDBMS. Thus, this topic is beyond the scope of this book, although you are now aware of this important aspect of embedded SQL.

Dynamic SQL is used to generate appropriate SQL code on the fly while an application is processing. Most programmers write to an API, such as ODBC, which can then be passed through to any ODBC-compliant database. Dynamic SQL is central to most Internet applications. The developer is able to create a more flexible application because the exact SQL query is determined at run time, including the number of parameters to be passed, which tables will be accessed, and so forth. Dynamic SQL is very useful when an SQL statement shell will be used repeatedly, with different parameter values being inserted each time it executes.

Embedded and dynamic SQL code is vulnerable to malicious modification. Any procedure that has or especially constructs SQL statements should be reviewed for such vulnerabilities. A common form of such an attack involves insertion of the malicious code into user input variables that are concatenated with SQL commands and then executed. Alternatively, malicious code can be included in text stored in the database. As long as the malicious code is syntactically correct, the SQL database engine will process it. Preventing and detecting such attacks can be complicated, and this is beyond the scope of this text. The reader is encouraged to do an Internet search on the topic of SQL injection for recommendations. At a minimum, user input should be carefully validated, strong typing of columns should be used to limit exposure, and input data can be filtered or modified so that special SQL characters (e.g., ;) or words (e.g., DELETE) are put in quotes so they cannot be executed.

Currently, the Open Database Connectivity (ODBC) standard is the most commonly used API. SQL:1999 includes the SQL Call Level Interface (SQL/CLI). Both are written in C, and both are based on the same earlier standard. Java Database Connectivity (JDBC) is an industry standard used for connecting from Java. It is not yet an ISO standard. No new functionality has been added in SQL:200n.

As SQL:200n becomes implemented more completely, the use of embedded and dynamic SQL will become more standardized because the standard creates a computationally complete SQL language for the first time. Because most vendors have created these capabilities independently, though, the next few years will be a period in which SQL:1999-compliant products will exist side by side with older, but entrenched, versions. The user will need to be aware of these possibilities and deal with them.

Summary

This chapter continues from Chapter 6, which introduced the SQL language. Equi-joins, natural joins, outer joins, and union joins have been considered. Equi-joins are based on equal values in the common columns of the tables that are being joined and will return all requested results including the values of the common columns from each table included in the join. Natural joins return all requested results, but values of the common columns are included only once. Outer joins return all the values in one of the tables included in the join, regardless of whether a match exists in the other table or not. Union joins return a table that includes all data from each table that was joined.

Nested subqueries, where multiple SELECT statements are nested within a single query, are useful for more complex query situations. A special form of the subquery, a correlated subquery, requires that a value be known from the outer query before the inner query can be processed. Other subqueries process the inner query, return a result to the next outer query, and then process that outer query.

Other advanced SQL topics include the use of embedded SQL and the use of triggers and routines. SQL can be included within the context of many third-generation languages including COBOL, C, Fortran, and Ada and more modern languages such as C, PHP, .NET, and Java. The use of embedded SQL allows for the development of more flexible interfaces, improved performance, and improved database security. User-defined functions that run automatically when records are inserted, updated, or deleted are called triggers. Procedures are user-defined code modules that can be called to execute. OLTP and OLAP are used for operational transaction processing and data analysis respectively.

New analytical functions included in SQL:200n are shown. Extensions already included in SQL:1999 made SQL computationally complete and included flow control capabilities in a set of SQL specifications known as Persistent Stored Modules (SQL/PSM). SQL/PSM can be used to create applications or to incorporate procedures and functions using SQL data types directly. SQL-invoked routines, including triggers, functions, and procedures, were also included in SQL:1999. Users must realize that these capabilities have been included as vendor-specific extensions and will continue to exist for some time.

Dynamic SQL is an integral part of Web-enabling databases and will be demonstrated in more detail in Chapter 8. This chapter has presented some of the more complex capabilities of SQL and has created awareness of the extended and complex capabilities of SQL that must be mastered to build database application programs.

Chapter Review

Key Terms

Correlated subquery *305*
Dynamic SQL *328*
Embedded SQL *328*
Equi-join *293*
Function *325*
Join *292*
Natural join *294*
Outer join *295*
Persistent Stored Modules (SQL/PSM) *321*
Procedure *325*
Trigger *323*
User-defined data type (UDT) *319*

Review Questions

1. Define each of the following terms:
   a. dynamic SQL
   b. correlated subquery
   c. embedded SQL
   d. procedure
   e. join
   f. equi-join
   g. self join
   h. outer join
   i. function
   j. Persistent Stored Modules (SQL/PSM)
2. Match the following terms to the appropriate definition:

____ equi-join	a. undoes changes to a table
____ natural join	b. user-defined data type
____ outer join	c. SQL:1999 extension
____ trigger	d. returns all records of designated table
____ procedure	e. keeps redundant columns
____ embedded SQL	f. makes changes to a table permanent
____ UDT	g. process that includes SQL statements within a host language
____ COMMIT	h. process of making an application capable of generating specific SQL code on the fly
____ SQL/PSM	i. does not keep redundant columns
____ Dynamic SQL	j. set of SQL statements that execute under stated conditions
____ ROLLBACK	k. stored, named collection of procedural and SQL statements

3. When is an outer join used instead of a natural join?
4. Explain the processing order of a correlated subquery.
5. Explain the following statement regarding SQL: Any query that can be written using the subquery approach can also be written using the joining approach but not vice versa.
6. What is the purpose of the COMMIT command in SQL? How does commit relate to the notion of a business transaction (e.g., entering a customer order or issuing a customer invoice)?
7. Care must be exercised when writing triggers for a database. What are some of the problems that could be encountered?
8. Explain the structure of a module of code that defines a trigger.
9. Under what conditions can a UNION clause be used?
10. Discuss the differences between triggers and stored procedures.
11. Explain the purpose of SQL/PSM.
12. List four advantages of SQL-invoked routines.
13. When would you consider using embedded SQL? When would you use dynamic SQL?
14. When do you think that the CASE keyword in SQL would be useful?
15. Explain the use of derived tables.
16. Describe an example in which you would want to use a derived table.
17. What other Oracle object can be used in place of a derived table? Which approach do you think is better?
18. If two queries involved in a UNION operation contained columns that were data type incompatible, how would you recommend fixing this?
19. Can an outer join be easily implemented when joining more than two tables? Why or why not?
20. This chapter discusses the data dictionary views for Oracle 11g. Research another RDBMS, such as Microsoft SQL Server, and report on its data dictionary facility and how it compares with Oracle.
21. What is a subquery in an SQL SELECT statement?
22. Under what circumstances you would be using an Embedded SQL or a Dynamic SQL?
23. What are TRIGGERS? When is a TRIGGER ideally to be used?

Problems and Exercises

Problems and Exercises 1 through 5 are based on the class schedule 3NF relations along with some sample data in Figure 7-14. For Problems and Exercises 1 through 5, draw a Venn or ER diagrams and mark it to show the data you expect your query use to produce the results.

1. Write SQL retrieval commands for each of the following queries:
   a. Display the course ID and course name for all courses with an ISM prefix.
   b. Display all courses for which Professor Berndt has been qualified.
   c. Display the class roster, including student name, for all students enrolled in section 2714 of ISM 4212.
2. Write an SQL query to answer the following question: Which instructors are qualified to teach ISM 3113?
3. Write an SQL query to answer the following question: Is any instructor qualified to teach ISM 3113 and not qualified to teach ISM 4930?
4. Write SQL queries to answer the following questions:
   a. How many students were enrolled in section 2714 during semester I-2008?
   b. How many students were enrolled in ISM 3113 during semester I-2008?
5. Write an SQL query to answer the following question: Which students were not enrolled in any courses during semester I-2008?

Problems and Exercises 6 through 14 are based on Figure 7-15. This problem set continues from Chapter 6, Problems and Exercises 10 through 15, which were based on Figure 6-12.

6. Determine the relationships among the four entities in Figure 7-15. List primary keys for each entity and any foreign keys necessary to establish the relationships and maintain referential integrity. Pay particular attention to the data contained in TUTOR REPORTS when you set up its primary key.

STUDENT (StudentID, StudentName)

StudentID	StudentName
38214	Letersky
54907	Altvater
66324	Aiken
70542	Marra
...	

QUALIFIED (FacultyID, CourseID, DateQualified)

FacultyID	CourseID	DateQualified
2143	ISM 3112	9/1988
2143	ISM 3113	9/1988
3467	ISM 4212	9/1995
3467	ISM 4930	9/1996
4756	ISM 3113	9/1991
4756	ISM 3112	9/1991
...		

FACULTY (FacultyID, FacultyName)

FacultyID	FacultyName
2143	Birkin
3467	Berndt
4756	Collins
...	

SECTION (SectionNo, Semester, CourseID)

SectionNo	Semester	CourseID
2712	I-2008	ISM 3113
2713	I-2008	ISM 3113
2714	I-2008	ISM 4212
2715	I-2008	ISM 4930
...		

COURSE (CourseID, CourseName)

CourseID	CourseName
ISM 3113	Syst Analysis
ISM 3112	Syst Design
ISM 4212	Database
ISM 4930	Networking
...	

REGISTRATION (StudentID, SectionNo, Semester)

StudentID	SectionNo	Semester
38214	2714	I-2008
54907	2714	I-2008
54907	2715	I-2008
66324	2713	I-2008
...		

FIGURE 7-14 Class scheduling relations (for Problems and Exercises 1–5)

FIGURE 7-15 Adult literacy program (for Problems and Exercises 6–14)

TUTOR (TutorID, CertDate, Status)

TutorID	CertDate	Status
100	1/05/2008	Active
101	1/05/2008	Temp Stop
102	1/05/2008	Dropped
103	5/22/2008	Active
104	5/22/2008	Active
105	5/22/2008	Temp Stop
106	5/22/2008	Active

MATCH HISTORY (MatchID, TutorID, StudentID, StartDate, EndDate)

MatchID	TutorID	StudentID	StartDate	EndDate
1	100	3000	1/10/2008	
2	101	3001	1/15/2008	5/15/2008
3	102	3002	2/10/2008	3/01/2008
4	106	3003	5/28/2008	
5	103	3004	6/01/2008	6/15/2008
6	104	3005	6/01/2008	6/28/2008
7	104	3006	6/01/2008	

STUDENT (StudentID, Read)

StudentID	Read
3000	2.3
3001	5.6
3002	1.3
3003	3.3
3004	2.7
3005	4.8
3006	7.8
3007	1.5

TUTOR REPORT (MatchID, Month, Hours, Lessons)

MatchID	Month	Hours	Lessons
1	6/08	8	4
4	6/08	8	6
5	6/08	4	4
4	7/08	10	5
1	7/08	4	2

7. Write the SQL command to add MATH SCORE to the STUDENT table.
8. Write the SQL command to add SUBJECT to TUTOR. The only values allowed for SUBJECT will be Reading, Math, and ESL.
9. What do you need to do if a tutor signs up and wants to tutor in both reading and math? Draw the new ERD and write any SQL statements that would be needed to handle this development.
10. Write the SQL command to find any tutors who have not submitted a report for July.
11. Where do you think student and tutor information such as name, address, phone, and e-mail should be kept? Write the necessary SQL commands to capture this information.
12. List all active students in June by name. (Make up names and other data if you are actually building a prototype database.) Include the number of hours students received tutoring and how many lessons they completed.
13. Which tutors, by name, are available to tutor? Write the SQL command.
14. Which tutor needs to be reminded to turn in reports? Write the SQL command.

PINE VALLEY FURNITURE

Problems and Exercises 15 through 44 are based on the entire ("big" version) Pine Valley Furniture Company database. Note: Depending on what DBMS you are using, some field names may have changed to avoid conflicting with reserved words for the DBMS. When you first use the DBMS, check the table definitions to see what the field names are for the DBMS you are using. See the Preface and inside covers of this book for instructions on where to find this database, including on **www.teradatastudentnetwork.com**.

15. Write an SQL command that will find any customers who have not placed orders.
16. List the names and number of employees supervised (label this value HeadCount) for each supervisor who supervises more than two employees.
17. List the name of each employee, his or her birth date, the name of his or her manager, and the manager's birth date for those employees who were born before their manager was born; label the manager's data Manager and ManagerBirth.
18. Write an SQL command to display the order number, customer number, order date, and items ordered for order number 1.
19. Write an SQL command to display each item ordered for order number 1, its standard price, and the total price for each item ordered.
20. Write an SQL command to total the cost of order number 1.
21. Calculate the total raw material cost (label TotCost) for each product compared to its standard product price. Display product ID, product description, standard price, and the total cost in the result.
22. For every order that has been received, display the order ID, the total dollar amount owed on that order (you'll have to calculate this total from attributes in one or more tables; label this result TotalDue), and the amount received in

payments on that order (assume that there is only one payment made on each order). To make this query a little simpler, you don't have to include those orders for which no payment has yet been received. List the results in decreasing order of the difference between total due and amount paid.

23. Write an SQL query to list each salesperson who has sold computer desks and the number of units sold by each salesperson.

24. List, in alphabetical order, the names of all employees (managers) who are now managing people with skill ID BS12; list each manager's name only once, even if that manager manages several people with this skill.

25. Display the salesperson name, product finish, and total quantity sold (label as TotSales) for each finish by each salesperson.

26. Write a query to list the number of products produced in each work center (label as TotalProducts). If a work center does not produce any products, display the result with a total of 0.

27. The production manager at PVFC is concerned about support for purchased parts in products owned by customers. A simple analysis he wants done is to determine for each customer how many vendors are in the same state as that customer. Develop a list of *all* the PVFC customers by name with the number of vendors in the same state as that customer. (Label this computed result NumVendors.)

28. Display the order IDs for customers who have not made any payment, yet, on that order. Use the set command UNION, INTERSECT, or MINUS in your query.

29. Display the names of the states in which customers reside but for which there is no salesperson residing in that state. There are several ways to write this query. Try to write it without any WHERE clause. Write this query two ways, using the set command UNION, INTERSECT, or MINUS and not using any of these commands. Which was the most natural approach for you, and why?

30. Write an SQL query to produce a list of all the products (i.e., product description) and the number of times each product has been ordered.

31. Display the customer ID, name, and order ID for all customer orders. For those customers who do not have any orders, include them in the display once.

32. Display the EmployeeID and EmployeeName for those employees who do not possess the skill Router. Display the results in order by EmployeeName.

33. Display the name of customer 16 and the names of all the customers that are in the same zip code as customer 16. (Be sure this query will work for any customer.)

34. Rewrite your answer to Problem and Exercise 33 for each customer, not just customer 16.

35. Display the customer ID, name, and order ID for all customer orders. For those customers who do not have any orders, include them in the display once by showing order ID 0.

36. Show the customer ID and name for all the customers who have ordered both products with IDs 3 and 4 on the same order.

37. Display the customer names of all customer who have ordered (on the same or different orders) both products with IDs 3 and 4.

38. Review the first query in the "Correlated Subqueries" section. Can you identify a special set of standard prices for which this query will not yield the desired result? How might you rewrite the query to handle this situation?

39. Write an SQL query to list the order number and order quantity for all customer orders for which the order quantity is greater than the average order quantity of that product. (Hint: This involves using a correlated subquery.)

40. Write an SQL query to list the salesperson who has sold the most computer desks.

41. Display in product ID order the product ID and total amount ordered of that product by the customer who has bought the most of that product; use a derived table in a FROM clause to answer this query.

42. Display employee information for all the employees in each state who were hired before the most recently hired person in that state.

43. The head of marketing is interested in some opportunities for cross-selling of products. She thinks that the way to identify cross-selling opportunities is to know for each product how many other products are sold to the same customer on the same order (e.g., a product that is bought by a customer in the same order with lots of other products is a better candidate for cross-selling than a product bought by itself).

a. To help the marketing manager, first list the IDs for all the products that have sold in total more than 20 units across all orders. (These are popular products, which are the only products she wants to consider as triggers for potential cross-selling.)

b. Make a new query that lists all the IDs for the orders that include products that satisfy the first query, along with the number of products on those orders. Only orders with three or more products on them are of interest to the marketing manager. Write this query as general as possible to cover any answer to the first query, which might change over time. To clarify, if product X is one of the products that is in the answer set from part a, then in part b we want to see the desired order information for orders that include product X.

c. The marketing manager needs to know what other products were sold on the orders that are in the result for part b. (Again, write this query for the general, not specific, result to the query in part b.) These are products that are sold, for example, with product X from part a, and these are the ones that if people buy that product, we'd want to try to cross-sell them product X because history says they are likely to buy it along with what else they are buying. Write a query to identify these other products by ID and description. It is okay to include "product X" in your result (i.e., you don't need to exclude the products in the result of part a.).

44. For each product, display in ascending order, by product ID, the product ID and description, along with the customer ID and name for the customer who has bought the most of that product; also show the total quantity ordered by that customer (who has bought the most of that product). Use a correlated subquery.

45. Write SQL retrieval commands for the following: (Refer table on Chapter 6, P. 288, Q 45)

a. List the department names where there are no employees.

b. List employees in dept no. 110 having the same salary as anyone in the TESTING department.

c. Display the information about employees earning more than any employee in dept no. 130.

46. Write SQL retrieval commands for the following: (Refer table on Chapter 6, P. 288, Q 45)

a. List the name and department of the employee earning the highest salary.

b. Find the average compensation paid to employees as COMM.

c. List employees names whose COMM is 15% more than their SALARY.

Field Exercises

1. Conduct a search of the Web to locate as many links as possible that discuss SQL standards.
2. Compare two versions of SQL to which you have access, such as Microsoft Access and Oracle SQL*Plus. Identify at least five similarities and three dissimilarities in the SQL code from these two SQL systems. Do the dissimilarities cause results to differ?

References

DeLoach, A. 1987. "The Path to Writing Efficient Queries in SQL/DS." *Database Programming & Design* 1,1 (January): 26–32.

Eisenberg, A., J. Melton, K. Kulkarni, J. E. Michels, and F. Zemke. 2004. "SQL:2003 Has Been Published." *SIGMOD Record* 33,1 (March):119–126.

Gulutzan, P., and T. Pelzer. 1999. *SQL-99 Complete, Really!* Lawrence, KS: R&D Books.

Holmes, J. 1996. "More Paths to Better Performance." *Database Programming & Design* 9, 2 (February):47–48.

Mullins, C. S. 1995. "The Procedural DBA." *Database Programming & Design* 8,12 (December): 40–45.

Rennhackkamp, M. 1996. "Trigger Happy." *DBMS* 9,5 (May): 89–91, 95.

Zemke, F., K. Kulkarni, A. Witkowski, and B. Lyle. 1999. "Introduction to OLAP Functions." ISO/IEC JTC1/SC32 WG3: YGJ.068 ANSI NCITS H2–99–154r2.

Further Reading

American National Standards Institute. 2000. *ANSI Standards Action* 31,11 (June 2): 20.

Celko, J. 2006. *Analytics and OLAP in SQL*. San Francisco: Morgan Kaufmann.

Codd, E. F. 1970. "A Relational Model of Data for Large Shared Data Banks." *Communications of the ACM* 13,6 (June): 77–87.

Date, C. J., and H. Darwen. 1997. *A Guide to the SQL Standard.* Reading, MA: Addison-Wesley.

Itzik, B., L. Kollar, and D. Sarka. 2006. *Inside Microsoft SQL Server 2005 T-SQL Querying*. Redmond, WA: Microsoft Press.

Itzik B., D. Sarka, and R. Wolter. 2006. *Inside Microsoft SQL Server 2005: T-SQL Programming*. Redmond, WA: Microsoft Press.

Kulkarni, K. 2004. "Overview of SQL:2003." Accessed at **www.wiscorp.com/SQLStandards.html#keyreadings**.

Melton, J. 1997. "A Case for SQL Conformance Testing." *Database Programming & Design* 10,7 (July): 66–69.

van der Lans, R. F. 1993. *Introduction to SQL*, 2nd ed. Workingham, UK: Addison-Wesley.

Winter, R. 2000. "SQL-99's New OLAP Functions." *Intelligent Enterprise* 3,2 (January 20): 62, 64–65.

Winter, R. 2000. "The Extra Mile." *Intelligent Enterprise* 3,10 (June 26): 62–64.

See also "Further Reading" in Chapter 6.

Web Resources

www.ansi.org Web site of the American National Standards Institute. Contains information on the ANSI federation and the latest national and international standards.

www.coderecipes.net Web site that explains and shows examples for a wide range of SQL commands.

www.fluffycat.com/SQL/ Web site that defines a sample database and shows examples of SQL queries against this database.

www.iso.ch The International Organization for Standardization's (ISO's) Web site, which provides information about the ISO. Copies of current standards may be purchased here.

www.sqlcourse.com and www.sqlcourse2.com Web sites that provide tutorials for a subset of ANSI SQL with a practice database.

standards.ieee.org The home page of the IEEE standards organization.

www.tizag.com/sqlTutorial/ Web site that provides a set of tutorials on SQL concepts and commands.

http://troelsarvin.blogspot.com/ Blog that provides a detailed comparison of different SQL implementations, including DB2, Microsoft SQL, MySQL, Oracle, and PostGreSQL

www.teradatastudentnetwork.com Web site where your instructor may have created some course environments for you to use Teradata SQL Assistant, Web Edition, with one or more of the Pine Valley Furniture and Mountain View Community Hospital data sets for this text.

CASE

Mountain View Community Hospital

Case Description

Use the databases you implemented in Chapter 6 for Mountain View Community Hospital to complete the case questions and case exercises.

Case Questions

1. Does your SQL-based DBMS support dynamic SQL, functions, triggers, stored procedures, and UDTs?
2. HIPAA's privacy and security rules mandate audit controls "that record and examine activity in information systems that contain or use electronic protected health information" [§164.312(b)]. How can DDL triggers be used in support of this mandate?

Case Exercises

1. Using the small sample database you created for Dr. Z in Case Exercise 1 in Chapter 6, write queries that illustrate the more complex queries covered in this chapter:
   a. Select information from two or more tables (e.g., all the details of all the visits of a patient, etc.).
   b. Use subquery syntax (e.g., a listing of all the patients who reported pain that exceeded the average pain for all visits).
   c. Return a result table that could be used to produce a report, sorted by patient name or date, for a particular week or after a particular date, or a listing of patient visits for patients assigned to a specific social worker.
2. Review the exercises below and select several to attempt. You will probably need to add to your prototype and populate your tables with sample data in order to test your queries:
   a. For a given physician, which treatments has that physician performed on each patient referred by that physician to the hospital?
   b. For the query in part a, also include physicians who have not referred patients to the hospital.
   c. For each patient, what is the average number of treatments performed on him or her by each physician who has treated that patient?
   d. List all patients who have received no treatments.
   e. For each nurse in charge, what is the total number of hours worked by all employees who work in the care center which that nurse supervises?
   f. Which technicians have more than one skill listed? Which technicians have no skills listed?
   g. Determine whether any outpatients were accidentally assigned to resident beds.
   h. Determine which item is consumed most.
   i. Determine which physicians prescribe the most expensive item.
   j. Return a result table that could be used to produce a hospital report, such as nursing staff assigned to each care center.
   k. Use the UNION statement to provide a combined listing of care center names and their locations as well as laboratories and their location. The list should be sorted by location, in ascending order. (You should use aliases to rename the fields in this query.)

Project Assignments

P1. Write and execute the queries for the five reports you identified in Chapter 5.

P2. Identify opportunities for using triggers in your database and create at least one DDL trigger. For example, the claims manager at the hospital may need to know that a patient's health insurance has been updated.

CHAPTER

8

Database Application Development

Learning Objectives

After studying this chapter, you should be able to:

- Concisely define each of the following key terms: **client/server systems, fat client, database server, stored procedure, three-tier architecture, thin client, application partitioning, middleware, and application program interface (API), World Wide Web Consortium (W3C), Extensible Markup Language (XML), XHTML, XML Schema Definition, Extensible Stylesheet Language Transformation (XSLT), XPath, XQuery, Java servlet, Web services, Universal Description, Discovery, and Integration (UDDI), Web Services Description Language (WSDL), Simple Object Access Protocol (SOAP), and Service-oriented architecture (SOA).**
- Explain the three components of client/server systems: data presentation services, processing services, and storage services.
- Distinguish between two-tier and three-tier architectures.
- Describe how to connect to databases in a two-tier application in VB.NET and Java.
- Describe the key components of a Web application and the information flow between the various components.
- Describe how to connect to databases in a three-tier Web application using Java Server Pages (JSP), PHP, and ASP.NET.
- Explain the purpose of XML and its uses in standardizing data exchange across the Internet.
- Understand how XQuery can be used to query XML documents.
- Explain how XML has led to the spread of Web services and the emergence of service-oriented architectures.

LOCATION, LOCATION, LOCATION!

When looking for property to buy, at least one of your friends will say, "It's all about location, location, location." Storing data and applications comes down to making location decisions, too. No, we aren't talking about giving data an ocean view with a hot tub and proximity to good schools. But good database design is built on picking the right location to store data.

You studied the location concept for storing data on storage devices in Chapter 5, with such concepts as denormalization and partitioning. In addition, multitiered computer architectures offer storage possibilities at each tier, and there is no right answer for all situations. That's the beauty of the client/server approach: It can be tailored to optimize performance. As with most other major steps forward in computerization, the first client/server applications were tried in noncritical situations. By the mid-1990s, success stories began to be publicized, and the client/server approach moved up to handle business-critical applications. Now client/server has become old hat, and you may feel that this chapter is the most mundane one in the whole book. That may be, but you are urged to pay close attention anyway because the client/server approach continues to drive the newest directions in database computing. You will read about Web-enabled databases and learn about some of the newest acronyms, including service-oriented architecture (SOA) and Web services. Some authors will write as though these newest approaches are somehow different and beyond client/server technology. Actually, the clients may be fat or thin, and the servers can be connected in different ways, but the basic concepts included in this chapter underlie the newest approaches to distributed computing (for Web applications here and distributed databases in Chapter 12).

And it's mostly about location: what must be located on the client (think cellphone), what is stored on the server, and how much information should be moved from the server to the cellphone when a request for data (think SQL query) is made (think about locating a restaurant when you're traveling). Part of the answer to optimizing a particular architecture lies not in location but in quickly moving the information from one location to another location. These issues are critically important to mobile applications, such as those for smartphones. In addition to transmitting voice data, most phone services now include text messaging, content browsing, object/image downloading, and business applications. Just as we can make a voice phone call from any phone in the world to any other phone, we expect to use these newer services in the same way, and we want immediate response times. Addressing these problems requires a good understanding of the client/server principles you will learn in this chapter.

INTRODUCTION

Client/server system
A networked computing model that distributes processes between clients and servers, which supply the requested services. In a database system, the database generally resides on a server that processes the DBMS. The clients may process the application systems or request services from another server that holds the application programs.

Client/server systems operate in networked environments, splitting the processing of an application between a front-end client and a back-end processor. Generally, the client process requires some resource, which the server provides to the client. Clients and servers can reside in the same computer, or they can be on different computers that are networked together. Both clients and servers are intelligent and programmable, so the computing power of both can be used to devise effective and efficient applications.

It is difficult to overestimate the impact that client/server applications have had in the past 20 years. Advances in personal computer technology and the rapid evolution of graphical user interfaces (GUIs), networking, and communications have changed the way businesses use computing systems to meet ever more demanding business needs. Electronic commerce requires that client browsers be able to access dynamic Web pages attached to databases that provide real-time information. Personal computers linked through networks that support workgroup computing are the norm. Mainframe applications have been rewritten to run in client/server environments and take advantage of the greater cost-effectiveness of networks of personal computers and workstations. The need for strategies that fit specific business environments is being filled by client/server solutions because they offer flexibility, scalability (the ability to upgrade a system without having to redesign it), and extensibility (the ability to define new data types and operations). As businesses become more global in their operations, they must devise distributed systems (discussed in Chapter 12); their plans often include client/server architectures.

CLIENT/SERVER ARCHITECTURES

Client/server environments use a local area network (LAN) to support a network of personal computers, each with its own storage, that are also able to share common devices (such as a hard disk or printer) and software (such as a DBMS) attached to the LAN.

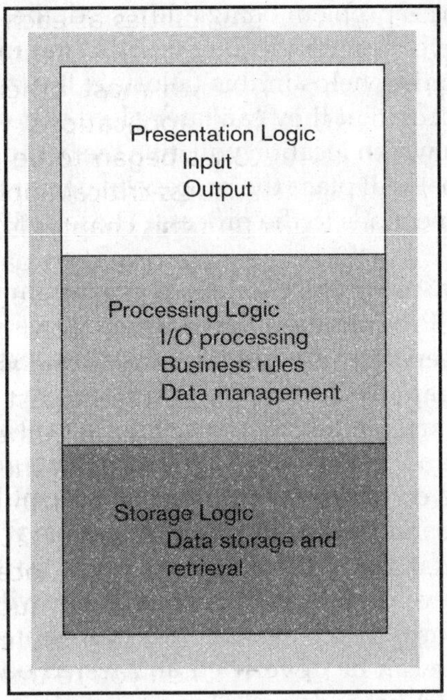

FIGURE 8-1 Application logic components

Each PC and workstation on a LAN is typically within 100 feet of the others; all PCs are usually within one mile of one another. A LAN may be hard-wired or it may be wireless. At least one PC is designated as a file server, on which the shared database is stored. The LAN modules of a DBMS add concurrent access controls, possibly extra security features, and query- or translation-queuing management to support concurrent access from multiple users of a shared database.

The various client/server architectures that have evolved can be distinguished by the distribution of application logic components across clients and servers. There are three components of application logic (see Figure 8-1). The first is the input/output (I/O), or presentation logic, component. This component is responsible for formatting and presenting data on the user's screen or other output device and for managing user input from a keyboard or other input device. The second component is the processing component. It handles data processing logic, business rules logic, and data management logic. Data processing logic includes such activities as data validation and identification of processing errors. Business rules that have not been coded at the DBMS level may be coded in the processing component. Data management logic identifies the data necessary for processing the transaction or query. The third component is storage, the component responsible for data storage and retrieval from the physical storage devices associated with the application. Activities of a DBMS occur in the storage component logic.

Partitioning an Application

There is no one optimal client/server architecture that is the best solution for all business problems. Rather, the flexibility inherent in client/server architectures offers organizations the possibility of tailoring their configurations to fit their particular processing needs. Figure 8-1 depicts the computing logics that must be distributed across the client and server(s). Presentation logic resides on the client, where the user interfaces with the system. Processing logic may be divided across clients and servers. Storage logic usually resides on the database server, close to the physical location of the data. Data integrity control activities, such as constraint checking, are typically placed there. Triggers, which will always fire when appropriate conditions are met, are associated with insert, modify, update, and delete commands. As these commands affect the data directly, triggers are also usually stored on the *database server*. Stored procedures that use the data directly are usually stored on the database server. Those that work with a query result may be stored on an application server or on the client. Depending on the nature of the business problem being addressed, these general rules may not be followed in order to achieve optimum throughput and performance.

Application partitioning
The process of assigning portions of application code to client or server partitions after it is written to achieve better performance and interoperability (ability of a component to function on different platforms).

Application partitioning helps in this tailoring. It gives developers the opportunity to write application code that they can later place either on a client workstation or on a server, depending on which location will give the best performance. It is not necessary to include the code that will place the process being partitioned or to write the code that will establish the connections to the process. Those activities are handled by application partitioning tools.

The objects created by using object-oriented programming are very appropriate for application partitioning. Programmers have tremendous control over each object's content, and it is easier to separate user interface code, business rules, and data. This separation supports today's rapidly developing *n*-tier systems. The strong business push toward Internet and e-commerce business solutions is causing application partitioning to develop more rapidly and in new ways. Web applications must be multitiered and partitioned. They require components that can be assembled on the fly, as they are requested by the browser, and they need to be compatible with different operating systems, user interfaces, and databases. Effective application partitioning is necessary in the Web environment to achieve desired performance along with acceptable maintainability, data integrity, and security in an unpredictable distributed environment.

The application code can be developed and tested on a client workstation, and decisions about partitioning that code and placing it can be made later. This capability is likely to increase developers' productivity. Application modules can be placed on a client or server late in the design phase. However, a developer must understand how and where each process will need to run in order to synchronize each process or transaction correctly across databases and platforms. Decisions about placing code on the application or database server will depend partly on the DBMS's capabilities. For example, a DBMS that supports static SQL (completely prewritten SQL code) through stored procedures and triggers that are located on the database server may create a performance decrement if dynamic SQL code (i.e., SQL code created at run time) is located on the application server. Each dynamic SQL statement will generate a dynamic bind (or links to database objects) at the database server as it is processed. The performance impact will depend on how intensively dynamic SQL statements are used. Whether to concentrate processing on the application server or the database server is a decision that must be made by the developer, who understands the hardware environment available, the interactions of the hardware and DBMS software, and the demands of the application.

It is also possible to add transaction processing monitors to client/server systems to improve performance. Where multiple application servers and database servers are available, TP monitors can balance the workload, directing transactions to servers that are not busy. TP monitors are also useful in distributed environments, where distributed transactions from a single unit of work can be managed across a heterogeneous environment.

To partition the environment to create a two-, three-, or *n*-tier architecture, decisions must be made about the placement of the processing logic. In each case, storage logic (the database engine) is handled by the server, and presentation logic is handled by the client.

Fat client
A client PC that is responsible for processing presentation logic, extensive application and business rules logic, and many DBMS functions.

Figure 8-2a depicts some possible two-tier systems, placing the processing logic on the client (creating a **fat client**), on the server (creating a thin client), or partitioned across both the server and the client (a distributed environment). It is the placement of the processing logic that is emphasized in the three scenarios. In the fat client, the application processing occurs entirely on the client, whereas in the thin client, this processing occurs on the server. In the distributed example, application processing is partitioned between the client and the server.

Figure 8-2b presents a typical three-tier architecture and an *n*-tier architecture. Again, some processing logic could be placed on the client, if desired. But, a typical client in a Web-enabled client/server environment will be a thin client, using a browser for its presentation logic. The middle tiers are typically coded in a portable language such as C or Java. The flexibility and easier manageability of the *n*-tier approaches account for its increasing popularity, in spite of the increased complexity of managing

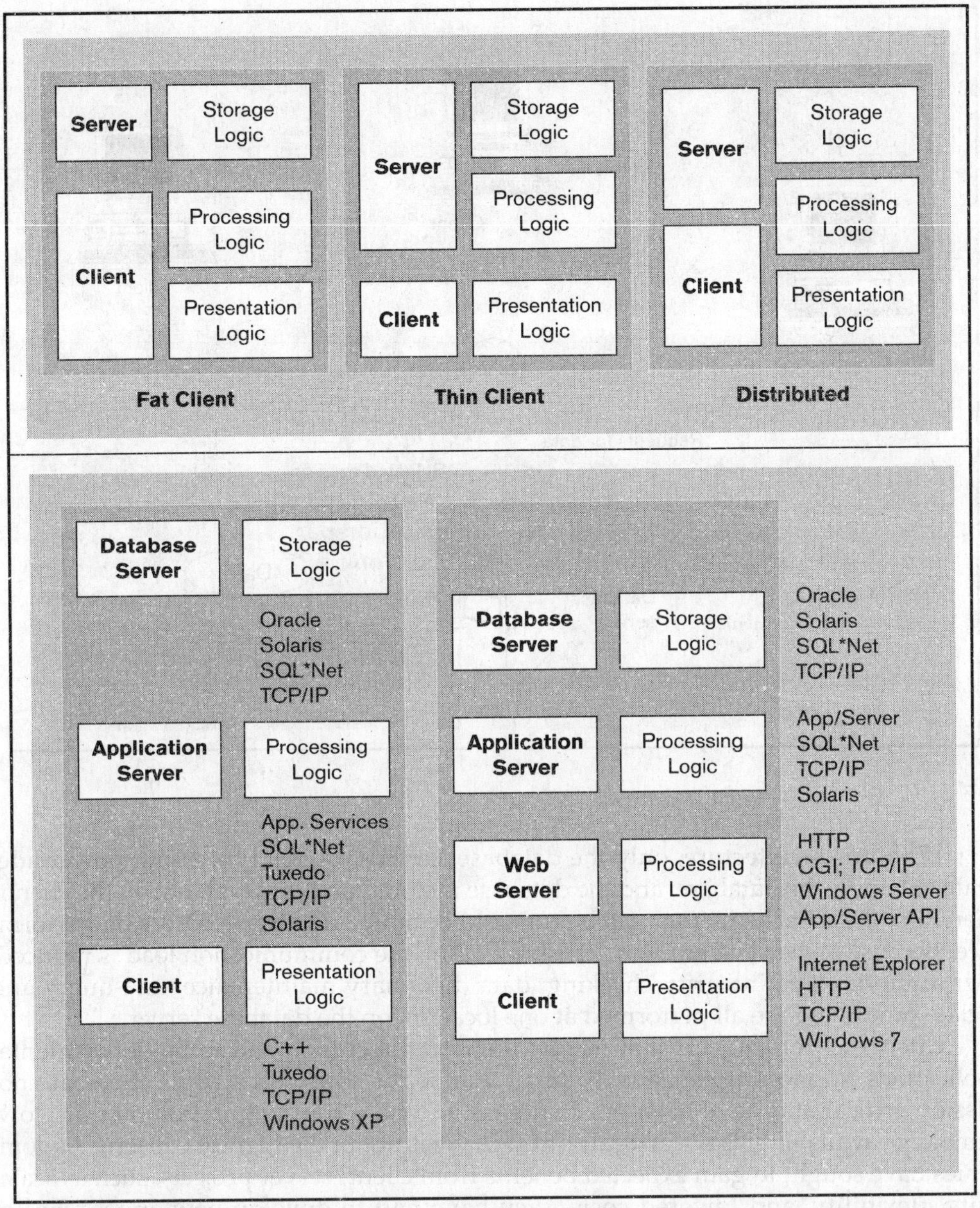

FIGURE 8-2 Common logic distributions

(a) Two-tier client/server environments

(b) Three-tier and *n*-tier client/server environments

communication among the tiers. The fast-paced, distributed, and heterogeneous environment of the Internet and e-commerce initiatives have also led to the development of many *n*-tier architectures.

Now that we have examined some of the key questions related to client/server architectures and their advantages and disadvantages in general, in the next two sections we show specific examples of the role of databases in these two types of architectures.

DATABASES IN A TWO-TIER ARCHITECTURE

In a two-tier architecture, a client workstation is responsible for managing the user interface, including presentation logic, data processing logic, and business rules logic, and a **database server** is responsible for database storage, access, and processing. Figure 8-3 shows a typical database server architecture. With the DBMS placed on the database server, LAN traffic is reduced because only those records that match the requested criteria are transmitted to the client station, rather than entire data files. Some people refer to the central DBMS functions as the *back-end functions*, whereas they call the application programs on the client PCs *front-end programs*.

Database server
A computer that is responsible for database storage, access, and processing in a client/server environment. Some people also use this term to describe a two-tier client/server applications.

FIGURE 8-3 Database server architecture (two-tier architecture)

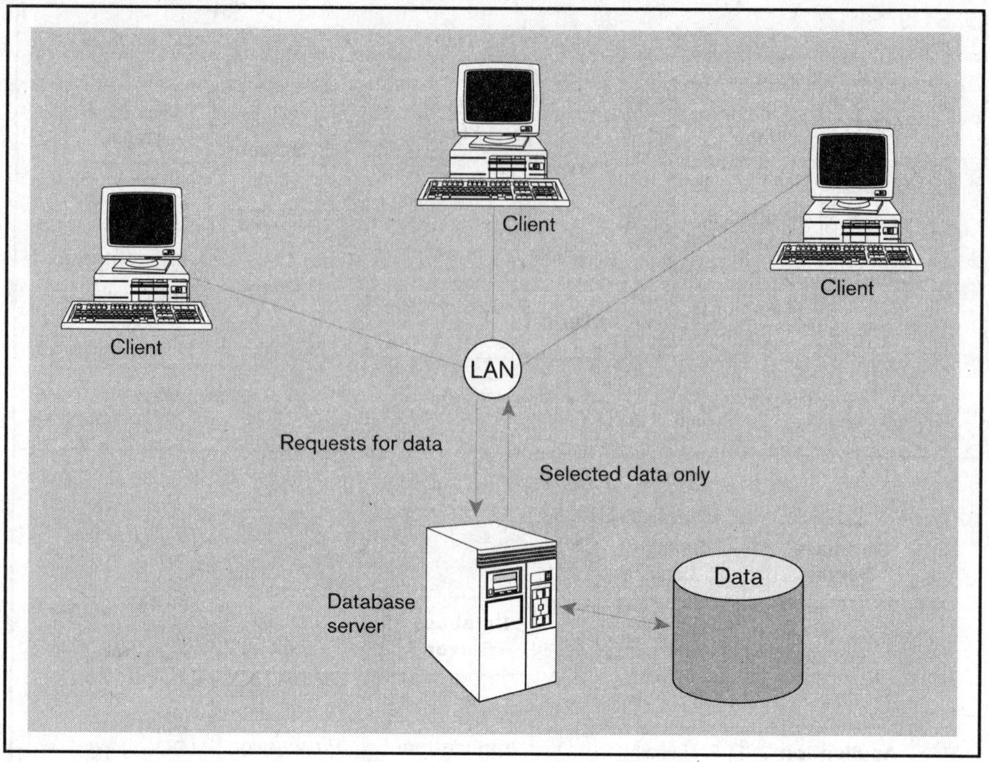

With this architecture, only the database server requires processing power adequate to handle the database, and the database is stored on the server, not on the clients. Therefore, the database server can be tuned to optimize database-processing performance. Because fewer data are sent across the LAN, the communication load is reduced. User authorization, integrity checking, data dictionary maintenance, and query and update processing are all performed at one location, on the database server.

Client/server projects that use two-tier architectures tend to be departmental applications, supporting a relatively small number of users. Such applications are not mission critical and have been most successful where transaction volumes are low, immediate availability is not critical, and security is not of the highest concern. As companies have sought to gain expected benefits from client/server projects, such as scalability, flexibility, and lowered costs, they have had to develop new approaches to client/server architectures.

Middleware
Software that allows an application to interoperate with other software without requiring the user to understand and code the low-level operations necessary to achieve interoperability.

Application program interface (API)
Sets of routines that an application program uses to direct the performance of procedures by the computer's operating system.

Open database connectivity (ODBC)
An application programming interface that provides a common language for application programs to access and process SQL databases independent of the particular DBMS that is accessed.

Most two-tier applications are written in a programming language such as Java, VB.NET, or C#. Connecting an application written in a common programming language, such as Java, VB.NET, or C#, to a database is achieved through the use of special software called *database-oriented middleware*. Middleware is often referred to as the glue that holds together client/server applications. It is a term that is commonly used to describe any software component between the PC client and the relational database in *n*-tier architectures. Simply put, **middleware** is any of several classes of software that allow an application to interoperate with other software without requiring the user to understand and code the low-level operations required to achieve interoperability (Hurwitz, 1998). The database-oriented middleware needed to connect an application to a database consists of two parts: an **application programming interface (API)** and a database driver to connect to a specific type database (e.g., SQL Server or Oracle). The most common APIs are **Open Database Connectivity (ODBC)** and ADO.NET for the Microsoft platform (VB.NET and C#) and Java Database Connectivity (JDBC) for use with Java programs.

No matter which API or language is used, the basic steps for accessing a database from an application remain surprisingly similar:

1. Identify and register a database driver.
2. Open a connection to a database.

3. Execute a query against the database.
4. Process the results of the query.
5. Repeat steps 3–4 as necessary.
6. Close the connection to the database.

A VB.NET Example

Let us take a look at these steps in action in the context of a simple VB.NET application. The purpose of the code snippet shown in Figure 8-4 is to insert a new record into a student database. For simplicity, we will not show code related to error handling. Also, while we show the password embedded in the code below, in commercial applications, other mechanisms to retrieve passwords are used.

The VB.NET code shown in Figure 8-4 uses the ADO.NET data access framework and .NET data providers to connect to the database. The .NET Framework has different data providers (or database drivers) that allow you to connect a program written in a .NET programming language to a database. Common data providers available in the framework are for SQL Server and Oracle.

The VB.NET code illustrates how a simple INSERT query can be executed against the Oracle database. Figure 8-4a shows the VB.NET code needed to create a simple form that allows the user input to a name, department number, and student ID. Figure 8-4b shows the detailed steps to connect to a database and issue an INSERT query. By reading the explanations presented in the text boxes in the figure, you can see how the generic steps for accessing a database described in the previous section are implemented in the context of a VB.NET program. Figure 8-4c shows how you would access the database and process the results for a SELECT query. The main difference is that use the ExecuteReader() method instead of ExecuteNonQuery() method. The latter is used for INSERT, UPDATE, and DELETE queries. The table that results from running a SELECT query are captured inside an OracleDataReader object. You can access each row in the result by traversing the object, one row at a time. Each column in the object can be accessed by a Get method and by referring to the column's position in the query result (or by name). ADO.NET provides two main choices with respect to handling the result of the query: DataReader (e.g., OracleDataReader in Figure 8-4c) and DataSet. The primary difference between the two options is that the first limits us to looping through the result of a query one row at a time. This can be very cumbersome if the

FIGURE 8-4 Sample VB.NET code that demonstrates an INSERT in a database (a) Setup form for receiving user input

```
Option Explicit On

Imports System

Imports System.Data

Imports System.Data.OracleClient

Public Class InsertForm

Private Sub Button1_Click (ByVal sender As System.Object, ByVal e As

System.EventArgs) Handles Button1.Click

Dim name As String = TextBox1.Text

Dim deptno As String = TextBox2.Text

Dim studentid As String = TextBox3.Text
```

> These two import statements allow VB.NET database functions to be made available for use in this program.
>
> This allows you to use the .NET data provider for Oracle.
>
> Retrieve the value for name from TextBox1.
>
> Retrieve the value for department number from TextBox2.
>
> Retrieve the value for student identification number from TextBox3.

(continued)

FIGURE 8-4 ***(continued)***
(b) Connecting to a database and issuing an INSERT query

```
Dim conn As New OracleConnection
Dim cmdQuery As String
conn.ConnectionString = "User Id=nisubram;Password=nisubram;
DataSource=oed1;"
cmdQuery = "INSERT INTO Student (name,deptno,student_id) VALUES (' " & name
& " ',' " & deptno
& " ',' " & studentid & " ')"
Dim cmd As OracleCommand = New OracleCommand(cmdQuery)
cmd.Connection = conn
conn.Open()
cmd.Connection = conn
Dim returnvalue As Integer
returnvalue = cmd.ExecuteNonQuery()
Label4.Text = "Success"
conn.Close()
End Sub
Private Sub InsertForm_Load(ByVal sender As System.Object, ByVal e As
System.EventArgs) Handles MyBase.Load
End Sub
End Class
```

This variable will be used to store a connection to an Oracle database.

Construct a valid SQL INSERTquery by using the values in the various text boxes.

Initialize a new variable with the INSERTquery as its value.

Make a connection to the database, using the details specified in ConnectionString.

Assign the connection to the current SQL command object that we want to execute.

Execute the INSERT query. returnvalue will contain a number greater than zero if the insert was successful.

(c) Sample code snippet for using a SELECT query

```
Dim queryReader As OracleDataReader
      cmdQuery = "Select * from Student"
queryReader = cmd.ExecuteReader()
      While queryReader.Read()
            Console.WriteLine(myReader.GetString(0))
End While
queryReader.Close()
```

Construct a valid SQL SELECT query.

Execute the SELECT query. Store the result in an OracleDataReader object.

Process the result one row at a time. GetString (0) refers to the first column in the result table.

result has a large number of rows. The DataSet object provides a disconnected snapshot of the database which we can then manipulate in our program using the features available in the programming language. Later in this chapter, we will see how .NET data controls (which use DataSet objects) can provide a cleaner and easier way to manipulate data in a program.

A Java Example

Let us now look at an example of how to connect to a database from a Java application (see Figure 8-5). This Java application is actually connecting to the same database as the VB.NET application in Figure 8-4. Its purpose is to retrieve and print the names of all students in the Student table. In this example, the Java program is using the JDBC API and an Oracle thin driver to access the Oracle database.

Notice that unlike the INSERT query shown in the VB.NET example, running an SQL SELECT query requires us to capture the data inside an object that can appropriately handle the tabular data. JDBC provides two key mechanisms for this: the ResultSet and RowSet objects. The difference between these two is somewhat similar to the difference between the DataReader and DataSet objects described in the VB.NET example.

The ResultSet object has a mechanism, called the cursor, that points to its current row of data. When the ResultSet object is first initialized, the cursor is positioned before the first row. This is why we need to first call the next() method before retrieving data. The ResultSet object is used to loop through and process each row of data and retrieve the column values that we want to access. In this case, we access the value in the name column using the rec.getString method, which is a part of the JDBC API. For each of the common database types, there is a corresponding *get* and *set* method that allows for retrieval and storage of data in the database. Table 8-1 provides some common examples of SQL-to-Java mappings.

It is important to note that while the ResultSet object maintains an active connection to the database, depending on the size of the table, the entire table (i.e., the result of the query) may or may not actually be in memory on the client machine. How and when data are transferred between the database and client is handled by the Oracle

```
import java.sql.*;
public class TestJDBC {
  public static void main(String[ ] args) {
  try {
  Driverd =
  (Driver)Class.forName("oracle.jdbc.driver.OracleDriver").newInstance( );
  System.out.println(d);
  DriverManager.registerDriver (new oracle.jdbc.driver.OracleDriver( ));
  Connection conn =
  DriverManager.getConnection ("jdbc:oracle:thin:@durga.uits.indiana.edu:1
  521:OED1", args[0], args[1]);

  Statement st = conn.createStatement( );
  ResultSet rec = st.executeQuery("SELECT * FROM Student");
  while(rec.next( )) {
    System.out.println(rec.getString("name"));}
  conn.close( );
  }
  catch (Exception e) {
System.out.println("Error — " + e);
  }
  }
}
```

Register the driver to be used.

Identify the type of driver to be used.

Open a connection to a database.

Create a Statement variable that can be used to issue queries against the database

Issue a query and get a result.

Process the result, one row at a time.

Close the connection.

FIGURE 8-5 Database access from a Java program

TABLE 8-1 Common Java-to-SQL Mappings

SQL Type	Java Type	Common Get/Set Methods
INTEGER	int	getInt(), setInt()
CHAR	String	getString, setString()
VARCHAR	String	getString, setString()
DATE	java.util.Date	getDate(), setDate()
TIME	java.sql.Time	getTime(), setTime()
TIMESTAMP	java.sql.Timestamp	getTimestamp(), setTimestamp()

driver. By default, a ResultSet object is read-only and can only be traversed in one direction (forward). However, advanced versions of the ResultSet object allow scrolling in both directions and can be updateable as well.

THREE-TIER ARCHITECTURES

Three-tier architecture
A client/server configuration that includes three layers: a client layer and two server layers. Although the nature of the server layers differs, a common configuration contains an application server and a database server.

In general, a **three-tier architecture** includes another server layer in addition to the client and database server layers previously mentioned (see Figure 8-6a). Such configurations are also referred to as *n*-tier, multitier, or enhanced client/server architectures. The additional server in a three-tier architecture may be used for different purposes. Often, application programs reside and are run on the additional server, in which case it is referred to as an application server. Or the additional server may hold a local database while another server holds the enterprise database. Each of these configurations is likely to be referred to as a three-tier architecture, but the functionality of each differs, and each is appropriate for a different situation. Advantages of the three-tier compared with the two-tier architecture, such as increased scalability, flexibility, performance, and reusability, have made three-layer architectures a popular choice for Internet applications and net-centric information systems. These advantages are discussed in more detail later.

FIGURE 8-6 Three-tier architecture
(a) Generic three-tier architecture

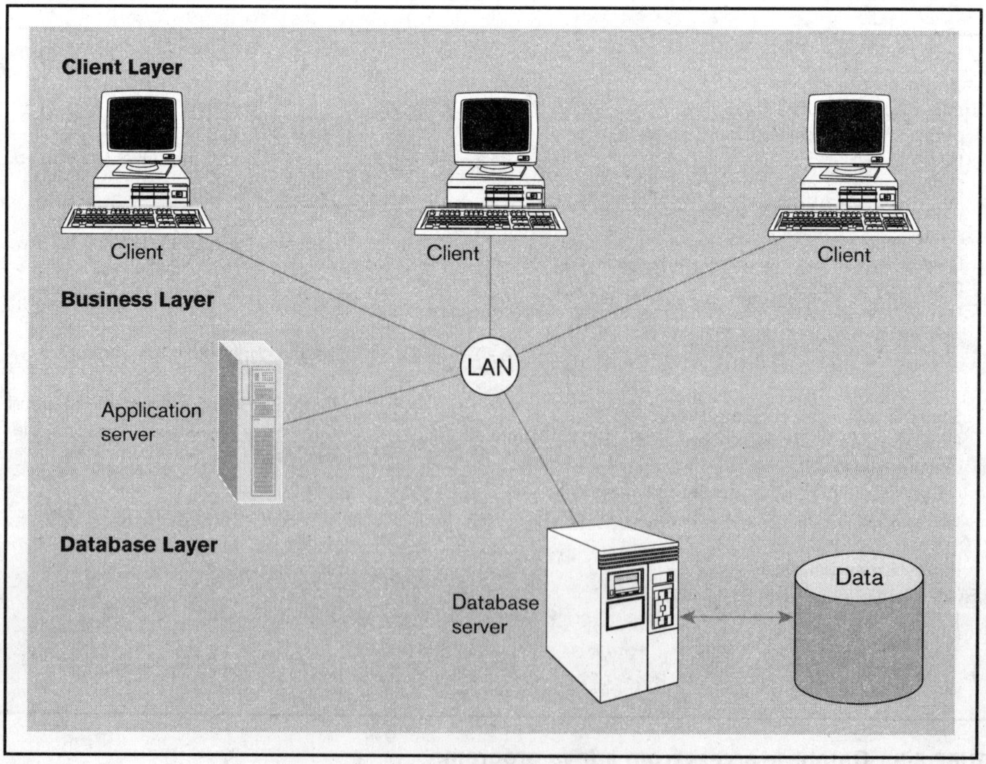

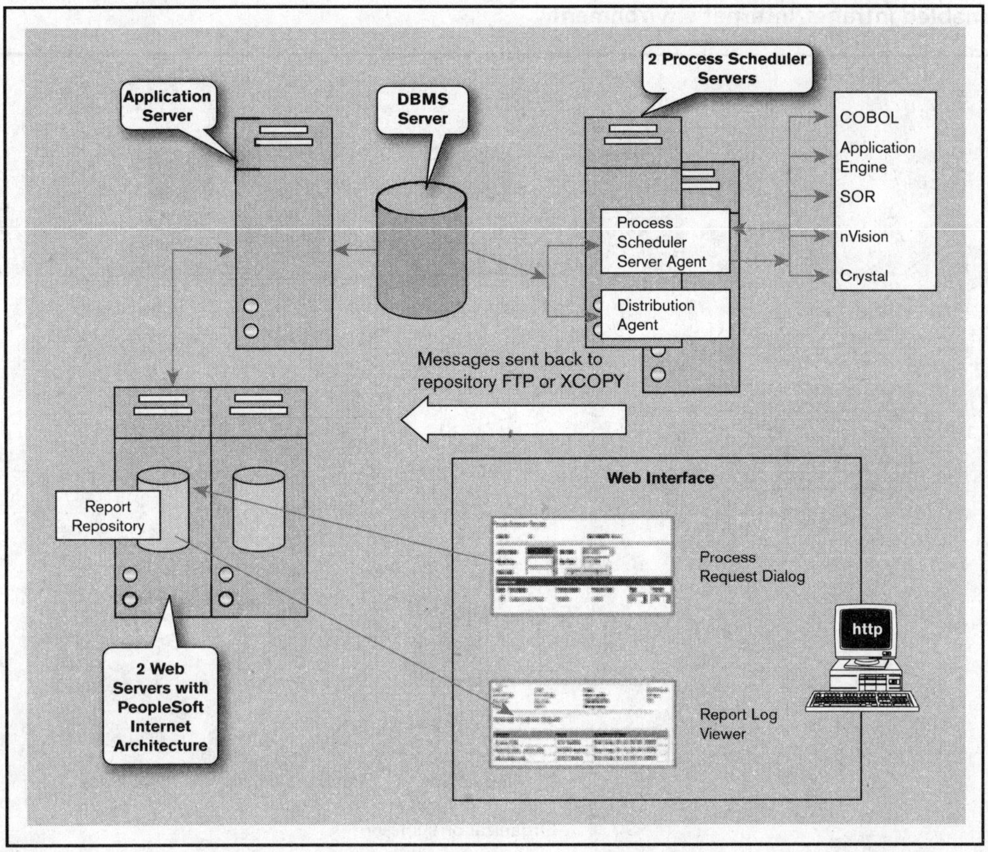

(b) Sample PeopleSoft Financials three-tier configuration

In some three-tier architectures, most application code is stored on the application server. This case realizes the same benefits as those that come from putting stored procedures on the database server in a two-tier architecture. Using an application server can also improve performance through the use of true machine code, easier portability of the application code to other platforms, and less reliance on proprietary languages such as SQL*Plus (Quinlan, 1995). In many situations, most business processing occurs on the application server rather than on the client workstation or database server, resulting in a **thin client**. The use of Internet browsers for accessing the Web is an example of a thin client. Applications that reside on a server and execute on that server without downloading to the client are becoming more common. Thus, upgrading application programs requires loading the new version only on the application server, rather than on client workstations.

Thin client
An application where the client (PC) accessing the application primarily provides the user interfaces and some application processing, usually with no or limited local data storage.

The most common type of three-tier application in use in modern organizations is a Web-based application. Such applications can be accessed from either the Internet or an intranet. Figure 8-7 depicts the basic environment needed to set up both intranet and Internet database-enabled connectivity. In the box on the right side of the diagram is a depiction of an intranet. The client/server nature of the architecture is evident from the labeling. The network that connects the client workstations, Web server, and database server uses TCP/IP. While multitier intranet structures are also used, Figure 8-7 depicts a simpler architecture, where a request from a client browser will be sent through the network to the Web server, which stores pages scripted in HTML to be returned and displayed through the client browser. If the request requires that data be obtained from the database, the Web server constructs a query and sends it to the database server, which processes the query and returns the results set when the query is run against the database. Similarly, data entered at the client station can be passed through and stored in the database by sending it to the Web server, which passes it on to the database server, which commits the data to the database.

The processing flow described here is similar when connecting from outside the company. This is the case whether the connection is available only to a particular customer or supplier or to any workstation connected to the Internet. However, opening up the Web server to the outside world requires that additional data security measures

FIGURE 8-7 A database-enabled intranet/Internet environment

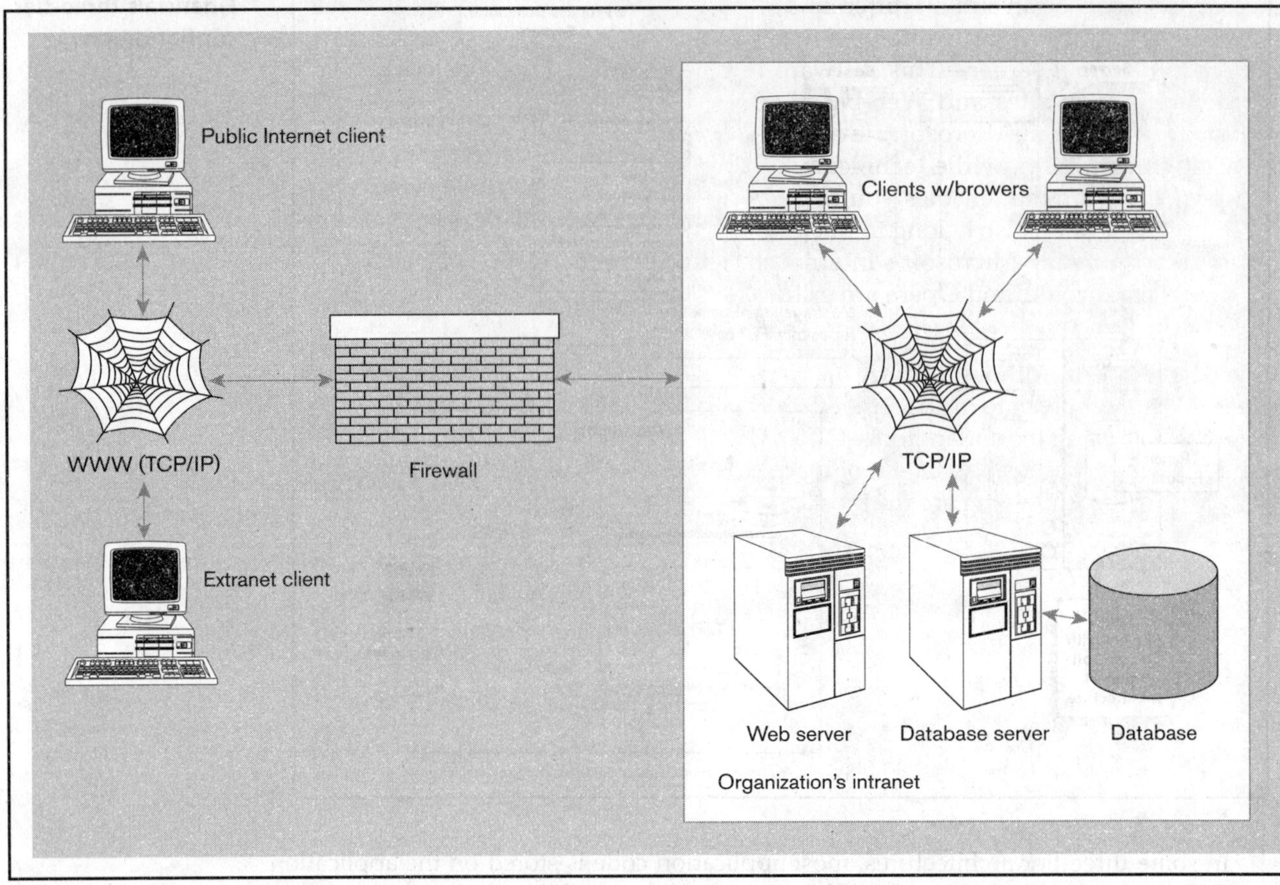

be in place. Security is central to the deployment of Web services and will be discussed in more detail in Chapter 11.

Internally, access to data is typically controlled by the database management system, with the database administrator setting the permissions that determine employee access to data. Firewalls limit external access to the company's data and the movement of company data outside the company's boundaries. All communication is routed through a proxy server outside of the organization's network. The proxy server controls the passage of messages or files through to the organization's network. It can also improve a site's performance by caching frequently requested pages that can then be displayed without having to attach to the Web server.

Given that the most common type of three-tier application is a Web application, in the next section we take a closer look at the key components of a Web application. We then present examples of simple Web applications written in three common languages: Java Server Pages (JSP), ASP.NET, and PHP.

WEB APPLICATION COMPONENTS

Figure 8-2 shows the various components of a typical Web application. Four key components must be used together to create a Web application site:

1. *A database server* This server hosts the storage logic for the application and hosts the DBMS. You have read about many of them, including Oracle, Microsoft SQL Server, Informix, Sybase, DB2, Microsoft Access, and MySQL. The DBMS may reside either on a separate machine or on the same machine as the Web server.
2. *A Web server* The Web server provides the basic functionality needed to receive and respond to requests from browser clients. These requests use HTTP or HTTPS as a protocol. The most common Web server software in use is Apache, but you

are also likely to encounter Microsoft's Internet Information Server (IIS) Web server. Apache can run on different operating systems, such as Windows, UNIX, or Linux. IIS is primarily intended to run on Windows servers.

3. ***An application server*** This software provides the building blocks for creating dynamic Web sites and Web-based applications. Examples include the .NET Framework from Microsoft; Java Platform, Enterprise Edition (Java EE); and ColdFusion. Also, while technically not considered an application server platform, software that enables you to write applications in languages such as PHP, Python, and Perl also belong to this category.
4. ***A Web browser*** Microsoft's Internet Explorer, Mozilla's Firefox, Apple's Safari, Google's Chrome, and Opera are examples.

As you can see, a bewildering collection of tools are available to use for Web application development. Although Figure 8-7 gives an overview of the architecture required, there is no one right way to put together the components. Rather, there are many possible configurations, using redundant tools. Often, Web technologies within the same category can be used interchangeably. One tool may solve the same problem as well as another tool. However, the following are the most common combinations you will encounter:

- IIS Web server, SQL Server/Oracle as the DBMS, and applications written in ASP.NET
- Apache Web server, Oracle/IBM as the DBMS, and applications written using Java
- Apache Web server, Oracle/IBM/SQL Server as the DBMS, and applications written using ColdFusion
- The Linux operating system, Apache Web server, a MySQL database, and applications written in PHP/Python or Perl (also sometimes referred to as the LAMP stack).

Your development environment is likely to be determined by your employer. When you know what environment you will be using, there are many alternatives available for becoming familiar and proficient with the tools. Your employer may send you to training classes or even hire a subject matter expert to work with you. You will find one or more books specific to each tool when you search online or in a bookstore. Figure 8-8 presents a visual depiction of the components necessary to create a dynamic Web site.

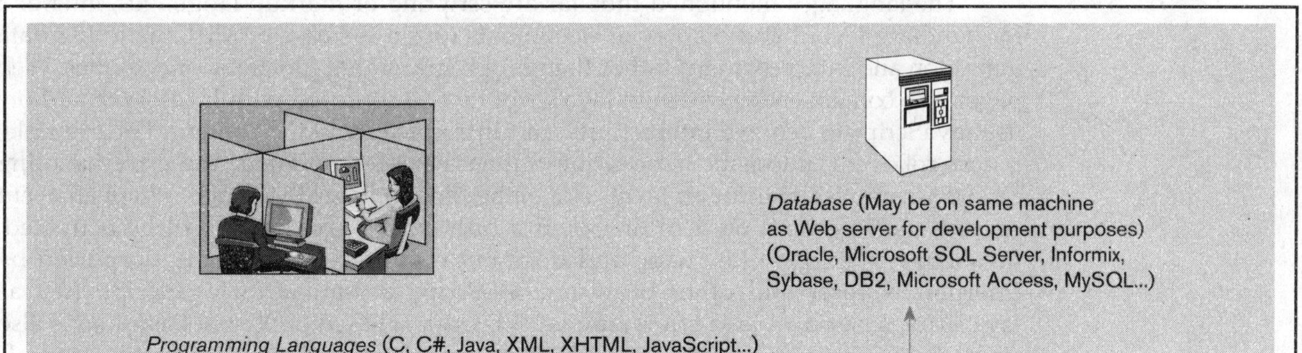

FIGURE 8-8 Dynamic Web development environment

Languages for Creating Web Pages

World Wide Web Consortium (W3C)
An international consortium of companies working to develop open standards that foster the development of Web conventions so that Web documents can be consistently displayed across all platforms.

The **World Wide Web Consortium (W3C)** is the chief standards body for HTTP and HTML. Founded in 1994 by Tim Berners-Lee, W3C is an international consortium of companies. W3C's intent is to develop open standards that foster the development of Web conventions so that Web documents can be consistently displayed across all platforms. The consortium organizes its work into four domains, each of which reports its current activities on the W3C Web site (**www.w3.org**). The four domains are Architecture, Interaction, Technology and Society, and the Web Accessibility Initiative.

The fundamental authoring language used to create documents for the Web is Hypertext Markup Language (HTML). HTML is similar to Standard Generalized Markup Language (SGML), which states the rules for tagging elements of a document so that they can be formatted in a standard way. HTML tag conventions are based on SGML rules. HTML is a scripting language, intended to define Web document structure and layout for display purposes, using a variety of tags and attributes. For example, an HTML document starts with the tags (document subject is entered here). The information to be displayed and additional formatting tags follow, and the document will end with the tags.

XML is a rapidly developing scripting language, also based on SGML, that has been widely accepted as a means of capturing data structure. XML is an acronym for Extensible Markup Language, a specification developed by the W3C. Designed especially for Web documents, XML allows the creation of customized tags. These tags can be used across organizations, enabling the definition, transmission, validation, and interpretation of data between applications and between organizations. XML has also proved useful for attaching legacy data to the Web because the XML tags can be used to define data as it is formatted in the legacy data store, thus eliminating the need to reformat it. We discuss XML in detail later in this chapter.

XHTML
A hybrid scripting language that extends HTML code to make it XML compliant.

W3C has issued specifications for a hybrid scripting language, **Extensible Hypertext Markup Language (XHTML)**, which extends HTML code to make it XML compliant. XHTML uses three XML namespaces that correspond to three HTML 4.0 data type definitions (DTDs): Strict, Transitional, and Frameset. Because the modules used in XHTML conform to certain standards, layout and presentation remain consistent across platforms. The W3C wants XHTML to replace HTML as the standard scripting language. It is recommended that the reader visit the W3C Web site to learn how close the organization is to accomplishing this objective.

The languages mentioned thus far are scripting or markup languages, intended for handling layout and display of documents (or, in the case of XML, handling data definition and interpretation) rather than for programming functions or activities. Web pages also contain code written in JavaScript (not be confused with Java). Web authors use JavaScript to achieve interactivity and introduce dynamic content. For example, mouse rollovers, automatic notices that content has been updated, and error handling can be accomplished through JavaScript embedded in the HTML code. When an event occurs, such as the mouse rolling over a button, the JavaScript will be activated. JavaScript is an open language and does not require a license. It is supported by Internet Explorer and other browsers. VBScript is similar to JavaScript. Just as JavaScript is based on Java but is simpler, VBScript is based on Visual Basic and is also simpler. VBScript can be used to add buttons, scrollbars, and other interactive controls to a Web page. Microsoft developed this scripting language, and it is supported by the Microsoft Internet Explorer browser.

Now that we have seen the technologies that can be used to create HTML pages, let us turn our attention toward understanding how a Web server, an application server, and a database server can be combined create a database-driven Web application. We will look at examples of such applications in three popular languages: JSP, ASP.NET, and PHP.

DATABASES IN THREE-TIER APPLICATIONS

Figure 8-9a presents a general overview of the information flow in a Web application. A user submitting a Web page request is unaware of whether the request being submitted is returning a static Web page or a Web page whose content is a mixture of static information and dynamic information retrieved from the database. The data returned

FIGURE 8-9 Information flow in a three-tier architecture

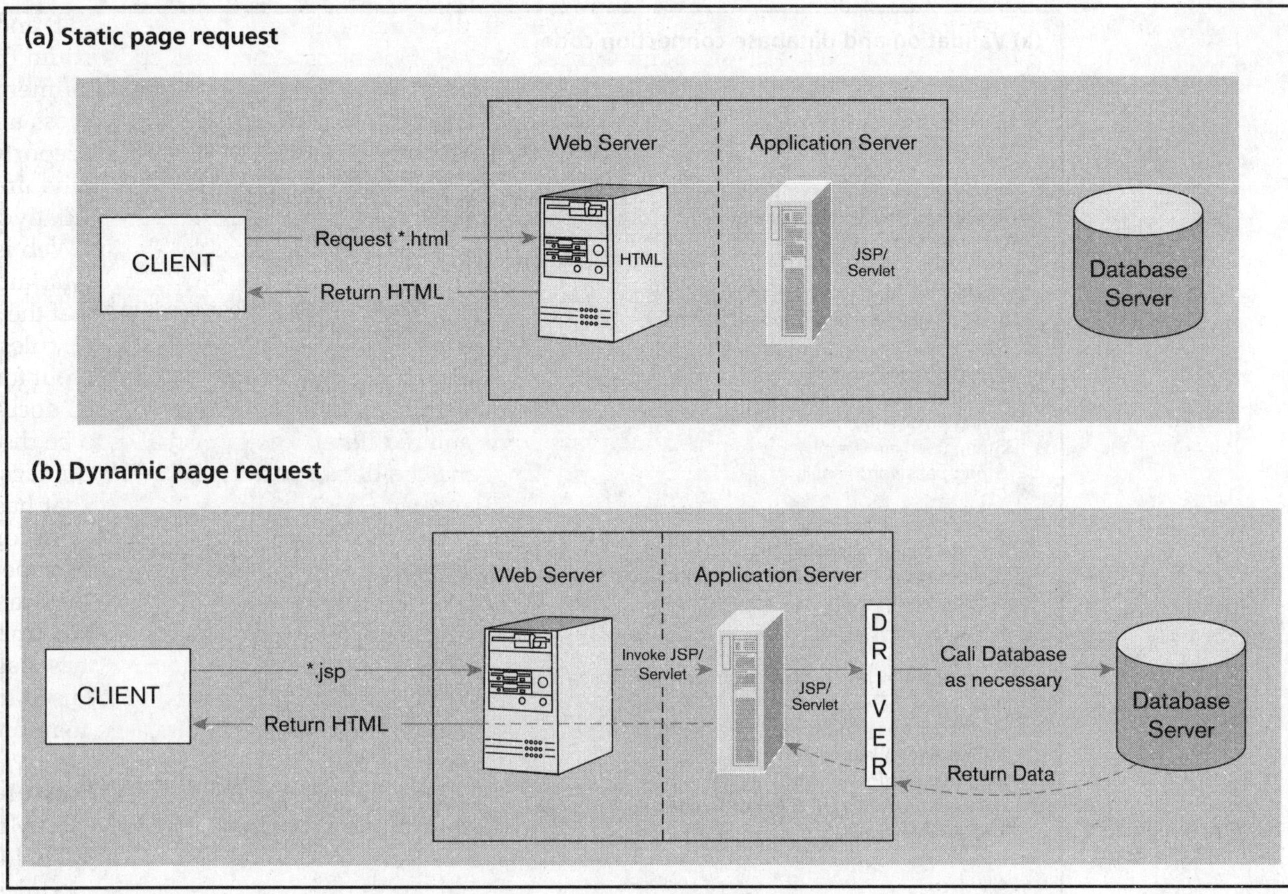

from the Web server is always in a format that can be rendered by the browser (i.e., HTML or XML).

As shown in Figure 8-9a, if the Web server determines that the request from the client can be satisfied without passing the request on to the application server, it will process the request and then return the appropriately formatted information to the client machine. This decision is most often based on the file suffix. For example, all .html and .htm files can be processed by the Web server itself.

However, if the request has a suffix that requires application server intervention, the information flow show in Figure 8-9b is invoked. The application invokes the database, as necessary, using one of the mechanisms described previously (ADO.NET or JDBC) or a proprietary one. While the internal details of how each of the popular platforms (JSP/Java servlets, ASP.NET, ColdFusion, and PHP) handle the requests are likely very different, the general logic for creating Web applications is very similar to what is shown in Figure 8.9b.

A JSP Web Application

As indicated previously, there are several suitable languages and development tools available with which to create dynamic Web pages. One of the most popular languages in use is Java Server Pages (JSP). JSP pages are a mixture of HTML and Java. The HTML parts are used to display information on the browser. The Java parts are used to process information sent from an HTML form.

The code in Figure 8-10 shows a sample JSP application whose purpose is to capture user registration information and store the data in a database. Let us assume that the name of the page is registration.jsp. This JSP page performs the following functions:

- Displays the registration form
- Processes the user's filled-in form and checks it for common errors, such as missing items and matching password fields

FIGURE 8-10 Sample JSP application

(a) Validation and database connection code

```
<%@ page import="java.sql.*" %>
<%

// Create an empty new variable
String message = null;

// Handle the form
if (request.getParameter("submit") != null)
{
  String firstName = null;
  String lastName = null;
  String email = null;
  String userName = null;
  String password = null;

  // Check for a first name
  if (request.getParameter("first_name")=="") {
     message = "<p>You forgot to enter your first name!</p>";
     firstName = null;
  }
else {
     firstName = request.getParameter("first_name");
  }

  // Check for a last name
  if (request.getParameter("last_name")=="") {
     message = "<p>You forgot to enter your last name!</p>";
     lastName = null;
  }
  else {
     lastName = request.getParameter("last_name");
  }

  // Check for an email address
  if (request.getParameter("email")=="") {
     message = "<p>You forgot to enter your email address!</p>";
     email = null;
  }
  else {
     email = request.getParameter("email");
  }

  // Check for a username
  if (request.getParameter("username")=="") {
     message = "<p>You forgot to enter your username!</p>";
     userName = null;
  }
  else {
     userName = request.getParameter("username");
  }

  // Check for a password and match against the confirmed password
  if (request.getParameter("password1")=="") {
     message = "<p>You forgot to enter your password!</p>";
     password = null;
  }
```

- The <%@ page %>directive applies to the entire JSP page. The import attribute specifies the Java packages that should be included within the JSP file.
- Check whether the form needs to be processed.
- Validate first nam.e
- Validate last name
- Validate e-mail address
- Validate username
- Validate the password

(continued)

(a) Validation and database connection code (continued)

```
else {
  if(request.getParameter("password1").equals(request.getParameter("password2"))) {
  password = request.getParameter("password1");
  }
  else {
  password = null;
  message = "<p>Your password did not match the confirmed password!</p>";
  }
}

// If everything's OK
PreparedStatement stmt = null;
Connection conn = null;
if (firstName!=null && lastName!=null && email!=null && userName!=null && password!=null) {

// Call method to register student
 try {
```

If all user information has been validated, the data will be inserted into the database (an Oracle Database in this case)

```
// Connect to the db
DriverManager.registerDriver(new oracle.jdbc.driver.OracleDriver( ));
conn=DriverManager.getConnection("jdbc:oracle:thin:@localhost:1521:xe","scott","tiger");
```

Connect to the Database :
Connection String : jdbc:oracle:thin:@localhost:1521:xe
Username : scott
Password : tiger

```
// Make the query
String ins_query="INSERT INTO users VALUES ('"+firstName+"','"+lastName+"','"
+email+"','"+userName+"','"+password+"')";
stmt=conn.prepareStatement(ins_query);

// Run the query
int result = stmt.executeUpdate(ins_query);
conn.commit();
message = "<p> <b> You have been registered ! </b> </p>";
```

Prepare and Execute INSERT query

If the INSERT was successful print message

```
// Close the database connection
stmt.close();
conn.close();
}
catch (SQLException ex) {
```

Close Connection and Statement

If the INSERT was not successful print error message

```
message = "<p> <b> You could not be registered due to a system error. We apologize
for any inconvenience. </b> </p>"+ex.getMessage()+"</p>";
stmt.close();
conn.close();
}
}
else {
  message = message+"<p>.Please try again</p>";
  }
}
%>
```

End of JSP code

(continued)

- If there is an error, redisplays the entire form, with an error message in red
- If there is no error, enters the user's information into a database and sends the user to a "success" screen.

Let us examine the various pieces of the code to see how it accomplishes the above functions. All Java code is found between <% and %> and is not displayed in the browser. The only items displayed in the browser are the ones enclosed in HTML tags.

When a user accesses the registration.jsp page in a browser by typing in a URL similar to **http://myserver.mydomain.edu/regapp/registration.jsp**, the value of

FIGURE 8-10 ***(continued)***

(b) HTML code to create a form in the JSP application

```
HTML code to create a form in the JSP application
<html>                                              <-- Beginning of HTML form
<head> <title> Register </title> </head>
<body>
<% if (message!=null) {%>
<font color ='red'> <%=message%> </font>
<%}%>
<form method="post">
<fieldset>
<legend>Enter your information in the form below:</legend>
<p> <b> First Name:      </b>
        <input type="text"    name="first_name"  size="15" maxlength ="15" value=""/> </p>
<p> <b> Last Name:       </b>
        <input type="text"    name="last_name"   size="30" maxlength ="30" value=""/> </p>
<p> <b> Email Address:   </b>
        <input type="text"    name="email"       size="40" maxlength ="40" value=""/> </p>
<p> <b> User Name:       </b>
        <input type="text"    name="username"    size="10" maxlength ="20" value=""/> </p>
<p> <b> Password:        </b>
        <input type="password" name="password1"  size="20" maxlength ="20" value=""/> </p>
<p> <b> Confirm Password: </b>
        <input type="password" name="password2"  size="20" maxlength ="20" value=""/> </p>
</fieldset>
<div align="center"> <input type="submit" name="submit" value="Register"/> </div>
</form> <!-- End of Form -->
</body>
</html>
```

(c) Sample form output from the JSP application

the message Web parameter is NULL. Because the IF condition fails, the HTML form is displayed without an error message. Notice that this form has a submit button and that the action value in the form indicates that the page that is going to process the data is also registration.jsp.

After the user fills in the details and clicks the submit button, the data are sent to the Web server. The Web server passes on the data (called parameters) to the application server, which in turn invokes the code in the page specified in the actions parameter (i.e., the registration.jsp page). This is the code in the page that is enclosed in the <% and %> and is written in Java. This code has several IF-ELSE statements for error checking purposes as well as a portion that contains the logic to store the user form data in a database.

If any of the user entries are missing or if the passwords don't match, the Java code sets the message value to something other than NULL. At the end of that check, the original form is displayed, but now an error message in red will be displayed at the top of the form because of the very first IF statement.

On the other hand, if the form has been filled correctly, the code segment for inserting the data into the database is executed. Notice that this code segment is very similar to the code we showed in the Java example before. After the user information is inserted into the database, <jsp:forward> causes the application server to execute a new JSP page called success.jsp. Notice that the message that should be displayed by this page is the value that is in the message variable and is passed to it in the form of a Web parameter. It is worthwhile to note that all JSP pages are actually compiled into **Java servlets** on the application server before execution.

Java servlet
A Java program that is stored on the server and contains the business and database logic for a Java-based application.

If you examine the segments of the application from a database access perspective (starting from the try block), you will notice that there is nothing fundamentally different about how the code inside a JSP page looks compared to the code in a the Java application, as described earlier. It still follows the same six steps identified earlier in the chapter. The primary difference is that in this case, the database access code is now part of a Java servlet that runs on the application server instead of the client.

A PHP Example

Java, C, C++, C#, and Perl are APIs that can be used with MySQL. PHP is one of the most popular APIs for several reasons. Support for MySQL has been built into PHP since PHP4. It has a reputation for ease of use, short development time, and high performance. PHP5, recently released, is more object oriented than PHP4 and includes several class libraries. It is considered to be relatively easy to learn. Intermediate-level programmers will learn it quickly.

Figure 8-11 includes a sample script from Ullman (2003) that demonstrates the integration of PHP with a MySQL database and HTML code. The script accepts a guest's registration on a Web site, including first name, last name, e-mail address, user name, and password. Once this information has been stored in the MySQL database, the database owner will want to retrieve it. Ullman also includes a sample script for retrieving the results and displaying them in good form. Reviewing Figure 8-11 will give you an overview of one approach to building a dynamic Web site with an attached database, as well as an appreciation for PHP's use of other language's syntax conventions that will make the script relatively easy for you to understand. As you review the figure, look for the embedded SQL code, necessary to establish a dynamic Web site.

The JSP and PHP examples presented above have several drawbacks associated with them. First, the HTML code, Java code, and SQL code are all mixed in together. Because the same person is unlikely to possess expertise in all three areas, creating large applications using this paradigm will be challenging. Further, even small changes to one part of an application can have a ripple effect and require that many pages be rewritten, which is inherently error prone. For example, if the name of the database needs to be changed from xe to oed1, then every page that makes a connection to a database will need to be changed.

To overcome this problem, most Web applications are designed using a concept known as the Model-View-Controller (MVC). Using this architecture, the presentation logic (view), the business logic (controller/model), and the database logic (model) are separated. Chapter 14 provides detailed examples of how this can be done in Java.

An ASP.NET Example

A final code segment that we will examine (Figure 8-12, page 357) shows how the registration page can be written in ASP.NET.

Notice that the ASP.NET code is considerably shorter than either the PHP or JSP code. This is partially because we have not included all the error checking aspects in this code. Further, we have used some powerful built-in controls available in ASP.NET

FIGURE 8-11 Sample PHP script that accepts user registration input

(a) PHP script initiation and input validation

```
<?php # Script 6.6 - register.php

// Set the page title and include the HTML header.
$page_title = 'Register';
include ('templates/header.inc');

//Handle the form.
if (isset($_POST['submit'])) {

        // Create an empty new variable.
        $message = NULL;

        // Check for a first name.
        if (empty($_POST['first_name'])) {
                        $fn = FALSE;
                        $message = '<p>You forgot to enter your first name!</p>';
        } else {
                        $fn = $_POST['first_name'];
        }

        // Check for a last name.
        if (empty($_POST['last_name'])) {
                        $ln = FALSE;
                        $message = '<p>You forgot to enter your last name!</p>';
        } else {
                        $ln = $_POST['last_name'];
        }

        // Check for an email address.
        if (empty($_POST['email'])) {
                        $e = FALSE;
                        $message = '<p>You forgot to enter your email address!</p>';
        } else {
                        $e = $_POST['email'];
        }

        // Check for a username.
        if (empty($_POST['username'])) {
                        $u = FALSE;
                        $message = '<p>You forgot to enter your username!</p>';
        } else {
                        $u = $_POST['username'];
        }

        // Check for a password and match against the confirmed password.
        if (empty($_POST['password1'])) {
                        $p = FALSE;
                        $message = '<p>You forgot to enter your password!</p>';
        } else {
                        if ($_POST['password1'] = $_POST['password2']) {
                                        $p = $_POST['password1'];
                } else {
                                        $p = FALSE;
                                        $message .= '<p>Your password did not match
                                                the confirmed password!</p>';
                }
        }
```

- PHP file named register.php begins.
- This file contains HTML code to set up a generic page, including its page title and header.
- Check whether to process form.
- Validate first name.
- Validate last name.
- Validate e-mail address.
- Validate username.
- Validate the password.

(continued)

(b) Adding user information to the database

```
//If everything's OK.
    if ($fn && $ln && $e && $u && $p) {

            // Register the user in the database.

            // Connect to the db.
            require_once ('../mysql_connect.php');

            // Make the query.
            $query = "INSERT INTO users (username, first_name, last_name, email, password,
            registration_date) VALUES ('$u', '$fn', '$ln', '$e', PASSWORD('$p'), NOW( ))";

            //Run the query.
            $result = @mysql_query ($query);

            //If it ran OK.
            if ($result) {

                    // Send an email, if desired.
                    echo '<p> <b>You have been registered!</b> </p>';

                    //Include the HTML footer.
                    include ('templates/footer.inc');

                    //Quit the script.
                    exit();

            // If it did not run OK.
            } else {

                    $message = '<p>You could not be registered due to a system error.
                    We apologize for any inconvenience.</p> <p>' . mysql_error() . '</p>';

            }

            //Close the database connection.
            mysql_close();

    } else {
            $message = '<p>Please try again.</p>';
    }

// End of the main Submit conditional.
}
```

- If all user information has been validated, the data will be inserted into the MySQL database.
- Establish connection to database.
- SQL query with encrypted password and current date.
- mysql_query( ) function sends SQL to MySQL.
- $result contains value returned by mysql_query. If TRUE, message is displayed, footer is required, script is halted.
- If $result FALSE, assign value to $message.
- Close connection to MySQL database.
- Completion of registration conditional.
- Completion of submit conditional.

(continued)

to perform the majority of the functions that we were writing code for ourselves in the other two languages. The DetailsView control, for example, automatically grabs data from the various text fields in the Web page and assigns the values to the corresponding data field variable in the control (e.g., the User Name form field is stored in the username data field). Further, the SqlDataSource control hides the details of the steps needed to connect to the database, issue SQL queries, and retrieve the results.

KEY CONSIDERATIONS IN THREE-TIER APPLICATIONS

In describing the database component of the applications in the preceding sections, we observed that the basics of connecting, retrieving, and storing data in a database do not change substantially when we move from a two-tier application to a three-tier application. In fact, what changes is where the code for accessing the database is located. However, there are several key considerations that application developers need to keep in mind in order to be able to create a stable high-performance application.

FIGURE 8-11 ***(continued)***

(c) Closing the PHP script and displaying the HTML form

If an error message exists, display it.

Begin HTML form.

```
// Print the message if there is one.
if (isset($message)) {
        echo '<font color="red">',$message, '</font>';
}
?>

<form action="<?php echo $_SERVER['PHP_SELF']; ?>" method="post">
<fieldset> <legend>Enteryour information in the form below:</legend>

<p> <b>FirstName:</b> <input type="text" name="first_name" size="15" maxlength="15"
value="<?php if (isset($_POST['first_name'])) echo $_POST['first_name']; ?>" /> </p>

<p> <b>LastName:</b> <input type="text" name="last_name" size="30" maxlength="30"
value="<?php if (isset($_POST['last_name'])) echo $_POST['last_name']; ?>" /> </p>

<p> <b>EmailAddress:</b> <input type="text" name="email" size="40" maxlength="40"
value="<?php if (isset($_POST['email'])) echo $_POST['email']; ?>" /> </p>

<p> <b>UserName:</b> <input type="text" name="username" size="10" maxlength="20"
value="<?php if (isset($_POST['username'])) echo $_POST['username']; ?>" > </p>

<p> <b>Password:</b><input type="password" name="password1" size="20" maxlength="20"/> </p>

<p> <b>ConfirmPassword:</b> <input type="password" name="password2" size="20" maxlength="20"

/></p>
</fieldset>

<div align="center"><input type="submit" name="submit" value="Register" /> </div>

</form> <!--End of Form -->

<?php
//Include the HTML footer.
include ('templates/footer.inc'); ?>
```

Source: Ullman, PHP and MySQL for Dynamic Web Sites, 2003, Script 6.6

Stored Procedures

Stored procedures (same as procedures; see Chapter 7 for a definition) are modules of code that implement application logic and are included on the database server. As pointed out by Quinlan (1995), stored procedures have the following advantages:

- Performance improves for compiled SQL statements.
- Network traffic decreases as processing moves from the client to the server.
- Security improves if the stored procedure rather than the data is accessed and code is moved to the server, away from direct end-user access.
- Data integrity improves as multiple applications access the same stored procedure.
- Stored procedures result in a thinner client and a fatter database server.

However, writing stored procedures can also take more time than using Visual Basic or Java to create an application. Also, the proprietary nature of stored procedures reduces their portability and may make it difficult to change DBMSs without having to rewrite the stored procedures. However, using stored procedures appropriately, can lead to more efficient processing of database code.

Figure 8-13a shows an example of a stored procedure written in Oracle's PL/SQL that is intended to check whether a user name already exists in the database. Figure 8-13b shows a sample code segment which illustrates that this stored procedure can be called from a Java program.

FIGURE 8-12 A registration page written in ASP.NET

(a) Sample ASP.NET code for user registration

```
<%@ Page Language="C#" AutoEventWireup="true" CodeFile="users.aspx.cs" Inherits="users" %>
<html xmlns="http://www.w3.org/1999/xhtml" >
<head runat="server">
   <title>Register</title>
</head>
<body>
<form id="form1" runat="server">
<div>
<asp:DetailsView ID="manageUsers" runat="server" DataSourceID="usersDataSource">
        <Fields>
                <asp:BoundField DataField="username" HeaderText="User Name" />
                <asp:BoundField DataField="first_name" HeaderText="First Name" />
                <asp:BoundField DataField="last_name" HeaderText="Last Name" />
                <asp:BoundField DataField="email" HeaderText="Email Address" />
                <asp:BoundField DataField="password" HeaderText="Password" />
                <asp:CommandField ShowInsertButton="True" ButtonType="Button" />
        </Fields>
        </asp:DetailsView>
<asp:SqlDataSource ID="usersDataSource" runat="server"
        ConnectionString="<%$ ConnectionStrings:StudentConnectionString %>"
        InsertCommand="INSERT INTO users(username, first_name, last_name, email, password,
        registration_date) VALUES (@username, @first_name, @last_name, @email, @password, GETDATE())"
        SelectCommand="SELECT [username], [first_name], [last_name], [email], [password] FROM [users]">
</asp:SqlDataSource>
</div>
</form>
</body>
</html>
```

(b) Form for the ASP.NET application

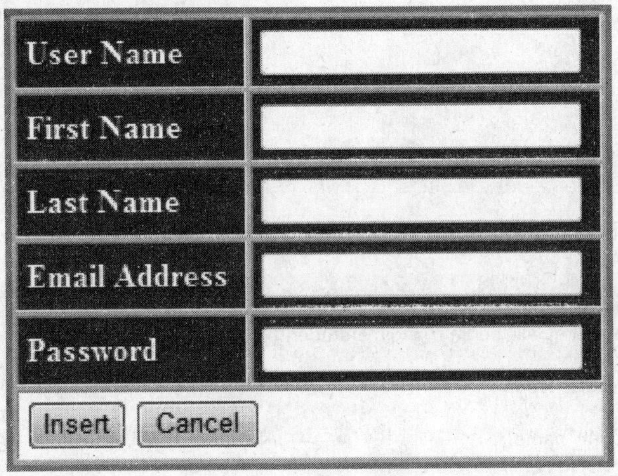

Transactions

In the examples shown so far, we have only examined code that consists of a single SQL action. However, most business applications require several SQL queries to complete a business transaction (refer to Figure 7-10). By default, most database connections assume that you would like to commit the results of executing a query to the database immediately. However, it is possible to define the notion of a business transaction in your program. Figure 8-14 shows how a Java program would execute a database transaction.

Given that there might be thousands of users simultaneously trying to access and/or update a database through a Web application at any given point time (think

FIGURE 8-13 Example Oracle PL/SQL stored procedure

(a) Sample Oracle PL/SQL stored procedure

```
CREATE OR REPLACE PROCEDURE p_registerstudent
(
 p_first_name   IN  VARCHAR2
 p_last_name    IN  VARCHAR2
 p_email        IN  VARCHAR2
 p_username     IN  VARCHAR2
 p_password     IN  VARCHAR2
 p_error        OUT VARCHAR2
)
IS
l_user_exists NUMBER := 0;
l_error       VARCHAR2(2000);

BEGIN

BEGIN
    SELECT COUNT(*)
    INTO  l_user_exists
    FROM  users
    WHERE  username = p_username;

  EXCEPTION
  WHEN OTHERS THEN
    l_error := 'Error: Could not verify username';
  END;

IF l_user_exists = 1 THEN
  l_error := 'Error: Username already exists !';
ELSE

  BEGIN
    INSERT INTO users VALUES(p_first_name,p_last_name,p_email,p_username,p_password,SYSDATE);

  EXCEPTION
    WHEN OTHERS THEN
      l_error := 'Error: Could not insert user';
  END;
END IF;

p_error = l_error;
END p_registerstudent;
```

Procedure p_registerstudent accepts first and last name, email, username, and password as inputs and returns the error message(if any).

This query checks whether the username entered already exists in the database.

If the username already exists, an error message is created for the user.

If the username does not exist in the database, the data entered are inserted into the database.

(b) Sample Java code for invoking the Oracle PL/SQL stored procedure

```
CallableStatement stmt =
    connection.prepareCall("begin p_registerstudent(?,?,?,?,?,?); end;");

// Binds the parameter types

stmt.setString(1, first_name);

    stmt.setString(2, last_name);

    stmt.setString(3, email);

    stmt.setString(4, username);

    stmt.setString(5, password);

    stmt.registerOutParameter(6, Types.VARCHAR);

stmt.execute();

error = stmt.getString(6);
```

Bind first parameter.

Bind second parameter.

Bind third parameter.

Bind fourth parameter.

Bind fifth parameter.

Bind sixth parameter.

Execute the callable statement.

Get error message.

FIGURE 8-14 Sample Java code snippet for an SQL transaction

```
connection.setAutoCommit(false);
try {
Statement st = connection.createStatement();

st.executeUpdate("UPDATE Order_T SET Quantity =(Quantity - 1) WHERE OrderID = "1001");

st.executeUpdate("UPDATE OrderLine_T SET Quantity = (Quantity - 1) WHERE OrderLineID = "100");
connection.commit();
}

catch (SQLException e) { connection.rollback(); }
finally { connection.setAutoCommit(true); }
```

Prevent the database driver from committing the query to the database immediately.

Cause the two updates to now be committed to the database as a group.

Rollback the database if either update doesn't succeed.

Reset the AutoCommit feature to true.

Amazon.com or eBay), application developers need to be well versed in the concepts of database transactions and need to use them appropriately when developing applications.

Database Connections

In most three-tier applications, while it is very common to have the Web servers and application servers located on the same physical machine, the database server is often located on a different machine. In this scenario, the act of making a database connection and keeping the connection alive can be very resource intensive. Further, most databases allow only a limited number of connections to be open at any given time. This can be challenging for applications that are being accessed via the Internet because it is difficult to predict the number of users. Luckily, most database drivers relieve application developers of the burden of managing database connections by using the concept of connection pooling. However, application developers should still be careful about how often they make connections to a database and how long they keep a connection open within their application program.

Key Benefits of Three-Tier Applications

The appropriate use of three-tier applications can lead to several benefits in organizations (Thompson, 1997):

- ***Scalability*** Three-tier architectures are more scalable than two-tier architectures. For example, the middle tier can be used to reduce the load on a database server by using a transaction processing (TP) monitor to reduce the number of connections to a server, and additional application servers can be added to distribute application processing. A TP monitor is a program that controls data transfer between clients and servers to provide a consistent environment for online transaction processing (OLTP).
- ***Technological flexibility*** It is easier to change DBMS engines, although triggers and stored procedures will need to be rewritten, with a three-tier architecture. The middle tier can even be moved to a different platform. Simplified presentation services make it easier to implement various desired interfaces such as Web browsers or kiosks.
- ***Lower long-term costs*** Use of off-the-shelf components or services in the middle tier can reduce costs, as can substitution of modules within an application rather than an entire application.
- ***Better match of systems to business needs*** New modules can be built to support specific business needs rather than building more general, complete applications.
- ***Improved customer service*** Multiple interfaces on different clients can access the same business processes.

- *Competitive advantage* The ability to react to business changes quickly by changing small modules of code rather than entire applications can be used to gain a competitive advantage.
- *Reduced risk* Again, the ability to implement small modules of code quickly and combine them with code purchased from vendors limits the risk assumed with a large-scale development project.

EXTENSIBLE MARKUP LANGUAGE (XML)

Extensible Markup Language (XML)
A text-based scripting language used to describe data structures hierarchically, using HTML-like tags.

Extensible Markup Language (XML) is a key development that is likely to continue to revolutionize the way data are exchanged over the Internet. As noted in an earlier section, HTML documents govern the display of information in a Web browser, whereas XML addresses the issue of representing data in a structure and format that can both be exchanged over the Internet and be interpreted by different components (i.e., browsers, Web servers, application servers). XML does not replace HTML, but it works with HTML to facilitate the transfer, exchange, and manipulation of data.

XML uses tags, short descriptions enclosed in angle brackets (< >), to characterize data. The use of angle brackets in XML is similar to their use for HTML tags. But whereas HTML tags are used to describe the appearance of content, XML tags are used to describe the content, or data, itself. Consider the following XML document stored in a file called PVFC.xml that is intended to provide the description of a product in PVFC:

```
<?xml version = "1.0"/>
<furniturecompany>
    <product ID="1">
        <description>End Table</description>
        <finish>Cherry</finish>
        <standard price>175.00</standard price>
        <line>1</line>
    </product>
</furniturecompany>
```

<description>, <finish>, and so on are examples of XML tags. <description>End Table</description> is an example of an element. Hence, an XML document consists of a series of nested elements. There are few restrictions on what can and cannot constitute tags in an XML element. However, an XML document itself must conform to a set of rules in terms of its structure. Three main techniques are used to validate that an XML document is structured correctly (i.e., follows all the rules for what constitutes a valid XML document): document structure declarations (DSDs), **XML Schema Definition (XSD)**, and Relax NG. All of these are alternatives to document type declarations (DTDs). DTDs were included in the first version XML but have some limitations. They cannot specify data types and are written in their own language, not in XML. In addition, DTDs do not support some newer features of XML, such as namespaces.

XML Schema Definition (XSD)
Language used for defining XML databases that has been recommended by the W3C.

To overcome these difficulties, theW3C published the XML Schema standard in May 2001. It defines the data model and establishes data types for the document data. The W3C XML Schema Definition (XSD) language uses a custom XML vocabulary to describe XML documents. It represents a step forward from using DTDs because it allows data types to be denoted. The following is very simple XSD schema that describes the structure, data typing, and validation of a salesperson record.

```
<?xml version="1.0" encoding="utf-8" ?>
<xsd:schema id="salespersonSchema"
xmlns:xsd="http://www.w3.org/2001/XMLSchema">
  <xsd:element name="Salesperson" type="SalespersonType" />
  <xsd:complexType name="SalespersonType">
      <xsd:sequence>
          <xsd:elementname="SalespersonID"
                type="xsd:integer"/>
```

```
            <xsd:elementname="SalespersonName"
                      type="xsd:string" />
            <xsd:element name="SalespersonTelephone"
                      type="PhoneNumberType">
            <xsd:element name="SalespersonFax"
                      type="PhoneNumber" minOccurs="0" />
            </xsd:element>
        </xsd:sequence>
    </xsd:complexType>
    <xsd:simpleType name="PhoneNumberType">
        <xsd:restriction base="xsd:string">
            <xsd:length value="12" />
            <xsd:pattern value="\d{3}-\d{3}-\d{4}" />
        </xsd:restriction>
    </xsd:simpleType>
</xsd:schema>
```

The following XML document conforms to the schema listed previously.

```
<?xml version="1.0" encoding="utf-8" ?>
<Salesperson xmlns:xsi=http://www.w3.org/2001/XMLSchema-instance
xsi:noNamespaceSchemaLocation="salespersonSchema.xsd">
    <SalespersonID>1</SalespersonID>
    <SalespersonName>Doug Henny</SalespersonName>
    <SalespersonTelephone>813-444-5555</SalespersonTelephone>
</Salesperson>
```

While it is possible to set up your own XML vocabulary, as we have just done, a wide variety of public XML vocabularies already exist and can be used to mark up your data. Many of them are listed at **http://wdvl.com/Authoring/Languages/XML/Specifications.html** and **www.service-architecture.com/xml/articles/xml_vocabularies.html**. Such vocabularies make it easier for an organization to exchange data with other organizations without having to engage in individual agreements with each business partner. Selecting the best XML vocabulary to use to describe a database is very important. As XML gains popularity, more libraries of external XML schemas should become available, but for now, Web searches and word of mouth are the most likely mechanisms for you to find the appropriate schemas for your application.

New XML-based vocabularies, such as Extensible Business Reporting Language (XBRL) and Structured Product Labeling (SPL), are emerging as open standards that will allow meaningful and unambiguous comparisons that could not be made easily previously. Financial organizations that adhere to XBRL may record up to 2,000 financial data points, such as cost, assets, and net income, using standard XBRL tag definitions. These data points may then be combined or compared across institutions' financial reports. As products that enable easier use of XBRL come to market, large financial institutions expect to spend much less time cleansing and normalizing their data and exchanging data with business partners. Smaller institutions can anticipate improved and more affordable access to financial analysis (Henschen, 2005). The FDA is also beginning to require the use of Structured Product Labeling (SPL), to record the information provided on drug labels, for both prescription and over-the-counter drugs.

Some sites are making standardization with their site easier for outside developers. For example, developers can use the eBay API via XML to display eBay listings on any third-party site. In addition, after downloading a developer's kit, creating an account, and obtaining a license key, developers can use Google APIs to query Google's database from within their own Web pages and applications. It is beyond the scope of this text to provide the reader with an in-depth understanding of XML. Nevertheless, the functionality provided by eBay and Google already make it clear that XML is an area that melds closely with traditional database content as e-commerce continues to develop.

Now that you have a basic understanding of what constitutes an XML document, we can turn our attention to how XML data can be used in the modern computing environment and the unique challenges they bring to the table.

Storing XML Documents

One of the biggest questions that needs to be answered as XML data becomes more prevalent is "Where do we store these data?" While it is possible to store XML data as a series of files, doing so brings back into play the same disadvantages with file processing systems that we discussed in Chapter 1. Luckily, we have several choices when it comes to storing XML data:

1. ***Store XML data in a relational database by shredding the XML document*** Shredding an XML document essentially means that we store each element of an XML schema independently in a relational table and use other tables to store the relationships among the elements. Modern databases such as Microsoft SQL Server and Oracle provide capabilities beyond standard SQL to help store and retrieve XML data.
2. ***Store an entire XML document in a field capable of storing large objects, such as a binary large object (BLOB) or a character large object (CLOB)*** This technique is not very useful if you have to actually search for data within the XML document.
3. ***Store the XML document using special XML columns that are made available as part of database*** These columns can be associated with an XSD, for example, to ensure that the XML document that is being inserted is a valid document.
4. ***Store the XML document using a native XML database*** These are non-relational databases designed specifically to store XML documents.

In general, the latter two options are used when the majority of the information being processed is originally in XML format. For example, many academic and practitioner conferences are beginning to require that authors submit their presentations and papers in XML format. On the other hand, the first two options are used primarily if XML is used as a data exchange format between a browser and an application server.

Retrieving XML Documents

XPath
One of a set of XML technologies that supports XQuery development. XPath expressions are used to locate data in XML documents.

Modern databases provide extensive support for retrieving information from databases in XML format. The key technologies behind XML data retrieval are **XPath** and XQuery. Each of the storage options listed above provides specific mechanisms by which you can retrieve data in XML format. For the first three options, these take the form of extensions to the SQL language (based on XPath and XQuery). In the case of a native XML database, the most likely choice is XQuery itself. XQuery helps in locating and extracting elements from XML documents; it can be used to accomplish such activities as transforming XML data to XHTML, providing information for use by Web services, generating summary reports, and searching Web documents.

XQuery
An XML transformation language that allows applications to query both relational databases and XML data.

The XML Query Working Group describes **XQuery** most simply in these words, published at **www.w3c.org/XML/Query**: "XQuery is a standardized language for combining documents, databases, Web pages and almost anything else. It is very widely implemented. It is powerful and easy to learn. XQuery is replacing proprietary middleware languages and Web Application development languages. XQuery is replacing complex Java or C++ programs with a few lines of code. XQuery is simpler to work with and easier to maintain than many other alternatives."

Built on XPath expressions, XQuery is now supported by the major relational database engines, including those from IBM, Oracle, and Microsoft.

Take a look at the XML document shown in Figure 8-15a. Now, consider the following XQuery expression that returns all product elements that have a standard price > 300.00:

```
for $p in doc("PVFC.xml")/furniture company/product
where $p/standardprice>300.00
order by $p/description
return $p/description
```

FIGURE 8-15 XML code segments
(a) XML schema

```
<?xml version = "1.0"?>
<furniture company>
    <product ID="1">
        <description>End Table</description>
        <finish>Cherry</finish>
        <standard price>175.00</standard price>
        <line>1</line>
    </product>
    <product ID="2">
        <description>Coffee Table</description>
        <finish>Natural Ash</finish>
        <standard price>200.00</standard price>
        <line>2</line>
    </product>
    <product ID="3">
        <description>Computer Desk</description>
        <finish>Natural Ash</finish>
        <standard price>375.00</standard price>
        <line>2</line>
    </product>
    <product ID="4">
        <description>Entertainment Center</description>
        <finish>Natural Maple</finish>
        <standard price>650.00</standard price>
        <line>3</line>
    </product>
    <product ID="5">
        <description>Writers Desk</description>
        <finish>Cherry</finish>
        <standard price>325.00</standard price>
        <line>1</line>
    </product>
    <product ID="6">
        <description>8-Drawer Desk</description>
        <finish>White Ash</finish>
        <standard price>750.00</standard price>
        <line>2</line>
    </product>
    <product ID="7">
        <description>Dining Table</description>
        <finish>Natural Ash</finish>
        <standard price>800.00</standard price>
        <line>2</line>
    </product>
    <product ID="8">
        <description>Computer Desk</description>
        <finish>Walnut</finish>
        <standard price>250.00</standard price>
        <line>3</line>
    </product>
</furniture company>
```

(continued)

You can see the similarities between XQuery and SQL in this example. It is often said that XQuery is to XML as SQL is to relational databases. This example demonstrates the ease with which you will become fluent in XQuery as your understanding of SQL increases. The XQuery expression shown previously is called a FLWOR expression. FLWOR is an acronym for For, LET, Where, Order by, and Return:

- The FOR clause selects all product elements from furniture company into the variable named $p.
- The WHERE clause selects all product elements with a standard price greater than $300.00.

FIGURE 8-15 ***(continued)***
(b) XSLT code

```
<?xml version = "1.0"?>
<xsl:stylesheet version="1.0" xmlns:xsl="http://www.w3.org/1999/XSL/Transform">
<xsl:template match="/">
    <html>
        <body>
        <h2>Product Listing</h2>
        <table border="1">
        <tr bgcolor="orange">
                <th>Description</th>
                <th>Finish</th>
                <th>Price</th>
        </tr>
        <xsl:for-each select="furniturecompany/product">
        <tr>
            <td> <xsl:value-of select="description"/> </td>
            <td> <xsl:value-of select="finish"/> </td>
            <td> <xsl:value-of select="price"/> </td>
        </tr>
        </xsl:for-each>
        </table>
        </body>
    </html>
</xsl:template>
</xsl:stylesheet>
```

(c) Output of XSLT tranformation

Product Listing

Description	Finish	Price
End Table	Cherry	175.00
Coffee Table	Natural Ash	200.00
Computer Desk	Natural Ash	375.00
Entertainment Center	Natural Maple	650.00
Writers Desk	Cherry	325.00
8-Drawer Desk	White Ash	750.00
Dining Table	Natural Ash	800.00
Computer Desk	Walnut	250.00

- The ORDER BY clause sets the sorting order of the results to be by the description element.
- The RETURN clause specifies that the description elements should be returned.

The results of the above XQuery are as follows:

```
<description>8-Drawer Desk</description>
<description>Computer Desk</description>
<description>Dining Table</description>
<description>Entertainment Center</description>
<description>Writer's Desk</description>
```

This example shows how to query data that is in XML format. Given the importance of XML as a data exchange format, many relational databases also provide mechanisms to return data from relational tables in an XML format. In Microsoft SQL Server, this can be achieved by adding the statement FOR XML AUTO or PATH to the end of a typical SELECT query. Essentially, the result table from the SELECT is converted into an XML form and returned to the calling program. Behind the scenes, many of these additional features use XPath as the basis for the queries.

Displaying XML Data

Notice that in the XML examples so far, we have provided little information about what to do with XML data. In fact, the separation of how data is formatted from how the data is displayed is one of the key reasons XML is gaining popularity over HTML, where the data and formatting are intermingled. The display of XML data on a Web browser is controlled by a stylesheet specified using the **Extensible Stylesheet Language Transformation (XSLT)**. Most modern browsers and programming languages provide support for XSLT. Thus, the transformation of the XML can happen either at the Web server layer or the application server layer. Figure 8-15b shows a sample XSLT specification for displaying the Salesperson data in the form of an HTML table. The resultant output is shown in Figure 8-15c.

Extensible Stylesheet Language Transformation (XSLT)
A language used to transform complex XML documents and also used to create HTML pages from XML documents.

One of the advantages of XSLT is that it can be used to handle the myriad devices that now use the Internet. Smartphone devices have built-in browsers that allow a user to access the Internet. Some of the browsers require that content delivered to them use the Wireless Application Protocol (WAP), using the Wireless Markup Language (WML). Others can handle HTML, as long as it has been appropriately transformed for optimal viewing on the screen size of a mobile device. By using XSLT, XML, and other technologies, the same set of data can be rendered onto the different devices without having to write a separate page for each device type.

XML and Web Services

The Internet has served as a powerful driver to encourage the integration of communication between the providers of software applications and the users of those applications. As the Internet evolves as a distributed computing platform, a set of emerging standards is affecting software development and distribution practices. Easing the automatic communication of software programs through the use of XML coding and Internet protocols such as HTTP and e-mail protocols, a new class of applications called **Web services** are improving the ability of computers to communicate over the Internet automatically, thus aiding the development and deployment of applications within a company or across an industry. Existing methods of establishing communication, such as electronic data interchange (EDI), are still being used, but the widespread availability of XML means that the Web services approach promises to make it much easier to create program application modules that execute in a distributed environment.

Web services
A set of emerging standards that define protocols for automatic communication between software programs over the Web. Web services are XML based and usually run in the background to establish transparent communication among computers.

The promise of Web services is the development of a standardized communication system among different applications, using XML based technologies at their core. Easier integration of applications is possible because developers need not be familiar with the technical details associated with the applications being integrated, nor must they learn the programming language of the application being integrated. Anticipation of increased business agility derived from significant reductions in the time and effort needed to establish enterprise application integration and B2B relationships is driving the interest in the Web services approach. Figure 8-16 is a very simple diagram of an order entry system that includes both internal Web services (Order Entry and Accounting) and Web services that are outsourced to companies that provide authentication and credit validation services over the Web (Newcomer, 2002).

There are some key additional terms that are associated with using Web services. Figure 8-17 depicts a common database/Web services protocol stack. The transformation and communication of data into and out of application programs and databases relies on a set of XML-based protocols. **Universal Description, Discovery, and Integration (UDDI)**

Universal Description, Discovery, and Integration (UDDI)
A technical specification for creating a distributed registry of Web services and businesses that are open to communicating through Web services.

FIGURE 8-16 A typical order entry system that uses Web services
Source: Based on Newcomer (2002).

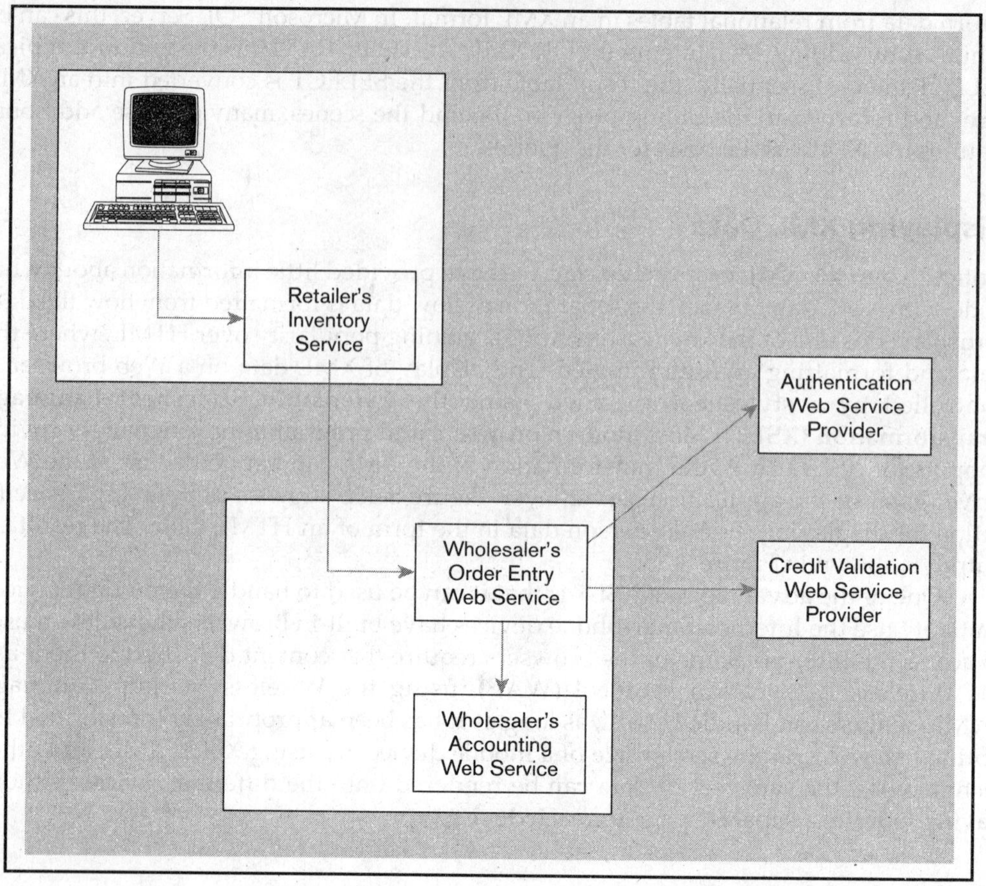

FIGURE 8-17 Web services protocol stack

Publish, Find, Use Services	UDDI	**U**niversal **D**escription, **D**iscovery, **I**ntegration
Describe Services	WSDL	**W**eb **S**ervices **D**escription **L**anguage
Service Interactions	SOAP	**S**imple **O**bject **A**ccess **P**rotocol
Data Format	XML	e**X**tensible **M**arkup **L**anguage
Open Communications	Internet	

Web Services Description Language (WSDL)
An XML-based grammar or language used to describe a Web service and specify a public interface for that service.

is a technical specification for creating a distributed registry of Web services and businesses that are open to communicating through Web services. **Web Services Description Language (WSDL)** is an XML-based grammar or language used to describe what a Web service can do and to specify a public interface for how to use that service. WSDL is used to create a file that automatically generates a client interface, allowing a developer to attend to the business logic rather than the communications requirements of an application. The definition of the public interface may indicate data types for XML messages, message format, location information for the specified Web service, the transport protocol to be used (HTTP, HTTPS, or e-mail), and so forth. These descriptions are stored in a UDDI repository.

Simple Object Access Protocol (SOAP) is an XML-based communication protocol used for sending messages between applications via the Internet. Because it is a language-independent platform, it enables communication between diverse applications. As SOAP moves toward becoming a W3C standard, it generalizes a capability that was previously established on an ad hoc basis between specific programs. Many view it as the most important Web service. SOAP structures a message into three parts: an optional header, a required body, and optional attachments. The header can support in-transit processing and can thus deal with firewall security issues.

Simple Object Access Protocol (SOAP)
An XML-based communication protocol used for sending messages between applications via the Internet.

The following is an example, adapted from an example displayed at **http://en.wikipedia.org/wiki/SOAP**, of how Pine Valley Furniture Company might format a SOAP message requesting product information from one of its suppliers. PVFC needs to know which product corresponds to the supplier's product ID 32879.

PINE VALLEY FURNITURE

```
<soap:Envelope xmlns:soap=http://schemas.xmlsoap.org/soap/envelope/>
  <soap:Body>
    <getProductDetails xmlns=http://supplier.example.com/ws
      <productID>32879</productID>
    </getProductDetails>
  </soap:Body>
</soap:Envelope>
```

The supplier's Web service could format its reply message, which contains the requested information about the product, in this way:

```
<soap:Envelope xmlns:soap=http://schemas.xmlsoap.org/soap/envelope/>
  <soap:Body>
    <getProductDetailsResponse xmlns="suppliers.example.com/ws">
      <getProductDetailsResult>
        <productName>Dining Table</productName>
        <Finish>Natural Ash</Finish>
        <Price>800</Price>
        <inStock>True</inStock>
      </getProductDetailsResult>
    </getProductDetailsResponse>
  </soap:Body>
</soap:Envelope>
```

Figure 8-18 shows the interaction of applications and systems with Web services. Note that as a transaction flows from one business to another or from a customer to a business, a SOAP processor creates a message envelope that allows the exchange of formatted XML data across the Web. Because SOAP messages connect remote sites, appropriate security measures must be implemented in order to maintain data integrity.

Web services, with their promise of automatic communication between businesses and customers, whether they are other businesses or individual retail customers, have generated much discussion and anticipation in the past few years. Concerns about adopting a Web services approach focus on transaction speed, security, and reliability. The open system implied in establishing automatic communication among computers attached to the Web must be further developed before the security and reliability match those of traditional business applications.

FIGURE 8-18 Web services deployment

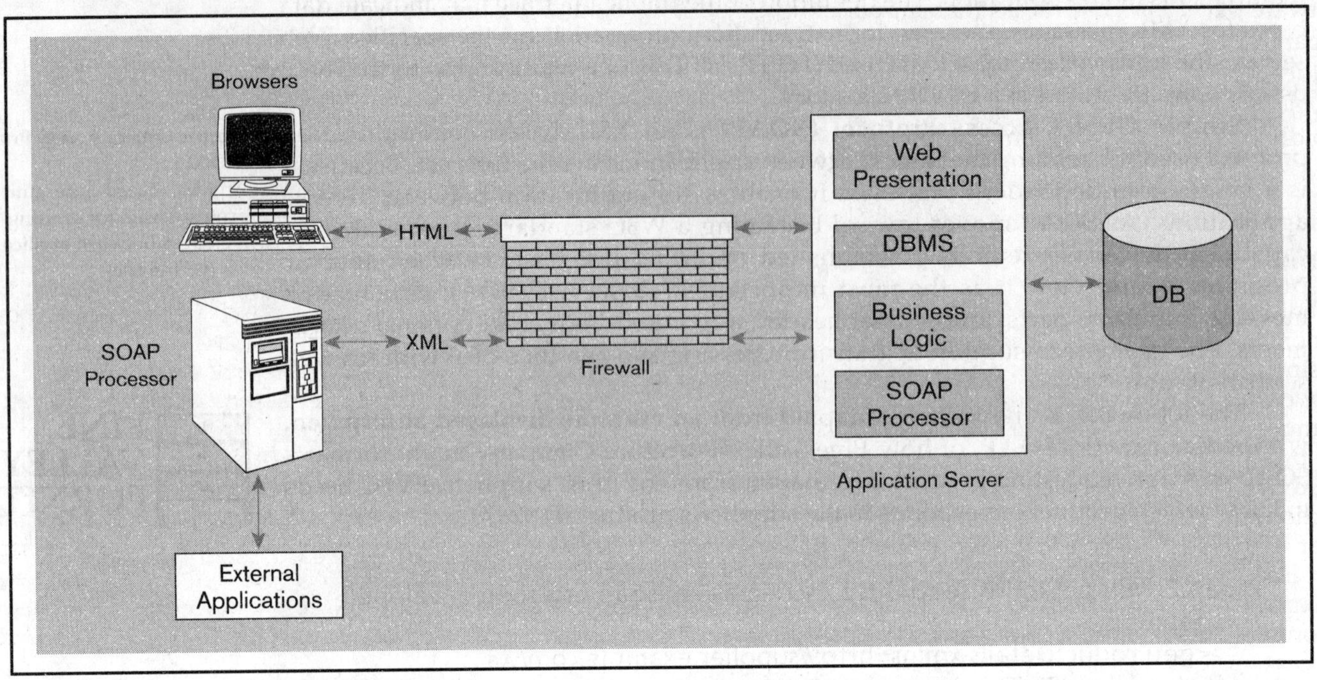

Source: Based on Newcomer (2002).

However, it is clear that Web services are here to stay. Several organizations have already attracted attention by their use of Web services. Both Amazon.com and Google, two companies with high-profile Web presence, use Web services extensively. Google began its program in April 2002, allowing developers to access its search database directly for noncommercial uses and to create their own interfaces to the data. Access to Amazon.com's inventory database was made available in July 2002. Combining the service with a blog tool, an API allows bloggers to create a link to a relevant Amazon.com product in one step. Programmers benefit from improved ease of access, customers conduct more efficient searches, and Amazon.com and Google continue to spread and support their brands. Google "Amazon Web services documentation" or "Google Web services" to become more familiar with these free opportunities.

Others charge for using their Web services. Microsoft .NET developers can use Microsoft's MapPoint Web Service to provide location-based services (LBS) from their Web sites. MapPoint Web Service provides both location and mapping capabilities that may be accessed over any HTTPS connection. MapQuest offers similar capabilities. After paying a setup fee, users may elect to pay on an annual or monthly basis. Charges depend on transaction count. Topographic and satellite images are available through MSR Maps (see **http://msrmaps.com**).

Service-oriented architecture (SOA)
A collection of services that communicate with each other in some manner, usually by passing data or coordinating a business activity.

The growing popularity and availability of Web services is also leading to a change in the way organizations think about developing their IT applications and capabilities. A new paradigm called **service-oriented architecture (SOA)** is gaining a foothold. An SOA is a collection of services that communicate with each other in some manner, usually passing data or coordinating a business activity. While these services do not have to be Web services, Web services are the predominant mechanism used. SOAs differ from traditional object-oriented approaches in that the services are loosely coupled and very interoperable. The software components are very reusable and operate across different development platforms, such as Java and .NET. Using XML, SOAP, and WSDL eases the establishment of necessary connections.

Using an SOA approach leads to the establishment of a modeling, design, and software development process that supports the efficient development of applications. Organizations that have adopted such an approach have found their development time reduced by at least 40 percent. Not only are the organizations experiencing shorter development time, they also hope to demonstrate more flexibility in responding to the rapidly changing business environment.

Summary

Client/server architectures have offered businesses opportunities to better fit their computer systems to their business needs. Establishing the appropriate balance between client/server and mainframe DBMSs is a matter of much current discussion. Client/server architectures are prominent in providing Internet applications, including dynamic data access. Application partitioning assigns portions of application code to client or server partitions after it is written in order to achieve better performance and interoperability. Application developer productivity is expected to increase as a result of using application partitioning, but the developer must understand each process intimately to place it correctly.

In a two-tier architecture, the client manages the user interface and business logic, while the database server manages database storage and access. This architecture reduces network traffic, reduces the power required for each client, and centralizes user authorization, integrity checking, data dictionary maintenance, and query and update processing on the database server. We looked at examples of a two-tier application written in VB.NET and Java and examined the six key steps needed to retrieve data from a database.

Three-tier architectures, which include another server in addition to the client and database server layers, allow application code to be stored on the additional server. This approach allows business processing to be performed on the additional server, resulting in a thin client. Advantages of the three-tier architecture can include scalability, technological flexibility, lower long-term costs, better matching of systems to business needs, improved customer service, competitive advantage, and reduced risk. But higher short-term costs, advanced tools and training, shortages of experienced personnel, incompatible standards, and lack of end-user tools are some of the challenges related to using three-tier or *n*-tier architectures.

The most common type of three-tier application is the Internet-based Web application. In its simplest form, a request from a client browser is sent through the network to the Web server. If the request requires that data be obtained from the database, the Web server constructs a query and sends it to the database server, which processes the query and returns the results. Firewalls are used to limit external access to the company's data.

Common components of Internet architecture are certain programming and markup languages, Web servers, applications servers, database servers, and database drivers and other middleware that can be used to connect the various components together. To aid in our understanding of how to create a Web application, we looked at examples of three-tier applications written in JSP, PHP, and ASP.NET and examined some of the key database-related issues in such applications.

Finally, we discussed the role of XML as a data exchange standard on the Internet. We examined issues related to the storage of XML documents in databases, retrieval of XML using languages such as XQuery and XPath, as well transformation of XML data into presentation formats such as HTML. We also examined various XML-based technologies, UDDI, WSDL, and SOAP, which are all fueling the interest in SOA and Web services. These allow disparate applications within a company or around the globe to be able to talk to each other.

Chapter Review

Key Terms

Application partitioning *340*
Application program interface (API) *342*
Client/server system *338*
Database server *341*
Extensible Markup Language (XML) *362*
Fat client *340*
Java servlet *355*
Middleware *342*
Open Database Connectivity (ODBC) *342*
Thin client *347*
Three-tier architecture *346*
Service-oriented architecture (SOA) *370*
Simple Object Access Protocol (SOAP) *369*
Universal Description, Discovery, and Integration (UDDI) *367*
Web services *367*
Web Services Description Language (WSDL) *368*
World Wide Web Consortium (W3C) *350*
XHTML *350*
XML Schema Definition (XSD) *362*
XPath *364*
XQuery *364*
Extensible Stylesheet Language Transformation (XSLT) *367*

Review Questions

1. Define each of the following terms:
   a. application partitioning
   b. application program interface (API)
   c. client/server system
   d. middleware
   e. stored procedure
   f. three-tier architecture
   g. Java Database Connectivity (JDBC)
   h. XML Schema
   i. Web services
   j. XSLT
   k. SOAP
2. Match each of the following terms with the most appropriate definition:

____ client/server system	a. a client that is responsible for processing, including application logic and presentation logic
____ application program interface (API)	b. World Wide Web Consortium
	c. a PC configured for handling the presentation layer and some business logic processing for an application
____ fat client	d. a collection of services that communicate with each other in some manner
____ database server	e. software that facilitates interoperability, reducing programmer coding effort
____ middleware	f. device responsible for database storage and access
____ three-tiered architecture	g. systems where the application logic components are distributed
____ thin client	h. software that facilitates communication between front-end programs and back-end database servers
____ XSD	i. three-layer client/server configuration
____ SOA	j. language used for defining XML databases
____ W3C	

3. List several major advantages of the client/server architecture compared with other computing approaches.
4. Contrast the following terms:
   a. two-tier architecture; three-tier architecture
   b. fat client; thin client
   c. ODBC; JDBC
   d. XHTML; XSLT
   e. SQL; XQuery
   f. Web services; SOA
5. Describe the advantages and disadvantages of two-tier architectures.
6. Describe the advantages and disadvantages of three-tier architectures.
7. Describe the common components needed to create a Web-based application.
8. What database APIs are commonly used to access databases from various programming languages?
9. What are the six common steps needed to access databases from a typical program?
10. If you were charged with developing a client/server application, how would you ensure success?
11. Research the Web for information on trends in migrating from mainframe systems to client/server architecture. What percentage of U.S. companies have migrated? Highlight success stories that you encounter, as well as difficulties. A good Web site to start with is **www.cs.wisc.edu/arch/www**.
12. What are the four common approaches to storing XML data?
13. What components must a PHP program that enables a dynamic Web site contain?
14. Explain why using XML Schema is a step forward from using document type declarations (DTDs).
15. What is XSLT, and how does it differ from XML? What role does it play in the creation of a Web application?
16. Discuss UDDI. Compare and contrast it with the white, yellow, and green pages of the telephone book. (If your telephone book does not have green pages, you will need to research this feature found in some telephone books.)
17. What is SOA? How would you, in your viewpoint, logically relate it to database application development?
18. What are the XML-based protocols used in Web services?
19. Explain why eXtensible Markup Language is a major development that has happened for data exchange over the Internet?

Problems and Exercises

1. You have been asked to prepare a report that evaluates possible client/server solutions to handle a new customer application system for all branch offices. What business characteristics would you evaluate? What technology characteristics would you evaluate? Why?
2. Explain the difference between a static Web site and a dynamic one. What are the characteristics of a dynamic Web site that enable it to better support the development of e-business?
3. Historically, what types of applications have moved quickly to client/server database systems? What types have moved more slowly, and why? What do you think will happen in the future to the ratio of client/server database systems versus mainframe database systems?
4. Discuss some of the languages that are associated with Internet application development. Classify these languages according to the functionality they provide for each application. It is not necessary that you use the same classification scheme used in the chapter.
5. Find some dynamic Web site code such as that included in Figures 8-10, 8-11, and 8-12. Annotate the code, as is done in these figures, to explain each section, especially the elements that involve interaction with the database. (Hint:

Google "JSP," "ASP.NET," or "PHP MySQL Examples" to find a rich set of sample code to explore.)

6. Rewrite the example shown in Figure 8-5 using VB.NET.
7. Rewrite the example show in Figure 8-4 using Java.
8. Construct a simple XML schema that describes a tutor. Include the tutor's last name, first name, phone, e-mail address, and certification date as child elements of the TUTOR element.
9. Using your schema from Question 8, write an FLWOR XQuery expression that lists only the tutors' names and lists them alphabetically by last name.
10. Using your schema from Question 8, write an XSLT program to display the tutor information in the form of an HTML table.
11. Discuss how Web services can be used to effectively integrate business applications and data. Search the Web for resources on current Web services that employ XML, SOAP, UDDI, and WSDL. Find at least three and discuss how each is used, including examples from industry.

Field Exercises

1. Investigate the computing architecture of your university. Trace the history of computing at your university and determine what path the university followed to get to its present configurations. Some universities started early with mainframe environments; others started when PCs became available. Can you tell how your university's initial computing environment has affected today's computing environment?
2. On a smaller scale than in Question 1, investigate the computing architecture of a department within your university. Try to find out how well the current system is meeting the department's information-processing needs.
3. Locate three sites on the Web that have interactive database systems attached to them. Evaluate the functionality of each site and discuss how its interactive database system is likely to affect that functionality. If you're not sure where to start, try **www.amazon.com**.
4. Determine what you would have to do to use PHP, JSP, or ASP.NET on a public Web site owned either by you or by the organization for which you work.
5. Outline the steps you would take to conduct a risk assessment for your place of employment with regard to attaching a database to your public site. If possible, help with the actual implementation of the risk assessment.
6. According to your own personal interests, use one of the common combinations PHP and MySQL, JSP and Oracle, or ASP.NET and Microsoft Access to attach a database to your personal Web site. Test it locally and then move it to your public site.
7. Identify a Web site that extensively describes XML technologies. What other XML technologies besides the ones described in this chapter do you see being discussed? What purpose do they serve? If you're not sure where to start, try **www.xml.com** or **www.w3.org**.

References

Henschen, D. 2005. "XBRL Offers a Faster Route to Intelligence." *Intelligent Enterprise 8, 8* (August): 12.

Hurwitz, J. 1998. "Sorting Out Middleware." *DBMS* 11,1 (January): 10–12.

Newcomer, E. 2002. *Understanding Web Services, XML, WSDL, SOAP, and UDDI*. Boston: Addison-Wesley.

Quinlan, T. 1995. "The Second Generation of Client/Server." *Database Programming & Design* 8,5 (May): 31–39.

Thompson, C. 1997. "Committing to Three-Tier Architecture." *Database Programming & Design* 10,8 (August): 26–33.

Ullman, L. 2003. *PHP and MySQL for Dynamic Web Sites*. Berkeley, CA: Peachpit Press.

Further Reading

Anderson, G., and B. Armstrong. 1995. "Client/Server: Where Are We Really?" *Health Management Technology* 16,6 (May): 34, 36, 38, 40, 44.

Cerami, E. 2002. *Web Services Essentials*. Sebastopol, CA: O'Reilly & Associates, Inc.

Frazer, W. D. 1998. "Object/Relational Grows Up." *Database Programming & Design* 11,1 (January): 22–28.

Innocenti, C. 2006. "XQuery Levels the Data Integration Playing Field." *DM Review* accessed at *DM Direct*, **http://www.information-management.com/infodirect/20061201/1069184-1.html** (December).

Koenig, D., A. Glover, P. King, G. Laforge, and J. Skeet. 2007. *Groovy in Action*. Greenwich, CT: Manning Publications.

Mason, J. N., and M. Hofacker. 2001. "Gathering Client-Server Data." *Internal Auditor* 58:6 (December): 27–29.

Melton, J., and S. Buxton.2006. *Querying XML, XQuery, XPath, and SQL/XML in Context*. Morgan Kaufmann Series in Data Management Systems. San Francisco: Morgan Kaufmann.

Morrison, M., and J. Morrison. 2003. *Database-Driven Web Sites*, 2nd ed. Cambridge, MA: Thomson-Course Technologies.

Richardson, L., S. Ruby, and D. H. Hansson. 2007. *RESTful Web Services*. Sebastopol, CA: O'Reilly Media, Inc.

Valade, J. 2006. *PHP & MySQL: Your Visual Blueprint for Creating Dynamic, Database-Driven Web Sites*. Hoboken, NJ: Wiley & Sons.

Wamsley, P. 2007. *XQuery*. Sebastopol, CA: O'Reilly Media, Inc.

Web Resources

www.javacoffeebreak.com/articles/jdbc/index.html "Getting Started with JDBC" by David Reilly.

http://www.w3schools.com/ASPNET/default.asp Tutorial on ASP.NET.

www.cs.wisc.edu/arch/www The WWW Computer Architecture site, maintained by the Computer Architecture Group in the Computer Sciences area at the University of Wisconsin.

www.w3.org/html/wg W3C's home page for HTML.

www.w3.org/MarkUp W3C's home page for XHTML.

www.w3.org/XML/Query W3C's home page for XQuery.

www.w3.org/XML/1999/XML-in-10-points The W3C article "XML in 10 points," which presents basic XML concepts.

www.netcraft.com The Netcraft Web Server survey, which tracks the market share of different Web servers and SSL site operating systems.

www.projectliberty.org The home page of the Liberty Alliance. Open standards specifications and drafts of specifications may be downloaded here.

www.w3schools.com/default.asp A Web developers' site that provides Web-building tutorials on topics from basic HTML and XHTML to advanced XML, SQL, databases, multimedia, and WAP.

www.ws-i.org The home page of the Web Services Interoperability Organization (WS-I).

www.oasis-open.org/home/index.php The home page of the Organization for the Advancement of Structured Information Standards (OASIS).

xml.apache.org/cocoon The Cocoon project, a Java Web publishing framework that separates document content, style, and logic, allowing the independent design, creation, and management of each.

CASE

Mountain View Community Hospital

Case Description

In Chapter 1, you learned about the Mountain View Community Hospital (MVCH) special study team that is developing a long-term strategic plan, including an information systems plan for MVCH. In assessing the future technology needs of the hospital, the planning team of Mr. Heller, Mr. Lopez, Dr. Jefferson, and a consultant has taken a close look at issues with existing systems as well as trends in the health-care IT industry.

You may recall that MVCH has systems for many different areas, including patient accounting, administrative services, and financial management. Most of the computer applications are implemented using relational database and client/server technology. Some systems were developed internally, while others were acquired from outside vendors. Responding to a recent survey of health-care CIOs, Mr. Heller chose the term *limited integration* to describe the hospital's current IT infrastructure: best-in-class systems in some areas, stand-alone systems in other areas, and some remaining manual or paper-based processes. Such limited integration is affecting virtually all of the hospital's stakeholders.

Physicians often have to log on to multiple applications to retrieve patient-related information or read e-mail. Some doctors have expressed an interest in being able to access clinical systems remotely while working outside the hospital. Patients must negotiate a maze of health plans, administrators, physicians, and clinics in their encounters with the hospital. The hospital's heterogeneous environment of platforms and applications, as well as the paper-based systems, has made exchange of patient data between the clinical systems and administrative/financial applications a challenge. At the same time, the managed-care environment and the needs to contain costs and simultaneously improve clinical outcomes, patient satisfaction, and efficiency require MVCH to closely track and analyze its clinical and financial data related to patient care services and provide those data to its administrative and clinical decision makers. Oftentimes, accurate data need to be available in real time.

In addition to these concerns, some important developments in the health-care IT industry factor into the study team's analysis. One is the trend toward using electronic medical record systems that require various clinical information systems to work together to provide a complete patient record. Hospitals concerned about moving patients through the hospital more efficiently and effectively have begun adopting workflow automation (or business process management) technology and Web technologies are making inroads. Web portals, for example, allow both patients and physicians to communicate online. Health-care alliances are extending their member and patient services beyond their organizational boundaries, to the workplace, schools, and homes. Health plan members can check their claim status, send messages to service representatives, and review coverage. Patients can even make their own appointments by accessing appointment schedules.

Given these issues and trends, the study team has concluded that better and more centralized access to operational, financial, and clinical information should be a top priority for the hospital. Specifically, the team would like MVCH to implement a system that integrates all of these data—data from health plans, physicians, and hospital systems—so that accurate real-time information is available.

MVCH's planning committee believes the adoption of Web-based solutions may greatly improve the hospital's operations, extend customer service and marketing functions, speed up and improve the quality of patient care, and allow physicians to be more responsive to their patients. The committee specifically sees Web services as a way of addressing many of the hospital's challenges.

For one thing, given the widespread access to the Internet these days, patients are increasingly demanding online capabilities, such as making appointments, booking surgeries, making payments, and so on. In response, hospitals have begun to implement patient portals that can even provide patients with access to their medical records. Another issue at MVCH is the heterogeneous environment of platforms and applications. As stated in previous chapters, MVCH has applications and software from many different vendors. Consequently, the IT department has been struggling to interface the many different systems and exchange patient data between the clinical systems and software that is not health-care specific, such as reporting and billing applications. Mr. Heller, MVCH's CIO, believes that Web services would provide an efficient means of making the diverse systems work together.

Such a solution would also be beneficial for the medical staff. Currently, physicians have to log on to multiple applications to retrieve diagnostic information such as radiology reports and digital images, access the latest medical literature regarding a patient condition, or read e-mail. Some doctors have also expressed an interest in accessing clinical systems remotely while working outside of the hospital. A physician's portal accessed from a standard Web browser could provide faster access to information regardless of location, and doctors could open and navigate multiple applications to extract information. Web services could even push relevant new information regarding a patient's condition. At a recent conference for health-care CIOs, Mr. Heller also learned from presentations and conversations with peers that Web services could potentially be rolled out in a relatively short time frame—three to six months.

In considering where Web services and other Web-based solutions could be developed for MVCH's health-care systems, several issues have been raised:

- Privacy and security concerns are of primary importance. Patient health information requires high levels of confidentiality because it is sensitive by nature and because of HIPAA's privacy and security mandates.
- Data entry questions are also significant. Doctors, nurses, and other health-care workers must be able and willing to enter the data into any system that is provided.
- Given that Web services are built on a foundation of HTTP, system availability and reliability would be crucial if a decision were made to implement a Web-enabled system, particularly for key business processes.
- How would a browser-based system integrate with the systems already in existence at MVCH?
- Would MVCH have the funding and staffing resources to go forward with a Web services project? Would it be

necessary to hire an external service provider? Could it be done in-house with existing IT staff?
- How would MVCH demonstrate that the proposed system is cost-effective?
- How will MVCH predict and handle changes in work patterns that may occur?
- What organizational policies and procedures will need to be changed or modified as system changes are implemented?

Case Questions

1. Do you think that MVCH IT staff under Mr. Heller should and could undertake the project of moving MVCH toward an integrated environment? Should MVCH outsource such a project? Why or why not?
2. Can you think of any other approaches to integration (besides the Web-based approach) that the study team has not considered? If so, what are some alternatives to address the issues at hand?
3. Discuss the extent and nature of security and privacy issues that the planning committee should consider when evaluating any decisions to provide more information that is critical to patients over the Web. Why would systems integration be important in terms of addressing HIPAA's privacy and security concerns?
4. The health-care industry has not embraced Web services as quickly as other industries for integrating diverse systems. Why do you think that's the case? What would be critical success factors for making Web services solutions a success at MVCH and other health-care organizations?
5. Should MVCH treat the potential implementation of Web-based solutions and Web services as a technology issue or a strategy issue? Please explain.

Case Exercises

1. Outline the advantages and risks/disadvantages of moving toward an integrated Web-based environment based on a three-tier architecture. What do you think would be the most significant challenges with this integration approach? Which specific technologies would you recommend for implementing this solution?
2. An alternative approach that has been suggested is to look for a single integrated solution. The study team is examining the Global Care Solutions Hospital 2000 system, a fully integrated hospital information system (HIS). What advantages do you see in adopting a fully integrated health information/ERP system? What do you think would be the most significant challenges with this integration approach?
3. Using the information developed in the first two case exercises, do you think MVCH has arrived at the right decision? Defend your answer. Indicate what additional information you would like to have to help you with your analysis.
4. Outline some of the benefits of using thin clients in a hospital setting such as MVCH. Which thin client devices would be most beneficial? Would thin client hardware make it easier to comply with the privacy and security requirements of HIPAA? Why or why not? Would you recommend that MVCH pursue a thin client strategy?
5. The MVCH planning committee is considering several business functions to be accessed via the Web: (1) submitting insurance claims online, (2) providing clinical information to patients online, (3) implementing supply chain management online, (4) providing medical records to other facilities, and (5) implementing an online medical knowledge base. Which of these five possibilities do you recommend implementing first? Why? In your answer, address the following issues for each option being considered:
   a. Security and confidentiality concerns: Who would need to access the data? How would access be restricted? How likely is the proposed security system to be compromised?
   b. Data entry requirements: Which job functions would enter data? How much resistance is expected from each function, and how is this resistance to be handled?
   c. The benefits that MVCH could expect and the expected costs.
6. Use the MVCH files you have prototyped to complete this exercise.
   a. Provide the PATIENT data as an XML file.
   b. Use XQuery to provide a query related to the PATIENT table.
   c. Generate a report and, using the XML capabilities in Microsoft Access (e.g., ReportML and an XSLT file), transform the report so that it can be displayed inside a browser view to look like the report in the Print Preview of Access.

Project Assignments

P1. Assume that the MVCH hospital database you developed in SQL Server (or another DBMS designated by your instructor) will be made available to several desktop client applications at the hospital.
   a. What client and connectivity components are needed in order for the applications to access the database?
   b. What types of client applications can access the database? How do the different types of clients connect to the database server?
   c. Which APIs are supported for building Web-based applications?
   d. What client tools are available? Describe their function.
   e. Would you use more than one database server? For what purposes? How would you add another server?

P2. Assume that Dr. Z's MS management system uses the same RDBMS that you used for your MVCH database but is currently located on a different database server.
   a. How could you establish a link to that database?
   b. What would you need to do to place the database on the same server as the MVCH database you created? How would client applications access the MS management system database?

P3. Web-enable the MVCH database you developed earlier and develop one or more functionalities such as the following:
   - Online patient registration (e.g., for ambulatory surgery, for Dr. Z's MS Center, etc.)
   - Online volunteer application
   - Login for employees or physicians with a user name and password

P4. Using the MVCH database you created earlier, identify one or two tables and provide the data as XML files.

P5. Using the MVCH database you created earlier, identify one or two queries and return the data as an XML stream.

CHAPTER

9

Data Warehousing

Learning Objectives

After studying this chapter, you should be able to:

- Concisely define each of the following key terms: **data warehouse, operational system, informational system, data mart, independent data mart, dependent data mart, enterprise data warehouse (EDW), operational data store (ODS), logical data mart, real-time data warehouse, reconciled data, derived data, transient data, periodic data, star schema, grain, conformed dimension, snowflake schema, online analytical processing (OLAP), relational OLAP (ROLAP), multidimensional OLAP (MOLAP), data visualization, and data mining.**
- Give two important reasons why an "information gap" often exists between an information manager's need and the information generally available.
- List two major reasons most organizations today need data warehousing.
- Name and briefly describe the three levels in a data warehouse architecture.
- Describe the two major components of a star schema.
- Estimate the number of rows and total size, in bytes, of a fact table, given reasonable assumptions concerning the database dimensions.
- Design a data mart using various schemes to normalize and denormalize dimensions and to account for fact history, hierarchical relationships between dimensions, and changing dimension attribute values.
- Develop the requirements for a data mart from questions supporting decision making.

INTRODUCTION

PMPL is a pioneer in the perfume industry in India. The company which began in 1940s as a cottage industry has now grown into a company with an annual turnover of Rs. 300 crore. It has its headquartered in Hassan, Karnataka. The company has over 2,500 employees and has operations in seven countries and in almost all states of India. The company has different business units for manufacturing, packaging, and marketing and sales.

Its marketing and sales unit operate independently and is responsible for sales plan, budget, advertising, sales promotion, and invoicing. The business unit is supported by a state-of-art data warehouse running of MS-SQL Analysis Services. The data warehouse incorporates daily sales from the company depots to its wholesalers, and its inventory data, plus country-wise data and data from external sources regarding finance and market data. It provides decision support milieu to the sales managers who manage regional sales territories to re-align the territories, if needed. The market specialists need the data warehouse for analyzing market potential. The data warehouse is also used as an executive information system by the corporate managers to create reports of the company's quarterly results.

In light of this strong emphasis on information and the recent advances in information technology, you might expect most organizations to have highly developed systems for delivering information to managers and other users. Yet this is often not the case. In fact, despite having mountains of data (as in petabytes—1000 terabytes, or 1000^5 bytes), and often many databases, few organizations have more than a fraction of the information they need. Managers are often frustrated by their inability to access or use the data and information they need. This situation contributes to why some people claim that "business intelligence" is an oxymoron.

Modern organizations are said to be drowning in data but starving for information. Despite the mixed metaphor, this statement seems to portray quite accurately the situation in many organizations. What is the reason for this state of affairs? Let's examine two important (and related) reasons why an information gap has been created in most organizations.

The first reason for the information gap is the fragmented way in which organizations have developed information systems—and their supporting databases—for many years. The emphasis in this text is on a carefully planned, architectural approach to systems development that should produce a compatible set of databases. However, in reality, constraints on time and resources cause most organizations to resort to a "one-thing-at-a-time" approach to developing islands of information systems. This approach inevitably produces a hodgepodge of uncoordinated and often inconsistent databases. Usually databases are based on a variety of hardware, software platforms, and purchased applications and have resulted from different organizational mergers, acquisitions, and reorganizations. Under these circumstances, it is extremely difficult, if not impossible, for managers to locate and use accurate information, which must be synthesized across these various systems of record.

The second reason for the information gap is that most systems are developed to support operational processing, with little or no thought given to the information or analytical tools needed for decision making. *Operational processing*, also called transaction processing, captures, stores, and manipulates data to support daily operations of the organization. It tends to focus database design on optimizing access to a small set of data related to a transaction (e.g., a customer, order, and associated product data). *Informational processing* is the analysis of data or other forms of information to support decision making. It needs large "swatches" of data from which to derive information (e.g., sales of all products, over several years, from every sales region). Most systems that are developed internally or purchased from outside vendors are designed to support operational processing, with little thought given to informational processing.

Bridging the information gap are *data warehouses* that consolidate and integrate information from many internal and external sources and arrange it in a meaningful format for making accurate and timely business decisions. They support executives, managers, and business analysts in making complex business decisions through applications such as the analysis of trends, target marketing, competitive analysis, customer relationship management, and so on. Data warehousing has evolved to meet these needs without disturbing existing operational processing.

The proliferation of Web-based customer interactions has made the situation much more interesting and more real-time. The activities of customers and suppliers on an organization's Web site provide a wealth of new clickstream data to help understand behaviors and preferences and create a unique opportunity to communicate the right message (e.g., product cross-sales message). Extensive details, such as time, IP address, pages visited, context from where the page request was made, links taken, elapsed time on page, and so forth, can be captured unobtrusively. These data, along with customer transaction, payment, product return, inquiry, and other history consolidated into the data warehouse from a variety of transaction systems, can be used to personalize pages. Such reasoned and active interactions can lead to satisfied customers and business partners and more profitable business relationships. A similar proliferation of data for decision making is resulting from the growing use of RFID and GPS-generated data to track the movement of packages, inventory, or people.

This chapter provides an overview of data warehousing. This exceptionally broad topic normally requires an entire text, especially when the expansive topic of business intelligence is the focus. This is why most texts on the topic are devoted to just a single aspect, such as data warehouse design or administration, data quality and governance, or business intelligence. We focus on the two areas relevant to a text on database management: data architecture and database design for data warehousing. You will learn first how a data warehouse relates to databases in existing operational systems. Described next is the three-tier data architecture, which characterizes most data warehouse environments. Next, we show special database design elements frequently used in data warehousing. Finally, you will see how users interact with the data warehouse, including online analytical processing, data mining, and data visualization. This last topic provides the bridge from this text to the broader context in which data warehousing is most often applied—business intelligence.

Data warehousing requires extracting data from existing operational systems, cleansing and transforming data for decision making, and loading them into a data warehouse—what is often called the extract–transform–load (ETL) process. An inherent part of this process are activities to ensure data quality, which is of special concern when data are consolidated across disparate systems. Data warehousing is not the only method organizations use to integrate data to gain greater reach to data across the organization. Thus, we devote Chapter 10, the first chapter in the next section of this text, to issues of data quality, which apply to data warehousing as well as other forms of data integration, which are also introduced in Chapter 10.

BASIC CONCEPTS OF DATA WAREHOUSING

A **data warehouse** is a subject-oriented, integrated, time-variant, nonupdateable collection of data used in support of management decision-making processes and business intelligence (Inmon and Hackathorn, 1994). The meaning of each of the key terms in this definition follows:

Data warehouse
A subject-oriented, integrated, time-variant, nonupdateable collection of data used in support of management decision-making processes.

- ***Subject-oriented*** A data warehouse is organized around the key subjects (or high-level entities) of the enterprise. Major subjects may include customers, patients, students, products, and time.
- ***Integrated*** The data housed in the data warehouse are defined using consistent naming conventions, formats, encoding structures, and related characteristics gathered from several internal systems of record and also often from sources external to the organization. This means that the data warehouse holds the one version of "the truth."
- ***Time-variant*** Data in the data warehouse contain a time dimension so that they may be used to study trends and changes.
- ***Nonupdateable*** Data in the data warehouse are loaded and refreshed from operational systems, but cannot be updated by end users.

A data warehouse is not just a consolidation of all the operational databases in an organization. Because of its focus on business intelligence, external data, and time-variant data (not just current status), a data warehouse is a unique kind of database.

Data warehousing is the process whereby organizations create and maintain data warehouses and extract meaning and inform decision making from their informational assets through these data warehouses. Successful data warehousing requires following proven data warehousing practices, sound project management, strong organizational commitment, as well as making the right technology decisions.

A Brief History of Data Warehousing

Data warehousing emerged as a result of advances in the field of information systems over several decades. The following were some key advances:

- Improvements in database technology, particularly the development of the relational data model and relational database management systems (RDBMSs)
- Advances in computer hardware, particularly the emergence of affordable mass storage and parallel computer architectures
- The emergence of end-user computing, facilitated by powerful, intuitive computer interfaces and tools
- Advances in middleware products that enable enterprise database connectivity across heterogeneous platforms (Hackathorn, 1993)

The key discovery that triggered the development of data warehousing was the recognition (and subsequent definition) of the fundamental differences between operational (or transaction processing) systems (sometimes called *systems of record* because their role is to keep the official, legal record of the organization) and informational (or decision-support) systems. Devlin and Murphy (1988) published the first article describing the architecture of a data warehouse, based on this distinction. In 1992, Inmon published the first book describing data warehousing, and he has subsequently become one of the most prolific authors in this field.

The Need for Data Warehousing

Two major factors drive the need for data warehousing in most organizations today:

1. A business requires an integrated, company-wide view of high-quality information.
2. The information systems department must separate informational from operational systems to improve performance dramatically in managing company data.

NEED FOR A COMPANY-WIDE VIEW Data in operational systems are typically fragmented and inconsistent, so-called silos, or islands, of data. They are also generally distributed on a variety of incompatible hardware and software platforms. For example, one file containing customer data may be located on a UNIX-based server running an Oracle DBMS, whereas another may be located on an IBM mainframe running the DB2 DBMS. Yet, for decision-making purposes, it is often necessary to provide a single, corporate view of that information.

To understand the difficulty of deriving a single corporate view, look at the simple example shown in Figure 9-1. This figure shows three tables from three separate systems of record, each containing similar student data. The STUDENT DATA table is from the class registration system, the STUDENT EMPLOYEE table is from the personnel system, and the STUDENT HEALTH table is from a health center system. Each table contains some unique data concerning students, but even common data (e.g., student names) are stored using different formats.

FIGURE 9-1 Examples of heterogeneous data

STUDENT DATA

StudentNo	LastName	MI	FirstName	Telephone	Status	•••
123-45-6789	Enright	T	Mark	483-1967	Soph	
389-21-4062	Smith	R	Elaine	283-4195	Jr	

STUDENT EMPLOYEE

StudentID	Address	Dept	Hours	•••
123-45-6789	1218 Elk Drive, Phoenix, AZ 91304	Soc	8	
389-21-4062	134 Mesa Road, Tempe, AZ 90142	Math	10	

STUDENT HEALTH

StudentName	Telephone	Insurance	ID	•••
Mark T. Enright	483-1967	Blue Cross	123-45-6789	
Elaine R. Smith	555-7828	?	389-21-4062	

Suppose you want to develop a profile for each student, consolidating all data into a single file format. Some of the issues that you must resolve are as follows:

- ***Inconsistent key structures*** The primary key of the first two tables is some version of the student Social Security number, whereas the primary key of STUDENT HEALTH is StudentName.
- ***Synonyms*** In STUDENT DATA, the primary key is named StudentNo, whereas in STUDENT EMPLOYEE it is named StudentID. (We discussed how to deal with synonyms in Chapter 4.)
- ***Free-form fields versus structured fields*** In STUDENT HEALTH, StudentName is a single field. In STUDENT DATA, StudentName (a composite attribute) is broken into its component parts: LastName, MI, and FirstName.
- ***Inconsistent data values*** Elaine Smith has one telephone number in STUDENT DATA but a different number in STUDENT HEALTH. Is this an error, or does this person have two telephone numbers?
- ***Missing data*** The value for Insurance is missing (or null) for Elaine Smith in the STUDENT HEALTH table. How will this value be located?

This simple example illustrates the nature of the problem of developing a single corporate view but fails to capture the complexity of that task. A real-life scenario would likely have dozens (if not hundreds) of files and thousands (or millions!) of records.

Why do organizations need to bring data together from various systems of record? Ultimately, of course, the reason is to be more profitable, to be more competitive, or to grow by adding value for customers. This can be accomplished by increasing the speed and flexibility of decision making, improving business processes, or gaining a clearer understanding of customer behavior. For the previous student example, university administrators may want to investigate if the health or number of hours students work on campus is related to student academic performance, if taking certain courses is related to the health of students, or whether poor academic performers cost more to support, for example, due to increased health care as well as other costs. In general, certain trends in organizations encourage the need for data warehousing; these trends include the following:

- ***No single system of record*** Almost no organization has only one database. Seems odd, doesn't it? Remember our discussion in Chapter 1 about the reasons for using a database compared to using separate file-processing systems? Because of the heterogeneous needs for data in different operational settings, because of corporate mergers and acquisitions, and due to the sheer size of many organizations, multiple operational databases exist.
- ***Multiple systems are not synchronized*** It is difficult, if not impossible, to make separate databases consistent. Even if the metadata are controlled and made the same by one data administrator (see Chapter 11), the data values for the same attributes will not agree. This is because of different update cycles and separate places where the same data are captured for each system. Thus, to get one view of the organization, the data from the separate systems must be periodically consolidated and synchronized into one additional database. We will see that there can be actually two such consolidated databases—an operational data store and an enterprise data warehouse, both of which we include under the topic of data warehousing.
- ***Organizations want to analyze the activities in a balanced way*** Many organizations have implemented some form of a balanced scorecard—metrics that show organization results in financial, human, customer satisfaction, product quality, and other terms simultaneously. To ensure that this multidimensional view of the organization shows consistent results, a data warehouse is necessary. When questions arise in the balanced scorecard, analytical software working with the data warehouse can be used to "drill down," "slice and dice," visualize, and in other ways mine business intelligence.
- ***Customer relationship management*** Organizations in all sectors are realizing that there is value in having a total picture of their interactions with customers across all touch points. Different touch points (e.g., for a bank, these touch points include ATMs, online banking, tellers, electronic funds transfers, investment portfolio management, and loans) are supported by separate operational systems. Thus, without a data warehouse, a teller may not know to try to cross-sell a customer one of the bank's mutual funds if a large, atypical automatic deposit transaction appears on the teller's screen. Having a total picture of the activity with a given customer requires a consolidation of data from various operational systems.
- ***Supplier relationship management*** Managing the supply chain has become a critical element in reducing costs and raising product quality for many organizations. Organizations want to create strategic supplier partnerships based on a total picture of their activities with suppliers, from billing, to meeting delivery dates, to quality control, to pricing, to support. Data about these different activities can be locked inside separate operational systems (e.g., accounts payable, shipping and receiving, production scheduling, and maintenance). ERP systems have improved this situation by bringing many of these data into one database. However, ERP systems tend to be designed to optimize operational, not informational or analytical, processing, which we discuss next.

Operational system
A system that is used to run a business in real-time, based on current data. Also called a system of record.

NEED TO SEPARATE OPERATIONAL AND INFORMATIONAL SYSTEMS An **operational system** is a system that is used to run a business in real-time, based on current data. Examples of operational systems are sales order processing, reservation systems, and patient registration systems. Operational systems must process large volumes of relatively simple

TABLE 9-1 Comparison of Operational and Informational Systems

Characteristic	Operational Systems	Informational Systems
Primary purpose	Run the business on a current basis	Support managerial decision making
Type of data	Current representation of state of the business	Historical point-in-time (snapshots) and predictions
Primary users	Clerks, salespersons, administrators	Managers, business analysts, customers
Scope of usage	Narrow, planned, and simple updates and queries	Broad, ad hoc, complex queries and analysis
Design goal	Performance: throughput, availability	Ease of flexible access and use
Volume	Many constant updates and queries on one or a few table rows	Periodic batch updates and queries requiring many or all rows

read/write transactions and provide fast response. Operational systems are also called *systems of record*.

Informational system
A system designed to support decision making based on historical point-in-time and prediction data for complex queries or data-mining applications.

Informational systems are designed to support decision making based on historical point-in-time and prediction data. They are also designed for complex queries or data-mining applications. Examples of informational systems are systems for sales trend analysis, customer segmentation, and human resources planning.

The key differences between operational and informational systems are shown in Table 9-1. These two types of processing have very different characteristics in nearly every category of comparison. In particular, notice that they have quite different communities of users. Operational systems are used by clerks, administrators, salespersons, and others who must process business transactions. Informational systems are used by managers, executives, business analysts, and (increasingly) by customers who are searching for status information or who are decision makers.

The need to separate operational and informational systems is based on three primary factors:

1. A data warehouse centralizes data that are scattered throughout disparate operational systems and makes them readily available for decision support applications.
2. A properly designed data warehouse adds value to data by improving their quality and consistency.
3. A separate data warehouse eliminates much of the contention for resources that results when informational applications are confounded with operational processing.

Data Warehousing Success

"If you build it, they will come" might work in a classic baseball movie. Data warehousing success, however, is not guaranteed. Data warehousing projects fail about 40 percent of the time (Whiting, 2003). Data warehousing is complex and requires cooperation across an organization. For example, when errors are discovered in data being loaded into the warehouse, the right place to fix the errors is in the source systems so erroneous data are not loaded again later. But the errors may be acceptable in the source system or not even considered errors by the business unit for the source system.

Several professional organizations sponsor annual award programs to highlight the best data warehousing practices. One of the most prestigious is the Data Warehousing Institute Awards. The winners for 2003 and 2006 illustrate many of the reasons success is becoming more common (TDWI, 2006; Whiting, 2003). The following is a summary of some of these award winners:

- ***Continental Airlines—Best Enterprise Data Warehouse*** The Continental data warehouse has a real-time architecture and automated data transformations. This *simplifies consolidating data from different source systems*. A cross-business-unit steering committee develops *standard data definitions (metadata)*. Uses of and changes to the warehouse must be *justified by revenue and profitability projections*.

- ***Bank of America—Data Warehouse Integration*** Separate well-established data warehouses had to be integrated when NationsBank and Bank of America merged in 1998. Links between the existing data warehouses created significant *performance issues* and encouraged departments to create separate work-arounds, with *independent systems (called data marts)* negating the value of the data warehouse. Top leadership designated the *data warehouse consolidation as high priority, appropriate resources were allocated, and extensive user requirements planning was completed*.
- ***Royal Bank of Canada—Enterprise Data Warehousing*** The enterprise data warehouse architecture was designed from the outset to enable *scalability, reliability, flexibility, and adaptability over the long term*. In particular, the enterprise information management team took a disciplined approach to data structure definition, providing an *integrated data and metadata* that enables efficient management and fast, cost-effective reuse of data. The EDW currently executes more than a million queries and up to 25,000 extract-transform-load batch processes every month. It houses more than 30 terabytes of business data, and supports more than 33,000 users.
- ***Toyota Motor Sales USA—Metadata Management*** A metadata repository improves the performance of Toyota's data warehouse by helping IT workers and business users *access the meaning of warehouse data* and hence the meaning of information in reports generated from the warehouse. It also makes it easier to *identify the impact of changes to data specifications*.
- ***Iowa Department of Revenue—Government or Nonprofit Organization*** The department managers felt that there were many companies and individuals who did not file tax returns or who underreported earnings. The data to uncover such problems were buried in many different mainframe applications, file extracts, and 20 disparate systems. The data warehouse was *funded from business improvements* from the additional $10 million per year in tax revenue that it now generates.

Based on these award winners, success is more likely when there is high-level support, adequate resources are committed, real business value is apparent, well-managed metadata exist, the organization has an enterprise vision, and changes are anticipated and well managed. Technology is important, and high-performance technologies enable successful data warehousing. But the organization-related factors outlined here are more important than technical factors. As one data warehousing executive from a consumer products company told the authors, "The technology is easy; it's the organizational issues that are tough." Thus, the tone of the rest of the chapter is to make sound database management decisions for the data warehouse within an organizational context.

DATA WAREHOUSE ARCHITECTURES

The architecture for data warehouses has evolved, and organizations have considerable latitude in creating variations. We will review here two core structures that form the basis for most implementations. The first is a three-level architecture that characterizes a bottom-up, incremental approach to evolving the data warehouse; the second is also a three-level data architecture that appears usually from a more top-down approach that emphasizes more coordination and an enterprise-wide perspective. Even with their differences, there are many common characteristics to these approaches.

Independent Data Mart Data Warehousing Environment

The independent data mart architecture for a data warehouse is shown in Figure 9-2. Building this architecture requires four basic steps (moving left to right in Figure 9-2):

1. Data are extracted from the various internal and external source system files and databases. In a large organization, there may be dozens or even hundreds of such files and databases.
2. The data from the various source systems are transformed and integrated before being loaded into the data marts. Transactions may be sent to the source systems

FIGURE 9-2 Independent data mart data warehousing architecture

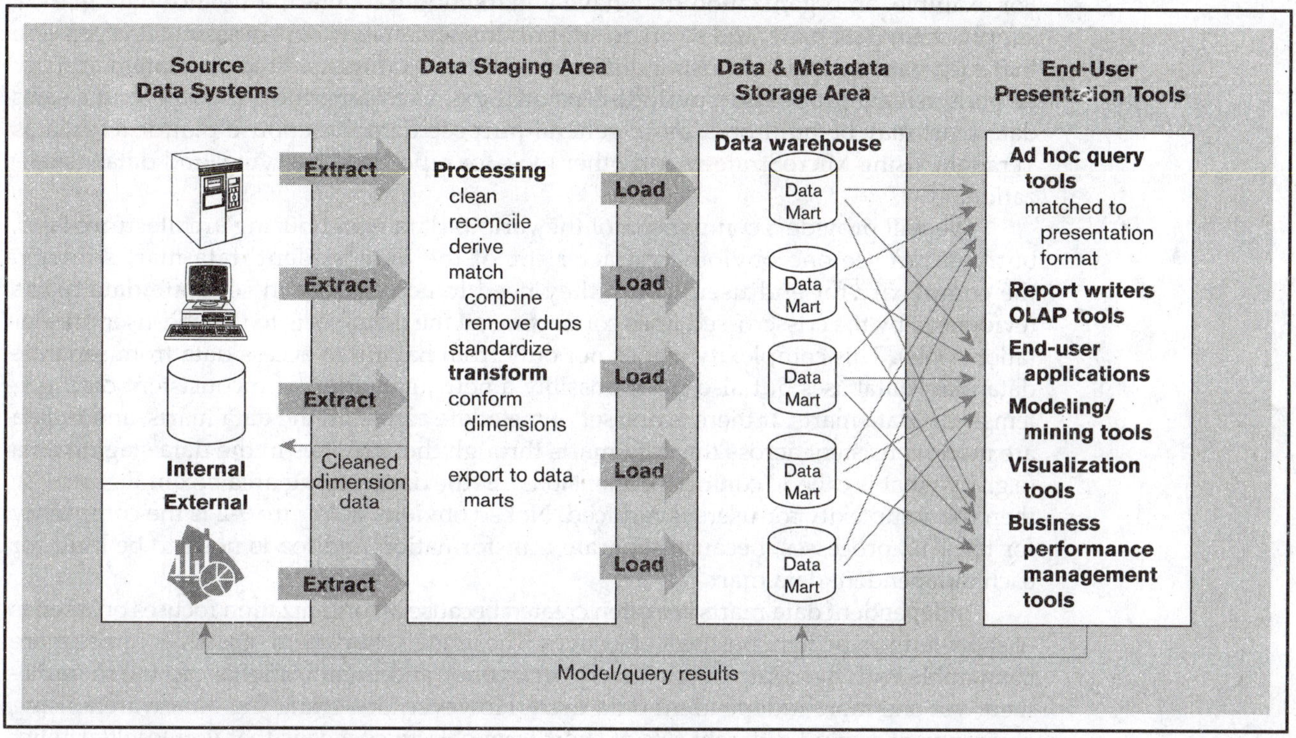

to correct errors discovered in data staging. The data warehouse is considered to be the collection of data marts.

3. The data warehouse is a set of physically distinct databases organized for decision support. It contains both detailed and summary data.
4. Users access the data warehouse by means of a variety of query languages and analytical tools. Results (e.g., predictions, forecasts) may be fed back to data warehouse and operational databases.

We will discuss the important processes of extracting, transforming, and loading (ETL) data from the source systems into the data warehouse in more detail in Chapter 10. We will also overview in a subsequent section various end-user presentation tools.

Extraction and loading happen periodically—sometimes daily, weekly, or monthly. Thus, the data warehouse often does not have, nor does it need to have, current data. Remember, the data warehouse is not (directly) supporting operational transaction processing, although it may contain transactional data (but more often summaries of transactions and snapshots of status variables, such as account balances and inventory levels). For most data warehousing applications, users are not looking for a reaction to an individual transaction but rather for trends and patterns in the state of the organization across a large subset of the data warehouse. At a minimum, five fiscal quarters of data are kept in a data warehouse so that at least annual trends and patterns can be discerned. Older data may be purged or archived. We will see later that one advanced data warehousing architecture, real-time data warehousing, is based on a different assumption about the need for current data.

Contrary to many of the principles discussed so far in this chapter, the independent data marts approach does not create one data warehouse. Instead, this approach creates many separate data marts, each based on data warehousing, not transaction processing database technologies. A **data mart** is a data warehouse that is limited in scope, customized for the decision-making applications of a particular end-user group. Its contents are obtained either from independent ETL processes, as shown in Figure 9-2 for an **independent data mart**, or are derived from the data warehouse, which we will discuss in the next two sections. A data mart is designed to optimize the performance for

Data mart
A data warehouse that is limited in scope, whose data are obtained by selecting and summarizing data from a data warehouse or from separate extract, transform, and load processes from source data systems.

Independent data mart
A data mart filled with data extracted from the operational environment, without the benefit of a data warehouse.

well-defined and predicable uses, sometimes as few as a single or a couple of queries. For example, an organization may have a marketing data mart, a finance data mart, a supply chain data mart, and so on, to support known analytical processing. It is possible that each data mart is built using different tools; for example, a financial data mart may be built using a proprietary multidimensional tool like Hyperion's Essbase, and a sales data mart may be built on a more general-purpose data warehouse platform, such as Teradata, using MicroStrategy and other tools for reporting, querying, and data visualization.

We will provide a comparison of the various data warehousing architectures later, but you can see one obvious characteristic of the independent data mart strategy: the complexity for end users when they need to access data in separate data marts (evidenced by the crisscrossed lines connecting all the data marts to the end-user presentation tools). This complexity comes not only from having to access data from separate data mart databases but also from possibly a new generation of inconsistent data systems—the data marts. If there is one set of metadata across all the data marts, and if data are made consistent across the data marts through the activities in the data staging area (e.g., by what is called "conform dimensions" in the data staging area box in Figure 9-2), then the complexity for users is reduced. Not so obvious in Figure 9-2 is the complexity for the ETL processes, because separate transformation and loads need to be built for each independent data mart.

Independent data marts are often created because an organization focuses on a series of short-term, expedient business objectives. The limited short-term objectives can be more compatible with the comparably lower cost (money and organizational capital) to implement yet one more independent data mart. However, designing the data warehousing environment around different sets of short-term objectives means that you lose flexibility for the long term and the ability to react to changing business conditions. And being able to react to change is critical for decision support. It can be organizationally and politically easier to have separate, small data warehouses than to get all organizational parties to agree to one view of the organization in a central data warehouse. Also, some data warehousing technologies have technical limitations for the size of the data warehouse they can support—what we will call later a scalability issue. Thus, technology, rather than the business, may dictate a data warehousing architecture if you first lock yourself into a particular data warehousing set of technologies before you understand your data warehousing requirements. We discuss the pros and cons of the independent data mart architecture compared with its prime competing architecture in the next section.

Dependent Data Mart and Operational Data Store Architecture: A Three-Level Approach

The independent data mart architecture in Figure 9-2 has several important limitations (Marco, 2003; Meyer, 1997):

1. A separate ETL process is developed for each data mart, which can yield costly redundant data and processing efforts.
2. Data marts may not be consistent with one another because they are often developed with different technologies, and thus they may not provide a clear enterprise-wide view of data concerning important subjects such as customers, suppliers, and products.
3. There is no capability to drill down into greater detail or into related facts in other data marts or a shared data repository, so analysis is limited, or at best very difficult (e.g., doing joins across separate platforms for different data marts). Essentially, relating data across data marts is a task performed by users outside the data warehouse.
4. Scaling costs are excessive because every new application that creates a separate data mart repeats all the extract and load steps. Usually, operational systems have limited time windows for batch data extracting, so at some point, the load on the operations systems may mean that new technology is needed, with additional costs.
5. If there is an attempt to make the separate data marts consistent, the cost to do so is quite high.

The value of independent data marts has been hotly debated. Kimball (1997) strongly supports the development of independent data marts as a viable strategy for a phased development of decision support systems. Armstrong (1997), Inmon (1997, 2000), and Marco (2003) point out the five fallacies previously mentioned and many more. There are two debates as to the actual value of independent data marts:

1. One debate deals with the nature of the phased approach to implementing a data warehousing environment. The essence of this debate is whether each data mart should or should not evolve in a bottom-up fashion from a subset of enterprise-wide decision support data.
2. The other debate deals with the suitable database architecture for analytical processing. This debate centers on the extent to which a data mart database should be normalized.

The essences of these two debates are addressed throughout this chapter. We provide an exercise at the end of the chapter for you to explore these debates in more depth.

One of the most popular approaches to addressing the independent data mart limitations raised earlier is to use a three-level approach represented by the dependent data mart and operational data store architecture (see Figure 9-3). Here the new level is the operational data store, and the data and metadata storage level is reconfigured. The first and second limitations are addressed by loading the **dependent data marts** from an **enterprise data warehouse (EDW)**, which is a central, integrated data warehouse that is the control point and single "version of the truth" made available to end users for decision support applications. Dependent data marts still have a purpose to provide a simplified and high-performance environment that is tuned to the decision-making needs of user groups. A data mart may be a separate physical database (and different data marts may be on different platforms) or can be a logical (user view) data mart instantiated on the fly when accessed. We explain logical data marts in the next section.

Dependent data mart
A data mart filled exclusively from an enterprise data warehouse and its reconciled data.

Enterprise data warehouse (EDW)
A centralized, integrated data warehouse that is the control point and single source of all data made available to end users for decision support applications.

A user group can access its data mart, and then when other data are needed, users can access the EDW. Redundancy across dependent data marts is planned, and redundant data are consistent because each data mart is loaded in a synchronized way from one common source of data (or is a view of the data warehouse). Integration of data is

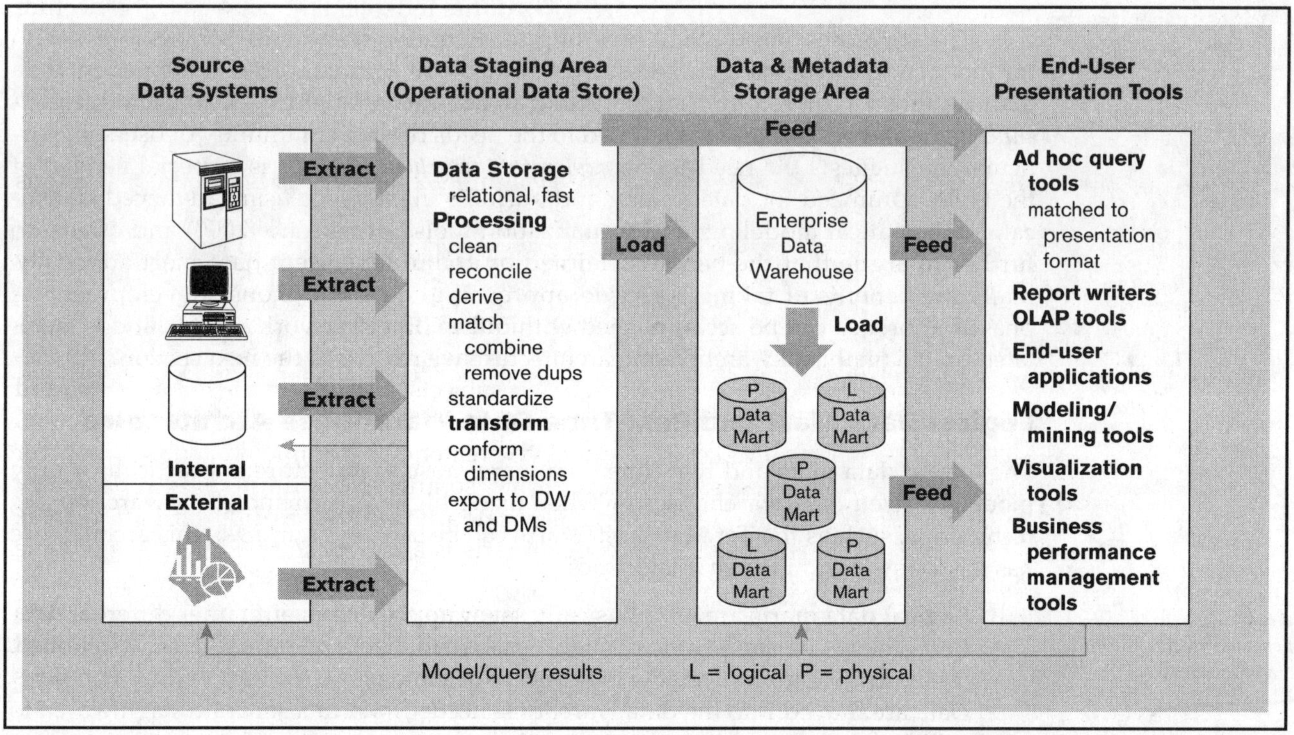

FIGURE 9-3 Dependent data mart and operational data store: A three-level architecture

the responsibility of the IT staff managing the enterprise data warehouse; it is not the end users' responsibility to integrate data across independent data marts for each query or application. The dependent data mart and operational data store architecture is often called a "hub and spoke" approach, in which the EDW is the hub and the source data systems and the data marts are at the ends of input and output spokes.

Operational data store (ODS)
An integrated, subject-oriented, continuously updateable, current-valued (with recent history), enterprise-wide, detailed database designed to serve operational users as they do decision support processing.

The third limitation is addressed by providing an integrated source for all the operational data in an operational data store. An **operational data store (ODS)** is an integrated, subject-oriented, continuously updateable, current-valued (with recent history), organization-wide, detailed database designed to serve operational users as they do decision support processing (Imhoff, 1998; Inmon, 1998). An ODS is typically a relational database and normalized like databases in the systems of record, but it is tuned for decision-making applications. For example, indexes and other relational database design elements are tuned for queries that retrieve broad groups of data, rather than for transaction processing or querying individual and directly related records (e.g., a customer order). Because it has volatile, current, and only recent history data, the same query against an ODS very likely will yield different results at different times. An ODS typically does not contain "deep" history, whereas an EDW holds typically a multiyear history of snapshots of the state of the organization. An ODS may be fed from the database of an ERP application, but because most organizations do not have only one ERP database and do not run all operations against one ERP, an ODS is usually different from an ERP database. The ODS also serves as the staging area for loading data into the EDW. The ODS may receive data immediately or with some delay from the systems of record, whichever is practical and acceptable for the decision-making requirements that it supports.

The dependent data mart and operational data store architecture is also called a *corporate information factory (CIF)* (see Imhoff, 1999). It is considered to be a comprehensive view of organizational data in support of all user data requirements.

Different leaders in the field endorse different approaches to data warehousing. Those that endorse the independent data mart approach argue that this approach has two significant benefits:

1. It allows for the concept of a data warehouse to be demonstrated by working on a series of small projects.
2. The length of time until there is some benefit from data warehousing is reduced because the organization is not delayed until all data are centralized.

The advocates of the CIF (Armstrong, 2000; Inmon, 1999) raise serious issues with the independent approach; these issues include the five limitations of independent data marts outlined earlier. Inmon suggests that an advantage of physically separate *dependent* data marts is that they can be tuned to the needs of each community of users. In particular, he suggests the need for an *exploration warehouse*, which is a special version of the EDW optimized for data mining and business intelligence using advanced statistical, mathematical modeling, and visualization tools. Armstrong (2000) and others go further to argue that the benefits claimed by the independent data mart advocates really are benefits of taking a phased approach to data warehouse development. A phased approach can be accomplished within the CIF framework as well, and is facilitated by the final data warehousing architecture we review in the next section.

Logical Data Mart and Real-Time Data Warehouse Architecture

The logical data mart and real-time data warehouse architecture is practical for only moderate-sized data warehouses or when using high-performance data warehousing technology, such as the Teradata system. As can be seen in Figure 9-4, this architecture has the following unique characteristics:

Logical data mart
A data mart created by a relational view of a data warehouse.

1. **Logical data marts** are not physically separate databases but rather different relational views of one physical, slightly denormalized relational data warehouse. (Refer to Chapter 6 to review the concept of views.)
2. Data are moved into the data warehouse rather than to a separate staging area to utilize the high-performance computing power of the warehouse technology to perform the cleansing and transformation steps.

FIGURE 9-4 Logical data mart and real-time data warehouse architecture

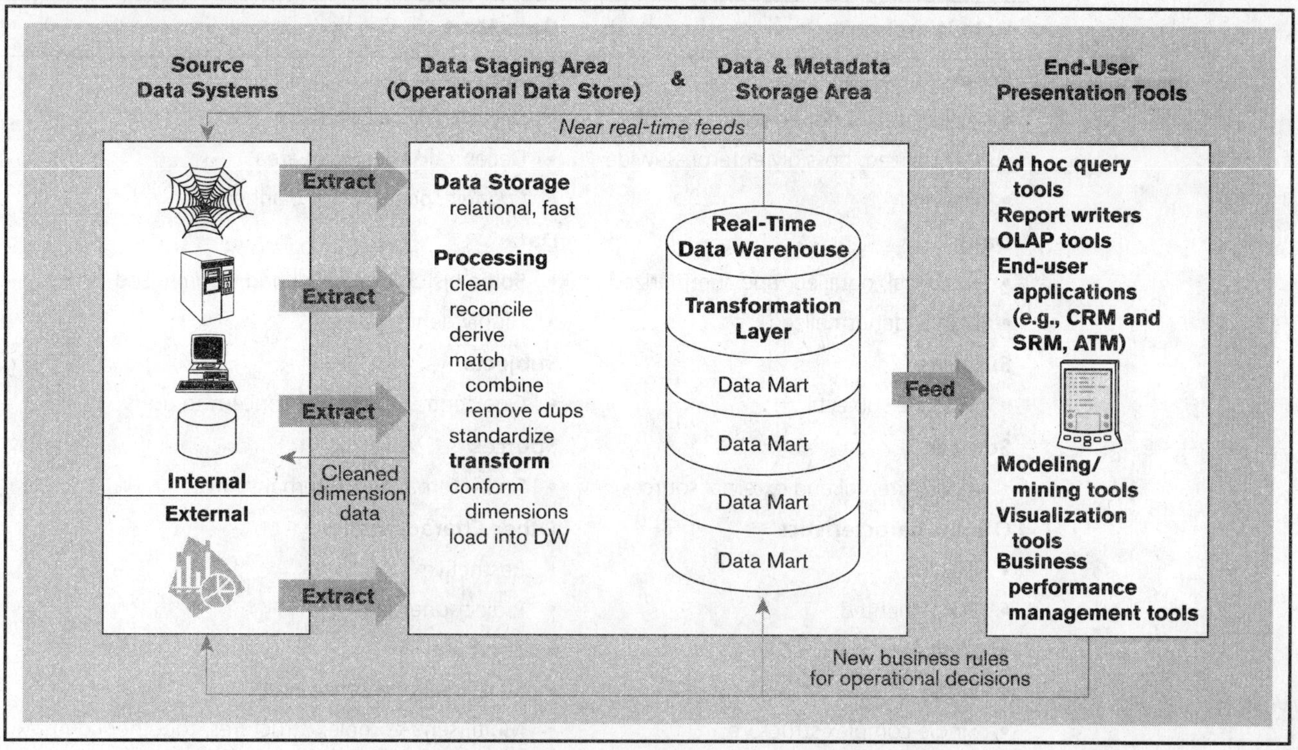

3. New data marts can be created quickly because no physical database or database technology needs to be created or acquired and no loading routines need to be written.
4. Data marts are always up to date because data in a view are created when the view is referenced; views can be materialized if a user has a series of queries and analysis that need to work off the same instantiation of the data mart.

Whether logical or physical, data marts and data warehouses play different roles in a data warehousing environment; these different roles are summarized in Table 9-2. Although limited in scope, a data mart may not be small. Thus, scalable technology is often critical. A significant burden and cost is placed on users when they themselves need to integrate the data across separate physical data marts (if this is even possible). As data marts are added, a data warehouse can be built in phases; the easiest way for this to happen is to follow the logical data mart and real-time data warehouse architecture.

The **real-time data warehouse** aspect of the architecture in Figure 9-4 means that the source data systems, decision support services, and the data warehouse *exchange* data and business rules at a *near*-real-time pace because there is a need for rapid response (i.e., action) to a current, comprehensive picture of the organization. The purpose of real-time data warehousing is to know what is happening, when it is happening, and to make desirable things happen through the operational systems. For example, a help desk professional answering questions and logging problem tickets will have a total picture of the customer's most recent sales contacts, billing and payment transactions, maintenance activities, and orders. With this information, the system supporting the help desk can, based on operational decision rules created from a continuous analysis of up-to-date warehouse data, automatically generate a script for the professional to sell what the analysis has shown to be a likely and profitable maintenance contract, an upgraded product, or another product bought by customers with a similar profile. A critical event, such as entry of a new product order, can be considered immediately so that the organization knows at least as much about the relationship with its customer as does the customer.

Real-time data warehouse
An enterprise data warehouse that accepts near-real-time feeds of transactional data from the systems of record, analyzes warehouse data, and in near-real-time relays business rules to the data warehouse and systems of record so that immediate action can be taken in response to business events.

TABLE 9-2 Data Warehouse Versus Data Mart

Data Warehouse	Data Mart
Scope	**Scope**
• Application independent	• Specific DSS application
• Centralized, possibly enterprise-wide	• Decentralized by user area
• Planned	• Organic, possibly not planned
Data	**Data**
• Historical, detailed, and summarized	• Some history, detailed, and summarized
• Lightly denormalized	• Highly denormalized
Subjects	**Subjects**
• Multiple subjects	• One central subject of concern to users
Sources	**Sources**
• Many internal and external sources	• Few internal and external sources
Other Characteristics	**Other Characteristics**
• Flexible	• Restrictive
• Data oriented	• Project oriented
• Long life	• Short life
• Large	• Start small, becomes large
• Single complex structure	• Multi, semi-complex structures, together complex

Source: Based on Strange (1997).

Another example of real-time data warehousing (with real-time analytics) would be an express mail and package delivery service using frequent scanning of parcels to know exactly where a package is in their transportation system. Real-time analytics, based on this package data, as well as pricing, customer service level agreements, and logistics opportunities, could automatically reroute packages to meet delivery promises for their best customers. RFID technologies are allowing these kinds of opportunities for real-time data warehousing (with massive amounts of data) coupled with real-time analytics to be used to greatly reduce the latency between event data capture and appropriate actions being taken.

The orientation is that each event with, say, a customer, is a potential opportunity for a customized, personalized, and optimized communication based on a strategic decision of how to respond to a customer with a particular profile. Thus, decision making and the data warehouse are actively involved in guiding operational processing, which is why some people call this active data warehousing. The goal is to shorten the cycle to do the following:

- Capture customer data at the time of a business event (what did happen)
- Analyze customer behavior (why did something happen) and predict customer responses to possible actions (what will happen)
- Develop rules for optimizing customer interactions, including the appropriate response and channel that will yield the best results
- Take immediate *action* with customers at touch points based on best responses to customers as determined by decision rules in order to make desirable results happen

The idea is that the potential value of taking the right action decays the longer the delay from event to action. The real-time data warehouse is where all the intelligence comes together to reduce this delay. Thus, real-time data warehousing moves data warehousing from the back office to the front office. For a thorough status report on real-time data warehousing, see Hackathorn (2002). Other authors refer to real-time data warehousing as action-oriented or active (@ctive) data warehousing.

The following are some beneficial applications for real-time data warehousing:

- Just-in-time transportation for rerouting deliveries based on up-to-date inventory levels
- E-commerce where, for instance, an abandoned shopping cart can trigger an e-mail promotional message before the user signs off
- Salespeople who monitor key performance indicators for important accounts in real-time
- Fraud detection in credit card transactions, where an unusual pattern of transactions could alert a sales clerk or online shopping cart routine to take extra precautions

Such applications are often characterized by online user access 24/7. For any of the data warehousing architectures, users may be employees, customers, or business partners.

With high-performance computers and data warehousing technologies, there may not be a need for a separate ODS from the enterprise data warehouse. When the ODS and EDW are one and the same, it is much easier for users to drill down and drill up when working through a series of ad hoc questions in which one question leads to another. It is also a simpler architecture, because one layer of the dependent data mart and operational data store architecture has been eliminated.

Three-Layer Data Architecture

Figure 9-5 shows a three-layer data architecture for a data warehouse. This architecture is characterized by the following:

1. Operational data are stored in the various operational systems of record throughout the organization (and sometimes in external systems).
2. Reconciled data are the type of data stored in the enterprise data warehouse and an operational data store. **Reconciled data** are detailed, current data intended to be the single, authoritative source for all decision support applications.
3. Derived data are the type of data stored in each of the data marts. **Derived data** are data that have been selected, formatted, and aggregated for end-user decision support applications.

Reconciled data
Detailed, current data intended to be the single, authoritative source for all decision support applications.

Derived data
Data that have been selected, formatted, and aggregated for end-user decision support applications.

We discuss reconciled data in the next chapter because the processes for reconciling data across source systems is a part of a topic larger than simply data warehousing: data quality and integration. Pertinent to data warehousing is derived data, which we cover

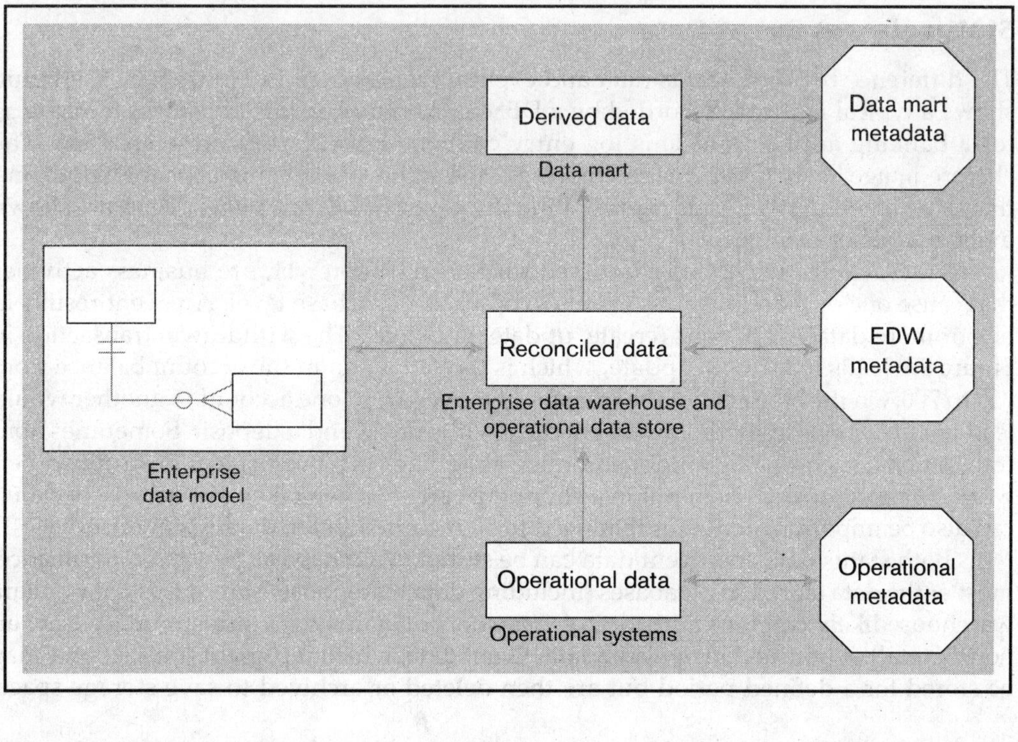

FIGURE 9-5 Three-layer data architecture for a data warehouse

in a subsequent section of the current chapter. Two components shown in Figure 9-5 play critical roles in the data architecture: the enterprise data model and metadata.

ROLE OF THE ENTERPRISE DATA MODEL In Figure 9-5, we show the reconciled data layer linked to the enterprise data model. Recall from Chapter 1 that the enterprise data model presents a total picture explaining the data required by an organization. If the reconciled data layer is to be the single, authoritative source for all data required for decision support, it must conform to the design specified in the enterprise data model. Thus, the enterprise data model controls the phased evolution of the data warehouse. Usually the enterprise data model evolves as new problems and decision applications are addressed. It takes too long to develop the enterprise data model in one step, and the dynamic needs for decision making will change before the warehouse is built.

ROLE OF METADATA Figure 9-5 also shows a layer of metadata linked to each of the three data layers. Recall from Chapter 1 that metadata are technical and business data that describe the properties or characteristics of other data. Following is a brief description of the three types of metadata shown in Figure 9-5.

1. *Operational metadata* describe the data in the various operational systems (as well as external data) that feed the enterprise data warehouse. Operational metadata typically exist in a number of different formats and unfortunately are often of poor quality.
2. *Enterprise data warehouse (EDW) metadata* are derived from (or at least consistent with) the enterprise data model. EDW metadata describe the reconciled data layer as well as the rules for extracting, transforming, and loading operational data into reconciled data.
3. *Data mart metadata* describe the derived data layer and the rules for transforming reconciled data to derived data.

For a thorough review of data warehouse metadata, see Marco (2000).

SOME CHARACTERISTICS OF DATA WAREHOUSE DATA

To understand and model the data in each of the three layers of the data architecture for a data warehouse, you need to learn some basic characteristics of data as they are stored in data warehouse databases.

Status Versus Event Data

The difference between status data and event data is shown in Figure 9-6. The figure shows a typical log entry recorded by a DBMS when processing a business transaction for a banking application. This log entry contains both status and event data: The "before image" and "after image" represent the status of the bank account before and then after a withdrawal. Data representing the withdrawal (or update event) are shown in the middle of the figure.

Transactions, which are discussed further in Chapter 11, are business activities that cause one or more business events to occur at a database level. An event results in one or more database actions (create, update, or delete). The withdrawal transaction in Figure 9-6 leads to a single update, which is the reduction in the account balance from 750 to 700. On the other hand, the transfer of money from one account to another would lead to two actions: two updates to handle a withdrawal and a deposit. Sometimes nontransactions, such as an abandoned online shopping cart, busy signal or dropped network connection, or an item put in a shopping cart and then taken out before checkout, can also be important activities that need to be recorded in the data warehouse.

Both status data and event data can be stored in a database. However, in practice, most of the data stored in databases (including data warehouses) are status data. A data warehouse likely contains a history of snapshots of status data or a summary (say, an hourly total) of transaction or event data. Event data, which represent transactions, may be stored for a defined period but are then deleted or archived to save storage space.

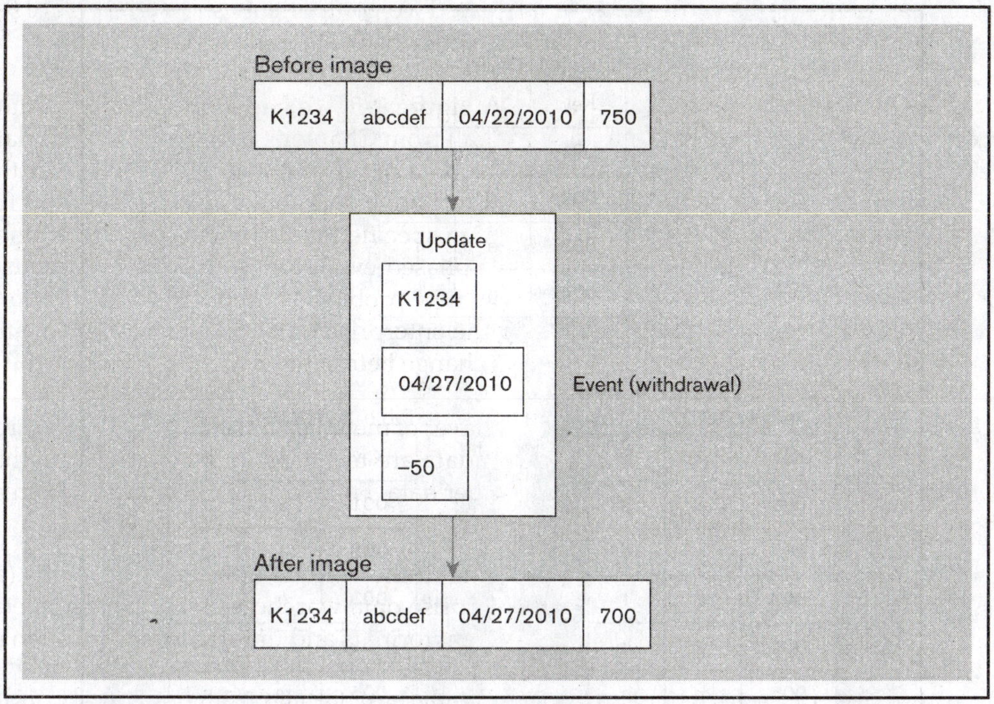

FIGURE 9-6 Example of a DBMS log entry

Both status and event data are typically stored in database logs (as represented in Figure 9-6) for backup and recovery purposes. As will be explained later, the database log plays an important role in filling the data warehouse.

Transient Versus Periodic Data

In data warehouses, it is typical to maintain a record of when events occurred in the past. This is necessary, for example, to compare sales or inventory levels on a particular date or during a particular period with the previous year's sales on the same date or during the same period.

Most operational systems are based on the use of transient data. **Transient data** are data in which changes to existing records are written over previous records, thus destroying the previous data content. Records are deleted without preserving the previous contents of those records.

Transient data
Data in which changes to existing records are written over previous records, thus destroying the previous data content.

You can easily visualize transient data by again referring to Figure 9-6. If the after image is written over the before image, the before image (containing the previous balance) is lost. However, because this is a database log, both images are normally preserved.

Periodic data are data that are never physically altered or deleted once added to the store. The before and after images in Figure 9-6 represent periodic data. Notice that each record contains a time stamp that indicates the date (and time, if needed) when the most recent update event occurred. (We introduced the use of time stamps in Chapter 2.)

Periodic data
Data that are never physically altered or deleted once they have been added to the store.

An Example of Transient and Periodic Data

A more detailed example comparing transient and periodic data is shown in Figures 9-7 and 9-8.

TRANSIENT DATA Figure 9-7 shows a relation (Table X) that initially contains four rows. The table has three attributes: a primary key and two nonkey attributes, A and B. The values for each of these attributes on the date 10/09 are shown in the figure. For example, for record 001, the value of attribute A on this date is a.

On date 10/10, three changes are made to the table (changes to rows are indicated by arrows to the left of the table). Row 002 is updated, so the value of A is changed from c to r. Row 004 is also updated, so the value of A is changed from g to y. Finally, a new row (with key 005) is inserted into the table.

FIGURE 9-7 Transient operational data

Table X (10/09)

Key	A	B
001	a	b
002	c	d
003	e	f
004	g	h

Table X (10/10)

Key	A	B
001	a	b
002	r	d
003	e	f
004	y	h
005	m	n

Table X (10/11)

Key	A	B
001	a	b
002	r	d
003	e	t
005	m	n

Table X (10/09)

Key	Date	A	B	Action
001	10/09	a	b	C
002	10/09	c	d	C
003	10/09	e	f	C
004	10/09	g	h	C

Table X (10/10)

Key	Date	A	B	Action
001	10/09	a	b	C
002	10/09	c	d	C
002	10/10	r	d	U
003	10/09	e	f	C
004	10/09	g	h	C
004	10/10	y	h	U
005	10/10	m	n	C

Table X (10/11)

Key	Date	A	B	Action
001	10/09	a	b	C
002	10/09	c	d	C
002	10/10	r	d	U
003	10/09	e	f	C
003	10/11	e	t	U
004	10/09	g	h	C
004	10/10	y	h	U
004	10/11	y	h	D
005	10/10	m	n	C

FIGURE 9-8 Periodic warehouse data

Notice that when rows 002 and 004 are updated, the new rows replace the previous rows. Therefore, the previous values are lost; there is no historical record of these values. This is characteristic of transient data.

More changes are made to the rows on date 10/11 (to simplify the discussion, we assume that only one change can be made to a given row on a given date). Row 003 is updated, and row 004 is deleted. Notice that there is no record to indicate that row 004 was ever stored in the database. The way the data are processed in Figure 9-7 is characteristic of the transient data typical in operational systems.

PERIODIC DATA One typical objective for a data warehouse is to maintain a historical record of key events or to create a time series for particular variables such as sales. This often requires storing periodic data, rather than transient data. Figure 9-8 shows the table used in Figure 9-7, now modified to represent periodic data. The following changes have been made in Figure 9-8:

1. Two new columns have been added to Table X:
   a. The column named Date is a time stamp that records the most recent date when a row has been modified.
   b. The column named Action is used to record the type of change that occurred. Possible values for this attribute are C (Create), U (Update), and D (Delete).
2. Once a record has been stored in the table, that record is never changed. When an update operation occurs on a record, both the before image and the after image are stored in the table. Although a record may be *logically* deleted, a historical version of the deleted record is maintained in the database for as much history (at least five quarters) as needed to analyze trends.

Now let's examine the same set of actions that occurred in Figure 9-7. Assume that all four rows were created on the date 10/09, as shown in the first table.

In the second table (for 10/10), rows 002 and 004 have been updated. The table now contains both the old version (for 10/09) and the new version (for 10/10) for these rows. The table also contains the new row (005) that was created on 10/10.

The third table (for 10/11) shows the update to row 003, with both the old and new versions. Also, row 004 is deleted from this table. This table now contains three versions of row 004: the original version (from 10/09), the updated version (from 10/1010), and the deleted version (from 10/11). The D in the last row for record 004 indicates that this row has been logically deleted, so that it is no longer available to users or their applications.

If you examine Figure 9-8, you can see why data warehouses tend to grow very rapidly. Storing periodic data can impose large storage requirements. Therefore, users must choose very carefully the key data that require this form of processing.

OTHER DATA WAREHOUSE CHANGES Besides the periodic changes to data values outlined previously, six other kinds of changes to a warehouse data model must be accommodated by data warehousing:

1. ***New descriptive attributes*** For example, new characteristics of products or customers that are important to store in the warehouse must be accommodated. Later in the chapter we call these attributes of dimension tables. This change is fairly easily accommodated by adding columns to tables and allowing null values for existing rows (if historical data exist in source systems, null values do not have to be stored).
2. ***New business activity attributes*** For example, new characteristics of an event already stored in the warehouse, such as a column C for the table in Figure 9-8, must be accommodated. This can be handled as in item 1, but is more difficult when the new facts are more refined, such as a data associated with days of the week, not just month and year, as in Figure 9-8.
3. ***New classes of descriptive attributes*** This is equivalent to adding new tables to the database.
4. ***Descriptive attributes become more refined*** For example, data about stores must be broken down by individual cash register to understand sales data. This change

is in the grain of the data, an extremely important topic, which we discuss later in the chapter. This can be a very difficult change to accommodate.

5. *Descriptive data are related to one another* For example, store data are related to geography data. This causes new relationships, often hierarchical, to be included in the data model.
6. *New source of data* This is a very common change, in which some new business need causes data feeds from an additional source system or some new operational system is installed that must feed the warehouse. This change can cause almost any of the previously mentioned changes, as well as the need for new extract, transform, and load processes.

It is usually not possible to go back and reload a data warehouse to accommodate all of these kinds of changes for the whole data history maintained. But it is critical to accommodate such changes smoothly to enable the data warehouse to meet new business conditions and information and business intelligence needs. Thus, designing the warehouse for change is very important.

THE DERIVED DATA LAYER

We turn now to the derived data layer. This is the data layer associated with logical or physical data marts (see Figure 9-5). It is the layer with which users normally interact for their decision support applications. Ideally, the reconciled data level is designed first and is the basis for the derived layer, whether data marts are dependent, independent, or logical. In order to derive any data mart we might need, it is necessary that the EDW be a fully normalized relational database accommodating transient and periodic data; this gives us the greatest flexibility to combine data into the simplest form for all user needs, even those which are unanticipated when the EDW is designed. In this section, we first discuss the characteristics of the derived data layer. We then introduce the star schema (or dimensional model), which is the data model most commonly used today to implement this data layer. A star schema is a specially designed, denormalized relational data model. We emphasize that the derived data layer can use normalized relations in the enterprise data warehouse; however, most organizations still build many data marts.

Characteristics of Derived Data

Earlier we defined *derived data* as data that have been selected, formatted, and aggregated for end-user decision support applications. In other words, derived data are information instead of raw data. As shown in Figure 9-5, the source of the derived data is the reconciled data, created from what can be a rather complex data process to integrate and make consistent data from many systems of record inside and outside the organization. Derived data in a data mart are generally optimized for the needs of particular user groups, such as departments, workgroups, or even individuals, to measure and analyze business activities and trends. A common mode of operation is to select the relevant data from the enterprise data warehouse on a daily basis, format and aggregate those data as needed, and then load and index those data in the target data marts. A data mart typically is accessed via online analytical processing (OLAP) tools, which we describe and illustrate in a later section of this chapter.

The objectives that are sought with derived data are quite different from the objectives of reconciled data. Typical objectives are the following:

- Provide ease of use for decision support applications
- Provide fast response for predefined user queries or requests for information (information usually in the form of metrics used to gauge the health of the organization in areas such as customer service, profitability, process efficiency, or sales growth)
- Customize data for particular target user groups
- Support ad hoc queries and data mining and other analytical applications

To satisfy these needs, we usually find the following characteristics in derived data:

- Both detailed data and aggregate data are present:
  a. Detailed data are often (but not always) periodic—that is, they provide a historical record.
  b. Aggregate data are formatted to respond quickly to predetermined (or common) queries.
- Data are distributed to separate data marts for different user groups.
- The data model that is most commonly used for a data mart is a dimensional model, usually in the form of a star schema, which is a relational-like model (such models are used by relational online analytical processing [ROLAP] tools). Proprietary models (which often look like hypercubes) are also sometimes used (such models are used by multidimensional online analytical processing [MOLAP] tools); these tools will be illustrated later in this chapter.

The Star Schema

A **star schema** is a simple database design (particularly suited to ad hoc queries) in which dimensional data (describing how data are commonly aggregated for reporting) are separated from fact or event data (describing business activity). A star schema is one version of a dimensional model (Kimball, 1996a). Although the star schema is suited to ad hoc queries (and other forms of informational processing), it is not suited to online transaction processing, and therefore is not generally used in operational systems, operational data stores, or an EDW. It is called a star schema because of its visual appearance, not because it has been recognized on the Hollywood Walk of Fame.

Star schema
A simple database design in which dimensional data are separated from fact or event data. A dimensional model is another name for a star schema.

FACT TABLES AND DIMENSION TABLES A star schema consists of two types of tables: one fact table and one or more dimension tables. *Fact tables* contain factual or quantitative data (measurements that are numerical, continuously valued, and additive) about a business, such as units sold, orders booked, and so on. *Dimension tables* hold descriptive data (context) about the subjects of the business. The dimension tables are usually the source of attributes used to qualify, categorize, or summarize facts in queries, reports, or graphs; thus, dimension data are usually textual and discrete (even if numeric). A data mart might contain several star schemas with similar dimension tables but each with a different fact table. Typical business dimensions (subjects) are Product, Customer, and Period. Period, or time, is always one of the dimensions. This structure is shown in Figure 9-9, which contains four dimension tables. As we will see shortly, there are variations on this basic star structure that provide further abilities to summarize and categorize the facts.

Each dimension table has a one-to-many relationship to the central fact table. Each dimension table generally has a simple primary key, as well as several nonkey attributes. The primary key, in turn, is a foreign key in the fact table (as shown in Figure 9-9). The primary key of the fact table is a composite key that consists of the concatenation of all of the foreign keys (four keys in Figure 9-9), plus possibly other components that do not correspond to dimensions. The relationship between each dimension table and the fact table provides a join path that allows users to query the database easily, using SQL statements for either predefined or ad hoc queries.

By now you have probably recognized that the star schema is not a new data model, but instead a denormalized implementation of the relational data model. The fact table plays the role of a normalized *n*-ary associative entity that links the instances of the various dimensions, which are in second, but possibly not third, normal form. To review associative entities, see Chapter 2, and for an example of the use of an associative entity, see Figures 2-11 and 2-14. The dimension tables are denormalized. Most experts view this denormalization as acceptable because dimensions are not updated and avoid costly joins; thus the star is optimized around certain facts and business objects to respond to specific information needs. Relationships between dimensions are not allowed; although such a relationship might exist in the organization (e.g., between employees and departments), such relationships are outside the scope of a star schema. As we will see later, there may be other tables related to dimensions, but these tables are never related directly to the fact table.

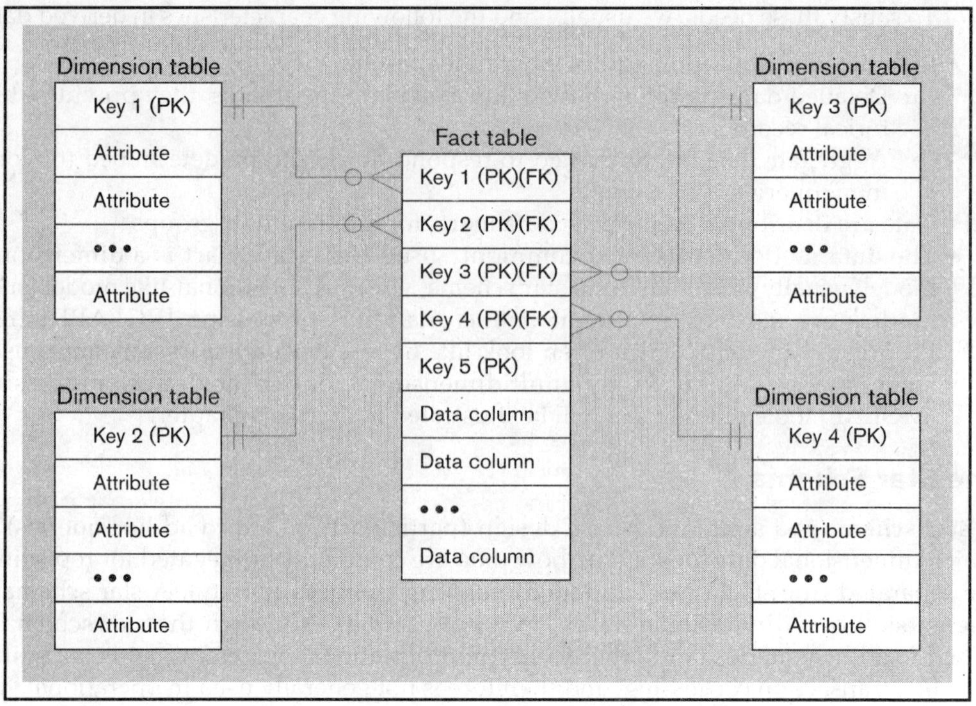

FIGURE 9-9 Components of a star schema

EXAMPLE STAR SCHEMA A star schema provides answers to a domain of business questions. For example, consider the following questions:

1. Which cities have the highest sales of large products?
2. What is the average monthly sales for each store manager?
3. In which stores are we losing money on which products? Does this vary by quarter?

A simple example of a star schema that could provide answers to such questions is shown in Figure 9-10. This example has three dimension tables: PRODUCT, PERIOD, and STORE, and one fact table, named SALES. The fact table is used to record three business facts: total units sold, total dollars sold, and total dollars cost. These totals are recorded for each day (the lowest level of PERIOD) a product is sold in a store.

Could these three questions be answered from a fully normalized data model of transactional data? Sure, a fully normalized and detailed database is the most flexible, able

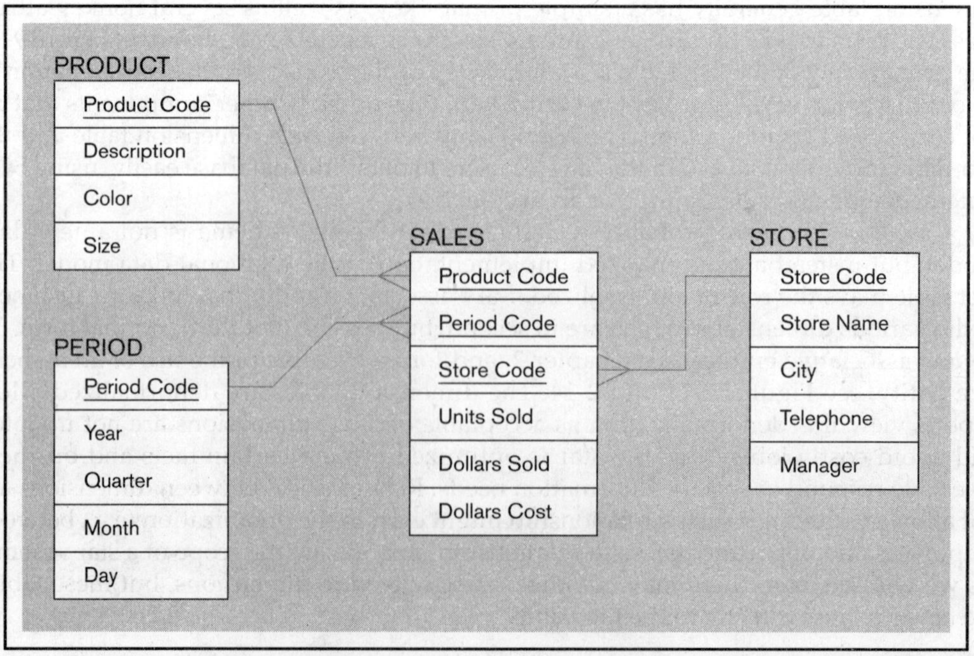

FIGURE 9-10 Star schema example

to support answering almost any question. However, more tables and joins would be involved, data need to be aggregated in standard ways, and data need to be sorted in an understandable sequence. These tasks might make it more difficult for the typical business manager to interrogate the data (especially using raw SQL), unless the business intelligence (OLAP) tool they use can mask such complexity from them (see sections later in this chapter on the user interface). And sufficient sales history would have to be kept, more than would be needed for transaction processing applications. With a data mart, the work of joining and summarizing data (which can cause extensive database processing) into the form needed to directly answer these questions has been shifted to the reconciliation layer, and processes in which the end user does not need to be involved. However, exactly what range of questions will be asked must be known in order to design the data mart for sufficient, optimal, and easy processing. Further, once these three questions become no longer interesting to the organization, the data mart (if it is physical) can be thrown away, and new ones built to answer new questions, whereas fully normalized models tend to be built for the long term to support less dynamic database needs (possibly with logical data marts that exist to meet transient needs). Later in this chapter, we will show some simple methods to use to determine how to determine a star schema model from such business questions.

Some sample data for this schema are shown in Figure 9-11. From the fact table, we find (for example) the following facts for product number 110 during period 002:

1. Thirty units were sold in store S1. The total dollar sale was 1500, and total dollar cost was 1200.
2. Forty units were sold in store S3. The total dollar sale was 2000, and total dollar cost was 1200.

FIGURE 9-11 Star schema sample data

Product

Product Code	Description	Color	Size
100	Sweater	Blue	40
110	Shoes	Brown	10 1/2
125	Gloves	Tan	M
•••			

Period

Period Code	Year	Quarter	Month
001	2010	1	4
002	2010	1	5
003	2010	1	6
•••			

Sales

Product Code	Period Code	Store Code	Units Sold	Dollars Sold	Dollars Cost
110	002	S1	30	1500	1200
125	003	S2	50	1000	600
100	001	S1	40	1600	1000
110	002	S3	40	2000	1200
100	003	S2	30	1200	750
•••					

Store

Store Code	Store Name	City	Telephone	Manager
S1	Jan's	San Antonio	683-192-1400	Burgess
S2	Bill's	Portland	943-681-2135	Thomas
S3	Ed's	Boulder	417-196-8037	Perry
•••				

Additional detail concerning the dimensions for this example can be obtained from the dimension tables. For example, in the PERIOD table, we find that period 002 corresponds to year 2010, quarter 1, month 5. Try tracing the other dimensions in a similar manner.

SURROGATE KEY Every key used to join the fact table with a dimension table should be a surrogate (nonintelligent, or system-assigned) key, not a key that uses a business value (sometimes called a natural, smart, or production key). That is, in Figure 9-10, Product Code, Store Code, and Period Code should all be surrogate keys in both the fact and dimension tables. If, for example, it is necessary to know the product catalog number, engineering number, or inventory item number for a product, these attributes would be stored along with Description, Color, and Size as attributes of the product dimension table. The following are the main reasons for this surrogate-key rule (Kimball, 1998a):

- Business keys change, often slowly, over time, and we need to remember old and new business key values for the same business object. As we will see in a later section on slowly changing dimensions, a surrogate key allows us to handle changing and unknown keys with ease.
- Using a surrogate key also allows us to keep track of different nonkey attribute values for the same production key over time. Thus, if a product package changes in size, we can associate the same product production key with several surrogate keys, each for the different package sizes.
- Surrogate keys are often simpler and shorter, especially when the production key is a composite key.
- Surrogate keys can be of the same length and format for all keys, no matter what business dimensions are involved in the database, even dates.

The primary key of each dimension table is its surrogate key. The primary key of the fact table is the composite of all the surrogate keys for the related dimension tables, and each of the composite key attributes is obviously a foreign key to the associated dimension table.

GRAIN OF THE FACT TABLE The raw data of a star schema are kept in the fact table. All the data in a fact table are determined by the same combination of composite key elements; so, for example, if the most detailed data in a fact table are daily values, then all measurement data must be daily in that fact table, and the lowest level of characteristics for the period dimension must also be a day. Determining the lowest level of detailed fact data stored is arguably the most important and difficult data mart design step. The level of detail of this data is specified by the intersection of all of the components of the primary key of the fact table. This intersection of primary keys is called the **grain** of the fact table. Determining the grain is critical and must be determined from business decision-making needs (i.e., the questions to be answered from the data mart). There is always a way to summarize fact data by aggregating using dimension attributes, but there is no way in the data mart to understand business activity at a level of detail finer than the fact table grain.

Grain
The level of detail in a fact table, determined by the intersection of all the components of the primary key, including all foreign keys and any other primary key elements.

A common grain would be each business transaction, such as an individual line item or an individual scanned item on a product sales receipt, a personnel change order, a line item on a material receipt, a claim against an insurance policy, a boarding pass, or an individual ATM transaction. A transactional grain allows users to perform analytics such as a market basket analysis, which is the study of buying behavior of individual customers. A grain higher than the transaction level might be all sales of a product on a given day, all receipts of a raw material in a given month at a specific warehouse, or the net effect of all ATM transactions for one ATM session. The finer the grain of the fact table, the more dimensions exist, the more fact rows exist, and often, the closer the data mart model is to a data model for the operational data store.

With the explosion of Web-based commerce, clicks become the possible lowest level of granularity. An analysis of Web site buying habits requires clickstream data (e.g., time spent on page, pages migrated from and to). Such an analysis may be useful to understand Web site usability and to customize messages based on navigational paths taken. However, this very fine level of granularity actually may be too low to be useful. It has been estimated that 90 percent or more of clickstream data are worthless (Inmon, 2006); for example, there is no business value to knowing a user moved a cursor when such movements are due to irrelevant events such as exercising the wrist, bumping a mouse, or moving a mouse to get it out of the way of something on the person's desk.

Kimball (2001) and others recommend using the smallest grain possible, given the limitations of the data mart technology. Even when data mart user information requirements imply a certain level of aggregated grain, often after some use, users ask more detailed questions (drill down) as a way to explain why certain aggregated patterns exist. You cannot "drill down" below the grain of the fact tables (without going to other data sources, such as the EDW, ODS, or the original source systems, which may add considerable effort to the analysis).

DURATION OF THE DATABASE As in the case of the EDW or ODS, another important decision in the design of a data mart is the amount of history to be kept; that is, the duration of the database. The natural duration is about 13 months or 5 calendar quarters, which is sufficient to see annual cycles in the data. Some businesses, such as financial institutions, have a need for longer durations. Older data may be difficult to source and cleanse if additional attributes are required from data sources. Even if sources of old data are available, it may be most difficult to find old values of dimension data, which are less likely than fact data to have been retained. Old fact data without associated dimension data at the time of the fact may be worthless.

SIZE OF THE FACT TABLE As you would expect, the grain and duration of the fact table have a direct impact on the size of that table. We can estimate the number of rows in the fact table as follows:

1. Estimate the number of possible values for each dimension associated with the fact table (in other words, the number of possible values for each foreign key in the fact table).
2. Multiply the values obtained in the first step after making any necessary adjustments.

Let's apply this approach to the star schema shown in Figure 9-11. Assume the following values for the dimensions:

Total number of stores = 1000
Total number of products = 10,000
Total number of periods = 24 (2 years' worth of monthly data)

Although there are 10,000 total products, only a fraction of these products are likely to record sales during a given month. Because item totals appear in the fact table only for items that record sales during a given month, we need to adjust this figure. Suppose that on average 50 percent (or 5000) items record sales during a given month. Then an estimate of the number of rows in the fact table is computed as follows:

Total rows = 1000 stores × 5000 active products × 24 months
= 120,000,000 rows (!)

Thus, in our relatively small example, the fact table that contains two years' worth of monthly totals can be expected to have well over 100 million rows. This example clearly illustrates that the size of the fact table is many times larger than the dimension tables. For example, the STORE table has 1000 rows, the PRODUCT table 10,000 rows, and the PERIOD table 24 rows.

If we know the size of each field in the fact table, we can further estimate the size (in bytes) of that table. The fact table (named SALES) in Figure 9-11 has six fields. If each of these fields averages four bytes in length, we can estimate the total size of the fact table as follows:

Total size = 120,000,000 rows × 6 fields × 4 bytes/field
= 2,880,000,000 bytes (or 2.88 gigabytes)

The size of the fact table depends on both the number of dimensions and the grain of the fact table. Suppose that after using the database shown in Figure 9-11 for a short period of time, the marketing department requests that *daily* totals be accumulated in the fact table. (This is a typical evolution of a data mart.) With the grain of the table changed to daily item totals, the number of rows is computed as follows:

$$\text{Total rows} = 1000 \text{ stores} \times 2000 \text{ active products} \times 720 \text{ days (2 years)}$$
$$= 1{,}440{,}000{,}000 \text{ rows}$$

In this calculation, we have assumed that 20 percent of all products record sales on a given day. The database can now be expected to contain well over 1 *billion* rows. The database size is calculated as follows:

$$\text{Total size} = 1{,}440{,}000{,}000 \text{ rows} \times 6 \text{ fields} \times 4 \text{ bytes/field}$$
$$= 34{,}560{,}000{,}000 \text{ bytes (or 34.56 gigabytes)}$$

Many large retailers e.g., Wal-Mart, Kmart, Sears) and e-businesses (e.g., Travelocity.com, MatchLogic.com) now have data warehouses (or data marts). The size of most of these data warehouses is in the multiple-terabyte range and growing rapidly as marketing people continue to press for more dimensions and an ever-finer grain in the fact table.

MODELING DATE AND TIME Because data warehouses and data marts record facts about dimensions over time, date and time (henceforth simply called *date*) is always a dimension table, and a date surrogate key is always one of the components of the primary key of any fact table. Because a user may want to aggregate facts on many different aspects of date or different kinds of dates, a date dimension may have many nonkey attributes. Also, because some characteristics of dates are country or event specific (e.g., whether the date is a holiday or there is some standard event on a given day, such as a festival or football game), modeling the date dimension can be more complex than illustrated so far.

Figure 9-12 shows a typical design for the date dimension. As we have seen before, a date surrogate key appears as part of the primary key of the fact table and is the primary key of the date dimension table. The nonkey attributes of the date dimension table include all of the characteristics of dates that users use to categorize, summarize, and group facts that do not vary by country or event. For an organization doing business in several countries (or several geographical units in which dates have different characteristics), we have added a Country Calendar table to hold the characteristics of each date in *each country*. Thus, the Date key is a foreign key in the Country Calendar table, and each row of the Country Calendar table is unique by the combination of Date key and Country, which form

FIGURE 9-12 Modeling dates

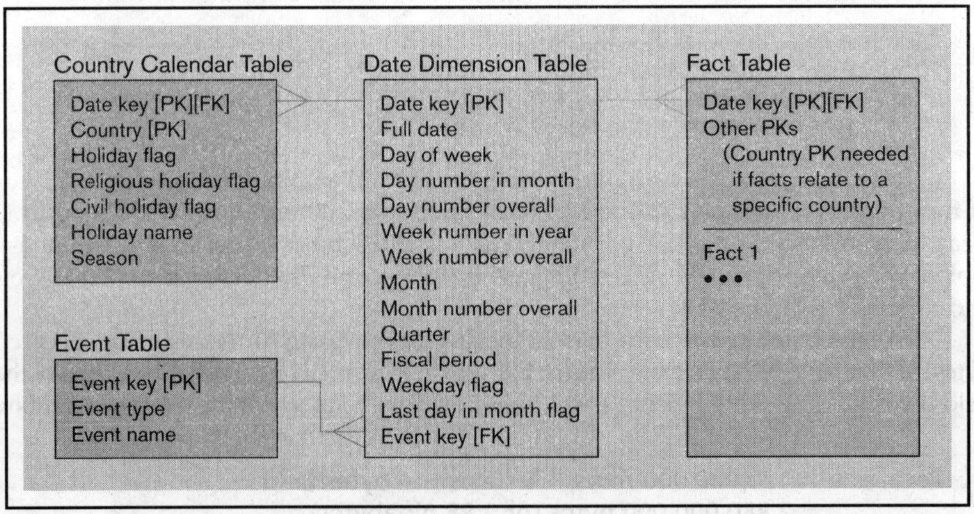

the composite primary key for this table. A special event may occur on a given date. (We assume here, for simplicity, no more than one special event may occur on a given date.) We have normalized the Event data by creating an Event table, so descriptive data on each event (e.g., the "Strawberry Festival" or the "Homecoming Game") are stored only once.

It is possible that there will be several kinds of dates associated with a fact, including the date the fact occurred, the date the fact was reported, the date the fact was recorded in the database, and the date the fact changed values. Each of these may be important in different analyses.

Variations of the Star Schema

The simple star schema introduced earlier is adequate for many applications. However, various extensions to this schema are often required to cope with more complex modeling problems. In this section, we briefly describe several such extensions: multiple fact tables with conformed dimensions and factless fact tables. For a discussion of additional extensions and variations, see subsequent sections, Poe (1996), and **www.ralphkimball.com**.

MULTIPLE FACT TABLES It is often desirable for performance or other reasons to define more than one fact table in a given star schema. For example, suppose that various users require different levels of aggregation (in other words, a different table grain). Performance can be improved by defining a different fact table for each level of aggregation. The obvious trade-off is that storage requirements may increase dramatically with each new fact table. More commonly, multiple fact tables are needed to store facts for different combinations of dimensions, possibly for different user groups.

Figure 9-13 illustrates a typical situation of multiple fact tables with two related star schemas. In this example, there are two fact tables, one at the center of each star:

1. Sales—facts about the sale of a product to a customer in a store on a date
2. Receipts—facts about the receipt of a product from a vendor to a warehouse on a date

As is common, data about one or more business subjects (in this case, Product and Date) need to be stored in dimension tables for each fact table, Sales and Receipts. Two approaches have been adopted in this design to handle shared dimension tables. In one case, because the description of product is quite different for sales and receipts, two separate product dimension tables have been created. On the other hand, because users want the same descriptions of dates, one date dimension table is used. In each case, we have created a **conformed dimension**, meaning that the dimension means the same

Conformed dimension
One or more dimension tables associated with two or more fact tables for which the dimension tables have the same business meaning and primary key with each fact table.

FIGURE 9-13 Conformed dimensions

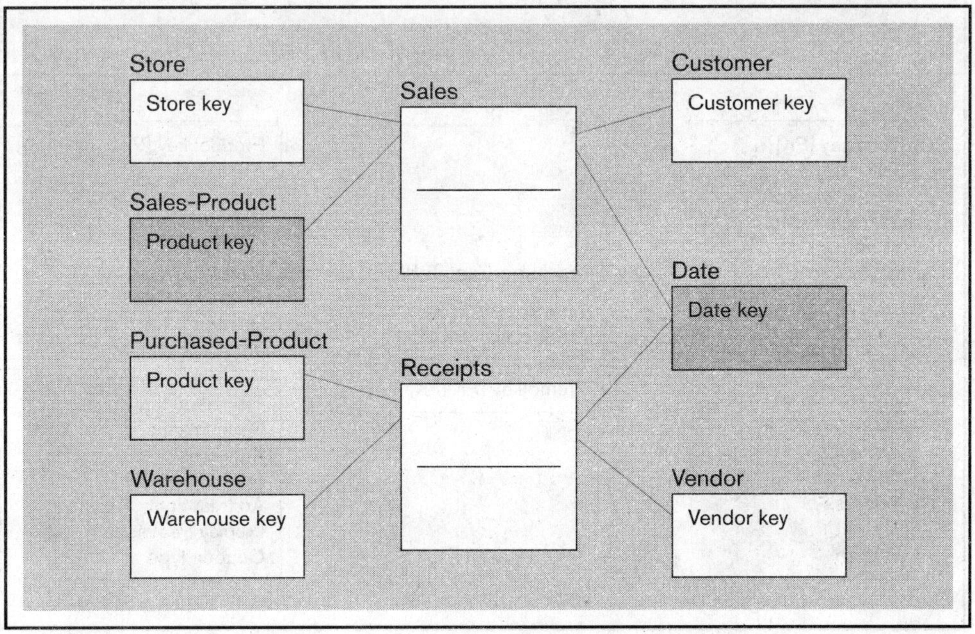

thing with each fact table, and hence, uses the same surrogate primary keys. Even when the two star schemas are stored in separate physical data marts, if dimensions are conformed, there is a potential for asking questions across the data marts (e.g., Do certain vendors recognize sales more quickly, and are they able to supply replenishments with less lead time?). In general, conformed dimensions allow users to do the following:

- Share nonkey dimension data
- Query across fact tables with consistency
- Work on facts and business subjects for which all users have the same meaning

FACTLESS FACT TABLES As strange as it may seem, there are applications for fact tables that do not have nonkey (fact) data but do have foreign keys for the associated dimensions. The two general situations in which factless fact tables may apply are tracking events (see Figure 9-14a) and taking inventory of the set of possible occurrences (called coverage) (see Figure 9-14b). The star schema in Figure 9-14a tracks which students attend which courses at which time in which facilities with which instructors. All that needs to be known is whether this event occurs, represented by the intersection of the five foreign keys. The star schema in Figure 9-14b shows the set of possible sales of a

FIGURE 9-14 Factless fact tables
(a) Factless fact table showing occurrence of an event
(b) Factless fact table showing coverage

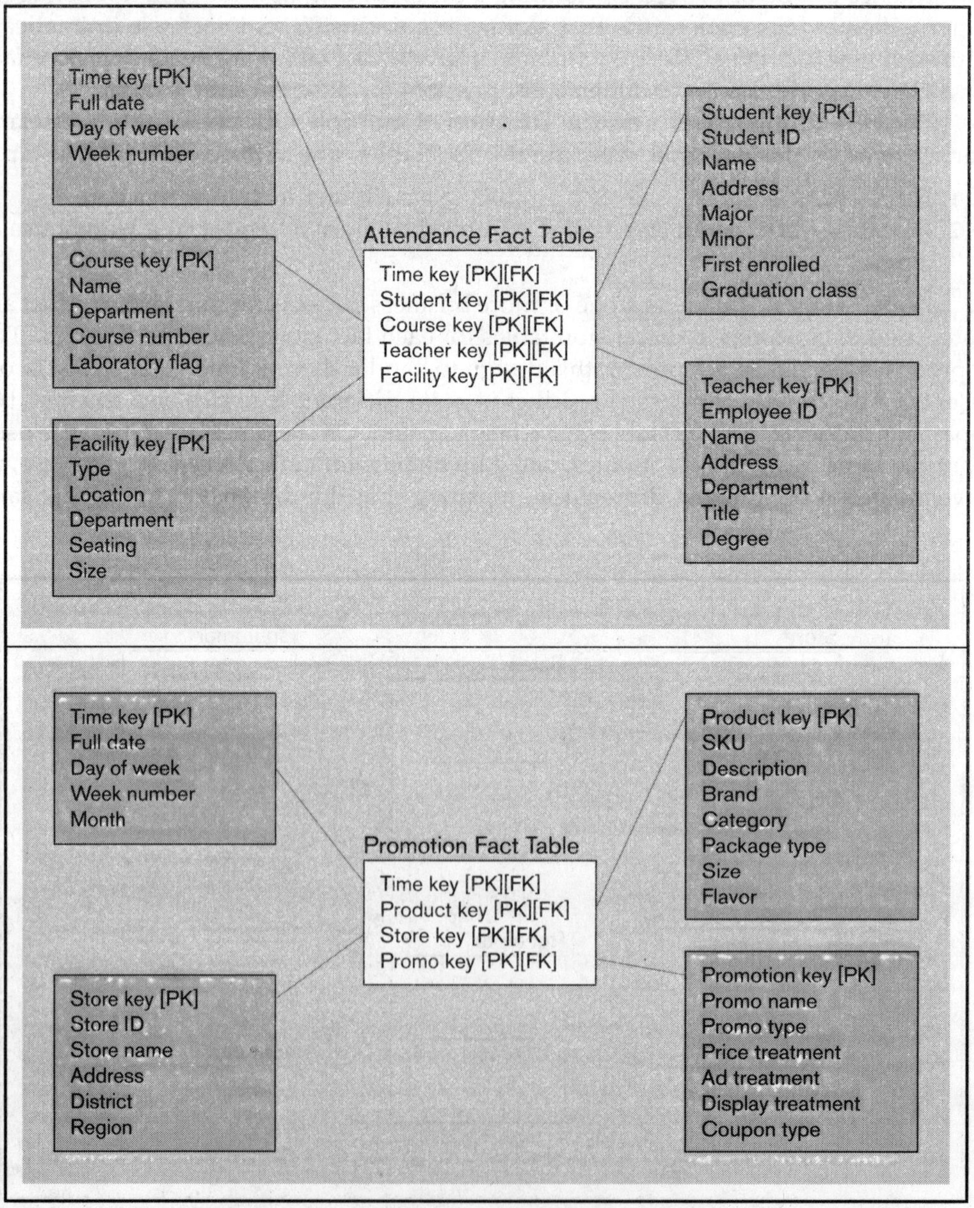

product in a store at a particular time under a given promotion. A second sales fact table, not shown in Figure 9-14b, could contain the dollar and unit sales (facts) for this same combination of dimensions (i.e., with the same four foreign keys as the Promotion fact table plus these two nonkey facts). With these two fact tables and four conformed dimensions, it is possible to discover which products that were on a specific promotion at a given time in a specific store did not sell (i.e., had zero sales), which can be discovered by finding a combination of the four key values in the promotion fact table, which are not in the sales fact table. The sales fact table, alone, is not sufficient to answer this question because it is missing rows for a combination of the four key values, which has zero sales.

Normalizing Dimension Tables

Fact tables are fully normalized because each fact depends on the whole composite primary key and nothing but the composite key. However, dimension tables may not be normalized. Most data warehouse experts find this acceptable for a data mart optimized and simplified for a given user group, so that all the dimension data are only one join away from associated facts. (Remember that this can be done with logical data marts, so duplicate data do not need to be stored.) Sometimes, as with any other relational database, the anomalies of a denormalized dimension table cause add, update, and delete problems. In this section, we address various situations in which it makes sense or is essential to further normalize dimension tables.

MULTIVALUED DIMENSIONS There may be a need for facts to be qualified by a set of values for the same business subject. For example, consider the hospital example in Figure 9-15. In this situation, a particular hospital charge and payment for a patient on a date (e.g., for all foreign keys in the Finances fact table) is associated with one or more diagnoses. (We indicate this with a dashed *M:N* relationship line between the Diagnosis and Finances tables.) We could pick the most important diagnosis as a component key for the Finances table, but that would mean we lose potentially important information about other diagnoses associated with a row. Or, we could design the Finances table with a fixed number of diagnosis keys, more than we think is ever possible to associate with one row of the Finances table, but this would create null components of the primary key for many rows, which violates a property of relational databases.

The best approach (the normalization approach) is to create a table for an associative entity between Diagnosis and Finances, in this case the Diagnosis group table. (Thus the dashed relationship in Figure 9-15 is not needed.) In the data warehouse database world, such an associative entity table is called a "helper table," and we will see more examples of helper tables as we progress through subsequent sections. A helper table may have nonkey attributes (as can any table for an associative entity); for example, the weight

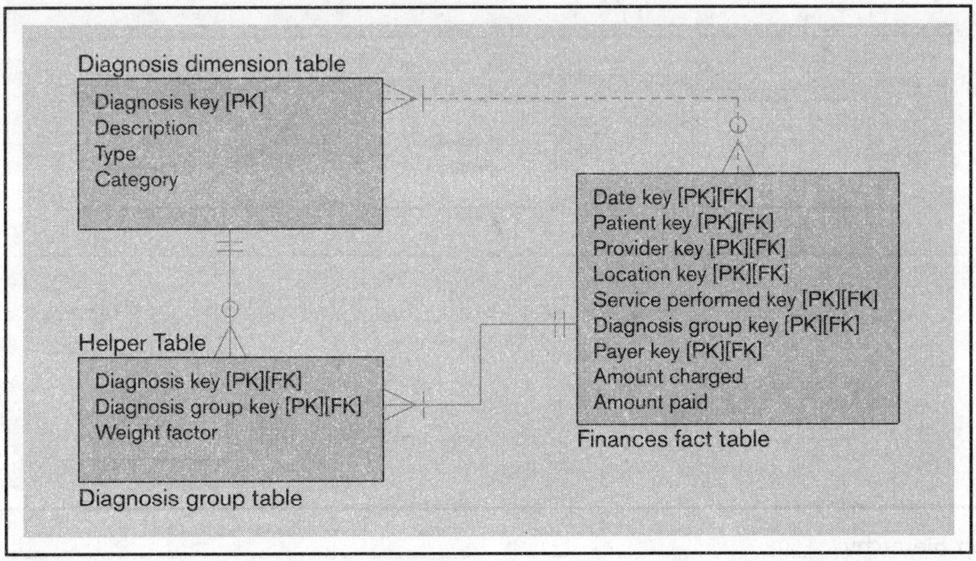

FIGURE 9-15 Multivalued dimension

factor in the Diagnosis group table of Figure 9-15 indicates the relative role each diagnosis plays in each group, presumably normalized to a total of 100 percent for all the diagnoses in a group. Also note that it is not possible for more than one Finances row to be associated with the same Diagnosis group key; thus, the Diagnosis group key is really a surrogate for the composite primary key of the Finances fact table.

HIERARCHIES Many times a dimension in a star schema forms a natural, fixed depth hierarchy. For example, there are geographical hierarchies (e.g., markets with a state, states within a region, and regions within a country) and product hierarchies (packages or sizes within a product, products within bundles, and bundles within product groups). When a dimension participates in a hierarchy, a database designer has two basic choices:

1. Include all the information for each level of the hierarchy in a single denormalized dimension table for the most detailed level of the hierarchy, thus creating considerable redundancy and update anomalies. Although it is simple, this is usually not the recommended approach.
2. Normalize the dimension into a nested set of a fixed number of tables with 1:*M* relationships between them. Associate only the lowest level of the hierarchy with the fact table. It will still be possible to aggregate the fact data at any level of the hierarchy, but now the user will have to perform nested joins along the hierarchy or be given a view of the hierarchy that is prejoined.

In the situation when the depth of the hierarchy can be fixed, each level of the hierarchy is a separate dimensional entity. Some hierarchies can more easily use this scheme than can others. Consider the product hierarchy in Figure 9-16. Here each product is part of a product family (e.g., Crest with Tartar Control is part of Crest), and a product family is part of a product category (e.g., toothpaste), and a category is part of a product group (e.g., health and beauty). This works well if every product follows this same hierarchy. Such hierarchies are very common in data warehouses and data marts.

Now, consider the more general example of a typical consulting company that invoices customers for specified time periods on projects. A revenue fact table in this situation might show how much revenue is billed and for how many hours on each invoice, which is for a particular time period, customer, service, employee, and project. Because consulting work may be done for different divisions of the same organization, if we want to understand the total role of consulting in any level of a customer organization, we need a customer hierarchy. This hierarchy is a recursive relationship between organizational units. As shown in Figure 4-17 for a supervisory hierarchy, the standard way to represent this in a normalized database is to put into the company row a foreign key of the Company key for its parent unit.

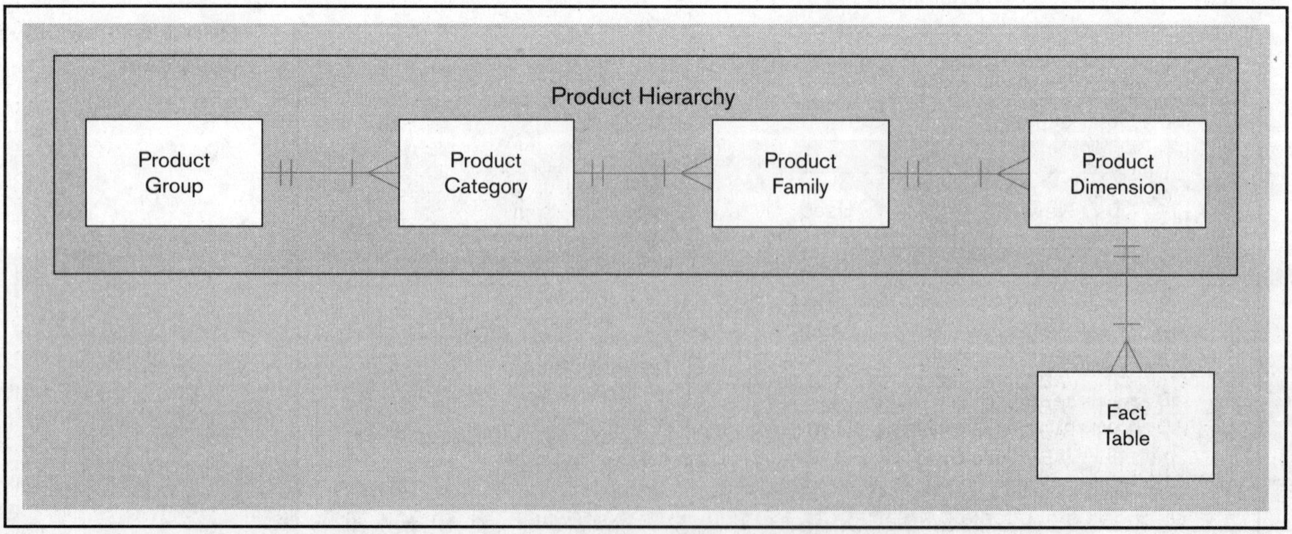

FIGURE 9-16 Fixed product hierarchy

Recursive relationships implemented in this way are difficult for the typical end user because specifying how to aggregate at any arbitrary level of the hierarchy requires complex SQL programming. One solution is to transform the recursive relationship into a fixed number of hierarchical levels by combining adjacent levels into general categories; for example, for an organizational hierarchy the recursive levels above each unit could be grouped into enterprise, division, and department. Each instance of an entity at each hierarchical level gets a surrogate primary key and attributes to describe the characteristics of that level needed for decision making. Work done in the reconciliation layer will form and maintain these instances.

Another simple but more general alternative appears in Figure 9-17. Figure 9-17a shows how this hierarchy is typically modeled in a data warehouse using a helper table (Chisholm, 2000; Kimball, 1998b). Each customer organizational unit the consulting firm serves is assigned a different surrogate customer key and row in the Customer dimension table, and the customer surrogate key is used as a foreign key in the Revenue fact table; this foreign key relates to the Sub customer key in the Helper table because the revenue facts are associated at the lowest possible level of the organizational hierarchy. The problem with joining in a recursive relationship of arbitrary depth is that the user has to write code to join an arbitrary number of times (once for each level of subordination) and these joins in a data warehouse, because of its massive size, can be very time-consuming

(a) Use of a helper table

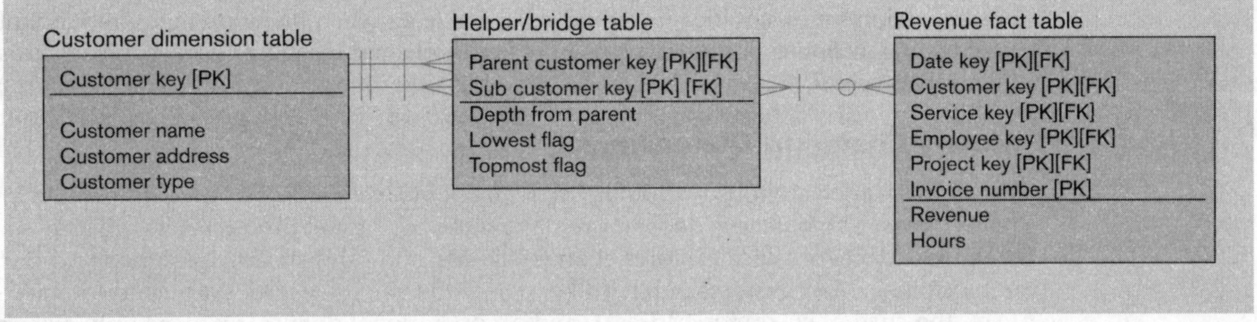

(b) Sample hierarchy with customer and helper tables

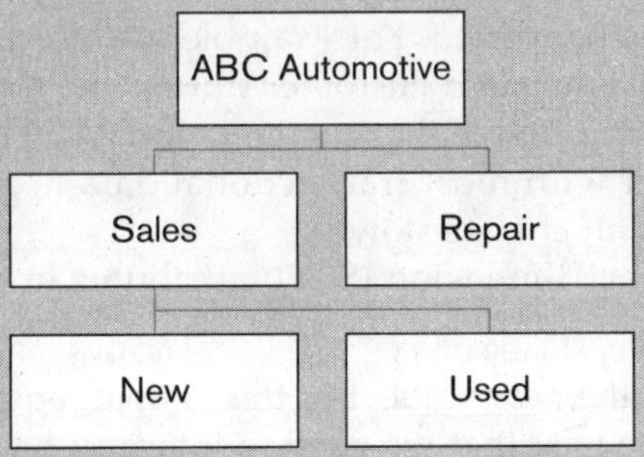

Hierarchy Helper Table

Parent key	Sub key	Depth	Lowest	Topmost
C0000001	C0000001	0	N	Y
C0000001	C0000002	1	N	N
C0000001	C0000003	1	N	N
C0000001	C0000004	2	Y	N
C0000001	C0000005	2	Y	N
C0000002	C0000002	0	N	N
C0000002	C0000004	1	Y	N
C0000002	C0000005	1	Y	N
C0000003	C0000003	0	Y	N
C0000004	C0000004	0	Y	N
C0000005	C0000005	0	Y	N

Customer Table

Customer key	Name	Address	Type
C0000001	ABC Automotive	100 1st St.	Dealer
C0000002	ABC Auto Sales	110 1st St.	Sales
C0000003	ABC Repair	130 1st St.	Service
C0000004	ABC Auto New Sales	110 1st St.	Sales
C0000005	ABC Auto Used Sales	110 1st St.	Sales

FIGURE 9-17 Representing hierarchical relationships within a dimension

(except for some high-performance data warehouse technologies that use parallel processing). To avoid this problem, the helper table flattens out the hierarchy by recording a row for each organizational subunit and each of its parent organizational units (including itself) all the way up to the top unit of the customer organization. Each row of this helper table has three descriptors: the number of levels the subunit is from its parent unit for *that* table row, a flag indicating whether this subunit is the lowest in the hierarchy, and a flag indicating whether this subunit is the highest in the hierarchy. Figure 9-17b depicts an example customer organizational hierarchy and the rows that would be in the helper table to represent that total organization. (There would be other rows in the helper table for the subunit-parent unit relationships within other customer organizations.)

The Revenue fact table in Figure 9-17a includes a primary key attribute of Invoice number. Invoice number is an example of a *degenerative dimension*, which has no interesting dimension attributes. (Thus no dimension table exists and Invoice number is not part of the table's primary key.) Invoice number also is not a fact that will be used for aggregation because mathematics on this attribute has no meaning. This attribute may be helpful if there is a need to explore an ODS or source systems to find additional details about the invoice transaction or to group together related fact rows (e.g., all the revenue line items on the same invoice).

Snowflake schema
An expanded version of a star schema in which dimension tables are normalized into several related tables.

When the dimension tables are further normalized by using helper tables (sometimes called *bridge tables*, or *reference tables*), the simple star schema turns into a **snowflake schema**. A snowflake schema resembles a segment of an ODS or source database centered on the transaction tables summarized into the fact table and all of the tables directly and indirectly related to these transaction tables. Many data warehouse experts discourage the use of snowflake schemas because they are more complex for users and require more joins to bring the results together into one table. A snowflake may be desirable if the normalization saves significant redundant space (e.g., when there are many redundant, long textual attributes) or when users may find browsing through the normalized tables themselves useful.

Slowly Changing Dimensions

Recall that data warehouses and data marts track business activities over time, often for many years. The business does not remain static over time; products change size and weight, customers relocate, stores change layouts, and sales staff are assigned to different locations. Most systems of record keep only the current values for business subjects (e.g., the current customer address), and an operational data store keeps only a short history of changes to indicate that changes have occurred and to support business processes handling the immediate changes. But in a data warehouse or data mart, we need to know the history of values to match the history of facts with the correct dimensional descriptions at the time the facts happened. For example, we need to associate a sales fact with the description of the associated customer during the time period of the sales fact, which may not be the description of that customer today. Of course, business subjects change slowly compared with most transactional data (e.g., inventory level). Thus, dimensional data change, but change slowly.

We might handle slowly changing dimension (SCD) attributes in one of three ways (Kimball, 1996b, 1999):

1. Overwrite the current value with the new value, but this is unacceptable because it eliminates the description of the past that we need to interpret historical facts. Kimball calls this the Type 1 method.
2. For each dimension attribute that changes, create a current value field and as many old value fields as we wish (i.e., a multivalued attribute with a fixed number of occurrences for a limited historical view). This schema might work if there were a predictable number of changes over the length of history retained in the data warehouse (e.g., if we need to keep only 24 months of history and an attribute changes value monthly). However, this works only under this kind of restrictive assumption and cannot be generalized to any slowly changing dimension attribute. Further, queries can become quite complex because which column is needed may have to be determined within the query. Kimball calls this the Type 3 method.

3. Create a new dimension table row (with a new surrogate key) each time the dimension object changes; this new row contains all the dimension characteristics at the time of the change; the new surrogate key is the original surrogate key plus the start date for the period when these dimension values are in effect. A fact row is associated with the surrogate key whose attributes apply at the date/time of the fact (i.e., the fact date/time falls between the start and end dates of a dimension row for the same original surrogate key). We likely also want to store in a dimension row the date/time the change ceases being in effect (which will be the maximum possible date or null for the current row for each dimension object) and a reason code for the change. This approach allows us to create as many dimensional object changes as necessary. However, it becomes unwieldy if rows frequently change or if the rows are very long. Kimball calls this the Type 2 method, and it is the one most often used.

Changes in some dimensional attributes may not be important. Hence, the first policy can be used for these attributes. The Type 2 scheme is the most frequently used approach for handling slowly changing dimensions for which changes matter. Under this scheme, we likely also store in a dimension row the surrogate key value for the original object; this way, we can relate all changes to the same object. In fact, the primary key of the dimension table becomes a composite of the original surrogate key plus the date of the change, as depicted in Figure 9-18. In this example, each time an attribute of Customer changes, a new customer row is written to the Customer dimension table; the PK of that row is the original surrogate key for that customer plus the date of the change. The nonkey elements are the values for all the nonkey attributes at the time of the change (i.e., some attributes will have new values due to the change, but probably most will remain the same as for the most recent row for the same customer). Finding the dimension row for a fact row is a little more complex; the SQL WHERE clause would include the following:

```
WHERE Fact.CustomerKey = Customer.CustomerKey
AND Fact.DateKey BETWEEN Customer.StartDate and Customer.EndDate
```

For this to work, EndDate for the last change to the customer dimension data must be the largest date possible. If not, the EndDate for the last change could be null, and the WHERE clause can be modified to handle this possibility. Another common feature of the Type 2 approach is to include a reason code (Kimball, 2006) with each new dimension row to document why the change occurred; in some cases, the reason code itself is useful for decision making (e.g., to see trends in correcting errors, resolve recurring issues, or see patterns in the business environment).

As noted, however, this schema can cause an excessive number of dimension table rows when dimension objects frequently change or when dimension rows are large "monster dimensions." Also, if only a small portion of the dimension row has changing values, there are excessive redundant data created. Figure 9-19 illustrates one approach, dimension segmentation, which handles this situation as well as the more general case of subsets of dimension attributes that change at different frequencies. In this example, the Customer dimension is segmented into two dimension tables; one segment may

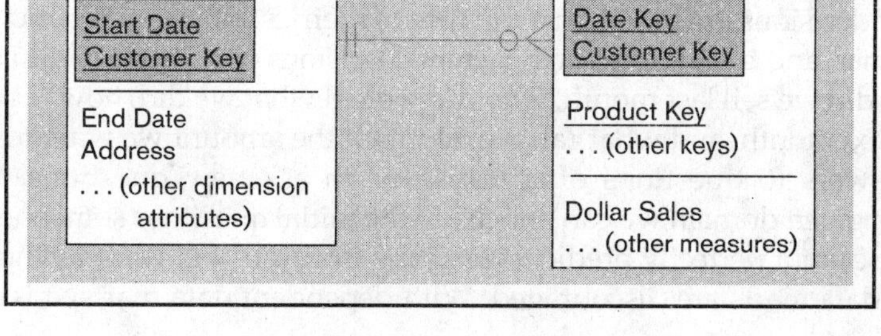

FIGURE 9-18 Example of Type 2 SCD Customer dimension table

FIGURE 9-19 Dimension segmentation

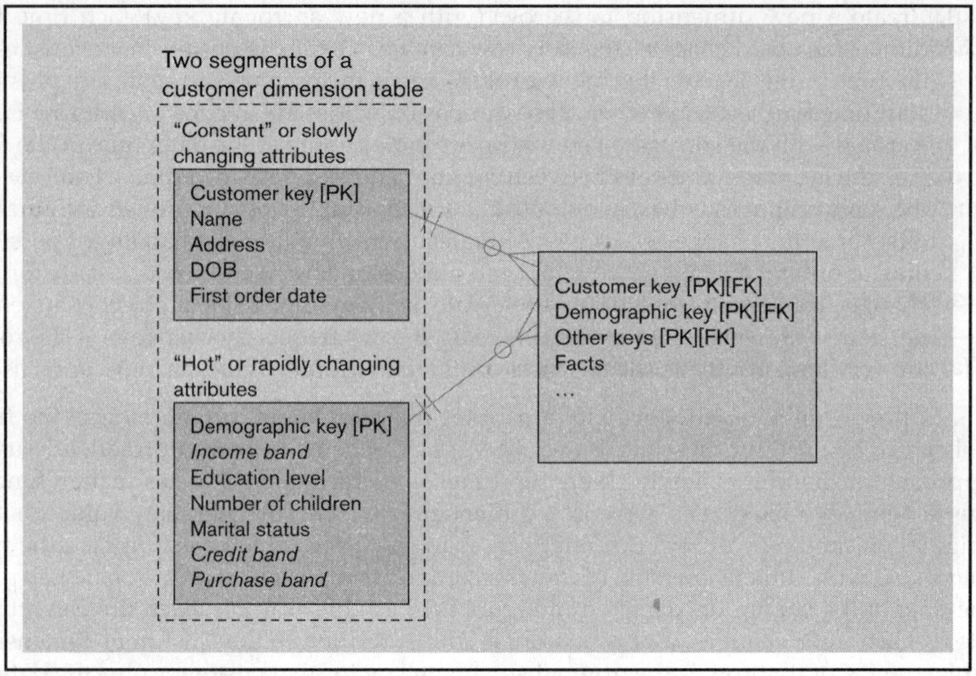

hold nearly constant or very slowly changing dimensions and other segments (we show only two in this example) hold clusters of attributes that change more rapidly and, for attributes in the same cluster, often change at the same time. These more rapidly changing attributes are often called "hot" attributes by data warehouse designers.

Another aspect of this segmentation is that for hot attributes, we changed individual dimension attributes, such as customer income (e.g., $75,400/year), into an attribute for a band, or range, of income values (e.g., $60,000–$89,999/year). Bands are defined as required by users and are as narrow or wide as can be useful, but certainly some precision is lost. Bands make the hot attributes less hot, because a change within a band does not cause a new row to be written. This design is more complex for users because they now may have to join facts with multiple dimension segments, depending on the analysis.

One other common variation for handling slowly changing dimensions is to segment the dimension table horizontally into two tables, one to hold only the current values for the dimension entities and the other table to hold all the history, possibly including the current row. The logic to this approach is that many queries need to access only the current values, which can be done quickly from a smaller table of only current rows; when a query needs to look at history, the full dimension history table is used. Another version of this same kind of approach is to use only the one dimension table but to add a column (a flag attribute) to indicate whether that row contains the most current or out-of-date values. See Kimball (2002) for additional ideas on handling slowly changing dimensions.

Determining Dimensions and Facts

Which dimensions and facts are required for a data mart is driven by the context for decision making. Each decision is based on specific metrics to monitor the status of some important factor (e.g., inventory turns) or to predict some critical event (e.g., customer churn). Many decisions are based on a mixture of metrics, balancing financial, process efficiency, customer, and business growth factors. Decisions usually start with questions such as how much did we sell last month, why did we sell what we did, how much do we think we will sell next month, and what can we do to sell the amount we want to sell?

The answers to questions often cause us to ask new questions. Consequently, although for a given domain we can anticipate the initial questions someone might ask of a data mart, we cannot perfectly predict everything the users will want to know. This is why independent data marts are discouraged. With dependent data marts, it is much easier to expand an existing data mart or for the user to be given access to other data marts or to the EDW when their new questions require data in addition to what is in the current data mart.

The starting point for determining what data should be in a data mart are the initial questions the users want answered. Each question can be broken down into discrete items of business information the user wants to know (facts) and the criteria used to access, sort, group, summarize, and present the facts (dimension attributes). An easy way to model the questions is through a matrix, such as that illustrated in Figure 9-20a. In this figure the

FIGURE 9-20 Determining dimensions and facts

(a) Fact-qualifier matrix for sales and customer service tracking

1. What was the dollar sales of health and beauty products in North America to customers over the age of 50 in each of the past three years?
2. What is the name of the salesperson who had the highest dollar sales of each product in the first quarter of this year?
3. How many European customer complaints did we receive on pet food products during the past year? How has it changed from month to month this year?
4. What is the name of the stores that had the highest average monthly quantity sales of casual clothing during the summer?

	dollar sales	number of complaints	avg. qty. sales
product category	1	3	4
customer territory	1	3	
customer age	1		
year	1	3	
salesperson name	2		
product	2		
quarter	2		
month		3	
store			4
season			4

(b) Star schema for sales and customer service tracking

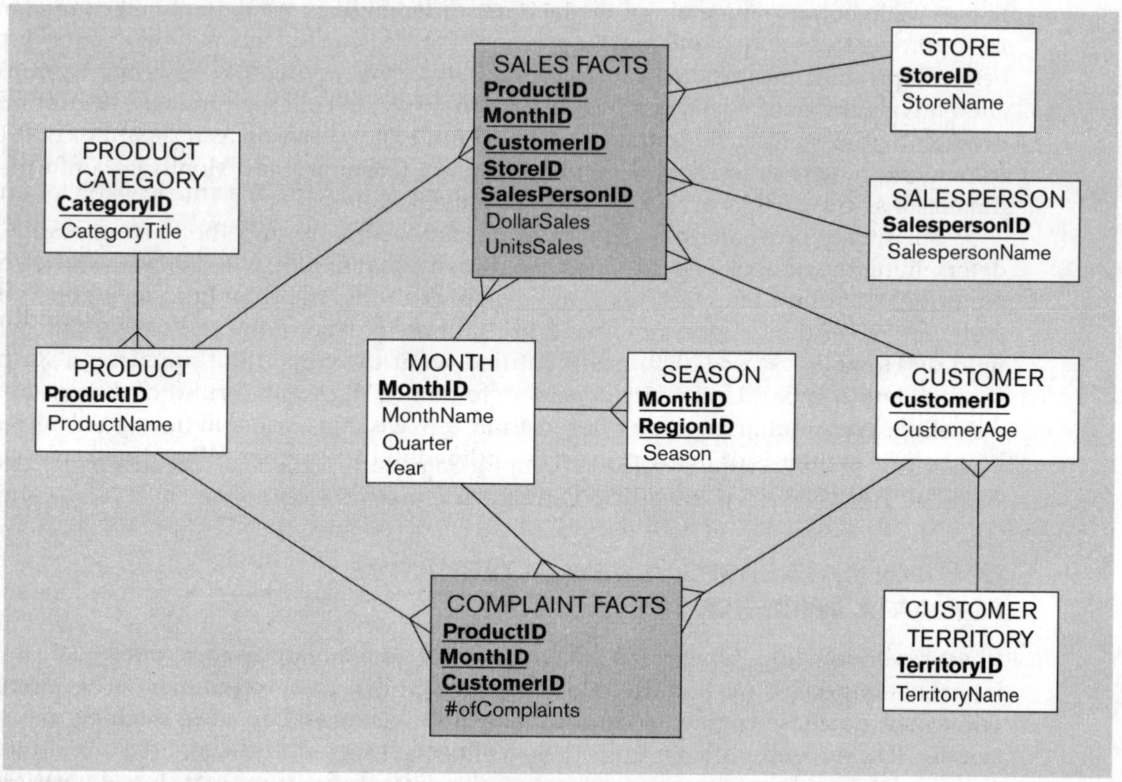

TABLE 9-3 Ten Essential Rules of Dimensional Modeling

1. **Use atomic facts:** Eventually, users want detailed data, even if their initial requests are for summarized facts.
2. **Create single-process fact tables:** Each fact table should address the important measurements for one business process, such as taking a customer order or placing a material purchase order.
3. **Include a date dimension for every fact table:** A fact should be described by the characteristics of the associated day (or finer) date/time to which that fact is related.
4. **Enforce consistent grain:** Each measurement in a fact table must be atomic for the same combination of keys (the same grain).
5. **Disallow null keys in fact tables:** Facts apply to the combination of key values, and helper tables may be needed to represent some *M:N* relationships.
6. **Honor hierarchies:** Understand the hierarchies of dimensions and carefully choose to snowflake the hierarchy or denormalize into one dimension.
7. **Decode dimension tables:** Store descriptions of surrogate keys and codes used in fact tables in associated dimension tables, which can then be used to report labels and query filters.
8. **Use surrogate keys:** All dimension table rows should be identified by a surrogate key, with descriptive columns showing the associated production and source system keys.
9. **Conform dimensions:** Conformed dimensions should be used across multiple fact tables.
10. **Balance requirements with actual data:** Unfortunately, source data may not precisely support all business requirements, so you must balance what is technically possible with what users want and need.

Source: Based on Ross (2009).

rows are the qualifiers (dimension or dimension attributes) and the columns are the metrics (facts) referenced in the questions. The cells of the matrix contain codes to indicate which qualifiers and metrics are included in each question. For example, question 3 uses the fact number of complaints and the dimension attributes of product category, customer territory, year, and month. One or several star schemas may be required for any set of questions. For the example in Figure 9-20a we have designed two fact tables, shown in Figure 9-20b because the grain of the facts are different (e.g., we determined complaints have nothing to do with stores or salespersons). We also created hierarchical relationships between product and product category and between customer and customer territory; alternatively it would have been possible, for example, to collapse product category into product, with resulting redundancy. We also understood season as a separate concept from month, and to be territory dependent. Product, Customer, and Month are conformed dimensions because they are shared by two fact tables.

So, if the type of analysis depicted in Figure 9-20 represents the starting point for determining the dimensions and facts of a dimensional model, when do you know you are done? We don't know of a definitive answer to this question (and let's hope you really are never done, but simply need to continue to expand the coverage of the data model). However, Ross (2009) has identified what the consulting practice for Ralph Kimball and Kimball University considers to be the 10 essential rules of dimensional modeling. We summarize these rules in Table 9-3; we think you will find these rules to be a helpful synthesis of many principles outlined in this chapter. When these rules are satisfied, you are done (for the time being).

COLUMN DATABASES: A NEW ALTERNATIVE FOR DATA WAREHOUSES

RDBMS vendors (e.g., Oracle, IBM) have typically added features to accommodate analytical query processing, and RDBMS vendors (e.g., Teradata, Netezza) have developed whole new database engines to handle data warehousing and business intelligence processing. These vendors have built their technologies around the standard relational data model of tables of rows and columns and physical structures that store data as files of records for rows, with columns as fields in each record. Emerging, but viable, vendors claim different storage structures are needed for analytical queries—ones that store data on a column basis rather than a row basis. That is, values are stored in sequence for one column, followed by the values for another column, and so on, thus virtually turning a table of data 90 degrees.

Data warehousing and business intelligence (BI) queries typically access many rows based on common values for a few columns, such as summarizing sales data to find the top 10 selling products in the Northwest region. This tends to be the opposite of transaction processing tasks, which seek values for many of the columns but for one row and some related rows, such as a particular customer order and its related customer record, line items, and associated product details. Vendors of column-based products claim to reduce storage space (because a value is stored only once) and to speed query processing time because the data are physically organized to support analytical queries. The conceptual and logical data models for the data warehouse do not change. SQL is still the query language, and you don't have to write queries any differently; the DBMS simply stores and accesses the data differently than in traditional row-oriented RDBMSs.

Column database technologies trade off storage space savings (data compression of over 70 percent is common) for computing time. For example, a customer ID might be stored only once in the database for all the places it appears, such as the identifier of customer data but also as foreign keys associated with customer orders, payments, product returns, service visits, and other activities. This would be true for any column of data, such as city names, street names, names of all types of parties, etc. Internal encoding of data is used to associate the business data value with physical database references to that value throughout the database. A query can then search rapidly through very condensed storage space for the codes associated with the column value used in the query. The claims for the advantage of column databases over row-based relational databases are based on the assumption that disk storage space and the bandwidth to access disk storage are more expensive than CPU time to reconstruct the business data from compressed storage. And, with compressed storage, overall query processing time is reduced.

Details about column database technology are beyond the scope of this book because the discussion would address the design of a DBMS rather than the design of a database. However, it is important for you to understand that new DBMS technologies designed from the ground up for analytical queries are emerging and should be considered in the overall architecture design of a data warehousing environment. Major vendors of column-based databases include Sybase and Vertica, and there is an open source option from Infobright that works with MySQL.

THE USER INTERFACE

Although we have covered most of what you need to know to get started designing a data warehouse, you may still wonder "what can I do with it?" Even a well-designed data mart or enterprise data warehouse, loaded with relevant data, may not be used unless users are provided with a powerful, intuitive interface that allows them to access and analyze those data easily. In this section, we provide a brief introduction to contemporary interfaces for data warehouses and marts.

A variety of tools are available to query and analyze data stored in data warehouses and data marts. These tools may be classified as follows:

- Traditional query and reporting tools
- OLAP, MOLAP, and ROLAP tools
- Data visualization tools
- Business performance management and dashboard tools
- Data-mining tools

Traditional query and reporting tools include spreadsheets, personal computer databases, and report writers and generators. For reasons of space (and because they are covered elsewhere), we do not describe these tools in this chapter. We describe the remaining four categories of tools after discussing the role of metadata.

Role of Metadata

The first requirement for building a user-friendly interface is a set of metadata that describes the data in the data mart in business terms that users can easily understand. We show the association of metadata with data marts in the overall three-level data architecture in Figure 9-5.

The metadata associated with data marts are often referred to as a "data catalog," "data directory," or some similar term. Metadata serve as kind of a "yellow pages" directory to the data in the data marts. The metadata should allow users to easily answer questions such as the following:

1. What subjects are described in the data mart? (Typical subjects are customers, patients, students, products, courses, and so on.)
2. What dimensions and facts are included in the data mart? What is the grain of the fact table?
3. How are the data in the data mart derived from the enterprise data warehouse data? What rules are used in the derivation?
4. How are the data in the enterprise data warehouse derived from operational data? What rules are used in this derivation?
5. What reports and predefined queries are available to view the data?
6. What drill-down and other data analysis techniques are available?
7. Who is responsible for the quality of data in the data marts, and to whom are requests for changes made?

SQL OLAP Querying

The most common database query language, SQL (see Chapters 6 and 7), is being extended to support some types of calculations and querying needed for a data warehousing environment. In general, however, SQL is not an analytical language (Mundy, 2001). At the heart of analytical queries is the ability to perform categorization (e.g., group data by dimension characteristics), aggregation (e.g., create averages per category), and ranking (e.g., find the customer in some category with the highest average monthly sales). Consider the following business question:

Which customer has bought the most of each product we sell? Show the product ID and description, customer ID and name, and the total quantity sold of that product to that customer; show the results in sequence by product ID.

Even with the limitations of standard SQL, this analytical query can be written without the OLAP extensions to SQL. One way to write this query, using the large version of the Pine Valley Furniture database provided with this textbook, is as follows:

```
SELECT P1.ProductId, ProductDescription, C1.CustomerId,
  CustomerName,SUM(OL1.OrderedQuantity) AS TotOrdered
  FROM Customer_T AS C1, Product_T AS P1, OrderLine_T
    AS OL1, Order_T AS O1
  WHERE C1.CustomerId = O1.CustomerId
    AND O1.OrderId = OL1.OrderId
    AND OL1.ProductId = P1.ProductId
  GROUP BY P1.ProductId, ProductDescription,
    C1.CustomerId, CustomerName
  HAVING TotOrdered >= ALL
  (SELECT SUM(OL2.OrderedQuantity)
  FROM OrderLine_T AS OL2, Order_T AS O2
  WHERE OL2.ProductId = P1.ProductId
    AND OL2.OrderId = O2.OrderId
    AND O2.CustomerId <> C1.CustomerId
  GROUP BY O2.CustomerId)
ORDER BY P1.ProductId;
```

This approach uses a correlated subquery to find the set of total quantity ordered across all customers for each product, and then the outer query selects the customer whose total is greater than or equal to all of these (in other words, equal to the maximum of the set). Until you write many of these queries, this can be very challenging to develop, and is often beyond the capabilities of even well-trained end users. And even this query is rather simple because it does not have multiple categories, does not ask for changes over time, or does not want to see the results graphically, Finding the second in rank is even more difficult.

Some versions of SQL support special clauses that make ranking questions easier to write. For example, Microsoft SQL Server and some other RDBMSs support clauses of FIRST n, TOP n, LAST n, and BOTTOM n rows. Thus, the query shown previously could be greatly simplified by adding TOP 1 in front of the SUM in the outer query and eliminating the HAVING and subquery. TOP 1 was illustrated in Chapter 7, in the section on "More Complicated SQL Queries."

Recent versions of SQL include some data warehousing and business intelligence extensions. Because many data warehousing operations deal with categories of objects, possibly ordered by date, the SQL standard includes a WINDOW clause to define dynamic sets of rows. (In many SQL systems, the word OVER is used instead of WINDOW, which is what we illustrate next.) For example, an OVER clause can be used to define three adjacent days as the basis for calculating moving averages. (Think of a window moving between the bottom and top of its window frame, giving you a sliding view of rows of data.) PARTITION BY within an OVER clause is similar to GROUP BY; PARTITION BY tells an OVER clause the basis for each set, an ORDER BY clause sequences the elements of a set, and the ROWS clause says how many rows in sequence to use in a calculation. For example, consider a SalesHistory table (columns TerritoryID, Quarter, and Sales) and the desire to show a three-quarter moving average of sales. The following SQL will produce the desired result using these OLAP clauses:

```
SELECT TerritoryID, Quarter, Sales,
  AVG(Sales) OVER (PARTITION BY TerritoryID
    ORDER BY Quarter ROWS 2 PRECEDING) AS 3QtrAverage
FROM SalesHistory;
```

The PARTITION BY clause groups the rows of the SalesHistory table by TerritoryID for the purpose of computing 3QtrAverage, and then the ORDER BY clause sorts by quarter within these groups. The ROWS clause indicates how many rows over which to calculate the AVG(Sales). The following is a sample of the results from this query:

TerritoryID	Quarter	Sales	3QtrAverage
Atlantic	1	20	20
Atlantic	2	10	15
Atlantic	3	6	12
Atlantic	4	29	15
East	1	5	5
East	2	7	6
East	3	12	8
East	4	11	10
. . .			

In addition, but not shown here, a QUALIFY clause can be used similarly to a HAVING clause to eliminate the rows of the result based on the aggregate referenced by the OVER clause.

The RANK windowing function calculates something that is very difficult to calculate in standard SQL, which is the row of a table in a specific relative position based on some criteria (e.g., the customer with the third-highest sales in a given period). In the case of ties, RANK will cause gaps (e.g., if there is a two-way tie for third, then there is no rank of 4, rather the next rank is 5). DENSE_RANK works the same as RANK but creates no gaps.

The CUME_DIST function finds the relative position of a specified value in a group of values; this function can be used to find the break point for percentiles (e.g., what value is the break point for the top 10 percent of sales or which customers are in the top 10 percent of sales?).

Different DBMS vendors will implement some or all of the SQL:1999 OLAP extension commands and possibly others specific to their products. For example, Teradata supports a SAMPLE clause, which allows samples of rows to be returned for the query. Samples can be random, with or without replacement, a percentage or count of rows can be specified for the answer set, and conditions can be placed to eliminate certain rows from the sample. SAMPLE is used to create subsets of a database that will be, for example, given different product discounts to see consumer behavior differences, or one sample will be used for a trial and another for a final promotion. SQL:1999 still is not a full-featured data warehouse querying and analysis tool, but it is a start at recognizing the special querying needs of decision support systems and business intelligence.

Online Analytical Processing (OLAP) Tools

A specialized class of tools has been developed to provide users with multidimensional views of their data. Such tools also usually offer users a graphical interface so that they can easily analyze their data. In the simplest case, data are viewed as a simple three-dimensional cube.

Online analytical processing (OLAP)
The use of a set of graphical tools that provides users with multidimensional views of their data and allows them to analyze the data using simple windowing techniques.

Relational OLAP (ROLAP)
OLAP tools that view the database as a traditional relational database in either a star schema or other normalized or denormalized set of tables.

Online analytical processing (OLAP) is the use of a set of query and reporting tools that provides users with multidimensional views of their data and allows them to analyze the data using simple windowing techniques. The term *online analytical processing* is intended to contrast with the more traditional term *online transaction processing (OLTP)*. The differences between these two types of processing were summarized in Table 9-1. The term *multidimensional analysis* is often used as a synonym for OLAP.

An example of a "data cube" (or multidimensional view) of data that is typical of OLAP is shown in Figure 9-21. This three-dimensional view corresponds quite closely to the star schema introduced in Figure 11-10. Two of the dimensions in Figure 9-21 correspond to the dimension tables (PRODUCT and PERIOD) in Figure 9-10, whereas the third dimension (named measures) corresponds to the data in the fact table (named SALES) in Figure 9-10.

OLAP is actually a general term for several categories of data warehouse and data mart access tools (Dyché, 2000). **Relational OLAP (ROLAP)** tools use variations of SQL

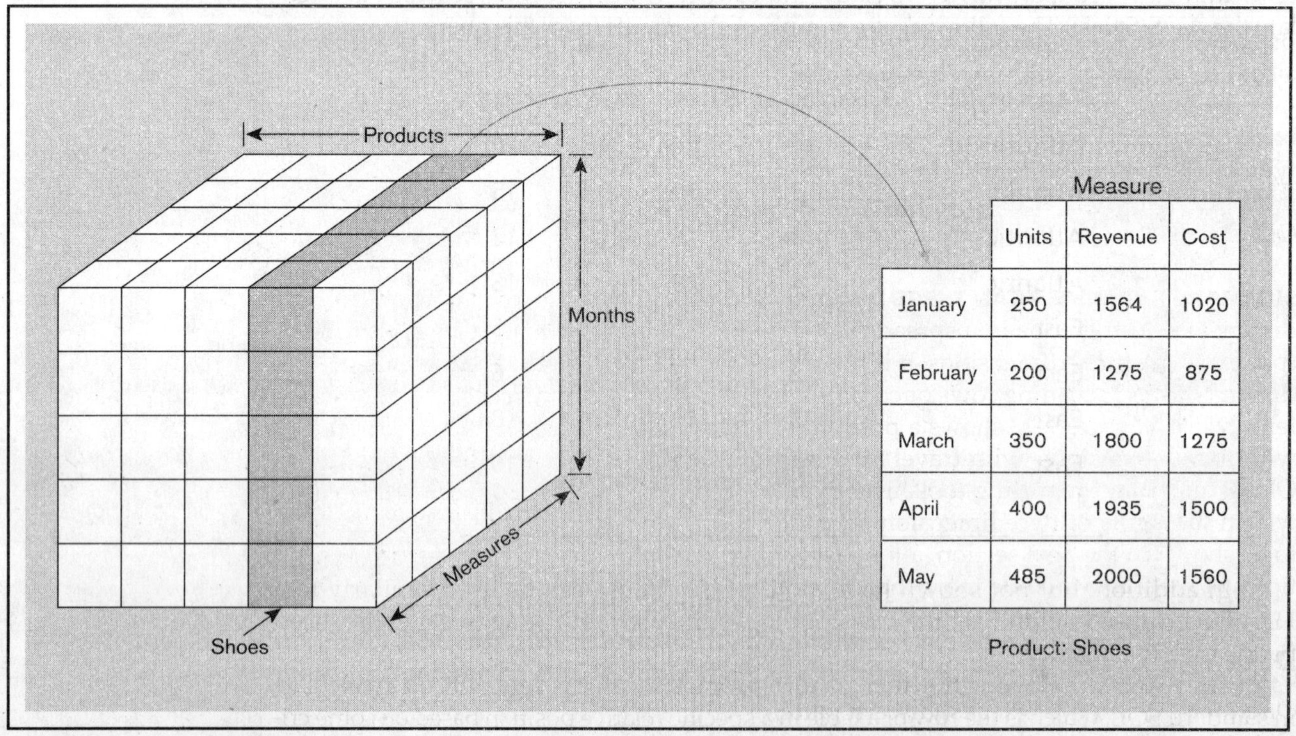

FIGURE 9-21 Slicing a data cube

and view the database as a traditional relational database, in either a star schema or another normalized or denormalized set of tables. ROLAP tools access the data warehouse or data mart directly. **Multidimensional OLAP (MOLAP)** tools load data into an intermediate structure, usually a three- or higher-dimensional array (hypercube). We illustrate MOLAP in the next few sections because of its popularity. It is important to note with MOLAP that the data are not simply viewed as a multidimensional hypercube, but rather a MOLAP data mart is created by extracting data from the data warehouse or data mart and then storing the data in a specialized separate data store through which data can be viewed only through a multidimensional structure. Other, less-common categories of OLAP tools are database OLAP (DOLAP), which includes OLAP functionality in the DBMS query language (there are proprietary, non-ANSI standard SQL systems that do this), and hybrid OLAP (HOLAP), which allows access via both multidimensional cubes or relational query languages.

Multidimensional OLAP (MOLAP)
OLAP tools that load data into an intermediate structure, usually a three- or higher-dimensional array.

SLICING A CUBE Figure 9-21 shows a typical MOLAP operation: slicing the data cube to produce a simple two-dimensional table or view. In Figure 9-21, this slice is for the product named shoes. The resulting table shows the three measures (units, revenues, and cost) for this product by period (or month). Other views can easily be developed by the user by means of simple "drag and drop" operations. This type of operation is often called *slicing and dicing* the cube.

Another operation closely related to slicing and dicing is data pivoting (similar to the pivoting possible in Microsoft Excel). This term refers to rotating the view for a particular data point to obtain another perspective. For example, Figure 9-21 shows sales of 400 units of shoes for April. The analyst could pivot this view to obtain (for example) the sales of shoes by store for the same month.

DRILL-DOWN Another type of operation often used in multidimensional analysis is *drill-down*—that is, analyzing a given set of data at a finer level of detail. An example of drill-down is shown in Figure 9-22. Figure 9-22a shows a summary report for the total sales of three package sizes for a given brand of paper towels: 2-pack, 3-pack, and 6-pack. However, the towels come in different colors, and the analyst wants a further breakdown of sales by color within each of these package sizes. Using an OLAP tool, this breakdown can be easily obtained using a "point-and-click" approach with a mouse device.

The result of the drill-down is shown in Figure 9-22b. Notice that a drill-down presentation is equivalent to adding another column to the original report. (In this case, a column was added for the attribute color.)

Executing a drill-down (as in this example) may require that the OLAP tool "reach back" to the data warehouse to obtain the detail data necessary for the drill-down. This type of operation can be performed by an OLAP tool (without user participation) only if an integrated set of metadata is available to that tool. Some tools even permit the OLAP tool to reach back to the operational data if necessary for a given query.

SUMMARIZING MORE THAN THREE DIMENSIONS It is straightforward to show a three-dimensional hypercube in a spreadsheet-type format using columns, rows, and sheets (pages) as the three dimensions. It is possible, however, to show data in more than three dimensions by cascading rows or columns and using drop-down selections to show different slices. Figure 9-23 shows a portion of a report from a Microsoft Excel pivot table with four dimensions, with travel method and number of days in cascading columns. OLAP query and reporting tools usually allow this way to handle sharing dimensions within the limits of two-dimension printing or display space. Data visualization tools, to be shown in the next section, allow using shapes, colors, and other properties of multiples of graphs to include more than three dimensions on the same display.

Data Visualization

Often the human eye can best discern patterns when data are represented graphically. **Data visualization** is the representation of data in graphical and multimedia formats for human analysis. Benefits of data visualization include the ability to better observe

Data visualization
The representation of data in graphical and multimedia formats for human analysis.

FIGURE 9-22 Example of drill-down
(a) Summary report

Brand	Package size	Sales
SofTowel	2-pack	$75
SofTowel	3-pack	$100
SofTowel	6-pack	$50

(b) Drill-down with color attribute added

Brand	Package size	Color	Sales
SofTowel	2-pack	White	$30
SofTowel	2-pack	Yellow	$25
SofTowel	2-pack	Pink	$20
SofTowel	3-pack	White	$50
SofTowel	3-pack	Green	$25
SofTowel	3-pack	Yellow	$25
SofTowel	6-pack	White	$30
SofTowel	6-pack	Yellow	$20

Country	(All)

Average of Price	Travel Method	No. of Days												
	Coach			Coach Total	Plane									Plane Total
Resort Name	4	5	7		6	7	8	10	14	16	21	32	60	
Aviemore			135	135										
Barcelona														
Black Forest	69			69										
Cork							269							269
Grand Canyon													1128	1128
Great Barrier Reef												750		750
Lake Geneva							699							699
London														
Los Angeles						295			375					335
Lyon									399					399
Malaga										234				234
Nerja					198				255					226.5
Nice						289								289
Paris–Euro Disney														
Prague		95		95										
Seville								199						199
Skiathos											429			429
Grand Total	69	95	135	99.66666667	198	292	484	199	343	234	429	750	1128	424.5384615

FIGURE 9-23 Sample pivot table with four dimensions: Country (pages), Resort Name (rows), Travel Method, and No. of Days (columns)

FIGURE 9-24 Sample data visualization with small multiples

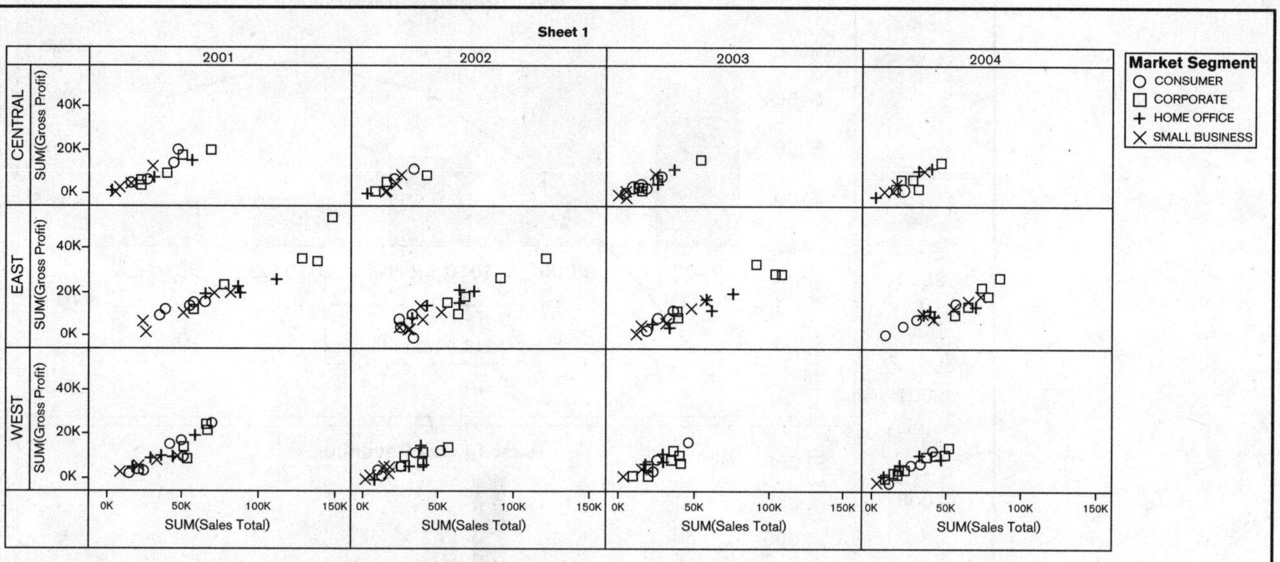

Note: Sum of Sales Total versus sum of Gross Profit broken down by Order Date Year versus Region. Shape shows details about Market Segment. Details are shown for Order Priority.

trends and patterns and to identify correlations and clusters. Data visualization is often used in conjunction with data mining and other analytical techniques.

In essence, data visualization is a way to show multidimensional data not as numbers and text but as graphs. Thus, precise values are often not shown, but rather the intent is to more readily show relationships between the data. As with OLAP tools, the data for the graphs are computed often from SQL queries against a database (or possibly from data in a spreadsheet). The SQL queries are generated automatically by the OLAP or data visualization software simply from the user indicating what he or she wants to see.

Figure 9-24 shows a simple visualization of sales data using the data visualization tool Tableau. This visualization uses a common technique called small multiples, which places many graphs on one page to support comparison. Each small graph plots metrics of SUM(Total Sales) on the horizontal axis and SUM(Gross Profit) on the vertical axis. There is a separate graph for the dimensions region and year; different market segments are shown via different symbols for the plot points. The user simply drags and drops these metrics and dimensions to a menu and then selects the style of visualization or lets the tool pick what it thinks would be the most illustrative type of graph. The user indicates what he or she wants to see and in what format, not how to retrieve the data from the data mart or data warehouse.

Business Performance Management and Dashboards

A business performance management (BPM) system allows managers to measure, monitor, and manage key activities and processes to achieve organizational goals. Dashboards are often used to provide an information system in support of BPM. Dashboards, just as those in a car or airplane cockpit, include a variety of displays to show different aspects of the organization. Often the top dashboard, an executive dashboard, is based on a balanced scorecard, in which different measures show metrics from different processes and disciplines, such as operations efficiency, financial status, customer service, sales, and human resources. Each display of a dashboard will address different areas in different ways. For example, one display may have alerts about key customers and their purchases. Another display may show key performance indicators for manufacturing, with "stoplight" symbols of red, yellow, and green to indicate if the measures are inside or outside tolerance limits. Each area of the organization may have its own dashboard to determine health of that function. For example, Figure 9-25 is a simple dashboard for one financial measure, revenue. The left panel shows dials about revenue over the past three years, with needles indicating where these measures fall within a desirable range. Other panels show more details to help a manager find the source of out-of-tolerance measures.

FIGURE 9-25 Sample dashboard

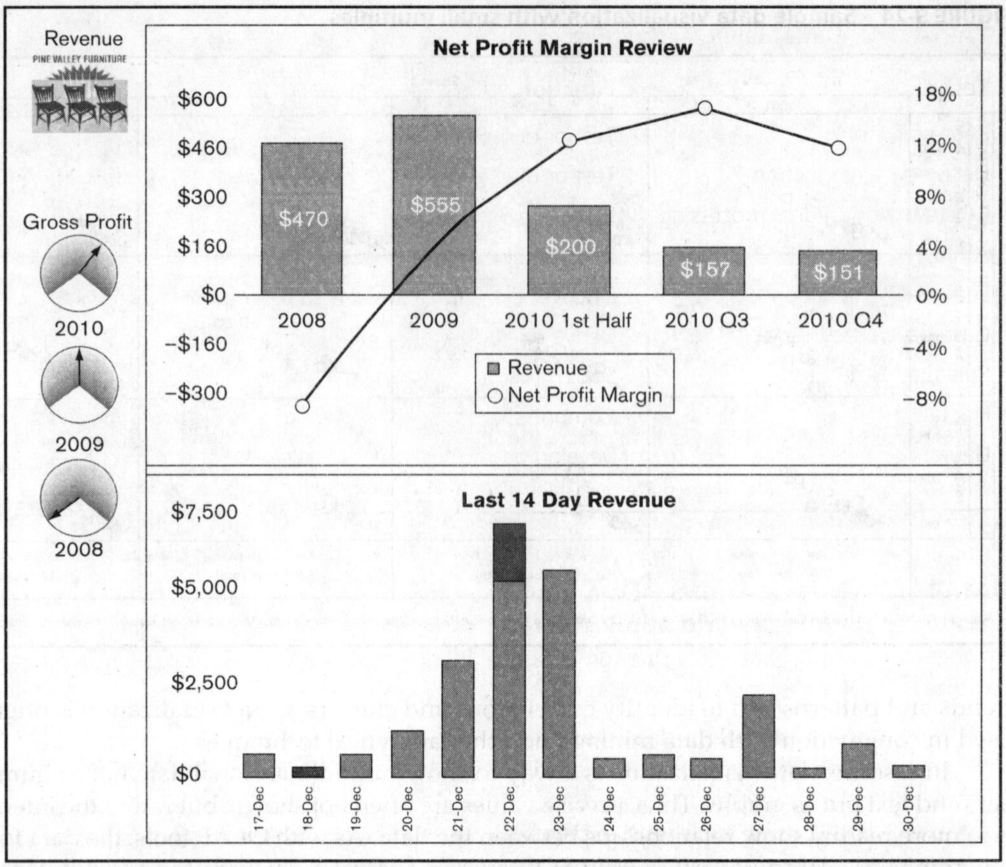

Each of the panels is a result of complex queries to a data mart or data warehouse. As a user wants to see more details, there often is a way to click on a graph to get a menu of choices for exploring the details behind the icon or graphic. A panel may be the result of running some predictive model against data in the data warehouse to forecast future conditions (so-called predictive modeling).

Integrative dashboard displays are possible only when data are consistent across each display, which requires a data warehouse and dependent data marts. Stand-alone dashboards for independent data marts can be developed, but then it is difficult to trace problems between areas (e.g., production bottlenecks due to higher sales than forecast).

Data-Mining Tools

With OLAP, users are searching for answers to questions, such as "Are health-care costs greater for single or married persons?" With data mining, users are looking for patterns or trends in a collection of facts or observations. **Data mining** is knowledge discovery using a sophisticated blend of techniques from traditional statistics, artificial intelligence, and computer graphics (Weldon, 1996).

Data mining
Knowledge discovery, using a sophisticated blend of techniques from traditional statistics, artificial intelligence, and computer graphics.

The goals of data mining are threefold:

1. *Explanatory* To explain some observed event or condition, such as why sales of pickup trucks have increased in Colorado
2. *Confirmatory* To confirm a hypothesis, such as whether two-income families are more likely to buy family medical coverage than single-income families
3. *Exploratory* To analyze data for new or unexpected relationships, such as what spending patterns are likely to accompany credit card fraud

DATA-MINING TECHNIQUES Several different techniques are commonly used for data mining. See Table 9-4 for a summary of the most common of these techniques. The choice of an appropriate technique depends on the nature of the data to be analyzed, as well as the size of the data set. Data mining can be performed against either the data marts or the enterprise data warehouse (or both).

TABLE 9-4 Data-Mining Techniques

Technique	Function
Regression	Test or discover relationships from historical data
Decision tree induction	Test or discover if . . . then rules for decision propensity
Clustering and signal processing	Discover subgroups or segments
Affinity	Discover strong mutual relationships
Sequence association	Discover cycles of events and behaviors
Case-based reasoning	Derive rules from real-world case examples
Rule discovery	Search for patterns and correlations in large data sets
Fractals	Compress large databases without losing information
Neural nets	Develop predictive models based on principles modeled after the human brain

DATA-MINING APPLICATIONS Data-mining techniques have been successfully used for a wide range of real-world applications. A summary of some of the typical types of applications, with examples of each type, is presented in Table 9-5. Data-mining applications are growing rapidly, for the following reasons:

- The amount of data in data warehouses and data marts is growing exponentially. Users need the type of automated techniques provided by data-mining tools to mine the knowledge in these data.
- New data-mining tools with expanded capabilities are continually being introduced.
- Increasing competitive pressures are forcing companies to make better use of the information and knowledge contained in their data.

For thorough coverage of data mining and all analytical aspects of business intelligence from a data warehousing perspective, see Turban et al. (2008).

TABLE 9-5 Typical Data-Mining Applications

Data-Mining Application	Example
Profiling populations	Developing profiles of high-value customers, credit risks, and credit-card fraud.
Analysis of business trends	Identifying markets with above-average (or below-average) growth.
Target marketing	Identifying customers (or customer segments) for promotional activity.
Usage analysis	Identifying usage patterns for products and services.
Campaign effectiveness	Comparing campaign strategies for effectiveness.
Product affinity	Identifying products that are purchased concurrently or identifying the characteristics of shoppers for certain product groups.
Customer retention and churn	Examining the behavior of customers who have left for competitors to prevent remaining customers from leaving.
Profitability analysis	Determining which customers are profitable, given the total set of activities the customer has with the organization.
Customer value analysis	Determining where valuable customers are at different stages in their life.
Upselling	Identifying new products or services to sell to a customer based upon critical events and life-style changes.

Source: Based on Dyché (2000).

Summary

Despite the vast quantities of data collected in organizations today, most managers have difficulty obtaining the information they need for decision making. Two major factors contribute to this "information gap." First, data are often heterogeneous and inconsistent as a result of the piecemeal systems development approaches that have commonly been used. Second, systems are developed (or acquired) primarily to satisfy operational objectives, with little thought given to the information needs of managers.

There are major differences between operational and informational systems and between the data that appear in those systems. Operational systems are used to run the business on a current basis, and the primary design goal is to provide high performance to users who process transactions and update databases. Informational systems are used to support managerial decision making, and the primary design goal is to provide ease of access and use for information workers.

The purpose of a data warehouse is to consolidate and integrate data from a variety of sources and to format those data in a context for making accurate business decisions. A data warehouse is an integrated and consistent store of subject-oriented data obtained from a variety of sources and formatted into a meaningful context to support decision making in an organization.

Most data warehouses today follow a three-layer architecture. The first layer consists of data distributed throughout the various operational systems. The second layer is an enterprise data warehouse, which is a centralized, integrated data warehouse that is the control point and single source of all data made available to end users for decision support applications. The third layer is a series of data marts. A data mart is a data warehouse whose data are limited in scope for the decision-making needs of a particular user group. A data mart can be independent of an enterprise data warehouse (EDW), derived from the EDW, or a logical subset of the EDW.

The data layer in an enterprise data warehouse is called the reconciled data layer. The characteristics of this data layer (ideally) are the following: It is detailed, historical, normalized, comprehensive, and quality controlled. Reconciled data are obtained by filling the enterprise data warehouse or operational data store from the various operational systems. Reconciling the data requires four steps: capturing the data from the source systems, scrubbing the data (to remove inconsistencies), transforming the data (to convert it to the format required in the data warehouse), and loading and indexing the data in the data warehouse. Reconciled data are not normally accessed directly by end users.

The data layer in the data marts is referred to as the derived data layer. These are the data that are accessed by end users for their decision support applications.

Data are most often stored in a data mart using a variation of the relational model called the star schema, or dimensional model. A star schema is a simple database design where dimensional data are separated from fact or event data. A star schema consists of two types of tables: dimension tables and fact tables. The size of a fact table depends, in part, on the grain (or level of detail) in that table. Fact tables with over one billion rows are common in data warehouse applications today. There are several variations of the star schema, including models with multiple fact tables and snowflake schemas that arise when one or more dimensions have a hierarchical structure. The emerging technology of column-based databases provide new options for storing and accessing data warehouse and data mart data.

A variety of end-user interfaces are available to access and analyze decision support data. Online analytical processing (OLAP) is the use of a set of graphical tools that provides users with multidimensional views of their data (data are normally viewed as a cube). Increasingly data visualization tools make multidimensional data easier to understand. OLAP facilitates data analysis operations such as slice and dice, data pivoting, and drill-down. Dashboards and business performance monitoring provide high-level views to assist managers in identifying into which areas to drill-down or where to pivot data. Data mining is a form of knowledge discovery that uses a sophisticated blend of techniques from traditional statistics, artificial intelligence, and computer graphics.

Chapter Review

Key Terms

Conformed dimension *403*
Data mart *385*
Data mining *420*
Data visualization *417*
Data warehouse *379*
Dependent data mart *387*
Derived data *391*
Enterprise data warehouse (EDW) *387*
Grain *400*
Independent data mart *385*
Informational system *383*
Logical data mart *388*
Multidimensional OLAP (MOLAP) *417*
Online analytical processing (OLAP) *416*
Operational data store (ODS) *388*
Operational system *382*
Periodic data *393*
Real-time data warehouse *389*
Reconciled data *391*
Relational OLAP (ROLAP) *416*
Snowflake schema *408*
Star schema *397*
Transient data *393*

Review Questions

1. Define each of the following terms:
   a. data warehouse
   b. data mart
   c. reconciled data
   d. derived data
   e. online analytical processing
   f. data mining
   g. star schema
   h. snowflake schema
   i. grain
   j. conformed dimension
2. Match the following terms and definitions:

____ periodic data	a.	lost previous data content
____ data mart	b.	detailed historical data
____ star schema	c.	data not altered or deleted
____ data mining	d.	data warehouse of limited scope
____ reconciled data	e.	dimension and fact tables
____ dependent data mart	f.	form of knowledge discovery
____ data visualization	g.	data filled from a data warehouse
____ transient data	h.	structure that results from hierarchical dimensions
____ snowflake schema	i.	data represented in graphical formats

3. Contrast the following terms:
   a. transient data; periodic data
   b. data warehouse; data mart; operational data store
   c. reconciled data; derived data
   d. fact table; dimension table
   e. star schema; snowflake schema
   f. independent data mart; dependent data mart; logical data mart
4. List the five major trends that necessitate data warehousing in many organizations today.
5. Briefly describe the major components of a data warehouse architecture.
6. List the three types of metadata that appear in a three-layer data warehouse architecture and briefly describe the purpose of each.
7. List four characteristics of a data warehouse.
8. List five claimed limitations of independent data marts.
9. List two claimed benefits of independent data marts.
10. Briefly describe three types of operations that can easily be performed with OLAP tools.
11. List four objectives of derived data.
12. Is a star schema a relational data model? Why or why not?
13. Explain how the volatility of a data warehouse is different from the volatility of a database for an operational information system.
14. Explain the pros and cons of logical data marts.
15. What is a helper table, and why is it often used to help organize derived data?
16. Describe the characteristics of a surrogate key as used in a data warehouse or data mart.
17. Why is time almost always a dimension in a data warehouse or data mart?
18. What is the purpose of conformed dimensions for different star schemas within the same data warehousing environment?
19. Can a fact table have no nonkey attributes? Why or why not?
20. In what ways are dimension tables often not normalized?
21. What is a hierarchy as it relates to a dimension table?
22. What is the meaning of the phrase "slowly changing dimension"?
23. Explain the most common approach used to handle slowly changing dimensions.
24. One of the claimed characteristics of a data warehouse is that it is nonupdateable. What does this mean?
25. In what ways are a data staging area and an enterprise data warehouse different?
26. How are logical data marts more helpful under certain circumstances?
27. What are the applications for real-time data warehouses? What factors characterize the usage of real-time data warehouses?
28. How is dimension modeling different from E-R modeling? Can E-R modeling system be applied to data warehouse?

Problems and Exercises

1. Examine the three tables with student data shown in Figure 9-1. Design a single-table format that will hold all of the data (nonredundantly) that are contained in these three tables. Choose column names that you believe are most appropriate for these data.
2. The following table shows some simple student data as of the date 06/20/2010:

Key	Name	Major
001	Amy	Music
002	Tom	Business
003	Sue	Art
004	Joe	Math
005	Ann	Engineering

The following transactions occur on 06/21/2010:

- Student 004 changes major from Math to Business.
- Student 005 is deleted from the file.
- New student 006 is added to the file: Name is Jim, Major is Phys Ed.

The following transactions occur on 06/22/2010:

- Student 003 changes major from Art to History.
- Student 006 changes major from Phys Ed to Basket Weaving.

Your assignment involves two parts:

a. Construct tables for 06/21/2010 and 06/22/2010, reflecting these transactions; assume that the data are transient (refer to Figure 9-7).
b. Construct tables for 06/21/2010 and 06/22/2010, reflecting these transactions; assume that the data are periodic (refer to Figure 9-8).

3. Millennium College wants you to help design a star schema to record grades for courses completed by students. There are four dimension tables, with attributes as follows:

CourseSection	Attributes: CourseID, SectionNumber, CourseName, Units, RoomID, and RoomCapacity. During a given semester, the college offers an average of 500 course sections.
Professor	Attributes: ProfID, ProfName, Title, DepartmentID, and DepartmentName. There are typically 200 professors at Millennium at any given time.
Student	Attributes: StudentID, StudentName, and Major. Each course section has an average of 40 students, and students typically take five courses per period.
Period	Attributes: SemesterID, and Year. The database will contain data for 30 periods (a total of 10 years).

The only fact that is to be recorded in the fact table is CourseGrade.

a. Design a star schema for this problem. See Figure 9-10 for the format you should follow.
b. Estimate the number of rows in the fact table, using the assumptions stated previously.
c. Estimate the total size of the fact table (in bytes), assuming that each field has an average of 5 bytes.
d. If you didn't want to or didn't have to stick with a strict star schema for this data mart, how would you change the design? Why?
e. Various characteristics of sections, professors, and students change over time. How do you propose designing the star schema to allow for these changes? Why?

4. Having mastered the principles of normalization described in Chapter 4, you recognize immediately that the star schema you developed for Millennium College (Problem and Exercise 3) is not in third normal form. Using these principles, convert the star schema to a snowflake schema. What impact (if any) does this have on the size of the fact table for this problem?
5. You are to construct a star schema for Simplified Automobile Insurance Company (see Kimball, 1996b, for a more realistic example). The relevant dimensions, dimension attributes, and dimension sizes are as follows:

InsuredParty	Attributes: InsuredPartyID and Name. There is an average of two insured parties for each policy and covered item.
CoverageItem	Attributes: CoverageKey and Description. There is an average of 10 covered items per policy.
Agent	Attributes: AgentID and AgentName. There is one agent for each policy and covered item.
Policy	Attributes: PolicyID and Type. The company has approximately 1 million policies at the present time.
Period	Attributes: DateKey and FiscalPeriod.

Facts to be recorded for each combination of these dimensions are PolicyPremium, Deductible, and NumberOfTransactions.

a. Design a star schema for this problem. See Figure 9-10 for the format you should follow.
b. Estimate the number of rows in the fact table, using the assumptions stated previously.
c. Estimate the total size of the fact table (in bytes), assuming an average of 5 bytes per field.

6. Simplified Automobile Insurance Company would like to add a Claims dimension to its star schema (see Problem and Exercise 5). Attributes of Claim are ClaimID, ClaimDescription, and ClaimType. Attributes of the fact table are now PolicyPremium, Deductible, and MonthlyClaimTotal.
   a. Extend the star schema from Problem and Exercise 5 to include these new data.
   b. Calculate the estimated number of rows in the fact table, assuming that the company experiences an average of 2000 claims per month.
7. Millennium College (see Problem and Exercise 3) now wants to include new data about course sections: the department offering the course, the academic unit to which the department reports, and the budget unit to which the department is assigned. Change your answer to Problem and Exercise 3 to accommodate these new data requirements. Explain why you implemented the changes in the star schema the way you did.
8. As mentioned in the chapter, Kimball (1997), Inmon (1997, 2000), and Armstrong (2000) have debated the merits of independent and dependent data marts and normalized versus denormalized data marts. Obtain copies of these articles from your library or from online sources and summarize the arguments made by each side of this debate. See also **www.intelligententerprise.com/030917/615warehouse1_1.shtml** for a 2003 article clarifying the Kimball position.
9. A food manufacturing company needs a data mart to summarize facts about orders to move goods. Some orders transfer goods internally, some are sales to customers, some are purchases from vendors, and some are returns of goods from customers. The company needs to treat customers, vendors, plants, and storage locations as distinct dimensions that can be involved at both ends of a movement event. For each type of destination or origin, the company wants to know the type of location (i.e., customer, vendor, etc.), name, city, and state. Facts about each movement include dollar volume moved, cost of movement, and revenue collected from the move (if any, and this can be negative for a return). Design a star-type schema to represent this data mart. Hint: After you design a typical star schema, think about how you might simplify the design through the use of generalization.
10. Visit **www.ralphkimball.com** and locate Kimball University Design Tip 37. Study this design tip and draw the dimensional model for the recommended design for a "pipeline" application for university admissions.
11. Visit **www.teradatastudentnetwork.com** and download the dimensional modeling tool located under the downloadable software section. (Your instructor will have to give you the current password to access this site.) Use this tool to draw your answers to Problems and Exercises 3, 5, 6, and 9. Write a report that comments on the usefulness of this modeling tool. What other features would you like the tool to have?

PINE VALLEY FURNITURE

12. Pine Valley Furniture wants you to help design a data mart for analysis of sales. The subjects of the data mart are as follows:

Salesperson	Attributes: SalespersonID, Years with PVFC, SalespersonName, and SupervisorRating.
Product	Attributes: ProductID, Category, Weight, and YearReleasedToMarket.
Customer	Attributes: CustomerID, CustomerName, CustomerSize, and Location. Location is also a hierarchy over which they want to be able to aggregate data. Each Location has attributes LocationID, AverageIncome, PopulationSize, and NumberOfRetailers. For any given customer, there is an arbitrary number of levels in the Location hierarchy.
Period	Attributes: DayID, FullDate, WeekdayFlag, and LastDay of MonthFlag.

Data for this data mart come from an enterprise data warehouse, but there are many systems of record that feed this data to the data warehouse. The only fact that is to be recorded in the fact table is Dollar Sales.

a. Design a typical multidimensional schema to represent this data mart.
b. Among the various dimensions that change is Customer information. In particular, over time, customers may change their location and size. Redesign your answer to part a to accommodate keeping the history of these changes so that the history of DollarSales can be matched with the precise customer characteristics at the time of the sales.

Problems 13 through 18 are based upon the Fitchwood Insurance Company case study, which is described next.

Fitchwood Insurance Company, which is primarily involved in the sale of annuity products, would like to design a data mart for its sales and marketing organization. Presently, the OLTP system is a legacy system residing on a Novell network consisting of approximately 600 different flat files. For the purposes of our case study, we can assume that 30 different flat files are going to be used for the data mart. Some of these flat files are transaction files that change constantly. The OLTP system is shut down overnight on Friday evening beginning at 6 P.M. for backup. During that time, the flat files are copied to another server, an extraction process is run, and the extracts are sent via FTP to a UNIX server. A process is run on the UNIX server to load the extracts into Oracle and rebuild the star schema. For the initial loading of the data mart, all information from the 30 files was extracted and loaded. On a weekly basis, only additions and updates will be included in the extracts.

Although the data contained in the OLTP system are broad, the sales and marketing organization would like to focus on the sales data only. After substantial analysis, the ERD shown in Figure 9-26 was developed to describe the data to be used to populate the data mart.

From this ERD, we get the set of relations shown in Figure 9-27. Sales and marketing is interested in viewing all sales data by territory, effective date, type of policy, and face value. In addition, the data mart should be able to provide reporting by individual agent on sales as well as commissions earned. Occasionally, the sales territories are revised (i.e., zip codes are added or deleted). The Last Redistrict attribute of the Territory table is used to store the date of the last revision. Some sample queries and reports are listed here:

- Total sales per month, by territory, by type of policy
- Total sales per quarter by territory, by type of policy
- Total sales per month by agent, by type of policy
- Total sales per month by agent, by zip code
- Total face value of policies, by month of effective date
- Total face value of policies by month of effective date, by agent
- Total face value of policies, by quarter of effective date
- Total number of policies in force, by agent
- Total number of policies not in force, by agent
- Total face value of all policies sold by an individual agent
- Total initial commission paid on all policies to an agent

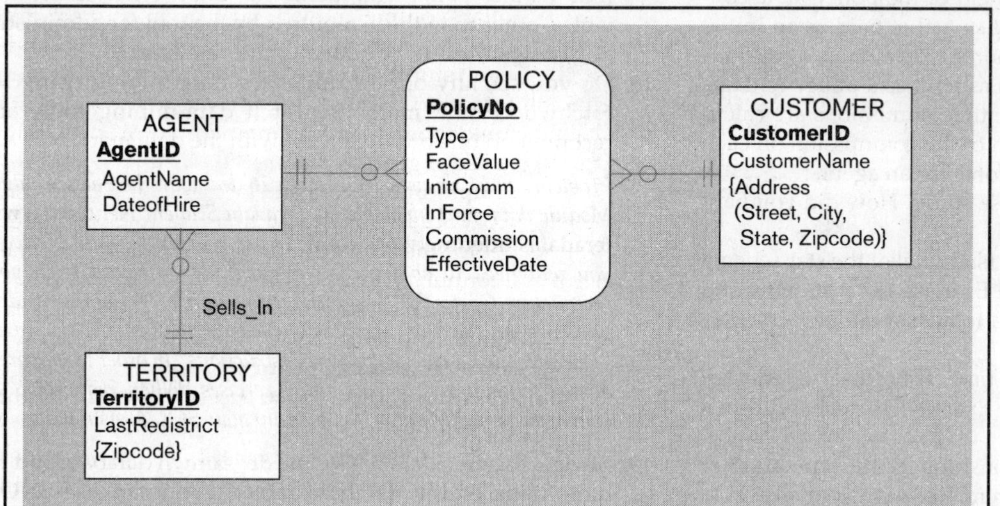

FIGURE 9-26 Fitchwood Insurance Company ERD

FIGURE 9-27 Relations for Fitchwood Insurance Company

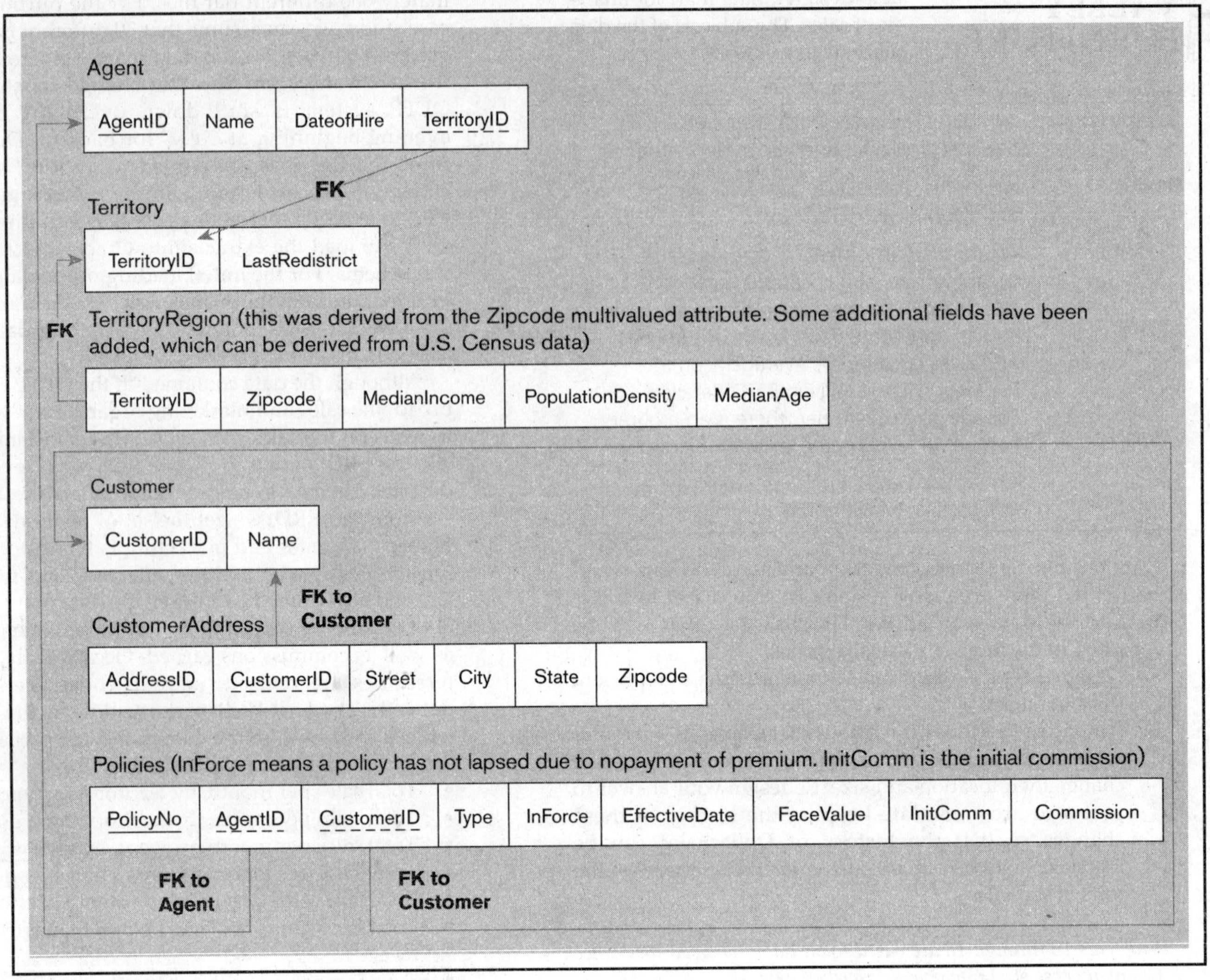

- Total initial commission paid on policies sold in a given month by agent
- Total commissions earned by month, by agent
- Top-selling agent by territory, by month

Commissions are paid to an agent upon the initial sale of a policy. The InitComm field of the policy table contains the percentage of the face value paid as an initial commission. The Commission field contains a percentage that is paid each month as long as a policy remains active or in force. Each month, commissions are calculated by computing the sum of the commission on each individual policy that is in force for an agent.

13. Create a star schema for this case study. How did you handle the time dimension?

14. Would you prefer to normalize (snowflake) the star schema of your answer to Problem and Exercise 13? If so, how and why? Redesign the star schema to accommodate your recommended changes.

15. Agents change territories over time. If necessary, redesign your answer to Problem and Exercise 14 to handle this changing dimensional data.

16. Customers may have relationships with one another (e.g., spouses, parents and children). Redesign your answer to Problem and Exercise 15 to accommodate these relationships.

17. Management would like to use the data mart for drill-down online reporting. For example, a sales manager might want to view a report of total sales for an agent by month and then drill down into the individual types of policies to see how sales are broken down by type of policy. What type of tool would you recommend for this? What additional tables, other than those required by the tool for administration, might need to be added to the data mart?

18. Do you see any opportunities for data mining using the Fitchwood data mart? Research data-mining tools and recommend one or two for use with the data mart.

*Problems and Exercises 19 through 26 deal with the Sales Analysis Module data mart available on Teradata Student Network (***www.teradatastudentnetwork.com***). To use Teradata Student Network, you will need to obtain the current TSN password from your instructor. Go to the Assignments section of Teradata Student Network or the this textbook's Website to find the document "MDBM 10e SAM Assignment Instructions" in order to prepare to do the following Problems and Exercises. When requested, use course password MDBM10e to set up your SQL Assistant account.*

19. Review the metadata file for the db_samwh database and the definitions of the database tables. (You can use SHOW TABLE commands to display the DDL for tables.) Explain the methods used in this database for modeling hierarchies. Are hierarchies modeled as described in this chapter?

20. Review the metadata file for the db_samwh database and the definitions of the database tables. (You can use SHOW TABLE commands to display the DDL for tables.) Explain what dimension data, if any, are maintained to support slowly changing dimensions. If there are slowly changing dimension data, are they maintained as described in this chapter?
21. Review the metadata file for the db_samwh database and the definitions of the database tables. (You can use SHOW TABLE commands to display the DDL for tables.) Are dimension table conformed in this data mart? Explain.
22. The database you are using was developed by MicroStrategy, a leading business intelligence software vendor. The MicroStrategy software is also available on TSN. Most business intelligence tools generate SQL to retrieve the data they need to produce the reports and charts and to run the models users want. Go to the Apply & Do area on the Teradata Student Network main screen and select MicroStrategy, then select MicroStrategy Application Modules, and then the Sales Force Analysis Module. Then make the following selections: Shared Reports → Sales Performance Analysis → Quarterly Revenue Trend by Sales Region → 2005 → Run Report. Go to the File menu and select the Report Details option. You will then see the SQL statement that was used, along with some MicroStrategy functionality, to produce the chart in the report. Cut and paste this SQL code into SQL Assistant and run this query in SQL Assistant. (You may want to save the code as an intermediate step to a Word file so you don't lose it.) Produce a file with the code and the SQL Assistant query result (answer set) for your instructor. You have now done what is called *screen scrapping* the SQL. This is often necessary to create data for analysis that is beyond the capabilities of a business intelligence package.
23. Take the query you scrapped from Problem and Exercise 22 and modify it to show only the U.S. region grouped by each quarter, not just for 2005 but for all years available, in order by quarter. Label the total orders by quarter with the heading TOTAL and the region ID simply as ID in the result. Produce a file with the revised SQL code and the answer set for your instructor.
24. Using the MDIFF "ordered analytical function" in Teradata SQL (see the Functions and Operators manual), show the differences (label the difference CHANGE) in TOTAL (which you calculated in the previous Problem and Exercise) from quarter to quarter. Hint: You will likely create a derived table based on your query above, similar to what is shown in examples in the Functions and Operators manual; when you do so, you will need to give the derived table an alias name and then use that alias name in the outer select statement when you ask to display the results of the query. Save your query and answer set to a file to give your instructor. (By the way, MDIFF is not standard SQL; this is an analytical SQL function proprietary to Teradata.)
25. Because data warehouses and even data marts can become very large, it may be sufficient to work with a subset of data for some analyses. Create a sample of orders from 2004 using the SAMPLE SQL command (which is standard SQL); put a randomized allocation of 10% of the rows into the sample. Include in the sample results the order ID, product ID, sales rep region ID, month description, and order amount. Show the results, in sequence, by month. Run the query two times to check that the sample is actually random. Put your SQL query and a portion of the two answer sets (enough to show that they are different) into a file for your instructor.
26. GROUP BY by itself creates subtotals by category, and the ROLLUP extension to GROUP BY creates even more categories for subtotals. Using all the orders, do a rollup to get total order amounts by product, sales region, and month and all combinations, including a grand total. Display the results sorted by product, region, and month. Put your query and the first portion of the answer set, including all of product 1 and a few rows for product 2, into a file for your instructor. Also, do a regular GROUP BY and put this query and the similar results from it into the file and then place an explanation in the file of how GROUP BY and GROUP BY with ROLLUP are different.
27. The marketing arm of PMPL, a FMCG company, needs data warehousing for its sales data. The company's sales distribution channel is mainly with pre-identified wholesalers. The company has several depots all over the country, from where the sales data is collated over their country-wise enterprise intranet over VPN, at their corporate office in Bangalore. The following are the dimension tables with their attributes:

    Product Attributes:
    ProdID, ProductName, ProdCategory, ProdCostPrice, ProdSellPrice (There typical 25 products on offer)

    Invoice Attributes:
    Invno, InvDate, WholesalerID, DepotID, Qty, ProdID, PrdRate, TotalAmount, PriceDiscount
    (Around 700–800 invoices are generated countrywide across depots)

    Wholesaler Attributes:
    WholesalerID, Wholesaler_Owner, WS_Address, WS_Phone, WS_DepotID
    (The FMCG has around 500 distributors spread across the country and depots)

    Depot Attributes:
    DepotID, DepotRegion, DepotManager
    (There are around 15 depots in different regions of the country)

    a. Design a star schema for this problem.
    b. Describe the OLAP uses of this data warehouse.
    c. Estimate the numbers of rows in the fact table.

Field Exercises

1. Visit an organization that has developed a data warehouse and interview the data administrator or other key participant. Discuss the following issues:
    a. How satisfied are users with the data warehouse? In what ways has it improved their decision making?
    b. Does the warehouse employ a three-tier architecture?
    c. Does the architecture employ one or more data marts? If so, are they dependent or independent?
    d. What end-user tools are employed? Is data mining used?
    e. What were the main obstacles or difficulties overcome in developing the data warehouse environment?

2. Visit the following Web sites. Browse these sites for additional information on data warehouse topics, including case examples of warehouse implementations, descriptions of the latest warehouse-related products, and announcements of conferences and other events.
   a. The Data Warehousing Institute: **www.tdwi.org**
   b. Knowledge Discovery Mine: **www.kdnuggets.com**
   c. Data Mining Institute: **www.datamining.org**
   d. An electronic data warehousing journal: **www.tdan.com**
3. Visit **www.teradatastudentnetwork.com** and use the various business intelligence software products available on this site. Compare the different products, based on the types of business intelligence problems for which they are most appropriate. Also, search the content of this Web site for articles, case studies, podcasts, training materials, and other items related to data warehousing. Select one item, study it, and write an executive briefing on its contents.

References

Armstrong, R. 1997. "A Rebuttal to the Dimensional Modeling Manifesto." A white paper produced by NCR Corporation.

Armstrong, R. 2000. "Avoiding Data Mart Traps." *Teradata Review* (Summer): 32–37.

Chisholm, M. 2000. "A New Understanding of Reference Data." *DM Review* 10,10 (October): 60, 84–85.

Devlin, B., and P. Murphy. 1988. "An Architecture for a Business Information System." *IBM Systems Journal* 27,1 (March): 60–80.

Dyché, J. 2000. *e-Data: Turning Data into Information with Data Warehousing*. Reading, MA: Addison-Wesley.

Hackathorn, R. 1993. *Enterprise Database Connectivity*. New York: Wiley.

Hackathorn, R. 2002. "Current Practices in Active Data Warehousing," available at **www.teradata.com** under White Papers.

Hays, C. 2004. "What They Know About You." *New York Times*. November 14: section 3, page 1.

Imhoff, C. 1998. "The Operational Data Store: Hammering Away." *DM Review* 8,7 (July) available at **www.dmreview.com/article_sub.cfm?articleID=470**.

Imhoff, C. 1999. "The Corporate Information Factory." *DM Review* 9,12 (December), available at **www.dmreview.com/article_sub.cfm?articleID=1667**.

Inmon, B. 1997. "Iterative Development in the Data Warehouse." *DM Review* 7,11 (November): 16, 17.

Inmon, W. 1998. "The Operational Data Store: Designing the Operational Data Store." *DM Review* 8,7 (July), available at **www.dmreview.com/article_sub.cfm?articleID=469**.

Inmon, W. 1999. "What Happens When You Have Built the Data Mart First?" *TDAN* accessed at **www.tdan.com/i012fe02.htm** (no longer available as of June, 2009).

Inmon, W. 2000. "The Problem with Dimensional Modeling." *DM Review* 10,5 (May): 68–70.

Inmon, W. 2006. "Granularity of Data: Lowest Level of Usefulness." *B-Eye Network* (December 14) available at **www.b-eye-network.com/view/3276**.

Inmon, W., and R. D. Hackathorn. 1994. *Using the Data Warehouse*. New York: Wiley.

Kimball, R. 1996a. *The Data Warehouse Toolkit*. New York: Wiley.

Kimball, R. 1996b. "Slowly Changing Dimensions." *DBMS* 9,4 (April): 18–20.

Kimball, R. 1997. "A Dimensional Modeling Manifesto." *DBMS* 10,9 (August): 59.

Kimball, R. 1998a. "Pipelining Your Surrogates." *DBMS* 11,6 (June): 18–22.

Kimball, R. 1998b. "Help for Hierarchies." *DBMS* 11,9 (September) 12–16.

Kimball, R. 1999. "When a Slowly Changing Dimension Speeds Up." *Intelligent Enterprise* 2,8 (August 3): 60–62.

Kimball, R. 2001. "Declaring the Grain." from Kimball University, Design Tip 21, available at **www.ralphkimball.com**.

Kimball, R. 2002. "What Changed?" *Intelligent Enterprise* 5,8 (August 12): 22, 24, 52.

Kimball, R. 2006. "Adding a Row Change Reason Attribute." from Kimball University, Design Tip 80, available at **www.ralphkimball.com**.

Marco, D. 2000. *Building and Managing the Meta Data Repository: A Full Life-Cycle Guide*. New York: Wiley.

Marco, D. 2003. "Independent Data Marts: Stranded on Islands of Data, Part 1." *DM Review* 13,4 (April): 30, 32, 63.

Meyer, A. 1997. "The Case for Dependent Data Marts." *DM Review* 7,7 (July–August): 17–24.

Mundy, J. 2001. "Smarter Data Warehouses." *Intelligent Enterprise* 4,2 (February 16): 24–29.

Poe, V. 1996. *Building a Data Warehouse for Decision Support*. Upper Saddle River, NJ: Prentice Hall.

Ross, M. 2009. "Kimball University: The 10 Essential Rules of Dimensional Modeling." (May 29), available at **www.intelligententerprise.com/showArticle.jhtml?articleID=217700810**.

TDWI. 2006. "What Works: Best Practice Awards 2006." (November), available at **www.tdwi.org/Publications/WhatWorks/display.aspx?id=8209**.

Turban, E., R. Sharda, J. Aronson, and D. King 2008. *Business Intelligence*. Upper Saddle River, NJ: Prentice Hall.

Weldon, J. L. 1996. "Data Mining and Visualization." *Database Programming & Design* 9,5 (May): 21–24.

Whiting, R. 2003. "The Data-Warehouse Advantage." *InformationWeek* 648 (July 28): 63–66.

Further Reading

Gallo, J. 2002. "Operations and Maintenance in a Data Warehouse Environment." *DM Review* 12,12 (2003 Resource Guide): 12–16.

Goodhue, D., M. Mybo, and L. Kirsch. 1992. "The Impact of Data Integration on the Costs and Benefits of Information Systems." *MIS Quarterly* 16,3 (September): 293–311.

Jenks, B. 1997. "Tiered Data Warehouse." *DM Review* 7,10 (October): 54–57.

Mundy, J., W. Thornthwaite, and R. Kimball. 2006. *The Microsoft Data Warehouse Toolkit: With SQL Server 2005 and the Microsoft Business Intelligence Toolset*. Hoboken, NJ: Wiley.

Web Resources

www.teradata.com/tdmo Web site of *Teradata* magazine, which contains articles on the technology and application of the Teradata data warehouse system. (This magazine recently changed its name. Articles under the magazine's new and previous names can be found at **www.teradatamagazine.com**.)

www.dmreview.com Web site of *DM Review*, a monthly trade magazine that contains articles and columns about data warehousing.

www.tdan.com An electronic journal on data warehousing.

http://www.inmoncif.com/home/ Web site of Bill Inmon, a leading authority on data management and data warehousing.

www.ralphkimball.com Web site of Ralph Kimball, a leading authority on data warehousing.

www.tdwi.org Web site of The Data Warehousing Institute, an industry group that focuses on data warehousing methods and applications.

www.datawarehousing.org The Data Warehousing Knowledge Center, which contains links to many vendors.

www.olapreport.com Web site that provides detailed information about OLAP products and applications.

www.information-quality.com Web site for Larry English, one of the leaders in data quality management.

www.teradatastudentnetwork.com A portal to resources for databases, data warehousing, and business intelligence. Data sets from this textbook are stored on the software site, from which you can use SQL, data mining, dimensional modeling, and other tools. Also, some very large data warehouse databases are available through this site to resources at the University of Arkansas. New articles and Webinars are added to this site all the time, so visit it frequently or subscribe to its RSS feed service to know when new materials are added. You will need to obtain a password to this site from your instructor.

CASE
Mountain View Community Hospital

Case Description

In most respects, Mountain View Community Hospital (MVCH) has followed a carefully planned approach to designing, selecting, and installing its information systems. The organization developed an enterprise data model to guide its database development (Chapters 2–7). The hospital installed computer systems to support most of the routine operations in the organization. For example, there are systems for patient accounting, administrative services, and financial management. Many systems were acquired from outside vendors after a careful selection process.

Despite this careful planning, management is aware that there are some deficiencies and limitations in the present hospital information systems. In addition to the challenge of interfacing systems in MVCH's heterogeneous environment of platforms and applications, two further problems have been noted:

1. Data are often duplicated in different files and databases, in different formats, and even in different media. For example, one set of patient data (used for billing purposes) resides in a patient accounting system based on a relational database. On the other hand, many patient medical records are maintained in a manual system (one folder per patient), or other applications, such as Dr. Z's MS management system.
2. The systems are designed primarily to support operational (or transaction) processing but are not generally well suited to providing management information or to support analytical studies that are increasingly required for modern hospital management.

Management feels that these problems must be addressed, and that better and more centralized access to the hospital's operational, financial, and clinical information is a strategic necessity for two reasons. First, like many other hospitals, MVCH is being driven by the trend to managed care and the resulting need to contain costs while maintaining or improving clinical outcomes. As a consequence, MVCH must closely track and analyze its clinical and financial data related to patient care services and provide that data to its administrative and clinical decision makers in a timely fashion. Second, Sarbanes-Oxley is beginning to have an impact. MVCH, as a not-for-profit organization, is not a covered entity under SOX. However, both Mr. Lopez, MVCH's CFO, and Ms. Baker, the hospital's CEO, have come under pressure from board members from the corporate world to certify the accuracy of financial statements, certify the accuracy of the hospital's annual information return filed with the IRS, and provide timely reports. As a result, both Mr. Lopez and Ms. Baker have begun to demand more timely access to financial data for decision making, business intelligence, and financial reporting. The board of directors is also asking that reports include trend information and graphic presentations. In light of these issues, management wishes to investigate whether the techniques of data warehousing might be successfully applied in their organization.

A typical hospital data warehouse often contains four types of data: patient records; doctor, clinic, and hospital records; drug and pharmaceutical company records; and HMO and insurance company records. However, the small size of the hospital may not justify a large-scale data warehouse development project. Instead, several smaller data marts may be more feasible. After some investigation, MVCH plans to test the concept with two small prototype data marts:

1. A data mart that will record summary information regarding tests and procedures performed by physicians at the hospital.
2. A more detailed data mart that will record the details of tests and procedures performed by physicians for individual patients.

Case Questions

1. What are some of the advantages that a hospital such as MVCH might realize from a data warehouse and/or data mart(s)? How can a data warehouse/ data mart help with improving the following?
   - Operational efficiency
   - Treatment efficiency
   - Clinical outcomes
   - Patient safety
   - Clinical research
2. How could a data mart be used to improve the quality of emergency room care?
3. Should MVCH consider developing data marts (such as those proposed) without an established data warehouse? What are the risks associated with that approach? Do you think that an organization can develop a prototype data mart to investigate "proof of concept" without an established data warehouse? Discuss some of the likely advantages and disadvantages of this approach.
4. How would you address concerns about security and HIPAA's privacy mandates that prohibit unauthorized use of patient-identifiable information?
5. If MVCH were to develop a data mart, do you think that OLAP tools should be used? If yes, which type (OLAP, ROLAP, or MOLAP)?
6. What types of data-mining operations could be used (e.g., predictive modeling, cluster analysis, etc.)? For what purposes?
7. The case segment mentions the Sarbanes-Oxley Act (described in Chapter 5). How can a data warehouse or data mart help Ms. Baker and Mr. Lopez respond to pressures from the board of directors for the following:
   a. Ensuring the accuracy of financial data
   b. Providing reports in a timely manner
   c. Providing reports that include trend information and graphic presentations

Case Exercises

1. MVCH Table 9-1 provides some details regarding the two data marts MVCH is considering.
   a. Design a star schema for each data mart.
   b. Calculate the expected number of rows in each fact table and its estimated size (bytes).

MVCH TABLE 9-1 MVCH Prototype Data Mart Details

	Summary Data Mart	Detailed Data Mart
Physician dimension	PhysicianID (pk): 5 bytes PhysicianName: 10 bytes Specialty: 5 bytes PhysicianAddress: 10 bytes PhysicianTelephone: 5 bytes	Same as summary data mart
Treatment dimension	TreatmentID (pk): 3 bytes TreatmentDescription: 6 bytes	Same as summary data mart
Period dimension	PeriodID (pk): 2 bytes Month: 1 byte Year: 2 bytes	PeriodID (pk): 3 bytes Date: 5 bytes
Patient dimension	none	PatientID (pk): 5 bytes PatientName: 10 bytes PatientAddress: 10 bytes PatientTelephone: 5 bytes
Treatment (fact) table	*Grain: Monthly summary of treatments and average treatment costs, by physician and treatment* MonthlyTotal: 3 bytes AverageCost: 5 bytes	*Grain: Detail for each treatment occurrence administered to a patient by a physician* TreatmentCost: 4 bytes TreatmentResult: 20 bytes
Assumptions	• Treatments: Approximately 500 different treatments are performed at the hospital. During a typical month, approximately 30 percent (or 150 different treatments) are performed. • Physicians: Each treatment is performed by one physician. • Periods: If a full-scale data mart is developed, it is anticipated that 36 periods (or 3 years) of data will be accumulated.	• Treatments: An average of 200 total treatments are performed for patients on a given day (this is based on an average patient census of 200, and an average of 2 treatments per patient per day). • Patients: Each treatment is performed for one patient. To simplify matters, assume that a given treatment may only be performed once by a given physician and for a particular patient on a given day. • Physicians: Each treatment is performed by one physician. • Periods: If a full-scale data mart is developed, it is anticipated that approximately 1,000 days (nearly 3 years) of data will be collected.

c. For the detailed data mart, why is it necessary to assume that a given treatment may be performed only once by a given physician for a given patient on a given day? Suggest a way to overcome this.

d. Would you recommend that MVCH implement both data marts? Why or why not? If yes, then what should MVCH do to ensure consistency across the two data marts?

e. Using SQL, create two star queries for each of the data marts.

2. After hearing about the data mart prototypes, Dr. Jefferson, chief of surgery, expresses an interest in a surgery data mart. Some of the reports he wishes to receive include the number of surgeries, by surgeon; the number of inpatient and outpatient surgeries per week and per month; the number of canceled surgeries, by reason, surgeon, and month; surgeries per week, operating room (MVCH has a suite of six operating rooms), and surgeon; mortality rates by surgeon; average surgery time, by type of surgery;

average surgery time, by OR; and number of negative patient reactions to blood transfusions by surgeon and by patient gender and age. Dr. Jefferson also wishes to analyze surgeries in terms of the duration of anesthesia, total time in the operating room, and amount of time in the operating room before the start and after the end of the surgery. He wants to be able to slice and dice the surgery data by diagnosis, patient age, gender, insurance company, acuity code (patient acuity at MVCH is rated on a five-point scale, with 1 reflecting the highest acuity and 5 the lowest acuity), operating room, and surgeon.

Given this information, you have the following tasks:

a. Identify the dimensions and facts for this data mart.

b. Create the star schema.

c. Use SQL to create three queries that satisfy some of Dr. Jefferson's information requirements.

d. Develop a business case for this data mart.

3. Identify dimensions and facts for two other possible data marts at MVCH: an emergency room data mart and a data mart for Dr. Z's MS Center. Use Microsoft Visio (or a similar tool) to draw the star schema.

PART

V

Advanced Database Topics

Chapter 10
Data Quality and Integration

Chapter 11
Data and Database Administration

Chapter 12
Overview: Distributed Databases

Chapter 13
Overview: Object-Oriented Data Modeling

Chapter 14
Overview: Using Relational Databases to Provide Object Persistence

AN OVERVIEW OF PART FIVE

Parts II through IV have prepared you to develop useful and efficient databases. Part V introduces some additional important database design and management issues. These issues include preserving data quality (including complying with regulations for accuracy of data reporting) and integrating across decentralized organizational databases (Chapter 10); database security, backup, recovery, and control of concurrent access to data, and advanced topics in database performance tuning (Chapter 11); distributed databases (Chapter 12) and object-oriented databases (Chapter 13); and using relational databases with object-oriented systems development environments (Chapter 14). Chapters 10 and 11 are included in their entirety in the printed text; full versions of Chapters 12 through 14 are included on the textbook's Web site, and summaries of these chapters are included in the printed text. Following Part V are three appendices, covering alternative E-R notations (Appendix A, complementing Chapters 2 and 3), advanced normal forms (Appendix B, supplementing Chapter 4), and data structures (Appendix C, supplementing Chapter 5).

Modern organizations are quickly realizing that one of their most prized assets is data and that effectively governing and managing data across an enterprise can be a potential source of competitive advantage. Chapter 10 ("Data Quality and Integration") focuses on key topics that are critical to enterprise data management: data governance, data quality, master data management, and data integration. Today data quality has become a major organizational issue for two reasons: Data quality is poor in many organizations, and new U.S. and international regulations impose criminal penalties for reporting erroneous financial and health data. Although data quality has been a theme throughout this book, Chapter 10 gives special attention to processes organizations can use (including data stewardship and governance) to systematically deal with data quality. Another major issue for data management is providing consistent and transparent access for users to data from multiple databases. Data warehousing, covered in the last chapter of Part IV, is one approach to achieving this goal. Other data integration strategies are outlined in Chapter 10. Data quality is a special concern when integrating disparate data sources.

You are likely to conclude from reading this text that data are corporate resources that are too valuable to be managed casually. In Chapter 11 ("Data and Database Administration"), you will learn about the roles of the following:

- ***A data administrator***—a person who takes overall responsibility for data, metadata, and policies about data use

- ***A database administrator***—a person who is responsible for physical database design and for dealing with the technical issues—such as security enforcement, database performance, and backup and recovery—associated with managing a database

Specialized data and database administrator roles for Web-based data warehouses and mobile systems are also defined in Chapter 11. Finally, in Chapter 11 you will learn about the challenges in managing security of data in a database and techniques that are available to help overcome these challenges. You will learn about views, integrity controls, authorization rules, encryption, and authentication—all key mechanisms to help manage data security. You will also understand the role of databases in Sarbanes-Oxley compliance, a hot topic in publicly traded companies in the United States. Finally, you will learn about open source DBMSs, concurrency control, deadlock, information repositories, locking, database recovery and backup, system catalogs, transactions, and versioning—all core topics today for managing data resources.

In larger organizations, a database may be distributed across multiple computers and locations. Special issues arise when an organization tries to manage distributed data as one database rather than as many decentralized, separate databases. In Chapter 12 ("Distributed Databases"), you learn about homogeneous and heterogeneous distributed databases, the objectives and trade-offs for distributed databases, and several alternative architectures for such databases. You learn about the important concepts of data replication and partitioning and how to synchronize multiple instances of the same data across a distributed database. You also study the special features of a distributed DBMS, including distributed transaction controls (such as commit protocols). There is a review of the evolution of distributed DBMSs and of the range of distributed DBMS products.

Chapter 13 ("Object-Oriented Data Modeling") introduces an alternative to E-R modeling. Object-oriented models of data and other system aspects are becoming increasingly popular because of their ability to represent complex ideas using highly related modeling notations. This chapter uses the Unified Modeling Language (UML), a standard in this field, particularly focusing on one of the static diagrams, the class diagram. In UML, an object is an entity that has three properties: state, behavior, and identity. The behavior of an object is determined by one or more operations that are encapsulated in the object. Associations, generalization, inheritance, and polymorphism are important concepts. This chapter presents an object-oriented version (in the form of a class diagram) of the Pine Valley Furniture Company case from Chapter 2.

Chapter 14 ("Using Relational Databases to Provide Object Persistence") addresses issues related to making relational databases, still the standard for organizational database management systems, available as a data repository for object-oriented systems development environments. This is necessary because true object-oriented DBMSs have never become mainstream, yet the object-oriented development approach and the relational data model are not directly compatible. This chapter addresses the mismatches between the relational and object-oriented models of data and systems and different approaches to dealing with the mismatches when building information systems using Java EE, .NET, and other object-oriented development environments. Several object-relational technologies are discussed and illustrated (including JDBC), with in-depth examples of Hibernate, one of the most common object-relational mapping frameworks.

CHAPTER

10

Data Quality and Integration

Learning Objectives

After studying this chapter, you should be able to:

- Concisely define each of the following key terms: **data governance, data steward, master data management (MDM), changed data capture (CDC), data federation, static extract, incremental extract, data scrubbing, refresh mode, update mode, data transformation, selection, joining,** and **aggregation**.
- Describe the importance of data governance and identify key goals of a data governance program.
- Describe the importance of data quality and list several measures to improve quality.
- Define the characteristics of quality data.
- Describe the reasons for poor-quality data in organizations.
- Describe a program for improving data quality in organizations, including data stewardship.
- Describe the purpose and role of master data management.
- Describe the three types of data integration approaches.
- Describe the four steps and activities of the ETL process for data integration for a data warehouse.
- Explain the various forms of data transformations needed to prepare data for a data warehouse.

INTRODUCTION

Quality data are the foundation for all of information processing and are essential for well-run organizations. Consider the following:

> This past February [2001], a war of words erupted between shoe and apparel manufacturer Nike Inc. and i2 Technologies, the software developer that provided Nike with a new demand and supply inventory system. Nike cited order problems that led to expensive manufacturing problems during deployment of the new system.
>
> For example, some shoe orders were placed twice, once each in the old and new systems, while the new system allowed other orders to fall through the cracks. This resulted in overproduction of some models and underproduction of others. Nike was even forced to make some shoes at the last minute and ship them via air to meet buyers' deadlines.

> Ultimately Nike blames these system problems for a $80 million to $100 million cut in third-quarter sales that caused the company to miss earnings estimates by as much as 13 cents. The day that Nike announced this, its stock price dropped 25 percent in value from $49.17 to $38.80. On the other side, i2's senior management claimed that their software was not responsible for Nike's shortfalls. (Loshin, 2001)

We have addressed data quality throughout this book, from designing data models that accurately represent the rules by which an organization operates, to including data integrity controls in database definitions, to data security and backup procedures that protect data from loss and contamination. However, with the increased emphasis on accuracy in financial reporting, the burgeoning supply of data inside and outside an organization, and the need to integrate data from disparate data sources for business intelligence, data quality deserves special attention by all database professionals.

Quality data is in the eye of the beholder. Data may be of high quality within one information system, meeting the standards of users of that system. But when users look beyond their system to match, say, their customer data with customer data from other systems, the quality of data can be called into question. Thus, data quality is but one component of a set of highly related enterprise data management topics that also includes data governance, master data management, and data integration.

This chapter on data quality and integration reviews the major issues related to the four topics identified above. First, we present an overview of data governance and how it lays the foundation for enterprise-wide data management activities. We then review why data quality is important and how to measure data quality, using seven important characteristics of quality data: identity uniqueness, accuracy, consistency, completeness, timeliness, currency, conformance, and referential integrity. Next, we explain why many organizations have difficulty achieving high-quality data, and then we review a program for data quality improvement that can overcome these difficulties. Part of this program involves creating new organizational roles of data stewards and organizational oversight for data quality via a data governance process. We then examine the topic of master data management and its role as a critical asset in enabling sharing of data across applications.

Managers and executives increasingly need data from many data systems and require this data in a consistent and consolidated way that makes the data appear to come from one database. Data integration methods of consolidation, federation, and propagation, along with master data management, make this possible. Data warehousing (see Chapter 9), a significant data management approach used to support decision making and business intelligence, often uses one consolidation approach called extract–transform–load (ETL); we explain ETL in detail in this chapter. First, the four major steps of ETL—mapping source to target and metadata management, extract, load, and finally transformation—are explained. The chapter illustrates the two types of extracts: static and incremental. Data cleansing is the ETL step most related to achieving quality data from the perspective of the data warehouse, so the chapter explains special data quality concerns for data warehousing. Then different types of data transformations are reviewed at the record and field levels. Finally, we introduce a few selected tools to assist in ETL.

Data governance
High-level organizational groups and processes that oversee data stewardship across the organization. It usually guides data quality initiatives, data architecture, data integration and master data management, data warehousing and business intelligence, and other data-related matters.

DATA GOVERNANCE

Data governance is a set of processes and procedures aimed at managing the data within an organization with an eye toward high-level objectives such as availability, integrity, and compliance with regulations. Data governance oversees data access policies by measuring risk and security exposures (Leon, 2007). Data governance provides a mandate for dealing with data issues. According to a TDWI 2005 (Russom, 2006) survey, only about 25 to 28 percent of organizations (depending on how the question was asked) have a data governance approach. Certainly, broad-based data governance programs are still emerging. Data governance is a function that has to be jointly owned by IT and the business. Successful data governance will require support from upper management in the firm. A key role in enabling success of data governance in an organization is that of a data steward.

The Sarbanes-Oxley Act of 2002 has made it imperative that organizations undertake actions to ensure data accuracy, timeliness, and consistency (Laurent, 2005). Although not mandated by regulations, many organizations require the CIO as well as the CEO and CFO to sign off on financial statements, recognizing the role of IT in building procedures to ensure data quality. Establishment of a business information advisory committee consisting of representatives from each major business unit who have the authority to make business policy decisions can contribute to the establishment of high data quality (Carlson, 2002; Moriarty, 1996). These committee members act as liaisons between IT and their business unit and consider not only their functional unit's data needs but also enterprise-wide data needs. The members are subject matter experts for the data they steward and hence need to have a strong interest in managing information as a corporate resource, an in-depth understanding of the business of the organization, and good negotiation skills. Such members (typically high-level managers) are sometimes referred to as **data stewards**, people who have the responsibility to ensure that organizational applications properly support the organization's enterprise goals.

Data steward
A person assigned the responsibility of ensuring that organizational applications properly support the organization's enterprise goals for data quality.

A data governance program needs to include the following:

- Sponsorship from both senior management and business units
- A data steward manager to support, train, and coordinate the data stewards
- Data stewards for different business units, data subjects, source systems, or combinations of these elements
- A governance committee, headed by one person, but composed of data steward managers, executives and senior vice presidents, IT leadership (e.g., data administrators), and other business leaders, to set strategic goals, coordinate activities, and provide guidelines and standards for all data management activities

The goals of data governance are transparency—within and outside the organization to regulators—and increasing the value of data maintained by the organization. The data governance committee measures data quality and availability, determines targets for quality and availability, directs efforts to overcome risks associated with bad or unsecured data, and reviews the results of data audit processes. Data governance is best chartered by the most senior leadership in the organization.

Data governance also provides the key guidelines for the key areas of enterprise data management identified in the introduction section: data quality initiatives, data architecture, master data management, data integration, data warehousing/business intelligence, and other data-related matters (Russom, 2006). We have already examined data warehousing issues in Chapter 9. In the next few sections, we examine the key issues in each of the other areas.

MANAGING DATA QUALITY

The importance of high-quality data cannot be overstated. According to Brauer (2002):

> Critical business decisions and allocation of resources are made based on what is found in the data. Prices are changed, marketing campaigns created, customers are communicated with, and daily operations evolve around whatever data points are churned out by an organization's various systems. The data that serves as the foundation of these systems *must be good data*. Otherwise we fail before we ever begin. It doesn't matter how pretty the screens are, how intuitive the interfaces are, how high the performance rockets, how automated the processes are, how innovative the methodology is, and how far-reaching the access to the system is, *if the data are bad—the systems fail*. Period. And if the systems fail, or at the very least provide inaccurate information, every process, decision, resource allocation, communication, or interaction with the system will have a damaging, if not disastrous impact on the business itself.

This quote is, in essence, a restatement of the old IT adage "garbage-in, garbage-out" (GIGO), but with increased emphasis on the dramatically high stakes in today's environment.

High-quality data—that is, data that are accurate, consistent, and available in a timely fashion—are essential to the management of organizations today. Organizations must strive to identify the data that are relevant to their decision making to develop business policies and practices that ensure the accuracy and completeness of the data, and to facilitate enterprise-wide data sharing. Managing the quality of data is an organization-wide responsibility, with data administration (the topic of Chapter 11) often playing a leading role in planning and coordinating the efforts.

What is your data quality ROI? In this case, we don't mean *return on investment*; rather, we mean *risk of incarceration*. According to Yugay and Klimchenko (2004), "The key to achieving SOX (Sarbanes-Oxley) compliance lies within IT, which is ultimately the single resource capable of responding to the charge to create effective reporting mechanisms, provide necessary data integration and management systems, ensure data quality and deliver the required information on time". Poor data quality can put executives in jail. Specifically, SOX requires organizations to measure and improve metadata quality; ensure data security; measure and improve data accessibility and ease of use; measure and improve data availability, timeliness, and relevance; measure and improve accuracy, completeness, and understandability of general ledger data; and identify and eliminate duplicates and data inconsistencies. According to Informatica (2005), a leading provider of technology for data quality and integration, data quality is important to

- ***Minimize IT project risk*** Dirty data can cause delays and extra work on information systems projects, especially those that involve reusing data from existing systems.
- ***Make timely business decisions*** The ability to make quick and informed business decisions is compromised when managers do not have high-quality data or when they lack confidence in their data.
- ***Ensure regulatory compliance*** Not only is quality data essential for SOX and Basel II (Europe) compliance, quality data can also help an organization in justice, intelligence, and antifraud activities.
- ***Expand the customer base*** Being able to accurately spell a customer's name or to accurately know all aspects of customer activity with your organization will help in up-selling and cross-selling new business.

Characteristics of Quality Data

What, then, are quality data? Redman (2004) summarizes data quality as "fit for their intended uses in operations, decision making, and planning." In other words, this means that data are free of defects and possess desirable features (relevant, comprehensive, proper level of detail, easy to read, and easy to interpret). Loshin (2006) and Russom (2006) further delineate the characteristics of quality data:

- ***Uniqueness*** Uniqueness means that each entity exists no more than once within the database, and there is a key that can be used to uniquely access each entity. This characteristic requires identity matching (finding data about the same entity) and resolution to locate and remove duplicate entities.
- ***Accuracy*** Accuracy has to do with the degree to which any datum correctly represents the real-life object it models. Often accuracy is measured by agreement with some recognized authority data source (e.g., one source system or even some external data provider). Data must be both accurate and precise enough for their intended use. For example, knowing sales accurately is important, but for many decisions, knowing sales only to the nearest $1000 per month for each product is sufficient. Data can be valid (i.e., satisfy a specified domain or range of values) and not be accurate.
- ***Consistency*** Consistency means that values for data in one data set (database) are in agreement with the values for related data in another data set (database). Consistency can be within a table row (e.g., the weight of a product should

have some relationship to its size and material type), between table rows (e.g., two products with similar characteristics should have about the same prices, or data that are meant to be redundant should have the same values), between the same attributes over time (e.g., the product price should be the same from one month to the next unless there was a price change event), or within some tolerance (e.g., total sales computed from orders filled and orders billed should be roughly the same values). Consistency also relates to attribute inheritance from super- to subtypes. For example, a subtype instance cannot exist without a corresponding supertype, and overlap or disjoint subtype rules are enforced.

- ***Completeness*** Completeness refers to data having assigned values if they need to have values. This characteristic encompasses the NOT NULL and foreign key constraints of SQL, but more complex rules might exist (e.g., male employees do not need a maiden name but female employees may have a maiden name). Completeness also means that all data needed are present (e.g., if we want to know total dollar sales, we may need to know both total quality sold and unit price, or if an employee record indicates that an employee has retired, we need to have a retirement date recorded). Sometimes completeness has an aspect of precedence. For example, an employee in an employee table who does not exist in an applicant table may indicate a data quality issue.
- ***Timeliness*** Timeliness means meeting the expectation for the time between when data are expected and when they are readily available for use. As organizations attempt to decrease the latency between when a business activity occurs and when the organization is able to take action on that activity, timeliness is becoming a more important quality of data characteristic (i.e., if we don't know in time to take action, we don't have quality data). A related aspect of timeliness is retention, which is the span of time for which data represent the real world. Some data need to be time-stamped to indicate from when to when they apply, and missing from or to dates may indicate a data quality issue.
- ***Currency*** Currency is the degree to which data are recent enough to be useful. For example, we may require that customers' phone numbers be up-to-date so we can call them at any time, but the number of employees may not need to be refreshed in real-time. Varying degrees of currency across data may indicate a quality issue (e.g., if the salaries of different employees have drastically different updated dates).
- ***Conformance*** Conformance refers to whether data are stored, exchanged, or presented in a format that is as specified by their metadata. The metadata include both domain integrity rules (e.g., attribute values come from a valid set or range of values) and actual format (e.g., specific location of special characters, precise mixture of text, numbers, and special symbols).
- ***Referential integrity*** Data that refer to other data need to be unique and satisfy requirements to exist (i.e., satisfy any mandatory one or optional one cardinalities).

These are high standards. Quality data requires more than defect correction; it also requires prevention and reporting. Because data are frequently updated, achieving quality data requires constant monitoring and measurement as well as improvement actions. Quality data are also not perfectly achievable nor absolutely necessary in some situations (there are obvious situations of life and death where perfection is the goal); "just enough quality" may be the best business decision to trade off costs versus returns.

Table 10-1 lists four important reasons why the quality of data in organizational databases has deteriorated in the past few years; we describe these reasons in the following sections.

EXTERNAL DATA SOURCES Much of an organization's data originates outside the organization, where there is less control over the data sources to comply with expectations of the receiving organization. For example, a company receives a flood of data via the Internet from Web forms filled out by users. Such data are often inaccurate or incomplete, or even purposely wrong. (Have you ever entered a wrong phone number in a Web-based form because a phone number was required and you didn't want to

TABLE 10-1 Reasons for Deteriorated Data Quality

Reason	Explanation
External data sources	Lack of control over data quality
Redundant data storage and inconsistent metadata	Proliferation of databases with uncontrolled redundancy and metadata
Data entry problems	Poor data capture controls
Lack of organizational commitment	Not recognizing poor data quality as an organizational issue

divulge your actual phone number?) Other data for B2B transactions arrive via XML channels, and these data may also contain inaccuracies. Also, organizations often purchase data files or databases from external organizations, and these sources may contain data that are out-of-date, inaccurate, or incompatible with internal data.

REDUNDANT DATA STORAGE AND INCONSISTENT METADATA Many organizations have allowed the uncontrolled proliferation of spreadsheets, desktop databases, legacy databases, data marts, data warehouses, and other repositories of data. These data may be redundant and filled with inconsistencies and incompatibilities. Data can be wrong because the metadata are wrong (e.g., a wrong formula to aggregate data in a spreadsheet or an out-of-date data extraction routine to refresh a data mart). Then if these various databases become sources for integrated systems, the problems can cascade further.

DATA ENTRY PROBLEMS According to a TDWI survey (Russom, 2006), user interfaces that do not take advantage of integrity controls—such as automatically filling in data, providing drop-down selection boxes, and other improvements in data entry control—are tied for the number-one cause of poor data. And the best place to improve data entry across all applications is in database definitions, where integrity controls, valid value tables, and other controls can be documented and enforced.

LACK OF ORGANIZATIONAL COMMITMENT For a variety of reasons, many organizations simply have not made the commitment or invested the resources to improve their data quality. Some organizations are simply in denial about having problems with data quality. Others realize they have a problem but fear that the solution will be too costly or that they cannot quantify the return on investment. The situation is improving; in a 2001 TDWI survey (Russom, 2006), about 68 percent of respondents reported no plans or only considering data quality initiatives, but by 2005 this percentage had dropped to about 58 percent.

Data Quality Improvement

Implementing a successful quality improvement program will require the active commitment and participation of all members of an organization. Following is a brief outline of some of the key steps in such a program (see Table 10-2).

GET THE BUSINESS BUY-IN Data quality initiatives need to be viewed as business imperatives rather than as an IT project. Hence, it is critical that the appropriate level of executive sponsorship be obtained and that a good business case be made for the improvement. In addition, it is important to identify and define key performance indicators and metrics that can quantify the results of the improvement efforts.

With the competing demands for resources today, management must be convinced that a data quality program will yield a sufficient ROI (in this case, we do mean *return on investment*). Fortunately (or unfortunately), this is not difficult to do in most organizations today. There are two general types of benefits from such a program: cost avoidance and avoidance of opportunity losses.

TABLE 10-2 Key Steps in a Data Quality Program

Step	Motivation
Get the business buy-in	Show the value of data quality management to executives
Conduct a data quality audit	Understand the extent and nature of data quality problems
Establish a data stewardship program	Achieve organizational commitment and involvement
Improve data capture processes	Overcome the "garbage in, garbage out" phenomenon
Apply modern data management principles and technology	Use proven methods and techniques to make more thorough data quality activities easier to execute
Apply TQM principles and practices	Follow best practices to deal with all aspects of data quality management

Consider a simple example. Suppose a bank has 500,000 customers in its customer file. The bank plans to advertise a new product to all of its customers by means of a direct mailing. Suppose the error rate in the customer file is 10 percent, including duplicate customer records, obsolete addresses, and so on (such an error rate is not unusual). If the direct cost of mailing is $5.00 (including postage and materials), the expected loss due to bad data is 500,000 customers × .10 × $5, or $250,000.

Often, the opportunity loss associated with bad data is greater than direct costs. For example, suppose the average bank customer generates $2000 revenue annually from interest charges, service fees, and so on. This equates to $10,000 over a five-year period. Suppose the bank implements an enterprise-wide data quality program that improves its customer relationship management, cross-selling, and other related activities. If this program results in a net increase of only 2 percent new business (an educated guess), the results over five years will be remarkable: 500,000 customers × $10,000 × .02, or $50 million. This is why it is sometimes stated that "quality is free."

CONDUCT A DATA QUALITY AUDIT An organization without an established data quality program should begin with an audit of data to understand the extent and nature of data quality problems. A data quality audit includes many procedures, but one simple task is to statistically profile all files. A profile documents the set of values for each field. By inspection, obscure and unexpected extreme values can be identified. Patterns of data (distribution, outliers, frequencies) can be analyzed to see if the distribution makes sense. (An unexpected high frequency of one value may indicate that users are entering an easy number or a default is often being used, thus accurate data are not being recorded.) Data can be checked against relevant business rules to be sure that controls that are in place are effective and somehow not being bypassed (e.g., some systems allow users to override warning messages that data entered violates some rule; if this happens too frequently, it can be a sign of lax enforcement of business rules). Data quality software, such as the programs mentioned later in this chapter for ETL processes, can be used to check for valid addresses, find redundant records due to insufficient methods for matching customer or other subjects across different sources, and violations of specified business rules.

Business rules to be checked can be as simple as an attribute value must be greater than zero, or can involve more complex conditions (e.g., loan accounts with a greater than zero balance and open more than 30 days must have an interest rate greater than zero). Rules can be implemented in the database (e.g., foreign keys), but if there are ways for operators to override rules, there is no guarantee that even these rules will be strictly followed. The business rules are reviewed by a panel of application and database experts, and the data to be checked are identified. Rules often do not have to be checked against all existing data, rather a random but representative sample is usually sufficient. Once the data are checked against the rules, a panel judges what actions should be taken to deal with broken rules, usually addressed in some priority order.

Using specialized tools for data profiling makes a data audit more productive, especially considering that data profiling is not a one-time task. Because of changes to the database and applications, data profiling needs to be done periodically. In fact, some organizations regularly report data profiling results as critical success factors for the information systems organization. Informatica's PowerCenter tool is representative of the capabilities of specialized tools to support data profiling. PowerCenter can profile a wide variety of data sources and supports complex business rules in a business rules library. It can track profile results over time to show improvements and new problem areas. Rules can check on column values (e.g., valid range of values), sources (e.g., row counts and redundancy checks), and multiple tables (e.g., inner versus outer join results). It is also recommended that any new application for a database, which may be analyzing data in new ways, could benefit from a specialized data profile to see if new queries, using previously hidden business rules, would fail because the database was never protected against violations of these rules. With a specialized data profiling tool, new rules can be quickly checked and inventoried against all rules as part of a total data quality audit program.

An audit will thoroughly review all process controls on data entry and maintenance. Procedures for changing sensitive data should likely involve actions by at least two people with separated duties and responsibilities. Primary keys and important financial data fall into this category. Proper edit checks should be defined and implemented for all fields. Error logs from processing data from each source (e.g., user, workstation, or source system) should be analyzed to identify patterns or high frequencies of errors and rejected transactions, and actions should be taken to improve the ability of the sources to provide high-quality data. For example, users should be prohibited from entering data into fields for which they are not intended. Some users who do not have a use for certain data may use that field to store data they need but for which there is not appropriate field. This can confuse other users who do use these fields and see unintended data.

ESTABLISH A DATA STEWARDSHIP PROGRAM As pointed out in the section on data governance, stewards are held accountable for the quality of the data for which they are responsible. They must also ensure that the data that are captured are accurate and consistent throughout the organization, so that users throughout the organization can rely on the data. Data stewardship is a role, not a job; as such, data stewards do not own the data, and data stewards usually have other duties inside and usually outside the data administration area.

Seiner (2005) outlines a comprehensive set of roles and responsibilities for data stewards. Roles include oversight of the data stewardship program, managers of data subject areas (e.g., customer, product, etc.), stewards for data definitions of each data subject, stewards for accurate and efficient production/maintenance of data for each subject, and stewards for proper use of data for each subject area.

There is debate about whether data steward roles should report through the business or IT organizations. Data stewards need to have business acumen, understand data requirements and usage, and understand the finer details of metadata. Business data stewards can articulate specific data uses and understand the complex relationships between data from a grounded business perspective. Business data stewards emphasize the business ownership of data and can represent the business on access rights, privacy, and regulations/policies that affect data. They should know why data are the way they are and can see data reuse possibilities.

But, as Dyché (2007) has discovered, a business data steward often is myopic, seeing data from only the depths of the area or areas of the organization from which he or she comes. If data do not originate in the area of the data steward, the steward will have limited knowledge, and may be at a disadvantage in debates with other data stewards. Dyché argues also for source data stewards, who understand the systems of record, lineage, and formatting of different data systems. Source data stewards can help to determine the best source for user data requirements by understanding the details of how a source system acquires and processes data.

IMPROVE DATA CAPTURE PROCESSES As noted earlier, lax data entry is a major source of poor data quality, so improving data capture processes is a fundamental step in a data quality improvement program. Inmon (2004) identifies three critical points of data entry: where data are (1) originally captured (e.g., a customer order entry screen), (2) pulled into a data integration process (e.g., an ETL process for data warehousing), and (3) loaded into an integrated data store, such as a data warehouse. A database professional can improve data quality at each of these steps. For simplicity, we summarize what Inmon recommends only for the original data capture step (and we discuss the process of cleansing data during ETL in a later section of this chapter):

- Enter as much of the data as possible via automatic, not human, means (e.g., from data stored in a smart card or pulled from a database, such as retrieving current values for addresses, account numbers, and other personal characteristics).
- Where data must be entered manually, ensure that it is selected from preset options (e.g., drop-down menus of selections pulled from the database), if possible.
- Use trained operators when possible (help systems and good prompts/examples can assist end users in proper data entry).
- Follow good user interface design principles (see Hoffer et al., 2010, for guidelines) that create consistent screen layouts, easy to follow navigation paths, clear data entry masks and formats (which can be defined in DDL), minimal use of obscure codes (full values of codes can be looked up and displayed from the database, not in the application programs), etc.
- Immediately check entered data for quality against data in the database, so use triggers and user-defined procedures liberally to make sure that only high-quality data enter the database; when questionable data are entered (e.g., "T for gender), immediate and understandable feedback should be given to the operator, questioning the validity of the data.

APPLY MODERN DATA MANAGEMENT PRINCIPLES AND TECHNOLOGY Powerful software is now available that can assist users with the technical aspects of data quality improvement. This software often employs advanced techniques such as pattern matching, fuzzy logic, and expert systems. These programs can be used to analyze current data for quality problems, identify and eliminate redundant data, integrate data from multiple sources, and so on. Some of these programs are discussed later in this chapter, under the topic of data extract, transform, and load.

Of course, in a database management book, we certainly cannot neglect sound data modeling as a central ingredient in a data quality program. Chapters 3 through 6 introduced the principles of conceptual to physical data modeling and design that are the basis for a high-quality data model. Hay (2005) (drawing on prior work) has summarized these into six principles for high-quality data models.

APPLY TQM PRINCIPLES AND PRACTICES Data quality improvements should be considered as an ongoing effort and not treated as one-time projects. With this mind, many leading organizations are applying total quality management (TQM) to improve data quality, just as in other business areas. Some of the principles of TQM that apply are defect prevention (rather than correction), continuous improvement of the processes that touch data, and the use of enterprise data standards. For example, where data in legacy systems are found defective, it is better to correct the legacy systems that generate that data than to attempt to correct the data when moving it to a data warehouse.

TQM balances a focus on the customer (in particular, customer satisfaction) and the product or service (in our case, the data resource). Ultimately, TQM results in decreased costs, increased profits, and reduced risks. As stated earlier in this chapter, data quality is in the eye of the beholder, so the right mix of the seven characteristics of quality data will depend on data users. TQM builds on a strong foundation of measurements, such as what we have discussed as data profiling. For an in-depth discussion of applying TQM to data quality improvement, see English (1999a, 1999b, 2004).

Summary of Data Quality

Ensuring the quality of data that enters databases and data warehouses is essential if users are to have confidence in their systems. Users have their own perceptions of the quality of data, based on balancing the characteristics of uniqueness, accuracy, consistency, completeness, timeliness, currency, conformance, and referential integrity. Ensuring data quality is also now mandated by regulations such as the Sarbanes-Oxley Act and the Basel II Accord. Many organizations today do not have proactive data quality programs, and poor-quality data is a widespread problem. We have outlined in this section a proactive data quality program that employs the use of data audits and profiling, best practices in data capture and entry, data stewards, proven TQM principles and practices, modern data management software technology, and appropriate ROI calculations.

MASTER DATA MANAGEMENT

If one were to examine the data used in applications across a large organization, one would likely find that certain categories of data are referenced more frequently than others across the enterprise in operational and analytical systems. For example, almost all information systems and databases refer to common subject areas of data (people, things, places) and often enhance those common data with local (transactional) data relevant to only the application or database. The challenge for an organization is to ensure that all applications that use common data from these areas, such as customer, product, employee, invoice, and facility, have a "single source of truth" they can use. **Master data management (MDM)** refers to the disciplines, technologies, and methods to ensure the currency, meaning, and quality of reference data within and across various subject areas (Imhoff and White , 2006). MDM ensures that everyone knows the current description of a product, the current salary of an employee, and the current billing address of a customer. Master data can be as simple as a list of acceptable city names and abbreviations. MDM does not address sharing transactional data, such as customer purchases. MDM can also be realized in specialized forms. One of the most discussed is customer data integration (CDI), which is MDM that focuses just on customer data (Dyché and Levy, 2006). Another is product data integration (PDI).

Master data management (MDM) Disciplines, technologies, and methods used to ensure the currency, meaning, and quality of reference data within and across various subject areas.

MDM has become more common due to active mergers and acquisitions and to meet regulations, such as the Sarbanes-Oxley Act. While many vendors (consultants and technology suppliers) exist to provide MDM approaches and technologies, it is important for firms to acknowledge that master data is a key strategic asset for a firm. It is therefore imperative that MDM projects have the appropriate level of executive buy-in and be treated as enterprise-wide initiatives. MDM projects also need to work closely with ongoing data quality and data governance initiatives.

No one source system usually contains the "golden record" of all relevant facts about a data subject. For example, customer master data might be integrated from customer relationship management, billing, ERP, and purchased data sources. MDM determines the best source for each piece of data (e.g., customer address or name) and makes sure that all applications reference the same virtual "golden record." MDM also provides analysis and reporting services to inform data quality managers about the quality of master data across databases (e.g., what percentage of city data stored in individual databases conforms with the master city values). Finally, because master data are "golden records," no application owns master data. Rather, master data are truly enterprise assets, and business managers must take responsibility for the quality of master data.

There are three popular architectures for master data management: identity registry, integration hub, and persistent. In the *identity registry* approach, the master data remains in their source systems, and applications refer to the registry to determine where the agreed upon source of particular data (e.g., customer address) resides. The registry helps each system match its master record with corresponding master records in other source systems by using a global identifier for each instance of a subject area. The registry maintains a complete list of all master data elements and knows which source system to access for the best value for each attribute. Thus, an application may have to access several databases to retrieve all the data it needs, and a database may need to allow more applications to access it. This is similar to the federation style of data integration.

In the *integration hub* approach, data changes are broadcast (typically asynchronously) through a central service to all subscribing databases. Redundant data are kept, but there are mechanisms to ensure consistency, yet each application does not have to collect and maintain all of the data it needs. When this style of integration hub is created, it acts like a propagation form of data integration. In some cases, however, a central master data store is also created for some master data, thus it may be a combination of propagation and consolidation. However, even with consolidation, the systems of record or entry—the distributed transaction systems—still maintain their own databases including the local and propagated data they need for their most frequent processing.

In the *persistent* approach, one consolidated record is maintained, and all applications draw on that one "golden record" for the common data. Thus, considerable work is necessary to push all data captured in each application to the persistent record so that the record contains the most recent values and to go to the persistent record when any system needs common data. Data redundancy is possible with the persistent approach because each application database may also maintain a local version of any data elements at its discretion, even those maintained in the persistent consolidated table. This is a pure consolidated data integration approach for master data.

It is important to realize that MDM is not intended to replace a data warehouse, principally because only master data and usually only current master data are integrated, whereas a data warehouse needs a historical view of both master and transactional data. MDM is strictly about getting a single view of data about each instance for each master data type. A data warehouse, however, might be (and often is) one of the systems that uses master data, either as a source to feed the warehouse or as an extension of the warehouse for the most current data when warehouse users want to drill through to source data. MDM does do data cleansing, similar to what is done with data warehousing. For this reason, MDM also is not an operational data store (see Chapter 9 for a description of ODSs). MDM is also considered by most people to be part of the data infrastructure of an organization, whereas an ODS, and even data warehousing, are considered application platforms.

DATA INTEGRATION: AN OVERVIEW

Many databases, especially enterprise-level databases, are built by consolidating data from existing internal and external data sources possibly with new data to support new applications. Most organizations have different databases for different purposes (see Chapter 1), some for transaction processing in different parts of the enterprise (e.g., production planning and control and order entry); some for local, tactical, or strategic decision making (e.g., for product pricing and sales forecasting); and some for enterprise-wide coordination and decision making (e.g., for customer relationship management and supply chain management). Organizations are diligently working to break down silos of data, yet allow some degree of local autonomy. To achieve this coordination, at times data must be integrated across disparate data sources.

It is safe to say that you cannot avoid dealing with data integration issues. As a database professional or even a user of a database created from other existing data sources, there are many data integration concepts you should understand to do your job or to understand the issues you might face. This is the purpose of the following sections of this chapter.

We have already studied one such data integration approach, data warehousing, in Chapter 9. Data warehousing creates data stores to support decision making and business intelligence. We will review in a subsequent section how data are brought together through an ETL process into what we called in Chapter 9 the *reconciled data layer* of the data warehousing approach to data integration. But before we dig in to this approach in detail, it is helpful to overview the two other general approaches, data federation and data propagation, that can be used for data integration, each with a different purpose and each ideal approaches under different circumstances.

General Approaches to Data Integration

Data integration creates a unified view of business data. This view can be created via a variety of techniques, which we will outline in the following subsections. However, data integration is not the only way data can be consolidated across an enterprise. Other ways to consolidate data are as follows (White, 2005):

- ***Application integration*** Achieved by coordinating the flow of event information between business applications (a service-oriented architecture can facilitate application integration)
- ***Business process integration*** Achieved by tighter coordination of activities across business processes (e.g., selling and billing) so that applications can be shared and more application integration can occur
- ***User interaction integration*** Achieved by creating fewer user interfaces that feed different data systems (e.g., using an enterprise portal to interact with different data reporting and business intelligence systems)

Changed data capture (CDC) Technique that indicates which data have changed since the last data integration activity.

Core to any method of data integration are techniques to capture changed data (**changed data capture [CDC]**), so only data that have changed need to be refreshed by the integration methods. Changed data can be identified by flags or a date of last update (which, if it is after the last integration action, indicates new data to integrate). Alternatively, transaction logs can be analyzed to see which data were updated when.

Three techniques form the building blocks of any data integration approach: data consolidation, data federation, and data propagation. Data consolidation is exemplified by the ETL processes used for data warehousing; we devote later sections of this chapter to an extensive explanation of this approach. The other two approaches are overviewed here. A detailed comparison of the three approaches is presented in Table 10-3.

Data federation A technique for data integration that provides a virtual view of integrated data without actually creating one centralized database.

DATA FEDERATION **Data federation** provides a virtual view of integrated data (as if they were all in one database) without actually bringing the data all into one physical, centralized database. Rather, when an application wants data, a federation engine (no, not from the *Starship Enterprise*!) retrieves relevant data from the actual sources (in real-time) and sends the result to the requesting application (so the federation engine looks like a database to the requesting application). Data transformations are done dynamically as needed. Enterprise information integration (EII) is one common term used to apply to data federation approaches. XML is often used as the vehicle for transferring data and metadata between data sources and application servers.

A main advantage of the federation approach is access to current data: There is no delay due to infrequent refreshes of a consolidated data store. Another advantage is that this approach hides the intricacies of other applications and the way data are stored in them from a given query or application. However, the workload can be quite burdensome for large amounts of data or for applications that need frequent data integration activities. Federation requires some form of a distributed query to be composed and run, but EII technology will hide this from the query writer or application developer. Federation works best for query and reporting (read-only) applications and when security of data, which can be concentrated at the source of data, is of high importance. The federation approach is also used as a stop-gap technique until more tightly integrated databases and applications can be built.

DATA PROPAGATION This approach duplicates data across databases, usually with near-real-time delay. Data are pushed to duplicate sites as updates occur (so-called event-driven propagation). These updates can be synchronous (a true distributed database technique in which a transaction does not complete until all copies of the data are updated; see Chapter 12) or asynchronous, which decouples the updates

TABLE 10-3 Comparison of Consolidation, Federation, and Propagation Forms of Data Integration

Method	Pros	Cons
Consolidation (ETL)	• Users are isolated from conflicting workloads on source systems, especially updates. • It is possible to retain history, not just current values. • A data store designed for specific requirements can be accessed quickly. • It works well when the scope of data needs are anticipated in advance. • Data transformations can be batched for greater efficiency.	• Network, storage, and data maintenance costs can be high. • Performance can degrade when the data warehouse becomes quite large (with some technologies).
Federation (EII)	• Data are always current (like relational views) when requested • It is simple for the calling application. • It works well for read-only applications because only requested data need to be retrieved. • It is ideal when copies of source data are not allowed. • Dynamic ETL is possible when one cannot anticipate data integration needs in advance or when there is a one-time need.	• Heavy workloads are possible for each request due to performing all integration tasks for each request. • Write access to data sources may not be supported.
Propagation (EAI & ERD)	• Data are available in near real-time. • It is possible to work with ETL for real-time data warehousing. • Transparent access is available to the data source.	• There is considerable (but background) overhead associated with synchronizing duplicate data.

to the remote copies. Enterprise application integration (EAI) and enterprise data replication (EDR) techniques are used for data propagation.

The major advantage of the data propagation approach to data integration is the near-real-time cascading of data changes throughout the organization. Very specialized technologies are needed for data propagation in order to achieve high performance and to handle frequent updates. Real-time data warehousing applications, which were discussed in Chapter 9, require data propagation (what are often called "trickle feeds" in data warehousing).

DATA INTEGRATION FOR DATA WAREHOUSING: THE RECONCILED DATA LAYER

Now that you have studied data integration approaches in general, let's look at one approach in detail. Although we detail only one approach, there are many activities in common across all approaches. These common tasks include extracting data from source systems, identity matching to match records from different source systems that pertain to the same entity instance (e.g., the same customer), cleansing data into a value all users agree is the true value for that data, transforming data into the desired format and detail users want to share, and loading the reconciled data into a shared view or storage location.

As indicated in Figure 9-5 for data warehousing, we use the term *reconciled data* to refer to the data layer associated with the operational data store and enterprise data warehouse. This is the term IBM used in 1993 to describe data warehouse architectures. Although the term is not widely used, it accurately describes the nature of the data that should appear in the enterprise data warehouse and the way they are derived. More commonly, reconciled data are referred to as the result of the ETL process. An EDW or ODS usually is a normalized, relational database because it needs the flexibility to support a wide variety of decision support needs.

Characteristics of Data After ETL

The goal of the ETL process is to provide a single, authoritative source for data that support decision making. Ideally, this data layer has the following characteristics:

1. ***Detailed*** The data are detailed (rather than summarized), providing maximum flexibility for various user communities to structure the data to best suit their needs.
2. ***Historical*** The data are periodic (or point-in-time) to provide a historical perspective.
3. ***Normalized*** The data are fully normalized (i.e., third normal form or higher). (We discussed normalization in Chapter 4.) Normalized data provide greater integrity and flexibility of use than denormalized data do. Denormalization is not necessary to improve performance because reconciled data are usually accessed periodically using batch processes. We will see, however, that some popular data warehouse data structures are denormalized.
4. ***Comprehensive*** Reconciled data reflect an enterprise-wide perspective, whose design conforms to the enterprise data model.
5. ***Timely*** Except for real-time data warehousing, data need not be (near) real-time, but data must be current enough that decision making can react in a timely manner.
6. ***Quality controlled*** Reconciled data must be of unquestioned quality and integrity because they are summarized into the data marts and used for decision making.

Notice that these characteristics of reconciled data are quite different from the typical operational data from which they are derived. Operational data are typically detailed, but they differ strongly in the other four dimensions described earlier:

1. Operational data are transient rather than historical.
2. Operational data are not normalized. Depending on their roots, operational data may never have been normalized or may have been denormalized for performance reasons.
3. Rather than being comprehensive, operational data are generally restricted in scope to a particular application.
4. Operational data are often of poor quality, with numerous types of inconsistencies and errors.

The data reconciliation process is responsible for transforming operational data to reconciled data. Because of the sharp differences between these two types of data, data reconciliation clearly is the most difficult and technically challenging part of building a data warehouse. The Data Warehousing Institute supports this claim, finding that 60 to 80 percent of work on a business intelligence project, often the reason for data warehousing, is spent on ETL activities (Eckerson and White, 2003). Fortunately, several sophisticated software products are available to assist with this activity. (See Krudop, 2005, for a summary of why ETL tools are useful and how to successfully implement them in an organization.)

The ETL Process

Data reconciliation occurs in two stages during the process of filling an enterprise data warehouse:

1. During an initial load, when the EDW is first created
2. During subsequent updates (normally performed on a periodic basis) to keep the EDW current and/or to expand it

Data reconciliation can be visualized as a process, shown in Figure 10-1, consisting of five steps: mapping and metadata management (the result shown as a metadata repository in Figure 10-1), capture, scrub, transform, and load and index. In reality, the steps may be combined in different ways. For example, data capture and scrub might be combined as a single process, or scrub and transform might be combined. Typically, data rejected from the cleansing step cause messages to be sent to the appropriate

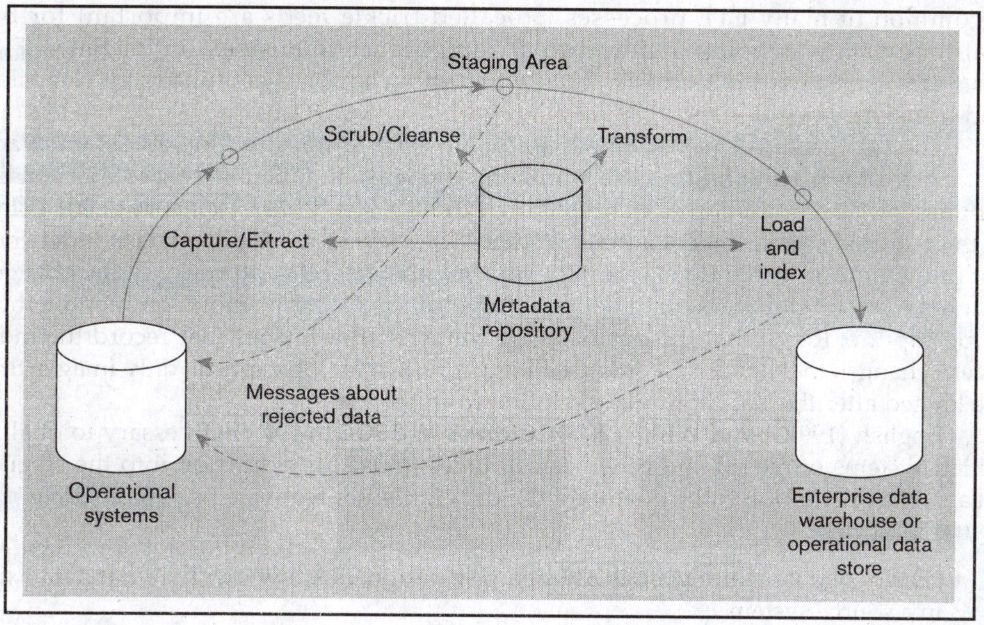

FIGURE 10-1 Steps in data reconciliation

operational systems to fix the data at the source and to be resent in a later extract. Figure 10-1 actually simplifies ETL considerably. Eckerson (2003) outline seven components of an ETL process, whereas Kimball (2004) outlines 38 subsystems of ETL. We do not have space to detail all of these subsystems. The fact that there are as many as 38 subsystems highlights why so much time is spent on ETL for data warehousing and why selecting ETL tools can be so important and difficult. We discuss mapping and metadata management, capture, scrub, and load and index next, followed by a thorough discussion of transform.

MAPPING AND METADATA MANAGEMENT ETL begins with a design step in which data (detailed or aggregate) needed in the warehouse are mapped back to the source data to be used to compose the warehouse data. This mapping could be shown graphically, or in a simple matrix with rows as source data elements, columns as data warehouse table columns, and the cells as explanations of any reformatting, transformations, and cleansing actions to be done. The process flows take the source data through various steps of consolidation, merging, de-duping, and simply conversion into one consistent stream of jobs to feed the scrubbing and transformation steps. And to do this mapping, which involves selecting the most reliable source for data, one must have good metadata sufficient to understand fine differences between apparently the same data in multiple sources. Metadata are then created to explain the mapping and job flow process. This mapping and any further information needed (e.g., explanation of why certain sources were chosen, the timing and frequencies of extracts needed to create the desired target data) are documented in a metadata repository. Choosing among several sources for target warehouse data is based on the kinds of data quality characteristics discussed earlier in this chapter.

EXTRACT Capturing the relevant data from the source files and databases used to fill the EDW is typically called *extracting*. Usually, not all data contained in the various operational source systems are required; just a subset are required. Extracting the subset of data is based on an extensive analysis of both the source and target systems, which is best performed by a team directed by data administration and composed of both end users and data warehouse professionals.

Technically, an alternative to this classical beginning to the ETL process is supported by a newer class of tools called enterprise application integration (EAI), which we outlined earlier in this chapter. EAI tools enable event-driven (i.e., real-time) data to be captured and used in an integrated way across disparate source systems. EAI can be used to capture data when they change not on a periodic basis, which is common of many ETL processes. So-called trickle feeds are important for the real-time data warehouse architecture to support active business intelligence. EAI tools can also be used to feed ETL tools, which often have richer abilities for cleansing and transformation.

The two generic types of data extracts are static extract and incremental extract. Static extract is used to fill the data warehouse initially, and incremental extract is used for ongoing warehouse maintenance. **Static extract** is a method of capturing a snapshot of the required source data at a point in time. The view of the source data is independent of the time at which it was created. **Incremental extract** captures only the changes that have occurred in the source data since the last capture. The most common method is log capture. Recall that the database log contains after images that record the most recent changes to database records (see Figure 9-6). With log capture, only images that are logged after the last capture are selected from the log.

Static extract
A method of capturing a snapshot of the required source data at a point in time.

Incremental extract
A method of capturing only the changes that have occurred in the source data since the last capture.

English (1999a) and White (2000) address in detail the steps necessary to qualify which systems of record and other data sources to use for extraction into the staging area. A major criterion is the quality of the data in the source systems. Quality depends on the following:

- Clarity of data naming, so the warehouse designers know exactly what data exist in a source system
- Completeness and accuracy of business rules enforced by a source system, which directly affects the accuracy of data; also, the business rules in the source should match the rules to be used in the data warehouse
- The format of data (Common formats across sources help to match related data.)

It is also important to have agreements with the owners of source systems so that they will inform the data warehouse administrators when changes are made in the metadata for the source system. Because transaction systems frequently change to meet new business needs and to utilize new and better software and hardware technologies, managing changes in the source systems is one of the biggest challenges of the extraction process. Changes in the source system require a reassessment of data quality and the procedures for extracting and transforming data. These procedures map data in the source systems to data in the target data warehouse (or data marts). For each data element in the data warehouse, a map says which data from which source systems to use to derive that data; transformation rules, which we address in a separate section, then state how to perform the derivation. For custom-built source systems, a data warehouse administrator has to develop customized maps and extraction routines; predefined map templates can be purchased for some packaged application software, such as ERP systems.

Extraction may be done by routines written with tools associated with the source system, say, a tool to export data. Data are usually extracted in a neutral data format, such as comma-delimited ANSI format. Sometimes the SQL command SELECT . . . INTO can be used to create a table. Once the data sources have been selected and extraction routines written, data can be moved into the staging area, where the cleansing process begins.

CLEANSE It is generally accepted that one role of the ETL process (as with any other data integration activity) is to identify erroneous data, not fix them. Experts generally agree that fixes should be made in the appropriate source systems, so such erroneous data, created by systematic procedural mistakes, do not reoccur. Rejected data are eliminated from further ETL steps and will be reprocessed in the next feed from the relevant source system. Some data can be fixed by cleansing so that loading data into the warehouse is not delayed. In any case, messages need to be sent to the offending source system(s) to prevent future errors or confusions.

Poor data quality is the bane of ETL. In fact, it is the bane of all information systems ("garbage in, garbage out"). Unfortunately, this has always been true and remains so. Eckerson and White (2003) found that ensuring adequate data quality was the number-one challenge of ETL, followed closely by understanding source data, a highly related issue. Procedures should be in place to ensure data are captured "correctly" at the source. But what is correct depends on the source system, so the cleansing step of

ETL must, at a minimum, resolve differences between what each source believes is quality data. The issue may be timing; that is, one system is ahead of another on updating common or related data. (As you will see later, time is a very important factor in data warehouses, so it is important for data warehousing to understand the time stamp for a piece of data.) So there is a need for further data quality steps to be taken during ETL.

Data in the operational systems are of poor quality or are inconsistent across source systems for many common reasons, including data entry errors by employees and customers, changes to the source systems, bad and inconsistent metadata, and system errors or corrupted data from the extract process. You cannot assume that data are clean even when the source system works fine (e.g., the source system may have used default but inaccurate values). Some of the errors and inconsistencies typical of these data that can be troublesome to data warehousing are as follows:

1. Misspelled names and addresses, odd formats for names and addresses (e.g., leading spaces, multiple spaces between words, missing periods for abbreviations, use of different capitalizations like all caps instead of upper- and lowercase letters)
2. Impossible or erroneous dates of birth
3. Fields used for purposes for which they were not intended or for different purposes in different table rows (essentially, multiple meanings for the same column)
4. Mismatched addresses and area codes
5. Missing data
6. Duplicate data
7. Inconsistencies (e.g., different addresses) in values or formats across sources (e.g., data could be kept at different levels of detail or for different time periods)
8. Different primary keys across sources

Thorough data cleansing involves both detecting such errors and repairing them and preventing them from occurring in the future. Some of these types of errors can be corrected during cleansing, and the data can be made ready for loading; in any case, source system owners need to be informed of errors so that processes can be fixed in the source systems to prevent such errors from occurring in the future.

Let's consider some examples of such errors. Customer names are often used as primary keys or as search criteria in customer files. However, these names are often misspelled or spelled in various ways in these files. For example, the name The Coca-Cola Company is the correct name for the soft-drink company. This name may be entered in customer records as Coca-Cola, Coca Cola, TCCC, and so on. In one study, a company found that the name McDonald's could be spelled 100 different ways!

A feature of many ETL tools is the ability to parse text fields to assist in discerning synonyms and misspellings, and also to reformat data. For example, name and address fields, which could be extracted from source systems in varying formats, can be parsed to identify each component of the name and address so they can be stored in the data warehouse in a standardized way, and can be used to help match records from different source systems. These tools can also often correct name misspellings and resolve address discrepancies. In fact, matched records can be found through address analysis.

Another type of data pollution occurs when a field is used for purposes for which it was not intended. For example, in one bank, a record field was designed to hold a telephone number. However, branch managers who had no such use for this field instead stored the interest rate in it. Another example, reported by a major UK bank, was even more bizarre. The data-scrubbing program turned up a customer on their files whose occupation was listed as "steward on the *Titanic*" (Devlin, 1997).

You may wonder why such errors are so common in operational data. The quality of operational data is largely determined by the value of data to the organization responsible for gathering them. Unfortunately, it often happens that the data-gathering organization places a low value on some data whose accuracy is important to downstream applications, such as data warehousing.

Given the common occurrence of errors, the worst thing a company can do is simply copy operational data to the data warehouse. Instead, it is important to improve the

Data scrubbing
A process of using pattern recognition and other artificial intelligence techniques to upgrade the quality of raw data before transforming and moving the data to the data warehouse. Also called data cleansing.

quality of the source data through a technique called data scrubbing. **Data scrubbing** (also called data cleansing) involves using pattern recognition and other techniques to upgrade the quality of raw data before transforming them and moving the data to a data warehouse. How to scrub each piece of data varies by attribute, so considerable analysis goes into the design of each ETL scrubbing step. Also, the data scrubbing techniques must be reassessed each time changes are made to the source system. Some scrubbing will reject obviously bad data outright, and the source system will be sent a message to fix the erroneous data and get them ready for the next extract. Other results from scrubbing may flag the data for more detailed manual analysis (e.g., why did one salesperson sell more than three times any other salesperson?) before rejecting the data.

Successful data warehousing requires that a formal program in TQM be implemented. TQM focuses on defect prevention rather than defect correction. Although data scrubbing can help upgrade data quality, it is not a long-term solution to the data quality problem. (See the earlier section in this chapter on TQM in data quality management.)

The type of data cleansing required depends on the quality of data in the source system. Besides fixing the types of problems identified earlier, other common cleansing tasks include the following:

- Decoding data to make them understandable for data warehousing applications.
- Parsing text fields to break them into finer components (e.g., breaking apart an address field into its constituent parts).
- Standardizing data, such as in the prior example for variations on customer names; standardization involves even simple actions such as using fixed vocabularies across all values (e.g., Inc. for incorporated and Jr. for junior).
- Reformatting and changing data types and performing other functions to put data from each source into the standard data warehouse format, ready for transformation.
- Adding time stamps to distinguish values for the same attribute over time.
- Converting between different units of measure.
- Generating primary keys for each row of a table. (We discuss the formation of data warehouse table primary and foreign keys later in this chapter.)
- Matching and merging separate extractions into one table or file and matching data to go into the same row of the generated table. (This can be a very difficult process when different keys are used in different source systems, when naming conventions are different, and when the data in the source systems are erroneous.)
- Logging errors detected, fixing those errors, and reprocessing corrected data without creating duplicate entries.
- Finding missing data to complete the batch of data necessary for subsequent loading.

The order in which different data sources are processed may matter. For example, it may be necessary to process customer data from a sales system before new customer demographic data from an external system can be matched to customers.

Once data are cleansed in the staging area, the data are ready for transformation. Before we discuss the transformation process in some detail, however, we briefly review in the next section the procedures used to load data into the data warehouse or data marts. It makes sense to discuss transformation after discussing load. There is a trend in data warehousing to reformulate ETL into ELT, utilizing the power of the data warehouse technology to assist in the cleansing and transformation activities.

LOAD AND INDEX The last step in filling an enterprise data warehouse (see Figure 10-1) is to load the selected data into the target data warehouse and to create the necessary indexes. The two basic modes for loading data to the target EDW are refresh and update.

Refresh mode
An approach to filling a data warehouse that involves bulk rewriting of the target data at periodic intervals.

Refresh mode is an approach to filling a data warehouse that involves bulk rewriting of the target data at periodic intervals. That is, the target data are written initially to fill the warehouse. Then, at periodic intervals, the warehouse is rewritten, replacing the previous contents. This mode has become less popular than update mode.

Update mode is an approach in which only changes in the source data are written to the data warehouse. To support the periodic nature of warehouse data, these new records are usually written to the data warehouse without overwriting or deleting previous records (see Figure 9-8).

Update mode
An approach to filling a data warehouse in which only changes in the source data are written to the data warehouse.

As you would expect, refresh mode is generally used to fill a warehouse when it is first created. Update mode is then generally used for ongoing maintenance of the target warehouse. Refresh mode is used in conjunction with static data capture, whereas update mode is used in conjunction with incremental data capture.

With both refresh and update modes, it is necessary to create and maintain the indexes that are used to manage the warehouse data. Two types of indexing, called *bit-mapped indexing* and *join indexing* (see Chapter 5), are often used in a data warehouse environment.

Because a data warehouse keeps historical data, integrated from disparate source systems, it is often important to those who use the data warehouse to know where the data came from. Metadata may provide this information about specific attributes, but the metadata, too, must show history (e.g., the source may change over time). More detailed procedures may be necessary if there are multiple sources or if knowing which specific extract or load file placed the data in the warehouse or what transformation routine created the data. (This may be necessary for uncovering the source of errors discovered in the warehouse.) Variar (2002) outlines the intricacies of tracing the origins of warehouse data.

Westerman (2001), based on the highly publicized and successful data warehousing at Wal-Mart Corporation, discusses factors in determining how frequently to update the data warehouse. His guideline is to update a data warehouse as frequently as is practical. Infrequent updating causes massive loads and requires users to wait for new data. Near-real-time loads are necessary for active data warehousing but may be inefficient and unnecessary for most data-mining and analysis applications. Westerman suggests that daily updates are sufficient for most organizations. (Statistics show that 75 percent of organizations do daily updates.) However, daily updates make it impossible to react to some changing conditions, such as repricing or changing purchase orders for slow-moving items. Wal-Mart updates its data warehouse continuously, which is practical given the massively parallel data warehouse technology it uses. The industry trend is toward updates several times a day, in near-real-time, and less use of more infrequent refresh intervals, such as monthly (Agosta, 2003).

Loading data into a warehouse typically means appending new rows to tables in the warehouse. It may also mean updating existing rows with new data (e.g., to fill in missing values from an additional data source), and it may mean purging identified data from the warehouse that have become obsolete due to age or that were incorrectly loaded in a prior load operation. Data may be loaded from the staging area into a warehouse by the following:

- SQL commands (e.g., INSERT or UPDATE)
- Special load utilities provided by the data warehouse vendor or a third-party vendor
- Custom-written routines coded by the warehouse administrators (a very common practice, which uses the previously mentioned two approaches)

In any case, these routines must not only update the data warehouse but must also generate error reports to show rejected data (e.g., attempting to append a row with a duplicate key or updating a row that does not exist in a table of the data warehouse).

Load utilities may work in batch or continuous mode. With a utility, you write a script that defines the format of the data in the staging area and which staging area data maps to which data warehouse fields. The utility may be able to convert data types for a field in the staging area to the target field in the warehouse and may be able to perform IF . . . THEN . . . ELSE logic to handle staging area data in various formats or to direct input data to different data warehouse tables. The utility can purge all data in a warehouse table (DELETE * FROM *tablename*) before data loading (refresh mode) or can append new rows (update mode). The utility may be able to sort input data so that rows are appended before they are updated. The utility program runs as would any stored procedure for the DBMS, and ideally all the controls of the DBMS for concurrency as well as restart and recovery in case of a DBMS failure during loading will work. Because the execution of a load can be very time-consuming, it is critical to be able to restart a load from a checkpoint in case the DBMS crashes in the middle of executing a load. See Chapter 11 for a thorough discussion of restart and recovery of databases.

DATA TRANSFORMATION

Data transformation
The component of data reconciliation that converts data from the format of the source operational systems to the format of the enterprise data warehouse.

Data transformation (or transform) is at the very center of the data reconciliation process. **Data transformation** involves converting data from the format of the source operational systems to the format of the enterprise data warehouse. Data transformation accepts data from the data capture component (after data scrubbing, if it applies), maps the data to the format of the reconciled data layer, and then passes the data to the load and index component.

Data transformation may range from a simple change in data format or representation to a highly complex exercise in data integration. Following are three examples that illustrate this range:

1. A salesperson requires a download of customer data from a mainframe database to her laptop computer. In this case, the transformation required is simply mapping the data from EBCDIC to ASCII representation, which can easily be performed by off-the-shelf software.
2. A manufacturing company has product data stored in three different legacy systems: a manufacturing system, a marketing system, and an engineering application. The company needs to develop a consolidated view of these product data. Data transformation involves several different functions, including resolving different key structures, converting to a common set of codes, and integrating data from different sources. These functions are quite straightforward, and most of the necessary software can be generated using a standard commercial software package with a graphical interface.
3. A large health-care organization manages a geographically dispersed group of hospitals, clinics, and other care centers. Because many of the units have been obtained through acquisition over time, the data are heterogeneous and uncoordinated. For a number of important reasons, the organization needs to develop a data warehouse to provide a single corporate view of the enterprise. This effort will require the full range of transformation functions described next, including some custom software development.

The functions performed in data scrubbing and the functions performed in data transformation blend together. In general, the goal of data scrubbing is to correct errors in data *values* in the source data, whereas the goal of data transformation is to convert the data *format* from the source to the target system. Note that it is essential to scrub the data before they are transformed because if there are errors in the data before they are transformed, the errors will remain in the data after transformation.

Data Transformation Functions

Data transformation encompasses a variety of different functions. These functions may be classified broadly into two categories: record-level functions and field-level functions. In most data warehousing applications, a combination of some or even all of these functions is required.

RECORD-LEVEL FUNCTIONS Operating on a set of records, such as a file or table, the most important record-level functions are selection, joining, normalization, and aggregation.

Selection
The process of partitioning data according to predefined criteria.

Selection (also called subsetting) is the process of partitioning data according to predefined criteria. For data warehouse applications, selection is used to extract the relevant data from the source systems that will be used to fill the data warehouse. In fact, selection is typically a part of the capture function discussed earlier. When the source data are relational, SQL SELECT statements can be used for selection. (See Chapter 6 for a detailed discussion.) For example, recall that incremental capture is often implemented by selecting after images from the database log that have been created since the previous capture. A typical after image was shown in Figure 9-6. Suppose that the after images for this application are stored in a table named AccountHistory_T Then the after images that have been created after 12/31/2010 can be selected with the following statements:

```
SELECT *
FROM AccountHistory_T
WHERE CreateDate > 12/31/2010;
```

Joining combines data from various sources into a single table or view. Data joining is an important function in data warehouse applications because it is often necessary to consolidate data from various sources. For example, an insurance company may have client data spread throughout several different files and databases. When the source data are relational, SQL statements can be used to perform a join operation. (See Chapter 6 for details.)

Joining
The process of combining data from various sources into a single table or view.

Joining is often complicated by factors such as the following:

- Often the source data are not relational (the extracts are flat files), in which case SQL statements cannot be used. Instead, procedural language statements must be coded or the data must first be moved into a staging area that uses an RDBMS.
- Even for relational data, primary keys for the tables to be joined are often from different domains (e.g., engineering part number versus catalog number). These keys must then be reconciled before an SQL join can be performed.
- Source data may contain errors, which makes join operations hazardous.

Normalization is the process of decomposing relations with anomalies to produce smaller, well-structured relations. (See Chapter 4 for a detailed discussion.) As indicated earlier, source data in operational systems are often denormalized (or simply not normalized). The data must therefore be normalized as part of data transformation.

Aggregation is the process of transforming data from a detailed level to a summary level. For example, in a retail business, individual sales transactions can be summarized to produce total sales by store, product, date, and so on. Because (in our model) the enterprise data warehouse contains only detailed data, aggregation is not normally associated with this component. However, aggregation is an important function in filling the data marts, as explained next.

Aggregation
The process of transforming data from a detailed level to a summary level.

FIELD-LEVEL FUNCTIONS A field-level function converts data from a given format in a source record to a different format in the target record. Field-level functions are of two types: single-field and multifield functions.

A *single-field* transformation converts data from a single source field to a single target field. Figure 10-2a is a basic representation of this type of transformation (designated by the letter *T* in the diagram). An example of a single-field transformation is converting a textual representation, such as Yes/No, into a numeric 1/0 representation.

As shown in Figures 10-2b and 10-2c, there are two basic methods for performing a single-field transformation: algorithmic and table lookup. An algorithmic transformation is performed using a formula or logical expression. Figure 10-2b shows a conversion from Fahrenheit to Celsius temperature using a formula. When a simple algorithm does not apply, a lookup table can be used instead. Figure 10-2c shows the use of a table to convert state codes to state names. (This type of conversion is common in data warehouse applications.)

A *multifield* transformation converts data from one or more source fields to one or more target fields. This type of transformation is very common in data warehouse applications. Two multifield transformations are shown in Figure 10-3.

Figure 10-3a is an example of a many-to-one transformation. (In this case, two source fields are mapped to one target field.) In the source record, the combination of employee name and telephone number is used as the primary key. This combination is awkward and may not uniquely identify a person. Therefore, in creating a target record,

FIGURE 10-2 Single-field transformations
(a) Basic representation
(b) Algorithmic
(c) Table lookup

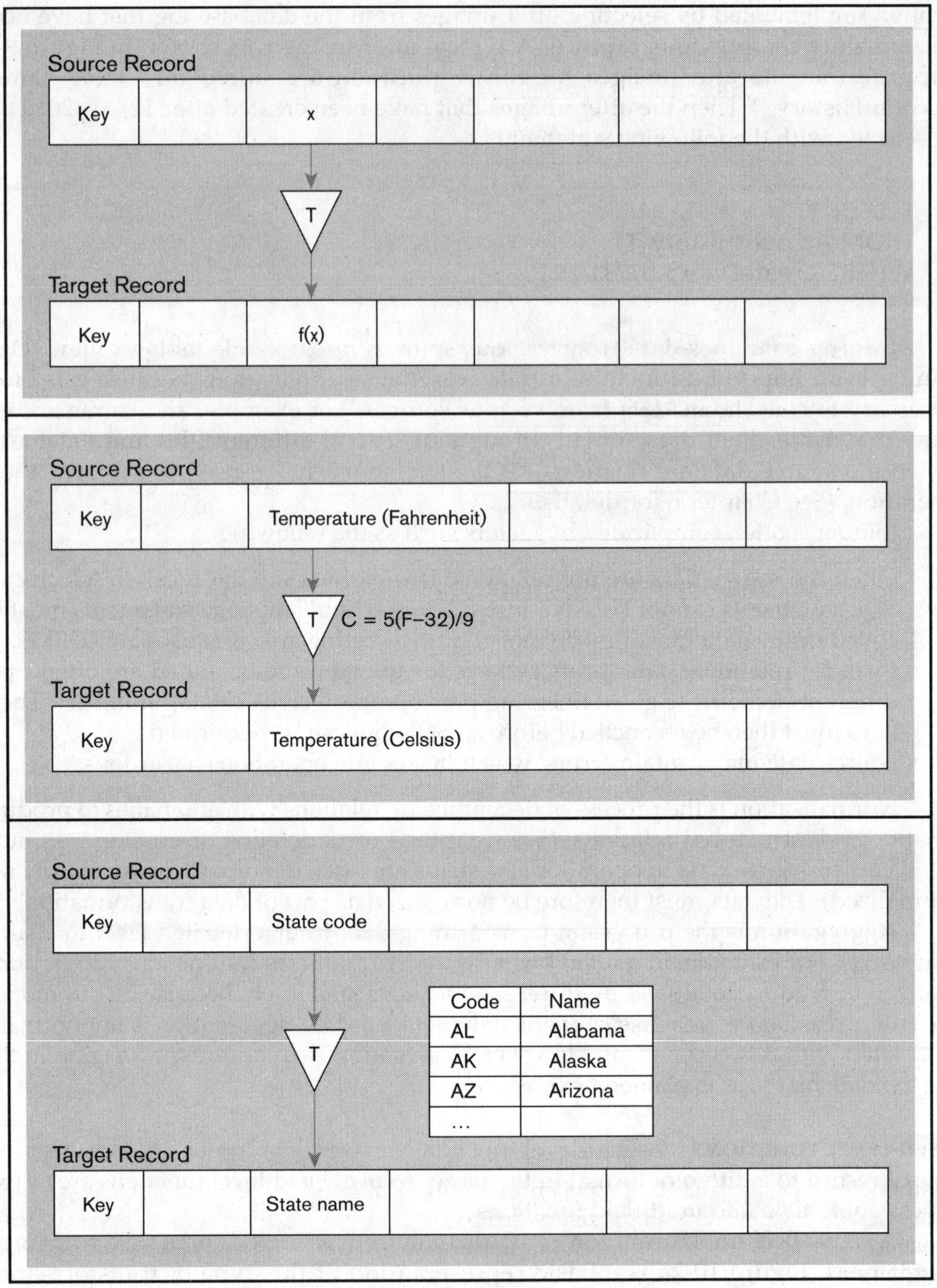

the combination is mapped to a unique employee ID (EmpID). A lookup table would be created to support this transformation. A data scrubbing program might be employed to help identify duplicates in the source data.

Figure 10-3b is an example of a one-to-many transformation. (In this case, one source field has been converted to two target fields.) In the source record, a product code has been used to encode the combination of brand name and product name. (The use of such codes is common in operational data.) However, in the target record, it is desired to display the full text describing product and brand names. Again, a lookup table would be employed for this purpose.

In Figure 10-3, the multifield transformations shown involve only one source record and one target record. More generally, multifield transformations may involve more than one source record and/or more than one target record. In the most complex cases, these records may even originate in different operational systems and in different time zones (Devlin, 1997).

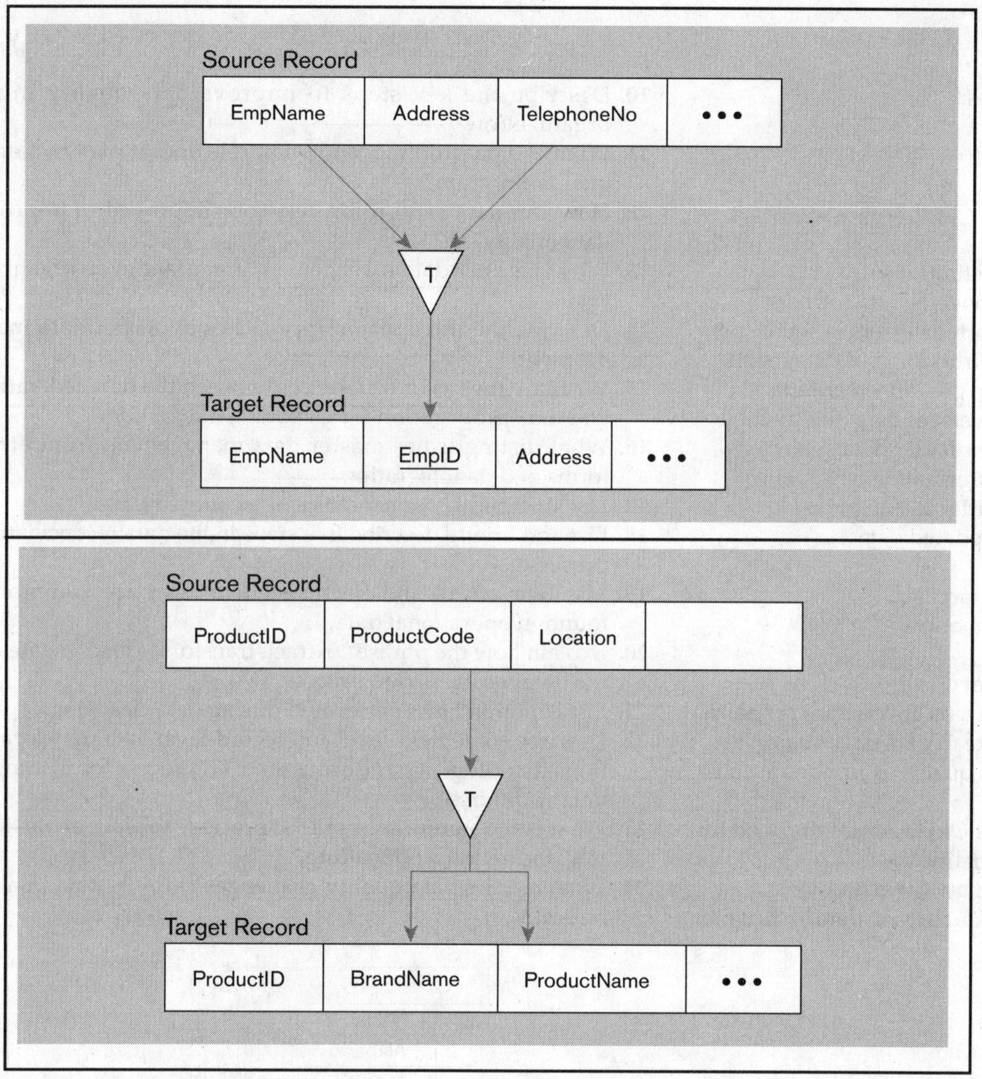

FIGURE 10-3 Multifield transformations
(a) Many sources to one target
(b) One source to many targets

Summary

Ensuring the quality of data that enter databases and data warehouses is essential if users are to have confidence in their systems. Ensuring data quality is also now mandated by regulations such as the Sarbanes-Oxley Act and the Basel II Accord. Data quality is often a key part of an overall data governance initiative. Data governance is often the backbone of enterprise-wide data management initiatives in an organization.

Many organizations today do not have proactive data quality programs, and poor quality data is a widespread problem. A proactive data quality program will start with a good business case to address any organizational barriers, be a part of an overall data governance program, employ the use of data stewards, apply proven TQM principles and practices, and use modern data management software technology. Data quality is of special concern when data are integrated across sources from inside and outside the organization. Fairly modern techniques of data integration—consolidation (including ETL for data warehouses), federation, propagation, and master data management—are vastly improving opportunities for sharing data while allowing for local controls and databases optimized for local uses.

Chapter Review

Key Terms

Aggregation *455*
Changed data capture (CDC) *446*
Data federation *446*
Data governance *436*
Data scrubbing *452*
Data steward *437*
Data transformation *454*
Incremental extract *450*
Joining *455*
Master data management (MDM) *444*
Refresh mode *452*
Selection *454*
Static extract *450*
Update mode *453*

Review Questions

1. Define each of the following terms:
   a. static extract
   b. incremental extract
   c. data steward
   d. master data management
   e. refresh mode
2. Match the following terms and definitions:

____ data transformation	a. converts data formats
____ data scrubbing	b. corrects errors in source data
____ selection	c. partitioning of data based on predefined criteria
____ data steward	d. oversees data quality for a particular data subject
____ changed data capture	e. information needed in order to integrate updated data

3. Contrast the following terms:
   a. static extract; incremental extract
   b. data scrubbing; data transformation
   c. consolidation; federation
   d. ETL; master data management
4. What are the key components of a data governance program?
5. How does data stewardship relate to data governance?
6. What are four reasons why data quality is important to an organization?
7. Explain the effect of the Sarbanes-Oxley Act on the need for organizations to improve data quality.
8. Define the eight characteristics of quality data.
9. Explain four reasons why the quality of data is poor in many organizations.
10. Describe the key steps to improve data quality in an organization.
11. What is data profiling, and what role does it play in a data quality program?
12. How can data capture processes be improved to improve data quality?
13. Why is master data management important in an organization?
14. Describe the three major approaches to master data management.
15. What are the major differences between the data federation and data propagation forms of data integration?
16. What distinguishes master data management from other forms of data integration?
17. List six typical characteristics of reconciled data.
18. List and briefly describe five steps in the data reconciliation process.
19. List five errors and inconsistencies that are commonly found in operational data.
20. Explain how the phrase "extract–transform– load" relates to the data reconciliation process.
21. List common tasks performed during data cleansing.
22. Describe some field-level and record-level data transformations that often occur during the ETL process for loading a data warehouse.
23. What is the significance of ETL process? Explain extraction, transformation, and loading.
24. What are the data quality challenges? Why is data quality critical?

Problems and Exercises

Problems 1 through 5 are based on the Fitchwood Insurance Company case study, which was described in the Problems and Exercises for Chapter 9, and the associated Figure 9-26.

1. The OLTP system data for the Fitchwood Insurance Company is in a series of flat files. What process do you envision would be needed in order to extract the data and create the ERD shown in Figure 9-26? How often should the extraction process be performed? Should it be a static extract or an incremental extract?
2. What types of data pollution/cleansing problems might occur with the Fitchwood OLTP system data?
3. Research some tools that perform data scrubbing. What tool would you recommend for the Fitchwood Insurance Company?
4. What types of data transformations might be needed in order to build the Fitchwood data mart?
5. After some further analysis, you discover that the commission field in the Policies table is updated yearly to reflect changes in the annual commission paid to agents on existing policies. Would knowing this information change the way in which you extract and load data into the data mart from the OLTP system?

PINE VALLEY FURNITURE

6. The Pine Valley databases for this textbook (one small version illustrated in queries throughout the text and a larger version) are available to your instructor to download from the book's Web site. Your instructor can make those databases available to you. Alternatively, these and other databases are available at **www.teradatastudentnetwork.com** (your instructor will tell you the login password, and you will need to register and then create an SQL Assistant log-in for the parts of this question). There may actually be another database your instructor wants you to use for this series of questions. Regardless of how you gain access to a database, answer the following exercises for that database.
   a. Develop a plan for performing a data profile analysis on this database. Base your plan on the eight characteristics of quality data, on other concepts introduced in the chapter, and on a set of business rules you will need to create for this database. Justify your plan.
   b. Perform your data profile plan for one of the tables in the database (pick the table you think might be the most vulnerable to data quality issues). Develop an audit report on the quality of data in this table.
   c. Execute your data profile plan for a set of three or four related tables. Develop an audit report on the quality of data in these tables.
   d. Based on the potential errors you discover in the data to the previous two exercises (assuming that you find some potential errors), recommend some ways the capture of the erroneous data could be improved to prevent errors in future data entry for this type of data.

e. Evaluate the ERD for the database. (You may have to reverse-engineer the ERD if one is not available with the database.) Is this a high-quality data model? If not, how should it be changed to make it a high-quality data model?

f. Assume that you are working with a Pine Valley Furniture Company (PVFC) database in this exercise. Consider the large and small PVFC databases as two different source systems within PVFC. What type of approach would you recommend (consolidation, federation, propagation, master data management), and why, for data integration across these two databases? Presume that you do not know a specific list of queries or reports that need the integrated database; therefore, design your data integration approach to support any requirements against any data from these databases.

7. Perform a search of companies and products that are available to help with data reconciliation and integration. Document your results by filling in the table below. We have provided a sample example:

Product Name	Company	Data Integration Steps Supported
Data Bridger	Taurus Software	Extract, transform, load, and index

8. Refer to the Problems and Exercises in Chapter 9 – PMPL:
   a. What could be the problems with respect to data cleansing and data pollution?
   b. In case the finance department of PMPL needs a data mart from the dimension tables, what transformations are required for the data?

Field Exercises

1. Master data management and the related specialty customer data integration are rapidly changing disciplines. Find a recent article or book on these topics (or some other specialty area for master data management, such as in health care, operations, or human resources) and prepare a summary of new ideas introduced in that resource that expand on the discussion from this chapter.
2. Access the resources at Teradata Student Network (**www.teradatastudentnetwork.com**) for a Webinar or Webcast (produced after 2007) on the topic of data integration or master data management that was. Prepare a summary of new ideas introduced in that Webcast that expand on the discussion from this chapter.
3. Interview data warehouse managers in an organization where you have contacts about their ETL processes. What lessons did you learn from your interviews about the design of sound ETL processes?
4. Interview a data administrator in an organization that has established a data governance committee and data stewards. Document the different roles provided by the data administrator(s), data stewards, and data governance committee members. What is the charter for the data governance committee? How are issues about data planning, quality, security, and ownership resolved? What would the data administrator like to change about the data governance process, and why?

References

Agosta, L. 2003. "Data Warehouse Refresh Rates." *DM Review* 13,6 (June): 49.

Brauer, B. 2002. "Data Quality—Spinning Straw into Gold," **www2.sas.com/proceedings/sugi26/p117-26.pdf**.

Carlson, D. 2002. "Data Stewardship Action," *DM Review* 12,5 (May): 37,62.

Devlin, B. 1997. *Data Warehouse: From Architecture to Implementation*. Reading, MA: Addison-Wesley Longman.

Dyché, J. 2007. "The Myth of the Purebred Data Steward." (February 22) available at **www.b-eye-network.com/print/3971**.

Dyché, J., and E. Levy. 2006. *Customer Data Integration: Reaching a Single Version of the Truth.* Hoboken, NJ: Wiley.

Eckerson, W. 2003. "The Evolution of ETL." *Business Intelligence Journal* (Fall): 4–8.

Eckerson, W., and C. White. 2003. *Evaluating ETL and Data Integration Platforms*. The Data Warehouse Institute, available at **www.tdwi.org**, under "Research Reports."

English, L. 1999a. *Business Information Quality: Methods for Reducing Costs and Improving Profits*. New York: Wiley.

English, L. P. 1999b. *Improving Data Warehouse and Business Information Quality*. New York: Wiley.

English, L. P. 2004. "Six Sigma and Total Information Quality Management (TIQM)." *DM Review* 14,10 (October): 44–49, 73.

Hay, D. C. 2005. "Data Model Quality: Where Good Data Begin." Published online at **www.tdan.com** (January).

Hoffer, J., J. George, and J. Valacich. 2010. *Modern Systems Analysis and Design*, 5th ed. Upper Saddle River, NJ. Prentice Hall.

Imhoff, C., and C.White. 2006. "Master Data Management: Creating a Single View of the Business," available at **www.beyeresearch.com/study/3360**.

Informatica. 2005. "Addressing Data Quality at the Enterprise Level." (October).

Inmon, B. 2004. "Data Quality." (June 24) available at **www.b-eye-network.com/view/188**.

Kimball, R. 2004. "The 38 Subsystems of ETL." *Intelligent Enterprise* 8,12 (December 4): 16, 17, 46.

Krudop, M. E. 2005. "Maximizing Your ETL Tool Investment." *DM Review* 15,3 (March): 26–28.

Laurent, W. 2005. "The Case for Data Stewardship." *DM Review* 15,2 (February): 26–28.

Leon, M. 2007. "Escaping Information Anarchy." *DB2 Magazine* 12,1: 23–26.

Loshin, D. 2001. "The Cost of Poor Data Quality." *DM Review* (June 29) available at **www.information-management.com/infodirect/20010629/3605-1.html**.

Loshin, D. 2006. "Monitoring Data Quality Performance Using Data Quality Metrics." A white paper from Informatica (November).

Moriarty, T. 1996. "Better Business Practices." *Database Programming & Design* 9,7 (September): 59–61.

Redman, T. 2004. "Data: An Unfolding Quality Disaster." *DM Review* 14,8 (August): 21–23, 57.

Russom, P. 2006. "Taking Data Quality to the Enterprise through Data Governance." *TDWI Report Series*. (March).

Seiner, R. 2005. "Data Steward Roles & Responsibilities," available at **www.tdan.com**, July, 2005.

Yugay, I., and V. Klimchenko. 2004. "SOX Mandates Focus on Data Quality & Integration." *DM Review* 14,2 (February): 38–42.

Variar, G. 2002. "The Origin of Data." *Intelligent Enterprise* 5,2 (February 1): 37–41.

Westerman, P. 2001. *Data Warehousing: Using the Wal-Mart Model*. San Francisco: Morgan Kaufmann.

White, C. 2000. "First Analysis." *Intelligent Enterprise* 3,9 (June): 50–55.

Further Reading

Eckerson, W. 2002. "Data Quality and the Bottom Line: Achieving Business Success Through a Commitment to Data Quality." **www.tdwi.org**.

Weill, P., and J. Ross. 2004. *IT Governance: How Top Performers Manage IT Decision Rights for Superior Results*. Boston: Harvard Business School Press.

Web Resources

www.informationintegrity.org Web site of a not-for-profit organization that promotes the awareness and understanding of information integrity.

www.knowledge-integrity.com Web site of David Loshin, a leading consultant in the data quality and business intelligence fields.

http://mitiq.mit.edu Web site for data quality research done at Massachusetts Institute of Technology.

www.tdwi.org Web site of The Data Warehousing Institute, which produces a variety of white papers, research reports, and Webinars that are available to the general public, as well as a wider array that are available only to members.

www.teradatastudentnetwork.com The Teradata Student Network (and the associated University Network for faculty), a free portal service to a wide variety of journal articles, training materials, Webinars, and other special reports on data quality, data integration, and related topics.

CASE

Mountain View Community Hospital

Case Description

At the end of Chapter 1, you learned about the Mountain View Community Hospital (MVCH) special study team that is developing a long-term strategic and information systems plan for the next five years. The team, composed of Mr. Heller, Mr. Lopez, Dr. Jefferson, and a consultant, is trying to devise a plan that will meet the hospital's goals of high-quality health care, cost containment, and expansion into new services, such as Dr. Browne's anticipated Geriatric Medicine department. Mr. Heller, MVCH's CIO, is a member of the Healthcare Information and Management Systems Society (HIMMS) and regularly reads IT-related magazines to keep up with developments and new technologies (e.g., *Computerworld*, *CIO Magazine*, *Health Management Technology*, *Health Data Management*, and *Healthcare Informatics*). He also attends health-care IT conferences that allow him to interact with his peers and find out what's new.

In response to issues with existing systems and recent trends in health-care IT (e.g., electronic medical records [EMRs], work-flow automation, etc.), the study team has been evaluating various options for integrating the hospital's operational, clinical, and financial information. An EMR system would allow physicians to access all medical information for a patient, even though that information is from different systems and locations, including various physician, hospital, laboratory, and insurance records. As part of a transition from the paper chart to EMRs, and as a way of addressing medical errors, hospitals, including MVCH, are also beginning to take a closer look at computerized physician order entry (CPOE) systems. (You may recall that the enterprise model developed by the study team included an ORDER entity.) Primarily implemented in large metropolitan areas and leading government hospitals at the present time, CPOE allows physicians to electronically enter their orders for labs, medications, radiology, and so on. CPOE not only eliminates problems stemming from illegible handwriting, it also provides decision support capabilities, intercepting medication errors at the time of order or alerting a physician to potential interactions with other medications a patient may be taking.

EMR and CPOE systems, however, represent a significant change in the way health-care information is collected and used. And change is often difficult. After a conversation with Dr. Z, who worked at a large hospital that used a CPOE system prior to joining MVCH, Mr. Heller realizes that physicians may not readily embrace such a system. For example, a physician who wants to prescribe an antibiotic for 10 days or 2 weeks may find that the default in the computer is 1 week. The physician would then have to manually override the default. Not only would this extra step consume extra time, it would also require greater knowledge of the computerized order system on the part of the physician. A handwritten order would have been more convenient. And, according to Dr. Z, this example is just one of a million little things that would be more difficult. While advocating the technology, Dr. Z believes that CPOE's steep learning curve and need for relearning can make the practice of medicine more difficult. Dr. Z also remembers a situation in which the pharmacy went into the system and unilaterally changed one of his orders.

In addition to his involvement with the hospital's special study team, Mr. Heller is facing a number of data management issues as a result of HIPAA's security rules to protect patient information. Contingency planning is one of them. HIPAA's contingency plan standard has five components: a data backup plan, a disaster recovery plan, an emergency mode operation plan, testing and revision procedures, and applications and data criticality analysis. The latter involves identifying all potential data security threats and determining their level of risk. HIPAA also has audit trail requirements that were briefly described in the Chapter 7 case segment.

Password management has become a huge issue lately. MVCH upgraded its security policies in response to HIPAA's information access management requirements. Users must have unique names and passwords for many applications and are required to change their passwords regularly. Physicians in particular are complaining about the many passwords they have to keep track of and the problems they have with logging on to an application when they forget a password. As a result, Mr. Heller's staff is working on making single sign-on (SSO) a reality at MVCH.

Other data management issues of concern to Mr. Heller include the hospital's data storage needs and data quality. Storage needs at MVCH continue to grow at an unprecedented rate as data (clinical and nonclinical) and diagnostic images are being created. HIPAA and other new regulations are increasing data volumes even more. HIPAA, for example, requires that some types of medical information be retained for many years—even beyond the lifetime of a patient. The study team's discussions of data warehousing technologies (see MVCH Chapter 9) have also brought data quality to the forefront. At one of the team's meetings, Mr. Lopez, the hospital's CFO, wanted to know just how much poor-quality data cost the hospital every year. He had read that poor data quality costs account for approximately 4 percent of a hospital's expenses.[1] Given the need for cost containment, Mr. Heller is beginning to feel the pressure to shift away from the current focus on fixing after the fact and moving toward proactively preventing data quality problems and building quality into the process.

Case Questions

1. Do you think that data quality at MVCH is a strategic issue? Why or why not?
2. In light of HIPAA and other regulations, securing and protecting patient records is a primary requirement for MVCH. Examine the organization chart for MVCH in Chapter 1 (MVCH Figure 1-1). Who would be the best choice for a data steward for patient data? Please explain your answer. What recommendations would you make for establishing a data governance committee for MVCH? Who should be on that committee?

---

[1]Barlow, R. D. 2005. "Routine Database Maintenance Can Lead to Hospital Treasure," *Health Care Purchasing News* 29:1 (January): 48-51.

3. Refer to the MVCH case in Chapter 9 and your answers to case questions and exercises there. How can a data warehouse help improve data quality at MVCH? Can it actually do so? Under what circumstance would a data warehouse improve data quality?
4. Refer to the MVCH case in Chapter 9 and your answers to case questions and exercises there. What data quality challenges may arise if MVCH develops a data warehouse and/or data mart(s)? Do you think that there is a need for data scrubbing? If so, is it necessary to scrub all tables or just some?
5. Commercial off-the-shelf (COTS) packages for EMR could replace all of the data systems that would have to be integrated to form an EMR system in-house at MVCH. (You might want to research a few as background to this question.) Develop a list of pros and cons for purchasing a COTS EMR system versus developing a program for data integration to provide EMR capabilities on top of the existing disparate data source systems within MVCH.

Case Exercises

1. Investigate data quality management in greater detail and outline a data quality strategy that would address the issues raised in the case description. What should be the first step? What would be considered high-quality data at MVCH? How could data quality be built into the process? Who should be part of it? What would be the ROI of a data quality initiative?
2. Assume that the result of an analysis to your answer to Case Question 5 is to develop an EMR system via data integration in-house. What approach to data integration would you recommend: consolidation, federation, propagation, or master data management? Justify your answer.

CHAPTER

11

Data and Database Administration

Learning Objectives

After studying this chapter, you should be able to:

- Concisely define each of the following key terms: **data administration, database administration, open source DBMS, database security, authorization rules, user-defined procedures, encryption, smart card, database recovery, backup facilities, journalizing facilities, transaction, transaction log, database change log, before image, after image, checkpoint facility, recovery manager, restore/rerun, transaction boundaries, backward recovery (rollback), forward recovery (rollforward), aborted transaction, database destruction, concurrency control, inconsistent read problem, locking, locking level (lock granularity), shared lock (S lock, or read lock), exclusive lock (X lock, or write lock), deadlock, deadlock prevention, two-phase locking protocol, deadlock resolution, versioning, data dictionary, system catalog, information repository, Information Resource Dictionary System (IRDS), data archiving,** and **heartbeat query.**
- List several major functions of data administration and of database administration.
- Describe the changing roles of the data administrator and database administrator in the current business environment.
- Describe the role of data dictionaries and information repositories and how they are used by data administration.
- Compare the optimistic and pessimistic systems of concurrency control.
- Describe the problem of database security and list five techniques that are used to enhance security.
- Understand the role of databases in Sarbanes-Oxley compliance.
- Describe the problem of database recovery and list four basic facilities that are included with a DBMS to recover databases.
- Describe the problem of tuning a database to achieve better performance, and list five areas where changes may be made when tuning a database.
- Describe the importance of data availability and list several measures to improve availability.

INTRODUCTION

Global Bank has branches worldwide and has many corporate accounts. The bank ran into deep problems because of its customers' data being compromised.

While the bank maintains that it servers were not hacked, the problems were rather caused by cyber criminals posing as legitimate business houses.

In certain cases, the accounts of HNI (High Net-worth Individuals) have been compromised and misused in stock market speculations leading to losses to the HNI. And it is shocking that in most cases, the fraud has been perpetuated by the internal staff of Global Bank.

The other HNIs have been alerted of such a fraud. Although the law enforcers have tracked down the criminals, the Global Bank had to bear the brunt of fraud as it had to compensate the HNI quite a large amount running to several millions of dollars.

The critical importance of data to organizations is widely recognized. Data are a corporate asset, just as personnel, physical resources, and financial resources are corporate assets. Like these other assets, data and information are too valuable to be managed casually. The development of information technology has made effective management of corporate data far more possible, but data are also vulnerable to accidental and malicious damage and misuse. Data and database administration activities have been developed to help achieve organizations' goals for the effective management of data.

Ineffective data administration, on the other hand, leads to poor data quality, security, and availability and can be characterized by the following conditions, which are all too common in organizations:

1. Multiple definitions of the same data entity and/or inconsistent representations of the same data elements in separate databases, making integration of data across different databases hazardous
2. Missing key data elements, whose loss eliminates the value of existing data
3. Low data quality levels due to inappropriate sources of data or timing of data transfers from one system to another, thus reducing the reliability of the data
4. Inadequate familiarity with existing data, including awareness of data location and meaning of stored data, thus reducing the capability to use the data to make effective strategic or planning decisions
5. Poor and inconsistent query response time, excessive database downtime, and either stringent or inadequate controls to ensure agreed upon data privacy and security
6. Lack of access to data due to damaged, sabotaged, or stolen files or due to hardware failures that eliminate paths to data users need
7. Embarrassment to the organization because of unauthorized access to data

Many of these conditions put an organization at risk for failing to comply with regulations, such as the Sarbanes-Oxley Act (SOX), the Health Insurance Portability and Accountability Act (HIPAA), and the Gramm-Leach-Bliley Act for adequate internal controls and procedures in support of financial control, data transparency, and data privacy. Manual processes for data control are discouraged, so organizations need to implement automated controls, in part through a DBMS (e.g., sophisticated data validation controls, security features, triggers, and stored procedures), to prevent and detect accidental damage of data and fraudulent activities. Databases must be backed-up and recovered to prevent permanent data loss. The who, what, when, and where of data must be documented in metadata repositories for auditor review. Data stewardship programs, aimed at reviewing data quality control procedures, are becoming popular. Collaboration across the organization is needed so data consolidation across distributed databases is accurate. Breaches of data accuracy or security must be communicated to executives and managers.

Morrow (2007) views data as the lifeblood of an organization. Good management of data involves managing data quality (as discussed in Chapter 10) as well as data security and availability (which we cover in this chapter). Organizations have responded to these data management issues with different strategies. Some have created a function called *data administration*. The person who heads this function is called the data administrator (DA), or information resource manager, and he or she takes responsibility for the overall management of data resources. A second function, *database administration*, has been regarded as being responsible for physical database design and for dealing with the technical issues, such as security enforcement, database performance, and backup and recovery, associated with managing a database. Other organizations combine the data administration and database administration functions. The rapidly changing pace of business has caused the roles of the data administrator and the database administrator (DBA) to change, in ways that are discussed next.

THE ROLES OF DATA AND DATABASE ADMINISTRATORS

Several new technologies and trends are driving the changes in the data administration and database administration roles (Mullins, 2001):

1. The proliferation of proprietary and open source technologies and databases on diverse platforms that must be managed concurrently in many organizations
2. Rapid growth in the size of databases, fueled by the storage of complex data types and the business intelligence needs of today's organizations
3. The embedding of business rules in databases in the form of triggers, stored procedures, and user-defined functions
4. The explosion of e-business applications that require linking corporate databases to the Internet and tracking Internet activity, thus making databases more open for unauthorized access from outside the organization

Against the background of these changes, it is important to understand traditional role distinctions. This will help us understand the ways in which the roles are being blended in organizations that have different information technology architectures.

Traditional Data Administration

Databases are shared resources that belong to the entire enterprise; they are not the property of a single function or individual within the organization. Data administration is the custodian of the organization's data, in much the same sense that the controller is custodian of the financial resources. Like the controller, the data administrator must develop procedures to protect and control the resource. Also, data administration must resolve disputes that may arise when data are centralized and shared among users and must play a significant role in deciding where data will be stored and managed. **Data administration** is a high-level function that is responsible for the overall management of data resources in an organization, including maintaining corporate-wide data definitions and standards.

Data administration
A high-level function that is responsible for the overall management of data resources in an organization, including maintaining corporate-wide definitions and standards.

Selecting the data administrator and organizing the function are extremely important organizational decisions. The data administrator must be a highly skilled manager capable of eliciting the cooperation of users and resolving differences that normally arise when significant change is introduced into an organization. The data administrator should be a respected, senior-level manager selected from within the organization, rather than a technical computer expert or a new individual hired for the position. However, the data administrator must have sufficient technical skills to interact effectively with technical staff members such as database administrators, system administrators, and programmers.

Following are some of the core roles of traditional data administration:

- ***Data policies, procedures, and standards*** Every database application requires protection established through consistent enforcement of data policies, procedures, and standards. Data policies are statements that make explicit the goals of data administration, such as "Every user must have a valid password." Data procedures are written outlines of actions to be taken to perform a certain activity. Backup and recovery procedures, for example, should be communicated to all involved employees. Data standards are explicit conventions and behaviors that are to be followed and that can be used to help evaluate database quality. Naming conventions for database objects should be standardized for programmers, for example. Increased use of external data sources and increased access to organizational databases from outside the organization have increased the importance of employees' understanding of data policies, procedures, and standards. Such policies and procedures need to be well documented to comply with the transparency requirements of financial reporting, security, and privacy regulations.
- ***Planning*** A key administration function is providing leadership in developing the organization's information architecture. Effective administration requires both an understanding of the needs of the organization for data and information and the ability to lead the development of an information architecture that will meet the diverse needs of the typical organization.
- ***Data conflict resolution*** Databases are intended to be shared and usually involve data from several different departments of the organization. Ownership of data is a ticklish issue at least occasionally in every organization. Those in data administration are well placed to resolve data ownership issues because they are not typically associated with a certain department. Establishing procedures for resolving such conflicts is essential. If the administration function has been given sufficient authority to mediate and enforce the resolution of the conflict, they may be very effective in this capacity.
- ***Managing the information repository*** Repositories contain the metadata that describe an organization's data and data processing resources. Information repositories are replacing data dictionaries in many organizations. Whereas data dictionaries are simple data element documentation tools, information repositories are used by data administrators and other information specialists to manage the total information processing environment. An information repository serves as an essential source of information and functionality for each of the following:
  1. Users who must understand data definitions, business rules, and relationships among data objects
  2. Automated CASE tools that are used to specify and develop information systems
  3. Applications that access and manipulate data (or business information) in the corporate databases
  4. Database management systems, which maintain the repository and update system privileges, passwords, object definitions, and so on
- ***Internal marketing*** While the importance of data and information to an organization has become more widely recognized within organizations, it is not necessarily true that an appreciation for data management issues—such as information architecture, data modeling, metadata, data quality, and data standards—has also evolved. The importance of following established procedures and policies must be proactively instituted through data (and database) administrators. Effective internal marketing may reduce resistance to change and data ownership problems.

When the data administration role is not separately defined in an organization, these roles are assumed by database administration and/or others in the IT organization.

Traditional Database Administration

Typically, the role of database administration is taken to be a hands-on, physical involvement with the management of a database or databases. **Database administration** is a technical function responsible for logical and physical database design and for dealing with technical issues, such as security enforcement, database performance, backup and recovery, and database availability. A database administrator (DBA) must understand the data models built by data administration and be capable of transforming them into efficient and appropriate logical and physical database designs (Mullins, 2002). The DBA implements the standards and procedures established by the data administrator, including enforcing programming standards, data standards, policies, and procedures.

Database administration
A technical function that is responsible for physical database design and for dealing with technical issues, such as security enforcement, database performance, and backup and recovery.

Just as a data administrator needs a wide variety of job skills, so does a DBA. Having a broad technical background, including a sound understanding of current hardware and software (operating system and networking) architectures and capabilities and a solid understanding of data processing is essential. An understanding of the database development life cycle, including traditional and prototyping approaches, is also necessary. Strong design and data modeling skills are essential, especially at the logical and physical levels. But managerial skills are also critical; a DBA must manage other information systems (IS) personnel while the database is analyzed, designed, and implemented, and the DBA must also interact with and provide support for the end users who are involved with the design and use of the database.

Following are some of the core roles assumed by database administration:

- ***Analyzing and designing the database*** The key role played by a DBA in the database analysis stage is the definition and creation of the data dictionary repository. The key task in database design for a DBA includes prioritizing application transactions by volume, importance, and complexity. Because these transactions are going to be most critical to the application, specifications for them should be reviewed as quickly as the transactions are developed. Logical data modeling, physical database modeling, and prototyping may occur in parallel. DBAs should strive to provide adequate control of the database environment while allowing the developers space and opportunity to experiment.
- ***Selecting DBMS and related software tools*** The evaluation and selection of hardware and software is critical to an organization's success. The database administration group must establish policies regarding the DBMS and related system software (e.g., compilers, system monitors, etc.) that will be supported within the organization. This requires evaluating vendors and their software products, performing benchmarks, and so on.
- ***Installing and upgrading the DBMS*** Once the DBMS is selected, it must be installed. Before installation, benchmarks of the workload against the database on a computer supplied by the DBMS vendor should be taken. Benchmarking anticipates issues that must be addressed during the actual installation. A DBMS installation can be a complex process of making sure all the correct versions of different modules are in place, all the proper device drivers are present, and the DBMS works correctly with any third-party software products. DBMS vendors periodically update package modules; planning for, testing, and installing upgrades to ensure that existing applications still work properly can be time-consuming and intricate. Once the DBMS is installed, user accounts must be created and maintained.
- ***Tuning database performance*** Because databases are dynamic, it is improbable that the initial design of a database will be sufficient to achieve the best processing performance for the life of the database. The performance of a database (query and update processing time as well as data storage utilization) needs to be constantly monitored. The design of a database must be frequently changed to meet new requirements and to overcome the degrading effects of many content

updates. The database must periodically be rebuilt, reorganized, and re-indexed to recover wasted space and to correct poor data allocation and fragmentation with the new size and use of the database.

- ***Improving database query processing performance*** The workload against a database will expand over time as more users find more ways to use the growing amount of data in a database. Thus, some queries that originally ran quickly against a small database may need to be rewritten in a more efficient form to run in a satisfactory time against a fully populated database. Indexes may need to be added or deleted to balance performance across all queries. Data may need to be relocated to different devices to allow better concurrent processing of queries and updates. The vast majority of a DBA's time is likely to be spent on tuning database performance and improving database query processing time.
- ***Managing data security, privacy, and integrity*** Protecting the security, privacy, and integrity of organizational databases rests with the database administration function. More detailed explanations of the ways in which privacy, security, and integrity are ensured are included later in the chapter. Here it is important to realize that the advent of the Internet and intranets to which databases are attached, along with the possibilities for distributing data and databases to multiple sites, have complicated the management of data security, privacy, and integrity.
- ***Performing data backup and recovery*** A DBA must ensure that backup procedures are established that will allow for the recovery of all necessary data should a loss occur through application failure, hardware failure, physical or electrical disaster, or human error or malfeasance. Common backup and recovery strategies are also discussed later in this chapter. These strategies must be fully tested and evaluated at regular intervals.

Reviewing these data administration and database administration functions should convince any reader of the importance of proper administration, at both the organizational and project levels. Failure to take the proper steps can greatly reduce an organization's ability to operate effectively and may even result in its going out of business. Pressures to reduce application development time must always be reviewed to be sure that necessary quality is not being forgone in order to react more quickly, for such shortcuts are likely to have very serious repercussions. Figure 11-1 summarizes how these data administration and database administration functions are typically viewed with respect to the steps of the systems development life cycle.

Trends in Database Administration

Rapidly changing business conditions are leading to the need for DBAs to possess skills that go above and beyond the ones described above. Here we describe three of these trends and the associated new skills needed:

1. ***Increased used of procedural logic*** Features such as triggers, stored procedures, and persistent stored modules (all described in Chapter 7) provide the ability to define business rules to the DBMS rather than in separate application programs. Once developers begin to rely on the use of these objects, a DBA must address the issues of quality, maintainability, performance, and availability. A DBA is now responsible for ensuring that all such procedural database logic is effectively planned, tested, implemented, shared, and reused (Mullins, 2002). A person filling such a role will typically need to come from the ranks of application programming and be capable of working closely with that group.
2. ***Proliferation of e-business applications*** When a business goes online, it never closes. People expect the site to be available and fully functional on a 24/7 basis. A DBA in such an environment needs to have a full range of DBA skills and also be capable of managing applications and databases that are Internet enabled (Mullins, 2001). Major priorities in this environment include high data availability

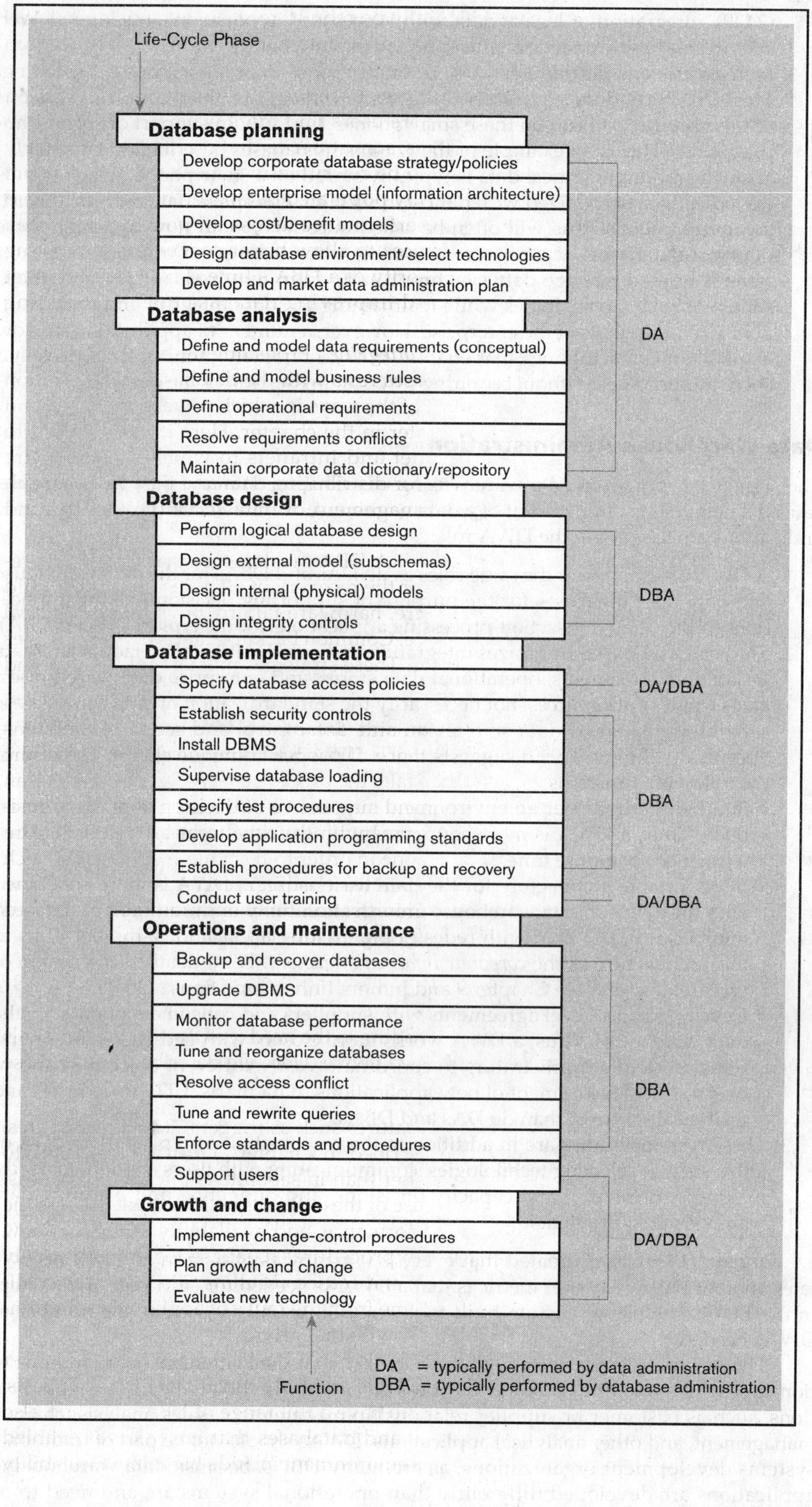

FIGURE 11-1 Functions of data administration and database administration

(24/7), integration of legacy data with Web-based applications, tracking of Web activity, and performance engineering for the Internet.

3. ***Increase use of smartphones*** Use of smartphones in organizations is exploding. Most DBMS vendors (e.g., Oracle, IBM, and Sybase) offer small-footprint versions of their products to run on these smartphones, typically in support of specific applications. (This is an example of the personal databases described in Chapter 1.) A small amount of critical data is typically stored on a smartphone, which then is periodically synchronized with data stored on the enterprise data servers. In such an environment, DBAs will often be asked questions about how to design these personal databases (or how to rescue users when they get in trouble). A greater issue is how to manage data synchronization from hundreds (or possibly thousands) of such smartphones while maintaining the data integrity and data availability requirements of the enterprise. However, a number of applications are now available on smartphones that enable DBAs to remotely monitor databases and solve minor issues without requiring physical possession of the devices.

Data Warehouse Administration

The significant growth in data warehousing (see Chapter 9) in the past five years has caused a new role to emerge: that of a data warehouse administrator (DWA). Two generalizations are true about the DWA role:

1. A DWA plays many of the same roles as do DAs and DBAs for the data warehouse and data mart databases for the purpose of supporting decision-making applications (rather than transaction-processing applications for the typical DA and DBA).
2. The role of a DWA emphasizes integration and coordination of metadata and data (extraction agreements, operational data stores, and enterprise data warehouses) across many data sources, not necessarily the standardization of data across these separately managed data sources outside the control and scope of the DWA. Specifically, Inmon (1999) suggests that a DWA has a unique charter to perform the following functions:
   - Build and administer an environment supportive of decision support applications. Thus, a DWA is more concerned with the time to make a decision than with query response time.
   - Build a stable architecture for the data warehouse. A DWA is more concerned with the effect of data warehouse growth (scalability in the amount of data and number of users) than with redesigning existing applications. Inmon refers to this architecture as the *corporate information factory*. For a detailed discussion of this architecture, see Chapter 9 and Inmon, Imhoff, and Sousa (2001).
   - Develop service-level agreements with suppliers and consumers of data for the data warehouse. Thus, a DWA works more closely with end users and operational system administrators to coordinate vastly different objectives and to oversee the development of new applications (data marts, ETL procedures, and analytical services) than do DAs and DBAs.
3. These responsibilities are in addition to the responsibilities typical of any DA or DBA, such as selecting technologies, communicating with users about data needs, making performance and capacity decisions, and budgeting and planning data warehouse requirements.

Inmon (1999)has estimated that every 100 gigabytes of data in an EDW necessitates another DWA. Another metric is that a DWA is needed for each year of data kept in the EDW. The use of custom-built tools for ETL usually increases the number of DWAs needed.

DWAs typically report through the IT unit of an organization but have strong relationships with marketing and other business areas that depend on the EDW for applications, such as customer or supplier relationship management, sales analysis, channel management, and other analytical applications. DWAs should not be part of traditional systems development organizations, as are many DBAs, because data warehousing applications are developed differently than operational systems are and need to be viewed as independent from any particular operational system. Alternatively, DWAs can be placed in the primary end-user organization for the EDW, but this runs the risk of creating many data warehouses or marts, rather than leading to a true, scalable EDW.

Summary of Evolving Data Administration Roles

The DA and DBA roles are some of the most challenging roles in any organization. The DA has renewed visibility with the recent enactment of financial control regulations and greater interest in data quality. The DBA is always expected to keep abreast of rapidly changing new technologies and is usually involved with mission-critical applications. A DBA must be constantly available to deal with problems, so the DBA is constantly on call. In return, the DBA position ranks among the best compensated in the IS profession.

Many organizations have blended together the data administration and database administration roles. These organizations emphasize the capability to build a database quickly, tune it for maximum performance, and restore it to production quickly when problems develop. These databases are more likely to be departmental, client/server databases that are developed quickly using newer development approaches, such as prototyping, which allow changes to be made more quickly. The blending of data administration and database administration roles also means that DBAs in such organizations must be able to create and enforce data standards and policies.

It is expected that the DBA role will continue to evolve toward increased specialization, with skills such as distributed database/network capacity, server programming, customization of off-the-shelf packages, and support for data warehousing DBAs (Dowgiallo et al., 1997) becoming more important. The ability to work with multiple databases, communication protocols, and operating systems will continue to be highly valued. DBAs who gain broad experience and develop the ability to adapt quickly to changing environments will have many opportunities. It is possible that some current DBA activities, such as tuning, will be replaced by decision support systems able to tune systems by analyzing usage patterns. Some operational duties, such as backup and recovery, can be outsourced and offshored with remote database administration services. Opportunities in large companies to continue working with very large databases (VLDBs) and opportunities in small and midsize companies to manage desktop and midrange servers should remain strong.

THE OPEN SOURCE MOVEMENT AND DATABASE MANAGEMENT

As mentioned previously, one role of a DBA is to select the DBMS(s) to be used in the organization. Database administrators and systems developers in all types of organizations have new alternatives when selecting a DBMS. Increasingly, organizations of all sizes are seriously considering open source DBMSs, such as MySQL and PostgreSQL, as viable choices along with Oracle, DB2, Microsoft SQL Server, Informix, and Teradata. This interest is spurred by the success of the Linux operating system and the Apache Web server. The open source movement began in roughly 1984, with the start of the Free Software Foundation. Today, the Open Source Initiative (**www.opensource.org**) is a nonprofit organization dedicated to managing and promoting the open source movement.

Why has open source software become so popular? It's not all about cost. Advantages of open source software include the following:

- A large pool of volunteer testers and developers facilitate the construction of reliable, low-cost software in a relatively short amount of time. (But be aware that only the most widely used open source software comes close to achieving this advantage; for example, MySQL has over 11 million installations.)
- The availability of the source code allows people to make modifications to add new features, which are easily inspected by others. (In fact, the agreement is that you do share all modifications for the good of the community.)
- Because the software is not proprietary to one vendor, you do not become locked into the product development plans (i.e., new features, time lines) of a single vendor, which might not be adding the features you need for your environment.

- Open source software often comes in multiple versions, and you can select the version that is right for you (from simple to complex, from totally free to some costs for special features).
- Distributing application code dependent on and working with the open source software does not incur any additional costs for copies or licenses. (Deploying software across multiple servers even within the same organization has no marginal cost for the DBMS.)

There are, however, some risks or disadvantages of open source software:

- Often there is not complete documentation (although for-fee services might provide quite sufficient documentation).
- Systems with specialized or proprietary needs across organizations do not have the commodity nature that makes open source software viable, so not all kinds of software lend themselves to being provided via an open source arrangement. (However, DBMSs are viable.)
- There are different types of open source licenses, and not all open source software is available under the same terms; thus, you have to know the ins and outs of each type of license (see Michaelson, 2004).
- An open source tool may not have all the features needed. For example, early versions of MySQL did not support subqueries (although it has now supported subqueries for several releases). An open source tool may not have options for certain functionality, so it may require that "one size fits all."
- Open source software vendors often do not have certification programs. This may not be a major factor for you, but some organizations (often software development contractors) want staff to be certified as a way to demonstrate competence in competitive bidding.

Open source DBMS
Free DBMS source code software that provides the core functionality of an SQL-compliant DBMS.

An **open source DBMS** is free or nearly free database software whose source code is publicly available. (Some people refer to open source as "sharing with rules.") The free DBMS is sufficient to run a database, but vendors provide additional fee-based components and support services that make the product more full featured and comparable to the more traditional product leaders. Because many vendors often provide the additional fee-based components, use of an open source DBMS means that an organization is not tied to one vendor's proprietary product.

A core open source DBMS is not competitive with IBM's DB2, Oracle, or Teradata, but it is more than competitive against Microsoft Access and other PC-oriented packages. As of this chapter's writing, the commercial version of MySQL is priced at $495 for one license, compared to $5,000 to $40,000 for Oracle, DB2, or Microsoft SQL Server, depending on the edition chosen. According to Hall (2003), a typical Oracle database annual license is $300,000, and a comparable MySQL annual subscription for bug fixes and code updates would be $4,000.

Open source DBMSs are improving rapidly to include more powerful features, such as the transaction controls described later in this chapter, needed for mission-critical applications. Open source DBMSs are fully SQL compliant and run on most popular operating systems. For organizations that cannot afford to spend a lot on software or staff (e.g., small businesses, nonprofits, and educational institutions), an open source DBMS can be an ideal choice. For example, many Web sites are supported by MySQL or PostgreSQL database back ends. Visit **www.postgresql.org** and **www.mysql.com** for more details on these two leading open source DBMSs.

When choosing an open source (or really any) DBMS, you need to consider the following types of factors:

- ***Features*** Does the DBMS include capabilities you need, such as subqueries, stored procedures, views, and transaction integrity controls?
- ***Support*** How widely is the DBMS used, and what alternatives exist for helping you solve problems? Does the DBMS come with documentation and ancillary tools?
- ***Ease of use*** This often depends on the availability of tools that make any piece of system software, such as a DBMS, easier to use through things like a GUI interface.

- ***Stability*** How frequently and how seriously does the DBMS malfunction over time or with high-volume use?
- ***Speed*** How rapid is the response time to queries and transactions with proper tuning of the database? (Because open source DBMSs are often not as fully loaded with advanced, obscure features, their performance can be attractive.)
- ***Training*** How easy is it for developers and users to learn to use the DBMS?
- ***Licensing*** What are the terms of the open source license, and are there commercial licenses that would provide the types of support needed?

MANAGING DATA SECURITY

Consider the following situations:

- At the university of one of this book's authors, anyone with access to the university's main automated system for student and faculty data can see everyone's Social Security number.
- A previously loyal employee is given access to sensitive documents, and within a few weeks leaves the organization, purportedly with a trove of trade secrets to share with competing firms.
- The FBI reports (Morrow, 2007) that there are 3,000 clandestine organizations in the United States whose sole purpose is to steal secrets and acquire technology for foreign organizations.
- Sarbanes-Oxley requires that companies audit the access of privileged users to sensitive data, and the payment card industry standards require companies to track user identity information whenever credit card data are used.

Database security
Protection of database data against accidental or intentional loss, destruction, or misuse.

The goal of **database security** is to protect data from accidental or intentional threats to their integrity and access. The database environment has grown more complex, with distributed databases located on client/server architectures and personal computers as well as on mainframes. Access to data has become more open through the Internet and corporate intranets and from mobile computing devices. As a result, managing data security effectively has become more difficult and time-consuming. Some security procedures for client/server and Web-based systems were introduced in Chapter 8.

Because data are a critical resource, all persons in an organization must be sensitive to security threats and take measures to protect the data within their domains. For example, computer listings or computer disks containing sensitive data should not be left unattended on desktops. Data administration is often responsible for developing overall policies and procedures to protect databases. Database administration is typically responsible for administering database security on a daily basis. The facilities that database administrators have to use in establishing adequate data security are discussed later, but first it is important to review potential threats to data security.

Threats to Data Security

Threats to data security may be direct threats to the database. For example, those who gain unauthorized access to a database may then browse, change, or even steal the data to which they have gained access. (See the news story at the beginning of this chapter for a good example.) Focusing on database security alone, however, will not ensure a secure database. All parts of the system must be secure, including the database, the network, the operating system, the building(s) in which the database resides physically, and the personnel who have any opportunity to access the system. Figure 11-2 diagrams many of the possible locations for data security threats. Accomplishing this level of security requires careful review, establishment of security procedures and policies, and implementation and enforcement of those procedures and policies. The following threats must be addressed in a comprehensive data security plan:

- ***Accidental losses, including human error, software, and hardware-caused breaches*** Establishing operating procedures such as user authorization, uniform software installation procedures, and hardware maintenance schedules are examples of actions that may be taken to address threats from accidental losses. As in any effort

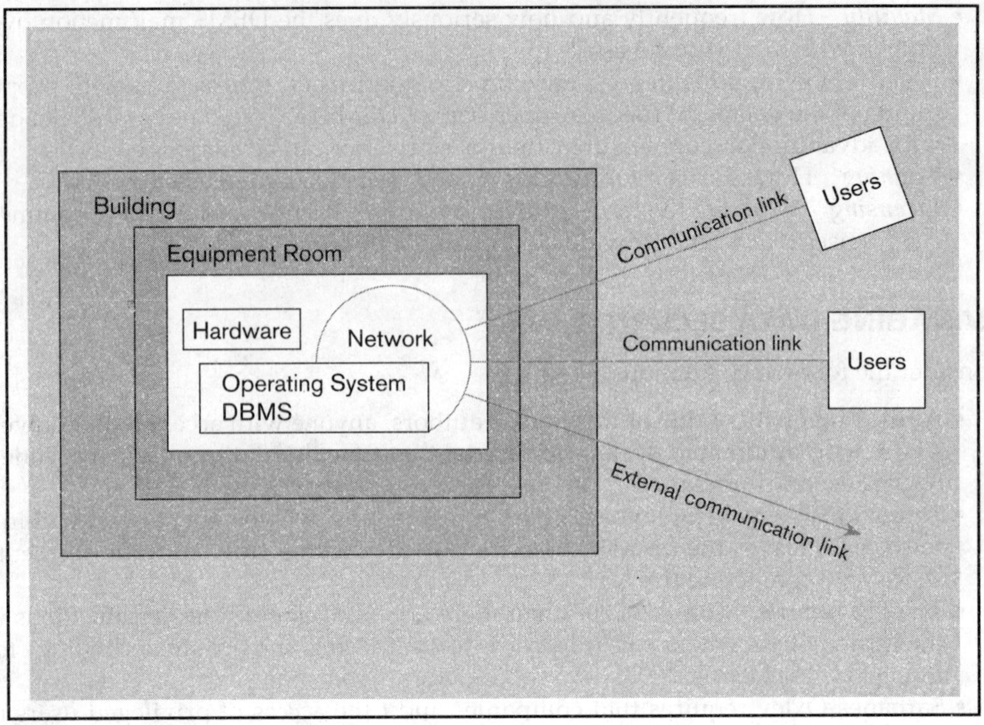

FIGURE 11-2 Possible locations of data security threats

that involves human beings, some losses are inevitable, but well-thought-out policies and procedures should reduce the amount and severity of losses. Of potentially more serious consequence are the threats that are not accidental.

- *Theft and fraud* These activities are going to be perpetrated by people, quite possibly through electronic means, and may or may not alter data. Attention here should focus on each possible location shown in Figure 11-2. For example, physical security must be established so that unauthorized persons are unable to gain access to rooms where computers, servers, telecommunications facilities, or computer files are located. Physical security should also be provided for employee offices and any other locations where sensitive data are stored or easily accessed. Establishment of a firewall to protect unauthorized access to inappropriate parts of the database through outside communication links is another example of a security procedure that will hamper people who are intent on theft or fraud.
- *Loss of privacy or confidentiality* Loss of privacy is usually taken to mean loss of protection of data about individuals, whereas loss of confidentiality is usually taken to mean loss of protection of critical organizational data that may have strategic value to the organization. Failure to control privacy of information may lead to blackmail, bribery, public embarrassment, or stealing of user passwords. Failure to control confidentiality may lead to loss of competitiveness. State and federal laws now exist to require some types of organizations to create and communicate policies to ensure privacy of customer and client data. Security mechanisms must enforce these policies, and failure to do so can mean significant financial and reputation loss.
- *Loss of data integrity* When data integrity is compromised, data will be invalid or corrupted. Unless data integrity can be restored through established backup and recovery procedures, an organization may suffer serious losses or make incorrect and expensive decisions based on the invalid data.
- *Loss of availability* Sabotage of hardware, networks, or applications may cause the data to become unavailable to users, which again may lead to severe operational difficulties. This category of threat includes the introduction of viruses intended to corrupt data or software or to render the system unusable. It is important to counter this threat by always installing the most current antivirus software, as well as educating employees on the sources of viruses. We discuss data availability later in this chapter.

As noted earlier, data security must be provided within the context of a total program for security. Two critical areas that strongly support data security are client/server security and Web application security. We address these two topics next, before outlining approaches aimed more directly at data security.

Establishing Client/Server Security

Database security is only as good as the security of the whole computing environment. Physical security, logical security, and change control security must be established across all components of the client/server environment, including the servers, the client workstations, the network and its related components, and the users.

SERVER SECURITY In a modern client/server environment, multiple servers, including database servers, need to be protected. Each should be located in a secure area, accessible only to authorized administrators and supervisors. Logical access controls, including server and administrator passwords, provide layers of protection against intrusion.

Most modern DBMSs have database-level password security that is similar to system-level password security. Database management systems, such as Oracle and SQL Server, provide database administrators with considerable capabilities that can provide aid in establishing data security, including the capability to limit each user's access and activity permissions (e.g., *select*, *update*, *insert*, or *delete*) to tables within the database. While, it is also possible to pass authentication information through from the operating system's authentication capability, this reduces the number of password security layers. Thus, in a database server, sole reliance on operating system authentication should not be encouraged.

NETWORK SECURITY Securing client/server systems includes securing the network between client and server. Networks are susceptible to breaches of security through eavesdropping, unauthorized connections, or unauthorized retrieval of packets of information that are traversing the network. Thus, encryption of data so that attackers cannot read a data packet that is being transmitted is obviously an important part of network security. (We discuss encryption later in the chapter.) In addition, authentication of the client workstation that is attempting to access the server also helps to enforce network security, and application authentication gives the user confidence that the server being contacted is the real server needed by the user. Audit trails of attempted accesses can help administrators identify unauthorized attempts to use the system. Other system components, such as routers, can also be configured to restrict access to authorized users, IP addresses, and so forth.

Application Security Issues in Three-Tier Client/Server Environments

The explosion of Web sites that make data accessible to viewers through their Internet connections raises new issues that go beyond the general client/server security issues just addressed. In a three-tier environment, the dynamic creation of a Web page from a database requires access to the database, and if the database is not properly protected, it is vulnerable to inappropriate access by any user. This is a new point of vulnerability that was previously avoided by specialized client access software. Also of interest is privacy. Companies are able to collect information about those who access their Web sites. If they are conducting e-commerce activities, selling products over the Web, they can collect information about their customers that has value to other businesses. If a company sells customer information without those customers' knowledge or if a customer believes that may happen, ethical and privacy issues are raised that must be addressed.

Figure 11-3 illustrates a typical environment for Web-enabled databases. The Web farm includes Web servers and database servers supporting Web-based applications. If an organization wishes to make only static HTML pages available, protection must be established for the HTML files stored on a Web server. Creation of a static Web page with extracts from a database uses traditional application development languages such as Visual Basic.NET or Java, and thus their creation can be controlled by using

FIGURE 11-3 Establishing Internet security

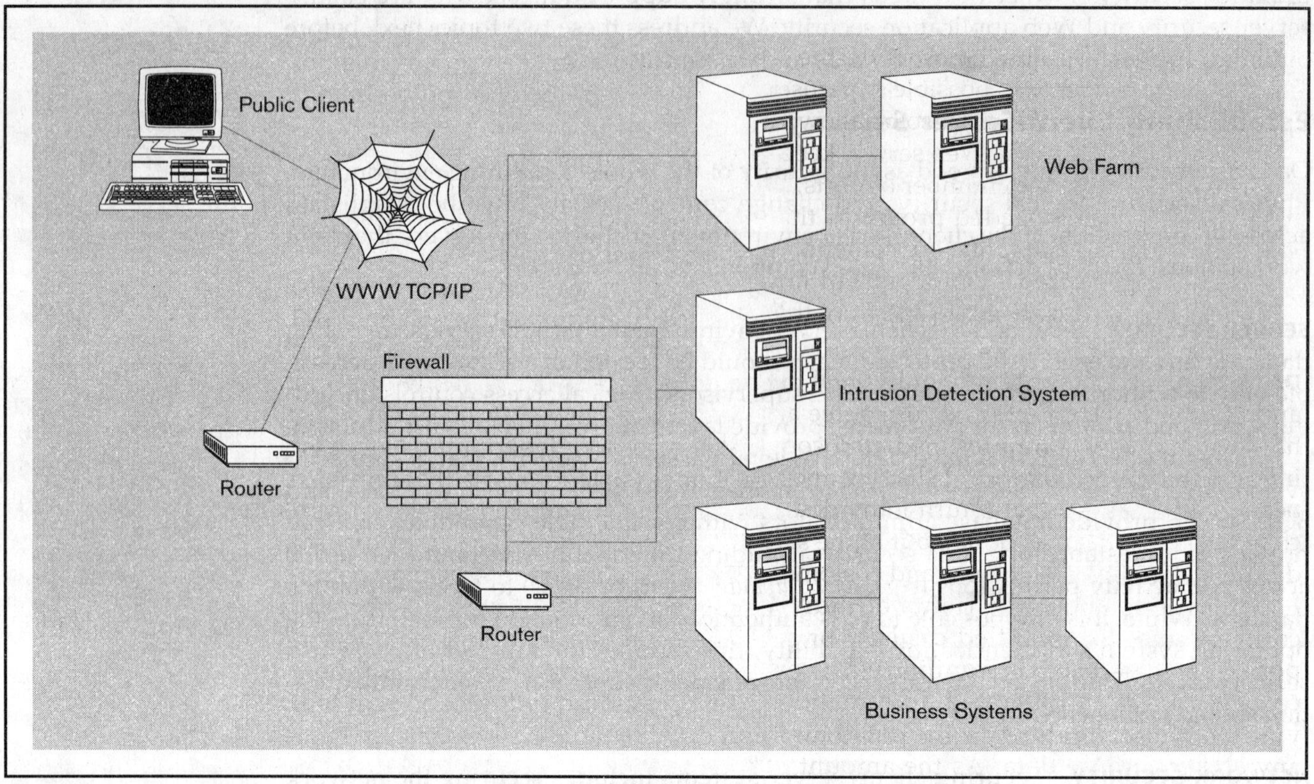

standard methods of database access control. If some of the HTML files loaded on the Web server are sensitive, they can be placed in directories that are protected using operating system security or they may be readable but not published in the directory. Thus, the user must know the exact file name to access the sensitive HTML page. It is also common to segregate the Web server and limit its contents to publicly browsable Web pages. Sensitive files may be kept on another server accessible through an organization's intranet.

Security measures for dynamic Web page generation are different. Dynamic Web pages are stored as a template into which the appropriate and current data are inserted from the database or user input once any queries associated with the page are run. This means that the Web server must be able to access the database. To function appropriately, the connection usually requires full access to the database. Thus, establishing adequate server security is critical to protecting the data. The server that owns the database connection should be physically secure, and the execution of programs on the server should be controlled. User input, which could embed SQL commands, also needs to be filtered so unauthorized scripts are not executed.

Access to data can also be controlled through another layer of security: user-authentication security. Use of an HTML login form will allow the database administrator to define each user's privileges. Each session may be tracked by storing a piece of data, or cookie, on the client machine. This information can be returned to the server and provide information about the login session. Session security must also be established to ensure that private data are not compromised during a session, because information is broadcast across a network for reception by a particular machine and is thus susceptible to being intercepted. TCP/IP is not a very secure protocol, and encryption systems, such as the ones discussed later in this chapter, are essential. A standard encryption method, Secure Sockets Layer (SSL), is used by many developers to encrypt all data traveling between client and server during a session. URLs that begin with https:// use SSL for transmission.

Additional methods of Web security include ways to restrict access to Web servers:

- Restrict the number of users on the Web server as much as possible. Of those users, give as few as possible superuser or administrator rights. Only those given these privileges should also be allowed to load software or edit or add files.
- Restrict access to the Web server, keeping a minimum number of ports open. Try to open a minimum number of ports, and preferably only http and https ports.
- Remove any unneeded programs that load automatically when setting up the server. Demo programs are sometimes included that can provide a hacker with the access desired. Compilers and interpreters such as Perl should not be on a path that is directly accessible from the Internet.

DATA PRIVACY Protection of individual privacy when using the Internet has become an important issue. E-mail, e-commerce and marketing, and other online resources have created new computer-mediated communication paths. Many groups have an interest in people's Internet behavior, including employers, governments, and businesses. Applications that return individualized responses require that information be collected about the individual, but at the same time proper respect for the privacy and dignity of employees, citizens, and customers should be observed.

Concerns about the rights of individuals to not have personal information collected and disseminated casually or recklessly have intensified as more of the population has become familiar with computers and as communications among computers have proliferated. Information privacy legislation generally gives individuals the right to know what data have been collected about them and to correct any errors in those data. As the amount of data exchanged continues to grow, the need is also growing to develop adequate data protection. Also important are adequate provisions to allow the data to be used for legitimate legal purposes so that organizations that need the data can access them and rely on their quality. Individuals need to be given the opportunity to state with whom data retained about them may be shared, and then these wishes must be enforced; enforcement is more reliable if access rules based on privacy wishes are developed by the DBA staff and handled by the DBMS.

Individuals must guard their privacy rights and must be aware of the privacy implications of the tools they are using. For example, when using a browser, users may elect to allow cookies to be placed on their machines, or they may reject that option. To make a decision with which they would be comfortable, they must know several things. They must be aware of cookies, understand what they are, evaluate their own desire to receive customized information versus their wish to keep their browsing behavior to themselves, and learn how to set their machine to accept or reject cookies. Browsers and Web sites have not been quick to help users understand all of these aspects. Abuses of privacy, such as selling customer information collected in cookies, has helped increase general awareness of the privacy issues that have developed as use of the Web for communication, shopping, and other uses has developed.

At work, the individual needs to realize that communication executed through their employer's machines and networks is not private. Courts have upheld the rights of employers to monitor all employee electronic communication.

On the Internet, privacy of communication is not guaranteed. Encryption products, anonymous remailers, and built-in security mechanisms in commonly used software help to preserve privacy. Protecting the privately owned and operated computer networks that now make up a very critical part of our information infrastructure is essential to the further development of electronic commerce, banking, health care, and transportation applications over the Web.

The W3C has created a standard, the Platform for Privacy Preferences (P3P), that will communicate a Web site's stated privacy policies and compare that statement with the user's own policy preferences. P3P uses XML code on Web site servers that can be fetched automatically by any browser or plug-in equipped for P3P. The client browser or plug-in can then compare the site's privacy policy with the user's privacy preferences and inform the user of any discrepancies. P3P addresses the following aspects of online privacy:

- Who is collecting the data?
- What information is being collected, and for what purpose?
- What information will be shared with others, and who are those others?
- Can users make changes in the way their data will be used by the collector?
- How are disputes resolved?
- What policies are followed for retaining data?
- Where can the site's detailed policies be found, in readable form?

Anonymity is another important facet of Internet communication that has come under pressure. Although U.S. law protects a right to anonymity, chat rooms and e-mail forums have been required to reveal the names of people who have posted messages anonymously. A 1995 European Parliament directive that would cut off data exchanges with any country lacking adequate privacy safeguards has led to an agreement that the United States will provide the same protection to European customers as European businesses do. This may lead Congress to establish legislation that is more protective than that previously enacted.

DATABASE SOFTWARE DATA SECURITY FEATURES

A comprehensive data security plan will include establishing administrative policies and procedures, physical protections, and data management software protections. Physical protections, such as securing data centers and work areas, disposing of obsolete media, and protecting portable devices from theft, are not covered here. We discuss administrative policies and procedures later in this section. All the elements of a data security plan work together to achieve the desired level of security. Some industries, for example health care, have regulations that set standards for the security plan and, hence, put requirements on data security. (See Anderson, 2005, for a discussion of the HIPAA security guidelines.) The most important security features of data management software follow:

1. Views or subschemas, which restrict user views of the database
2. Domains, assertions, checks, and other integrity controls defined as database objects, which are enforced by the DBMS during database querying and updating
3. Authorization rules, which identify users and restrict the actions they may take against a database
4. User-defined procedures, which define additional constraints or limitations in using a database
5. Encryption procedures, which encode data in an unrecognizable form
6. Authentication schemes, which positively identify persons attempting to gain access to a database
7. Backup, journaling, and checkpointing capabilities, which facilitate recovery procedures

Views

In Chapter 6, we defined a view as a subset of a database that is presented to one or more users. A view is created by querying one or more of the base tables, producing a dynamic result table for the user at the time of the request. Thus, a view is always based on the current data in the base tables from which it is built. The advantage of a view is that it can be built to present only the data (certain columns and/or rows) to which the user requires access, effectively preventing the user from viewing other data that may be private or confidential. The user may be granted the right to access the view, but not to access the base tables upon which the view is based. So, confining a user to a view may be more restrictive for that user than allowing him or her access to the involved base tables.

For example, we could build a view for a Pine Valley employee that provides information about materials needed to build a Pine Valley furniture product without providing other information, such as unit price, that is not relevant to the employee's work. This command creates a view that will list the wood required and the wood available for each product:

```
CREATE VIEW MATERIALS_V AS
  SELECT Product_T.ProductID, ProductName, Footage,
      FootageOnHand
  FROM Product_T, RawMaterial_T, Uses_T
  WHERE Product_T.ProductID = Uses_T.ProductID
  AND RawMaterial_T.MaterialID = Uses_T.MaterialID;
```

The contents of the view created will be updated each time the view is accessed, but here are the current contents of the view, which can be accessed with the SQL command:

```
SELECT * FROM MATERIALS_V;
```

ProductID	ProductName	Footage	FootageOnHand
1	End Table	4	1
2	Coffee Table	6	11
3	Computer Desk	15	11
4	Entertainment Center	20	84
5	Writer's Desk	13	68
6	8-Drawer Desk	16	66
7	Dining Table	16	11
8	Computer Desk	15	9

8 rows selected.

The user can write SELECT statements against the view, treating it as though it were a table. Although views promote security by restricting user access to data, they are not adequate security measures because unauthorized persons may gain knowledge of or access to a particular view. Also, several persons may share a particular view; all may have authority to read the data, but only a restricted few may be authorized to update the data. Finally, with high-level query languages, an unauthorized person may gain access to data through simple experimentation. As a result, more sophisticated security measures are normally required.

Integrity Controls

Integrity controls protect data from unauthorized use and update. Often, integrity controls limit the values a field may hold and the actions that can be performed on data, or trigger the execution of some procedure, such as placing an entry in a log to record which users have done what with which data.

One form of integrity control is a domain. In essence, a domain can be used to create a user-defined data type. Once a domain is defined, any field can be assigned that domain as its data type. For example, the following PriceChange domain (defined in SQL) can be used as the data type of any database field, such as PriceIncrease and PriceDiscount, to limit the amount standard prices can be augmented in one transaction:

```
CREATE DOMAIN PriceChange AS DECIMAL
  CHECK (VALUE BETWEEN .001 and .15);
```

Then, in the definition of, say, a pricing transaction table, we might have the following:

```
PriceIncrease PriceChange NOT NULL,
```

One advantage of a domain is that, if it ever has to change, it can be changed in e place—the domain definition—and all fields with this domain will be changed omatically. Alternatively, the same CHECK clause could be included in a constraint both the PriceIncrease and PriceDiscount fields, but in this case, if the limits of the check were to change, a DBA would have to find every instance of this integrity control and change it in each place separately.

Assertions are powerful constraints that enforce certain desirable database conditions. Assertions are checked automatically by the DBMS when transactions are run involving tables or fields on which assertions exist. For example, assume that an employee table has the fields EmpID, EmpName, SupervisorID, and SpouseID. Suppose that a company rule is that no employee may supervise his or her spouse. The following assertion enforces this rule:

```
CREATE ASSERTION SpousalSupervision
  CHECK (SupervisorID < > SpouseID);
```

If the assertion fails, the DBMS will generate an error message.

Assertions can become rather complex. Suppose that Pine Valley Furniture has a rule that no two salespersons can be assigned to the same territory at the same time. Suppose a Salesperson table includes the fields SalespersonID and TerritoryID. This assertion can be written using a correlated subquery, as follows:

```
CREATE ASSERTION TerritoryAssignment
  CHECK (NOT EXISTS
    (SELECT * FROM Salesperson_T SP WHERE SP.TerritoryID IN
      (SELECT SSP.TerritoryID FROM Salesperson_T SSP WHERE
        SSP.SalespersonID < > SP.SalespersonID)));
```

Finally, *triggers* (defined and illustrated in Chapter 7) can be used for security purposes. A trigger, which includes an event, a condition, and an action, is potentially more complex than an assertion. For example, a trigger can do the following:

- Prohibit inappropriate actions (e.g., changing a salary value outside the normal business day)
- Cause special handling procedures to be executed (e.g., if a customer invoice payment is received after some due date, a penalty can be added to the account balance for that customer)
- Cause a row to be written to a log file to echo important information about the user and a transaction being made to sensitive data, so that the log can be reviewed by human or automated procedures for possible inappropriate behavior (e.g., the log can record which user initiated a salary change for which employee)

As with domains, a powerful benefit of a trigger, as with any other stored procedure, is that the DBMS enforces these controls for all users and all database activities. The control does not have to be coded into each query or program. Thus, individual users and programs cannot circumvent the necessary controls.

Assertions, triggers, stored procedures, and other forms of integrity controls may not stop all malicious or accidental use or modification of data. Thus, it is recommended (Anderson, 2005) that a change audit process be used in which all user activities are logged and monitored to check that all policies and constraints are enforced. Following this recommendation means that every database query and transaction is logged to record characteristics of all data use, especially modifications: who accessed the data, when it was accessed, what program or query was run, where in the computer network the request was generated, and other parameters that can be used to investigate suspicious activity or actual breaches of security and integrity.

Authorization Rules

Authorization rules are controls incorporated in a data management system that restrict access to data and also restrict the actions that people may take when they access data. For example, a person who can supply a particular password may be authorized to read any record in a database but cannot necessarily modify any of those records.

Authorization rules
Controls incorporated in a data management systems that restrict access to data and also restrict the actions that people may take when they access data.

Fernandez et al. (1981) have developed a conceptual model of database security. Their model expresses authorization rules in the form of a table (or matrix) that includes subjects, objects, actions, and constraints. Each row of the table indicates that a particular subject is authorized to take a certain action on an object in the database, perhaps subject to some constraint. Figure 11-4 shows an example of such an authorization matrix. This table contains several entries pertaining to records in an accounting database. For example, the first row in the table indicates that anyone in the Sales Department is authorized to insert a new customer record in the database, provided that the customer's credit limit does not exceed $5,000. The last row indicates that the program AR4 is authorized to modify order records without restriction. Data administration is responsible for determining and implementing authorization rules that are implemented at the database level. Authorization schemes can also be implemented at the operating system level or the application level.

Most contemporary database management systems do not implement an authorization matrix such as the one shown in Figure 11-4; they normally use simplified versions. There are two principal types: authorization tables for subjects and authorization tables for objects. Figure 11-5 shows an example of each type. In Figure 11-5a, for example, we see that salespersons are allowed to modify customer records but not delete these records. In Figure 11-5b, we see that users in Order Entry or Accounting can modify order records, but salespersons cannot. A given DBMS product may provide either one or both of these types of facilities.

Authorization tables, such as those shown in Figure 11-5, are attributes of an organization's data and their environment; they are therefore properly viewed as metadata. Thus, the tables should be stored and maintained in the repository. Because authorization tables contain highly sensitive data, they themselves should be protected by stringent security rules. Normally, only selected persons in data administration have authority to access and modify these tables.

For example, in Oracle, the privileges included in Figure 11-6 can be granted to users at the database level or table level. INSERT and UPDATE can be granted at the column level. Where many users, such as those in a particular job classification, need similar privileges, roles may be created that contain a set of privileges, and then all the privileges can be granted to a user simply by granting the role. To grant the ability to read the product table and update prices to a user with the log in ID of SMITH, the following SQL command may be given:

```
GRANT SELECT, UPDATE (UnitPrice) ON Product_T TO SMITH;
```

There are eight data dictionary views that contain information about privileges that have been granted. In this case, DBA_TAB_PRIVS contains users and objects for every user who has been granted privileges on objects, such as tables. DBA_COL_PRIVS contains users who have been granted privileges on columns of tables.

Subject	Object	Action	Constraint
Sales Dept.	Customer record	Insert	Credit limit LE $5000
Order trans.	Customer record	Read	None
Terminal 12	Customer record	Modify	Balance due only
Acctg. Dept.	Order record	Delete	None
Ann Walker	Order record	Insert	Order aml LT $2000
Program AR4	Order record	Modify	None

FIGURE 11-4 Authorization matrix

FIGURE 11-5 Implementing authorization rules
(a) Authorization table for subjects (salespersons)

	Customer records	Order records
Read	Y	Y
Insert	Y	Y
Modify	Y	N
Delete	N	N

(b) Authorization table for objects (order records)

	Salespersons (password BATMAN)	Order entry (password JOKER)	Accounting (password TRACY)
Read	Y	Y	Y
Insert	N	Y	N
Modify	N	Y	Y
Delete	N	N	Y

FIGURE 11-6 Oracle privileges

Privilege	Capability
SELECT	Query the object.
INSERT	Insert records into the table/view. Can be given for specific columns.
UPDATE	Update records in table/view. Can be given for specific columns.
DELETE	Delete records from table/view.
ALTER	Alter the table.
INDEX	Create indexes on the table.
REFERENCES	Create foreign keys that reference the table.
EXECUTE	Execute the procedure, package, or function.

User-Defined Procedures

User-defined procedures
User exits (or interfaces) that allow system designers to define their own security procedures in addition to the authorization rules.

Some DBMS products provide user exits (or interfaces) that allow system designers or users to create their own **user-defined procedures** for security, in addition to the authorization rules we have just described. For example, a user procedure might be designed to provide positive user identification. In attempting to log on to the computer, the user might be required to supply a procedure name in addition to a simple password. If valid password and procedure names are supplied, the system then calls the procedure, which asks the user a series of questions whose answers should be known only to that password holder (e.g., mother's maiden name).

Encryption

Encryption
The coding or scrambling of data so that humans cannot read them.

Data encryption can be used to protect highly sensitive data such as customer credit card numbers or account balances. **Encryption** is the coding or scrambling of data so that humans cannot read them. Some DBMS products include encryption routines that automatically encode sensitive data when they are stored or transmitted over communications channels. For example, encryption is commonly used in electronic funds transfer (EFT) systems. Other DBMS products provide exits that allow users to code their own encryption routines.

Any system that provides encryption facilities must also provide complementary routines for decoding the data. These decoding routines must be protected by adequate security, or else the advantages of encryption are lost. They also require significant computing resources.

Two common forms of encryption exist: one key and two key. With a one-key method, also called Data Encryption Standard (DES), both the sender and the receiver need to know the key that is used to scramble the transmitted or stored data. A two-key method, also called asymmetric encryption, employs a private and a public key. Two-key methods (see Figure 11-7) are especially popular in e-commerce applications to provide secure transmission and database storage of payment data, such as credit card numbers.

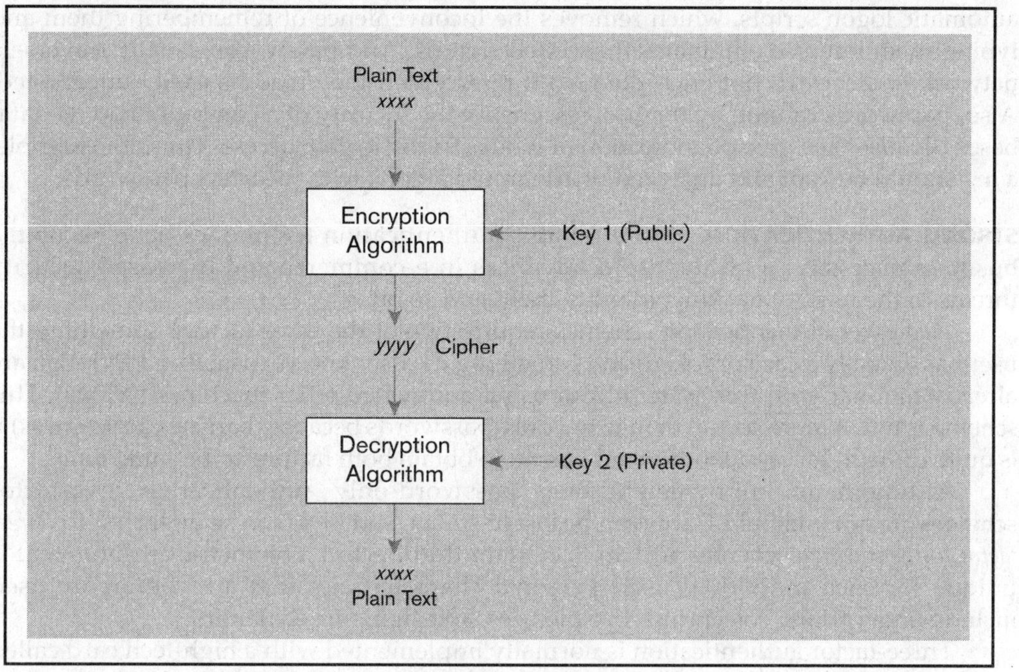

FIGURE 11-7 Basic two-key encryption

A popular implementation of the two-key method is Secure Sockets Layer (SSL), developed by Netscape Communications Corporation. SSL is built into most major browsers and Web servers. It provides data encryption, server authentication, and other services in a TCP/IP connection. For example, the U.S. banking industry uses a 128-bit version of SSL (the most secure level in current use) to secure online banking transactions.

Details about encryption techniques are beyond the scope of this book and are generally handled by the DBMS without significant involvement of a DBA; it is simply important to know that database data encryption is a strong measure available to a DBA.

Authentication Schemes

A long-standing problem in computer circles is how to identify persons who are trying to gain access to a computer or its resources, such as a database or DBMS. In an electronic environment, a user can prove his or her identity by supplying one or more of the following factors:

1. Something the user knows, usually a password or personal identification number (PIN)
2. Something the user possesses, such as a smart card or token
3. Some unique personal characteristic, such as a fingerprint or retinal scan

Authentication schemes are called one-factor, two-factor, or three-factor authentication, depending on how many of these factors are employed. Authentication becomes stronger as more factors are used.

PASSWORDS The first line of defense is the use of passwords, which is a one-factor authentication scheme. With such a scheme, anyone who can supply a valid password can log on to a database system. (A user ID may also be required, but user IDs are typically not secured.) A DBA (or perhaps a system administrator) is responsible for managing schemes for issuing or creating passwords for the DBMS and/or specific applications.

Although requiring passwords is a good starting point for authentication, it is well known that they this method has a number of deficiencies. People assigned passwords for different devices quickly devise ways to remember these passwords, ways that tend to compromise the password scheme. The passwords get written down, where others may find them. They get shared with other users; it is not unusual for an entire department to use one common password for access. Passwords get included in automatic logon scripts, which removes the inconvenience of remembering them and typing them but also eliminates their effectiveness. And passwords usually traverse a network in cleartext, not encrypted, so if intercepted they may be easily interpreted. Also, passwords cannot, by themselves, ensure the security of a computer and its databases because they give no indication of who is trying to gain access. Thus, for example, a log should be kept and analyzed of attempted logons with incorrect passwords.

STRONG AUTHENTICATION More reliable authentication techniques have become a business necessity, with the rapid advances in e-commerce and increased security threats in the form of hacking, identity theft, and so on.

Two-factor authentication schemes require two of the three factors: something the user has (usually a card or token) and something the user knows (usually a PIN). You are already familiar with this system from using automated teller machines (ATMs). This scheme is much more secure than using only passwords because (barring carelessness) it is quite difficult for an unauthorized person to obtain both factors at the same time.

Although an improvement over password-only authentication, two-factor schemes are not infallible. Cards can be lost or stolen, and PINs can be intercepted. *Three-factor authentication* schemes add an important third factor: a biometric attribute that is unique for each individual user. Personal characteristics that are commonly used include fingerprints, voiceprints, eye pictures, and signature dynamics.

Smart card
A credit card–sized plastic card with an embedded microprocessor chip that can store, process, and output electronic data in a secure manner.

Three-factor authentication is normally implemented with a high-tech card called a smart card (or smart badge). A **smart card** is a credit card–sized plastic card with an embedded microprocessor chip that can store, process, and output electronic data in a secure manner. Smart cards are replacing the familiar magnetic-stripe-based cards we have used for decades. Using smart cards can be a very strong means to authenticate a database user. In addition, smart cards can themselves be database storage devices; today smart cards can store well over 100MB bytes of data, and this number is increasing rapidly. Smart cards can provide secure storage of personal data such as medical records or a summary of medications taken.

All of the authentication schemes described here, including use of smart cards, can be only as secure as the process that is used to issue them. For example, if a smart card is issued and personalized to an imposter (either carelessly or deliberately), it can be used freely by that person. Thus, before allowing any form of authentication—such as issuing a new card to an employee or other person—the issuing agency must validate beyond any reasonable doubt the identity of that person. Because paper documents are used in this process—birth certificates, passports, driver's licenses, and so on—and these types of documents are often unreliable because they can be easily copied, forged, and so on, significant training of the personnel, use of sophisticated technology, and sufficient oversight of the process are needed to ensure that this step is rigorous and well controlled.

SARBANES-OXLEY (SOX) AND DATABASES

The Sarbanes-Oxley Act (SOX) and other similar global regulations were designed to ensure the integrity of public companies' financial statements. A key component of this is ensuring sufficient control and security over the financial systems and IT infrastructure in use within an organization. This has resulted in an increased emphasis on understanding controls around information technology. Given that the focus of SOX is on the integrity of financial statements, controls around the databases and applications that are the source of these data is key.

The key focus of SOX audits is around three areas of control:

1. IT change management
2. Logical access to data
3. IT operations

Most audits start with a walkthrough—that is, a meeting with business owners (of the data that fall under the scope of the audit) and technical architects of the applications and databases. During this walkthrough, the auditors will try to understand how the above three areas are handled by the IT organization.

IT Change Management

IT change management refers to the process by which changes to operational systems and databases are authorized. Typically any change to a production system or database has to be approved by a change control board that is made up of representatives from the business and IT organizations. Authorized changes must then be put through a rigorous process (essentially a mini systems development life cycle) before being put into production. From a database perspective, the most common types of changes are changes to the database schema, changes to database configuration parameters, and patches/updates to the DBMS software itself.

A key issue related to change management that was a top deficiency found by SOX auditors was adequate segregation of duties between people who had access to databases in the three common environments: development, test, and production. SOX mandates that the DBAs who have the ability to modify data in these three environments be different. This is primarily to ensure that changes to the operating environment have been adequately tested before being implemented. In cases where the size of the organization does not allow this, other personnel should be authorized to do periodic reviews of database access by DBAs, using features such as database audits (described in the next section).

Logical Access to Data

Logical access to data is essentially about the security procedures in place to prevent unauthorized access to the data. From a SOX perspective, the two key questions to ask are: Who has access to what? and Who has access to too much? In response to these two questions, organizations must establish administrative policies and procedures that serve as a context for effectively implementing these measures. Two types of security policies and procedures are personnel controls and physical access controls.

PERSONNEL CONTROLS Adequate controls of personnel must be developed and followed, for the greatest threat to business security is often internal rather than external. In addition to the security authorization and authentication procedures just discussed, organizations should develop procedures to ensure a selective hiring process that validates potential employees' representations about their backgrounds and capabilities. Monitoring to ensure that personnel are following established practices, taking regular vacations, working with other employees, and so forth should be done. Employees should be trained in those aspects of security and quality that are relevant to their jobs and encouraged to be aware of and follow standard security and data quality measures. Standard job controls, such as separating duties so no one employee has responsibility for an entire business process or keeping application developers from having access to production systems, should also be enforced. Should an employee need to be let go, there should be an orderly and timely set of procedures for removing authorizations and authentications and notifying other employees of the status change. Similarly, if an employee's job profile changes, care should be taken to ensure that his or her new set of roles and responsibilities do not lead to violations of separation of duties.

PHYSICAL ACCESS CONTROLS Limiting access to particular areas within a building is usually a part of controlling physical access. Swipe, or proximity access, cards can be used to gain access to secure areas, and each access can be recorded in a database, with a time stamp. Guests, including vendor maintenance representatives, should be issued badges and escorted into secure areas. Access to sensitive equipment, including hardware and peripherals such as printers (which may be used to print classified reports) can be controlled by placing these items in secure areas. Other equipment may be locked to a desk or cabinet or may have an alarm attached. Backup data tapes should be kept in fireproof data safes and/or kept offsite, at a safe location. Procedures that make explicit the schedules for moving media and disposing of media and that establish labeling and indexing of all materials stored must be established.

Placement of computer screens so that they cannot be seen from outside the building may also be important. Control procedures for areas external to the office building should also be developed. Companies frequently use security guards to control access to their buildings or use a card swipe system or handprint recognition system (smart badges) to automate employee access to the building. Visitors should be issued an identification card and required to be accompanied throughout the building.

New concerns are raised by the increasingly mobile nature of work. Laptop computers are very susceptible to theft, which puts data on a laptop at risk. Encryption and multiple-factor authentication can protect data in the event of laptop theft. Antitheft devices (e.g., security cables, geographic tracking chips) can deter theft or help quickly recover stolen laptops on which critical data are stored.

IT Operations

IT operations refers to the policies and procedures in place related to the day-to-day management of the infrastructure, applications, and databases in an organization. Key areas in this regard that are relevant to data and database administrators are database backup and recovery, as well as data availability. These are discussed in detail in later sections.

An area of control that helps to maintain data quality and availability but that is often overlooked is vendor management. Organizations should periodically review external maintenance agreements for all hardware and software they are using to ensure that appropriate response rates are agreed to for maintaining system quality and availability. It is also important to consider reaching agreements with the developers of all critical software so that the organization can get access to source code should the developer go out of business or stop supporting the programs. One way to accomplish this is by having a third party hold the source code, with an agreement that it will be released if such a situation develops. Controls should be in place to protect data from inappropriate access and use by outside maintenance staff and other contract workers.

DATABASE BACKUP AND RECOVERY

Database recovery
Mechanisms for restoring a database quickly and accurately after loss or damage.

Database recovery is database administration's response to Murphy's law. Inevitably, databases are damaged or lost or become unavailable because of some system problem that may be caused by human error, hardware failure, incorrect or invalid data, program errors, computer viruses, network failures, conflicting transactions, or natural catastrophes. It is the responsibility of a DBA to ensure that all critical data in a database are protected and can be recovered in the event of loss. Because an organization depends heavily on its databases, a DBA must be able to minimize downtime and other disruptions while a database is being backed up or recovered. To achieve these objectives, a database management system must provide mechanisms for backing up data with as little disruption of production time as possible and restoring a database quickly and accurately after loss or damage.

Basic Recovery Facilities

A database management system should provide four basic facilities for backup and recovery of a database:

1. ***Backup facilities,*** which provide periodic backup (sometimes called *fallback*) copies of portions of or the entire database
2. ***Journalizing facilities,*** which maintain an audit trail of transactions and database changes
3. ***A checkpoint facility,*** by which the DBMS periodically suspends all processing and synchronizes its files and journals to establish a recovery point
4. ***A recovery manager,*** which allows the DBMS to restore the database to a correct condition and restart processing transactions

Backup facility
A DBMS COPY utility that produces a backup copy (or save) of an entire database or a subset of a database.

BACKUP FACILITIES A DBMS should provide **backup facilities** that produce a backup copy (or save) of the entire database plus control files and journals. Each DBMS normally provides a COPY utility for this purpose. In addition to the database files, the backup facility should create a copy of related database objects including the repository (or system catalog), database indexes, source libraries, and so on. Typically, a backup copy is produced at least once per day. The copy should be stored in a secured location where it is protected from loss or damage. The backup copy is used to restore the database in the event of hardware failure, catastrophic loss, or damage.

Some DBMSs provide backup utilities for a DBA to use to make backups; other systems assume that the DBA will use the operating system commands, export commands, or SELECT . . . INTO SQL commands to perform backups. Because performing the nightly backup for a particular database is repetitive, creating a script that automates regular backups will save time and result in fewer backup errors.

With large databases, regular full backups may be impractical because the time required to perform a backup may exceed the time available. Or, a database may be a critical system that must always remain available; in such a case, a cold backup, where the database is shut down, is not practical. As a result, backups may be taken of dynamic data regularly (a so-called *hot backup*, in which only a selected portion of the database is shut down from use), but backups of static data, which don't change frequently, may be taken less often. Incremental backups, which record changes made since the last full backup, but which do not take so much time to complete, may also be taken on an interim basis, allowing for longer periods of time between full backups. Thus, backup strategies must be based on the demands being placed on the database systems.

Database downtime can be very expensive. The lost revenue from downtime (e.g., inability to take orders or place reservations) needs to be balanced against the cost of additional technology, primarily disk storage, to achieve a desired level of availability. To help achieve the desired level of reliability, some DBMSs will automatically make backup (often called fallback) copies of the database in real time as the database is updated. These fallback copies are usually stored on separate disk drives and disk controllers, and they are used as live backup copies if portions of the database become inaccessible due to hardware failures. As the cost of secondary storages steadily decreases, the cost to make redundant copies becomes more practical in more situations. Fallback copies are different from RAID storage, discussed in Chapter 5, because the DBMS is making copies of only the database as database transactions occur, whereas RAID is used by the operating system for making redundant copies of all storage elements as any page is updated.

JOURNALIZING FACILITIES A DBMS must provide **journalizing facilities** to produce an audit trail of **transactions** and database changes. In the event of a failure, a consistent database state can be reestablished, using the information in the journals together with the most recent complete backup. As Figure 11-8 shows, there are two basic journals, or logs. The first is the **transaction log**, which contains a record of the essential data for each transaction that is processed against the database. Data that are typically recorded for each transaction include the transaction code or identification, action or type of transaction (e.g., insert), time of the transaction, terminal number or user ID, input data values, table and records accessed, records modified, and possibly the old and new field values.

The second kind of log is a **database change log**, which contains before and after images of records that have been modified by transactions. A **before image** is simply a copy of a record before it has been modified, and an **after image** is a copy of the same record after it has been modified. Some systems also keep a security log, which can alert the DBA to any security violations that occur or are attempted. The recovery manager uses these logs to undo and redo operations, which we explain later in this chapter. These logs may be kept on disk or tape; because they are critical to recovery, they, too, must be backed up.

CHECKPOINT FACILITY A **checkpoint facility** in a DBMS periodically refuses to accept any new transactions. All transactions in progress are completed, and the journal files are brought up-to-date. At this point, the system is in a quiet state, and the database and transaction logs are synchronized. The DBMS writes a special record (called a *checkpoint record*) to the log file, which is like a snapshot of the state of the database. The checkpoint record contains information necessary to restart the system. Any dirty data blocks (i.e., pages of memory that contain changes that have not yet been written out to disk)

Journalizing facility
An audit trail of transactions and database changes.

Transaction
A discrete unit of work that must be completely processed or not processed at all within a computer system. Entering a customer order is an example of a transaction.

Transaction log
A record of the essential data for each transaction that is processed against the database.

Database change log
A log that contains before and after images of records that have been modified by transactions.

Before image
A copy of a record (or page of memory) before it has been modified.

After image
A copy of a record (or page of memory) after it has been modified.

Checkpoint facility
A facility by which a DBMS periodically refuses to accept any new transactions. The system is in a quiet state, and the database and transaction logs are synchronized.

FIGURE 11-8 Database audit trail

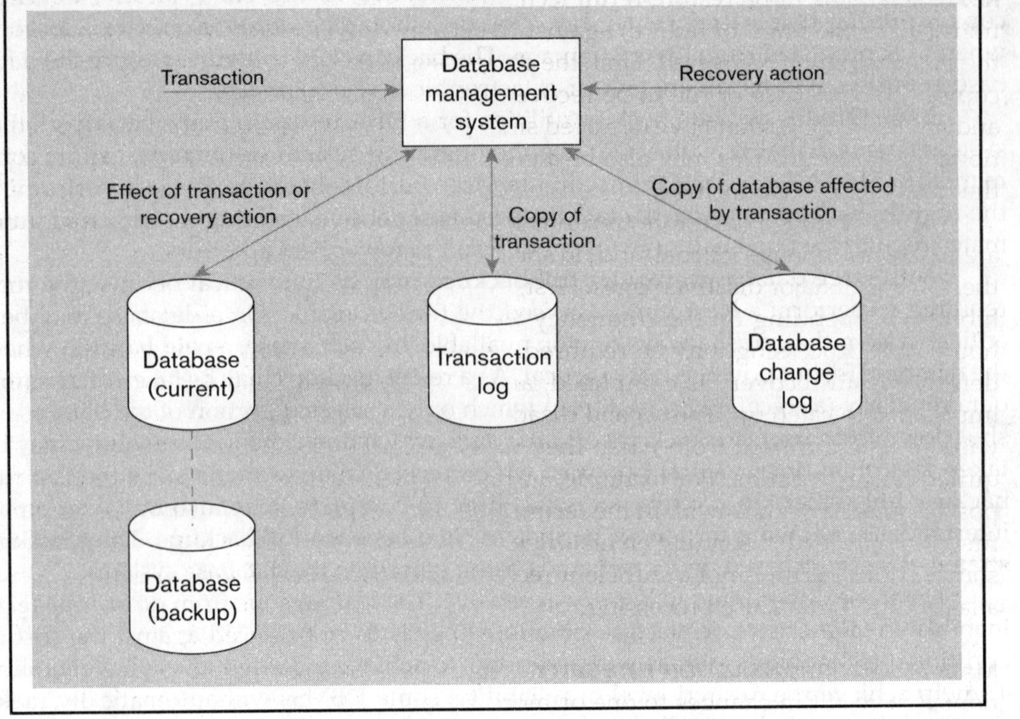

are written from memory to disk storage, thus ensuring that all changes made prior to taking the checkpoint have been written to long-term storage.

A DBMS may perform checkpoints automatically (which is preferred) or in response to commands in user application programs. Checkpoints should be taken frequently (say, several times an hour). When failures occur, it is often possible to resume processing from the most recent checkpoint. Thus, only a few minutes of processing work must be repeated, compared with several hours for a complete restart of the day's processing.

Recovery manager
A module of a DBMS that restores the database to a correct condition when a failure occurs and then resumes processing user questions.

RECOVERY MANAGER The **recovery manager** is a module of a DBMS that restores the database to a correct condition when a failure occurs and then resumes processing user requests. The type of restart used depends on the nature of the failure. The recovery manager uses the logs shown in Figure 11-8 (as well as the backup copy, if necessary) to restore the database.

Recovery and Restart Procedures

The type of recovery procedure that is used in a given situation depends on the nature of the failure, the sophistication of the DBMS recovery facilities, and operational policies and procedures. Following is a discussion of the techniques that are most frequently used.

DISK MIRRORING To be able to switch to an existing copy of a database, the database must be mirrored. That is, at least two copies of the database must be kept and updated simultaneously. When a media failure occurs, processing is switched to the duplicate copy of the database. This strategy allows for the fastest recovery and has become increasingly popular for applications requiring high availability as the cost of long-term storage has dropped. Level 1 RAID systems implement mirroring. A damaged disk can be rebuilt from the mirrored disk with no disruption in service to the user. Such disks are referred to as being *hot-swappable*. This strategy does not protect against loss of power or catastrophic damage to both databases, though. See Chapter 5 for a more detailed discussion of RAID.

RESTORE/RERUN The **restore/rerun** technique involves reprocessing the day's transactions (up to the point of failure) against the backup copy of the database or portion of the database being recovered. First, the database is shut down, and then the most recent copy of the database or file to be recovered (say, from the previous day) is mounted, and all transactions that have occurred since that copy (which are stored on the transaction log) are rerun. This may also be a good time to make a backup copy and clear out the transaction, or redo, log.

Restore/rerun
A technique that involves reprocessing the day's transactions (up to the point of failure) against the backup copy of the database.

The advantage of restore/rerun is its simplicity. The DBMS does not need to create a database change journal, and no special restart procedures are required. However, there are two major disadvantages. First, the time to reprocess transactions may be prohibitive. Depending on the frequency with which backup copies are made, several hours of reprocessing may be required. Processing new transactions will have to be deferred until recovery is completed, and if the system is heavily loaded, it may be impossible to catch up. The second disadvantage is that the sequencing of transactions will often be different from when they were originally processed, which may lead to quite different results. For example, in the original run, a customer deposit may be posted before a withdrawal. In the rerun, the withdrawal transaction may be attempted first and may lead to sending an insufficient funds notice to the customer. For these reasons, restore/rerun is not a sufficient recovery procedure and is generally used only as a last resort in database processing.

MAINTAINING TRANSACTION INTEGRITY A database is updated by processing transactions that result in changes to one or more database records. If an error occurs during the processing of a transaction, the database may be compromised, and some form of database recovery is required. Thus, to understand database recovery, we must first understand the concept of transaction integrity.

A business transaction is a sequence of steps that constitute some well-defined business activity. Examples of business transactions are Admit Patient in a hospital and Enter Customer Order in a manufacturing company. Normally, a business transaction requires several actions against the database. For example, consider the transaction Enter Customer Order. When a new customer order is entered, the following steps may be performed by an application program:

1. Input the order data (keyed by the user).
2. Read the CUSTOMER record (or insert record if a new customer).
3. Accept or reject the order. If Balance Due plus Order Amount does not exceed Credit Limit, accept the order; otherwise, reject it.
4. If the order is accepted, increase Balance Due by Order Amount. Store the updated CUSTOMER record. Insert the accepted ORDER record in the database.

When processing transactions, a DBMS must ensure that the transactions follow four well-accepted properties, called the ACID properties:

1. ***Atomic,*** meaning that the transaction cannot be subdivided and, hence, it must be processed in its entirety or not at all. Once the whole transaction is processed, we say that the changes are *committed*. If the transaction fails at any midpoint, we say that it has aborted. For example, suppose that the program accepts a new customer order, increases Balance Due, and stores the updated CUSTOMER record. However, suppose that the new ORDER record is not inserted successfully (perhaps due to a duplicate Order Number key or insufficient physical file space). In this case, we want none of the parts of the transaction to affect the database.
2. ***Consistent,*** meaning that any database constraints that must be true before the transaction must also be true after the transaction. For example, if the inventory on-hand balance must be the difference between total receipts minus total issues, this will be true both before and after an order transaction, which depletes the on-hand balance to satisfy the order.
3. ***Isolated,*** meaning that changes to the database are not revealed to users until the transaction is committed. For example, this property means that other users

do not know what the on-hand inventory is until an inventory transaction is complete; this property then usually means that other users are prohibited from simultaneously updating and possibly even reading data that are in the process of being updated. We discuss this topic in more detail later under concurrency controls and locking. A consequence of transactions being isolated from one another is that concurrent transactions (i.e., several transactions in some partial state of completion) all affect the database as if they were presented to the DBMS in serial fashion.

4. ***Durable,*** meaning that changes are permanent. Thus, once a transaction is committed, no subsequent failure of the database can reverse the effect of the transaction.

Transaction boundaries
The logical beginning and end of a transaction.

To maintain transaction integrity, the DBMS must provide facilities for the user or application program to define **transaction boundaries**—that is, the logical beginning and end of a transaction. In SQL, the BEGIN TRANSACTION statement is placed in front of the first SQL command within the transaction, and the COMMIT command is placed at the end of the transaction. Any number of SQL commands may come in between these two commands; these are the database processing steps that perform some well-defined business activity, as explained earlier. If a command such as ROLLBACK is processed after a BEGIN TRANSACTION is executed and before a COMMIT is executed, the DBMS aborts the transaction and undoes the effects of the SQL statements processed so far within the transaction boundaries. The application would likely be programmed to execute a ROLLBACK when the DBMS generates an error message performing an UPDATE or INSERT command in the middle of the transaction. The DBMS thus commits (makes durable) changes for successful transactions (those that reach the COMMIT statement) and effectively rejects changes from transactions that are aborted (those that encounter a ROLLBACK). Any SQL statement encountered after a COMMIT or ROLLBACK and before a BEGIN TRANSACTION is executed as a single statement transaction, automatically committed if it executed without error, aborted if any error occurs during its execution.

Although conceptually a transaction is a logical unit of business work, such as a customer order or receipt of new inventory from a supplier, you may decide to break the business unit of work into several database transactions for database processing reasons. For example, because of the isolation property, a transaction that takes many commands and a long time to process may prohibit other uses of the same data at the same time, thus delaying other critical (possibly read-only) work. Some database data are used frequently, so it is important to complete transactional work on these so-called hotspot data as quickly as possible. For example, a primary key and its index for bank account numbers will likely need to be accessed by every ATM transaction, so the database transaction must be designed to use and release this data quickly. Also, remember, all the commands between the boundaries of a transaction must be executed, even those commands seeking input from an online user. If a user is slow to respond to input requests within the boundaries of a transaction, other users may encounter significant delays. Thus, if possible, collect all user input before beginning a transaction. Also, to minimize the length of a transaction, check for possible errors, such as duplicate keys or insufficient account balance, as early in the transaction as possible, so portions of the database can be released as soon as possible for other users if the transaction is going to be aborted. Some constraints (e.g., balancing the number of units of an item received with the number placed in inventory less returns) cannot be checked until many database commands are executed, so the transaction must be long to ensure database integrity. Thus, the general guideline is to make a database transaction as short as possible while still maintaining the integrity of the database.

Backward recovery (rollback)
The backout, or undo, of unwanted changes to a database. Before images of the records that have been changed are applied to the database, and the database is returned to an earlier state. Rollback is used to reverse the changes made by transactions that have been aborted, or terminated abnormally.

BACKWARD RECOVERY With **backward recovery** (also called **rollback**), the DBMS backs out of or undoes unwanted changes to the database. As Figure 11-9a shows, before images of the records that have been changed are applied to the database.

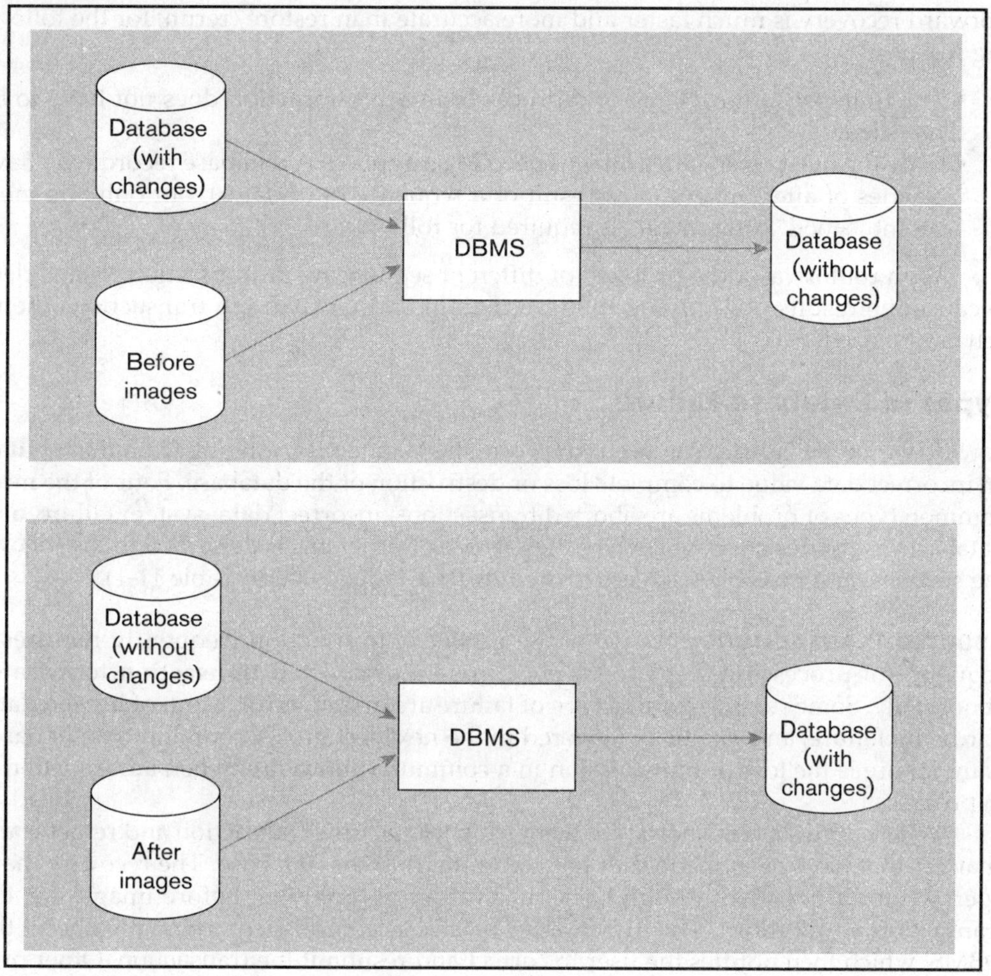

FIGURE 11-9 Basic recovery techniques
(a) Rollback
(b) Rollforward

As a result, the database is returned to an earlier state; the unwanted changes are eliminated.

Backward recovery is used to reverse the changes made by transactions that have aborted, or terminated abnormally. To illustrate the need for backward recovery (or UNDO), suppose that a banking transaction will transfer $100 in funds from the account for customer A to the account for customer B. The following steps are performed:

1. The program reads the record for customer A and subtracts $100 from the account balance.
2. The program then reads the record for customer B and adds $100 to the account balance. Now the program writes the updated record for customer A to the database. However, in attempting to write the record for customer B, the program encounters an error condition (e.g., a disk fault) and cannot write the record. Now the database is inconsistent—record A has been updated but record B has not—and the transaction must be aborted. An UNDO command will cause the recovery manager to apply the before image for record A to restore the account balance to its original value. (The recovery manager may then restart the transaction and make another attempt.)

FORWARD RECOVERY With **forward recovery** (also called **rollforward**), the DBMS starts with an earlier copy of the database. Applying after images (the results of good transactions) quickly moves the database forward to a later state (see Figure 11-9b).

Forward recovery (rollforward) A technique that starts with an earlier copy of a database. After images (the results of good transactions) are applied to the database, and the database is quickly moved forward to a later state.

Forward recovery is much faster and more accurate than restore/rerun, for the following reasons:

- The time-consuming logic of reprocessing each transaction does not have to be repeated.
- Only the most recent after images need to be applied. A database record may have a series of after images (as a result of a sequence of updates), but only the most recent, "good" after image, is required for rollforward.

With rollforward, the problem of different sequencing of transactions is avoided, because the results of applying the transactions (rather than the transactions themselves) are used.

Types of Database Failure

A wide variety of failures can occur in processing a database, ranging from the input of an incorrect data value to complete loss or destruction of the database. Four of the most common types of problems are aborted transactions, incorrect data, system failure, and database loss or destruction. Each of these types of problems is described in the following sections, and possible recovery procedures are indicated (see Table 11-1).

Aborted transaction
A transaction in progress that terminates abnormally.

ABORTED TRANSACTIONS As we noted earlier, a transaction frequently requires a sequence of processing steps to be performed. An **aborted transaction** terminates abnormally. Some reasons for this type of failure are human error, input of invalid data, hardware failure, and deadlock (covered in the next section). A common type of hardware failure is the loss of transmission in a communications link when a transaction is in progress.

When a transaction aborts, we want to "back out" the transaction and remove any changes that have been made (but not committed) to the database. The recovery manager accomplishes this through backward recovery (applying before images for the transaction in question). This function should be accomplished automatically by the DBMS, which then notifies the user to correct and resubmit the transaction. Other procedures, such as rollforward or transaction reprocessing, could be applied to bring the database to the state it was in just prior to the abort occurrence, but rollback is the preferred procedure in this case.

INCORRECT DATA A more complex situation arises when the database has been updated with incorrect, but valid, data. For example, an incorrect grade may be recorded for a student, or an incorrect amount could be input for a customer payment.

Incorrect data are difficult to detect and often lead to complications. To begin with, some time may elapse before an error is detected and the database record (or records)

TABLE 11-1 Responses to Database Failure

Type of Failure	Recovery Technique
Aborted transaction	Rollback (preferred)
	Rollforward/return transactions to state just prior to abort
Incorrect data (update inaccurate)	Rollback (preferred)
	Reprocess transactions without inaccurate data updates
	Compensating transactions
System failure (database intact)	Switch to duplicate database (preferred)
	Rollback
	Restart from checkpoint (rollforward)
Database destruction	Switch to duplicate database (preferred)
	Rollforward
	Reprocess transactions

corrected. By this time, numerous other users may have used the erroneous data, and a chain reaction of errors may have occurred as various applications made use of the incorrect data. In addition, transaction outputs (e.g., documents and messages) based on the incorrect data may be transmitted to persons. An incorrect grade report, for example, may be sent to a student or an incorrect statement sent to a customer.

When incorrect data have been processed, the database may be recovered in one of the following ways:

- If the error is discovered soon enough, backward recovery may be used. (However, care must be taken to ensure that all subsequent errors have been reversed.)
- If only a few errors have occurred, a series of compensating transactions may be introduced through human intervention to correct the errors.
- If the first two measures are not feasible, it may be necessary to restart from the most recent checkpoint before the error occurred, and subsequent transactions processed without the error.

Any erroneous messages or documents that have been produced by the erroneous transaction will have to be corrected by appropriate human intervention (letters of explanation, telephone calls, etc.).

SYSTEM FAILURE In a system failure, some component of the system fails, but the database is not damaged. Some causes of system failure are power loss, operator error, loss of communications transmission, and system software failure.

When a system crashes, some transactions may be in progress. The first step in recovery is to back out those transactions, using before images (backward recovery). Then, if the system is mirrored, it may be possible to switch to the mirrored data and rebuild the corrupted data on a new disk. If the system is not mirrored, it may not be possible to restart because status information in main memory has been lost or damaged. The safest approach is to restart from the most recent checkpoint before the system failure. The database is rolled forward by applying after images for all transactions that were processed after that checkpoint.

DATABASE DESTRUCTION In the case of **database destruction**, the database itself is lost, destroyed, or cannot be read. A typical cause of database destruction is a disk drive failure (or head crash).

Database destruction
The database itself is lost, destroyed, or cannot be read.

Again, using a mirrored copy of the database is the preferred strategy for recovering from such an event. If there is no mirrored copy, a backup copy of the database is required. Forward recovery is used to restore the database to its state immediately before the loss occurred. Any transactions that may have been in progress when the database was lost are restarted.

Disaster Recovery

Every organization requires contingency plans for dealing with disasters that may severely damage or destroy its data center. Such disasters may be natural (e.g., floods, earthquakes, tornadoes, hurricanes) or human-caused (e.g., wars, sabotage, terrorist attacks). For example, the 2001 terrorist attacks on the World Trade Center resulted in the complete destruction of several data centers and widespread loss of data.

Planning for disaster recovery is an organization-wide responsibility. Database administration is responsible for developing plans for recovering the organization's data and for restoring data operations. Following are some of the major components of a recovery plan (Mullins, 2002):

- Develop a detailed written disaster recovery plan. Schedule regular tests of the plan.
- Choose and train a multidisciplinary team to carry out the plan.
- Establish a backup data center at an offsite location. This site must be located a sufficient distance from the primary site so that no foreseeable disaster will disrupt both sites. If an organization has two or more data centers, each site may

serve as a backup for one of the others. If not, the organization may contract with a disaster recovery service provider.

- Send backup copies of databases to the backup data center on a scheduled basis. Database backups may be sent to the remote site by courier or transmitted by replication software.

CONTROLLING CONCURRENT ACCESS

Databases are shared resources. Database administrators must expect and plan for the likelihood that several users will attempt to access and manipulate data at the same time. With concurrent processing involving updates, a database without **concurrency control** will be compromised due to interference between users. There are two basic approaches to concurrency control: a pessimistic approach (involving locking) and an optimistic approach (involving versioning). We summarize both of these approaches in the following sections.

Concurrency control
The process of managing simultaneous operations against a database so that data integrity is maintained and the operations do not interfere with each other in a multiuser environment.

If users are only reading data, no data integrity problems will be encountered because no changes will be made in the database. However, if one or more users are updating data, then potential problems with maintaining data integrity arise. When more than one transaction is being processed against a database at the same time, the transactions are considered to be concurrent. The actions that must be taken to ensure that data integrity is maintained are called *currency control actions*. Although these actions are implemented by a DBMS, a database administrator must understand these actions and may expect to make certain choices governing their implementation.

Remember that a CPU can process only one instruction at a time. As new transactions are submitted while other processing is occurring against the database, the transactions are usually interleaved, with the CPU switching among the transactions so that some portion of each transaction is performed as the CPU addresses each transaction in turn. Because the CPU is able to switch among transactions so quickly, most users will not notice that they are sharing CPU time with other users.

The Problem of Lost Updates

The most common problem encountered when multiple users attempt to update a database without adequate concurrency control is lost updates. Figure 11-10 shows a common situation. John and Marsha have a joint checking account, and both want to withdraw some cash at the same time, each using an ATM terminal in a different location. Figure 11-10 shows the sequence of events that might occur in the absence of a concurrency control mechanism. John's transaction reads the account balance (which is $1,000) and he proceeds to withdraw $200. Before the transaction writes the new account balance ($800), Marsha's transaction reads the account balance (which is still $1,000). She then withdraws $300, leaving a balance of $700. Her transaction then writes this account balance, which replaces the one written by John's transaction. The effect of John's update has been lost due to interference between the transactions, and the bank is unhappy.

Another similar type of problem that may occur when concurrency control is not established is the **inconsistent read problem**. This problem occurs when one user reads data that have been partially updated by another user. The read will be incorrect, and is sometimes referred to as a *dirty read* or an *unrepeatable read*. The lost update and inconsistent read problems arise when the DBMS does not isolate transactions, part of the ACID transaction properties.

Inconsistent read problem
An unrepeatable read, one that occurs when one user reads data that have been partially updated by another user.

Serializability

Concurrent transactions need to be processed in isolation so that they do not interfere with each other. If one transaction were entirely processed before another transaction, no interference would occur. Procedures that process transactions so that the outcome is the same as this are called *serializable*. Processing transactions using a serializable schedule will give the same results as if the transactions had been processed one after the other.

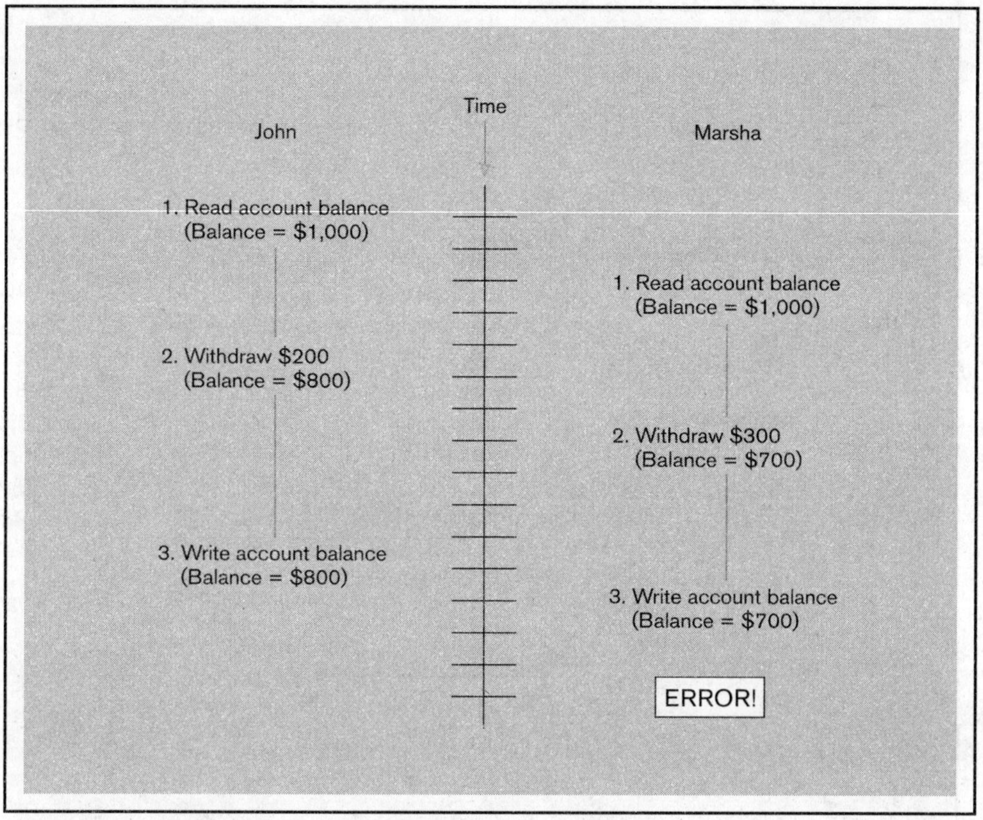

FIGURE 11-10 **Lost update (no concurrency control in effect)**

Schedules are designed so that transactions that will not interfere with each other can still be run in parallel. For example, transactions that request data from different tables in a database will not conflict with each other and can be run concurrently without causing data integrity problems. Serializability is achieved by different means, but locking mechanisms are the most common type of concurrency control mechanism. With **locking**, any data that are retrieved by a user for updating must be locked, or denied to other users, until the update is complete or aborted. Locking data is much like checking a book out of the library; it is unavailable to others until the borrower returns it.

Locking
A process in which any data that are retrieved by a user for updating must be locked, or denied to other users, until the update is completed or aborted.

Locking Mechanisms

Figure 11-11 shows the use of record locks to maintain data integrity. John initiates a withdrawal transaction from an ATM. Because John's transaction will update this record, the application program locks this record before reading it into main memory. John proceeds to withdraw $200, and the new balance ($800) is computed. Marsha has initiated a withdrawal transaction shortly after John, but her transaction cannot access the account record until John's transaction has returned the updated record to the database and unlocked the record. The locking mechanism thus enforces a sequential updating process that prevents erroneous updates.

LOCKING LEVEL An important consideration in implementing concurrency control is choosing the locking level. The **locking level** (also called **lock granularity**) is the extent of the database resource that is included with each lock. Most commercial products implement locks at one of the following levels:

Locking level (lock granularity)
The extent of a database resource that is included with each lock.

- ***Database*** The entire database is locked and becomes unavailable to other users. This level has limited application, such as during a backup of the entire database (Rodgers, 1989).
- ***Table*** The entire table containing a requested record is locked. This level is appropriate mainly for bulk updates that will update the entire table, such as giving all employees a 5 percent raise.

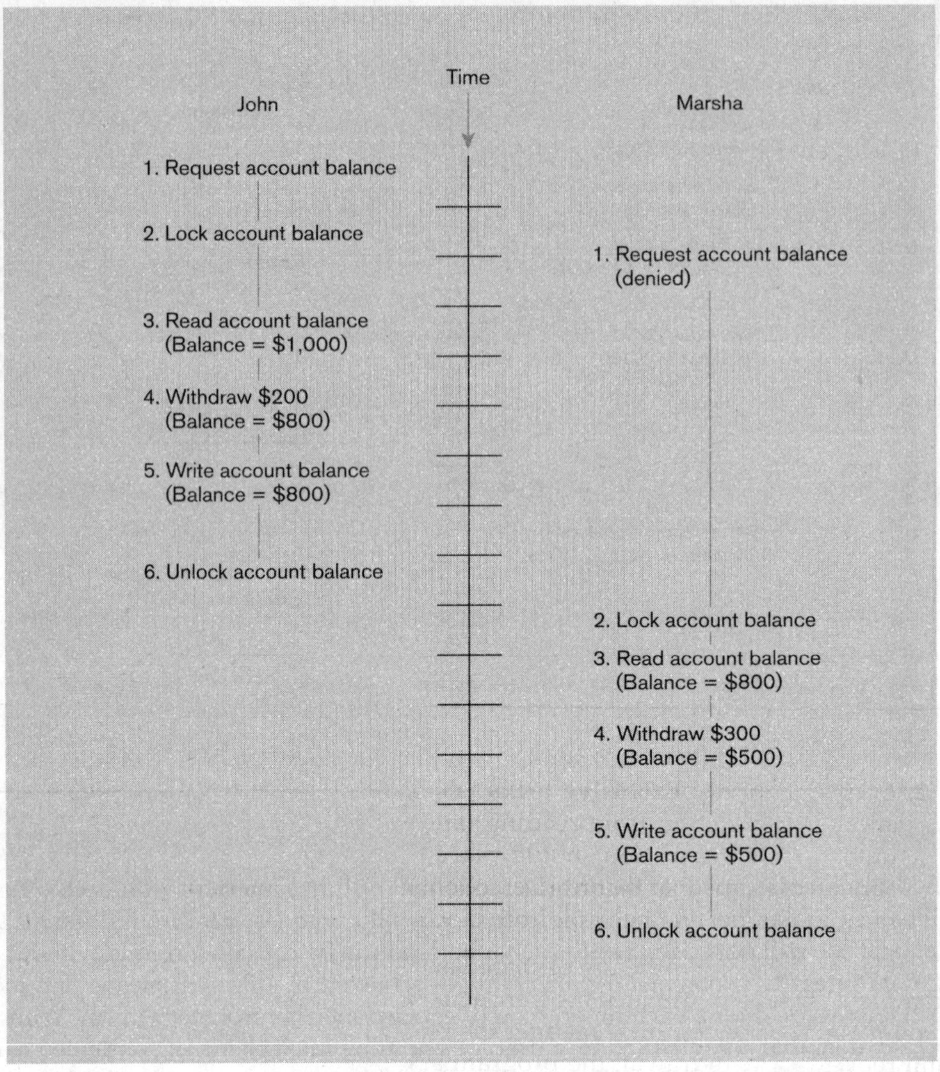

FIGURE 11-11 Updates with locking (concurrency control)

- ***Block or page*** The physical storage block (or page) containing a requested record is locked. This level is the most commonly implemented locking level. A page will be a fixed size (4K, 8K, etc.) and may contain records of more than one type.
- ***Record*** Only the requested record (or row) is locked. All other records, even within a table, are available to other users. It does impose some overhead at run time when several records are involved in an update.
- ***Field*** Only the particular field (or column) in a requested record is locked. This level may be appropriate when most updates affect only one or two fields in a record. For example, in inventory control applications the quantity-on-hand field changes frequently, but other fields (e.g., description and bin location) are rarely updated. Field-level locks require considerable overhead and are seldom used.

TYPES OF LOCKS So far, we have discussed only locks that prevent all access to locked items. In reality, a database administrator can generally choose between two types of locks:

Shared lock (S lock, or read lock) A technique that allows other transactions to read but not update a record or another resource.

1. ***Shared locks*** **Shared locks** (also called **S locks**, or **read locks**) allow other transactions to read (but not update) a record or other resource. A transaction should place a shared lock on a record or data resource when it will only read but not update that record. Placing a shared lock on a record prevents another user from placing an exclusive lock, but not a shared lock, on that record.

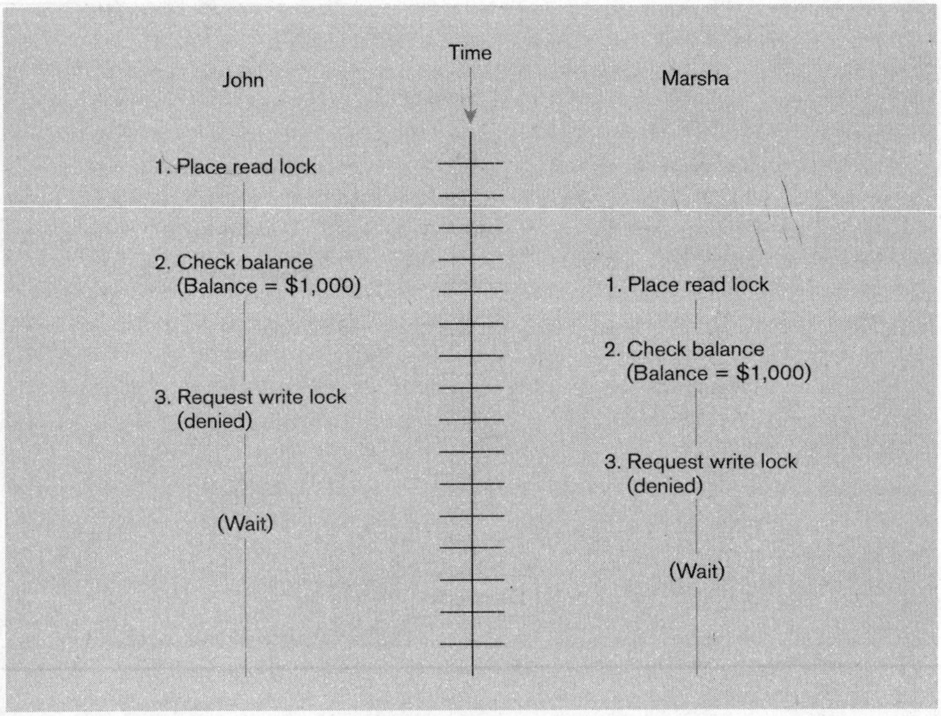

FIGURE 11-12 The problem of deadlock

2. *Exclusive locks* **Exclusive locks** (also called **X locks**, or **write locks**) prevent another transaction from reading (and therefore updating) a record until it is unlocked. A transaction should place an exclusive lock on a record when it is about to update that record (Descollonges, 1993). Placing an exclusive lock on a record prevents another user from placing any type of lock on that record.

Exclusive lock (X lock, or write lock)
A technique that prevents another transaction from reading and therefore updating a record until it is unlocked.

Figure 11-12 shows the use of shared and exclusive locks for the checking account example. When John initiates his transaction, the program places a read lock on his account record, because he is reading the record to check the account balance. When John requests a withdrawal, the program attempts to place an exclusive lock (write lock) on the record because this is an update operation. However, as you can see in the figure, Marsha has already initiated a transaction that has placed a read lock on the same record. As a result, his request is denied; remember that if a record is a read lock, another user cannot obtain a write lock.

DEADLOCK Locking solves the problem of erroneous updates but may lead to a problem called **deadlock**—an impasse that results when two or more transactions have locked a common resource, and each must wait for the other to unlock that resource. Figure 11-12 shows a simple example of deadlock. John's transaction is waiting for Marsha's transaction to remove the read lock from the account record, and vice versa. Neither person can withdraw money from the account, even though the balance is more than adequate.

Deadlock
An impasse that results when two or more transactions have locked a common resource, and each waits for the other to unlock that resource.

Figure 11-13 shows a slightly more complex example of deadlock. In this example, user A has locked record X, and user B has locked record Y. User A then requests record Y (intending to update), and user B requests record X (also intending to update). Both requests are denied, because the requested records are already locked. Unless the DBMS intervenes, both users will wait indefinitely.

MANAGING DEADLOCK There are two basic ways to resolve deadlocks: deadlock prevention and deadlock resolution. When **deadlock prevention** is employed, user programs must lock all records they will require at the beginning of a transaction, rather than one at a time. In Figure 11-13, user A would have to lock both records X and Y before processing the transaction. If either record is already locked, the

Deadlock prevention
A method for resolving deadlocks in which user programs must lock all records they require at the beginning of a transaction (rather than one at a time).

FIGURE 11-13 Another example of deadlock

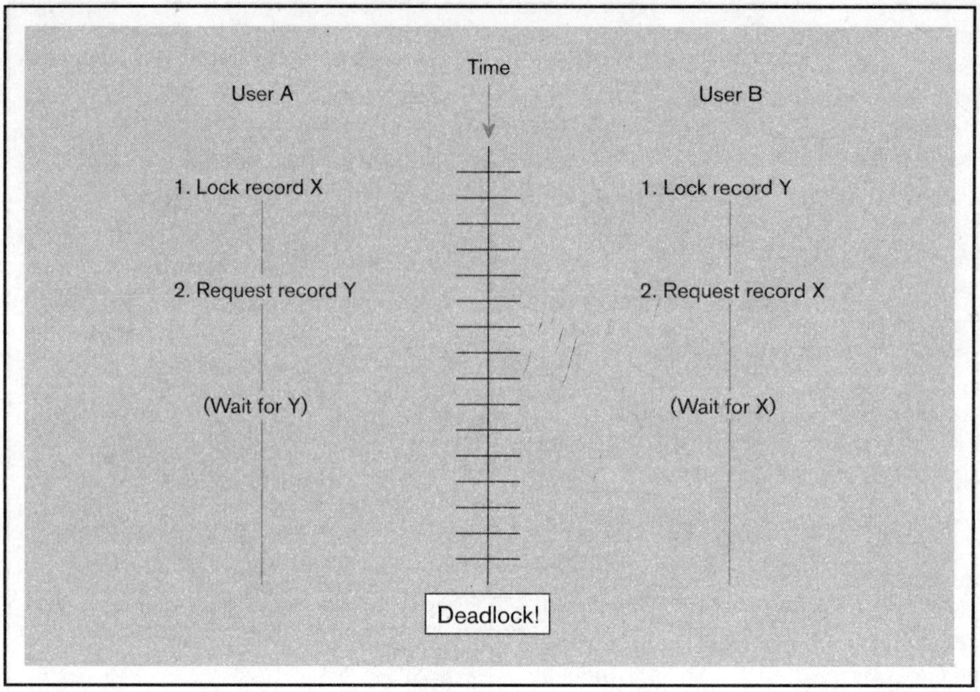

program must wait until it is released. Where all locking operations necessary for a transaction occur before any resources are unlocked, a **two-phase locking protocol** is being used. Once any lock obtained for the transaction is released, no more locks may be obtained. Thus, the phases in the two-phase locking protocol are often referred to as a growing phase (where all necessary locks are acquired) and a shrinking phase (where all locks are released). Locks do not have to be acquired simultaneously. Frequently, some locks will be acquired, processing will occur, and then additional locks will be acquired as needed.

Two-phase locking protocol
A procedure for acquiring the necessary locks for a transaction in which all necessary locks are acquired before any locks are released, resulting in a growing phase when locks are acquired and a shrinking phase when they are released.

Locking all the required records at the beginning of a transaction (called *conservative two-phase locking*) prevents deadlock. Unfortunately, it is often difficult to predict in advance what records will be required to process a transaction. A typical program has many processing parts and may call other programs in varying sequences. As a result, deadlock prevention is not always practical.

Two-phase locking, in which each transaction must request records in the same sequence (i.e., serializing the resources), also prevents deadlock, but again this may not be practical.

The second, and more common, approach is to allow deadlocks to occur but to build mechanisms into the DBMS for detecting and breaking the deadlocks. Essentially, these **deadlock resolution** mechanisms work as follows: The DBMS maintains a matrix of resource usage, which, at a given instant, indicates what subjects (users) are using what objects (resources). By scanning this matrix, the computer can detect deadlocks as they occur. The DBMS then resolves the deadlocks by "backing out" one of the deadlocked transactions. Any changes made by that transaction up to the time of deadlock are removed, and the transaction is restarted when the required resources become available. We will describe the procedure for backing out shortly.

Deadlock resolution
An approach to dealing with deadlocks that allows deadlocks to occur but builds mechanisms into the DBMS for detecting and breaking the deadlocks.

Versioning

Locking, as described here, is often referred to as a pessimistic concurrency control mechanism because each time a record is required, the DBMS takes the highly cautious approach of locking the record so that other programs cannot use it. In reality, in most cases other users will not request the same documents, or they may only want to read them, which is not a problem (Celko, 1992). Thus, conflicts are rare.

A newer approach to concurrency control, called **versioning**, takes the optimistic approach that most of the time other users do not want the same record, or if they do, they only want to read (but not update) the record. With versioning, there is no form of

Versioning
An approach to concurrency control in which each transaction is restricted to a view of the database as of the time that transaction started, and when a transaction modifies a record, the DBMS creates a new record version instead of overwriting the old record. Hence, no form of locking is required.

locking. Each transaction is restricted to a view of the database as of the time that transaction started, and when a transaction modifies a record, the DBMS creates a new record version instead of overwriting the old record.

The best way to understand versioning is to imagine a central records room, corresponding to the database (Celko, 1992). The records room has a service window. Users (corresponding to transactions) arrive at the window and request documents (corresponding to database records). However, the original documents never leave the records room. Instead, the clerk (corresponding to the DBMS) makes copies of the requested documents and time stamps them. Users then take their private copies (or versions) of the documents to their own workplace and read them and/or make changes. When finished, they return their marked-up copies to the clerk. The clerk merges the changes from marked-up copies into the central database. When there is no conflict (e.g., when only one user has made changes to a set of database records), that user's changes are merged directly into the public (or central) database.

Suppose instead that there is a conflict; for example, say that two users have made conflicting changes to their private copy of the database. In this case, the changes made by one of the users are committed to the database. (Remember that the transactions are time-stamped, so that the earlier transaction can be given priority.) The other user must be told that there was a conflict, and his work cannot be committed (or incorporated into the central database). He must check out another copy of the data records and repeat the previous work. Under the optimistic assumption, this type of rework will be the exception rather than the rule.

Figure 11-14 shows a simple example of the use of versioning for the checking account example. John reads the record containing the account balance, successfully withdraws $200, and the new balance ($800) is posted to the account with a COMMIT statement. Meanwhile, Marsha has also read the account record and requested a withdrawal, which is posted to her local version of the account record. However, when the transaction attempts to COMMIT, it discovers the update conflict, and her transaction is aborted (perhaps with a message such as "Cannot complete transaction at this time"). Marsha can then restart the transaction, working from the correct starting balance of $800.

The main advantage of versioning over locking is performance improvement. Read-only transactions can run concurrently with updating transactions, without loss of database consistency.

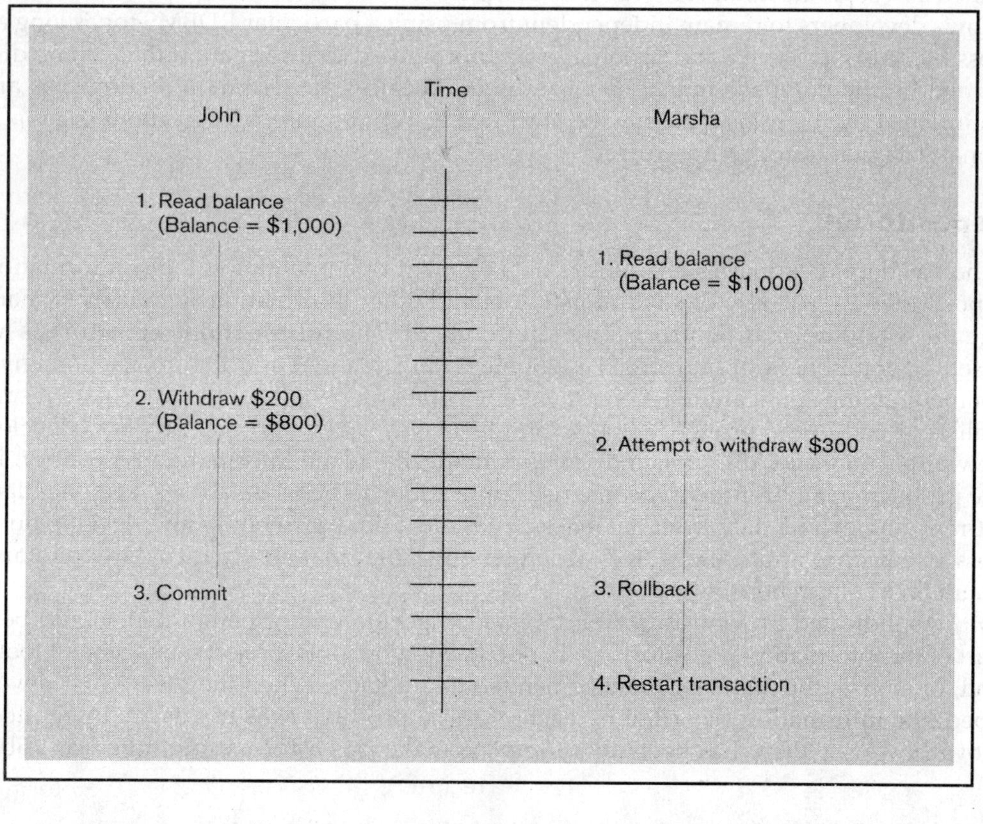

FIGURE 11-14 The use of versioning

DATA DICTIONARIES AND REPOSITORIES

In Chapter 1, we defined *metadata* as data that describe the properties or characteristics of end-user data and the context of that data. To be successful, an organization must develop sound strategies to collect, manage, and utilize its metadata. These strategies should address identifying the types of metadata that need to be collected and maintained and developing methods for the orderly collection and storage of that metadata. Data administration is usually responsible for the overall direction of the metadata strategy.

Metadata must be stored and managed using DBMS technology. The collection of metadata is referred to as a *data dictionary* (an older term) or a *repository* (a modern term). We describe each of these terms in this section. Some facilities of RDBMSs to access the metadata stored with a database were described in Chapter 7.

Data Dictionary

Data dictionary
A repository of information about a database that documents data elements of a database.

System catalog
A system-created database that describes all database objects, including data dictionary information, and also includes user access information.

An integral part of relational DBMSs is the **data dictionary**, which stores metadata, or information about the database, including attribute names and definitions for each table in the database. The data dictionary is usually a part of the **system catalog** that is generated for each database. The system catalog describes all database objects, including table-related data such as table names, table creators or owners, column names and data types, foreign keys and primary keys, index files, authorized users, user access privileges, and so forth. The system catalog is created and maintained automatically by the database management system, and the information is stored in systems tables, which may be queried in the same manner as any other data table, if the user has sufficient access privileges.

Data dictionaries may be either active or passive. An *active* data dictionary is managed automatically by the database management software. Active systems are always consistent with the current structure and definition of the database because they are maintained by the system itself. Most relational database management systems now contain active data dictionaries that can be derived from their system catalog. A *passive* data dictionary is managed by the user(s) of the system and is modified whenever the structure of the database is changed. Because this modification must be performed manually by the user, it is possible that the data dictionary will not be current with the current structure of the database. However, the passive data dictionary may be maintained as a separate database. This may be desirable during the design phase because it allows developers to remain independent from using a particular RDBMS for as long as possible. Also, passive data dictionaries are not limited to information that can be discerned by the database management system. Because passive data dictionaries are maintained by the user, they may be extended to contain information about organizational data that is not computerized.

Repositories

Information repository
A component that stores metadata that describe an organization's data and data processing resources, manages the total information processing environment, and combines information about an organization's business information and its application portfolio.

Whereas data dictionaries are simple data element documentation tools, information repositories are used by data administrators and other information specialists to manage the total information processing environment. The **information repository** is an essential component of both the development environment and the production environment. In the application development environment, people (either information specialists or end users) use CASE tools, high-level languages, and other tools to develop new applications. CASE tools may tie automatically to the information repository. In the production environment, people use applications to build databases, keep the data current, and extract data from databases. To build a data warehouse and develop business intelligence applications, it is absolutely essential that an organization build and maintain a comprehensive repository.

As indicated previously, CASE tools often generate information that should be a part of the information repository, as do documentation tools, project management tools, and, of course, the database management software itself. When they were first developed, the information recorded by each of these products was not easily integrated. Now, however, there has been an attempt to make this information more accessible

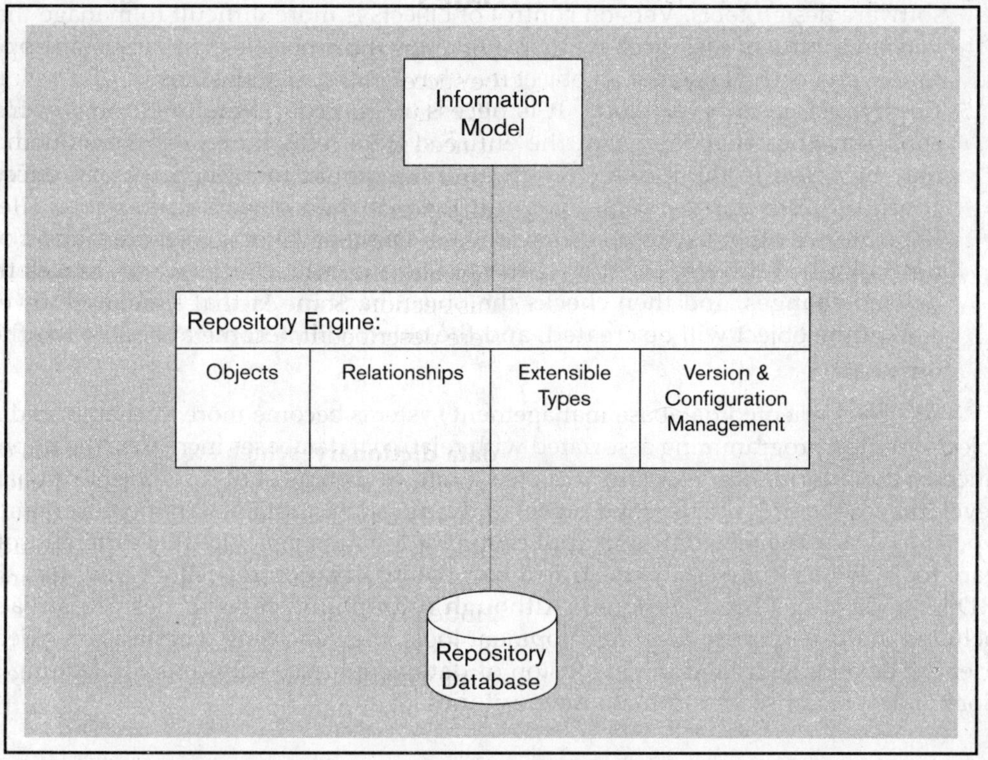

FIGURE 11-15 Three components of repository system architecture

Source: Based on Bernstein (1996)

and shareable. The **Information Resource Dictionary System (IRDS)** is a computer software tool that is used to manage and control access to the information repository. It provides facilities for recording, storing, and processing descriptions of an organization's significant data and data processing resources (Lefkovitz, 1985). When systems are compliant with IRDS, it is possible to transfer data definitions among the data dictionaries generated by the various products. IRDS, which has been adopted as a standard by the International Standards Organization as the ISO/IEC 10027 standard **www.iso.org/iso/catalogue_detail.htm?csnumber=17985** includes a set of rules for storing data dictionary information and for accessing it.

Information Resource Dictionary System (IRDS)
A computer software tool that is used to manage and control access to the information repository.

Figure 11-15 shows the three components of a repository system architecture (Bernstein, 1996). First is an information model. This model is a schema of the information stored in the repository, which can then be used by the tools associated with the database to interpret the contents of the repository. Next is the repository engine, which manages the repository objects. Services, such as reading and writing repository objects, browsing, and extending the information model, are included. Last is the repository database, in which the repository objects are actually stored. Notice that the repository engine supports five core functions (Bernstein, 1996):

1. ***Object management*** Object-oriented repositories store information about objects. As databases become more object oriented, developers will be able to use the information stored about database objects in the information repository. The repository can be based on an object-oriented database or it can add the capability to support objects.
2. ***Relationship management*** The repository engine contains information about object relationships that can be used to facilitate the use of software tools that attach to the database.
3. ***Dynamic extensibility*** The repository information model defines types, which should be easy to extend, that is, to add new types or to extend the definitions of those that already exist. This capability can make it easier to integrate a new software tool into the development process.
4. ***Version management*** During development, it is important to establish version control. The information repository can be used to facilitate version control for

software design tools. Version control of objects is more difficult to manage than version control of files, because there are many more objects than files in an application, and each version of an object may have many relationships.

5. ***Configuration management*** It is necessary to group versioned objects into configurations that represent the entire system, which are also versioned. It may help you to think of a configuration as similar to a file directory, except configurations can be versioned and they contain objects rather than files. Repositories often use checkout systems to manage objects, versions, and configurations. A developer who wishes to use an object checks it out, makes the desired changes, and then checks the object back in. At that time, a new version of the object will be created, and the object will become available to other developers.

As object-oriented database management systems become more available, and as object-oriented programming associated with relational databases increases, the importance of the information repository is also going to increase because object-oriented development requires the use (and reuse) of the metadata contained in the information repository. Also, the metadata and application information generated by different software tools will be more easily integrated into the information repository now that the IRDS standard has been accepted. Although information repositories are already included in the enterprise-level development tools, the increasing emphasis on object-oriented development and the explosion of data warehouse solutions are leading to more widespread use of information repositories.

OVERVIEW OF TUNING THE DATABASE FOR PERFORMANCE

Effective database support results in a reliable database where performance is not subject to interruption from hardware, software, or user problems and where optimal performance is achieved. Tuning a database is not an activity that is undertaken at the time of DBMS installation and/or at the time of implementation of a new application and then disregarded. Rather, performance analysis and tuning is an ongoing part of managing any database, as hardware and software configurations change and as user activity changes. Five areas of DBMS management that should be addressed when trying to maintain a well-tuned database are addressed here: installation of the DBMS, memory and storage space usage, input/output contention, CPU usage, and application tuning. The extent to which the database administrator can affect each of these areas will vary across DBMS products. Oracle 11g will be used as the exemplar DBMS throughout this section, but it should be noted that each product has its own set of tuning capabilities.

Tuning a database application requires familiarity with the system environment, the DBMS, the application, and the data used by the application. It is here that the skills of even an experienced database administrator are tested. Achieving a quiet environment, one that is reliable and allows users to secure desired information in a timely manner, requires skills and experience that are obtained by working with databases over time. The areas discussed next are quite general and are intended to provide an initial understanding of the scope of activities involved in tuning a database rather than providing the type of detailed understanding necessary to tune a particular database application.

Installation of the DBMS

Correct installation of the DBMS product is essential to any environment. Products often include README files, which may include detailed installation instructions, revisions of procedures, notification of increased disk space needed for installation, and so on. A quick review of any README files may save time during the installation process and result in a better installation. Failing to review general installation instructions may result in default parameter values being set during installation that are not optimal for the situation. Some possible considerations are listed here.

Before beginning installation, the database administrator should ensure that adequate disk space is available. You will need to refer to manuals for the specific DBMS to be able to translate logical database size parameters (e.g., field length, number of table rows, and estimated growth) into actual physical space requirements. It is possible that the space allocation recommendations are low, as changes made to a DBMS tend to make it larger, but the documentation may not reflect that change. To be safe, allocate at least 20 percent more space than suggested by standard calculations. After installation, review any log files generated during the installation process. Their contents will reveal installation problems that were not noticed or provide assurance that the installation proceeded as expected.

Allocation of disk space for the database should also receive consideration. For example, some UNIX backup systems have trouble with data files that exceed a gigabyte in size. Keeping data files under one gigabyte will avoid possible problems. Allocation of data files in standard sizes will make it easier to balance I/O, because data file locations can be swapped more easily should a bottleneck need to be resolved.

Memory and Storage Space Usage

Efficient usage of main memory involves understanding how the DBMS uses main memory, what buffers are being used, and what needs the programs in main memory have. For example, Oracle has many background processes that reside in memory and handle database management functions when a database is running. Some operating systems require a contiguous chunk of memory to be able to load Oracle, and a system with insufficient memory will have to free up memory space first. Oracle maintains in main memory a data dictionary cache that ideally should be large enough so that at least 90 percent of the requests to the data dictionary can be located in the cache rather than having to retrieve information from disk. Each of these is an example of typical memory management issues that should be considered when tuning a database.

Storage space management may include many activities, some of which have already been discussed in this book, such as denormalization and partitioning. One other activity is **data archiving**. Any database that stores history, such as transaction history or a time series of values for some field, will eventually include obsolete data—data that no longer has any use. Database statistics showing location access frequencies for records or pages can be a clue that data no longer has a purpose. Business rules may also indicate that data older than some value (e.g., seven years) does not need to be kept for active processing. However, there may be legal reasons or infrequently needed business intelligence queries that suggest data should simply not be discarded. Thus, database administrations should develop a program of archiving inactive data. Data may be archived to separate database tables (thus making active tables more compact and, hence, more likely to be more quickly processed) or to files stored outside the database (possibly on magnetic tape or optical storage). Archive files may also be compressed to save space. Methods also need to be developed to restore, in an acceptable time, archived data to the database if and when they are needed. (Remember, archived data are inactive, not totally obsolete.) Archiving reclaims disk space, saves disk storage costs, and may improve database performance by allowing the active data to be stored in less expansive space.

Data archiving
The process of moving inactive data to another storage location where it can be accessed when needed.

Input/Output (I/O) Contention

Database applications are very I/O intensive; a production database will usually both read and write large amounts of data to disk as it works. While CPU clock speeds have increased dramatically, I/O speeds have not increased proportionately, and increasingly complex distributed database systems have further complicated I/O functioning.

Understanding how data are accessed by end users is critical to managing I/O contention. When hot spots (physical disk locations that are accessed repeatedly) develop, understanding the nature of the activity that is causing the hot spot affords the database administrator a much better chance of reducing the I/O contention being experienced. Oracle allows the DBA to control the placement of tablespaces, which contain data files. The DBA's in-depth understanding of user activity facilitates her or his ability to reduce I/O contention by separating data files that are being accessed together. Where possible, large database objects that will be accessed concurrently may be striped across disks to reduce I/O contention and improve performance. An overall objective of distributing I/O activity evenly across disks and controllers should guide the DBA in tuning I/O.

CPU Usage

Most database operations will require CPU work activity. Because of this, it is important to evaluate CPU usage when tuning a database. Using multiple CPUs allows query processing to be shared when the CPUs are working in parallel, and performance may be dramatically improved. DBAs need to maximize the performance of their existing CPUs while planning for the gains that may be achieved with each new generation of CPUs.

Monitoring CPU load so that typical load throughout a 24-hour period is known provides DBAs with basic information necessary to begin to rebalance CPU loading. The mixture of online and background processing may need to be adjusted for each environment. For example, establishing a rule that all jobs that can be run in off-hours must be run in off-hours will help to unload the machine during peak working hours. Establishing user accounts with limited space will help manage the CPU load also.

Application Tuning

The previous sections have concentrated on activities to tune a DBMS. Examining the applications that end users are using with the database may also increase performance. While normalization to at least 3NF is expected in many organizations that are using relational data models, carefully planned denormalization (see Chapter 5) may improve performance, often by reducing the number of tables that must be joined when running an SQL query.

Examination and modification of the SQL code in an application may also lead to performance improvement. Queries that do full table scans should be avoided, for example, because they are not selective and may not remain in memory very long. This necessitates more retrievals from long-term storage. Multitable joins should be actively managed when possible with the DBMS being used, because the type of join can dramatically affect performance, especially if a join requires a full table join. A general rule of thumb is that any query whose ratio of CPU to I/O time exceeds 13:1 is probably poorly designed. Active monitoring of queries by the DBMS can be used to actually terminate a query of job that exhibits exceeding this ratio. Alternatively, such queries may be put into a "penalty box" to wait until the job scheduler determines that sufficient CPU time is available to continue processing the query.

Similarly, statements containing views and those containing subqueries should be actively reviewed. Tuning of such statements so that components are resolved in the most efficient manner possible may achieve significant performance gains. Chapter 5 discussed a variety of techniques a DBA could use to tune application processing speed and disk space utilization (e.g., re-indexing, overriding automatic query plans, changing data block sizes, reallocating files across storage devices, and guidelines for more efficient query design). A DBA plays an important role in advising programmers and developers which techniques will be the most effective.

The same database activity may take vastly different amounts of time, depending on the workload mix at the time the query or program is run. Some DBMSs have job schedulers that look at statistics about the history of running queries and will schedule batch jobs to achieve a desirable mix of CPU usage and I/O. A DBA can actively monitor query processing times by running so called "heartbeat" or "canary" queries. A **heartbeat query** is a very simple query (possibly SELECT * FROM table WHERE some condition) that a DBA runs many times during the day to monitor variations in processing times. When heartbeat queries are taking extraordinarily long to run, there is probably either an inappropriate mix of jobs running or some inefficient queries are consuming too many DBMS resources. A heartbeat query may also be exactly like certain regularly run user queries for which there are service-level agreements (SLAs) with users on maximum response times. In this case, the heartbeat query is run periodically to make sure that if the user were to submit this query, the SLA goals would be met.

Heartbeat query
A query submitted by a DBA to test the current performance of a database or to predict the response time for queries that have promised response times. Also called a canary query.

Another aspect of application tuning is setting realistic user expectations. Users should be trained to realize that more complex queries, especially if submitted ad hoc, will take more processing and response time. Users should also be trained to submit queries first using the EXPLAIN or similar function that will not actually run the query but rather estimate the time for query processing from database statistics. This way, many poorly written queries can be avoided. To effectively set realistic user expectations, the DBA needs to realize that database statistics (e.g., number of table rows and distribution of values for certain fields often used for qualifications) must to be recalculated frequently. Recalculation of statistics should occur at least after every batch load of a table, and more frequently for tables that are constantly being updated online. Statistics affect the query optimizer, so reasonable up-to-date statistics are essential for the DBMS to develop a very good query processing plan (i.e., which indexes to use and in which order to execute joins).

The preceding description of potential areas where database performance may be affected should convince you of the importance of effective database management and tuning. As a DBA achieves an in-depth understanding of a DBMS and the applications for which responsibility is assigned, the importance of tuning the database for performance should become apparent. Hopefully this brief section on database tuning will whet your appetite for learning more about one or more database products in order to develop tuning skills.

DATA AVAILABILITY

Ensuring the availability of databases to their users has always been a high-priority responsibility of database administrators. However, the growth of e-business has elevated this charge from an important goal to a business imperative. An e-business must be operational and available to its customers 24/7. Studies have shown that if an online customer does not get the service he or she expects within a few seconds, the customer will take his or her business to a competitor.

Costs of Downtime

The costs of downtime (when databases are unavailable) include several components: lost business during the outage, costs of catching up when service is restored, inventory shrinkage, legal costs, and permanent loss of customer loyalty. These costs are often difficult to estimate accurately and vary widely from one type of business to another.

A DBA needs to balance the costs of downtime with the costs of achieving the desired availability level. Unfortunately, it is seldom (if ever) possible to provide 100 percent service levels. Failures may occur (as discussed earlier in this chapter) that may interrupt service. Also, it is necessary to perform periodic database reorganizations or other maintenance activities that may cause service interruptions. It is the responsibility of database administration to minimize the impact of these interruptions. The goal is to provide a high level of availability that balances the various costs involved.The cost of downtime escalates annually as and when the availability time decreases, although the worst downtime could be as low as 1 percent.

Measures to Ensure Availability

A new generation of hardware, software, and management techniques has been developed (and continues to be developed) to assist database administrators in achieving the high availability levels expected in today's organizations. We have already discussed many of these techniques in this chapter (e.g., database recovery) or in earlier ones (e.g., RAID storage); in this section we provide only a brief summary of potential availability problems and measures for coping with them. A number of other techniques, such as component failure impact analysis (CFIA), fault-tree analysis (FTA), CRAMM, and so on, as well as a wealth of guidance on how to manage availability are described in the IT Infrastructure Library (ITIL) framework (**www.itil-officialsite.com**).

HARDWARE FAILURES Any hardware component, such as a database server, disk subsystem, power supply, or network switch, can become a point of failure that will disrupt service. The usual solution is to provide redundant or standby components that replace a failing system. For example, with clustered servers, the workload of a failing server can be reallocated to another server in the cluster.

LOSS OR CORRUPTION OF DATA Service can be interrupted when data are lost or become inaccurate. Mirrored (or backup) databases are almost always provided in high-availability systems. Also, it is important to use the latest backup and recovery systems (discussed earlier in this chapter).

HUMAN ERROR "Most . . . outages . . . are not caused by the technology, they're caused by people making changes" (Morrow, 2007, p. 32). The use of standard operating procedures, which are mature and repeatable, is a major deterrent to human errors. In addition, training, documentation, and insistence on following internationally recognized standard procedures (see, for example, COBIT [**www.isaca.org/cobit**] or ITIL [**www.itil-officialsite.com**]) are essential for reducing human errors.

MAINTENANCE DOWNTIME Historically, the greatest source of database downtime was attributed to planned database maintenance activities. Databases were taken offline during periods of low activity (nights, weekends) for database reorganization, backup, and other activities. This luxury is no longer available for high-availability applications. New database products are now available that automate maintenance functions. For example, some utilities (called *nondisruptive utilities*) allow routine maintenance to be performed while the systems remain operational for both read and write operations, without loss of data integrity.

NETWORK-RELATED PROBLEMS High-availability applications nearly always depend on the proper functioning of both internal and external networks. Both hardware and software failures can result in service disruption. However, the Internet has spawned new threats that can also result in interruption of service. For example, a hacker can mount a denial-of-service attack by flooding a Web site with computer-generated messages. To counter these threats, an organization should carefully monitor its traffic volumes and develop a fast-response strategy when there is a sudden spike in activity. An organization also must employ the latest firewalls, routers, and other network technologies.

Summary

The importance of managing data was emphasized in this chapter. The functions of data administration, which takes responsibility for the overall management of data resources, include developing procedures to protect and control data, resolving data ownership and use issues, conceptual data modeling, and developing and maintaining corporate-wide data definitions and standards. The functions of database administration, on the other hand, are those associated with the direct management of a database or databases, including DBMS installation and upgrading, database design issues, and technical issues such as security enforcement, database performance, data availability, and backup and recovery. The data administration and database administration roles are changing in today's business environment, with pressure being exerted to maintain data quality while building high-performing systems quickly.

Threats to data security include accidental losses, theft and fraud, loss of privacy, loss of data integrity, and loss of availability. A comprehensive data security plan will address all of these potential threats, partly through the establishment of views, authorization rules, user-defined procedures, and encryption procedures.

Databases, especially data security, play a key role in an organization's compliance with Sarbanes-Oxley (SOX). SOX audits focus on three key areas: IT change management, logical access to data, and IT operations.

Database recovery and backup procedures are another set of essential database administration activities. Basic recovery facilities that should be in place include backup facilities, journalizing facilities, checkpoint facilities, and a recovery manager. Depending on the type of problem encountered, backward recovery (rollback) or forward recovery (rollforward) may be needed.

The problems of managing concurrent access in multiuser environments must also be addressed. A DBMS must ensure that database transactions possess the ACID properties: atomic, consistent, isolated, and durable. Proper transaction boundaries must be chosen to achieve these properties at an acceptable performance. If concurrency controls on transactions are not established, lost updates may occur, which will cause data integrity to be impaired. Locking mechanisms, including shared and exclusive locks, can be used. Deadlocks may also occur in multiuser environments and may be managed by various means, including using a two-phase locking protocol or other deadlock-resolution mechanism. Versioning is an optimistic approach to concurrency control.

Managing the data dictionary, which is part of the system catalog in most relational database management systems, and the information repository help the DBA maintain high-quality data and high-performing database systems. The establishment of the Information Resource Dictionary System (IRDS) standard has helped with the development of repository information that can be integrated from multiple sources, including the DBMS itself, CASE tools, and software development tools.

Ensuring the availability of databases to users has become a high priority for the modern DBA. Use of batch windows to perform periodic maintenance (e.g., database reorganization) is no longer permissible for mission-critical applications. A new generation of hardware, software, and management techniques is being introduced to assist the DBA in managing data availability.

Effective data administration is not easy, and it encompasses all of the areas summarized here. Increasing emphasis on object-oriented development methods and rapid development are changing the data administration function, but better tools to achieve effective administration and database tuning are becoming available.

Chapter Review

Key Terms

Aborted transaction *492*
After image *487*
Authorization rules *481*
Backup facility *486*
Backward recovery (rollback) *490*
Before image *487*
Checkpoint facility *487*
Concurrency control *494*
Data administration *465*
Data archiving *503*
Data dictionary *500*
Database administration *467*
Database change log *487*
Database destruction *493*
Database recovery *486*
Database security *473*
Deadlock *498*
Deadlock prevention *497*
Deadlock resolution *498*
Encryption *482*
Exclusive lock (X lock, or write lock) *497*
Forward recovery (rollforward) *491*
Heartbeat query *505*
Inconsistent read problem *494*
Information repository *500*
Information Resource Dictionary System (IRDS) *501*
Journalizing facility *487*
Locking *495*
Locking level (lock granularity) *495*
Open source DBMS *472*
Recovery manager *488*
Restore/rerun *489*
Shared lock (S lock, or read lock) *496*
Smart card *484*
System catalog *500*
Transaction *487*
Transaction boundaries *490*
Transaction log *487*
Two-phase locking protocol *498*
User-defined procedures *482*
Versioning *498*

Review Questions

1. Define each of the following terms:
   a. data administration
   b. database administration
   c. two-phase locking protocol
   d. information repository
   e. locking
   f. versioning
   g. deadlock
   h. transaction
   i. encryption
   j. data availability
   k. data archiving
   l. heartbeat query
2. Match the following terms to the appropriate definitions:

____ backup facilities	a. protects data from loss or misuse
____ biometric device	b. reversal of abnormal or aborted transactions
____ checkpoint facility	c. describes all database objects
____ database recovery	d. automatically produces a saved copy of an entire database
____ database security	e. application of after images
____ granularity	f. might analyze your signature
____ recovery manager	g. restoring a database after a loss
____ rollback	h. DBMS module that restores a database after a failure
____ rollforward	i. extent to which a database is locked for transaction
____ system catalog	j. records database state at moment of synchronization

3. Compare and contrast the following terms:
   a. data administration; database administration
   b. repository; data dictionary
   c. deadlock prevention; deadlock resolution
   d. backward recovery; forward recovery
   e. active data dictionary; passive data dictionary
   f. optimistic concurrency control; pessimistic concurrency control
   g. shared lock; exclusive lock
   h. before image; after image
   i. two-phase locking protocol; versioning
   j. authorization; authentication
   k. data backup; data archiving
4. What is an open source DBMS?
5. Indicate whether data administration or database administration is typically responsible for each of the following functions:
   a. Managing the data repository
   b. Installing and upgrading the DBMS
   c. Conceptual data modeling
   d. Managing data security and privacy
   e. Database planning
   f. Tuning database performance
   g. Database backup and recovery
   h. Running heartbeat queries
6. Describe the changing roles of a data administrator and database administrator in the current business environment.
7. List four common problems of ineffective data administration.
8. List four job skills necessary for data administrators. List four job skills necessary for database administrators.
9. Briefly describe four new specialized DBA roles that are emerging today.
10. What changes can be made in data administration at each stage of the traditional database development life cycle to deliver high-quality, robust systems more quickly?
11. List and discuss five areas where threats to data security may occur.
12. Explain how creating a view may increase data security. Also explain why one should not rely completely on using views to enforce data security.
13. List and briefly explain how integrity controls can be used for database security.
14. What is the difference between an authentication scheme and an authorization scheme?
15. What are the key areas of IT that are examined during a Sarbanes-Oxley audit?
16. What are the two key types of security policies and procedures that must be established to aid in Sarbanes-Oxley compliance?
17. What is the advantage of optimistic concurrency control compared with pessimistic concurrency control?
18. What is the difference between shared locks and exclusive locks?
19. What is the difference between deadlock prevention and deadlock resolution?
20. Briefly describe four DBMS facilities that are required for database backup and recovery.
21. What is transaction integrity? Why is it important?
22. List and describe four common types of database failure.
23. Briefly describe four threats to high data availability and at least one measure that can be taken to counter each of these threats.
24. What is an Information Resource Dictionary System (IRDS)?
25. List and briefly explain the ACID properties of a database transaction.
26. Explain the two common forms of encryption.
27. Briefly describe four components of a disaster recovery plan.
28. Explain the purpose of heartbeat queries.
29. How can views be used as part of data security? What are the limitations of views for data security?
30. What is the purpose of the GRANT and REVOKE SQL commands? List some actions that can be granted to or revoked from a user.
31. What is concurrency control? What are the repercussions of not having a concurrency control? Using your own example (other than the one provided in the text), explain "inconsistent read"?
32. What is pessimistic concurrency control? How does Versioning help in solving the problems of locking?
33. What type of problems do the forward recovery and backward recovery help solve? How does mirroring a database relate to these two recovery concepts?
34. What is a journal or a log? Explain the different types of logs and their purposes.

Problems and Exercises

1. Fill in the two authorization tables for Pine Valley Furniture Company below, based on the following assumptions (enter Y for yes or N for no):

Authorizations for Inventory Clerks

	Inventory Records	Receivables Records	Payroll Records	Customer Records
Read				
Insert				
Modify				
Delete				

Authorizations for Inventory Records

	Salespersons	A/R Personnel	Inventory Clerks	Carpenters
Read				
Insert				
Modify				
Delete				

- Salespersons, managers, and carpenters may read inventory records but may not perform any other operations on these records.
- Persons in Accounts Receivable and Accounts Payable may read and/or update (insert, modify, delete) receivables records and customer records.
- Inventory clerks may read and/or update (modify, delete) inventory records. They may not view receivables records or payroll records. They may read but not modify customer records.

2. Five recovery techniques are listed below. For each situation described, decide which of the following recovery techniques is most appropriate.
   - Backward recovery
   - Forward recovery (from latest checkpoint)
   - Forward recovery (using backup copy of database)
   - Reprocessing transactions
   - Switch

   a. A phone disconnection occurs while a user is entering a transaction.
   b. A disk drive fails during regular operations.
   c. A lightning storm causes a power failure.
   d. An incorrect amount is entered and posted for a student tuition payment. The error is not discovered for several weeks.
   e. Data entry clerks have entered transactions for two hours after a full database backup when the database becomes corrupted. It is discovered that the journalizing facility of the database has not been activated since the backup was made.

3. Whitlock Department Stores runs a multiuser DBMS on a LAN file server. Unfortunately, at the present time, the DBMS does not enforce concurrency control. One Whitlock customer had a balance due of $250.00 when the following three transactions related to this customer were processed at about the same time:
   - Payment of $250.00
   - Purchase on credit of $100.00
   - Merchandise return (credit) of $50.00

   Each of the three transactions read the customer record when the balance was $250.00 (i.e., before any of the other transactions were completed). The updated customer record was returned to the database in the order shown in the bulleted list above.

   a. What balance will be included for the customer after the last transaction was completed?
   b. What balance should be included for the customer after the three transactions have been processed?

4. For each of the situations described below, indicate which of the following security measures is most appropriate:
   - Authorization rules
   - Encryption
   - Authentication schemes

   a. A national brokerage firm uses an electronic funds transfer (EFT) system to transmit sensitive financial data between locations.
   b. An organization has set up an offsite computer-based training center. The organization wishes to restrict access to the site to authorized employees. Because each employee's use of the center is occasional, the center does not wish to provide the employees with keys to access the center.
   c. A manufacturing firm uses a simple password system to protect its database but finds it needs a more comprehensive system to grant different privileges (e.g., read, versus create or update) to different users.
   d. A university has experienced considerable difficulty with unauthorized users accessing files and databases by appropriating passwords from legitimate users.

5. Metro Marketers, Inc., wants to build a data warehouse for storing customer information that will be used for data marketing purposes. Building the data warehouse will require much more capacity and processing power than they have previously needed, and they are considering Oracle and Red Brick as their database and data warehousing products. As part of their implementation plan, Metro has decided to organize a data administration function. At present, they have four major candidates for the data administrator position:

   a. Monica Lopez, a senior database administrator with five years of experience as an Oracle database administrator managing a financial database for a global banking firm, but no data warehousing experience.
   b. Gerald Bruester, a senior database administrator with six years of experience as an Informix database administrator managing a marketing-oriented database for a *Fortune* 1000 food products firm. Gerald has been to several data warehousing seminars over the past 12 months and is interested in being involved with a data warehouse.
   c. Jim Reedy, currently project manager for Metro Marketers. Jim is very familiar with Metro's current systems environment and is well respected by his coworkers. He has been involved with Metro's current database system but does not have any data warehousing experience.

d. Marie Weber, a data warehouse administrator with two years of experience using a Red Brick–based application that tracks accident information for an automobile insurance company.

Based on this limited information, rank the four candidates for the data administration position. Support your rankings by indicating your reasoning.

6. Referring to Problem and Exercise 5, rank the four candidates for the position of data warehouse administrator at Metro Marketing. Again, support your rankings.
7. Referring to Problem and Exercise 5, rank the four candidates for the position of database administrator at Metro Marketing. Again, support your rankings.
8. What concerns would you have if you accept a job as a database administrator and discover that the database users are entering one common password to log on to the database each morning when they arrive for work? You also learn that they leave their workstations connected to the database all day, even when they are away from their machines for extended periods of time.
9. During the Sarbanes-Oxley audit of a financial services company, you note the following issues. Categorize each of them into the area to which they belong: IT change management, logical access to data, and IT operations.
   a. Five database administrators have access to the sa (system administrator) account that has complete access to the database.
   b. Several changes to database structures did not have appropriate approval by management.
   c. Some users continued to have access to the database even after having been terminated.
   d. Databases are backed up on a regular schedule, using an automated system.
10. Revisit the four issues identified in Problem and Exercise 9. What risk, if any, do each of them pose to the firm?
11. An organization has a database server with three disk devices. The accounting and payroll applications share one of these disk devices and are experiencing performance problems. You have been asked to investigate the problem and tune the databases. What might you suggest to reduce I/O contention?
12. You take a new job as a database administrator at an organization that has a globally distributed database. You are asked to analyze the performance of the database, and as part of your analysis, you discover that all of the processing for regional monthly sales reports is being conducted at the corporate headquarters location. Operations are categorized by five regions: Eastern United States, Western United States, Canada, South America, and Mexico. Data for each region are kept on a server located at the regional headquarters. What would you try to improve the time needed to create the monthly sales reports?
13. An e-business operates a high-volume catalog sales center. Through the use of clustered servers and mirrored disk drives, the data center has been able to achieve data availability of 99.9 percent. Although this exceeds industry norms, the organization still receives periodic customer complaints that the Web site is unavailable (due to data outages). A vendor has proposed several software upgrades as well as expanded disk capacity to improve data availability. The cost of these proposed improvements would be about $25,000 per month. The vendor estimates that the improvements should improve availability to 99.99 percent.
    a. If this company is typical for a catalog sales center, what is the current annual cost of system unavailability? (You will need to refer to Tables 11-2 and 11-3 to answer this question.)
    b. If the vendor's estimates are accurate, can the organization justify the additional expenditure?
14. The mail order firm described in Problem and Exercise 13 has about 1 million customers. The firm is planning a mass mailing of its spring sales catalog to all of its customers. The unit cost of the mailing (postage and catalog) is $6.00. The error rate in the database (duplicate records, erroneous addresses, etc.) is estimated to be 12 percent. Calculate the expected loss of this mailing due to poor-quality data.
15. The average annual revenue per customer for the mail order firm described in Problems and Exercises 13 and 15 is $100. The organization is planning a data quality improvement program that it hopes will increase the average revenue per customer by 5 percent per year. If this estimate proves accurate, what will be the annual increase in revenue due to improved quality?
16. Referring to the Fitchwood Insurance Company case study at the end of Chapter 9, what types of security issues would you expect to encounter when building a data warehouse? Would there be just one set of security concerns related to user access to the data warehouse, or would you also need to be concerned with security of data during the extracting, cleansing, and loading processes?
17. How would Fitchwood's security have to be different if the data mart were made available to customers via the Internet?
18. What security and data quality issues need to be addressed when developing a B2B application using Web services?
19. Research available data quality software. Describe in detail at least one technique employed by one of these tools (e.g., an expert system).
20. Visit some Web sites for open source databases, such as **www.postgresql.org** and **www.mysql.com**. What do you see as major differences in administration between open source databases, such as MySQL, and commercial database products, such as Oracle? How might these differences come into play when choosing a database platform? Summarize the DBA functions of MySQL versus PostgreSQL.
21. Compare the concurrency issues that must be dealt with when developing an OLTP system versus a data warehouse.
22. The Indian Railways (IR) is the largest rail network in Asia and the world's second largest under single management. It spans over 6,000 stations and carries 17 million passengers everyday. The Indian Railways has a portal for booking passenger tickets and cargo freights online. The passengers, needless to say, can book their tickets from any source to destination. The passengers are given a login and password to book online. The ticket booking transactions are stored onto a mainframe server at their regional hub, in Hyderabad and New Delhi. If you were hired as the database consultant, how would you design the following:
    a. An all-inclusive set of data security measures to protect the Railways data
    b. A concurrency control mechanism
    c. Disaster recovery techniques from a wide range of failures from natural calamity to human errors

Field Exercises

1. Visit an organization that has implemented a database approach. Evaluate each of the following:
   a. The organizational placement of data administration, database administration, and data warehouse administration
   b. The assignment of responsibilities for each of the functions listed in part a
   c. The background and experience of the person chosen as head of data administration
   d. The status and usage of an information repository (passive, active-in-design, active-in-production)
2. Visit an organization that has implemented a database approach and interview an MIS department employee who has been involved in disaster recovery planning. Before you go for the interview, think carefully about the relative probabilities of various disasters for the organization you are visiting. For example, is the area subject to earthquakes, tornadoes, or other natural disasters? What type of damage might the physical plant be subject to? What is the background and training of the employees who must use the system? Find out about the organization's disaster recovery plans and ask specifically about any potential problems you have identified.
3. Visit an organization that has implemented a database approach and interview individuals there about the security measures they take routinely. Evaluate each of the following at the organization:
   a. Database security measures
   b. Network security measures
   c. Operating system security measures
   d. Physical plant security measures
   e. Personnel security measures
4. Identify an organization that handles large, sporadic data loads. For example, organizations that have implemented data warehouses may have large data loads as they populate their data warehouses. Determine what measures the organization has taken to handle these large loads as part of its capacity planning.
5. Databases tend to grow larger over time, not smaller, as new transaction data are added. Interview at least three companies that use databases extensively and identify their criteria and procedures for purging or archiving old data. Find out how often data are purged and what type of data are purged. Identify the data each organization archives and how long those data are archived.
6. Visit an organization that relies heavily on e-commerce applications. Interview the database administrator (or a senior person in the organization) to determine the following:
   a. What is the organizational goal for the system availability?
   b. Has the system estimated the cost of system downtime (Rs./hour)?
   c. What is the greatest obstacle to achieve high data availability for this organization?
   d. What measures has the organization taken to ensure high availability? What measures are planned for the future?
7. Visit an organization that uses an open source DBMS. Why did the organization choose open source software? Does it have other open source software besides a DBMS? Has it purchased any fee-based components or services? Does it have a DA or DBA staff, and, if so, how do these people evaluate the open source DBMS they are using? (This could especially provide insight if the organization also has some traditional DBMS products, such as Oracle or DB2.)

References

Anderson, D. 2005. "HIPAA Security and Compliance," available at **www.tdan.com** (July).

Bernstein, P. A. 1996. "The Repository: A Modern Vision." *Database Programming & Design* 9,12 (December): 28–35.

Celko, J. 1992. "An Introduction to Concurrency Control." *DBMS* 5,9 (September): 70–83.

Descollonges, M. 1993. "Concurrency for Complex Processing." *Database Programming & Design* 6,1 (January): 66–71.

Dowgiallo, E., H. Fosdick, Y. Lirov, A. Langer, T. Quinlan, and C. Young. 1997. "DBA of the Future." *Database Programming & Design* 10,6 (June): 33–41.

Fernandez, E. B., R. C. Summers, and C. Wood. 1981. *Database Security and Integrity*. Reading, MA: Addison-Wesley.

Hall, M. 2003. "MySQL Breaks into the Data Center," available at **www.computerworld.com/printthis/2003/0,4814,85900,00.html**.

Inmon, W. H. 1999. "Data Warehouse Administration." Found at **www.billinmon.com/library/other/dwaadmin.asp** (no longer available).

Inmon, W. H., C. Imhoff, and R. Sousa. 2001. *Corporate Information Factory*, 2nd ed. New York: Wiley.

Lefkovitz, H. C. 1985. *Proposed American National Standards Information Resource Dictionary System*. Wellesley, MA: QED Information Sciences.

Michaelson, J. 2004. "What Every Developer Should Know About Open Source Licensing." *Queue* 2,3 (May): 41–47. (Note: This whole issue of *Queue* is devoted to the open source movement and contains many interesting articles.)

Morrow, J. T. 2007. "The Three Pillars of Data." *InfoWorld* (March 12): 20–33.

Mullins, C. 2001. "Modern Database Administration, Part 1." *DM Review* 11,9 (September): 31, 55–57.

Mullins, C. 2002. *Database Administration: The Complete Guide to Practices and Procedures*. Boston: Addison-Wesley.

Rodgers, U. 1989. "Multiuser DBMS Under UNIX." *Database Programming & Design* 2,10 (October): 30–37.

Further Reading

Loney, K. 2000. "Protecting Your Database." *Oracle Magazine*. 14,3 (May/June): 101–106.

Surran, M. 2003. "Making the Switch to Open Source Software." *THE Journal*. 31,2 (September): 36–41. (This journal is available at **www.thejournal.com**)

Quinlan, T. 1996. "Time to Reengineer the DBA?" *Database Programming & Design* 9,3 (March): 29–34.

Web Resources

http://gost.isi.edu/publications/kerberos-neuman-tso.html A guide to the Kerberos method of user authentication.

www.abanet.org/scitech/ec/isc/dsg-tutorial.html An excellent guide to digital signatures from the American Bar Association Section of Science and Technology, Information Security Committee.

http://tpc.org Web site of the Transaction Processing Performance Council, a nonprofit corporation founded to define transaction processing and database benchmarks and to disseminate objective, verifiable transaction processing performance data to the industry. This is an excellent site for learning more about evaluating DBMSs and database designs through technical articles on database benchmarking.

CASE

Mountain View Community Hospital

Case Description

Refer to the case presented for Mountain View Community Hospital (MVCH) in Chapter 10.

Case Questions

1. Do EMR and CPOE systems seem to have the potential to help MVCH achieve its goals of achieving high-quality care and cost containment? Support your answers with examples of how you think these goals may or may not be achieved.
2. In light of HIPAA and other regulations, securing and protecting patient records is a primary requirement for MVCH.
   a. What data security issues would you expect MVCH to encounter if an EMR system is implemented that is accessible by physicians in the community, by laboratories, and by health-care organizations?
   b. What data security techniques described in this chapter could be used to address these issues?
3. If MVCH decides to implement a CPOE system, how could access problems such as the one that Dr. Z experienced at another hospital be prevented?
4. Given that the MVCH database you developed in SQL Server already includes tables for physicians, orders, and so on, do you think a full-fledged CPOE system could or should be developed internally? Why or why not?
5. Dr. Z indicated that physicians might resist the implementation of a CPOE system. Do you think that would also be true for an EMR system? Why or why not? What would be critical success factors for implementing an electronic medical record at MVCH?
6. Should MVCH adopt a continuous data protection (CDP) system? Why or why not? What other backup strategies might the hospital pursue?
7. Do you think data storage at MVCH should be treated as a strategic issue? Why or why not?
8. Which data and database administration issues described in this chapter should be addressed by MVCH's special study team as part of the long-range business and information systems plan? Why?

Case Exercises

1. List all the possible types of users who would need authorization to use (a) an ERM system and (b) a CPOE system at MVCH. Include user groups external to the hospital that may need to be included.
2. For each user type you listed in Case Exercise 1, indicate what permissions (read, insert, delete, modify) you would grant.
3. Investigate how a hospital such as MVCH could use RFID in connection with an EMR system. How would that affect data storage requirements?
4. In light of HIPAA's security rules (data backup, access to data, data retention, etc.) and the tremendous growth of data at MVCH, outline the pros and cons of various data storage options that the hospital may be using. Are there storage media that can potentially lead to violations under HIPAA? Which ones? Why?
5. Access HIPAA's security requirements online and outline a contingency plan for MVCH.

Project Assignments

P1. Password protect the MVCH database you created in SQL Server (or other database management systems required by your instructor).

P2. Create a matrix to indicate the permissions (read, insert, delete, modify) you would grant to different users of the database you identify.

P3. Create at least two different users and implement their permissions using SQL statements.

CHAPTER

12

Overview: Distributed Databases

Learning Objectives

After studying this chapter, you should be able to:

- Concisely define the following key terms: **distributed database, decentralized database, location transparency, local autonomy, synchronous distributed database, asynchronous distributed database, local transaction, global transaction, replication transparency, transaction manager, failure transparency, commit protocol, two-phase commit, concurrency transparency, time-stamping,** and **semijoin.**
- Explain the business conditions that are drivers for the use of distributed databases in organizations.
- Describe the salient characteristics of a variety of distributed database environments.
- Explain the potential advantages and risks associated with distributed databases.
- Explain four strategies for the design of distributed databases, options within each strategy, and the factors to consider in selecting among these strategies.
- State the relative advantages of synchronous and asynchronous data replication and partitioning as three major approaches for distributed database design.
- Outline the steps involved in processing a query in a distributed database and several approaches used to optimize distributed query processing.
- Explain the salient features of several distributed database management systems.

OVERVIEW

Distributed database
A single logical database that is spread physically across computers in multiple locations that are connected by a data communication link.

When an organization is geographically dispersed, it may choose to store its databases on a central database server or to distribute them to local servers (or a combination of both). A **distributed database** is a single logical database that is spread physically across computers in multiple locations that are connected by a data communications network. We emphasize that a distributed database is truly a database, not a loose collection of files. The distributed database is still centrally administered as a corporate resource while providing local flexibility and customization. The network must allow the users to share the data; thus a user (or program) at location A must be able to access (and perhaps update) data at location B. The sites of a distributed system may be spread over a large area (e.g., the United States or the world) or over a small area (e.g., a building or campus). The computers may range from PCs to large-scale servers or even supercomputers.

A distributed database requires multiple instances of a database management system (or DBMSs) running at each remote site. The degree to which these different DBMS instances cooperate, or work in partnership, and whether there is a master site that coordinates requests involving data from multiple sites distinguish different types of distributed database environments.

Various business conditions encourage the use of distributed databases: distribution and autonomy of business units, data sharing, data communications costs and reliability, environments with multiple applications and vendors, database recovery, and the satisfying of both transaction and analytical processing.

Objectives and Trade-offs

A major objective of distributed databases is to provide ease of access to data for users at many different locations. To meet this objective, the distributed database system must provide **location transparency**, which means that a user (or user program) using data for querying or updating need not know the location of the data. Any request to retrieve or update data from any site is automatically forwarded by the system to the site or sites related to the processing request. Ideally, the user is unaware of the distribution of data, and all data in the network appear as a single logical database stored at one site. In this ideal case, a single query can join data from tables in multiple sites as if the data were all in one site.

Location transparency
A design goal for a distributed database, which says that a user (or user program) using data need not know the location of the data.

A second objective of distributed databases is **local autonomy**, which is the capability to administer a local database and to operate independently when connections to other nodes have failed (Date, 2003). With local autonomy, each site has the capability to control local data, administer security, log transactions, recover when local failures occur, and provide full access to local data to local users when any central or coordinating site cannot operate. In this case, data are locally owned and managed, even though they are accessible from remote sites. This implies that there is no reliance on a central site.

Local autonomy
A design goal for a distributed database, which says that a site can independently administer and operate its database when connections to other nodes have failed.

Compared with centralized databases, either form of a distributed database has numerous advantages. The most important are increased reliability and availability, local control, modularity, lower communication costs, and faster response. A distributed database system also faces certain costs and disadvantages: software cost and complexity, processing overhead, data integrity, and slow response (if the data are not distributed properly).

Options for Distributing a Database

How should a database be distributed among the sites (or nodes) of a network? We discussed this important issue of physical database design in Chapter 5, which introduced an analytical procedure for evaluating alternative distribution strategies. In that chapter, we noted that there are four basic strategies for distributing databases: data replication, horizontal partitioning, vertical partitioning, and combinations of the above.

There are many forms of *data replication*, which are discussed in detail in the complete online version of this chapter. There are five advantages to data replication: reliability, fast response, possible avoidance of complicated distributed transaction integrity routines, node decoupling, and reduced network traffic at prime time. Replication has three primary disadvantages: storage requirements, complexity, and cost of updating.

With *horizontal partitioning* (see Chapter 5 for a description of different forms of table partitioning), some of the rows of a table (or relation) are put into a base relation at one site, and other rows are put into a base relation at another site. More generally, the rows of a relation are distributed to many sites. Horizontal partitions for a distributed database have four major advantages: efficiency, local optimization, security, and ease of querying. Thus, horizontal partitions are usually used when an organizational function is distributed, but each site is concerned with only a subset of the entity instances (frequently based on geography). Horizontal partitions also have two primary disadvantages: *inconsistent access speed* and *backup vulnerability*.

Distributed DBMS

To have a distributed database, there must be a database management system that coordinates the access to data at the various nodes. We will call such a system a *distributed DBMS*. Although each site may have a DBMS managing the local database at that site, a distributed DBMS will perform the following functions (Buretta, 1997; Elmasri and Navathe, 2006):

1. Keep track of where data are located in a distributed data dictionary. This means, in part, presenting one logical database and schema to developers and users.
2. Determine the location from which to retrieve requested data and the location at which to process each part of a distributed query without any special actions by the developer or user.
3. If necessary, translate the request at one node using a local DBMS into the proper request to another node using a different DBMS and data model and return data to the requesting node in the format accepted by that node.
4. Provide data management functions, such as security, concurrency and deadlock control, global query optimization, and automatic failure recording and recovery.
5. Provide consistency among copies of data across the remote sites (e.g., by using multiphase commit protocols).
6. Present a single logical database that is physically distributed. One ramification of this view of data is global primary key control, meaning that data about the same business object are associated with the same primary key no matter where in the distributed database the data are stored, and different objects are associated with different primary keys.
7. Be scalable. Scalability is the ability to grow, reduce in size, and become more heterogeneous as the needs of the business change. Thus, a distributed database must be dynamic and be able to change within reasonable limits and without having to be redesigned. Scalability also means that there are easy ways for new sites to be added (or to subscribe) and to be initialized (e.g., with replicated data).
8. Replicate both data and stored procedures across the nodes of the distributed database. The need to distribute stored procedures is motivated by the same reasons as those for distributing data.
9. Transparently use residual computing power to improve the performance of database processing. This means, for example, the same database query may be processed at different sites and in different ways when submitted at different times, depending on the particular workload across the distributed database at the time of query submission.
10. Permit different nodes to run different DBMSs. Middleware (see Chapter 8) can be used by the distributed DBMS and each local DBMS to mask the differences in query languages and nuances of local data.
11. Allow different versions of application code to reside on different nodes of the distributed database. In a large organization with multiple, distributed servers, it may not be practical to have each server/node running the same version of software.

A distributed DBMS provides location transparency (defined earlier), **replication transparency**, **failure transparency**, and **concurrency transparency**. A distributed DBMS uses a **commit protocol** to ensure data integrity for real-time, distributed update operations. The most common commit protocol is **two-phase commit** (which is detailed in the complete online version of this chapter).

Replication transparency
A design goal for a distributed database, which says that although a given data item may be replicated at several nodes in a network, a programmer or user may treat the data item as if it were a single item at a single node. Also called fragmentation transparency.

Failure transparency
A design goal for a distributed database, which guarantees that either all the actions of each transaction are committed or else none of them is committed.

Concurrency transparency
A design goal for a distributed database, with the property that although a distributed system runs many transactions, it appears that a given transaction is the only activity in the system. Thus, when several transactions are processed concurrently, the results must be the same as if each transaction were processed in serial order.

Commit protocol
An algorithm to ensure that a transaction is either successfully completed or aborted.

Two-phase commit
An algorithm for coordinating updates in a distributed database.

Query Optimization

With distributed databases, the response to a query may require a DBMS to assemble data from several different sites (although with location transparency, the user is unaware of this need). A major decision for the DBMS is how to process a query, which is affected by both the way a user formulates a query and the intelligence of the distributed DBMS to develop a sensible plan for processing. Several plausible query-processing strategies are detailed in the complete chapter. Depending on the choice of strategy, the time required to satisfy a query might range from one second to several days!

One technique used to make processing a distributed query more efficient is to use a **semijoin** operation (Elmasri and Navathe, 2006). In a semijoin, only the joining attribute is sent from one site to another, and then only the required rows are returned. If only a small percentage of the rows participate in the join, the amount of data being transferred is minimal.

Semijoin
A joining operation used with distributed databases in which only the joining attribute from one site is transmitted to the other site, rather than all the selected attributes from every qualified row.

Chapter Review

For coverage of key terms, review questions, problems and exercises, and field questions, see the complete chapter on the textbook's Web site. The following are the full set of references for the chapter, followed by information about additional sources of information on distributed databases.

References

Bell, D., and J. Grimson. 1992. *Distributed Database Systems*. Reading, MA: Addison-Wesley.

Buretta, M. 1997. *Data Replication: Tools and Techniques for Managing Distributed Information*. New York: Wiley.

Date, C. J. 2003. *An Introduction to Database Systems*, 8th ed. Reading, MA: Addison-Wesley.

Edelstein, H. 1993. "Replicating Data." *DBMS* 6,6 (June): 59–64.

Edelstein, H. 1995. "The Challenge of Replication, Part I." *DBMS* 8,3 (March): 46–52.

Elmasri, R., and S. Navathe. 2006. *Fundamentals of Database Systems*, 5th ed. Menlo Park, CA: Benjamin Cummings.

Froemming, G. 1996. "Design and Replication: Issues with Mobile Applications—Part 1." *DBMS* 9,3 (March): 48–56.

Koop, P. 1995. "Replication at Work." *DBMS* 8,3 (March): 54–60.

McGovern, D. 1993. "Two-Phased Commit or Replication." *Database Programming & Design* 6,5 (May): 35–44.

Özsu, M. T., and P. Valduriez. 1992. "Distributed Database Systems: Where Were We?" *Database Programming & Design* 5,4 (April): 49–55.

Thé, L. 1994. "Distribute Data without Choking the Net." *Datamation* 40,1 (January 7): 35–38.

Thompson, C. 1997. "Database Replication: Comparing Three Leading DBMS Vendors' Approaches to Replication." *DBMS* 10,5 (May): 76–84.

Further Reading

Edelstein, H. 1995. "The Challenge of Replication, Part II." *DBMS* 8,4 (April): 62–70, 103.

Web Resources

http://databases.about.com Web site that contains a variety of news and reviews about various database technologies, including distributed databases.

http://dsonline.computer.org The IEEE Web site, which provides material regarding various aspects of distributed computing, including distributed databases in a section that focuses on this topic area. The newest material is available through IEEE's Computing Now (**http://computingnow.computer.org**).

CHAPTER

13

Overview: Object-Oriented Data Modeling

Learning Objectives

After studying this chapter, you should be able to:

- Concisely define each of the following key terms: **class, object, state, behavior, class diagram, object diagram, operation, encapsulation, constructor operation, query operation, update operation, class-scope operation, association, association role, multiplicity, association class, abstract class, concrete class, class-scope attribute, abstract operation, method, polymorphism, overriding, multiple classification, aggregation,** and **composition.**
- Describe the activities in the different phases of the object-oriented development life cycle.
- State the advantages of object-oriented modeling vis-à-vis structured approaches.
- Compare the object-oriented model with the E-R and EER models.
- Model a real-world domain by using a Unified Modeling Language (UML) class diagram
- Provide a snapshot of the detailed state of a system at a point in time, using a UML object diagram.
- Recognize when to use generalization, aggregation, and composition relationships.
- Specify different types of business rules in a class diagram.

OVERVIEW

In Chapters 2 and 3, you learned about data modeling using the E-R and EER models. In those chapters, you discovered how to model the data needs of an organization using entities, attributes, and a wide variety of relationships. In this chapter, you will be introduced to the object-oriented model, which is becoming increasingly popular because of its ability to thoroughly represent complex relationships, as well as to represent data and system behavior in a consistent, integrated notation. Fortunately, most of the concepts you learned in those chapters correspond to concepts in object-oriented modeling, but the object-oriented model has even more expressive power than the EER model.

An object-oriented model is built around *objects*, just as the E-R model is built around entities. An object *encapsulates* both data *and* behavior, implying that we can use the object-oriented approach not only for data modeling, but also for modeling system behavior. To thoroughly model any real-world system, you need to model both the data, and the processes and behavior that act on the data (recall the discussion in Chapter 1 about information planning objects). By allowing you to capture them together within a common representation, and by offering benefits such as *inheritance* and code reuse, the object-oriented modeling approach provides a powerful environment for developing complex systems.

Coad and Yourdon (1991) identify several motivations and benefits of object-oriented modeling: the ability to tackle more challenging problem domains; improved communication between the users, analysts, designers, and programmers; increased consistency among analysis, design, and programming activities; explicit representation of commonality among system components; robustness of systems; reusability of analysis, design, and programming results; and increased consistency among all the models developed during object-oriented analysis, design, and programming.

In this chapter, we present object-oriented data modeling as a high-level conceptual activity. As you will learn in Chapter 14, a good conceptual model is invaluable for designing and implementing an object-oriented application that uses a relational database for providing persistence for the objects.

Unified Modeling Language

Unified Modeling Language (UML) is a set of graphical notations backed by a common metamodel that is widely used both for business modeling and for specifying, designing, and implementing software systems artifacts. For representing a complex system effectively, the model you develop must consist of a set of independent views or perspectives. UML allows you to represent multiple perspectives of a system by providing different types of graphical diagrams, such as the use-case diagram, class diagram, state diagram, sequence diagram, component diagram, and deployment diagram. If these diagrams are used correctly together in the context of a well-defined modeling process, UML allows you to analyze, design, and implement a system based on one consistent conceptual model.

Because this text is about databases, we will describe only the *class diagram*, which is one of the static diagrams in UML, addressing primarily structural characteristics of the domain of interest. The class diagram allows us also to capture the responsibilities that classes can perform, without any specifics of the behaviors. We will not describe the other diagram types because they provide perspectives that are not directly related to a database system, for example, the dynamic aspects of a system. Keep in mind that a database system is usually part of an overall system, whose underlying model should encompass all the different perspectives. For a discussion of other UML diagrams, see Hoffer et al. (2010) and George et al. (2007). It is important to note that the UML class diagrams can be used for multiple purposes at various stages of the life cycle model.

Object-Oriented Data Modeling

A **class** is an entity type that has a well-defined role in the application domain about which the organization wishes to maintain state, behavior, and identity. A class is a concept, an abstraction, or a thing that makes sense in an application context (Blaha and Rumbaugh, 2005). A class could represent a tangible or visible entity type (e.g., a person, place, or thing); it could be a concept or an event (e.g., Department, Performance, Marriage, Registration, etc.); or it could be an artifact of the design process (e.g., User Interface, Controller, Scheduler, etc.). An **object** is an instance of a class (e.g., a particular person, place, or thing) that encapsulates the data and behavior we need to maintain about that object. A class of objects shares a common set of attributes and behaviors.

The **state** of an object encompasses its properties (attributes and relationships) and the values those properties have, and its **behavior** represents how an object acts and reacts (Booch, 1994). Thus, an object's state is determined by its attribute values and links to other objects. An object's behavior depends on its state and the operation being performed. An operation is simply an action that one object performs in order to give a

Class
An entity that has a well-defined role in the application domain about which the organization wishes to maintain state, behavior, and identity.

Object
An instance of a class that encapsulates data and behavior.

State
An object's properties (attributes and relationships) and the values those properties have.

Behavior
The way in which an object acts and reacts.

response to a request. You can think of an operation as a service provided by an object (supplier) to its clients. A client sends a message to a supplier, which delivers the desired service by executing the corresponding operation.

Consider an example of the Student class and a particular object in this class, Mary Jones. The state of this object is characterized by its attributes, say, name, date of birth, year, address, and phone, and the values these attributes currently have. For example, name is "Mary Jones," year is "junior," and so on. The object's behavior is expressed through operations such as calcGpa, which is used to calculate a student's current grade point average. The Mary Jones object, therefore, packages its state and its behavior together. Every object has a persistent identity; that is, no two objects are the same, and an object maintains its own identity over its life. For example, if Mary Jones gets married and, thus, the values of the attributes name, address, and phone change for her, she will still be represented by the same object.

Class diagram
A diagram that shows the static structure of an object-oriented model: the object classes, their internal structure, and the relationships in which they participate.

You can depict the classes graphically in a class diagram as in Figure 13-2a. (Note: figure numbers are not continuous in this overview because only selected figures from the complete chapter on the textbook's Web site are included in this overview). A **class diagram** shows the static structure of an object-oriented model: the object classes, their internal structure, and the relationships in which they participate. The figure shows two classes, Student and Course, along with their attributes and operations. All students have in common the properties of name, dateOfBirth, year, address, and phone. They also exhibit common behavior by sharing the calcAge, calcGpa, and registerFor(course) operations.

Operation
A function or a service that is provided by all the instances of a class.

Encapsulation
The technique of hiding the internal implementation details of an object from its external view.

An **operation**, such as calcGpa in Student (see Figure 13-2a), is a function or a service that is provided by all the instances of a class. Typically, other objects can access or manipulate the information stored in an object only through such operations. The operations, therefore, provide an external interface to a class; the interface presents the outside view of the class without showing its internal structure or how its operations are implemented. This technique of hiding the internal implementation details of an object from its external view is known as **encapsulation**, or information hiding. So although we provide the abstraction of the behavior common to all instances of a class in its interface, we encapsulate within the class its structure and the secrets of the desired behavior.

FIGURE 13-2 UML class and object diagrams
(a) Class diagram showing two classes
(b) Object diagram with two instances

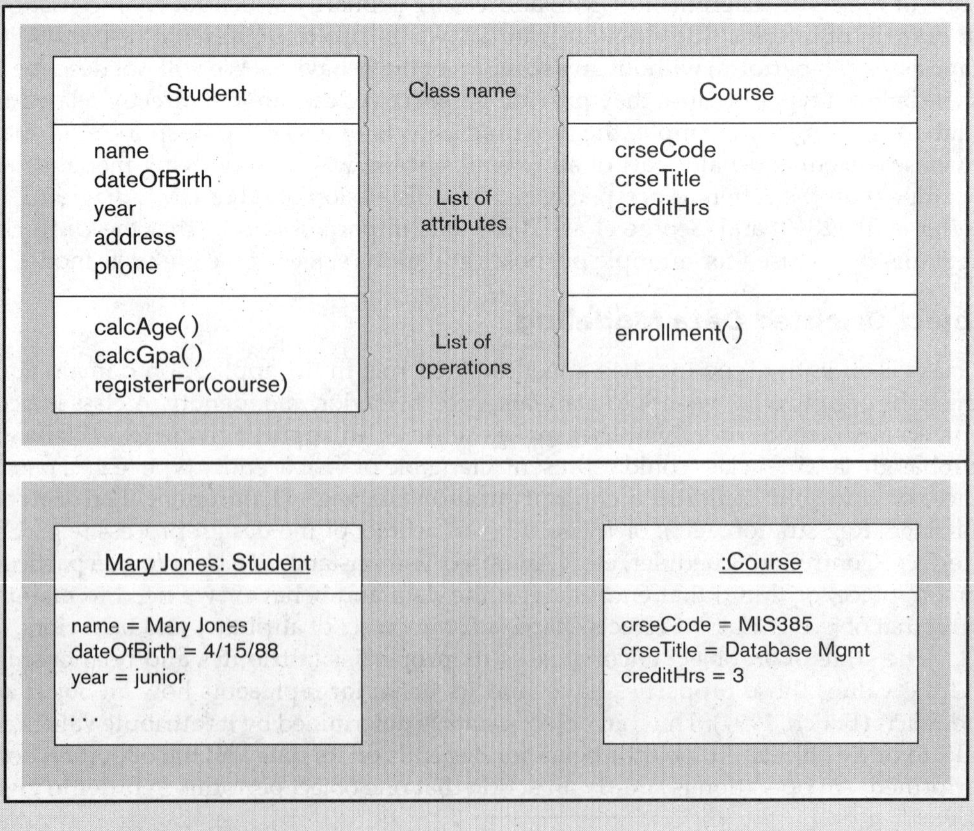

Parallel to the definition of a relationship for the E-R model, an **association** is a named relationship between or among instances of object classes. In Figure 13-3, we use examples from Figure 3-12 to illustrate how the object-oriented model can be used to represent association relationships of different degrees. The end of an association where it connects to a class is called an **association role** (Rumbaugh et al., 2004). A role may be explicitly named with a label near the end of an association (see the "manager" role in Figure 13-3a).

Association
A named relationship between or among object classes.

Association role
The end of an association, where it connects to a class.

Each role has a **multiplicity**, which indicates the number of objects that participate in a given relationship. In a class diagram, a multiplicity specification is shown as a text string representing an interval (or intervals) of integers in the following format:

Multiplicity
A specification that indicates how many objects participate in a given relationship.

lower-bound..upper-bound

In addition to integer values, the upper bound of a multiplicity can be a star character (*), which denotes an infinite upper bound. If a single integer value is specified, it means that the range includes only that value.

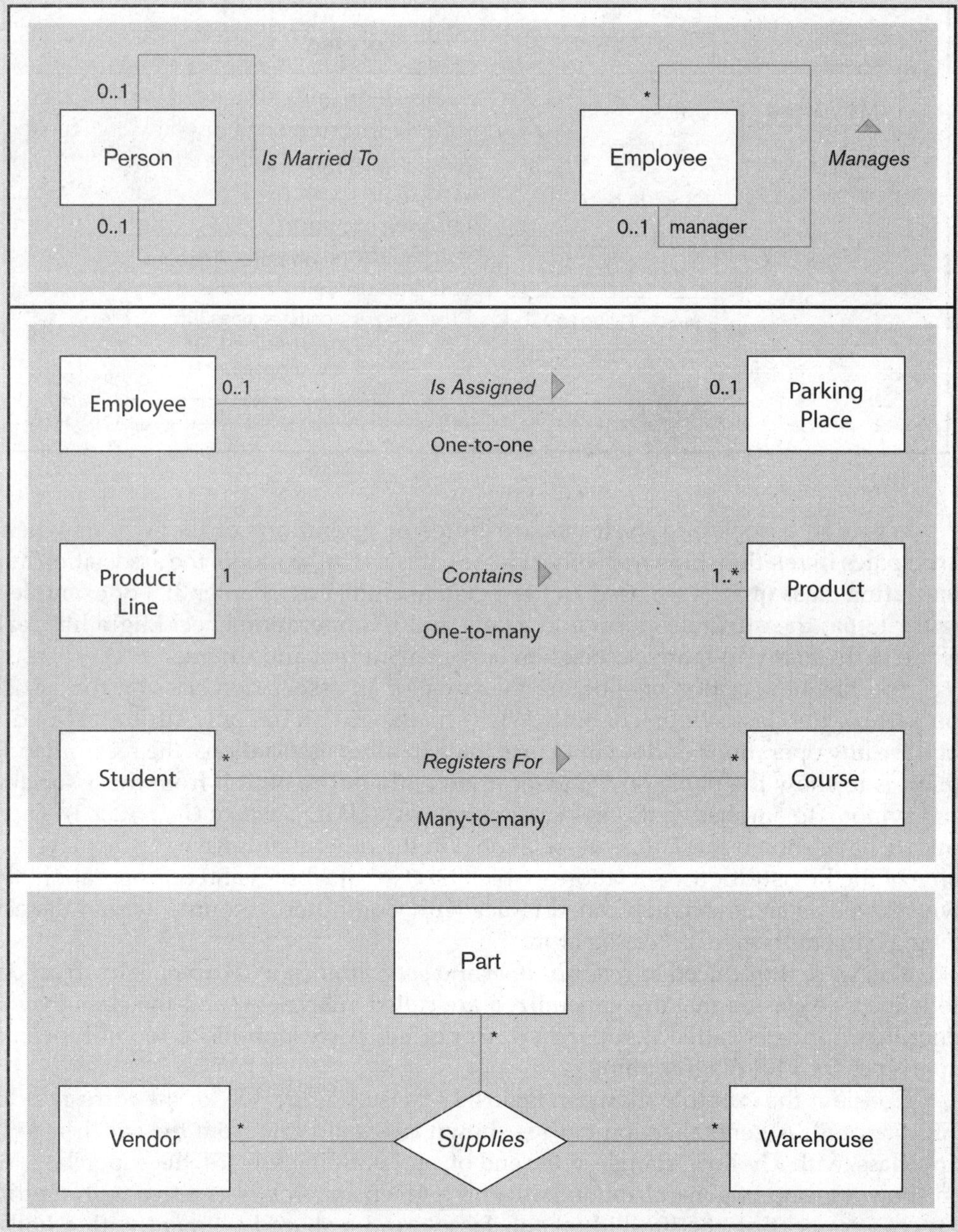

FIGURE 13-3 Examples of association relationships of different degrees
(a) Unary relationships
(b) Binary relationships
(c) Ternary relationship

FIGURE 13-6 Association class and link object
(a) Class diagram showing association classes
(b) Object diagram showing link objects

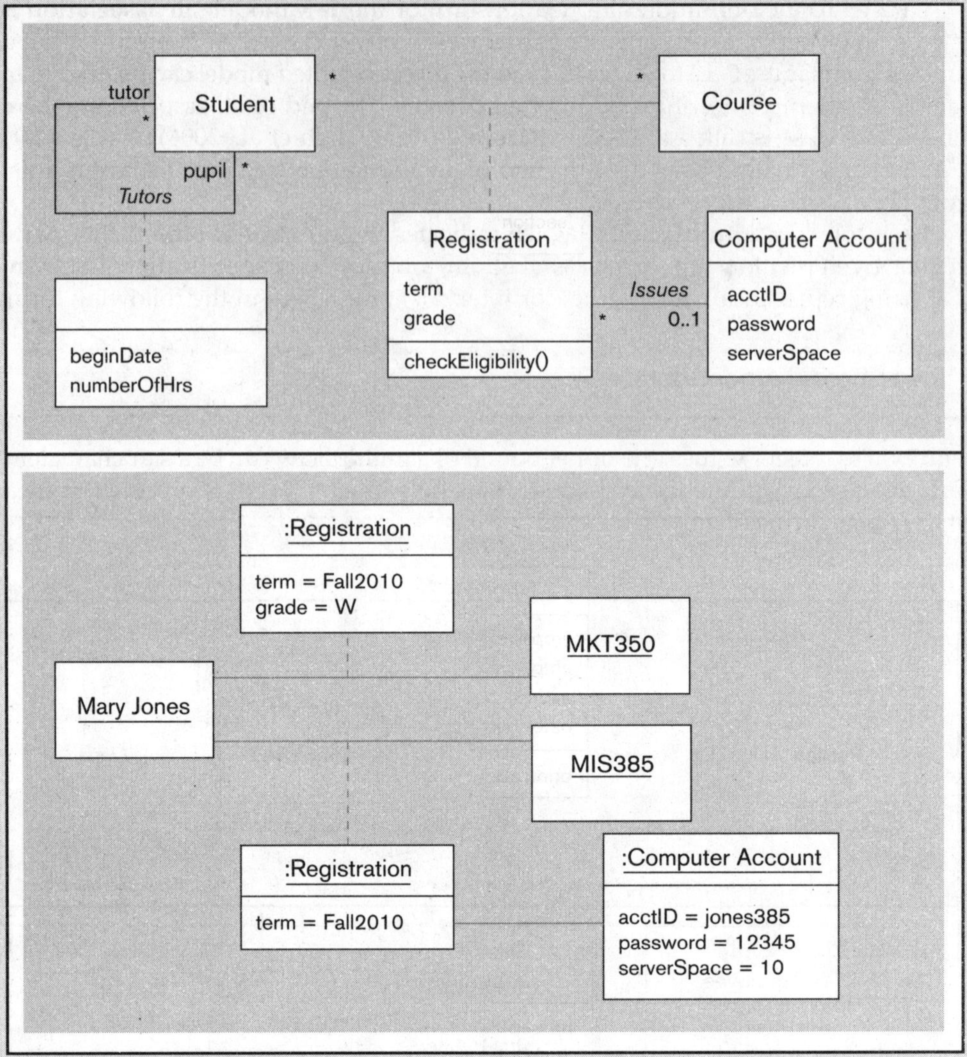

Association class
An association that has attributes or operations of its own or that participates in relationships with other classes.

When an association itself has attributes or operations of its own, or when it participates in relationships with other classes, it is useful to model the association as an **association class** (just as we used an "associative entity" in Chapter 3). For example, in Figure 13-6a, the attributes term and grade and the operation checkEligibility really belong to the many-to-many association between Student and Course.

You have the option of showing the name of an association class on the association path, or the class symbol, or both. When an association has only attributes but does not have any operations or does not participate in other associations, the recommended option is to show the name on the association path, but to omit it from the association class symbol, to emphasize its "association nature" (*UML Notation Guide*, 2003). That is how we have shown the Tutors association. On the other hand, we have displayed the name of the Registration association—which has two attributes and one operation of its own, as well as an association called Issues with Computer Account—within the class rectangle to emphasize its "class nature."

You were introduced to *generalization* and *specialization* in Chapter 3. In object data modeling, the classes that are generalized are called subclasses, and the class they are generalized into is called a superclass, in perfect correspondence to subtypes and supertypes for EER diagramming.

Consider the example shown in Figure 13-9a (see Figure 3-8 for the corresponding EER diagram). A generalization path is shown as a solid line from the subclass to the superclass, with a hollow triangle at the end of, and pointing toward, the superclass. You can show a group of generalization paths for a given superclass as a tree with multiple branches connecting the individual subclasses, and a shared segment with a hollow

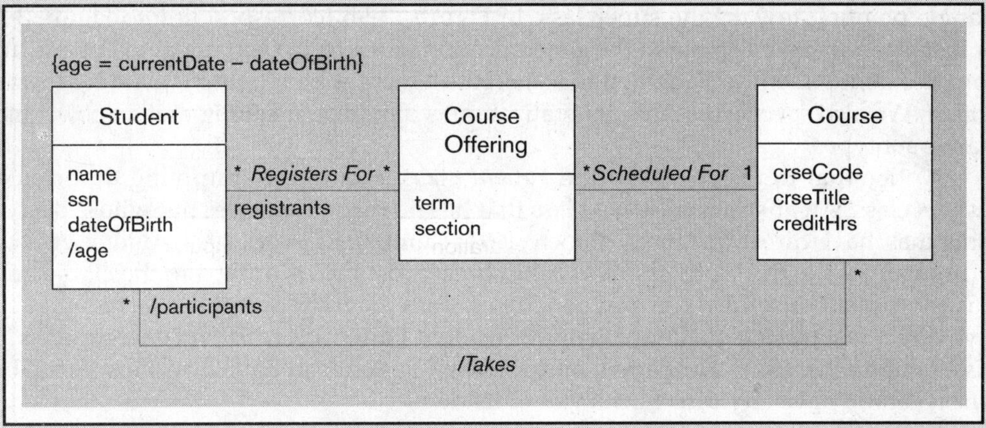

FIGURE 13-8 Derived attribute, association, and role

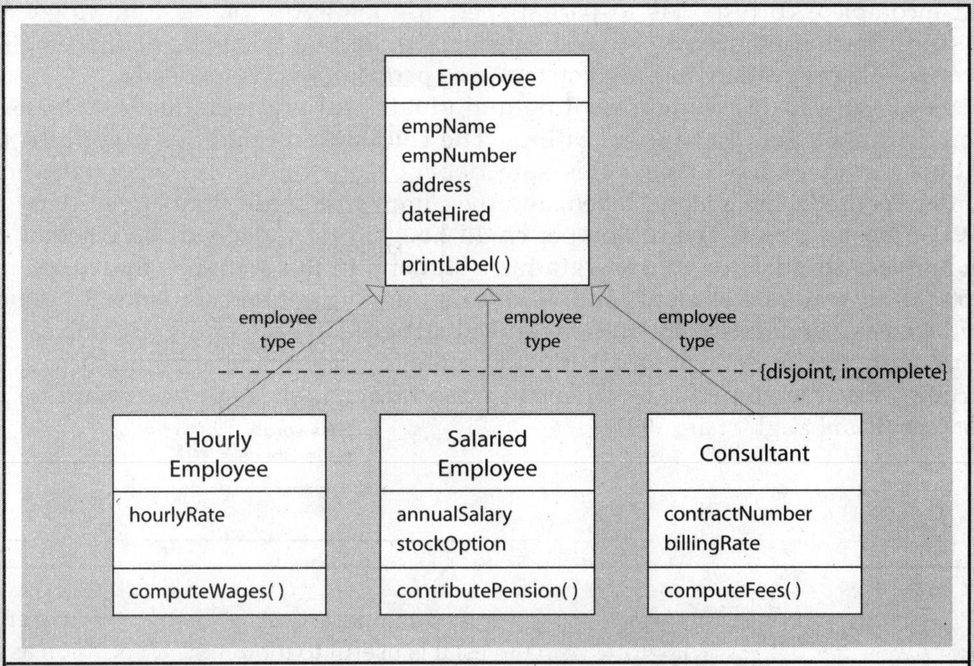

FIGURE 13-9 Examples of generalization, inheritance, and constraints

(a) Employee superclass with three subclasses

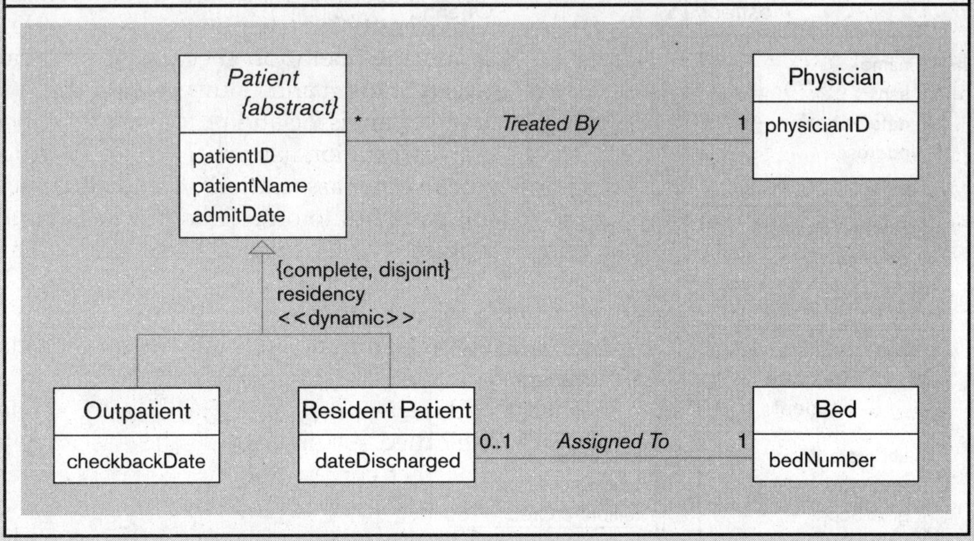

(b) Abstract Patient class with two concrete subclasses

triangle pointing toward the superclass. In Figure 13-9b (corresponding to Figure 3-3), for instance, we have combined the generalization paths from Outpatient to Patient, and from Resident Patient to Patient, into a shared segment with a triangle pointing toward Patient. We also specify that this generalization is dynamic, meaning that an object may change subtypes.

Abstract class
A class that has no direct instances but whose descendants may have direct instances.

Concrete class
A class that can have direct instances.

Notice that in Figure 13-9b the *Patient* class is in italics, implying that it is an abstract class. An **abstract class** is a class that has no direct instances but whose descendants may have direct instances (Booch, 1994; Rumbaugh et al., 1991). (Note: You can additionally write the word *abstract* within braces just below or next to the class name. This is especially useful when you generate a class diagram by hand.) A class that can have direct instances (e.g., Outpatient or Resident Patient) is called a **concrete class**. In this example, therefore, Outpatient and Resident Patient can have direct instances, but *Patient* cannot have any direct instances of its own.

In Figures 13-9a and 13-9b, the words "complete," "incomplete," and "disjoint" have been placed within braces, next to the generalization. They indicate semantic constraints among the subclasses. (In the EER notation, complete corresponds to total specialization, and incomplete corresponds to partial specialization.) Any of the following UML keywords for constraints may be used: overlapping, disjoint, complete, and incomplete, corresponding to overlapping, disjoint, total, and partial from EER modeling.

Class-scope attribute
An attribute of a class that specifies a value common to an entire class rather than a specific value for an instance.

In Figure 13-11, we represent both graduate and undergraduate students in a model developed for student billing. The calcTuition operation computes the tuition a student has to pay; this sum depends on the tuition per credit hour (tuitionPerCred), the courses taken, and the number of credit hours (creditHrs) for each of those courses. The tuition per credit hour, in turn, depends on whether the student is a graduate or an undergraduate student. In this example, that amount is $900 for all graduate students and $750 for all undergraduate students. To denote that, we have underlined the tuitionPerCred attribute in each of the two subclasses, along with its value. Such an attribute is called a **class-scope attribute** because it specifies a value common to an entire class rather than a specific value for an instance (Rumbaugh et al., 1991).

FIGURE 13-11 Polymorphism, abstract operation, class-scope attribute, and ordering

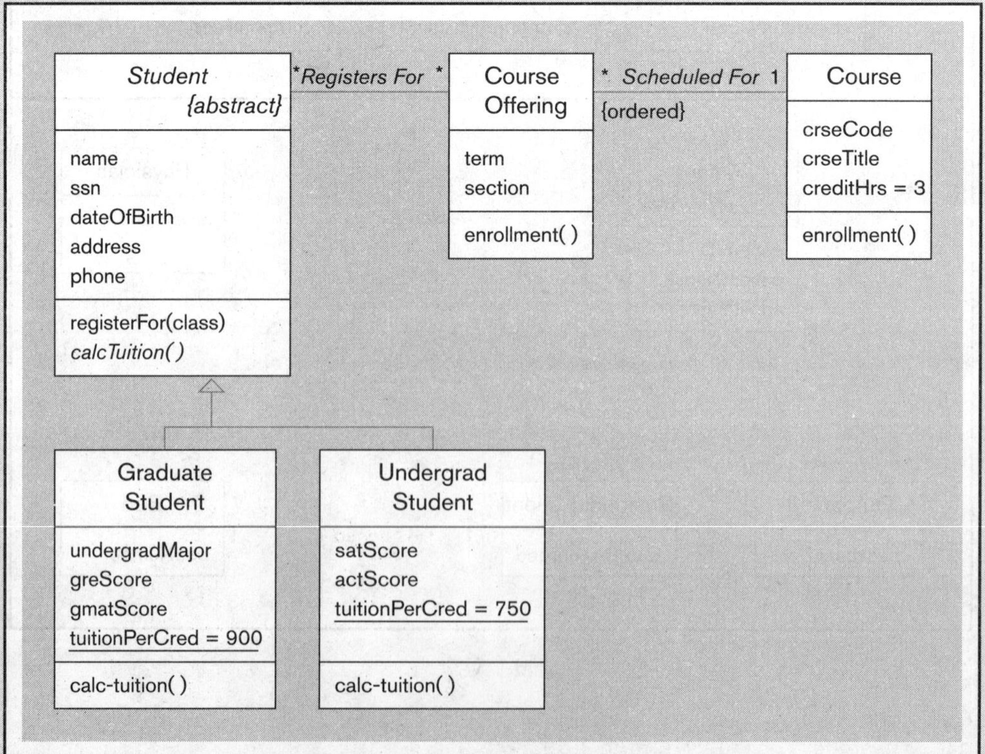

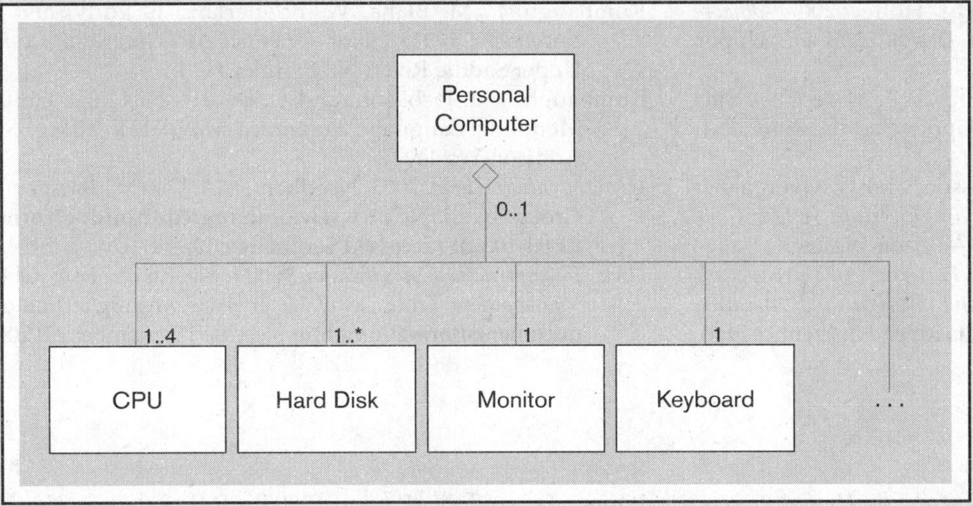

FIGURE 13-14 Example of aggregation

It is important to note that although the Graduate Student and Undergraduate Student classes share the same calcTuition operation, they might implement the operation in quite different ways. For example, the method that implements the operation for a graduate student might add a special graduate fee for each course the student takes. The fact that an operation with the same name may respond in different ways depending on the class context is known as polymorphism, a key concept in object-oriented systems. The enrollment operation in Figure 13-11 illustrates another example of **polymorphism**. While the enrollment operation within Course Offering computes the enrollment for a particular course offering or section, an operation with the same name within Course computes the combined enrollment for all sections of a given course.

Polymorphism
The ability of an operation with the same name to respond in different ways depending on the class context.

Representing Aggregation

An **aggregation** expresses a *Part-of* relationship between a component object and an aggregate object. It is a stronger form of association relationship (with the added "part-of" semantics) and is represented with a hollow diamond at the aggregate end. For example, Figure 13-14 shows a personal computer as an aggregate of CPU (up to four for multiprocessors), hard disks, monitor, keyboard, and other objects (a typical bill-of-materials structure). It is also possible for component objects to exist without being part of a whole (e.g., there can be a Monitor that is not part of any PC). In **composition**, a part object belongs to one and only one whole object; for example, a room is part of only one building and cannot exist by itself.

Aggregation
A part-of relationship between a component object and an aggregate object.

Composition
A part-of relationship in which parts belong to only one whole object and live and die with the whole object.

Chapter Review

For coverage of key terms, review questions, problems and exercises, and field questions, see the complete chapter on the textbook's Web site. The following is the full set of references for the chapter, followed by information about additional sources of information on object data modeling.

References

Blaha, M., and Rumbaugh, J. 2005. *Object-Oriented Modeling and Design with UML*, 2nd ed. Upper Saddle River, NJ: Prentice Hall.

Booch, G. 1994. *Object-Oriented Analysis and Design with Applications*, 2nd ed. Redwood City, CA: Benjamin/Cummings.

Coad, P., and E. Yourdon. 1991. *Object-Oriented Design*. Upper Saddle River, NJ: Prentice Hall.

Fowler, M. 2003. *UML Distilled: A Brief Guide to the Standard Object Modeling Language*, 3rd ed. Reading, MA: Addison-Wesley-Longman.

George, J., D. Batra, J. Valacich, and J. Hoffer. 2007. *Object-Oriented Systems Analysis and Design*, 2nd ed. Upper Saddle River, NJ: Prentice Hall.

Hoffer, J., J. George, and J. Valacich. 2010. *Modern Systems Analysis and Design*, 6th ed. Upper Saddle River, NJ: Prentice Hall.

Jacobson, I., M. Christerson, P. Jonsson, and G. Overgaard. 1992. *Object-Oriented Software Engineering: A Use Case Driven Approach*. Reading, MA: Addison-Wesley.

Larman, C. 2004. *Applying UML and Patterns: An Introduction to Object-Oriented Analysis and Design and Iterative Development*, 3rd ed. Upper Saddle River, NJ: Prentice Hall.

Rumbaugh, J., M. Blaha, W. Premerlani, F. Eddy, and W. Lorensen. 1991. *Object-Oriented Modeling and Design*. Upper Saddle River, NJ: Prentice Hall.

Rumbaugh, J., I. Jacobson, and G. Booch. 2004. The Unified Modeling Language Reference Manual. Reading, MA: Addison-Wesley.

UML Notation Guide. 2003. Needham, MA: Object Management Group, available at **www.omg.org/cgi-bin/doc?formal/03-03-10.pdf** (accessed September 12, 2009).

UML Superstructure Specification. 2009. Needham, MA: Object Management Group, available at **www.omg.org/technology/documents/formal/uml.htm** (accessed September 12, 2009).

Further Reading

Arlow, J., and I. Neustadt. 2005. *UML 2 and the Unified Process: Practical Object-Oriented Analysis and Design*, 2nd ed. Reading, MA: Addison-Wesley.

Pilone, D., and N. Pitman. 2005. *UML 2.0 in a Nutshell*. Sebastopol, CA: O'Reilly.

Web Resources

www.omg.org Web site of the Object Management Group, a leading industry association concerned with object-oriented analysis and design.

www.omg.org/technology/documents/formal/uml.htm OMG's official UML Web site.

CHAPTER

14

Overview: Using Relational Databases to Provide Object Persistence

Learning Objectives

After studying this chapter, you should be able to:

- Concisely define each of the following terms: **persistence, serialization, object-relational mapping (ORM), object-relational impedance mismatch, object identity, accessor method, call-level application programming interface, transparent persistence, separation of concerns, pooling of database connections, entity class, fetching strategy, *N*+1 selects problem, declarative mapping schema,** and **value type.**
- Understand the fundamental mismatch between the object-oriented paradigm and the relational model and the consequences of this mismatch for the use of relational databases with object-oriented development environments.
- Understand the similarities and differences between the approaches that are used to address the object-relational impedance mismatch.
- Create a mapping between core object-oriented structures and relational structures using Hibernate.
- Identify the primary contexts in which the various approaches to addressing the object-relational impedance mismatch can be most effectively used.
- Understand possible effects of the use of the object-relational mapping approaches on database performance, concurrency control, and security.
- Use HQL to formulate various types of queries.

OVERVIEW

One of the key characteristics of the object-oriented development approach is that the same core concepts can be applied at all stages of development. The same domain model that is identified at the conceptual level during requirements specification and analysis (as you learned in Chapter 13) will be directly transformed into a model of interconnected software objects. Many of the core object-oriented concepts (modeling the world with classes of objects, integrating behavior and data, inheritance, encapsulation, and polymorphism) can be applied seamlessly at different levels of abstraction. The object-oriented principles are applied across a broad spectrum of systems development activities, except in data management. For a long time, it was widely believed that object-oriented database management systems (OODBMSs) would gradually become very popular. These systems were intended to provide direct, transparent persistence for objects in object-oriented applications, and they were expected to become as widely used as object-oriented languages and systems analysis and design methods are. For a variety of reasons, they never took off.

It is not practical for object-oriented applications to maintain all relevant objects in run-time memory all the time. Therefore, object-oriented development environments need a mechanism for storing object states between the application execution sessions (i.e., provide **persistence** to the objects). In practice, relational database management systems have to be used to provide persistence because of their dominant role in organizational data management. There are, however, significant conceptual differences between the object-oriented and relational approaches; these differences, often collectively called **object-relational impedance mismatch**, have been summarized in Table 14-1.

Persistence
An object's capability to maintain its state between application execution sessions.

Object-relational impedance mismatch
The conceptual differences between the object-oriented approach to application design and the relational model for database design and implementation.

Thus, system architects and application developers currently face a significant challenge: In application development, the object-oriented approach has gradually reached a dominant position, and a large percentage of software projects that include development of new applications is based on the object-oriented philosophy in some way. The most commonly used application development frameworks, Java EE and Microsoft .NET, are both object-oriented. At the same time, relational databases are almost invariably used as the mechanism to provide long-term persistence for organizational data. This is unlikely to change any time soon. Also, we have no choice but to provide long-term object persistence for any realistic organizational application; the key reason we have information systems in organizations is to maintain long-term information about the objects that are important for the business. Object-oriented applications need object persistence, and in the foreseeable future, the only technology that will provide that in a reliable, scalable way in the enterprise context are relational database management systems. Therefore, solutions for closing the gap between these two approaches are an essential component of the modern computing infrastructure.

Providing Persistence for Objects Using Relational Databases

Many different approaches have been proposed for addressing the need to provide persistence for objects using relational databases. Most modern relational database management systems offer object-oriented extensions, which are typically used for dealing with nonstandard, complex, and user-defined data types. In this chapter, however, our focus is on mechanisms that provide persistence support to a genuine object-oriented design and implementation model, and we will review the most common of those.

TABLE 14-1 Elements of the Object-Relational Impedance Mismatch

- Nature and granularity of data types
- Structural relationships:
  - Inheritance structures
  - Representation of associations
- Defining the identity of objects/entity instances
- Methods of accessing persistent data
- Focus on data (relational databases) versus integrated data and behavior (the object-oriented approach)
- Architectural styles
- Support for managing transactions

CALL-LEVEL APPLICATION PROGRAMMING INTERFACES Since the early days of Java, Java Database Connectivity (JDBC) has been an industry standard for a **call-level application programming interface (API)** with which Java programs can access relational databases. If you are developing software using Microsoft's .NET Framework, ADO.NET provides similar types of capabilities for providing access to relational databases. Open database connectivity (ODBC) is another widely used API for accessing data stored in relational databases from different types of application programs. All of these mechanisms are based on the same idea: An SQL query hand-coded by a developer is passed as a string parameter to the driver, which passes it on to the DBMS, which, in turn, returns the result as a set of rows consisting of (untyped) columns. The mechanisms have their differences (e.g., ADO.NET provides an intermediate DataSet construct), but conceptually they are very similar.

Call-level application programming interface
A mechanism that provides an application program with access to an external service, such as a database management system.

SQL QUERY MAPPING FRAMEWORKS The next category of tools provides additional support and a higher level of abstraction for using a relational database to provide object persistence by linking classes in an object-oriented solution to parameters and results of SQL queries (instead of database tables). These tools are not full-blown object-relational mapping tools because they do not generate the needed SQL based on a mapping between descriptions of tables and classes. They are, however, an "elegant compromise" (in the words of Tate and Gehtland, 2005) that hide some of the complexity of a pure JDBC or ADO.NET solution but still give the developers full access to SQL. The best-known tools in this category are iBATIS and iBATIS.NET. They consist of two components: iBATIS Data Mapper/SQL Maps, which are structures used to create a bridge between an SQL query and a Java object, and iBATIS Data Access Objects, which form an abstraction layer between the details of your persistence solution and the actual application.

OBJECT-RELATIONAL MAPPING FRAMEWORKS Comprehensive **object-relational mapping (ORM)** frameworks, such as the Java Persistence API (JPA) specification and its implementations Hibernate, OpenJPA, and EclipseLink, hide the relational data access methods from the object-oriented applications and provide an entirely transparent persistence layer. These frameworks, when integrated with an object-oriented application, move the management of the concerns related to persistence outside the core structure of the object-oriented applications. They provide a **declarative mapping schema** that links domain classes needing persistence to relational tables and mechanisms for managing database transactions, security, and performance in ways that are hidden from the applications. The classes for which an ORM framework provides persistence do not know that they are persistent: Persistent objects in these classes are created, loaded, and deleted by the ORM framework. Many ORM frameworks also include a query language, improve performance by optimizing the time when objects are loaded from the database, use caching to manage performance, and allow applications to detach objects that can be modified and, at a suitable time, made persistent again (Richardson 2006). The number of options in this category is quite large. The most widely used of them is Hibernate (and its .NET counterpart NHibernate), which is one of several implementations of the JPA. In addition to Hibernate, Apache's OpenJPA and Eclipse Foundation's EclipseLink (together with Oracle's older, closely related TopLink) are widely used JPA implementations. The past few years have seen the parallel development of multiple ORM frameworks. At this time, JPA has emerged as the overall framework specification and Hibernate as the most popular implementation. In this chapter, we have chosen to use Hibernate as our vehicle for presenting the examples because of its long-standing status as the most widely used ORM framework and because its XML-based mapping specifications provide us with more visibility to the internal mapping structures.

Object-relational mapping
Definition of structural relationships between object-oriented and relational representations of data, typically to enable the use of a relational database to provide persistence for objects.

Declarative mapping schema
A structure that defines the relationships between domain classes in the object-oriented model and relations in the relational model.

PROPRIETARY APPROACHES Finally, there are many proprietary approaches for integrating data access directly into object-oriented environments and languages, such as Microsoft's Language Integrated Query (LINQ), which is a component of the .NET Framework. The goal of LINQ is to very closely integrate data access queries into programming languages, not limiting the access to relational databases or XML but offering access any type of data store. The first version of LINQ, titled LINQ to SQL, was released as part of the first version of the .NET Framework 3.5; a more sophisticated but also more complex version of the technology, called LINQ to Entities, was released with .NET 3.5 SP1. LINQ to Entities is significantly closer to offering a full set of comprehensive ORM framework capabilities than LINQ to SQL, and it appears to form the foundation of Microsoft's future efforts in this area.

SELECTING THE RIGHT APPROACH Which one of the four principal approaches to providing persistence for objects using relational databases should be used in a specific project? To help you understand the issues affecting this decision, Tables 14-2, 14-3, and 14-4 summarize the advantages and disadvantages of the first three approaches. We will not include the proprietary approaches in the comparison because no one of them has yet become widely used, but we encourage you to follow developments in this area. All of the approaches have strengths and weaknesses, and at the detailed level, they will change over time. Therefore, a detailed comparison of any specific products is

TABLE 14-2 Advantages and Disadvantages of the Call-Level API Approach

Advantages	Disadvantages
• Low overhead • Highest level of control over the details of the database connection	• Proliferation of code related to database connectivity • Need to write a lot of detailed code • Little reuse of code • Developers need a detailed understanding of DBMS capabilities and the database schema • SQL code not generated automatically • The approach does not provide transparent persistence

TABLE 14-3 Advantages and Disadvantages of the SQL Query Mapping Frameworks

Advantages	Disadvantages
• Direct access to all DBMS capabilities provided through SQL • Mapping to legacy database schemas easier • Amount of code required significantly less than with call-level APIs • Database access code easier to manage than with call-level APIs	• More overhead than with call-level APIs • Developers need a detailed understanding of DBMS capabilities and the database schema • SQL code not generated automatically • The approach does not provide transparent persistence

TABLE 14-4 Advantages and Disadvantages of the Object-Relational Mapping Frameworks

Advantages	Disadvantages
• They provide the highest level of persistence transparency • Developers do not need to have a detailed understanding of the DBMS or the database schema • The implementation of persistence is fully separated from the rest of the code • They enable true object-oriented design	• There is more overhead than with call-level APIs and with query mapping frameworks • Complex cases often need detailed attention • Legacy databases lead to difficulties

beyond the scope of this text. It is, however, important that you know what the most important implementation options are and continuously evaluate their fit with your own development environment and projects.

Object-Relational Mapping Example

In this section, we will present a brief overview of mapping between a relational database schema and an object-oriented model. Figure 14-4 includes a UML class diagram that represents an object-oriented design model of our area of interest. (Note: figure numbers are not continuous in this overview because only selected figures from the complete chapter on the textbook's Web site are included in this overview). Figure 14-5 presents a Java representation of the design model included in Figure 14-4. Note that each of the classes would also need a constructor without parameters (so called no-arg constructor) and getter and setter methods; Hibernate requires these to operate correctly. Figure 14-6, in turn, includes a possible relational model for a database serving this application. With both the object solution and the relational solution defined, we can now analyze the characteristics of the solution that links the two using Hibernate as the object-relational mapping tool.

MAPPING FILES The core element of Hibernate that defines the relationship between the object-oriented classes and relational tables is XML mapping files, which are typically named <Class name>.hbm.xml. The following example appears to be relatively simple, but it reveals interesting mapping challenges.

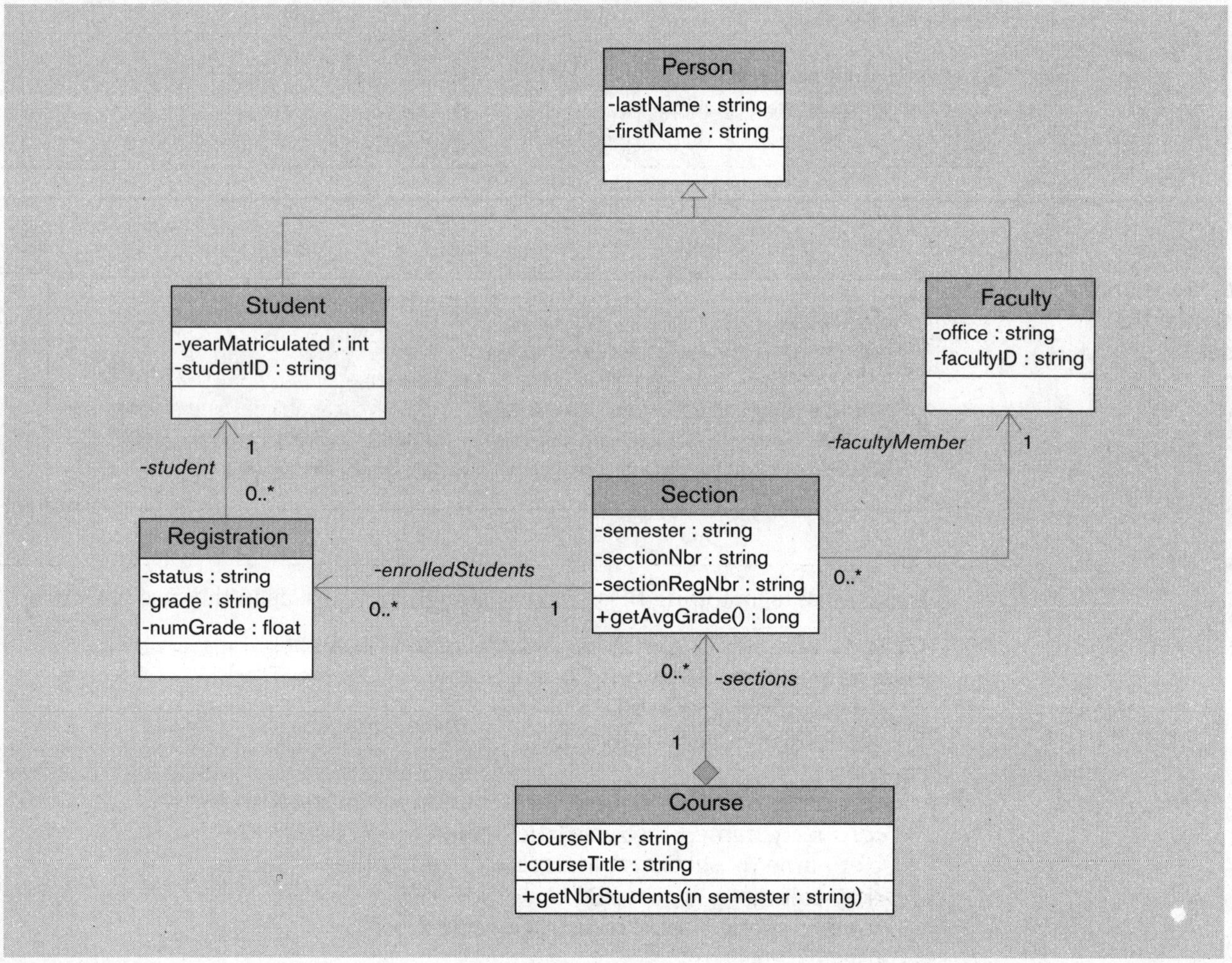

FIGURE 14-4 Object-oriented design model

FIGURE 14-5 Java implementation of the design model

```
public abstract class Person {
        private Long id;

        private String lastName;
        private String firstName;

}

public class Student extends Person {
        private int yearMatriculated;
        private String studentID;
}

public class Faculty extends Person {

        private String office;
        private String facultyID;
}

public class Course {

        private Long id;

        private String courseNbr;
        private String courseTitle;
        private Set<Section> sections;

        public int getNbrStudents(String semester) {
        // the body of the method is intentionally missing
        }
}

public class Section {

        private Long id;

        private String sectionRegNbr;
        private String sectionNbr;
        private String semester;
        private Faculty facultyMember;
        private Set<Registration> enrolledStudents;

        public double getAvgGrade() {
        // the body of the method is intentionally missing
        }
}

public class Registration {

        private Long id;

        private Student student;
        private String status;
        private String grade;
        private float numGrade ;
}
```

FIGURE 14-6 Relational representation of the design model

PERSON (PersonID, LastName, FirstName)
FACULTY (FacultyPersonID, FacultyID, Office)
STUDENT (StudentPersonID, StudentID, YearMatriculated)
COURSE (CourseID, CourseNbr, CourseTitle)
SECTION (SectionID, SectionRegNbr, SectionNbr, Semester, CourseID, FacultyPersonID)
REGISTRATION (SectionID, StudentPersonID, Status, Grade, NumGrade)

In some cases, mapping files are very straightforward, as in the case of Course:

```
<class name = "registrations.Course" table = "Course_T">
    <id column = "courseID">
    <generator class="native"/>
    </id>
    <property name = "courseNbr" column = "courseNbr"/>
    <property name = "courseTitle" column = "courseTitle"/>
    <set name = "sections" inverse = "true" table = "Section_T">
    <key column = "courseID"/>
    <one-to-many class="registrations.Section"/>
    </set>
</class>
```

Note that the mapping is based on the classes in the programming language (in this case, Java), not on the database structure. Therefore, the fundamental element is the class, followed by its attributes name and table, specifying the name of the programming language class (Course) and the corresponding table (Course_T). The <id> element specifies the primary key of the database table, which in this case is a nonintelligent key, Course_ID. The <generator> element gives the DBMS instructions regarding how to create the primary key values. The <property> tags specify a relationship between an attribute of the programming language class and the name of the database column. Finally, we need to specify that a course has multiple sections (maintained in the Java attribute sections) and that those sections are persistently stored in table Section_T.

In the same way, we will specify the mapping for the class Section:

```
<class name = "registrations.Section">
    <id name = "id" column = "sectionID">
        <generator class = "native"/>
    </id>
    <property name = "sectionRegNbr" column = "sectionRegNbr"/>
    <property name = "sectionNbr" column = "sectionNbr"/>
    <property name = "semester" column = "semester"/>

    <many-to-one name = "course" class = "registrations.Course" column =
    "courseID"/>

    <many-to-one name = "faculty" class = "registrations.Faculty" column =
    "facultyID" not-null = "true"/>

    <set name = "enrolledStudents" table = "Registration_T">
      <key column = "sectionID"/>
      <composite-element class = "registrations.Registration">
        <parent name="Section"/>

        <many-to-one name = "student" column = "studentPersonID" class =
        "registrations.Student" not-null = "true"/>

        <property name = "status" column = "status"/>
        <property name = "grade" column = "grade"/>
        <property name = "numGrade" column = "numGrade"/>

      </composite-element>
    </set>
</class>
```

In this mapping, we are using the <many-to-one> tags to tell Hibernate that there is one course and there is one faculty member per course but that a course can have multiple sections, and a faculty member can be responsible for multiple sections. In addition, we are mapping the table Registration_T to the class Registration. They both represent the many-to-many relationship between Student and Section. In the Hibernate configuration file, this structure is called *composite-element*.

The final configuration file that is needed for mapping the original Java representation to relational tables describes the mapping for the abstract superclass Person and its two subclasses, Student and Faculty. It is as follows:

```
<class name = "registrations.Person" table = "Person_T">
  <id name = "id" column = "personID">
    <generator class = "native"/>
  </id>
```

```
    <property name = "firstName" column = "firstName"/>
    <property name = "lastName" column = "lastName"/>

    <joined-subclass name="registrations.Student" table = "Student_T">
      <key column = "studentPersonID"/>

      <property name = "studentID" column="studentID"/>
      <property name = "yearMatriculated" column="yearMatriculated"/>
    </joined-subclass>
    <joined-subclass name="registrations.Faculty" table = "Faculty_T">
      <key column = "facultyPersonID"/>

      <property name = "facultyID" column="facultyID"/>
      <property name = "office" column="office"/>
    </joined-subclass>
  </class>
```

Hibernate offers multiple ways to take care of the mapping of an inheritance hierarchy. In this case, we have chosen to use an approach often called "table per subclass." This name is somewhat misleading because the approach requires a table for each class and subclass that requires persistence. The configuration file first specifies the way the superclass is mapped and then uses the <joined-subclass> tab to map the subclasses. Note that you do not need a separate configuration file for the Student or Faculty subclasses; this is all that is needed to map them.

A more comprehensive explanation of these mapping files is included in the complete version of this chapter, available on the book's Web site.

Responsibilities of Object-Relational Mapping Frameworks

This section summarizes the responsibilities of the ORM frameworks in greater detail.

First, an ORM framework provides a layer of abstraction that separates object-oriented applications from the details of a specific database implementation. The manipulation of the persistence status of objects takes place using statements of the programming language, not with a separate database language.

Second, although one should not use the ORM frameworks without understanding the characteristics of the underlying databases and DBMSs, the frameworks have the responsibility for generating the SQL code for database access, which means application developers do not have to worry about that. An added benefit is that the code for database access does not have to be written for each of the classes separately, but the relationships between the class structures and the database schema are systematically and centrally defined.

Third, the ORM frameworks include tools for managing database performance in the context of object-oriented applications. A typical ORM framework is capable of using the services of a connection pool (e.g., C3P0) for the efficient management of expensive database connections. Another performance-related issue that is central in the use of ORM frameworks is the specification of fetching strategies, which define when and how the framework retrieves persistent objects to run-time memory during a navigation process. A specific issue that has to be addressed is the ***N*+1 selects** problem, which refers to a situation in which a poorly defined **fetching strategy** might lead to a separate SELECT statement for each associated object in a one-to-many relationship. For example, Hibernate uses, by default, so-called lazy loading, in which objects are retrieved from a database only when they are needed. The alternative is eager loading, in which all associated objects are always retrieved together with the object to which they are linked. Careful design of fetching strategies is very important from the perspective of achieving a high level of performance in applications based on an ORM framework.

_N_+1 selects problem
A performance problem caused by too many SELECT statements generated by an ORM framework.

Fetching strategy
A model for specifying when and how an ORM framework retrieves persistent objects to the run-time memory during a navigation process.

Fourth, the ORM frameworks provide support for transactions and transaction integrity. This topic was covered in Chapter 11, so we will not discuss it again here in detail. The transaction support mechanisms in the ORM frameworks work together with standard transaction management tools, such as Java Transaction API (JTA), that are provided by many application servers (e.g., JBoss and WebSphere). The development of enterprise-level applications would not, in general, be possible without transaction support. It is particularly important in the ORM world because, in many cases, a change in a persistent object leads to cascading changes in the database, which all have to be either accepted or rejected.

The ORM frameworks provide services for concurrency control, which was also covered in Chapter 11. Hibernate uses, by default, optimistic concurrency control, but its behavior can be modified when more stringent isolation guarantees are needed. The highest level of isolation in Hibernate is fully serializable isolation, which ensures—with a performance penalty—that transactions are executed one after another.

Finally, the ORM frameworks often include a custom query language, such as HQL in Hibernate, and other mechanisms to run queries, such as direct SQL and the Criteria application programming interface (API) in Hibernate. HQL, the query language in Hibernate, resembles SQL in many ways. Based on what you have learned about SQL in Chapters 6 and 7, you will be able to learn HQL easily.

Summary

The object-oriented approach has become very popular in application development and systems analysis and design, but object-oriented database management systems never gained widespread acceptance. Instead, relational database management systems continue to maintain their dominant role as the primary data management technology. Therefore, it is essential that relational databases be used effectively with object-oriented application development approaches.

In this chapter, we first reviewed the reasons underlying the object-relational impedance mismatch—that is, the conceptual conflict between the object-oriented and relational models. These reasons include differences in the representation of complex data types and structural relationships (including inheritance and associations), representation of object/entity instance identity, importance and implementation of the transaction concept, and methods of accessing persistent data. In addition, the approaches have a different core focus because the relational model focuses entirely on data, whereas the object-oriented approach, by definition, integrates data and behavior. Also, the predominant architectural styles within each approach are different. It is essential that the gap between the two approaches be closed because, in practice, both will be used widely in the foreseeable future.

There are four basic categories of mechanisms through which relational databases can be used to provide persistence to objects. Call-level application programming interfaces (APIs), such as Java Database Connectivity (JDBC), require that application developers embed SQL statements in the program code through a low-level interface. SQL query mapping frameworks, such as iBATIS, raise the level of abstraction by providing a mechanism for declaring links between class specifications and SQL queries and by hiding the details of the call-level APIs. Object-relational mapping (ORM) frameworks, such as Java Persistence API and its implementations Hibernate, EclipseLink, and OpenJPA provide a transparent persistence solution by creating declarative mapping between classes and database tables. They hide the database structure and the relational query language from developers. Finally, there are many proprietary persistence solutions that intend to integrate data access directly into object-oriented environments and languages, such as Microsoft's LINQ. Each of the approaches has strengths and weaknesses, and it is essential that you carefully evaluate the specific needs of your project before selecting a tool for linking relational databases to an object-oriented development environment.

Object-relational mapping frameworks have multiple responsibilities: They provide a layer of abstraction between object-oriented applications and a database schema implemented with a DBMS to provide transparent persistence for the applications. They generate the SQL code that is needed for database access, and they centralize this code so that it does not proliferate throughout the application. These frameworks provide support for concurrency control and transaction integrity and management. They also typically include a query language (such as HQL in Hibernate) that provides capabilities similar to those of SQL.

Understanding the mechanisms used for linking object-oriented applications and relational databases is very important for both those whose specialty is data management and those who focus on application development. For data management specialists, an increasing number of the applications that they support are developed using the object-oriented approach. To provide high-quality service to these applications (and their developers), it is essential that data specialists understand how these applications connect to relational databases. Application developers, on the other hand, benefit greatly from understanding at least the principles of the mechanisms that provide persistence for the objects in their solutions. It is particularly important that both sides be able to communicate effectively with each other. The quality of the object-relational connection solution directly affects application performance, reliability, and security.

Chapter Review

For coverage of key terms, review questions, problems and exercises, and field questions, see the complete chapter on the textbook's Web site. The following is the full set of references for the chapter.

References

Ambler, S. 2006. *Mapping Objects to Relational Databases: O/R Mapping in Detail*. Available at **www.agiledata.org/essays/mappingObjects.html**. (accessed September 19, 2009).

Bauer, C., and G. King. 2006. *Java Persistence with Hibernate*. Greenwich, CT: Manning.

Neward, T. 2005. *Comparing LINQ and Its Contemporaries*. Available at **http://msdn2.microsoft.com/en-us/library/aa479863.aspx** (accessed September 19, 2009).

Richardson, C. 2006. *POJOs in Action*. Greenwich, CT: Manning.

Tate, B., and J. Gehtland. 2005. *Spring: A Developer's Notebook*. Sebastopol, CA: O'Reilly.

Further Reading

Elliott, J., T. O'Brien, and R. Fowler. 2008. *Harnessing Hibernate*. Sebastopol, CA: O'Reilly.

Keith, M., and M. Schincariol. 2006. *Pro EJB 3: Java Persistence API*. Berkeley, CA: Apress.

Minter, D., and J. Linwood. 2006. *Beginning Hibernate: From Novice to Professional*. Berkeley, CA: Apress.

Panda, D., R. Rahman, and D. Lane. 2007. *EJB 3 in Action*. Greenwich, CT: Manning.

Web Resources

www.java-source.net/open-source/persistence A collection of links to various open source persistence frameworks.

www.hibernate.org The Hibernate Web site.

http://java.sun.com/javaee/overview/faq/persistence.jsp An official Sun site that provides a description of the persistence standard in Java EE.

APPENDIX

A

Data Modeling Tools and Notation

Chapters 2 and 3 present several common notations for representing conceptual data models. Depending on the software tool available for depicting a data model, your ability to replicate these notations will vary. Just as business rules and policies are not universal, neither are the symbols and notation used in the various data modeling tools. Each uses different graphical constructs and methodologies that may or may not be able to convey the meaning of a particular business rule.

This appendix is intended to help you compare the book's notations with your modeling tool's notation. Four commonly used tools are covered: CA ERwin Data Modeler r7.3, Oracle Designer 10g, Sybase PowerDesigner 15, and Microsoft Visio Pro 2003. Table A-1a and Table A-1b chart samples of the notation used in each tool for entities, relationships, attributes, rules, constraints, and so forth.

Figure 2-22, a data modeling diagram for Pine Valley Furniture Company (PVFC), is the basis for the examples pictured in this appendix. That figure shows the data model drawn from the narrative of PVFC business rules included in Chapter 2, using the Visio notation system, which is very similar to the notation used in this textbook. Figure A-1, included here, is this same figure. Table A-1 shows a comparison of the textbook notation with that available in the four software tools.

COMPARING E-R MODELING CONVENTIONS

As can be seen from Table A-1, modeling tools can differ significantly in the notation available to create a data model. While not intended as an in-depth comparison of the various tools, the following explanation provides a means to analyze the tools' differences, using the PVFC data model depicted in Figures 2-22 and A-1. Pay particular attention to differences in depicting many-to-many relationships, cardinalities and/or optionalities, foreign keys, and supertype/subtype relationships. Each tool offers multiple sets of notation. We have chosen entity/relationship sets of symbols for each tool. Note, in particular, how associative entities are drawn; the foreign key relationships are included.

Visio Professional 2003 Notation

The Professional version of Visio includes a database diagramming tool for modeling a conceptual or physical diagram. Visio provides three database modeling templates. Selecting Database Model Diagram for a new data model allows a further choice of relational or IDEF1X symbols. Both of these choices allow reverse engineering of existing physical databases. The two other template choices are Express-G and ORM, which allow you to use the notation associated with each of those methods, and do not provide for

TABLE A-1 A Comparison of Hoffer, Ramesh, and Topi Modeling Notation with Four Software Tools
(a) Common modeling tools, notations

	Hoffer-Ramesh-Topi Notation	*Visio PRO 2003*	*CA ERWin Data Modeler r7.3*	*Sybase PowerDesigner 15*	*Oracle Designer 10g*
Basic Entity	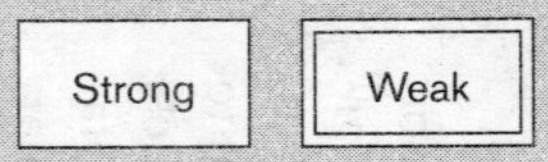	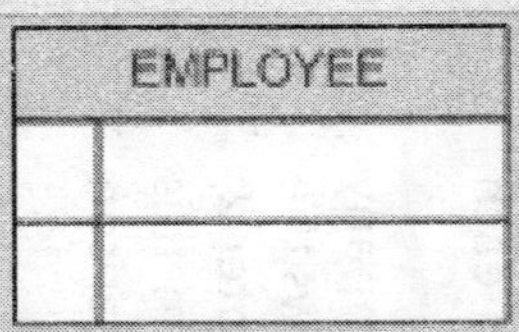	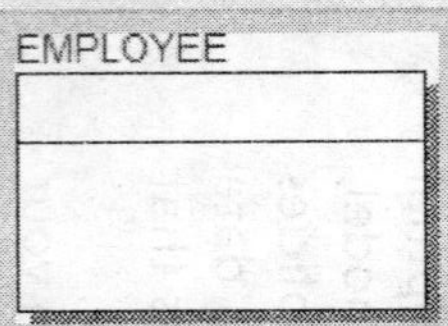	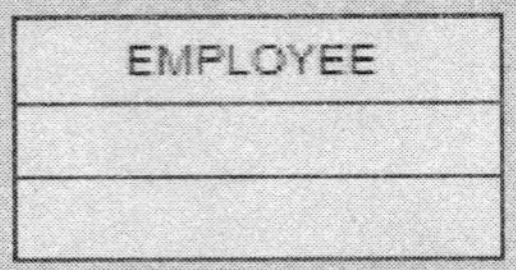	
Associative Entity	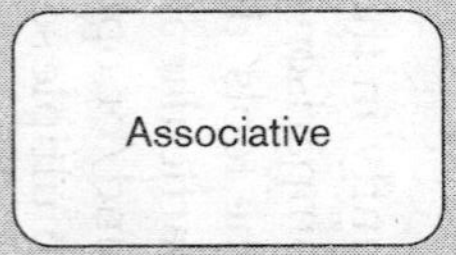	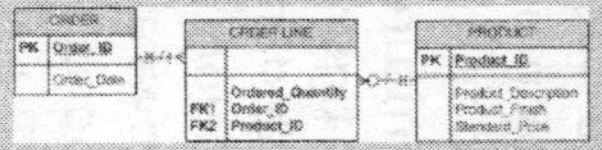	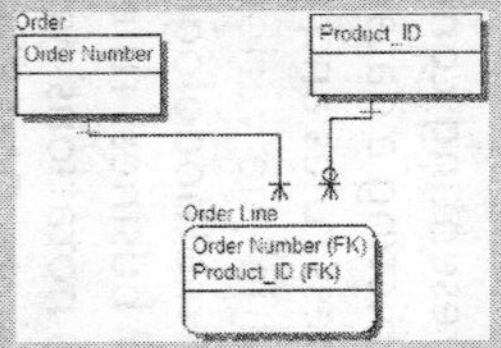	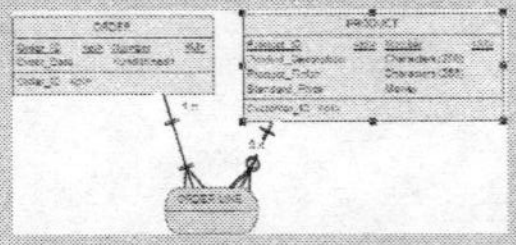	(No special symbol. Uses regular Entity symbol.)
Subtypes	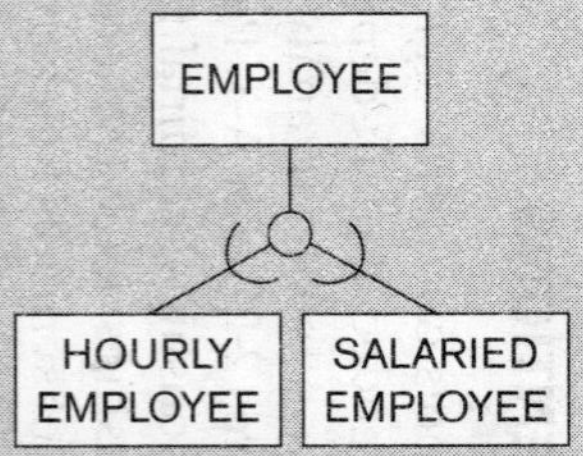	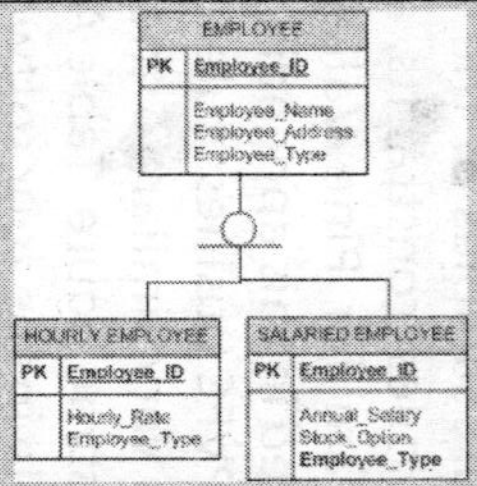	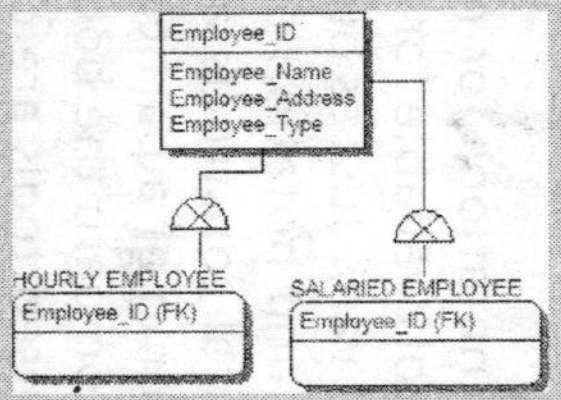	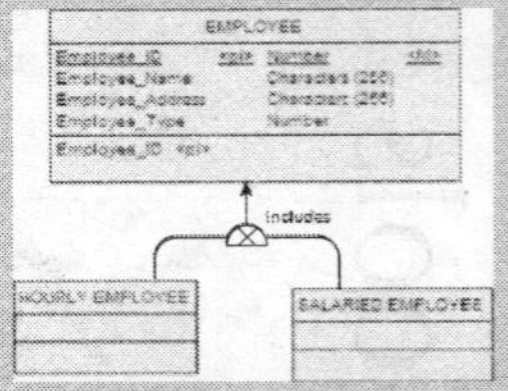	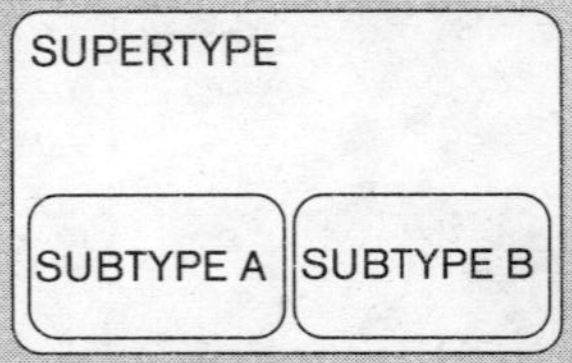
Recursive Relationship	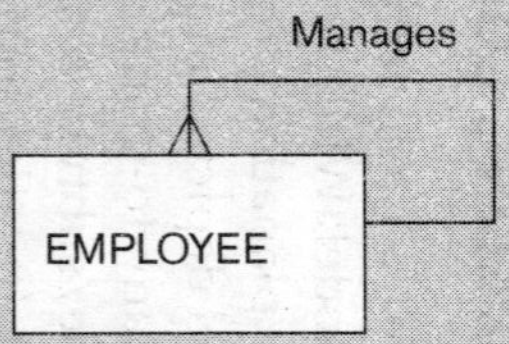	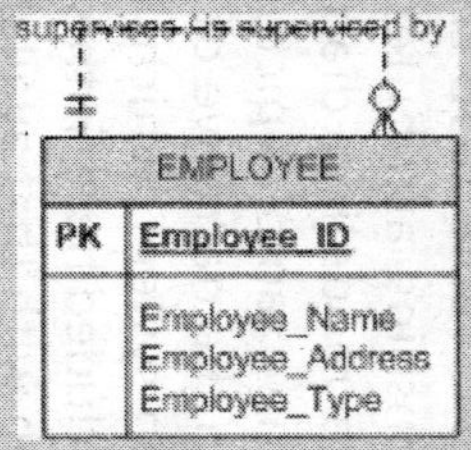	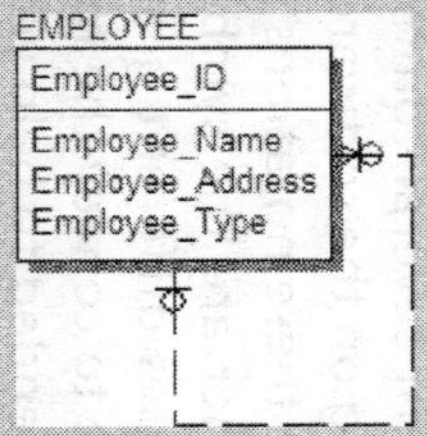	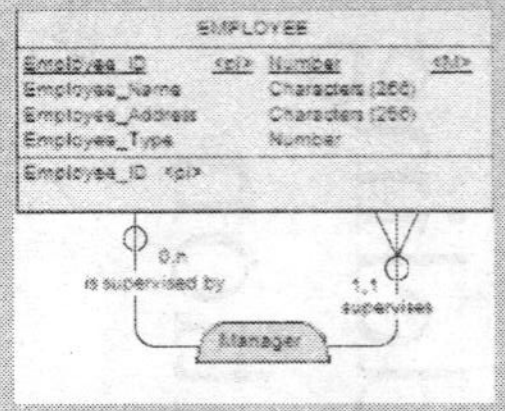	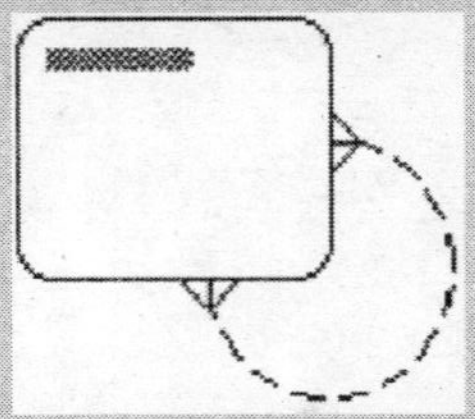
Attributes	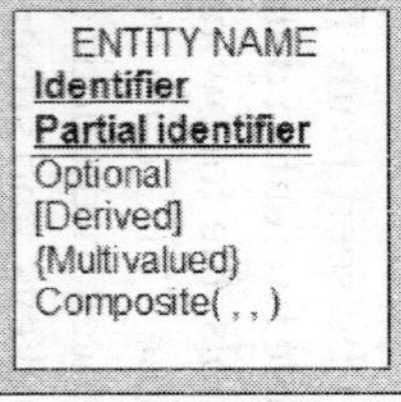	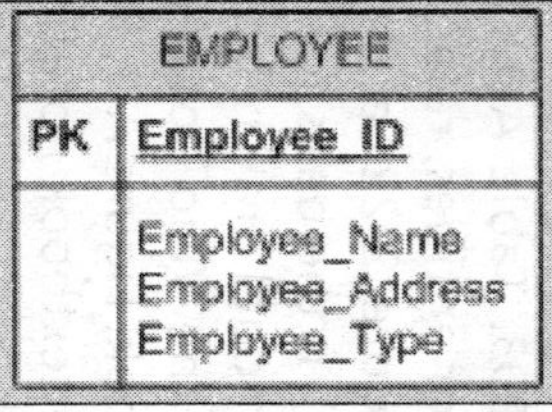	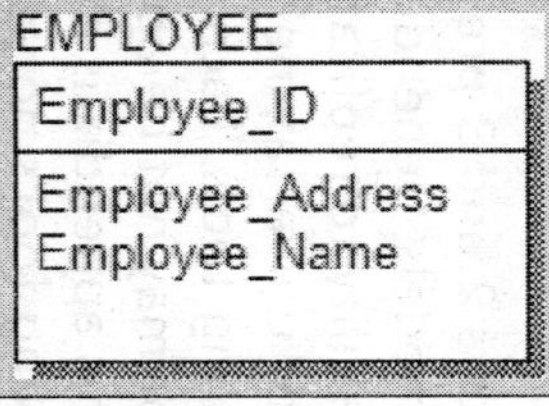	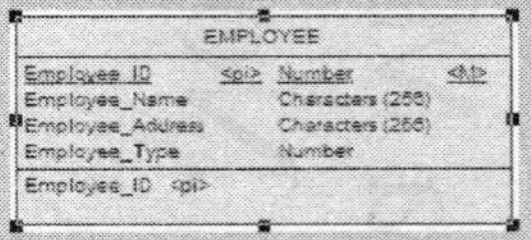	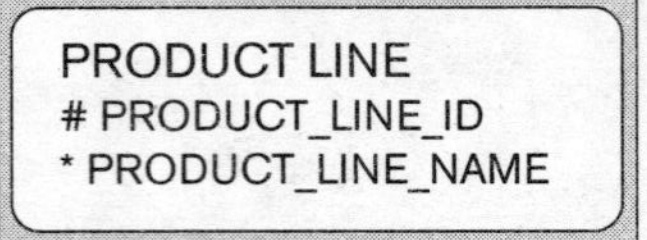

(continued)

TABLE A-1 (continued) (b) Common modeling tools' cardinality/optionality notations

	Hoffer-Ramesh-Topi Notation	*Visio PRO 2003*	*CA ERWin Data Modeler r7.3*	*Sybase PowerDesigner 15*	*Oracle Designer 10g*
1:1		(Not available without cardinality)	(Not available without cardinality)	 0,1 0,1	
1:M		(Not available without cardinality)	(Not available without cardinality)	 0,1 0,n	
M:N		(Not allowed)	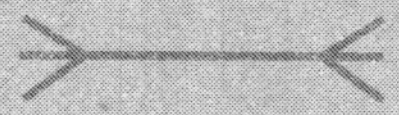	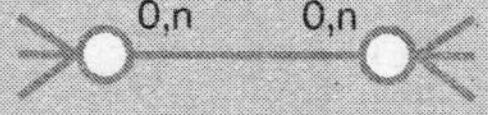 0,n 0,n	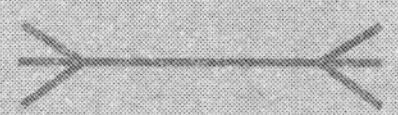
Mandatory 1:1			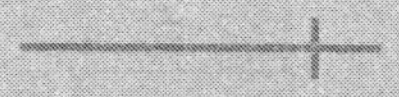 1		
Mandatory 1:M			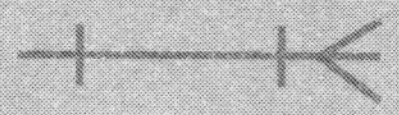 P		
Optional 1:M	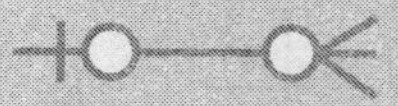	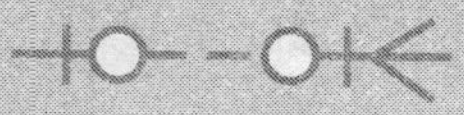		 0,1 0,n	

FIGURE A-1 Visio PRO 2003 model

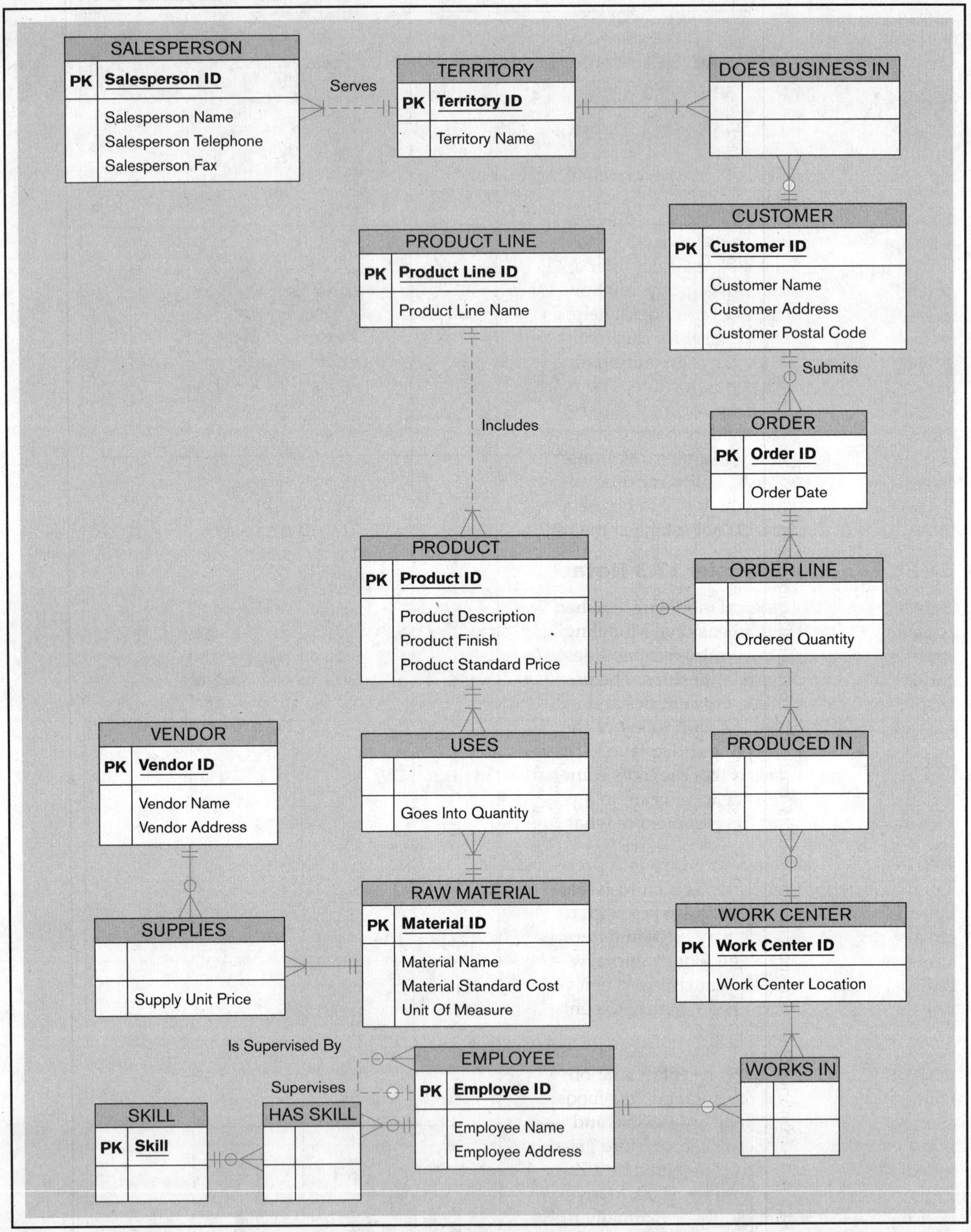

reverse engineering unless you are using Visio Enterprise. Each template may be customized to indicate primary key (PK), foreign keys (FK), secondary indexes, nonkey fields, data types, and so on. You can also elect to display the primary key fields at the top of each entity or in their actual physical order. This text uses the relational template.

ENTITIES All entities are depicted as square rectangles with optional horizontal and vertical lines used to partition entity information. Keys (primary, alt, foreign), nonkey attributes, referential integrity, and so on can be optionally displayed within the entity box. Subtype/supertype connectors are available.

RELATIONSHIPS Lines can be labeled in one or both directions or neither, and the relationship types are either identifying (solid line) or nonidentifying (dashed line). Cardinality and optionality notation differ according to the symbol set chosen, relational or IDEF1X. Notation samples for the relational symbol set chosen for our diagram can be seen in Table A-1b. This tool provides a helpful "range" option, where a minimum and a maximum value can also be set for cardinality. When identifying or nonidentifying relationships are established, keys are automatically migrated above or below, respectively, the entity's horizontal separator line. The recursive Supervises relationship shows the business rule that a supervisor may supervise none or any number of employees, but cannot show that the president has no supervisor, only that each employee has exactly one supervisor. A many-to-many relationship between two entities cannot be established; a new (associative) entity must be added to resolve it. The many and varied line connectors provided by the tool can be used to draw a many-to-many relationship, but these connector objects do not establish the functional relationship within the tool.

CA ERwin Data Modeler r7.3 Notation

Here, for physical or logical modeling, one has the choice among IDEF1X, IE (Information Engineering), or DM (Dimensional Modeling) notation. The examples used here demonstrate IE. ERwin has very robust capabilities for adding many types of metadata to the entities, attributes, and relationships. The user can choose to display the model in several Display Levels, including only entities and relationships, entities with key attributes, and fully attributed entities. As with many of the other tools, both logical and physical data models can be developed and displayed. The key difference between most conceptual and logical data models is that the tools want to resolve all primary keys in a logical data model, which is necessary to migrate to a physical data model. Thus, many tools, like ERwin, do not support development of what is purely a conceptual data model.

ENTITIES An independent entity is represented as a box with a horizontal line and square corners. If an entity is a child (weak) entity in an identifying relationship, it appears as a dependent entity—a box with rounded corners. Associative entity symbols are also represented this way. ERwin determines the entity type based on the relationship in which it is involved. For example, when you initially place an entity in a model, it displays as an independent entity. When you connect it to another entity using a relationship, ERwin determines whether the entity is independent or dependent, based on the relationship type selected.

RELATIONSHIPS ERwin represents a relationship as a solid or dashed line connecting two entities. Depending on the notation you choose, the symbols at either end of the line may change. Cardinality options are flexible and may be specified unambiguously. A parent may be connected to "Zero, One, or More," signified by a blank space; "One or More," signified by a P; "Zero or One," signified by a Z; or "Exactly," some number of instances; P or Z may optionally appear on the ERD. Many-to-many relationships can be depicted or the user may opt to automatically or manually resolve them. Figure 2-22 (A-1) does not have any many-to-many relationships because it already shows all possible ones as associative entities (e.g., DOES BUSINESS IN). (Visio does not support *M:N* relationships.) In Figure A-2 we show what would result from manually telling ERwin to resolve each *M:N* by creating an associative entity. For example, consider the many-to-many SUPPLIES relationship between Vendor and Raw Materials. The user selects a "Show Association Entity" option on the relationship line that then automatically eliminates the many-to-many

FIGURE A-2 CA ERwin Data Modeler r7.3 model

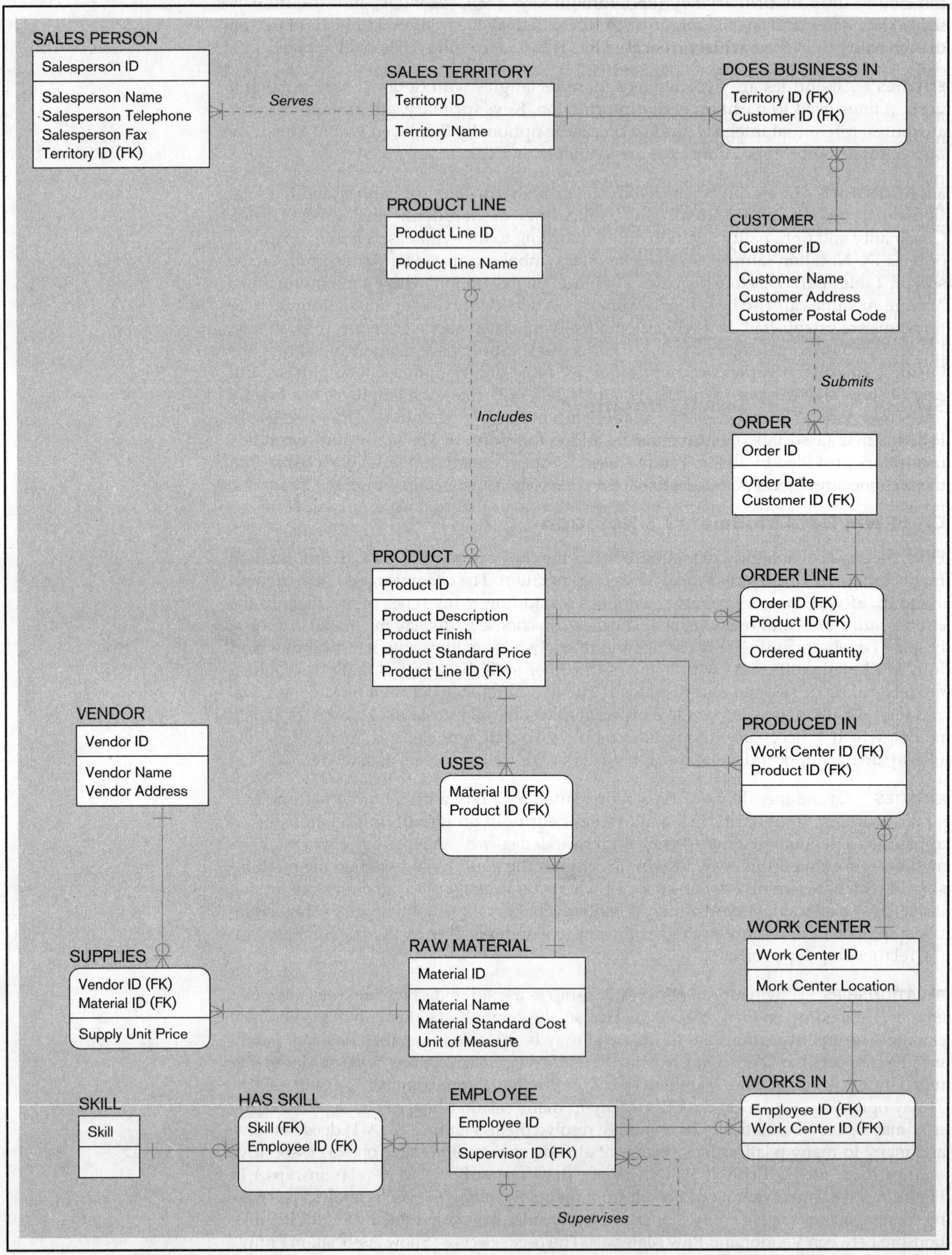

relationship, establishes new ones with cardinality and optionality notations, creates the associative entity, and allows the "Supply Unit Price" attribute for the SUPPLIES relationship to be displayed in the diagram. SUPPLIES would not be the name automatically given this associative entity, so we have renamed it. ORDER LINE is also shown as an associative entity by ERwin. The recursive nonidentifying Supervises relationship, where parent and child are shown as the same entity, shows that an Employee (a Supervisor) may supervise many employees, but not all employees are supervisors. The notation also indicates that nulls are allowed, which shows that a supervisor may have no employees and an employee (the president) may have no supervisor. The diagram introduces a Role Name (Supervisor ID) for the PK attribute in its role as a nonkey FK attribute for the Supervises relationship. Keys migrate automatically when relationships are established, and foreign keys are notated "FK." In an identifying relationship, the FK migrates above the horizontal line in the entity and becomes part of the primary key of the child entity. In a nonidentifying relationship, the foreign key migrates below the line and becomes a nonkey attribute in the child entity. In ERwin, a dashed line represents a nonidentifying relationship.

The chart captured from ERwin's online help and shown in Figure A-3 depicts the range of cardinality symbols for different ER notation sets that may be used from this product.

Sybase PowerDesigner 15 Notation

PowerDesigner projects are contained within a workspace that can be customized and includes a hierarchy of folders and models. Links to model files, report files, and external files are also stored in the workspace. Where a data modeler is working on multiple projects or on a part of a project with different requirements, multiple workspaces may be defined as needed. Each is kept locally and is reusable. It is only possible to work in one workspace at a time. PowerDesigner 15 includes various integrated modeling tools

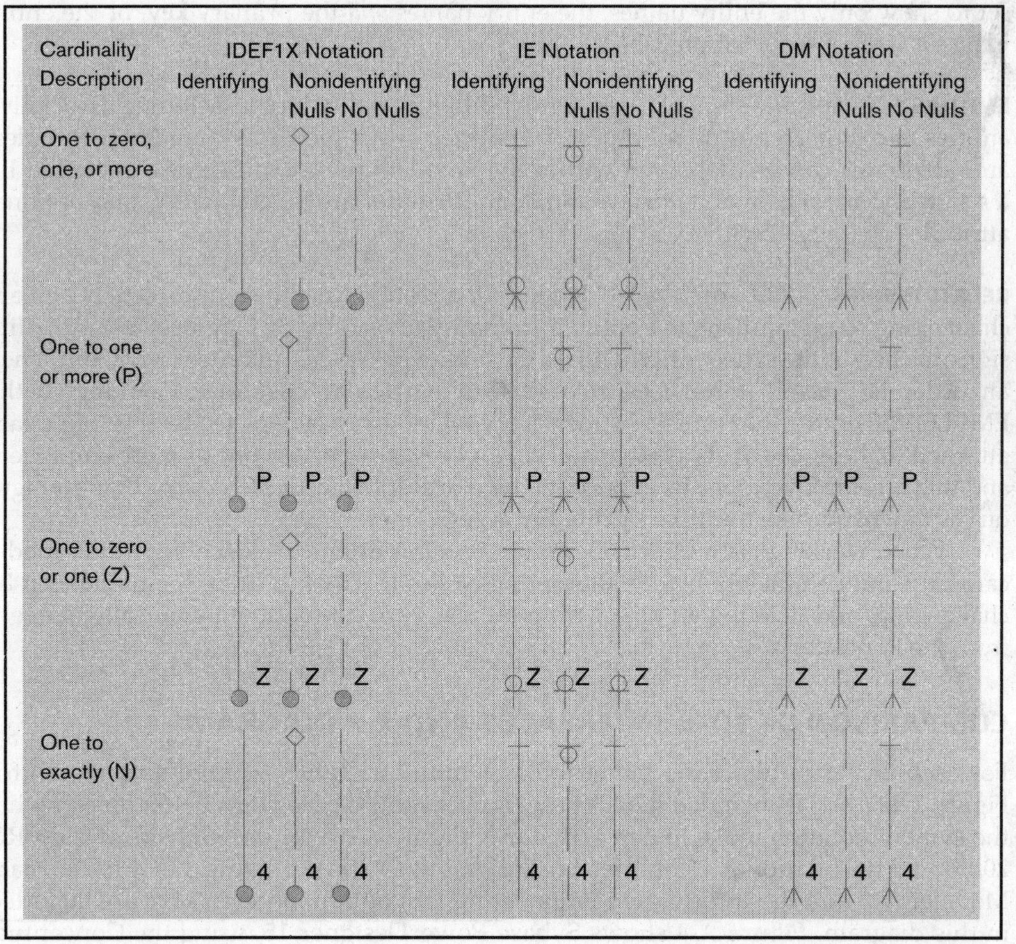

FIGURE A-3 ERwin cardinality/optionality symbols

besides data modeling, including XML modeling, data movement modeling, and various enterprise information architecture tools.

The examples in this appendix use the Conceptual Data Model graphics with the Information Engineering notation. Other conceptual modeling notations supported are Barker and IDEF 1/x. Conceptual designs can be used to generate first logical and then physical data models. Further, PowerDesigner 15 has added data warehouse design capabilities, including the ability to identify dimension and fact tables, and generate cubes.

ENTITIES The amount of detail that is displayed in the data model is selected by the modeler and may include primary identifiers, a predetermined number of attributes, data type, optionality, and/or domain. A double-click of the entity allows access to the entity's property sheet. Properties shown include name, technical code name, a comment field that contains a descriptive label if desired, stereotype (subclassification of entity), estimated number of occurrences, and the possibility of generating a table in the physical data model. Additional entity properties include attributes, identifiers, and rules. Each of these properties has its own property sheet.

RELATIONSHIPS PowerDesigner uses a solid line between entities to establish any relationship. Crows foot notation is used to establish cardinality and the circle and line establish optionality, similar to the Hoffer notation. Relationship properties include name, technical code name, comment, stereotype, the related pair of entities (only binary and unary relationships are supported), and a generation capability. It is possible to model a many-to-many relationship without breaking it down to include the associative entity. If desired, however, an associative entity may be modeled and displayed. Recursive (reflexive) relationships may be modeled easily, and subtypes may also be presented.

Oracle Designer Notation

Diagrams drawn using Oracle Designer's Entity Relationship Diagrammer tool can be set to show only the entity names, the entity names *and* the primary key, or the entity names *and* all of the attribute labels.

ENTITIES No specific symbols exist for the different entity types, including associative entities and supertypes or subtypes. All entities are depicted as rounded rectangles, and attributes can be displayed within the box. Unique identifiers are preceded by a # sign and must be mandatory, mandatory attributes are tagged with *, and optional attributes are tagged with ∘.

RELATIONSHIPS Lines must be labeled in *both* directions, not just one direction, and are challenging to manipulate and align. Cardinality is read by picking up the cardinality sign attached to the other entity. Thus, a Customer *may* place an order or not, but when an order is placed, it must be related to a particular customer. Looking at the EMPLOYEE entity, the recursive supervisory relationship is depicted by the "pig's ear" attached to the entity. It shows that an Employee *may* supervise one or more employees and that an employee *must* be supervised by one employee, or supervisor. It is ambiguous as to whether the multiple cardinality is zero, one, or many.

When working with Oracle Designer, it is important to sketch your data model carefully and completely before attempting to use the tool. Editing the model can be challenging, and deleting an object from the diagram does not automatically delete it from the Repository.

COMPARISON OF TOOL INTERFACES AND E-R DIAGRAMS

For each of the software modeling tools included in Table A-1, the data model for Figure 2-22 (A-1) is included here. These figures should give you a better idea of what the symbol notation looks like in actual use. Figure A-1 was drawn using Visio PRO 2003 and its relational template. Figure A-2 was drawn using CA ERwin Data Modeler r7.3 and the Information Engineering (IE) option. Foreign keys are included in this diagram. Figure A-4 shows Sybase PowerDesigner 15, using the Conceptual

FIGURE A-4 Sybase PowerDesigner 15 model

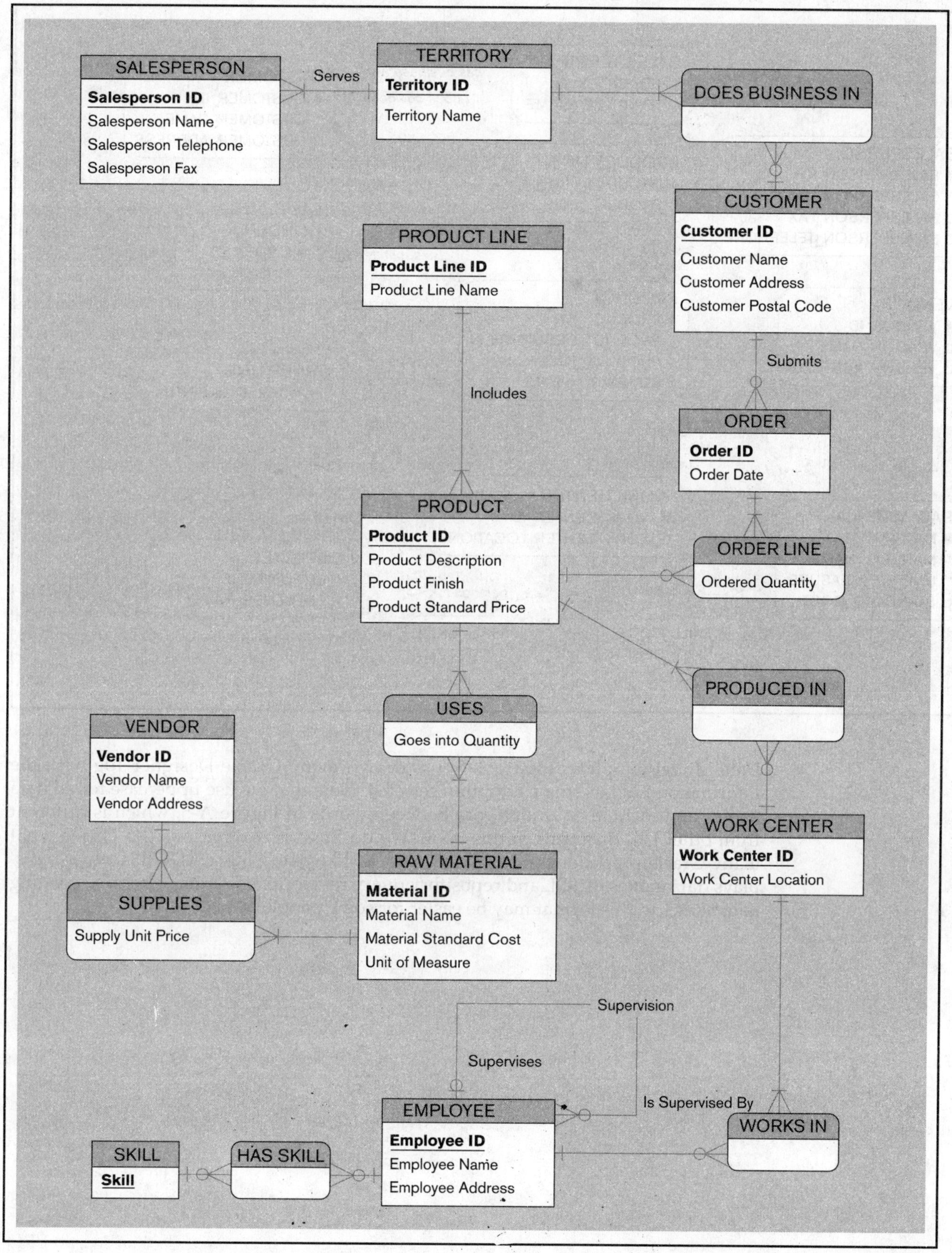

FIGURE A-5 Oracle Designer 10g model

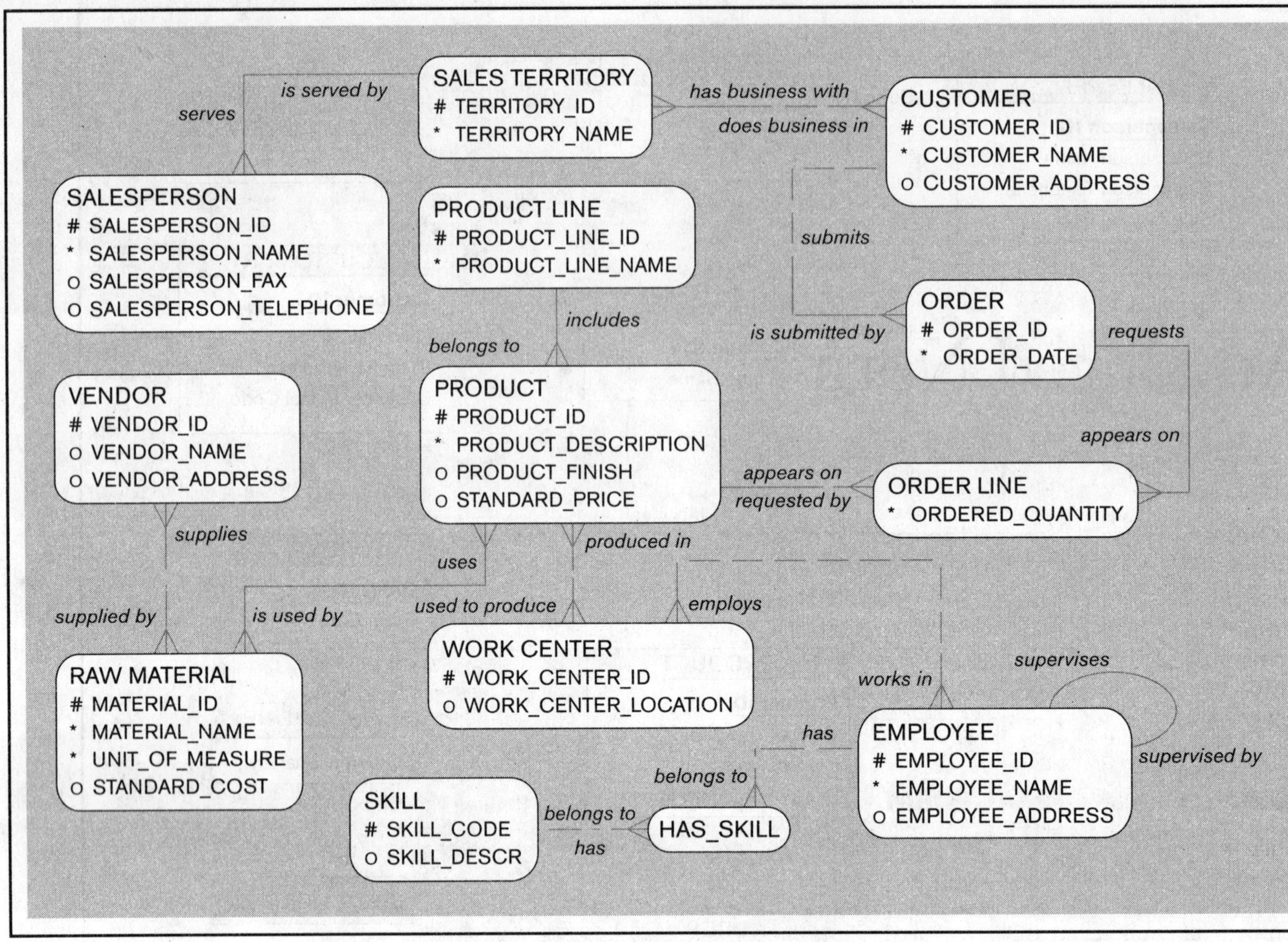

Data Model template. Figure A-5 was drawn using Oracle Designer 10g with the Information Engineering (IE) option selected. Note that we use uppercase for all data names and include an underscore between words in Figure A-5, which is different from other E-R diagrams in this book. We do this for two reasons: (1) This is what many Oracle practitioners do, and (2) Oracle, like many other RDBMSs, always displays data names in SQL and repository query results in all-capital letters, so creating data names in this format may be easier for some people to read.

APPENDIX

B

Advanced Normal Forms

In Chapter 4, we introduced the topic of normalization and described first through third normal forms in detail. Relations in third normal form (3NF) are sufficient for most practical database applications. However, 3NF does not guarantee that all anomalies have been removed. As indicated in Chapter 4, several additional normal forms are designed to remove these anomalies: Boyce-Codd normal form, fourth normal form, and fifth normal form (see Figure 4-22). We describe Boyce-Codd normal form and fourth normal form in this appendix.

BOYCE-CODD NORMAL FORM

When a relation has more than one candidate key, anomalies may result even though that relation is in 3NF. For example, consider the STUDENT ADVISOR relation shown in Figure B-1. This relation has the following attributes: SID (student ID), Major, Advisor, and MajGPA. Sample data for this relation are shown in Figure B-1a, and the functional dependencies are shown in Figure B-1b.

As shown in Figure B-1b, the primary key for this relation is the composite key consisting of SID and Major. Thus, the two attributes Advisor and MajGPA are functionally dependent on this key. This reflects the constraint that although a given student may have more than one major, for each major a student has exactly one advisor and one GPA.

There is a second functional dependency in this relation: Major is functionally dependent on Advisor. That is, each advisor advises in exactly one major. Notice that this is not a transitive dependency. In Chapter 4, we defined a transitive dependency as a functional dependency between two nonkey attributes. In contrast, in this example a key attribute (Major) is functionally dependent on a nonkey attribute (Advisor).

Anomalies in STUDENT ADVISOR

The STUDENT ADVISOR relation is clearly in 3NF, because there are no partial functional dependencies and no transitive dependencies. Nevertheless, because of the functional dependency between Major and Advisor, there are anomalies in this relation. Consider the following examples:

1. Suppose that in Physics, the advisor Hawking is replaced by Einstein. This change must be made in two (or more) rows in the table (update anomaly).
2. Suppose we want to insert a row with the information that Babbage advises in Computer Science. This, of course, cannot be done until at least one student majoring in Computer Science is assigned Babbage as an advisor (insertion anomaly).
3. Finally, if student number 789 withdraws from school, we lose the information that Bach advises in Music (deletion anomaly).

FIGURE B-1 Relation in 3NF but not in BCNF
(a) Relation with sample data

STUDENT ADVISOR

SID	Major	Advisor	MajGPA
123	Physics	Hawking	4.0
123	Music	Mahler	3.3
456	Literature	Michener	3.2
789	Music	Bach	3.7
678	Physics	Hawking	3.5

(b) Functional dependencies in STUDENT ADVISOR

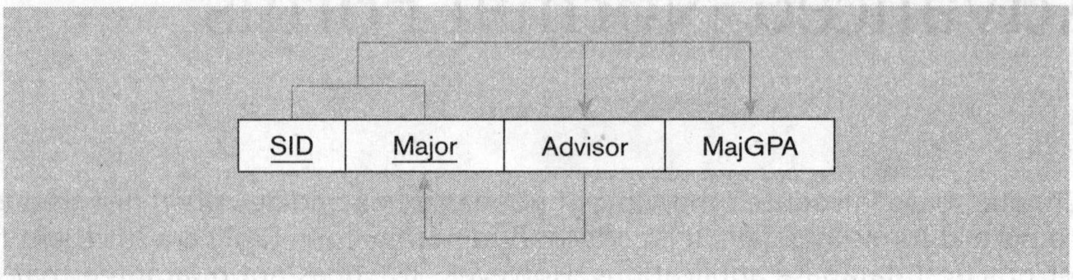

Definition of Boyce-Codd Normal Form (BCNF)

Boyce-Codd normal form (BCNF) A normal form of a relation in which every determinant is a candidate key.

The anomalies in STUDENT ADVISOR result from the fact that there is a determinant (Advisor) that is not a candidate key in the relation. R. F. Boyce and E. F. Codd identified this deficiency and proposed a stronger definition of 3NF that remedies the problem. We say a relation is in **Boyce-Codd normal form (BCNF)** if and only if every determinant in the relation is a candidate key. STUDENT ADVISOR is not in BCNF because although the attribute Advisor is a determinant, it is not a candidate key. (Only Major is functionally dependent on Advisor.)

Converting a Relation to BCNF

A relation that is in 3NF (but not BCNF) can be converted to relations in BCNF using a simple two-step process. This process is shown in Figure B-2.

In the first step, the relation is modified so that the determinant in the relation that is not a candidate key becomes a component of the primary key of the revised relation. The attribute that is functionally dependent on that determinant becomes a nonkey attribute. This is a legitimate restructuring of the original relation because of the functional dependency.

The result of applying this rule to STUDENT ADVISOR is shown in Figure B-2a. The determinant Advisor becomes part of the composite primary key. The attribute Major, which is functionally dependent on Advisor, becomes a nonkey attribute.

If you examine Figure B-2a, you will discover that the new relation has a partial functional dependency. (Major is functionally dependent on Advisor, which is just one component of the primary key.) Thus the new relation is in first (but not second) normal form.

The second step in the conversion process is to decompose the relation to eliminate the partial functional dependency, as we learned in Chapter 4. This results in two relations, as shown in Figure B-2b. These relations are in 3NF. In fact, the relations are also in BCNF because there is only one candidate key (the primary key) in each relation. Thus, we see that if a relation has only one candidate key (which therefore becomes the primary key), 3NF and BCNF are equivalent.

The two relations (now named STUDENT and ADVISOR) with sample data are shown in Figure B-2c. You should verify that these relations are free of the anomalies

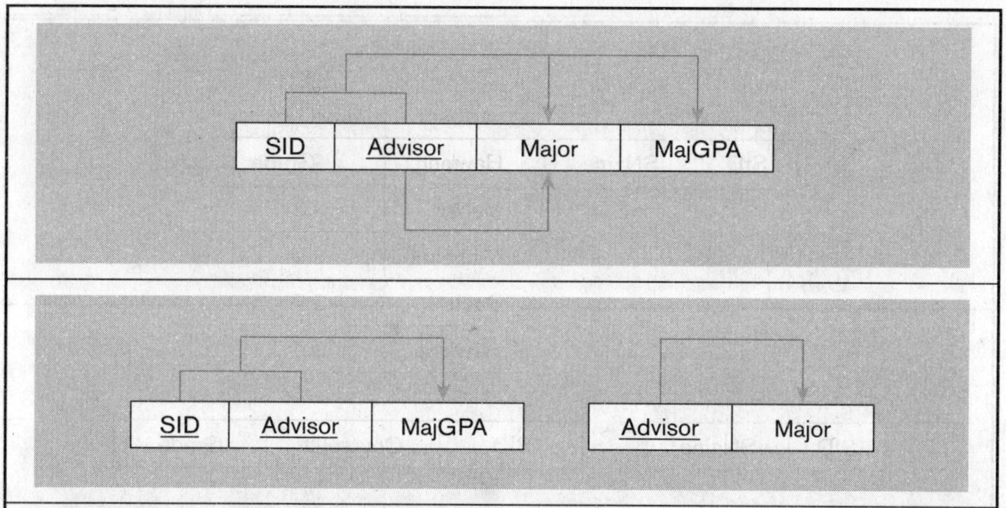

FIGURE B-2 Converting a relation to BCNF relations
(a) Revised STUDENT ADVISOR relations (1NF)
(b) Two relations in BCNF
(c) Relations with sample data

STUDENT

SID	Advisor	MajGPA
123	Hawking	4.0
123	Mahler	3.3
456	Michener	3.2
789	Bach	3.7
678	Hawking	3.5

ADVISOR

Advisor	Major
Hawking	Physics
Mahler	Music
Michener	Literature
Bach	Music

that were described for STUDENT ADVISOR. You should also verify that you can recreate the STUDENT ADVISOR relation by joining the two relations STUDENT and ADVISOR.

Another common situation in which BCNF is violated is when there are two (or more) overlapping candidate keys of the relation. Consider the relation in Figure B-3a. In this example, there are two candidate keys, (SID, CourseID) and (SName, CourseID), in which CourseID appears in both candidate keys. The problem with this relationship is that we cannot record student data (SID and SName) unless the student has taken a course. Figure B-3b shows two possible solutions, each of which creates two relations that are in BCNF.

FOURTH NORMAL FORM

When a relation is in BCNF, there are no longer any anomalies that result from functional dependencies. However, there may still be anomalies that result from multivalued dependencies (defined in the next section). For example, consider the user view shown in Figure B-4a. This user view shows for each course the instructors who teach that course and the textbooks that are used. (These appear as repeating groups in the view.) In this table view, the following assumptions hold:

1. Each course has a well-defined set of instructors (e.g., Management has three instructors).
2. Each course has a well-defined set of textbooks that are used (e.g., Finance has two textbooks).
3. The textbooks that are used for a given course are independent of the instructor for that course (e.g., the same two textbooks are used for Management regardless of which of the three instructors is teaching Management).

FIGURE B-3 Converting a relation with overlapping candidate keys to BCNF
(a) Relation with overlapping candidate keys
(b) Two alternative pairs of relations in BCNF

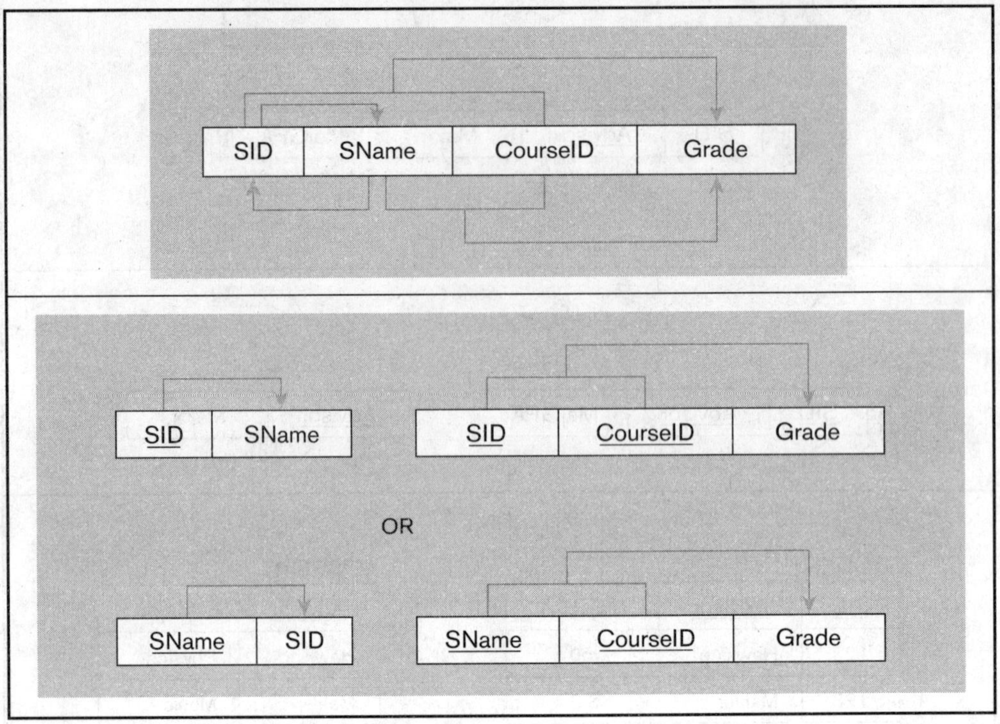

FIGURE B-4 Data with multivalued dependencies

(a) View of courses, instructors, and textbooks

COURSE STAFF AND BOOK ASSIGNMENTS

Course	Instructor	Textbook
Management	White Green Black	Drucker Peters
Finance	Gray	Jones Chang

(b) Relation in BCNF

OFFERING

Course	Instructor	Textbook
Management	White	Drucker
Management	White	Peters
Management	Green	Drucker
Management	Green	Peters
Management	Black	Drucker
Management	Black	Peters
Finance	Gray	Jones
Finance	Gray	Chang

In Figure B-4b, this table view has been converted to a relation by filling in all of the empty cells. This relation (named OFFERING) is in 1NF. Thus, for each course, all possible combinations of instructor and text appear in OFFERING. Notice that the primary key of this relation consists of all three attributes (Course, Instructor, and Textbook). Because there are no determinants other than the primary key, the relation is actually in BCNF. Yet it does contain much redundant data that can easily lead to update anomalies. For example, suppose that we want to add a third textbook (author: Middleton) to the Management course. This change would require the addition of three new rows to the relation in Figure B-4b, one for each Instructor (otherwise that text would apply to only certain instructors).

Multivalued Dependencies

The type of dependency shown in this example is called a **multivalued dependency,** and it exists when there are at least three attributes (e.g., A, B, and C) in a relation, and for each value of A there is a well-defined set of values of B and a well-defined set of values of C. However, the set of values of B is independent of set C, and vice versa.

Multivalued dependency
The type of dependency that exists when there are at least three attributes (e.g., A, B, and C) in a relation, with a well-defined set of B and C values for each A value, but those B and C values are independent of each other.

To remove the multivalued dependency from a relation, we divide the relation into two new relations. Each of these tables contains two attributes that have a multivalued relationship in the original relation. Figure B-5 shows the result of this decomposition for the OFFERING relation of Figure B-4b. Notice that the relation called TEACHER contains the Course and Instructor attributes, because for each course there is a well-defined set of instructors. Also, for the same reason, TEXT contains the attributes Course and Textbook. However, there is no relation containing the attributes Instructor and Course because these attributes are independent.

A relation is in **fourth normal form (4NF)** if it is in BCNF and contains no multivalued dependencies. You can easily verify that the two relations in Figure B-5 are in 4NF and are free of the anomalies described earlier. Also, you can verify that you can reconstruct the original relation (OFFERING) by joining these two relations. In addition, notice that there are fewer data in Figure B-5 than in Figure B-4b. For simplicity, assume that Course, Instructor, and Textbook are all of equal length. Because there are 24 cells of data in Figure B-4b and 16 cells of data in Figure B-5, there is a space savings of 33 percent for the 4NF tables.

Fourth normal form (4NF)
A normal form of a relation in which the relation is in BCNF and contains no multivalued dependencies.

HIGHER NORMAL FORMS

At least two higher-level normal forms have been defined: fifth normal form (5NF) and domain-key normal form (DKNF). Fifth normal form deals with a property called "lossless joins." According to Elmasri and Navathe (2006), 5NF is not of practical significance because lossless joins occur very rarely and are difficult to detect. For this reason (and also because 5NF has a complex definition), we do not describe 5NF in this text.

Domain-key normal form is an attempt to define an "ultimate normal form" that takes into account all possible types of dependencies and constraints (Elmasri and Navathe, 2006). Although the definition of DKNF is quite simple, its practical value is minimal. For this reason, we do not describe DKNF in this text.

For more information concerning these two higher normal forms see Elmasri and Navathe (2006) and Dutka and Hanson (1989).

FIGURE B-5 Relations in 4NF

TEACHER

Course	Instructor
Management	White
Management	Green
Management	Black
Finance	Gray

TEXT

Course	Textbook
Management	Drucker
Management	Peters
Finance	Jones
Finance	Chang

Appendix Review

Key Terms

Boyce-Codd normal form (BCNF) *548*

Fourth normal form (4NF) *551*

Multivalued dependency *551*

References

Dutka, A., and H. Hanson. 1989. *Fundamentals of Data Normalization*. Reading, MA: Addison-Wesley.

Elmasri, R., and S. Navathe. 2006. *Fundamentals of Database Systems*, 5th ed. Reading, MA: Addison-Wesley.

Web Resource

www.bkent.net/Doc/simple5.htm A simple, understandable guide to first through fifth normal forms.

APPENDIX

C

Data Structures

Data structures are the basic building blocks of any physical database architecture. No matter what file organization or DBMS you use, data structures are used to connect related pieces of data. Although many modern DBMSs hide the underlying data structures, the tuning of a physical database requires understanding the choices a database designer can make about data structures. This appendix addresses the fundamental elements of all data structures and overviews some common schemes for storing and locating physical elements of data.

POINTERS

The concept of pointers was introduced in Chapter 5. As described in that chapter, a pointer is used generically as any reference to the address of another piece of data. In fact, there are three types of pointers, as illustrated in Figure C-1:

1. ***Physical address pointer*** Contains the actual, fully resolved disk address (device, cylinder, track, and block number) of the referenced data. Using a physical pointer is the fastest way to locate another piece of data, but it is also the most restrictive: If the address of the referenced data changes, all pointers to it must also be changed. Physical pointers are commonly used in legacy database applications with network and hierarchical database architectures.
2. ***Relative address pointer*** Contains the relative position (or "offset") of the associated data from some base, or starting, point. The relative address could be a byte position, a record, or a row number. A relative pointer has the advantage that when the whole data structure changes location, all relative references to that structure are preserved. Relative pointers are used in a wide variety of DBMSs; a common use is in indexes in which index keys are matched with row identifiers (a type of relative pointer) for the record(s) with that key value.
3. ***Logical key pointer*** Contains meaningful data about the associated data element. A logical pointer must be transformed into a physical or relative pointer by some table lookup, index search, or mathematical calculation to actually locate the referenced data. Foreign keys in a relational database are often logical key pointers.

Table C-1 summarizes the salient features of each of these three types of pointers. A database designer may be able to choose which type of pointer to use in different situations in a database. For example, a foreign key in a relation can be implemented using any of these three types of pointers. In addition, when a database is damaged, a database administrator who understands what types of pointers are used may be able to rebuild broken links between database contents.

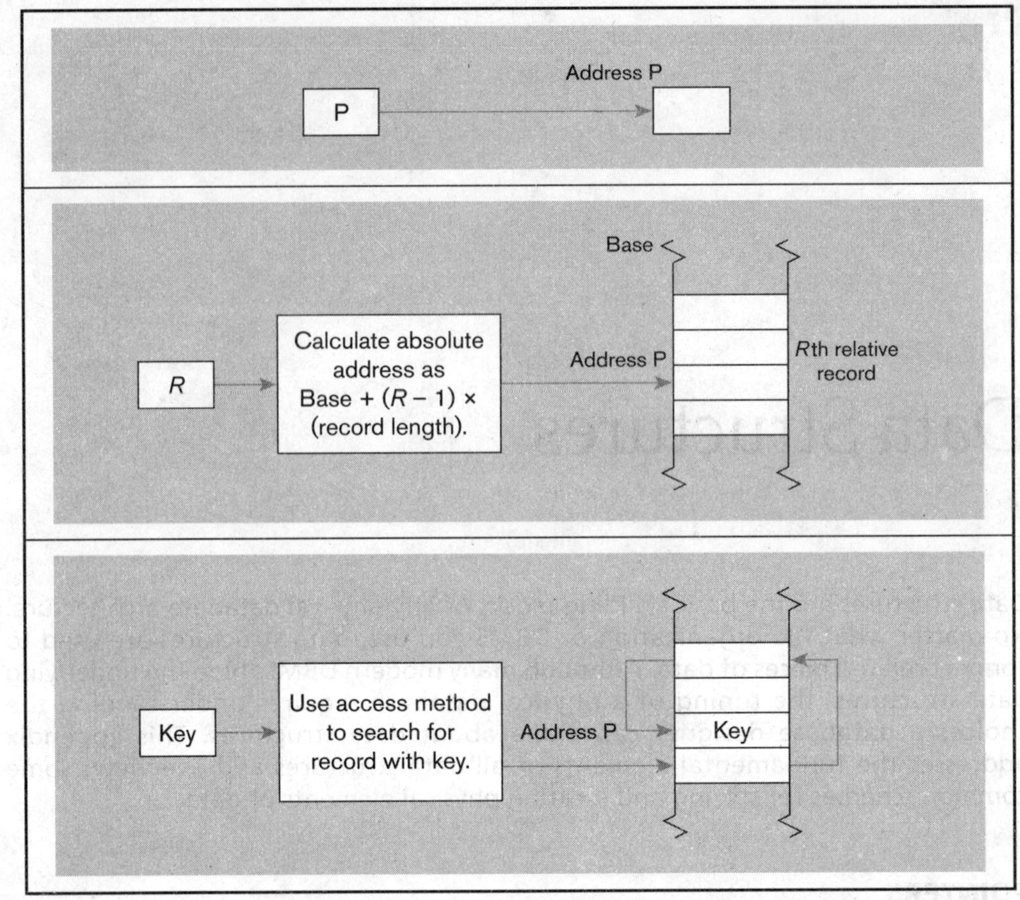

FIGURE C-1 Types of pointers
(a) Physical address pointer
(b) Relative address pointer for *R*th record in file
(c) Logical key pointer for record with key

TABLE C-1 Comparison of Types of Pointers

	Type of Pointer		
Characteristic	**Physical**	**Relative**	**Logical**
Form	Actual secondary memory (disk) address	Offset from reference point (beginning of file)	Meaningful business data
Speed of access	Fastest	Medium	Slowest
Sensitivity to data movement	Most	Only sensitive to relative position changes	Least
Sensitivity to destruction	Vary	Vary	Often can be easily reconstructed
Space requirement	Fixed, usually short	Varies, usually shortest	Varies, usually longest

DATA STRUCTURE BUILDING BLOCKS

All data structures are built from several alternative basic building blocks for connecting and locating data. Connecting methods allow movement between related elements of data. Locating methods allow data within a structure to first be placed or stored and then found.

There are only two basic methods for *connecting* elements of data:

1. ***Address-sequential connection*** A successor (or related) element is placed and located in the physical memory space immediately following the current element (see Figures C-2a and C-2c). Address-sequential connections perform best for reading the entire set of data or reading the next record in the stored sequence. In contrast, address-sequential structures are inefficient for retrieving arbitrary

FIGURE C-2 Basic location methods

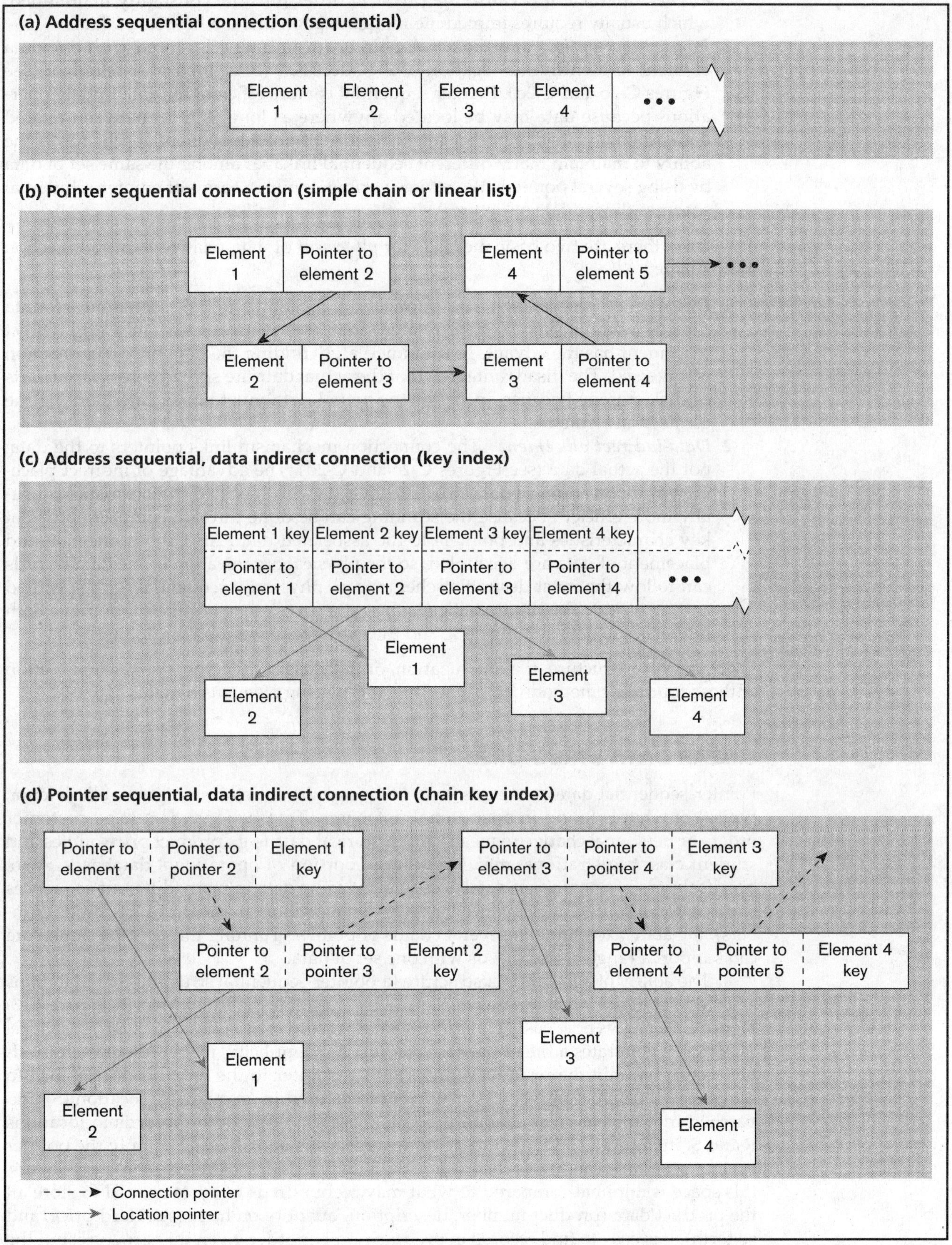

records and data update (add, delete, and change) operations. Update operations are also inefficient because the physical order must be constantly maintained, which usually requires immediate reorganization of the whole set of data.

2. ***Pointer-sequential connection*** A pointer (or pointers) is stored with one data element to identify the location of the successor (or related) data element (see Figures C-2b and C-2d). Pointer sequential is more efficient for data update operations because data may be located anywhere as long as links between related data are maintained. Another major feature of pointer-sequential schemes is the ability to maintain many different sequential linkages among the same set of data by using several pointers. We review various common forms of pointer-sequential schemes (linear data structures) shortly.

Also, there are two basic methods for *placement* of data relative to the connection mechanism:

1. ***Data-direct placement*** The connection mechanism links an item of data directly with its successor (or related) item (see Figures C-2a and C-2b). Direct placement has the advantage of immediately finding the data once a connection is traversed. The disadvantage is that the actual data are spread across large parts of disk storage because space for the actual data must be allocated among the connection elements.
2. ***Data-indirect placement*** The connection mechanism links pointers to the data, not the actual data (see Figures C-2c and C-2d). The advantage of indirect placement is that scanning a data structure for data with specified characteristics is usually more efficient because the scanning can be done through compact entries of key characteristics and pointers to the associated data. Also, the connection and placement of data are decoupled, so the physical organization of the data records can follow the most desirable scheme (e.g., physically sequential for a specified sorting order). The disadvantage is the extra access time required to retrieve both references to data and the data, and the extra space required for pointers.

Any data structure, file organization, or database architecture uses a combination of these four basic methods for connecting and placing elements of data.

LINEAR DATA STRUCTURES

Pointer-sequential data structures have been popular for storing highly volatile data, typical of what is found in operational databases. Transactional data (e.g., customer orders or personnel change requests) and historical data (e.g., product price quotes and student class registrations) make up a large portion of operational databases. Also, because users of operational databases want to view data in many different sequences (e.g., customer orders in sequence by order date, product numbers, or customer numbers), the ability to maintain several chains of pointers running through the same data can support a range of user needs with one set of data.

The ability of a linear data structure (a pointer-sequential structure that maintains a sorted sequence on the data) to handle data updates is illustrated in Figure C-3. Figure C-3a shows how easy it is to insert a new record into a linear (or chain) structure. This figure illustrates a file of product records. For simplicity, we represent each product record by only the product number and a pointer to the next product record in sequence by product number. A new record is stored in an available location (S) and patched into the chain by changing pointers associated with the records in locations R and S. In Figure C-3b the act of deleting a record is equally easy, as only the pointer for the record in location R is changed. Although there is extra space to store the pointers, this space is minimal compared to what may be hundreds of bytes needed to store all the product data (product number, description, quantity on hand, standard price, and so forth). It is easy to find records in product number order given this structure, but the actual time to retrieve records in sequence can be extensive if logically sequential records are stored far apart on disk.

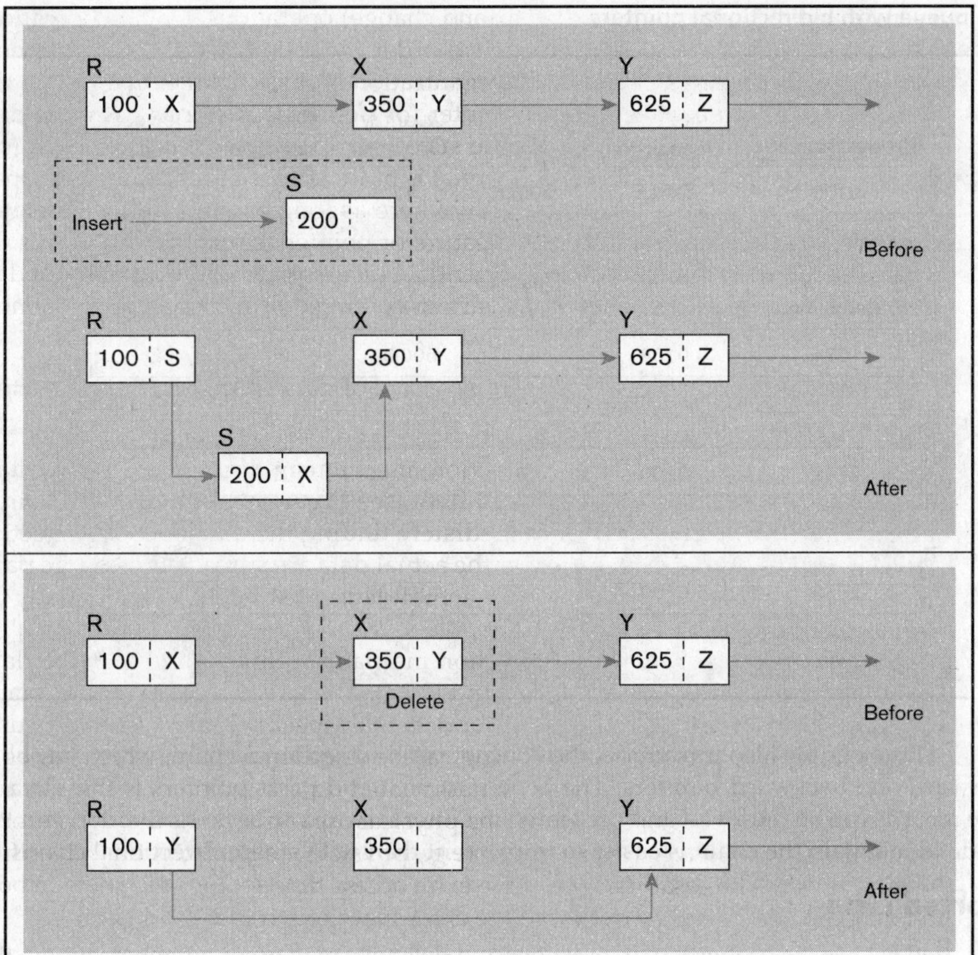

FIGURE C-3 Maintaining a pointer sequential data structure
(a) Insertion
(b) Deletion

With this simple introduction to linear data structures, we now consider four specific versions of such structures: stacks, queues, sorted lists, and multilists. We conclude this section with some cautions about linear, chain data structures.

Stacks

A stack has the property that all record insertions and deletions are made at the same end of the data structure. Stacks exhibit a last-in/first-out (LIFO) property. A common example of a stack is a vertical column of plates in a cafeteria. In business information systems, stacks are used to maintain non-prioritized or unsorted records (e.g., the line items associated with the same customer order).

Queues

A queue has the property that all insertions occur at one end and all deletions occur at the other end. A queue exhibits a first-in/first-out (FIFO) property. A common example of a queue is a checkout lane at a grocery store. In business information systems, queues are used to maintain lists of records in chronological order of insertion. For example, Figure C-4 illustrates a chained queue of Order Line records kept in order of arrival for a common Product record in Pine Valley Furniture.

In this example, the Product record acts as the head-of-chain node in the data structure. The value of the OldestOrderLine field is a pointer to the oldest (first entered) Order Line record for product 0100. The NextOrderLine field in the OrderLine record contains the pointers to the next record in reverse chronological sequence. The value Ø in a pointer is called a null pointer and signifies the end of the chain.

FIGURE C-4 Example of a queue with bidirectional pointers

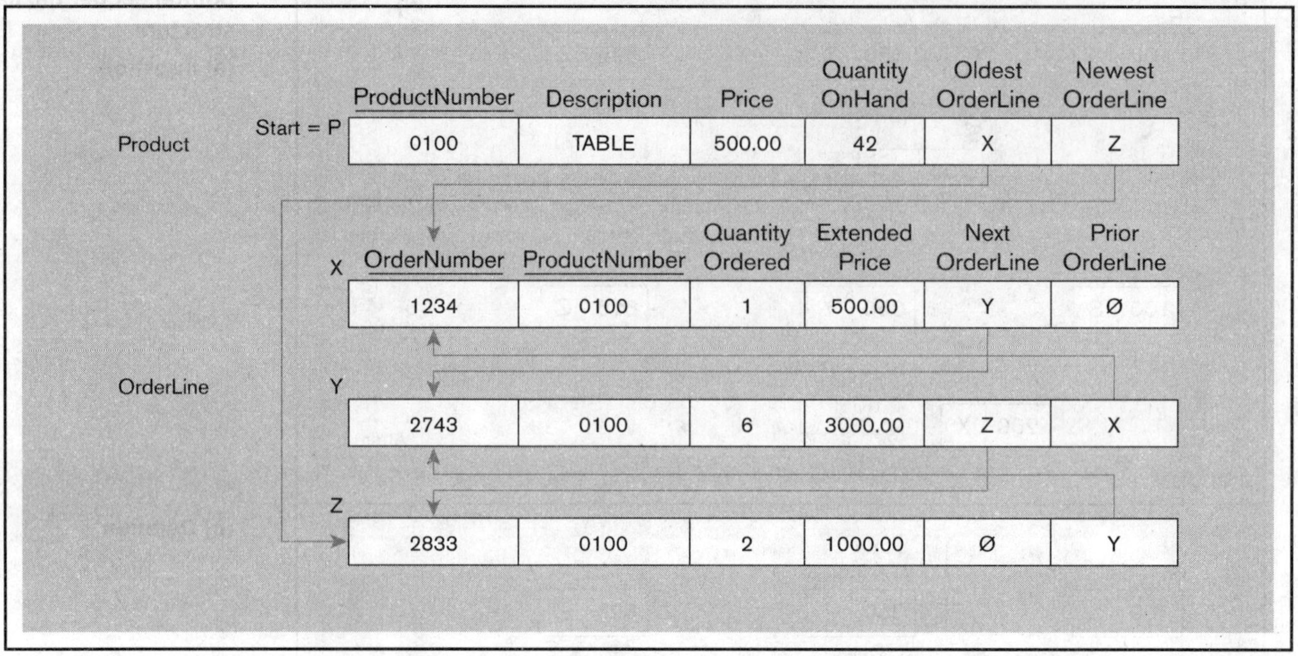

This example also introduces the concept of a bidirectional chain, which has both forward and backward pointers. The benefit of next and prior pointers is that data in the records can be retrieved and presented in either forward or backward order, and the code to maintain the chain is easier to implement than with single-directional chains.

Sorted Lists

A sorted list has the property that insertions and deletions may occur anywhere within the list; records are maintained in logical order based on a key field value. A common example of a sorted list is a telephone directory. In business information systems, sorted lists occur frequently. Figure C-5a illustrates a single-directional, pointer sequential sorted list of Order records related to a Customer record, in which records are sorted by DeliveryDate.

Maintaining a sorted list is more complex than maintaining a stack or a queue because insertion or deletion can occur anywhere in a chain, which may have zero or

FIGURE C-5 Example of a sorted list

(a) Before new Order record insertion and without dummy first and dummy last Order records

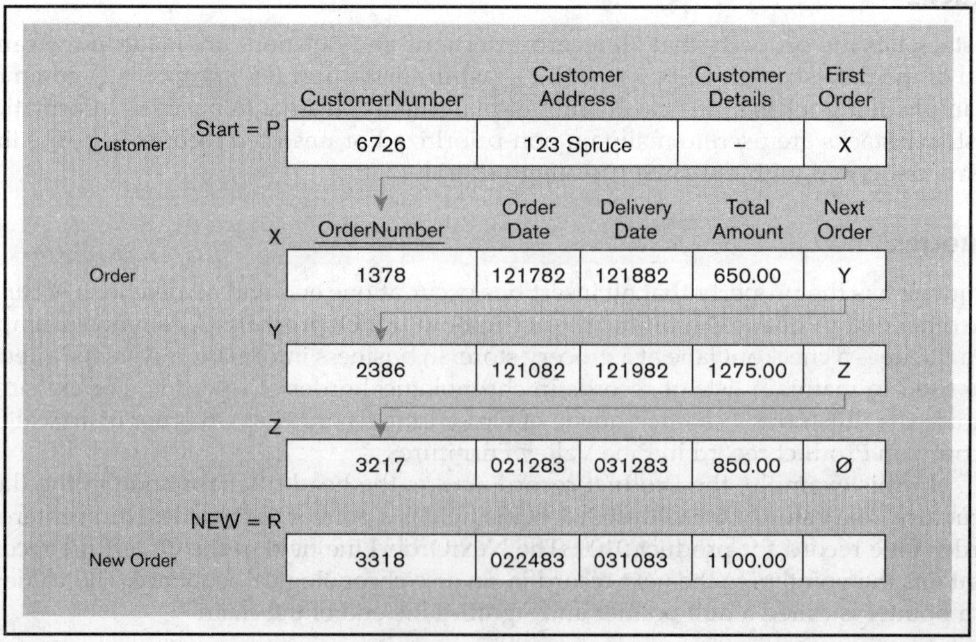

(continued)

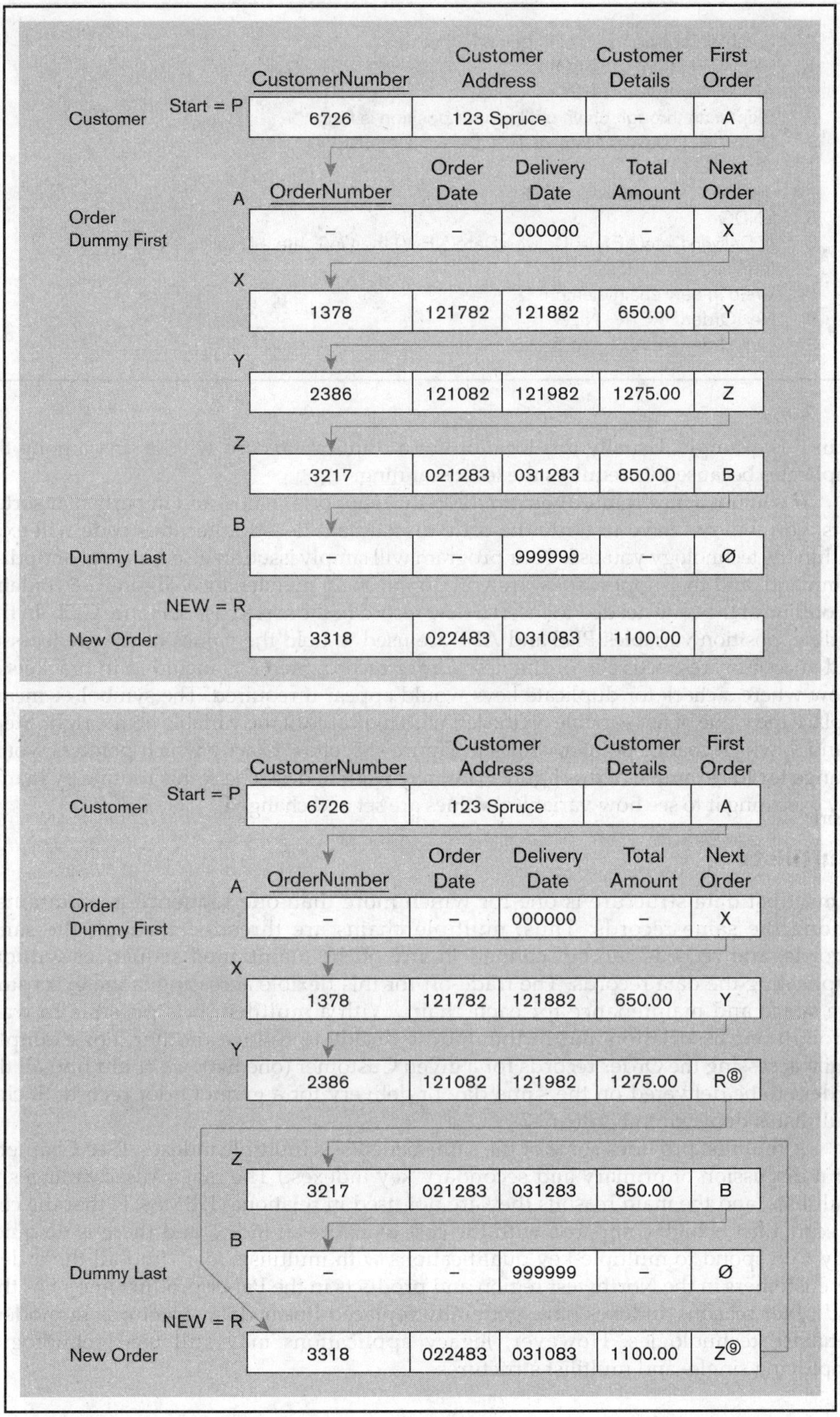

(b) Before new Order record insertion and with dummy first and dummy last Order records

(c) After new Order record insertion (Circled numbers next to pointers indicate the step number in the associated maintenance procedure of Figure C-6 that changes pointer value.)

many existing records. To guarantee that insertions and deletions always occur in the interior of the chain, "dummy" first and last records are often included (see Figure C-5b). Figure C-5c shows the result of inserting a new Order record into the sorted list of Figure C-5b. To perform the insertion, the list is scanned starting from the address in the pointer FirstOrder. Once the proper position in the chain is found, there must be a rule for deciding where to store a record with a duplicate key value, if duplicates are allowed,

FIGURE C-6 Outline of record insertion code

```
/*  Establish position variables beginning values */
1   PRE ← FirstOrder(START)
2   AFT ← NextOrder(PRE)
/*  Skip/scan through chain until proper position is found */
3   DO WHILE DeliveryDate(AFT) < DeliveryDate(NEW)
     4  PRE ← AFT
     5  AFT ← NextOrder(AFT)
6   ENDO
7   [If DeliveryDate(AFT) = DeliveryDate(NEW) then indicate a Duplicate Error and
    terminate procedure]
/*  Weld in new chain element */
8   NextOrder(PRE) ← NEW
9   NextOrder(NEW) ← AFT
```

as in this example. Usually this location for a duplicate record will be first among the duplicates because this requires the least scanning.

If you use a file organization or DBMS that supports chains, and in particular sorted lists, you will not have to write the code to maintain lists. Rather, this code will exist within the technology you use. Your program will simply issue an insert, delete, or update command, and the support software will do the chain maintenance. Figure C-6 contains an outline of the code needed to insert a new record in the sorted list of Figure C-5b. In this outline, position variables PRE and AFT are used to hold the values of the predecessor and successor, respectively, of the new Order record. Step 7 is included in brackets to show where a check for duplicate keys would appear if required. The symbol ← means replace the value of the variable on the left with the value of the variable on the right. Steps 8 and 9, which change pointer values in Figure C-5, show exactly which pointers would change for the example of this figure. You may want to desk check this routine by manually executing it to see how variables' values are set and changed.

Multilists

A multilist data structure is one for which more than one sequence is maintained among the same records. Thus, multiple chains are threaded through the same records, and records can be scanned in any of the maintained sequences without duplicating the data records. The trade-off for this flexible accessing is the extra storage space and maintenance for each chain. With a multilist, it is possible to walk through one association and in the middle decide to follow another. For example, while accessing the Order records for a given Customer (one list), we could find all the Orders to be delivered on the same day of delivery for a given Order record. Such a multilist is depicted in Figure C-7.

A multilist provides some of the same benefits as multiple indexes. (See Chapter 6 for a discussion of primary and secondary key indexes.) The major disadvantages of multilists, and the main reasons they are not used in relational DBMSs, is that the cost to scan a list is high compared with the cost to access an index, and there is no quick way to respond to multiple-key qualifications with multilists (e.g., find all the orders for customers in the Northwest region and products in the Paper product line). For this and other reasons, indexes have generally replaced linear data structures in modern database technologies. However, legacy applications may still use technologies employing single- and multilist structures.

HAZARDS OF CHAIN STRUCTURES

Besides the limitation of chains that prohibits their use in quickly responding to multiple-key qualifications, chains also have the following hazards and limitations:

1. Long chains can take an enormous amount of time to scan because records in sequence are not necessarily stored physically close to one another.

FIGURE C-7 Example of multilist structures

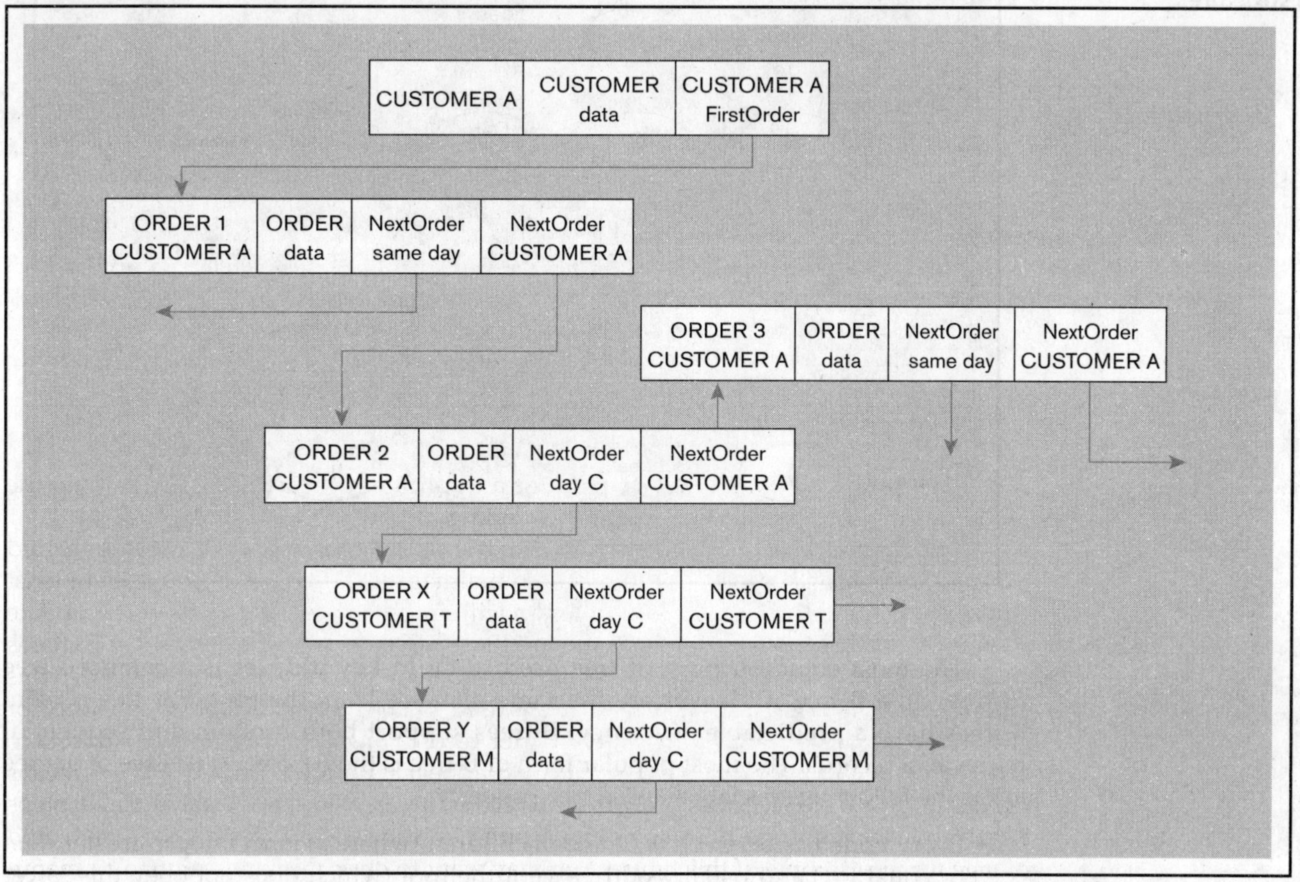

2. Chains are vulnerable to being broken. If an abnormal event occurs in the middle of a chain maintenance routine, the chain can be partially updated, and the chain becomes incomplete or inaccurate. Some safety measures can be taken to cope with such mistakes, but these measures add extra storage or processing overhead.

TREES

The problem that a linear data structure may become long, and hence time-consuming to scan, is an inherent issue with any linear structure. Fortunately, nonlinear structures, which implement a divide-and-conquer strategy, have been developed. A popular type of nonlinear data structure is a tree. A tree (see Figure C-8) is a data structure that consists of a set of nodes that branch out from a node at the top of the tree (thus the tree is upside down!). Trees have a hierarchical structure. The root node is the node at the top of a tree. Each node in the tree, except the root node, has exactly one parent and may have zero, one, or more than one child nodes. Nodes are defined in terms of levels: the root is level zero, and the children of this node are at level one, and so on.

A leaf node is a node in a tree that has no child nodes (e.g., nodes J, F, C, G, K, L, and I in Figure C-8). A subtree of a node consists of that node and all the descendants of that node.

Balanced Trees

The most common use of trees in database management systems today is as a way to organize the entries within a key index. As with linear data structures, a database programmer does not have to maintain the tree structure because this is done by the DBMS software. However, a database designer may have the opportunity to control the structure of an index tree to tune the performance of index processing.

FIGURE C-8 Example of a tree data structure

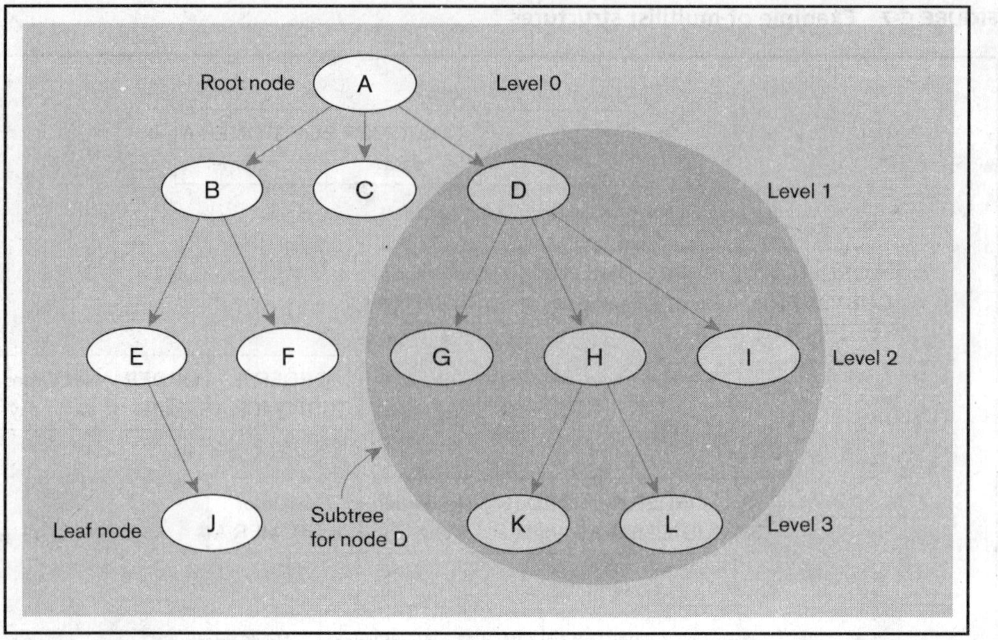

The most common form of tree used to build key indexes is a balanced tree (B-tree). In a B-tree, all leaves are the same distance from the root. For this reason, B-trees have a predictable efficiency. B-trees support both random and sequential retrieval of records. The most popular form of B-tree is the B+-tree. A B+-tree of degree *m* has the following special balanced tree property:

- Every node has between $m/2$ and m children (where m is an integer greater than or equal to 3 and usually odd), except the root (which does not obey this lower bound).

It is this property that leads to the dynamic reorganization of nodes, which we illustrate later in this section.

Virtual sequential access method (VSAM), a data access method supported by many operating systems, is based on the B+-tree data structure. VSAM is a more modern version of indexed sequential access method (ISAM). There are two primary differences between ISAM and VSAM: (1) The locations of index entries under ISAM are limited by the physical boundaries of a disk drive, whereas in VSAM index entries may span the physical boundaries, and (2) an ISAM file needs to be occasionally rebuilt when its structure becomes inefficient after many key additions and deletions, whereas in VSAM the index is dynamically reorganized in incremental ways when segments of the index become unwieldy.

An example of a B+-tree (of degree 3) appears in Figure C-9 for the Product file of Pine Valley Furniture Company. In this diagram, each vertical arrow represents the path followed for values that are equal to the number to the left of the arrow but less than the number to the right of the arrow. For example, in the nonleaf node that contains the values 625 and 1000, the middle arrow leaving the bottom of this node is the path followed for values equal to 625 but less than 1000. Horizontal arrows are used to connect the leaf nodes so that sequential processing can occur without having to move up and down through the levels of the tree.

Suppose you wanted to retrieve the data record for product number 1425. Notice that the value in the root node is 1250. Because 1425 is greater than 1250, you follow the arrow to the right of this node down to the next level. In this node you find the target value (1425), so you follow the middle arrow down to the leaf node that contains the value 1425. This node contains a pointer to the data record for product number 1425, so this record can now be retrieved. You should trace a similar path to locate the record for product number 1000. Because the data records are stored outside the index, multiple B+-tree indexes can be maintained on the same data.

FIGURE C-9 Example of a B+-tree of degree 3

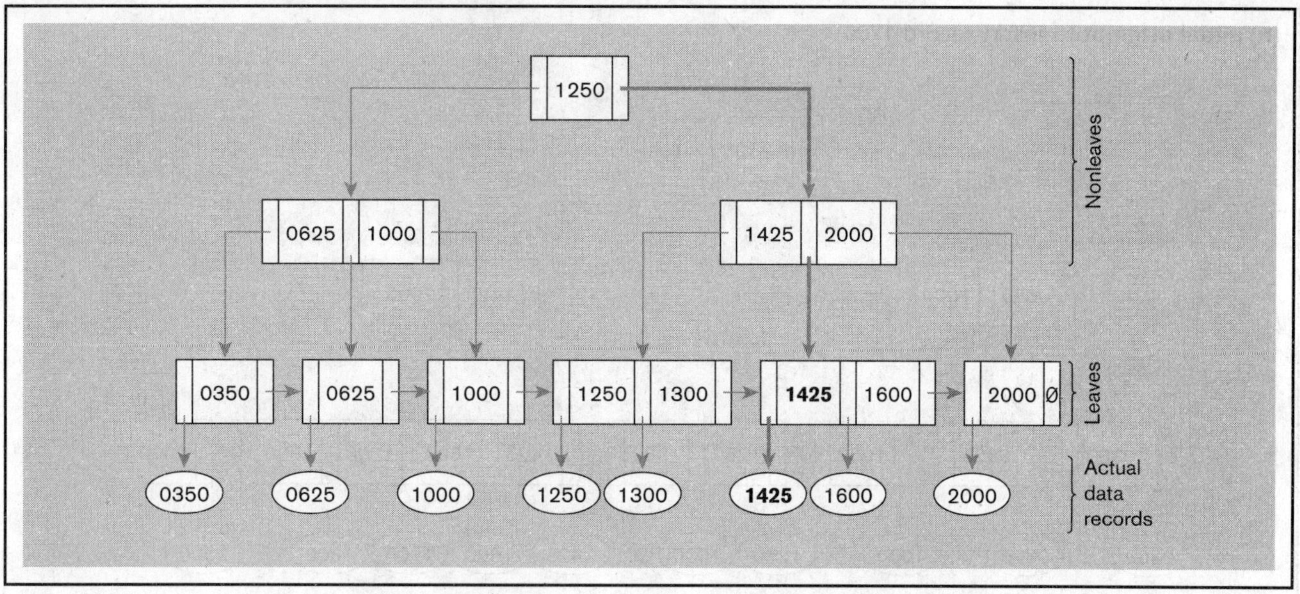

A B+-tree also easily supports the addition and deletion of records. Any necessary changes to the B+-tree structure are dynamic and retain the properties of a B+-tree. Consider the case of adding a record with key 1800 to the B+-tree in Figure C-9. The result of this addition is shown in Figure C-10a. Because node 1 still has only three children (the horizontal pointer does not count as a child pointer), the B+-tree in Figure C-10a still satisfies all B+-tree properties. Now consider the effect of adding another record, this time with key 1700, to the B+-tree in Figure C-10a. An initial result of this insertion appears in Figure C-10b. In this case, node 1 violates the degree limitation, so this node must be split into two nodes. Splitting node 1 will cause a new entry in node 2, which then will make this node have four children, one too many. So, node 2 must also be split, which will add a new entry to node 3. The final result is shown in Figure C-10c.

An interesting situation occurs when the root becomes too large (has more than m children). In this case, the root is split, which adds an additional level to the tree.

FIGURE C-10 Inserting records in a B+-tree

(a) Insertion of record 1800

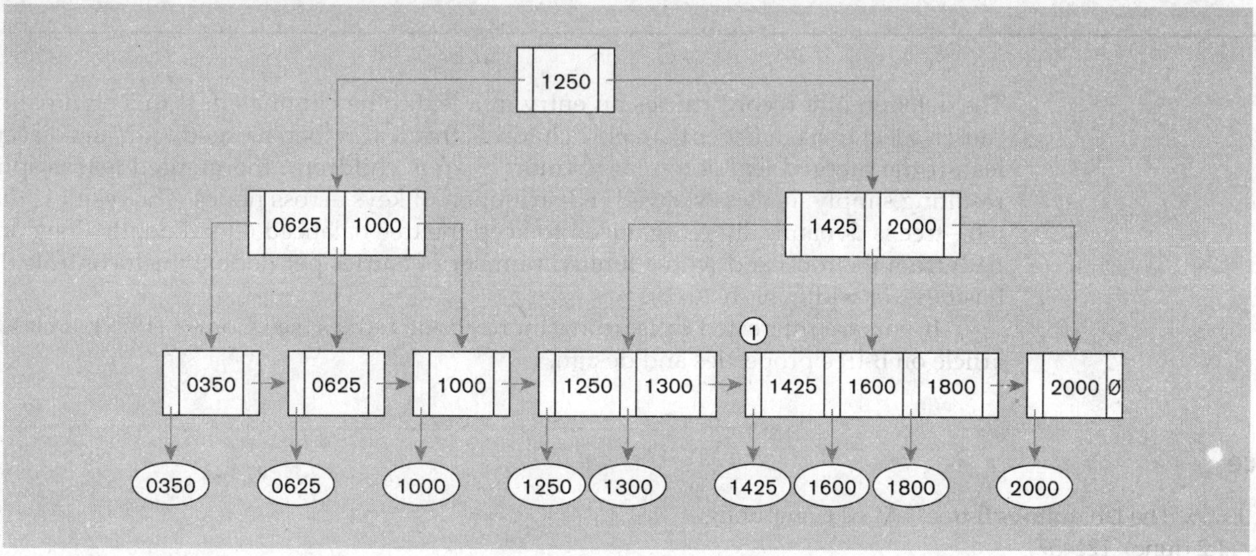

(continued)

FIGURE C-10 ***(continued)***

(b) Initial attempt to insert record 1700

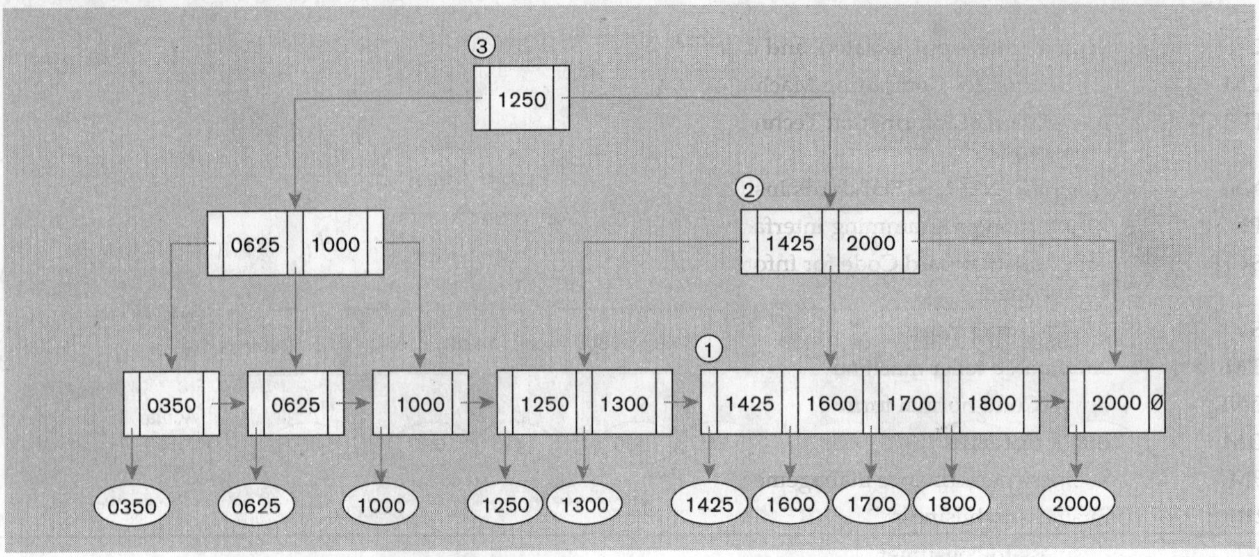

(c) Final B+-tree after insertion of record 1700

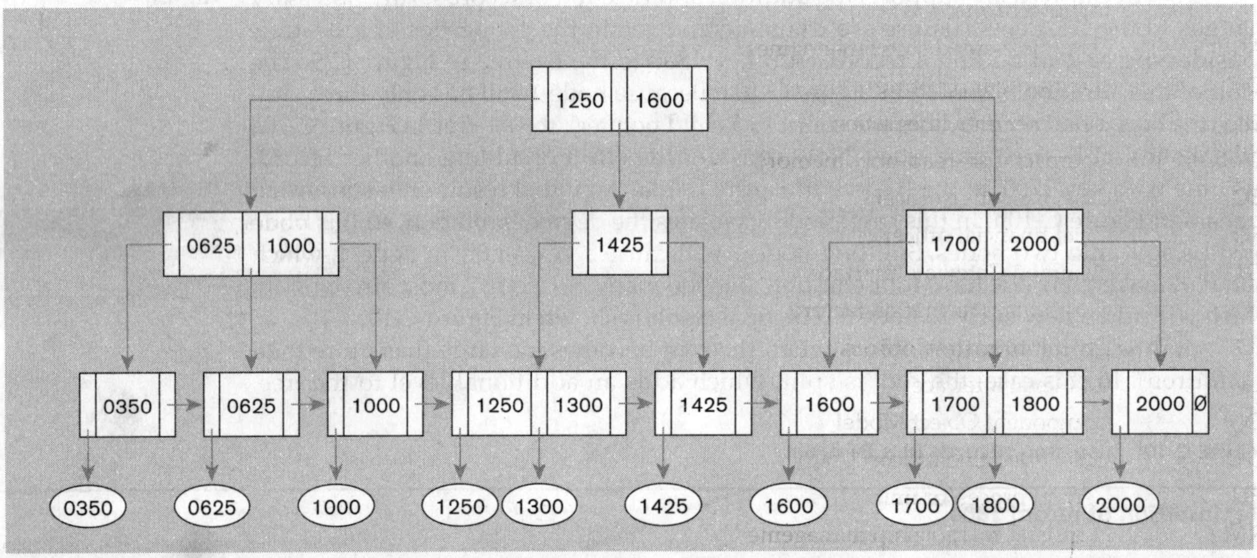

The deletion of a record causes an entry in a leaf to be eliminated. If this elimination causes a leaf to have fewer than $m/2$ children, that leaf is then merged with an adjacent leaf; if the merged leaf is too large (more than m children), the merged leaf is split, resulting simply in a less skewed redistribution of keys across nodes. The result is that a B+-tree is dynamically reorganized to keep the tree balanced (equal depth along any path from the root) and with a limited number of entries per node (which controls the business, or width, of the tree).

If you are interested in learning more about B-trees, see Comer (1979), a classic article on B-tree properties and design.

Reference

Comer, D. 1979. "The Ubiquitous B-tree." ACM Computing Surveys 11,2 (June): 121–37.

GLOSSARY OF ACRONYMS

ACID	Atomic, consistent, isolated, and durable
ACM	Association for Computing Machinery
AITP	Association of Information Technology Professionals
ANSI	American National Standards Institute
API	Application programming interface
ASCII	American Standard Code for Information Interchange
ASP	Active Server Pages
ATM	Automated teller machine
BCNF	Boyce-Codd normal form
BOM	Bill of materials
BPM	Business performance management
B2B	Business-to-business
B2C	Business-to-consumer
CAD/CAM	Computer-aided design/computer-aided manufacturing
CASE	Computer-aided software engineering
CDC	Changed data capture
CDI	Customer data integration
CD-ROM	Compact disc–read-only memory
CEO	Chief executive officer
CFO	Chief financial officer
CGI	Common Gateway Interface
CIF	Corporate information factory
CIO	Chief information officer
CLI	Call-level interface
COM	Component Object Model
COO	Chief operating officer
CPU	Central processor unit
CRM	Customer relationship management
C/S	Client/server
CSF	Critical success factor
DA	Data administrator (or data administration)
DBA	Database administrator (or database administration)
DBD	Database description
DBMS	Database management system
DB2	Data Base2 (an IBM Relational DBMS)
DCL	Data control language
DDL	Data definition language
DES	Data Encryption Standard
DFD	Data flow diagram
DKNF	Domain-key normal form
DML	Data manipulation language
DNS	Domain Name System
DSS	Decision support system
DTD	Data type definitions
DWA	Data warehouse administrator
DVD	Digital versatile disc
EAI	Enterprise application integration
EDI	Electronic data interchange
EDW	Enterprise data warehouse
EDR	Enterprise data replication
EER	Extended entity-relationship
EFT	Electronic funds transfer
EII	Enterprise information integration
EJB	Enterprise JavaBeans
E-R	Entity-relationship
ERD	Entity-relationship diagram
ERP	Enterprise resource planning
ETL	Extract–transform–load
FDA	Food and Drug Administration
FK	Foreign key
FTC	Federal Trade Commission
FTP	File Transfer Protocol
GPA	Grade point average
GUI	Graphical user interface
HIPAA	Health Insurance Portability and Accountability Act
HQL	Hibernate Query Language
HTML	Hypertext Markup Language
HTTP	Hypertext Transfer Protocol
IBM	International Business Machines
I-CASE	Integrated computer-aided software engineering
ID	Identifier
IDE	Integrated development environment
IE	Information engineering
INCITS	International Committee for Information Technology Standards
I/O	Input/output
IP	Internet Protocol
IRDS	Information Resource Dictionary System
IRM	Information resource management
IS	Information system
ISAM	Indexed sequential access method
ISO	International Standards Organization
IT	Information technology
ITAA	Information Technology Association of America
J2EE	Java 2 Enterprise Edition
JDBC	Java Database Connectivity
JDO	Java Data Objects

JPA	Java Persistence API
JSP	Java Server Pages
LAN	Local area network
LDB	Logical database
LDBR	Logical database record
LDM	Logical data model
LINQ	Language Integrated Query
MB	Megabytes (million bytes)
MDM	Master data management
MIS	Management information system
M:N	Many-to-many
M:1	Many-to-one
MOLAP	Multidimensional online analytical processing
MMS	Multi-messaging service
MOM	Message-oriented middleware
MRN	Medical record number
MRP	Materials requirements planning
MS	Microsoft
MVCH	Mountain View Community Hospital
NIST	National Institute of Standards and Technology
ODBC	Open database connectivity
OODBMS	Object-oriented database management system
ODL	Object definition language
ODS	Operational data store
OLAP	Online analytical processing
OLTP	Online transaction processing
OO	Object-oriented
OODM	Object-oriented data model
OQL	Object Query Language
O/R	Object/relational
ORB	Object request broker
ORDBMS	Object-relational database management system
ORM	Object-relational mapping
P3P	Platform for Privacy Preferences
PC	Personal computer
PDA	Personal digital assistant
PIN	Personal identification number
PK	Primary key
PL/SQL	Programming Language/SQL
PVFC	Pine Valley Furniture Company
RAD	Rapid application development
RAID	Redundant array of inexpensive disks
RAM	Random access memory
RDBMS	Relational database management system
ROI	Return on investment
ROLAP	Relational online analytical processing
RPC	Remote procedure call
SCD	Slowly changing dimension
SDLC	Systems development life cycle
SGML	Standard Generalized Markup Language
SOA	Service-oriented architecture
SOAP	Simple Object Access Protocol
SOX	Sarbanes-Oxley Act
SPL	Structured Product Labeling
SQL	Structured Query Language
SQL/CLI	SQL/Call Level Interface
SQL/DS	Structured Query Language/Data System (an IBM relational DBMS)
SQLJ	SQL for Java
SQL/PSM	SQL/Persistent Stored Modules
SSL	Secure Sockets Layer
TCP/IP	Transmission Control Protocol/Internet Protocol
TDWI	The Data Warehousing Institute
TQM	Total quality management
UDDI	Universal Description, Discovery, and Integration
UDF	User-defined function
UDT	User-defined data type
UML	Unified Modeling Language
URI	Universal resource identifier
URL	Uniform resource locator
VLDB	Very large database
W3C	World Wide Web Consortium
WSDL	Web Services Description Language
WYSIWYG	What you see is what you get
WWW	World Wide Web
XBRL	Extensible Business Reporting Language
XHTML	Extensible Hypertext Markup Language
XML	Extensible Markup Language
XSL	Extensible Style Language
XSLT	XML Stylesheet Language Transformation
1:1	One-to-one
1:M	One-to-many
1NF	First normal form
2NF	Second normal form
3GL	Third-generation language
3NF	Third normal form
4NF	Fourth normal form
5NF	Fifth normal form

GLOSSARY OF TERMS

Note: Number (letter) in parenthesis corresponds to the chapter (appendix) in which the term is found. Terms in Chapters 12 through 14 will best be found in the full versions of the chapters on the book's Web site.

Aborted transaction A transaction in progress that terminates abnormally. (11)

Abstract class A class that has no direct instances but whose descendants may have direct instances. (13)

Abstract operation An operation whose form or protocol is defined but whose implementation is not defined. (w13)

Accessor method A method that provides other objects with access to the state of an object. (w14)

After image A copy of a record (or page of memory) after it has been modified. (11)

Aggregation A part-of relationship between a component object and an aggregate object. (w13) The process of transforming data from a detailed level to a summary level. (10)

Agile software development An approach to database and software development that emphasizes **"individuals and interactions** over processes and tools, **working software** over comprehensive documentation, **customer collaboration** over contract negotiation, and **response to change** over following a plan." (1)

Alias An alternative name used for an attribute. (4)

Anomaly An error or inconsistency that may result when a user attempts to update a table that contains redundant data. The three types of anomalies are insertion, deletion, and modification anomalies. (4)

Application partitioning The process of assigning portions of application code to client or server partitions after it is written to achieve better performance and interoperability (ability of a component to function on different platforms). (8)

Application program interface (API) Sets of routines that an application program uses to direct the performance of procedures by the computer's operating system. (8)

Association A named relationship between or among object classes. (13)

Association class An association that has attributes or operations of its own or that participates in relationships with other classes. (13)

Association role The end of an association, where it connects to a class. (13)

Associative entity An entity type that associates the instances of one or more entity types and contains attributes that are peculiar to the relationship between those entity instances. (2)

Asynchronous distributed database A form of distributed database technology in which copies of replicated data are kept at different nodes so that local servers can access data without reaching out across the network. (12)

Attribute A property or characteristic of an entity or relationship type that is of interest to the organization. (2)

Attribute inheritance A property by which subtype entities inherit values of all attributes and instances of all relationships of their supertype. (3)

Authorization rules Controls incorporated in a data management systems that restrict access to data and also restrict the actions that people may take when they access data. (11)

Backup facility A DBMS COPY utility that produces a backup copy (or save) of an entire database or a subset of a database. (11)

Backward recovery (rollback) The backout, or undo, of unwanted changes to a database. Before images of the records that have been changed are applied to the database, and the database is returned to an earlier state. Rollback is used to reverse the changes made by transactions that have been aborted, or terminated abnormally. (11)

Base table A table in the relational data model containing the inserted raw data. Base tables correspond to the relations that are identified in the database's conceptual schema. (6)

Before image A copy of a record (or page of memory) before it has been modified. (11)

Behavior The way in which an object acts and reacts. (13)

Binary relationship A relationship between the instances of two entity types. (2)

Boyce-Codd normal form (BCNF) A normal form of a relation in which every determinant is a candidate key. (B)

Business rule A statement that defines or constrains some aspect of the business. It is intended to assert business structure or to control or influence the behavior of the business. (2)

Call-level application programming interface A mechanism that provides an application program with access to an external service, such as a database management system. (14)

Candidate key An attribute, or combination of attributes, that uniquely identifies a row in a relation. (4)

Cardinality constraint A rule that specifies the number of instances of one entity that can (or must) be associated with each instance of another entity. (2)

Catalog A set of schemas that, when put together, constitute a description of a database. (6)

Changed data capture (CDC) Technique that indicates which data have changed since the last data integration activity. (10)

Checkpoint facility A facility by which a DBMS periodically refuses to accept any new transactions. The system is in a quiet state, and the database and transaction logs are synchronized. (11)

Class An entity type that has a well-defined role in the application domain about which the organization wishes to maintain state, behavior, and identity. (13)

Class diagram A diagram that shows the static structure of an object-oriented model: the object classes, their internal structure, and the relationships in which they participate. (13)

Class-scope attribute An attribute of a class that specifies a value common to an entire class rather than a specific value for an instance. (13)

Class-scope operation An operation that applies to a class rather than to an object instance. (w13)

Client/server system A networked computing model that distributes processes between clients and servers, which supply the requested services. In a database system, the database generally resides on a server that processes the DBMS. The clients may process the application systems or request services from another server that holds the application programs. (8)

Commit protocol An algorithm to ensure that a transaction is either successfully completed or aborted. (12)

Completeness constraint A type of constraint that addresses whether an instance of a supertype must also be a member of at least one subtype. (3)

Composite attribute An attribute that has meaningful component parts (attributes). (2)

Composite identifier An identifier that consists of a composite attribute. (2)

Composite key A primary key that consists of more than one attribute. (4)

Composition A part-of relationship in which parts belong to only one whole object and live and die with the whole object. (13)

Computer-aided software engineering (CASE) tools Software tools that provide automated support for some portion of the systems development process. (1)

Conceptual schema A detailed, technology-independent specification of the overall structure of organizational data. (1)

Concrete class A class that can have direct instances. (13)

Concurrency control The process of managing simultaneous operations against a database so that data integrity is maintained and the operations do not interfere with each other in a multiuser environment. (11)

Concurrency transparency A design goal for a distributed database, with the property that although a distributed system runs many transactions, it appears that a given transaction is the only activity in the system. Thus, when several transactions are processed concurrently, the results must be the same as if each transaction were processed in serial order. (12)

Conformed dimension One or more dimension tables associated with two or more fact tables for which the dimension tables have the same business meaning and primary key with each fact table. (9)

Constraint A rule that cannot be violated by database users. (1)

Constructor operation An operation that creates a new instance of a class. (w13)

Correlated subquery In SQL, a subquery in which processing the inner query depends on data from the outer query. (7)

Data Stored representations of objects and events that have meaning and importance in the user's environment. (1)

Data administration A high-level function that is responsible for the overall management of data resources in an organization, including maintaining corporate-wide definitions and standards. (11)

Data archiving The process of moving inactive data to another storage location where it can be accessed when needed. (11)

Data control language (DCL) Commands used to control a database, including those for administering privileges and committing (saving) data. (6)

Data definition language (DDL) Commands used to define a database, including those for creating, altering, and dropping tables and establishing constraints. (6)

Data dictionary A repository of information about a database that documents data elements of a database. (11)

Data federation A technique for data integration that provides a virtual view of integrated data without actually creating one centralized database. (10)

Data governance High-level organizational groups and processes that oversee data stewardship across the organization. It usually guides data quality initiatives, data architecture, data integration and master data management, data warehousing and business intelligence, and other data-related matters. (10)

Data independence The separation of data descriptions from the application programs that use the data. (1)

Data manipulation language (DML) Commands used to maintain and query a database, including those for updating, inserting, modifying, and querying data. (6)

Data mart A data warehouse that is limited in scope, whose data are obtained by selecting and summarizing data from a data warehouse or from separate extract, transform, and load processes from source data systems. (9)

Data mining Knowledge discovery, using a sophisticated blend of techniques from traditional statistics, artificial intelligence, and computer graphics. (9)

Data model Graphical systems used to capture the nature and relationships among data. (1)

Data scrubbing A process of using pattern recognition and other artificial intelligence techniques to upgrade the quality of raw data before transforming and moving the data to the data warehouse. Also called data cleansing. (10)

Data steward A person assigned the responsibility of ensuring that organizational applications properly support the organization's enterprise goals for data quality. (10)

Data transformation The component of data reconciliation that converts data from the format of the source operational systems to the format of the enterprise data warehouse. (10)

Data type A detailed coding scheme recognized by system software, such as a DBMS, for representing organizational data. (5)

Data visualization The representation of data in graphical and multimedia formats for human analysis. (9)

Data warehouse A subject-oriented, integrated, time-variant, nonupdateable collection of data used in support of management decision-making processes. (9) An integrated decision support database whose content is derived from the various operational databases. (1)

Database An organized collection of logically related data. (1)

Database administration A technical function that is responsible for physical database design and for dealing with technical issues, such as security enforcement, database performance, and backup and recovery. (11)

Database application An application program (or set of related programs) that is used to perform a series of database activities (create, read, update, and delete) on behalf of database users. (1)

Database change log A log that contains before and after images of records that have been modified by transactions. (11)

Database destruction The database itself is lost, destroyed, or cannot be read. (11)

Database management system (DBMS) A software system that is used to create, maintain, and provide controlled access to user databases. (1)

Database recovery Mechanisms for restoring a database quickly and accurately after loss or damage. (11)

Database security Protection of database data against accidental or intentional loss, destruction, or misuse. (11)

Database server A computer that is responsible for database storage, access, and processing in a client/server environment. Some people also use this term to describe a two-tier client/server applications. (8)

Deadlock An impasse that results when two or more transactions have locked a common resource, and each waits for the other to unlock that resource. (11)

Deadlock prevention A method for resolving deadlocks in which user programs must lock all records they require at the beginning of a transaction (rather than one at a time). (11)

Deadlock resolution An approach to dealing with deadlocks that allows deadlocks to occur but builds mechanisms into the DBMS for detecting and breaking the deadlocks. (11)

Decentralized database A database that is stored on computers at multiple locations; these computers are not interconnected by network and database software that make the data appear in one logical database. (w12)

Declarative mapping schema A structure that defines the relationships between domain classes in the object-oriented model and relations in the relational model. (14)

Degree The number of entity types that participate in a relationship. (2)

Denormalization The process of transforming normalized relations into non-normalized physical record specifications. (5)

Dependent data mart A data mart filled exclusively from an enterprise data warehouse and its reconciled data. (9)

Derived attribute An attribute whose values can be calculated from related attribute values. (2)

Derived data Data that have been selected, formatted, and aggregated for end-user decision support applications. (9)

Determinant The attribute on the left side of the arrow in a functional dependency. (4)

Disjoint rule A rule that specifies that an instance of a supertype may not simultaneously be a member of two (or more) subtypes. (3)

Disjointness constraint A constraint that addresses whether an instance of a supertype may simultaneously be a member of two (or more) subtypes. (3)

Distributed database A single logical database that is spread physically across computers in multiple locations that are connected by a data communication link. (12)

Dynamic SQL Specific SQL code generated on the fly while an application is processing. (7)

Dynamic view A virtual table that is created dynamically upon request by a user. A dynamic view is not a temporary table. Rather, its definition is stored in the system catalog, and the contents of the view are materialized as a result of an SQL query that uses the view. It differs from a materialized view, which may be stored on a disk and refreshed at intervals or when used, depending on the RDBMS. (6)

Embedded SQL Hard-coded SQL statements included in a program written in another language, such as C or Java. (7)

Encapsulation The technique of hiding the internal implementation details of an object from its external view. (13)

Encryption The coding or scrambling of data so that humans cannot read them. (11)

Enhanced entity-relationship (EER) model A model that has resulted from extending the original E-R model with new modeling constructs. (3)

Enterprise data modeling The first step in database development, in which the scope and general contents of organizational databases are specified. (1)

Enterprise data warehouse (EDW) A centralized, integrated data warehouse that is the control point and single source of all data made available to end users for decision support applications. (9)

Enterprise key A primary key whose value is unique across all relations. (4)

Enterprise resource planning (ERP) A business management system that integrates all functions of the enterprise, such as manufacturing, sales, finance, marketing, inventory, accounting, and human resources. ERP systems are software applications that provide the data necessary for the enterprise to examine and manage its activities. (1)

Entity A person, a place, an object, an event, or a concept in the user environment about which the organization wishes to maintain data. (1, 3)

Entity class A class that represents a real-world entity. (w14)

Entity cluster A set of one or more entity types and associated relationships grouped into a single abstract entity type. (3)

Entity instance A single occurrence of an entity type. (2)

Entity integrity rule A rule that states that no primary key attribute (or component of a primary key attribute) may be null. (4)

Entity type A collection of entities that share common properties or characteristics. (2)

Entity-relationship diagram (E-R diagram, or ERD) A graphical representation of an entity-relationship model. (2)

Entity-relationship model (E-R model) A logical representation of the data for an organization or for a business area, using entities for categories of data and relationships for associations between entities. (2)

Equi-join A join in which the joining condition is based on equality between values in the common columns. Common columns appear (redundantly) in the result table. (7)

Exclusive lock (X lock, or write lock) A technique that prevents another transaction from reading and therefore updating a record until it is unlocked. (11)

Extensible Markup Language (XML) A text-based scripting language used to describe data structures hierarchically, using HTML-like tags. (8)

Extensible Stylesheet Language Transformation (XSLT) A language used to transform complex XML documents and also used to create HTML pages from XML documents. (8)

Extent A contiguous section of disk storage space. (5)

Fact An association between two or more terms. (2)

Failure transparency A design goal for a distributed database, which guarantees that either all the actions of each transaction are committed or else none of them is committed. (12)

Fat client A client PC that is responsible for processing presentation logic, extensive application and business rules logic, and many DBMS functions. (8)

Fetching strategy A model for specifying when and how an ORM framework retrieves persistent objects to the run-time memory during a navigation process. (14)

Field The smallest unit of application data recognized by system software. (5)

File organization A technique for physically arranging the records of a file on secondary storage devices. (5)

First normal form (1NF) A relation that has a primary key and in which there are no repeating groups. (4)

Foreign key An attribute in a relation that serves as the primary key of another relation in the same database. (4)

Forward recovery (rollforward) A technique that starts with an earlier copy of a database. After images (the results of good transactions) are applied to the database, and the database is quickly moved forward to a later state. (11)

Fourth normal form (4NF) A normal form of a relation in which the relation is in BCNF and contains no multivalued dependencies. (B)

Function A stored subroutine that returns one value and has only input parameters. (7)

Functional dependency A constraint between two attributes in which the value of one attribute is determined by the value of another attribute. (4)

Generalization The process of defining a more general entity type from a set of more specialized entity types. (3)

Global transaction In a distributed database, a transaction that requires reference to data at one or more nonlocal sites to satisfy the request. (w12)

Grain The level of detail in a fact table, determined by the intersection of all the components of the primary key, including all foreign keys and any other primary key elements. (9)

Hash index table A file organization that uses hashing to map a key into a location in an index, where there is a pointer to the actual data record matching the hash key. (5)

Hashed file organization A storage system in which the address for each record is determined using a hashing algorithm. (5)

Hashing algorithm A routine that converts a primary key value into a relative record number or relative file address. (5)

Heartbeat query A query submitted by a DBA to test the current performance of a database or to predict the response time for queries that have promised response times. Also called a canary query. (11)

Homonym An attribute that may have more than one meaning. (4)

Horizontal partitioning Distribution of the rows of a logical relation into several separate tables. (5)

Identifier An attribute (or combination of attributes) whose value distinguishes instances of an entity type. (2)

Identifying owner The entity type on which the weak entity type depends. (2)

Identifying relationship The relationship between a weak entity type and its owner. (2)

Inconsistent read problem An unrepeatable read, one that occurs when one user reads data that have been partially updated by another user. (11)

Incremental extract A method of capturing only the changes that have occurred in the source data since the last capture. (10)

Independent data mart A data mart filled with data extracted from the operational environment, without the benefit of a data warehouse. (9)

Index A table or other data structure used to determine in a file the location of records that satisfy some condition. (5)

Indexed file organization The storage of records either sequentially or nonsequentially with an index that allows software to locate individual records. (5)

Information Data that have been processed in such a way as to increase the knowledge of the person who uses the data. (1)

Information repository A component that stores metadata that describe an organization's data and data processing resources, manages the total information processing environment, and combines information about an organization's business information and its application portfolio. (11)

Information Resource Dictionary System (IRDS) A computer software tool that is used to manage and control access to the information repository. (11)

Informational system A system designed to support decision making based on historical point-in-time and prediction data for complex queries or data-mining applications. (9)

Java servlet A Java program that is stored on the server and contains the business and database logic for a Java-based application. (8)

Join A relational operation that causes two tables with a common domain to be combined into a single table or view. (7)

Join index An index on columns from two or more tables that come from the same domain of values. (5)

Joining The process of combining data from various sources into a single table or view. (10)

Journalizing facility An audit trail of transactions and database changes. (11)

Local autonomy A design goal for a distributed database, which says that a site can independently administer and operate its database when connections to other nodes have failed. (12)

Local transaction In a distributed database, a transaction that requires reference only to data that are stored at the site where the transaction originates. (w12)

Location transparency A design goal for a distributed database, which says that a user (or user program) using data need not know the location of the data. (12)

Locking A process in which any data that are retrieved by a user for updating must be locked, or denied to other users, until the update is completed or aborted. (11)

Locking level (lock granularity) The extent of a database resource that is included with each lock. (11)

Logical data mart A data mart created by a relational view of a data warehouse. (9)

Logical schema The representation of a database for a particular data management technology. (1)

Master data management (MDM) Disciplines, technologies, and methods used to ensure the currency, meaning, and quality of reference data within and across various subject areas. (10)

Materialized view Copies or replicas of data, based on SQL queries created in the same manner as dynamic views. However, a materialized view exists as a table and thus care must be taken to keep it synchronized with its associated base tables. (6)

Maximum cardinality The maximum number of instances of one entity that may be associated with each instance of another entity. (2)

Metadata Data that describe the properties or characteristics of end-user data and the context of those data. (1)

Method The implementation of an operation. (w13)

Middleware Software that allows an application to interoperate with other software without requiring the user to understand and code the low-level operations necessary to achieve interoperability. (8)

Minimum cardinality The minimum number of instances of one entity that may be associated with each instance of another entity. (2)

Multidimensional OLAP (MOLAP) OLAP tools that load data into an intermediate structure, usually a three- or higher-dimensional array. (9)

Multiple classification A situation in which an object is an instance of more than one class. (w13)

Multiplicity A specification that indicates how many objects participate in a given relationship. (13)

Multivalued attribute An attribute that may take on more than one value for a given entity (or relationship) instance. (2)

Multivalued dependency The type of dependency that exists when there are at least three attributes (e.g., A, B, and C) in a relation, with a well-defined set of B and C values for each A value, but those B and C values are independent of each other. (B)

***N*+1 selects problem** A performance problem caused by too many SELECT statements generated by an ORM framework. (14)

Natural join A join that is the same as an equi-join except that one of the duplicate columns is eliminated in the result table. (7)

Normal form A state of a relation that requires that certain rules regarding relationships between attributes (or functional dependencies) are satisfied. (4)

Normalization The process of decomposing relations with anomalies to produce smaller, well-structured relations. (4)

Null A value that may be assigned to an attribute when no other value applies or when the applicable value is unknown. (4)

Object An instance of a class that encapsulates data and behavior. (13)

Object diagram A graph of objects that are compatible with a given class diagram. (w13)

Object identity A property of an object that separates it from other objects based on its existence. (w14)

Object-relational impedance mismatch The conceptual differences between the object-oriented approach to application design and the relational model for database design and implementation. (14)

Object-relational mapping Definition of structural relationships between object-oriented and relational representations of data, typically to enable the use of a relational database to provide persistence for objects. (14)

Online analytical processing (OLAP) The use of a set of graphical tools that provides users with multidimensional views of their data and allows them to analyze the data using simple windowing techniques. (9)

Open database connectivity (ODBC) An application programming interface that provides a common language for application programs to access and process SQL databases independent of the particular DBMS that is accessed. (8)

Open source DBMS Free DBMS source code software that provides the core functionality of an SQL-compliant DBMS. (11)

Operation A function or a service that is provided by all the instances of a class. (13)

Operational data store (ODS) An integrated, subject-oriented, continuously updateable, current-valued (with recent history), enterprise-wide, detailed database designed to serve operational users as they do decision support processing. (9)

Operational system A system that is used to run a business in real-time, based on current data. Also called a system of record. (9)

Optional attribute An attribute that may not have a value for every entity (or relationship) instance with which it is associated. (2)

Outer join A join in which rows that do not have matching values in common columns are nevertheless included in the result table. (7)

Overlap rule A rule that specifies that an instance of a supertype may simultaneously be a member of two (or more) subtypes. (3)

Overriding The process of replacing a method inherited from a superclass by a more specific implementation of that method in a subclass. (w13)

Partial functional dependency A functional dependency in which one or more nonkey attributes are functionally dependent on part (but not all) of the primary key. (4)

Partial specialization rule A rule that specifies that an entity instance of a supertype is allowed not to belong to any subtype. (3)

Periodic data Data that are never physically altered or deleted once they have been added to the store. (9)

Persistence An object's capability to maintain its state between application execution sessions. (14)

Persistent Stored Modules (SQL/PSM) Extensions defined in SQL:1999 that include the capability to create and drop modules of code stored in the database schema across user sessions. (7)

Physical file A named portion of secondary memory (such as a hard disk) allocated for the purpose of storing physical records. (5)

Physical schema Specifications for how da'a from a logical schema are stored in a computer's secondary memory by a database management system. (1)

Pointer A field of data indicating a target address that can be used to locate a related field or record of data. (5)

Polymorphism The ability of an operation with the same name to respond in different ways depending on the class context. (13)

Pooling of database connections The process of using a limited number of database connections that are shared by multiple applications and users. (w14)

Primary key An attribute or a combination of attributes that uniquely identifies each row in a relation. (4)

Procedure A collection of procedural and SQL statements that are assigned a unique name within the schema and stored in the database. (7)

Project A planned undertaking of related activities to reach an objective that has a beginning and an end. (1)

Prototyping An iterative process of systems development in which requirements are converted to a working system that is continually revised through close work between analysts and users. (1)

Query operation An operation that accesses the state of an object but does not alter the state. (w13)

Real-time data warehouse An enterprise data warehouse that accepts near-real-time feeds of transactional data from the systems of record, analyzes warehouse data, and in near-real-time relays business rules to the data warehouse and systems of record so that immediate action can be taken in response to business events. (9)

Reconciled data Detailed, current data intended to be the single, authoritative source for all decision support applications. (9)

Recovery manager A module of a DBMS that restores the database to a correct condition when a failure occurs and then resumes processing user questions. (11)

Recursive foreign key A foreign key in a relation that references the primary key values of the same relation. (4)

Referential integrity constraint A rule that states that either each foreign key value must match a primary key value in another relation or the foreign key value must be null. (4)

Refresh mode An approach to filling a data warehouse that involves bulk rewriting of the target data at periodic intervals. (10)

Relation A named two-dimensional table of data. (4)

Relational database A database that represents data as a collection of tables in which all data relationships are represented by common values in related tables. (1)

Relational DBMS (RDBMS) A database management system that manages data as a collection of tables in which all data relationships are represented by common values in related tables. (6)

Relational OLAP (ROLAP) OLAP tools that view the database as a traditional relational database in either a star schema or other normalized or denormalized set of tables. (9)

Relationship instance An association between (or among) entity instances where each relationship instance associates exactly one entity instance from each participating entity type. (2)

Relationship type A meaningful association between (or among) entity types. (2)

Replication transparency A design goal for a distributed database, which says that although a given data item may be replicated at several nodes in a network, a developer or user may treat the data item as if it were a single item at a single node. Also called fragmentation transparency. (12)

Repository A centralized knowledge base of all data definitions, data relationships, screen and report formats, and other system components. (1)

Required attribute An attribute that must have a value for every entity (or relationship) instance with which it is associated. (2)

Restore/rerun A technique that involves reprocessing the day's transactions (up to the point of failure) against the backup copy of the database. (11)

Scalar aggregate A single value returned from an SQL query that includes an aggregate function. (6)

Schema A structure that contains descriptions of objects created by a user, such as base tables, views, and constraints, as part of a database. (6)

Second normal form (2NF) A relation in first normal form in which every nonkey attribute is fully functionally dependent on the primary key. (4)

Secondary key One field or a combination of fields for which more than one record may have the same combination of values. Also called a nonunique key. (5)

Selection The process of partitioning data according to predefined criteria. (10)

Semijoin A joining operation used with distributed databases in which only the joining attribute from one site is transmitted to the other site, rather than all the selected attributes from every qualified row. (12)

Separation of concerns The approach of dividing an application or a system into feature or behavior sets that overlap with each other as little as possible. (w14)

Sequential file organization The storage of records in a file in sequence according to a primary key value. (5)

Serialization The writing of an object onto a storage medium or a communication channel as a data stream. (w14)

Service-oriented architecture (SOA) A collection of services that communicate with each other in some manner, usually by passing data or coordinating a business activity. (8)

Shared lock (S lock, or read lock) A technique that allows other transactions to read but not update a record or another resource. (11)

Simple (or atomic) attribute An attribute that cannot be broken down into smaller components that are meaningful to the organization. (2)

Simple Object Access Protocol (SOAP) An XML-based communication protocol used for sending messages between applications via the Internet. (8)

Smart card A credit card-sized plastic card with an embedded microprocessor chip that can store, process, and output electronic data in a secure manner. (11)

Snowflake schema An expanded version of a star schema in which dimension tables are normalized into several related tables. (9)

Specialization The process of defining one or more subtypes of the supertype and forming supertype/subtype relationships. (3)

Star schema A simple database design in which dimensional data are separated from fact or event data. A dimensional model is another name for a star schema. (9)

State An object's properties (attributes and relationships) and the values those properties have. (13)

Static extract A method of capturing a snapshot of the required source data at a point in time. (10)

Strong entity type An entity that exists independently of other entity types. (2)

Subtype A subgrouping of the entities in an entity type that is meaningful to the organization and that shares common attributes or relationships distinct from other subgroupings. (3)

Subtype discriminator An attribute of a supertype whose values determine the target subtype or subtypes. (3)

Supertype A generic entity type that has a relationship with one or more subtypes. (3)

Supertype/subtype hierarchy A hierarchical arrangement of supertypes and subtypes in which each subtype has only one supertype. (3)

Surrogate primary key A serial number or other system-assigned primary key for a relation. (4)

Synchronous distributed database A form of distributed database technology in which all data across the network are continuously kept up to date so that a user at any site can access data anywhere on the network at any time and get the same answer. (w12)

Synonyms Two (or more) attributes that have different names but the same meaning. (4)

System catalog A system-created database that describes all database objects, including data dictionary information, and also includes user access information. (11)

Systems development life cycle (SDLC) The traditional methodology used to develop, maintain, and replace information systems. (1)

Tablespace A named logical storage unit in which data from one or more database tables, views, or other database objects may be stored. (5)

Term A word or phrase that has a specific meaning for the business. (2)

Ternary relationship A simultaneous relationship among the instances of three entity types. (2)

Thin client An application where the client (PC) accessing the application primarily provides the user interfaces and some application processing, usually with no or limited local data storage. (8)

Third normal form (3NF) A relation that is in second normal form and has no transitive dependencies. (4)

Three-tier architecture A client/server configuration that includes three layers: a client layer and two server layers. Although the nature of the server layers differs, a common configuration contains an application server and a database server. (8)

Time stamp A time value that is associated with a data value, often indicating when some event occurred that affected the data value. (2)

Time-stamping In distributed databases, a concurrency control mechanism that assigns a globally unique time stamp to each transaction. Time-stamping is an alternative to the use of locks in distributed databases. (w14)

Total specialization rule A rule that specifies that each entity instance of a supertype must be a member of some subtype in the relationship. (3)

Transaction A discrete unit of work that must be completely processed or not processed at all within a computer system. Entering a customer order is an example of a transaction. (11)

Transaction boundaries The logical beginning and end of a transaction. (11)

Transaction log A record of the essential data for each transaction that is processed against the database. (11)

Transaction manager In a distributed database, a software module that maintains a log of all transactions and an appropriate concurrency control scheme. (w12)

Transient data Data in which changes to existing records are written over previous records, thus destroying the previous data content. (9)

Transitive dependency A functional dependency between the primary key and one or more nonkey attributes that are dependent on the primary key via another nonkey attribute. (4)

Transparent persistence A persistence solution that hides the underlying storage technology. (w14)

Trigger A named set of SQL statements that are considered (triggered) when a data modification (i.e., INSERT, UPDATE, DELETE) occurs or if certain data definitions are encountered. If a condition stated within a trigger is met, then a prescribed action is taken. (7)

Two-phase commit An algorithm for coordinating updates in a distributed database. (12)

Two-phase locking protocol A procedure for acquiring the necessary locks for a transaction in which all necessary locks are acquired before any locks are released, resulting in a growing phase when locks are acquired and a shrinking phase when they are released. (11)

Unary relationship A relationship between instances of a single entity type. (2)

Universal data model A generic or template data model that can be reused as a starting point for a data modeling project. (3)

Universal Description, Discovery, and Integration (UDDI) A technical specification for creating a distributed registry of Web services and businesses that are open to communicating through Web services. (8)

Update mode An approach to filling a data warehouse in which only changes in the source data are written to the data warehouse. (10)

Update operation An operation that alters the state of an object. (w13)

User view A logical description of some portion of the database that is required by a user to perform some task. (1)

User-defined data type (UDT) A data type that a user can define by making it a subclass of a standard type or creating a type that behaves as an object. UDTs may also have defined functions and methods. (7)

User-defined procedures User exits (or interfaces) that allow system designers to define their own security procedures in addition to the authorization rules. (11)

Value type A class specification for objects that exist for storing the value of a property of another object. (w14)

Vector aggregate Multiple values returned from an SQL query that includes an aggregate function. (6)

Versioning An approach to concurrency control in which each transaction is restricted to a view of the database as of the time that transaction started, and when a transaction modifies a record, the DBMS creates a new record version instead of overwriting the old record. Hence, no form of locking is required. (11)

Vertical partitioning Distribution of the columns of a logical relation into several separate physical tables. (5)

Virtual table A table constructed automatically as needed by a DBMS. Virtual tables are not maintained as real data. (6)

Weak entity type An entity type whose existence depends on some other entity type. (2)

Web services A set of emerging standards that define protocols for automatic communication between software programs over the Web. Web services are XML based and usually run in the background to establish transparent communication among computers. (8)

Web Services Description Language (WSDL) An XML-based grammar or language used to describe a Web service and specify a public interface for that service. (8)

Well-structured relation A relation that contains minimal redundancy and allows users to insert, modify, and delete the rows in a table without errors or inconsistencies. (4)

World Wide Web Consortium (W3C) An international consortium of companies working to develop open standards that foster the development of Web conventions so that Web documents can be consistently displayed across all platforms. (8)

XHTML A hybrid scripting language that extends HTML code to make it XML compliant. (8)

XML Schema Definition (XSD) Language used for defining XML databases that has been recommended by the W3C. (8)

XPath One of a set of XML technologies that supports XQuery development. XPath expressions are used to locate data in XML documents. (8)

XQuery An XML transformation language that allows applications to query both relational databases and XML data. (8)

INDEX